A HISTORY OF PHILOSOPHY

A HISTORY OF
PHILOSOPHY

Third Edition

BY

B. A. G. FULLER

Professor Emeritus of Philosophy
University of Southern California

REVISED BY

STERLING M. McMURRIN

Professor of Philosophy
University of Utah

NEW YORK

HENRY HOLT AND COMPANY

22960-0615

PRINTED IN THE

UNITED STATES OF AMERICA

PREFACE TO THE THIRD EDITION

The third edition of Fuller's *A History of Philosophy* is published primarily in the interest of a more complete and effective presentation of philosophical developments during the past half century and to permit the inclusion of historical materials commonly neglected in the study of philosophy in the universities. The first volume has been changed only by occasional minor alterations or brief additions. Revisions in the second volume have been more frequent, and this volume has been entirely reconstructed for the period from 1900 to the present. Extensive additions have been made to most of the existing material on recent schools and trends and on American Philosophy, and new chapters have been added on Latin-American Philosophy, Spanish Philosophy, Neo-Scholasticism, Logical Empiricism, and Existentialism. The bibliography, chronology, and glossary have been revised and enlarged, and reading lists added.

From his home in Mexico, Professor Fuller has graciously condoned, and perhaps thereby encouraged, my incursions into his excellent work. He has written the materials on Latin-American and Spanish philosophy, and has rewritten the section on Santayana. He has also contributed Latin-American data for the chronology and bibliography and has read parts of the revised manuscript. For all of this I am greatly indebted to him.

Several of my colleagues have commented critically on sections of the text or have otherwise made valuable suggestions: Professors W. P. Read, James L. Jarrett, Obert C. Tanner, William P. Kent, and George T. Boyd. Professor Louis C. Zucker kindly prepared the bibliography on the history of Jewish thought. Finally, I am especially indebted to my wife, Natalie McMurrin, for preparing the manuscript and assisting with the proof.

S. M. McM.

University of Utah
Salt Lake City
January 12, 1955

PREFACE TO REVISED EDITION OF
A HISTORY OF PHILOSOPHY

I have revised my *History of Philosophy* at the request of my publishers, who have made it because of the numerous criticisms and suggestions for improvement provoked by the earlier edition. These have been sent to me, anonymously, of course, to give me an idea of the faults found with the first edition, and of the ways proposed for bettering it, especially for classroom use. I expected to find them helpful in the work of revision, but this hope has been disappointed. The universal opinion that the *History* should be condensed and broken into more chapters and sections, I already shared. But when it came to specific advice regarding improvements, I found that the criticisms and suggestions largely canceled one another out, and left me still in the dark and to my own devices as to what to do.

For example, although everyone felt that the book as a whole should be made much shorter, almost everyone complained that some philosopher or philosophic movement had been slighted and wished some chapter or chapters to be lengthened. And with two exceptions, which I shall mention in a moment, there was almost complete disagreement as to what should be given more space. Again, I was taken to task, on the one hand, for including too many lesser lights, and, on the other, for not including more. In short, almost everyone was insistent that I should rob Peter to pay Paul, but none could agree as to which was which.

The quality of the various chapters proved also a bone of contention. One critic, for instance, found the chapter on Spinoza "comparatively lucid and gratifying"; another said it "is not well organized and does this thinker a disservice." Again, while one wished the chapter on Christian philosophy expanded, another found it so bad that he felt it had better be omitted altogether unless completely rewritten in the light of a sympathetic and intelligent reading of the original sources. With the exception of the dropping of the demolition bomb above-mentioned, the chapter drew no fire save for a couple of suggestions for a clearer exposition of the controversy over universals and the doctrine of substantial forms.

Enough, however, to constitute a quorum voted for a more extensive account of the Pre-Socratics and of dialectical materialism and
the Marxian theory. Indeed, one critic was so dissatisfied with my
meager coverage of the Pre-Socratics that he wondered whether it
might not be attributable to a desire on my part not to displace Vol.
I of my *History of Greek Philosophy* which deals with early Greek
thought at length. And the others, without invoking the economic
interpretation of history as a possible explanation of my shortcomings,
were equally insistent that the exposition should be lengthened. This
I have done, not only because I agreed with them that more space
should be given the period, but because I felt that the discussion of
the Pre-Socratics in the present edition, as well as in the first volume
of the *History of Greek Philosophy,* was in many respects incorrect.
I have also enlarged the exposition of dialectical materialism and the
Marxian theory. In addition I have revised and added to the discussion of Nietzsche, whom I felt I had treated inadequately. There were
also one or two suggestions that I ought to amplify the account of
personalism, particularly in its European phases. This I have done.
I have, however, held it within the restrictions imposed upon both
this and the earlier edition and mentioned no living thinkers.

Since it was obviously impossible to make the revised *History* all
things to all teachers of philosophy and to suit everybody's taste, I
decided to proceed as follows. All material errors in the old book I
would, of course, correct. Since everybody, including myself, agreed
that the *History* should be condensed and broken up into more
chapters and sections, I would, with the exceptions just noted, ignore
all appeals for lengthier exposition of this or that philosophic system
or epoch. Under no circumstances would I carry the *History* further
into the present or include any philosopher not already touched upon.
In abbreviating it I would, however, take into consideration all the
specific suggestions as to what should be shortened. Also I would even
condense some chapters certain critics wished lengthened. But that I
would do only incidentally to a final improvement of the book as a
whole. Throughout the text I would, of course, try further to ac-
centuate the clarity of my exposition as well as to improve the writing
as a whole where possible.

In reading over the data at my disposal I soon began to suspect
that what some of the critics most disliked about the book was myself.
There were complaints that I was unsympathetic, that I played favor-
ites, and above all that I betrayed the fact that I found some episodes
in the history of philosophy amusing and treated lightly and even

flippantly those that amused me. Therefore, out of deference to these critics I have tried to expurgate the text of all comments, interpretations, and opinions of my own. Particularly I have endeavored to suppress all expressions of the amusement I get from the philosophic spectacle. I have tried, in short, to go the Cheshire Cat one better and to fade from the scene without leaving so much as the trace of a smile —or a frown—behind me.

I do not, of course, claim complete success in this effort. Every philosopher has his particular bias, which cannot but distort and accent somewhat his survey and account of the history of human speculation about the nature of the Real and of man's place in and attachments to it. My bias is naturalistic—and I probably cannot prevent a certain after-image of naturalism persisting even if the smile and the frown have disappeared. I hope, however, that, all things considered, the revised edition of the *History* will be found a much improved text for classroom use.

In conclusion I wish to thank Mr. John W. Weber for his careful reading of the galley proof, and also Mr. Emerson Buchanan for his final proofreading of the page proof. I am also most grateful to Professor Hunter Mead of San Diego State College, who not only has read the galley proof and made many helpful suggestions for the improvement of the text, but has also overhauled and expanded the bibliography that appeared in the earlier edition of the *History*.

B. A. G. F.

Tasco, Gro.
Mexico,
March 15, 1945.

CONTENTS—I

CONTENTS

CONTENTS—II

CONTENTS

CONTENTS

ANCIENT AND MEDIEVAL

Chapter I

INTRODUCTION

I. WHAT IS PHILOSOPHY?

Meaning of the Term. The word "philosophy" has from the beginning been loosely used. Apparently it, or rather the word "philosopher," was coined, or at least first given publicity by the Greek philosopher Pythagoras, in the sixth century B.C., who spoke of himself as a "philosophos" or lover of wisdom. After that, we find the term and its derivatives knocking about in everyday Greek to indicate a love of thinking about things and the possession of a thoughtful and reflective attitude towards life in general. This incidentally is the popular significance of "philosopher" and "philosophy" today.

It was Plato, however, who gave a specific and technical meaning to words of this group, when he described the "philosopher" as one whose attention was fixed on reality rather than appearance and whose characteristic interest lay in grasping the essential being and nature of things. Since his time "philosophy" in its widest and broadest sense has meant *a reflective and reasoned attempt to infer the character and content of the universe, taken in its entirety and as a single whole, from an observation and study of the data presented by all its aspects.*

Inconclusiveness of the Subject. We may say at once that this attempt has never succeeded in reaching a conclusion upon which all philosophers agree. The total nature of the universe remains an unknown quantity—a mystery—and no satisfactory piecing together of even those aspects of it with which we are acquainted has ever been accomplished. There always have been, are now, and probably ever will be, a number of opposed philosophic systems in the field, each one claiming that it makes more sense than the others. We must not, however, assume from its inconclusiveness that the history of philosophy is simply an account of one vain speculation after another—between which no connection can be established and in whose sequence no progress can be discerned. For a number of reasons it does not revolve in a circle, but revolves in a spiral.

1

Nature of Philosophic Progress. In the first place, the evidence at hand upon which systems are based is always being enlarged by further exploration and more detailed analysis of every aspect of the world. The human intellect may, indeed, be no keener than it was twenty-five hundred years ago when European philosophy began in Greece. But it certainly has today not only much more material to work with than had the Greeks, but also a material that has been more thoroughly sifted and is better understood. Consequently, philosophic speculation today has at its disposal the results of a completer exploration, both telescopic and microscopic, so to speak, of every aspect of the universe, including the phenomena of human life.

Again, there has been a steady improvement in organizing philosophic procedure. Techniques have been developed and clarified. Fields of investigation have been more accurately mapped and delimited. Above all, the human mind and its powers, limitations and idiosyncrasies have been scrutinized with greater care and efficiency. Then, too, philosophy is always learning from its own accumulating history; negatively, from the pitfalls into which it has fallen and the blind alleys up which it has turned in the past; positively, from suggestions in earlier speculations that can be followed up and utilized in the development of new hypotheses. Hence it has become increasingly better equipped, not only to examine the case presented by the universe and to detect new symptoms, but also to diagnose what it finds.

Everlasting Disagreement. Future philosophers will doubtless be much more skilled in both these respects than we are. Nevertheless, it is doubtful whether their diagnosis of the situation with which they will be confronted, five or ten, or twenty thousand years hence, will be any more unanimous than ours is today. Probably philosophy must expect to the end of human time to find its doctors disagreeing. But this means that, in growing, it will never grow old, and that it will continue to exasperate, delight, and tempt the human mind as long as man exists.

II. WHY DO WE PHILOSOPHIZE?

But why should speculation about the nature of the universe perpetually fascinate us? Why should "all men naturally desire to know," as Aristotle puts it in the opening sentence of his *Metaphysics*? To attempt to answer this question, at least to the extent that we are here concerned with it, we may note that this desire is complex and has its sources in two somewhat different groups of human interests which we may call the *practical* and the *contemplative,* or we might say, the *self-centered* and the *self-transcending*. By "self" we mean here not the individual but the race. Both groups are of course *self-centered* in the sense that both have their sources in human nature, satisfy human nature, and constitute a human point of view. But, as we shall see in a moment, their objects and their satisfactions differ so much that we may contrast them. At the same time, in disentangling and contrasting them for the purpose of analysis, we must always keep in mind that in our thought and our action they are inextricably intertwined. Let us now discuss all this more in detail.

III. THE PRACTICAL INCENTIVES TO KNOWLEDGE

Human Betterment. Man, like the other animals, has to struggle for existence, and survives, like them, by both adapting himself to his environment and his environment to himself. But whereas they have a limited capacity for manipulating their surroundings to suit their special needs and desires, he has developed it so greatly that we may almost call it a distinctively human characteristic. Consequently a large part of our *practical activities* are devoted to *bettering* ourselves and our place in the world, and this not only by preserving, but by constantly expanding and enriching our life—something which the other animals seem unable to do.

Furthermore the development of man's power of imagination has enabled him to translate his natural drives and desires into fixed and detailed pictures of a world that would be congenial to them. Hence, his capacity for improving the human situation in the world, which would otherwise find only hand-to-mouth and hit-and-miss expressions, becomes guided by *definite ideals* and *fixed purposes*. These supply the motive power and the directives of the evolution of the *social, economic, and moral orders,* and of the *applied* sciences that serve them.

Natural Limitations. But this power of man to alter, improve, and enrich both his environment and himself is exercised within limitations to which his practical activities have to submit. Much of this adjustment of himself to his own fixed organic structure and to a fixed order in the external world is frictionless and satisfying. The universe brings him into being, and permits him to live, and to live happily, within the limitations it imposes upon him. It is in part friendly to him, and abounds in much that he finds beautiful and good, and it presents itself to him as an object of religious experience from communion with which he draws a profound satisfaction and peace. At the same time the universe does not seem *wholly* or even, it may be, *intentionally* friendly to him. Many of the limitations imposed upon him by his own make-up and that of external nature not only retard and often positively obstruct the realization of his ideals, but inflict pain and disaster upon him and are a constant threat to the continued existence both of the individual and the race. Hence much of man's adjustment of himself to nature, and of nature to himself, is a laborious and disagreeable process with which he is dissatisfied, against which he rebels, and which he seeks to circumvent.

Imaginary Ideal Worlds. Once more, however, imagination comes to his rescue. Although his practical activities cannot overcome and abolish the harsh limitations that distress and defeat him, his fancy can. Not only can he picture goals that his practical activities can actually achieve within the fixed frame of the apparent nature of the universe, but he can also dream of a universe remade according to the heart's desire, freed from what he finds evil, and wholly in accord and even actively sympathetic with his vision of human perfection. And in imagination he can substitute the universe he wants for the universe he has on his hands. Of this universe his art and his religion are two great prophets. Art seeks to repicture the face of things in such wise that its features are wholly beautiful. Religion in its highest reaches remolds the heart of things in forms expressive in various and widely different ways of the peace religious experience brings and of the support man finds in it for his pursuit of human good.

But man can go further than dream about the better world suggested by esthetic and moral and religious experience and depict that dream in moral vision, and art, and articulate religion. He can also attempt to *think* such a world into existence. After all, the universe as it appears, seems also to be not the whole universe, or even the real nature of as much of it as lies within his ken. May it not be, then, that if only he could *know* everything there is to know about the world, he would find that its harsh and restrictive aspects are only seeming? Might he not find that the wholly good and beautiful universe of which he dreams, responsive in all respects to moral and religious aspirations, is really the *true* universe as well?

Avoidance of Useless and Disagreeable Knowledge. Now it is under such auspices, as instruments of survival and betterment, and as means to perfecting the world and making our dreams come true, that the human need and desire to know have in large part been evolved. Therefore it is not unnatural that in everything pertaining to man we tend to ignore and even to despise knowledge that is not of practical use and *good for something,* and that cannot be immediately *applied* and *utilized* in securing and improving the human situation in the world. Nor is it unnatural that in theorizing about the true nature of the world, man should also be not only inclined to ignore and disparage any knowledge which suggests that the universe is not as he desires it to be, but inclined as well to resent and condemn such knowledge as "disillusioning" and dangerous to his happiness, and to dismiss it as short-sighted and fallacious.

IV. THE BASES OF DISINTERESTED CURIOSITY AND CONTEMPLATION

Curiosity. But this is only half the story of our natural desire to know and of our dealings with the world. The other half has to do with a human characteristic that differs widely in some respects from the interests we have just been describing. This characteristic, which man shares with many other animals and perhaps particularly with the anthropoids, is *inquisitiveness.* Man is endowed with an insatiable curiosity.

In the lower animals curiosity seems to be associated almost entirely with special interests and occasions, to explode in puffs of activity, and to come and go by fits and starts. Man, however, has developed over and above these intermittent curiosities a *sustained general curiosity,* which is excited by no particular occasion but by any and every occasion. Though a valuable instrument of survival and betterment, it is such only incidentally. It exercises itself simply for the sake of the satisfaction it gets out of just poking and prying about in the universe at large, and from just contemplating whatever it may unearth.

Satisfactions of Contemplation and Explanation. It displays and realizes itself on two levels, so to speak. In the first place, it is interested in *surveying* the content of all space and time; in watching equally what is taking place on earth and in the outer galaxies; in reconstructing the past from its findings; and perhaps in forecasting the future both of the race and of the universe. Secondly, it is insatiable in its desire to *explain* things, to co-ordinate the whole content of space and of time, so that the procession of events which constitutes the world-process shall fall into as *intelligible* a pattern as possible. In a word, if our practical and moral interests are always asking "what good is it?" our general curiosity is always asking "what is it?" "why is it?" "what makes its wheels go around?" We naturally desire not only to *better* the world from the human point of view, but to *understand* it as it is.

Were it not for this characteristic of *general curiosity,* it is doubtful whether we should wonder much about things or speculate very persistently about the nature of the Real. We should probably rather live happily by satisfactory rules of thumb learned from experience, without bothering to inquire into the *reasons* for their validity. For that matter, we should probably take no interest in *explaining* anything at all. It is interesting to note in passing that had the line of our evolution been feline rather than simian, *general curiosity* and philosophic speculation would very likely be almost non-existent. We should be purring rather than prying our way through life, making the best of the world as we found it, and letting it go at that.

General Curiosity Disinterested. Now, *general curiosity* [1] has features that are disconcerting to our special, human, moral and religious interests and to our tendencies to *think* in accordance with them. In the first place, it can be exercised without ulterior motive, and without practical goal, or moral end in view. Just the activity of exploration and explanation is enjoyable in itself, irrespective of what it discovers. Secondly, our *general curiosity* is not interested in the practical and moral bearings upon human life of its subject-matter, its investigations, and its findings. It feeds equally upon what we consider desirable and undesirable, good and evil, sin and sanctity, and finds them all equally palatable. Although its findings may prove useful in promoting the one and abolishing the other, it is not concerned with their possible uses. It is dissatisfied only when it cannot size up a situation, and it is satisfied when it feels it has sized it up. Plainly, then, in so far as we are actuated by general curiosity and nothing else, we are quite indifferent to the moral and religious results of our speculations. All that matters is that our curiosity regarding the nature of the universe should be satisfied by *making sense* of its behavior.

General Curiosity and the Pure Sciences. Just as our special, centripetal activities animate and direct our practical and moral life and the reflection of that life in religious experience and vision, so our centrifugal, roving, *general curiosity* animates and sustains what we may call the *theoretic* exercise of the intellect in a disinterested pursuit

[1] I am indebted to Lundholm for the terms *special interests* and *general curiosity* and for suggestions as to the relations between them.

of what we call *true*. Without *general curiosity* there would be no dispassionate scientific and philosophic inquiry, no *pure* science, no pursuit of learning for its own sake, no voyages of intellectual, or for that matter of geographical discovery, undertaken in the spirit and for the sake of sheer adventure. There would be no historians, no ethnologists, no archaeologists, no "ologists" at all, no higher mathematicians, no ultra-physicists, probing the constitution of the physical world, no astronomers sweeping the outer reaches of space through their telescopes—all for the joy such research brings. Nothing would be pursued beyond the point where it ceased to pay cash dividends of immediate usefulness, and there would be no enrichment of human experience over and above that which can be measured in terms of practical utility, social adaptation, moral uplift, and somewhat earth-bound spiritual consolation.

Imagination, too, could do no more than flutter and falter, if it had not general curiosity to unfold its wings, to expand its horizon and its ceiling, and to sustain it in its flights.

General Curiosity and Art. For that matter, there might be no art, for art is the re-picturing of nature in objects created for the mere satisfaction of contemplating them, or at least, in the case of objects created primarily for utilitarian purposes or for moral and social propaganda, it adds to their functional aspects a capacity for affording this satisfaction as well.[2] To be sure, esthetic and intellectual enjoyment are not identical, since our *general curiosity* may take pleasure in exploring and sizing up situations that are esthetically uninteresting or even distasteful. But art shares the indifference of our general curiosity towards the practical and moral desirability or undesirability of its subject-matter. It is concerned only with dramatic and esthetic possibilities and with their elucidation for the sole purpose of pleasurably contemplating the result; just as pure science is concerned only with the intellectual problem presented by a given situation, and with a solution with which, however much it may disappoint us morally, our curiosity with respect to that situation will be satisfied. In short, the peace that is given by the contemplation of beauty, like that which attends the contemplation of truth, is neither given nor taken away by ethical approbation or disapproval.

No other animal, so far as we know, creates objects just to look at them or listen to them—although the ants, we are told, treat some of

[2] Cf. Lundholm's interesting discussion of the relation of art to general curiosity, *The Aesthetic Sentiment,* Ch. IX.

their domesticated insects in a contemplative rather than a practical way, getting no apparent use from them save the pleasure of having them about. Indeed, if I am not mistaken, some entomologists have suggested that the ants must either keep them as pets, or venerate them much as part of mankind venerates sacred animals.

V. THE INTERWEAVING OF PRACTICAL AND CONTEMPLATIVE ACTIVITY

We must not think, however, that our disinterested curiosity about things as they are and our special human interests in having things as they are also as we want them to be, flow side by side in our minds as two separate and distinct currents. On the contrary, they are intermingled to the extent of confusion in all our behavior and all our thinking. Curiosity may be occasioned, and its indulgence may be directed, by practical and moral needs; and, even when aroused and indulged with no ulterior, practical motive, it may generate by-products that contribute greatly to practical and moral improvement of the human situation. Much of our applied science has come into existence in this way.

Action a Means to Contemplation. Conversely, our practical activities may be regarded and used as means to ensuring an opportunity for the indulgence of disinterested curiosity and contemplation. Certainly we *act,* economically, socially and morally, in part at least, for the purpose of achieving the conditions necessary to surveying and enjoying, as spectators, the panorama and the plan of all time and existence. Furthermore, practical activity may be enjoyable in itself. In that case it becomes in a way an object of contemplation, in the mere experience of which we come to rest, without seeking further justification for it—just as we do when we have satisfied our curiosity.

Thus the scientist deliberately bent on benefiting humanity satisfies incidentally his general curiosity at the same time. Or, whatever our particular "practical" job in life may be, we may love it just for itself, irrespective of what it pays us or of what service it may be to society. Indeed, if we could not suffuse our everyday work with a contemplative enjoyment of it for its own sake, purified of all pre-occupation with the service it may render practical and moral ends, it would be mere drudgery, worthless except for its results. The same suffusion keeps moral endeavor from becoming self-conscious and self-righteous. Life would indeed be a dreary and priggish affair, if everything we did had to be done consciously and deliberately from a worthy motive

and with a worthy goal in view, and never could be justifiably contemplated and enjoyed as an end in itself.

Religion, too, besides being a way of practical and moral living
directed by the ideal of the human good and aimed at its attainment,
is also contemplative, and its satisfactions are akin to those of our
general curiosity. For, in the first place, the mere presence of its vision,
like the presence of what strikes us as beautiful, and of what we
suppose to be true, brings peace and contentment, quite apart from its
possible practical applications. For that matter, just the presence of
these visions is a partial solution of the problem of life for those who
entertain them. In the second place, in so far as these visions are regarded as *explanations,* and as religion claims to be *intelligible,* they
must be satisfactions of our general curiosity as well as of our spiritual
aspirations.

Fusion in Thought of Truth and Goodness. This brings us to our
final point—that in our conscious thinking and philosophizing all the
component drives of our desire to know are so fused that we are
scarcely aware of a possible antagonism between them. Undoubtedly
we want to find *true* what we find *good* in other respects, and conversely we cannot find an interpretation of the universe wholly *good*
unless we believe it to be *true.* Indeed, minds dominated by moral
and religious insistencies go so far as to regard the satisfaction of
these demands as a positive sign of truth, and to feel that any conclusion that defeats their realization must by that very token be false.
On the other hand, a mind dominated by curiosity feels that moral
and religious ideals and concepts, however lofty, are not only untrue
but also bad religion and bad morals if they do not make sense in
its eyes. And a thinker so minded seems to accommodate without
friction his ethics and theology to whatever hypothesis seems most
plausible in the light of disinterested investigation.

Internal Unity of Philosophic Systems. In no case is there much
creaking and groaning within a philosophic system. It is generally
so completely lubricated throughout either by disinterested curiosity
or by our special interests, as the case may be, that in the mind of its
author its parts all glide into place, and fit together, and click smoothly
and noiselessly, so that either what looks good seems true, or what
seems true looks good. No thinker proclaims his philosophy to be
profoundly acceptable in the one respect, profoundly unacceptable in
the other. On the contrary, whatever his interpretation of the universe
may be, every philosopher shows every sign of getting an all-round,

even satisfaction from it as a whole, and of being quite at peace with and within himself. But he may be and often is at war with other philosophers. To this conflict we now turn.

VI. WHY PHILOSOPHERS DISAGREE

Temperamental Bias. The investigation of the desire to know has shown us that the continued accumulation, both telescopic and microscopic, of new data for the mind to reflect upon is not the only reason for the disagreements regarding the nature of the universe which have agitated philosophers since the beginning. We have now to add other reasons internal to the human intellect. Chief among these is the inevitable bias, with which thinkers of different temperaments, differently conditioned by education and environment, undertake the task of interpreting the behavior of the world. The deepest cleavage seems to be between those who are on the whole inclined to be swayed in their thinking by disinterested curiosity and those who are inclined to be governed on the whole by moral and religious motives. Indeed, as we shall see in a moment, philosophers may be roughly grouped according as they stand squarely, or at least have the balance of their weight, on the one foot or the other.

Conflicting Moral and Religious Preferences. But this is not all. The inclination to interpret the behavior of the universe in a fashion favorable to human moral and religious interests is itself torn by disagreements as to what kind of universe would be morally and religiously the most desirable sort for human beings to live in. For that matter, people are quite as much at loggerheads over what is really good and really divine as they are over what is true—witness the conflicting theories of how human life should be lived to the best advantage, the varieties of religious experience, and the different kinds of gods these varieties suggest. If, then, the universe is to be morally and divinely ordered and governed, in accordance with whose moral ideals is it to be directed, and in the image of whose religious craving is the divine to be conceived? We must therefore supplement a general bias towards interpreting the world along lines suggested either by curiosity or by our special interests, with a host of particular preferences reflecting individual variations of moral and religious aspiration.

The universe itself smiles inscrutably upon the confusion its presence inspires in the minds which are part of it. At any rate, it has dropped them no prior hint, by way of logical possibility or impossibility, as to which bias, if any, is correct. There is no *logical* reason why a universe should not completely satisfy both our general curiosity and our special interests. A universe morally and divinely ordered for the good and happiness of mankind is quite conceivable. It contains no self-contradictions and might just as well exist as not. The same is true of the innumerable universes reflecting the varieties of religious and moral preferences. There is no *logical* reason against the existence of any one of them or against its satisfying our desire to know the truth about things, unless it contains some internal absurdity.

But, on the other hand, there is no *logical* reason why a universe *should* satisfy our moral and religious aspirations—or the aspirations of one moral or religious system rather than another. A universe indifferent, or partially hostile, or even wholly antagonistic to individual or racial human preferences, is quite conceivable. It, too, contains no self-contradictions. It might just as well exist as not, and it might satisfy our general curiosity quite as completely.

The Nature of Things Inferred from Their Behavior. Deprived, then, of any hints, in the shape of *a priori* necessities of thought, as to whether and to what extent and in accordance with whose views the universe is or is not morally and divinely constructed, our minds are thrown back upon an observation of its actual behavior as the only base upon which to build and verify philosophic hypotheses. This, however, is not without its compensation, since it frees our special interests from any *logical* obstacles to having the universe as they wish it, as long as their hypotheses regarding its nature are not internally self-contradictory and therefore self-stultifying.

Again, the evidence is such as to permit at least the hope that the actual universe may be one of the many possible ones upon which the various moral and religious aspirations of different individuals and groups have set their hearts. The world, as we have already pointed out, shows us great kindness in many ways. Much of it comes ready-made in patterns that seem good and beautiful and divine to human eyes. The only difficulty, then, that stands in the way of philosophic hypotheses satisfactory alike to our general curiosity and our special interests arises over the answer to be given to the following question. We must ask ourselves whether, and to what extent, and how, the seeming indications that the universe is also in many respects *indifferent* and even *hostile* to human moral and religious aspirations can be made *intelligible* on the supposition that in reality it satisfies them. It is over this point among others that the philosophies dominated by curiosity and by our special interests part company.

Incidentally, this divergence would occur even if all human minds agreed that the behavior of the universe could be made intelligible on the supposition that it is morally and divinely ordered and governed. For in that case general curiosity would be called in to arbitrate the dispute between the adherents of different moral systems and different religious experiences and theologies, by deciding whose views were more *credible*—that is, more satisfactory to curiosity itself. And each different moral and religious point of view would *argue* that it alone satisfied general curiosity, and each would reject similar arguments on the part of the others.

Most Systems Dominated by Special Human Interests. The majority of the systems we are about to study are motivated by our special interests. They are attempts to reconcile the observed behavior of the universe and the inferences our disinterested curiosity, if left to itself, might draw from it, with the hypothesis that the world is constituted and governed, in whole, or at least in part, in accordance with those interests. They are quite frankly anthropocentric and anthropomorphic and display much energy and ingenuity in defending and justifying their point of view. The history of philosophy is in large part the chronicle of an unremitting struggle to bring within the same focus the good, the beautiful, and the true, and to contemplate them all as a single, self-consistent, all-explanatory object in which all our aspirations, including our yearning to satisfy our curiosity, find equal and complete fulfillment.

That this should be the case is not surprising. Our moral and religious preferences, like our other special interests, reflect the fundamental organic impulse of every form of life to preserve and perpetuate itself at all costs, and to behave as if it were the sole form that mattered in the universe and the only measure of good and evil. Man would not exist unless, in all his active and practical relations with the world and in the ideals generated by them, he were implacably anthropocentric and determined at all costs to have the world as *he* wishes it to be. We might expect, then, to find this determination gritting the teeth of his philosophizing as well, and spitting out as false and illusory whatever is too hard or too harsh for them to crack.

Some Systems Dominated by General Curiosity. However, in some cases the urge of general curiosity is so strong as to discount rather than reinforce the claims of the special interests, and as to permit their indulgence only within the limitations imposed upon them by its disinterested findings. So it is that there has also been a persistent philosophical minority, predisposed by temperament, education, environment, etc., to take its stand neither here nor there, but, as it were, everywhere, for viewing existence and for seeking to make out its pattern.

This minority tends to decentralize the universe in its thinking, and to find *all* aspects and events equally interesting, equally important, and equally deserving of attention, and equally valuable sources of information regarding the nature of the Real, no matter how they affect our special interests. To this minority, human life and its attachments to the universe are one phenomenon among others to be impartially studied and appraised. The place of man in the scheme of things is not to be determined by *a priori* assumptions of centrality and special importance shared with, and incidentally contested by, all other living beings. It is rather to be determined by the position that the total context of events in which man occurs, and the total behavior of the universe towards him, seem to assign him.

Starting from a point of view that discounts man's pretensions to be a center or an apex, pending at least further investigation of these claims in the light of the total situation, the minority finds unsatisfactory the arguments brought forward by the majority for exalting him to such a position. It has contended from the beginning that the behavior of the universe, dispassionately considered, will not admit of an interpretation agreeable in all respects both to our desire to know the truth and to our desire to have the truth what our special, human interests would like it to be. It charges the majority with ignoring, or suppressing, or *explaining away* instead of explaining, such evidence as does not bear out their hypotheses. In a word, it finds that these hypotheses are, in a phrase of Dr. Kallen's, "compensations in discourse for disappointments in experience," rather than intelligible *explanations* of why these disappointments occur.

Conflict between Satisfaction of Curiosity and of Special Interests. The majority retort, not unnaturally, that only the existence of what would satisfy our religious and moral needs can possibly explain them:—to which the minority replies that this is another assumption, like that of man's central position, which must be tested by taking into equal account all that makes against it as well as what makes for it, and by weighing the *pros* and the *cons* as impartially as possible. If those aspects of the universe that suggest its being morally and religiously constructed are to be taken at their face value and regarded as *prima facie* evidence of the nature of Reality, then those aspects that might seem to indicate the contrary must be given equal weight—or lack of weight—in influencing our conclusions. And, whatever our conclusions may be, we should be as ready to accept the bitter in them as we are to embrace the sweet.

This dispute, which excites deep-rooted human passions and emotions and involves man's right to extend in theory the self-importance he must practice if he is to survive and progress, naturally expresses itself in invective as well as argument. It has been especially acrimonious in modern philosophy. For only since the time of the early Christian philosophers have our special human interests insisted that both the *existence* and the *total behavior* of the *whole* universe must be *completely explained* in terms *entirely* satisfactory to them. Ancient philosophy, with the exception of the Stoics, permitted the disappointing aspects of the world to be explained by ultimate factors in the nature of things that were *really* obstructive to a complete moral, rational and divine government of the world. Consequently it found the problem of reconciling the satisfaction of our special interests with that of our general curiosity less difficult to handle. At the moment, it looks also as if the contemporary philosophies dominated by our special interests were becoming less exacting in their demands that the Real should *completely* support and satisfy our human preferences as to its nature.

Permanence of the Conflict. We may expect temperamental differences among philosophers to continue till the end to divide them along the lines we have been discussing. We may expect, also, that philosophies inspired and directed by our special interests will always be in the majority and will have the upper hand in human thinking. But we may believe that a minority of thinkers, instigated and guided by general curiosity, will also persist, and will continue to dispute the conclusions of the majority.

We must remember, too, that just as the evidence from which our conclusions are drawn is always accumulating and changing, so our special interests may also be expected to change in response to altered practical conditions—as indeed they have changed in the past. Different economic, social, moral and religious interests and preferences have come and gone, creating in their transit the ideal worlds they demanded that our curiosity should disclose and verify in the actual world of their experience. And so we may expect it to be in the future. Moreover, however they may change and whatever they may be, the special interests and preferences of different individuals and groups will go on fighting with one another and with general curiosity over the question of which is to have the say in interpreting whatever the evidence is at the moment.

VII. PHILOSOPHY AND THE SPECIAL SCIENCES

We are accustomed to think of philosophy as a kind of clearinghouse for the reports of the various sciences, whose business it is to analyze, criticize, and combine the information they turn in, smoothing out, as best it can, the contradictions in and between their conclusions, and filling in the gaps with surmises of its own as to how they hang together. For example, how are we to dovetail the description of the physical aspects of the universe given by the physical sciences, with the results of the study of its mental aspects by psychology? To answer this question is one of the major tasks of philosophy.

Origination of the Sciences by Philosophy. This may be the relation of philosophy to the sciences today. But to think that such has been the case from the beginning, and that philosophy has been developed out of the sciences, and has been built up on bases provided by them, is to reverse the original and, in a way, still essential relation between them. Man began by dealing wholesale with the world. In the beginning he faced the universe *en masse,* wondered indiscriminately about all those aspects of it that most struck him at the moment, and indulged in speculations about both its general nature and behavior, and the nature and occurrence of particular events, without separating "scientific" and "philosophical" fields and methods of investigation from one another. We shall have occasion to remark this again and again in the next few chapters.

It was only as this original, massive wonder about the world as a whole began also to be engaged by and directed upon different groups of events, that the spirit of universal inquiry subdivided into specialized investigations devoted to fields of research deliberately set off from one another. Then, one by one, the special sciences, like runners from a parent plant, slowly took root for themselves and became independent and self-supporting. Only, they have never severed their connection with their original source, but have kept sending back to feed it part of the nourishment they take from their various fields. And conversely philosophy, in its turn, still makes valuable suggestions to the special sciences.

Progressive Separation of the Sciences from Philosophy. Astronomy and medicine and logic set up for themselves at a fairly early date, whereas physics and chemistry did not take firm independent root until after the Renaissance. And it is only in our own day that psychology has ceased to be a branch of philosophy and, freed from prior metaphysical hypotheses regarding the nature of consciousness, has made a separate science of the study of that subject-matter. Research, however, into human relationships would seem to be still mixed to some extent with philosophical speculations, and to be largely at the mercy of emotion and passion and prejudice, although we have begun to speak of the social *sciences*. Ethics, for example, is particularly under the influence of metaphysical theories. But we are already talking of a *scientific* ethics, and moving towards standards and directives of conduct based upon independent investigation of the field of human behavior rather than upon philosophical and other preoccupations with it. So, too, attempts are being made to work out a science of economics and a science of sociology. It may be that in the future these infant sciences will attain to the same detached status as the physical sciences enjoy, and instead of being unduly influenced by antecedent presuppositions, will begin, not only to furnish scientific data for philosophic meditation, but also have some effect upon human conduct.

Chapter II

THE RELIGIOUS AND ETHICAL BACKGROUND OF GREEK PHILOSOPHY

I. GENERAL CHARACTER OF GREEK RELIGION

As we have seen, religious interpretations of the appearance and behavior of the universe, and reflections upon human happiness and the best way to attain it, precede, as a rule, philosophic speculation, and play an important part in molding it. Hence it will be well for us to examine briefly the characteristic Greek religious and moral atmosphere in which Western philosophy drew its first breath and uttered its first cries.

Absence of Heresy in Greek Religion. By way of introduction, we should mention the almost complete absence of *heresy* from Greek religion. This was due in part to the fact that the Greeks had no powerful and well organized and entrenched clergy, and no definitely formulated creeds. They looked to Homer or Hesiod, to be sure, for information on points of theology, but they did not regard them as divinely inspired, or consider their accounts to be last words on the subject.

Furthermore, as we shall see in a moment, the Greek gods were so conceived that philosophic speculation, unless it denied their existence, could not easily offend religious sentiment. A profession of atheism or agnosticism, or even the suspicion of worshiping other than the Olympian deities could, and for a while did, get philosophers into difficulties and even danger—particularly at Athens, which was religiously conservative. But in the Greek cities in Asia Minor, and Sicily and southern Italy, where philosophy first appeared, a considerable freedom of religious and irreligious thinking seems to have existed from the beginning.

This was of great advantage to the rapid and untrammeled development of early science and philosophy. Their growth was almost entirely unhampered by the conflict with religious sentiment and belief, and by the repressions and persecutions, that were later to im-pede their progress. Nor was Greek religion itself divided by sectarian-ism and agitated by the bickerings and hostilities of opposed groups within its fold. The variety and richness of the godhead it adored and the temples and festivals built and celebrated in honor of this multiple divinity, gave everyone a chance and left everyone free to worship pretty much as he chose, without incurring the ire of his neighbors.

General Characteristics of Greek Religion. Passing now to the gen-eral characteristics of Greek theology, we may note the following points.

1. The idea of a gradual evolution of the universe was a common-place of Hellenic religious thought. All the creation stories tell of a development by slow stages out of earlier, more chaotic conditions. The notion of a universe created out of nothing by the fiat of a divine will never occurred to the Greeks.

2. The gods were not regarded as creators of the world-process, or as directors of its course, but as products of it along with everything else. Nor were they brought into being in a completed state. They had a family tree, and rose generation by generation, as the world evolved. Even the Olympian deities, in which the divine genealogy culminated, progressed and grew wiser and better and more civilized, as the world in general became more stable and more orderly.

3. The gods were always part of a larger scheme which allotted to them their places and limited their powers. They were not regarded as omnipotent or as omniscient in the modern sense of these terms. They simply had the power and the knowledge appropriate to their superior but not totalitarian situation in the universe.

4. Hence their relation to man was not so much that of creator and father as of elder brothers. Gods and men were alike children of the same mother, sharers of the same heritage, and members of the same family, as the poet Pindar sang. But to the gods alone nature had allotted easy and everlasting life. Deathlessness and carefree living were the divine prerogatives that marked their difference from men. For man to seek to become or even to dream of becoming as one of them, was to disobey the law of the universe and was insolence of the worst sort. "Seek not to become Zeus, mortal things befit a mortal." Though, as we shall see in a moment, there were movements in Greek religion that defied this warning of Pindar's, the idea that the universe imposes upon each form of being a *moira* or plot, or lot, within which

it must remain, and with which it should be content, is dominant in both Greek religious and ethical thinking.

5. **Kinship of Man and Nature.** In a universe so conceived it was natural that there should be little distinction between the animate and the inanimate. We have been accustomed to think of a universe, composed of dead matter and inhabited by a few living beings, which has been created out of nothing to serve as staging and scenery for the all-important drama of human life. But to the Greek mind nature was living and companionable through and through. All her phenomena could be interpreted in terms of human feelings and motives, and, in her physical laws, were subjected to moral restraints akin to those laid upon human beings in their dealings with one another and with the gods. Hence man found himself on a familiar and friendly footing with the whole of nature, at home in the world, and unabashed, self-respecting, and at ease in the presence of the divine.

It is very difficult for us with our conditioning to enter into this fellow-feeling for the universe. The imaginative child perhaps still enjoys it. And it has been suggested that it was, and for that matter still is, the attitude of the Pueblo civilization of the American Southwest. "The native American," we are told, "like the Oriental," and, we should add, like the early Greeks, "viewed nature as the great source of all existence, found in contemplating its orderly processes the principle for the ordering of his life, sought in its mysterious forces not something to be captured and made to serve him, but harmonies that he might share to the profound satisfaction of his soul." [1]

6. **Greek Religion Extroverted not Introverted.** A race so happily and completely at one with the rest of nature might also be expected to look outwards rather than inwards for its religious experience. Hellenic religion was essentially extroverted. It was not preoccupied with the inner life of man, and given to introspection and searchings of the soul, and to finding God by withdrawing from the world. The Greek was comparatively selfless, absorbed in the communal life of his city and in the larger social life of the universe. He had only to go out from himself and immerse himself in the divinity of external nature, to submit himself to her order and her laws, and to live the life she had ordained for human beings, in order to find his gods waiting halfway to meet him. Indeed, his language had no equivalents for such introverted terms as "person," "personality," "individual," the "self," "selfhood," "self-consciousness," the "ego," the "I," "conscience," and

[1] Hewett, *Ancient Life in the American Southwest,* p. 61.

the like, which figure so prominently in our modern religious and philosophic vocabulary.

7. Again, the Greeks did not ascribe to human life an undue importance in the universe. Greek religion, though anthropomorphic and accenting the humanity of the gods, was not anthropocentric. Man was only an incident in the larger life of nature. Human society was only part of the great cosmic society to which men and gods alike belonged. And the ascent and redemption of man was but an episode in a cosmic progress from disorder to order, from barbarism to civilization, in which not only human beings, but all things, even the very gods, participated.

8. **The Orthodox Doctrine of Immortality.** The idea of immortality played a small and not particularly agreeable part in the orthodox Greek tradition. To be sure, it was believed that the individual survived death, but the future life was a vague and shadowy affair—a flitting, bat-like, so Homer says, down into the dark house of Hades, of a shade bereft of wits and memory and everything save a pale flicker of life. All that made a man a man and life worth living was bound up with the body. Indeed, so drab and dull was the after-life that in Homer's story of the descent of the living Odysseus into Hades, the ghost of Achilles says he had rather "live on ground as the hireling of another, with a landless man who had no great livelihood, than bear sway among all the dead that be departed." [2]

II. GENERAL CHARACTERISTICS OF THE MYSTERIES

Pre-Olympian Deities and Cults. Besides these "orthodox" aspects of Greek religion, associated with the cult of the Olympians, there were other currents entering into it, derived from a different source. The Olympian gods, like the Greeks themselves, were late-comers in Hellas. They accompanied the migrations of the invading tribes from the north who overran the country and conquered the earlier inhabitants. There they grafted themselves upon and became assimilated to the deities of the conquered race, whose religion seems to have been a primitive worship of the inexhaustible fertility of nature and of her recurrent cycles of life and death in the changing seasons. Its gods were gods who died and rose again from the dead, of whose divinity and death-defying essence their worshipers might partake by initiation and sacrament.

[2] *Odyssey,* XI, 489-491 (trans. Butcher and Lang).

The cult of these deities ran counter to the orthodox tradition, and broke down the barrier that separated the human from the divine, by enabling man to overcome death and even to become God. But in so doing it satisfied the desire for a happy immortality and the mystical yearning to unite with the godhead, for which Olympianism found little place. Moreover, whereas the orthodox tradition left man to work out his own salvation, the dying and the rising gods were saviors, who offered to those who joined in their worship divine aid in escaping from mortality and the limitations of human nature. Two of these cults were of special appeal and furnished material for two powerful and widespread religious movements which emphasized man's immortality and quasi-divine destiny.

III. THE ELEUSINIAN MYSTERIES

First, there was the story of Demeter, goddess of the crops, and her daughter Persephone. Persephone was carried off by Hades, god of the underworld, to be his bride, and the sorrowing Demeter wandered over the whole earth in search of her. Meantime all vegetation died, winter descended upon the land, and man was about to die of starvation. Then the gods decreed that Persephone should spend half the year beneath the earth with Hades and half in the world above with her mother. Each autumn she descends to Hades, leaving death and desolation behind her, each spring she rises, bringing greenery and warmth and life.

An important cult of these goddesses had established itself at Eleusis near Athens in the seventh century B.C. After Eleusis was annexed by Athens this cult became part of the Athenian state religion, and finally pan-Hellenic in its scope. Its power lay in the promise of a happy immortality, far away in the Islands of the Blest, which it held out to its adherents and to its adherents alone. Outsiders were excluded from salvation. Joining it involved long and solemn rites of initiation, culminating in a celebration of "Mysteries," whose secret had to be kept by the communicants under pain of death. Still, something of their nature has leaked out, and it would appear that they centered about some sort of re-enactment of the descent into Hades and the resurrection of Persephone, either by the neophyte himself or in his presence. The impressiveness, the secrecy, the sense of brotherhood and of enjoyment of special privileges, and the assurance of a blessed immortality denied to non-communicants, gave to the Eleusinian Mysteries an immense popularity and prestige throughout the Greek world.

IV. THE ORPHIC MYSTERIES

Their Origin. This cult, however, did not so immediately and profoundly affect philosophical speculation, as did the story of the god Dionysus elaborated in the Orphic Mysteries. Originally a Thracian deity of vegetation, and particularly of the vine and wine, and of the sense of liberation from human bondage and of access to divinity that intoxication bestows, he was worshiped in the beginning by orgiastic rites of frenzied dancing and drunkenness. Probably in the beginning his priest, in whom he was supposed to be incarnate, was sacrificed and eaten by his worshipers, who thus partook of the *mana* or strength of their god. But before the cult entered Greece, the sacrifice of the priest had given way to that of a sacred animal, the wild bull, which now became the vehicle for communicating the divine substance of the god to his devotees.

Theology and Ritual. Brought down into Greece from the north, his cult became more civilized, and developed a complicated theology. First begotten by Zeus from a divine mother, Persephone, he was slain in the form of a wild bull by the evil Titans, and was torn to pieces and devoured by them. But his heart was saved. This Zeus ate, and begot him a second time from a human mother, Semele. She, demanding to see her divine lover face to face, was consumed by a thunderbolt. Her unborn child was preserved and placed in the thigh of Zeus from which in the fullness of time it was brought forth and made Lord of the world. The Titans, also, Zeus slew with a thunderbolt, and formed man from their ashes. Hence man is a dual creature, a mixture of the evil substance of the Titans and of the divine substance of the god they had devoured. His soul or mind is a fragment of Dionysus, his body a heritage from the Titans. Salvation consists in freeing the divine within us from the bondage of the body. This can only be accomplished by a long series of reincarnations, at the end of which, if she has sufficiently purified herself, the soul may escape from the wheel of birth and rebirth and be reunited with her divine source.

This purification, however, could only be effected by joining the Orphic cult, assisting at its Mysteries, and following its rule of life. The exact nature of the Mysteries it is difficult to make out, but they seem, like the Eleusinian, to have centered about a dramatic representation of the death of their god and his restoration to life, and to have assigned a great importance to the "omophagia" or partaking of the flesh and blood of the sacred bull. Also, a theoretically ascetic regime

was prescribed, which, however, amounted to little more than absten-
tion from animal food and the observance of certain technicalities of
purification.

Influence. The Orphic Mysteries, though never incorporated in the
state religion, and always looked at somewhat askance as eccentric
and perfervid, enjoyed a great vogue. As we shall presently see, they
influenced the Pythagoreans, probably Socrates, Plato, and the later
mystical Neo-Platonic and Neo-Pythagorean movements. Also, they
contained certain ideas that were given new focus and form by the
later mystery religions and Christianity.

V. THE MORAL BACKGROUND

Contrast of Greek with Christian Ethics. A final point remains—
the background of moral tradition and attitude from which Greek
ethical speculation emerged. Our modern ethical systems, however
independent and strictly scientific they may have wished to be, have
developed willy-nilly in the shadow of Christianity, with its spirit of
introspection, its preoccupation with the inner life, and its propensity
to a dualistic contrast of the spirit with the flesh. We hear a great deal
of the will, of conscience, and duty, of sin, the conviction of sin, of
this life as merely a preparation for a life to come, and as therefore
without final value and justification in itself. Sin is regarded as essentially an alienation of the human will from the divine, and its consequences and punishments in this world are held to be of little importance in comparison with its "spiritual" results.

Moreover, sin has nothing in common with virtue. The motives
that provoke it spring from entirely different sources, and move us in
diametrically opposed directions. The moral life is a life of conflict
between an essentially "higher" and an essentially "lower" nature.
For our guidance in this conflict we are bidden not so much to use
our reason as to be on the alert for the whispering of some "still small
voice" within us whose utterances acquaint us directly with the difference between right and wrong.

Naturalism of Greek Ethics. Except in the attenuated form in which
it appeared in the Orphic Mysteries, this way of looking at life is absent from early Greek religious and moral meditation. To the Hellenic
mind man was primarily a natural fact, allotted, along with all other
facts, his specific nature and place in the universe, and enabled by
the world-process which had produced him to live happily and completely within the bounds imposed by that place and nature. Super-

natural sanctions and a supernatural destiny were not necessary to right living and well-being. Nor, on the other hand, was there any conflict between an essentially lower and an essentially higher nature to oppose a fundamental obstacle to self-fulfillment and happiness. Man had a single though composite character. Nothing with which nature had endowed him was alien to his best interests or a stumbling block to his perfection. His good lay in as complete and as generous as possible an adjustment of the claims of all his various instincts and desires and interests. All were entitled to contribute their due part to his happiness and to receive their due share in it.

Some conflict, of course, there had to be since the various impulses got in one another's way and could not be all satisfied together. Moreover any one interest might seek more than was its due, or even might efface itself overmuch and not demand enough. But this conflict did not array one set of impulses against another. The same activities figured in both rightdoing and wrongdoing. The difference between virtue and vice was not one of kind but simply of degree and direction. Any activity kept within bounds was good. But the moment it got out of hand and tried to usurp a larger share of the individual life than was befitting it was evil.

Greek Rationalism. The adjustment of all these different amounts of activity so as to yield a balanced, harmonious, and happy life, demanded the exercise of intelligence and reason. The moral problem was an intellectual problem.—the problem of determining in the first place how much space and scope it was suitable for each interest to have, and then of devising the rules for keeping each within its proper limits. Since man was a social animal, this problem could not be solved apart from social considerations. Individual self-realization must be attained in such a way, and subject to such restrictions, that it harmonized with the general life of the community. The exercise of virtue lay in working out your life within the confines laid upon it by nature and society. The fundamental vice, on the other hand, was "insolence," which consisted in climbing over the fence and trespassing upon other people's lots.

From this point of view, sin was not primarily an aberration of the will but an error of intellectual judgment. The Greek word for it was drawn from athletics, and meant "to miss the mark." The sinner was a poor shot when it came to hitting the bull's-eye of a well-balanced and harmonious life. He had a bad eye which failed to distinguish the limitations laid upon him by society and nature. Hence his actions went wild and either overshot or fell short of the mark of virtuous behavior. Unless his mental eye was corrected by retribution its defective vision would grow on him and become a vicious habit. But once corrected, his vision was as good as ever. No scar or taint remained upon it that could only be removed by divine grace. Sin, then, was to the Greek a functional, not an organic disorder. It could be avoided to a large extent by the use of ordinary intelligence, which was quite sufficient to keep a man reasonably straight. And human society was competent, without divine aid, to effect a cure by punitive and compensatory methods. All in all, we have in this objective and "healthy-minded" moral attitude the ethical partner of the extroverted, outward-looking character of Greek religious experience. Naturally, growing as it does out of a background so different from ours, Greek ethics will impress us in many respects as quite unlike some of our modern systems.

But, after all, we have told only part of the story, though perhaps the larger part. The Orphic Mysteries with their dualism of soul and body, their belief in reincarnation, and their hope of an ultimate escape of the spirit from the bondage, as they considered it, of the flesh, fostered a moral point of view more in line with ours. This point of view is reflected to some extent in Plato's ethics, and plays an important part in the rebellion against the world and the flesh that we find in the later mystical systems. Still, it is under the influence of the tradition of the good life as a harmonious development of all the faculties and exercise of all the functions with which nature has endowed man, that Greek ethics made its great contribution to moral theory.

Chapter III

THE MILESIAN SCHOOL

I. BACKGROUND

Life at Miletus. At Miletus at the beginning of the sixth century B.C. the native brilliance, broad-mindedness, and insatiable intellectual curiosity of the Ionian Greeks conspired with time and place to produce the first European philosophy. Miletus was long established, large, and powerful. Her great sea-borne trade and her commerce with the Asiatic hinterland had given her the wealth and the resultant leisure which, as Aristotle pointed out, is a prerequisite of philosophy and, we might add, of civilization in general. And it had also made her metropolitan and cosmopolitan, a city of the world, traveled, sophisticated, at ease in the presence of new ideals and ideas. Then, too, the age was one of unrest—political and social, moral, religious, and intellectual. Old orders were being overturned, old traditions challenged. Revolutions were in the air. Kingship and aristocracy were being supplanted, amid much disorder, by cycles of oligarchy, democracy, and tyranny.

Under the protection and patronage of the new despots who were coming to the front the artistic and scientific genius that lay smoldering in the race burst into full flame. Architecture, sculpture, and poetry took on new forms and were put to fresh uses. Alcaeus and Sappho loved and sang at the brilliant court of Lesbos, and Solon and Theognis in their poetry voiced the intellectual skepticism and unrest of the age by attacking the very gods and calling them to account for their misgovernment of the world. In short, man was awakening to new possibilities both in himself and outer nature, and was reaching out to realize them, groping and experimenting, exploiting and reforming, discovering beauty and enlightenment, and creating art and science for their service. Human life had come to one of its sudden flowerings, and had borne once and for all the marvelous fruit of Greek civilization.

Into, or out of, such a city and such times Greek philosophy was born in the last half of the seventh century B.C. in a group of thinkers known as the Milesian School.

II. GENERAL CHARACTERISTICS OF THE MILESIAN SCHOOL

Difficulty of Reconstructing the Milesians' Teaching. Reconstruction of the Milesians' teaching is difficult. We have only disconnected fragments of their sayings for the most part, and are forced to rely to a great extent upon the reports and criticisms of their systems by later ancient thinkers. These accounts frequently exhibit the tendency of most philosophers to seek and to see prophets and forerunners of their own ideas in the doctrines of their predecessors. Hence they have always to be distilled as clear as possible of the proverbial grain of salt before they can be trusted.

But in trying to organize the original fragments and to strain from later accounts what has been read into the earlier systems, we have also to discount our own prejudices and ways of thinking. To judge correctly the Milesian School we should have to throw ourselves back into their world, to perceive it as they perceived it, and to feel about it as they felt about it. This is almost impossible for us to do. We may indeed note their differences from ourselves, but to note them is not to feel and perceive as the Milesians did.

Milesian Reliance on the Senses. We have already indicated their moral and religious background. We have now to add a word about the data at their command, from which their theories had to be inferred. We must remember that they faced the world with a naked and an innocent eye. They perceived only what their unaided senses permitted them to perceive. They lacked entirely those devices for sharpening our powers of perception which have enabled us to see far into space and into past and future time, and more and more deeply into the inner structures and workings of physical and mental events. Hence in their philosophic interpretation of the sum and substance of all things and of the general behavior of the universe they naturally used the stuffs, and the qualities, and the processes with which their physical sense-organs acquainted them. These, moreover, they seem to have accepted quite naïvely at their face value, and probably knew nothing of the more sophisticated and esoteric meanings sometimes read into their stock-in-trade by later commentators. They meant what they said, and what they said expressed the spirit and the knowledge of their own times.

Basic Problems. Before taking up the individual thinking of the School, let us review briefly some of its general characteristics. It is all the more interesting to do this, since the Milesians were immediately

confronted by two of the fundamental questions that beset all philosophers, and dealt with them in some ways after a fashion that has
never become outmoded.

1. The two basic problems which they recognized and sought to
solve were (a) What is the real nature of the universe like? and (b)
How is the universe as we perceive it generated by the universe as it
actually is? The asking of these questions presupposes a suspicion that
the universe is not altogether what it seems to be, and a consequent
recognition of a difference and even an opposition between *appearance*
and *reality*. But this distinction did not mean to them an opposition of
illusion or *sense deception* to *fact* and *truth*. The sensible world was
to them just as real and truly existent as that of which it was composed. The suspicion that the apparent world deceives us as to its
true nature was indeed soon to occur, but it is absent from Milesian
thought. Indeed, because of the innocence of their senses the Milesians
had to conceive reality in terms of appearance, and the problem of
discovering what it was like was the problem of finding some one
perceptible substance or quality, or mixture of such substances and
qualities, to which the sensible world might be reduced and from
which it could conceivably be derived.

The solution of this problem went hand in hand with finding some
observed process of generation in nature in terms of which the production of the rest of the world from the world-principle might be
most easily conceived.

2. **Religious Terminology.** It has been pointed out as most interesting and noteworthy that in dealing with these problems the Milesians
discarded entirely the current theology and the current theological
explanation of the generation of the world.[1] They seem indeed scarcely
to have heard of the gods. They almost never mention them, and never
introduce them as explanatory principles. They speak, however, frequently of God and the divine, which they identify with the universe
as a whole. This was quite in keeping with the tendency that we have
already noted of the Greeks to think of the world as animate through
and through, but it is an evidence of Greek broadmindedness and
an example of the absence of "heresy" that the Milesians could so
completely ignore the theology of the day in their systems.

From the Milesian, and for that matter from the whole Pre-Socratic
use of the terms "God," "divine," "divinity," and the like, we must,
however, exclude a large part of the significance they have come to

[1] Cf. Heinrich Gomperz, *Problems and Methods of Early Greek Science*, to
which I am much indebted for my discussion of the Milesians.

have for us. We have become so accustomed to a personal God, that for us their first association is that of a personal being. It is highly improbable that they had any such association for the Pre-Socratics. Personality, as we have already seen, does not appear to have had any very great interest for the early Greeks. Certainly it was not a philosophic concept, and presented no philosophic problem. The "divinity" of the universe, like that of the gods, lay rather for the Milesians and other Pre-Socratics, in its exemption from human limitations—in its immortality, its agelessness, its fullness and ease of life, and in its possession and exercise of power. These were awesome and majestic things to be reverenced and worshiped wherever they were made manifest. Whatever exhibited them was divine.

3. **The Soul.** We must make similar reservations with regard to the Milesian use of the word "soul." Here again we have a term whose first connotation for us is that of a self-conscious, personal entity that perceives and feels and thinks and possesses moral character. The Milesians, however, seem to have used the word much as Homer did. It meant to them little more than the *animate* character of a thing. Anything that *lived* had a *soul,* but not necessarily a mind or a personality. This principle of animation was *deathless* and survived the extinction of the individual thing to which it had given life, but its survival did not involve what we today call personal immortality.

4. **Use of Analogies.** In their solutions of the problems we have just mentioned, the Milesians resorted to analogies drawn from experience. In so doing they were merely setting the pace for subsequent philosophy. Almost all systems have an analogy at their core. We say that the universe behaves as if it were a machine, or an organism, or a work of art. Modern idealism, indeed, has added the analogy of a personal career and tells us that the universe behaves as if it were a cosmic individual living out his life and fulfilling his possibilities. And the Greeks humanized the organic analogy—by thinking of the universe as a political organization modeled after their city states.

All these analogies—except of course that of a personal career—were used by the Milesians. But whereas we commonly use one and the same analogy and seek to reduce everything in the universe to terms of it, the Milesians used a number of analogies in dealing with different groups of phenomena, and did so frequently, as we shall see, in an inconsistent manner and with confusing results. For example, the organic, political and "plan" analogies were employed in interpreting the general structure and operations of the universe, but when it came to particular processes and phenomena, the mechanical analogy was applied and the cause of the occurrence was sought simply in antecedent natural events.

"Acts of God" Explained Mechanically. This curiously enough was the case where we should least expect it to be so, as in the explanation of portentous, unusual and catastrophic phenomena. We still traditionally call such events "acts of God," and many people still believe that they are the results of divine intervention—just as the Greeks were wont to attribute them directly to the thunderbolt of Zeus, the trident of Poseidon, the forge of Hephaestus, or the loosing of the captive winds of Aeolus. Here, then, we might expect to find the Milesians appealing at least to the quasi-moral and social considerations of balance and harmony and justice by which the world as a whole was supposed to be steered and by which its basic processes, like the movements of the heavenly bodies and the alternation of generation and decay, were supposed to be directed. But although the universe in general may behave as it does because such behavior is meet, right, fitting and logical, we hear next to nothing of propriety, moral, legal or logical, as a reason for the occurrence of extraordinary phenomena. Earthquakes, tempests, eclipses, and other extraordinary events, like the usual ones, are regarded as caused mechanically by prior natural phenomena.

5. Generalizations founded upon this mechanical linkage and sequence of particular events, became incipient *laws of nature,* as distinguished from *philosophical hypotheses*. And these were inferred from a wide range of data, which later were divided up among the various sciences. To put it in modern terms, the Milesians were greatly interested not only in philosophy, but in geometry, astronomy, meteorology, physics, biology and psychology, and in problems we now regard as belonging to the theory of knowledge. Many of their theories in these fields we should now regard as crude and wild, but some of them are prophetic of later scientific developments.

6. Mechanical analogies were also used, not only by the Milesians but by the Pre-Socratic philosophers generally, to show how the universe was built up out of its constituent principle or principles. Two analogies in particular were employed, (a) that of the condensation and rarefaction of a definite substance, and (b) that of a turgid and nondescript mixture separating itself into distinct elements and qualities frequently conceived as emerging in pairs of opposites. The analogy of rarefaction and condensation was prophetic. It contained the seed of the theory that all qualitative variety can be expressed in terms of purely quantitative difference, and that all change can be

expressed in terms of movement in space—a theory that in the next century came to full flower in the teaching of Leucippus and Democritus and has since borne continual fruit as a basic concept of modern science.

7. Hylozoism. By Aristotle the Milesians, and for that matter the other Pre-Socratics as well, were called *physicists* and *physiologists,* not however in the specialized, modern sense of the words, but because of their preoccupation with the *physis* or nature and source of things in general. They are nowadays also called *hylozoists,* because of their view that the universe was as essentially animate as it was material. The term is derived from the Greek word for stuff (*hylé*) and life (*zoé*) and was apparently coined by the British philosopher Cudworth in the seventeenth century to describe early Greek philosophy. It is still used of theories that regard the physical universe as animate and organic.

8. Milesian Philosophy Motivated by General Curiosity. We today, reflecting upon the Milesians and, for that matter, the other Pre-Socratics in the light of our earlier discussion of the motivations of philosophy, can safely say, I think, that they were actuated by a general, disinterested curiosity regarding the nature of the universe rather than by any special moral interest in showing it to be congenial with and congealed about prior human preferences as to its make-up. Their primary interest was, as Aristotle said, in *physis*—in the sum and substance and general lay-out and behavior-pattern of all things—of which man was but one. They were not anthropocentric; nor were they anthropomorphic except perhaps in their extension of the social analogy of propriety and equity to the behavior of the universe. But this cosmic "justice" that held all things within their proper bounds and would redress any wrong done it by any overstepping of these bounds on the part of anything, was as dehumanized as human justice is, or tries to be, impersonal in its dealings with human individuals. Furthermore, as we have already noted, and shall soon have occasion to observe in detail, the Pre-Socratics either simply ignore or actively criticize personal gods created in man's image and apply the term "divine" without personal connotations to the stuff of which all things equally are made and to a world-structure that has no particular apex.

III. THALES

Thales was the founder of the Milesian School and the father of Western philosophy. Born at Miletus in the last half of the seventh century B.C., he was a statesman of great wisdom and vision, a successful businessman who is said to have established a monopoly in olive oil, and a mathematician and astronomer of note in his day— as well as the first European philosopher. Indeed his attainments won him a place among the famed Seven Sages of Greece.

The World-Stuff is Water. Our knowledge of his philosophic and scientific speculations is scanty. We have no direct quotations from him, and do not even know whether he ever wrote down his opinions. Aristotle, however, reports that Thales believed *water* to be the stuff of which all things are made, that he taught that the earth floats on water, and that he said that all things are full of gods, and that the power of the lodestone to move iron shows that it must have a soul— or in other words that it is a living thing.

How he came to the conclusion that *water,* rather than some other substance, is the world-stuff we do not know. Neither do we know how he conceived the derivation of other substances and things from *water,* although the analogy of rarefaction and condensation might well have suggested itself to him. Water could be seen apparently transforming itself into vapor, and even, in the phenomenon of "the sun drawing water," into fire. Then, too, the process of evaporation was reversed in falling rain, and fire and air might seem to be returning to water. Again, it froze solid before one's eyes, and it was thought to turn to earth in the silt it deposited at the mouth of the Nile and of other rivers. So, too, people believed that the springs that bubbled up and the mists that rose from the ground were earth becoming water again. The existence of water beneath the earth, as evidenced by springs, might also have suggested the opinion that the earth floats on water. Then, too, there were theological creation-stories that the ocean was the source from which the world arose. Water, moreover, was the giver of life to all animate things. Animals and vegetables alike depended on it. The seed of all animals was wet.

But these are only conjectures of later commentators.

The World-Stuff Divine. The remarks that all things are full of gods, and that magnetism is evidence of life in the objects that possess it are probably no more than expressions of Thales' "hylozoism." It goes without saying that for him, as for the whole Milesian School, the world-stuff, whatever it was, was as profoundly moving, changing, living, and perhaps thinking, as it was material and tangible. Later philosophers, to be sure, tried to read into Thales a belief in a world-soul, or even in a divine mind—but this attempt throws light upon their opinions rather than upon his.

Scientific Achievements. Thales is credited with having introduced geometry from Egypt, speculated about the causes of the seasonal rise and fall of the Nile, and predicted an eclipse of the sun that according to the calculation of modern astronomers took place in May, 585 B.C. He is also said to have been an inventor and engineer and a city-planner, to have applied the geometry he learned in Egypt or elsewhere to the measurement of the height of buildings and the calculation of the distances of ships at sea, and to have taught sailors how to navigate by observations of the constellation of the Big Bear. The eclipse he may very well have predicted, for the Babylonians had already noted the intervals separating eclipses both of the sun and the moon, and were therefore able to predict roughly the times at which they were likely to occur, though not their path. Very likely, then, he knew that an eclipse was due, and was lucky in that it was actually visible in Miletus.

IV. ANAXIMANDER

The World-Stuff Is an Indefinite Something. Of the teaching of Thales' pupil, Anaximander, who flourished in Miletus about 546 B.C. we have more information. The world-stuff he described as an Indefinite Something, from which pairs of opposites like hot and cold, wet and dry, were continually being separated out, and into which they were continually relapsing. Just how Anaximander conceived this world-stuff we do not know. But since those of his successors who used his analogy of separation to describe the generation of the universe from it, regarded it as a confused mixture of elements and qualities, it is not unlikely that he thought of the Indefinite Something, not as homogeneous, but as a heterogeneous mass.

This mass he apparently conceived as infinite in space and time, as full of gods, whom he may have identified with the stars, and as perhaps encompassing a plurality of co-existent worlds coming into and passing out of being. He appears, in that case, to have broken away from the popular notion of the heavens as an enclosing vault within which the whole universe was compressed, and to have envisaged in his way our modern view of a space indefinitely sprinkled with galaxies which in their turn are filled with suns and solar systems, of which ours is one.

Plurality of Worlds. This doctrine of a plurality of worlds coming into and passing out of being throughout all space is, if it can be attributed to Anaximander, evidence of a daring and adventurous imagination. Though the solar system remained geocentric, it and with it the earth were detached from a central position in the universe and became incidental to a grander cosmology. All this is largely conjecture, and in any case Anaximander's interest was mainly in the geocentric world in which we live. The theory, however, proved to be but a flash in the pan. It was, to be sure, revived by Leucippus and Democritus. But the earth was made again the center of the whole universe, and the heavens were contracted once more to an enclosing vault, by Plato and Aristotle, whose opinions were followed by the Scholastics, and prevailed till the new astronomy of the Renaissance recaptured Anaximander's vision of an infinite space in which a plurality of systems was dispersed.

The process of separation from and relapse into the Indefinite Something, although described after the mechanical analogy, is also explained in terms of social and ethical propriety and fitness. The separated opposites conflict with and reciprocally destroy one another eventually "as is ordained; for they give satisfaction and reparation to one another for their injustice according to the ordering of time." [2] There has been conjecture as to whether Anaximander meant this to be taken literally, and as to what he meant by it if he did. But at least he seems to have felt that any cessation of the alternation of opposites and final victory of one over the other would have disturbed a certain fitness and fair apportionment of things and upset the balance of the world-process, which ordains for each member of the pair its turn at existing.

Cosmology. Anaximander gives us quite a detailed account of how a world is formed within the Indefinite Something. In the beginning "something capable of begetting hot and cold was separated off," and began to revolve, like an eddy or vortex. The flaming heat swirled around and enclosed the cold and moist, which became differentiated into earth, water, and air, and formed a cylinder in which the one was superimposed upon the other. The earth itself is shaped like a drum and is suspended in the Indefinite at the center of the vortex and was probably conceived as sharing in its rotation.

Astronomy. The air, expanding under the influence of the surrounding fire, disrupts it and breaks it into revolving wheels. These wheels of flame, however, are obscured by the air which envelops them, except for "breathing-places—certain pipe-like passages at which the heavenly bodies show themselves. That is why, when the breathing holes are stopped, eclipses take place. And the moon appears now to

---

[2] Trans. Burnet, *Early Greek Philosophy,* 3rd ed., p. 52, from which almost all the translations of the fragments of the Pre-Socratics are taken.

wax and now to wane, because of the stopping and opening of these passages. . . . The sun is the highest of all, and lowest are the wheels of the stars." These "hoop-like compressions of air, full of fire, breathing out flames at a certain point through orifices" [3] revolve about the earth in such wise that these orifices are carried beneath it—hence the rising and the setting of the sun and moon, the planets and the constellations of the stars. Thunder and lightning also are due to the violent and sudden rending of the envelope of air and the flaming out through the rents of the enclosed flame.

Anaximander also speculated about the comparative sizes of the solar and lunar wheels with respect to the size of the earth. His views were somewhat numerological in character, and were probably influenced by the view that some numbers—especially the multiples of three—were sacred.

Biology. On our earth, we are told, "Living creatures arose from the moist element, as it was evaporated by the sun." They were "enclosed in prickly bark. As they advanced in age they came out upon the drier part. When the bark broke off they survived for a short time."

As for man, he "was like another animal, namely a fish in the beginning. . . . He was born from animals of another species. The reason for this is that while other animals quickly find food for themselves, man alone requires a lengthy period of suckling. Hence, had he been originally as he is now, he would never have survived." More specifically, "at first human beings arose in the inside of fishes, and after having been reared like sharks" (whose gestation somewhat resembles that of mammals) "and become capable of protecting themselves, they were finally cast ashore and took to land." [4]

V. ANAXIMENES

The World-Stuff Is Vapor or Air. Anaximander's successor, Anaximenes, who taught at Miletus during the last half of the sixth century B.C., reverted towards the teaching of Thales, in that he chose a particular and homogeneous element for his world-stuff. This element is *Breath,* a concept which includes both air and vapor. "From it, he said, the things that are, and have been, and shall be, the gods and things divine took their rise, while other things come from its offspring." [5] *Air-vapor,* like water, could be observed, it might seem, assuming liquid and then solid form, and according to the teaching

[3] Trans. Burnet, *op. cit.,* pp. 66-67.   [5] Trans. Burnet, p. 73.
[4] Trans. Burnet, pp. 70-71.

of Anaximander was half-way between the dry and the hot on the one hand and the moist and the cold on the other. Moreover, all animate things were dependent on it for life, and Anaximenes extended this dependence to the whole universe. "First . . . as our soul, being air, holds us together, so do breath and air encompass the whole world." [6] Air, then, was a suitable candidate for the world-principle.

Cosmology. The "offspring" of the divine Air, which in their turn produce the rest of the universe, are generated by condensation and rarefaction—a view that, as we have already pointed out, may have been held also by Thales, and that was prophetic of modern scientific theory. When Air "is dilated so as to become rarefied, it becomes fire; while winds on the other hand are condensed Air, Cloud is formed from Air by felting [an analogy drawn from making wool into cloth], and this still further condensed becomes water. Water condensed still more turns to earth, and when condensed as much as it can be, to stones." [7]

Our world is produced as follows. "As air was felted, the earth first came into being. It is very broad and is accordingly supported by the air . . . and is shaped like a table. . . . The heavenly bodies were produced from the earth by the moisture rising from it. When this is rarefied fire comes into being, and the stars are composed of the fire thus raised aloft" and are broad, fiery leaves, as it were. There are also bodies of earthy substance in the region of the stars, revolving along with them. "However, the heavenly bodies do not move under the earth," as Anaximander had maintained, "but round it, as a cap turns round our head. The sun is hidden from sight, not because it goes under the earth, but because it is concealed by the higher parts of the earth, and because its distance from us becomes greater."

Lightning, hail, snow, the rainbow and earthquakes were also treated by Anaximenes. Lightning is due to sudden rarefactions of Air. "Hail is produced when water freezes in falling, snow when there is some air imprisoned in the water. The rainbow is produced when the beams of the sun fall on thick, condensed Air (Vapor). . . . The cause of earthquakes was the dryness and moisture of the earth, occasioned by droughts and heavy rains respectively." [8] It is interesting to note that Anaximenes could ignore with impunity the theological teaching of his day that the thunderbolt is cast by the hand of Zeus, that the rainbow (Iris) is a goddess, and that earthquakes are expressions of the divine wrath of Poseidon.

[6] Trans. Burnet, p. 73.
[7] Trans. Burnet, *op. cit.*, p. 76.
[8] Trans. Burnet, *op. cit.*, p. 76.

Prestige of His Teaching. It is a pity that we have not more knowledge of Anaximenes. His teaching seems tame and provincial in comparison with the bold and truly cosmic flight of Anaximander's imagination, which broke through the "flaming ramparts" of our world into illimitable space, and peopled it with systems like our own. Yet he enjoyed far greater prestige with the philosophers of antiquity, and exerted far more influence.

His doctrine had, to be sure, two advantages over that of Anaximander. His reversion to a simple, homogeneous, determinate world-principle was more in line with the tendency of the human mind to seek a single explanation of the multiplicity of the universe, than was Anaximander's doctrine of an indeterminate and somewhat cloudy world-stuff. And his analogy of condensation and rarefaction showed how one simple and homogeneous substance might conceivably give rise to a plurality and variety of other substances, and was generally a clearer and neater way of deriving the universe from the world-principle than the analogy of a "separating out" of a medley of constituents that lay fused and confused within it. However that may be, Anaximenes' system was regarded as the "last word," figuratively as well as literally, of the Milesian School, and it is he who was invoked as the great exponent of the early Ionian philosophy.

VI. XENOPHANES

Life and Character. In 494 B.C. Miletus was conquered by the Persians. Anaximenes was probably dead by this time. At any rate, we hear no more of a Milesian School. Ionia, however, had still two more thinkers to contribute to the history of philosophy, Xenophanes and Heraclitus. As Xenophanes is said to have been a pupil of Anaximander, and shows signs of having been influenced by him, as well as by the general outlook of the School, we may well deal with him at this point.

He was born at Colophon near Ephesus, probably about the middle of the sixth century B.C., but spent much of his life in Sicily. He lived, it is said, to be ninety-two years old. At that time there was considerable reaction against the over-civilization and luxury of the age, as well as a religious revival, and Xenophanes is best understood in the light of these movements. He was essentially a reformer, and we find him inveighing against all sorts of things—against the cult of the athletic hero and of brawn instead of brains, against over-dressing and over-perfuming, and getting drunk at dinner parties, and indulging in empty conversation. Besides being a reformer he was a poet, and vented his criticisms in the form of satirical elegies in which it is sometimes difficult to distinguish satire and poetic license from plain statement.

Attack on Orthodox Theology. The revived interest in religion, however, did not bring Xenophanes into the orthodox fold or the mystery cults. On the contrary, it inspired a thorough and unsparing assault on contemporary theology, upon which his fame is chiefly based.

"Homer and Hesiod," he tells us, "have ascribed to the gods all things that are a shame and a disgrace among mortals, stealings, and adulteries, and deceivings of one another. . .

"But mortals deem that the gods are begotten as they are, and have clothes like theirs, and voice and form.

"Yes, and if oxen or lions had hands and could paint with their hands, and produce works of art as men do, horses would paint the forms of the gods like horses, and oxen like oxen, and make their bodies in the image of their several kinds.

"The Ethiopians make their gods black and snub-nosed; the Thracians say theirs have blue eyes and red hair. . . .

"There never was, nor will be a man who has certain knowledge about the gods and about all the things I speak of. But all may have their fancy.

"Let these be taken as fancies something like the truth."

There is "one god, the greatest among gods and men, neither in form like unto mortals nor in thought.

"He sees all over, thinks all over, and hears all over.

"But without toil he swayeth all things by the thought of his mind.

"And he abideth ever in the self-same place, moving not at all; nor doth it befit him to go about now hither now thither." [9]

This attack on the current theology based upon Homer and Hesiod, which was later to be repeated by Plato, and the substitute for it proposed by Xenophanes, suggest to us, with our religious background, an abandonment of polytheism for monotheism. It certainly discarded polytheism, but if taken, as it probably should be, in connection with the philosophy of Xenophanes' times rather than with the thought of our own, it is at least doubtful whether it indicates a belief in monotheism, as we understand the word. It looks more like a restate-

[9] Burnet, *op. cit.,* pp. 119-121.

ment in more detailed terms and theological phraseology of the "hylozoism" of the Milesian School. The "one god" was, many scholars think, identified with the universe, and the seeing, thinking, and hearing all over, and "the swaying of all things by the thought of his mind" were very likely little more than a re-affirmation of the active, living character of the Milesian world-stuff, and of the organic and social analogies which the earlier philosophers had invoked in describing the behavior of the *physis,* or nature, of all things.

Cosmology. We have also some reputed speculations of Xenophanes regarding the nature of the world-stuff and the generation of the universe. "All things come from earth and in earth all things end . . . all things are earth and water that come into being and grow . . . for we are all born of earth and water." Earth is "being gradually dissolved by the moisture." Marine life arose when all things were mud, as is attested by the imprints of seaweed and fishes found in rock. "All human beings are destroyed when the earth has been carried down into the sea and turned to mud. This change takes place for all the worlds."

As for our earth, its limit "above is seen at our feet in contact with the air; below it reaches down without a limit." The air extends infinitely upward, and the surface of the earth stretches horizontally to infinity. The heavenly bodies are ignited clouds, which move in a straight line to infinity above the terrestrial plain. Hence it would appear that the heavenly bodies of one day are not those of the preceding, but are a completely new solar and sidereal outfit. So far as the usefulness of the heavenly bodies is concerned, the sun may help generate and sustain life, but the moon doesn't do a thing and is quite superfluous.

This account is obviously somewhat influenced by the speculations of Anaximander. But it seems so naïve and inconsistent in various points that it has been suggested [10] that it is meant more as satire than as a serious theory. In any case, it plays ducks and drakes with Greek theology, stripping, it might seem, with malice aforethought, heaven and earth and ocean and all the heavenly bodies of their divinity, and substituting natural for supernatural entities and operations. In other words, it may be a "scientific" reinforcement of Xenophanes' attack upon orthodox religion, and perhaps an extension of his "Let these be taken as fancies something like the truth" to philosophical as well as theological systems.

[10] Cf. Burnet, *op. cit.,* pp. 120 ff.

Xenophanes appears also to take a little fling at the doctrine of re-incarnation taught by the Orphics and by Pythagoras. "Once they say that he [Pythagoras] was passing by when a dog was being beaten, and spoke this word, 'Stop! don't beat it! For it is the soul of a friend that I recognized when I heard its voice.'" [11]

[11] Burnet, *op. cit.*, p. 118.

Chapter IV

PYTHAGORAS AND THE PYTHAGOREANS

I. THE PYTHAGOREAN BROTHERHOOD

Life of Pythagoras. We turn now to an interesting movement in Greek philosophy which contributed greatly to its future course. The founder of this movement, Pythagoras, was a man to whom many legends attributed semi-divine powers and supernatural adventures. Born at Samos, and possibly at one time a pupil of Anaximander, he emigrated to Croton in southern Italy, somewhere about 530 B.C., and there founded a brotherhood whose rule, taboos, and religious beliefs appear to have been influenced by the Orphic Mysteries. The Order grew rapidly and exercised considerable moral and political influence wherever it established its lodges. In the struggle then in progress between aristocracy and the democratic movement, the Pythagoreans allied themselves with the aristocratic party. Hence, when the aristocratic governments of the south Italian cities were overthrown in the middle of the fifth century B.C., the Pythagoreans shared their fate. Many of the order were killed and many had to flee for their lives, some of them to Greece. Others, however, managed to stick it out in Italy, particularly at Rhegion (Reggio) on the Straits of Messina. Later, under the threat of the growing power of Syracuse, they, too, found it advisable to emigrate. Tarentum, however, which successfully defied Syracuse, remained a Pythagorean center of some importance. There the liberal tyrant of Tarentum, Archytas, who was a friend of Plato's, belonged to the Order.

Religious Teachings. On the religious side Pythagoras and the early Pythagoreans emphasized the doctrine of reincarnation, and practiced a rule of life calculated in their opinion to purify the soul. But just how they conceived the soul and reincarnation is obscure. There is some ground for supposing that they followed the Orphic belief in a wheel of birth and rebirth from which the soul, after sufficient purification, for the most part ritual in character, might hope eventually to escape to reunion with the divine. But there is also reason for

41

holding that they regarded reincarnation as simply an automatic re-currence, every so often, of the same old person, repeating in every detail the same old life, and so on *ad infinitum*. In any case Pytha-goreanism disregarded entirely the elaborate theology built up about the person of Dionysus, and, for that matter, considered Apollo as its patron god.

Scientific Attainments. The members of the Order were also sci-entists of no mean rank, especially in the fields of mathematics, music, astronomy and medicine. To them we owe, for example, the formula-tion of the so-called "Pythagorean" proposition in geometry. Also, they had made important observations on the arithmetical proportions that govern musical harmony. Their belief that the movements of the heavenly bodies produce concordant notes was later expressed in Eng-lish in our well-known phrase "the music of the spheres." To them we owe also the first intimation that the earth is not the center of the solar system.

II. THE NUMBER THEORY

Dualism of Limit and the Unlimited. In his philosophical specula-tions Pythagoras is apparently influenced by Anaximander and An-aximenes. At any rate, he considers that the universe is ultimately divisible into two opposed principles, one of which he describes as Unlimited Breath. The other principle is Limit. It is with the nature and operations of Limit that the famous Pythagorean teaching that all things are Numbers is concerned.

This teaching is an extension of Pythagoras' interest in mathematics, and is perhaps also bound up with a "numerological" belief in the sacredness and magical efficacy of certain numbers. In considering the mathematics of the day, we must remember that the Greeks lacked the symbol *o*, as well as the arithmetical notation that enables us to perform on paper the operations of addition, subtraction, multiplica-tion, and division. They commonly used the letters of the alphabet, as did the Romans, to symbolize numerical quantities, which did not lend themselves to arithmetical manipulation by such means. At the same time, being ten-fingered, they naturally reckoned in groups of tens. And it appears that already in Pythagoras' time mathematicians were looking for better and more maneuverable symbols than those provided by letters.

Greek System of Notation Geometrical not Arithmetical. These they found by an adaptation of geometry, in which arrangements of dots, or of the letter *alpha,* were used. Pythagoras' fame is said to rest on his new arrangement of these dots in the form of a triangle tapering from a base of *four,* through *three* and *two* to *one,* to represent the *dekad* or number *ten.* This was called the *tetraktys,* or aggregate of four, expressing the fact that $1 + 2 + 3 + 4 = 10$. The sum of $1 + 2 + 3 + 4 + 5$ and so on *ad infinitum* could also be expressed by similar triangles, formed by a similar tapering down, one less dot to each line, from a base containing a number of dots equal to the last number of the series. Such sums of series of integers were therefore known as triangular numbers. So, too, the sums of series of odd numbers, of any length, e.g., $1 + 3 + 5 = 9$; $1 + 3 + 5 + 7 = 16$ can be expressed in squares of three rows of three, or in four rows of four, and so on indefinitely. These are called square numbers. And, stop the series of even numbers where you will, its sum can always be arranged in an oblong in which the number of dotted lines is one less than the number of dots in the line. For example,

$$2 + 4 + 6 = 12 = \quad 3 \text{ rows of } \quad 4 \text{ dots}$$

$$2 + 4 + 6, \text{ etc.} + 28 = 210 = 14 \text{ rows of } 15 \text{ dots}$$

$$2 + 4 + 6, \text{ etc.} + 46 = 552 = 23 \text{ rows of } 24 \text{ dots}$$

Hence such series were known as oblong numbers.

Points, Lines, Planes and Solids. Again, the minimum requirement for outlining or, we might say, composing, a line, a plane, and a solid was respectively two, three, and four dots or points. That is, the line is made of two units or the number 2, the plane, of three units or the number 3, the solid, of four units or the number 4. With the introduction of solids into the scheme, the way was open for pyramidal and cubic arrangements of dots, but although later Pythagoreans entered this field, we do not know whether Pythagoras himself pushed his study of sums of number series into the third dimension. Finally Pythagoras' interest in music probably led him to the discovery of the octave and the proportions of harmonic intervals—a discovery that might suggest that sounds, or at least musical notes, were made by, and of, numbers.

All Things Are Numbers. However this may be, the Pythagoreans concluded that things are really Numbers. How far and into what detail they carried this doctrine we do not know—but some of them certainly pushed it apparently at an early date to the somewhat fantastic extent of reducing not only objects, but moral qualities, and political and social institutions to Numbers. Thus justice is a square number, perhaps because it involves harming him who has harmed.

or taking the doer and the "done by" twice over, and 5, which is the union of the first even with the first odd combination of units, is the nature of marriage.

III. THE GENERATION OF THE UNIVERSE

Cosmology. In the beginning, the unit-dot-point, or number one, was formed in the Unlimited. Then, if we may trust Aristotle's account of the Pythagoreans, "the nearest part of the unlimited began to be constrained and limited by the limit,"[1] and to separate and distinguish units from one another, "as if it were like what separates and distinguishes the terms of a series."[2] Thus Numbers came into existence. Given the geometrical nature of their arithmetical thinking, the Pythagoreans may have envisaged the initial situation as emptiness dotted at intervals with points. Furthermore, in view of their interest in astronomy, their known assimilation of the opposites, light and darkness, to Limit and the Unlimited, and their possible actual identification of the Unlimited with darkness and the Limited with Fire, they may have imagined the first state of the universe as a limitless black void of mist or breath teeming with star-like points of light. Groups of different quantities and different arrangements of these points might constitute the Numbers that defined and distinguished the basic elements and different classes of things. Indeed, we are told by Aristotle that one Pythagorean went so far as to decide "what was the number of what (e.g., of man or of horse), viz., by imitating the figures of living things with pebbles, as some people bring numbers into the forms of triangle and square."[3]

Pairs of Opposites. In any case, the opposition of Limit to the Unlimited was reflected in an opposition of light to darkness, and in eight other pairs of contrasts, odd and even, one and many, right and left, male and female, resting and moving, straight and curved, good and bad, square and oblong. And there was a tendency to extend such pairs to other contrarieties. Furthermore, the members of these pairs were set over against each other as the better to the worse. Limit, light, odd, male, etc., are *right*. The Unlimited, darkness, even, female, etc., are *wrong*. Or at any rate the one set is superior, the other inferior. We must remember that the unlimited suggested to the Greek mind not perfection, as it does to us, but obscurity and haziness;

---

[1] *Metaphysics*, XIV, 3, 1091*a*13 ff. (Trans. Ross).
[2] *Physics*, IV, 6, 213*b*22 ff.
[3] Aristotle, *Metaphysics*, XIV, 5, 1092*b*10 ff.

whereas limit suggested clearness and intelligibility. Limit might seem, then, the source of the "virtues" of the universe, the Unlimited the source of its "vices." Religiously, too, the Pythagoreans were disposed, as we have seen, to dualism.

IV. ASTRONOMY, PHYSICS, ETC.

Proceeding now to the further stages of the formation of the universe, we find Pythagoras possibly adopting Anaximander's new theory of the nature of the heavenly bodies, though this is uncertain. He seems, however, to have rejected the vortex theory. The earth he probably regarded not as flat but as spherical, and placed it at the center of the universe with the sun. The moon, the known planets, and a heaven of fixed stars revolved about it. At an early date, too, the Pythagoreans had noted that, whereas the whole heaven seemed to revolve daily about the earth from east to west, the sun, moon and planets had also a reverse, slower, varying and wobbling movement from west to east, and exhibited other departures from uniform circular motion—to explain which they may have evolved some sort of theory of component motions.

The doctrine that the movements of the heavenly bodies gave off sounds at harmonic intervals from one another, may go back to Pythagoras himself. Later it was considerably elaborated.

Sooner or later, too, the Pythagoreans are said to have displaced the earth from its central position and to have made it revolve, along with the other heavenly bodies, about a "central-fire," whose light is reflected by them. And the idea that the earth also rotates on its own axis has been attributed to them. In any case, ideas appear to have been afloat that eventually made port in the heliocentric system of the astronomer Aristarchus. Also, the existence of a new planet, the *antichthon* or "counter-earth" was assumed to explain eclipses, which Anaximenes also had explained by the intervention of dark planets. We do not see either the "counter-earth" or the "central-fire" because our part of the earth is turned away from it. The introduction of the *antichthon* raised the number of bodies, including the heaven of fixed stars, revolving about the central fire to ten, the sacred *tetraktys;* and Aristotle adduced this fact as a reason for the assumption of the new planet. That he meant this to be taken seriously has been questioned.

It is possible, also, that Pythagoras accepted Anaximander's view of a plurality of worlds. At any rate, an early Pythagorean is said to have held that there were a hundred and eighty-three worlds disposed in the form of a triangle, which is, we may recollect, the geometrical form of the *tetraktys*.

Development of Pythagoreanism. As time went on and the Pythagoreans had to deal with new mathematical discoveries and philosophic speculations, the number-theory was developed to meet the situation. Specific geometrical arrangements, for example, were assigned to the four elements. Fire was perhaps regarded by them, as it was by Plato, as a composition of pyramidal particles, earth possibly as composed of cubes, water of icosahedrons, and air of octahedrons—while the dodecahedrons formed the frame for the enclosing sphere of the heavens.

Another later development was the theory that the soul is an attunement of the elements and pairs of opposites present in the body. This view is destructive of the earlier doctrine of the immortality and reincarnation of souls. Whether and how the two teachings were held together we do not know. It may be also that the attunement was conceived musically as constructed according to the intervals of the fourth, the fifth, and the octave—a conjecture that would support the attribution of Plato's doctrine of the tripartite soul, to which we shall presently come, to the Pythagoreans.

V. FINAL CONSIDERATIONS

It should be pointed out that the reconstruction of the Pythagorean philosophy is attended with very great difficulties and has given rise to much controversy. We have no original fragments. It is hard to say what is early doctrine and what is later elaboration. It is also hard to determine what has been misunderstood by later commentators, and what they have read into or added to the teaching because of their own bias, or to suit their own purposes. These points are in dispute among modern scholars. Hence the above account should be read, as it has been written, with considerable suspicion as to its accuracy.

Contributions to Philosophy. However, we may note in the Pythagorean system several pretty well-established points of importance to the history of philosophy. The parts played by Limit and the Unlimited influenced Plato, and contributed to the eventual distinction between Form and Matter stressed by both the Platonic and the Aristotelian systems. Again, not only did the theory that things are really Numbers greatly affect Plato, but it also hit in its way upon a cardinal point of modern science. We, too, do not think we have grasped the essence of a thing till we can express its nature by a mathematical formula. In chemistry, for instance, substances are defined and distinguished by the numbers that indicate the arithmetical proportions borne by their constituent elements to one another. And the so-called models constructed by physics to illustrate the nature of the actual world or of possible universes, boil down, when their pictorial content has been precipitated from them, to strings of equations. Indeed, it is not entirely a misnomer to refer to the modern mathematical physicist as a kind of Pythagorean. Moreover, there are today those who are even more explicitly Pythagorean in their philosophy, attempting to employ number theory in every possible analysis, in art, for instance, as well as in physics.

Pythagoreanism and Methodology. An interesting point of argument regarding the Pythagoreans is whether they should be regarded as rationalists or empiricists in the typical modern usage of those terms. The matter in their case is difficult to decide and is probably in fact ambiguous. They were at times involved in both observation and experimentation, and yet their concern for mathematics, particularly geometry, as demonstrative deductive argument, indicates an interest, at least, in arriving at knowledge of matters of fact independently of experience. Whether this is possible has proved to be one of the foremost questions of philosophy, involving logic, mathematics, metaphysics, and the natural sciences. It was not until the development of non-Euclidean geometry in the nineteenth century and its application in physics that the empiricists were able to counter the argument of the rationalists that in geometry is found an example of *a priori* factual knowledge. It has been held by some that the religious interests of the Pythagoreans, particularly their concern for purification, may have inclined them to favor knowledge that is not gained from contact with the material world, and may therefore have been an important factor in their contributions to geometry. At any rate, mathematics was for them the basic factor in an intellectual mysticism that was to leave a permanent imprint on philosophic method.

Chapter V

HERACLITUS

I. GENERAL CONSIDERATIONS

The Problem of Change. By the beginning of the fifth century B.C. philosophy had acquired more sophistication. Apparently it had become acquainted with certain problems and difficulties which were inherent in the earlier systems, but which the Milesians seem not to have realized. Foremost among these problems was that of the nature and possibility of *change*. To the Milesians it seems not to have occurred that there were any difficulties in the idea of the transformation of a single homogeneous world-stuff or of distinct, homogeneous opposites into a world of heterogeneous, changing, shifting phenomena. But sooner or later the question was bound to arise whether any such transformation was really conceivable. How could Water, or an Indeterminate Something, or Vapor be *really* changed into a lot of things they apparently were not? And how could they remain *really* the same in spite of, and throughout, all their transformations? How could Water *become* a flower, and yet remain Water? How could the Indefinite Something *become* a pair of definite opposites quite different from it and from each other, and how could they become a world of particular things different from themselves? Furthermore, how could a flower really *become* a fruit, if both flower and fruit were really made of Water or Air? For the apparent transformation of one into the other would be really a transformation of Water into Water, or Vapor into Vapor—which was equivalent to no transformation at all. Was it, then, thinkable that opposites and differences should be really identical? Was it conceivable that one thing should turn into another?

At any rate both Heraclitus and the Eleatics were agitated by such questions, and in attempting to answer them were led to very different philosophical conclusions.

II. HERACLITUS' LIFE

Sense of Superiority. Heraclitus comes on the scene just a hundred years after Thales. Born at Ephesus, he was in his prime about 500 B.C., and lived to see the repulse of the Persians by the Greeks at Marathon in 490, and again at Salamis in 480. He belonged to the aristocratic party and despised the common herd. His fellow Ephesians he told in so many words to go hang themselves, for having cast out one of their best citizens, saying, "We will have none that is best among us; if there be any such, let him be so elsewhere and among others." [1] He also had little use for Homer and Hesiod, and still less for the Orphic Mysteries, which he denounced as mad and unholy. He condemned the worship of images and ridiculed the rites of atonement for blood-guilt. He was contemptuous, too, of the philosophy of his day, and spoke disparagingly of both Pythagoras and Xenophanes, chiding them with having failed to understand what they had investigated and learned. He felt that he had attained a novel and superior philosophic insight, and was setting forth truths that no one else had grasped.

Obscurity of Style. To clarify and restate these truths is difficult because of the obscurity of his style. Indeed in antiquity he was known as "the dark." This obscurity was probably in part deliberate, since it was fashionable in those days to write for the "intelligentsia," above the head of the ordinary man. However that may be, the fragments of Heraclitus "have first of all, a literal and often somewhat trivial meaning behind which, however, there looms an indefinite number of more general and also more profound meanings." [2] Furthermore, he illustrates his *logos* or discourse with startling paradoxes in which he seeks to drive home the point of his new discovery. Naturally his double meanings and his paradoxes have proved a happy hunting ground for commentators and interpreters who have perhaps credited him with much that never entered his head.

III. RECONCILIATION OF IDENTITY, DIFFERENCE, AND CHANGE

Identity of Opposites. At the same time, Heraclitus proclaims clearly the gist of his discovery. It is that *opposites are in reality identical* and that "all things are one." [3] Upon the existence of opposites and upon

[1] Fr. 114 (Burnet, p. 141).
[2] H. Gomperz, *Heraclitus of Ephesus*. Athens, 1939.
[3] Fr. 1 (Burnet, p. 132).

the tendency of phenomena in general to fall into groups of contrasted pairs he is even more insistent than Anaximander and the
Pythagoreans. As we shall see in a moment, he expands indefinitely
their lists of opposed entities. But whereas the Pythagoreans had regarded opposition as fundamental, and the members of Anaximander's
pairs of opposites were essentially and irreconcilably *different* from
each other, Heraclitus had discovered that *different things were also
one and the same thing.* By this, however, he did not mean that *difference* is merely *apparent,* whereas *identity* is *real.* Difference and
sameness are equally real, and where the one is, there must the other
be also.

At first sight, it might appear that Heraclitus was merely reaffirm-
ing the doctrine of Thales and Anaximenes. For they, too, had proclaimed, implicitly at least, the identity of opposites and of all things,
when they made Water and Vapor the stuffs of which all things were
made. Why, then, should Heraclitus boast of the novelty of his doctrine?

We do not know what Heraclitus had to say about them, but we can
see what he might have said. Thales and Anaximenes had taught that
all things are *made* of one thing, to which opposites may be reduced.
The hot and the cold, the light and the dark, etc., were both *Water* or
both *Vapor.* To Heraclitus, however, it had occurred that all things
are one thing, that they are *made*—not of Vapor or Water—but of
one another, that the hot *is*—not Water or Vapor—but the cold, and
vice versa, that light and dark are the same, not by virtue of being
aspects or derivations of the same thing, but by virtue of being themselves the same thing.

The Flux. Again it is certain that *change* was very much on Heraclitus' mind, and that his new *logos,* in his opinion, accounted for its
existence and nature—which other philosophers had left unexplained
and inexplicable. To his eyes the universe was above all things a
process, a *becoming.* In a famous fragment he tells us that "you cannot step into the same river twice, for fresh waters are ever flowing
in upon you." [4] And later philosophers are unanimous in recording
his insistence upon the moving, shifting, restless, transitory character
of phenomena. "All things are in flux" became the tag universally
attached to his system. Even if we do not credit him with the extreme
views the phrase suggested to some of his successors—views that reduced the universe to a flux so rapid that you could not even step

[4] Fr. 41, 42 (Burnet. p. 136).

into the same river once—we can be sure that he was sure of the
reality and central importance of *becoming* and of the necessity of
finding a place for it in any philosophic system.

The World-Stuff a Process. Now reflection upon the nature of
change might have suggested to Heraclitus that its reality depended
upon a world-stuff that was *inherently* and *in and of itself* in a process
of becoming, and whose essential nature lay in being both the *same
as itself* and *different from itself*. For, in order to change, a thing must
become *different* from itself. If it remains the *same as itself,* it has not
changed. But also, after it has changed it must still be the *same* thing,
otherwise there has been no change but simply the substitution of one
object for another. A *changing* thing is, then, an *identity* of *opposites*.
It both is and is not what it was and what it will be.

Search for a Visibly Changing Stuff. We must remind ourselves at
this point that Heraclitus, like the Milesians, thought almost entirely
in terms of sense-perception. Hence in facing and attempting to solve
these problems, he had, like them, at his command only *perceptible*
substances, qualities, and changes. Moreover, the line between qualities and things was thinly drawn. Philosophy knew nothing as yet
of what we should call chemical and physical substructures and processes. To be sure, thinking in terms of the imperceptible was not far
off, but in Heraclitus' day it had not arrived. Still further away were
philosophic concepts like that of a substance or substructure to and
from which qualities attached and detached themselves without altering its essence.

For him, then, as for the Milesians, the world-stuff did not underlie
phenomena and exist, so to speak, at a deeper and more fundamental
level than they did. It existed on the same perceptible level as other
sensible substances, and its claim to be the one substance of which
all others were made, lay in the fact that it was the *only* substance that
could be seen by the naked eye undergoing transformation into them.
Heraclitus' universe, like that of the Milesians, was, so to speak,
without depth. His problem was to find among sensible phenomena
something that actually *displayed* both identity and difference, and was
perceptibly a stuff that was also a process rather than one like Water,
or Vapor, or the Indeterminate, which was not visibly in a state of
continuous transformation and *becoming,* but apparently at times inert
and unchanging.

Any *real* transformation of such stuffs or principles into a universe
was impossible—not to speak of a transformation undertaken at their
own initiative and expressive of their nature. They could be trans-

formed, to be sure, but they were not themselves processes of transformation. The only possible world-stuff was one whose *being* lay in
becoming.

Discovery of this Stuff in Fire. This was the *logos* other philosophers
had not understood and even now could not understand. Their blindness now was all the more inexcusable, Heraclitus thought, because
the truth of his *logos* was palpable. The real world-stuff, the stuff
whose *being* lay in *becoming*, the stuff that was both *identical* and
different, that was itself when in the act of becoming not itself, and
that was ever changing and yet ever the same, was all about them,
perceptible to eye and touch. It was *Fire*.

IV. THE EVER-LIVING FIRE

Fire a Process. *Fire* was always "on the go," flickering, flaring, waxing, waning, flaming hotter and brighter, dying down and cooling
to glowing embers. Still, brighter or dimmer, hotter or cooler, it was
the same Fire. We could see it burning up all sorts of things and apparently transforming them, in the process of combustion, into itself.
We could see it becoming in that process embers and ashes, and
smoke and vapor. Fire was just combustion, and combustion was
conversion. Its burning, which was its substance, was a changing of
things different from itself into itself, and of itself into things different from itself, throughout which it remained the same self-identical
Fire. Here, then, in Fire we had a world-stuff whose distinctive nature,
unlike that of Water or Vapor, would be just to change of its own
initiative into a universe, without losing its own identity or changing
its own character in the process. Since its nature was a process of
transformation, it was not transformed by being transformed.

These, of course, are not reasons that Heraclitus himself gave as
inspirations of his discovery. They are our reasons for feeling that
he had good reason to believe his *logos* true and novel. Still, it is
not improbable that some of these considerations influenced his train
of thought.

Fire the World-Stuff. But, however Heraclitus was led to his conclusion, it is that "this world, which is the same for all, no one of
gods or men has made; but it was ever, is now, and ever shall be an
ever-living Fire, with measures of it kindling and measures going out.
All things are an exchange for Fire, and Fire for all things, even as
wares for gold, and gold for wares." [5]

[5] Frs. 20, 22 (Burnet, pp. 134, 135).

Whether Heraclitus thought of Fire in terms primarily of heat or of light is an interesting question. We generally visualize fire, but as the process of combustion which constitutes its essence, and in which it is exchanged for other things and other things for it, is associated with its heat rather than with its light, it may be that Heraclitus considered its tactual quality primary, and its brightness as something secondary and derivative.[6]

Heraclitus regarded Fire as animate, and as the principle of animation—of soul—of all living things. And, like the Milesians, he regarded the world-stuff as divine, and like Xenophanes, called it God.

Fire an Identity of Opposites. That it is a process of becoming in which opposites are identical, and sameness and difference are merged, he emphasizes at some length.

> Fire is want and surfeit. Fire lives the death of air, and air lives the death of fire; water lives the death of earth, earth that of water.
>
> God is day and night, winter and summer, war and peace, surfeit and hunger. . . .
>
> Cold things become warm, and what is warm cools; what is wet dries, and the parched is moistened. . . .
>
> It scatters and it gathers; it advances and retires.
>
> The straight and the crooked path of the fuller's comb is one and the same.
>
> Couples are things whole and things not whole, what is drawn together and what is torn asunder, the harmonious and the discordant. The one is made up of all things, and all things issue from the one.
>
> To God all things are fair and good and right but men hold some things wrong, and some right.
>
> Good and ill are one.
>
> Mortals are immortals, and immortals are mortals, the one living the others' death, and dying the others' life.
>
> And it is the same thing in us that is quick and dead, awake and asleep, young and old; the former are shifted and become the latter, and the latter in turn are shifted and become the former.[7]

V. THE LAW OF CHANGE

Orderly Behavior of the Universe. But the discovery of a world-stuff that solves the problem of change and of the identity of opposites implied in change, was by no means the whole of Heraclitus' novel *logos*. He had discovered something else, which also, in his opinion,

---

[6] On this point cf. H. Gomperz, *op. cit.,* p. 55.
[7] Frs. 24, 25, 36, 39, 40, 50, 57, 59, 61, 67, 78 (Burnet. pp. 135-139).

lay plain as day to anyone who would use his powers of observation and would reflect upon what he observed. The exchanges of Fire for all things and of all things for Fire are not haphazard and capricious. They follow a fixed rule and exhibit a fixed order. The ever-living Fire displays an invariable habit of transformation, and its behavior can be summed up and described in a definite *formula*. In short, there is a *Law of Change,* which makes the world-process an intelligible and rational affair.

The orderly character of the transformation that constitutes the world-process is called by Heraclitus a kind of *wisdom* inherent in the world-stuff. And the fact that this characteristic designates a pattern and rule of behavior common to all things alike, displayed everywhere and at all times by the universe, is expressed by his saying that "the wise" is something different from any of the phenomena that exemplify it. It is, however, not one of a pair of different, opposed entities like day and night, summer and winter, war and peace, but is itself present in all opposites, harmonizing them, and governing their transformations into one another, as "the thought by which all things are steered through all things." [8] It seems, then, to be, like Fire, the one thing that is not transformed in the process of transformation. In a word, the Law of Change does not change. "The wise is one only. . . ." Furthermore, Heraclitus adds, "it is willing and unwilling to be called by the name of Zeus." [9]

Difficulties of a Theistic Interpretation. This ascription of wisdom and thought, or "insight," to the ever-living Fire not unnaturally suggests a theistic interpretation, which some later commentators adopted. Such an interpretation, however, is now rejected by many scholars, who believe that Heraclitus was merely distinguishing in his way what we should today call the form or order of the universe from its stuff. "The wise" is the lawfulness and intelligibility exhibited by the ever-living Fire. It does not exist apart from the world-stuff, but in the world-stuff as the unvarying habit of its behavior. Its willingness to be called Zeus is simply an affirmation that the Law of Change in the ever-living Fire is divine; its unwillingness to be called Zeus is perhaps a warning that the divine law like the divine world-stuff is not *a* god, after the personal style of the Olympian deities.[10]

Use of the Political Analogy. However, Heraclitus would seem to conceive the law and order in the universe after the political and legal analogy. For that matter, we today still speak of natural laws as laws

[8] Fr. 19 (Burnet, p. 134). [10] Cf. H. Gomperz, *op. cit.,* p. 60.
[9] Fr. 65 (Burnet, p. 138).

governing the behavior of phenomena, as if they *prescribed* rather than simply *described* the general course events follow and the conduct common to and universally characteristic of them. But whereas we have become aware that we are speaking metaphorically, Heraclitus undoubtedly felt that the Law of Change really *directed* and *controlled* the world process, much as the laws of a city compel and control the actions of its citizens.[11]

Any deviation from the universal law would, moreover, be a kind of immorality on the part of phenomena, analogous to human disobedience to civic rules and regulations. It would upset the order of the universe just as lawlessness among human beings would upset the constitution of the city-state. And just as infraction of civil and moral regulations is rectified, and the stability of the body politic is restored, by punishment, so wayward phenomena will be overtaken by a cosmic retribution. "The sun," we are told, "will not overstep his measures; if he does, the Erinyes, the handmaids of Justice, will find him out." [12] To act *justly,* he must mete out day and night, summer and winter, according to their established measures and the law of their alternation. In the same way, the general rhythmic pulsation and alternation of opposites in which Fire now scatters, now gathers, now advances, now retires, throughout the entire universe, was subject to a just measure, to exceed or disturb which would somehow be a *wrong* that deserved to be chastised. Anaximander, it will be remembered, also spoke of the world-process in terms of injustice and reparation.

The Logos. The word "logos" is never used by Heraclitus to designate the Law of Change, at least in any of the fragments that have been preserved. Nor is there any certain evidence that he ever so used it. In any case, in the Greek of his time the word had no metaphysical significance, and signified "discourse" or "teaching." Hence, if he did use it, he could have meant by it no more than he meant by "wisdom" and "the wise." However, later philosophers used the word metaphysically to designate a divine, personal or quasi-personal Reason immanent in the universe and directing the world-process. And in this sense it was read back into Heraclitus. Hence we must be prepared to hear the law and order inherent in the transformations of the ever-living Fire frequently referred to as the Heraclitean Logos, and sometimes invested with the attributes of a personal God.

However, this misunderstanding really makes Heraclitus in a sense, at least, one source of the doctrine of the Logos. In the meaning given

[11] Cf. Fr. 91*b* (Burnet, p. 139).
[12] Fr. 29 (Burnet, p. 135).

the term by the Stoics and read back into him, the word was used
also by some of the Neo-Platonists to designate the Divine Intellect,
and was taken over by the author of the Fourth Gospel to describe
what later became the second person of the Christian Trinity. Whether,
however, the author in using it was influenced directly by contemporary Graeco-Roman philosophy, or indirectly through the Hellenizing
Jews, or applied the term to a purely Hebrew concept, is an open
question.[13]

VI. THE UPWARD AND THE DOWNWARD WAY

Statement of the Law of Change. What now is the nature and law
of the world-process? In the first place, Fire is always varying in intensity, becoming hotter and colder "with measures of it kindling and
measures going out." And the contrast and conflict of opposites reflects the fundamental opposition of Fire flaring up and Fire dying
down. In a word, Fire ceaselessly travels an Upward and a Downward
Way. But "the way up and the way down is the same,"[14] because
Fire is always both kindling and going up and also going out and
down. Again, the kindling and cooling expresses itself in a rhythmic
alternation in the world-process. Fire is burning more hotly in day,
and summer, and life, and waking, less hotly at night, and in winter,
and death, and sleep. But day and night, summer and winter, waking
and sleeping, living and dying, succeed each other in perpetual recurrence, as Fire now flares up, now dies down.

The measures of some of the rhythmic alternations of the Upward
and the Downward Way, Heraclitus appears to have computed in a
somewhat "numerological" fashion. Attaching special importance to
the number seven, he, seemingly, tried to relate it to the number thirty
—thirty days being the period of the waxing and waning of the moon,
and thirty years being regarded by him as the period of a human
generation. Also he felt, apparently, that the so-called Great Year, a
period of 10,800 years, played some part in the rhythmic process. But
this is all really very obscure. It is also a question whether he believed
in recurrent world-conflagrations in which all things are destroyed by
Fire and resolved into it and then re-created, or held that the Upward
and the Downward Ways are always both in operation and everlastingly counterbalance one another.

[13] Cf. Burnet, p. 133, *note*.
[14] Fr. 69 (Burnet, p. 138).

VII. "WAR IS THE FATHER OF ALL"

Stability Rests on Tension. "Homer was wrong in saying: 'Would that strife might perish from among gods and men!' He did not see that he was praying for the destruction of the universe; for, if his prayer were heard, all things would pass away. . . .

"War is the father of all and the king of all; and some he has made gods and some men, some bond and some free. . . . We must know that war is common to all, and strife is justice, and that all things come into being and pass away through strife." [15]

In these fragments Heraclitus expresses in vivid language his theory that the universe is kept in existence by a kind of *tension* or *struggle* between the Upward and the Downward Ways. Upon this strife of opposites the stability and structure of the universe depend, just, we might say, as the rigidity, or the slow swaying, of a pair of wrestlers is due to the effort either one is making to throw his opponent. Tension, then, constitutes equilibrium, and equilibrium is tension. Stability is instability, and instability is stability. Things hold together because they are held together. War is the same as peace, peace is the same as war Harmony and discord are identical. "Men do not know how what is at variance with itself agrees with itself. It is an attunement of opposite tensions, like that of the bow and the lyre," [16] in which one and the same string pulls in two opposite directions at the same time. The structure of the universe is a *taut* structure. "It rests by changing." [17] But "the hidden attunement is better than the open." [18] It is more perfect than that of the bow or the lyre, or of any other of its visible examples.

VIII. THE GENERATION AND STRUCTURE OF THE UNIVERSE

Cosmology. Our material for reconstructing Heraclitus' theory of the generation and structure of the universe in any detail is somewhat scanty. Heraclitus himself tells us that "the transformations of Fire are first of all sea; and half of the sea is earth, half whirlwind," [19] by which he means apparently either a hurricane attended by waterspouts and thunder storms, or exhalations of shimmering vapor from the sea.

[15] Frs. 43, 44, 62 (Burnet, pp. 136-137).   [18] Fr. 47 (Burnet, p. 136).
[16] Fr. 45 (Burnet, p. 136).   [19] Fr. 21 (Burnet, p. 135).
[17] Fr. 83 (Burnet, p. 139).

Whether this fiery phenomenon, whatever it may be, is to be regarded as Fire descending into sea, or sea ascending into Fire, seems to be a disputed point. In any case, half of the sea ascends firewards, and half of it changes into earth, and water is equally changing both into fire and into earth. Earth is both downwardly precipitated from water, and upwardly resolved back into water, as it returns by the Upward Way of water to the Fire, from which by the Downward Way of water it is derived. An early historian of philosophy, Diogenes Laertius, also tells us that Heraclitus said that Fire becomes water, water earth, earth water again, and that water evaporates in bright exhalations that nourish Fire.

IX. THE PHYSICAL WORLD

Astronomy. We have already seen that Heraclitus draws largely upon physical phenomena, particularly those of astronomy and meteorology, to illustrate his *logos*. But for a more specific and co-ordinated description of his views of the structure of the physical universe we have to rely largely upon later commentators. We can perhaps do no better than quote the account given by Diogenes Laertius.

He held, too, that exhalations arose both from the sea and the land; some bright and pure, others dark. Fire was nourished by the bright ones, and moisture by the others.

He does not make it clear what is the nature of that which surrounds the world. He held, however, that there were bowls in it with the concave sides turned towards us, in which the bright exhalations were collected and produced flames. These were the heavenly bodies.

The flame of the sun was the brightest and warmest; for the other heavenly bodies were more distant from the earth; and for that reason gave less light and heat. The moon, on the other hand, was nearer the earth; but it moved through an impure region. The sun moved in a bright and unmixed region and at the same time was at just the right distance from us. That is why it gives more heat and light. The eclipses of the sun and moon were due to the turning of the bowls upwards, while the monthly phases of the moon were produced by a slight turning of its bowl.

Day and night, months and seasons and years, rains and winds, and things like these were due to the different exhalations. The bright exhalation, when ignited in the circle of the sun, produced day, and the preponderance of the opposite exhalations produced night. The increase of warmth proceeding from the bright exhalation produced summer, and the multiplication of moisture from the dark exhalation produced winter. He assigns the causes of other things in conformity with this.

As to the earth he makes no clear statement about its nature, any more than he does about that of the bowls.[20]

Sensible Evidence of the Transformations of Fire. To this we might add that probably Heraclitus, like his predecessors, thought that we could actually perceive water turning into earth in the silting of the mouths of rivers, and earth turning back into water in the springs issuing from the ground. Together with the heavenly bodies, the shimmering exhalations from the sea, waterspouts, and the electric disturbances frequently accompanying them, they gave him a complete visible demonstration of the entire cycle of the Upward and the Downward Ways.

X. THE SOUL

Psychology. Fire, we may remember, is animate and the principle of life in all living things. Our souls, then, are the element of pure Fire in us—or, in other words, that part of us which is hottest and in the most intense combustion. The hotter and the more intense that process is, the better are our minds and characters. "The dry soul is the wisest and the best." [21] Any dulling of the soul is due to its becoming damper, when the Downward Way towards water preponderates in its Fire. Thus drunkenness and sleep are moderate dampenings of the soul, in which we lose hold of the real, waking world. "The waking have one common world, but the sleeping turn aside, each into a world of his own." [22] And in our cups it is hard to conceal folly.[23] Pleasure, too, is a moistening, perhaps because its pursuit is a lapse from wisdom. And when the Downward Way prevails as far as it can, and the Fire in us becomes water, then we die, and all that is left of us is the water and earth of which our bodies are composed.

Possible Belief in Immortality. But there is also the reverse process of the Upward Way in us. When we sober up or wake up in the morning, the Fire in us which has been undergoing a minor setback, rekindles. Also, it has been suggested that Heraclitus thought we could, so to speak, die upwards as well as downwards, in which case our souls became purer fire. Deaths such as this are perhaps the "greater deaths" that win "greater portions." [24] Then, too, the statement that "mortals are immortals and immortals are mortals, the one living the others'

[20] Diogenes Laertius (trans. Burnet, pp. 147-148).
[21] Frs. 74-76 (Burnet, p. 138).
[22] Fr. 95 (Burnet, p. 140).
[23] Cf. Frs. 108, 109 (Burnet, p. 140).
[24] Fr. 101 (Burnet, p. 140. Cf. pp. 153-154).

death, and dying the others' life," [25] might mean that human souls on
the Upward Way finally become so fiery that they die to the body
and become gods, and that gods, when the Downward Way prevails
in them, and they descend towards the earth and become cooler, become human souls.[26] This smacks of Orphic-Pythagorean doctrine.

In any case, however, soul that dies downwards into water is being
also continually raised again from the dead. For after the death of soul
by becoming water, and the death of water by becoming earth, "water
comes from earth" again "and from water, soul," as the Upward Way
reasserts itself. For "it is the same thing in us that is quick and dead,
awake and asleep, young and old; the former are shifted and become
the latter, and the latter in turn are shifted and become the former." [27]
Hence "you will not find the boundaries of soul by traveling in any
direction, so deep is the measure of it." [28] Wherever Fire is, there it
is also.

Intelligence a Degree of Heat. In its fiery, waking state the soul is
rational and wise. For Fire, as we may remember, is infused with
"the wise," or, in other words, is an orderly process, the behavior of
which exhibits and is governed by fixed habits and rules. Hence, in
proportion as soul is hot and dry, its waking life, also, is infused with
"the wise," and governed by reason. Furthermore, in proportion as
this state prevails, soul not only perceives the sensible phenomena of
the process of combustion—which it may do even when moistened by
drunkenness and sleep—but is aware of "the wise," that is, of the
orderly and intelligible character of the process. Dry soul is an *understanding* of the world.

But even in the driest and wisest human soul Fire is not at its hottest
and its brightest, and man's understanding of the world-order falls
far short of grasping the whole nature and law of change and of ex-
hausting their capacity for being understood. At any rate, we are told
that "the way of man has no wisdom, but that of God has. Man is
called a baby by God, even as a child by a man. The wisest man is
an ape compared to God, just as the most beautiful ape is ugly compared to man." [29]

[25] Fr. 67 (Burnet, p. 138).   [28] Fr. 71 (Burnet, p. 138).
[26] Cf. H. Gomperz, *op. cit.,* p. 66.   [29] Frs. 96-99 (Burnet, p. 140).
[27] Fr. 78 (Burnet, p. 139).

Chapter VI

THE ELEATICS

I. PARMENIDES

The conclusion reached by Heraclitus encountered the violent opposition of Parmenides of Elea, or Velia, a city south of present-day
Naples, not far from Paestum. Born of a rich and powerful family,
and himself a person of political prominence, he "flourished" early in
the fifth century B.C. Plato tells us that he visited Athens at the age
of sixty-five and was interviewed by the youthful Socrates. And he
enjoyed a great reputation in antiquity. His first philosophical instruction was received apparently from the Pythagoreans.

The Way of Truth. Hitherto philosophers had merely announced
their theories and let them go at that. But Parmenides supports his
with logical reasoning. He uses hexameter verse to convey his argument and entitles his work *The Way of Truth*. His primary care is to
lay down the rules of the game. Reason is the ultimate judge of truth,
and where and when the senses conflict with it, their evidence must
be false. Moreover, it is a fundamental law of thought that a self-
contradictory concept cannot be valid.

Change Logically Impossible. Proceeding on these premises, Parmenides launches an attack on the reality of *change*. It may be that
this attack was directly inspired by the teaching of Heraclitus. In any
case, it seems to have been directed against him, in part at least, although it would apply equally to all earlier Greek philosophy, which
had taken *change* for granted, without, however, analyzing its implications as Heraclitus had done. The gist of Parmenides' criticism
was that a thing cannot both be itself and not itself, as Heraclitus had
explicitly maintained in his doctrine of the identity of opposites, and
as the Milesians had implicitly taught in their theories of a single
homogeneous world-stuff turning into a multiple, heterogeneous universe. "Undiscerning crowds," he exclaims, "who hold that it is and
is not the same and not the same; and that all things travel in opposite
directions." [1] *A thing must either be or not be.* There is no middle

[1] Fr. 6 (Burnet, p. 174).

way. Furthermore what *is,* cannot change. Hence change cannot *be,* but is non-existent.

The Unity, Self-identity and Changelessness of the Real. From these premises Parmenides deduces that the existent, the Real, or as Parmenides calls it, *what is,* must be one, eternal, illimitable, homogeneous, without multiplicity or variety of any sort, and devoid of motion or alteration. Logic demands this, as we shall see in a moment, and where logic conflicts with the testimony of the senses, the senses are wrong. Multiplicity, variety, generation and destruction, change of any sort, are deceitful opinions we entertain about the universe, not the truth. The sensible world does not *really* exist. It is a false appearance only.

This thesis Parmenides defends at length. The existent, he tells us, cannot be conceived as coming into being or passing out of being. "There are very many tokens that what is, is uncreated and indestructible; for it is complete, immovable, and without end. Nor was it ever, nor will it be; for now *it is,* all at once, a continuous one. For what kind of origin for it wilt thou look for? In what way and from what source could it have drawn its increase? . . . I shall not let thee say nor think that it came from what is not; for it can neither be thought nor uttered that anything is not. And if it came from nothing, what need could have made it arise later rather than sooner?" Moreover, how "can what *is* be going to be in the future? Or how could it come into being? If it came into being, it is not; nor is it, if it is going to be in the future. Thus is becoming extinguished and passing away not to be heard of.

"Nor is it divisible, since it is all alike, and there is no more of it in one place than another to hinder it from holding together, nor less of it, but everything is full of what is. Wherefore it is wholly continuous, for what is, is in contact with what is.

"Moreover it is immovable. . . . It is the same and it rests in the self-same place abiding in itself. And thus it remaineth constant in its place." It cannot be "infinite; for it is in need of nothing, while if it were infinite, it would stand in need of everything."

Finally, thinking depends upon the existent and cannot be set up as a separate principle. "The thing that can be thought and that for the sake of which the thought exists is the same, for you cannot find thought without something that is, as to which it is uttered. And there is not, and never shall be, anything besides what is, since fate has chained it so as to be whole and immovable." [2]

[2] Fr. 8 (Burnet, pp. 174-176).

Change, Variety, etc., Are False Opinions. Hence, Parmenides concludes, multiplicity, variety, motion, transformation, generation and
destruction are erroneous human opinions regarding the nature of the
Real. "All these things are but names which mortals have given, believing them to be true—coming into being and passing away, being
and not-being, change of place and alteration of bright colour." [3]

At the same time, Parmenides asserts that the truly existent is
corporeal. It is extended, solid, and continuous, contiguous with itself,
a *plenum,* and spherical in shape. "Since . . . it has a furthest limit,
it is complete on every side, like the mass of a rounded sphere, equally
poised from the center in every direction; for it cannot be greater or
smaller in one place than in another. For there is no nothing that
could keep it from reaching out equally, nor can aught that is be
more here or less there than what is, since it is all inviolable. For the
point from which it is equal in every direction tends equally to the
limits." [4]

Summary of the Nature of the Real. In short, we may picture *what
really is,* all sensible evidence and human opinions to the contrary
notwithstanding, as a single, eternal, solid, absolutely compact, motionless, changeless ball of completely transparent and homogeneous
world-stuff, without crack or flaw or differentiation or quality of any
sort within its substance. There is not even nothing—in the sense of
a void or emptiness—outside and beyond and surrounding this ball,
since there is no such thing as nothing or emptiness or a void. Logic,
in Parmenides' opinion, demands that we so picture it, and there is no
gainsaying logic.

The Way of Opinion. To *The Way of Truth,* Parmenides adds a
Way of Opinion, which gives us a picture of the nature of the universe, such as might be inspired from an unreasoned observation of
sensible phenomena. "Henceforward learn the beliefs of mortals, giving
ear to the deceptive ordering of my words." Of this "deceptive ordering" we possess only a few scattered fragments—which, however, we
may eke out with reports given of his views by other Greek philosophers. The picture thus pieced together is influenced by the cosmology
of the Pythagoreans, from whom, it will be remembered, Parmenides
received his first philosophic instruction.

"Mortals," he tells us, "have made up their minds to name two
forms . . . opposite in form, and have assigned to them marks distinct from one another. To the one they allot the fire of heaven, gentle,
very light. . . . The other is just the opposite to it, dark night, a

[3] *Ibid.*   [4] *Ibid.*

compact and heavy body." [5] Of these two, light and dark night, all things are compounded. The universe is a series of concentric bands or rings, of which the outer one, which walls in the world, and the inner one at its center—the earth—are composed of the dark solid principle. Between these revolve rings of mingled light and darkness, possibly also interspersed with rings of pure fire and pure darkness—though the point is obscure. The heavenly bodies, apparently, are light shining out of the mixed rings—which reminds us of Anaximander. The revolution of the mixed rings is the source of motion and change in the universe. Somewhere in the universe there resides a "divinity that directs the course of all things"—Necessity—who contrived Eros, the first of all the gods, from whom the succeeding generations of the gods proceeded. [6]

We have also one fragment dealing with thinking and knowledge. "Just as thought stands at any time to the mixture of its erring organs, so does it come to men; for that which thinks is the same, namely, the substance of the limbs, in each and every man; for their thought is that of which there is more in them." [7] And we are told by a later commentator, Simplicius, that Parmenides believed that men were wise or foolish according as the principle of light or that of darkness was preponderant in the composition of their bodies.

Possible Reasons for Adding the "Way of Opinion." Why Parmenides wrote a *Way of Opinion* and expounded a theory of the universe he believed to be false has perplexed commentators both ancient and modern. It has been said that he meant to set forth and systematize the vulgar views "of the many"; that he was seriously describing the structure of the world of appearance, much as Kant and Spencer in modern times discussed the principles and laws by which phenomena are governed, while maintaining that the nature of Reality is inscrutable and unknowable; and that he was setting forth Pythagorean views, accepted by himself in his youth, but now rejected, for the express purpose of acquainting his disciples with, and warning them against, his earlier opinions. [8]

Parmenides' Influence. The reasoning of Parmenides seems to have created a stir in the contemporary philosophic world, and it continued to exert considerable influence, direct or indirect, on subsequent Greek thinking. There is ground for believing that the Pythagoreans retorted immediately by attempting to show that his concept of the absolute unity and homogeneity of Being was as self-contradictory and mathe-

---

[5] Fr. 8 (Burnet, p. 176).   [7] Fr. 16 (Burnet, pp. 177-178).
[6] Frs. 12, 13 (Burnet, p. 177).   [8] On this point, cf. Burnet, p. 182 ff.

matically impossible as he had tried to prove the concept of multiplicity to be. And apparently, a generation later, Empedocles and Anaxagoras and Leucippus, to whom we shall come in the next chapter, while accepting in the main Parmenides' logic and his conclusions regarding the nature of the Real, attempted also to save the reality of the sensible world and of its apparent multiplicity, variety, motion and change by means which we shall presently describe. Indeed, it has been suggested that the arguments of Parmenides' disciple, Zeno, were a counter-blast to the Pythagorean attack on his master's teaching, and that another disciple, Melissus, was largely concerned to show that the compromises suggested by Empedocles and Anaxagoras would not hold water.[9] To the teachings of these disciples we now turn.

II. ZENO

Originator of Dialectic. Zeno (b. at Elea circ. 490 B.C., d. circ. 430 B.C.), who succeeded Parmenides as head of the Eleatic School, initiated a new form of logical argument. It consisted in admitting for the moment the truth of the views of one's opponent, and then developing the logical absurdities of his position. This method of argument, called by the Greeks "dialectic," was used by Socrates in his development of a position by question and answer, and was perfected as a literary as well as a logical device by Plato, who also used the word to describe reasoning about first principles.

Absurdities in the Conception of the Real. Suppose, says Zeno, that Reality instead of being one and unbroken, as Parmenides asserted, is really broken into many parts. In that case, it will have to be both finite and infinite—which is absurd. On the one hand, it must be composed of a finite number of indivisible parts, if we are to talk of real, ultimate parts at all. But, on the other, every part must be conceived as divisible into smaller parts, and so on *ad infinitum*. Again, the Real must be thought of as both infinitely large and infinitely small. If composed of indivisible parts it must be infinitely small, since its parts, to be conceived as indivisible, must be conceived as without magnitude. But if it is infinitely divisible, it will have an infinite number of parts and therefore will be infinitely large. Finally, the total effect of a Reality that is many ought logically to be no more than the sum of the separate effects produced by its different parts. And yet, drop a single grain of millet seed and you will not hear it

[9] On these points, cf. Burnet, *op. cit.,* pp. 314, 328; H. Cherniss, *Aristotle's Criticism of Presocratic Philosophy,* pp. 398, 402 ff.

But drop a whole bushel and there will be a noise. How is this possible? How can a noise be a sum total of silences? How can the audible
be composed of inaudible parts? It cannot. A Reality, therefore, made
up of many parts is once more shown to be logically self-contradictory.[10]

Or, take Parmenides' theory that Reality is a sphere outside of
which there is no space. Suppose that he is wrong, as the Pythagoreans
were arguing, and that such an external space does exist. This space,
once that we are outward bound, will require another space to contain it, and so on *ad infinitum*. But in that case we shall never reach
a final space which contains all things. We shall simply go on and
on, looking for the space in which all things exist—that is, for real
space—and never finding it. The notion, then, of infinite space is at
least as absurd as the Parmenidean conception of a finite, spherical
space, if not more so.[11]

Paradoxes Proving Motion Inconceivable in a Pluralistic Reality.
Finally Zeno points out that motion is by no means saved by supposing
that Being is multiple and made up of parts. On the contrary, it remains as self-contradictory and logically impossible in a world in
which multiplicity is real, as it is in the Parmenidean concept of the
nature of Reality. To drive home the inconceivability of motion in
a universe that is divisible into many units, he brings forward four
paradoxes.

In the first place it will prove impossible to pass from one fixed
point to another, as, for example, to cross a race-course. For to traverse
any given distance, you must first traverse half of it, and again half
of that half and so on *ad infinitum*. Since the space you must traverse
will, on the pluralistic hypothesis, be infinitely divisible, you can never
come to the end of it; and it will always separate you, by however
infinitesimal an amount, from your goal.

Again, Achilles, however swiftly he may run, can never overtake
the tortoise. For by the time he has reached the place from which the
tortoise started, the tortoise will have covered some ground. And by
the time Achilles himself has traversed the same ground, the tortoise
will have traveled a little further. And so on, once more *ad infinitum,*
with Achilles always gaining, but the tortoise always ahead.

Or, take the arrow apparently in flight. In reality it is at rest. For
at every moment in its flight it must be occupying a space equal to
itself. But when anything is occupying a space equal to itself it is at
rest.

[10] Cf. Frs. 1, 2, 3 (Burnet, pp. 315-316). Simplicius, 255 (trans. Fairbanks,
The First Philosophers of Greece, p. 117).
[11] Cf. Burnet, p. 317.

Finally, let us suppose three lines of an equal number of bodies, say chariots, on the track of a stadium. One line is stationary, the other two, equally distant from it, are approaching it from opposite directions with equal speeds. Hence both the moving lines will take the same number of moments to pass it. But in so doing, either moving line will pass twice as many chariots in the line going in the opposite direction as it does in the line of chariots at rest. In short the moving lines will pass each other twice as fast as they do the stationary line. In that case at any given moment they will both be moving with two different speeds one of which is half or twice the other, according as we look at it. Hence we are obliged to say that each of the moving chariots is going at every moment both twice and half as fast as it is moving at that moment—which is absurd. It is, then, as logically impossible to move from one moment to another as it is to move from one point in space to the next.[12]

All in all, Zeno concludes, no matter from what angle we view the problem, those who maintain that the Real is a moving Many make certainly no more sense, and, if anything, much less sense, than those who assert that the Real is a motionless indivisible One.

Persistence of the Paradoxes till Modern Times. These paradoxes remained unsolved by mathematics and logic for some twenty-two hundred years. As long as space and time were conceived as divisible *ad infinitum* into discrete points and instants, no way of satisfactorily answering them could be found. It is only recently that a solution has been offered by new mathematical theories regarding the nature of the infinitesimal, the infinite, and the continuous from which the notions of discreteness and infinite divisibility have been banished.[13]

III. MELISSUS

The last important member of the Eleatic School was Melissus of Samos, a somewhat younger contemporary of Zeno's. He was a prominent statesman, and, as admiral of the fleet during the rebellion of Samos against the Athenian Empire, he inflicted a defeat upon the enemy forces, which happened at the moment to be commanded by the poet Sophocles.

Attack on Anaxagoras. By this time the philosophers Empedocles and Anaxagoras had appeared upon the scene, both of whom, while

---

[12] For the paradoxes of Zeno, cf. Aristotle, *Phys.* VI, 9, 239 *b*.
[13] Cf. Russell, *Mysticism and Logic,* Chap. V.

in agreement with Parmenides' conclusions regarding the nature of Reality, were trying to reconcile with them the multiple, variegated, moving and changing characteristics it seemed to exhibit. This they were doing by breaking up the Real into a number of elementary substances, each one of which complied with Parmenides' specifications, except for that of immobility, and by attributing variety and alteration to different mixings of these primary elements. They both followed Parmenides, however, in maintaining that there was no void and that the substances of which the Real was composed were completely compacted, with no empty space between them.

Reiteration of Parmenides' Argument. The arguments of Melissus, as we have already noted, seem to have been excited by and directed against these attempts at compromise—particularly, perhaps, by and against the system of Anaxagoras. Melissus reiterates the views of Parmenides. The truly existent must be one and continuous, without motion, alteration, development, divisibility, multiplicity or variety of any sort, and there can be neither more nor less of it. Moreover, even if the Real were multiple and composite, its constituent parts would have to be conceived along Eleatic lines as simple, unchanging, uncreated and indestructible units. By no stretch of thought could they be conceived as coming into being or ceasing to be, or growing out of anything else. This, incidentally, both Empedocles and Anaxagoras admitted.

But, continues Melissus, in that case there can be no mixings and rearrangements (such as Empedocles and Anaxagoras resorted to). For rearrangement is alteration, and, if it takes place, "then the real must needs not be all alike, but what was before must pass away, and what was not must come into being. . . .

"Further it is not possible that its order should be changed; for the order which it had before does not perish, nor does that which was not come into being. But since nothing is either added to it or passes away or is altered, how can any real thing have its order changed? For if anything became different, this would amount to a change in its order." [14]

Motion Impossible Without a Void. Again, if there is no void, and the Real is completely compact (as Empedocles and Anaxagoras admitted), how can the parts into which they divided the Real move and commingle? A compact Reality cannot move, "for it has nowhere to betake itself to, but is full. For if there were aught empty it would

[14] Fr. 7 (Burnet, pp. 322-323).

betake itself to the empty. But since there is naught empty, it has nowhere to betake itself to. . . . It must needs be full if there is naught empty, and if it is full it does not move." [15]

Furthermore, if the Real has many constituents, these constituents must be distinguishable and separated from one another. But to be separated they must have moved away from one another. Motion, however, is impossible. "If what is real is divided, it moves; but if it moves, it cannot be." [16]

Change and Motion. Finally things certainly seem to change into one another. If, however, this seeming transformation is *really* nothing but a rearrangement of unchangeable constituents, then transformation is no less unreal and illusory in a pluralistic Reality than it is in the Real of Parmenides. [17] The implication is perhaps that the pluralists have no reason for accepting the reality of motion when they do not accept the reality of change, and that, if they admit the unreal character of the one, they might as well admit the illusory nature of the other—in which case their systems fall to the ground. [18] For in any case they would not be seeing aright, since the many that we see would not be the many principles to which they reduce the multiplicity and variety of the sensible world. Hence they must admit that the plurality of the sensible world, as well as its apparent change, is a matter of false opinion. And when we examine the many principles or elements to which they reduce the multiplicity and variety of phenomena, we shall find that these elements are nothing but a multiplication of Parmenidean Ones. "So then, if there were many things they would have to be just of the same nature as the one." [19]

Melissus on Infinity of the Real. There was, however, one point in which Melissus differed from Parmenides. He denied that the Real was spherical in shape, and held that it "must ever be infinite in magnitude. But nothing which has a beginning or end is either eternal or infinite." [20] No void exists outside it to contain and limit it. It is then infinitely extended in space, just as it is without temporal beginning or end.

We pass now to the systems of Empedocles and Anaxagoras which Melissus seems to have been criticizing.

[15] *Ibid.* (Burnet, p. 323).
[16] Fr. 10 (Burnet, p. 324).
[17] Cf. Fr. 8 (Burnet, p. 323).
[18] On all these points, cf. Cherniss, *op. cit.,* pp. 402 ff.
[19] Fr. 8 (Burnet, p. 324).
[20] Frs. 3, 4 (Burnet, p. 322).

Chapter VII

THE PLURALISTS

I. GENERAL CHARACTERISTICS

Attempted Reconciliation of Sense-data with Logic. The Pluralists, as we have already pointed out, all sought by one device or another to reconcile the reality of multiplicity, variety, and change with the existence of a world-stuff of whose essentially unchanging and unvaried nature the logic of Parmenides had convinced them. They all set about this task in the same way, though the details of their schemes differed greatly. They all smashed the Parmenidean sphere of motionless, simple, and single Being to bits, each one of which retained most or all of the Eleatic characteristics—eternity, indestructibility, simplicity, unalterableness, and the like. Then, affirming the possibility of change of place, though not of quality and nature, they proceeded to move these bits about in space, to fit them together in different ways, and to regard all seeming alteration as in reality merely a rearrangement of them in different proportions and figures. Thus apparent qualitative change did not affect or contradict the real, immutable being of the particles of world-stuff, although there was a real change in their external and spatial relations to one another.

II. EMPEDOCLES

Life. The first of these philosophers, Empedocles, was born at Agrigentum in Sicily about 490 B.C., and died in southern Italy or Greece about 435 B.C. He came of one of the richest and most aristocratic families of his native city. His father was one of the leaders of the recently established democratic government there, and Empedocles himself, for a while, exerted great political influence. He was also a doctor and a scientist as well as a philosopher, and was much under the spell of the religious beliefs of the Pythagoreans and the Orphics. Like Pythagoras, he was credited with supernatural powers, in his possession of which he himself apparently believed. And there were stories that instead of dying, he disappeared at the summons of a great voice and in the midst of a great light from heaven. Other sensational reports had him jump into the crater of Etna, hang himself, be killed by falling out of a chariot, and die by drowning. Abundant fragments of his writings have come down to us. They are couched in a somewhat florid hexameter verse, in which it is sometimes difficult to disentangle fact from poetic license.

Attack on Current Theology. Like Xenophanes, Empedocles revolted against the orthodox Greek theology with its gods created in man's own image. And like Xenophanes and his other predecessors he transferred the idea of the divine to the world-stuff:

"It is not possible," he tells us, "to set God before our eyes or lay hold of him with our hands, which is the broadest way of persuasion that leads into the heart of man.

"For he is not furnished with a human head on his body, two branches do not sprout from his shoulders, he has no feet, no swift knees nor hairy parts; but he is only a sacred and unutterable mind flashing through the whole world with rapid thoughts." [1] The gods of the popular theology may exist, to be sure. Empedocles speaks of them, and uses their names to designate and symbolize natural forces and elements. But they are sprung from the same elements and produced by the same forces as have brought the rest of the world into being. "For out of these (sources) have sprung all things that were and are and shall be—trees and men and women, beasts and birds and the fishes that dwell in the waters, and the gods that live long lives and are exalted in honour." [2]

This description of God as "a sacred and unutterable mind" should in the opinion of many scholars not be interpreted in a monotheistic or personalistic way. For, in the philosophic portion of his poem he speaks of the universe as God, and of its constituent elements as divine, and tells us that mind and thought are a property of all things and that it is the world-stuff that does the thinking.

Doctrine of Reincarnation. Empedocles also proclaims his belief in reincarnation. Men, he tells us, are fallen daemons who have sinned, and for punishment must "wander thrice ten thousand seasons from the abodes of the blessed, being born throughout the time in all manner of mortal forms, changing one toilsome path of life for another." He himself is "one of these, an exile and a wanderer from the gods. . . . For I have been ere now a boy and a girl, a beast and a bird and

[1] Frs. 133, 134 (Burnet, p. 225).
[2] Fr. 21 (Burnet, p. 209).

a dumb fish in the sea. . . . From what honour, from what height of bliss have I fallen to go about among mortals here on earth." [3] This view is inconsistent with what he has to say later on about death.

Fire, Air, Water and Earth Fill the Universe. In his philosophy proper, Empedocles quarters the Parmenidean sphere of undifferentiated Being into four elements: the Fire, Water, and Earth of his predecessors, to which he adds Air, whose corporeal nature had by his time been recognized. Each one of these elements is uncreated, indestructible, and internally simple, homogenous and incapable of change and alteration. Of these four elements or "roots," as Empedocles calls them, all things in the universe are composed. Individual things possess no proper substance of their own. "They are only a mingling and interchange of what has been mingled. Substance is but a name given to these things by men." [4]

The four "roots" he so closely compacted that there is no such thing as empty space. In denying the existence of the void, Empedocles is as emphatic as Parmenides. "In the all there is naught empty." [5] At the same time, he does not find that a lack of empty space to move in makes change of place impossible—an opinion that, as we have just seen, was attacked by Melissus. Perhaps he relied on sensible experience, in which substances seem to interpenetrate one another without perceptible interstices, as when solids dissolve in liquids, and liquids seep through solids, and fire springs directly from the materials it is consuming. Perhaps, too, the discovery that the "empty air" is corporeal helped, since solids and liquids and fire could apparently move through "solid" air and "solid" air could interpenetrate them. We might remember, too, that in the seventeenth century, the philosopher Descartes, who was also an eminent mathematician and physicist of his time, upheld the possibility of locomotion within a *plenum*. However that may be, Empedocles believed that space is full, and found no difficulty in reconciling the possibility and reality of change of place with this concept.

The Four Elements Moved by Love and Strife. There was, however, one difficulty that apparently he did find in explaining the occurrence of motion in a universe composed of elements that measured up to the Parmenidean specifications of real being. To make the four "roots" the sources of their own movement, and to say that each was inherently, and naturally, and of its own self in motion, might seem to threaten their inner immobility and to make change of place an essen-

[3] Frs. 115, 117, 119 (Burnet, p. 223).   [5] Frs. 13, 14 (Burnet, p. 207).
[4] Fr. 8 (Burnet, p. 206).

tial characteristic of them. In that case it would be difficult, if not impossible, to think of them as in themselves the static entities that Eleatic logic demanded they should be. In any case, whether or not Empedocles felt this difficulty, we find him conceiving them as in themselves inert, and attributing their change of place and their consequent commingling to two further factors, which he calls Love and Strife, or we might say, attraction and repulsion.[6]

Just how he conceived these two factors we do not know. There is good ground for believing that he did not regard them as incorporeal "forces," as such a concept would have been out of keeping with his time and background. Rather, we are told, they were considered by him to be corporeal.[7] Certainly he himself describes them as equal in weight, length and breadth to the four "roots." He also calls Love, Aphrodite, and regards sexual desire as a manifestation of it. For that matter, he frequently uses sexual terms and analogies to describe its cosmic workings and results.

The Alternation of Love and Strife. Love and Strife alternate in moving the four "roots." The world-process, then, moves in recurrent cycles of four periods. There is a stage in which the influence of Love is complete, and Fire, Air, Water and Earth are completely commingled. Then Strife begins to prevail, and there is a gradual separation of the roots from one another until, when Strife is completely triumphant and Love has been overcome, the four elements lie wholly separated out from one another and apart. Finally, Love makes itself felt again, the elements begin to interpenetrate one another, and the commingling continues till their fusion is once more complete.

Obviously no universe such as we inhabit can exist at the poles of this process, when the Fire, Air, Water and Earth are wholly fused or wholly isolated. The formation and destruction of a world can recur only in the intermediate periods of the cycle, when Love and Strife are contending with each other and the "roots" are only partially commingled or separated. "There is a double becoming of perishable things, and a double passing away. The coming together of all things brings one generation into being and destroys it; the other grows up and is scattered as things become divided. And these things never cease continually changing places, at one time all uniting in one through Love, at another borne in different directions by the repulsion of Strife."[8]

[6] Cf. Cherniss, *op. cit.,* p. 399.
[7] Cf. Zeller, *Pre-Socratic Philosophy,* II, p. 138; Burnet, *op. cit.,* p. 232.
[8] Fr. 17 (Burnet, p. 207). Cf. Fr. 26, Burnet, p. 210.

Cosmology. There is some question as to whether Empedocles believed our world to belong to the period in which Love is casting out Strife, or to that in which Strife is casting out Love.[9] The fragments we possess are not decisive, nor do they give a clear picture of his cosmology. By later commentators we are told that Air was first separated out, then Fire, and then Earth. Fire rushed up and solidified a portion of the Air into a sort of crystalline eggshell surrounding the universe—an idea possibly connected with the Orphic world-egg from which the god, Phanes, was hatched. Immediately within this shell of crystallized Air a hemisphere of Fire formed, and the displaced Air, mixed with Fire, sank down below the earth and became a dark hemisphere in which the Fire appears as the fixed stars attached to the Air, and as free-moving planets.

The upward rush of Fire and the downward rush of the displaced Air set the cosmic egg rotating about the earth and presenting now the sphere of star-studded Air, now the sphere of pure Fire. The sun, Empedocles thought, was a spot of light reflected back upon the heavens by the earth from the radiance of the fiery hemisphere. The moon was a disc of frozen air, shining with light reflected from the sun. The darkness of night was caused by the disappearance of the fiery sphere beneath the earth, and the consequent obscuration of the earth's upper surface by its own shadow. Solar eclipses were caused by the moon cutting off the sun's rays "as he goes above her" and casting "a shadow on as much of the earth as is the breadth of the pale-faced moon." [10] These last assertions were founded on contemporary astronomical discoveries of the true nature of the moon's light, of the darkness of night, and of solar eclipses.

The separated Earth and Water were precipitated to the center of the universe, where the Water was squeezed out of the Earth by pressure. "Sea" is "the sweat of earth." Wind is caused by the movement of the two hemispheres; rain by the compression of Air squeezing out the Water mixed with it; lightning by the squeezing of the Fire out of the clouds. The Earth shares in the general rotation of the universe, whose rapid spinning keeps it and the heavens in their proper places and prevents them from falling. Empedocles is said to have illustrated this by the whirling of a cup of water at the end of a string.

The Origin and Development of Life. Of the origin and development of life on earth, Empedocles gives an interesting account. A

[9] Zeller advocates Love, Burnet, Strife. Cf. Burnet, pp. 234 ff.
[10] Fr. 42 (Burnet, p. 213).

certain mixture of the four elements agitated by both Love and Strife forms the primitive organic compound from which all living beings arise. First come plants, to which Empedocles attributed bi-sexuality as well as sensation, pleasure, pain, and desire. They are followed by the evolution of animals and man.

In the period in which Strife is casting out Love, this evolution proceeds as follows. "Whole natured forms first arose from the earth, having a portion both of water and fire. These did the fire, desirous of reaching its like, send up, showing as yet neither the charming form of the limbs, nor yet the voice and parts that are proper to men." [11] The sex and species of these primitive forms were unrecognizable, but the continued operation of Strife separated them into species and into males and females. Such species as were "better suited to it took to the water; others were wafted up into the air for such time as they possessed more of the fiery matter, and the heavier remained on earth." [12] Meantime there was sufficient Love in the mixture to keep living bodies and species fairly fixed in structure and to insure perpetuation of the species by reproduction.

When a universe is formed by the reverse process of Love casting out Strife, life begins with the production of disjointed and scattered animal parts. "Many heads sprung up without necks, and arms wandered bare and bereft of shoulders. Eyes strayed up and down in want of foreheads. Solitary limbs wandered seeking union. But as divinity was mingled still further with divinity [i.e., Love with Strife] these things joined together as each might chance, and many other things arose. Shambling creatures with faces and breasts looking in different directions were born; some offspring of oxen with faces of men, while others again, arose as offspring of men with the heads of oxen, and creatures in whom the nature of women and men was mingled, furnished with sterile parts." [13]

In this as in the other process of evolution, Empedocles taught, according to Aristotle, that those forms survived which were suited to their environment, while the unfit were weeded out. "Certain things have been preserved because they had spontaneously acquired a fitting structure, while those which were not so put together have perished and are perishing, as Empedocles says of the oxen with human faces." [14]

Evolution and Physiology. Empedocles supplemented his theories of evolution by noting the analogies in the structure of different living species. He thought, for example, that "hair and leaves and thick

[11] Fr. 62 (Burnet, p. 215).   [13] Frs. 57-61 (Burnet, p. 214).
[12] Aetius, V, 19.   [14] *Phys.* II, 8, 198 *b* (Burnet, p. 243).

feathers of birds and scales that grow on mighty limbs are the same thing." He studied the nature of reproduction and of nutrition, and has left a long passage on respiration in which he remotely foresaw the circulation of the blood. The blood, he says, pulses to and fro between the surface and the interior of the body, pulling in the air after it through the pores of the body as well as the nose and mouth, when it recedes from the surface, and driving them out again when it returns. He also studied the structure of the eye and the nature of vision.

Consciousness and Perception. To his biological and physiological studies Empedocles added investigations in what we today should call the field of psychology. He does not seem, any more than his predecessors, to have made conscious and mental activity a separate principle. "All things," he tells us, "have wisdom and a share of thought," [15] and in ourselves it is the basic "roots" mixed in our bodies which "think, and feel pleasure and pain." [16] Our consciousness, furthermore, is more or less localized in the heart and the surrounding blood, "for the blood round the heart is the thought of men." [17] He chose the blood, we are told, because "in it of all parts of the body, all the elements are most completely mingled." [18] Incidentally, the different capacities, temperaments, and humors displayed by different individuals are the expressions of varying conditions and proportions of the mixture.[19] Sleep is due to a partial separation of Fire from the other elements, which gives rise to "a moderate cooling of the blood." If the Fire becomes wholly separated, and the blood becomes completely cold, we die.[20] Then the organic mixture is dissolved and the constituent elements combine in new ways, or merge, each with its kindred "root." Such views are quite inconsistent with his Orphic doctrine of reincarnation.

Empedocles also discussed perception at some length, which he found to be bound up with the affinity of the particles of the four elements, each for its own kind, and with their tendency, expressed in Strife, to seek out their fellows. Hence the elements commingled in our bodies are sensitive to the corresponding "roots" mixed in external bodies. These bodies are continually giving off effluences,

[15] Fr. 110 (Burnet, p. 221).
[16] Fr. 107 (Burnet, p. 220).
[17] Fr. 105 (Burnet, p. 220).
[18] Theophrastus, *De Sensu,* 10 (Burnet, p. 247).
[19] *Ibid.* (Aetius, V, 24, 25).
[20] Cf. Burnet, pp. 244-245.

which strike the body, enter the sense-organ best fitted to receive them, and are amalgamated with the kindred element within.

The Operation of the Senses. Thus, in seeing, light is perceived by the Fire within the eye, darkness by the Water, and differences of ability to see by day or by night are explained by the preponderance of one of these elements in the organ of vision. "Hearing," he holds, "is produced by sound outside, when the air moved by the voice sounds inside the ear; for the sense of hearing is a sort of bell sounding inside the ear. . . . When the air is set in motion it strikes upon the solid part, and produces a sound." Smell, he holds, arises from respiration. As to touch and taste, he does not lay down how, nor by what means they arise, except that he gives us an explanation applicable to all: that sensation is produced by adaptation to the pores. Pleasure is produced by what is like in its elements and their mixture; pain, by what is opposite.

"And he gives a precisely similar account of thought and ignorance. Thought arises from what is like, and ignorance from what is unlike, thus implying that thought is the same, or nearly the same, as perception. . . ." [21]

III. ANAXAGORAS

Life. Anaxagoras, the next philosopher on our list, was born about 500 B.C. at Clazomenae near present-day Smyrna. But he spent the larger part of his life at Athens as an intimate of the statesman Pericles, the builder of the Athenian Empire. And he was an adornment to the brilliant circle of artists, sculptors, architects, musicians, and poets that Pericles gathered about himself to his own and Athens' great glory. Among them were the sculptor Phidias, who carved the frieze of the Parthenon; Ictinus and Callicrates, the supervising architects of the building; Mnesicles, who planned the Propylaea leading up the slope of the Acropolis; the historians Herodotus and Thucydides; Damon, one of the most intelligent and cultivated men in Athens, and the great musician of the day; and the poets Sophocles and Euripides. So Anaxagoras moved in good company. But he himself was no mean contributor to the splendor of the Periclean Age.

Towards the end of his life, however, he got into trouble. The Athenians were conservative in matters religious, and in this respect differed from the liberal, free-thinking, tolerant Ionian Greeks. Pericles himself was accused by the opposition party of being pro-

[21] Theophrastus, *De Sensu*, 7 ff. (Burnet, pp. 246-247).

Ionian and un-Athenian in his views, and his court, and especially his Milesian mistress, the brilliant and emancipated Aspasia, were in disfavor with the fundamentalists of the day. The opposition lost no opportunity to wound him through his friends, and the publication of Anaxagoras' philosophical system gave them an excellent opening. In his book Anaxagoras had declared that the sun was not a god, but a piece of fiery stone about the size of the Peloponnesus. The moon, too, was not a goddess but was made "of earth and had plains and ravines in it." For these assertions he was tried for blasphemy, convicted, and thrown into prison. He escaped, however, perhaps with Pericles' aid, and fled back to Ionia. He settled at Lampsacus, where he died, mourned by his adopted countrymen, who erected an altar dedicated to mind and truth in his memory.

Pluralistic Treatment of Eleatic Being. Anaxagoras seems to have received his first lessons in philosophy from disciples of Anaximenes. He was, however, impressed, like Empedocles, with the Parmenidean logic, and accepted the Eleatic dictum that what is real can be neither created nor destroyed nor internally altered, and that it must be a *plenum,* packed solid and with no emptiness within it. But, like Empedocles, he felt that the absence of empty space, and the completely continuous character of the Real, did not exclude the possibility of multiplicity and variety and change of place within it. He, too, dealt with the Parmenidean sphere by smashing it to bits to which he attributed different but unalterable characteristics, and he explained the diversity and alteration of the sensible world in terms of the spatial combination, separation, and rearrangement of these particles. Furthermore, he explicitly proclaimed that the world-stuff is infinitely divisible. "Nor is there a least of what is small, but there is always a smaller; for it cannot be that what is should cease to be by being cut. Hence it is impossible that there should be a least thing." [22] With Melissus' criticism of this dictum we are already familiar.

Advance over Empedocles. Anaxagoras, however, was unwilling to stop with the division of Parmenidean Being into four stuffs. It has been suggested that he felt that the rearrangements of Fire, Air, Earth and Water in the variety of sensible substances really involved the occurrence in the Real of new *qualities*—just, we might say, as a mixture of red and yellow would be no longer just red *plus* yellow, but a new color, orange. But Parmenides had shown to Anaxagoras'

[22] Frs. 3, 6 (Burnet, pp. 258, 259).

satisfaction, and, for that matter, to Empedocles', that the appearance of new qualities was impossible. What is real is what it always was. In that case variety and apparent alteration could, in Anaxagoras' opinion, be reconciled with the immutable character of Reality only by supposing that as many different elements really exist as there are sensible examples of qualitative difference.[23] There must be ultimate particles of hair and flesh, for example, just as there are ultimate particles of fire, air, water, and earth. For "how can hair come from what is not hair, or flesh from what is not flesh?"[24]

The "Seeds" and Their Mixed Nature. So it is that we find Anaxagoras pulverizing the Parmenidean sphere of being into an indefinite number of kinds of qualitatively different "seeds," as he called them, each one of which is quantitatively infinitely divisible. Reality, according to him, is a mixture of these seeds, and sensible variety and alteration are the result of their coming together in different combinations which are eventually dissolved.

However, and this is one of the most distinctive marks of his system, the "seeds" themselves, instead of being homogeneous after their kind, like Empedocles' particles of Fire, Air, Water and Earth, are themselves mixtures, and remain such, no matter how minutely they are divided. Each kind of "seed" contains a portion of every other kind, or at least of all opposed qualities.[25] "The things that are in the world are not divided nor cut off one from another with a hatchet, neither the warm from the cold, nor the cold from the warm." So, too, there is a mixture "of the moist and the dry . . . and the light and the dark and of a multitude of innumerable seeds in no way like each other. For none of the other things either is like any other." All things, then, "will be in everything; nor is it possible for them to be apart, but all things have a portion of everything."[26]

Everything, however, is not equally present in all the seeds. In some, one quality predominates, in others, another. Hence we have various sorts of seeds, whose different kinds are determined by the nature preponderant in them, as, for example, hot, cold, moist, dry, light, dark, hair, flesh. But mixed with cold in the seeds of cold there is some hot, and it may be some hair and flesh, while a seed of flesh contains some hair and some light, etc., though in such small proportions that they do not adulterate its essentially fleshly character.

In this way, perhaps, by attributing mixture to the qualitatively different seeds themselves, Anaxagoras may have felt that he was

[23] Cf. Cherniss, *op. cit.,* pp. 400-401. [25] Cf. Burnet, pp. 263 ff.
[24] Fr. 10 (Burnet, p. 259). [26] Frs. 4, 6, 8 (Burnet, pp. 258-259).

avoiding what he apparently considered the weakness of the Emped-
oclean philosophy—the danger that mixtures of unmixed Fire, Air,
Water and Earth might produce new qualities in the nature of the
Existent and thus destroy the unalterable character of the Real. If
every kind of seed always possessed to some degree the distinctive
characteristics of all the other kinds, no matter how far the process
of quantitative division was pushed, then plainly no new qualities not
already contained in the seeds could be produced by, or in, any mixture of them. On the contrary, each seed of the truly Existent would
already possess, immutably and to and from eternity, all the qualities
that ever could appear in the universe as the result of any mixture
whatsoever.

The "Seeds" Imperceptible to the Senses. Again, whereas Empedocles, like Heraclitus and the Milesians, found the world-stuff in elements apparent to the senses, the seeds of which Anaxagoras constructs his world-stuff, though possessed of qualities perceptible *en
masse,* are not individually perceptible like Fire or Air or Water or
Earth. We do not, then, immediately experience the true nature of
the Real. "From the weakness of our senses we are not able to judge
the truth. What appears is a vision of the unseen." [27] In short, Anaxagoras, like Parmenides, invokes reason to indicate what Reality is
like, and demonstrates by argument the character of the world-stuff.
He supports, however, his trust in the power of reason to figure out
what escapes the senses by his account of the nature of mind, to
which we shall come in a moment.

Melissus' Criticism of Anaxagoras. These views, however, did not
save Anaxagoras from censure by the Eleatics. Melissus seems to have
argued that the doctrine that "all things have a portion of everything"
made the seeds themselves composite and variegated, and thus open
to the objections Parmenides had made to the reality of multiplicity
and variety. And the qualitative differences, like those of the sensible
world, were only seeming. What really *was* in each one of them was its
"being," and hence, since the "being" of one was in no wise different
from the "being" of the other, they were in reality identical, and their
multiplicity became as much a matter of false opinion as their variety.

Furthermore, in affirming that *what is* is not perceived by the senses
but discovered by reason, Anaxagoras had admitted the unreality of
sensible characteristics, and by the same token the worthlessness of
our sensible experience of multiplicity, variety, and motion as evi-

[27] Frs. 21, 21 *a* (Burnet, p. 261).

dence of the nature of the Real, and had thus given his case away.[28]
We turn back now to Anaxagoras' views about mind.

The "Unmixed" Nature of Mind. Mind is the one exception to the
rule that "all things have a portion of everything." All other things,
he tells us, "partake in a portion of everything, while *Nous* [mind] is
infinite and self-ruled and is mixed with nothing, but is alone, itself
by itself. . . . It is the thinnest of all things and the purest." It
permeates the cosmic mixture. It "is certainly there where everything
else is, in the surrounding mass, and in what has been united with it,
and separated off from it." Furthermore, "it has knowledge about
things. . . . And all the things that are mingled together and separated off and distinguished are all known by Nous." [29] We might,
then, perhaps say that Mind, by virtue of being diffused throughout
the "unseen" mixture and in contact with it, can know what the senses
cannot perceive.

Mind the Only "Self-moving Seed." Again, Mind seems to be the
one element among the seeds that possesses an inherent activity and
motion of its own, in contrast to the other ingredients of the mixture
which are in themselves static and inert. Mind has "the greatest
strength; and Nous has power over all things, both greater and smaller,
that have life." [30] To the exertion of this power is due the evolution
of the cosmic mixture into a universe.

The evolution of the world begins as follows. Mind sets up a whirling motion, or vortex in the mixture. "And Nous had power over the
whole revolution, so that it began to revolve in the beginning. And it
began to revolve first from a small beginning; but the revolution now
extends over a larger space, and will extend over a larger still. And
Nous set in order all things that were to be, and all things that were
and are not now, and are, and this revolution in which now revolve
the stars, and the sun and the moon and the air and the aether that
are separated off." [31]

Just how Anaxagoras thought of Mind and how he conceived the
method by which it sets the mixture revolving and orders things is
uncertain. Some modern commentators have felt that he regarded it
as incorporeal, or at least that he was on his way towards conceiving
it as an immaterial principle. Indeed, some suggest a personalistic,
theistic interpretation. Others, however, argue that his description of
it as thin, and unmixed, and diffused throughout the mixture, and

---

[28] Cf. Cherniss, *op. cit.,* pp. 402 ff.   [30] Fr. 12 (Burnet, p. 260).
[29] Frs. 12, 14 (Burnet, p. 260).   [31] *Ibid.*

"alike, both the greater and the smaller," in contrast to the mixed character of the other seeds, will not permit of such an interpretation. From this point of view, there are corporeal mind-seeds, just as there are material seeds of everything else.

The Activity of Mind Probably Not Conceived as Teleological. Again, some commentators envisage Mind as exercising its power over the seeds in a purposive and teleological manner, and ordering the course of events in accordance with a plan. Others think, on the contrary, that Anaxagoras was simply perpetuating the Ionian, hylozoist tradition in which he was educated, according to which the world-stuff "thinks all over," and by which no distinction between teleological and other kinds of activity and movement had been drawn. According to this point of view he probably thought of the mind-seeds as communicating their inherent movement to the inert constituents of the mixture in the same way that physical bodies in motion impart their movement to others with which they come in contact. If Anaxagoras really had broken so completely with the Ionian tradition and had thought up such innovations as the immaterial nature of Mind and its purposive planning of the world-process, we might expect him to have proclaimed explicitly and to have emphasized these new ideas. But, as we have seen, we find no such unequivocal declarations in the fragments we possess. And the ancient historians of philosophy make no mention of his ever having made them.

Platonic and Aristotelian Criticisms of Mind. Indeed, Plato, either using Socrates as a mouthpiece, or, it may be, reporting Socrates' own views, expresses disappointment at finding that Anaxagoras, for all that he said Mind caused and ordered all things, "ascribed no causal power whatever to it in the ordering of things, but to airs, aethers, and waters, and to a host of other strange things." [32] And Aristotle, while praising him for saying that "reason was present—as in animals so throughout nature—as the cause of the world and of all its order," [33] complained that he used it "as a *deus ex machina* to account for the formation of the world," invoking it only when he was at a loss for "some other explanation, and generally speaking, ascribing events to anything rather than to mind." [34]

The Anaxagorean Cosmology. But, by whatever means Mind set the mixture whirling, and whether or no it continued to guide teleologically the vortex thus produced, the first effect of the revolution of the mixture was a separation of opposites. "And this revolution

[32] *Phaedo*, 97 B, 8 (Burnet, p. 267).   [34] *Ibid.*, 4, 985 B, 18 ff.
[33] *Met.* I, 3, 984 B, 15 ff.

caused the separating off, and the rare is separated from the dense, the warm from the cold, the light from the dark, and the dry from the moist." But, Anaxagoras hastens to remind us, "nothing is altogether separated off, nor distinguished from anything else, except Nous." [35]

Next, "the dense and the moist and the cold and the dark came together where earth is now, while the rare and the warm and the dry [and the bright] went out towards the further part of the aether."

From "these" (i.e., the dense, moist, etc.) "as they separated off earth is solidified, for from mists water is separated off, and from water earth. From the earth stones are solidified by the cold, and these rush outwards more than water." [36] The stones may be the great rocks, which, according to the description of Anaxagoras' cosmology by ancient commentators, were hurled off by the rotation of the earth and, becoming incandescent by their rapid motion, went on revolving about the earth in the spinning ether, and constituted the heavenly bodies. We may at this point remember that Anaxagoras was tried by the Athenians for impiety on the ground that he held that the sun and the moon were not deities but huge masses of stone. The sun, we are told, he regarded as larger than the Peloponnesus. The moon is sometimes spoken of as incandescent, sometimes as shining with a reflected light and as possessed of plains and ravines. Eclipses he explained as due to the interposition of the earth between the sun and the moon, and of the moon between the sun and the earth. [37] The Milky Way was the reflection of the light of the stars that were not illuminated by the sun.

The earth itself "is flat in shape and remains suspended because of its size and because there is no vacuum. For this reason the air is very strong, and supports the earth which is borne up by it." The "sea arose from the waters in the earth . . . and from the rivers that flow into it. Rivers take their being both from rains, and from the waters of the earth; for the earth is hollow and has waters in its cavities. . . . Winds arose when the air was rarefied by the sun. . . . Thunder and lightning were produced by heat striking on the clouds. Earthquakes were caused by the air above striking on that beneath the earth; for the movement of the latter caused the earth which floats on it to rock." [38]

[35] Fr. 12 (Burnet, p. 260).
[36] Frs. 15, 16 (Burnet, p. 260).
[37] Hippolytus, Ref. 1, 8, 3 (Burnet, p. 271).
[38] Ibid. (Burnet, pp. 270, 271).

Plurality of Worlds. Apparently Anaxagoras believed that a plurality of worlds like ours arises from the revolution of the mixture and the separation of the seeds. And we must suppose, he says, "that men have been formed in them, and other animals that have life, and that these men have inhabited cities and cultivated fields as with us; and that their earth brings forth for them many things of all kinds of which they gather the best together into their dwellings, and use them. This much have I said with regard to separating off to show that it will not be only with us that things are separated off, but elsewhere, too." [39]

Development of Life. As regards the development of the living beings arising with the mixture, we are told by later commentators that Anaxagoras held that the seeds from which vegetables and animals arose were precipitated from the air by rain and thus brought to earth, and that animals were generated in the beginning in the moist element. He is also said to have attributed pain and pleasure to plants and to have called them "animals fixed in the earth." [40]

Theory of Sensation. In his theory of the nature of sensation he differs radically from Empedocles. Instead of like perceiving like, "perception is produced by opposites, for like things cannot be effected by like." Thus in seeing, he tells us, the colors in the pupil of the eye are picked up by the colors within the eye different from them, "because the prevailing color casts an image more readily upon its opposite." Most animals see better by day than by night because the difference of the colors in the pupil from those in the external world is then more marked.

Night is more of the same color with the eyes than day. . . .

It is in the same way that touch and taste discern their objects. . . . We know cold by warm, fresh by salt, and sweet by sour in virtue of our deficiency in each. . . . And we smell and hear in the same manner; the former by means of the accompanying respiration, the latter by the sound penetrating to the brain. . . .

And all sensation implies pain, a view which would seem to be the consequence of the first assumption, for all unlike things produce pain by their contact. And this pain is made perceptible by the long continuance or by the excess of a sensation. Brilliant colors and excessive noises produce pain, and we cannot dwell long on the same things. And generally sensation is proportionate to the size of the organs of sense. [41]

[39] Fr. 4 (Burnet, p. 258).
[40] Cf. Burnet, p. 272.
[41] Theophrastus, *De sensu*, 27 ff. (Burnet, pp. 273-274).

IV. ARCHELAUS OF ATHENS

Anaxagoras had gathered a number of disciples about him in Lampsacus, and at his death, one of them, Archelaus of Athens, suc ceeded him as head of the school he had founded. It is also said that Socrates studied with him.

Archelaus differed in some respects from his master. "He spoke of the mixture of matter in a similar way to Anaxagoras and of the first principles likewise. He held, however, that there was a certain mixture immanent even in Nous (Mind). And he held that there were two efficient causes which were separated off from one another, namely, the warm and the cold. The former was in motion, the latter at rest."

Cosmology. The universe arose by the flowing of water to the center of the vortex, where "being burnt up it turned to earth and air, the latter of which was borne up, while the former took its position below. . . . The earth is at rest," and "lies in the centre, being no appreciable part of the universe." From the original combustion of air

comes the substance of the heavenly bodies. Of these the sun is the largest, and the moon second; the rest are of various sizes. He says that the heavens were inclined, and that then the sun made light upon the earth, made the air transparent, and the earth dry; for it was originally a pond, being high at the circumference and hollow in the centre. He adduces as proof of this hollowness that the sun does not rise and set at the same time for all peoples, as it ought to do if the earth were level.

As to animals, he says that when the earth was first being warmed in the lower part where the warm and the cold were mingled together, many living creatures appeared, and especially men, all having the same manner of life, and deriving their sustenance from the slime; they did not live long, and later on generation from one another began. And men were distinguished from the rest, and set up leaders, and laws, and arts, and cities and so forth. And he says that Nous [Mind] is implanted in all animals alike; for each of the animals, as well as man, makes use of Nous [Mind], but some quicker, some slower.[42]

V. LEUCIPPUS AND DEMOCRITUS

Life of Leucippus. The last steps of the attempt to reconcile the reality of multiplicity, variety, and change with the exigencies of Eleatic logic were taken by Leucippus and Democritus.

[42] Hippolytus, Ref. 1, 9 (Burnet, pp. 359-360).

Of Leucippus' life we know little. He was born, according to a varying tradition, at Abdera, at Elea, at Melos, and at Miletus. The date
of his birth is unknown, but apparently he was a contemporary of
Empedocles and Anaxagoras. He is reputed to have been a disciple
of Parmenides and even of Zeno. Whether or not he committed his
views to writing is not known, and we have only one direct quotation
of his teaching. Our knowledge of him is wholly derived from the
comments of ancient writers, by whom he is always mentioned in
conjunction with his pupil Democritus.

Life of Democritus. Of Democritus we know somewhat more. He
was born about 460 B.C. at Abdera in Thrace, where he spent a considerable portion of his life teaching and building up a group of
disciples. He was rich and independent, and apparently traveled extensively. He wrote voluminously—and was rated as second only to
Aristotle in his literary fecundity by the historian Diogenes Laertius,
who gives a long catalogue of his works on physics, astronomy, biology,
psychology, mathematics, and grammar, as well as treatises on agriculture, painting, tactics, law, coughing, fever, and the like. In Graeco-
Roman times he enjoyed a reputation almost as great as those of Plato
and Aristotle, not only because of his learning and his philosophic
genius, but because of a literary style, comparable, in ancient opinion,
with that of the Platonic dialogues.

Identity of Their Views. Unfortunately, his works have all been lost,
"the most lamentable [loss] that has happened to the original documents of ancient philosophy," [43] and many of such purported fragments as have come down to us are of doubtful authenticity. For his
views, as for those of Leucippus, we are obliged to rely largely upon
later commentators. They seem, however, to have so nearly coincided
with those of Leucippus that we may count the philosophies of master
and pupil as a single system. This system, as we are about to see, not
only clarified, crystallized, and brought to a head and a conclusion
the work of their predecessors, but also, in so doing, it laid down the
fundamental principles of the atomic and mechanistic hypothesis which
has been the basis of all scientific advance up to the present day.

Attempt to Reconcile Pluralism with Eleatic Logic. Leucippus, like
Empedocles and Anaxagoras, accepted the Eleatic teaching that whatever really *is* must be uncreated and indestructible, and internally
homogeneous, immutable, invariable, and unalterable. Like them, too,

[43] Windelband, *History of Ancient Philosophy* (Eng. trans., 1889), p. 172.

he conceived the Real as a multiplicity of constituent elements each one of which possessed these characteristics. And like them he maintained that these constituents could change their place and reduced the qualitative varieties and alterations, as well as the spatial movement perceived by the senses, to terms of such change. Like Anaxagoras, moreover, he pulverized the Parmenidean sphere into a powder whose particles were too minute to be perceived as they are in themselves. And like Anaxagoras, heedful, too, it may be, of the criticisms of Melissus, he admitted the infinite divisibility, mathematically, at least, of these particles.

1. The "Atoms" Stripped of Secondary Sensible Qualities. But Leucippus also made four important novel modifications of the pluralistic hypothesis. In the first place, influenced it may be by the arguments of Melissus, he distilled the constituent elements of his Reality clear of what we should today call their secondary qualities—color, taste, smell, temperature, tactile characteristics, etc., and left them possessed of magnitude alone. "And he made their forms infinite in number since there was no reason why they should be of one kind rather than another." Democritus tells us that they differed in size as well as shape—whether repeating Leucippus' teaching or adding to it we do not know. These particles, moreover, are absolutely solid, and internally homogeneous. Each one is a *plenum,* with no emptiness within it—intrinsically an Eleatic "one" in all respects. In substance the particles are absolutely alike—made of the same identical stuff, so to speak. Since they possess spatial magnitude, they are divisible in mathematical theory, but, being completely solid, compact, and internally continuous, they are, as a matter of physical fact, indivisible. To split them there would have to be interstices between their parts for a knife to enter. But they have no parts between which such interstices can exist. They are incapable of being cut—in Greek *a* (not) and *tomé* (cut, separation). Hence Democritus called them *atoma* or, as we say, *atoms.*

All qualitative differences are expressive of the different shapes, and, with Democritus, sizes, of the atoms, and of the different spatial positions and arrangements they assume. All change of quality is *really* nothing but change of place as the atoms shift their positions and pass from one spatial arrangement to another. This is explicitly asserted by Democritus, and there is reason to believe he got it from Leucippus. In short, all qualitative difference was reduced to and explained in terms of quantitative difference, and all qualitative change was reduced to and explained in terms of movement in space. This is one of the cardinal principles of science today.

2. Assertion of the Evidence of Empty Space. In the second place, Leucippus parted company with both Empedocles and Anaxagoras over the question of the possibility of motion in a *plenum*. They, it will be remembered, had followed Parmenides in his denial that empty space—or the void—can exist, and had packed their "roots" and "seeds" into an absolutely continuous mass. But they had held, nevertheless, that in spite of there being no free space to move in, the particles into which they had pulverized the Parmenidean sphere could change their place. This view, as we have seen, was attacked by Melissus. Leucippus agreed with Melissus' criticism, it would seem, but he refused to abandon with the Eleatics the reality of motion. On the contrary, he rejected the Eleatic conclusion on this point, took the bull by the horns and proclaimed that empty space—or the void—exists and that the atoms move in it. This was a revolutionary assertion for his day, since it was tantamount, in the language and thought of the times, to maintaining the existence of that in which nothing exists.

3. Motion Universally Inherent in All the Atoms. In the third place, Leucippus refused to segregate the sources of motion in special principles, like Empedocles' Love and Strife and the mind-seeds of Anaxagoras, and declined to attribute the origin of the movement of the other constituents of the Real to their activity. *All* the atoms, he declared, are and have always been naturally and inherently in motion. Their motion, like themselves, is uncreated and indestructible, and it is no more necessary to seek an explanation for its existence than it is for their existence. There is, then, no need of any external agent to set them in motion in the beginning or to keep them moving. They just move, even as they are just there, and that is all there is to it. To ask why Being is in motion is like asking why Being *is*.

4. Motion and Causation Mechanistic in Character. Finally Leucippus thinks that the atoms change their places and arrangements in a purely "mechanical" manner. Their movements and situations at any given moment are the necessary outcome of antecedent situations and movements, and it is in those antecedent conditions only that we should seek and that we can find the explanations of their patterns and motions at that moment. In the one direct quotation of his opinions that has come down to us—a quotation, it should be said, that has also been attributed to Democritus—it is affirmed that "naught happens for nothing, but everything from a ground and of necessity." [44]

---

[44] Aetius, 1, 25, 4 (Burnet, p. 340).

This would seem to rule out not only chance, but purpose and design as well from the movement of the atoms.[45]

Here, again, we have two basic principles of modern science. Physics deals with a universe already in motion and does not seek to go behind that fact. For it, as for Leucippus and Democritus, movement, activity, occurrence, are simply there and require no explanation. Again science proceeds on the assumption that at any rate gross physical events do not happen at random,[46] and it has ruled out design and purpose as scientific explanations of their occurrence. It, too, regards events as necessary effects of antecedent situations, and seeks their causes there.

Concept of the Atom. There has been considerable discussion among modern commentators as to whether Leucippus and Democritus thought of the atoms as inherently possessed of weight, and whether they regarded the native motion of the atoms as a perpendicular fall through space or as a flying-about in all directions. Epicurus, who, as we shall presently see, made the views of Democritus the basis of his system, attributed weight and an inherent falling motion to them. But even ancient evidence is contradictory as to the origination of these concepts by Democritus himself, and there is ground for believing that they were modifications introduced by Epicurus. The consensus of modern opinion would seem to be that the motion of the atoms as conceived by Leucippus at any rate, and probably by Democritus, was simply a hurtling about hither and thither. It has also been pointed out that the phenomenon of weight did not particularly interest earlier Greek philosophers, and was generally ascribed by them to a tendency of the particles of the different elements to attract their like and to come together, rather than associated with the idea of a perpendicular fall.[47]

The Real in Relation to the Atom. We may now sum up Leucippus' view of the nature of the Real and describe how he conceived the generation of the worlds, and particularly of our world, within it, in the words of the ancient historian Diogenes Laertius, based upon an earlier account of the commentator Theophrastus.

He says that the All is infinite, and that it is in part void, in part full. These [the full and the empty], he says, are the elements. From them

[45] Cf. Zeller, *Pre-Socratic Philosophy,* II, pp. 237 ff.

[46] The possible tychistic or undetermined and chance character of the "goings on" within the atom does not appear to interfere with our conducting our scientific dealings with nature on a deterministic basis.

[47] Cf. Burnet, pp. 341 ff.

arise innumerable worlds and are resolved into them. The worlds come into being thus. There were borne along by "abscission from the infinite" many bodies of all sorts of figures "into a mighty void," and they being gathered together, produce a single vortex. In it, as they came into collision with one another and were whirled round in all manner of ways, those which were alike were separated apart and came to their likes. But, as they were no longer able to revolve in equilibrium owing to their multitude, those of them that were fine went out to the external void, as if passed through a sieve; the rest stayed together and becoming entangled with one another, ran down together and made a first spherical structure. This was in substance like a membrane or skin containing in itself all kinds of bodies.

And, as these bodies were borne round in a vortex, in virtue of resistance of the middle, the surrounding membrane became thin, as the contiguous bodies kept flowing together from contact with the vortex. And in this way the earth came into being, those things which had been borne towards the middle abiding there. Moreover, the containing membrane was increased by the further separating out of bodies from the outside; and, being itself carried round in a vortex, it got further possession of all with which it had come in contact. Some of these becoming entangled, produce a structure, which was at first moist and muddy; but, when they had been dried and were revolving about with the vortex of the whole, they were then ignited and produced the substance of the heavenly bodies. The circle of the sun is the outermost, that of the moon is the nearest to the earth, and those of the others are between these. And all the heavenly bodies are ignited because of the swiftness of their motion; while the sun is also ignited by the stars. But the moon receives only a small portion of fire. The sun and the moon are eclipsed (and the obliquity of the zodiac is produced) by the earth being inclined towards the south; and the northern parts of it have constant snow and are cold and frozen. And the sun is eclipsed rarely, and the moon continually, because their circles are unequal. And just as there are comings into being of the world, so there are growths and decays and passings away in virtue of a certain necessity, of the nature of which he gives no clear account.[48]

Astronomical Views. In addition to this account, we have reports that Democritus—whether on the authority of Leucippus or out of his own head we do not know—supposed that at first the earth moved about within the vortex, while it was still small and of little density, but later on, as it grew bigger and more solid, settled in its place at the center. Again the Epicurean notion that the winds and the influences of the stars forced the smaller atoms to the surface of the earth where they became water, while the earth in consequence con-

[48] Diogenes Laertius, ix, 31 ff. (Burnet, pp. 338-339).

densed and grew solid may perhaps have originated with Democritus. The earth itself, he—and possibly Leucippus—taught was not round but a large thin disc, half again as long as it was broad, upheld by the air. Leucippus, as we have just seen, said the earth was tilted. The sun and moon were represented as big bodies, and Democritus regarded the lunar markings as shadows cast by mountains on it. There was also a question whether they belonged originally to our vortex or had been caught in from the outside by the bodies revolving within it.

Religious Views. We also have fragments and accounts of Democritus showing that he explored philosophic fields that we have no evidence ever were entered by Leucippus. For instance, we know a good deal about his religious views. Like most of the early philosophers he called the world-stuff divine. Particularly he applied the term to fire and to the heavenly bodies as well as to the soul-atoms which, he thought, were responsible for animation and consciousness in living bodies. The individual, personal gods of Greek theology he explained as personifications of natural phenomena and moral qualities. But he treated them with reverence. Also he felt that there were sound philosophic reasons for believing in the existence of divine, man-like beings in our world. Only on such a supposition could we explain, in his opinion, the dreams and apparitions, foreboding both good and ill, in which godlike figures appeared to mankind. But these beings, though more powerful and longer-lived than ourselves, were made of the same atomic stuff as we are, and like us eventually perished.

Biology. Democritus denied personal immortality—which brings us to his biology, physiology and psychology and his ideas regarding the nature of the soul. His biology and physiology seem to have been chiefly concerned with man, whom he described as a little world. He tells us that life originated in mud or slime, and we have scattered fragments about plants and animals. He was much struck by the adaptation of animal and particularly of human organs to their uses, and ascribed it to the workings of some hidden principle.

The Soul and Its Relation to the Body. The soul is atomic in character. Its particles are like if not identical with those of fire, and are very fine, round, smooth, polished, and mobile, and are diffused throughout the void. When they cluster together in a mass of other atoms, that mass becomes living and conscious. Consciousness, indeed, is nothing but their quivering and dancing. They are spread throughout the entire body, and are continually inhaled and exhaled by it. As long as the quantity of them in the body remains approximately constant, life and consciousness continue. A slight deficiency in their number produces sleep, a more serious one causes fainting or coma, and at times apparent death, and a complete loss of them means real death to the body which their presence has animated. Once out of the body they disperse and are lost in the crowd of soul-atoms with which the universe as a whole is suffused, and the body they have deserted disintegrates into its constituent atoms. Hence there is no such thing as individual immortality.

Theory of Sensation. Sensation is caused by the impact upon the sense-organs of effluences from the atomic clusters of which material objects are composed. These effluences are miniature atomic copies of the bodies that exude them. Penetrating through the sense-organs, they set the soul-atoms moving, and their various sizes, shapes, and degrees of roughness and smoothness set up the correspondingly different vibrations that compose our various color, sound, taste, smell, temperature, and touch sensations. Sensation is modified in different people by the individual peculiarities of their sense-organs. Also, damage done the atomic miniatures by the friction of the air and by collision among themselves helps to account for the distortions and variations that occur in our perception of objects at a distance.

Epistemology. But obviously the senses do not show us things as they really are. The colors, sounds, tastes, smells, and the like that constitute sensible experience are not in the atoms outside us, or even in the soul-atoms, but are vibrations of the mind-particles. Reason alone—and here Democritus is in complete agreement with the Eleatics and Anaxagoras—can see through the deception of the senses and make out the true nature of Reality.

However, the power of reason to reach the truth could no longer be taken for granted, as it had been by the earlier thinkers. Democritus lived in a period of intense skeptical distrust of the capacities and results of our reasoning process. The ability of thought to reach any universally true conclusions on any subject whatsoever was being challenged, and metaphysical systems especially were being riddled with objections by critics of no mean caliber. Democritus, then, found himself obliged to validate the possibility of knowledge.

This he did as follows. The senses, he said, were not our only means of contact with the external world. Some of the images given off by the atomic clusters penetrated directly to the soul-atoms, instead of being indirectly conveyed by the sense-organs. The images that reached the soul-atoms in this way were not confused by the sense vibrations which blurred the pictures forwarded *via* sight, sound, touch, and the like. Hence they could set the mind moving in a way indicative of the true nature of their originals, and by imparting to it an unfalsified impression of the external world could give it real and trustworthy knowledge of the unseen structure of Reality.

Ethics. Finally, we find in Democritus the first attempt to construct not only a theory of knowledge, but a reasoned ethics as well. Unfortunately we have only the scantiest fragments of his moral theory. Enjoyment, he seems to have taught, is the end naturally sought by all men; pain the thing naturally and universally avoided. The useful and the harmful are defined in terms of pleasure and pain. All enjoyment, however, is not equally good. The pleasures of the senses, which are short-lived, agitating, and productive of surfeit or pain, are not so desirable as the calm, enduring, painless pleasures of the mind. Wellbeing and cheerfulness are the ends to be sought above all. Their attainment is dependent not upon wealth and good fortune and other external circumstances, but upon the cultivation of the resources of the soul, the treading of the middle path between excess and deficiency, and the contemplation of noble things. To distinguish, however, the true good from the false, a man must be wise. Virtue for Democritus was essentially a matter of the exercise of intelligence.

Metrodorus and Anaxarchus. Of the fortunes of the school founded by Leucippus and Democritus we know next to nothing. History has preserved the names of a few disciples and some scattered references to their views. The most prominent members were Metrodorus of Chios and Anaxarchus of Abdera. The latter was a teacher of Pyrrho, the founder of an important revival of skepticism that followed upon the close of the constructive period of Plato and Aristotle.

VI. DIOGENES OF APOLLONIA

Reassertion of the Homogeneity of the World-Stuff. Perhaps we should not end this chapter without mentioning Diogenes of Apollonia—not that his system was original or particularly important, but because it illustrates, along with that of Archelaus of Athens, a tendency to combine the ideas of the newer with those of earlier philosophies. His view, he tells us, "is, to sum it all up, that all things are differentiations of the same thing and are the same thing . . . they take different forms at different times, and return again to the same thing."

The orderly character of the process by which the world-stuff is divided into many things and the balance and rhythm and regular alternation which they display, and their disposal "in the best possible manner," prove that the world-stuff possesses intelligence.

And my view is that that which has intelligence is what men call air and that all things have their course steered by it, and it has power over all things. For this very thing I hold to be a god, and to reach everywhere, and to dispose everything and to be in everything . . . but there are many modes both of air and of intelligence. For it undergoes many transformations. . . . And the soul of all living things is the same, namely, air warmer than that outside us and in which we are, but colder than that near the sun. . . . And this warmth is not alike in any two kinds of living creatures, nor, for the matter of that, in any two men; but it does not differ much. . . . At the same time it is not possible for any of the things which are differentiated to be exactly like one another, till they all once more become the same. . . .

At the same time they all live, and see, and hear by the same thing and have their intelligence from the same source.

And this itself is an eternal and undying body, but of those things some come into being, and some pass away.

But this too appears to me to be obvious, that it is both great, and mighty, and eternal, and undying and of great knowledge.[49]

And further, there are still the following great proofs. Men and all animals live upon air by breathing it, and this is their soul and their intelligence. . . . While, when this is taken away, they die and their intelligence fails.[50]

Cosmology. We are also told that he believed the universe originated by the denser air massing to form the earth, which is round, by which he probably means disc-like, not spherical—while the lighter portions formed the other things, and the lightest of all the sun. The heavenly bodies were like red-hot pumice stones, through the pores of which our universe breathes. Meteors he accounted for on the supposition that besides the visible heavenly bodies there revolve invisible stones, which often fall and are extinguished on the earth.

VII. REVIEW

We now review briefly the ideas developed by Greek philosophy up to date.

1. What Is the World-Stuff? Occidental philosophy began in Europe, when in the sixth century B.C. the idea appeared that all things are

---

[49] Frs. 3-8 (Burnet, pp. 354-355).
[50] Fr. 4 (Burnet, p. 354).

parts of a single Reality, and that there is a world-stuff in which they all participate, and of which they are all made. The occurrence of this idea was accompanied by speculation as to the nature of the world-stuff. Early speculation consisted in picking out some one sensible thing, like the water of Thales, the general, undeterminate, boundless stuff of Anaximander, and the vapor of Anaximenes, which could be *seen* apparently changing into other things.

2. How Does the Universe Arise from It? At the same time, in the Milesian School the question arose as to how the universe was generated from and by the world-stuff. We do not know whether Thales touched on this point, or if so, how he dealt with it. But Anaximander suggested a process of separation and dissolution of opposites of whose interaction the world is the result; and Anaximenes proposed a process of condensation and rarefaction of the original vapor.

This hypothesis of Anaximenes, we noted, was prophetic of the view, soon to be developed, that all qualitative difference and alteration can be reduced to purely quantitative terms.

3. Pythagorean Dualism and Number Theory. Towards the end of the sixth century B.C. we saw Pythagoras and the early Pythagoreans, inspired by their interest and their discoveries in geometry, "mathematicizing" the world-stuff. They split it into two opposed fundamental principles, Limit and the Unlimited, whose interaction produced an indefinite number of geometrical points, different quantities and arrangements of which constituted different kinds of objects. This view they expressed by saying all things are Numbers. They also emphasized the difference between the odd and even series of numbers, in which they found the basis not only of physical but of moral opposites.

4. The Problem of Change. By this time the problem of change had become a philosophic issue, and doubts were being raised as to whether any *real* transformation of a single, homogeneous world-stuff, like that of the Milesians, into a multiple world full of a variety of things different both from it and from one another, was thinkable. Diametrically opposed attempts to solve this problem were made by Heraclitus on the one hand, and Parmenides and his Eleatic School on the other.

5. The Heraclitean World-Stuff. Heraclitus, defending the reality of change, multiplicity and variety, maintained that the world-stuff was essentially a process of transformation, and, seeking a world-stuff in itself volatile and in constant movement and alteration, he found it in Fire, whose essence is the process of combustion. Analyzing the implications of change, he proclaimed the identity of opposites, and, noting the regular and rhythmic character of the world-process, he formulated a law or "wisdom" obeyed by Fire in its cycle of trans-formations, which he called the Upward and the Downward Ways. To the tension set up by the pull of these ways against one another he attributed the stability of the cosmic structure, and to the alterna-tion of their prevalence over each other, the tendency of nature to oscillate between opposites.

6. The Eleatic View of Reality. Parmenides and the other Eleatics, Zeno and Melissus, denied the reality of change on the ground that existence as such cannot be logically conceived as coming into being or passing out of being, or altering or varying or multiplying the fact that it *is*. Since it alone exists, it cannot come from anything, be divided by anything, change into anything or be destroyed by anything except itself—which is tantamount to saying that it is uncreated, indestructible, invariable, single, and homogeneous throughout. Nor can it move spatially since there is no emptiness for it to move in. It is a com-pact, continuous *plenum*—a spatially extended, solid sphere, in Parmenides' opinion. Hence variety, multiplicity, change of quality and place, generation and destruction are all *false* opinions men hold regarding the nature of the Real.

Parmenides' pupil Zeno defended his master's position in a series of famous paradoxes showing the self-contradictory consequences that followed from admitting the reality of motion. And Zeno's follower, Melissus, argued against attributing variety and multiplicity, as well as spatial movement, to the Real by showing up the logical absurdities that resulted.

7. Pluralistic Attempts to Reconcile Sensible Phenomena with Eleatic Logic. Meantime, inspired by a respect for Eleatic logic, as well as by a desire to find a *real* place in the universe for multiplicity, variety, and change of quality and place, others were proposing systems that adopted different forms and degrees of one and the same ex-pedient. This expedient was that of dividing the simple, homogeneous, continuous, unchanging, and motionless Reality of Parmenides into a number of elements, incapable of internal division, variegation and change, but capable of spatial movement and arrangement in dif-ferent combinations in terms of which the qualitative differences and transformations of the sensible world could be expressed and under-stood. These systems were those of Empedocles, of Anaxagoras, and of Leucippus and Democritus.

8. The Four Elements Moved by Love and Strife. Empedocles quar-tered the Parmenidean sphere into four elements, Fire, Air, Water, and Earth. The formation of worlds, he argued, was due to the alternating commingling and separation of these elements under the influence of the two principles of Love and Hate. Universes occur in the intermediary stages of conflict and relative balance between Love and Strife, before either complete separation or complete commingling has been accomplished. Empedocles regarded the Real as a *plenum,* a fact, however, he thought compatible with movement.

9. Elements Moved by Mind. Anaxagoras pulverized Eleatic Being into as many constituents as there are different qualities and classes of things, or, at any rate, as there are fundamental opposites. None of these kinds of particles, however, were completely pure, with the exception of those of Mind. The others each contained some slight admixture of everything else. Mind, however, was not only unmixed, but was the only thing whose particles were inherently in motion. And it set the other elements moving. Like Empedocles, Anaxagoras thought of Reality as compact, continuous and completely full, and like him felt that under these conditions change of place and of arrangement of its constituents was still possible.

10. Elements Reduced to Atoms. Leucippus and Democritus pulverized "what really is" into an infinite number of atoms, Eleatic in their internal character, and devoid of all qualities and differences except those of size and shape. All the atoms are everlastingly in motion of their own nature, flying about hither and thither, and it is due to their clusterings and dispersions and to the formation of vortices by the component motion of their collisions that universes are generated. This generation is entirely "mechanical" and unpurposive, controlled and directed only by impact, with resultant agglomeration and modification of movement. Unlike Empedocles and Anaxagoras, Leucippus and Democritus considered change of place in a *plenum* impossible, and asserted the equal reality of the void or empty space.

11. Various Religious Views. Along with these theories of the nature of the universe, we find interesting views about religion and speculation in the fields of astronomy, biology, physiology, psychology, and the theory of knowledge, and in the case of Democritus in ethics. All the philosophers so far treated appear to have been skeptical of the orthodox theology. All applied the term *divine* to the world-stuff and the universe, and seem to have attributed to the Real mental and animate qualities (soul) suffused throughout it. The Pythagoreans and Empedocles were also influenced by the Orphics and taught the transmigration of souls—a doctrine out of step with their other teachings regarding the soul. The others either ignored the question, so far as we know, or constructed systems with which personal immortality was inconsistent—with the possible exception of Heraclitus, if we can interpret his allusion to a "greater death" and to men being cooled-off gods and to gods being heated-up men as indicating a belief in transmigration.

12. Astronomical Speculations. We noted also interesting astronomical speculations. These, for the most part, were alike in their essentials, and proved to be blind alleys, so far as the future was concerned. But the Pythagoreans asserted that the earth was spherical, not flat, displaced it from a central position in the universe, and had it revolving, not about the sun to be sure, but, along with the sun and the other heavenly bodies, about a "central fire." Besides these astronomical speculations we found many meteorological observations.

13. Biological and Physiological Studies. Biology and physiology as well came in for their share of investigation. Theories in line with the modern doctrine of evolution, deriving life from a primeval slime, and asserting the slow *development* of species into their present forms, were proposed, most notably by Anaximander and Empedocles. The structure and operations of the human body were studied, and the process of reproduction was discussed at some length, and Empedocles' theory of respiration was prophetic of the later discovery of the circulation of the blood.

14. Psychological Theories. We found also the beginnings of psychology. Sensation and thinking, at first referred to the world-stuff in general, became objects of special study. The Pythagoreans taught that the soul is a "harmony" of the body, but held also the doctrine of the transmigration of souls. Empedocles, while also holding that doctrine, connected sensation and thought with the blood, particularly the blood nearest the heart. Anaxagoras and Leucippus and Democritus segregated them in soul-particles, purer, finer, and more mobile than the other constituents of the world-stuff. These last three also had well-developed theories of the nature of sensation, and of the operation of the sense-organs, Empedocles maintaining that perception is of like by like, Anaxagoras, that it is of unlike by unlike, and Leucippus and Democritus, that it is due to the impact of atoms upon the sense-organs and the consequent vibrations set up in the soul-atoms in the body.

15. Theories of Knowledge. The nature of knowledge, too, was being discussed. The Eleatics set up logical tests of truth and reality, which determined the trustworthiness of perceptual evidence, and these standards were generally accepted by the later philosophers we have so far mentioned. And Democritus made an explicit attempt to defend the validity of knowledge against skeptical attacks. He also had, apparently, elaborated a system of ethics.

16. Prevalence of General Curiosity over Special Interests. Finally, we may repeat of all the systems we have described what we said in discussing the general characteristics of the Milesian School—that they were motivated by general curiosity about the nature of Reality rather than by a desire to satisfy their religious or moral preferences by their description of the Real.

Chapter VIII

THE SOPHISTS

I. THE RISE OF SKEPTICISM

Distrust of the Senses and Reason. Periods of intense philosophic speculation and feverish constructive activity, like the one we have just been recording, are apt to be followed by skeptical reactions in which the achievements of the past are riddled by a fire of hostile criticism, and the established beliefs and standards of the day tend to collapse, temporarily, at least. Metaphysical inquiry, being the biggest gamble of all the philosophic industries, generally suffers first and worst, and little or no stock is taken, for the time being, in its results or possibilities. A philosophic reaction of this sort occurred in Greek thought towards the middle of the fifth century B.C. The constructive cycle was at an end, and a period of salutary criticism and deflation of metaphysical pretensions was needed before the work of rehabilitation could begin on a sounder, a more comprehensive, and a grander scale.

There were many causes of this skeptical turmoil in which not only metaphysics but all established beliefs and standards, religious, scientific, moral and political, were called to account. There had been only too obvious difficulties and self-contradictions in each of the older systems, and all those systems had flatly contradicted one another. The untrustworthiness of the senses had become notorious, and the ability of reason to correct their deceptions was doubtful. Moreover, reason, as exercised by different thinkers of apparently equal eminence, led to diametrically opposed conclusions. So its prospects of reaching and grasping the truth by the exercise of its own, native ability did not appear particularly bright.

The sense of relativity that might well have been provoked by contemplation of the philosophic scene could not but have been reinforced by the temper of the times. The growth of trade, the increase of travel, and the awakening interest in the geography and history of other lands disclosed the difference, and even the opposition of religious beliefs, political and social conventions and institutions, standards of taste and ideas of moral right and wrong, all of which seemed to work equally well in their respective communities and times. And this disclosure was bound to make men skeptical of the absoluteness or even the superiority of the particular views and ways to which they had happened to be born and bred.)

Rise of Athenian Democracy. Nor was any assurance of permanence or universality to be had from the spectacle of affairs at Athens, to which the center of philosophic gravity had now shifted from Ionia and Magna Graecia. There, after the death of Pericles, democracy had run riot, with the inevitable results—results intensified if anything by the long drawn-out agony of the Peloponnesian War. The rich and the poor were busy cutting each other's throats in the name of the same immutable justice, and the Assembly and the Law Courts were swayed from day to day by contradictory and reversible passions and prejudices in the name of the same everlasting right and truth. There was, then, no need of the disagreements of the philosophers, or the lessons of history and geography to teach the lesson that nothing is certain or universal or lasting or absolutely valid. A day in his own courts or town-meeting was enough to show any Athenian that.

The philosophic formulation of this skeptical attitude fell to a class of men that conditions of modern life at Athens were fast bringing to the fore. The Athenian democracy governed both the city and the empire directly in town-meeting, not through elected representatives. Moreover, there were no lawyers, and each citizen had to plead his own case in court. In such circumstances skill in debating was an urgent necessity for any man who wished to defend his property, his interests, and perhaps his life against hostile forces; not to speak of a man who wanted to forge ahead, impose his views and his will upon his fellow-citizens, and succeed in the struggle for existence. Practical issues were to the fore, and teaching had to turn practical to meet them. The dominant art was now the art of worldly success, and instruction in this became the Alpha, and only too often the Omega, of education.

Rhetoric and Its Teachers, the Sophists. So it was that there arose in Greece a class that devoted itself to the teaching of *rhetoric,* or the art of persuasion, upon the mastery of which worldly success so largely depended. The ministers of this new gospel of utility and "business first" were known as *Sophists,* or "wise ones"—a term also rather indiscriminately applied to philosophers, bards, music teachers, poets, and prose writers. But they lived up to the name, in theory at any rate, for, in order to prepare their pupils for success in the rough-

and-tumble of business and political life, they had themselves to be thoroughly conversant, not only with rhetoric in all its branches, such as grammar, diction, logical argument, and appeal to the emotions, but also with constitutional, civil, and criminal law, and parliamentary procedure. Furthermore, they must keep their ear to the ground and know everything that was going on behind the scenes, if they were to give expert advice to their clients.

For their services the Sophists charged fat fees, and to this custom we may trace a part of their unpopularity in antiquity, and of the general opprobrium that hangs about the terms "sophist," "sophistry," "sophistic" and the like in modern times. To the Greek way of thinking the acceptance of pay for teaching was an "unethical" practice; just as today the taking of contingent fees by a lawyer or the patenting of a medical discovery by a physician is viewed with disfavor. Moreover, it must be remembered that the prejudice against receiving money for literary production lingered in Europe well into the nineteenth century.

Unscrupulousness of the Sophists. Again, this habit turned the Sophists into servants of the rich, and allied them with the classes against the masses, since naturally they put themselves at the disposition of the highest bidder. The irritation that they thus aroused was intensified, at Athens at least, by the fact that so many of them were aliens. Nor was their influence upon the youth of the day—whom they seemed to be infecting with their irony, their cynicism, their sharp tongues, and their suspected "foreign" broad-mindedness and irreligion—calculated to enhance their reputation with the conservative Athenian elders. Finally, they were exercising their talents and drawing their pay in a field that lay closest to the Greek heart—the field of politics—and were professionalizing an activity that had hitherto been regarded as an amateur sport. To rely upon a paid coach for help in winning a case or getting a law passed was not fair play.

To our eyes, however, the worst part of the charge against the Sophists lies in the accusation that they were corrupters of youth in that they made the worse cause appear the better and the better the worse; in other words, that they were unscrupulous in their methods and taught their pupils how to win at all costs and by whatsoever means. This indictment, which used to be accepted as generally true by historians of philosophy, is now largely discredited, so far, at any rate, as the more eminent members of the profession are concerned. Undoubtedly, there were small fry who were willing to help win shady cases and to resort to dishonest tricks to gain their ends. It was their behavior, probably, that brought the whole profession into disrepute. Certainly, no reproach of that sort ever attached to the two great philosophers, Protagoras and Gorgias, whom the group produced.

Sophists and Morality. Nevertheless, even these men succeeded in giving an artificial and superficial look to moral conduct. Protagoras felt that moral behavior could be taught much as grammar or arithmetic could. A set of precepts telling you how to act to your own best advantage could be memorized and applied. However admirable these precepts might be, they sat rather loosely upon the mind. Morality was just one subject among many, on a par with mathematics or correct speech, and it could be taught a man by rote, as they could. Furthermore, Gorgias insisted that moral precepts had no essential unity and no general applicability. Their suitability was not the same for child and adult, slave and free, rich and poor. The different stations in life had each its appropriate code. Virtue was many, not one. We could speak of the virtues, but not of virtue in general. On the whole, then, Protagoras and Gorgias tended to undermine the authority of moral standards, even though their conduct and their teaching of what actually constituted right action were exemplary.

II. PROTAGORAS

Protagoras, born in the early part of the fifth century, was a fellow townsman of Democritus, somewhat the older of the two. He began life as a porter, but his intelligence and his ability to read and write soon enabled him to become an itinerant teacher. When he was about thirty he left Abdera and wandered through Sicily and Magna Graecia, gathering fame as he went. Eventually he turned up in Athens, where his success was great and immediate. He became an intimate of the Periclean circle, and quickly amassed a large fortune by his lectures, not to speak of an enthusiastic band of pupils and disciples. His last years are somewhat obscure. It used to be thought that his views got him into difficulties and that, exiled from Athens, he was drowned on his way to Sicily. His writings, too, were said to have been burned by public order. But there is also an alternative theory that he lived and died in good enough odor, and that his works were read long after his death.

Man the Measure of All Things. However that may be, of all his writings scarcely a dozen fragments have come down to us, and of these two only are important. One of them, from his treatise *On the*

Gods, simply states that with regard to the gods he "cannot feel sure that they are, or that they are not, nor what they are like in figure, for there are many things that hinder sure knowledge, the obscurity of the subject and the shortness of human life." The other, the more famous, amplifies this religious agnosticism into a denial of the existence of any absolute and universal truth, one and the same for all individuals in all times and places. *"Man,"* he says, *"is the measure of all things, of things that are that they are, and of things that are not that they are not."* In other words, truth is a purely relative and subjective affair. What *seems* true or false to a man *is* the only truth or falsehood he can know anything about. What *appears* to him to be real or unreal *is* real or unreal so far as he is concerned. And that is all there is to it. There is no means of measuring my truth against yours, and no warrant for saying that what seems true to me is truer than what seems true to you. Each man is his own final court of appeal. There is no higher authority to which the claims of conflicting views can be submitted for a binding decision.

The Relativity of Truth. Moreover, as his opinions change, so each man's truth will change. What appeared true yesterday looks false today. Very well, what *was* true for the individual *is* now false for him. Not only, then, is truth that which appears true to the individual, but that which appears true to him at the moment. And just as there is no ground for asserting that one man's truth is truer than another's, so in the same individual there is no possible means of measuring the truth of one moment against that of the next. Whatever it is that seems true is true so long as it seems so and no longer. All of my shifting opinions are equally true for me during the time that I hold them and equally false after I have discarded them. From the instant, as from the individual, there can be no appeal to any permanent and universal standard of what is so and what is not.

Since, then, what seems true to a man is the only truth he can possess, and since this truth is at variance both with the truths of other men and, from moment to moment, with itself, metaphysical speculation is idle, and its results are worthless. There is no "reality" that reason can know except the ever-changing flux of sensible experience, and even if there were, there would be no way of knowing which philosophical system most closely approximated it. All systems appear equally true to their respective adherents for equally convincing reasons, and men are continually changing their systems and clinging with equal tenacity and conviction now to this philosophy, and at the next moment to another.

These conclusions were apparently reinforced by, if not actually based upon the Heraclitean teaching. If everything was in flux, then perceiver and perceived alike were in constant change. Sensation was due to a momentary contact between them which gave rise to a flash of sensation. But the instant the collision between sense-organ and perceived object was over, the sensation in the perceiver disappeared and so did the corresponding quality in the object. The next minute both subject and object had altered their characters. Hence in both of them, the sensation or the idea of the moment was true only of the instant in which it took place.

III. GORGIAS

The skepticism of Protagoras was ably seconded by the other great Sophist philosopher, Gorgias, from Leontini in Sicily. Prominent in his native town as a master of the art of persuasion in its most eloquent and flowery form, he was chosen by his fellow citizens to head an embassy sent in 427 B.C. to Athens to enlist aid in the struggle of Leontini against her powerful neighbor, Syracuse. Once arrived, he was so taken with the charm of the city that he settled there, and, by virtue of his gift of silver-tongued oratory, his statesmanlike vision, and his general culture, became a bright star in the twilight of the Periclean Age. He was also greatly interested in science and ethical problems. Later on, it is said, he went to the court of Jason of Pherae in Thessaly, where he lived to be nearly a hundred years old.

Knowledge of Reality Beyond Sense-Experience. Of metaphysical speculation regarding world-stuffs and "ultimate realities," Gorgias was no less suspicious and critical than Protagoras. In a work called *On Nature or the Non-existent,* he challenged the power of reason to discover any reality beyond the flux of sensible experience. To support his thesis he fell back on the self-contradictions that arise from the logical necessity of conceiving the Real as both one and many, created and uncreated, finite and infinite in space and time. The only escape from these paradoxes lay, he said, in supposing that Reality is neither one nor many, infinite nor finite, created nor uncreated—which is equally absurd. Hence the Real cannot exist. Furthermore, if a world-stuff existed, we could never know what it was like. It is not what it appears to be, since the senses are notorious liars. Nor need it be what reason thinks it is, since thought can conceive the non-existent as readily as it can the existent, and possesses in itself no criterion for distinguishing such of its ideas as may refer to real existence from those that may be pure creations of fancy.

Finally, even if Reality could be known, knowledge of it could not be communicated to others. For we are dependent upon language for sharing our ideas, and language is mere noise. But how can a noise transfer from one mind to another knowledge of a reality that is not a noise? How can the optical sensation *red,* for example, be communicated by the audible sensation of the spoken word "red"? The word is quite different from the color. In the same way, whatever my concept of the truth may be, the words by which I seek to convey it are quite unlike it, and I cannot be sure that they arouse in my neighbor's mind a concept in any way similar to my own.

IV. ETHICAL AND POLITICAL IMPLICATIONS

No Universal Moral Standards. The arguments advanced by Protagoras and Gorgias were destructive not only of metaphysical speculation; in the field of ethics they were equally destructive of the authority of all moral and social standards and institutions. For, if each man is the measure of all things, he must be the final arbiter of what is good, as well as of what is true. What seems right or wrong to him *is* right or wrong so far as he is concerned, and there can be no valid ground for quarreling with him. No one can lay down the moral law to another, since there is no moral law to lay down. Universal and authoritative standards of right and wrong are as nonexistent as universal truths. Each man has the same right to do what seems good to him as he has to believe what seems true to him. No one has any right or reason to reprimand him. The only argument is force.

Callicles. Might Is Natural Right. There is no evidence that Protagoras and Gorgias ever applied the logical consequences of their doctrine to ethics. Indeed, they were apparently highly respectable and respected pillars of the established moral and social order. But there were plenty of people to make the application, and presently we shall find Socrates and Plato combating ethical and political views directly derived from the Sophistic skepticism. For instance, the Athenian politician, Callicles, argues that conventional morality is designed by the inferior, "the many weak," to keep the superior, "the few strong," in check; "whereas nature herself intimates that it is just for the better to have more than the worse, the more powerful than the weaker." True morality, the ethics sanctioned by nature, teaches that justice, or as we should perhaps say today, righteousness, "consists in the superior ruling over and having more than the inferior."[1]

Thrasymachus and Nature of Right. The Sophist, Thrasymachus, was even more extreme in his deductions. Callicles, after all, had maintained that there was such a thing as a natural morality, a standard of right and wrong countenanced by nature, though this standard reversed the ordinary ideals of good conduct. But for Thrasymachus there is not even a natural right that the superior should rule over and have more than the inferior. Whoever happens to be on top is so by accident, not by right, and the arbitrary will of those in power decides what shall be considered virtuous and what vicious. Moral principles are obviously determined with a view to the pleasure and profit of the ruling party, so that righteousness is "nothing else than the interest of the stronger."[2] Good and evil are simply legislated into existence at the caprice of the lawmakers and have no being apart from their say-so. Different groups or forms of government lay down different rules suited to their different advantages, and as a result the saint of one day is the sinner of the next, and *vice versa*.

Plainly, then, if philosophy was to be rehabilitated, new and sound foundations had to be discovered for an authoritative truth and right. Plainly, too, man's attention had been shifted from the spectacle of external existence to himself so far, at least, as knowledge is concerned. His mind was the measure of all things, and the relative and inaccurate nature of that measure had been exposed. Not only had the hope of reaching a common truth been blighted, but faith in the ordinary standards and institutions of human life had been called upon to justify itself and had failed to do so. Was there, then, any way of standardizing the mind that measured all things and of restoring confidence in the value of its judgments? Socrates and Plato thought there was. To their work of reconstruction we now turn.

[1] Plato, *Gorgias,* 483 B ff. (trans. Jowett).
[2] Plato, *Republic,* I, 339 A.

Chapter IX

SOCRATES

I. LIFE

Socrates (born about 470 B.C.), the first Athenian-born philosopher, was the son of a respectable and well-to-do bourgeois couple, a sculptor and a midwife. Brought up probably with a view to following in his father's footsteps, he showed at an early age the dreamy and mystical temperament and the unbusinesslike proclivities of his later life. He was in the habit of falling into "brown studies" or trances, which sometimes lasted a long time, and he believed he possessed a sort of familiar spirit whose warning voice admonished him when he was about to do anything wrong. He was a man of great moral courage, whom no arguments or threats could turn from the course he believed right. Twice he defied the government in power at the risk of his own life—once when as presiding officer he refused to sanction the trial *en masse* of the Athenian generals who had abandoned the dead after the battle of Arginusae; and again later when he declined to enforce an illegal order of the Thirty Tyrants. And in the campaigns in which he fought he showed himself a brave soldier. But, for all his high principles and strength of mind and purpose, he was no prude or prig or ascetic. Temperance in all things was for him the rule of right and happy living. He loved human life and especially the city streets and the market place. He was gay, kindly, genial, witty, a great talker and a famous diner-out. And most of his friends he could drink under the table without so much as turning a hair himself.

His Disciples. Of his philosophic education we know little for certain. He seems to have had a fair acquaintance with the work of the preceding thinkers and to have been particularly impressed by the religious, Orphic side of Pythagoreanism. His own temperament predisposed him to a belief in the immortality of the soul and in the existence of a divine Providence which ordered all things for the best. At an early age, apparently, he had already gathered about himself a circle of disciples to whom he expounded his views. This circle numbered at one time or another the beautiful Charmides, an uncle of Plato's, who eventually introduced his nephew to Socrates; Critias, a cousin of Plato's mother, and later a leader in the usurpation of power by the Thirty Tyrants; the brilliant and shifty Alcibiades; Xenophon, the leader of the Anabasis; and a number of Pythagoreans of some note.

The Socratic Method. Also, it would appear that by this time he had developed his own peculiar and famous method, the method of question and answer. This lay in buttonholing passers-by, asking them questions, picking their answers to pieces, demanding more and more clear and definite replies, and thus slowly wringing from the wretched victims of the inquisition either a confession of ignorance or a final definition of the subject under discussion that would hold water. As Socrates was accustomed to try out his method on those who considered themselves exceptionally wise, and frequently made fools of the elders in the presence of their children, he did not add to his popularity with the older generation. But he attracted crowds of young men, who loved to trail about the streets with him and to be in at the death when he engaged in conversation and discomforted some self-important citizen.

By the time he was thirty-five this habit had become a kind of religious mania with him. An admirer of his, inquiring of the Delphic oracle, had been told that there was no man wiser than Socrates; and Socrates, conscious of his own ignorance, had interpreted the reply as meaning that wisdom lies in knowing how little one really knows. It was his duty, as he conceived it, to drive home this lesson to the Athenian people. It was his mission, laid upon him by Apollo, to be a kind of gadfly stinging his fellow-citizens to a realization of their shortcomings. So he set about his preaching with a new and mystical fervor, inspired by a sense of divine favor and command.

His Growing Unpopularity. The Athenian people, however, were not in the best mood to be stung, exasperated as they were by the interminable Peloponnesian War which ended in the collapse of the Empire. And Socrates' stinging found their tenderest spot—their form of democratic government. Day in and day out he exposed and ridiculed the follies and vices of the popular regime. Not only that, but his affiliations were largely with men who had earned the hatred of their fellow-citizens; such as Alcibiades, the instigator and leader of that final catastrophe, the Sicilian Expedition, and Critias, the leader of the Thirty Tyrants, who had seized the power when the city eventually capitulated to Sparta. Moreover, religiously he had come to be suspect. His voices and his trances, and his ideas regarding the immortality and transmigration of the soul might be forgiven him. But it was possible that he was mixed up with some secret, international Orphic-Pythagorean cult at variance with the established religion. Nor could one forget that some of his most intimate friends had been suspected of the blasphemous mutilation of the hermae, or statues of Hermes, erected as a kind of wayside shrine at the corners of the city-streets, and again of parodying and profaning the Eleusinian Mysteries in their houses. All in all, he was an undesirable citizen, a nuisance to the old and a danger to the young.

His Arrest, Trial, and Death. As the weight of all this resentment accumulated against him, Socrates became more and more unpopular, and the charges that were eventually brought against him slowly crystallized in men's minds. He was worshiping strange gods, and he was corrupting the youth of the city by his non-conformist and particularly by his anti-democratic teachings. The storm broke shortly after the Thirty were overthrown, and the democracy returned to power. In 399 B.C. he was arrested and formally charged with impiety and corruption of the young. Behind these accusations lay thirty years of growing dislike and irritation and of very real alarm at his influence. To this, rather than to any specific evidence, his condemnation was due. He was sentenced to death, but given the option of proposing another penalty. He retorted that if he were to get what he deserved, he ought to be maintained for life at the public expense like the winner of a chariot-race at Olympia. He could not afford to pay a large fine, but his friends had scraped together a small amount. Would a fine of that size satisfy the court? He was promptly sentenced to death. In the two months that elapsed between the sentence and its execution, Socrates could easily have escaped. But he refused to do so on the ground that it was wrong to disobey even an unjust law. Of his last hours, spent in conversing about immortality with his friends, and of his drinking of the fatal hemlock, Plato has given us an account in the *Phaedo*.

II. OPPOSED PICTURES OF THE SOCRATIC TEACHING

Socrates' Interest in Metaphysics a Disputed Point. Whether or not, and to what extent Socrates shared the Sophists' disdain of metaphysics and world-stuffs is a moot point, which involves the question, also disputed, of Plato's relation to the doctrines he puts into Socrates' mouth in the earlier dialogues. Until recently it has been supposed that Plato merely used Socrates as a vehicle to express his own views, and

that we must look to the *Memorabilia* of Xenophon—the leader and
historian of the Anabasis, and also one of the Socratic circle, for the
most reliable account of the Socratic teaching. Lately, however, this
view has been challenged, and it has been suggested that Plato for
a long time acted merely as a historian, and that the teachings put
into Socrates' mouth in all the earlier dialogues, including even the
Phaedo, the *Symposium,* and the *Republic,* were really Socratic rather
than Platonic in origin.[1]

If we adhere to the former view, we must think of Socrates as primarily a moralist rather than a metaphysician, preoccupied with ethical
problems and with determining the kind of conduct most conducive
to the best interests of mankind, and possessed, at the best, of only a
moderate and derivative interest in metaphysical questions, if not of
the Sophists' disdain of them. If, however, we believe that the earlier
Platonic dialogues are an account of Socrates' own teaching, then we
must regard him not only as a moralist but as a metaphysician with a
well-developed system, yet largely influenced by ethical considerations.
To these possible metaphysical views, we shall return in a moment,
after describing his ethics. And in any case, we may be reasonably
sure that even if he shared the metaphysical skepticism of the Sophists,
he did not follow them in their religious agnosticism. Though apparently he did not take literally the orthodox theology, he was religious
in temperament and believed, as we have seen, in immortality and in
a beneficent Providence ordering all things for the best.

III. SOCRATES' ETHICS

Denial of Sophistic Relativism. Moreover, as a moralist, vitally interested in discovering the true human good, he could not for a moment accept the ethical implications of the dictum that the individual man is the measure of all things. Superficially, to be sure,
moral standards might seem conflicting and relative, with no hint of
universal validity and authority beneath their hopeless variance and
antagonism. But apply the Socratic method to the situation by sufficiently analyzing, comparing, and redefining the differing standards
of different individuals, and you would find these standards all slowly
converging towards points of agreement, and would eventually extract
from them a definition of virtue common to them all, and a universal
rule of right and wrong, applicable to all individuals in all times

[1] This is the view of Burnet.

and places. Good and evil, right and wrong, looked purely conventional, arbitrary, and relative, simply because men were over-hasty in their conclusions, and did not stop to weigh their answers and expound their exact meaning when they sought to define justice or temperance or any other virtue. Universal ideas, standards, and laws were there, if only men would stop long enough and take sufficient pains to discover them.

The prerequisite of such discovery was a rigorous self-examination. The celebrated inscription on the temple of Apollo at Delphi, "Know Thyself," was the beginning of wisdom. The first fruits of its application were to clear away ignorance and folly and superstition and prejudice, and to lead a man to realize how second-hand and second-rate most of his so-called knowledge really was. Then would come the work of reconstruction of a true wisdom founded upon notions that had been found to be common and acceptable to all men alike.

The Metaphor of the Midwife. The discovery through conversation and argument of such basic universal ideas lying hidden in the human mind beneath the welter of prejudice, partisanship, and bigotry, might be well pictured as a kind of begetting and bringing of these ideas to birth; and Socrates, influenced perhaps by his mother's profession, described his part as that of a midwife. It was his business to help deliver the mind of the true definitions, with which it was always pregnant and which it was forever laboring to bring forth. The travail must necessarily be long and halting, obstructed by self-assurance and self-righteousness, but the wider good, the right and wrong upon which all men could agree, lay in the womb of every man's soul, waiting to be born.

Virtue a Natural Endowment. Virtue, then, was a natural endowment, an innate propensity in mankind, not an artificial convention or habit of action to be acquired through education, as the Sophists had maintained. It could indeed be taught, but only if we regarded instruction in it, not as an introduction from without of a course of behavior foreign to our nature, but as a revelation to the soul of her own inborn disposition. In showing a man how to be virtuous, you showed him how to be true to his own self; you did not show him how to be untrue to it for reasons of expediency.

Again, the several virtues could not be a mere disconnected set of precepts, as Gorgias had taught, differing in their applicability according to age, sex, and station in life. They all could be boiled down to knowledge of one's own best interests, and this knowledge was one and identical in all individuals under all conditions. Virtue, in short, was one, not many, and the seemingly different virtues were merely different aspects of a single thing.

If, however, self-knowledge was the beginning of wisdom and virtue, it might also be regarded as the end thereof. Since man was a rational being, and presumably actuated by self-interest, he would naturally do what was best for him if he but knew what that best was. Virtue, then, from start to finish depended on knowledge, and could be defined as such. So we reach the famous Socratic assertion that *virtue is knowledge,* and that if only men can be brought to see what the better course is they will spontaneously follow it.

In this definition and this confidence Socrates was a victim, perhaps, of the rationalistic attitude of the Greeks toward ethical problems. He did not give sufficient weight to the power of instinct, and passion, and the desire of the moment, to fly in the face of the true good, even when our best interests in the long run are clearly perceived. Over and over again, we do wrong knowingly. As the poet Ovid sings, we know and approve the better course, but follow the worse.

But there is also another, graver difficulty with Socrates' saying that virtue is knowledge. Knowledge, we instinctively retort, of what? Knowledge, Socrates replies, of what is good for us. But what is good for us? If we answer, as we are tempted to do, that virtuous behavior is good for us, then we are simply saying that virtue is knowledge of what is virtuous, and have fallen into the vicious circle of defining a thing by itself. To extricate ourselves, we must determine what it is that constitutes goodness and makes knowledge of it virtuous.

In dealing with this question we come up against the dispute as to whether Xenophon or Plato gives the truer picture of Socrates.

Dispute over Socrates' View of the Good. If we look only to the *Memorabilia* for Socrates' real views, we shall feel that he answered the question, What is the good? in terms of practical utility. Virtue is knowledge of what is useful for man, and man finds useful that which gives him the greatest pleasure and benefits him most in the long run. Law and order, we are told, are better than lawlessness and disorder because they make the state and the individual more prosperous and more secure and "more honored at home and abroad." Continence and temperance are good, because self-control alone has "the power to give us any pleasure worth remembering," whereas through lack of it we are "cut off from the full fruition of the more obvious and constantly recurring pleasures." [2] Even beauty lay essentially in appropriateness and service to a particular use.

From this point of view virtuous behavior is behavior calculated to ensure us security, comfort, prosperity and respectability. Much, too, in the Platonic account of Socrates countenances such an interpretation. There he is depicted as insensitive to the beauties of nature and as regarding art and literature as worthless and even dangerous except as they point a moral lesson.

If, however, we accept Plato as a historian of Socrates' real teaching, we can amplify the picture. His attention is now fixed, not upon the profits of virtue here below, but upon righteousness as the means of opening the eyes of the soul to the glories of a realm of being that transcends sense. This realm is not one of world-stuffs, but of immaterial and intelligible Forms, the absolute natures of Temperance and Justice and Beauty in themselves, laid up in a heaven from which the soul has descended and to which, after the suitable discipline and preparation of virtuous living, she may eventually return. The universal and immutable notions of right and wrong, which it is Socrates' business to discover in and elicit from men's minds, are of divine origin. They are memories of the soul's converse before birth with the bright and perfect Forms of what is absolutely and wholly good. In this realm of real and perfect being the soul's true home lies. Thither she must bend all her efforts to repair, resisting the allurements of sensible beauty and contemplating those things and doing those deeds only that will speed her on her journey.

But, in any case, whether we regard Socrates as a metaphysician or as interested only in ethics and logic and willing to take immortality and the existence of a divine Providence on simple faith, the fact remains that he seems to have left the nature of the human good a wide-open question and to have bequeathed a problem rather than a solution to his disciples. For immediately upon his death the questions "What is virtue? What is the human good?" became burning ones, to which his followers gave diametrically opposed answers, all claiming to be the true interpreters of the real meaning of his teaching. To these divergent interpretations we now pass.

[2] *Mem.,* IV, 4, 13 ff. (trans. Dakyns).

Chapter X

THE LESSER SOCRATICS

I. THE MEGARICS

One of the most fervent disciples of Socrates was Euclid, a citizen of the neighboring and hostile town of Megara. Because of the enmity existing between Megara and Athens, which culminated in an Athenian decree forbidding any Megarian to enter not only the capital but any port in the Empire, Euclid had to visit Socrates secretly, disguised, it is said, as a woman. He was present at Socrates' execution, and afterwards many of the Socratic group, including Plato, sought refuge at his house when Athens for a time, because of anti-Socratic feeling, proved too dangerous for them to live in.

Euclid's Identification of the Socratic Good with Eleatic Being. Euclid had been philosophically "raised" in the Eleatic tradition, and had a great veneration for Parmenides. His association with Socrates did not alter his earlier views, but only served to confirm them, and indeed threw new light for him upon the nature of Being. For the Socratic "good," to which all the seemingly different virtues could be reduced, possessed all the earmarks of Eleatic Being. It was one, simple, homogeneous, unalterable, indestructible, the same in all times and places, for all sorts and conditions of men. "What really is," then, is the good. Men might call it by different names, to be sure, such as wisdom, God, mind, and the like, but these were mere tricks of speech. Nothing but the Good could really exist, since it alone lived up to all the specifications laid down for what is real, and anything opposed to or different from it was a matter of false opinion and illusion.[1] Of anything further that Euclid may have said about the nature of either Eleatic Being or the Socratic Good we have no record.

Continuance of the Eleatic Tradition by Euclid's Followers. The followers of Euclid delighted in logical hair-splitting, and in raising questions like our familiar catches, Have you left off beating your

---

[1] Cf. Diogenes Laertius, II, x, 116; Zeller, *Socrates and the Socratic Schools,* pp. 222 ff.; Gomperz, *Griechische Denker,* IV, 8, § 2.

grandmother yet? How many hairs must a man lose to be bald? How many grains does it take to make a heap? They also carried on the Eleatic polemic against the reality of the many. Since you cannot tell where the few leave off and the many begin, and, since there can be no limit to them, where the many end, there can be no logical definition and hence no existence of the many. Motion, chance, creation and annihilation, and even the concept of possibility itself were subjected in like manner to a rigorous and skeptical overhauling.

II. THE CYNICS

Antisthenes. Antisthenes, the founder of the Cynic School, was born at Athens early in the fourth century. He was by nature a rough customer. Uncouth, disdainful of the amenities of life, and in many respects stupid, he began early in his career to affect the rude and unconventional ways for which his School was afterwards famous. He defiantly carried the beggar's staff and wallet to signalize his independence of spirit, and persisted in ostentatiously confining his dress to a coarse woolen mantle so ragged that Socrates once twitted him with the remark, "I can see your vanity through your cloak." [2] But he was a faithful disciple and stood by his master to the death.

After Socrates' execution Antisthenes gathered about himself a band of disciples of his own. The name Cynic is perhaps derived from the spot where they used to gather, a school called Cynosarges open to the children of Athenians and foreigners, who were technically illegitimate. Or it may come from the Greek word for dog, because of the "dog's life" he imposed upon his followers. Indeed, he discouraged them in every possible way, by personal harshness and brutality as well as by the discipline to which he subjected them. In spite of it all, however, he attracted to himself a large number of adherents.

Diogenes. Of these the best known is Diogenes, famed for living in a tub and walking the streets by daylight, lantern in hand, looking for someone worthy to be called a man. He was originally a young counterfeiter who had run away from his native town of Sinope and taken refuge at Athens. His adventures, however, were by no means over. Captured by pirates one day, while crossing to the island of Aegina, he was sold into slavery, bought by a rich Corinthian, and made the tutor of his purchaser's children. He was later freed and took to expounding his views and living the simple life in Corinth,

[2] Diogenes Laertius, IV, i, 4, § 8.

of which he quickly became one of the chief sights and boasts. The story of his meeting with Alexander the Great is well known. Alexander, when visiting Corinth, went to see the old man, whom he found basking in the sun. "Can I do anything for you?" he asked. "Stand a bit out of my light, will you?" was the answer. The king did as he was told, remarking, "If I were not Alexander, I'd like to be Diogenes." Both men died on the same day in 323 B.C.

Cynic View of Virtue. First hand information regarding the Cynic tenets is almost entirely lacking. The works of Antisthenes, which were so voluminous that he was called a "universal chatterbox," have all been lost. But from contemporary reports we can gather that his surly and independent character responded to the hardy, self-sufficient, and self-controlled side of Socrates' nature, and that he found in these traits the key to the true nature of the Socratic idea of the good. What was supremely useful, nay, indispensable, to man was just the possession of Socrates' qualities of indifference to external conditions and composure in the face of adverse circumstances. Virtue lay in cultivating serenity and independence of mind, and in thus fortifying the inner life against both the blows and the smiles of fickle fortune. Only by freeing his happiness from dependence upon worldly things and even human ties, could a man render it truly secure and unassailable. But to cultivate these qualities was to possess them. Virtue, then, was not a means to anything beyond itself. It was an end in itself. To be virtuous was to be happy. Thus "virtue for virtue's sake" became the famous watchword of the sect.

Attack on Socratic and Platonic Universals. This centering of the moral life and good in the self-sufficiency of the individual was intensified by views drawn from the Sophists' teaching. Antisthenes violently disagreed with Plato's exaltation of the common definitions or "universals" discovered by Socrates into absolute Forms existing in and for themselves, independent of the particular instances that exemplified them. Nor could he accept even the relative importance attributed to them by Socrates. Each individual was unique. Its nature or "form" belonged to it alone and was not shared with anything else. So-called "classes," then, and, for that matter, all standards, institutions, and organizations that implied the real existence of a common tie or interest, were wholly artificial constructions resting on superficial and incidental similarities. "Synthetic" judgments, which tried to knit together subjects and predicates, were logically impossible, since all you were entitled to say of any subject was that it was itself and nothing else. You could not, for instance, say that the apple was red, for then you put it in a class different from itself. All you could properly say of it was that it was an apple. "Synthetic" behavior, which rested upon an identification of different men's activities in a common cause, was equally absurd. It had no basis or justification in the nature of things, which had created each individual a unique being and a "class" and a law unto himself.

Attack on Social Conventions and Institutions. The good life consisted in stripping human existence of everything that was artificial, and in freeing the self-sufficiency of the particular man from external props and supports. The material conditions of human life, and all our political and social forms, conventions, and institutions were unnatural, and dependence upon them was fatal to happiness. Salvation lay in getting back to nature and in reducing our external needs and our satisfactions to an irreducible minimum. Prosperity, wealth, glory, social position and prominence, and all the enormous complications, generally, of what we mistakenly call "civilization" were hindrances, not helps to real well-being.

Marriage, for example, was necessary neither for satisfying duly the wants of sex nor for propagating the species. All forms of government were equally artificial and therefore bad. Nationality and patriotism were false sentiments. A man's true country was the whole world. So, too, the economic order was vicious. Property and money were evils. The popular religion, also, was a trumped-up affair. Its gods, images, temples, and cults were silly and superfluous.

But worst of all was the pleasure man took in all these complications. For that matter the very sensation of pleasure should be suppressed so far as possible, even in connection with elementary and "natural" activities, since in any form it compromised the inner dignity of man. "I had rather go mad than experience pleasure," Antisthenes is reported to have exclaimed.

The practice of these precepts, to which the Cynics applied themselves with missionary zeal, naturally got for Antisthenes and his school a reputation for unconventionality. And their flouting, not only of the amenities, but of what we should call the decencies of life shocked even the tolerant and easy-going ancients. However, the members of the School do not seem to have carried their social and moral anarchy to a point where it seriously conflicted with the established order, and the chief response to their propaganda appears to have been a good-natured derision of their eccentricities.

III. THE CYRENAICS

Aristippus and the Pleasure Principle. Quite different from Antisthenes in most respects was his fellow pupil, Aristippus, the founder
of the Cyrenaic School. Born of a rich and influential family of the
African city of Cyrene, when that town was at the height of her prosperity in the middle of the fifth century, he was by nature a genial,
clever, sweet-tempered youth, a great wit, a "good mixer," and a *bon
vivant* addicted to the pursuit of pleasure. It was only to be expected
that, when he finally fell in with Socrates and attached himself to the
group of disciples, it should be his master's genial, human, pleasure-
loving side that attracted him and suggested to him the true nature
of the good of which virtue is the knowledge. Moreover, if Xenophon's
Memorabilia is to be trusted, it looks very much as if Socrates really
did justify virtue on the ground that the pleasures it ensured were
greater than those procured by vice.

After Socrates' death Aristippus traveled for a while, visiting en
route the court of Dionysius I at Syracuse, of whom we shall have
more to say when we come to Plato. There is a story to the effect
that once the king, whose manners were not his strong point, spat in
Aristippus' face, and that the philosopher took the incident calmly
with the remark that one must expect to get splashed sometimes when
landing a big fish.

Eventually, Aristippus returned to Cyrene, where he started a school
of philosophy. Pleasure, he proclaimed, is the real good which all men
seek—the good of which virtue is the knowledge and to which it is a
means. This fact is obvious. All sentient beings from the moment of
their birth strive after pleasure and shun pain. Hence pleasure and
pain are the good and evil indicated to all her creatures by nature.
Enjoyment is the right end to pursue; the disagreeable is the proper
thing to avoid.

Attack on Socratic and Platonic Universals. In amplifying his theory, Aristippus, like Antisthenes, was greatly influenced by the Sophists.
He, too, felt that the universals by which Socrates and Plato laid such
store were surface and chance resemblances, and that each individual
was a class and a law unto himself. They were mere names, which
failed to indicate any real common nature in the things to which they
were applied. Hence Aristippus and Antisthenes together may perhaps claim to be the founders of the "nominalistic" theory of universals
in contradistinction to the so-called realism of Plato.

But Aristippus went further than his Cynic confrère. Not only did the common or class name applied to several objects stand for no common nature resident in them, but it did not necessarily denote a common impression made upon the minds of the onlookers. Take, for example, the word "red," which we use in connection with roses, apples, blood, etc. It does not express a quality of redness in general which exists in all those objects and which at the same time has a nature of its own independent of them. But neither can it imply that these things impress you and me in the same way. Since I cannot get inside of your head, I have no means of knowing whether the word "red" suggests to your mind the same color-sensation it suggests to mine. For all I know your "red" may be quite different. As a matter of fact, if you are color-blind it means to you a sensation I should call grayish green.

So it is with all universals. There is no guarantee that the class-name "man," or "horse," or "table," or "justice," or "temperance" paints the same picture before our respective eyes. "Common" names, then, can no more draw universality from agreement in the minds of percipients, than they can from agreement in natures of the objects perceived. Not only is there no namable, definable, objective world, which can be known, but there can be no comparison of the experiences of different subjects. All that the individual can know is his own sensations, and all he can know of them is how they appear at the moment.

No Universal Standard of Pleasurableness. The bearings of all this on Aristippus' theory that pleasure is the good are plain, and he does not hesitate to draw the logical conclusion. Since no comparison of the pleasures experienced by different individuals is possible, any universal agreement as to what pleasures are pleasantest, and therefore best, is out of the question. Again, there is no reason for considering some pleasures "higher" than others. Pleasure is pleasure, from whatever source it may be derived. Moreover, that source is always the body, since even so-called mental pleasures are physical sensations. Finally, pleasure is always experienced at its best and fullest in the present moment. The pleasures of memory and of anticipation are pale in comparison with immediate enjoyment.

The moral good, then, is to be found in the pleasure of the moment alone. It "has nothing to do with the recollection of past enjoyments or with the hope of future ones." [3] Hence, in estimating the worth of pleasure, the factor of duration can be ignored. Immediacy and intensity are the only measures of its value. The most immediate and

[3] Athenaeus, XII, 544 (trans. Yonge).

intense pleasures are those of the senses. Therefore they are the best, and are the end at which all moral activity, so far as it is truly moral, is aimed.

Practical Difficulties of This Theory. This theory, though, proved impossible of application, as the Cyrenaics soon found. The consequences of a pleasure, and the amount of pains needed to procure it, simply had to be taken into account in estimating its goodness. Some pleasures, however good they might be at the moment, were not worth the suffering that resulted; and some were not worth the bother involved in attaining them. Some pains, too, were better undergone because of the later enjoyment to which they were a means. There was no dodging the factors of duration and consequences in estimating the goodness and badness of pleasure and pain.

As a result the Cyrenaics now found themselves constructing willy-nilly the universal and objective standards of moral conduct the existence of which they had denied. It is true, indeed, that nothing is "naturally and intrinsically just or honorable or disgraceful," but "the good man will do nothing out of the way because of the punishments which are imposed upon, and the discredit which is attached to such actions." [4] Furthermore, the moment that other factors than the mere pleasurableness of pleasure enter into the computation of its goodness, the so-called mental pleasures prove to be more satisfactory than those of the senses. They last longer, and they are not so apt to bring satiety or suffering in their train.

The Comparative Value of Pleasures Determined by Intelligence. But the theory required still further amendment. It is difficult to compare the pleasurableness of one pleasure with that of another, and decide which is better. Again, it is almost as difficult to make up one's mind whether a pleasure is worth the trouble of procuring it or warrants the disagreeable consequences that may follow from it. To deal with these problems and bring them to a happy solution, an outside judge, wisdom or reason, is needed. Intelligence, then, is an indispensable factor in virtue and a necessary means to happiness, just as Socrates said.

On the whole the Cyrenaics ended by giving away most of their original case. They slipped rapidly towards something not unlike the "enlightened self-interest" of the modern utilitarians. But they improved upon Socrates, in that they defined more clearly than he did the end towards which intelligent behavior should be directed.

So, too, their practice belied their preaching. Like the Cynics, they

[4] Diogenes Laertius, II, viii, 10, 97 (trans. Yonge).

taught independence, cosmopolitanism, indifference to external circumstances, cheerfulness, self-control, and an even mind both in success and adversity. But they prized the amenities and refinements of
life, which the Cynics despised, and they conformed with good-natured
tolerance to the world and society as they found it, where the Cynics
were inclined to defiance.

The Later Cyrenaics. The School lasted a long time, and the more
rational aspects of its teaching were eventually taken over by the
Epicureans. Aristippus' successors wobbled in various directions in
their efforts to keep the pleasure theory intact. Thus, Theodosius maintained that a man can do exactly what he pleases and be moral, provided only he is clever enough to escape evil consequences. Hegesias,
however, came to the pessimistic conclusion that pleasure is so rarely
attained as to make life not worth living. And this conclusion he defended so eloquently at Alexandria that he was forbidden to lecture,
because he incited some of his pupils to suicide. Finally, Anniceris
tried to reinstate the pleasure of the moment as the good. But he believed also in an inborn social nature and innate benevolence in man,
which made altruistic action, not a means to pleasure, but an important ingredient in enjoyment and an end in itself.

Reversion of the Cynics and the Cyrenaics Towards the Sophists.
The Cyrenaics and Cynics taken together demonstrate an important
fact which otherwise might be overlooked. They show that in the
eyes of some of his pupils Socrates by no means triumphantly refuted
the Sophists. He stimulated his disciples' interest in ethics and made
them reflect upon the nature of the good. But the fruits of their interest and reflection were in some cases a reversion to the Sophist
doctrine and an attempt to answer the question, "What is the good?"
in its light, rather than along Socratic lines. Neither Antisthenes nor
Aristippus had any use for Socrates' universals, or for standards of
right and wrong common to all men lying innate in the human mind
waiting to be brought to birth. Their centering of the moral good in
the individual, and their doctrine of independence and self-sufficiency,
reflected in moral form Protagoras' saying that "man is the measure
of all things."

The greatest of Socrates' pupils, however, shared not only his
master's interest in ethics but the belief in common and universal
moral standards as well. Indeed, in the Socratic general definitions of
the virtues, which could be discovered underlying apparently irreconcilable differences of individual opinion, he found the key to the
nature of Reality itself. That pupil was Plato.

Chapter XI

PLATO

Birth and Education. Plato was born at Athens in 427 B.C., two years after the death of Pericles. On both sides he sprang from the old Athenian aristocracy. Through his father he could claim descent from Codrus, the last king of Athens, and through his mother from Solon, the great lawgiver and author of the first Athenian constitution. His father had been a supporter of Pericles, and his stepfather and his mother's relatives were prominent in contemporary affairs.

Though he grew up during the long years of the Peloponnesian War and the slow collapse of the Athenian Empire, his family escaped the financial ruin that overtook so many of his class, and were in a position to give him the best possible education. Later, he did his military training with the cavalry, and very likely saw active service in the war. The universality of his nature was early apparent. He was a good athlete, and tried his hand at painting, music, writing verses and, it is said, at composing an epic and a tragedy.

His first philosophy was learned from Cratylus, a follower of Heraclitus of the extreme type, who maintained that you could not step into the same river even once, so rapid was the flux, and who refused to speak because words could not convey the meaning of the fleeting instant. Socrates, of whom his uncle Charmides was an intimate friend, must have been familiar to him from early youth, though there is some doubt whether Plato ever became a member of the intimate Socratic circle. As a young man he had no particular flair for philosophy, but thought rather of entering politics, where his high connections and "pull" would have ensured him success. Still, as time went on he was falling more and more under Socrates' influence and becoming more and more attached to him personally.

Conversion to Philosophy. It was Socrates' death that turned him once and for all into a philosopher. There could be no further thought of serving a government that had just committed so unforgivable a crime. Then, too, in the flood of his grief and anger his other literary and artistic interests were submerged. His mission was at length plain to him—to follow in Socrates' footsteps and to vindicate and exalt his memory. Henceforth the whole of Plato's nature was impressed in the service of this ideal, and we may remind ourselves that it is an open question whether for some time he did not write primarily as a chronicler of Socrates' opinions and only later develop his own system.

Travels and Dialogues. The anti-Socratic feeling ran so high in Athens that after the execution Plato found it prudent to leave the city. He went first to visit Euclid at Megara in whose house a number of his fellow-disciples also found refuge. For the next ten years he seems to have traveled. To this decade also probably belong the early dialogues, including even a part of the *Republic*. We may note here that the exact order in which the dialogues were composed is a disputed point. The sequence prepared by Campbell and Lutoslawski is perhaps the most authoritative. It places first, in a so-called "Socratic" group, the *Apology, Euthyphro, Crito, Charmides, Laches, Protagoras, Meno, Euthydemus, Gorgias,* and *Lysis.* There follows a first Platonic series composed of the *Cratylus, Symposium,* the *Phaedo,* and the earlier books of the *Republic.* Then comes a "middle Platonic" group comprising the rest of the *Republic,* the *Phaedrus,* and the *Theaetetus* and the *Parmenides;* and finally we have, as late dialogues, the *Sophist, Politicus* or *Statesman, Philebus, Timaeus, Critias,* and the *Laws.*

Twelve years or so after Socrates' death we find Plato in Italy. He had gone there apparently to acquaint himself at first hand with Pythagoreanism, with which he had become fascinated either through association with the Pythagoreans from Thebes who had joined the Socratic circle, or it may be through the teaching of Socrates himself. The revolution that had driven the Order from Italy and Greece was long since over, the proscription had been withdrawn, and they had re-established themselves at Tarentum. Especially prominent at the moment was Archytas, the virtual ruler of the city, a man of noble character and universal genius. With him Plato became fast friends.

Another friend that he made at this time was destined to play a prominent part in his life. Dion, the brother-in-law of the reigning tyrant of Syracuse, Dionysius I, became deeply attached to him and procured for him an invitation to visit the Syracusan Court. The visit turned out badly, however, as Plato could not stand his host, who, for all his ability, was a vulgar parvenu of the most objectionable sort. They quarreled, and Dionysius handed Plato over to the Spartan ambassador—Sparta and Athens being then at war—by whom the philosopher was sent off to Aegina and offered for sale in the slave-market. A friend recognized him, bought him, and sent him home.

Foundation of the Academy. By this time the Socrates affair was forgotten, and Plato, who was now about forty and comfortably off, could settle down to teach in a congenial atmosphere. He had a house and garden outside the gates on the road to Eleusis, near a playground and athletic field known as Hecademus Park. Here he founded his school, known from its location as the *Academy*. New buildings in the shape of a common dining hall and a chapel dedicated to the Muses were added, and eventually his nephew Speusippus and an early pupil of his called Menedemus joined him as a "staff." The method of instruction was the Socratic one of friendly conversation interspersed with question and answer. Problems in mathematics, astronomy, and logic were set the pupils, and formal lectures were also given.

The Academy was primarily a school, not of philosophy, but of political science, and the greater number of Plato's pupils were the sons of ruling or prominent families in the towns of northern Greece, Macedon, and the Propontis and the Black Sea, who had been sent by their parents to Athens to learn the art of government. Among them we may note the Prince Dion, who had followed his beloved Plato to Athens, three young men who were destined for high positions in Arcadia, Elis, and Byzantium, and the Prince of Atarneus, the friend and future uncle-in-law or brother-in-law of Aristotle. Nor should we forget Aristotle himself, who joined the school at the age of eighteen.

Educational Curriculum. The venture flourished exceedingly, and the next twenty years of Plato's life were devoted to its development. Unwittingly he was founding the first university in Europe, and thanks to his success Pericles' dream of Athens as the "School of Hellas" was in a fair way to be realized. As the fame of the Academy grew, foreigners no longer came as in the old days to give instruction but to receive it.

Of the curriculum we may perhaps gain some idea from the scheme of education set forth in the *Republic*. During the first years of the School, Plato was putting the finishing touches to his picture of an ideal commonwealth, of whose constitution it was a fundamental article that the rulers should be men of philosophic training and vision, conversant with the immutable principles upon which all real being and all right action rest. As a means to this end, he advocated a thoroughgoing instruction in mathematics, capped by a stiff course in "dialectic." Such, he thought, were the subjects best calculated to instill the impersonality, the breadth, the soundness, and the justice of out-look indispensable to a man who would govern wisely and well. Specific information in the practical details of the art of government would, he seems to have felt, come of itself through practice and might be left to one side to be picked up along the way. It was the habit of mind inculcated by mathematics and philosophy that was the all-important thing.

Later, Plato became less visionary and more practical. He extolled as the best form of government obtainable under earthly conditions a limited monarchy in which the rule of the sovereign was checked by a constitution and the consent of the governed. This political philosophy he preached to his pupils. And as a matter of fact he turned out so many future law-givers, governors, military leaders, and even would-be despots that he was accused of having founded a school for making tyrants.

Second Visit to Syracuse. For twenty years Plato presided in peace and quiet over the growth of the Academy. He finished the *Republic*, wrote the *Theaetetus* and some, at least, of the so-called "critical" dialogues, the *Parmenides, Sophist, Politicus (Statesman)* and *Philebus*. And then the calm was suddenly interrupted. In 367 B.C. his old acquaintance, Dionysius I of Syracuse, died, leaving the throne to his son. The second Dionysius, however, had been so neglected and suppressed by his father that when he acceded he was wholly unprepared for his job. Not unnaturally he turned for advice to his uncle Dion, Plato's friend and pupil, who thus became virtually regent. The young ruler, however, was keen on being educated and learning how to rule for himself. Dion, who had no political ambitions of his own, seconded the project, and proposed that Plato should be invited to Syracuse as the royal tutor. The invitation was sent and was accepted by Plato, who must have seen in it an opportunity to put his theories to the test by training with his own hand a "philosopher-king" of the first magnitude.

For a time the visit went well. Dionysius proved an amenable pupil, and the study of mathematics became the rage at court. But the innovation was not popular with a large party, who did their best to discredit both Plato and Dion in the sovereign's eyes. Their efforts succeeded in making the king so jealous and suspicious of his uncle that he banished him from Sicily. His affection for Plato, however, they could not shake, though Plato himself must have been disgusted with events and eager to get away. Finally a war interfered. The studies had to be abandoned, and Plato was permitted to leave on condition that he would return when hostilities had ceased. He promised, but insisted that Dion should be allowed to return also.

Third Visit to Syracuse. The next five years Plato spent at the Academy. He finished the "critical" dialogues, and perhaps made a beginning with the *Laws,* his last work. But his peace was again interrupted. In Syracuse the war was over, and Dionysius was reminding him of his promise and clamoring for him to come back. But the king would not hear of his uncle's return. In view of this refusal Plato might have flatly declined to stir, had not Dion, eager for a reconciliation with his nephew, urged him to go. Then, too, there were reports that Dionysius was a changed man and had carried on his studies in mathematics by himself during the war. Perhaps there was still hope of turning him into a philosopher-king after all. So Plato went.

But he went only to court more immediate and complete disaster. His efforts to reconcile uncle and nephew only irritated Dionysius into confiscating Dion's property. Plato wanted to go home, but the king would not allow it. They quarreled, and the philosopher was shut up in the palace gardens, virtually a prisoner, for a year. Eventually he was released and allowed to depart, as the result of diplomatic representations made by his old friend Archytas and the Tarentine government.

Old Age and Death. Once back in Athens, he settled down again to his teaching and writing. To this period belong apparently the *Timaeus,* the unfinished *Critias,* the *Laws,* and if it be genuine, the *Epinomis.* Life went on the whole peacefully, but he still had one great grief to suffer. Dion, with Plato's consent, enlisted a number of his friends at the Academy in an effort to seize Syracuse and expel Dionysius. The expedition was at first a brilliant success. Dionysius fled to Italy, and Dion was received with acclamation. But his reign was short-lived. He was stabbed by a fellow Academician, one Callippus, who maintained himself in power for a precarious year, and then was overthrown. The whole episode, apart from the personal grief it caused Plato, involved the Academy in scandal and disrepute. Nevertheless, we find him still willing to give sound political advice to the avengers of Dion.

In 347 B.C., Plato died at the age of eighty. Cicero tells us he was hard at work writing, up to the end. And the story is that he died swiftly and easily one day, while at the marriage feast of a friend.

II. THE PLATONIC TEST OF REALITY

Reality Not Sense-Experience. The Platonic philosophy is a child of many fathers. Its paternity, to be sure, is commonly ascribed to Socrates, but other strains enter into its composition, inherited from Pythagoras, Heraclitus, the Eleatics, and the Sophists, to mention only the more dominant. The Heraclitean flux, for example, Plato accepted as an accurate description of the outstanding feature of the sensible world. All particular, concrete objects, of whatsoever kind, come into and pass out of being. Generation after generation of them appear, hesitate a moment between existence and non-existence, and are gone. The first and last state of the sensible world is one, not of *being* anything but of unremitting restlessness, passage, and *becoming*. It fails, therefore, to measure up to the specifications laid down by Parmenides for real being, such as indestructibility, changelessness, homogeneity, and the like—specifications that Plato was inclined, for the moment at any rate, to accept.

Furthermore, its failure is equally conspicuous if we approach the question of its reality by the road of *knowledge*. The sensible world cannot possibly be an object of knowledge, if there is nothing to it but a chaotic flow of dissolving sensations. In that case it will present no *things* to know, nothing that can be named, nothing of which it can be said "it *is*." At the most, we can have of it only individual and shifting *opinions,* and these will not shift rapidly enough to keep up with the swiftness of the change they represent. It would look, then, as if we might as well abandon at the outset any hope of knowledge, science, and philosophy, and turn Protagorean once and for all.

Structure More Real than Stuff. Before adopting this counsel of despair, however, let us turn back once more to the flux. Is it really as hopeless as the Sophists thought? If we look more closely we shall see that it is not an undifferentiated flow of chaotic qualities in which no patterns can be discerned. Its whole surface is pitted, as it were, with whirlpools, which never shift their positions in the stream and never alter their different sizes and shapes. These whirlpools arrest the onward rush of the flux. They suck its waters in, constrain them to revolve for an instant about a fixed point and to assume a definite form, and then discharge them back into the stream, where they are immediately caught in a new vortex. So thoroughly pitted is the stream that there is not a drop of its content but is revolving about some point of arrest. To leave one whirlpool is to enter another. To put off an old form is to put on a new. There is no relapse in change, even for an instant, into sheer formlessness.

To put it in Platonic terms, the sensible world of *becoming* is a mixture of the principle of *being,* on the one hand, and of *not-being,* on the other. The two elements are always present in it. *Not-being* makes the object *run; being* makes it run true to form. *Being* gives it its outlines, and makes it what it *is; not-being* is forever blurring and erasing those outlines, and rubbing out whatever it is that the object may happen to be.

Immaterial Character of the Real. The direction in which we must look, if we are to discover the nature of Reality, must now be plain. We must seek and shall find the Real, not in the sensible, tangible, corporeal world-*stuffs* of the earlier philosophers, but in an intelligible world-*structure.* For all stuffs, in spite of their seemingly hard and solid character, have a "being" that is but skin-deep. The only really enduring and "solid" features in the kaleidoscope of change prove, paradoxically enough, to be its most immaterial, non-concrete, in-corporeal aspects—the laws it obeys, the forms it exemplifies, the general definitions or ideas that remain constantly applicable to its behavior. These are the things that make the universe what it is, and give it backbone and rigidity. These are the things that endure, that are reliable, that can be leaned upon without their giving way, that are the same yesterday, today and forever. It is, then, not individual bodies, or yet the matter composing them, but rather these bodiless types and natures, lifted clear of space and time and birth and death, and approached not by sense-perception but by the mind's eye, which alone fulfill the specifications of real being.

Universals, Not Particulars, Are the Realities. The Socratic teaching, too, led Plato to this conclusion and threw further light upon the nature of the Real. Socrates, we may remember, had sought for common and authoritative definitions underlying the confusion and conflict of individual opinions regarding the nature of the moral good. And he had discovered, as he believed, universal truths in the field of ethics upon which all men could be brought to agree. These definitions could be *known* for certain, and thus raised the mind above sense-impression and opinion and set it upon surer ground. But, unless we accept the theory that attributes to him the teaching of the earlier Platonic dialogues and makes of him a metaphysician as well as a moralist, he never read into them any cosmic and metaphysical significance. Euclid of Megara, however, had, as we have seen, been quick to do so, and had pointed out that the Socratic general idea of a single self-identical good, expressing itself in different ways in the different virtues, passed all the tests of real existence set up by Parmenides, and therefore constituted the nature of the Real.

Plato was quick to parallel, if not to follow, Euclid's footsteps. That in a thing which gave it character and existence was not its particular but its universal element. The common nature which it shared with others of the same class was the only aspect of it that defied the process of its growth and decay and survived the catastrophe of its death. Specific acts of temperance and courage and justice were over in a moment, swept by the flux into the dead past. But Temperance in itself, Courage in itself, and Justice in itself, or, as Plato calls them, the *Ideas* or *Forms* of temperance, courage and justice, were immutable and deathless essences ever present in the course of history to inspire fresh instances of themselves. They were the true "stuff" of which noble and heroic deeds were formed, just as human nature in general was the real "stuff" of which individual human beings were composed. The universal, then, not the particular and the concrete, constituted the nature of Reality.

III. THE PLATONIC IDEAS

Nature of the Ideas. By these converging avenues of approach, leading from the Pythagoreans, Heraclitus, the Eleatics, and Socrates, we reach at last, the Forms or Ideas—the "unseen" Reality, of which, in Anaxagoras' phrase, "what appears is the vision." Incidentally, we may remark that "Form" is a more accurate description for us of what Plato meant than "Idea." The term "Idea" suggests to us something mental, a concept conceived by and having its existence in a consciousness. But there is no ground in the earlier dialogues for attributing such a notion to Plato, and later we shall find him expressly combating it. Whether he came finally to adopt it, as some critics maintain, is doubtful. The "Idea," apparently for him, was as little dependent upon mind for its existence as it was upon the material world. It had a kind of being all its own which would not be disturbed, were all the intellects entertaining, as well as all the particular objects enacting, it to be destroyed.

Let us listen now to Plato's own description of the Forms. They are, he tells us, eternal and immutable, present always and everywhere, self-identical, self-existent, absolute, separate, simple, without beginning or end. They are complete, perfect, existent in every respect. They are without taint of sense or imagery, invisible to the eye, accessible only to the mind. Furthermore, now that they were trans-figured into metaphysical principles, or at least, into logical essences, they escaped, not only the comparatively humble status assigned to them by Socrates, but also the comparatively narrow field of ethics to which he had confined them. Forming as they now did the in-telligible structure of the entire universe, their scope had to be cor-respondingly extended. Wherever two or three data of sense are gathered together under a common name, there a Form is present also. Hence there must be as many Forms as there are possibilities of grouping things under headings and applying to them a common term.

So it is that besides Ideas of the virtues, we find Plato mentioning Forms of esthetic values like beauty, and of physical qualities such as health and strength, color, shape, and sound, swiftness and slowness. Also, there are Forms of natural objects, and of artificial objects like beds and tables, and of categories and relations such as sameness and difference, equality, greatness and smallness, and even perhaps of evil and negative things.

The Ideas a Single System. At the same time, these Forms all fit together like the pieces of a picture-puzzle, and present, when prop-erly grasped and arranged by the intellect, a single coherent system, or vision of Reality as a whole. Just as the place and significance of each separate piece is determined by the picture it helps compose, so the different Forms get the general quality of intelligibility that char-acterizes them from the total system of which they are a part. From the Form of the Whole they derive the light which they shed upon the sensible universe. If they did not all together compose a single rational order, they would make confusion worse confounded by add-ing to the chaos of sense a further intellectual chaos of isolated laws, and types, and values, which could not be related or even reconciled to one another. They would be like random bits from different puzzles, which could not possibly be fitted together to give a picture of any sort. Therefore, over and above the different Ideas there must be a Form of Forms or essence of general rationality in the universe, from which comes the power of the mind to assemble the Ideas in a con-sistent, comprehensible picture of the Real.

The Ideas as Ideals. Moreover, in the deepest sense of the word, all the Forms remained moral principles and continued to wear the Socratic halo. From the beginning, the Platonic Ideas were ideals. They were not averages but archetypes or models. They were "typical" only in the sense that the breeder of fancy stock uses the term. They possessed all the "points" which the fancier seeks to reproduce. The Idea of man, for instance, was not a composite photograph but an idealized portrait. It was human nature as it would be if relieved of all shortcomings and disabilities. The Form of the horse was not any old nag, but thoroughbred. The Idea of the bed had no lumps in its mattress. The true nature of health was not ordinary but perfect physical and mental well-being.

Being ideals, the Forms were objects of adoration. They were not coldly scientific, post-mortem reports of the nature and content of beauty and holiness and truth. They were not a map, but an idealized panorama of the universe, painted with all the colors of the soul's yearning towards perfection. Union with them gave both heart and mind a peace that the sensible world could neither give nor take away, akin to the peace of God.

Divinity of the Ideas. Indeed the Forms, synthesized and organized under the all-inclusive Form of the Whole, perhaps occupied in Plato's philosophy much the same position that a God holds in a theistic system.[1] They were the core of Reality. They set the standard and the goal for moral and esthetic aspiration and activity. And until they were apprehended, the ceaseless struggle of the mind to know the truth could never come to rest. Later we shall find Plato introducing into his scheme a God apart from them, and shall see that he had sound metaphysical reasons for so doing. But even then, they were not to be shaken from their supreme position. They remained the inspiration of the divine thinking and creative activity as they are of ours. They were God's ideals as well as man's. Hence it is not surprising to find him speaking of the completed picture puzzle, or Form of the whole, into which all the other Forms fit, and from which they receive their meaning, as the *Idea of the Good*.

The Idea of the Good. Nor is it surprising, since the whole is more than the sum of its parts and has a nature of its own, to find Plato apparently conceiving the Idea of the Good as a metaphysical principle different from and higher than the other Forms. Euclid of Megara had already pointed the way in this direction when he identified the Good that in Socrates' eyes unified all the virtues with the pure Being that for Parmenides underlay the seeming existence of particular beings. The relation of the Idea of the Good to the other

[1] On this point cf. Zeller, *Plato and the Older Academy*, pp. 279 ff.; Adam, *Republic of Plato*, II, pp. 50-51; Nettleship, *Lectures on the Republic of Plato*, pp. 232-233; Burnet, *Greek Philosophy*, Part I, 232; More, *Religion of Plato*, pp. 119 ff.

Ideas in the intelligible world, is, Plato tells us, that of the sun in the sensible world to the landscape it illuminates and makes visible. As the sun enables the eye to see and the physical object to be seen, so the Idea of the Good imparts truth to the known and the power of knowledge to the knower. Again just as the sun is neither the perceiving eye nor the perceived object, but is higher than both, so the Good is neither knowledge nor truth but higher than either of them. Finally, just as visible objects depend upon the sun not only for visibility but for life and growth, so the Ideas depend for their very existence, as well as for intelligibility, upon the Good, which in itself "is not essence, but far beyond essence in dignity and power." [2]

Modern Dispute over Plato's Concept of the Ideas. In spite of the piety displayed by Plato towards the Forms and the language he uses in describing them, considerable doubt has arisen lately as to the exact status he ascribed to them. By most philosophers from Aristotle on, this language has been taken at its face value, and the Forms have figured as metaphysical principles, existing in and for themselves apart from the sensible world which enacts them, and possessing, roughly speaking, the incorporeal yet quasi-substantial sort of being commonly attributed by theologians to the Deity.

Certainly, our first impression of them is of models and archetypes, laid up in heaven and imperfectly copied and exemplified by the things of sense. In that case we have what we may call a three-story universe. Beginning at the top, we have the Idea of the Good, from which the light of pure being and intelligibility proceeds. Next we find this light broken into the various Forms, Laws, Types, Values and the like, the presence and apprehension of which in our experience transform it from a chaos of disorderly sensation into an orderly and intelligible world. Finally, we have the world of sensible objects, which is understandable and permanently existent only in so far as it catches and retains the likeness of the Forms.

Of late years, however, this view of Plato's meaning has been challenged by a group of eminent scholars,[3] who regard the Forms, not as *metaphysical principles* existing in and for themselves apart from the sensible world, but as *logical essences* which are enacted nowhere save in the particular objects exemplifying them. For instance, the law of gravitation has a real being of its own apart from physical objects. It exists, but it is not a concrete thing, like the falling apple.

[2] *Rep.*, VI, 527 A-529 D.
[3] Notably Natorp and J. A. Stewart.

Apart, however, from the gravitating objects, it has no *enacted* existence. It might, indeed, be conceived as continuing to exist as a formula, not only if all physical objects, but even if all minds were destroyed. For it was valid, and "held" for the behavior of bodies, long before any minds discovered it. Nor would the disappearance of all bodies annihilate its essence any more than the extinction of all individual dinosaurs and dodos annihilated the types or Forms that these creatures once assumed. Nevertheless, in spite of its independence in one sense of its material embodiments, the Idea gets all its punch and substantial being from the bodies that incorporate and enact it.

Or again, take a value like beauty or moral goodness. It is what it is, whether or not it is ever realized in thought or deed or fact. It points the way, though there are none to follow. It exists, as an ideal, independent of the sensible world. But this does not mean that it realizes itself by some metaphysical method and on some metaphysical level, apart from the sensible order. Apart from that order it is an unrealized value. It can only be met and dealt with in its particular instances.

The Ideas Perhaps Not Metaphysical Models but Architectural Plans. If we apply these considerations to the relation of the Platonic Ideas as a whole to the sensible world, we find ourselves not in a three-story but in a one-story universe. The Forms do not constitute a model of the universe, composed of a substance different from the stuff of sense and existing side by side with the material objects; they give the "layout" of the house of life, the sizes and shapes of its rooms and their relations to one another. Take away the bricks and mortar provided by the sensible order, and the plan continues to exist to be sure, but not as another *thing*. It is no longer enacted or incorporated anywhere in heaven or earth. It exists only on the logical plane, as a Form or set of Forms that perhaps some architect might happen upon and embody concretely. Nowhere save in the material, tangible, sensible house has it substantial, enacted existence.

So, too, the Idea of the Good is merely the plan of the universe viewed not in detail but in its entirety. This plan is, to be sure, more than the sum of the plans of the rooms. It is those plans so connected as to show how the whole house is constructed. But it does not need to be drawn on a separate sheet of paper. It is not a second plan. And, like the drawings for the different rooms, the plan of the whole house can be realized only in the material of which the edifice is built.

It is further pointed out that there is really nothing in Plato's praise of the Forms that conflicts with such an interpretation. Laws, types,

standards, and norms, regarded as logical essences and moral and
esthetic ideals enacted in the world of sense alone, pass the Eleatic
tests of true being as easily as they do when turned into self-enacting
metaphysical principles. They are no less true, no less valuable, no
less the goals of scientific and moral activity, for being realizable only
in the material stuff of the sensible universe.

Whether the "logical essence" view really represents the Platonic
teaching is an open question. There is much to be said both for it and
against it. But it is so important and has been so ably championed that
it cannot be ignored in any description of Plato's doctrine.

IV. PLATONIC LOVE

The Origin and Significance of Love. Whatever kind of being Plato
ascribed to the Forms, every department of experience attested the
vital necessity of their existence. Take, for example, the whole affectional side of our nature—the fact that we like and dislike—of which
the most intense and characteristic manifestation is our love of our
fellow-beings. In one of the earliest dialogues, the *Lysis,* Plato had
suggested that friendship cloaks a profound aspiration towards some
absolute and final good, which is prized for its own sake. At the
famous dinner-party described in the *Symposium* this suggestion is
taken up and developed in a series of speeches about the nature and
the meaning of love. Love, we are told, is a glorious thing, inspiring
deeds of self-sacrifice in beloved and lover alike. It must, however, be
divided into two sorts, a sacred and a profane love, the one occupied
with the body of the beloved, the other with his mind and character.
Only through the higher love can true happiness be found. The sense
of completion of one's own self in union with the beloved—and here
Plato puts a half-serious, half-jesting explanation into the mouth of the
poet Aristophanes, who figures as a guest at the dinner—comes from
the fact that in the beginning each human being was double, with
two faces, four arms and four legs. In some of these creatures the
halves were of the same sex, in others male and female were joined
together. Zeus, fearing their strength and agility, cut them in two
and rearranged each half in our present human form. The severed
halves go about seeking for each other, and, when they have found
them and united with them, feel "rounded out" and completed again.
Thus the love of man for woman and of members of the same sex
for one another and the satisfaction that comes from consummating it
are explained.

Love a Longing for Union with Absolute Beauty and Immortality.
Socrates now takes up the tale. Love is the mediator between God and
man. It is the child of want and plenty, the aspiration of the incomplete towards that which completes it. The other half, of which Aristophanes spoke, can only be found in some final good which is desired for its own sake alone. Towards this good we mount step by
step, first loving the beloved's body, then all physical loveliness, then
the beauties of mind and soul, and finally the pure Form or essence
of loveliness in itself, "absolute, separate, simple and everlasting, which
without diminution and without increase, or any change, is imparted
to the ever growing and perishing beauties of all things." [4]

In the embrace of this absolute beauty we fulfill also our longing
for immortality. Reproduction, to be sure, rescues the race from the
mortality of the individual life, and nutrition and memory enable
the particular body and soul to survive the passing moment and attain
the comparative immortality of a lifetime and a career. So, too, noble
thoughts and deeds, which live after us, save us from oblivion as no
children of our body can. But the mind that here and now becomes
one with the Form of pure beauty, and thus identifies itself with the
eternal, is lifted clear of time altogether and becomes deathless in another, higher sense of the word. In its union with a timeless and eternal
object it has lost all sense of the passage of time and all interest in the
temporal; just as we, when engrossed in an absorbing book or occupation, are made one with the story or the problem, and take no account
of the ticking clock and the lengthening shadows of the outside world.
Time has ceased to exist for us also, and when we return to earth
we note with a start how late the hour is. But, whereas we are eventually aroused from our timeless reverie by the claims of the sensible
world, the soul, Plato feels, may become so sunk in and attached to
the eternal, that her liberation from time and sense may become almost
complete in this life and be wholly completed by death. Side by side
with this view, we shall also find another theory of immortality as everlastingness or going on in time, instead of salvation from temporal
continuance. But of this more anon.

The Dual Nature of the Soul. In the *Phaedrus* Plato takes up again
the subject of love. There, in a famous "myth" or allegory, he likens
the soul to a charioteer driving two winged steeds. The one is thoroughbred and gentle, eager to bear the soul upward into the presence
of the ideal, the other vicious and refractory, forever bolting in pursuit

[4] *Symposium,* 211 B.

of physical satisfaction. The discipline of love lies in training the unruly steed to run in harmony with its thoroughbred mate, and, if successful, bears lover and beloved away from the world of sense to the vision of that absolute loveliness which alone makes them truly lovely and lovable in each other's eyes. To this myth we shall have occasion to return once more at greater length.

For the moment enough said. The existence of affection of any sort, we now see, can only be explained on the hypothesis that there exists a pure essence or Form of loveliness whose presence in sensible objects renders them desirable to one another. All the forms of love, down to the primitive drives of hunger and sex, are seen to be at heart aspirations towards the eternal, which can only reach their true goal when they have raised the soul altogether out of time and becoming, and have united her with a beauty that is universal and absolute, existent in itself and lovable for itself alone.

V. THE PLATONIC ETHICS AND POLITICS

As was to be expected of so ardent a disciple of Socrates, Plato found the field of ethics and politics rich in indications of the existence of the Forms. Moral values and right action and social organization could no more be explained and justified, if there were no absolute good, than could the sense and the love of the beautiful in the absence of a Form of absolute beauty. He agreed with Socrates that virtue lay in knowing what this good was, and that right conduct spontaneously flowed from such knowledge. The determination of its nature was for him, as it was for his fellow-disciples Antisthenes and Aristippus, a major philosophical problem, but he could not be put off with the superficial answers that had satisfied them. In pressing for a further and deeper solution of the question he was led to the Ideas.

The Good Not Pleasure. Plato was particularly opposed to hedonism, or the teaching that the good is pleasure. He attacked it again and again in the *Gorgias* and the *Protagoras,* in the ninth book of the *Republic,* and in a later dialogue, the *Philebus.* In the *Protagoras* he disposes to his own satisfaction of the doctrine that the good is the pleasure of the moment, by exposing our instinctive unwillingness to admit that all pleasures are *ipso facto* good, and all pains necessarily evil. The teaching, however, that the good may lie in the balance of pleasure in the long run he is willing to admit for the moment, only to smash it in the *Gorgias* by pointing out that, even if it could be shown that the maximum of enjoyment in the long run was to be had from continually itching and scratching, such a good would be repugnant to human nature. To determine what pleasures are really preferable we must appeal to something beyond their pleasurableness, and this something Plato finds in wisdom or reason.

Later, in the ninth book of the *Republic,* he returns to the charge, this time to show that pleasures are deceptive, that mere cessation of pain or anticipation of enjoyment are often mistaken for them, and that intelligence is needed to distinguish not only what pleasures are preferable, but what are really pleasures. To make this distinction the sources of enjoyment must be taken into account, since the enjoyments derived from the less real and permanent parts of our nature, such as the body, will have less reality than those connected with the soul whose delight is in contemplating the changeless and the eternal. Finally, in the *Philebus,* Plato, provoked perhaps by an advocacy of the pleasure theory by some of his own pupils, sums up the whole matter. Pleasure and intelligence are both indispensable ingredients in the good life. To make pleasure alone the criterion of the good, as the Cyrenaics were fain to do, would reduce human life to the level of the oyster's existence. On the other hand, an austere life of pure thought, such as the Cynics advocated, from which all pleasure was banished as evil, would not be worth living. Still, reason must be the dominant factor and the final judge both of the quality and quantity of pleasure necessary to a well-balanced moral diet.

The recurrence at intervals of these attacks upon different aspects of the pleasure theory shows, perhaps, that hedonism remained a burning issue during Plato's lifetime, and that while constructing his own system he had constantly to ward off repeated assaults from his adversaries.

Virtue One Not Many, Innate Not Acquired. But there was other preliminary work to do, in the way of clearing the ground. In the *Protagoras* Plato also refutes the Sophists' teaching that the several virtues have no unified principle of goodness underlying them. This he does by showing that all the virtues, however different they may seem, have a common opposite, *ignorance,* and therefore imply in their various ways a *knowledge* of what is best for man. Furthermore, this knowledge cannot be taught in the Sophists' use of the word "teaching," as an instilling into the mind from without of a set of artificial precepts which take no real root there. But it can be taught, if by "teaching" we mean a revelation to the soul from within of principles grounded in her essential nature. That the mind possesses such innate principles or ideas he demonstrates in the *Meno* by showing that even an untutored mind, totally ignorant of geometry, will recognize instinctively the truth of the Pythagorean proposition. Mathematical knowledge is, then, latent in the mind from the beginning and needs only to be awakened. In the same way, ideas of right and wrong are innate.

The Nature of Right and of Morality. Thus, at the very outset, Plato established the existence of moral standards of some sort, which drew their authority not from the pleasure of the moment, or even from pleasure in the long run, but rather from the use of intelligence directed towards some broader end. There were, however, still foes to be dealt with. There were, for instance, the politician Callicles, and the Sophist Thrasymachus whose political inferences from the teaching of the Sophists we mentioned in a former chapter. Callicles, we may remember, advocated the extravagant view that conventional morality is entirely artificial and at variance with natural morality which supports the right of the stronger to rule the weaker as they choose. To this Plato replies that the possession of power in itself is no advantage; nay, that power in the hands of a fool is only an instrument of self-destruction. The strong must also be wise and just if they are to be really strong. The pursuit of pleasure and self-aggrandizement on their part not only corrupts them but leads to their downfall. The truly strong exhibit their strength by showing themselves able to improve mankind. Indeed, it is *better* to suffer injustice than to commit it, and those who perpetrate it would do well to seek out the judge and ask for remedial punishment at his hands, just as the sick man goes to the doctor and asks to be made well again, even by an unpleasant cure.

Much the same argument is advanced in the first book of the *Republic* against the contention of Thrasymachus that there is not even a natural right, and that so-called morality is merely the interest of the party in power at the moment. That party may mistake its own interests, in which case its edicts can be obeyed only to its own disadvantage. Its real advantage, like that of the doctor or the shepherd, is identical with the well-being of those over whom it rules. The physician or the herdsman, so far as he is skillful and a true doctor or shepherd, is primarily concerned with his patients or his flock. He loves and takes pride in his work for its own sake. That it also pays him is secondary. Pay is an extra reward bestowed upon him by society for work well done. Nor does the successful practitioner of any art try to circumvent its restrictions, as the man seeking only his own advantage tries to get around the restrictions laid upon him by the art of government. Moreover, when each pursues only his own private interest, there is strife, which makes for weakness, not for strength. All in all, selfishness impedes the proper functioning of human nature and stands in the way of happiness instead of furthering it.

The Nature of Goodness. Still, the suspicion will not down that morality is really artificial and a matter of expediency pure and simple. Are not men naturally inclined to pursue their private ends and to war upon one another, and are they not merely constrained to deal justly with their neighbors from fear of retaliation, human or divine, or because they consider honesty the best policy? It is in reply to this question that Plato abandons his tactics of telling us what the good is not, and undertakes a positive description of the nature of righteousness, or as he calls it, of "justice."

Such an undertaking, he says, may best be conducted in capital letters, that is, in describing the ideal State, in order that we may the more readily recognize righteousness when we find it writ small in the individual. So our search is raised to the political level and becomes an inquiry into the constitution of the perfect commonwealth. Any State, he continues, that has developed beyond the primitive, Arcadian stage, will require a *working class* given to many, varied occupations, an *army* to defend it against its foes and to ensure its growth, and a *governing class* to administer it. At the same time, no State can be perfect if it is too large or too rich. Hence its size and wealth must be strictly limited. But too great poverty must also be avoided, since it breeds discontent and inefficiency.

Equality of Men and Women. The all-important thing, however, is the breeding and training of the class entrusted with government, for, if it be wise and good, the well-being of the State as a whole will follow as a matter of course. In outlining the ideal method of reproduction and education, Plato makes three startling proposals. In the first place women should receive the same training as men, so far as their weaker and somewhat less intelligent nature permits. They should even undergo military training. Here Plato seems to be influenced by the movement for the emancipation of women already afoot in Athens, as well as by the example of Sparta where women already shared to a large extent the life of the men.

Abolition of the Family and of Private Property. Secondly, individual marriage should be abolished and all the women and children should be held in common. The governing class should be bred eugenically like prize stock among the other animals. Only men between twenty-five and fifty-five should be allowed to beget, only women between twenty and forty to bear. Union should be by lot, but the dice should be so loaded that the best and bravest men pair with the strongest and fairest woman. Inferior children should be put out of the way at birth. The others should be at once separated from their mothers and brought up by the State in a kind of government nursery, ignorant of the identity of their parents. Only in this way can the opposition to the common good of the private interest created by the family be abolished. Inbreeding, however, will be supplemented by recruiting from the ranks the abler children of the lower classes. And the less brilliant offspring of the governors will be allowed to sink to their proper levels. The ownership of private property by the governing class must also be strictly forbidden, since it, too, is a dis tracting influence.

The Philosophers as Governors. The greatest innovation in Plato's eyes is, however, that the rulers must be philosophers. "Until philos ophers are kings, or the kings and princes of this world have the spirit and power of philosophy, and political greatness and wisdom meet in one . . . cities will never rest from their evils . . . and then only will this our State have a possibility of life and behold the light of day." [5] It matters not that philosophers have the reputation of being impractical and unbusinesslike. They alone are the spectators of all time and existence, and are able to see through the superficialities and shams of the world of appearance to the truth of things. Under actual conditions, where the art of government consists in humoring the whims and blind prejudices of that great beast, the people, and in dodging its furies, the philosopher, naturally, seems to be either a knave or a fool. He is like an expert navigator on a ship, who finds himself at the mercy of a stupid captain and an ignorant crew, each one of whom thinks himself capable of steering the vessel and there- fore berates the trained pilot as a mere star-gazer. No wonder that in these circumstances the true philosopher prefers to shelter himself in obscurity from the insults of the crowd, and to "live his own life and be pure from evil and unrighteousness, and depart in peace and good will." [6] Still, although his nature, being finer, is perhaps sub- ject to deeper corruption than more ordinary characters, and although there are many second-rate imitators of his wisdom, to him and to him alone the guidance of the State must be entrusted, if the ideal commonwealth is to be realized.

[5] *Rep.,* V, 473 C-D.
[6] *Ibid.,* VI, 496 D.

Education of the Governing Class. The education of such a man must necessarily be long, painstaking, and subject to every edifying influence. It will begin, naturally, with "music," or the general cultural training in poetry and in playing upon some musical instrument, to which all the Athenian youth of Plato's time were subjected. But "music" as it stood must be thoroughly expurgated before it could be made a suitable element in the discipline of a philosopher-king. In suggesting the necessary changes, Plato involved himself in a remarkable theory of the relation of art to morality.

Homer and Hesiod, who heretofore had been the backbone of Greek cultural and religious training, must, he tells us, be banned, since they frequently portray the gods as immoral, death as fearful, and the apportionment of reward to merit as non-existent. These are ideas from which youth should be carefully shielded. The budding philosopher-king, especially, must hear and believe nothing that is not morally edifying and a model of virtuous thought. Nor can the run of dramatic poetry be permitted. Dramatic poetry is imitative, and unworthy situations and sayings are attributed directly to the characters in the plays. If imitation is to be allowed at all, it must always be of the good. Even the epic poet must never speak of vice in terms of which a strict moralist would not approve.

So, too, with singing and playing. The sentimental Lydian harmonies and the soft Ionian melodies used as accompaniments for drinking songs must be forbidden. The sterner Dorian and Phrygian modes which reflect the high seriousness of life are the only ones to pass the censor. New-fangled, many-stringed, curiously harmonized instruments, and strange, complicated scales have no place in the heavenly choir. The flute, particularly, is very demoralizing. Only the old-fashioned lyre, the harp, and the shepherd's pipe are ethical. Rhythm, too, must be carefully scrutinized and rigorously cleansed of anything that might excite an unworthy mood. The other arts, weaving, embroidery, painting, sculpture, and architecture, must be purified in like manner. Extreme severity and simplicity must be the order of their day, and in their works they must not aim at anything but moral edification.

In the tenth book, Plato renews his crusade. All art is intrinsically poor stuff. It imitates the sensible world, which in its turn is but an imitation of the Ideas. Its productions are a third step away from reality, and belong to the world of illusion. Poets and painters know less about true being than do practical men of affairs who, by making and using the objects the artist only depicts, learn more about their real natures. Imitative art is an inferior who marries an inferior and has inferior offspring. Poetry is particularly low-born. Once more, Homer must be politely invited to leave the ideal State, where hymns to the gods and praises of famous men are the only poetry that is permissible.

Gymnastics, Military Service, and Mathematics. The foundations of a strong mind laid by "music" must be reinforced by a strong and healthy body which "gymnastics" will build up by exercise, diet, hygiene, and the like. The two disciplines reinforce and counterbalance each other, since "music" without gymnastics breeds softness and effeminacy, and gymnastics unrefined by music favors harshness and savagery and turns out a race of boors. These two studies, it would seem, are prescribed for the youth of the entire community. The recruiting and education of the governing class begins with the selection of the strongest and most intelligent individuals, apparently both from the children of the lower classes and from those of the governors, for military service. From the professional army of auxiliaries or warriors thus mobilized, the most patriotic, intelligent, and morally courageous will be sifted out and submitted to the special curriculum calculated to make philosopher-kings of them. The studies prescribed to this end are first arithmetic, which makes for clearness of thought, and is also indispensable to the military art. Then will come plane geometry, which besides its practical uses impels the mind to recognize the difference between the perishable, sensible order and the world of eternal truth. The focusing of the attention upon changeless and imperishable realities is furthered by the study of solid geometry, which in Plato's time was in its infancy, and of astronomy which investigates the eternal laws governing the movements of the heavenly bodies and presents to the mind universal and immaterial natures like absolute swiftness and slowness. To this must be added harmonics, or the science dealing with the absolute relations of harmonious sounds.

Dialectics. By the time the pupil is thirty, the course of preliminary studies should be completed, and the next five years must be devoted to dialectic, or philosophy. Great care, however, must be taken to prevent dialectic from degenerating into mere arguing for the sake of argument. At the end of the period, the chosen few will be put to a fifteen-year test of practical life and of governing the State in accordance with the principles of real being with which they have been inculcated. Finally, when they are fifty, those who have passed the test will be released from their duties and allowed to retire to a life of contemplation, though even then they will be required at intervals to return to the world for brief periods and to assume again the responsibilities of government.

Nature of Political Justice. Having thus completed his picture of the ideal State, Plato is ready to apply its lessons to the discovery of the nature of justice, or righteousness in general. Obviously each of the three classes in the commonwealth has its particular function, in the proper performance of which its excellence or virtue consists. The function and virtue of the *governing class* lie in the possession and exercise of *wisdom;* of the *military class,* in *courageous behavior* inspired by a knowledge of the things that are truly to be feared; and of the *masses,* in a recognition of the superior ability of the wise to rule and in *obedience* to their behests. This last virtue may be called self-control or temperance. When each part of the State is displaying its proper excellence, and is not trespassing upon the functions of the others, the *commonwealth as a whole* is in excellent shape. Its general virtue is *harmony* and *balance.*

Here at last, then, we have the nature of political justice or righteousness. It is constituted by each class sticking to its own job, minding its own business, doing what it is fitted to do, and not meddling with the business or aspiring to take on the job of the others. So, too, in the good State every individual, whatever his class, will also mind his own particular business, cultivate his proper talents, and not try to do things for which he is not suited.

The Righteous Individual. The righteous individual character is only political justice writ small. Like the State, each man is divided into three parts. He has a governing part, *intelligence,* which corresponds to the ruling class in the State, and whose distinctive virtue also is wisdom; and he has *passions and appetites* connected with the economy of bodily life, which correspond to the economic classes in the body politic. This element shows itself virtuous in so far as it exhibits temperance by submitting to the control of intelligence and wisdom. Again, the individual has a *spirited or willful faculty* in him which can be either stampeded by the desires or harnessed in the service of reason. This element corresponds to the warriors in the State and, like them, displays its specific excellence of courage when it is guided by reason rather than by passion in its estimate of what things are truly to be feared. Finally, in the individual as in the commonwealth, justice, or righteousness, will lie in a harmonious co-operation of all faculties and functions in which each tends its own job, minds its own business, and refrains from encroaching upon the others.

In the righteous man reason rules, the desires and passions obey, and will or "spirit" is guided by intelligence, not misguided by impulse.

Inferior Types of the State and the Individual. The nature of righteousness is further illustrated by the picture, drawn by Plato in the eighth book of the *Republic,* of the progressive deterioration of the State and the individual from the ideal of perfect justice. The first stage in the lapse from *aristocracy,* or the unfettered rule of the whole by the best part of both the commonwealth and the particular citizen, is called *timocracy.* Politically this means the passing of government from the hands of the philosopher-kings to men of rougher caliber, disciplined and respectful of authority, to be sure, but *covetous of worldly power and distinction instead of wisdom.* Individually, it means a similar shift in the private interest from *governance by reason* to *the sway of worldly ambitions.* Indeed, intelligence, which should rule, now becomes the mere servant of the will to power and glory. Interest, however, does not remain long at this level. It is soon diverted from prowess and fame to the more vulgar end of wealth. The direction of the State falls into the hands of the rich, and the individual citizen, intent now only on making money, becomes avaricious instead of ambitious. In this way we sink to the level of *plutocracy* and *the miser.*

In the State this condition opens a gulf between the rich and the poor, breeds discontent, and leads to a revolution which brings the *masses* into power and sets up *democratic rule.* Democracy, however, is worse than plutocracy, since it lacks any unifying and restraining force whatsoever, such as even the rule of the rich imposed, and abandons the direction of the commonwealth to a "free" play of random and conflicting impulses, in which the crowd is swayed blindly hither and thither by the whim of the moment. Respect for superior wisdom and ability has disappeared, authority of any sort is flouted, and everyone does what he pleases regardless of whatever may happen to be the law. In the individual, a similar deterioration takes place. The restraining ideal of *avarice* gives way to an *unbridled self-indulgence* in which the appetites let themselves loose in a free-for-all, rough-and-tumble scrimmage. All cohesion and unity is lost from his life, which, instead of being a career of some, if even of the meanest, sort, is plunged into moral chaos.

Finally, in the State a single person takes advantage of the situation, seizes the power, and makes himself *tyrant* over the rest. And in the individual some one besetting passion, generally lust, becomes a mania and obsesses his entire nature. Freed from even the check imposed

on the "democratic" person by the variety and the conflict of his many
wants, he speedily turns criminal and is swept away to ruin. Than
tyranny as a political institution, and the tyranny of some single passion in the individual soul, nothing could be worse—except the combination of the two in the person of a criminally inclined despot.

The Moral Life and the Absolute Good. In this description of the
nature of political and individual righteousness, and of the progressive
lapses from it, we can see that Plato is preaching his doctrine of the
Forms. He is asserting that there is an absolute and universal moral
law and order, which is not dependent upon human opinion or caprice,
but is part and parcel of the constitution of the Real. We may never
be able to enact on earth either the perfect commonwealth or the perfect human being. But they are nevertheless laid up from all eternity
in heaven, as patterns and standards, increasing conformity with which
means the progressive approach of both the State and the individual
towards their *real* natures. If these ideals had no *real* existence they
could have no *real* authority, and the Sophists would be right. Socrates
was short-sighted in not perceiving that even the common consent of
mankind was not sufficient to give validity to his universal definitions.
Common consent made of them only universal *opinions* which, after
all, might change with time. To become universal *truths,* their foundations had to be sunk beneath the unstable ground of human experience,
and set upon the changeless bedrock of Reality.

The metaphysical implications of a political and moral order are
more explicitly set forth in a later dialogue, the *Philebus,* to which
we have already had occasion to refer. There, we may remember,
Plato tried to settle the dispute between the Cynic and the Cyrenaic
theories of the good by determining the proportions in which wisdom
and pleasure should be mixed in the righteous life. This mixture, he
now tells us, must be determined by the ideal of symmetry and measure, or, in other words, of harmony. But the attainment in human
experience of the symmetry and measure necessary to make it good,
depends upon the existence of an absolute formula which prescribes
with mathematical rigidity the relations that the ingredients of the
good life must bear to one another. Unless an eternal Form or Idea
of symmetry exists, it cannot be applied to the moral problem, and
there will be no way of knowing just which proportion is really best.
In short, unless there is such a thing as absolute righteousness and a
universally valid Form of social organization, equally authoritative
in all times and places, moral standards will be matters of opinion,
and ethics and politics can never be exact sciences.

VI. THE PLATONIC THEORY OF KNOWLEDGE

Since a sound morality rests upon true knowledge of the good, and not upon mere opinions about its nature, we are led to ask how the two differ and how true knowledge is acquired. There are, Plato tells us, four stages in the passage from blank ignorance to comprehension of the truth, two of which belong to the realm of opinion, two to that of knowledge. The two that fall within the sphere of opinion, are (1) *vain imagining* and *wild guessing* and (2) *assurance* or *confidence*.

Opinion. 1. In the first stage the mind scarcely distinguishes fact from fancy, dreaming from waking, the shadow from the substance, the reflection from the original. It reacts at random to sensations as they come.

2. The more tutored mind, however, learns to distinguish these things from one another, and to distinguish the so-called real and reliable aspects of sense-experience from the deceptive and "imaginary" ones. Inspired by observation, it passes from hit-and-miss guesswork in dealing with the world to rough-and-ready rules of thumb and predictions that prove trustworthy. But, though these are sufficient for carrying on everyday life, and, indeed, are the guides which most people are content to follow, they are empirical rules, drawn roughly from scattered, particular events and objects and accepted on faith. We do not as yet *understand* why or how the substance differs from the shadow, waking from dreaming, the real from the imaginary. Nor do we know the *reasons* for the trustworthiness of the rules of thumb we follow.

So far, then, we have not begun to think. We have merely noted certain regularities and recurrences in the flux of sensible events and developed a blind trust in them. We have come to have *opinions* about things, but we as yet have no foundation for them.

Knowledge. We pass now to the third and fourth stages, which belong to the realm of knowledge. These are (3) *thinking through* and *understanding,* and (4) *dialectic* or *philosophic wisdom.*

3. We enter upon the third stage when we begin to back up our views by *thinking through* situations and seeking *reasons* for our opinions about them. We are thus led to the discovery of general principles and universal laws in the flux of events, and come, as we say, to *understand why* things occur as they do and what they really are. Our opinions now have foundation, and our predictions can now

be made with certainty. For we have now crossed the line that divides mere *opinion* from *true knowledge*.

In so doing, we have, moreover, entered another realm of existence. We have passed from the multiple, moving world of particular concrete objects to an immutable, eternal order of universal Types and Laws and Values, which the flux of sense-experience invariably displays in all times and places and throughout all its changes. These Forms and formulae are, however, not perceived by the senses. They are apprehended and entertained by the intellect, whose function it is to grasp the general pattern and plan that particular objects enact in a sensible medium.

Knowledge and Absolute Truth. Now, if these Forms have no real existence, or, in other words, if the universe has no definite, intelligible constitution but is wholly formless and lawless and nothing but an unordered flux of sense-data, then so-called understanding and knowledge are from start to finish an abortive and meaningless pursuit of something that does not exist. Hence, if there is to be anything to knowledge, and we are ever to get beyond the stage of unfounded and unverifiable opinions in dealing with the world, the immutable Types and Laws which knowledge is forever seeking, and the discovery of which alone can satisfy the mind—in other words, the Platonic Ideas—must have a real existence of their own.

4. We come at last to the final stage in the acquisition of knowledge. *Thinking through* the world of sense to the world of eternal Forms and laws exemplified in the flux, does not bring our mental activities to their final goal. Before we can be really said to *know,* we must bind into a single, organized *whole* the different Forms and laws discovered by thinking through and understanding phenomena. Only in such a unified vision of Reality can the aspiration toward knowledge and truth come to rest. Furthermore, we must also rid ourselves of the imagery, as, for instance, the visible diagrams and written equations, upon which scientific explanation and demonstration lean. Knowledge must dispense with such aids, abstain from pictures and metaphors altogether, and rely solely upon pure reasoning, before it can rid itself of every type of uncertainty and be absolute. This final stage, in which the mind passes from the Forms discovered by the sciences "to the first principle of the whole; and then clinging to this, and to that which depends upon this, by successive steps . . . descends again without the aid of any sensible object, from ideas, through ideas, and ends in ideas," [7] is *dialectic* or *philosophy.*

---

[7] *Rep.,* VI, 511 B.

The Divided Line. These four stages, Plato says, may be illustrated by dividing a line into two and then subdividing the resulting sections, making four in all. The first act of division separates the sensible from the intelligible world and opinion from knowledge. The furthest subdivision of the sensible section stands for our perceptions and the imaginings and guessings to which they give rise, the nearer for the external world of sensible objects of which our perceptions are copies, and for the confidence they engender. Crossing the line to the intelligible world, we come first to the separate Ideas, and to scientific understanding of them, and finally to the unified system of the Ideas, expressed in the single all-embracing and all-explaining Idea of the whole embraced by philosophy.

The Prisoners in the Cave. Or again, we may think of mankind as prisoners in an underground cave (the sensible world), doomed to watch by firelight the flickering shadows (sensible data) cast by figures (physical objects) behind them copied from objects (The Ideas) existing in the sunlight above, on the surface of the earth (the intelligible world). What the prisoners see and take for truth is really nothing but the shadow of an image. Turn them round, and, dazzled by the firelight, they will have hard work to see the figures in the first place, and then to believe that the figures are more real than the shadows to which they have been accustomed. Take them up into the sunlight and they will be even more dazzled and blinded. It will take them a long time, and will require a gradual habituation of the eye to the new light, before they can distinguish the objects of which the figures are the copies—or in other words, the Ideas—and still longer before they can bear to look with a philosophically trained eye upon the Idea of the Good, of which the sun in the sensible world may be regarded as the visible counterpart.

Indeed, Plato feels, the attainment of this final vision of the truth, the whole truth, and nothing but the truth, can scarcely be realized by the mind while it is still imprisoned in the body. In any case, it involves a complete "conversion" of the whole mind from the sensible to the intelligible realm, and, like the experience of the soul yielding herself to the embrace of absolute beauty, can only be described in mystical terms. Knowledge, like love, is consummated in an ineffable ecstasy. But even so, knowledge like love has meaning only if its object—the universal and the absolute—has real being.

Knowledge or Reminiscence. At this point, however, we are confronted with a difficulty. After all, here and now, the mind is in the body, and is dependent upon the senses, it would seem, for its contact with external reality. But the senses never acquaint us with the universal and the absolute. They present the mind only with particular, concrete data. We do not *perceive* redness, or mankind in general, or the law of gravitation. We perceive this or that individual man, this or that particular object. How then can the mind ever come by general ideas and universal truths at all? It cannot get them from the senses, and yet, apparently, there is no other source save the senses for any experience whatsoever.

This difficulty Plato meets with his famous doctrine of Reminiscence or Recollection. In the *Phaedrus,* to which we have already referred in discussing the nature of love, we are told that before birth the soul, living in heaven with the gods, saw the Ideas face to face. Fallen from heaven and born in the body, she retains a faint recollection of the Forms she has seen, and is *reminded* of them by their sensible embodiments with which the senses acquaint her. It is by virtue of being thus "reminded" that the soul is able to find similarity in sensible objects, to single out in them features they have in common, to classify them according to their "type," and to give them group names. In the *Meno* also, we may remember, the untutored slave-boy's ability to recognize the truths of mathematics was attributed to his conversance with them before birth. Generally speaking, then, the growth of knowledge is simply clearer and clearer recollection of the Form of which the particular sensible object "reminds" us.

Particular Objects and Universal Ideas. There was, however, another difficulty not so intimately connected with knowledge, but still quite closely related. We recognized the Form in the sensible particular because of our previous acquaintance with it, but how did the Form get into the particular object? What was the relation between the universal Idea or type and its individual instances, between the abstract nature of redness and particular splotches of red, between human nature in general and individual men? Plato might seem to have so completely severed the Form and the concrete things exemplifying it that there was no hope of getting them together again. Indeed, he was accused by Aristotle of having done so. He seems to have felt the difficulty and to have tried to deal with it, for we find him now suggesting that particular objects are *copies* of their archetypes, and again that they somehow *participate* or *share* in the universals of which they are instances. But neither of these suggestions patched up the difference, as Aristotle was soon to point out. Not only did they leave the Idea and the particular as disconnected as ever, but the relationship of copying or participating raised fresh perplexities. Some modern apologists, particularly advocates of the "one-story theory," have tried to make the notion or metaphor of participation plausible. But others feel that here we have a real and enduring weakness in the Platonic system, which was never satisfactorily overcome. We shall find Plato again struggling with this problem in a later dialogue.

VII. PLATO'S THEORY OF IMMORTALITY

Reasons for Believing the Soul Survives Death. As we have just seen, the possibility of recognizing the Form in the particular object and of recapturing it in the process of knowledge is bound up with the pre-existence, and by implication with the immortality, of the soul. In the *Phaedo,* Socrates' conversation with his disciples in the hours preceding his execution is devoted to proving that the soul survives death. The interdependence of opposites and their generation out of one another are invoked to show that as life turns to death, so death must return to life once more. So, too, death means decomposition, and therefore cannot touch a simple and unalterable and therefore indissoluble entity. The soul is such an entity, since her natural affinity is not with the changing sensible world but with the changeless and eternal objects of thought. Nor can the soul be a harmony of the body, as the Pythagoreans taught, and hence dependent upon the body as music is upon the lyre. On the contrary, she directs and sometimes opposes the body, and is therefore independent of it. And since she is invariable in nature, there is no reason to fear that, after wearing out several bodies and passing through a number of reincarnations, she may eventually herself run down and stop. Finally, the essential nature of the soul is to live. That is, she participates in the Idea or principle of life. But this Idea logically excludes its opposite, which is death. Therefore, she can never be dead, any more than what participates in the nature of the odd can ever be even, or of the hot, cold.

Again, in the *Phaedrus,* it is pointed out that the soul, being self-moving, cannot be started or stopped by anything outside herself. Hence she must also be without beginning and immortal.

Doctrine of Reincarnation. These arguments are supplemented in the *Phaedo,* the *Gorgias,* and the *Republic,* by vivid pictures of the after-life, drawn from Orphic and Pythagorean sources. After death the soul preserves for a time her personality and is punished or rewarded for her evil or good deeds on earth. But this retention of personality lasts for only a thousand years. At the end of each thousand-year period there comes what we should call a real death, involving a complete extinction of personality, so far, at least, as continuity of memory is concerned. All the souls are assembled and are told to choose the lives they are to live in their new reincarnation. Their choice is proclaimed to be free, that theirs may be the responsibility and that God may not be blamed. But it is determined as a matter of fact by the preferences developed in them by their past existences. The souls of animals are also free to choose, and some animals select human, and some men animal, lives. Having chosen, the soul passes through the waters of Lethe, forgets her past, and enters upon her new incarnation with a clean slate, except for one thing. All personal ties with her past existences have been obliterated. She is a new person, with no inkling of the other lives, animal and human, she has lived. But her disposition for good and evil, and her moral fortunes for better or for worse in her new career, are a heritage from her behavior in her former lives. This and this alone, except for the equally impersonal reminiscence of the Forms, links the individual with a pre-natal past and a post-mortem future.

Reunion with the Divine. But there is more to Platonic immortality than an endless repetition of death and rebirth. For Plato the proper destiny of the soul is to regain her birthright of reunion with the eternal to which she is akin, and from which somehow she has become separated. This destiny she may fulfill by repeatedly renouncing the world of sense and taking refuge in the intelligible and the timeless, until she has at length sufficiently purified herself from the dross of earth. Then, when the moment of her release arrives, she escapes from the revolving wheel of reincarnation, passes out of time altogether, ceases to be everlasting, and becomes one with the eternal. With this mystical, timeless, super-personal immortality as Plato conceives it, his discussion of love in the *Symposium* has already made us familiar.

Chapter XII

PLATO (CONTINUED)

I. FURTHER PROBLEMS

Critical Character of the Later Dialogues. We have now reviewed the teaching set forth in the dialogues that are regarded by some critics as a description by Plato of Socrates' teaching rather than as an exposition of his own views. In the dialogues to which we are about to turn we have certainly Plato's own philosophy. We shall see in them, if we regard the earlier work also as essentially Platonic rather than Socratic, an amplification and revision of his position. Otherwise, we shall think of Plato as now launching upon his own system, which develops and corrects in a more critical spirit the ideas of Socrates. In either case, we shall find in the dialogues we are about to discuss both a further and more critical treatment of questions already raised in the earlier dialogues and an exploration of new problems, as yet scarcely touched upon. This later work seems also to have been provoked in part by objections raised by his opponents. We must remind ourselves that Plato did not do his thinking in an intellectual vacuum, but in an atmosphere of excited and bitter philosophic controversy, in which his views were under constant attack.

The chief problems raised in the later dialogues are as follows: (1) the relation of the Forms to the concrete objects that enact them and to the minds that entertain them; (2) the difference between truth and error; (3) the nature and place in the universe of Soul and of God; (4) the mathematical aspect of the Forms; (5) the generation of the universe; (6) the nature of the world-stuff; (7) the imperfection of the universe; and (8) final reflections upon politics. Let us take up these points one by one.

II. THE RELATION OF THE IDEAS TO CONCRETE OBJECTS

Criticism of Participation. In the *Parmenides* Plato tackles the difficulties he now finds in the first of the problems just mentioned. After noting that there ought by rights to be ideal archetypes of ugly and evil particular objects, as well as of good and beautiful ones, he goes on to criticize his earlier suggestion that the relation of sensible objects to the Forms they exemplify may be described as one of *participating* in the Idea, or of *resembling* and being a *copy* of it. Neither of these ways of expressing the relation, he now tells us, will work.

The trouble with *participation*, he continues, is this. Either one and the same Form must be present at one and the same time in many particular objects—which is absurd; or else the many particular objects possessing one and the same Form only possess a part of it, and are therefore only partly what they are—which is equally absurd. How, for example, can you and I both be in exclusive possession of the whole nature or Idea of Man? On the other hand, how, if we are both human beings, can we fail, either one of us, wholly to possess the human Form in its entirety? If that Form is shared between us, and either one of us possesses only a portion of it, then neither you nor I is *completely* human.

Criticism of Resemblance. We fare no better, however, if we say that particular objects *resemble* and are *copies* of the Forms they exemplify. To do so, involves us at once in an infinite regress—the difficulty of what Plato calls "the third man." For suppose we say that human beings resemble one another by virtue of *resembling* and being *copies* of the Form of man. In that case, by virtue of what do they resemble the human Form? If *resemblance* means exhibiting one and the same Form, then the likeness of human individuals to the Idea of Man must mean that both they and it resemble and are copies of still another Form—a "third man," of which the Idea of Man and the individual man are both examples. And this process of explaining resemblance by invoking further resemblance must be carried on to infinity.

III. THE RELATION OF IDEAS TO MINDS

The Ideas Are Not Thoughts. Turning now to the puzzling question of the relation of the Forms to the minds which entertain them, Plato encounters further difficulties. Are the Ideas *thoughts* either of individual minds or of a divine mind? This question he answers in the negative. The Forms are not thoughts but the objects of thought, and exist independently of whether and what we think about them. If they were thoughts, then the concrete objects which exemplify them would also be thoughts; in which case all sensible objects would be thinking beings, or else there would be such things as unthought thoughts.

How Then Can We Entertain Ideas? But if the Forms are not our thoughts, and if they exist *outside* and independently of our minds, how can we entertain them in our minds and think about them? Apparently they cannot be reached by our minds at all, and the resemblances and typical features we perceive in concrete objects have nothing to do with, and give us no knowledge of, the Forms as they are in themselves. To say that the Forms are thoughts of a divine mind only complicates matters. It makes them no less independent of our minds and inaccessible to them. And, if they are what God thinks about, then what *we* think about is as unknown to him as what *he* thinks about is unknown to us. In any case, we apparently cannot escape the conclusion that the Forms, if they exist in themselves independently of the particular minds that entertain them, can "have nothing to do with us, or we with them; they are concerned with themselves only, and we with ourselves." [1]

Plato's Dilemma and Possible Escape. So we end in a dilemma. If the Forms are objects common to many minds, they cannot be just the thoughts of any one of these minds, but must exist apart from and independent of all minds whatsoever. On the other hand, if they are what we think about, they must somehow be present in our minds. Otherwise we could not think about them—nor unless they were somehow present in sensible objects could those objects enact them.

Whether Plato ever succeeded to his own satisfaction in extricating himself from this dilemma we do not know. But it has been suggested that we may perhaps see an escape in the last part of the *Parmenides*, which is devoted to a very difficult and seemingly paradoxical demonstration of the interdependence of Unity and Plurality. This might be construed, we are told, as signifying a similar interdependence of the Forms on the one hand, and of particular things and minds on the other. Just, we might say, as the concept of Unity is meaningless apart from that of Plurality, so one and the same Form is neither one, nor the same, nor even a Form in any significant sense of the word, apart from the many concrete objects to which it gives character and unity, and the many individual minds to which it gives a common object of thought. Without objects to enact it, and minds to entertain it, it would have no place or function in the scheme of things.

Conversely, just as plurality cannot be conceived apart from unity,

---

[1] *Parmenides,* 134 A.

so objects, if they are to be even objects, must be some *sort* or *class* of objects. And minds, if they are to be intelligences, must think about something in common. Individual objects, then, and individual minds could not exist without the Forms to give character to the one and point to the other.

In short, real being is a one-in-many and a many-in-one whose unity depends upon its multiplicity, and whose multiplicity depends upon its unity.[2]

This, however, is a suggestion of modern scholars. Whether Plato himself so intended the last part of the *Parmenides* is an open question.

IV. WHAT IS KNOWLEDGE?

Granting, however, that Plato had solved to his own satisfaction the problems raised in the *Parmenides,* he was by no means out of the woods. For now the question arose how the mind, if it could really entertain the true Forms of things, could entertain false Ideas about them, as it obviously did when it was in error. This question Plato takes up in the *Theaetetus* and the *Sophist.*

Truth Not Relative to the Individual. In the *Theaetetus* he discusses what knowledge is, or rather what it is not. He first attacks the Protagorean doctrine, to which both the Cynics and Cyrenaics also subscribed, that knowledge is perception, and that the truth is what seems true to the individual at the moment. This doctrine, he tells us, gives us no ground for preferring waking to dreaming, or the experience of the human being to that of the pig or the baboon, or the perception of one man to that of another, as a criterion of truth. For that matter, Protagoras' own doctrine is self-contradictory. It proclaims as absolute truth that there is no such thing as absolute truth, and confesses that it is false to those who believe it false. Finally, knowledge means relating and formulating our sense-experience according to certain categories, such as being and not-being, likeness and difference, unity and plurality, etc., which are not given directly in our perceptions, but by some other faculty of the soul.

Truth and Falsehood Not Matters of Opinion. Shall we, then, define knowledge as *true opinion?* But how are we to distinguish true opinions from false, and how, moreover, can we hold *false* opinions? An opinion that we hold, we believe to be *true,* as long as we hold it. Nor can error arise from indistinct perceptions, like blurred impressions

---

[2] Cf. Burnet, *Greek Philosophy,* Part I, p. 272. Stewart, *Plato's Doctrine of Ideas,* pp. 80-81. Horn, *Platonstudien,* II, pp. 120, 155.

on a wax tablet, since we can make mistakes in abstract, mathematical thinking, as in the wrong addition of numbers. Again, error cannot consist in getting hold of the wrong Idea, as one might reach into a birdcage and grab the wrong bird. For we cannot mistake the "feel" of the bird of ignorance or falsity for the "feel" of the bird of knowledge. Then, too, opinions may just *happen* to be true. For example, judges in the law courts may *happen* to hand down perfectly sound opinions without having any real knowledge of the case whatsoever.

If we enlarge our definition, and say that knowledge is *true opinion, for which reasonable ground may be given,* we are no better off. For, paradoxically enough, the final grounds and reasons for our opinions, being *ultimate* explanations, cannot themselves be explained. All opinions, then, rest finally upon grounds for which no reasons can be adduced. Yet for all our inability to find explanations of these ultimate principles, we feel we *know* them better than the inferences we draw from them. How can this be? As Plato himself says, we would seem to have discovered rather what knowledge is not than what it is.

V. THE NATURE OF ERROR

Self-Contradictions in Predication and Negation. Perhaps, however, we can learn what knowledge is, if we first examine the nature of *error.* This Plato does in the *Sophist.* He begins by analyzing what we mean by *sophistry,* which, he tells us, consists in making people believe that what *is* is not and *vice versa.* But to assert the *non-existence* of the *existent* or the *existence* of the *non-existent* would seem to involve a contradiction in terms. Furthermore to predicate non-existence is to predicate nothing, and the existent itself seems to be a self-contradictory affair since it is both in motion and at rest, both the same and different, at the same time. All the philosophers so far—the Eleatics, the Heracliteans, the "friends of the Ideas" and the materialists—have stumbled over this block, since all have maintained that the Real at least seems to be both changing and unchanging, active and static. But how can the universe be, or seem to be, both in motion and at rest, or neither in one state nor the other?

The answer, says Plato, lies in the fact that while every Form is different from every other and is *not* any other, some Forms can be combined with one another, whereas some cannot. Hence the fact that one thing is *not* another does not necessarily preclude the possibility—denied by the Cynics, we may remember—of predicating one thing of another. We cannot, indeed, predicate Motion of Rest, or

Sameness of Difference, and *vice versa;* but these Ideas, although *not* the Idea of Existence, can be predicated of and combined with it. So, too, the fact that Motion and Rest are *different* from each other does not prevent either one of them from being the *same* as itself. Hence the *existent* can be both in *motion* and at *rest,* the *same* and *different,* without contradiction, although, of course, Motion and Rest, Sameness and Difference, cannot both be predicated of it conjointly.

Difference Between Truth and Error. The nature of truth and error is now fairly clear. Truth and knowledge lie in combining in our thinking and discourse Forms that will go together, and in combining them as they are really combined in the structure of the universe. Error comes from our failure to distinguish the Ideas that are both different and uncombinable from those which, in spite of their difference from one another and their *not* being one another, can nevertheless be combined. Such failure results in our asserting the existence of non-existent combinations of Forms and *vice versa.* It is the business of philosophy to distinguish clearly between the "not" that forbids and the "not" that permits the conjunction of Ideas, and thus to discover what Forms can be predicated of one another, and what cannot.

VI. THE REALITY OF THE SENSIBLE WORLD

The Sensible World and Unreality. Possibly these considerations threw further light upon the relation of the sensible world to the Forms. It will be remembered that in the earlier dialogues Plato had described the moving, changing world of particular things—the realm of *Becoming*—as a mixture of the *Being* of the Forms with *Not-Being.* The latter term, however, he had left almost without further definition, and it might seem to imply that the whole multiple, sensible, concrete, changing aspect of the universe, lacking as it did the characteristics of the true Being possessed by the Forms, was therefore unreal and illusory. The Eleatics, we may recall, had come to that conclusion for much the same reasons. However, if the "not" in Not-Being, instead of meaning non-existence, meant merely a kind of existence different *from* and *not* possessed by the Forms, then the sensible world was by no means reduced to illusion by not being the Ideas. Its reality, to be sure, was not the same as that of the Forms, but it was not thereby prevented from having a reality *other than* theirs. In the *Parmenides,* as we have just seen, Plato had argued that Unity and Multiplicity, far from excluding and annulling each other, not only were combinable, but could not *exist* without each other. In the same way he may now be contending that, generally speaking, the formal and the sensible, the universal and the concrete, aspects of the universe, although not the same, are not only logically combinable but actually combined in the totality of Existence. In a moment we shall find him in the *Timaeus* trying to tell us what kind of being Not-Being really possesses.

VII. THE SOUL

Meantime another question was pressing for an answer—the problem of getting the Forms into dynamic, creative relation to the sensible world, and accounting for the changing, moving, "becoming" aspect of Reality. Here *soul* or *mind,* to which Plato paid no great metaphysical attention in the earlier dialogues, came in handy. The existence of the soul to be sure he had taken for granted, and had already made of her the knowing subject in the process of knowledge. And her uncreated and immortal nature he had proclaimed in the *Phaedo* and the *Phaedrus.* Also he had analyzed her in a rudimentary way in the *Republic.* And in the *Phaedrus* he had made her the self-moving and self-animating source of the life and movement of the body, and asserted her uncreated and indestructible nature. But he had not as yet found her particular niche in his universe.

At last, however, she was called upon to act as the natural intermediary between the Forms and the sensible world, and to that end she was elevated into a cosmic principle. For this service and this dignity she was naturally fitted, linked as she was through the senses to the world of sensible particulars, and through her intellectual activities to the Forms. She was bathed in change, and yet she was changeless. She was everlasting, but she could also become eternal. She was at the same time uncreated and creative, constant and variable, static and dynamic. It was to her, then, that Plato finally looked as the proper agent to put the Forms into effect and to enact and embody them in a physical world.

VIII. GOD

The growing metaphysical importance of soul is paralleled by that of God. In the earlier dialogues God figures little and casually. The Forms occupy the entire stage. Now he comes to the fore. He is located by Plato, not among the Forms, but in the soul-mind section of Reality. Indeed, in the *Parmenides,* we may remember, it is pointed out that his too intimate association with the Forms would deprive him of all concern and contact with the sensible world. He is rather the supreme mind, the king of souls, whose function is to create and sustain the sensible universe and to direct all things for the best in his infinite wisdom and providence.[3] Nay more, in the *Laws,* Plato's last work, God, as we shall soon see, appears to have supplanted the Forms in Plato's affections and thought.

Plato's Views of God. Much of Plato's talk about God is highly ornate, figurative, and poetical; so much so indeed that many critics are inclined to regard his picture of a personal creator as a purely fanciful and "mythological" way of stating that the Forms are dynamic and formative, not purely static and self-contained principles. Indeed, there is no point more disputed and no question more open than the problem of just what Plato really does mean by God.

However that may be, in the *Philebus* and the *Timaeus* God appears in sober metaphysical guise. In the *Philebus,* we are told, Reality may be divided into four parts: the Determinate, the Indeterminate, the Mixture of the two, and the Cause of the Mixture. Though the coincidence is not perfect, the determinate would seem to correspond to the Forms, the indeterminate to the principle of "Not-Being," and the mixture of the two to the sensible world. The cause of the mixture lies, we are told, not in chance or unreason but in the "marvelous intelligence and wisdom" of a supreme living mind. To the part played by God in the *Timaeus,* we shall turn in a moment.

IX. THE IDEAS AS NUMBERS

Mathematical Approach to the Ideas. But, if the description in the *Philebus* of the cause of the mixture throws light upon the increasing importance of theology in Plato's system, the appearance of the Pythagorean terms, limit and the unlimited, the determinate and the indeterminate, as designations respectively for the Forms and Not-Being suggests another no less interesting development of his thought. Plato was a scientist as well as a mystic and poet, and mathematics and the mathematical philosophy of the Pythagoreans had always fascinated him. We have already seen how prominent a place he assigns to arithmetic and geometry in his plan of education. In the *Philebus* we may also remember that he was seeking an exact mathematical statement of the *ratio* the ingredients of the good life should bear to one another. Moreover, limit, or the determinate, is essentially a mathematical concept. To give the precise nature of a thing is to state its *formula.*

[3] Cf. *Sophist,* 265 C-E; *Statesman,* 269 A-274 E.

Margins of variation and error in description introduce an element of uncertainty and indeterminateness.

Basic Character of Ideas of Numbers. The independent evidence of the *Philebus* suggests, then, that Plato was busy attacking the Ideas from a new angle and was seeking to develop their mathematical implications as the objects and guides of exact scientific method. This evidence is borne out by a statement of Aristotle's that Plato believed the Forms to be essentially Number-Forms. Aristotle adds, moreover, that Plato considered these Number-Forms to be "unaddible," or incapable of mathematical manipulation, and that he interpolated between them and the world of sensible objects a third world of mathematical entities, our ordinary numbers, which unlike their prototypes could be added, subtracted, multiplied, and divided. This statement of Aristotle's has given rise to much conjecture and controversy, but many modern critics find in it perfectly good sense, and see in Plato a prophet of our latest and most up-to-date scientific thought.

Let us take first the statement that the Ideas are numbers, and examine it in the light of modern science. The chemist of today gives the formula, or Platonic Idea, of water as H_2O. But the Form of water as such evidently lies in the 2, rather than in the H or the O, since hydrogen and oxygen combined in other proportions would not give water. Again, the physicist of today tells us that the difference between the hydrogen atom and the oxygen atom lies in the fact that the one consists of a single electron revolving about a nucleus, the other of eight—so that here again the *number* of electrons is the determining factor in the nature or Form of the element in question. For that matter, the differences of all the chemical elements are differences of nothing but number and geometrical arrangement. Plato, then, would seem to be merely anticipating modern science, when he seeks to resolve all Forms into basic Number-Ideas.

Moreover, Plato would seem to be right in asserting that these Number-Forms, though the bases of mathematics and hence of scientific knowledge and description, are themselves incapable of mathematical manipulation. The nature, or definition, or, in other words, the Form of a number cannot be added to, subtracted from, multiplied, or divided. Nor can the Form of the circle be divided into two definitions of the semicircle, or be intersected, or segmented. For instance, to repeat four times the definition of the number one does not give us the nature or Form of the number four, nor can we inscribe the definition of the triangle within that of the circle, and *vice versa*.

The "Addible" Numbers. Turning now to the statement that there is a realm of mathematical entities, which are "addible," and that these addible numbers mediate between the Idea-Numbers and the multiplicity and extension of the sensible world, we find that this, too, is not a fancy but a fact. The numbers used by mathematics can be added, subtracted, multiplied, and divided. And they really do hover midway between the Number-Forms and the sensible objects. The mathematical number two—or 2—is not Twoness.[4] It is expressive of a given pair of objects, whereas Twoness is the nature or Form of all pairs. But neither is the number two to be identified with two particular things. It is "any old" two, equally applicable to all pairs of all sorts wherever we come across them. And yet, in spite of the fact that it is general, it is still always *a* two, not *the* Two. For *the* Two is the definition or Form of *a* two; that is, of any old two. The same is the case with the circle, for instance, of geometry. It is not circularity, or the Idea of the circle, and yet it is not any one particular circular thing. It, too, is *a* circle, not *the* circle. In a sense general in nature, it can be still intersected and subdivided like a concrete thing, although in so handling it we do not have to break up or interlock two particular sensible circles like this plate or that wheel. Plato is then making the best of sense when he distinguishes the "figures" of our geometry books and the 1, 2, 3, 4, etc., of our arithmetics from the Number-Forms on the one hand, and from the sensible instances of number and of geometrical figure on the other.

Derivation of the Number Series. Our difficulties, however, are not over. How can even mere mathematical numbers be addible? The unit and the point would seem to be the basic elements from which arithmetical and geometrical processes start. But both the unit and the point are in themselves incapable of self-propagation. The unit will not spontaneously reproduce or subdivide, the point will not spontaneously repeat itself or flow into a line. Something more is necessary, if we are to derive plurality from the unit, extension from the point, the many from the one.

This something, Aristotle tells us, Plato found in the "indeterminate dyad" or principle of "the-great-and-the-small." But if we mean by the dyad just Twoness, or the nature of plurality, as Aristotle interpreted the term, the result is nonsense. The Number-Form of twoness *plus* 1 would bear no fruit. For that matter we could not speak of

---

[4] It must be remembered that the Greeks were without our system of arithmetical notation, introduced later into Europe from India *via* Arabia.

"and" or *"plus"* unless we first had a pair of objects to unite, and therefore the number two already present. But, if we follow some modern critics who regard the dyad as Plato's way of saying "twice," the difficulty is cleared up. Twiceness is not a Number-Form, just as "twice" is not a number or limit. It is rather a signal to go on and expand to an indeterminate extent. If then we combine the number one with twiceness we get twice one = two; if two with twiceness, $2 \times 2 = 4$, and so on *ad infinitum*. In this way the whole series of even numbers can be produced from the number one.

Generation of the Odd Numbers. The odd numbers, Plato said, were generated by the "equalizing" or "stabilizing" of the dyad by the unit. This is somewhat blind, but we may remark that if we tip twiceness on its back, it becomes one halfness. 2×1 inverted becomes $\frac{1}{2} \times 1$. And if we apply one halfness to the sum of any two adjacent even numbers, we get the odd number sandwiched between them. Thus $2 + 4 = 6$, and one half of $6 = 3$. Or $4 + 6 = 10$ and $1\frac{1}{2} = 5$; $6 + 8 = 14$, and $1\frac{4}{2} = 7$, etc. According to this theory, we see, the "dyad" stands for the *plus* and *minus,* the *times* and *divided by* aspect of mathematics.

The Continuum and Fluxion. The suggestion has also been made that in describing the dyad as the-great-and-the-small Plato was on his way towards the theory of the *continuum* and of *"fluxion,"* according to which the line is formed, not by the addition of discrete points, but by the continuous flowing of its starting-point, and the plane, not by the laying down of separate lines side by side, but by pushing the whole line at an angle to its length. If this be so, Plato had solved the paradoxes of Zeno, which remained insoluble as long as space was regarded as divisible into discrete parts, and had forestalled our modern mathematical union of arithmetical and geometrical concepts. Nay more, he had mathematicized not only the realm of Being but that of Becoming as well, and had identified the principle of change and motion with that of numerical plurality and geometrical extension. In a moment we shall find him also "mathematicizing" the realm of Not-Being, and, by reducing it to pure space, showing how it necessitates mathematically flux and multiplicity.

X. THE CREATION OF THE UNIVERSE

Chaos into Cosmos. We now return to the *Timaeus.* There we find a highly picturesque account of the creation and structure of the phys-

ical world. Incidental to it, we have also the attempt we have just
mentioned to define the principle of Not-Being and Matter in terms of
pure extension. In the beginning, we are told, God was confronted
with unformed chaos agitated by disorderly and irrational motion.
Being good, he desired to impart and share his goodness, and to that
end he sought to bring chaos into conformity with the world of perfect and eternal Forms, to which he looked as guiding models. Working from the top down, he fashioned first a principle of life and animation by mixing the natures of Being and Not-Being (or, as Plato
now calls them, the Same and the Other). This principle, which, because of its dual nature, was capable of bringing Form and Matter
together and of transforming mechanical and random movement into
purposive and living activity, was the World-Soul.

The World-Soul was then cut up into the fundamental activities of
the universe—an outer circular movement, uniform in character, designed to animate the heaven of fixed stars, and seven divergent, irregular motions within, to carry the planets. This "astral" framework
was clothed with material made of the four elements, whose rudiments
were thrashing aimlessly about in the original chaos. The stars and
planets were created for the particular purpose of measuring time,
whose everlasting flow is the moving image of eternity. The earth was
set at the center of the universe.

Creation of Souls. For the stars the maker created divine souls, and
to these lesser gods he entrusted the contriving of animate creatures,
which the universe still lacked. However, he himself made the souls
of these creatures out of the World-Soul well diluted. And he dispersed
them among the stars and arranged for their incarnation in men and
animals.

And so the visible universe was at length complete. It was a perfect
sphere, uniting soul and body, in which the whole system of Forms,
or Idea of the perfect living being, was given as complete concrete
expression as the nature of Not-Being, or Matter, as Plato now calls it,
permitted.

We may note in passing that Plato here admits that the soul is not
the cause of all motion. He attributes to Matter a blind or random
movement of its own, for which the soul-principle is not responsible.
But in the *Laws,* as we shall see, he reverts with emphasis to the position that all movement and activity of every sort must be caused by
soul.

XI. THE NATURE OF MATTER

The most significant portion of the *Timaeus* is perhaps that in which Plato deals with the nature of Matter, or Not-Being. Such a principle, he says, must exist. Obviously the sensible world is in part *other* than the Forms, and its difference must rest upon a principle that is different from them. Moreover, sensible objects keep *changing* their Forms, and change requires a substratum—a something which is no more *this* Form than it is that, but is simply "thus and thus."

Matter Formless and Void. This "something," however, can have no Form of its own, since, if it had, it would not be different from Form and could not change. Hence the "otherness" of the sensible world from the world of Ideas does not lie in its possession of any other *Form* of Being. It must lie rather in the projection of the Forms into a "formless" dimension of Reality, which somehow imparts to them the appearance of a moving, changing world of particular objects. How can this be?

Plato's reply to the question is that their combination with *space* gives them multiple, sensible, moving embodiment.

In other words Not-Being, considered as the substratum of Becoming, is empty space—space so empty and blank that not even dimensions or geometrical configuration can be ascribed to it, since even the most primitive geometrical structure would imply the presence of Form. This sheer emptiness can be neither perceived nor conceived. And yet we are haunted by its presence and have a kind of "bastard" concept of it, to use the Platonic phrase, just as we somehow "see" darkness which is, logically speaking, utter absence of visibility. When all form and content have been thought away, we still retain the sense of their *place*—the spot *where* they were and *where* they may reappear.

This formless space is the "receptacle and in a manner the nurse of all generation" [5] in which the Ideas father the sensible world. It "is stirred and informed by them, and appears different from time to time by reason of them." [6] As a matter of fact, it was never without their impress. The stuff that God confronted in the beginning was space already laid out geometrically, exhibiting tri-dimensionality and the rudimentary solid figures characteristic of the four elements.

[5] 49 A.
[6] 50 B.

Space Makes Participation and Resemblance Intelligible. This spatial interpretation of the principle of Not-Being or "Otherness" which made the sensible world of Becoming different from the Forms and accounted for its spread-out, multiple, changing, solid, and concrete character, may have provided Plato with a final solution of the problem of the relation of the sensible world to the Forms, and have cleared up for once and all the questions of participation and resemblance. For it was now possible to see that sensible objects, although different from their archetypes, need not be copies of them, and that the Forms need not be parceled out among their instances, but could be present in their entirety in each one of their multiple embodiments.

Being formless and void, Space had no Form of its own, but was simply another dimension, so to speak, of Being in which the Forms were projected. It added no new Form to them, in embodying them, nor did it in any way duplicate or copy them or divide them up in so doing. In the same way, we might say, a stereoscope imparts the dimension of depth to a photograph without adding or subtracting anything from it, and without reduplicating it or copying it. And if the stereoscope were also kaleidoscopic, and multiplied the photograph and imparted to its multiple projections motion as well as depth, then each one of the solid, moving images perceived by the eye would show not a part of the photograph but the whole of it. So, too, space in presenting the Forms as a multiplicity of solid, moving images allows each Form to be wholly present in each one of its instances.

Physical Space and Mathematical Law. Physical matter, or physical space, is the result of impressing upon blank *place* the simplest of all geometrical plane figures, the Form of the triangle, and then producing the solid by the projection or juxtaposition of these planes. In this way, the material principle had already been impressed in a rudimentary fashion with the Forms of the four elements before God took a hand in the process of creation. His work simply lay in refining these elements, in introducing rationality and purpose into their movements, and in combining them according to the pattern of the higher Forms.

It will be noticed that by thus "geometrizing" pure space or Not-Being Plato supplemented his "mathematicizing" of the world of Forms. Not only were the Ideas expressible in mathematical formulae, but Not-Being was now reduced to terms of extension pure and simple, and all Becoming could be interpreted as essentially change of place. Mathematical law at last reigned supreme throughout Reality. This accomplishment of Plato's has been hailed by some critics as comparable with our modern extension of mathematical concepts to the physical sciences.[7]

XII. THE PROBLEM OF EVIL

Variety of Plato's Answers. Plato, however, had still another problem on his hands—that of explaining why the sensible world was such a poor expression of the world of Forms. The particular object blurred the Idea. The universe, in spite of the rationalizing of its movements, still went wrong. Ugliness existed side by side with beauty, and human institutions, individuals, and behavior fell woefully short of their ideal prototypes.

To this question Plato gives no consistent answer. For the most part, perhaps, he tends to attribute the imperfection of the universe to the intractability of the material principle. Matter, for all its essential formlessness and passive receptiveness of all Forms, somehow resists the process of formulation, and to this resistance, or element of "necessity," in things, ugliness and evil are due. But in the *Parmenides,* as we have seen, Plato suggests that there ought rightly to be Forms of ugly and evil things, as well as of the beautiful and good. Again, moral shortcomings are, as in the *Phaedrus,* now assigned to some coarseness existent from all eternity in the soul, and now, as in the tenth book of the *Republic,* to the misuse of free-will. Finally, as we are about to see, in the *Laws,* in which Soul is proclaimed the one and only source of all motion and activity whatsoever, the necessity of accounting on this hypothesis for irrational, disorderly, and subversive movement leads Plato to the doctrine of a quasi-personal devil.

Theological Character of the Laws. By the time Plato wrote the *Laws,* his philosophy had apparently become theological. The doctrine of the Ideas seems to have retreated into the background, and God monopolizes the picture of real Being. His majesty and glory are celebrated in terms that remind us of the Hebrew prophets. He is a divine mind and reason governing all things, as is shown by the orderliness and rationality of his handiwork. He is just, good, a champion of righteousness, forever at war with evil and disorder, dispensing punishment and reward to men according to their deserts. His commandments are the foundation of the State, and all law is in essence the enactment of his commands. Atheism is the root of all evil, and dis-

[7] Notably by Taylor, Robin, Natorp, and Zeller.

believers and heretics should be spied out, denounced, and punished
with the utmost severity. Since Soul is the source of all life and motion,
the opposition to the divine will must originate in a soul or souls opposed to God. There is an evil world-soul, whether it be one or many,
that fights the divine purpose, and with which God is incessantly at
war.

This doctrine, it has been suggested, was influenced by Plato's inclination to dramatize and magnify to cosmic proportions the struggle
between good and evil. It was perhaps also fed by his acquaintance
with Zoroastrian dualism, which depicted the universe as the scene of
an everlasting struggle between the powers of light and darkness. It
was, moreover, a logical conclusion of his teaching that all cosmic
life and activity originate in Soul and are purposively directed by
Mind.

XIII. LAST WORDS ON POLITICS

We pass now to Plato's last words on politics. Bitter experience
would seem to have disillusioned him of the practicability of the political constitution set forth in the *Republic,* and we find in the later
dialogues a more realistic attitude. In the *Statesman,* for example, he
is willing to concede that as long as statesmanship is displayed in government, the kind of constitution a state adopts is of minor importance. At the same time, statesmanship is best exercised by a single
person under constitutional restraints. Hence limited monarchy is the
best practicable form of government. Next comes aristocracy, bridled
by law, and after that constitutional democracy. Tyranny, oligarchy,
and mob-rule are the lawless forms of the three limited types. Mob-
rule in which the will of the majority is free from legal restraint is,
however, better than oligarchy or tyranny, since it is on the whole
less oppressive.

The Best Practicable Form of Government. The best practicable
type of citizen is one in whom antagonistic virtues offset one another
in such a way as to produce a harmonious balance of temperance and
courage, peacefulness and high spirit, reflection and action. It is one
of the chief tasks of a statesman to breed and educate this blend of
qualities in the people.

In the *Laws* Plato assigns even more importance to law and less to
the particular kind of political constitution. The great thing is that
the divine commandments shall be enforced, for God is the head and
the foundation of the State. A combination of constitutional democracy and limited monarchy is the most practicable form of government

for putting divine law into effect. Plato dispenses, however, with a single king and replaces him with a supreme council elected by the people. Towards the end of the Dialogue he does, to be sure, revert towards the philosopher-kings of the *Republic,* and suggests that the duty of preserving the constitution and the laws intact shall be entrusted to a "nocturnal council" composed of ten elders of wide experience, and ten young men chosen by them, all of whom shall have received a special education in right action, correct theology, and the mathematical exactitude of thought inculcated by astronomy. But this is something of an afterthought.

Legal Code. The greater part of the *Laws* is devoted to enumerating the rules and regulations of which Plato approves and feels that God approves. These were probably gathered from the codes of various Greek cities and especially from contemporary Athenian law. The civil and criminal fields are covered at length, and the machinery, political and judicial, necessary for running the State and preserving law and order is described in detail. Rules, for example, dealing with marriage and the family, with the ownership and transference of property, and with the conduct of business, are laid down in the civil field, and crimes are enumerated and their punishment prescribed. Punishment, Plato insists, should be remedial rather than vindictive. Education is provided for very much along the lines suggested in the *Republic,* and the arts are again attacked for their demoralizing effect. Methods of election and the nature and number of magistracies are provided for, as are the organization of law-courts and the selection of judges. International relations are also discussed.

Into the detail of all this we have no time to penetrate. But we may note in general the theocratic, austere, puritanical, and even at times fanatical tone that characterizes the dialogue and makes us feel that Plato, in spite of his genius, did not, like good wine, mellow as he grew old. We turn now to Plato's pupil, Aristotle, who ranks with his master as one of the greatest and most influential philosophers of all time.

Chapter XIII

ARISTOTLE

I. ARISTOTLE'S LIFE

Education. Born in 384 B.C. in Stagira, a town in the peninsula of Chalcidice in Thrace, Aristotle entered the world surrounded by none of the pomp and circumstance to which Plato fell heir. He came, rather, of a long line of provincial doctors and emerged from a comparatively middle-class background. But his father must have been a man of more than average ability and prominence, for, while Aristotle was still a child, he became court physician to Amyntas of Macedon, the grandfather of Alexander the Great. This meant the removal of his family from Stagira to Pella, the newly established and somewhat unkempt capital of the Macedonian kingdom, where a portion, at least, of Aristotle's boyhood was spent. His parents died while he was still young, and he was given a home and an education by a friend of the family named Proxenus. At the age of eighteen he went to Athens to study at Plato's Academy, where, we are told, his affected ways and the care he lavished upon his personal appearance caused the college authorities some concern. There are also stories of disputes with his masters and of strained personal relationship, but these are probably gossip. How far he actually differed from Plato while still at the Academy is an open question. The fragments of works written during his discipleship are seemingly thoroughly Platonic in tone.

At Plato's death the leadership of the Academy passed to his nephew and legal heir, Speusippus, who was a second-rate man. Aristotle's tutelage was at an end. Being somewhat at loose ends, he accepted an invitation from a college friend, Hermeias, who had bought the towns of Atarneus and Assos in the Troad and the title of Prince from the Persian government. He stopped for a while at Atarneus, also at Mytilene, where he devoted himself to biological research. At this time he married Hermeias' sister or niece, Pythias, by whom he had a daughter.

Tutor to Alexander the Great. Amyntas of Macedon was now dead, and his son Philip, with whom Aristotle had perhaps played as a child, had become king, and had begotten in his turn a son, Alexander. Interested in science and art, in touch with Athens and the Academy, and acquainted with Aristotle's brilliant career, Philip offered him the job of tutoring the boy, now twelve years old. Aristotle accepted, and in 343-342 B.C. returned to Pella—which had become a bustling, spick-and-span, up-to-date city, and the garrison town of the most powerful army in the western world. Here Aristotle spent the next four years, educating Alexander, and seeking to imbue him with the reverence for Greek ideals and institutions and the contempt for "barbarians" or, in other words, non-Hellenes, that he himself felt so keenly.

His tutorship was interrupted and virtually brought to an end, by the appointment of Alexander, then sixteen years of age, as regent, while the king carried on the campaign that ended in the subjection of all Greece at the battle of Chaeronea in 339 B.C. Three years later Philip was assassinated and Alexander ascended the throne. Aristotle was free once more, and his inclination was to go back to Athens, which was full of old memories and old friends, and by far the most stimulating place for literary and scientific work. During the war it would have been unwise for him, because of his Macedonian affiliations, to return there, but now the city was "pacified" and safe.

Return to Athens. So the spring of 334 B.C.—the same spring that Alexander was off to Asia on his conquest of the world—saw Aristotle back in his old haunts. He could not, of course, re-enter the Academy, of which Xenocrates, an old friend, but, like Speusippus, second-rate, was now president. He was too big a man and too conscious of his own powers for that. He had, moreover, a new philosophic system to expound, innumerable scientific researches in various fields to occupy him, and perhaps large collections of data on his hands. The only solution was to set up a school of his own.

Foundation of the Lyceum. This he did by first gathering his pupils about him in a park near Mt. Lycabettus, dedicated to the Muses and Apollo Lyceus, and called after Apollo's title, the Lyceum. By this name his school came to be known, and from his habit of walking up and down with his pupils as he lectured, the group was called "Peripatetic"—a label that became the official designation of the Aristotelian system. His more technical lectures were given in the morning, but afternoons he held crowded classes in rhetoric and oratory. Meantime he carried on his scientific researches, subsidized, it would appear, by Alexander. He rented land and built buildings to house his collections and his manuscripts. Residential halls also sprang up, a college chapel was erected and dedicated to the Muses, and there was a commons where his pupils dined together and held "symposia" or convivial meetings devoted to food, drink, and philosophic converse. The Lyceum quickly outstripped the Academy, but Aristotle seems always to have kept on pleasant and friendly terms with his Alma Mater.

Aristotle's Genius. In the next twelve years of his life he completed a prodigious amount of work—all his extant writings, not to speak of many lost ones, as well as a profound and detailed research in every field of knowledge. Physics, astronomy, biology, physiology, anatomy, natural history, psychology, politics, ethics, logic, rhetoric, art, theology and metaphysics were all explored and mapped by him. He is probably the only human intellect that has ever compassed at first hand and assimilated the whole body of existing knowledge on all subjects, and brought it within a single focus—and a focus, at that, which after more than two thousand years still stands as one of the supreme achievements of the mind of man.

The fruits that have come down to us of all this study and meditation comprise the great work on logic known as the *Organon;* the *Physics,* the *De Caelo,* the *De Generatione et Corruptione,* and the *Meteorologica* in the field of the physical sciences; in biology, physiology and psychology, the *De Anima,* the *Parva Naturalia,* the *Historia Animalium,* and other treatises on natural history; and finally the *Metaphysics,* the *Nicomachean* and the *Eudemian Ethics,* the *Politics,* the *Rhetoric,* the *Poetics,* and the *Constitutions,* a chapter of which on the *Constitution of Athens* has been lately recovered from an Egyptian papyrus.

He had been back in Athens but a short time when his wife died. Soon afterwards he formed a lasting liaison with a lady named Herpyllis, who survived him. She bore him one son, Nicomachus.

Estrangement from Alexander. To this period belongs also the beginning of his estrangement from Alexander. On the one hand, Aristotle was annoyed and disturbed by the king's behavior. Alexander, after his conquest of Persia, had assumed the diadem, the robes, and the state of the fallen Darius. His court was conducted with Oriental pomp and ceremony. The oracle of Ammon in Egypt had proclaimed him son of Zeus, and he demanded that divine honors be paid him by all who entered the Presence. He had married one Bactrian and two Persian princesses, and it looked as if Macedonia and Greece would eventually be ruled by a half-breed, Eurasian despot. He had moved the capital of the empire to Babylon, mated his soldiers with native women, appointed Persians to positions of honor and responsibility, both civil and military, and generally fraternized with the "barbarian." All this must have been gall and wormwood to Aristotle. His teaching had been in vain. Alexander had proved renegade to the ideals of Hellenic moral superiority and political supremacy with which his tutor had been at such pains to imbue him.

The king, on the other hand, had grown intensely suspicious, though without reason, of the loyalty of his regent, Antipater, whom he had left behind in Macedon to keep Greece in order. And this suspicion had come to embrace all of Antipater's friends, among whom Aristotle was counted one of the staunchest and most intimate. It was, however, the behavior and fate of Aristotle's nephew, Callisthenes, that brought the latent animosity to an open breach. He was a very worthy and rather dreary young man for whom his uncle had procured the post of historian to the expedition. He soon gained the king's ill will by his open disapproval of Alexander's Oriental proclivities and pref- erences. Eventually he was accused of complicity in a plot against the king's life. He seems to have been innocent of any connection with it, but he was tortured and put to death. Alexander suspected Aristotle of being privy to the conspiracy, and wrote an angry letter of denun- ciation to Antipater. Fortunately, he was too taken up with his pro- jected invasion of India to make good his threats. But Aristotle's feel- ing for his erstwhile charge can scarcely have been sweetened by the unjust execution of his nephew and the equally unjust charges against himself.

Death of Alexander and Aristotle. In the spring of 323 Alexander died suddenly, apparently from getting drunk while down with a bad attack of malaria. He was not quite thirty-three and had reigned for nearly thirteen years. Though his death was due to natural causes, the slander was soon abroad that he had been poisoned at the behest of Aristotle and Antipater. Thanks to the energy of Perdiccas, to whom he had left the regency of the empire pending the birth of the child with whom the Bactrian wife, Roxanna, was pregnant, things held together for a short time after his death. But Greece was in immediate and open rebellion, inspired by the fanatically anti-Macedonian orator, Demosthenes, and it was a full year before Antipater could put down the uprising.

Aristotle, because of his Macedonian connections and his friendship with Antipater, had found it imperative to leave Athens at once. He was accused like Socrates, for want of any better reason, of offending against the established religion. Not wanting, as he said, "to give the Athenians a second chance of sinning against philosophy," he retired to a country estate in Chalcis on the island of Euboea, which he had inherited from his mother. A year later he died there of a disease of the stomach from which he had been suffering for some time. He was sixty-three years old.

II. ARISTOTLE'S SCIENTIFIC OUTLOOK

Aristotle's Temperament Different from Plato's. As we have already noted, it is an open question how early in his career Aristotle parted company with his master's teachings. Accounts of certain writings [1] dating back to his Academy days, would seem to indicate that for a time he accepted Plato's idealism and theism, doctrine of immortality, dualistic ethics and anti-worldly scheme of salvation. But his whole temperament and outlook on life were fundamentally at variance with Plato's. He was not addicted to causes and reforms, and his heart rarely, if ever, got the better of his head. He was a spectator, not an actor; cool, analytical, judicial and unpartisan, not easily stampeded by enthusiasm or disgust. Essentially a scientist and a realist, he was intent on discovering the true rather than establishing the good. And this impartial, unsqueamish, scientific temper, hospitable to all data, and equally receptive of any reasoned conclusion to which investigation of them might lead, became more marked as he grew older.

Plato's death and Aristotle's departure from the Academy appear to have unleashed these tendencies. From the dialogue *On Philosophy*, probably written at Assos or during the early years at the Macedonian court, both the Platonic Ideas and the Platonic creator, which figured in his first writings, have been erased. The universe is proclaimed to be uncreated—a cardinal point in Aristotle's system. And God has apparently been already shifted from his previous, Platonic task of actively fashioning and ruling all things for the best, to his distinctively Aristotelian role of inspiring motion and activity in the universe through no will or effort of his own, but simply by the attraction of his supreme perfection. To this point we shall return in a moment.

III. CRITICISM OF PLATO

Universals Not Independent Substances. Aristotle seems to have broken with Plato over the question of the relations of the Ideas to

[1] The *Eudemus* and *Protrepticus*.

the sensible world. He felt that by separating the Ideas from their sensible instances, and by attributing to them an independent existence of their own, Plato had rendered them powerless to explain either the existence or the moving, changing character of particular objects. For that matter, it was impossible to conceive the Ideas as having even a being of their own apart from the individual things that embodied them. How, for example, could we conceive of a human-nature-in-itself existing outside of and independent of individual human beings? Where and what would the Idea of the bed be, if there were no such *things* as beds. Moreover, Aristotle felt, when Plato asserted the independent existence of the Idea, he turned the Idea itself into a thing. He thought of human-nature-in-general, as if it were a sort of gigantic, deified particular man—existing side by side with ordinary human beings, who imitated its perfection, so far as they could, in their appearance and behavior. But to attribute particular, concrete existence to the universal, which was abstract and general, was a contradiction in terms. These difficulties became especially glaring in Aristotle's opinion, when Plato reduced the Ideas to numbers. With the "mathematicizing" tendencies of his master, which later were pushed to extremes by the Academy under the leadership of Speusippus and Xenocrates, he had no patience whatsoever.

If the advocates of the "one-story" interpretation of the Ideas are right, Aristotle misunderstood Plato, and the criticisms we have just been recounting are beside the point. But whether to the point or beside it, they started Aristotle off on his own philosophic adventure.

The Concrete and Individual Character of Substance. If the Platonic Ideas or Forms proved to have no vitality or punch of their own when divorced from particular things, one conclusion was plain. Real Being was not to be sought and found in universals—human nature and courage-in-itself, and the character all beds have in common, as Plato had maintained. It was located and could be discovered only in the particular, the individual, and the concrete. The real was always a concrete thing. *Substance,* Aristotle insists, *is primarily and essentially individual.* Whenever we come across it, we find it to be a determinate, particular *thing,* and a thing that is *essentially* itself and nothing else. Universals, to be sure, or general types, which classify individuals and define their essential and distinctive properties, may be called "substances" in a secondary sense and by courtesy. And the species and subspecies that more and more closely define the individual thing and set it apart from all other things have even more right to the title.

But in its full and primary sense the term is applicable to the individual alone.[2]

At the same time, Aristotle was quick to realize that there was much to be said for the Platonic position. In the first place, though the universal can never be found or dealt with except in particular things, it really is separable from them for the purposes of thought and knowledge. We can abstract from a class of individual objects what they have in common, and entertain a general notion about them. Indeed, *knowing* a thing means knowing *what* it is, and knowing *what* it is means classifying it under the general type or law that it exemplifies. Here we may note that Aristotle created for himself a dilemma from which he never succeeded in extricating himself. The object of *knowledge* was the universal. Science meant the reduction of the individual to general terms. And yet, the individual as such was the only true substance and reality. Hence it looked as if knowledge and science were not concerned with Reality. This disparity between the real and the knowable was never overcome.[3]

IV. FORM AND MATTER

The Universal Essential to the Particular. Again, the Platonic Idea, though it had no existence outside of the particular, was a very vital and forceful element *in* the particular. It was decidedly not accidental or superficial, as the Cynics and Cyrenaics maintained. Remove it from the individual and the individual itself perished. For any concrete, particular thing, if it was to exist as such, had to be not only this particular object rather than that, but also this *sort* of object rather than that sort. Unless it were some *kind* of thing, it was not a thing at all.

In every sensible substance, then, two elements or aspects are fused. On the one hand, there is *Form,* which makes it the kind of particular it is; on the other, there is *Matter,* which makes it particular and concrete, and individuates it from all other particular, concrete objects of its kind. These two aspects cannot be separated from each other as Plato, in Aristotle's opinion, had maintained. On the contrary, they can never be found and cannot exist apart from one another. Absolutely formless Matter or matterless Form is never met with in the sensible universe. Hence the Aristotelian dictum—*No Form without*

---

[2] *Met.,* V, 8; VII, 3-4.
[3] Cf. Zeller, *Aristotle,* pp. 334 ff., 377 ff. Ross, *Aristotle,* p. 171.

Matter, no Matter without Form, so far, at least, as the sensible world is concerned.

Identity and Relativity of Form and Matter. Moreover, Aristotle feels, the two aspects of Form and Matter, which everything displays, are not even two separate sides of a substance. They denote rather two different directions in which each particular thing points. On the one hand, every sensible object exists by virtue of realizing and giving new Form to possibilities latent in other substances. On the other, no sensible substance completely exhausts and realizes within itself its own capacities. It is also a stuff of which other things can be made— a possible something else. It is, then, at the same time both Form and Matter, Form relatively to what has made its existence possible, Matter relatively to what its existence, in its turn, makes possible.

Take grass, for example. It could not grow without earth, and in its growth it realizes and gives Form to the ability of the soil to support vegetable life. It is a Form, of which earth is the Matter. But grass is also fodder for cattle, and is capable of being transformed into beef. In other words, its substance is a stuff or Matter to which beef gives a new Form. Grass, then, is at the same time Form relatively to the earth that it feeds on and transforms into its own substance, and Matter relatively to the cattle which can feed on it and turn it into the Form of beef.

To express more clearly this relation between Form and Matter and their inseparable and interchangeable character in the same object, Aristotle uses the terms Actuality and Potentiality.[4] Every sensible object is an actualization of potentialities resident in other substances, and in the act of actualizing them it also acquires new potentialities of its own which make the actualization of further Forms of concrete existence possible. In short, each new Actuality is also a new Potentiality. In the language of Form and Matter, it is both a new Form in which other objects have been cast, and a new Matter for recasting in the Forms of still other substances.

The Actual Nature of an Object and Its Potentialities. Hence it is the actual nature or Form of an object that determines the object's potentialities and what it shall be suitable Matter for. For instance, only when the potentialities of earth have been actualized in vegetable life, do the potentialities of cattle or of ships—in the Forms of fodder and timber—come into existence. Cattle cannot browse on earth, neither can ships be built of it. Nor can cattle browse on wood or

---

[4] For Aristotle on Actuality and Potentiality, cf. *Met.,* IX.

ships be constructed out of grass. Earth, then, though it is potentially fodder and trees, is not potentially ships and cows. It is the actualized Form of grass that is potential beef, and the actualized Form of wood that is potential ships.[5]

We can now see that Aristotle means by Matter something quite different from what we ordinarily mean by it. To us Matter signifies primarily physical matter—something extended and solid. To Aristotle, however, it signifies anything, physical, mental, moral, or spiritual, that can contribute to the existence and make-up of anything else. We today still speak of human passions, emotions, and interests as good "material" for a novel, or of a man as having good "stuff" in him, or as being good Presidential timber. This meaning of the word, which has become secondary and metaphorical for us, was its primary meaning for Aristotle. Physical matter was for him simply one of innumerable "stuffs" and potentialities.

V. CHANGE AND ITS CAUSES

The process of Becoming in all its phases—motion, change, growth and decay, generation and dissolution and the like—can, Aristotle thinks, be defined as a process of actualizing the potential and of turning what is relatively Matter into what is relatively Form, or conversely of relapsing from comparative actuality to comparative potentiality.[6] In the creative processes of Nature, the fashioning of artificial objects, and even in the movement of bodies in space, the earlier stages and positions make possible the later, and the later actualize the potentialities provided by the earlier.

The Four Causes of Change. Further inspection of the situation reveals that all change and motion involve four factors or causes. There must be (1) something to be moved (a *material cause*), (2) something to move it (an *efficient cause*), (3) a line of development (a *formal cause*) and (4) a goal at which the movement is aimed, and towards which its line of movement proceeds (a *final cause*). To produce a work of art like a statue, for example, there must be (1) bronze, (2) a sculptor, (3) a form envisaged by the sculptor, and (4) a purpose to enact and embody that form. Again animal reproduction requires (1) material for the embryo (provided in Aristotle's opinion by the female), (2) the male seed to set the process of gestation going, (3) a pattern or form for the process to follow, and (4) an aim or purpose,

[5] For Aristotle on this point, cf. *Met.*, VII, 17; VIII, 6; *Phys.*, II, 2.
[6] *Met.*, XI, 9; *Phys.*, III, 1; VIII, 1.

latent in the process, to breed true to the form in question, and produce offspring of the same species as the parent. Finally, the same
four causes are present in mere mechanical motion. There must be
(1) a body to move, (2) something to set it in motion, (3) a trajectory
for it to follow, and (4) an inclination or purpose in the body to
follow it, instead of going off at a tangent.[7]

We may, however, at once rule out the *material cause,* so far as the
source of change and movement is concerned. A moment's reflection
shows us that the Potential is without power to actualize itself or
determine the Forms in which it shall be actualized. Earth cannot
become grass by itself, nor could it become grass unless there were
such a thing as the Form of grass for it to assume. Nor does it contain
within itself the reason why it now becomes grass and now a tree.
The cause, then, of any given change or movement is to be found in
the *final-formal-efficient cause.*

The Priority of the Actual. This at first looks somewhat startling.
It implies that the later, more actualized and formulated stages of any
process are somehow prior to its earlier, less formulated and less actualized ones. The statue is prior to the bronze of which it is cast, the
man is prior to the child that is to become him. But, after all, the
plan or Form of the completed object must somehow be really present
from the beginning in the process of which it is, relatively speaking,
the end, causing the process to take place and guiding it in the direction of the plan or Form in question. Otherwise, there would be nothing to set any particular process going or to prevent change and
motion from going every which way.

Even supposing, for example, that bronze could set about casting
itself of its own initiative, it might just as well become a bowl or a
candlestick, as far as it is concerned, as a statue. And if an animal
embryo is to develop into one species of animal rather than another,
the Form and Actuality of that species must be present in the process
of gestation from the outset, molding the foetus into the kind of
animal it is to become. Even in the movement of an arrow as it leaves
the bow, the target must be in a sense present to give aim and direction to its flight. Causally, then, the Actual must be prior to the
Potential. To describe the Form and Actuality of an object in their
role of the cause of their own self-realization, Aristotle coins the word
"entelechy," probably derived from the Greek word for "to be absolute" or "finished." [8]

---

[7] Cf. *Met.,* V, 2, 1013 *a* 25-1014 *a* 25; *Phys.,* II, 7, 198 *a* 14-198 *b* 5.
[8] Cf. *Met.,* IX, 8; *Phys.,* II, 8.

VI. THE FIRST CAUSE OF MOTION

The existence of all this change and motion in the universe calls for some final explanation. To be sure, the fact that there is a universe and that it exhibits the general structure and specific Forms it does, need not be accounted for. It is a fact that we have to accept as ultimate and behind which we cannot and need not go. The universe, then, must be regarded as uncreated and eternal. It never began and it will never end, and from everlasting to everlasting its formal structure is the same. Aristotle had come, we may remember, to this conclusion, when, as a young man he wrote the dialogue *On Philosophy,* and he found no reason to change his opinion on this point as his system developed. But the fact that the universe exhibits not only an eternal fixed formal structure but also an everlasting process of constant movement and change and passage from one Form to another could not be taken for granted. For that a Cause had to be found.

There must, then, be a First Cause of Motion, and it now becomes our business to discover what its nature is and how it keeps the world on the go.

The Nature of a First Cause. Some light has already been thrown on the nature of a First Cause by the reduction of the four factors present in all change to two, and by the discovery that it is the factor of Form and Actuality which initiates and directs movement of every sort. Plainly, then, a First Cause of Motion must be a completely actualized, formulated substance standing in the same relation to the world-process as a whole as any particular final-formal-efficient cause within the process stands to the particular change of which it is the immediate source. Furthermore, it is equally plain that a First Cause of Motion cannot itself be subject to change or movement of any sort. For if it were, its motion and alteration would have to be explained, and it would then be not a First Cause but in part an effect.

It follows that a First Cause cannot be a Form of existence that either depends for its actualization upon potentialities provided by other substances, or that itself provides Matter which it takes Forms other than its own to actualize. For actualization is a process—is a movement and change from what is relatively Matter and Potentiality towards what is relatively Actuality and Form. The original source of all change can take no part in, and must have no contact with, the movement and alteration it originates. It must be self-existent, self-sustaining, and self-explaining. And to be this, it must actualize only its own potentialities and actualize them in a Form that is not Matter for anything else. Only so can it be, to use Aristotle's own phrase, an "Unmoved Mover" imparting motion without participating in it.

The existence of such a substance, Aristotle feels, is not inconsistent with his assertion that in the universe we never find Matter without Form or Form without Matter. Pure Actuality is not Form without Matter in the sense of being empty Form. On the contrary, it is a concrete individual thing, in which Form and Matter, the Actual and the Potential, have completely coincided and been indistinguishable from one another from all eternity.

VII. THE LOGICAL NECESSITY OF PURE ACTUALITY

The Pyramidal Structure of the Universe. Apart from the necessity of assuming such a substance to account for change and motion, its existence is logically implied in the plan of the Aristotelian universe, which would lack logical conclusion without it. The universe, we can now see, rises in successive tiers or platforms of being, each one of which is characterized by a decrease of unrealized Potentiality and unformulated Matter, and by an increase of actualized Form, relatively to the tier on which it rests.

At its base we have five primitive formulations of Prime Matter—the physical elements of earth, water, air, and fire; to which Aristotle adds a fifth, the ether, partly to guard against a too great preponderance of fire in the universe, and partly because the exalted and semi-divine nature of the heavenly bodies seemed to demand a finer substance than the grosser stuffs of which earthly things are compounded. The diffuse potentialities of the four elements are given further actualization by the Forms of the terrestrial physical substances composed of them; the potentialities of the ether are realized in the movement of the heavenly bodies.

The Successive "Set-Backs" to a Necessary Apex. From the extended and variegated platform of the terrestrial physical substances rises, with considerable set-back, a smaller platform of organic bodies which actualize the potentialities of life possessed by certain combinations of physical matter; and from this again a still smaller platform actualizing the capacity some organic and living matter has for becoming sentient and conscious. Finally, at least one sentient living physical substance possesses potentialities of which thinking is the actualization. This substance is man, whose mind expresses the maximum of actualized Form and the minimum of unrealized Potentiality and Matter that a physical substance can attain. Thus the human mind stands at the end of a series of actualizations, each one of which is made possible by the level below it, and makes possible the level above it. For, in the sensible world at least, only physical bodies can live, only living physical bodies can be conscious, and only conscious living physical bodies can think.

This pyramidal convergence of the universe from a base of unformed Matter and unrealized possibilities towards completely realized and specific Form can come to a point and a logical conclusion only in a substance from which all unrealized Potentiality has disappeared, and which is, therefore, pure Actuality and Form containing no residue of Matter whatsoever. Without such an apex the formal structure of the universe would be decapitated and unfinished. The demands of logic, then, coincide with those of dynamics. What fulfills the one, answers the requirements of the other.

VIII. THE UNMOVED MOVER AND MOTION

An Unmoved Mover Cannot Exert Force or Volition. We have now laid down certain general specifications to which the nature of an Unmoved Mover must conform. But in so doing, we have gained little information as to what a substance complying with these specifications would be like, and hence are far from having discovered the nature of the First Cause. Moreover, what little we have discovered greatly complicates the question of how motion itself is imparted to the universe by the Unmoved Mover. Obviously, it cannot be imparted by any exertion of energy or even exercise of volition on the part of the First Cause. For an outflow of energy or power implies that its source is bestirring itself and is therefore in process and movement, and volition is a process of satisfying a desire and realizing an end. Hence both the application of power and the expression of will have to be ruled out as methods of causing motion, since both involve a passage from the Potential to the Actual, and are therefore characteristic of a moved mover—that is, of a link in the chain of cause and effect—rather than of an Unmoved Mover and a First Cause.

We still have, then, our two original questions on our hands, though they have now become more specific. We have first to look the universe over more thoroughly to see if we can anywhere find anything that in any way measures up to pure Form and Actuality. To be sure, we can be pretty certain that the substance we are seeking will not be found within the universe itself, since the human mind, in which all the potentialities of Matter are realized to the highest possible extent, still needs a body to keep it going and an external world to give it something to think about. Nevertheless, it may be that within the universe we shall find hints as to the nature of the Unmoved Mover. And we may also perhaps find there suggestions as to how such a Mover can impart motion without doing violence to its own nature. Let us, then, rapidly review Aristotle's physics, biology, and psychology.

IX. PHYSICS AND ASTRONOMY

Physical bodies, as we have already seen, are simply one form of Matter in the wide sense of the word in which Aristotle uses it. But the four, or rather the five, physical elements out of which all bodies are made are the first and fundamental actualizations of the potential, without which further actualization would be impossible and upon which it is based. Were there no physical bodies to move and change, live, feel, and think, there would be no activity, no life, no sentience, no thought in the universe.

Space and Time. The distinguishing characteristics of physical or corporeal matter would seem to be its possession of *position* or *place*— in a word, its occupation of *space*. Every body occupies a place, which is defined relatively to its nearest stationary surroundings. Hence the universe, which has no surroundings, cannot be conceived as in space. On the contrary, space is in it. Nor can there be such a thing as the empty space or void preached by Leucippus and Democritus. For, apart from the bodies occupying it, space is nothing. Nor again can space or body be infinite, since such a concept involves us in innumerable difficulties and paradoxes. Space, therefore, must be finite and, for reasons connected with Aristotle's astronomy, spherical.[9]

Time, the Siamese-twin of space, is united to it by motion. Space is a prerequisite of motion, and motion implies time. All passage from place to place is also passage from moment to moment. The points in a body's trajectory that lie spatially to the *fore* of it, lie also *before* it in time; those that are spatially aft are also temporally *behind* it. Time measures out the beat, the *now, now, now,* the *one, two, three,* involved in the sense of transition. According as we can count more or less of these beats in passing from one place or state to another,

---

[9] For Aristotle's discussion of space and time, cf. *Phys.,* IV.

movement is slower or faster. *Time,* then, says Aristotle, is *the meas-ure,* or *"number of motion in respect of the 'before' and 'after.'"* [10]

The Three Kinds of Motion. There are three kinds of motion—rectilinear and circular movement and the motion resulting from their combination. Rectilinear movement is the motion native to the four elements. Since it cannot return upon itself, it must have a definite and separate starting-point and end, and cannot be continuous, as circular movement can. Furthermore, unlike rotation, it cannot be self-starting, self-perpetuating, and everlasting. In obedience to their native rectilinear motion, earth and water tend straight towards the center, air and fire straight towards the circumference of the terrestrial sphere. Hence our distinctions of up and down, high and low, light and heavy and the like. Their tendencies, however, are interfered with by the influence of the movements of the heavenly bodies, and notably of the sun, which keep earthly elements mixed and earthly affairs muddled by seasons, climate, weather, and the processes of generation and decay.

Circular motion is the natural movement of the fifth element, the ether, of which the heavenly bodies are composed. When undisturbed, its direction and rate are uniform, and, since it involves no displace-ment of its center, in a certain sense it involves no change of place. It is, therefore, free from any possibility of alteration in its quality, like slowing down or halting. Its only taint of potentiality lies in its possession of the capacity for "whence" and "whither"; that is, for the change of place involved in revolution about a fixed point.

Astronomy. Holding, as he did, to a geocentric astronomy, and convinced, as he was, that the heavenly bodies, being composed of ether, moved in circles, Aristotle found himself confronted with the necessity of explaining the observed aberrations in the orbits of the planets and the sun's ecliptic. This difficulty he dealt with by adapting the theory of *component motions,* proposed by his fellow-pupil at the Academy, Eudoxus of Cnidus, and amplified by the astronomer, Cal-lippus. To make a long story short, he thought the universe to be a nest of hollow etheric or "crystalline" spheres, fitted one inside the other. Each sphere was not only carried in the revolution of its container, but also possessed a circular motion of its own, oblique to the con-tainer's movement, much as a revolving hoop may also be rotated sideways upon its axis. In certain of these spheres, the planets, the

---

[10] *Phys.,* IV, 11, 220 *a,* ll. 24-25. The italics are mine. The translations of Aristotle are all taken from the Oxford translation of his works.

sun, and the moon were embedded, and the outermost globe was studded with the fixed stars.

The component motions of fifty-five such spheres were necessary, in Aristotle's opinion, to explain the apparent eccentricity of the planetary, solar and lunar orbits, and to account for their divergence both from one another and from the all-inclusive rotation of the outer heaven in which they were carried. This system, in the final shape given to it by the Alexandrian scientist, Ptolemy, persisted for nearly two thousand years till Galileo and Copernicus established the revolution of the earth about the sun and its rotation upon its own axis, and Kepler early in the seventeenth century showed that the planets, including now the earth, move not in circles but in ellipses.

No Unmoved Mover on the Inorganic Level. Plainly, however, pure Actuality and the Unmoved Mover are not lurking anywhere on the inorganic level of the universe. All terrestrial substances are thoroughly infected with Potentiality. The ether, to be sure, freed from all possibility of qualitative changes or generation and dissolution, and naturally endowed with a self-repetitive activity of circular motion to which no beginning or end in space or time can be set, comes very near to filling the bill. But it is disqualified by its capacity for movement. Let us, then, explore the level of organic matter and see what we can find there.

X. BIOLOGY. THE VEGETATIVE SOUL

The Nature of the Soul and Its Relation to Organic Bodies. Aristotle's chief interest lay in biology, and it is in that field that he chiefly shone. Indeed, he ranks as one of the great biologists of all time. The transition from inorganic to organic bodies, he tells us, is marked by the appearance of *soul,* which is an actualization of capacities provided by certain combinations of the four elements in conjunction with pneuma, or "breath," akin to the ether and the carrier of life in the sperm. In Aristotle's own words soul is "the first actuality [entelechy] of a natural body furnished with organs." [11] Its relation to the body may be likened to that of cutting to the ax or of vision to the eye. Without the body it could not exist. And just as it is in its entirety dependent upon the body, so our various emotional and mental states are forms and actualizations for which different bodily states afford the stuff and potentiality. This dependence of the soul upon the body for its existence does not, however, mean that the

[11] *De Anima,* II, 1, 412 *b.*

soul is a physical substance, as Democritus maintained, or yet that it is a state of the body like the harmony of the Pythagoreans. It is the actuality of an organic body, and forms with it a single, indivisible living creature, just as wax and the form into which it is molded make up a single indivisible object.

The capacities of soul are not actualized all at once, but progressively in three steps. First appear living bodies, then sentient living bodies, and finally both sentient and intelligent animate bodies. Common to all organic forms of Matter is the power of self-development and self-direction. The most primitive expressions of this power, common to vegetables and animals alike, are the functions of nutrition and reproduction. These constitute what Aristotle calls the *vegetative soul*.

The vegetative soul makes possible the appearance of a new activity, *sensation*. Bodies must live before they can perceive and feel. The vegetative soul is therefore the Potentiality, or Matter, of which the *sensitive soul,* as Aristotle calls it, is the Form and Actuality. It is the addition of sensation in its various forms that raises animal above purely vegetable life. The difference between the sensitive and the vegetative soul is signalized by an important difference in their relations to the external world. Nutrition extracts and assimilates the *Matter* from external objects, but spits out the Form, whereas sensation takes over their *Form* without their Matter.

Extent of Aristotle's Biological Research. Aristotle's researches into the distinctive structures and functions of organic matter are so extensive, observant, and exhaustive that we have not the space to follow them even in their main lines.[12] Suffice it to say that he was acquainted with five hundred or more different species of animals, had dissected and investigated in detail some fifty kinds ranging over the whole animal kingdom, and, besides many conclusions that now appear primitive and fanciful, had drawn others that have stood the test of time or at least command the admiration of modern biologists. Among these we may mention his insistence that whales are mammals; his descriptions of the mechanism of locomotion, of the process of digestion in ruminants, and of the habits of bees; his discussion of the mechanism of animal reproduction; his exposition of analogous structures in living bodies; and the methods of biological classification he proposed.

[12] Aristotle's chief works on biology are the *Historia Animalium, De Partibus Animalium, De Motu Animalium, De Incessu Animalium*, and *De Generatione Animalium*.

The Nature of Sensation. The same thoroughness and brilliance characterize Aristotle's investigation of the sensitive level of the soul, which raises animals above plants.[13] The distinctive mark of sensation lies, we may remember, in its power to absorb the qualities and Forms of things without ingesting their Matter; in much the same way, Aristotle remarks, that wax takes the seal of a signet-ring without absorbing the metal of which the ring is made. Sensation, however, is not a passive reception of impressions from without. It is a process of actualizing complementary potentialities resident both in the perceiving sense-organ and the thing perceived. For example, when the eye is shut, color is present only potentially in the external object. But the moment one has one's eye on the object, it becomes colored.

This double actualization, which involves a reciprocal action of the organ upon the object and the object upon the organ, takes place in all perception. And it is the actual imbuing of the percipient with the quality perceived that constitutes perception. Thus, the sensation red is the actual reddening of the eye that occurs in the act of seeing a red object. When the sense-organ is turned off, the perceived quality lapses from an actual to a potential state in both the perceiving and the perceived body. But in the perceiving body traces of the actualized condition linger on as actual memories and images.

The Different Senses and Sense-Organs. The basic sense, which all animals possess, is touch. It absorbs primarily the properties common to all bodies. The other senses specialize, and are important in proportion to the thoroughness with which they suck from objects the Forms and qualities to which they are sensitive. The most important perceptual activity is sight, though hearing is a more indispensable condition for thinking than vision is.

In order to actualize in themselves so many different and even opposite forms, the sense-organs must be composed of a simple, neutral material, actually none of the qualities they assume, but potentially all of them; inclined, moreover, to no one more than to another, but occupying a mid-way position with respect to them.

Perception is never in direct contact with its object. It always sucks in the qualities of the external world through a straw, as it were—the ear through the air, the eye through a luminous medium existing both in water and in the atmosphere, smell through moisture.

[13] For Aristotle's psychology, cf. the *De Anima* and the *Parva Naturalia*.

Even taste and touch are only transmitted by the tongue and the skin to the heart where the sensations actually occur.

The Common Sense. Now, our different senses intercommunicate. Although actualized by different organs in different parts of the body, they refer to the same object and give us not five external worlds but one. In short, our senses experience a wide range of what Aristotle calls "common sensibles."

In dealing with these "common sensibles," however, we come across contradictions and fall into error. A cavity in a tooth that feels big, may look small. Yet the separate reports of the senses never lie. They are what they are. The cavity actually does *look* small and *feel* big.

To explain all these phenomena, as well as the fact that in sleep all our senses lapse into unconsciousness together, Aristotle supposes that over and above the five senses there is a "common sense," resident in the heart, which operates through the different organs of perception, and organizes and unifies, sometimes erroneously, their reports. The existence of such a sense is also necessary to account for self-consciousness. For, although perceptions are actualized in the particular sense-organ, our further awareness that we perceive cannot be located there. The eye sees. But it is not conscious that it sees. All that it is conscious of is sights. Nor is our awareness that we are seeing or hearing, a *seeing* that we see, or a *hearing* that we hear. The consciousness then of seeing, and hearing, which accompanies our consciousness of sights and sounds, cannot be located in our eyes and ears, in so far as they are exercising their specific functions of vision and hearing. It can be located in them, if at all, only in so far as they may be also exercising an additional function of perception in general whose real seat is elsewhere.

Imagination and Memory. The sensible qualities actualized in the sense-organs at the moment of perception linger on, as we have seen, after the perception is over, as images and memories. Most of these memories exist only potentially and are merely actualized or recovered from time to time, often at random, without apparent rhyme or reason, but sometimes deliberately and with conscious effort. In dreams these images, cut loose from their sources, are mistaken for present experiences; but our ability when we are awake to trace the image *back* to the sensible impression responsible for it, makes it a *memory* of the *past*. This sense of the past and, generally, of time is, Aristotle thinks, the work of the "common sense." When we try to remember, deliberately and for a purpose, we have *recollections*. But even our seemingly haphazard trains of memories and daydreams are often guided by certain laws of association, such as contrast or similarity, or contiguity in space or time.

Behavior of Organisms. We pass now to the motor aspects of consciousness, or, as we might say, to the behavior of the organism. Living bodies are self-moving and self-directing. Moreover, their movements are not random, but definitely motivated. This motivation is supplied by sensation, which is not neutral, but pleasurable or painful, and therefore an incentive to behavior. Just as the organism of its own nature lives and feels, so of its own nature it feels pleasure and pain and instinctively likes and seeks the one and dislikes and shuns the other, whether they are presented in immediate experience or in image and memory. The consciousness of liking and seeking a thing is *desire* for a thing. The desirability of a thing naturally inspires movement towards it and *vice versa*. The organic counterpart of its desirability is purposive movement directed towards it. Without desire to motivate it, motion would be purposeless.

Desire is the offspring of the sensitive activities of the soul, and is particularly bound up with imagination. But the images of fulfilled desire, and therefore the purposes of the organism, do not all move on the same level. Some, indeed, anticipate the pleasures connected with the physical activities of the body, and constitute our appetites. But some may also commend themselves to reason more than others, and thus constitute an ascending series of objects of rational wish—or of what is good for us in the long run rather than pleasurable at the moment.

No Unmoved Mover on the Vegetative or Sensitive Levels. Obviously, a wholly actual, Unmoved Mover is no more to be discovered among living, feeling, and desiring substances than among inorganic ones. For all such substances actualize potentialities provided by lower stages of existence, and in their actual form possess capacities requiring higher forms of being to bring to full fruition. At the same time, the vegetative and sensitive levels of the soul have important implications for metaphysics. In organisms the priority of the Actual and the dominance of the final cause, obscurely indicated by the behavior of inorganic bodies, are plainly displayed. The explanation of organic structure, Aristotle feels, lies in the functions it performs. The eye exists and is fashioned as it is *in order to* see, the ear *in order to* hear, the animal body as a whole *in order to* live and to perpetuate its species. Everywhere, then, process is caused, not by antecedent events, but by subsequent ones, and finds its real reason in its result.

Teleological Character of Nature. In short, on the organic level, the end to be realized—the prior Actual and the final cause—is every-where visibly originating and directing the movement leading towards it. In this respect, living processes are but striking samples of the universal operations of nature. The rectilinear motions of the four elements, their tendencies to return, each to its appointed place, and the revolutions of the celestial spheres are really just as purposive and just as teleological in character as the animal functions of nutrition and reproduction are. They are strivings towards an end, and their why and wherefore can be found only by discovering what that end is.

So, too, with all the levels of the universe. The lower exist *for the purpose* of giving rise and support to the higher. The end, then, we might say, of the whole world-process, and the reason for it, is the creation of intelligence, and all the lower stages are but means to carrying out this final purpose fulfilled in human beings.

Perhaps, here, we should speak a word of warning. The Aristotelian world-process, though evolutionary in the sense that it exhibits a ladder of Forms culminating in man, is not an evolution in time. The higher Forms are not produced *after* the lower. The human level is not *later* than the inorganic level. All the stages, superimposed upon each other in due order, have existed together from all eternity—the universe just as it is, ever was and ever shall be, world without end. The process of evolution lies simply in the constant ascending movement from the potential to the actual involved in the support and nourishment of the higher levels of existence by the lower.

The general purposive, upward thrust of the world-process is broken by checks and distortions. Factors of "necessity" and absolute chance, apparently bound up, in Aristotle's opinion, with the taint of potentiality, make nature's aims sometimes fly wide of their marks and mar and thwart the realization of her purposes. In this way all the malformations, deformations, failures, and other apparent contra-indications of purpose that occur in natural processes are accounted for.

A Mover Can Attract Without Itself Being Moved. The sensitive soul, all in all, shows us how the prior actual can instigate the process of realization in the potential, how purpose can actuate nature, and how motion can be caused by an Unmoved Mover. Plainly the actual, being *ahead of* the movement that actualizes it, cannot push it into being *from behind,* and plainly an Unmoved Mover, as we have seen, cannot exert effort or even volition in setting things going. But *the object of desire* lies not behind but ahead of the movement pursuing it, and, nevertheless, causes the various means and successive stages of attaining it. Furthermore, in causing them it puts forth no force.

Nor does it *will* the pursuit of itself to take place. It may be even quite oblivious to the fact that the pursuit is taking place. May not, then, this desirability be the secret of the prior Actual's power to actualize the Potential, and of Form to inspire and guide its realization by Matter? Indeed, why should not some supreme object of the world's desire cause, just by its attraction, the heavenly spheres to turn round and round in a kind of cosmic lovesickness? In any case, we can now explain how a First Cause that neither pushes, nor pulls, nor wills, nor anywhere or in any way is in contact with its effect, can still produce it.

XII. EPISTEMOLOGY. THE RATIONAL SOUL

We pass now to the activity of rational thought,[14] exercised by man alone of all the animals, in our search for the Unmoved Mover. Here, too, there is the same gradual transition from animal to specifically human consciousness that marks the passage from the organic to the inorganic and from vegetable to distinctively animal life. The child begins on the "sensitive" stage and develops reason only as it grows older, and many of the higher animals are capable of a limited degree of intelligence.

Again, just as sensation extracts their sensible qualities from things, so reason absorbs their abstract, intelligible Forms. And just as the sense-organ is potentially all the qualities it can become in the process of perceiving, so the intellect is potentially inscribed with all the Forms that can be actualized in the process of knowledge, much as space is potentially inscribed with all geometrical figures. Since reason is capable of grasping *any* truth, it is therefore potentially *all* truth—i.e., the whole system of intelligible Forms that constitute the structure of the universe.

Error. The Forms are actualized by the intellect, not bit by bit, but all at once, in their entirety, in a single instant of time. They "flash" upon us, as we say, all complete. Nor can there be any more doubt or error with respect to what Form we are thinking at the moment than there is with respect to what sensation we are experiencing. Unfortunately, however, all the Forms are not actualized together by the intellect, or interlocked like the pieces of a wholly, or of even a partially, completed picture-puzzle. They are rather poured into the

---

[14] For Aristotle's account of the activities of the rational soul and his discussion of the potential and the active intellect cf. *De Anima,* III.

mind as the pieces of the puzzle are dumped upon the table, disconnected and in confusion. The intellect has the task of fitting them together and solving the puzzle they present. This task is called *synthetic judgment* or *thought,* as contrasted with *analytic judgment* which lies in simply stating that each different Form is what it is. "Man is human" or "a cow is a cow" are examples of analytic judgments, "man is an animal," or "cows chew cuds," of synthetic ones.

It is in fitting different Forms together, and in suggesting how perhaps they may be related and where they may belong in the puzzle, that error arises. Liability to mistakes is increased by the fact that all Forms given to the mind are stuffed with sensible content, and that we cannot think without images. For sensible objects, being infected with potentiality, *need* not be what they are, and do not indicate precisely what their true natures or Forms are. It is very difficult, for example, to know whether certain Forms of life are animal or vegetable. Time, too, complicates the problem, since it transforms our picture-puzzle into a sort of kaleidoscope, and forces us to figure out, not merely how Forms *are* related here and now, but how they once *were,* and how in the future they *will be* connected.

The Unmoved Mover Not a Being that Reasons. Human reasoning, then, is a *process,* a means towards an end, an actualization of the Potential; not an end in itself containing its own reward. Not only does it depend upon the body for its existence, and need images provided by the sensitive soul to help nourish and sustain it, but it is actualized by "flashes" of insight that seem to come from a higher level of being. It is not, then, the pure actuality and Unmoved Mover of our search.

At the same time there are signs that we are now hot on the scent and have almost cornered our quarry. In the first place, in contrast to sensation, thought, Aristotle believes, has no specific physical basis. There must, to be sure, be a physical organism before human thinking can occur, but reason is not an actualization of bodily capacities in the sense that sight, hearing, etc., are. *Its potentialities lie within itself,* and, unlike other potentialities, do not imply a Matter different from itself, but merely the *absence* of its own activity. For example, break up a statue and you have still on your hands the bronze or marble of which it is composed. But banish a concept from your mind, and you have nothing on your hands except the blank possibility of thinking of it again.

Identity of Actual and Possible Concepts. In short, a concept when it lapses from the actual to the potential state does not relapse into another stuff, as the statue does. So, too, in becoming actual a concept does not change its nature and name, as bronze does when it becomes a statue. It remains the same concept, whether it is actually present or only latent in the mind. In other words, *the potential and the actual reason are not two things but one*. Or as Aristotle puts it, the intellect "is nothing at all before it thinks." [15]

Again, when the intellect does think, it is nothing at all actually except *what* it thinks. It has no Form of its own in addition to and different from the Forms it entertains. There is nothing to the mind apart from its intelligible content. Remove that content, and thinking itself has ceased. "For," says Aristotle, "where the objects are immaterial," as intelligible Forms are, "that which thinks and that which is thought are identical." (Speculative knowledge and its object are identical.) [16]

Meaning of the Potential Intellect. The *potential intellect* means, then, simply that we are not able to retain our grasp upon the Forms that constitute our thinking, but are subject to long intervals when they are not actually apprehended. In these intervals they are merely knowable, and as such become objects to be sought for and reasoned out. For Potentiality implies the possibility of not thinking as well as thinking, of thinking more or less accurately, and of thinking this rather than that. Hence truth can never be wholly or continuously present to the human organism, and the flashes in which it is revealed to us must necessarily be flickering, intermittent and partial.

A second point to be noted is this. In contrast to the sensitive and vegetative activities, and, for that matter, to the processes of discursive reasoning and the potential intellect, all of which are parceled out among different organisms, the flashes of insight in which reason is actualized are super-individual in character. When you and I *perceive* one and the same object, *two* bodies are active, and *two* pairs of eyes duplicate its qualities in the act of perceiving it. But when you and I *conceive* what an object is, there are not two Forms, or natures, of the object, one in your mind, the other in mine. The same identical form flashes upon us both.

Truth Enters the Mind from Above. Nay more, since thinking and what is thought are identical, in one and the same super-individual act of thinking the Form in question is present in both our organisms, actualizing our two processes of discursive reasoning and turning what is knowledge to both of us into what is true and intelligible in

---

[15] *De Anima*, III, 4, 429, i. 24.
[16] *De Anima, loc. cit.*, 22 ff.

itself, independent of us both. Though you and I may work out a problem independently, the solution, when it occurs to us, is one and the same in us both. It is therefore not thought by us severally, but thinks itself in us universally. And, unlike all other actualizations of the Potential, it comes not as a *transformation* of an alien subject matter, partially actualized on the lower levels of nature, but as a kind of "supernatural" burst of *information* from above.

XIII. THE ACTIVE REASON

Identity of Thought and Truth in the Active Reason. Our inspection of human reason, then, suggests the existence of a still higher Form and activity of being—an activity of intellect which is one with and nothing but the whole truth about the universe. By this supreme act of thought the entire system of Forms constitutes itself the intelligible structure of the world. This activity floats free of all material conditions and supports. It is self-existent and self-sustaining. The truth, the intelligible structure of things, is still there and is still rational, whether *we* think it or not. But by her higher actualizations of the potential, nature has prepared, in the intellect of man, a place for it which it may inhabit now and then for a brief moment, and reveal there the truth for which the potential, distinctively *human* intellect is an unremitting search.

In what Aristotle now calls the *Active Reason,* we have also all that is immortal in man. On this point he is specific. The potential, or *passive reason,* he tells us, can no more exist without the body than loving and hating, memory, imagination, sensation and life can. Hence it disappears along with them when the body returns to dust. The Active Reason alone is separable from the body, immortal and eternal. But in that timeless, deathless, all-comprehending act of thought there is nothing of *us*. It is impersonal in its essence, and, even while we live, so far as it succeeds in entering into us it abolishes our personalities and separate individualities, and merges our minds in a single registration of the one and only truth. Its survival of our death has nothing of personal immortality about it. In surviving our bodies it survives *us* also. For all that makes you, you, and me, me, is bound up with our emotions and feelings, our images, perceptions, and organic structures. It is to them that we are bound, so far as we are *we* and have separate personalities, and we share their mortality and meet their fate. Only the apprehension of truth, of which we were for a brief space the fragile and ephemeral receptacles, defies our passing, and, heedless of our destruction, continues throughout all eternity to enlighten the minds of successive generations of men.

The Active Reason an Unmoved Mover. At last, in this *Active Reason*, contrasted by Aristotle with the distinctively human, *passive* intellect, we have a form of being that fulfills all the specifications laid down for pure Actuality and the Unmoved Mover. For the Active Reason neither is produced out of anything lower than itself nor produces anything higher than itself. It depends upon nothing outside itself for either its existence or its completion. Nothing else is capable of becoming it, and it is capable of becoming nothing else. In it the distinction between the Potential and the Actual has been from all eternity abolished and meaningless. It is therefore pure Actuality.

The Unmoved Mover, then, can only be found in this activity. Moreover, inspection of the universe shows us that the Active Reason actually is the supreme object of the world's desire. All nature aspires towards man and aims at his production, and all the activities of man, Aristotle feels, are subordinated to, and have as their indirect or direct goal, the exercise of the intellect in and for itself, or, in other words, the attainment of the vision of truth. Hence this exercise and this attainment are at once the climax and the driving power of the world-process. By the sheer attraction of its finished and perfect Form the Active Reason lifts the whole universe towards itself, with no expenditure of energy and without occurrence of change or movement within it. Love of its perfect activity makes the world go round, and the successive actualizations of the Potential proceed onward and upward forever in a ceaseless effort to compass and possess the beloved.

XIV. THEOLOGY

The Active Reason and God. Whether the Active Reason can without further refinement qualify for Godhead is, however, a disputed point. Aristotle's pupil, Eudemus, and many later commentators, both ancient and modern, believed it could. Their views receive some support from a passage in the *Metaphysics* stating that the universe, like an army, has its good both outside and inside itself; outside, in the person of a commander, inside, in its discipline and order. This might be taken to imply that God in one aspect, at least, is the whole intelligible structure of the world, or the content of the Active Reason. Still, Aristotle insists that the transcendent aspect of God is more important than the immanent. And the identification of the Active Reason with the divine mind would suggest that, when it enlightens our intellects with its flashes of insight and unites them with the truth, it actually merges and makes us one with the divine essence. But Aristotle explicitly declares that, wonderful as these flashes are, they are only somewhat *like* the life of God, which is a state of existence still more wonderful.

Again, the content of the Active Reason, being the whole system of Forms which constitutes the intelligible framework of the universe, is a multiple content, in which degrees of higher and lower also exist. God, on the other hand, can have as the object of his thought nothing higher or lower than himself. He can have nothing higher because such an object does not exist. He can have nothing lower because such an object would be unworthy of his thought. Moreover, since "that which thinks and that which is thought are identical," he would be identified with something other and less perfect than himself—which is absurd. Hence God can think and be only his own Form. And that Form must be simply the nature of the activity of thinking in itself, distilled clear of the Forms that diversify it. In God, Aristotle concludes, "it must be itself that thought thinks (since it is the most excellent of all things) and its thinking is thinking on thinking." [17] In short, God would seem to be a special and the most perfect instance of the activity of the Active Reason.

However this may be, the Aristotelian God does not seem to be a personal deity. He has no love, no hate, no will, no aim, no moral qualities or activities. Indeed, in another place Aristotle expressly declares that he is not a moral being in the sense, at least, of possessing and practicing the moral and social virtues. [18] For that matter he cannot even so much as know that the universe, or that anything besides him, exists, so completely confined is he by his perfection to meditation upon himself.

Relation of the Active Reason to God. Now, if the Active Reason is not God, the question arises of its relation to him. Here we have another obscure and disputed point. One opinion is that Aristotle regarded it as mediating between the divine and human intellects—a supposition that led the Arabian commentator, Averrhoes, to suggest a whole hierarchy of intellectual levels culminating in the Active Reason, which link the mind of man with the divine intellect and enable us to attain to knowledge of God and union with him.

Again, we cannot but ask what meaning or content we can ascribe to just "thinking about thinking." Thinking, we say, about thinking

[17] *Met.*, XII, 9, 1074 *b*, 32 ff.
[18] *Ethica Nic.*, X, 8. *Pol.*, I, 2, 1253 *a*, 28 ff.

what? St. Thomas Aquinas tried to answer this question by suggesting that whereas the human intellect knows itself incidentally to the knowing of its objects, the divine mind does just the reverse. God knows himself first in the pure act of "thinking about thinking" posited by Aristotle. But in "thinking about thinking" he thinks incidentally all that is thinkable, i.e., the whole intelligible structure of the universe. This suggestion has been followed by a number of scholars both modern and medieval. But it seems to be not so much a description of Aristotle's thought as an attempt to rescue him from the consequences of it.

The Nature of God. Aristotle, however, is not troubled by these difficulties. He has discovered to his own satisfaction the nature of the Unmoved Mover and pure Actuality that moves the world, "even as the beloved moves the lover, unmoved itself." [19] "On such a principle," he declares, "depend the heavens and the world of nature. And its life is such as the best we enjoy, and enjoy but for a short time. For it is ever in this state (which we cannot be). . . . If then God is always in that good state in which we sometimes are, this compels our wonder; and if in a better state, this compels it yet more. And God *is* in a better state. And life also belongs to God, for the actuality of thought is life, and God is that actuality; and God's essential actuality is life most good and eternal. We say therefore that God is a living being, eternal, most good, so that life and duration continuous and eternal belong to God; for this *is* God." [20]

Astronomical Objections to Monotheism. Still, there was one difficulty that did bother Aristotle. The failures to fulfill purpose and achieve Form, and the flagrant shortcomings of every sort that marked the upward and onward striving of the world-process, might be set down to the hesitancy, the indirection, and the tendency to incompleteness inherent in the nature of the Potential. The imperfection of all terrestrial life was thus easily accounted for. But the movements of the heavenly spheres exhibited a perplexing peculiarity for which Potentiality could not be held responsible. Their motions were all regular, uniform and unremitting throughout all time, and were perfect in every respect except for the potentiality of "whence" and "whither."

But—and here came the question—why were the inner spheres out of step with the procession of the fixed stars, and revolving every

---

[19] *Met.*, XII, 7, 1072 *b.*
[20] *Met.*, XII, 7, 1072 *b*, 12 ff.

which way with respect to it and to one another? Since this maze of oblique revolutions was without so much as a hint of imperfection—all circular movements being equally perfect irrespective of direction—it could not be laid at the door of Potentiality. Neither could it be derived from the outer heaven, which transmitted only the direction of its own revolution to the inner spheres; or directly from the Unmoved Mover, which could scarcely be expected to attract—or rather to distract—the fifty-five spheres in fifty-five different directions.

One God, or Fifty-five Gods? The only possible explanation of this sidereal situation was that each sphere must be in love with a different beloved and have its special Unmoved Mover, to which the particular direction, as well as the fact, of its revolution was due. In a word, there must be not one but fifty-five principles upon which "depend the heavens and the world of Nature," fifty-five divine intellects engaged in "thinking about thinking," fifty-five Gods of co-equal divinity and exactly alike in all respects.

Just how Aristotle tried to smooth things over, we do not know. His pupil Eudemus tells us that he accepted the fifty-four new additions and decided that there were as many First Causes of motion as there were spheres. And a modern scholar has suggested that, starting out as a monotheist, he finally came to see that a single source of movement was not sufficient to explain the running of the universe, and frankly adopted, in writings now lost, a polytheistic hypothesis.[21] His own last extant words on the subject are non-committal. In a late passage in the *Physics,* we find him merely asserting that there must be a First Cause of motion "whether the cause be one or more than one." [22]

---

[21] Jaeger, *Aristotle,* pp. 379-380.
[22] *Phys.,* VIII, 6, 258 *b,* 10 ff.

Chapter XIV

ARISTOTLE (CONTINUED)

I. LOGIC

The Categories. At the same time that Aristotle was reasoning out his conclusions regarding the nature of the universe, he was busy reflecting upon the character and validity of the mental processes by which he arrived at them. The results of these reflections have come down to us in his *Logic,* which is not only the first systematic work on the subject, but one of the great contributions to the philosophy of all time.[1] There is, he saw, a "grammar" governing correct thinking, which the grammar of language follows and expresses. Just as all the profusion of speech may be reduced to a limited number of "parts of speech," so all our reasoning makes use of eight or, at the most, of ten *categories.* These categories are: *substance, quantity, quality, relation, place, time, action, being acted upon or affected* and perhaps *state* and *position.* There is nothing we can think about that does not fall under one or another of these headings.

Substance the Primary Category. *Substance* is the fundamental category. Without it—without *things* to have quantity or quality or relation or to act or be acted upon—the others are meaningless. As we have already seen, it stands primarily for individual concrete objects, but it may be used in a secondary sense, of the smallest and closest *species* by which the individual is defined for the purpose of knowing *what* it is. Distinguishing marks of *substance* are that it is always a *subject,* never a *predicate,* and that it cannot be more or less itself or other than itself, although it may assume more or less of a given predicate and take on properties different from itself and contrary to one another. A man, for example, is never more or less a human being or other than one, but he may be black or white, more or less cold, and hot at one time, cold at another.

Into Aristotle's discussion of the other categories we need not enter. Suffice it to say that he feels that, since they are ultimate and un-

---

[1] Aristotle's logic or *Organon* comprises the *Prior* and *Posterior Analytics,* the *Topics,* the *Sophistici Elenchi,* the *Categories,* and the *De Interpretatione.*

analyzable, they present themselves to the mind with the same immediacy as sense perceptions do. We no more *judge* that a man is a
substance, or that white is a quality, or that large is a quantity, than
we *judge* that an apple is a sense-datum, or red or large. In the one
case we just *know* it, in the other we just *perceive* it. Behind that
knowledge, as behind that perception, we cannot go.

Propositions and Predication. When we talk and think, however,
we join categories together in sentences and predicate one thing of
another. And the truth or falsehood of our statements is largely a
matter of asserting or denying predicates according as they are, or
are not, in actual fact united with their subjects. Predicates, according
to Aristotle, are of three sorts.

1. They may denote accidents, or, in other words, qualities of the
subject that add little or nothing to our knowledge of what it really
it—as when we say "man is hairy."

2. Or they may denote properties which, although co-extensive with
the species or genus to which the subject belongs and expressive of its
true nature, are not ultimate definitions of that nature—as when we
say "man talks."

3. Finally they may denote the essential characteristics of a thing,
which set it apart from all others and constitute its distinctive species—
as when we say "man is rational."

For example, man's hairiness has nothing to do with his rationality;
his ability to talk is expressive of and follows from his rationality;
but his rationality expresses and depends upon nothing more profoundly human than itself, and is itself the final and distinctive characteristic, or essence, of human nature.

Species and Genera. From this final and distinctive characteristic, or
infima species, as a center we may move out in a series of widening
concentric circles towards the *summum genus,* or most general class
within which the species falls. In the case of man the *summum genus*
is the class of "living beings" in general. We have, however, to observe
a given order in proceeding from the *infima species* to the *summum
genus,* and *vice versa,* arranging the classes we predicate of the subject in such wise that each new predicate we apply modifies all the
preceding predicates. We must, that is, be able to write our description with no commas separating the descriptive adjectives.

For instance, man is distinguished from other living beings, by his
two-footed, viviparous, rational, and mammalian characteristics, and
loosely speaking we may and do predicate these properties of him in
any order we choose. But to give an accurate and scientific description

of him we must invest him with them in the order in which the different classes predicated of him enclose one another, and must define
him as a rational (kind of) two-footed (kind of) mammalian (kind
of) viviparous (kind of) animal (kind of) living being. Any other
order of arranging the descriptive adjectives would be incorrect. And
the same order must be observed in reverse in passing from the
summum genus of living beings in general to the *infima species* of a
human living being.

Definition. As we thus enclose within one another in their proper
order the classes that intervene between the *infima species* and the
summum genus, we disentangle those characteristics of each successive class, "commensurate" with the class in question, or in other
words, present in all its instances and differentiating it from all other
species. In this wise the essential characteristic, or *differentia,* is distinguished not only from accidental qualities but from secondary
though universal properties. The sum total of the *differentiae* of all
the classes from the *infima species* to the *summum genus* inclusive
gives us the complete definition of the object. For we have then discovered "the number of attributes that are severally of wider extent
than the subject, but collectively co-extensive with it," [2] or in other
words, the precise number of qualities that though shared with other
species, exist *together* only in the species in question.

Thus man, who is the only rational species of living beings, shares
his two-footedness with the birds, his suckling of his young with the
other mammals, his bringing forth his young alive not only with the
mammals but with some snakes and fishes, and the characteristic of
being alive with the vegetables as well as with the animals. But he
alone combines all these properties. "Hence this synthesis must be
the substance of the thing." [3]

Much loose thinking, Aristotle feels, comes from inattention to the
difference between "essence," "accident," "property," "species," "genus"
and the like, as well as from carelessness in distinguishing those qualities that are "commensurately universal" with a thing from those that
are not. This results in our misunderstanding the true nature of things.

Correct Inference. To return, however, to the proposition. Even the
simplest statement, which is that of a noun and a verb, leads us far
afield and suggests new possibilities. Thus "man walks" makes us
think of beings that are not men, and of actions that are not walking,
and leads us to combine our four terms diagonally as well as directly,

[2] *An. Post.,* II, 7, 92 *b,* 32 ff.
[3] *Ibid.,* 90 *a,* 32 ff.

so that we get four possible suggestions. "Man or not-man walks or walks not."

If we add another qualification and say "man is not tall," our four propositions beget eight, since the "not" may imply either that he is actually *short,* the *contrary* of tall, or that he is merely middle-sized or hairy or something to which neither of the contrasts applies. In that case "not" indicates simply the *contradictory,* but not the contrary of tall. Furthermore, the proposition as it stands does not indicate beyond doubt whether we are using either subject or predicate in the sense of "some" or of "all." And when we try to see into what other propositions it can be correctly converted by reversing the subject and the predicate, and still more when we attempt by "opposition" to infer the falsity or the truth of the negative propositions implied in it, the double sense of "not," and the difference between "some" and "all" dig many a pitfall for us. Only by observing a complicated set of rules governing correct inference can we avoid falling into logical error.

The Syllogism. But our troubles are only beginning. We habitually join our statements by such words as "hence," and "therefore," and so run on from thought to thought, developing our argument and pursuing lines of reasoning. In so doing, however, we frequently make statements based upon long and complicated trains of thought and lines of reasoning from which, in making our final assertions, we have dropped, for the sake of brevity and convenience, the intermediate steps leading from the subject to the predicate. For example, if I assert that "Socrates is mortal," I have really argued as follows:— "Socrates is a man; all men are mortal; therefore Socrates is mortal." Otherwise I could not have asserted the predicate of the subject with any certainty.

But in stating my final conclusion, I have altogether suppressed the middle term "man" and the *major premise* "all men are mortal." I have merely linked the predicate of the *major premise* "mortal" to the subject of the *minor premise* "Socrates," and said "Socrates is mortal." Most of our condensed statements of this sort may be expanded in the same way into what is known as the *syllogism.*

The Figures of the Syllogism. This simple form—or first figure, as it is called—of the syllogism is subject to an even more complicated set of inferences than the proposition. We may invert the order of the subject and predicate of either or both of the premises, and we may further elaborate them with the implications of "some" and "all," and of "no" and "not." As a result, we get twenty-four logically

valid variations, of which five, however, give us partial or weak conclusions elsewhere demonstrated in full. To ensure correct inference
and reasoning we must be careful to indicate whether we are thinking of our subjects and predicates in terms of "all" or "some," and to
what extent we are carrying the process of exclusion when we use
"not" and "no." The mechanism of the syllogism has, with some
additions and modifications, remained the basis of our formal logic
until very recently.

Before we desert the syllogism, a final point must be mentioned.
The validity of the syllogism is independent of the truth or falsehood
of its content. For example, the syllogisms "all centaurs are half horse,
half man; Cheiron was a centaur; therefore Cheiron was half horse,
half man," and "all Scots are Mongolian; Robert Bruce was Scotch;
therefore Robert Bruce was Mongolian" are perfectly good syllogisms
and capable of twenty-four logically correct variations, though the
one deals with a myth and the other starts with a lie.

Induction. So far we have been dealing with the correct deduction
of conclusions from propositions whose truth is taken for granted.
We have now to face about and ask ourselves if and how the truth
of the propositions from which we deduce consequences can be established. Plainly such a question has to do with the inferring of general
rules from the observation of particular data—or with what we call
induction.

Many philosophers today feel that it is impossible to infer infallible
general rules and propositions of this sort, and are inclined to regard
all scientific and philosophical theories as speculative hypotheses whose
certainty is always open to doubt. But Aristotle, who believed that the
formal structure of the universe is eternal and immutable, and that
we have an immediate intuition of its Forms and categories, was
troubled by no such suspicions. Knowledge of the universal, he felt,
was given along with our perception of particulars, since a substance
is always some sort of substance, and the mind can proceed immediately, step by step, to the *summum genus* under which a thing falls.
The individual man, for example, is at once known to be a human
being, human beings are apprehended as two-footed mammals, mammals as viviparous living beings, and so on "until the indivisible concepts, the true universals, are established," and we reach the final
Forms with which we describe and explain the universe. Hence,
clearly "we must get to know the primary premises by induction." [4]

[4] *An. Post.*, II, 19, 99 *b*, 32 ff, 100 *a*, 14 ff.

These ideas, which provide us with the primary assumptions of scientific thought and investigation, cannot themselves be demonstrated or reasoned out. They have to be taken for granted, since the concepts that explain and make all things clear cannot themselves be explained or further clarified. Moreover, Aristotle assumes that things cannot both be and not be (the law of self-contradiction), that they must either be or not be (the law of excluded middle), that our words have meaning, and that objects corresponding to them exist.

Scientific Demonstration. Scientific method, outfitted with these assumptions and with the logical procedures of deduction and induction, aims at discovering the true definitions or essences of things. Mere definition, however, does not prove that a thing exists, and, as science is interested only in the existent, a scientific definition must show why and how the event comes to pass. For until we have discovered the cause of an event we are unable to place it. We do not know for sure whether it is a dream or an illusion or a so-called objective occurrence. A scientific definition, then, must include the cause among the essential attributes.

We cannot, of course, demonstrate a substance into concrete existence or into being the kind of substance it is. We can only intuit and observe its presence and its qualities. But we can demonstrate why and how it occurs, and thus give a reason for the presence and the pecularities of what we experience.

Inclusion of the Cause in the Definition. The discovery of the cause and the inclusion of the cause in the definition of an event can be made by the application of logic and of syllogistic procedure to the situation in question. Aristotle gives as an example the definition of a lunar eclipse, which, he says, to be scientific must comprise not only the descriptive phrase "privation of the moon's light," but the reason why the light is cut off. To find this reason we must look for a middle term between "moon" and "privation of light" which is "commensurately universal" with eclipses, just as in arguing that Socrates is mortal, we had to find a middle term connecting Socrates with mortality. We discover this middle term by experimenting with various concepts till we hit upon one that fills the bill. It proves to be the idea of the passage of the earth between the sun and the moon, since this idea alone will fit and explain all the aspects of all lunar eclipses. Our scientific, all-inclusive definition of a lunar eclipse will therefore be "a privation of the moon's light by the interposition of the earth," because "all" (not some) "interpositions of the earth give rise to eclipses." [5] For then, and then only, have we so defined a lunar eclipse that the statement of why it occurs is also a statement of what it is in essence, and thus demonstrated that the cause is essential to the effect. Any seeming plurality of causes means that the class of phenomena under investigation has not been analyzed into all its aspects, and is therefore incompletely defined.

Danger of Regarding Effects as Causes and Vice Versa. In establishing the causes of events, we must, Aristotle tells us, be careful not to confuse two uses of the word "because." For instance, he says, we can demonstrate scientifically both that the planets are nearer than the fixed stars because they do not twinkle, and that they do not twinkle because they are nearer. But, in the first case "because" denotes merely a reason for our believing the planets to be comparatively near, whereas in the second it denotes an objective, physical effect of their nearness. The steadiness of the planets' light does not cause them to be near. It merely causes us to think them near. At the same time it is the necessary effect of their nearness. And the cause of our belief that the planets are near (their untwinkling light) must be shown to be the inevitable consequence of their proximity to the earth, before we can be said to have scientific knowledge of the essence of the phenomenon in question.

Unless we take care to distinguish these two meanings of "because" we are likely to regard effects as causes and causes as effects, and thus to fall into error.

Induction and scientific method are as tricky and full of pitfalls as deduction is, and Aristotle warns the would-be scientist as well as the formal logician against erroneous reasoning. At the same time he enumerates certain very general forms of argument which, though specious, are plausible enough to take in not only those who hear but those who use them. We may use words ambiguously, or punctuate our sentences and thoughts so as to give false emphasis and impression. Or we may palm off an accidental quality as an essential property, or a special case as a general rule (*a dicto secundum quid ad dictum simpliciter*). Again, we may befuddle ourselves as well as our opponents by substituting false for true causes (*non causa pro causa*), or by simply begging the question and assuming the point at issue (*petitio principii*).

[5] *An. Post.*, II, 90 *a*, 3 ff.

II. ETHICS

Early Platonic Influence. Aristotle's first meditations upon ethics, like those upon metaphysics, seem to have been dominated by Plato's influence. In the early dialogue, the *Protrepticus,* ethics is regarded as an exact science which acquaints us with standards of right conduct built into the fundamental structure of the universe. But in the *Eudemian Ethics,* whether it marks a progress in Aristotle's own thought or the revolt of some disciple against the final, more naturalistic conclusions of his master, the notion has been abandoned that ethics rests upon absolute knowledge of a transcendent good. The nature of right and wrong is rather to be inferred by "using perceived facts as evidence and illustration." But traces of Plato still linger in the substitution of religious insight for the intuition of the good, in the feeling that God sets the moral pace for man, and that morality is essentially a service and imitation of a divine model. And the Platonic dualism persists in the belief that morality lies in freeing ourselves from the world of sense and all our attachments to it, and in raising ourselves from earth towards heaven.

From the *Nicomachean Ethics,* however, the Platonic influence has almost entirely disappeared. The highest in us is, to be sure, still akin to the divine, but the divine activity is no longer a moral but a purely intellectual ideal which is imitated by us most perfectly when, in our most detached, disinterested, impartial, and scientific moods, we are most deeply concerned, not with good and evil, but with truth. Such dualism as remains is not that of a higher and a lower within the moral sphere, but of the lower, moral activities as a whole with the higher, intellectual activities of pure contemplation.

Ethics Concerned with the Human Good. Ethics, Aristotle now tells us, is concerned with the human being as we find him, remembering always that he is a composite being with body, passions and parts, which determine the nature of his good and underpin his moral character. It is the business of ethics to determine on a purely scientific basis the kind of life that is best for such a being. This in its turn will be determined by its capacity to produce *happiness,* which is the end at which all our activities aim, and to which they strive to become the means. It is highly important for us to know in what happiness consists, but such knowledge, considering the variety and variability of human nature, can never be exact. In short, ethics is doomed from the start to be an inexact and approximative science and therefore, incidentally, a less agreeable and less worthy object of intellectual study than an exact science like mathematics.

Popular and Platonic Views of the Good Criticized. How, then, are we to define human happiness? Candidates for the position, like riches, honor, virtue, amusement and the like, are immediately rejected on the ground that they are desired not for themselves but for the happiness they bring. And the Platonic notion of an absolute good laid up in heaven proves to be open to all the objections urged against the Ideas in general. Pleasure, however, is a formidable candidate, and to combating its claims Aristotle devotes considerable space.

Plato's attack on hedonism, however, he regards as unsuccessful and unjust. Pleasure is not in itself bad. Very few pleasures, even the violent physical ones, are base or harmful unless carried to excess. That pleasure is the better for wise guidance does not prevent it from being in itself *a* good if not *the* good. Neither does the fact that it is not a quality, or admits of degrees of intensity. Moreover, it is not a process of becoming, as Plato maintained, rather than a goal; nor, if it were, would that be anything against it. It cannot be a process, for it is neither quick nor slow nor divisible nor at times incomplete like motion. It is simply *there* in its entirety when it occurs. It is not a "becoming" for it comes from nowhere and goes away nowhere. It is not a physiological process. It merely accompanies processes, and mental as well as physical ones, at that.

Untenability of Hedonism. Nevertheless it is not *the* good. It is only good when it accompanies activities conducive to happiness. Its goodness is not determined solely by its pleasurableness but by its sources and its results. It is not preferable at any price. Nay more, it could be removed and the functioning of the organism would continue without its stimulus. "It seems clear, then, that neither is pleasure the good nor is all pleasure desirable . . . though some pleasures are desirable in themselves, differing in kind or in their sources from the others." [6]

Pleasure really is the completion or crown of an activity—the reward bestowed by nature for proper functioning. It is, indeed, a work of supererogation on her part, since our activities would go on and complete themselves without it. It rests upon healthy functioning as the "bloom of youth does on those in the flower of their age." It is therefore inseparable from our activities, and we cannot avoid it or help feeling it, as the Cynics would fain have done. Accompanying morally desirable and morally undesirable activities alike, it is itself morally

[6] *Eth. Nic.,* X, 3, 1174 *a*, 4-12.

neutral. And though entangled with happiness, it is not itself happiness.

Happiness, however, like pleasure is involved in action and bound up with it. Though the goal of activity, it does not put an end to the activity that attains it. But, unlike pleasure, it must last more than a moment to be realized. It needs a certain length of time for its fruition. No one dead in childhood can be called happy. For that matter it is doubtful whether an individual can be called truly happy even at the end of a long life, if he is not honored after his death, or if his descendants meet with great misfortunes.

Happiness the Rationally Organized Activity of the Whole Man. How then are we to find and define human happiness? The answer is not so difficult. Just as each organ of the body has its distinctive function, and measures its well-being, or "happiness," by the degree of excellence or "virtue" with which it exercises that function, so man's happiness will go hand in hand, primarily with the excellent or "virtuous" operation of his distinctive activity, which is reason, and secondarily with the harmonious exercise of the other activities of his composite and complicated nature. In short the "human good turns out to be activity of the soul in accordance with virtue, and, if there be more than one virtue, in accordance with the best and most complete." [7] Moreover, for that best and most complete operation of our total human nature, in which human happiness lies, not only is completeness of life necessary, but certain external conditions like friends, money, children, good birth and good looks are highly conducive, if not absolutely indispensable. "For it is impossible, or not easy to do noble acts without proper equipment." [8]

Again, the excellent, or happy, functioning of the human organism presupposes on its intellectual side education and enlightenment, and on its ethical side the inculcation of habits, or rather, the actualization of potentialities already present within us. Moral principles are neither inborn, as Socrates and Plato maintained, nor artificial and conventional as the Sophists taught. They are *developed*. The aim of education and of the inculcation of habits is to make virtuous functioning as nearly spontaneous as possible.

The Golden Mean. But what is the mark of excellent or "virtuous" activity? How are we to know whether or not we are on the road to happiness? The test of excellence and the guarantee of happiness are to be found, Aristotle replies, in the *degree* to which activities are

[7] *Eth. Nic.,* I, 7, 1097 *b,* ff.
[8] *Ibid.,* 8, 1099 *a,* ff.

exercised. Activity is *virtuous* when it is exercised neither insufficiently nor excessively, but in moderation. Over-indulgence and over-suppression of any activity are both *vicious*. Right conduct is just enough, wrong conduct is too much or too little, of a given function. This is the famous Aristotelian doctrine of virtue as the "golden mean"—a doctrine characteristic of the Greek passion for balance and reasonableness already set forth by the poets Theognis and Pindar in the phrase "nothing in excess," and expressed philosophically and politically by the Pythagoreans and Plato.

The mean, however, is not absolute but relative, differing as it must with respect to the individual and to the object, time, place, and circumstances of the action. Indeed, it takes great intelligence and great excellence to hit it exactly. But the confines of morally satisfactory behavior are spacious and flexible enough to allow for a certain amount of swing in one direction or the other. In determining the amount of permissible deviation, experience and good taste are important factors. Experience also shows us that on the whole it is preferable to swing towards underdoing rather than towards overdoing. It should be noted that there is no opposition here of intrinsically higher to intrinsically lower activities. All the functions with which ethics is concerned are in themselves morally neutral. Their goodness or badness, or in other words, their bearing upon human happiness, is wholly determined by the *degree* of their exercise. Precisely the same function is virtuous in moderation as is vicious in excess or defect.

Illustrations of the Golden Mean. This doctrine of virtue as the golden mean is illustrated by Aristotle at length. He arranges a long list of moral qualities in triads of virtuous means between vicious extremes. For example, courage is the right or mean amount of the same activity as in deficiency constitutes cowardice, in excess, rashness. Temperance is a moderate love and pursuit of the physical pleasures; insensibility is too little interest in them, and self-indulgence or sensuality, too great a one. Liberality is the golden mean between stinginess and prodigality; magnificence, between ostentatious and niggardly living; greatness of soul, between humility and vainglory; and so the list goes. Acts like theft, adultery, murder, and the like, and emotions like shamelessness, envy, and spite, Aristotle deals with by pointing out that they are in themselves already either excesses or defects, and therefore cannot exist in moderation.

The virtue of justice is important in that it links moral with legal considerations and also introduces into ethics the question of the *intention* with which an act is committed. It deals with rewards and punishments and with the fair treatment of one individual by another. The accommodation of justice to the particular case is notoriously difficult, and gives rise to the distinction between justice and equity. Equity lies in being scrupulously fair even when considerations of legal justice do not force you to be so.

Voluntary Action and Moral Freedom. In last resort, however, both the moral and the legal justice or injustice of an act, or, in other words, the propriety of its social and legal reward or punishment, are determined by the *intention* with which it is committed. An act committed under compulsion or because of ignorance is neither praiseworthy nor reprehensible. To be one or the other it must be *voluntary;* that is, it must have its "moving principle" wholly within the agent himself. No man can be held morally responsible for an act which he is compelled to perform by an external force and contrary to his own inclination. At the same time, no man can claim exemption from responsibility for acts committed on the spur of the moment or from considerations of pleasure and pain. For such acts arise from within himself, and nothing could be more "voluntary" and "free" than the drive of the organism toward the ends imposed upon it by its own nature. As long as one is self-determined, one is free and responsible.

Still, the situation is complex. Is a drunken person free? Is a man acting under terror of a threat free? Is a man free who sacrifices his own honor in order to save those dear to him? We have, as Aristotle realizes, and as morality and the law have always recognized, a vast area of borderline cases, where the voluntary and the involuntary are hopelessly entangled.

The same is true of acts committed ignorantly. They are not voluntary, but neither are they involuntary unless afterwards we feel remorse. Again, we must distinguish acts committed *in* ignorance from those done *from* ignorance. When drunk, for instance, we act *in* ignorance of the consequences of our behavior. But we do not act *from* ignorance of them, since drunkenness, not ignorance, is the reason for our behavior. Acts done *from* ignorance are usually involuntary and excusable, whereas acts done *in* ignorance frequently are not. However, to act *from* ignorance of general moral principles does not excuse the evil-doer whose eyes are open to the consequences of his particular deed. It is only acts resulting *from* ignorance of *particular* results that can be considered *involuntary*.

Intention, Preference, and Choice. *Intention,* or the self-determination of the moving principle within us to a particular course of action when faced with a particular set of circumstances, involves *preference* and results in *choice*. These are narrower in their scope than volition or appetite (which we find also in inconsequential and impulsive acts), and than wishing and opining (which concern themselves not only with the practicable but with the impossible and the inevitable). Nor have they to do with the ends of action (which, after all, are prescribed for us by our nature and are stated by our wishes) but rather with the means to those ends. Then, too, choice involves weighing and deliberating. In short, it may be defined as "deliberate desire of things in our power."

Since that is the case, obviously the Cynic contention that virtue is the good, is exercised for its own sake, and is its own reward, will not stand. On the contrary, "the exercise of virtue is concerned with means" to the good. Moreover, this good rests not upon a moral foundation but upon a natural one. Nature has made us the kind of beings we are, has molded us in the human form and no other, and has outfitted us with the wishes, aspirations, and ideals appropriate to our particular structure. We can no more help wishing to be healthy and happy, to eat, to procreate, to think, to live socially and rationally, than we can help being human beings. There is nothing to be ashamed or proud of in this, no virtue and no vice, no occasion for praising or blaming either nature or ourselves. Moral conduct begins and ends in the measures we take to realize our natural ends, and these measures are virtuous or vicious, right or wrong, solely as they are calculated to ensure or to defeat the attainment of these ends. Far, then, from moral standards determining what we *ought* to aim at, what we naturally *do* aim at determines moral standards.

At the same time, Aristotle avoids the Protagorean and morally anarchistic implications that might be drawn from this position. Each man is not a law unto himself, justified in taking himself as he finds himself and in pursuing his ends, whatever they may happen to be. For all men are *human* and actualize the same Form. In disclosing to us the outline of this form, observation of human nature also discloses the approximate limits of a "natural object of wish," revealed to us in the wishes and ends of the run of healthy, typical individuals. It allows for some latitude, to be sure, but where the variation of individual wishes goes beyond the limit, we are dealing with warped instances of the species, whose ends are no longer *human,* and therefore are not properly held or pursued by *human* beings. Although, then, the wishes and ideals of every individual man *seem* good to *him,* whether they really *are* good depends upon their agreement with the "natural object of wish" of mankind in general. In short, it is not the individual but the species that determines the *natural* good of the individual belonging to that species.

Moral Responsibility. We turn now to the question of moral responsibility. Since our choices are determined in last resort by the moving principle within us, we are responsible for them and for their success or failure in hitting the golden mean. Evil-doing, then, is not involuntary, as Socrates thought. It is just as voluntary as virtue is, since we are as much the "moving principle" of our bad acts as we are of our good ones. If vice is involuntary, so is virtue, and deserves praise as little as vice deserves blame. Nor can we plead ignorance as an excuse, since for the most part it is avoidable. We are not forced by any power outside ourselves to be careless or unacquainted with the law, or to fly into such a passion or get so drunk that we do not know what we are doing. We possess the "power of taking care," and it is not our misfortune but our fault if, by a failure to exercise that power, we allow ourselves to be blinded temporarily or permanently to the consequences of our acts.

Nay more, the individual is not only responsible for pursuing his ends. He is also partially responsible, at least, for *having* them. He can be morally censured even for *wishing* the things he wishes. To be sure, to good and bad alike "the end appears and is fixed by nature." Nevertheless, one's nature is to some degree a matter of training, and the "natural object of wish" can be inculcated, if a man takes himself in hand before his character has become set. Although then "the end appears to each man in a form answering to his character," still he, "being somehow responsible for his state of mind . . . will also be somehow responsible for the end appearing to him as it does." [9] Indeed, if we had no right to reprove a vicious man for his low ideals, the virtuous man would deserve no credit for his high ones. And in any case, even if a man's propensities were thrust upon him, as physical beauty or deformity are, he could still be held to account for acting or not acting in accordance with them, since, at any rate, that power would be his.

Moral Virtue Based on Intellectual Excellence. Selecting the golden mean involves deliberation, as we have seen, and deliberation brings intelligence into play. Thus we pass from moral virtue, or excellence of conduct, to intellectual virtue, or correctness of understanding, from which alone right behavior can proceed. [10] The function of rea-

---

[9] *Eth. Nic.,* III, 5, 1114 *a,* 31-1114 *b,* 3. (I have slightly expanded the Ross translation.)

[10] For the "intellectual virtues," cf. *Eth. Nic.,* VI.

son in the moral life is twofold; first to discover the natural aims of the human organism and then to devise the best means for realizing them. When the intellect meditates upon human nature and understands *what* will make us happy, it is exercising in the sphere of ethics its essential "philosophizing," scientific, *contemplative* activity of grasping the truth. When it is calculating *how* to attain what will make us happy, it displays itself as *practical reason* which is the basis and guide of distinctively moral *action*. Indeed, morality in last resort is nothing but *intelligent conduct*—conduct that flows logically, and even after the fashion of the syllogism, from the assumption a correct understanding of the human organism permits us to make with respect to the nature of the human good. Rightly directed, desire must pursue just what reasoning asserts. Conversely, individual departures from the "natural object of wish," and ill-chosen means to its attainment, are due to the "being untrue," or the false understanding, in which intellectual vice consists. The virtue and vice of both contemplative and practical reason are identical. Morally virtuous behavior is reasonable conduct; morally vicious behavior is a symptom of irrationality.

Hence Socrates, Aristotle feels, was both right and wrong in his assertion that the virtues are one, and that the one virtue is knowledge. There are as many different virtues as there are human activities, no one of which (except reason) can pretend to have knowledge of itself. But the moral attitude is the same towards every activity and does consist in *knowing* the golden mean in each.

Incontinence and Vice. Again, Socrates is wrong in supposing that right action must necessarily follow from correct knowledge of the end to be pursued and of the means to its attainment. He failed to reckon with *incontinence,* as Aristotle calls it, which is the habitual and deliberate flouting by desire of the knowledge of good and evil.[11] Such flouting, however, is not a mere triumph of passion over clear knowledge and of sheer irrationality over the moral logic of practical reason. That logic, being moral and therefore infected with desire, suffers from a defect peculiar to itself. Desire has an argument of its own, with which it stifles the counsels of prudence. In the first place, it opposes the certain major premise of practical reason, that acts of a given sort are bad for us, with the equally certain major premise that they are acts we *want* to do. So far honors are equal. But when it comes to the minor premise, desire may hold the winning hand. For the minor premise of practical reason, that the particular act under contemplation is of the bad sort, admits of uncertainty and engenders

[11] Incontinence is discussed in *Eth. Nic.,* VII, 1-10.

doubt and hesitation, because our knowledge of particulars is never exact and complete; whereas there can be no uncertainty about the minor premise of desire, that the act in question belongs among the acts I *want* to do. The minor premise of desire, then, may be stronger logically than that of reason and give rise to the stronger syllogism. In other words, the fact that we *want* to do the thing may carry more weight with us than does our hesitation as to whether the thing is to our advantage in the long run. In that case, the morally unsound conclusion is logically bound to be drawn.

The out-and-out vicious man, however, differs from the merely incontinent individual in feeling no hesitation in the minor premise of his calculation. He feels with equal certainty both that he wants to commit the evil deed and that it is to his advantage to do so. Such a man is incurable. But the incontinent person may be cured of his hesitancy and may be established in the habit of refusing on rational grounds to give way to wants whose morality is questionable. Unless this hesitancy is overcome, the incontinent attitude becomes habitual and hardens into criminality.

Friendly Association. So far Aristotle has been studying morality "in that form which is concerned with a man himself—with the individual." But he is also insistent that the individual is by nature a "political animal" to whom social and political life and organization are instinctive and essential. The social side of morality, its bases and developments, he discusses in Books VIII and IX of the *Nicomachean Ethics,* which deal with friendship, and in the *Politics.* Friendly association, he points out, is necessary to the welfare of the individual and indispensable to the development of many of his virtues. There are three types of such association, according as they exist for the purpose of pleasure, utility, or the permanent enrichment of the individual's character and life. The first two types are selfish, treat other people as means to enjoyment or profit, and establish only passing relationships. But the parties to the third type, "the friendship of the good," as Aristotle calls it, treat one another as ends and seek to give as much as they receive. Their friendship for one another is disinterested and is aroused by intrinsic excellence.

Identity of Self-Love and Love of Others. However, even this sort of friendship is a kind of self-love. For, "men love what is good for themselves; for the good man in becoming a friend becomes a good to his friend. Each then loves what is good for himself," and regards his friends as a sort of extension of himself. Still, there is nothing "selfish," in the bad sense of the word, about such self-love. For the object of one's affection, as in the case of a child or a brother, is identified with one's self not as a mere plaything or possession, but as "a sort of other self," leading "a separate existence." Moreover, "friendship of the good" would "seem to lie in loving rather than in being loved." From self-love of this sort the opposition between egoism and altruism has disappeared. The self a man loves is the wider, social self. It is only when the self is identified with "wealth, honor, and bodily pleasures," rather than with our friends, and is cultivated at other people's expense, that self-love becomes a term of reproach. The good man is willing to lay down wealth, honor, position, the opportunity to do noble deeds and win renown, nay life itself, for the sake of his friends and his country; realizing, as he does, that it is the quality rather than the quantity of life that counts, and preferring "a twelve month of noble life to many years of humdrum existence, and one great and noble action to many trivial ones." In the case, then, of men actuated by the "friendship of the good" there is no sense in raising the question "whether a man should love himself most or someone else." [12]

III. POLITICS

The Family and the State. In the *Politics,* which is a compilation of different treatises rather than an organic whole, Aristotle discusses the two great institutions, the family and the state, produced by the instinctively social nature of man. The family is the primitive human unit and owes its existence to the sexual nature of human reproduction. It quickly expands so as to include slaves and property—both of which institutions are as natural and as imbedded in the constitution of the universe as the distinction of sex itself. Nature has created man an acquisitive animal, and has established different degrees of ability in human beings that mark out some for masters, some for slaves. Fundamentally, however, slavery is a matter of character rather than of legal institution, and the institution is wrong when it runs counter to natural distinctions and makes slaves of those whom nature has created worthy of a higher position.

Property arises out of the natural propensity of the human animal to hunt, fish, till the soil, and lay up sustenance for himself. This is the root of the whole economic system with its trade, its medium of exchange, its banking and lending. As long as the economic system, like slavery, follows the lines indicated by nature, it is unobjectionable.

[12] On friendship as self-love, cf. *Eth. Nic.,* IX, 8.

But wealth regarded as an end in itself and many of the means of procuring wealth are unnatural and to be deplored. One of the means which Aristotle particularly condemns is putting money out at interest.

From the union of several families springs the village, and "when several villages are united in a single complete community large enough to be nearly or quite self-sufficing, the state comes into existence, originating in the bare needs of life, and continuing in existence for the sake of the good life." Since "the earlier forms of society are natural . . . it is evident that the state is a creation of nature and that man is by nature a political animal." Nay more, since man is naturally a political animal and dependent upon the state both for his individual and family life, "the state is by nature prior [logically] to the family and the individual." [13]

Criticism of Plato's Social Theory. In his theory of the state as in his ethics, Aristotle apparently began as a good Platonist. In the *Protrepticus,* for example, he urges the statesman to look, in framing a constitution, not to existing human institutions but to the divine and enduring ideal of what a perfect state should be. And in the earlier portions of the *Politics* we find him engaged, like Plato, in depicting the ideal commonwealth. But his Utopia sharply differs from Plato's, which he subjects to a searching criticism. He particularly attacks the rigidity and unity of the Platonic republic and the confinement of the exercise of government to a closed corporation like the guardians. He favors rather the greatest degree of flexibility, division of labor, and variety of interest consistent with social stability, and the rotation of all the citizens in positions of authority. Against Plato's scheme for communizing property, women, and children he urges as a fundamental objection that the individual himself can never be communized and freed from the distinction between mine and thine. Public interest, then, must always rest upon private interest, and public spirit must consist in freely placing at the service of the community something that the individual instinctively considers his own. For the state deliberately to deprive the individual of what he regards as *his* is to create an artificial opposition between private and public interest, and to make a forced sacrifice of what should be a free gift. It can only embitter his natural propensity to share his own with his fellows, and thus poison the impulse from which society springs. "It is clearly better," then, "that property should be private but the use of it common; and the special business of the legislator is to create in men this

[13] *Pol.,* I, 2.

benevolent disposition."[14] Furthermore, it is always better to have an eye upon past history and actual conditions in planning one's reforms.

The Test of a Good State. The test of a good state is its service of the common interest in accordance with strict principles of justice. Such service may exist under the conditions of kingship, aristocracy, or constitutional democracy; and ceases equally to exist under tyranny, plutocratic oligarchy, or an unbridled democracy in which the poor and the lower classes are favored at the expense of the common interest. One thing, however, is certain—whatever the form of government, it must be constitutional. Law must be supreme.

Under ideal conditions, the public interest would be perhaps best served by an enlightened absolute monarch. By virtue of his isolated and unpartisan position he would be well fitted to frame and administer the laws, and to mitigate their inflexibility, which is the great vice of legal enactments, by modifying their application to suit individual cases. At the same time, under actual conditions absolute monarchy has its disadvantages. It is too apt to degenerate into tyranny; the load it puts upon the shoulders of one man is too great, and the delegation of power to others leads to the abandonment in fact, if not in theory, of the advantages and principle of a single absolute ruler.

All in all, what shall be the best form of government depends upon the temperament of the people. A highly civilized race "superior in the virtue needed for political rule is fitted for kingly government." But aristocracy is better adapted for a race that lays stress upon freedom and at the same time produces a class of superior individuals. Constitutional democracy best suits the needs of a warlike community in which discipline universally prevails, and which is accustomed to rotation of command.

But in any case, whatever constitution it may adopt, that form of government is best in which every man, whoever he is, can act best and live happily. The test of ideal government is not its particular organization, but the results of that organization in promoting the welfare and happiness, not of any one class, but of all classes. There is nothing to the objection that government of any and every sort interferes with the liberty and self-development of the individual. This may be true of tyranny, be it the tyranny of a king, an oligarchy, or a democracy. But constitutional government does not suppress but rather expresses the political nature of man, engages rather than im-

[14] *Pol.*, II, 4-5.

pedes his practical and moral activities, and is an aid rather than a detriment to the rational life and the contemplation of truth. Nor will such a government interfere with those individual values and activities that are private, cannot be communized, and are exercised in isolation.

Physical Circumstances of the Ideal State. Aristotle now turns his attention to the physical circumstances of an ideal state. It must not be larger than the conditions of a prosperous and happy life demand and permit. "A great city is not to be confounded with a populous one." Size breeds disorder and ugliness. The ideal state must, however, be able to produce everything its citizens need, and be easy of defense. It should be near the sea, in order to facilitate trade. Its site must be healthy and include an abundant supply of pure water. Its streets should be laid out in rectangular fashion and with an eye to beauty. The territories of the state should be so divided among the freemen that each has a country as well as a town estate. In this way the opposition of rural to urban interests is avoided in times of peace, and all are equally exposed to the hazards of war.[15]

Citizenship will be denied to merchants and tradesmen, since "their life is ignoble and inimical to virtue," and to husbandmen because they lack the leisure that "is necessary both for the development of virtue and the performance of political virtue." As far as possible these functions will be performed by slaves—who must be kindly treated and should be encouraged to work by the hope of gaining their freedom.

Education in the Ideal State. The freemen, themselves, should live as communal a life as possible. In the absence of the impracticable ideal of an absolute monarchy, "all the citizens alike should take their turn of governing and being governed." But if democracy, also, is not to be impracticable, a sound system of education must be established, calculated to train all citizens both to rule and to obey. This system must be realistic and based upon a knowledge of the kind of animal man is in general, and of the "diversities of human lives and actions."[16]

Education will begin before birth by the practice of eugenics and birth control, supplemented by the destruction at birth of deformed children. The development both of body and of mind must begin at birth. Both the physical and the mental diet of the child must be carefully supervised. At seven he will go to school, where he will learn

[15] *Pol.,* VII, 4-6.
[16] *Pol.,* VII, 10.

reading and writing and arithmetic and gymnastic and "music" (in the Greek sense of the word). To the objection that "music" is not "practical," Aristotle replies that the end of education is not so much to fit a man for a vocation as to teach him to value leisure and make it conduce to his welfare and happiness. To place the accent of education upon professional training is the mark of an illiberal mind. "To be always seeking after the useful does not become free and exalted souls." For "leisure itself gives pleasure and happiness and enjoyment of life, which are experienced not by the busy man but by those who have leisure." There is then "a sort of education in which parents should train their sons, not as being useful or necessary, but because it is liberal or noble." [17]

The Best Government and Revolution. Aristotle's description of the ideal commonwealth here breaks off abruptly. Apparently either the rest of it is lost, or he left it unfinished. In any case, his earlier interest in ideal states was short-lived, for the portions of the *Politics* presumably written after his return to Athens are quite non-utopian. His concern is now with the best practicable form of government, and this he finds in "polity"—a happy mean between oligarchy and democracy, in which the bearing of arms and the franchise is restricted to property-owners, and a large, prosperous middle class holds the balance of power between the upper class and the proletariat. And he lays down a few rules of political hygiene. The spirit of obedience to law should be inculcated. The authorities should be men of ability, integrity, and loyalty to the established constitution. They should be fair to and considerate of the governed, and should be quick to discern and reward superior talent. Above all, every state should be so administered and so regulated by law that its magistrates cannot possibly make money. For rich and poor alike are irritated at the thought that they are being bled by grafters.

Yet, even so, these better forms of government are threatened by revolution, which is the bane of all states, good or bad. Its causes are manifold and its occasions often trivial. No matter how well governed a state may be, there is always a tendency of the many to resent the dominance of the few. Each political type has its special precautions to take. The king should avoid despotic ways and, still more, despotic airs, and should welcome and observe constitutional restrictions upon his authority, if he wishes to avoid revolution and preserve the monarchy. Aristocracies should be on their guard against plutocracy and

[17] *Pol.*, VII, 17; VIII, 3.

the oligarchic substitution of the welfare of a special class for the public weal. The bane of constitutional democracy lies in too little leisure for politics among the upper classes or too much leisure among the lower. Democracy, for all its theory of equality, the rule of the people, and government by the will of the majority, can only work if the more able have the time and are given the opportunity to direct affairs. This may happen sometimes in simple, contented agricultural or pastoral communities, where there is little political ambition or corruption, and the people are willing to leave the actual administration of the state to an upper, leisured class. But if the upper as well as the lower classes are immersed in business, as is the case in industrial and commercial communities, the constitution is apt to be allowed to take care of itself, and, though plenty of laws may be passed, little heed is paid their administration and application to special cases.

Dangers of Unbridled Democracy. Still, this is far less dangerous than the presence of so much leisure among the lower classes that they acquire the taste and have the time to occupy themselves overmuch with legislation. In that case the "people," not the constitution, "becomes the monarch," and "demagogues make the decrees of the people override the laws, by referring all things to the popular assembly." The result is a tyrannical rule of the majority. For "the decrees of the *demos* correspond to the edicts of the tyrant; and the demagogue is to the one what the flatterer is to the other." Such a state is ripe for revolution, either by rebellion of the oppressed classes against the oppressing masses, or by the assumption of despotic power by some demagogue.

These warnings, however, are, as Aristotle recognizes, counsels of perfection. All governments tend to degenerate towards the substitution of private for public interest, class—or mass—domination, and the tyranny of a part over the whole. Yet, even so, the resultant, diseased political types may succeed in preserving themselves by exercising certain precautions. Democracies, even if unrestrained by constitutions and governed by the whim of majorities, will do well not to attack the eminent, or to confiscate the property or the incomes of the rich. Nor should they embark on a policy of doles and compensations to the poor. "Such help is like water poured into a leaky cask," since "the poor are always receiving and wanting more and more." The rich can do their part in averting the development of these dangers by being generous and wise and using their surplus wealth in providing employment for the poor by setting them up to little farms and helping them "make a beginning in trade or husbandry."

Oligarchies and Tyrants. Oligarchy may get on well enough if it avoids lawlessness, sees that the citizens exceed in strength the non-citizens, makes the higher offices too expensive for the ordinary man, and keeps the people amused by magnificent spectacles and soothed by splendid public donations of one sort or another that may serve as "memorials of its munificence." It would be well advised also to train and maintain a strongly armed force, preferably of cavalry, since "this service is better suited to the rich than to the poor." Above all, it should avoid recruiting troops from the masses, since such a force is apt to prove a boomerang.

To tyranny, which combines all the vices of oligarchy and democracy, two courses are open. On the one hand a despot may play the heavy tyrant, cutting off the heads of all men of spirit; prohibiting clubs, assemblies, education, and discussion; establishing a system of espionage; encouraging private and clan jealousies; impoverishing his subjects, and keeping them hard at work; and, if need be, indulging in a foreign war, in order to rally them about himself as their leader. On the other hand, he may hide the mailed fist within the velvet glove by clinging to the appearance of constitutional government and affecting financial honesty. He should also defer, outwardly, to religion and morality, refrain from outraging or insulting his subjects, and flatter the upper classes into contentment with his rule. His punishments should seem to come, not from him, but legally through the courts of justice. And above all he should give the impression of being a great military leader. Tyranny and oligarchy, however, are in their very nature the weakest kinds of government and the most liable to revolution.[18]

The Art of Oratory. In his *Rhetoric* Aristotle discusses the art of oratory, so important to the would-be successful politician or litigant in the law-courts. Success in winning a case or promoting a cause, be it good or bad, is the only measure of a telling speech. Since oratorical flights are not necessary in matters that are self-evident, and since their object is to make the merely probable and dubious seem absolutely certain and convincing, their appeal is primarily to the emotions rather than to the reason. Indeed, the test of a good orator is his ability to arouse the prejudices of his audience and to enlist them on his side. In accomplishing this the sentimentalities and moral aversions and convictions of his hearers are the orator's best friends, and by skillfully stringing together platitudes and maxims that reflect their

[18] On causes of, and prophylactics against, revolution, cf. *Rhet.*, I, 8; *Pol.*, V.

outlook on life he can win for himself the reputation of being "a man of sound moral character," and hence a sound thinker, and can give to his discourse a counterfeit logic and make those to whom he is speaking exclaim, "How true!" This assumption of a high moral purpose is far more important than any display of intelligence. The latter shows only horse sense, but a high moral tone suggests that the speaker has a noble nature—a suggestion that carries all the more weight, the less intelligent and more subject to emotional appeal the audience itself is.

The oration itself has two parts. "You must state your case and prove it." You should begin with an impassioned exhortation of some sort or other, which need have "nothing to do with the speech itself," but appeals to "the weak-minded tendency of the hearer to listen to what is beside the point." Then you state your case in such a way as to create an impression favorable to yourself and derogatory to your opponent. Here the "moral purpose" comes in handy. Proof is really not necessary. So-called argument will consist in discrediting your adversary and his proposals on emotional and moral grounds. And if you happen by chance to be reasoning, you should, if logic falters and good reasons fail, "fall back upon moral discourse" in the place of "argument." There should follow an epilogue, whose business is to fan to fever heat all the emotions and prejudices you have created.

Rules of Style. Naturally, political, legal, and ceremonial speeches will employ different means and be couched in different styles. The pleader in the law-courts, for example, must be expert in handling evidence, minimizing or exaggerating the importance of the witnesses' testimony, and suggesting perjury in his opponents and incorruptible honesty in himself. And the politician must know his subject, in order to represent or misrepresent it to his own advantage, and must be able to gauge and to sway the temper of the assembly.

So far as style is concerned, all orations should be clear, appropriate, natural, and suited to the kind of subject under discussion and the kind of people addressed. The speaker's periods should be well-rounded, but should avoid poetical rhythms. They should be short and compact, vivid and sparkling, and interspersed with epigrams and elements of surprise to capture and to hold the listeners' attention.

IV. THEORY OF THE FINE ARTS

Art an Imitation of Nature. Save for a short but important passage in the *Politics,* our knowledge of Aristotle's views about art is drawn almost entirely from his *Poetics,* the first book of which, dealing with tragedy, has alone come down to us. His theory, as we shall see in a moment, is quite different from Plato's. All the fine arts, he tells us, in their several ways are essentially imitations of nature. The imitative character of art is deeply rooted in human psychology. Man is an imitative animal, and not only are his senses pleased but his intellect is stimulated by the act of imitation. This is true, even if the subject imitated be in other respects painful. Music, dancing, declaiming, singing, poetry, etc., express also man's native love of harmony and rhythm.

Art a Divination of the Universal in the Particular. Artistic imitation is not, however, as Plato maintained, of the sensible and the particular. Its medium, to be sure, is sensuous stuff, and its works are sensible objects. But it is a divination of what is universal and eternal in the particular—of what nature is trying, as it were, to say—and a work of art expresses in sensible terms the ideal after which she is striving.

Art and Esthetic Pleasure. Again, the business of art is not, as Plato taught, to edify and teach a moral lesson. Its justification does not lie outside itself. Its purpose is to give pleasure, and in proportion as it gives esthetic enjoyment it is good art. For that matter, to demand that art should always "teach a lesson" by exhibiting, for example, vice always punished and virtue triumphant, is the mark of a second-rate audience. To the enlightened and cultivated man endings that are invariably happy and moral appear ridiculous and titillate only his comic sense.

Again, it is the function of art to excite pleasurably the passions and the emotions; for such excitement, instead of harming the soul as Plato thought, purges, lightens, delights, and heals it. Finally, art is not under even an esthetic obligation to give us enjoyment of the "higher" sort. The greatest art, to be sure, stimulates us and makes us think. But man needs recreation as well as serious endeavor, and, if he is to exercise his faculties at their best, he must have intervals of amusements and relaxation. It is the function of the lighter works of art to provide such intervals—nor are they less desirable because they are light. The lower classes, too, who are as a rule incapable of appreciating art of the more serious sort, are entitled to the less serious forms in which they can find entertainment and repose. It is better that they should enjoy art of some kind than be cut off altogether from esthetic pleasure.

Good and Bad Art. The "higher" and the "lower" in art, then, have little to do with morality. They are essentially matters of esthetics. This even is true of the choice of a subject-matter. To be sure, the subject must not be one that so outrages us in other respects as to prevent our enjoying it esthetically. But idealistic art does not lie in selecting and depicting morally superior subjects. It lies in choosing subjects, not necessarily ideal or desirable from the moral point of view, that can be manipulated so as to produce the most esthetic pleasure, and in bringing out their dramatic and artistic values. If moral goodness is chosen, then that goodness must be made esthetically interesting before art itself can be called good. Otherwise, it is photographic and mediocre, however "moral" its material. In the same way, "low" art lies not so much in choosing a morally "low" subject as in failing to bring out the highest *esthetic* values of one's material, whatever that material may be. A good example of "low" art is caricature. Nevertheless, such distortion of material in the interests of ridicule and laughter is quite permissible, as long as it does not cause pain or harm. Indeed, art of this sort, so far as it affords amusement, is good art of the lighter type.

The same tendency to free art from moralistic supervision is suggested by Aristotle's insistence that no one-sided person of narrow interests and outlook, even though it be the artist himself, is competent to judge of the all-round goodness or badness of a work of art. It is not for the maker but for the user of the rudder to estimate its real worth; not for the cook but for the *bon viveur* to say whether the dinner is excellent or poor. In like manner the test of fine art lies in the effect it makes, not upon the esthete or the puritan, but upon the "free and educated audience," composed of the "better public." It is in the enjoyment or displeasure a work of art produces in this "free and educated audience" that the only proper ground of approbation or censure lies.[19]

Expurgation of the Classics Ill-Advised. Judged by these standards, an expurgation of the classics in the interest of morality is, Aristotle apparently feels, hasty and misguided. The stories of the gods and heroes that shock the moral sense "may," he remarks, "be as wrong as Xenophanes says, neither true nor the better thing to say; but they are certainly in accord with opinion." [20] They are suitable material for the artist, and in spite of their ethical inferiority may be idealized

[19] On the freeing of art from moralistic standards and supervision, cf. Butcher, *Aristotle's Theory of Poetry and Fine Art*, pp. 215 ff.

[20] *Poetics*, 25, 1460 *b*, 36 ff.

and ennobled by artistic treatment, as they stand. Generally speaking, too, before we accuse an artist, or at least a writer, of immoral art, we should consider the objectionable passage, or scene, not in isolation, but in its relations to the plot as a whole and the total dramatic effect. Moral objections are only too often hasty and unintelligent as literary criticism.

At the same time, Aristotle insists that the artist is justified in depicting moral evil only when it contributes to the dramatic value of his work, and even then should confine it to minor roles and incidents. There is no excuse for portraying "depravity of character where it is not necessary and no use is made of it." Some critics, indeed, have maintained that he would have condemned on these grounds the Satan of *Paradise Lost,* and Macbeth.

The Nature of Tragedy. Turning now to poetry, Aristotle tells us that its subject is human character and action considered in their universal aspects. It is therefore the greatest of all the fine arts. In tragedy it finds its highest expression. Tragedy, using song and dance as accessories, sets forth in dramatic, not narrative, form some "serious" and complete human episode, accomplished preferably "within a single circuit of the sun"; and so presents it as to arouse the emotions of pity and fear upon which the sense of tragedy is based, and at the same time to purge them of their unpleasantness.

From the first part of this description flowed the famous doctrine of the "three unities" of plot, time, and place, which dominated, often with absurd results, many French and Italian playwrights of the sixteenth and seventeenth centuries. Aristotle, however, seems to have meant literally only the unity of plot, and to have advised restricting the episode to a single day and a single spot, partly because this practice was common, though not invariable, on the Greek stage, and partly as a warning against prolixity and disjointedness.

A good, unified plot must tell a complete and self-contained story. It must be selective, "with its several incidents so closely connected that the transposal or withdrawal of any one of them will disjoin and dislocate the whole." [21] It may embroider and alter the legendary or historical material from which the Greek tragedians habitually took their plots, but it must always be plausible. It must, however, select and manipulate its subject with an eye to extraordinary surprises and coincidences. Such incidents occurring "unexpectedly, and at the same time in consequence of one another," have "an appearance of design,"

[21] *Ibid.,* 8, 1451 *a,* 30 ff.

and seem to be "not without a meaning," which arouse wonder and awe in the spectator. And since the story as a whole is one that drives home the fickleness of fortune, the furtiveness of destiny, and the uncertainty of human life and happiness, it surcharges us with the pity and the terror that reflection upon our lot must inspire in every thoughtful man.

The Catharsis of the Emotions Effected by Tragedy. But, to be truly tragic rather than merely horrible, a plot must do more than bring these emotions to a head. It must relieve us of their painfulness; not by ridding us of them altogether, since that would destroy the sense of tragedy and render us simply callous, but by turning them into pleasurable experiences. This "catharsis" of the emotions, as Aristotle calls it, is effected by transferring them from our own predicament to the sufferings of the tragic hero. In him, to be sure, we see ourselves, and in his fate our possible doom, and we weep and shudder accordingly. But since his fate does not threaten us immediately, our tears and apprehension are shifted from ourselves to him. This transference from fact to fiction, and from our particular lot to universal human destiny, detaches us from ourselves, releases us from our individual burdens, and, momentarily at least, substitutes for self-pity and personal fear a nobler, all-embracing, impersonal sympathy and compassion. So it is that the depiction of great misfortunes and disasters can and does give *pleasure,* that we *enjoy* the tears we shed at the theater, that we come away saying we have seen a *good* play.

Nay more, this "purging" of pity and terror not only gives esthetic pleasure but raises us for the moment to a higher moral level. We leave the theater feeling the better ourselves for what we have seen. But the moral exaltation his work happens to produce in us is an accidental by-product, so far as the tragedian is concerned. His business is simply to turn the pitiful and the horrible into a thing of *beauty.* In so far as he deliberately aims at teaching us a lesson and improving our characters, he ceases to be an artist and becomes a preacher.

The Tragic Hero. To turn a normally painful situation into an esthetically pleasurable or, in other words, into a *beautiful* one, requires careful handling of the tragic hero. To begin with, he must be a person of eminence and in enjoyment of marked good fortune, if his fall is to be striking and truly tragic. The misfortunes, however pitiful, of an obscure or mediocre man are not sufficiently impressive to produce the desired effect. Again, the evils that befall the hero must not be due to pure mischance. Neither must they be the wages of sin pure and simple. The sufferings of the absolutely innocent, or the execution of an out-and-out criminal, are not tragic; they are merely odious. The hero must be neither too good nor too bad, and his misfortunes must appear "brought upon him not by vice or depravity, but by some error in judgment," due to inexcusable carelessness, or a fit of passion, or some other weak spot in an otherwise upright character. These requirements, critics have pointed out, are too strict from the modern point of view, since they would bar from tragedy the sufferings of a blameless character like Cordelia, or of an essentially evil one like Richard III, Macbeth, and Milton's Satan.

Again, to produce the best tragic effect, the downfall of the hero must be sudden and unlooked for, and accompanied, if possible, by an unforeseen "discovery" or "change from ignorance to knowledge, and thus to either love or hate, in the personages marked for good or evil fortune." At the same time, the *dénouement* must be logically approached by a series of incidents that are caused by one another and also expressive of and true to the psychology of the characters. The more intimately related the characters are, the more tragic the wrongs they do one another. For instance, parricide, matricide, and fratricide, either consciously or unconsciously committed, are especially good material for tragedy.

Needless to say, the tragedian must be a great poet and playwright. He must be a master of poetic diction "at once clear and not mean," and of meter and rhythm. And he must know how to choose and construct a plot, and how to weld both the dialogue and the choral songs and dances into a single compact whole.

Epic Poetry. The book ends with a brief discussion of epic poetry. Epic poetry differs from tragedy in not being adapted to stage presentation, in its different meter, and in its greater length. Otherwise its plot should follow the rules laid down for a good tragedy, displaying the same unity, and using much the same devices of catastrophe, surprise, discovery, heroic suffering, and the like. Its freedom from stage restrictions, its superior ability to make the improbable and even the impossible seem plausible, and its employment of the hexameter, give it certain advantages over tragedy. And yet tragedy is really the finer of the two. It is more unified and more concentrated, and the fact that it can be staged and embellished with a song and dance give it a vividness and poetic effect to which epic narration cannot attain. Hence it is the higher form of art.

The second book of the *Poetics,* in which Aristotle discussed comedy, is lost.

Chapter XV

THE HELLENISTIC WORLD. THE OLDER ACADEMY AND THE LYCEUM

I. THE HELLENISTIC WORLD

The Silver Age. Aristotle and Alexander the Great, dead almost within the same twelve months, were scarcely cold in their graves before the realms that each had subdued and consolidated were falling to pieces. The Empire, which for a tense moment had not only unified Greece and imposed Hellenic rule upon Asia Minor and Egypt, but had promised a synthesis of East and West in a new Alexandrian civilization, was partitioned by the kings and generals, and collapsed into a number of hostile kingdoms ever at war with one another. These, in their turn, gave way to the universal dominion of Rome. In the same way, the philosophic synthesis effected by the genius of Aristotle, who, no less than Alexander, might have wept because he too had no more worlds to conquer, dissolved and was replaced by a medley of lesser systems, which eventually disappeared before the triumphant onslaught of Christianity. Again, both the new politics and the new philosophies had this in common—both were cosmopolitan and eclectic, and in them different races and speculations mingled freely, interchanging and combining different customs and institutions, different points of view, moral, religious and philosophical. Both, moreover, though fecund in talent, were sterile in great genius. The men of gold were gone, and Hellenism had entered upon its silver age. The world was to wait three hundred years for Julius and Augustus Caesar, and nearly three hundred more for Plotinus—the one philosopher of high eminence in post-Aristotelian ancient philosophy.

It is well to dwell for a moment upon the great length of the period we are about to study. Otherwise, seeing it in the perspective of the distant past, and half-blinded to its true duration by the brief brilliance of the preceding epoch, we are likely to foreshorten it unduly.

Greek philosophy flowered and bore its ripest fruit in slightly less than three hundred years—within less time, that is, than separates us from the ascension of the Stuarts in England or the landing of the Pilgrims in America. But from 322 B.C., the year of Aristotle's death, till the closing of the schools of philosophy at Athens in 529 A.D., is a span of eight and a half centuries, which in retrospect takes us today back to the Norman Conquest. All these years philosophy lay dying, in contrast to its swift leap to its extraordinary prime.

Accumulation of Wealth. Though the epoch ushered in by the death of Alexander was of silver rather than gold, it was nevertheless lustrous. The loot of Persia and the exploitation of the new conquests had brought great wealth to Greece, produced a class of *nouveaux riches,* and established many large fortunes. Hence, in spite of the consequent depreciation of the value of money and the rise in the cost of living, which, to be sure, bore heavily upon the poor, the new world on the whole was rich. And within forty-five years of Alexander's death the partition of the Empire was complete, and the four great kingdoms of Macedonia, Syria, Egypt, and Pergamus had established a new political stability and equilibrium, and entered upon the path of power and prosperity.

Like their later "cousins," the Italian despots of the Renaissance, these new kings were great patrons of the arts, which now entered upon a second, though comparatively decadent, flowering. Sculpture produced the Victory of Samothrace, the Apollo Belvedere, the Venus of Melos, the Altar at Pergamus. Apelles, the court painter of Alexander, was followed by Protogenes of Rhodes, and by an outburst of portrait, *genre,* and allegorical painting. Statues and pictures now for the first time appeared in private houses as part of the rich and luxurious furnishing and interior decoration that the recent and rapid acquisition of wealth had made possible. Literature too did not lag behind, as Theophrastus with his *Characters* and Menander and the rise of the New Comedy testify. But art like philosophy had become imitative rather than creative, and looked to the past or to the foreigner for its inspiration.

Alexandria vs. Athens. Of the cities of the new epoch, Alexandria, founded by Alexander and made by Ptolemy the capital of Egypt, was perhaps the most brilliant. Embellished by the king and his successors, it rapidly became one of the most beautiful and luxurious cities of the age, and the foundation by Ptolemy II of the university and the museum, and of the library whose accidental burning by Julius

Caesar was a major disaster in the history of civilization, made of
it a center of learning and culture that vied with Athens, and indeed,
in scientific activity, surpassed her. For Athens, though her political
importance had disappeared, was still supreme as a seat of learning.
She had not only fulfilled the destiny of which Pericles had dreamed
—that she should be the school of Hellas; but she was and remained
the school of the whole Hellenistic world. To her students and scholars
flocked for education and for research, in spite of the rival charms of
Alexandria. Even after the Romans had pillaged her, they still looked
to her for light. And though philosophers might emigrate to the banks
of the Tiber, they still dwelt beneath the shadow of the Acropolis.

Post-Aristotelian Philosophies. An outstanding mark of the post-
Aristotelian systems is their tendency to become primarily guides to
human living and ways of human salvation rather than pursuits of
truth for its own sake. The reasons for this reversal are not far to
seek. All crystallized theologies and ethics arouse skepticism as well
as belief, and Greek theology and ethics were no exception to the rule.
Ionia and Magna Graecia, where European philosophy was born and
cradled, were free-thinking, and, as early as the time of Xenophanes,
the Olympian gods could be criticized and disavowed with impunity,
at least in Asia Minor and the Italian cities, and were evidently no
longer taken too literally by the philosophers. The Sophistic movement was frankly agnostic regarding the existence of the gods, and
had devastating implications for the traditional morality as well. Moreover, in spite of Athenian religious conservatism, the deities of religious orthodoxy were apparently none too seriously regarded by
Socrates, and had become poetry for Plato, and for Aristotle not even
that. So, too, the ethical reconstructions undertaken by these three
philosophers bears witness to the demoralization of traditional standards of conduct.

The Growth of Theological Skepticism. After Aristotle, certainly,
the growth of skepticism with regard to the religious and moral
orthodoxies of the past was irresistible, overwhelming first the educated and thence seeping down to the masses. Fifty years later,
Eudemus of Messene was suggesting for the consumption, not of the
few, but of the populace, that the gods had a human and historical
origin in forgotten kings and conquerors, the tradition of whose greatness lingered on in religious myths. And at an even earlier date the
Athenians had welcomed Demetrius Poliorcetes, King of Macedon,
with a song in which he was likened to "a true god, not one of wood

and stone" in contrast to "the other gods" who "are a long way off, or have no ears, or no existence, or take no care of us." [1]

But the failing hold of the Olympians upon the imagination and belief of antiquity did not mean a decay of religious and moral aspirations and needs. These needs and interests, choked and dried up in their orthodox channels, worked out new courses for themselves, first by invading the field of philosophy and later by mingling with the influx of oriental cults into Rome.

Philosophers in Politics. An interesting concomitant of this change in the temper of philosophy was the restoration of philosophers to political prestige. The Pre-Socratic thinkers, to be sure, had almost all been men who played prominent parts in the government of their cities. But Socrates and Plato had taught, the one in an open and eventually fatal hostility to the political conditions of his times, the other in a more theoretic and less active though in reality no less bitter antagonism to them. Aristotle, in spite of his exceptional opportunities, carefully kept out of politics, and developed his own theory of the state with objectivity and detachment. Now, however, as philosophy was invoked to do the work of religion, the philosopher was called upon to perform the offices of the priest. It was to him that people turned for consolation, advice and encouragement. He began to have his flock to whose spiritual needs he ministered. Even Alexander had had philosophic court chaplains in his train, to whom on one occasion he came to confess and to receive absolution after he had killed his friend Clitus in a fit of rage.

So it was that the philosopher began to assume once more a leading position in the political life of the community, and to be enlisted in the service of the state. Just as in former days Leontini had chosen the Sophist, Gorgias, to head the mission sent to beg help from the Athenians against Syracuse, so now we find heads of the Academy, like Xenocrates and Crates, chosen by the Athenians as special ambassadors to the court of Macedon, and later the presidents of the Academy, the Lyceum, and the more recently founded Stoa, despatched as envoys to Rome.

The re-entrance, however, of philosophers into political life exposed them once more to political vicissitudes. In fact, the Athenian democracy, under the measure of self-government granted it by Macedon, at one time forbade the existence of philosophic schools unless licensed by the Assembly, and went so far as to banish the Peripatetics. But

[1] Ferguson, *Greek Imperialism*, p. 143.

the city suffered so severely from the loss of the money ordinarily spent in the town by the students that the law had to be repealed and the philosophers restored. Thereafter, till the final closing of the Schools, no successful attempt was made to interfere with their freedom of thought and speech.

Appeal of Philosophy to the Masses. The rise of the philosophers and their assumption of a priestly role also gave them a larger and more diversified audience. Their appeal to the masses was perhaps due in part to the more popular character of their teachings. The moral support and religious consolation they served up was not fresh and deepcut, like the ethics of Plato and Aristotle, but warmed-over; and, at that, a re-hash not of Platonic or Aristotelian strong meat but rather of the more easily digested ethics of the Cynics and the Cyrenaics. These, again, were fortified and flavored for popular consumption with the simpler and more easily understood portions of the metaphysics of Heraclitus and Democritus. Perhaps, too, the flavorless quality of the immediate followers of both Plato and Aristotle and of their presentation of their masters' doctrines had something to do with the failure of the two great philosophers to become the leaders of the new age. In any case, it is a fact that they both suffered immediate and almost total eclipse, for the moment, as soon as they were dead. Upon their eclipse we shall do well to meditate a moment before taking up the more positive aspects of post-Aristotelian philosophy.

II. THE OLDER ACADEMY

Upon Plato's death the leadership of the Academy fell to his pupil and nephew, Speusippus, not because of the latter's philosophic merits but because he was the natural heir to Plato's considerable estate. It was, we may recall, his succession that led to Aristotle's withdrawal from the Academy and to the foundation of the Lyceum.

Speusippus and Xenocrates. Both Speusippus and the next head of the Academy, Xenocrates, were, like Aristotle, primarily concerned with bridging the gulf left, in their opinion, by Plato between the intelligible and the sensible worlds. Plato himself, it will be remembered, had had misgivings on this score, and had tried to bring the Forms and the sensible world into communication by using soul as a stop-gap. For this single span both Speusippus and Xenocrates substituted several arches, some of which extended back into the intelligible world itself. Thus Speusippus broke into three separate principles the interconnected, organized, and unified character of the world of Forms, which for Plato merely indicated its perfection and intelligibility. First came the One or Unity, then, proceeding from it, the Good, and finally, Reason, which Speusippus identified with the Platonic world-soul and the Pythagorean central fire. In this division the Forms disappear altogether, and their place is taken by number, which replaces soul as the connecting link between the intelligible and the sensible orders. The material world itself is founded upon the principle of plurality, or the Platonic the-great-and-the-small. With number Speusippus toyed in a thoroughly Pythagorean and somewhat fantastic manner. He seems, along with Xenocrates, completely to have missed in Plato's discussion of the subject the anticipation of the scientific method of stating the natures of things as mathematical formulae.

Xenocrates treated this hierarchy of principles in a more theological and out-and-out Pythagorean manner than did Speusippus. He regarded unity and plurality as not only metaphysically and mathematically but morally opposed, and from their interaction he derived not only numbers but also the soul. And he carried out in detail the idea of a hierarchy of beings endowed with different degrees of perfection. The heavens, the stars, the Olympian gods, demons or angels, men, animals, and even the material elements partake in a descending scale of the divine soul-principle. He also emphasized the immaterial character of the soul, and accepted, along with Speusippus, the theory of transmigration. Finally, following the lead given by Plato in the *Laws,* he even believed in evil spirits.

Academy Ethics. In their ethics both men seem to have moved in the same direction as did Aristotle. Though Speusippus shared Plato's suspicion of pleasure and would not even admit that it played any part in the good, he taught like Aristotle, and like Plato at times, that happiness lay in the perfect and harmonious functioning of all the activities with which nature has endowed us, and that it was dependent to some extent upon external advantages like health, freedom from worry, and the like. Again, like Aristotle, he insisted upon the importance of virtue or human excellence as a means to happiness and an essential ingredient in it. These views were shared by Xenocrates, who developed them at greater length, and also gave to them a theological and Orphic twist by expressing moral conflict as a struggle between the Dionysus within us and our evil heritage from the Titans.

Other Members and Tendencies. Other interesting contemporaneous members of the Academy are Heraclides of Pontus and Eudoxus of

Rhodes. Heraclides is noteworthy chiefly for his physics and astronomy. These tended towards an atomism not unlike that of Democritus, and recognized the immobility of the fixed stars, the spherical shape of the earth, and its rotation upon its axis. Eudoxus is best known for his acceptance, even as a member of the Academy, of the Cyrenaic hedonism, which Plato was doing his utmost to combat.

With Polemo, Crates, and Crantor the School fell more and more under the moralizing tone of the age, but remained on the whole true to the ethics taught by Speusippus and Xenocrates. Finally, under the leadership of Arcesilaus, it became, ironically enough, a champion of the same destructive and skeptical attitude as Socrates and Plato had done their best to oppose in Protagoras and his followers. We must, however, postpone for a moment our discussion of this new phase, and hie us back to the fortunes of the Lyceum.

III. THE LYCEUM

Theophrastus. Were Theophrastus, Aristotle's immediate successor, not so overshadowed by his master, he would probably cut a larger figure in the history of philosophy than he does. He shared to the full Aristotle's universality of interest, insatiable and omnivorous curiosity, unflagging devotion to scientific inquiry and to the pursuit of truth, tireless zeal in collecting and reviewing evidence of all sorts from all sources, and power of keen and discriminating analysis and inference. He wrote voluminously on logic, metaphysics, physics, natural history, botany, zoology, psychology, ethics, politics, rhetoric, art, and music. In conjunction with his fellow-Peripatetic, Eudemus (to whom the *Eudemian Ethics* is attributed by many critics), he was the first to amplify the syllogism into its hypothetical and disjunctive forms. The difficulties he found in the Aristotelian metaphysics bear witness to his ability as a critic and as a speculative thinker. His treatises on botany are considered by some to surpass in scope and method all other studies of the subject both in ancient and medieval times, and his famous *Characters* testify to his eminence as a man of letters. But in the end he contributed little that was new to either Aristotle's scientific research or philosophy.

Criticism of Aristotle. At the same time, we may perhaps find some evidence of the changing conditions and attitude towards life in Theophrastus' criticism of Aristotle. In the doubts, for example, that he casts upon the major role assigned by Aristotle to design and purpose in the course of events, and in his inclination to make the soul even more dependent upon the body than did his master, we may detect a more naturalistic spirit. His ethics, too, dwelt more upon external circumstances, not indeed as necessary elements in happiness, but as real disturbers of peace and quiet and as obstructions to the pursuit of knowledge and the living of the contemplative life in which happiness consists.

Eudemus. Of Theophrastus' contemporary, Eudemus, we need not speak further. His fame rests upon his reputed authorship of the *Eudemian Ethics,* which, however, is regarded by some critics as a youthful work of Aristotle's, and of which we have already treated in discussing the Aristotelian theory of morals.

Strato. The next head of the Lyceum was Strato of Lampsacus, a scientist of much the same universal interest as Theophrastus, and, perhaps, of even greater ability. In him the naturalistic spirit implicit in Aristotle, and more explicit in Theophrastus, comes into the open. The Aristotelian Unmoved Mover, however, disappears altogether from the scene, and his place is taken by nature, regarded, in the manner of Democritus, as a mechanism actuated by necessity. For Democritus' atoms, however, Strato substituted heat and cold as the elements of which all things are made. Furthermore, he denied Aristotle's distinction between the sensitive and the rational souls, and, if his criticisms of Plato's *Phaedo* had any effect upon his own opinion, he can scarcely have believed in immortality. The soul is, to be sure, a force, with a distinctive character of its own, but it is a force lodged in the body, without which it cannot be exercised.

After Strato, the Lyceum deteriorated rapidly. It fell a victim to the ethical and practical spirit of the times, and lost even its leading position as a school of scientific research. But it was still of value as a repository of the scientific knowledge accumulated in the past, and it kept alive the spirit and the letter of Aristotle's moral teaching.

Chapter XVI

THE EPICUREANS

I. LEADERS OF THE SCHOOL .

Epicurus. Epicurus, though the son of an Athenian citizen, was born on the island of Samos, in 342 or 341 B.C. He was, then, twenty years old when Aristotle died. He claimed that he was entirely self-taught and self-made, but tradition has it that his father was a schoolmaster, and gives the names of the philosophers under whom he studied the systems of Democritus and Plato. It is said, too, that he was for a time a pupil of Xenocrates. His poor literary style, however, his almost Socratic scorn of the higher reaches of education, and his ignorance in many matters make us suspect that his early training, wherever it may have been obtained, was not all it might have been.

After several years of teaching school in various towns of Asia Minor, he moved to Athens (about 306 B.C.), where he purchased a garden, destined, as the famous Garden of Epicurus, to take its place in the history of philosophy beside the Academy of Plato and the Lyceum of Aristotle. There he began to expound his system and to gather about himself disciples. There, too, walled also within the garden of thought he had constructed, full of cool and quiet and peace of mind, he spent the rest of his life not only teaching, but writing with a diligence that made him one of the most voluminous writers of antiquity. Unfortunately only fragments of his work, and these for the most part unimportant, have come down to us.[1] In 270 B.C. he died of a painful illness which he bore calmly and courageously.

The charm of Epicurus' personality, his kind and friendly disposition, the liberal character of his ethics, and the consolations his teaching not only promised but seems to have afforded, gave him a large and immediate following. They imparted, too, a vitality and a power of survival to the school that enabled it to meet with success and equanimity the bitter attacks, both of the other philosophies and later

[1] Our knowledge of Epicurus himself is chiefly derived from Diogenes Laertius, Cicero, Seneca, and Plutarch. Epicureanism is fully expounded by Lucretius.

of Christianity, and to remain intact until ancient philosophy itself came to an end. It was in Rome that Epicureanism achieved its greatest fame. Transferred thither within fifty years of its founder's death, it rapidly gained numerous disciples, and within another two hundred had inspired Lucretius' poem *De Rerum Natura* ("On the Nature of Things"), which contains, in spite of the difficulties of the subject, some of the finest poetry not only in Latin literature but in the literature of all time.

Lucretius. Of Lucretius, who ranks with Epicurus himself in the history of the sect, we unfortunately know very little. He was born early in the first decade of the first century, b.c., of unknown parents, and lived his own life in retirement and obscurity. He was an invalid, and suffered, it is said, from intermittent fits of insanity provoked by the use of love-philters. Eventually, when scarcely forty, he committed suicide, leaving his poem almost but not quite finished. Either he, or his friends, brought the *De Rerum Natura* to the attention of Cicero, whom Lucretius seems greatly to have admired, and by him, after the poet's death, it was edited and published as it stood in 54 b.c. Of the immediate reception it was accorded we know nothing. But in the next generation we find it recognized as a masterpiece and constantly imitated by Virgil and studied by Horace and Ovid.

II. THE EPICUREAN ETHICS

Epicureanism a Philosophic Substitute for Religion. Epicureanism, being a philosophy of salvation, was primarily interested in offering for a fading religious faith and a failing traditional morality a philosophical substitute founded upon reason and natural sanctions. Its end was to give a peace that the world as it stood could not give, and that, whatever it might bring, it could not take away. With any other goal than the securing of human happiness—with metaphysical or even scientific speculation, with the arts, with learning and culture, even with mathematics—Epicurus had no patience whatsoever. Philosophy is first and last a practical activity—is behaving, speaking, and thinking in the way that makes you happiest.

To discover, however, the happiest way of life, we must first ask again the old question—What is happiness? His answer, Epicurus liked to think, was without debt to the past, but the influence of the Cyrenaics is too obvious to be denied. With Aristippus' doctrine that pleasure is the end at which all moral activities aim, we are already familiar, as we are also with his effort to maintain the goodness of pleasure apart from its sources and consequences, and to uphold the impossibility of comparing pleasures as better or worse. In this Epicurus followed him, accepting pleasure as the end to which all else, including virtue itself, is only a means. Furthermore, he believed that all pleasure was in the end physical, and, indeed, being himself somewhat dyspeptic, considered the most fundamental enjoyment to be the pleasures of a good digestion.

Happiness and Pleasure. But Epicurus could not see eye to eye with Aristippus in so far as the equality of all pleasures in point of goodness and their detachment from their sources and consequences were concerned. For that matter, neither could the later Cyrenaics. Happiness, Epicurus said, is a matter of the greatest amount of pleasure in the long run. The attainment of this balance will often involve both the enduring of pain for the sake of pleasure to come and the sacrifice of such present enjoyments as are more than offset by their painful results. Furthermore, intelligence and reasoning are necessary to weigh pleasures against pains and *vice versa,* and to determine what are and what are not worth foregoing or enduring. This appeal to reason rather than to sensation as the criterion of pleasures and pains that are worth while was also allowed by the later Cyrenaics, and was for them, as for Epicurus, the mark of the wise as contrasted with the foolish man.

Pleasure as Absence of Pain. So far, then, Epicurus follows the disciples of Aristippus in their correction and development of their master's teaching. Now he diverges from them, and Epicureanism as distinct from Cyrenaicism begins. Curiously enough, the signpost at this parting of the ways is to be found in his insistence that the greatest of all pleasures is the enjoyment of a sound digestion. For when is digestion at its best? Precisely when we are least aware that it is in progress. The pleasures of digestion lie in *an absence of pain* rather than in anything positive. This negative twist Epicurus gives to the concept of pleasure in general. Pleasure is essentially absence of pain.

His reasons for so conceiving enjoyment are not far to seek. Positive pleasures are enjoyed only at intervals—and we have often to wait a long while for them to occur. Between times we jog along in a condition that is neither positively pleasurable nor painful. If happiness lies in the experience of even a balance of positive pleasure, it is a spotty and sporadic affair, separated by long stretches of unhappiness. But, as a matter of fact, we do not feel unhappy when we are not experiencing pleasure. On the contrary, we are quite content. Hence if the human good is to be identified with pleasure, we must extend the

meaning of pleasure in general so as to cover these long neutral intervals, and must define it more broadly as absence of pain. Enjoyment,
then, is essentially comfort. When we are not uncomfortable we are
in a pleasurable condition. Nay more, positive and, more particularly,
violent pleasure tends to be upsetting and disturbing, and is therefore
often more destructive than conducive to happiness.

Ataraxia. To pleasure thus defined as absence of desire, of physical
discomfort, and of mental disturbance, Epicurus gives the name of
ataraxia, which we may translate as "serenity," or peace of mind and
body. It has, he seems to feel, a sounder psychological and physiological
basis than positive pleasure, for it denotes a state of repose and equilibrium in the organism, whereas keen enjoyment is based upon motion and unrest. Furthermore, it is something that does not lie at the
end of a long struggle for attainment, but may be ever present and
immediately enjoyed. It is supremely worth while, and it is within
the reach of all. The good is not a distant or a difficult goal, accessible,
if at all, only to a few. All men can be happy, almost without effort,
if only they will. For all men can cultivate the amenities of life, and
to a large extent can avoid its disagreeable aspects. Furthermore, when
the disagreeable cannot be dodged, it can at least be endured with
cheerfulness and equanimity.

The Sheltered Garden of Epicurus. The Garden of Epicurus is,
therefore, a fitting symbol of his ethics. Happiness for him is a walled
and sheltered thing, attained by shutting one's self away from all that
is harsh and uncomfortable and upsetting in existence. This we can
accomplish both by practical measures and by the cultivation of a
mental attitude. Courage and temperance are the two great wind-
breaks that protect the garden of the soul from the rude and icy
blasts of life. Friendship and conviviality are its flowers. Upon the
place of friendship in happiness Epicurus set great store. Not only
must his disciples love one another, but they should have a philan-
thropic feeling for all mankind. This insistence upon devotion to one
another and upon general amiability was, if anything, overdone by the
school, which was reproached with a somewhat too sugary sweetness
and gentleness of attitude.

In spite, however, of the importance he attached to sociability,
Epicurus discouraged participation in political life. The wise man will
disdain wealth, worldly honors, prestige, and the plaudits of the
crowd. He will prefer to live in quiet retirement, avoiding the burdens
of the citizen, and taking no part in the affairs of the state. Even wife

and child may be distracting, though here, as in other relations imposed upon him by membership in society, he must perhaps gamble on their not too greatly interfering with his peace of mind.

III. THE EVILS OF RELIGION

But the disturbers of human peace are not altogether of the natural order and of this life. Above all, man is haunted and his *ataraxia* is hounded by two supernatural and superstitious terrors—the fear of what may lie beyond this life and that of the spying, prying eye and heavy, interfering hand of the gods. These terrors are the arch-destroyers of man's happiness. Some of the most dramatic passages in Lucretius are devoted to reciting and depicting the evils that follow in their train—the cringing before the supernatural, the sense of being spied upon, the uncertainty of what the gods may do, the dread of what may befall us in an unknown after-world. Others are consecrated to reassuring us, and to removing our uneasiness, our sense of helplessness in the grip of supernal powers, our panics of prayer and placation, and our fears of what death may bring, by showing us the groundlessness of the belief in immortality and in a divine government of the world. The horrors of death do not exist for the dead, but only for those they have left behind. The dead know nothing of the funeral pyre or the grave, nothing of the mourning and the lamentation. They rather sleep a sleep from which nothing can arouse them. Why, then, should we find death terrible? It is as natural as life. It is the gate to unbroken peace. It is the road down which high and low alike have gone for countless generations. Why should we shrink from treading it, too, and from entering with them into everlasting rest?

IV. METAPHYSICS

If man is to be freed from the superstitious fears engendered by religion, the non-existence of a providential government of the world and of a life beyond the grave must be established beyond doubt. For doubt on any subject is itself a disagreeable sensation, threatening to our peace of mind. Particularly disturbing is the suspense aroused by a sneaking suspicion that religion may after all be really right, for all we *know*. Hence if we are to be happy, we must have *scientific proof* that its teachings are groundless. Such proof Epicurus finds in the philosophy of Democritus, whose mechanical and atomistic system left no place, we may remember, for a moral government of the world or an after-life. This system Epicurus took largely on faith because it suited his scheme of salvation.

Epicurean Modifications of Atomism. In taking it over, however, Epicurus made several changes in it. In the first place, it seems probable that he added the characteristic of *weight* to the two characteristics of size and shape to which Leucippus and Democritus apparently had limited the atoms.

Again, whereas Leucippus and Democritus apparently conceived the atoms as moving helter-skelter in all directions, Epicurus thought that, because of their weight, they would naturally fall perpendicularly through space. This view, however, involved him in difficulties. Since, in his opinion, empty space would offer no resistance to the falling atoms, there was, he felt, no reason for the larger and heavier atoms to fall faster than the smaller and lighter ones. But in that case, the heavier could not overtake the lighter, and collisions between them could not take place. Hence there could be no clusterings of the atoms to form larger masses, nor, without collisions and the consequent deviations from the perpendicular, could atomic whirlpools be set up in the Void, and worlds be brought into being.

The Spontaneous Deviation of the Atoms. To get round this difficulty, and it may be in part for moral motives to which we shall come in a moment, Epicurus advances the idea that besides a natural tendency to fall vertically, expressive of their weight, the atoms also possess a characteristic of *spontaneous deviation* from the perpendicular. This characteristic is independent of the fixed properties of the atom, such as its size, shape, and weight. The spontaneous swerving of the atoms, moreover, introduces an element of freedom into their movements and collisions and into the resultant world-systems. For their clusterings and motions are not absolutely determined by their fixed properties and by their antecedent situations and lines of movement, as they were in the systems of Leucippus and Democritus. The course they will follow cannot be computed since they are not bound absolutely by the laws of mechanical motion, and move to some extent in an unaccountable way. In short, Epicurus rejects the absolute *necessity* and the *determinism* to which Leucippus and Democritus had subjected all movement and change, and injects into the behavior of the atoms a factor undetermined by their antecedent arrangements and movements.

As we have just said, Epicurus may have had moral as well as scientific reasons for his doctrine of *spontaneous deviation* as it stood. The philosophy of Leucippus and Democritus might indeed liberate

us from the fear of God and of death, but as it stood it also substituted for the tyranny of a divine providence that minded and managed all our business for us another tyranny no less irksome and
terrible—the rule of an inexorable necessity which held us in an iron
grip, determined all our acts, ran our lives in every detail, and blindly
dispensed to us happiness or misery. It is preferable, he thinks, to
believe in the fables about the gods than to be enslaved to the determinism of the physicists. These fables leave us some hope of
wheedling the gods by prayer and placation, but necessity is implac-
able. The terrors aroused by the idea of blind destiny are even more
disturbing to our *ataraxia* than are those inspired by belief in a divine
providence.

The spontaneity of atomic behavior, moreover, validates man's feeling of freedom and his desire to manage his own affairs. It liberates
him, as it does the atom itself, from the heavy hand of destiny. His
sense of being actuated and directed by himself alone proves to be
no illusion. It springs rather from the very heart of things of whose
ungoverned and irregular beating it is the conscious expression.

V. THE FREEDOM OF THE WILL

Upon the human freedom and moral responsibility to which he
considers himself to be thus giving a physical basis, Epicurus cannot
insist too strongly. Of two contradictory propositions, particularly
when they refer to the future, neither, he tells us, is necessarily true
at the present moment. One of them may *become* true, to be sure,
but it is not necessarily so before the event. Prediction, prophecy, sooth-
saying, are vain. There is no foretelling how men will act or what
will befall them. So, too, we alone, not God or necessity, are the
causes of our acts. Nor can any external event or person invade our
privacy, infringe upon our liberty, or rob us of our happiness. We
are masters of our fate, immune alike to destiny and chance. Chance,
to be sure, springs from the same source as does freedom. External
events are to some extent incalculable, because they, too, reflect the
spontaneous deviation of the atoms. Their incalculable character makes
us speak of the fickleness of *fortune,* and of *luck,* good or bad. But
our inner liberty, in which the same spontaneity displays itself, is not
a thing of inexplicable vagaries. It is power over ourselves, ability to
will and act on our own initiative. This power is at the mercy neither
of inner caprice nor of external hazards.

VI. EPICUREAN RELIGION

In denying the existence of divine beings to whom the secrets of all hearts were known and who directed human affairs, Epicurus did not, however, banish gods from the universe. Like Democritus, he seems to have accepted their apparition in dreams and visions as sufficient proof of their existence. For him as for Democritus these visitations could be explained only as a stirring of the soul-atoms by effluences from existent external objects. There were, then, gods in the worlds—at any rate in our world. But they were powerless to interfere with human destinies; if indeed they so much as knew that man existed. But if we had nothing to hope from them, at least we had nothing to fear. They dwelt far off in the serene interstellar spaces, leading there the happy, carefree, amply provided life of which man dreams. Spun like ourselves from the whirling atoms—though from a finer stuff than ours—they were not uncreated and indestructible, but their existence was everlasting compared with the brief span of human life.[2]

Furthermore Lucretius seems to have found religious value in the spectacle of infinite atoms falling through infinite space throughout infinite time, forever generating and destroying in the Void by their falling an infinity of worlds. "The walls of the world," he says, "part asunder. I see things in operation throughout the whole void. . . . At all this a kind of godlike delight mixed with shuddering awe comes over me to think that nature . . . is laid thus visibly open, is thus unveiled on every side."[3] And the *De Rerum Natura* is infused with religious veneration for the vision he has been vouchsafed of the true nature of things, and with exultation that it has cast out fear from man's heart and given him peace.

VII. THEORY OF KNOWLEDGE

To defend his system against the attacks of the skeptics Epicurus had to show how the mind could know the nature of things, and to do this he had to develop a theory of knowledge. Here he is influenced both by the Cyrenaics and by Democritus himself, who had developed his philosophy under fire, and had sought to entrench it in rational grounds against attack. With the Cyrenaics, Epicurus agrees that

[2] Cf. Lucretius, *De Rerum Natura*, I, 1014 ff.; III, 18 ff.; V, 146 ff.
[3] *Ibid.*, III, 15 ff.

sensation is the test of truth, as it is of good and evil. For, if perception cannot be trusted, what can be? Impressions are what they are, and there can be no gainsaying them. Moreover, the rest of our thinking is derived from sense. Repetition of the same impression gives rise to a remembered image, which we call a notion. Notions give rise to opinions. And those opinions are true that are in correspondence with the external world.

To establish such correspondence Epicurus invokes Democritus. Impressions are produced by the impact upon the sense-organs of miniature copies or pictures of external objects, which these objects are continually throwing off from themselves. If the pictures arrive intact, we get true and faithful images. If, however, they meet with accidents *en route,* by collision or otherwise, they present us with false or distorted pictures. Further than this Epicurus does not go.

VIII. THEORY OF SOCIETY

Primitive Human Social Conditions. The fifth book of Lucretius' *De Rerum Natura* is devoted to setting forth the Epicurean view of the origins of life, of man, and of human society. First the earth grew vegetation, much as animals grow hair, and heat and moisture generated animals. Then she brought forth man from innumerable wombs of her contriving. Monstrous forms of life died out because they were unsuited to their environment and unable to perpetuate their species. The monsters of mythology, however, never existed, and are fables pure and simple. In the beginning, man led a purely animal existence, completely at the mercy of natural forces. After a while he got control of fire, learned to cook and to fabricate clothes and shelter, and transformed little by little his inarticulate cries into speech. To this epoch belongs the dawning of tribal and social existence. Agriculture was now undertaken, animals were domesticated, the use of metals was discovered, and wealth came into being and began to accumulate. Social organization grew, and government evolved as natural inequalities in strength and talent fostered class distinctions and brought about the rule of chiefs and kings. Then music appeared, modeled on the songs of birds, and mirth and merry-making, and the appeal of beauty. And so, step by step, men advanced to their present state of civilization.

The Epicureans felt that the state, and with it law and the concept of justice, appeared as natural developments of social evolution. In this, they were opposed to popular contemporary theories, dating back to the Sophists, and advanced by politicians like Callicles and Thrasymachus in Plato's *Republic,* by the Cynics and Cyrenaics, and by the new Skepticism to which we shall soon be turning. According to these views there is no such thing as natural right, and the lawful and the unlawful are mere matters of convention, founded upon and backed by might. To these assertions the Epicureans replied that the state is in a sense artificial in that it is a conscious creation, organized with an end in view. But the creation, the end, and the means are indicated by nature. In their primitive state men do, to be sure, prey upon each other. But it takes little reflection to see that such a condition is contrary to man's self-interest, which is best subserved by a reciprocal agreement among individuals to live at peace with one another. So, in the common interest, a compact is made not to injure, in return for not being injured. This compact is the basis of what we call natural right,[4] and of what we call justice, and of law. Apart from such a compact, none of these terms would have any meaning. In that sense they are conventional. But the compact is a natural product, growing out of the natural desire for self-preservation and self-assertion inherent in the individual, and for protection in the pursuit of his own ends.

The Nature of Right and Wrong. It follows that right- and wrongdoing are entirely a matter of consequences. Hence law is primarily concerned with preventing the suffering of evil rather than the doing of it, and takes heed of the wrong-doer only in so far as his deeds affect others. Nevertheless, the individual is well advised not to do wrong even if he thinks he can avoid the consequences. For, though punishment is not certain, it is always possible, and the lawbreaker, although he may escape, must live in perpetual suspense and fear of detection and arrest. Hence the wise man, who values his peace of mind, will steer clear of the police by observing the law and refraining from acts considered unjust.

Justice, however, is not a fixed but a fluid thing. It varies with time and place and circumstance. In a sense it is the same for all, since it represents a common social need. But what is just for one man is not necessarily just for another. Nor is what is just at one epoch necessarily always so. Law, if it is to command respect and obedience, must follow and reflect the changing standards of changing times. Otherwise it does not prescribe what is right but may even enjoin what is wrong. For right and wrong are relative to whatever happens to be

[4] Diogenes Laertius, X, 150.

the organization and interest of society as it is, not as it was, or as it perhaps will be.

In this fashion, it has been pointed out, the Epicureans took a middle and sensible path between the moral conservatives and the moral radicals of their age. Since individuals have in all times and places much the same make-up, there will always be a fund of enduring interests and standards handed down from generation to generation in the form of unchanging conventions and laws. But there will also be diversities of interest, and hence of justice and law, varying with time and place and adapted to special circumstances.[5]

Lucretius was the last Epicurean of any note, but Epicureanism was still so strong in the second century A.D. that it was established as one of the Schools of Athens.

[5] Cf. Guyau, *La Morale d'Epicure,* p. 149.

Chapter XVII

THE STOICS

I. THE GREEK FOUNDERS. THE OLD STOA

In contrast to Epicureanism the history of Stoicism presents a confused and varying spectacle. The doctrines of the one were simple and consistent, and, once promulgated, descended unchanged through the centuries. The teachings of the other allowed of wide diversities of opinion on fundamental problems, and underwent important alterations in the course of time.[1] Like Epicureanism, however, Stoicism was primarily a scheme of salvation and a way of life, concerned first of all with defining the nature of human happiness and discovering the means to its attainment.

Zeno. In its case, moreover, the moralizing tendency was perhaps intensified at the beginning by the personality of Zeno, the founder of the School. A native of Cyprus, he emigrated to Athens about 320 B.C., where he, like Epicurus, studied under Xenocrates. His temperament was attracted to the Cynic doctrines of virtue for virtue's sake, the unconquerable soul, and the independence of happiness on external conditions. These teachings, and the sect's missionary zeal in trying to reform what they considered the wickedness of the world, were congenial to his severe, didactic and proselytizing temperament.

He was, however, dissatisfied with his first teacher, Crates, and with the unadulterated Cynicism taught by him. But he found what he desired in the Cynic Stilpo, who had come under the influence of the Megaric school, adopted its Eleatic method of logical argument, and accepted its identification of the Socratic Good with Eleatic Being. After some twenty years of study he launched out for himself, delivering his lectures in a colonnade known as the Stoa Poikile, or

---

[1] The fragments of the writings of the older Stoics have been collected and published by J. von Arnim (Leipzig, 1903-1905). Valuable sources may also be found in Diels's *Doxographi Graeci*. The teachings of Panaetius and Posidonius have been preserved, thanks largely to Cicero's translations or adaptations in his *De Officiis* and his *De Deorum Natura*. The works of the later Stoics are for the most part extant. No attempt at detailed references has been made in this chapter, except in the case of direct translations.

Painted Porch, whence the name Stoic is derived. The uprightness of his character and life won for him great respect both in Athens and abroad. Eventually, having received a physical injury, he felt that his hour had come and committed suicide. The exact date of his death is unknown. Only a few of his prolific writings have come down to us.

Cleanthes. At his death, the leadership of the School fell to Cleanthes, from Assos in the Troad, the sister or niece of whose reigning prince, we may remember, Aristotle married. He is said to have been originally a prize-fighter, and was distinguished more for solid worth than for keenness of intellect. He embraced the teaching of Zeno with religious fervor, gave to it a theological twist, and has left us an important legacy in his *Hymn to Zeus*. By this time the School was well established, and history mentions many of its adherents, of whom the most prominent was perhaps Eratosthenes the Grammarian, head of the great Library at Alexandria and tutor to the crown-prince, under Ptolemy III.

Chrysippus. Cleanthes was succeeded by his pupil Chrysippus, born in 280 B.C. in Cilicia, near Tarsus. Though he lacked originality, he was a man of great learning and a master of argument. He ably defended Stoicism against all comers, and particularly against the Epicureans and the attacks of the new, skeptical Academy. It is to him we owe the consolidation of Stoic doctrine along the lines that characterized it for the rest of its existence. With him the first period of Stoicism, known as the Old Stoa, came to a culmination and an end. At the same time, we shall find that Stoicism could not hold its lines absolutely intact against the pressure of its critics and the exigencies of practical life. In the course of time, as we shall see, its sharper salients were flattened by the Epicurean teaching, and the common cause that it found itself making, willy-nilly, with the Academy against this common foe also helped modify its more extreme positions. The result was that it tended, particularly after it had gone over to Rome, to become self-critical and eclectic, and to be accepted by its later disciples in part and in combination with elements from other systems.

II. THE STOIC ETHICS

Divergence from Epicureanism. Let us, however, pause at this point to survey the doctrines established by the Greek founders of the school, before tracing their further history. And, since Stoicism like Epicureanism was primarily a way of life, let us begin with its ethical aspects. At the outset we may note its wide divergence from the way chosen by Epicurus. He had sought peace by assiduously cultivating the amenities of life and shunning its disagreeable aspects as far as possible, though he was prepared to bear evil with a courageous and even mind when it could not be avoided. But his rule was to dodge the disagreeable rather than to face it. The Stoics, to be sure, also strove for freedom from disturbance, but the calm they tried to attain was of a different sort, and was to be reached by different means. Cultivation of the pleasant and avoidance of the painful were not conducive to it. On the contrary, they were detrimental. For both alike made happiness to some extent dependent on external circumstances. They put man in the power of the world and deprived him of self-mastery. Peace of mind lay rather in absolute independence of fortune, good or bad, and the secret of independence lay in the cultivation of an absolutely indifferent attitude towards both her caresses and her stings. Thus and thus only, by an unyielding, unruffled endurance of the vicissitudes of life, can we triumph over them and preserve ourselves intact, whatever may occur.

Apathy. This "apathy," as the Stoics called it, is fostered for its own sake and is its own reward. It is an end, not a means, to anything beyond it. Nay more, it is *the* end—the supreme goal towards which all human activity, if rightly disciplined, is directed. Happy, then, he who possesses it, since happiness also is that which is desired in and for itself, and is the target at which moral conduct is aimed. In a word, to be virtuous is to be happy and *vice versa*. Happiness and virtue are one and the same thing.

Furthermore, this attitude is that of the wise and reasonable man. It is the *rational* way of meeting life, and the independence and indifference that go with it are in their deepest aspects an indifference of the rational part of us, or *ruling principle,* as the Stoics call it, to the passions, desires, and emotions aroused by our contact with other persons and external objects, including our own bodies. Hence virtue, happiness, and rational living are identical.

Again, though "apathy" is a passive acceptance on our part of whatever befalls us, it is a state maintained only by constant effort and tension. We have to *will* the independence dictated by reason, and constantly to oppose that will to the innumerable forces that tend ceaselessly to break it down. The ruling principle in each man is, then, also a *strength* of mind, a *determination* to remain untroubled. This, in its turn, implies a conviction that nothing is really evil or to be avoided except as we allow it to become so through a weakening of that determination.

Stoic Austerity. The teaching that virtue lies in insensibility or "apathy," that it is desired for its own sake, and that it is identical with happiness and the good, led the Stoics, as it led the Cynics, to austere conclusions, in theory at least. Cleanthes, like Antisthenes, found himself obliged to include in his denunciation of all pleasure as contrary to nature even the pleasure of being good. All the emotions were equally taboo, since they were all irrational, and therefore ran counter to the ruling principle, whose right estimate of good and evil they tended to confuse with false images of pleasure and desire, and anxiety and fear. This theoretical suppression of all feeling, including as it did generous emotions like sympathy and pity, aroused immediate criticism, and invited the charge that Stoicism was hard-hearted.

Furthermore, the Stoic was forced to maintain that whatever a man did was right, granted his heart, so to speak, was pure, or, in other words, insensible. Virtue was a matter of the will, not of the deed. Conversely, no matter how excellent in its consequences an act might be, unless it was performed with an absolutely right intention, that is, with absolute indifference, it was wholly wicked. This view also was criticized, and ridiculed as well. Was it right, for example, to commit adultery in a disinterested manner, and therefore with honorable intentions? Was it a deed of darkness to follow the irrational impulse to save a life you saw in danger?

No Variety or Degrees of Virtue. Again, logically speaking, there could be no such thing as a number of different virtues. It was not merely that the virtues were one in the Socratic sense of being all reducible to knowledge of what is best. To misjudge in one department of conduct was to betray an incapacity for right judgment in any and all departments, and marked a man as a fool and a knave all over. You were either ruled by reason and therefore virtuous in all respects, or you were not ruled by reason and therefore vicious through and through. So, too, there could be no *degrees* of virtue or vice. You could not be more or less rational, more or less insensible, more or less independent. You either possessed the good will, the right intention, the Stoic attitude, or you did not. To be sensible of so much as a pin-prick was to be not insensible, and therefore not good, and therefore simply wicked. You were completely saved or wholly damned. And that was that.

It followed that there could be no such thing as real moral progress and improvement. There could be only sudden and total *conversion* from absolute folly and wickedness to complete righteousness and wisdom. We are changed from evil to good, not slowly, but in the twinkling of an eye; and until then, we still belong to the ranks of the lost, no matter how valiantly we may be struggling to be good.

Total Depravity. Like the Cynics, the Stoics were also obliged by their theory to take a pessimistic view of the condition of mankind. Social institutions and the conventions and standards of so-called moral behavior between individuals were all contrary to nature, and menaced rather than supported the maintenance of that inner "apathy" in which true virtue and happiness alone consisted. Those who allowed their conduct to be influenced by these standards and conventions were all wandering in outer darkness. Salvation was reserved to the Stoic sage alone. The human race was almost entirely in a state of total depravity, utter folly, and complete unhappiness.

Naturally such a theory could no more stand up against hard fact than could Aristippus' devotion to the pleasure of the moment as the highest good. Almost immediately we find the Stoics engaged in the concessions and modifications that made of their philosophy, in the end, a workable system by which human beings were inspired and consoled in their dealings with themselves and with the world.

Concessions to the World. The unity and the self-sufficiency of virtue remained, indeed, a persistent and cardinal principle of the School. But Zeno himself had been forced to mitigate the doctrine by recognizing that the four classic virtues of temperance, courage, wisdom and justice were at least four distinct ways of exhibiting one and the same righteousness. And both Zeno and Cleanthes had described the "daily duties," or proper performance of "that which it comes in one's way to do," which are incumbent upon the sage as the result of living and moving in a surrounding world. Indeed, by the time Stoicism passed over to Rome, temperance, or propriety in human relations, had taken precedence over the self-centered courage preached by the Cynics and the private wisdom emphasized by Zeno, as the most revealing expression of the rightly directed will.

Moreover, even the individual man, being after all human, had instinct and feelings as well as reason, and lived not in a vacuum but in a material environment. The concept of the right attitude had, therefore, to be broadened in its inner aspects by admitting that the instincts and the emotions were not always antagonistic to right living, and that external circumstances might have value, provided that they were kept in submission to the ruling principle and not allowed to get the upper hand.

A Middle Ground Recognized. Again, the uncompromising distinction between good and evil, wisdom and folly, was softened by the admission of a third class of things—those that are neither good nor bad but merely indifferent, and have no bearing upon virtuous or vicious conduct. To this class belong a host of trivial actions, whose performance demands no examination of the conscience, and also many things which in some circumstances are to be preferred, in others to be avoided. Consequently it had to be admitted that there were real *degrees* of virtue and of vice, and that instead of having to be suddenly converted from a state of total depravity to one of perfect goodness, a man could progress step by step from the one condition to the other. Nor could a hard and fast line easily be drawn between advance towards virtue and attainment of it, since moral improvement is itself a good thing. For that matter, though Cleanthes still maintained that once saved a man could not fall from grace, Chrysippus admitted that the sage was capable of backsliding and could never be too sure he was not doing so.

The concessions made by the Stoics to political and social organization seem to belong largely to the later, Roman period. Zeno adhered to the Cynic view that such organization is altogether artificial and conventional and that in an ideal society composed of perfectly virtuous men there would be no marriage, no family organization, no church, no judicial procedure, no government, no money. And Chrysippus advised abstinence from all political activity. Nor did Stoicism, even under Roman influence, ever give ground to the point of admitting any positive worth to social institutions. At the best they were to be shouldered as part of the human burden. What Roman Stoicism did do, as we shall soon see, was to give real content and value to the incipient notion of the brotherhood of man, inherited from the Cynics.

III. THE STOIC METAPHYSICS

Rationality of the Universe. But if it is reasonable for us to accept with an untroubled mind everything that occurs—and this remained till the end the essence of the Stoic way of life—it must be reasonable for everything to happen as it does. To regard external events as irrational would be to regard them as evil in themselves, irrespective of our attitude towards them. In that case, our acceptance of them would not be a willing one. It would be rather a forced compliance, which would make man the victim, not the master of his fate, shackle his inner life to the chain of external circumstances, and deprive him of his inner, essential freedom and dignity.

The Stoics, then, had to feel that the universe responded to our reason's voluntary acceptance of it, by being itself a rational affair. To support their attitude, they needed like the Epicureans a congenial metaphysics. This they found in the system of Heraclitus, just as the Epicureans took refuge in the philosophy of Democritus. What chiefly attracted the School to Heraclitus was his doctrine that the ever-changing Fire was infused with "the wise" and exhibited in its ceaseless alterations an order which reason could discover and grasp.

The Stoic Logos and Pantheism. This intelligibility of the world-process the Stoics interpreted in terms of a quasi-personal mind, akin to human reason, omnipresent in the universe and governing the course of events. To designate the rational ruling principle of the world they took over from Heraclitus the word "logos" to which, however, he himself, as we have seen, very likely never attached any cosmic or metaphysical significance. And then, apparently, they read back into him their own use of the term, and attributed to him the concept of a Logos or cosmic Mind immanent in the ever-living Fire.

In any case, the Stoics erected upon Heraclitean foundations an elaborate pantheism. The Logos and the ever-living Fire were amalgamated into a single, living, moving, thinking world-stuff, which they called indifferently God, Ether, Fire, Nature, and the Universe. And the world-process they variously described as the expression of Reason, Mind, Soul, Providence, Destiny, and Fate. All these are really one. Mind is essentially material, fiery breath, and matter is essentially living and thinking and rational in its behavior. All that occurs, although it proceeds by inexorable necessity from the nature of the universe, is also dictated by a cosmic Reason, directed by divine Providence, and determined by a wise purpose, since the nature of the universe is rational, and all that occurs is for the best.

In developing this pantheism, the Stoics appealed to the analogy of the human being, who is both body and soul. Narrowly speaking, God may be called the Soul of the universe, the universe the body of God. But since neither can be conceived or exist without the other, the two are essentially identical. God is the universe, and the universe is God.

IV. STOICISM AND RELIGION

Piety of the Stoic Attitude. Of the essentially ethical and religious character of the Stoic pantheism there can be no doubt. The belief in the rationality of the world, the faith that the march of events is providential in character and that all things happen for the best, the serene acceptance of all that occurs as in accordance with the divine Reason, and the feeling that virtue and happiness lie in identifying the "ruling principle" within us with the "ruling principle" of the world—all these bespeak a profound piety and were a source of moral strength and consolation. Moreover, though the Stoics could not accept contemporary orthodox theology literally, their attitude towards it was not antagonistic, as was that of the Skeptics and the Epicureans. On the contrary, they recognized its poetic and symbolic value, and used the names and stories of its gods to designate different aspects and processes of the universe. Thus they identified Zeus with the universe as a whole, Poseidon with water, Demeter with the earth, Athena with the upper air, Ares with rashness, Aphrodite with love, Apollo with the sun, Artemis with the moon, etc. This symbology was developed to great and fantastic lengths.

Furthermore, they were ready to admit, following Plato and Aristotle, that the stars have souls superior to ours, possessed of a greater share of the divine Reason. Nor had they any fault to find with the cult of heroes, whom they regarded as outstanding manifestations of the divine nature. It is an open question, too, whether they did not also believe in spirits or "demons" intermediate between the spirits of the stars and human souls. At the same time they had no use for the temples, the ceremonies, or the propitiations and prayers of the established cult. Prayer could be only meditation upon the nature of the universe, or, at the most, the expression of the desire to attain virtue; and true worship lay in leading a life of reason in conformity with the rational constitution of the world.

The Immortality of the Soul. With regard to the immortality of the soul there were divergent opinions. Zeno seems to have left the question open, but to have leant towards the opinion that the souls of the virtuous, at any rate, survived death. Cleanthes extended survival to all men, but Chrysippus went Zeno one better and limited immortality to the Stoic sage alone. But all the Stoics agreed, at least down to Roman times, that eventually all souls, along with all the rest of the universe, would be reabsorbed into the ever-living Fire, in a world-conflagration. To this point we shall refer again in a moment.

V. THE PROBLEM OF EVIL

Stoic Insistence upon Perfection. Upon the unity and perfection of the universe in every respect the Stoics could not insist too strongly. Its parts play into one another's hands, and combine to realize the supreme end of providential activity, which is the production and support of rational beings like man and the lower gods. The universe exists for their sake, not only to be useful to them in every possible way, but also to delight them with its beauty—a quality upon which the Stoics laid great stress in arguing that this is the best of all possible worlds. Finally man was created to glorify God and enjoy him forever.

Conversely, this design expresses itself as a providence that not even the fall of a sparrow can escape. Nothing, Cleanthes says, can occur on earth, or in the heaven above, or in the sea, apart from God. Nothing, Chrysippus repeats, not even the least event, can happen except in accordance with the divine Reason and with law and justice and providence.

Perfection and Evil. However, the Stoics found it difficult to reconcile the perfection, the rationality, the beauty, and the providential direction of the universe in every respect with the seeming failure of its design along so many lines, and with the irrational, imperfect, ugly and evil character of so many of its aspects and workings. In short, they had on their hands the problem of evil in its acutest possible form. To solve it, they marshaled almost all the arguments that have ever before or since been employed by those who, believing in a God at the same time all-powerful and all good, have found themselves hard put to justify his ways to man.

Their main line of defense was that the seeming imperfection of the parts of the universe is in reality necessary and even advantageous to the perfection of the whole. In supporting this assertion the Stoics could ignore the occurrence of so-called physical evils like pain, disease, death, and natural catastrophes. Since none of these could shake our "apathy" unless we allowed them to do so, they were not evil in themselves but simply events as "natural" as any others. Nay, more, they might be advantageous in keeping the population down or as means for punishing or setting an example to the wicked, to whom alone they would be annoying. Even the bedbug, Chrysippus remarks, has its place in the moral economy. It serves to keep us from sleeping too late or too much.

The Interdependence of Opposites. Again, the Stoics fell back upon the Heraclitean doctrine of the interdependence of opposites. No day without night, no summer without winter, therefore no justice without injustice, no courage without cowardice, no truth without falsehood. Evil is the necessary foil to good.

To this argument they also gave an esthetic twist. Just as the comedy is improved by coarse wit, or the lights in the picture are enhanced by the shadows, so what we call imperfection is an integral part of the perfection of the all, for the absence of which the universe would be poorer. In these matters we must trust God, for he, as Cleanthes sings in his *Hymn to Zeus,* understands how to make the crooked straight, to bring order out of disorder, to make the unlovely lovely in his sight, and so to harmonize good and evil that they form a single rational whole.

Moral evil, however, could not be dealt with in this manner. The esthetic analogy might indeed be invoked again, and the sinner might be likened to the villain in the play, without whom the dramatic effect would be spoiled. But the fact remained that God was the playwright, and, in creating or permitting sin, he had apparently made himself responsible for something whose positively anti-moral and anti-perfect character could not be denied. For here was something that affected the essence of man himself, that sapped his reason and perverted his inner attitude. Furthermore, there was the disproportion between merit and reward to be reckoned with. The wicked flourished, the virtuous were cast down. Natural catastrophes, in curtailing population, failed to distinguish between the sheep and the goats.

Misfortune and Virtue. Upon the disproportion of reward to merit the Stoics first trained their old argument that no *real* misfortune can overtake the good man, and that conversely no *real* good fortune can happen to the vicious one. For that matter, misfortune may be an occasion for the display of virtue. Later, too, we find Seneca bringing forward a curious anticipation in inverted form of the Christian doctrine of original sin. The prosperity of the wicked, he suggests, may be explained as a sort of imputation to them of the merits, if not of their first parents, at least of some godly ancestors.

But the fact of sin could not be demolished by such means and to reduce it the Stoics finally advanced the argument from free-will. Virtue and vice are attitudes of the will which are not forced upon us from the outside. The adoption of them springs only from ourselves, and it is within our power to choose which one we will adopt. For this choice the individual alone, not God, is responsible. Hence God is not responsible for moral evil, which is the only evil.

Free-Will and Divine Foreordination. Such an explanation, however, was not consistent with their deterministic view that everything that happens, including our own actions, is providentially governed and directed for the best. Hence we find both Cleanthes and Chrysippus trying to reconcile human free-will with divine foreordination. This they attempted in a number of ways.

In the first place, Cleanthes suggested that foreordination, although it excludes chance, does not exclude the possibility either of our having acted differently in the past, or of acting in the future in any one of a number of ways, possible at the moment, which will always remain open to us. Chrysippus, however, though he agreed with Cleanthes as to the possibility of "might have beens," felt that future courses of action now possible and open to us may become impossible as time goes on. But both men saw in this idea of possibility a basis for free-will within a deterministic scheme.

Proximate and Principal Causes. Again, we find Chrysippus trying to reconcile moral responsibility with destiny by maintaining that destiny implies law, and law implies a distinction between right and wrong and meritorious and censurable behavior; and again, that destiny implies a universe, a universe a God, and a God goodness, which in its turn implies the distinction between good and evil. To the objection that if all things are fated, it can make no difference what we do, he retorted that events are predetermined not absolutely but contingently. Certain acts are bound to have certain results, but we are not bound to perform them. Furthermore, he distinguished between so-called "proximate" and "principal" causes of moral action, and regarded the one as determined, the other as free. A cylinder, for example, needs a push to set it rolling, but, once started, its course is guided by the inner necessity—or freedom—of its own nature. In the same way the will cannot act without the proximate cause of a motive, but assent to that motive, which is the "principal cause" of the act, lies with the will itself. Therefore this assent is undetermined by anything outside ourselves.

Limitations of God. Cleanthes, moreover, from the very beginning had had his doubt about the feasibility of identifying destiny and providence, and had tended to oppose "necessity" to the divine purpose, as an outer limitation upon the divine power responsible ultimately for evil. And Chrysippus was forced by the frequent failures of oracles and soothsayers to conclude that God cannot know everything, and to concede, under fire, that neither can God do everything but is confronted with necessities that even he cannot overcome.

Moreover, you cannot expect both to have your cake and eat it. For example, according to Chrysippus, if the human head is to conform to the best design it has to be built of easily broken bone. A fragile skull is a "necessary consequence" or disadvantage of a shapely one.

Later, at any rate, the doctrine of special providence, also, was undermined by the admission that though God controls events in the large he leaves minor matters to take care of themselves. By the time of Cicero and Seneca this incipient dualism was well on its way to develop into a doctrine of intractable matter, and God was cleared of responsibility for evil on the ground that he was doing the best that he could under difficult conditions, and must not be blamed for his inability to do better.

VI. STOIC COSMOLOGY, PHYSICS, AND ASTRONOMY

Cosmology. The main outlines of the Stoic cosmology were laid down by the Stoic version of the Heraclitean philosophy. Conceiving as they did the intelligible structure—or Logos—of the universe as an active, creative world-reason—or *logos spermatikos*—they regarded the world-process as the unfolding of a divine plan. But the Logos does not precede in time the universe in which it expresses itself. For it itself is not in time, but is the Form or Nature of all that takes place in the temporal process. Furthermore, it is an organization of all the myriad forms and laws that give natures and names to individual objects and inspire and govern their activities. These forms and laws are particular *logoi spermatikoi,* individual manifestations of the creative and all-ruling *logos spermatikos* of the universe.

The fundamental expression of the Logos is the Heraclitean law of the Upward and the Downward Way which the divine Fire follows in its cycle of successive transformations. The tension set up by the opposing ways gives stability to the material structure of the universe. Eventually, however, the Upward Way will prevail and give rise to a world-conflagration in which, as we have seen, all souls as well as all bodies will be destroyed. And then the world-process will begin all over again and repeat itself. This view, however, was rejected by many Stoics, particularly in Roman times, who inclined rather to the Aristotelian teaching that the universe is eternal.

Physics. In the development of their physics the Stoics were largely influenced by Aristotle. Like him, and in opposition to Democritus and the Epicureans, they taught that qualitative alteration could not be reduced to terms of movement in space, though they considered locomotion the primary form of change. Time and space are not found apart from body. The one is the extension occupied by a body, the other the "extension" occupied by its movement. Neither one exists in itself or outside the universe. The "empty" is neither spatial nor temporal. It is a kind of existent non-existent.

Motion, as with Aristotle, was divided into two sorts, rectilinear, pertaining to things of earth, and circular, natural to the heavens. Fire and air tend to move towards the circumference, water and earth towards the center of the universe. The Aristotelian fifth element, the super-fire or ether, which Aristotle had adopted as a kind of insurance against a world-conflagration, was rejected as unnecessary. The four causes of Aristotle were also dispensed with, and were reduced to variations of the single fundamental causal act by which the nature of things determines each thing to be what it is, to occur at the time and place it does, and to have the antecedents and the consequences it has.

Astronomy. The Stoic astronomy was in the main Aristotelian. Earth, water and air form at the center of the universe an immobile mass, about which, embedded in their respective spheres, the moon, the sun, the planets, and the heaven of fixed stars revolve. Incidentally, the Stoics were violently opposed to the doctrines that the earth turned upon its axis and revolved about the sun—two theories that were beginning to make headway even as early as Cleanthes' time. They denounced these views as impious, and their influence was instrumental in shelving them and in committing the world for so many centuries to the Ptolemaic system.

VII. THE STOIC PSYCHOLOGY

The Nature of the Soul. The Stoics' psychology reflects to a large extent their metaphysics. Man is a microcosm or small edition of the universe, just as the universe is a macrocosm or large edition of man. Like the universe he is both body and soul. His soul is part of the Soul of the world, and like the World-Soul and primal world-stuff is pure fire infused with reason. At the same time, the Stoics admitted that she might have some admixture of air, and even of the other elements—which would account for the four different types of temperament—hot and cold, dry and moist. In addition to these temperaments the soul has various parts or activities—the ruling principle, the five senses, the faculty of speech, and the ability to procreate.

The ruling principle is reason, which is a particular manifestation of the divine mind. It is also, Chrysippus tells us, the principle of personal identity. By it the activities of thought and will are sustained. From it all the other activities of the soul are derived. Its seat is in the heart, and thence its functions extend to the other organs and parts of the body, like the arms of an octopus from the central body.

Even feeling and desire have not separate regions and seats, as with Plato, but belong immediately to it. Through the sense-organs the ruling principle stretches out into the external world.

Nature of Sensation and of the Body. This outgoing activity is poured forth through the channels of the sense-organs. From the eye, for example, rays of light are emitted which meet those coming from the visible object. The same is true of hearing. The medium through which the ruling principle reaches out into the sense-organs, and the sense-organs reach out towards their objects, is breath or air.

Reproduction is not merely of the body but of the soul as well. The ruling principle projects itself into the organs of reproduction as it does into those of sense, and the resultant seed is a divine thing. It is a fragment of a sort of soul-plasm, torn, Zeno tells us, from the spirits of our ancestors. Reason, however, is not present in the embryo. It develops in the child after birth. Animals, also, lack it. Their behavior is governed by the impulses of desire and aversion. In man these impulses must be governed by reason. Otherwise they become irrational and harmful.

The body is composed mostly of earth and water. But as these elements are themselves forms assumed by the ever-living fire, so the body is a form of soul. It and the soul grow and develop as one thing. With the physiological details of bodily structure, however, the Stoics concerned themselves little.

VIII. THE STOIC EPISTEMOLOGY

The Nature of Knowledge. There remained the task of explaining how the ruling principle, stimulated by the external world, not only created sensations, but built out of those sensations, by the process that we call *knowledge,* abstract ideas and concepts that we call *true.* The mind at birth, the Stoics tell us, is like a blank page or an unmarked wax tablet, upon which both external objects and internal states of the body make actual physical impressions. Those impressions are preserved by memory, and thus give rise to lasting images or phantasms. Then, by the comparison, combination, and association of these images, trains of thought are initiated, sometimes spontaneously, sometimes artificially and deliberately, which terminate in general concepts. The spontaneous play of images is the basis of certain notions common to all mankind, such as truth, virtue, good, evil, and the like. But when our thinking is deliberately directed and subjected to the laws of logic, we acquire knowledge.

The Stoics, however, followed the Cynics in maintaining that general ideas have no counterpart in the external world. The existent is concrete and individual, and universals are merely names marking the superficial resemblances of particular things. Indeed, the Stoics went so far as to say that only bodies and their modifications have real existence.

Truth and Error. But how can we be sure that we have a true image or concept of things as they really are? What is the test for distinguishing a true idea from a false one? For that matter, how is it possible to entertain false ideas at all? We must, then, find a reliable criterion of truth and error.

Plainly this criterion cannot be found in our sensations, which are neither true nor false, but are simply there, are what they are, and cannot be mistaken for one another. But the case is different with the images built up out of sensations. These we do not have to accept for what they seem to be, as we do sensations. They may be hallucinations, or illusions, or false representations, as when we mistake one thing for another. Error consists in assenting to such images as if they represented external objects, when they do not. Or it may lie in accepting an image as corresponding to one thing, when in reality it corresponds to another. We are not forced to such assent and acceptance. To err or not to err lies within our power. It is an act of the will.

The Source of Error. But why does the will make wrong assents and acceptances? The reason for this may lie either in the will itself or in the nature of the images in the mind. The will may suffer from an inherent lack of tension, and therefore be unstable and inclined to be either too irritable and hasty or too flabby in its acceptances. Or a lack of clearness in the image itself may cause even a well-balanced will to accept a misleading image as a reliable one. Generally speaking, however, clear picturing and resolute willing go together, whereas cloudy images appeal to the weak or overhasty will. To clarify the picture and ensure right assent, the image must be carefully studied and thoroughly mastered before it is accepted. Such study may provoke either acceptance, or denial, or simply suspension of judgment.

The Criterion of Truth. The criterion of truth, then, is clearness. The clear image carries conviction and compels assent. It is *irresistible*. It feels true. Beyond this irresistible feeling of truth we cannot go. Any image that after prolonged and careful examination and weighing has this value simply has to be accepted as indicating that its counterpart really exists. This test of irresistible conviction was also set up for the "common notions" and for scientific and philosophic concepts.

Those ideas are true descriptions of the universe, which are so clear and make everything so plain that there is no getting away from them.

To bring, however, a scientific or philosophic concept to the point of irresistible clearness requires much more detailed and painstaking study than is necessary in the case of images and "common notions," whose convincing character is largely spontaneous and more immediately self-evident. Such concepts are established only by reasoning them out step by step through a process of logical thinking. In short, a sound logic is a necessary preliminary to sound science and philosophy.

IX. THE STOIC LOGIC

The Stoic logical inquiries led them first to investigate grammar, to whose crystallization they helped contribute. They then proceeded to inquire into the nature of propositions and judgments of truth and falsity. They found, however, that categorical affirmations and denials were of no great importance to the process of scientific and philosophical investigations, although the conclusions drawn from such inquiries could always be stated categorically. The process of inquiry itself is conducted rather by a series of hypothetical judgments, which take the form of "If this, then that; but not this, therefore that," and "Either this or that; but this, therefore not that." It is by using hypothetical and disjunctive syllogisms of this sort that we finally reach an "if," and a "therefore" that enable us to say that such and such *must* be the case.

The Stoics studied in considerable detail disjunctive and hypothetical syllogisms, of which, however, Chrysippus accepted only five forms as giving correct conclusions. These studies later exercised considerable influence on medieval logic.

In spite, however, of their efforts to create an ironbound logic and to establish scientific and philosophic thinking upon an infallible basis of absolutely clear, irresistible, and convincing concepts, the Stoics from the beginning began to backslide and to concede that probability, without complete certainty, was a sufficient reason for scientific and metaphysical conclusions. In so doing, they were perhaps influenced by the repeated attacks made by the Skeptics upon the possibility of being absolutely sure about anything, and particularly upon the doctrine of irresistible impressions as a test of truth.

X. THE MIDDLE STOA

Diogenes. By the beginning of the second century B.C. Stoicism was diffused throughout the Hellenistic world, and had even its outposts as far east as Babylon. In Athens meantime, the leadership of the School had devolved upon Diogenes, a native of Seleucia. In 155 B.C. he, along with Critolaus, the head of the Peripatetics, and Carneades, president of the Academy, were chosen by Athens as special ambassadors to Rome to plead for a remission of the fine imposed upon Athens by Roman arbitrators as a penalty for invading and plundering the state of Oropus. While the case was under consideration by the Roman Senate, all three took the opportunity to give public lectures on their respective philosophies.

Diogenes' way had already been prepared for him by the Stoic Crates, head of the great library recently founded by Eumenes II at Pergamus in emulation of the library at Alexandria. Four years earlier Crates had visited Rome and acquainted the intelligentsia with Stoic doctrine. So Diogenes did not have to lecture to a wholly uninstructed audience. He made a good impression, though he was completely overshadowed by the Skeptic, Carneades, a far abler man and more brilliant lecturer. The latter, indeed, created such a furor that Cato besought the Senate to render its decision at its earliest convenience and bid the three ambassadors godspeed before the beliefs of the Roman youth had been completely undermined by Academic agnosticism.

Panaetius and Posidonius. But it was Panaetius and Posidonius who brought Stoicism once and for all to Rome. Panaetius, born about 189 B.C. into a rich and prominent family of Rhodes, studied philosophy first at Pergamus, and then at Athens where he became an ardent disciple of the Stoic Diogenes. On a visit to Rome he formed a lasting friendship with Scipio Africanus, and became with him and the historian Polybius the center of a learned and aristocratic circle. In 129 B.C. Scipio died, and Panaetius, elected about the same time to the presidency of the Stoa, returned to Athens, where he spent the remaining twenty years of his life. He possessed great eloquence, and wrote in a forceful and polished literary style. And he had a thorough knowledge of Greek philosophy and was a devotee of Plato.

Posidonius, who was also born at Rhodes, about 135 B.C., was one of Panaetius' most gifted pupils. Although, after much traveling, he finally settled in Rhodes where he died about 51 B.C., he exercised through his writings an influence scarcely second to that of Panaetius upon the growing circle of noble Roman Stoics. He was one of the most learned men of his age, well versed not only in history and philosophy, but in the natural sciences as well, and he shared Panaetius' admiration of the Platonic teaching.

With them the narrowness and the traces of Cynic uncouthness, from which the Early Stoa had not shaken itself entirely free, disappeared, and the tone of Stoic teaching became more cultured and more catholic, and more attuned to the spiritual ear of the contemporary world. Moreover, at the hands of both men Stoic doctrine underwent further, though not parallel, modifications. Panaetius continued the humanization of Stoic ethics. He adopted Aristotle's definition of virtue as a golden mean, and admitted that external goods might be not only means to right living, but ends to be pursued for their own sake. Furthermore, he helped adapt Stoicism to Roman needs by emphasizing the virtue of temperance, or propriety in daily life, as the most important revelation of the good will, and by laying great stress upon the performance of the daily duties that result from contact with the world.

In his metaphysics he made even wider departures from the earlier teaching. He rejected the theory of a world-conflagration, and maintained with Aristotle, not only the eternity of the world, but the latter's sharp distinction between God and the universe. He was also suspicious of divination.

Reactionary Tendencies of Posidonius. From the views of Panaetius, Posidonius was somewhat reactionary. Apparently of a deeply religious temperament himself, he emphasized the religious aspects of Stoic doctrine in an old-fashioned way. His ethics reverted to the severity of Cleanthes. He clung to the reality of divination and to the theory of a world-conflagration, and was greatly shocked by the heliocentric theory. He was a firm believer in the divine origin of the soul, and in her pre-existence as well as her personal survival of death—beliefs that led him at times to contrast the soul to the body in a dualistic fashion. Historically, too, he played an important part in the philosophic ancestry of the second person of the Christian trinity. From him Philo Judaeus, who will presently engage our attention, took over the Stoic Logos, and made it part and parcel of the Neo-Platonic speculation that so influenced the early development of Christian theology.

Influence of Rome on Stoicism. The ball that Panaetius and Posidonius thus set rolling proved to be of snow and gathered momentum, prestige, and numbers as the years passed. Rome was henceforth the home and center of the school, and little more came from Athens. Under Roman influence Stoicism continued more rapidly than heretofore to develop the divergencies of opinion and the concessions to hard fact that had begun to appear so early in its history. It became more mellow, more urbane, more tolerant, more adapted generally to the needs of the mass of mankind. This was due in part to the worldliness and the sturdy political and social common sense of the Romans. In part, too, the change reflected the cosmopolitanism of the Empire, which fused and welded together many different countries and civilizations with all their variety of customs, manners, moralities and gods. This imperial atmosphere, which no Roman of the period could wholly escape, was unfavorable to the development of intellectual and moral dogmatism.

Again both the Academics and Epicureans, as we have already remarked, played no small part in the humanization of the Stoic school. The Academics, who were death on dogmatism of any sort, helped undermine the original Stoic assumption of intellectual certainty. And the Epicureans, their opponents, contributed not a little to the liberalization of the School.

XI. ROMAN STOICISM. THE LATE STOA

It is impossible for us to follow in any detail the intricate evolution of Stoicism in this later and third period, or to give all the names of its leaders and prominent adherents. The best we can do is to mention a few of the most eminent Romans who were either professed members of the sect, or sympathetic in the main to its teachings. Of Scipio Africanus we have already spoken. Horace and Virgil were both influenced by the School, and later, too, Hadrian, most fascinating and enigmatic of the Roman Emperors, was interested in it. Again, Cicero was officially an adherent of the old Academy, but found much in the very similar liberal wing of Stoicism to arouse his sympathies. Seneca, though professing independence, was a Stoic at heart. Attalus, who converted him, and Musonius, his contemporary, were evangelists and had a tremendous influence. And finally we have the slave Epictetus, and the philosopher-king Marcus Aurelius. To the translations and comments of Cicero and Seneca we owe most of our knowledge of the older school; to the discourses of the slave and the Emperor our most profound insight into what Stoic teaching might mean to men.

Seneca. Seneca illustrates both with his writings and his life the concessions that the Stoics were forced to make to the exigencies of hard fact, the worldliness of the Roman genius, and the spirit of the times. Austere and somewhat sanctimonious by nature, he was given to deploring human weaknesses and to bewailing the vanity and wickedness of the world, from which he professed himself to await impatiently release in a happier home beyond the grave. But at the same time he was far from averse to worldly success. He was a shrewd and energetic business man, who considerably increased the fortune he had inherited. And in his philosophic sermons he defended the righteousness of great wealth against the doubts cast upon it by the Cynics and the Epicureans. He succeeded also in rising to great political prominence and was tutor and later minister to Nero—whom, however, he so bored and irritated in the long run that he was eventually ordered by the Emperor to commit suicide.

Again, his feeling that reason is bankrupt and his willingness to accept in its place sentimental and moral needs as sufficient grounds for religious convictions bear witness to the changes Stoicism was undergoing in its final phase. Taken in connection with his general inclination to be skeptical of all certainty, his inclination to temporize, and his teaching that social and political hazards should be avoided rather than faced, they show how rapidly and to what lengths Stoicism was now departing from the doctrines of its founders.

Popularity and Persecution of Stoicism. By the time of Augustus Caesar, Stoicism had begun to seep from the upper classes to the masses, and under Tiberius it had obtained a considerable following among the people at large. Its growing popularity was perhaps due in part to its willingness, which we have already remarked, to accept the popular theology as an allegorical and pictorial expression of Stoic truth. This hospitable and sympathetic attitude was all the more marked by its contrast to the attacks launched by the Academics and the Epicureans upon the current orthodoxy. In Rome the work of reconciliation was carried on partly by Cicero, whose views were eclectic, and who translated and adapted in part the writings of Panaetius and Posidonius, and partly by Cornutus, who lived in the first century A.D. Although he contributed little to Stoic thought, he wrote a book in which every last detail of Graeco-Roman theology was given a Stoic meaning.

In the first century A.D., however, after the Republic had given way to the Empire, philosophy, and particularly Stoicism, fell for a time under a cloud. The leading philosophers, most of whom at the mo-

ment happened to be Stoics, were regarded by the Imperial government as menaces to Roman ideals and institutions, and were subjected
to frequent persecution and deportation. Under Nero, indeed, a determined effort was made to suppress all freedom of thought and expression, and Stoicism, since it was the most prominent champion of
free inquiry and discussion, bore the brunt of the attack. Many of its
leaders were put to death, and many others deported. The growing
sect of Christians was now also for the first time persecuted. Similar
though less drastic attempts at suppression were made by Vespasian
and Domitian. For a while, then, Stoicism had to take to cover, hold
its tongue, and bide its time. But that time was not long in coming.
Twenty years later, we find the Emperor Hadrian establishing public
teachers of philosophy at Rome, and his successor, Antoninus Pius,
extending the system to the provinces. And Hadrian's grandson by
adoption was the Stoic Emperor, Marcus Aurelius Antoninus.

Epictetus. Before turning, however, to the Emperor let us consider
for a moment the slave, the scarcely less distinguished Epictetus.
Slavery, it must be remembered, did not in Roman times necessarily
imply inferiority of intellect or even of birth. It was confined to the
population of the conquered races, and was often only an accident of
nationality or war. Hence, in the great Roman households the slaves
were frequently better educated, more talented, and more civilized
than their masters, and were entrusted with highly responsible and
confidential positions. They ran their masters' establishments, advised
them on all matters, educated the children, and in all but name were
trusted companions and friends rather than servants. Men of such
caliber were generally given their freedom as a reward for their
loyalty and efficiency, and sometimes rose afterwards to positions of
high political importance. The ministers of the Emperor Claudius,
for instance, were almost all of them freedmen.

Epictetus, himself, was a Phrygian. Born about 50 A.D., he started
life as a slave to a freedman formerly belonging to Nero, and was
sent by him to attend the lectures of Musonius. He proved an apt
pupil and quickly won recognition and reputation among contemporary Stoics. Indeed, before he was forty he had become important
enough to be deported by Domitian along with the other prominent
philosophers of the time. He retired to Nicopolis, where he continued
to lecture till his death in 130. Tradition has it that he and the Emperor Hadrian were friends.

A Moralist. The sayings of Epictetus, taken down by Arrian, and
transmitted to us in two books, the *Discourses* and the *Manual,* rank

with the *Meditations* of Marcus Aurelius among the great books of consolation. Philosophically, they reveal Epictetus as an old-fashioned Stoic in many respects, leaning towards Cynic austerity and concerned principally with the moral and religious aspects of the school's teaching. He concerned himself little with physical and metaphysical speculations, or with logic, all of which he regarded in true Cynic fashion as a waste of time. As he grew older, to be sure, he became reconciled to the necessity of some logic as indispensable to sound thinking, but his tendency was always to refute his opponents by simple appeals to what he considered the self-evident truth of his positions. For him the philosopher was primarily the healer of souls, whose message was more to the moral sense than to the intellect, and whose vocation was to arouse the conscience, to awaken a conviction of sin, to turn men from their wickedness and to point the way that led to happiness and peace.

The content of his message added little new to Stoic doctrine. Salvation was of the familiar sort. Its root and flower lay in the time-honored cultivation of independence on external circumstance. It was also stimulated and enriched by religious sentiment and conviction, and by an assurance that all is for the best.

The Brotherhood of Man. We have, however, no definite indications of his views on immortality. Certain passages suggest a dualistic opposition of the soul to the flesh, from the burden of which she is released by death. Others seem to substitute for personal survival the breaking up of the individual into the elements of which he is made, and a possible recombination in some new object of the particles that once composed him.

What does stand out in Epictetus, as also in Marcus Aurelius, is the doctrine of the brotherhood of man. The Cynics, we may remember, had proposed it in a rough and negative form, incidentally to their general denunciation of all political institutions, including national units, as artificial and contrary to nature. The Stoics fell heir to it, gave it positive content and meaning, and turned its purely destructive anti-nationalism into a constructive and civilized internationalism. All men, Epictetus tells us, are children of one Father. All men, irrespective of race or station, are brothers. All men equally are not only citizens of the world but of the universe, akin not only to one another but to all things. The Stoic will feel this kinship with them all, and particularly with his fellow men. He will love them like brothers, whatever their nationality, their race, or their station in life may be. The Christians, also, were by now developing the same doctrine in their own terms. Thanks to Stoicism, they found the way already prepared for it, increased in numbers and influence, and moved towards their eventual domination of the western world.

Marcus Aurelius. According to the historian Gibbon, the condition of the human race has never been more prosperous or more happy than it was at Rome for the greater part of the century following the assassination of the Emperor Domitian in 96 A.D. A series of rulers succeeded him, as excellent as he had been ignoble, culminating in the two Antonines in whom Plato might have felt that his dream of the philosopher-king was at last brought true. Born in 121 of an old Spanish family long eminent at Rome, Marcus Aurelius was adopted while still a youth, at Hadrian's behest, by his aunt's husband, Titus Annius Antoninus, whom the childless Emperor, now an old man, had lately designated as heir to the throne. Thus from an early age he was hedged by the divinity that would some day be his, and was educated with great care, and at the same time with extreme simplicity of life, for his future position. Philosophy was taught him by Junius Rusticus, at the time one of the most eminent Stoics in Rome and a follower of the teachings of Musonius and Epictetus. How great an influence his master's precepts and example had upon him he tells us in the *Meditations*.

Grave, studious, conscientious, physically never robust, disliking pomp and ceremony, he viewed his approaching responsibility with distaste rather than elation, and his rapid elevation to a quaestorship at seventeen, and, the next year, to a consulship and the title of Caesar, which carried with it a close association with Antoninus, now Emperor, failed to turn his head or to affect his native modesty and kindliness. At the same time, he was scrupulous in maintaining the dignity of his position and the outward show and state that it demanded.

A deep affection sprang up between him and his uncle and adopted father, strengthened by his marriage with Antoninus' daughter Faustina. To her and to the thirteen children she bore him he was devoted, and her death and the loss of eight of them in childhood and in youth, were a never-forgotten grief to him. He shared, too, the Emperor's love of the country and of country life, and of retiring to the villas at Lorium and at Lavinium in the Alban Hills where he could go boar-hunting to his heart's content.

Interest in Philosophy. In one respect, however, his family circle failed to satisfy him. It could not give him the intellectual companionship that his native intelligence and imagination, and his interest in

literature and philosophy, and particularly in Stoicism, craved. The
Emperor and Empress were not people of intellectual tastes, and
Faustina, however devoted a wife and mother she may have been,
malicious gossip to the contrary notwithstanding, was certainly not
overburdened with brains. This aspiration for wider horizons than
those disclosed by a happy home life, or at a purely moral elevation,
led to his friendship with Fronto, the leading spirit of a brilliant
literary circle which numbered among its members Lucian, Polemon,
Favorinus, and Aulus Gellius, and devoted itself especially to the
study of the Latin classicists of the Republic. A man of the world,
one of the most eminent lawyers of his time, and none too glad a
sufferer of philosophers, it may well be that Fronto did much to
infuse the Stoicism of his imperial friend and pupil with the breadth
and humanity of vision that characterize it.

Reign as Emperor. In 161 Antoninus Pius had died and Marcus had
come to the throne. The remaining nineteen years of his life called
for all his Stoicism. Death and disappointment within his family, the
plague that swept over the Empire and devastated Rome, the war
with the Parthians, the ceaseless efforts to beat back the ever more
menacing barbarian invasions from the north, the revolt of a trusted
general in command of the armies of the East—all these laid upon
him one by one a burden heavier than his none too robust constitution could bear. Almost all his reign was spent at the front, and it
was at headquarters in the field near present day Vienna and Budapest,
by candle-light in his tent, after long days of attending to all the civil
and military business of the Empire, that the *Meditations* were written.
Here, too, near Vienna he died in 180 A.D.

Faith in the Universe. Philosophically, Marcus Aurelius belongs
among those who were inclined to substitute the notion of probable
truth for the certainty and infallibility of Stoic teaching to which
some members of the school still clung. But he has no doubt that the
world-order is rational, and that all things and events are expressions
of a divine Reason which finds them all equally necessary and equally
perfect. Nor is there any uncertainty either in Aurelius' words or deeds
that living in the light of reason, both human and divine, means to
be firm and unyielding, to be patient, to be magnanimous, to be compassionate and forgiving, in the face of all that destiny may decree.

Death, he feels, more surely than Epictetus, is the end of the individual. It merges us with the elements from which we spring, and
re-unites the reason within us with the Logos of which it is a part.
It is as natural as birth and growth, as begetting and bearing, as ma-

turity and old age. It is not to be desired or dreaded, hastened or delayed. It is simply to be accepted along with all other natural facts and awaited with the same calmness that we await each new year of life. One thing is certain—no one has anything to fear from it.

The following quotation, jotted down in camp at Carnuntum on the Danube near Vienna (II, 17), is typical of the lonely heights from which he viewed all time and existence:

Of human life the time is a point, and the substance is in a flux, and the perception dull, and the composition of the whole body subject to putrefaction, and the soul a whirl, and fortune hard to divine, and fame a thing devoid of judgment. And, to say all in a word, everything which belongs to the soul is a dream and vapor, and life is a warfare and a stranger's sojourn, and after-fame is oblivion. What then is that which is able to conduct a man? One thing, and only one, philosophy. But this consists in keeping the daemon within a man free from violence and unharmed, superior to pains and pleasures, doing nothing without a purpose, nor yet falsely and with hypocrisy, not feeling the need of another man's doing or not doing anything; and besides, accepting all that happens, and all that is allotted, as coming from thence, wherever it is, from whence he himself came; and, finally waiting for death with a cheerful mind, as being nothing else than a dissolution of the elements of which every living being is compounded. But if there is no harm to the elements themselves in each continually changing into another, why should a man have any apprehension about the change and dissolution of all the elements? For it is according to nature, and nothing is evil which is according to nature.

Decay of Stoicism. At the death of Marcus Aurelius, Stoicism retired to the background of the philosophic stage, there to remain until its final extinction. It still had a large following, but it suffered from the competition of Christianity, which was now rapidly pushing to the fore, and was not only attracting to its ranks many who would otherwise have become Stoics, but also was recruiting its converts from within the School. But Christianity itself was in its early days merely one phase of a larger philosophic and religious movement, which will presently be reviewed. Since, however, this movement had important negative as well as positive causes, and was in part a reaction against a widespread, rapidly increasing and philosophically organized spirit of agnosticism, it will be well first to consider for a moment the skeptical attacks, with which, as we have seen, Epicureanism and Stoicism also had to contend.

Chapter XVIII

THE SKEPTICS

I. PYRRHO

Attack on the Possibility of Knowledge. The Platonic Academy, we may remember, had quickly succumbed to the moralizing temper of the times, and had abandoned metaphysical for ethical problems and discussions. This interlude of indifference to metaphysical speculations soon turned to positive dislike of them, and was succeeded by an active distrust of the mind's ability to know the nature of Reality. Before, however, this suspicion became articulate in the skepticism of the Academy under Arcesilaus, an independent onslaught upon the possibility of knowledge and the pretensions of metaphysics had been made by Pyrrho of Elis, born probably about 360 B.C. He is said to have accompanied the army of Alexander to India, and to have passed the last years of his life, poor but respected, in his native city. His skeptical attitude seems to have been derived in part from his acquaintance with the logical mazes in which the Megaric school delighted, and in part from the doctrine, accepted alike by Sophists, Cynics, Cyrenaics, Plato, and Democritus, that sense-experience is untrustworthy. But, whereas both Plato and Democritus believed that reason was able to see through the false reports of perception and to grasp the nature of the Real, Pyrrho extended their disbelief in the senses to thinking as well, and came to the conclusion, at which Protagoras and the skeptical followers of Socrates had arrived, that knowledge of anything absolute is unobtainable. The Sophists, it will be remembered, had gone so far as to deny categorically that there is any such thing as universal and absolute truth. Pyrrho, however, did not proceed to quite such lengths. He contented himself with pointing out that such truth, if it exists, cannot be known by the human mind.

The Relativity of Truth and Morality. As Pyrrho left no writings,[1] all our knowledge of him is secondhand and scanty at that. But he

---

[1] Almost all the original writings of the Skeptics, with the exception of those of Sextus Empiricus, have been lost. Fragments of Timon survive and have been

appears to have argued that individuals differ quite as hopelessly in what they think as in what they perceive. Philosophers disagree, each claiming that reason is on his side, and, as a matter of fact, bring forward equally convincing arguments for the most diametrically opposed conclusions. Every statement, then, about the nature of Reality may be countered with a contradictory statement no less well-founded. Even so-called moral verities, or in other words, universal and authoritative standards of human practice, turn out upon examination to be matters of tradition and convention, relative to time and place. The approved characters, institutions, and ways of one age and group are not those of another. No amount of thinking can decide between them and lay down which are best.

It follows that the only sound attitude in all questions is one of complete suspension of judgment. In pretending to know what is or is not really true or right, we are only expressing our private opinions of what seems true or false to you or me. At the same time, Pyrrho and his pupil Timon tried to avoid the objection, already made by Plato to Protagoras, that they were asserting as absolutely certain the non-existence of absolute certainty. They dodged the difficulty by maintaining that even their own position was not certain, but only probable. The most he can say, Pyrrho feels, is that in his opinion the probabilities are against the possibility of attaining certain knowledge and of arriving at indubitably certain conclusions on any subject.

Action Governed by Probability. Suspension of judgment, however, does not mean indecision in action. You must take chances, and the best bet is to play the numbers that most often turn up—in other words to follow the customs and traditions and to conform to the institutions that have succeeded in establishing themselves. But in so doing you will preserve your mental integrity by remembering that they are in no way God-given or authoritative. They may be right. They probably are. But you will not be fooled by that probability into mistaking it for certainty.

Timon. Pyrrho's outburst was in a way isolated. He had one pupil, Timon, and whether or not Timon left any disciples is a matter of dispute. In any case, the school, if such it can be called, did not last beyond the third generation. Already in Timon's day, and to his great disgust, the skeptically minded were flocking to the new Acad-

collected and published by Mullach, *Fragmenta Philosophorum Graecorum.* Otherwise, our chief sources of knowledge of the school are Diogenes Laertius, Cicero, Eusebius, and also Sextus Empiricus. Specific references to these sources have not been given, except in case of quotation.

emy, where Arcesilaus was conducting a detailed and skillfully planned campaign against both the Stoic and the Epicurean epistemologies and metaphysics.

II. ARCESILAUS

Arcesilaus, born at Pitane in Aeolia about 315 B.C., was some twenty years younger than Zeno and Epicurus. Brilliant, acute, critical, and witty by nature, he received an excellent education in mathematics, literature and philosophy, and at an early age identified himself with the Academy, of which he became the head after the death of Crates. A man of kindly, genial, and upright character, he was highly respected at Athens, even by those whom he attacked most bitterly.

It was the Stoic doctrine of "irresistible impressions" as the test of truth that aroused his philosophic ire, and against them and the trust in the senses they implied he launched all the time-honored arguments against the credibility of sense-perception. More particularly he urged against the Stoics that the false is often as convincing as the true, opinion as irresistible as so-called knowledge, and that therefore irresistible impressions are common property of the sage and the fool alike, hovering between knowledge and opinion, and devoid in themselves of any indication of truth or error. And, since all so-called knowledge is derived from impressions, it can set up no criterion as to which are trustworthy and which are not.

Probability, and here again Arcesilaus agrees with Pyrrho, is all we need as a warrant and a guide for action. As a matter of fact, we are always coming to decisions and putting our decisions into effect without waiting for irresistible convictions, and we are quite right in doing so. Common-sense behavior does not require certainty of knowledge. Morality does not need absolute standards. What is *probably* right is all we know and all we need to know. And, if the somewhat scanty account of Arcesilaus' ethics can be trusted, what is probably the right course to follow is the moderate, temperate, sensible middle path, neither over-lax nor over-severe.

III. THE NEW ACADEMY

Carneades. For some seventy-five years after the death of Arcesilaus, the Academy produced no noteworthy philosophers. Then suddenly Carneades appeared upon the scene. Born about 213 B.C. in Cyrene, he studied at Athens under Diogenes and Chrysippus, as well as under Hegesinus, the head of the Academy. But his Stoic teachers served only to antagonize him and to turn him into an ardent critic and opponent of their school. His abilities were such as to make him the rallying point of the contemporary skeptical movement, into which he infused so much fresh life that he was regarded by the ancients as the founder of a new Academy. We have already noted that he was one of the three philosopher-ambassadors despatched on a political mission by the Athenians to Rome, where Cato was so exercised over the corrupting influence of his immensely popular lectures upon the beliefs of Roman youth. He lived, himself, to a ripe old age, and died in 129 B.C.

Like Arcesilaus and Pyrrho he wrote little, and his views are known to us thanks to the labors of his disciple Cleitomachus, a Carthaginian by birth, who, it is said, devoted some four hundred books to his master's views, and thus perpetuated his memory.

Attack on Stoic Epistemology. Carneades added little if anything new to the critical method of his predecessors. He simply amplified their technique and extended Arcesilaus' criticism of the Stoic theory of "irresistible impressions" into a general attack upon the whole Stoic philosophy. To the Skeptic treatment of probability, however, he made important additions, as we shall see in a moment.

In his further development of the polemic against the Stoic theory of knowledge, Carneades pointed out the deceptiveness of all conviction, however firm. Dreams, illusions, and hallucinations are just as convincing at the time they are experienced as are the impressions of waking and sane perception, and the latter, however clear and irresistible, frequently misrepresents its objects, or, at the best, presents us with a series of contradictory impressions, all equally convincing and all equally relative. The same is the case with seemingly clear and convincing concepts. Many of them involve logical fallacies, and in any case logical correctness is no guarantee that a concept represents the real nature of things. Equally logical conclusions may contradict one another, and there is no way of deciding which of two equally irresistible and convincing ideas is true. Since, then, the supposed certainties of reasoning are as fallacious as those of sense and feeling, there can be no such thing as knowledge of the truth.

Attack on Stoic Theology. This conclusion, Carneades illustrated at length by exposing what he considered the absurdities of the Stoic system. Stoic theology offered the broadest target for attack, and bit by bit he set to work to demolish it. First, he discredited its arguments for the existence of God. The universality of the belief in a God, to which the Stoics appealed, he denied outright. Nor had he much difficulty in disposing of the so-called evidence from divination, omens, and prophecy. He insisted that the universe shows no signs of being intelligently planned and directed, and that it is the height of folly to regard it as designed expressly for the benefit of man when we con-sider the disasters and destruction it deals out to the human race. Again, in the face of all the misery, the folly, and the sin in the world, not to speak of the undeserved sufferings of the virtuous and prosperity of the wicked, where is there any ground for inferring the existence of a divine providence and a moral government of the universe?

Furthermore, even if the universe could be called rational and good in every respect, we should have no right to conclude that therefore it was the work or the expression of an intelligent and beneficent God. Its law and order and its subservience to human interests might just as well have been produced by natural causes. Nor have we any right to impose upon nature our views of what is higher and lower, and to argue that the rational is *better* than the irrational, or that the human mind must be derived from a universal reason because a thing cannot rise *higher* than its source. Granting that a higher and a lower exist in nature, how do we know what is higher and what is lower in her sight? Her standards may differ from ours.

Moreover, the Stoics make contradictory demands in their very idea of God. They proclaim him to be infinite, but at the same time they insist on investing him with characteristics, like life, conscious-ness, intelligence, and moral qualities, that imply limitations of one sort or another and make sense only in connection with finite beings. For that matter, the Stoic God cannot be conceived as either infinite *or* finite, immaterial *or* material, not to speak of trying to conceive him as both. The infinite cannot be a whole, and have any organiza-tion to support activity and soul. The finite cannot be a totality of existence. The immaterial has no stuff to it to be living and feeling and active. The material is only animate when it is composite. Life and thought are never found in connection with the simple elements which alone are stable and unchanging. But the composite is always subject to change and destruction. Quite apart, then, from the lack of any evidence for the existence of God, the Stoic concept of God is in itself nonsensical.

Attack on Stoic Ethics. The Stoic ethics Carneades attacked as vigor-ously as he did the Stoic theology. In his opinion it contradicted itself in one and the same breath by declaring both that virtue is a final good and end in itself and that it is a means towards living in conformity with nature, which thus turns out to be the real good which virtue subserves.

Again, Carneades continues, it can be argued that all morality is artificial, not natural; that the fundamental motive of human conduct is the self-interest of the individual; that all law is a device deliberately invented for the purpose of assuring the individual protection and security in the pursuit of his ends; and that therefore justice and righteousness are not valuable in themselves but are practiced always with an eye to the main chance. It can be maintained that laws and moral standards are relative to time and place, and that nations have grown great by preferring might to so-called right. We may, then, logically conclude that moral codes should never be allowed to stand in the way of self-interest when they can be safely circumvented—especially since we can never be sure that a moral precept or law really is just and good.

Our final conclusion must, then, be that clear, irresistible and convincing moral standards are as impossible of attainment as irresistible impressions and concepts in the field of knowledge, and that it is as impossible to assert absolute good as it is absolute truth.

Doctrine of Probability. So far, Carneades is purely critical and destructive. Now we turn back to his constructive development of the doctrine of probability. Maintaining, like Pyrrho and Arcesilaus, that the necessity of suspending our judgment as to what, if anything, is really true and really good does not incapacitate us for action, he proceeds to analyze at some length the reasons why this is so. After all, he points out, in spite of the absence of any reliable intellectual criterion for distinguishing true from false ideas, the fact remains that some ideas *seem* truer and more convincing than others, and that we habitually act upon them. It is, then, possible to set up standards for distinguishing different degrees of apparent truth, or, in other words, a scale for measuring probabilities.

The degrees of probability are three, and are distinguished as follows:

1. In the first place, we have *mere probability,* where we act with little or no observation of similar situations to help us, and where the chances therefore are about fifty-fifty, but seem worth taking in view of what we shall gain if we win.

2. Secondly, we have *undisputed probability,* where empirical observation shows us that other people have repeatedly taken the same chances successfully and to their advantage, and have never lost. Here the face-value of the probable truth and reliability of an impression is backed up by all the other impressions and notions related to it.

3. Finally, we may be able to act upon chances that not only look worth taking on a fifty-fifty basis and are uncontradicted and backed up by the experiences of other people, but have been thoroughly investigated and found to have solid reasons for taking them. In other words, we may be able to discover a "system" for life's gamble that mathematically, so to speak, ought to work. Then, says Carneades, we have a basis for action that is *probable, undisputed,* and *tested.*

According as the stakes for which we are playing are low or high, we take more or less chances in the game of life, and play it with an eye to greater or lesser degrees of probable success. We can afford to take greater risks in things of lesser importance, but the serious business of living should always be based upon the highest degree of probability where the chances of failure are least.

The Basis of Morality. Now, the most important activities of human life are comprised in what we call moral conduct. Moral behavior, then, should be based upon the highest degree of probability it is possible to ascertain, and to this end ethics must be thoroughly investigated and the most probable human good must be determined. Unfortunately, however, Carneades gives us no clear indications as to his conclusions on this point. Judging from his attitude towards Stoic ethics, he must have felt, like Aristotle, that virtuous living is not the good and is rewarded not by itself but by the happiness which it bestows. Happiness, he seems to have taught, is most probably to be found in the enjoyment of natural goods, among which he included the exercise of mental as well as physical functions and activities. In that case, he was in substantial agreement with the ethical teaching of Aristotle, the Academy, and the left wing of Stoicism, which was already much influenced by the Skeptics.

The doctrine of probability he also applied to theology. He believed, to be sure, that the existence of the gods could not be proved, and that the Stoic idea of God was quite absurd. But he was willing to allow that the existence of the divine was possible and even probable, and that religious belief had a fair chance of being well-founded.

IV. PHILO OF LARISSA AND ANTIOCHUS

Carneades was succeeded, as head of the Academy, by his pupil Cleitomachus, and Cleitomachus by Philo of Larissa (b. 148-140 B.C., d. 85-77 B.C.). Under the latter's presidency, one of his pupils, Antiochus of Ascalon (b. 127-124 B.C., d. 69 B.C.), made a vigorous attack on Carneades' doctrine of probability, which divided the Academy into two camps. The gist of his objection was that Carneades had involved himself in the self-contradiction of talking about apparently, or even probably, true and false impressions, while at the same time denying that any criterion of distinguishing truth from falsehood could be found. How, then, could Carneades distinguish greater from lesser degrees of probability without admitting the existence of an absolute standard by approximation to which the greater and the lesser were measured? How could he distinguish what was probably more or less true from what was probably more or less false, unless he used absolute truth as a yardstick? How could he say that one course of action was probably better than another, without some previous concept of what was really good?

This objection Philo tried to counter by conceding that there is such a thing as absolute truth, while maintaining that certain knowledge of it is impossible. To this Antiochus retorted by inquiring how, if we cannot know the truth, we can know that it exists or know that it is unknowable.

This quarrel embittered the last days of the Academy, which at Philo's death came to an end. The torch of Skepticism now passed across the sea into other hands.

V. AENESIDEMUS

The Skeptical point of view had already found favor and devoted adherents in Alexandria, which under the patronage of the Ptolemies, had rapidly become a brilliant center of philosophy, and particularly of science. Here the flame of Skepticism was rekindled to burn with an even greater brilliance in its next great disciple, Aenesidemus.

The exact period of Aenesidemus' life is unknown and has been the subject of considerable controversy. By some he has been placed as early as 80 B.C., by others as late as 130 A.D.[2] The preponderance of opinion seems to be in favor of the earlier date. We will accept it, then, provisionally, and regard him as a near contemporary of Philo and Antiochus. Born in Crete, he migrated to Alexandria, and apparently taught there the rest of his life. Skepticism now was established upon a broader and a sounder basis which has reminded some modern critics of the systems of Hume and Kant.

The Relativity of Standards. Aenesidemus began by exposing the relative and self-contradictory character of sensation and opinion. One

[2] Cf. Brochard, *Les Sceptiques Grecs*, pp. 242 ff.

and the same object, he pointed out, may produce different and opposed impressions upon different animals, including man; upon different individual men; upon the different sense-organs of the same
individual; and upon the same sense-organ of the same individual in
different conditions and situations. Moreover, institutions, moral standards, and religious beliefs vary in different times and places, and opposed philosophies seem equally convincing to different persons. So
far, then, we are obviously dealing with appearances rather than with
reality, and with opinion rather than with knowledge and with truth.

Finally, not only do both the percepts and concepts of the same
individual at different times, and of different individuals at the same
time contradict one another, but concepts in general frequently give
the lie to percepts and *vice versa*. Since there is no deciding these
various conflicts, no criterion can be found, and truth itself is non-
existent, at least so far as we are concerned.

Attack on Causation. Aenesidemus reinforces his position by a thoroughgoing attack upon the possibility of giving reasons or causes for
anything. We seek, he says, to explain phenomena in one of two ways.
We say either that one event is caused by another, or that sensible
phenomena are the manifestations of an underlying reality, invisible
to the senses but discoverable by the intellect, in terms of which the
behavior of phenomena may be interpreted and understood. In Aenesidemus' opinion, neither of these ways of explaining things will work.

The first method fails because physical causation is incomprehensible.
We never perceive the act of production of one physical body by another, or of one incorporeal being by another, or of the material by
the immaterial and *vice versa*. Nor is it possible to conceive how such
production can take place. Hence, since the causal link is both imperceptible and inconceivable, there is no such thing as the relation of
cause and effect.

Furthermore, even if it existed, it would be practically undiscoverable because of the difficulties of distinguishing true reasons from false
ones, and of disentangling the real explanation from the multitude of
seeming causes.

The second method employed by science and metaphysics is even
more fallacious. Sensible events no more indicate the existence of an
explanatory order outside and beyond them than they do that of a
causal linkage of one phenomenon to another. And certainly, even if
the sensible world could be regarded as a "sign" of an unseen reality
underlying phenomena, it could, because of its self-contradictory character, give us no hint as to what that reality was like. There are,

Aenesidemus concludes, "no visible signs revealing invisible things, and those who believe in their existence are the victims of a vain illusion." [3]

Attack on Stoic Ethics. Aenesidemus seems also to have brought the same sort of skepticism to bear upon ethics. After attacking particularly the Stoics, and showing that neither happiness nor pleasure nor wisdom can qualify as *the* good, he concludes that any final and absolute good is in the same boat with absolute truth.

It has greatly puzzled commentators to find Aenesidemus, in spite of his skepticism, also credited with having developed a metaphysical system inspired by Heraclitus. He believed, we are told, that air, which he identified with time and number, was the world-substance, out of which by the separation and the interaction of opposites the universe arose. Motion is of two sorts—qualitative alteration and movement in space. Reason is breathed into the body from the outside and uses the sense-organs as windows for perceiving what is going on inside. The universal character of reason accounts for the possession by different individuals of a common standard of truth.

These scraps of information do not suggest a weighty metaphysics. Its relation to the rest of his thought has received several explanations. By some critics Aenesidemus is represented as having been first a Heraclitean and then turned Skeptical. Others suppose that he is merely giving an account of the Heraclitean philosophy, which later was regarded as an exposition of his own views; still others that he is attributing the Heraclitean doctrine of the interaction and identity of opposites merely to the flow of sensible events, without abandoning his Skeptical attitude with respect to objective truth. Others, again, feel that he really changed his mind as he grew older, and abandoned Skepticism, or rather sought for his Skeptical attitude a congenial metaphysical basis.[4]

VI. AGRIPPA

For two centuries after Aenesidemus' death we have little or no knowledge of the history of Skepticism. There can be no doubt that the school grew and flourished, for the brilliant renaissance of the movement, which occurred about 200 A.D., shows signs of long preparation. But in that period, only one name, Agrippa, stands out with any distinction, and he is not included in the list of the leaders of

[3] Photius, *Myriob.*, 170 B, 12.
[4] For these differences of opinion cf. Brochard, *op. cit.*, pp. 277 ff.

the school compiled by Diogenes. Of Agrippa himself we know next to nothing. But the teaching attributed to him and his circle codified and gave a finishing touch to the Skeptics' position. We are, they said, confronted with a dilemma. Either we must grant at once the Skeptical contention that absolute truth is non-existent, or at least undiscoverable, and therefore suspend our judgment, or we must embark upon a course of investigation in the hope of discovering it. The latter course leads us nowhere except to an eventual suspension of judgment, since no first cause in a series of so-called causes and effects can ever be found, and no explanatory concept of the sensible world as a whole can ever be reached that does not itself have to be accounted for. In both cases we are involved in an infinite regress. Nor is there any such thing as self-evident truth—witness the deceptions of the senses and the quarrels of the philosophers. It is not only, then, impossible as a matter of fact to discover the truth, as the older Skeptics had shown; the search for truth is itself invalidated from the start by its logical difficulties. Why, then, should we waste our time and disturb our peace of mind by seeking what we know beforehand it is impossible to find? We had far better suspend our judgment at the beginning, cease from vain questionings, and settle down to live happily by probabilities alone.

VII. SEXTUS EMPIRICUS

The Empirical School of Medicine. We turn now to watch the last lap and the final spurt of ancient Skepticism. The runners were all doctors associated with the "empiric" school of medicine, which founded its practice directly upon the observation of individual cases and the inferences drawn therefrom, rather than upon general theories regarding the nature and causes of different diseases. This school was already very old, dating back, as it did, to the middle of the third century B.C.

By the middle of the first century A.D., it turned to philosophy, had become addicted to Skepticism, and had produced two thinkers of some note, Theiodas and Menodotus. But it remained for Sextus Empiricus, a couple of generations later, to combine the empirical attitude of his medical training with philosophic skepticism.

Sextus' Writings. The life of Sextus is obscure. He was a Greek. He taught about 200 A.D.—exactly where is unknown. Three of his works have been preserved: one, a general résumé of Skeptical arguments, the two others attacks respectively upon the scientists and the philosophers.

These books are a mine of interesting and valuable historical information, but they do not add much that is novel to the critical possibilities of Skepticism, which had already been pretty thoroughly probed and realized by Sextus' predecessors. To Aenesidemus' contention that the existence of an external world cannot be inferred from sensible experience, he does add, however, that even the attempt to infer universal characteristics of the sensible world from the observation of particular instances is likewise foredoomed to failure. For how can we know that any characteristic is universal until we have ransacked the entire universe—all space and all time—which we can never do? Hence so-called universal forms, types, laws, etc., are relative to time and place and to the range of our powers of observation.

Self-Contradictory Nature of Concepts. Again, Sextus continues, amplifying the position of Aenesidemus, not only is the concept of causation unintelligible, but so, too, are the concepts of body, space, time, generation, and the like, habitually used by philosophers. Upon examination all of them turn out to be riddled with self-contradictions. Even mathematics will not hold water.

But if logic, physics, and mathematics are full of contradictions and can give us no absolute truth, what shall we say of ethics? Ethics aims at discovering and defining the good. Confusion now becomes worse confounded—witness not only the diametrically opposed views of the nature of the good taken by the moralists, but the diverse and conflicting ethical practices of mankind. Certainly, then, there is no single, universal *natural* good, revealed to all men alike.

Again, pursuit and desire are the root of all evil. They involve dissatisfaction and discontent and disturbing hopes and fears. And their satisfaction, far from being desirable, only too often proves to be vicious. Virtue, too, involves unhappiness. It rests upon temptation and struggle.

All in all, we are left with the paradox that the good is at the same time bad. The good, then, does not exist. The pretense of ethics to discover what it is, and to teach men how to attain it, is a pretense and nothing more. In ethics, as elsewhere, complete suspension of judgment is the only sound attitude.

Adequacy of Empirical Rules of Behavior. But Sextus, like the other Skeptics, is quick to point out that suspension of judgment does not paralyze action. Empirical rules of life, like empirical rules of medicine, can be drawn from observation of individual cases. These rules make up the body of what we call common-sense. Nature indicates to us a certain way of life. She has given us as guides our senses, our instincts, and our intelligence. It is the part of the wise man to conform to ourselves as we find ourselves. It is sensible to accept and accommodate ourselves to the social organization into which we are born, to obey the laws, respect the institutions, including religion, and the conventions of the society in which we live. There is nothing transcendent or metaphysical about these things. They are facts of experience.

Nor should we merely conform. We should progress. Though truth and certainty in any matter are unobtainable, and dogmatic assertions of every sort are ridiculous, we may learn much from observation. By noting and studying similar cases we may establish provisional probabilities that are of great use. Methodical observation of this sort gives us arts and sciences to which a Skeptic may devote himself without infidelity to his basic suspension of judgment. Organized scientific investigations can be profitably undertaken with no other basis than the observation of phenomena, and with no further end than the establishment of probability. Absence of certainty and the necessity of suspending judgment with respect to ultimate questions do not render scientific investigation and speculation fruitless. Their theory and practice of medicine had given the Empirics an inkling of a new and fruitful line of approach. Indeed, it has been suggested that the inductive method of modern science, set forth by Bacon and developed in the last century by John Stuart Mill, had begun to dawn upon them.[5]

Contemporaneous Renewal of Speculative Philosophies. In following Skepticism straight through to its final phases we may have received a false impression of the history of philosophy as a whole. The blank intervals, we noted, so empty of any news about the development of the Skeptical movement, do not mean that philosophy itself was dormant. They represent merely moments when the fortunes of the Skeptical movement are obscure. But they are full of information about the progress of new currents of thought that originated long before Sextus Empiricus and were fast approaching their high-water mark in his time. As early as the first century B.C. these currents were in existence, and, when Skepticism was having its last great outburst, they had swollen to a flood of speculation and thinking that aimed at solving precisely the problems declared by Sextus and his predecessors to be insoluble. This renewed constructive activity looked back

[5] Cf. Brochard, *op. cit.,* pp. 375 ff.

to the Pythagoreans for its inspiration and guidance, as well as to
Plato, who after a period of eclipse which we have already remarked,
came into his own again and dominated both the rise of the new
secular philosophy and the formulation of Christian theology. Let us
then turn time backward in its flight and watch the growth of Neo-
Pythagoreanism and Neo-Platonism.

Chapter XIX

THE NEO-PYTHAGOREANS

I. THE ORIENTAL CULTS AND THEIR INFLUENCE UPON PHILOSOPHY

Revival of Religious Pythagoreanism. Pythagoreanism, we may remember, lasted but a short time as a distinct philosophic school. But it was more than a philosophy. It was a religious brotherhood inspired by the Orphic Mysteries, and retained, if not their elaborate theology, at least such essential tenets as the divine origin and the fall of the soul and perhaps, though this is disputable, her eventual escape from the wheel of birth and re-birth and reunion with the godhead from which she sprang. As a religious cult, Pythagoreanism seems to have lived on after its philosophical doctrines had become only a memory and a tradition, and, as early as the second century B.C., after a hundred and fifty years of obscurity, we find it emerging again as an active and an increasingly influential sect. By the beginning of the first century it was becoming philosophical again, harking back nominally to original Pythagorean doctrines for its inspiration, but also appropriating much from Platonic and contemporary Stoic thought. This revival of Pythagoreanism as a philosophy seems to have begun in Alexandria and to have spread from there to Rome. Among these early Neo-Pythagoreans we may mention Apollonius of Tyana, also celebrated as a magician and a soothsayer, and Moderatus of Gades.

Sterility of Roman Religion. The revival of the Orphic-Pythagorean religious cult was incidental to a rising tide of religious interest and fervor that was creeping into the Roman world from the Near East as early as the second century B.C., and that four hundred years later had completely engulfed the Empire. Since it swept philosophical speculation along with it, we shall do well to pause here for a moment and watch its progress. We may note at once that the religion of ancient Rome, grounded as it was in an unimaginative and practical temperament, had little to offer the devout. It promised no salvation, it held out no hope for a happy immortality in which wrongs might be redeemed and tears might be wiped away. It offered no consolation in time of sorrow and no support in the moral struggle of good against

evil. It knew nothing of an inner and direct communion of the soul
with the divine. It did indeed identify its principal deities with the
Olympian gods, but these serene and beautiful beings, deprived of
the passion for a perfected human life and of the worship of the ideal
by which they were fructified in Greece, were dwarfed and withered
when grafted on the Roman stock.

Influx and Popularity of the Oriental Cults. Roman religion had
already become mere lip-service for many people before the fall of
the Republic, and indifference to it became progressively more widespread and more profound under the Empire. And this, in spite of
strenuous attempts made from time to time by the state to rein-
vigorate the established cult and to stamp out its competitors. But
these were too strong and too appealing to be withstood. They offered
everything that the established cult could not give—salvation, immortality, direct communion with the divine, help in the struggle of
good against evil, and often, if not always, the intervention and the
aid of a redeemer, a dying and a rising god, whose death and resurrection not only guaranteed his worshipers against death, but held out
the hope of eventual triumph over evil and reunion with deity. Furthermore, these consoling theologies were presented in alluring and
impressive form, with a highly pictorial and often magnificent ceremonial and liturgy, and with sacramental rites of initiation and purification, and generally of union with the deity by partaking symbolically of his divine substance. Add to this the secrecy with which
some of these mysteries were celebrated and the sense of brotherhood
and of intimate relation with God that they fostered, and we have
every reason for understanding their fascination. To be sure, in both
their teachings and their rituals the Oriental cults continued to betray
the gross and barbaric origins from which they sprang. For example,
even to the end, the devotees of Mithra were literally bathed in the
blood of a bull actually slaughtered for their salvation. Nevertheless,
most of these sects gave to their doctrines and ceremonies, however
crude, a moral and spiritual significance.

The Various Mystery-Religions. Shortly after the Second Punic War
the cult of Dionysus appeared in Rome. But its Bacchanalian rites so
shocked the Romans, who suspected in them every sort of debauchery,
that they were rigorously suppressed by the government. The first
Oriental religion to be introduced was the worship of the Phrygian
goddess Cybele, the Great Mother, and of her lover Attis, a dying and
a rising god akin to Dionysus—at the instance, it is said, of the Sibyl-
line books, which prophesied that by her Rome might be saved from

Hannibal. A century later, we find in the Italian seaports an established cult of Isis and of her divine spouse Osiris, or Serapis, as he was re-baptized by the Ptolemies when they adopted him as the national god of their Hellenized Egypt. Slaves and merchants from Syria brought with them the goddess Atargatis, sometimes identified with the Phoenician Astarte, and from Phoenicia came also the worship of the dying and rising Adonis. Much later, from Syria, there was also to be introduced the adoration of *Sol Invictus,* the unconquerable Sun. Meantime, Persia had sent another sun-god, Mithra, the lover of truth and justice, who wages ceaseless warfare against the powers of darkness to the furtherance of the kingdom of Ormuzd, the lord of good and light. He was the soldier-god, adored by the far-flung Roman legions, and it is he whom, if Christianity had not won out in its long struggle with the other Oriental cults, the western world might perhaps be worshiping today.

These deities had so much in common not only with one another but with the Graeco-Roman gods, that they easily became confused and merged—Attis and Osiris, for example, with each other and with Dionysus; Isis and Atargatis with Aphrodite or Venus; Mithra with Apollo. Then, too, Mithra soon came to figure as the husband of the Great Mother, and their cults were, so to speak, in communion, if not actually amalgamated. Needless to say, all these affinities with the gods of Greece and Rome made the assimilation of the Oriental deities all the more rapid and the more easy, though it should be said that at first most of the new religions were viewed somewhat askance, and in some cases there were repeated attempts to suppress them. But in Imperial times they came into their own, and it was in them that the great mass of the religiously minded throughout the Empire, the educated and uneducated alike, sought and found peace and salvation.

Influence of the Mystery-Religions on Philosophy. It is not surprising that the revival of philosophic speculation, nurtured in the atmosphere created by these religious movements, was itself theological and mystical in character. Nor was it altogether out of keeping with the despair of reason, rampant in Skepticism and increasingly apparent in Stoicism, which had become a prevailing philosophic mood, that the new speculations should seek access to the Real more by feeling and intuition than by the processes of logical thought. At the same time, it should be said, these philosophies did not substitute feeling for thinking all along the line and ignore altogether the claims of logic. On the contrary, they followed reason as far as it could lead them, and under its guidance developed an elaborate and subtle metaphysics.

which converged from all sides upon the nature of the Real. It was only when rational thinking finally cracked its teeth upon a core of problems seemingly impenetrable by the power of the intellect that metaphysics turned for strength to immediate intuition and mystical "ecstasy" in which Reality was felt rather than known.

II. NEO-PYTHAGOREANISM

Diversity of Philosophic Speculations. Influenced as the new speculations also were by the whole history of philosophy up to date, they were highly eclectic in character and led to many divergent conclusions. The revived Pythagoreanism, for example, whose outlines we are about to sketch, was greatly influenced by Plato and Aristotle and the Stoics. It harked back, to be sure, to the original distinction drawn by the ancient Pythagoreans between unity and plurality, the odd and the even, the limited and the unlimited, and to their identification of the divine and the good with the one, of the evil and the earthly with the other, of these two fundamental principles. But with regard to the nature of God and of his relation to the world there was great diversity of opinion. Some, influenced by the Stoics, regarded him as the Soul of the universe, and incidentally identified him with the Platonic World-Soul. Others separated the godhead from the cosmos, and explained his relation to it after the fashion of Aristotle or of Plato in the *Timaeus*. Still others regarded God as a principle indescribable even in terms of being or thought or reason or unity, a mystical and ineffable "Monad" from which unity and plurality, the odd and the even, form and matter alike proceeded.[1]

By these last particularly, the Pythagorean Numbers, the Platonic Ideas, the divine workman in the *Timaeus* and the Stoic *logos spermatikos* were combined in a creative World-Reason, generated by God, which is both the intelligible structure of the universe and the creative power by which the world is called into being and given form and stability. The Platonic World-Soul was also invoked by them as a mediating principle.

The Four Principles. Metaphysically, then, the Neo-Pythagoreans present us with four principles—God, the World-Reason, the World-Soul, and Matter. The first three play an important part in the formulation of both the Plotinian and the Christian trinities. The status of

---

[1] The early Neo-Pythagorean sources have been collected and published by Mullach, *op. cit.* Cf. also Zeller, *Philosophie der Griechen* (4th ed.), III, ii, pp. 115 ff.

the fourth variously conceived as identical with God after the Stoic fashion, as co-eternal with him, or as derived from him, led to a long controversy which culminated in the Plotinian theory of emanation, on the one hand, and the Christian doctrine of creation out of nothing by divine fiat, on the other.

Needless to say, the necessity of explaining evil and imperfection loomed large in such speculations. Those who inclined to Stoic pantheism, or later to the theory of emanation, not unnaturally made much of the Stoic arguments for reconciling imperfection in the part with the perfection of the universe as a whole, while those who made a clear-cut distinction between God and the universe fell back upon Matter as a scapegoat. The general spirit of Neo-Pythagoreanism was, however, true to the metaphysical dualism of Pythagoras and Plato.

Epistemology and Physics. In their theory of knowledge and in their physics and geometry the Neo-Pythagoreans followed Plato for the most part. Like him they mounted from *sensation* to *opinion,* and from *opinion* through *understanding* to pure *reason* which simply contemplates the truth. As with Plato again, the sensible world is the image of the intelligible, and its manifest failure to imitate the perfection of its model is explained away by the means we have just been noting. Whether it had a beginning in time, as Plato intimated in the *Timaeus,* or was uncreated and eternal, as Aristotle maintained, appears to have been a disputed point.

Psychology. In psychology, the Neo-Pythagoreans combined, as the older Pythagoreans had done, the doctrine that the soul is essentially a harmony with the Orphic teaching that she is immaterial and immortal. But apparently they laid little stress on reincarnation. Also, they adopted Plato's division of the soul into three parts and identified her highest, rational part with the Aristotelian reason. Besides human souls there were also "daemons," or guardian angels, some good, some bad, who tempted human beings or protected them, as the case might be. The gods of the popular theology were also easily worked into this scheme, and the Neo-Pythagoreans had no quarrel with the established religion.

Ethics. For their moral guidance in this world the Neo-Pythagoreans developed an ethics that added little or nothing to the moral teachings of Plato and Aristotle. But, like Plato himself, they supplemented this ethics with an anti-worldly theory of the ultimate destiny and salvation of man, inherited from the Orphics. The world and the flesh were regarded as the enemies of the spirit, and redemption as a flight of the soul from the fetters of the body and the senses to her divine source. Their discipline for suppressing and escaping from the senses and bodily desires seems to have been only mildly ascetic. It consisted for the most part of ceremonial purifications, including abstinence from certain foods. But, unlike the rules governing the early Pythagoreans, it did not forbid the eating of meat or the drinking of wine. Nor did it advocate celibacy, though it did insist that sexual relations should be motivated, not by the promptings of nature, but solely by a due regard for propagating the species.

Veneration of Inspired Teachers. Like all religiously inclined philosophies, Neo-Pythagoreanism had leaders whom it venerated as teachers specially gifted and inspired from on high. Naturally it turned back to Pythagoras himself as the source of the truth and light of which it regarded itself the vehicle. Indeed, we owe to it most of the legends of magical powers and prophetic gifts and peculiar intimacy with the godhead that gathered about him and almost turned him into an incarnation of the deity. But it also found more contemporary inspiration in Apollonius of Tyana, whom it invested with the same superhuman experiences and powers. His biography, written many years later by Philostratus, is one of the most valuable documents we have relating to the Neo-Pythagorean movement.

As we must have already noticed, the Neo-Pythagoreans drew almost, if not quite, as much upon Plato as they did upon Pythagoras for inspiration. Indeed, except that the Platonic influence had not become so marked or so dominant as it became later, the new movement might be described as a revival of Plato. In Plutarch, however, to whom we are about to turn, the Platonic influence is so strong that we may describe him as even more inspired by it than by the Pythagoreans, and as therefore an important contributor to the development of Neo-Platonism. Moreover, he is the first philosopher to give a really extended and systematic expression to the speculative revival and to fuse the elements entering into it. As we shall see, the general characteristics of Neo-Pythagoreanism which we have just been describing almost all hold true of him.

III. PLUTARCH

Plutarch is already familiar to us as the author of the famous *Lives*. Born at Chaeronea about 48 A.D., he studied first mathematics, and then, at Athens, philosophy. Later he visited Rome on business connected with his native city, and there learned Latin, began his acquaintance with Roman literature, and also made many personal friends. He was chosen archon and priest at Chaeronea, and appointed one of the overseers of the Pythian Games. He died between 120-125 A.D. He was a prolific writer, and fortunately, besides fifty of his biographies, some eighty-three of his other writings and fragments of another twenty-four have been preserved for us.[2]

The Transcendency of God. Widely read in philosophy, he detested the Epicureans, disliked much in Stoicism, and was attracted by Plato, Aristotle, and the Pythagoreans, who appealed to his serious and religious temperament. For him, God is the only wholly actual and existent being, self-caused and self-sufficient, pure and undivided unity, the good that knows no jealousy, the reason that governs all things. Even these epithets, however, do not exhaust or describe his essence. When all is said and done, we can only know *that* he is, but not *what* he is, so far removed is he from the material and sensible universe and from the concepts and words at the command of our finite and fallible intellects.

Dualistic Solution of the Problem of Evil. So high and so holy a God cannot be regarded as in any way responsible for the evil and the imperfection in the world. The Stoic attempts to reconcile sin and suffering and the hostile activities of nature with the goodness, the omnipotence, and the universal providence of the deity are one and all rejected by him. Even a material principle distinct from and co-eternal with the divine cannot account for imperfection. For Matter is but clay in the potter's hands, and not from it but from them comes the good or evil form in which it is molded. In addition to Matter, then, there must be, as Plato taught in the *Laws,* a diabolic activity, or bad world-soul, positively opposed to God, whose workings are responsible for the shortcomings of the world.

It is possible that Plutarch's insistence upon an evil world-soul was inspired not only by Plato's arguments in the *Laws* but also by the Persian doctrine that two co-eternal principles, Ormuzd, the spirit of good and light, and Ahriman, the spirit of darkness and of evil, are ceaselessly at war in the universe.

To the Aristotelian view that the universe is uncreated and eternal Plutarch opposes the Platonic teaching that it had a definite beginning and creation at the hands of God. As with Plato, this act of creation is not direct. God is too remote for that. It is accomplished through the

[2] For Plutarch's metaphysics, cf. especially *De Isi et Osiride; De El apud Delphos; Non posse suaviter vivi secundum Epicurum; De defectu oraculorum; De animae procreatione in Timeo; Platonicae quaestiones; De Stoicorum repugnantiis; De fato; De facie in orbe lunae.*

agency of a good world-soul, like that in Plato's *Timaeus,* which God makes from his own divine essence and infuses into matter, and by the activities of lesser gods and angels.

The Lesser Gods and Souls. Besides the good and evil world-souls there are also individual spirits, some good, some bad. The stars, the nearest of all corporeal things to the divine, have, as with Plato and Aristotle, their presiding deities, and below them are ranks of angelic beings mediating between God and man. Through them God and the lesser gods exercise their moral government of the world, using them as instruments for punishing the wicked and rewarding the virtuous both in this life and the next. Some of these "daemons," however, like human souls, possess free will and may fall into evil ways, and may even be reduced to human estate. Contrariwise, good men may rise to the angelic level, and the angels may become equal to the lesser gods.

The human soul inherits from both the good and evil world-souls, and in her both dispositions are inextricably interwoven. From the one come the senses and the bodily desires and everything that knits us to the world and the flesh; from the other comes our reason, which is a "daemon" within us. The lower soul is divided Platonic-wise into spirit, or will, and appetite. At death the rational part of the souls of the good rejoins the angels, to remain with them forever, or to be reincarnated again in human bodies, according to its merits. The souls of the wicked may be incarnated as animals. Upon immortality Plutarch lays great stress.

The Freedom of the Will. The freedom of the will is also emphasized by Plutarch. He is untiring in his attacks on the Epicureans for denying it outright; apparently he took little stock in their championing of freedom, and in the doctrine of the deviation of the atoms they invented to accommodate it to Democritus' teaching. The Stoics, also, were upbraided for the destructive determinism that lurked, he felt, in their theory of a providential government of the world, and also for their pantheism and their attempt to reconcile the existence of evil with the omnipotence of God. All suffering, Plutarch thinks, is the just wages of sin, for which man is wholly responsible, since it lies within his power to withstand the promptings that arise from his lower nature and from the evil world-soul with which it is associated, and to follow the dictates of his higher, rational self.

Physics, Psychology, and Ethics. Plutarch's physics is in the main Platonic, and contains little that is new or noteworthy. He follows Aristotle, however, in adding a fifth element—ether—to the conventional four. He also argued for a plurality of worlds, both co-existent and successive. His psychology, too, is largely Platonic, with Aristotelian additions. He accepts Plato's division of the soul into three parts, and he adds the vegetative and sensitive functions ascribed to her by Aristotle.

In spite of his extreme metaphysical dualism, Plutarch's ethics has little or nothing of the asceticism that we might expect such a view to breed.[3] The morality that appealed to him was that of Aristotle, and his own teaching is derived largely from the *Nicomachean Ethics*. With the Epicurean insistence that pleasure is the good he had as little sympathy as with their supposed denial of free-will. But he was equally opposed to the Stoic doctrine that pleasure and external goods and the activities and fortunes of our bodies have no bearing upon human happiness. These things are not indifferent to us, neither is happiness obtainable by merely ignoring and rendering ourselves callous to them. Our instincts and desires, our passions and emotions, are part of the nature with which God has endowed us, and, freed from the promptings of the evil world-soul, directed by reason, and subjected to the rule of the golden mean, they are necessary and important elements in the good life. Nay more, man is a political animal, as Aristotle said. His happiness comes, not from withdrawing so far as possible from social and political activities, but from participating in them to the best of his ability. Politics or statesmanship is the noblest of human occupations. Great responsibilities are laid upon those entrusted with authority, who should labor unselfishly and wholeheartedly for the good of the community. Monarchy, Plutarch feels, is the best form of government, but the monarch must act as the representative and the servant of God. Still, when all is said and done, man attains his final peace and salvation not in good works alone but rather in an inner life of religious experience.

Religion. Atheism, which destroys this experience and knowledge of God and impoverishes man's spiritual nature, is one of the most terrible things that in Plutarch's eyes can befall a human soul. Equally bad is superstition, which is exemplified by the unworthy stories and ideas about the gods current in the popular theology. With polytheism itself, however, provided it is rightly understood, Plutarch has no quarrel. To be sure, there is only one true God, the God of all men and of the whole universe. But this God reveals himself in many ways, and the popular gods are simply the many aspects under which he is

[3] For Plutarch's ethics, cf. *De virtute morali; De profectibus in virtute; De communibus notitiis; De virtute et vitio; De tranquillitate animi.*

seen, as through a glass darkly, and the many names by which he is worshiped and glorified in different times and places. So, too, the theologies centering about the various divinities are all in their way intimations of the nature of the true God and of his ways with man.

Nor is the popular belief in the supernatural character of oracles and dreams wholly to be scorned. When we sleep, our souls are freed from the fetters of the senses and are in better condition to consort with the divine and to receive revelations from it. The same severance of the soul from the body with increased power of insight and prophecy may also be brought about by artificial means, as for example, the vapors that issue from the earth at Delphi. Hence, under these conditions, the priests and priestesses of oracles may also be considered to be divinely inspired, though the popular attitude towards them and trust in them is infected with superstition.

IV. THE LATER NEO-PYTHAGOREANS

Maximus of Tyre. The next philosopher of note after Plutarch to expound this mixture of Pythagoras and Plato was Maximus of Tyre, who taught in the first half of the second century A.D. In general outlines his system differs little from that of Plutarch.[4] God, however, he identifies with the pure reason that Aristotle had made the essence of the divine nature, and Matter he regards as a sufficient explanation of the imperfection of the universe, without bringing in an evil world-soul. Sin springs from misuse of free-will in following the promptings of our lower sensual nature rather than our reason. The soul is a spark of the divine, momentarily imprisoned in the body, but destined, if virtuous, for a happy release and reunion with her source. Between God and man there intervenes a hierarchy of lesser gods and spirits, or "daemons," who act as the guardian angels of men and servants of divine providence.

Apuleius. Along with Maximus we may also mention Apuleius of Madaura in Numidia, still famous as the author of the *Metamorphoses,* or *Story of the Golden Ass,* with its interlude describing the marriage of Cupid and Psyche. His metaphysics follows that of Maximus, but with greater elaboration of detail. Between God and Matter he inserts not only a hierarchy of gods and angels, but the Platonic Ideas and Reason. The hierarchy itself he expanded to include, not only the visible gods of the stars, but the Olympian deities and a descending

---

[4] For most of Maximus' philosophy we have original sources in his *Dissertations,* which are extant.

order of angelic beings terminating in the human soul. Salvation lies
in freeing the soul from the fetters of the world and the flesh in which
she is temporarily imprisoned. The story of Cupid and Psyche seems
to be used by Apuleius as an allegory of her fall and redemption.

Albinus and Atticus. The same multiplication of mediators between
God and the world is found in Albinus, who inserted the World-Soul
as well as the Platonic Ideas into the hierarchy, and also consigned
the creation of the world to the lesser gods and angels on the ground
that God himself was too far removed from material things to handle
them directly. With Aristotle, however, as against Plutarch, Albinus
maintained that the universe was not created in time but was eternal.

Atticus, however, another of the successors of Plutarch, upheld the
doctrine of creation in time, and also re-introduced the evil world-soul,
which Maximus and Apuleius had dropped from their systems.

Numenius. In Numenius of Apamea philosophy takes a quite appreciable step forward. Indeed, Plotinus was accused of having plagiarized
his teaching. Numenius deliberately casts aside Neo-Pythagoreanism
and Neo-Platonism up to date and goes back to the original sources
for his inspiration. But he finds that both Plato and Pythagoras were
themselves the interpreters of an earlier wisdom, which they found in
the teachings of the Brahmins, the Magi, the Egyptians, and the Jews.
For Moses he had a great veneration, and considered Plato a Greek
twin of the Hebrew prophet. It is said also that he spoke of the teaching of Jesus with respect. In that case, he differs from his contemporary and fellow Pythagorean-Platonist, Celsus, who, inspired also by
a strain of Stoic determinism and naturalism, accused Christianity of
being a superstitious and fantastic degradation of Platonic doctrine.

Numenius' system [5] is even more dualistic than that of Plutarch.
On the one hand, we have a God, identified with the Reason of Aristotle, the Monad of the Pythagoreans, and Plato's Idea of the Good,
so high and so remote as to be altogether inactive and out of contact
with the world. Hence he can have nothing whatsoever to do with
the act of creation. The universe is the work of a "Second God" derived from, but inferior to, the supreme Deity, and the universe itself
may be called the "Third God." We have, then, at this point, three
Gods, the Father, the Creative Agent generated by him, and the
Created World.

The Second and Third Gods, however, have a dual nature. The
Second, though sprung from pure spirit, is also in contact with Matter

[5] Our knowledge of Numenius is largely drawn from Eusebius, Porphyry,
Chalcidius, Iamblichus and Proclus.

and is the indwelling good soul of the universe. The Third God is a mixture of the divine soul and of Matter. But Matter is also animated by an active, evil principle that opposes the divine soul and is responsible for the imperfection of the universe. Hence to the three Gods we must add a sort of devil.

Man, being both spiritual and corporeal, rational and irrational, participates in both world-souls. Their conflict within him constitutes his moral life. At the same time, Numenius, like Plutarch in somewhat similar metaphysical circumstances, refuses to turn ascetic in his ethics. The activities of the body are not in themselves evil. They become so only when they cease to be governed by reason and fall a prey to the irrational and evil world-soul. Nevertheless, the descent of the rational part of the soul into the body represents a fall from a higher to a lower state. Salvation lies in an escape from corporeal and sensible existence and in a reabsorption of the soul into her divine source. This can be accomplished only through a long series of reincarnations. Meantime, it behooves us in this life to cultivate our reasons and to commune with God.

The Hermetic Writings. We may as well here glance at the so-called *Hermetic writings,* though they belong to the last half of the third century, and are therefore later even than Plotinus. However, they seem to reflect speculations of an earlier period and belong to the line of development we have been tracing. They purport to be the revelations of the god Hermes to his disciples. By whom they were written or assembled is uncertain. There is little that is novel in them. They push the exaltation of the First God to a point where it becomes almost completely mystical, though they still attribute to him reason and will. From him, intellect proceeds as light from the sun, and from intellect proceeds soul. The soul has need of a mediator between herself and Matter, which is supplied by air or breath. Matter is an inert and formless principle, but is so completely organized and molded by the divine that the universe may be called the Second God or the Son of God. In this connection the Christians are attacked for scorning and vilifying the world, and the Gnostic sects are berated for the teaching, which we have also found in Numenius, that God himself is too good to be its creator. At the same time, when it comes to explaining imperfection and evil, there is an inconsistent and even contradictory change of face. Matter is at the root of all that is bad. There can be no commerce between the spiritual and the material, between the changeable, sensible world and the divine. These two opposed points of view were left unreconciled.

The promotion of the universe to the rank of Second God leaves the position of Third God open for man himself. Our souls and reasons are derived from the divine, and may return to the deity if we practice piety and virtue here below.

In ethics, the inconsistency we have just noted in the Hermetic treatment of the sensible world reappears. On the one hand, we are told to turn our back upon the world and the senses and to seek direct inner communion with God. On the other, we are warned that to despise the world, in which we live, is sinful. Nay more, we are enjoined to follow the practices of the established religion, and even to set up for worship graven images of the gods, to which the Hermetic writings attributed magical powers such as prophecy and healing and the ability to evoke and exorcise spirits.

Chapter XX

THE HELLENIZING JEWS AND PHILO JUDAEUS

I. THE HELLENIZING JEWS

Of all the peoples with which Hellenic civilization and philosophy came in contact, the Jews might seem the most impermeable. Their social isolation, the intensity of their national, cultural, and religious antipathies, their uncompromising monotheism, their conviction that Jehovah was the only true God, their sense of being a chosen people favored by a divine revelation that was vouchsafed to them alone, their detestation of polytheism and their contempt for the gods of other peoples—all this was calculated to harden them against the dissolving influence of the Hellenic civilization in the midst of which they had lived engulfed since the conquests of Alexander, or, at any rate, since the Roman domination of the Mediterranean world. Still, the impact of the Graeco-Roman environment proved too much for them, and they became partially merged with, though not submerged by, the alien civilizations by which they were surrounded. There was, to be sure, a conservative, "orthodox" element which, still deep-rooted in its ancestral Palestine, clung stubbornly to the traditions, the mode of life, the way of thinking, and the disdainful isolation of the past. But this element seems to have been deeply fringed with what we call "liberal" Jews.

Influence of Plato on the Alexandrian Jews. In cosmopolitan Alexandria, where there had been a large Jewish colony since its foundation, these liberal tendencies were most marked; for here Hebrew thought and culture were in their most widespread and intimate contact with Hellenic influences, and particularly with Greek philosophy. So it is that possibly as early as the third century B.C. Jewish thinkers there had begun to read the Greeks, and especially Plato, and to find in them suggestions of their own doctrines. Indeed, it has been argued that the so-called Septuagint, or translation into Greek of the Old Testament made during the first half of the third century B.C., shows traces of Greek philosophic influence in some of the words and phrases used to render the Hebrew originals. In *Ecclesiastes,* probably written during approximately the same period, there are also hints of Stoicism. The *Book of Wisdom,* a work of the first century B.C., is clearly imbued with Greek philosophy, and its treatment of the divine wisdom as a reflection and mirror of God's glory, almost separate from him, is directly in line with the development of the doctrine of the Logos, soon to be expressly set forth by Philo, and later to be incorporated by Plotinus and Christian theology.

Philosophy Enlisted in the Service of Revelation. The Hebrews, however, approached philosophy in a spirit quite different from that of the Greeks. To the latter it was a free inquiry into the nature of the Real, whose results were the nearest approach to truth the human mind could make. But to the Jews the truth had already been revealed by Jehovah through the mouths of the Prophets. It needed no establishment by the exercise of reason. The most that reason and philosophy could do was to testify to the accuracy of the Old Testament revelation, and to defend it by rational and metaphysical argument against rationalistic and philosophical attacks. The Jewish thinkers then, who interested themselves in the Greek systems did not look to them for further light upon the nature of God and the world. They were fascinated rather by the hints they seemed to discover that the Greeks had seen as through a glass darkly what they themselves, by divine favor, had been permitted to see face to face. They were everywhere on the lookout for foreshadowings and analogies and agreements, which they often pressed to fantastic extremes. For instance, Aristobulus, an Alexandrian Jew of the second century B.C., in his eagerness to establish parallels and relations between Greek and Jewish thought, went so far as to claim that both Plato and Pythagoras had been influenced by an early Greek translation of the Old Testament. In him we see also another characteristic tendency of the times. Influenced apparently by the more abstract concepts and terms of the Greek thinkers, he finds philosophical equivalents for the pictorial and anthropomorphic expressions used by the Prophets in speaking of Jehovah. Thus "the hand of God" is a figurative way of referring to his power, and his appearance to Moses on Sinai in the form of fire is not to be taken literally, but should be regarded as a kind of vision or pictorial representation of an inner and invisible revelation.

Spread of Graeco-Roman Influence to Palestine. Meantime, even in Jerusalem and Palestine, which were the stronghold of orthodox Jewry, Hellenic influences were making themselves felt. Palestine was now a subordinate part of a larger world, not only politically, but culturally, to whose existence and character, to whose ways and whose thoughts, it could not blind itself. It was invaded year after year by "liberal," Hellenized Jews returning to the fatherland. It had to learn Greek. It had even to Hellenize its Hebrew names. Hence, as early as the second century B.C., there was already in the capital a considerable liberal, pro-Hellenic element.

It is also possible, though the point is in dispute, that acquaintance with the Neo-Pythagorean order had some influence upon the Essenes, a communistic, ascetic Jewish sect, already in existence by the middle of the second century B.C. This secret brotherhood, which exacted a long novitiate, held all property in common, condemned slavery, advocated the brotherhood of man, and not only preached but practiced virtuous living and love of God and of one's neighbor. Their tenets and their life so resembled that of the early Christians that it has been suggested that John the Baptist and even Jesus himself came in contact with them. In connection with the Essenes, we may mention, also, the Therapeutae, an ascetic, semi-mystical brotherhood of Egyptian Jews, who, like the Christian hermits of a later age, retired from the world to the desert to lead there in scattered communities a solitary life devoted to worship and contemplation.

II. PHILO JUDAEUS

Hebrew Theology Modified by Greek Philosophy. When we come to Philo, an Alexandrian Jew, born in the last quarter of the first century B.C., it looks as if Hellenic influence and the impact of Greek philosophy had succeeded in making a very real dent in the substance of Hebrew theology.[1] Philo considered himself orthodox, accepted the infallibility of Moses, and never doubted that the Old Testament was a direct and ultimate revelation of the truth on the part of God. At the same time, his wide and thorough acquaintance with the history of Greek philosophy and his sympathy with its teachings led him far beyond his predecessors in drawing parallels between Hellenic and Hebrew thought and in developing an allegorical interpretation of the words of the Prophets. Not only Plato and the Neo-Pythagoreans, but the earlier thinkers, contemporary Stoics, and even Skeptics had

[1] The main features of Philo's philosophy are set forth in his *De cherubim; De somniis; De allegoriis legium; De opificiis mundi; De sacrificiis Abelis et Caini; De migratione Abrahami; De Abrahamo; De providentia; Quod Deus sit immutabilis; Quis rerum divinarum heres sit; De eo quod deterius potiori insidiatur; De profugis; De vita contemplativa.*

all in their several ways guessed at the truth of which, in its fullness, the Scriptures were the chosen repository. Philosophers and prophets alike were all setting forth in different allegorical forms the same essential ideas. Even polytheism, so abhorrent to the orthodox Jew, was not to be condemned as wholly false. The Greek gods, far from being the evil spirits that the Hebrews generally considered them, were in part personifications of natural phenomena, in part, as Euhemerus had maintained, memories of ancient heroes. God is so high and so removed that he cannot be comprehended, but must reveal himself indirectly through myth and allegory to the finite human mind.

The Transcendency of God. Philo's system is of the dualistic sort with which Neo-Pythagoreanism has already made us so familiar, but it is obviously dominated by Platonic teaching, somewhat modified, however, by Stoic influence. Upon the transcendence of God and the consequent cleavage between God and the world Philo insists even more vehemently than his predecessors. God, like the Platonic Idea of the Good, escapes in the end every attempt to describe or define him, even by the highest and most abstract terms at our command. He is beyond goodness, beyond beauty, beyond holiness, beyond unity. Like Jehovah he is simply the "I am that I am." But he is essentially and incessantly creative, and his creative activity, like that of the Platonic divine workman in the *Timaeus,* springs from the desire to bring into being every possible form and degree of goodness.

The Mediating and Creative Logos. However, as in the Neo-Pythagorean systems, God is too high and too remote to be directly creative. He needs intermediaries, and to this end he generates "powers," which are not only forms and archetypes, like the Platonic Ideas, but forces, like the Stoic *logoi spermatikoi,* that create the universe in their own image.

The two fundamental *logoi* are God's goodness and potency, which, taken together constitute the *Logos,* or all-creating Form and Force by which the world is made and after which it is patterned. On the relation of the *Logos* to God Philo is not clear. At times, he seems to regard it as a being separate from the godhead and describes it variously in personal terms as the mediator, the vice-regent, the messenger, the high priest, the archangel, and the first-begotten of God. Again, it is described less personally as the image, the shadow, and the dwelling place of the Most High, and yet again as an attribute or manifestation of the divine nature, having no independent existence of its own.

There is a similar obscurity in Philo's views regarding the relation of the lesser *logoi* to the *Logos* and to God. Sometimes, they are spoken of as the servants and messengers and instruments of deity, mediating between God and the world; sometimes as simply the ideas and activities of the divine mind.

Mediation between God and man does not, however, stop with the *Logos* and the lesser *logoi*. The heavens are full of spirits or angels derived from the *Logos* who help carry on the government of the world. Some of them inhabit the stars and direct their courses; some, living in the lower atmosphere, are caught by the attraction of earth and sense, become incarnate in human bodies, and are made man. Every human soul is, then, a portion of the divine breath and spirit, an image and part of the divine mind, a power of God, estranged for the time being from its source by imprisonment in the body and the senses.

Matter a Cause of Evil. The physical and sensible world in which the human spirit is caught is in no way derived from the divine substance. It is, to be sure, created by God, but it is created by him out of a stuff which he finds already there, and for whose existence and whose character he is in no wise responsible. He has to accept it for what it is, and make the best he can of it. This stuff is Matter, which stands in eternal opposition to God and forever thwarts the plan and purpose of the *Logos*. It is to the inferior and intractable nature of Matter that all the shortcomings of the universe are due. It stands to reason, Philo thinks, that God, being good, can be the author of good only, and hence cannot account for the inertia, the conflict, the imperfection, and the evil which vitiate the material and sensible world.

Though Matter is co-eternal with God, the universe itself has a beginning, as Plato taught. It is not eternal, as Aristotle maintained. But its beginning is not a beginning in time, since time itself was created, again as Plato taught, when the world was formed.

In describing the nature of Matter, Philo vacillates somewhat inconsistently between Plato and the Stoics. Following Plato, he speaks of it as uncreated, formless, passive, chaotic, Not-Being pure and simple. It is wholly negative—a principle of privation. At the same time, like Plato, he finds it difficult not to regard Matter as a stuffing of some sort which gives spatial dimensions and solidity to corporeal things. Plato had dealt with the inconsistency, we may remember, by identifying Matter with empty space, but Philo is inclined, like the Stoics, to endow it with positive and substantial properties.

Free-Will and Sin. In any case, however, Philo is convinced that sin consists in the misuse of free-will. This misuse arises from listening to the solicitations of our lower nature which is bound up with the senses and the body and thus eventually with the material principle. The body Philo belabors in vigorous dualistic fashion. It is a loathsome dungeon, a corpse, a tomb, a grave, in which our higher nature lies imprisoned and dead, cut off from communion with the divine. We are, then, all infected with a kind of "original sin," by the very fact that we possess a body. Nay more, our possession of a body is due, as we have already seen, to a sinful tendency to dally with the flesh and the senses, which is somehow present in those disembodied spirits who inhabit the heavens nearest to the earth. But it is through an act of free-will that the spirit gives way to this tendency and becomes incarnate. Hence we enter the world already besmirched with an inclination to evil. To be sure, this extreme dualism is modified by the admission that the senses, and even the pleasures of the senses, are not necessarily evil in themselves, provided that they are controlled by our higher nature and dominated by reason. But even so, our higher nature, derived as it is from the divine, cannot fulfill itself as long as we lie captive in the body, and we can attain final redemption and happiness only by an eventual escape from its clutches.

Ethics. To effect this escape is the goal of the moral life. Hence the inner, contemplative life of withdrawing our interests from the world and fixing them through meditation and communion upon God is the way of salvation. In following it lie religion pure and undefiled, true wisdom, and true philosophy. But, though we should not be of the world, we are perforce in it, and, being in it, we are forced to have commerce with it. In dealing with it we should follow in the footsteps of the Stoics, shouldering cheerfully the burdens, social and political, life lays upon us, making the inevitable concessions to our physical environment and to our physical needs, practicing love and charity towards our fellow-men; but at the same time maintaining our inner life in independence of external circumstances, unspotted, untouched, and unshaken by our contact with outer things. For all other things are as nothing compared with the knowledge and the love of God.

The Vision of God. So, too, with our intellectual life and interests. Scientific pursuits and logical thinking have indeed their place, but they are incapable of reaching truth, and are at the best preparatory steps towards the self-examination and the moral discipline through which the soul makes herself ready to receive the divine illumination. The final vision of God, in which alone the soul can find peace, is, like God himself, ineffable and indescribable. It is a state of mystical ecstasy, transcending the utmost reaches of even our highest and most abstract thought.

Influence of Philo. After Philo, philosophic speculation was carried on and forwarded by the later Neo-Pythagoreans, with whom we have already dealt. Philo seems to have had no disciples of any note, and no direct influence on the content of philosophy during the century and a half that intervenes between his death and the birth of Plotinus. However, his allegorical method had an important influence on the techniques of antique theology, and the pattern of his thought, the reconciliation of biblical religion and Greek philosophy, affected the form of Christian theology and philosophy not only among the Alexandrian theologians but even into the medieval period. He had stated the large issue of the relation of religion in its institutionalized forms to scientifically oriented culture.

Chapter XXI

PLOTINUS

I. NEO-PLATONISM

We come now to a movement that is distinctly and consciously Platonic and Aristotelian in its inspiration, and that considers itself the reconciler of these two philosophies and the exponent of their true meaning. This movement is Neo-Platonism. Its originator seems to have been Ammonius Saccas, who taught at Alexandria in the first half of the third century A.D.

Contemporary History. The epoch in which he and his great pupil, Plotinus, lived was one of impending chaos, political, social, moral and religious, throughout the Roman world. To the north and east loomed the ever blacker and more rumbling storm clouds of the barbarian invasions. Within the Empire, upon which the last rays of the setting sun of ancient grandeur still lay, there reigned a spirit of political fatigue and lassitude, born of the countless wars and revolutions by which so much of the best blood of Rome had been slowly but surely drained. The government was maintained by a rapid succession of Emperors, some good, most bad or indifferent, who owed their rise and their fall to the intrigues and the support of the army. The Antonines had descended not only to the dust but to the dirt under the infamous Commodus, the son of Marcus Aurelius, murdered in 192. The next year, after two Caesars had been elevated and cast down by the soldiery, there came to the throne Septimus Severus, who administered the Empire with ability for eighteen years, and succeeded in dying in his bed. But his son Caracalla proved equal in infamy to Commodus, and after a short reign yielded by assassination to the amazing Emperor Elagabalus, than whom no youth probably has ever packed the years between fourteen and eighteen with more varied and intense dissipation. Elagabalus' cousin and adopted heir, Severus Alexander, proved, however, an excellent ruler, whose very virtues, after a brief reign of three years, proved his undoing. Between him and the accession of Aurelian, in 270—the year, incidentally, in which Plotinus died—ten emperors of small account came and went.

It was a kind of pernicious anemia, with its characteristic brief periods of remission, of which the body politic was dying. The end was not far off. The brief convulsions that preceded the dissolution of the Empire were beginning. Another sixty years and the division between the West and the East had occurred; another hundred, and Rome had been abandoned as the imperial residence for Ravenna on the one hand, Constantinople on the other.

Social Conditions. With the decay of political vigor went a decline of social and individual morals. The old-time virtues of the Romans had faded. Severity and self-discipline were a thing of the past. Their martial ardor was no more. Their native coarseness and brutality had turned effeminate. Criminal law had become more and more barbarous. The "third degree" was universal in the examination of the accused, and even free men were put to the torture. Burning at the stake was the common method of execution.

The wealth of the Empire had become concentrated in the hands of the great landowners—absentee landlords for the most part, who paid little or no attention to their estates, which were farmed by slave labor. The senatorial clan, forbidden to govern, to engage in business, or even to enter military service, became either dilettante or out-and-out soft, luxurious, and over-sensual. The populace had long since been debauched by the dole of free food and free amusement—*panem et circenses*. The population had been decimated by disease and a falling birth-rate, and the native stock had been largely replaced by immigrants of Teutonic and Semitic origin.

Cultural Decay. The realms of thought suffered no less severely. Latin literature had come to an end with Apuleius, and the revival of Greek in the second century, which found its most distinguished exponents in Plutarch and Lucian, was artificial and brief. Art was second rate and imitative, though there were still good portrait painters, architects, and engineers. The old theology, too, was by this time thoroughly decadent, and people had turned from it to the Oriental mystery-religions, whose rise we have already noted, and which were now in the heyday of their popularity. There was no longer any attempt to suppress them. The Christians and the Jews alone were persecuted, and they not on religious grounds, but because their conscience forbade them to take part in religious rites equivalent to saluting the flag and taking the prescribed oath of allegiance to the state.

Ammonius Saccas. Of Ammonius and his teachings we know next to nothing. He was born a Christian but was later converted to the Hellenic faith. He was highly respected both as a man and a teacher at Alexandria, and was held in great veneration by his pupils, who attributed to him almost supernatural insight, and especially by Plotinus, who could not too strongly insist on the debt he owed him. He was credited also with being the first philosopher to undertake a systematic reconciliation of Plato and Aristotle.

Longinus. Ammonius had a number of famous pupils besides Plotinus. There were the two Origens, one of whom later became a famous early Christian philosopher. There was Longinus, best known to us not as a philosopher, but as the reputed though not the probable author of the essay on impressiveness in literary style which figures in English as the *Treatise on the Sublime.* Longinus also wrote commentaries on the *Phaedo* and the first part of the *Timaeus,* and was familiar with and critical of the works of Plotinus. Like Ammonius, he attacked the Stoic view that the soul is a material thing, and he seems also to have been concerned with the relation of the Platonic Ideas to the Demiurge. Did the Ideas exist independent of and prior to the Demiurge, or were they simply thoughts of the Demiurge existing in his mind? Plotinus, as we shall see in a moment, made them the thoughts of the divine mind, but Longinus insisted that they existed independent and outside of the creative intellect, as the models or patterns to which it looked in its work of fashioning the world.

II. PLOTINUS

But, just as Aristotle overtopped so tremendously all the other pupils of Plato, so the disciples of Ammonius, the reviver of Plato, were all overtopped by Plotinus, by some critics regarded as an even greater metaphysician than Plato and Aristotle themselves.

Life. The first thirty years of Plotinus' life are almost blank. It is believed that he was born in Lycopolis about 204 A.D., of stock that had earlier emigrated to Egypt from Rome. At the age of twenty-eight, however, he appears at Alexandria as a pupil of Ammonius, with whom he remained for eleven years. At his master's death, eager to acquaint himself at first hand with the wisdom of the East, he attached himself to a military expedition which the Emperor Gordian was leading against the Persians. The campaign, however, came to an untimely end. It had scarcely reached the Euphrates when Gordian was murdered by his generals, and in the confusion that ensued Plotinus, barely escaping with his life, had to flee to Antioch.

The next year, 244 A.D., he betook himself to Rome, where his success was immediate. He quickly gathered about himself a band of eminent disciples, which came eventually to include the Emperor Gallienus and the Empress Salonina. His influence with the imperial couple was great. They granted him land on which to establish a city incorporating the principles of Plato's *Republic*—a scheme that fell through because of the intrigues of his enemies at court—and it has been suggested that Gallienus' toleration of the Christians and personal guarantee of protection were due to Plotinus' intercession on their behalf. Not that Plotinus had any love for the Christians. He never mentions them directly in his writings, and in what seems to be an indirect reference to them he passes them by with disdain. Against the Gnostics, parts of whose fantastic speculations had a Christian background, he is outspoken in his condemnation.

Religious Mysticism. By nature Plotinus was a religious mystic of the first order. Indeed, his pupil and biographer, Porphyry, tells us that four times in a state of ecstasy he was made one with God. He is also said to have been ashamed that he had a body, and to have considered his parentage and birthplace of so little importance that he never would speak of them. But this mysticism and piety were tempered by a justness and sanity of vision and an intellectual balance that made him dislike all forms of religious or philosophical vagary and excess. In his scheme of salvation there was no dodging the discipline of clear and exact thinking. Reasoning, to be sure, could not get you all the way to God. In the end he had to be directly felt. But the mind was not ready for the final "ecstasy" of immediate union with him till the discipline of close and reasoned thinking had been carried to its finish. Again, in spite of his piety, Plotinus would never affiliate himself with any of the organized worships. "The gods," he said, "must come to me, not I to them." Their dwelling was not in temples but in the human heart.

The last years of his life he suffered from a fatal illness which forced him to abandon his teaching and retire to the home of a friend at Minturnae, not far from Rome. There he died in the year 270 A.D., at the age of sixty-six.

The Enneads. It was not until he was fifty that he could be induced to put his thoughts down in writing. Hitherto all his teaching had been oral. His lectures, we are told, were clear and brilliant and held his audiences spellbound. But he had no love for writing and slapped his ideas down as they occurred to him, often obscurely and ungrammatically, with no effort at style. Moreover, his eyesight was so bad that he could not himself revise and correct what he had written, and his handwriting was so illegible that no one else could succeed at the task. His pupil Porphyry collected all these disconnected jottings, shook them down, and published them, not in the order in which they were written, but divided somewhat arbitrarily into six parts, each one of which contained nine monographs or books. The material in each book was to some extent shaken down and organized. From the division into nine comes the name *Enneads* by which the collected works of Plotinus are known.

III. THE PLOTINIAN REALITY

In interpreting Plato's doctrine Plotinus could not hope to escape the color and the distortion of his own temperament and the atmosphere of the times. Naturally he seized upon the religious and the mystical elements in the Platonic teaching, upon the allegories and myths, which Plato apparently did not mean his readers to take literally, and in general upon the most imaginative and pictorial and the least scientific aspects of the Platonic philosophy. The presentation of the Idea of the Good in the likeness of the sun shedding being and life throughout the universe; the theological drama of creation in the *Timaeus,* which portrays a cosmic workman fashioning Matter into a world in the image of a divine archetype or model; the doctrine of the fall and the reincarnation of the soul and of her possible release from the wheel of birth and rebirth and mystical reunion with her divine source; the opposition of the spirit to the flesh and its salvation by flight from the world to a higher sphere—these were the things that fascinated him most and that gave him his cue.

Adoption of the Eleatic-Platonic Standard of Reality. Again, the standard of Reality that Plato took from the Eleatics, Plotinus in his turn took from Plato. Only that can really *be,* in the fullest sense of the word, which is uncreated, indestructible, unchangeable, motionless, indivisible and therefore unextended, simple in quality, single in essence, without taint of variety, multiplicity, and alteration.

Applying this standard, he rejects, one by one, Matter, Soul, Mind, and even the Aristotelian Active Reason as suitable candidates for the position of ultimate Reality. The first three are notoriously infected with multiplicity, motion, and change, and even the Active Reason as conceived by Aristotle, is still the contemplation of a truth that is complex and that is the object of a contemplating subject. Hence it lacks the indivisibility and the unity that the ultimately Real must possess.

Reality, therefore, must lie beyond even the confines of the intelligible world—the world of Platonic Ideas—and slip through the fingers of reason at each effort our minds make to grasp it. Plato himself, Plotinus might feel, had hinted at this when he elevated the Idea of the Good above the system of Forms which constituted the intelligible structure of the universe, and had asserted that it was indescribable even in such ultimate terms as existence and essence. However that may be, Plotinus insists that the nature of the Real is unutterable in any of the categories of our finite experience, even though they be most high, like beauty, or goodness, or mind, or being. The Real is higher than all these things and is not to be described by their names. It is attainable only in a state of mystical ecstasy from which the last trace of sensible and intelligible experience has been erased. In that state there is no longer any multiplicity or division of any sort. The complexity of the truth contemplated by pure reason is dissolved, the distinction between thinking and being thought about is overcome, the difference between subject and object disappears, subject and object are one, and that One is absolute unity, simple, indivisible, homogeneous, unalterable, uncreated, indestructible, in which there is no shadow of multiplicity or variety or turning. Here at last we have something that measures up to the Eleatic and Platonic specifications of the Real.

IV. EMANATION

Having thus by analysis and rejection located the ground of all being in this ineffable One, inexpressible in any of the terms at the command of a finite being, but nevertheless accessible in rare moments of mystical ecstasy, Plotinus turns to the problem of deriving the universe from its source.[1]

To solve this problem Plotinus turns back once more to Plato. In the *Timaeus* he had read that God was good and that the good can never have any jealousy of anything, but rather desired that all things should be as like itself as possible. And in the *Republic* there were the passages, to which we have already referred, in which the Idea of the Good is portrayed as giving being and intelligibility to the world of Ideas even as the sun by its light turns the darkness by night into a landscape by day to which it gives visibility and being.

Here was the answer plain at hand. The One, like the Good, must spend itself, must pour from itself its essence till every possible form

[1] The account, in the next paragraphs, of the Divine Reason and the World-Soul, and of their derivation from the One is found in IV, 8; V, 1, 2, 3, 4, 9.

and degree of existence was actualized. Just, then, as light pours from the sun, so being emanates from the One. But the moment that the effulgence of being has separated itself from its source it becomes other than, different from, and less than the One. This separation gives rise to an act of what Plotinus calls "epistrophe" or turning back and yearning toward its source. By this act the light becomes aware that it has left the sun and is no longer one with it. Thus the distinction between subject and object is brought into being. Moreover, it also becomes aware of the nature of its separated self, which, since it is no longer the One, is multiple in nature, yet multiple in the way that most closely approaches absolute unity.

V. THE DIVINE INTELLECT

Union of the Intellect with the Intelligible. But what is the nearest approach of the many to pure unity? When is the distinction between subject and object only just drawn and ever on the point of being erased? The answer to these questions is found in the contemplative activity of pure reason. The nature of thought is essentially a striving toward unity, a search for the pure and undivided One, and it achieves the closest approach to pure unity that can be attained short of mystical ecstasy. It reduces all the variety and multiplicity of the universe to a single, interconnected, unified system of types and laws, over which it hovers and broods in self-sustained and motionless meditation, beholding and apprehending at a single glance the plan of all time and existence given in its entirety. It sees, then, the world-process not as a temporal succession of events, but under the aspect of eternity. Its act of knowing the truth knows once and for all everything that there is to know about the past, the present, and the future. It, like the truth upon which it meditates, is timeless.

Further than this, however, the activity of contemplative reason cannot soar. It reaches its "ceiling" in possessing and being the answer, good in all times and places, to all the questions that have and do and will beset all minds intent on discovering the truth about the world.

Not until Reason has emanated from the One have we anything of which we can say "it exists" or "it is." The One itself no more exists than it thinks or can be thought of. Such terms belittle its supreme majesty, which is higher than being, and higher than thinking even eternal truth. But existence can be predicated of the Divine Reason and of the rational order of the universe it enshrines. Indeed, the activity of contemplative reason and the immaterial Forms and Laws with which it occupies itself alone measure up to the specifications laid down by Plato and Aristotle for real existence. Real existence, then, and the intelligible structure of the universe are identical.

Ideas of Particulars. In expatiating upon the content and lay-out of the divine mind, Plotinus follows closely Plato's enumeration of the different sorts of Ideas. But in one important respect ne parts company with both Plato and Aristotle. They, it will be remembered, had said that all Ideas and Forms are general or universal in character. The particular objects exemplifying the Ideas are incomplete and multiple representations of them by the material principle, whose nature it is to refract the universal and to display it broken up into a myriad instances of itself. Plotinus, however, maintains that there are Ideas or Forms of particular men, as well as an Idea of mankind in general laid up in the divine mind. Our separate personalities are recognized and registered in the formal structure of the universe. So, too, as thinkers, our individual reasons are eternally separate parts of the Divine Reason.

VI. THE WORLD-SOUL

Emanation of the World-Soul from the Divine Intellect. Now, the universe is obviously more than a system of eternal Forms enshrined in a purely contemplative reason. It is a moving, living flow of many concrete, sensible phenomena, to which the Forms give structure and order. The Forms that contemplative reason thinks, are, as the Stoics would say, *logoi spermatikoi,* seminal forms, which also create, as nearly as possible in their own image, a further generation of being. Just, then, as the One overflowed, so now Reason in its turn overflows. And just as the light pouring out of the One looked back to its source and, recognizing its departure and difference from the One, became the nearest possible thing to the One, so the light emanated by con-templative Reason turns back in a similar "epistrophe" and, seeing that it is no longer Reason, becomes the nearest possible thing to contemplative Reason, which is Soul. So, too, the essence of Soul is a striving after that contemplative possession of truth which is the prerogative of the Divine Reason. But, once more, she could not attain her goal without being reabsorbed into the Divine Reason and ceasing to be herself. Her "ceiling" is reached in so-called discursive or syn-thetic thinking, which wrestles with problems, and puzzles and argues and reasons things out, and by so doing brings us to the moment, and leaves us at the moment, when the solution suddenly reveals itself to us and the truth is self-evident. Then the activity of contemplative Reason takes her place. Furthermore, and here Plotinus adopts the Platonic and the Aristotelian triple division of the soul, she possesses two other powers or capacities. She is the principle of sensation which man shares with the animals, and the giver of life and of the vital functions which both man and animals share with plants. The sensitive soul may be regarded as a sort of minor and internal overflow of the rational soul, and the vegetative soul as a similar emanation from the sensitive.

The Generation of Time. With the appearance of Soul, a new and important element comes upon the scene. In the generation of Reason from the One, and of Soul from Reason, there is no question of temporal succession. The three are co-eternal. But the operations of Soul take place in *time*. She thinks of one thing *after* another, she perceives one event *after* another, the vital functions she sustains *go on*. Time, says Plotinus, occupies the same relation to soul as does eternity to Reason. Whereas the activity of contemplative Reason is eternal, the activities of Soul are everlasting. Time, as Plato said, is the moving image of eternity. Time, however, cannot be abstracted from motion, and set up as a measure of motion, as Aristotle had maintained. It is, rather, inseparable from the synthetic and discursive or "running through" activity of the soul—of her having to pass from one thing to another instead of grasping all things at once. If the soul should succeed in identifying herself with contemplative Reason and in seeing all things together, then time would cease.

The Emanation of Individual Souls. The emanation of Soul from the Divine Reason takes place both in a general and particular manner. Just as the Divine Reason emerges from the One as a single, unified system of the many Forms that constitute the intelligible structure of the universe, so Soul emerges from Reason as a single, all-comprehending, all-unifying World-Soul containing within itself the particular souls of individual beings. Like Reason, it is a one-in-many.

Plotinus lays equal stress upon the unity of the World-Soul and the multiplicity and variety of individual souls. Individual souls must be separate and distinct, else we should all experience one another's sensations, desires, thoughts, and the like, and for that matter everything that occurred anywhere in the universe. On the other hand, all particular souls are interrelated, and all partake of the nature of Soul in general. They are then not only many, but one. But how can this be? How can individual souls proceed from the World-Soul, or be parts

ɔf it, without diminishing or dividing its nature? This difficulty disappears, Plotinus thinks, if we will think of derivation or division not
in a material but in a logical sense. Take, for example, a science. The
notions that spring from it do so without altering or impairing its
nature, and involve one another without losing their distinctive character. After the same fashion all particular souls can be interrelated,
and can be contained within and derived from the World-Soul without impairing its essential unity and without losing their separate
individualities.

VII. IMMORTALITY

The immortality of the individual soul is argued at great length.[2]
Plotinus attacks in succession the materialistic doctrine that the soul
can be reduced to physical atoms or their motions; the Pythagorean
teaching that she is a harmony of the body; and the Aristotelian contention that she is the entelechy or actualization of potentialities inherent in living organisms. Matter of itself cannot be conceived as
producing vital and conscious activities. The body can no more produce harmony by itself than the lyre can play itself. Nor could Aristotle locate the higher or even the lower activities of the soul anywhere
in the physical organism.

The truth is that the soul is an incorporeal essence, the source and
the substance of life and motion. Nothing can stop her going on forever, except possible reabsorption into the timeless and the eternal.
All human souls are everlasting expressions of the eternal *logoi
spermatikoi* of individual men. Not only, however, is ihe rational part
of our soul immortal, but also the sensitive and the vegetative parts,
which are portions of the sensitive and vegetative powers of the world-
soul, and at death return to their source.

Reincarnation. Being everlasting, our souls must exist before birth
as well as after death. Following the lead given by Plato in the
Phaedrus, Plotinus tells us that the heavens are full of souls, possessed
not only of reason but of the sensitive and vegetative faculties, and
dominated, as the case may be, by one or another of these three powers.
When these souls fall into the body and become incarnate, the pro-
pensities of the individual they inhabit are determined by their dominant characters. The process of reincarnation is directed in the same
way. Those who have abandoned themselves to their passions and
lived on the level of sense become wild and lustful animals; the stupid,
who have merely "vegetated" all their lives, become plants. Esthetes,

[2] On immortality and reincarnation, cf. III, 2, 3; IV, 4, 8.

he tells us, are reincarnated as song-birds, good tyrants turn into eagles, unsuccessful social reformers into busy bees, and absent-minded philosophers into soaring birds. Good all-round men become men again. Furthermore, things are so arranged that those who have done wrong to others are in their next life wronged in the same way. Malefactors of great wealth are reborn in poverty, and murderers are murdered.

But reincarnation for Plotinus is only episodic—like passing, he says, from dream to dream or sleeping each night in a new bed. How far he intends his descriptions to be taken literally it is hard to say. In any case, they are full of discrepancies, and are not worked together into anything like a systematic doctrine of immortality. The reason perhaps is not far to seek. To Plotinus as to Plato the *immortality* of the soul, in the usual sense of everlastingness, meant simply endless imprisonment in time, varied only by a shift from cell to cell. It was not something to be desired but something from which the soul should make every effort to escape. She must break her bars, awake from her dreaming, and stay awake without thought or desire of going back to bed. She must put off everlastingness and put on eternity. But to this point—the manner of the soul's redemption—we shall return anon.

VIII. THE PLOTINIAN TRINITY

So far, then, we have three divine principles. First we have the ineffable One, the source of all being, but itself above and beyond being, and indescribable in any term or category of human experience. Second, we have the Divine Intellect generated by and emanating from the One, as light is generated by the sun and proceeds from it. This principle enshrines, and contemplates, and is one with, the Form and intelligible structure of the existent. And finally we have the World-Soul which in its turn proceeds from the Divine Intellect and enacts and gives multiple and particular spatial and temporal expression to the content of the Divine Mind. Applying Plotinus' own metaphor, as embroidered by Dante, to the scene, we may envisage it as a central flame of intolerable light, which even the eye of reason cannot bear to look upon, surrounded by concentric, circular rainbows, the one at rest, the other revolving, aglow with the many, varied colors of the spectrum of existence and thought and sense and life. These three principles constitute the Plotinian trinity.

IX. THE PHYSICAL UNIVERSE

We pass now from the realm of pure spirit to the corporeal world of physical bodies spread out and in motion in space, and coming into and passing out of being in time, whose occurrence and movement are subjected to a law of mechanical cause and effect. Why, we ask, should such a universe exist, and how does it come to pass? [3]

The answer is that the generation of the physical universe is incidental to the same process of emanation as necessitates the generation of the World-Soul by the Divine Intellect, and of the Divine Intellect by the One. With the generation of the World-Soul the process of emanation has by no means exhausted itself or come to a logical conclusion, since there remain vast realms of unrealized possibilities of lower forms of being waiting to be actualized. Hence the World-Soul must overflow just as the One and the Divine Intellect overflow, and the further outpouring and extension of divinity is the physical universe. We should note incidentally that here Plotinus breaks with Plato, who regarded the universe as the handiwork of a creator, and with Aristotle, who regarded it as uncaused.

But if we look more deeply beneath the act of generation to its results, the picture changes. Now there is not merely difference in the divine light, there is diminution of it. There is a creeping shadow and a gathering dimness. The white light of the One is not merely split into many colors. It is beginning to *fade*. For the physical universe is corporeal and spatial. In a word, it is *material,* and the incipient twilight means the transition from a spiritual to a material world. Still, even so the universe, taken as a whole is a perfect body and represents the closest approach that light which has begun to fade can make to light in which as yet no shadow has occurred. The flawless constitution and frictionless running of the cosmos are a kind of "epistrophe" towards its source and mark the "ceiling" to which body may attain, but beyond which it cannot pass without ceasing to be body and returning to the spirit from which it came. Such lessening, then, of the divine light as occurs in the lapse from pure spirit to a physical order is not necessarily ominous.

When, however, we turn from the universe as a whole to an inspection of its parts, darkness suddenly looms as darkness and not simply as diminished light. The operations of the universe involve the birth

[3] For the generation of the universe by the World-Soul, and of individual bodies by individual souls, cf. IV, 8; V, 1, 2, 4, 9.

and death, the conflict, and the collision of its parts and their destruction by one another—a situation that brings suffering to sentient beings,
and defeat and despair to beings also conscious of their aims and
hopes and possibilities. Then, too, the generation of the individual
body by the individual soul is attended with labor and pain, and only
too often enslaves her to bodily desires and makes her the servant
rather than the master of that which she has created. In short, her
"descent" becomes a "fall," and sin enters the world.

X. THE PROBLEM OF EVIL

Plotinus now had on his hands the problem of evil. He had to
explain the sudden change the process of emanation took for the
worse after generating the physical universe, and to reconcile the imperfections of the world with the perfection of its source. And, so far as
human beings were concerned, he had to justify the misfortunes and
sufferings that befell the best of them and the prosperity frequently
enjoyed by the wicked. Moreover, he had, above all, to explain moral
evil, and to show how souls outpoured from the divine and themselves
parts of the divine World-Soul could and did sin.

In dealing with the problem of physical evil he employed, first of
all, most of the Stoic devices, with which we are already familiar and
which we need not repeat. The gist of his contention, as of theirs, was
that suffering and misfortune are not evil for the good man and that
for the sinner they are a just punishment and therefore good. In developing the latter point he had at his command the idea of individual
immortality and reincarnation, which for the most part the Stoics
lacked. Where suffering, he tells us, cannot be referred to sin committed here and now, it may be regarded as the fruit of evil deeds done
in past existences. The moral order is, if anything, to be praised for
the economy and ingenuity it displays in so arranging things that the
victims of crime in this life were always former criminals in past existences, and that they are being done by precisely as they did. Thus
evil-doing is impressed into the service of the moral government of
the world, and is always turned to a good purpose, without, however,
making the deed by which justice is done any the less criminal, and
the agent of the divine justice any the less wicked and deserving of
punishment in a future reincarnation.

The dramatic propriety of setting a thief to catch a thief is used by
Plotinus also to justify evil in general. The sinner is like the villain
in the play. For the want of him the cosmic drama would be the poorer.

Sin and suffering are like the shadows in the picture for the presence of which it is a finer work of art. Nay more, just as the shadows bring out the lights, so evil by its contrast enhances the good. Or again, good and evil are like the different and opposed tones which when combined produce a musical harmony. The harsher notes, and, for that matter, even the discords contribute to the perfection of the composition, and any instrument is better according as it produces the greatest variety of sounds.

We must not think, however, that providence deliberately generates sin and suffering for the express purpose of producing these artistic effects. Evil is simply utilized by divine providence when and where it happens in the course of events.

XI. FREE-WILL AND MORAL RESPONSIBILITY

The Soul a Free Agent. These arguments, however, could not explain why the individual soul went wrong, and how she could be justly held to account for her wrong-doing. The nature of sin, to be sure, lay, in Plotinus' opinion, in an "audacious" impulse conceived by the soul, after she had generated the body and entered into it, to free herself from the restraints laid upon her as part of the World-Soul, and to go her own way—a way that followed the solicitations of the body and of the physical universe. Thus a conflict arose within her between a lower nature expressive of these solicitations and a higher nature shared with the World-Soul and derived from her *logos spermatikos* in the Divine Intellect.

But where does this "audacious" inclination come from? And is the soul compelled to follow it, or is it within her power to resist it? These questions bring Plotinus face to face with the problem of free-will and moral responsibility. That the soul is a free agent, and that she, and she alone, is to blame for her fall, Plotinus cannot emphasize too strongly. However, to establish this fact, he feels that we must first define what we mean by freedom and then see if the soul can successfully exercise it.

The Process of Emanation. The nature of freedom can best be illustrated by reviewing the process of emanation. The emanation of the existent from the One is, Plotinus insists, a free act on the part of the One. Yet it is an act in which there is no exercise of will or choice, since the One is above choice and volition. Moreover, it is an act to which there is no possible alternative. The One *must* overflow, because it is its nature to do so, and it cannot abstain from being itself. The freedom, then, of the first act of emanation does not depend upon or imply an ability on the part of the free agent either to act otherwise or to refrain from action. It lies simply in the fact that the One is not compelled to overflow by anything outside itself, but only by its own nature. The freedom of the One, in short, is not a "free-will of indifference" but a freedom of self-determination.

So, too, the Divine Intellect is forced by itself alone to generate the World-Soul, and the World-Soul by herself alone to generate the physical universe. No alternative to emanation, no other course to choose, is open to them. But since their acts are determined by themselves and not performed under external compulsion, they, too, are free agents.

The freedom of the individual soul is of the same sort. She *must* generate the individual body and descend into it, because it is her nature to do so. No outer force either compels or opposes her act. The emanation of the body to which she is forced by her nature is at the same time a completely free expression of herself. Indeed, if she did not radiate a body and descend into it, her creative power would remain unmanifested and without fruit, to the curtailment of her own inner goodness and power, and to the impairment of her freedom.

The Soul Determined by Her Character. That her freedom also is not freedom of indeterminism but of self-determination Plotinus makes clear beyond any possible misunderstanding. Our choices and our acts, he insists, must always have a sufficient reason by which they are determined to be what they are. . . . "Causelessness is quite inadmissible; we can make no place here for unwarranted 'slantings,' sudden movements of bodies apart from any initiating power" (such as the Epicureans invoked as a basis of freedom), "for precipitate spurts in a soul with nothing to drive it into a new course of action. Such causelessness would bind the soul under an even sterner compulsion, no longer master of itself, but at the mercy of movements apart from will and cause. . . . On the assumption that all happens by cause, it is easy to discover the determinants of any particular act or state, and to trace it plainly to them." [4]

In the case of the soul, the determinants of her particular acts or states are to be found in her *character*. This character is composite. It consists of a central core, which proceeds from the particular form or *logos* of the individual soul laid up in the Divine Reason,[5] and of incidental accretions acquired during the process of reincarnation. The

---

[4] III, 1, § 1 (trans. Mackenna).
[5] Cf. V, 7; III, 3, § 3 ff.

soul has made herself what she is by the kind of life she has led in her past existences. The character she has thus built up may predispose her to vice. The wicked are wicked because it has become their nature to be wicked. Nevertheless the soul is essentially disposed to the good. She cannot deliberately and of herself *will* evil. When her choices and acts are determined by her essential nature and carried out in accordance with it, they are *free* acts. She is, to be sure, responsible also for the acts to which her acquired character may lead. But her responsibility for them rests upon the fact that, in Plotinus' opinion, she need not have acquired the character of which the deeds in question are the necessary outcome.[6]

We have now seen that the soul possesses a free will not of indeterminism but of self-determination, that her choices are expressions of her character, that her character is essentially self-determined to the good, and that her vicious tendencies and behavior are somehow acquired by her after she has generated and descended into the body. But we are as far as ever from explaining how the soul can sin. For how can a blameless character, self-determined to the good, acquire vicious tendencies and go wrong and fall into evil ways?

The Incarnate Soul Influenced by the Body. A possible answer suggests itself at this point. When the soul has descended into the body she is no longer without alternative courses of action open to her, and is no longer determined by herself alone. On the contrary, she is now attached to an individual body of her own with its passions and pleasures, and she is surrounded by a multiple, complex physical world which presses upon her from all sides, offers innumerable choices between alternative courses of behavior, and incites her to behave in all sorts of ways. In these circumstances her choices are dictated, in part at least, by the nature of the external situation by which she is confronted, and her actions are reactions whose nature is determined both by her own character and that of the external stimulus. In short, her behavior is now the result of a component of forces of which she herself is but one.

Is it not possible, then, that under such conditions her power of determining her conduct should be largely or completely blocked by a superior strength of external forces? May not these forces prevail over the force she contributes to the component? Must she not be carried at times helplessly in the stream of physical impulses and events? Nay more, if these events and impulses are themselves all

[6] Cf. IV, 8, §§ 3, 9; I, 8, § 4; III, 2, § 10.

providentially ordered, is not the fact that she succumbs to them also part of the divine order, and therefore something for which she is not responsible, and, for that matter, something that is not evil but good?

Self-Determination Possible. Plotinus, however, will not listen to such an excuse. The soul is emphatically *not* enslaved to external circumstance by her descent into the body. Nothing—call it fate, destiny, or divine providence—can deprive her of her power of self-determination. She may, indeed, choose to act in accordance with providence, but action in accordance with providence is not necessarily action to which the soul is determined by providence. "The act of the libertine is not done by providence or in accordance with providence; neither is the action of the good done by providence—it is done by the man—but it is done in accordance with providence."[7]

Furthermore, we must not forget that the soul is always a factor in the component of forces that determines each of her reactions to the physical world, and hence that her behavior must be at least partly determined by herself. And what she contributes is, in Plotinus' opinion, always the dominating factor in the reaction. Therefore, no combination of external forces, however strong, can take from her the power to control her behavior in any situation. She cannot be forced to sin by the incentives that beset her. When she sins, she and she alone is to blame.[8]

The freedom of self-determination of which nothing can deprive the soul, Plotinus, like the Stoics, considers a sufficient basis for moral and legal responsibility. We do not need to ask whether a man, being what he was and confronted with a situation such as faced him, could have acted otherwise. If he did at the moment what he wanted to do and in acting felt himself under no compulsion save that of his own nature, he can be held to account, legally and morally, for what he did, and can be justly punished for his criminal act.[9]

But the question of how the soul can sin still remains wide-open. She is self-determined to the good, and is the dominating factor in all her reactions. By rights, then, it would seem that she ought to exercise her freedom by withstanding her "audacious" inclination to cut loose from the World-Soul and yield herself to the body, and by resisting the temptations to which contact with the sensible world exposes her.

[7] III, 3, § 5 (trans. Mackenna).   [9] Cf. III, 2, § 10.
[8] Cf. IV, 3.

XII. MATTER

There remains, however, one further possible explanation of the soul's misuse of her freedom and her consequent fall into sin, that we have not yet explored. Even if she possesses an inalienable sovereignty over herself, and a power to withstand the temptations of the world and the flesh, the fact remains that it is only after she has generated and descended into the body, and has become enmeshed in the material universe, that sin occurs. It looks, then, as if sin must have its source, or at least its occasion, in the material principle. Perhaps if we examine the nature of Matter we shall find a solution of our problem.[10]

The Nature of Matter. Plotinus begins his inquiry into the nature of Matter by reviewing existing theories, and comes at once to the conclusion that physical matter is only one manifestation of the material principle. This principle is, as Plato taught, one of Not-Being as opposed to Being, and, as Aristotle maintained, one of formless and unrealized Potentiality as opposed to Form and Actuality. It is, as they also thought, the principle to which the multiple, restless, unfinished, unperfected, non-unified aspects of the universe are due. In terms of Plotinus' own central metaphor, Matter is the darkness which mingles with the light emanated by the One, as that light recedes from its source, and which dims its radiance and power and confuses the vision of which it is the vehicle.

The appearance of Matter is necessitated by the very nature of emanation and must occur in the primal act of generation on the part of the One. For emanation and generation mean separation of the generated from its source, and separateness means otherness and difference from the One, which, in its turn, implies deprivation of complete unity and perfection. Matter, then, is already present in the Divine Intellect, which is other than the One and therefore multiple in content, and other than the Perfect and therefore in a sense imperfect. But this "Intelligible Matter," as Plotinus calls it, which differentiates the Divine Intellect from the One and expresses itself as a substratum of general intelligibility in which many Forms participate, is innocuous and without evil in the ordinary sense of the word.

Matter a Diminution of Being. However, as the process of emanation continues, the divine light is gradually diffused and spent as it proceeds further and further from the One. In the Divine Intellect and the World-Soul it is broken into many colors and begins to

[10] For Plotinus on matter and its relation to evil, cf. I, 8; II, 4; III, 3.

---

shimmer, but it has not yet perceptibly begun to fade. But with the emanation of the corporeal universe, diminution appears along with difference. The light is perceptibly dimmer, and darkness begins to manifest itself. And slowly fullness of being wanes, and the twilight of distance from the One waxes, as we pass down the scale of animate creation to the lowest forms of life, and thence through progressively increasing formlessness to the faintly glowing rim of the most elemental formulations of Matter, which flicker on the verge of black night and at last expire into it.

Pure Matter, then, is for Plotinus, as for Aristotle, a negative limit approached but never reached by Being. It is the final darkness to which the dying light of Being gives rise by its extinction. It cannot be penetrated by the eye of either sense or thought. Nevertheless, as Plato found when dealing with the formless space of Not-Being, we can have a spurious or "bastard" concept of it, just as the eye can somehow "see" darkness, which is an absence of light and sight.[11]

XIII. MATTER AND EVIL

Since Matter is the source and principle of imperfection and evil, what is true of it will, by and large, be true of them. Neither Matter nor evil, as we now see, is a positive principle actively and stubbornly resistant to the good, either in the shape of an intractable world-stuff which God has difficulty in handling, as Plato thought, or of an ill-disposed animated world-stuff such as Numenius believed in. Again, Matter is not a purely neutral substratum for the domination of which God and an evil world-soul are contending, as Plutarch maintained, nor is the source of evil a malignant, quasi-personal power opposed to God, as the Persians and the Gnostics held.

Imperfection and Matter are rather a deforming or "unforming" of Form, as Aristotle believed. But this blurring and smudging of Form is not due, as he thought, to a kind of "drag" in a creative process of converting lower and more potential into higher and more actual Forms of being. On the contrary, says Plotinus, they are incidental to a creative process in which Actuality and Form dwindle away into the lower, less actual, and more formless degrees of existence. Evil in itself, "primal" evil, as Plotinus calls it, in which the degeneration of the Good terminates, is identical with pure Matter and utter darkness.

This curious negative-positive, "absence of light = presence of darkness" character of Matter and evil enables Plotinus to derive them

[11] Cf. I, 8, § 14.

from the One, without thereby making the One their cause. They are neither part of God, as the Stoics supposed, nor do they exist independently of God, as the Neo-Pythagoreans and the Gnostics held. They are derived from the One, just as darkness may be regarded as derived from the fading of light. But they are not caused by the One any more than the derivation of darkness from the fading of light makes light itself, whose nature it is to shine, the cause of darkness. All we can say is that just as the sun must radiate light, so the One must radiate being and goodness if it is not to remain non-creative and unfulfilled.[12] But just as light, once radiated, must fade, so being and goodness, once emanated, must diminish until they are wholly spent—that is, until they lapse into the complete absence of light and goodness and being which is at the same time a complete presence of darkness and evil and nothingness. God, then, being the source of emanation, is in a sense the source of Matter and evil but he is not, in Plotinus' opinion, therefore responsible for them.

XIV. THE RELATION OF SIN TO EVIL

Turning now to sin, we note first that it is itself not *the* bad. In the same way, virtue is not *the* good. Both virtue and vice are inclinations or movements, the one towards perfection, the other towards absolute evil. Sin, in Plotinus' own phrase, is "secondary evil," metaphysically speaking at least, although morally and for the soul it is primary, since it is the ultimate degradation she can endure, the least she can do and be, and still exist. To sink to absolute evil would mean annihilation.

Sin exhibits the same ambiguous, negative-positive character as does the primal evil of which it is the shadow. It is essentially, if we can speak of its having an essence, a *failure* to act virtuously, a *lack* of self-determination, an *absence* of good, in the soul. Wrongdoing is *not* doing right.[13] At the same time, *not* doing right is *doing* wrong. It is not inaction. It is performing deeds, but deeds that are deeds of darkness, not of light. Vice, then, like absolute evil, has its positive side and expression, and is treated positively by Plotinus.

We are now ready for our last word with regard to the soul's moral responsibility for her evil deeds. The moral struggle, we may say, is not against an outer force, but against a failure of the soul's own inner power. For the presence of that weakness neither she nor God is re-

[12] Cf. V, 3, §§ 14-16.
[13] Cf. I, 8, §§ 1-5.

sponsible, any more than the sun or the light that proceeds from it is responsible for that light's fading. At the same time, just as light, however diminished and spent it may be, is still light and retains till the moment of its extinction its luminous essence and its capacity for shining more brightly, so the soul's essential self-determination to the good and her capacity for salvation cannot be wholly lost as long as she continues to exist. In a word, no matter how low she sinks, she is always able and free *not* to sin, and *not* to acquire bit by bit the evil habit and character of failing to determine her own actions. Because, then, she is always free *not* to sin, she is morally responsible for her wrongdoing. Therefore, Plotinus feels, we can say with equal right that the fall of the soul is part and parcel of the process of emanation; that it is an act of free-will; and that it is a punishment for sin.[14]

But how a soul that can neither determine herself to evil nor be forced thereto by anything outside herself does or can sin, Plotinus does not answer. In last resort, he can only plead that we ought not ask too much of the lesser degree of goodness and existence that is hers because of her distance from the One.[15]

XV. THE WAY OF SALVATION

We turn now from the process of emanation to the way of salvation which the soul must tread if she is to be reunited with the One. The possibility of redemption is, as we have just seen, something that the soul can never lose, short of utter annihilation. There is no soul so degraded, no ray of light so spent, as to lose the power of returning through the vast abyss of metaphysical space to mingle with its source. For all the countless light-years of procession that remove the dying spark from the central sun, it is still "God out of God, Light out of Light." [16]

The way of redemption is long and gradual. It may take aeons of reincarnation to traverse it, and there are no short cuts in the long windings of its ascent. Sudden conversions, short-circuitings such as seemed to be promised by the mystery-religions, irrelevant and premature ecstasies, reunions with the One in outbursts of irrational emotion, have no place in the system. In the end, to be sure, the soul will be wrapt away and united with the divine in an indescribable ecstasy, but she must first fledge herself for that last flight by a long and

[14] Cf. IV, 8, § 5.
[15] I, 8, § 7, § 10 ff.; III, 2, § 8; IV, 8, § 6 ff.
[16] Cf. IV, 8, § 7 ff.; VI, 9, § 7 ff.; I, 6, § 5 ff.; III, 6, § 2; V, 1, § 3 ff.

rigorous discipline, not only moral but intellectual. Without this long and careful training she would not be strong enough to attain the heights upon which redemption dwells or to bear the splendors of the beatific vision there revealed to her.[17]

Moral Discipline. First, she must perfect herself in the practice of the ordinary social and practical virtues. The world may be something to be renounced, and salvation may involve renunciation of it, but that does not absolve us from the necessity of an upright and noble participation in worldly affairs and of honest, generous and friendly relations with our fellow-men.[18] The body and its needs are not to be despised and suppressed, but must be disciplined in such wise that they do not distract the soul from the contemplation of higher things.[19]

At the same time Plotinus shows little interest in social reform and apparently feels, like the Stoics, that the good man has done his whole duty if he as an individual leads a godly, sober, righteous life under the conditions that exist. The core of human virtue, with him as with them, lies in detachment from worldly goods and evils and in a basic indifference to them, which put him out of reach of their caresses and their stings. But, whereas with the Stoics this "apathy" was an end in itself and the essence of salvation, for Plotinus it was merely a means to the next step along the way of redemption. Having attained it, the soul was now free to turn and fix her attention upon the intelligible world, and thus to identify herself utterly with that "epistrophe" towards the Divine Reason in which her true being lies.[20]

The Discipline of Philosophic Thought. But this is to pass from one discipline to another, for now the soul is confronted with the necessity of hard and intricate and correct thinking. She must perfect her power of reasoning as well as her moral nature. To do this, she must philosophize and grasp the final categories of thought and being which pervade and organize the intelligible structure of the universe and provide the fundamental terms in which she reasons. In enumerating these categories, Plotinus follows Plato, rejecting the Aristotelian and Stoic lists as superficial and unanalyzed and sometimes contradictory. The most general and the most profound assertions that we can make about the rational structure of the universe are (1) that it exists (being); (2) that it is stable (rest); (3) that it is also instinct with life and creative energy (motion); (4) that it displays sameness (identity); and (5) that it at the same time exhibits variety (difference).[21]

---

[17] Cf. V, 3, §§ 1, 9; I, 6, § 9.

[18] Cf. I, 3, § 6, 4, § 1.

[19] Cf. I, 4, § 1.

[20] Cf. I, 3, §§ 1, 6; V, 9, § 1.

[21] Cf. V, 1, § 4; VI, 1; VII, 2.

The discipline of philosophy terminates in the contemplation of truth, in which the soul beholds the plan of all existence, not bit by bit, but all at once, in its entirety as a single eternal fact. Wrapt away from the sensible world, and all movement and change, by the vision of eternal and immutable truth, the soul herself is no longer conscious of sensible experience and time and space, but is lifted clear of them and united with the Divine Intellect from which she springs.

Now, too, for the first time, she becomes aware of her true self. She is no longer a separate individual, one person among other persons, viewing the universe from a particular location within it, and seeing herself as a part of it, surrounded by other parts. She has transcended personal self-consciousness and has become a contemplative and synoptic vision overarching and comprehending in a single act of thought the entire plan of all truth and all existence. Nor is she any longer aware of any separation of herself from what she sees. Subject and object, the knower and the known, have become one and the same thing in her.[22] Now and now only is she prepared for the final ecstasy of reunion with the One.

The ascent of the soul is accompanied by a progressive purification of her affections, which Plotinus describes in terms drawn directly from Plato's *Symposium*. Starting from the loveliness of the sensible world and the human body, the soul first learns to regard all earthly beauty as a shadow or image of a heavenly prototype. Step by step her love is directed from sensible loveliness to the loveliness of virtuous conduct and works, and thence to the beauty of noble souls. Then, when once she has withdrawn from discursive and synthetic thinking to contemplation of the truth, the beauty of the intelligible and the rational will engage her affections. This will lead her to the vision and the love of the essence or Form of loveliness in itself—the highest experience of which she is capable, short of the final ecstasy of reunion with the One.

Art a Revelation of the Divine. Plotinus, however, does not, like Plato, scorn the artist as a mere imitator, and the work of art as the copy of a copy and therefore further removed from reality than the sensible object it portrays. The loveliness of the sensible world is a direct revelation of the intelligible order that lies at its heart. Things are beautiful or ugly according as they reveal or obscure the Form within them.[23] The artist is one who is vouchsafed a greater sensitive-

[22] Cf. V, 3, §§ 1-6.
[23] Cf. I, 6, §§ 1-5; V, 9, §§ 2-3.

ness to the Form of which the object of sense is the copy, and who reveals that Form in his work more distinctly than it is revealed by the object itself. All imitative arts, then, such as painting, sculpture, dancing, acting, and music, not only copy sensible objects, but copy them in such a way as to make the intelligible structure within them more manifest, and to lead the soul to a perception of the higher beauty. This is also true of productive arts, like architecture and carpentry, and even of agriculture and medicine, and rhetoric, strategy, and political economy. All of them, in so far as they are arts, arouse and purify the esthetic sense,[24] and help raise the soul from the sensible to the intelligible world.

Finally we must note that Plotinus chooses esthetic rather than moral experience as the closest adumbration of the mystical ecstasy in which the soul is reunited with the One. The virtues are means of purification, not ends in themselves. As long as that purification is taking place, the soul desires God as the sovereign *good,* but, when it is accomplished, and she stands upon the brink of salvation, ready for her final ecstasy, she beholds and adores him as sovereign *beauty.* The attainment of this vision is the supreme end in comparison with which all other ends are naught. The love with which it fills her—a love that is not a search but a possession, a love that is of nothing beyond herself, but of herself transfigured and consummated by the beauty she embraces—is the truest foretaste of the bliss into which she is about to enter.[25]

The Final Ecstasy of Reunion with the One. And now the soul, strengthened and prepared by the discipline of right conduct, exact thinking and properly directed love, is ready for release from the wheel of birth and rebirth, from sensible experience and every other attachment to the body, from virtue, from thinking, from the vision of eternal truth and being and beauty, from self-consciousness, and even from existence. Her final state, in which she is at last one with the One is as indescribable and ineffable as is the One itself. No category of our experience can compass or define it. It can only be described negatively. The soul who has attained it is formless, unconscious of herself, not present to herself, void of movement, desire, passion, reason, and thought. It cannot be called a beatific vision. It is rather "some other kind of seeing, ecstasy, and simplification and self-surrender." It cannot even be called union with God in the ordinary

---

[24] Cf. V, 9, § 9.
[25] Cf. I, 6, § 7.

sense of the term, which implies a fusion of two separate entities. The soul is identical with God, as the centers of two concentric circles are identical. She and God are not together; they are one and the same thing. The tremendous arc of emanation and redemption has returned to its starting point and the One is all in all.[26]

[26] Cf. VI, 9, §§ 10-11.

Chapter XXII

THE LATER NEO-PLATONISTS

I. THE POST-PLOTINIAN TENDENCIES

It would have taken great speculative minds to sustain philosophy at the heights to which Plotinus had raised it, and these were notably lacking among his successors. His immediate disciples, though learned and zealous, were not, with the possible exception of Proclus, of profound and original thought. They were content to follow their master's teaching, and to expound it, with additional interpretations of his meaning and glosses of their own. Moreover, they tended to succumb to the fascinations of the mystery-religions from which Plotinus held himself aloof. The results were over-elaborated and subtilized systems, which the application of the allegorical method and the tendency to find theological parallels frequently made fantastic. Again, the moral outlook of the later philosophers reverted to the dualism and asceticism which Plotinus deplored, and were infused with gloom and pessimism in so far as the affairs of the world and man's earthly life were concerned.

Philosophically, a tendency to extend the trinitarian principle in describing the godhead and to multiply trinities within trinities in explaining the universe became characteristic of post-Plotinian speculation. Thus Aemilius, one of Plotinus' pupils, divided the Divine Intellect into three entities, the thought that is, the thinking that possesses this thought, and the thinking that participates in this possession and by means of it beholds the thought that is. The first entity wills the world to exist; the second expresses that will in a command; the third puts that command into effect. Individual souls, Aemilius reduced to aspects of the World-Soul. Apparently, too, he noted certain resemblances between his concept of the World-Soul and the views the Christians were at the time developing regarding the Logos.

II. PORPHYRY

His Extreme Dualism. Aemilius' fellow-pupil, Porphyry, we may remember, who wrote Plotinus' life and edited the *Enneads,* was the most distinguished of Plotinus' disciples.[1] A man of immense learning and a voluminous author, he composed among other things an *Introduction* to Aristotle's *Categories* which was regarded as authoritative in the Middle Ages, and which laid the foundation for all subsequent formal logic. In his *Sentences* he popularized Plotinus' system without any great departure from it, though he emphasized the distinction between the corporeal and the incorporeal. Nor could he permit the human soul in her reincarnations to sink to animal estate, as Plotinus did. But he prolonged the process of reincarnation and made of the flesh a heavier cross, harder to bear and to lay down. Indeed, the burden of the flesh is carried by us beyond the grave and to the very threshold of redemption, in the form of a more refined but still material body that survives death. Nor can union even with the divine reason, to say nothing of the final ecstasy, be attained here on earth. For the complete wisdom and goodness that prepare us for salvation, we must look to some future existence.

Attack on Morals and Popular Religion. This more pessimistic outlook is perhaps the result of Porphyry's more severe and fanatical moral attitude. His treatise on *Abstinence* reminds us of the prohibitions still advocated by some people. Pleasure of every description is sinful. Horse-racing, theater-going, dancing, sexual intercourse under any conditions, are abominations, and eating meat is scarcely less abhorrent in his eyes.

Furthermore, Porphyry was as pious as he was learned. He was an ardent opponent of the spirit and the practices of the popular religion, and he devoted fifteen treatises, of which we possess only a few fragments, to attacking the Christians, who by this time had become a serious menace to the established cults. The gods worshiped by the conflicting sects, the Olympians as the people conceived and worshiped them, were not in Porphyry's eyes the true gods. They were evil spirits (in whose existence, incidentally, he devoutly believed) masquerading as divinities, and pandering, through the prayers and sacrifices they demanded and the oracles they delivered, to the unholy desires and the material satisfactions of their devotees. True religion is the religion of the philosopher, who turns his back upon this devil-worship

---

[1] Besides the life of Plotinus, the *Introduction*, and the *De Abstinentia*, we possess Porphyry's *De Antro Nympharum, Ad Marcellam, Quaestiones Homericae,* and fragments of his *De Philosophia ex oraculis haurienda* and *Adversus Christianos.* Other information is drawn from Eunapius, Proclus, Suidas, Stobaeus, and Damascius.

and adores, in the persons of the Olympian godhead, the spiritual reality of which they are the symbols.

Plotinus, himself, had made a symbolic use of Hellenic theology, finding, for example, in the story of the overthrow of Ouranos by Cronos and of Cronos by Zeus, a pictorial version of the emanation of the Divine Reason from the One and of the World-Soul from the Divine Reason.[2] Porphyry carried the allegorical method to the extremes exhibited by Philo Judaeus in his treatment of the Old Testament stories, and illustrated every detail of Neo-Platonism with a picture drawn from Greek mythology. Apparently he, no more than Plotinus, took all this wealth of theology literally, and always saw through it to the philosophic truth it veiled. At the same time, the Olympians were the gods of religious experience and worship, the profoundest manifestations of the divine nature that it was vouchsafed to anyone except the philosopher to reach. The philosopher might have a still deeper, intellectual vision, but it was they that excited his religious emotions and satisfied his religious cravings. Porphyry truly loved them and out of that love sprang his hatred of the Christian deity who was already threatening to dethrone them and to reign in their stead.

Belief in Evil Spirits. The evil spirits, among whom the false gods worshiped by the populace were numbered, swarmed about the surface of the earth, and throughout all the sublunar sphere. Their power was tremendous to bewitch, to deceive, to tempt, and to seduce even the wisest and noblest of mankind. So it was that, however much Porphyry might deplore the rites, the sacrifices, the atonements, the placations, the exorcisations, the magic spells and practices, the charms and the amulets, in which the multitude placed its faith, he had no doubts as to their necessity or their actual efficacy in curbing, directing, and warding off the machinations of these malignant forces.

III. IAMBLICHUS

Philosophy a Defense of Theology. The rising wave of religious fervor upon which, as we have already noted, the whole Neo-Platonic movement was borne, became from this time on more and more frankly expressed in contemporary philosophy. With the Syrian Iamblichus, Porphyry's pupil, theology is no longer primarily an allegory and symbol of philosophic truth. Its figures have a metaphysical

[2] Cf. III, 6; IV, 3; V, 1, 8; VI, 9.

validity, and take their place among the entities emanated by the First Principle. At the same time the relations of philosophy and theology tend to become reversed. The metaphysical system of which the theology was formerly the symbol retreats into the background, and the gods come more and more to the fore. It is now the business of philosophy to define and relate and defend them in terms acceptable to the intellect.

The wealth and multiplicity of the Hellenic godhead, of which the deities also of the mystery-religions had by this time become persons, necessitated a more complicated philosophic background than that afforded by preceding systems. The means for its expansion were indicated by the trinitarian method of Plotinus and Porphyry, already amplified by Aemilius. Inspired by the Pythagorean theory of numbers, Iamblichus proceeded to multiply trinities within trinities. From the One, which is so transcendent as to be unable to communicate even its blank oneness to the universe, there proceeds the One that can communicate itself and generate number or multiplicity, and from the one-in-many thus produced the Divine Intelligence proceeds. This in its turn is a trinity of the knower, knowing, and the known, each term of which is subdivided into a triad. It is the intelligible model or paradigm of the world, the dwelling place of the numbers and Ideas. From it emanates the creative power, analagous to the divine workman of the *Timaeus* and the Plotinian World-Soul, and the gods who dwell outside the world. Finally come the gods within the universe, the gods of the Hellenic theology, who directly rule our destinies and with whom religious experience comes in contact. These are the gods who count. To them we build our temples and raise our altars, address our prayers, and dedicate our rites and sacraments. Their number is that of the planets, the signs of the zodiac, and the days of the year.

The Plight of the Human Soul. The human soul is immeasurably removed by all these intervening levels and kinds of being from the incommunicable source of all existence. Furthermore, she is beset on all sides by evil demons, in whose existence and power Iamblichus believed no less devoutly than did Porphyry. Nor is the ladder of salvation sufficient ever to unite her with God, or even with the Divine Reason. In the highest possible state to which she may attain, she is still in the toils of sensible experience and attachment to the body, which cling to her beyond the grave and weigh her down to all eternity. The space separating her from God, never so tremendous for

Plotinus that it might not be recrossed by the soul in search of him, has become an impassable gulf, which even redemption cannot bridge.

Nay more, the soul is no longer, as she was with Plotinus, able of her own self to turn away from evil and attain such salvation as is possible for her. She needs the help of the gods to enable her to escape the snares of the demons who plot her destruction, and she can invoke and obtain divine aid only by the rigid observance of prescribed rites and sacraments. Iamblichus was as firm a believer in the efficacy of magic as Porphyry, and is reputed himself to have possessed mediumistic and miraculous powers. It is said that he could levitate, perform materializations, and converse with the spirits of the dead.

IV. THE ESTABLISHMENT OF CHRISTIANITY

Iamblichus died about 330 A.D. Some twenty years earlier, Constantine, at the time one among six pretenders to the imperial throne, had had, it is said, a vision of the Christian cross, promising him victory in an impending battle with his rival, Maxentius, if he would adopt it as his standard. This he did, and Maxentius was not only defeated, but drowned as he fled the field of battle. Furthermore, Constantine's fortunes continued to prosper. He disposed of the other pretenders one by one, and in 324 became sole ruler of the Empire. He now proclaimed Christianity to be the official faith, though he was baptized formally into it only on his deathbed. The eventual success of the new religion was assured.

The Christian leaders, however, once in the saddle, aspired to political power and tried to control the Emperor. In spite of the Council of Nicaea and the promulgation of the Nicene Creed, they were still at loggerheads over points of theology. The Arians refused to accept the Council's decision that the Son was co-equal, co-eternal, and consubstantial with the Father and clung to their position that he was secondary in majesty and of similar rather than identical substance. Over this question of sameness or likeness a controversy continued to rage, inflamed by passions and marked by attempts at reciprocal persecution out of keeping with the peace, charity, and brotherly love which the Christians preached and promised to the world.

Their behavior in these respects was unlike that of the priests of the old religion, who were not politically ambitious, or desirous of influencing the administration of the Empire; and who, moreover, were tolerant of other religious faiths and willing to receive them hospitably and to live with them on friendly terms. Hitherto, civil life had been undisturbed by theological disputes, nor had the throne had to concern itself, in matters religious, with complaints, recriminations, propaganda, and demands for imperial intervention. Drawn into these quarrels, Constantine supported the decisions of the Council of Nicaea, but his son Constantius, to whom a portion of the Eastern Empire was left, and who eventually succeeded in making himself master of both East and West, favored the Arians.

V. THE DISESTABLISHMENT OF CHRISTIANITY BY JULIAN

Julian's Apostasy. In 361 Constantius was succeeded by Julian, Constantine's nephew. Brought up in the Christian faith, Julian seems in his early youth to have become dissatisfied with it, and though outwardly still professing it, to have inwardly turned back to the old religion for inspiration and support. On his accession to the throne, he openly proclaimed his allegiance to the ancient faith and disestablished Christianity. Because of this, the Christians called him "The Apostate."

Julian's abjuration of Christianity was due in part to a deep love and enthusiasm for ancient Greece and its way of life. It was also influenced by his interest in philosophy and his friendship with the Neo-Platonist teachers of the day. Among them he was particularly intimate with Maximus and with Sallust, the reputed author of an elaborate treatise *On the Gods*. Maximus seems to have been something of a charlatan, who impressed Julian with his display of mediumistic and magic powers. But the treatise *On the Gods* appears a sincere attempt to defend the existence of the Olympians, very much as Iamblichus had defended it, by fitting them into the hierarchy of emanated beings that intervened between the supreme deity and the sensible world. They are the objects of religious experience, of worship, and of ritual and sacramental approach. The higher orders of deity and the First Principle itself can be reached only by philosophic meditation.

Formal Disestablishment of Christianity. When Julian disestablished Christianity, he did not return persecution for persecution, and take against it the suppressive measures it had itself advocated against other faiths. Indeed, he issued an edict ordering universal religious toleration. But he did all he could to discourage the new religion, and went so far as to forbid the teaching of Christian doctrine in the schools and universities. Moreover, being himself not only a devout polytheist but a philosopher, he descended into the intellectual arena and argued at length against the Christian system.[3]

Julian's New Religion. But Julian saw also the vices of the ancient faith. He was a man not only of great intelligence and ability, but gentle and humane, and of a high morality, who hated the moral and political corruption with which he was surrounded, and dreamt of a new order in which the virtues preached by the Christians would be incorporated. It was, then, a polytheism reformed and purified, not only theologically, but ethically, that he sponsored—almost, indeed, a new religion of his own. He seems to have regarded the gods much as Porphyry did—not as metaphysical entities, but as symbols in which religious experience grasps the deeper philosophic reality behind them. So far as that experience is concerned, with Julian it centers upon the sun—the Sovereign Sun, as he calls it—the giver of life and light and goodness to the world. This exaltation of the sun in his new religion was perhaps due to his earlier adherence to the cult of Mithra of which we have already spoken.

Julian, however, not only tried to focus the whole polytheistic system about the divine figure of the hero sun-god, "mighty in strength, mighty ruler, greatest king of the gods . . . lord of heaven and earth, god of gods," but provided for his religion a philosophic support, characteristically Neo-Platonic, but much simpler than the foundations proposed by Porphyry and Iamblichus. The visible sun, in his opinion, incarnates and gives sensible form to an emanation, conceived after the fashion of the second person of the Neo-Platonic and Christian trinities, which rules and animates a world of pure intellects, or spirits, or gods. This emanation proceeds from the First Principle, the sovereign good, which rules and gives being to the world of Platonic Ideas.

In the same spirit, Julian interprets the cult of the mother of the gods and of her beloved, Attis. The Great Mother is the First Principle itself. Her love for Attis symbolizes the emanation of the divine intellect; Attis' infidelity to her means the creation of the material world; his emasculation indicates that creative power has reached limits beyond which it cannot go and by which it is turned back towards its source.

Scarcely less distasteful to Julian than the Christians were all those non-Christians who for one reason or other opposed his new inter-

[3] Of Julian's works we possess his *Orations, Symposium, Misopogon,* and numerous letters, the most important of which are addressed to Themistius, and to the Athenian Senate and people.

pretation of polytheism and refused to accept his reformed religion. In his *Discourse against Eraclius* we have his reply to their attacks, and a further defense of his symbolic polytheism. The ancient myths, he points out, are the ways in which the human mind grasps and represents to itself a divine reality too high and too pure to be envisaged except in the images they present, or to be approached except symbolically through the sacraments and ceremonies they prescribe

But for all his political and military ability, his intelligence, his high-mindedness, and his true piety, he was scarcely less a victim of the superstitions of his age than were Porphyry and Iamblichus. He was a firm believer in the efficacy of magic, with its formulae, its rules, its incantations, its divinations, its omens and its oracles.

Superior Strength of Christianity. Julian died in his early thirties in 363 A.D. By then Christianity was too widely diffused and too securely intrenched among all classes to be dislodged. It had already seized the cities and relegated the ancient cults to the rural communities or "pagi," and thus had enlisted in its service the snobbery with which the city-man is apt to regard the "country bumpkin." No more than five years after Julian's death, this social stigma was legalized by the Emperor Valentinian in an edict in which he refers to the non-Christian cults as "pagans," or, as we might say, "hayseeds."

It is not surprising, then, that Jovian, Julian's immediate successor, promptly re-established Christianity. Its restoration was attended by some sporadic persecution both of the non-Christian cults and of philosophy, of which the most notorious instance was the martyrdom, at the hands of a Christian mob, of the learned lady, Hypatia, head of the Neo-Platonic school at Alexandria. By and large, however, there was little forcible interference with either the old philosophy or the old religion. Both were left in comparative peace to die in each other's arms of inanition and old age. Within some thirty odd years, the great temple of Serapis at Alexandria had been torn down, various other temples of the ancient creed had been delivered over to the Christians, and the Roman Senate had been officially converted.

VI. THE END OF ANCIENT PHILOSOPHY

Last Days at Athens. But before Greek philosophy was finally and formally extinguished it had a brief moment, not of lucidity perhaps, but of such vigor as its senility could muster. Appropriately enough, its dying rally occurred in Athens, where even the Christian converts could not be persuaded to despise, or in their hearts to forsake, the ancient gods, and where reversion to polytheism under Julian had taken place without a qualm. For years, too, Greece had been a backwater, removed from the main currents of imperial life and activity, and Athens had been a quiet university town, of no political ambitions or account, living entirely on the memories of her past. The persistence there of the ancient creed and of non-Christian philosophy might, then, well be regarded as harmless. However that may be, the Schools at Athens remained unmolested by even such mild suppressions and persecutions as plagued the "pagan" philosophers elsewhere. They were still free to think and to teach as they choose, and their liberties were guaranteed them by imperial edicts respectful of their learning and of their great traditions, and quite conscious probably of their innocuousness.

Syrianus. The two principal figures in the revival of philosophy at Athens were Syrianus and Proclus. Of Syrianus' writings we possess only a commentary on Aristotle's *Metaphysics* in which he tries to reconcile Aristotle's doctrine that the individual alone is real with the Platonic teaching that all reality abides in the universal. Number, he tells us, overcomes this difficulty, since mathematical entities, as Plato said, are intermediate between the universal and the particular, and have the characteristics of both. It is, then, a form of existence intervening between and uniting the concrete being of Aristotle and the universal being of Plato.

Proclus. Needless to say, Syrianus' commentary on Aristotle was written with a Neo-Platonic background, which he developed in two lost treatises on the *Parmenides* and the *Timaeus*. The views he expressed there seem to have differed little from the teachings of his pupil Proclus, from whom we draw all our knowledge of them. Proclus was a thinker of great ability. He was also profoundly religious and an ardent supporter of the ancient creed. For this reason he was especially hated by the Christians, and, it is said, was forced at one time to leave Athens because of their hostility. In the conduct of his own life he was ascetic to a degree, and he was extremely punctilious in his observance of all the outward forms and ceremonies of his faith. With this religious zeal and severity of self-discipline he combined a lovable nature, great personal charm, and unusual physical beauty, of which, for all his unworldliness, he was not unconscious. Born in Constantinople in 412, of wealthy parents, he received as a youth the best of educations in Alexandria, and later in Athens under Syrianus, whom he succeeded there as head of the Neo-Platonic school. Among his pupils he quickly acquired a reputation not only for great sanctity, but for miraculous powers, which he used to heal the sick, to procure rain, to avert earthquakes, and to perform other magical feats.[4]

In his philosophizing, however, Proclus was meticulously logical. He adopted the dialectical method initiated by the Eleatics and developed by Socrates and Plato. Zeno, it will be remembered, argued negatively the truth of the Eleatic position by pointing out the absurdities involved in its falsity, and Socrates and Plato pressed their points by a process of progressive self-questioning and self-answering and increasingly definite analysis. In the same way Proclus' habit was to deduce and compare all the positive and negative consequences of both the truth and the falsity of a given proposition.

By this method of self-questioning, which is really an application of the maxim "know thyself," the mind, he said, is led to distinguish within itself two orders of experience, the sensible and the intellectual, whose objects are the physical and the intelligible worlds. The logical exploration of the first of these realms gives us "physiology," of the second, theology.

The Ineffable Nature of the One. The cause of all being is even more ineffable, indescribable, and incommunicable than it was for Plotinus. Not only is the One neither life, nor consciousness, nor thought, nor being; it is also beyond eternity and beyond godhead. All we can say of it is that it is both the source from which we spring, in which capacity the term *One* most nearly fits it, and the goal of all our striving, in which capacity it is best described as *good*. But Alpha and Omega, the beginning and the end, flow together, since unity is order and goodness is unity.

The One generates because of its goodness and without destroying its unity. The first emanation is not, as with Plotinus, the Divine Reason, but as with Iamblichus the realm of Numbers, an order of units each one of which images, as far as separate, existent and dependent entities can, the absolute oneness of its source. These units, like the Platonic Number-Ideas, are unaddible and therefore do not constitute a number series or afford a means of counting. Hence they do not constitute a many. Each one of these units, however, can communicate itself, and thus initiate a series of numbers participating in it—

---

[4] The extant philosophical works of Proclus comprise his *Commentaries* on various Platonic Dialogues; *In Platonis theologiam; Institutio theologica; Institutio physica sive de motu; De physica auscultatione; De providentia et fato; Decem dubitationes circa providentiam; De malorum subsistentia.* Besides these we have works on astronomy, mathematics, and grammar.

Plato's mathematical entities as distinguished from the Number-Ideas. From Numbers the Divine Intellect proceeds.

It will be noted here that we have a trinity of a One that is incommunicable, a One that can communicate itself (Idea-Number), and a One that can partake of communicable unity (mathematical number). This trinity of the unshared, the shared, and the sharer, already advanced by Aemilius and Iamblichus, became a veritable obsession for Proclus, who proceeds to repeat and multiply it *ad infinitum* in the Divine Intellect and the World-Soul.

The Divine Intellect, the World-Soul, Nature, and the Physical Universe. The World-Soul is the intermediary through which the Divine Intellect creates, and through which the goodness and rationality of the intelligible order are communicated to the sensible universe. The physical world is the body of the World-Soul, emanated from it, and united with it in such wise that the two constitute a single living organism. But this union also requires an intermediary—*Nature,* as Proclus calls it. Nature is the incorporeal principle of movement and alteration, which directs the ceaseless "becoming" of the sensible world in accordance with the intelligible model. But whereas the activities of the World-Soul are entirely rational, those of Nature spring in part from soul and reason and in part from the material character of the objects whose changes and motives she directs. Hence the world-process is a mixture of purpose and necessity.

The universe itself is, as Plato taught, a mixture of the definite and the indefinite, of Form and Matter. Because of its material character it is extended. It is also everlasting, without beginning and without end. It is orderly, since all the seeming disorder of its parts and movements conceals a hidden harmony and symmetry of the whole. It is also perfect and happy in its entirety, in spite of partial and particular appearances to the contrary. It is a sphere, or rather a nest of spheres, in which the heavenly bodies are carried. It is composed of fire, air, water, and earth.

The Problems of Evil and Matter. Needless to say, Proclus now finds himself confronted with the problem of reconciling evil in all its forms with the goodness of the creator and the perfection of his handiwork. His justification of the ways of God to man is more detailed and more subtle than that of Plotinus, but, since in the long run it does little more than rehearse the arguments of the Stoics and of Plotinus, we need not further concern ourselves with it.

Matter is as indefinable for Proclus as it was for Plato and Plotinus. It is beyond and *below* forms of being, just as the One is beyond and *above* them. But it has to be there to account for the existence of a sensible as well as an intelligible world. It is not, however, evil, as Plotinus maintained. It has about it some faint semblance of good and is therefore derived from the divine substance.

The Human Soul and Free-Will. The human soul is derived from the World-Soul. She has one foot in the intelligible world, the other in the sensible world. She therefore feels as well as thinks. Moral and spiritual progress consists in disengaging her rational part from the obscurations of sensible experience. In outlining the successive steps of this progress Proclus follows Aristotle and Plato and Plotinus.

Being derived from the World-Soul, the human soul is naturally good. When she acts according to her nature, or in other words freely, she will never sin. This freedom of self-determination is true freedom. Evil action is interference with her freedom, is incomplete freedom. The possibility of choosing the wrong course is a sign of imperfection. The divine *cannot* choose evil. On the other hand, man, being imperfect, *must* be capable of *not* acting according to his nature. This capacity exposes him to determination by external causes, and may make him, so to speak, a mere pawn in the play of outer forces. But since he *may,* though unlike God he *need,* not choose the good, he is morally responsible for not choosing it. However, even if he chooses evil, all seems to be ironed out in the end by providence, which weaves his evil deeds into the fabric of the universe in such wise that they do not detract from its perfection.

Furthermore, it is providence that keeps the soul from succumbing to the presence of external events and that gives her strength to resist temptation and to choose the right course. Abandoned to her own powers, she could not achieve redemption. To be saved she needs divine support.

Philosophy and Religion. It is into this system that Proclus works the ancient theology, supplementing the philosophic trinities with theological ones. Eventually Zeus is generated as a member of one of these trinities and from him proceed the other Olympians, arranged in descending triads dwelling within the World-Soul. Finally in the sensible world we find angels, spirits, heroes, and, lowest of all, human souls.

Since it is to these gods that man must look for salvation, the performance of his religious duties and the observance of all the ceremonies and rites of the church is of the utmost importance. Prayer is indispensable, for by prayer we are raised towards the divine and prepared for our final union with deity. But, Proclus insists, it must never be motivated by the desire for worldly benefits, or by fear and the desire to placate the gods.

The Successors of Proclus. Proclus died in 485 A.D. His successors, Damascius, Olympiodorus, and Simplicius, were men of little account, though their writings are invaluable for a knowledge of the period. Damascius, dissatisfied with both Plotinus and Proclus, re-attacked the problem of deriving the many from the One, not-being from being, the universe from God. He also sought to give a philosophical background, not only to Greek theology, but also to the Oriental religions, and to find least common denominators for their various gods.

With Olympiodorus the gods seem to have lost the theological and metaphysical status accorded them by Proclus, and to have relapsed once more into symbols. The learned Simplicius confined himself largely to commenting on Plato and Aristotle and the Stoics, and to endeavors to iron out their differences and reconcile their teachings.

Closing of the Schools at Athens. But Neo-Platonism and the ancient faith, both of them already sterile and incapable of producing by their union a new truth or life, were now in a state of coma. Brief convulsions marked their end. Justinian mounted the throne of Byzantium and became Emperor of the Eastern Empire in 527. Even before his accession measures were being taken to suppress paganism and the philosophers who supported it, and one of his first acts was to institute fresh persecution. Profession of the ancient faith was made a penal offense. In 529 the Schools at Athens were closed by imperial edict. The last Neo-Platonists, among them Damascius and Simplicius, fled to Persia for refuge. But their reception was not all that they had hoped, and they returned. Safety was assured them by the treaty of peace made between Justinian and the Persians in 533, which stipulated, among other things, that they should be unmolested and allowed to die in peace. With them died Greek religion and Greek philosophy. The famous prophecy uttered, it is said, by Julian on his death-bed had been fulfilled. The Galilean had conquered.

Chapter XXIII

CHRISTIAN PHILOSOPHY THROUGH BOETHIUS[1]

I. PHILOSOPHY, THE HANDMAID OF CHRISTIANITY

Philosophy as a Defense of Revealed Truth. We have now to retrace our steps some four hundred years or more and to record the beginnings and the development of another enlistment of philosophy in the service of religion.

The new religion, however, differed in one respect from the old. The service of the ancient gods was one of perfect philosophic freedom. As long as their existence was not denied—and even that could be safely challenged save in religiously conservative communities like Athens—freedom of criticism and speculation was untrammeled by interference from priest or populace. Heresy was a thing as yet unknown. But now the true version of the nature and the constitution of Reality, which in the past had been sought by the use and tested by the standards of reason, was made manifest once and for all to all mankind by God speaking through the Hebrew prophets and through Christ. There was no gainsaying the content of this revelation. Even to question it was heresy, and heresy might have disagreeable consequences.

Under Christianity, then, philosophy was deprived of her essential activity of inquiring freely into the nature of the Real and of fearlessly publishing the conclusions drawn from her investigations. Her task was now to expound and defend the content of revelation in terms acceptable to the intellect as far as this was possible, and, where it proved impossible, her only course was to bow before a mystery of faith too high for her understanding, and to incline without questioning before the wisdom and authority of Scripture and of the councils of the Church.

---

[1] I have no first-hand knowledge of Patristic and Scholastic thought and texts. The following chapters are founded for the most part upon the histories of Medieval and Scholastic philosophies by Gilson and De Wulf, and upon Ruggiero's *Filosofia del Cristianesimo*.

Plato and Aristotle. However, the situation in which she now found herself was partly of her own making. Bound to accept revelation, she also bound herself to interpret it, not by new and original thinking, but by calling in, first Plato and the Neo-Platonists, and then Aristotle, to bear the brunt of her new task. Thus she curtailed by her own action what freedom Christianity left her, and, in addition to the yoke imposed by the new religion, imposed upon herself the yoke of the ancient metaphysics.

From an epoch of double servitude, we ought not to expect too much in the way of original thinking. What to think about was determined by revelation; how to think about it by Plato and Aristotle. Still, there are mitigating circumstances that must be borne in mind. In the first place the transformation of the classic systems into an apology for revealed truth required ingenuity, in which philosophy was not found wanting, and there was still occasion for profundity in dealing with questions that did not trespass upon dogma. Even in the Middle Ages, after the details of revelation had been meticulously worked out and Christian doctrine had become crystallized, there still remained a large field in which philosophy could move comparatively freely without ecclesiastical interference.

Contribution of Philosophy to Revealed Truth. Again, we must not forget that the theological as well as the philosophic fetters by which she was gradually bound were largely of her own forging. What counted in the end as revelation was largely her work. Jesus and his immediate disciples had revealed very little in the way of metaphysics or theology. Like Socrates, they were not interested in such subjects, but intent rather on preaching a way of life, and were content to accept as the source of their inspiration and the background for their mission their national God moralized and universalized to accord with their higher ideals of what life and God should be. Whatever Jesus believed of himself and whatever his disciples believed of him, they believed simply and naïvely without analysis or speculation. Even at the end of the first century, after Jesus had become an incarnate, dying and rising God worshiped with the rites and approached through the sacraments characteristic of the mystery-religions, orthodoxy was still at a minimum. For that matter, there were still Christians who would have nothing to do with the deification of Christ and persisted in regarding him as simply a prophet of superior sanctity and attainments.

II. EVOLUTION OF CHRISTIAN DOGMA

The writings of Paul and documents like the Epistle to the Hebrews and the Fourth Gospel show, however, that Jesus' worshipers now included men of considerable talent prone to metaphysical speculation. They show, furthermore, that these men were interpreting his status as the incarnate Son of God in the light of contemporary Neo-Pythagorean and Neo-Platonic philosophy. But even so, the relation of the Son to the Father and of the Holy Ghost to the Father and the Son was still a wide-open question, and many other important theological problems were still more vaguely formulated and further from definite solution.

Conflicting Christian Views. The next two centuries of Christian thought abounded in conflicting speculations and conclusions, among which it would have been difficult to distinguish future heresy from future orthodoxy. Indeed, what was finally accepted as revealed truth was largely the product of a struggle between the most diverse points of view, the outcome of which was determined, in part at least, by philosophic considerations and on philosophic grounds. It was only as some philosophic hypotheses rather than others received in an Ecumenical Council a majority vote, believed by the Church to be inspired by the Holy Ghost, that they were regarded as revealed and became Christian verities.

The Gnostic Sects. It is impossible, however, for us to follow the development of the fortunes of all these diverse and conflicting speculations. As an example of their variety and reciprocally contradictory character, we may note a few of the more divergent. For instance, there were the various Gnostic Christian sects, which drew both upon the other Oriental cults and upon Neo-Platonism in formulating their doctrines. The Gnostics tried to treat Christianity much as Proclus tried to treat polytheism. The Valentinian Gnostics, for example, regarded it as a kind of terminal product of an incredibly complicated system of emanations and intermediary beings descending from the ineffable One to a sensible world whose imperfections and very existence are due to forces of evil rather than of good. This extreme dualism of God and the universe they paralleled with an equally extreme opposition of the human soul to the world and the flesh and the devil. The soul is fallen so low that her redemption would be impossible had not Jesus, the mightiest of the divine emanations or aeons, taken pity on her and descended into the sensible world to show her the way back to God. This return is effected by the observance of a system of rites and sacrifices, endowed with magic efficacy. Indeed, magic and astrology loomed as large as they did in contemporary non-Christian religion and philosophy.

Manichaeism. The dualistic and the diabolistic interpretation of the Gnostics persisted as a powerful movement, which in the form of Manichaeism we find still very much alive at the end of the fourth and the beginning of the fifth centuries. But, since this movement proved a blind alley and contributed little or nothing to the development of orthodoxy, save perhaps a belief in the objective and automatic efficacy of the sacraments, we may leave it to one side.

Controversy About the Trinity. Meantime, controversy that was helping formulate eventual Christian orthodoxy was centering in the question of the Trinity and particularly in the relations of the Son to the Father. For instance, at the other end of the scale from those who contended that Christ was simply a great prophet were the Patripassians who identified him with the Father and maintained that in his crucifixion the Father himself suffered death upon the cross. There were also the Sabellians who regarded Father, Son, and Holy Ghost as merely three aspects of one and the same divine person. Again, there was the party, later represented by Arius, who considered the Son a created being of different but similar substance. Still again, we have the Montanists who protested against the development both of worldliness and theology within the Church, and believed themselves to be the special beneficiaries of a new descent of the Holy Ghost, under whose leadership they were to restore primitive Christianity. Finally there were those who under the guidance of a saner Neo-Platonism than inspired the Gnostics were marching slowly but surely towards the formulation of the Nicene Creed.

III. CLEMENT AND ORIGEN

In keeping these last in step two men, Clement and Origen, played an indispensable part. Both were members of the church at Alexandria, learned in contemporary philosophy and sympathetic with other religions, which they regarded not as essentially false and diabolic but as such imperfect intimations of the nature of Reality as religious experience and reason unenlightened by revelation could achieve. Both were strongly influenced by Philo's doctrine of the Logos in their discussion of the relations of the Father and the Son, and were ardent advocates of his allegorical method of interpreting Scripture, which

Origen, at least, carried so far as almost to deny verbal inspiration and to reduce the outer and historic aspects of the Incarnation and Redemption to signs and symbols of an inner all-embracing cosmic process.

Clement's View of the Trinity and Redemption. Of the two thinkers Clement was perhaps the more dominated by Neo-Platonic thought. For example, he strikingly anticipates Plotinus in his doctrine of the transcendent and ineffable nature of the Father, and his teaching that the Son is the divine mind of the Father, through which the Father creates and in which he becomes conscious of what he creates. Neo-Platonic, too, is Clement's insistence that the fate of the soul is not determined in this life, but at the end of a process of probation and purification, terminated, in his opinion, only by the Last Judgment. Even though a man's sins be as scarlet and he die unrepentant, he cannot here and now exclude himself from the possibility of future redemption.

Sin Clement attributed, very much as Proclus did, to the misuse of man's power of choice between good and evil. But whereas Proclus and the Gnostics regarded the power to choose evil as a mark of imperfection, Clement felt it to be, in man at least, a sign of perfection. In this way he dealt with the Gnostics' argument that Adam was created imperfect and therefore must be, along with the rest of the universe, the work, not of God, but of an evil creator.

At the same time, Clement did not believe in "original sin." Mankind is not infected by Adam's fall. Each human soul comes into the world as perfect as Adam and suffers only for her own abuse of freewill. Finally Clement shows his Hellenic heritage by his opposition to excessive moral dualism. Indeed, the distinction that he does make between the higher and the lower life is founded on the Aristotelian opposition of the supermoral, contemplative activities to the "lower" activities of practical reason with which ethics deals.

Origen's Views on the Trinity. Origen, who was some thirty years younger than Clement and a fellow-pupil of Plotinus under Ammonius Saccas, was the greatest and most influential of Christian philosophers prior to Augustine. Brought up though he was under the influences that had produced Clement and were molding Plotinus, he did not share their extreme mysticism, but adopted a more rationalistic position.

The Father, in his opinion, though transcendent, is not beyond determination by the categories of our experience. Words like wisdom and goodness and power give us a true though incomplete picture of his essence. The Son and his relations to the Father were conceived, as with Clement, in the light of Philo's doctrine of the Logos. The Son is the wisdom or word of the Father. The divine will and intellect are made explicit and manifest in the work of creation and in the Christian revelation. To the Holy Ghost, Origen devotes more attention than did Clement, and attributes to it the special work of preparing the soul to accept Christian truth and of endowing her with the peculiar sanctity and the other gifts of the spirit that reward her acceptance of it.

To help him in wrestling with the difficulties involved in reconciling the three "persons" of the Trinity with the divine Unity, Origen took over the terms "hypostasis," used by the Stoics to designate what remains of a thing after its predicates have been stripped from it, and οὐσία, essence, or as the Latins translated it, substance. God is one essence, substance, or nature existing in three hypostases or individual determinations, or as the Latins said, "persons." But, as the Latins also translated "hypostasis" by "substantia," the term proved ambiguous, and its use provoked confusion and theological dispute.

The Eternity of the Universe. The three hypostases are declared by Origen to be co-eternal. Whether he regarded them as co-equal is a matter of dispute. By ancient theologians he was accused of "subordinating" the Son to the Father. Another occasion of scandal was his extension of co-eternity to the created universe. Since God is perfect and eternal, he argues, there can never have been a time when God's creative activity was not exerted, and hence never a time when creation did not exist. Furthermore, unless we are to regard God as at one time not wholly self-realized and therefore not wholly perfect, what he creates must exhaust once and for all his capacity for creation, and every possibility of existence must have been enacted before all time. Hence the universe is as immutable as God. God cannot change it or add to it, since any alteration would be incompatible with the eternal completeness of the divine power and wisdom.

On one point, however, both Clement and Origen, and with them future orthodox Christianity, broke completely with Neo-Platonism. For the Neo-Platonists the production of the universe, and in some cases even that of Matter, was an extension of the same process as produced the Divine Intellect and the World-Soul from the One. The human soul and the material world were lesser *degrees* of the divine substance, but did not differ from it in *kind*. This, however, Christian philosophy denied. The Son, the Christians said, is *begotten,* not *made.* The Holy Ghost is not *made* but *proceeds.* Human souls and the material universe are not *begotten,* neither do they *proceed.* They are *made.* They are not *emanations from* the divine. They are *created by* the divine, have a different substance from the divine, and therefore differ from it fundamentally in kind as well as in degree.

The Fall and Redemption of the Soul. The eternity of the created implied, however, that human souls were eternal and therefore existed before birth. Origen accepted pre-existence, though he denied reincarnation. Like Clement, he conceived salvation as a cosmic process of which human life here on earth is but an episode. The Father created through the Son a perfect universe and perfect souls to inhabit it, endowed with free-will. Some abused their freedom, among them Lucifer, and fell, never to rise again. Others, who used it to soar towards God, form the celestial hierarchy. Still others, more lightly sinning and not wholly separated from the love of God, became human beings who exchanged their ethereal raiment for gross physical bodies.

Sin, therefore, is in a sense original, because the very presence of the soul in a human body is the sign of a fall. It is also in a sense inherited from Adam, since the bodies descended from him were begotten after his expulsion from Paradise. But human freedom remains intact. It is beyond the reach of divine predestination, and the way it will be exercised escapes even the foreknowledge of God. Nor can divine grace do more than suggest and incite and support virtuous action. It cannot compel it.

The evil in the world, then, man has brought upon himself, and his sufferings here and now are the wages of his sin and the means of its purgation. But our earthly life is not sufficient to determine our damnation or salvation. Almost all human souls leave the body with that question undecided and in need of further testing. This period of probation and correction, as with Clement, will last till the Day of Judgment. Till then it is open and free to all souls to accept or to reject Christ and his salvation. Finally, on that day the redeemed and purified will return to their original state as pure intelligences. Then, too, the Son, having by the operation of the Holy Ghost subjected all things unto himself, will himself be subject to the Father, and God will be all in all.

IV. IRENAEUS AND TERTULLIAN

Irenaeus' Attack on Dualism. In the West, in the meanwhile, two men were playing a great part in those developments of Christianity of which the church at Rome was the center. They were Irenaeus and

Tertullian. Irenaeus, born at Smyrna about 135, and later made bishop of Lyons, devoted his energies to refuting Gnostic and other heresies—a work to which his great contribution to the crystallizing of orthodox Catholic dogma was incidental. The current metaphysical and mythological dualism he combated at some length, as well as the original Platonic dualism of the Ideas and the sensible objects patterned after them, from which he supposed these theories sprang. These dualisms, he argued, limit the power of God and make both God and the principle opposed to him part of a third, inclusive reality, and these three part of a fourth, and so on *ad infinitum*. The first principle, then, from which all things proceed, instead of being God, will lie at the end of an infinite regress, and can never be reached. Furthermore, if the world and man are essentially evil, and mankind is incapable of finding God, redemption is impossible and the Incarnation is futile. Man, however, can be reconciled to God by the aid of Christ. In him God became man in order that man, separated from God by a created and therefore imperfect nature, of which Adam's sin was the expression, might be raised to divine estate.

Tertullian. Tertullian, born at Carthage in 160, a fighter in temper and a lawyer by profession, offered to the Christian cause, which he embraced at the age of thirty-three, not only all the resources of a fanatical, passionate and uncompromising character, further fortified by an excellent classical education, but the superabundant zeal and devotion that so often mark the convert of mature years. His one aim was to show that everything in Catholic Christianity was superior to everything in any other religion, and to this task he brought all a lawyer's skill and frequently the speciousness of the special pleader. In his later years, disgusted with the growing worldliness and politics within the Catholic party, he deserted it and joined the Montanists.

Credo quia Absurdum. Tertullian is famous in the history of philosophy for his saying, made with reference to the Christian doctrine of God's sacrifice of himself on the cross, *"It is believable, because it is absurd; it is certain, because it is impossible."* [2] This remark, which contrasts with the view held by both Clement and Origen that revelation must be reasonable, is of double significance. On the one hand, it overstates Tertullian's conviction that the individual's immediate intuition of God in religious experience is the surest witness we have to the existence and nature of a deity—surer than rational proof, and surer even than Christian revelation whose purpose is to confirm the

[2] De Carne Christi, 5.

certitude and to enlarge the knowledge the soul already possesses. On the other hand, it testifies to the presence of the growing conflict between the claims of faith and reason.

But for all his intuitionism Tertullian was more than ready to argue about the mysteries of faith. His earlier doctrine of the Trinity points towards Plotinus in the teaching that the Son is an "extension" of the Father and in his illustration of his meaning by the analogy of the sun projecting itself unchanged and even amplified in the light proceeding from it. Later, however, in his eagerness to refute all antitrinitarian views he overemphasized, if anything, the distinction between the Son and Father and incidentally seems to have "subordinated" the one to the other.

Substitution of Intuition for Reason. We may note Tertullian's substitution of immediate intuition for reasoning as the primary source and the final judge of certitude respecting the existence of God. Moreover, we may remark that Tertullian's contention that the senses are to be trusted and that their reports can be accepted without the audit of reason is quite un-Platonic. Nor, he feels, is there any psychological ground for Plato's opposition between perception and thought and his attribution of them to different faculties and parts of the soul. Their objects, to be sure, differ, since the one is concerned with things apparent, the other with things unapparent, to sense. But it is the same hand that grasps both the sensible and the intelligible. Finally, Tertullian argues in a Stoic and certainly un-Platonic way that the soul, being created, is material. Nay more, she has need of the flesh to come to full fruition, display her powers, and exploit her possibilities of life and happiness. Matter, then, far from being evil, as the Gnostics maintain, is good, and all aspersions cast upon it are impious reflections upon the work of the Creator. The need of the body persists after death, wherefore the eventual resurrection of the body and its reunion with the soul.

V. AUGUSTINE

The Nicene Creed. In the interval that separates the epoch we have been studying from Augustine, there is no Christian philosopher of great note. Nevertheless it was a pregnant period. It gave birth to Plotinus, whose influence upon Christian thought, in the Eastern churches, at least, was immediate, widespread, and profound. His effect upon the West came later, largely through the influence of Augustine. But, once established, it became so powerful that the opinion has been advanced that even in the Middle Ages he, rather than

Aristotle, was the dominating figure.[3] In 325, as an incident in the prolonged Arian controversy to which we have already referred, the Nicene Creed was promulgated, and the doctrine of the Trinity was crystallized. The bone of contention among the orthodox now became the precise relation of the divine and human natures in Christ—a question that evoked as much discussion and produced as many heresies as those that had raged about the Trinity.

Augustine's Platonic Influences. Augustine was born in 354. After a youth whose profligacy his later repentance may have somewhat exaggerated, and after a period of skepticism and brief adherence to Manichaeism, he was converted to the Catholic faith. Eventually he became bishop of Hippo. He died in 430. He was a prolific writer and his works, of which the best known are his *Confessions* and the *City of God,* exercised great influence over subsequent developments of Christian thought.

His conversion to Catholicism, it is said, was due largely to his reading of Plotinus, whose *Enneads* had by this time been translated into Latin. However this may be, he is dominated by Platonic and Neo-Platonic influences, and we hear from him next to nothing of Aristotle. These influences led him to recoil from Tertullian's confidence in the senses and emphasis upon the body. He shared, to be sure, Tertullian's opinion that the primary source of our certainty of God's existence and nature lies in our inner intuition of the divine being. *We must first believe,* he tells us in one of his most famous assertions, *in order that we may know.* But this inner intuition is intellectual in character. The senses are not to be trusted, and the objects with which they present us are unreliable images of truth. The certainty of our intuition springs from the fact that it is of the very nature of reason to know the truth. Knowledge is an inner illumination of the soul by God. Hence whatever is *intelligible* is certain. But among things intelligible and therefore certain are the fact and the content of revelation. Knowledge, then, though it springs from intuition, confirms and amplifies the certainty of faith. We believe in order that we may know, but *we also know in order that we may believe.*

Arguments for the Existence of God. The essentially true character of the concepts of reason is the chief of the many witnesses to the existence of God, which is also attested by the necessity of a first cause, the rational character of the universe and the universal belief in his existence. Being true, these concepts must be necessary and unchange-

[3] Cf. Picavet, *Esquisse d'une Histoire Générale et Comparée des Philosophies Médiévales.*

able. Therefore that which gives rise to them, and to which they refer, must be equally necessary and immutable. There exists, then a necessary and unchangeable being—to wit, God. Such a being must be all and more than our reason says he is. Although his essence transcends all the categories of our experience (like the Plotinian One) yet our concepts of goodness, justice, wisdom, omnipotence, and the like approximate his nature (as Origen taught).

These qualities are unfolded, and his rational character is revealed in the person of the Son in whom he conceives the world of Platonic Ideas, which serves as the example or pattern of the universe, and through whom he creates the sensible world in its image. Incidentally this world of archetypes contains not only universals but Ideas of individuals, as Plotinus asserted. The Ideas form a single harmonious whole, and therefore the universe modeled upon the intelligible order is beautiful and good, appearances to the contrary and the Gnostic assertions of its evil nature, notwithstanding.

Theory of Creation. In his theory of creation, Augustine continues and strengthens the orthodox Christian view, already set forth by Clement and Origen and by this time generally accepted. The universe is not created out of a pre-existing matter co-eternal with God, as Plato taught. It did not emanate from God before all time and is not therefore consubstantial and co-eternal with God, as Plotinus maintained. Nor is it the eternal expression of an eternal act of creation as Origen believed. It was created out of nothing at a given moment by an act of God's free will. This given moment was, however, the first moment. Hence the universe and time are created together. This disposes of the objection that if the universe is not eternal, God's creative power must have been idle for a time before he exerted it. It disposes, too, of the argument that his will to create must be an after-thought and sudden whim. God's determination to create a universe, and to create this universe rather than some other is, like himself, eternal. There never was a *time* when it did not exist. It is not permissible to ask the reasons for this determination. That God was so determined of his own free will must be enough for us.

The Nature of the Soul. Augustine's proof of the existence of the soul is akin to that later used by Descartes. To doubt her existence is to assert it, since to doubt we must think, and if we think we must exist. We are then thinking beings or, in other words, souls.

The soul is not material, as Tertullian had taught, but an immaterial, spiritual entity. This, as well as her immortality, is witnessed by her power to grasp eternal and immaterial essences. She is not however pre-existent as Plato and Origen believed. With regard to her derivation, Augustine hesitates. He argues that she does not emanate from God, but, along with the material universe, is created by him. But he is uncertain whether she is derived in each particular case from the souls of the parents of the individual (traducianism) or is created directly by God and implanted by him in each new body that comes into the world. This question was discussed for some time in the Church before the doctrine of a special creation of each soul became the orthodox view.

Matter, also, created out of nothing by divine fiat, is conceived by Augustine somewhat as Aristotle conceived it. It is not primarily extended substance or body, but potentiality infused with seminal reasons which, upon the proper occasion, give effect to the Ideas in the divine mind and actualize particular sensible images. Thus every detail of the enactment of the divine plan in space and time, as well as the plan itself, is pre-conceived from all eternity.

Each soul is unique. Each one mirrors the nature of God in her possession of three faculties. Incidentally, Augustine finds everywhere triads that suggest the trinitarian character of the godhead. The soul's three faculties are intellect, will, and memory. The content of consciousness, however, all comes from without; sensible experience from the sensible world, knowledge of the intelligible order from the world of Ideas made manifest to us by the inner light vouchsafed us by God, and impressed upon us a priori quite independently of sensible experience. We do not then have to follow Plato and invoke pre-existence in order to explain our seemingly innate possession of intelligible truths. The growing, developing aspect of knowledge is due to the progressive nature of revelation on the part of God, or discovery on the part of the soul, of the truth with which he has endowed or is continually more fully endowing her.

Knowledge and Error. Error and uncertainty are to be explained as the results of Adam's fall and our heritage of sin from him. Because of the Fall the light of reason is obscured and we are no longer able to attain the truth by the use of our native powers. Hence the Incarnation had to take place and the truth had to be revealed visibly in Christ if the human race was to be redeemed and to be given back its lost birthright of knowledge of God.

Such knowledge is the goal not only of the intellectual but of the moral activities. In attaining it man finds his happiness and peace. His search for it reveals him as a member of the City of God. The stumbling and straying nature of that search betrays his citizenship in the lower, opposed, earthly city and his dependence upon divine grace for enlightenment. Increase in wisdom and virtue go hand in hand. Therefore the moral life must not be regarded as a *means* to happiness (as Aristotle and the Epicureans taught). Being identical with the life enlightened by knowledge of the divine, it is an end in itself (as the Stoics taught). The aim of moral discipline is (as with Plato) to convert all love and desire into love and desire of the true good—which is God.

In connection with this opposition and conflict between a higher and a lower nature in man, Augustine constructed in his *City of God* a philosophy of human history. Man, created in the beginning sinless and placed in a terrestrial Paradise as a suitable habitat by God, fell from his high estate by his misuse of free-will. Thus sin and evil entered the world, and henceforth the human race, now expelled from Eden, was infected with original sin and justly subject to total damnation. But God, in his mercy, planned to redeem such as would accept the salvation offered them, and selected the Hebrews as the forerunners and instruments of redemption.

Mankind, however, became so utterly corrupt and lost that God destroyed it by a flood, singling out only Noah and his family for survival. Nevertheless, the descendants of Noah reverted to the ancient wickedness, save for a small number of righteous men, who, living virtuously and according to God's will in the midst of the corruption by which they were surrounded, constituted a City of God as contrasted with a City of the Devil peopled by the great mass of sinful, unregenerate humanity. Among them were numbered the great prophets and reformers of the Old Testament who rebuked the prevailing corruption of the world and bore witness to the approach of the Incarnation and the Redemption, which would hold out to all men the opportunity to turn from their wickedness and be saved.

After the coming of Christ, those who accepted him and lived according to his precepts were numbered among the redeemed and accounted citizens of the City of God. Thenceforth human history was essentially a record of a ceaseless struggle between the two cities —between the Kingdom of God and the kingdoms of this world with their pomps and vanities and seductions and their lusts of the flesh and all else that prevents mankind from accepting and following the new dispensation. The outward and visible expressions of the two cities are on the one hand the Church, the vehicle and dispenser of the divine grace and the true home of the faithful, and, on the other, those mundane and secular and material interests and activities of mankind that oppose the living of a spiritual and Christian life.

The warfare between the City of God and the City of the Devil will continue to be the sum and substance of human history till the second coming of Christ and the Last Judgment, in which that history will culminate and end. Then, the righteous who have accepted Christ and repented their sins and walked with God will receive their just reward and live on in the celestial City of God in glory everlasting; whereas those who have rejected him and led worldly, sinful and un-repentant lives will be eternally damned and cast once and for all into hell.

The Pelagian Heresy. Augustine is also famous for the part he played in fighting the Pelagian heresy. Pelagius and his followers denied, like Clement of Alexandria, the doctrine of "original sin." According to this doctrine "In Adam's fall, we sinned all," and are punished by being born to a state of sin and death, physical and spiritual, from which only Christ's passion and saving grace can redeem us. To this view the Pelagians opposed the teaching that death is not a divine punishment for sin, but a natural event which has nothing to do with the Fall, and that each new human soul enters the world as sinless as Adam's before his transgression and becomes sinful only by her own act. Nay more, we can refrain from sin and preserve our pristine in-nocence without the aid of the Christian dispensation. Hence before Christ's coming there were men who lived without sin and attained salvation. Nor are souls of children who die unbaptized logically bound to go to hell.

These teachings were subversive of Christian orthodoxy. Among other things, they rendered the Incarnation and the Redemption un-necessary and superfluous. Augustine charged into the fray with an ardor that carried him even further than his objective—the formal condemnation of the heresy by the Council of Carthage in 411. For in fighting for original sin he asserted that God in his omniscience foresaw before the foundation of the world Adam's sin and its conse-quences, and therefore might be said to have elected from all eternity certain souls to be saved and others to be damned.

Foreknowledge and Foreordination. This argument raised the per-plexing question whether foreknowledge did not necessarily involve foreordination, and made it difficult for Augustine to maintain the existence of free-will in man, whether of indeterminism or self-deter-mination, not to speak of reconciling the omniscience and the omni-potence of God with the implications of human liberty. Immediate controversy arose, which still agitates Christian theologians. Nearly eleven hundred years later Luther drew from Augustine his doctrine of justification by divine grace rather than by good works, and Calvin and his disciples, following the same lead, developed their doctrine of predestination.

Another question, which aroused much controversy later on, was raised by Augustine. Which is primary in God, his will or his intellect? Does the divine will decide what an intelligible and perfect being shall be like, or does God's fundamentally moral and rational nature determine what a good will shall be like? In a word, is God's character the result and expression of his will, or is his will the expression and result of his character? Tertullian had inclined to the former of these alternatives, but Augustine argues for the latter. What God wills is not good simply because he wills it. He wills it because it is good. Right and wrong are not made by divine fiat; they inspire the divine decrees. This question, which also asks whether God's freedom means self-determination or lack of any determination whatsoever, was later fought over by Thomas Aquinas and Duns Scotus. The Thomistic doctrine of self-determination has become the official view of the Catholic Church.

VI. CHRISTIAN PHILOSOPHY FROM AUGUSTINE TO BOETHIUS

Christian Philosophy in the West. The death of Augustine in 430 marks the end of a creative epoch. Twenty years before, Rome had been sacked by Alaric, and twenty years later just escaped a similar fate at the hands of Attila. Another couple of decades and the last Emperor of the West was deposed, and a German mercenary reigned in his stead. Western Europe was entering the four centuries of chaos and darkness that intervened between the death of the Old World and the birth of the New.

Throughout this period the Church was the one stable and orderly institution in western Europe. She was the sole heir and repository of the ancient culture as well as of the Christian tradition, which, thanks to her, not only were implanted, as deeply as conditions permitted, in the rough and untilled but fallow soil of the new peoples, but were also conserved for posterity. She commented the philosophers and philosophies of antiquity. She codified and crystallized in anthologies and encyclopedias the knowledge of the day. She extended and strengthened the science of logic. She evolved a system of education. The work of consolidation performed throughout these centuries laid the foundation for the Scholastic movement.

Dionysius the Areopagite. In the East, always more inclined to speculation than the West, and thanks to the Byzantine Empire more securely entrenched against the forces of disorder and disruption, darkness did not descend so rapidly upon Christian philosophy. A full century after Augustine's death there appeared in Constantinople the works of a Christian thinker who concealed himself behind the name of Dionysius the Areopagite (a disciple of St. Paul's). These works, profoundly mystical in character and imbued with Neo-Platonism, reapplied to Christian theology the cardinal doctrines of Plotinus and Proclus—the ineffability of the One, the extension of emanation beyond the divine hypostases to the human soul and the universe, the triadic constitution of all things, and the conception of the world-process as an eternal and infinite outpouring of the divine essence and return of the divine essence to its source. Wiping out as they did the orthodox distinctions in kind between God and the created universe, they were pantheistic and heretical. But they exercised great influence upon all subsequent Christian mysticism, and helped embolden many a daring thinker to pass from orthodoxy to similar heresy. As it was, they immediately inspired another Byzantine, Maximus the Confessor, to an even more openly pantheistic interpretation of Christianity. Other eastern theologians of note, who followed a more orthodox line of thought, were John of Damascus and John Italus. They showed little originality, but did good service in codifying extant knowledge in encyclopedic form.

Eclipse of Byzantine Philosophy. After them the twilight engulfs also the eastern world. The Byzantine Empire was already at grips with the rising power of Mohammedanism, which was despoiling it of its richest and most civilized provinces preparatory to eventually destroying it altogether. Henceforth conditions in the East as in the West were not conducive to philosophizing. But the forces destined in the end to overthrow Constantinople and in the meantime to constitute a grave danger even to western Europe were also to render invaluable service to the development of Christian Scholasticism by their studies and translations of Aristotle and the Neo-Platonists.

VII. BOETHIUS

The Consolation of Philosophy. With the exceptions just noted, there are few names of philosophic significance to note anywhere in Christendom from the fifth to the ninth century. Best known is that of Boethius (480-524), the unfortunate minister of Theodoric, who from the heights of political eminence was suddenly cast into prison under suspicion of treason, and eventually executed. During his imprisonment he wrote his book, *The Consolation of Philosophy,* which ranks along with the *Meditations* of Marcus Aurelius, the *Encheiridion* of Epictetus and the *Imitation of Christ* as one of the great manuals of refuge and consolation of all times. Its influence, later, was widespread and profound. Alfred the Great translated it into Anglo-Saxon. Chaucer, Lydgate, and, it is said, Elizabeth translated it into English, and it appeared in German, French, Italian, Spanish and Greek in the early years of the Renaissance.

In it Boethius relates how philosophy visited him in prison in the guise of a fair lady and consoled him for the seeming harshness of his fate. God, she pointed out, rules the world, so all must be well. If Boethius rebels against fortune, it is because he has failed to understand in what the true good and true happiness consist. They lie not in the gifts of this world, with which Boethius has been liberally blest, but in the love and knowledge of God which the world can neither give nor take away. Nor is the existence of seeming evil any bar to trust in God's supreme goodness and justice. The wicked never really flourish, for their very wickedness deprives them of the only abiding good. They destroy their true selves, and, though they seem to live and prosper, they have really suffered spiritual death. The longer they succeed in their evil ways, the more prolonged is their agony. After death they will be punished or undergo a painful purgation of their sins. Boethius may rest assured that all things happen in accordance with the divine will and the divine plan. Providence, acting through what we call fate, sees to that. Fate is the instrument through which the divine intelligence makes the divine plan operative and conforms individual events to it. The interweaving of things may seem to us confused and capricious, but in God's sight the pattern is clear and harmonious.

Finally, God's providential direction of all things through the instrumentality of fate does not deprive man of his freedom. God, to be sure, foresees all things. In his mind past, present, and future are all grasped together, and the everlastingness of the universe is seen as a single eternal event. But this foreknowledge does not imply foreordination. God's knowledge of how we shall exercise our freedom in no way constrains or influences our choice, except in so far as our consciousness that we walk ever in the sight of God may turn us from the paths of wickedness to a sober, godly, and righteous life.

Boethius' Other Works. Throughout his life Boethius was an enthusiastic Greek scholar, and to his translations into Latin of Aristotle's logical treatises the medieval philosophers were greatly indebted.
He also wrote a number of books of his own on logic, which contributed much to the development of logical theory, and he compiled
manuals on arithmetic, music, geometry, and astronomy for use in
the schools. A long and thorough treatise of his on music is still a
valuable source of knowledge about ancient music.

Boethius a Christian? Whether Boethius was ever a Christian or
not is a moot point. The *Consolations* show little trace of Christian
influence. But there are a number of theological tracts attributed to
him, dealing with different points of Christian doctrine, which, if
genuine, prove that in his younger days, at least, he was a Catholic.

Cassiodorus. Along with Boethius, we ought also to mention Cassiodorus. Somewhat younger than Boethius, he also held high office
under Theodoric and lived to a ripe old age. His chief service lay in
his great erudition and encyclopedic knowledge, and in his foundation
of two monasteries dedicated specifically to the acquisition of knowledge and to the translation of the Greek authors into Latin. Incidentally he spent much money collecting manuscripts. He wrote profusely,
and his treatise on the seven liberal arts, grammar, rhetoric, and dialectic, as well as music, arithmetic, geometry and astronomy played a
principal part in helping organize medieval theory and practice. He
had also a knack for mechanical inventions—a talent, incidentally,
shared with Boethius—and occupied himself particularly with devising sun-dials and water-clocks.

The impetus he gave to the pursuit of learning was perpetuated
largely through the Benedictine order which had been established at
Monte Cassino near Naples some ten years before his own monasteries
were founded. Indeed, it has been suggested that Cassiodorus himself
joined the new brotherhood, but this is doubtful.

Isidore of Seville and the Venerable Bede. For the next two hundred years the Church was for the most part the graveyard of "mute
inglorious Miltons"—priests and monks whose patient and industrious
collection and compilation of knowledge went unrecognized. Two
names, however, should perhaps be singled out. Isidore of Seville, who
died in 630, left behind him an encyclopedia and a theological treatise
of some merit, and early in the century in England the Venerable Bede
wrote upon physics and astronomy, summarized and commented the
writings of Augustine, Jerome, and Isidore, and composed his *Ecclesiastical History of the English Nation.*

Chapter XXIV

EARLY MEDIEVAL PHILOSOPHY

I. PHILOSOPHIC EQUIPMENT OF THE TIMES

The Middle Ages are commonly dated from the end of the eighth and the beginning of the ninth centuries, and an Englishman, Alcuin, is regarded by some as the first of the distinctively medieval philosophers. However, before turning to the new outburst of philosophic activity, let us pause a moment and cast an eye over the materials collected in previous centuries for its use. We may note in the first place that ability to read Greek was almost extinct and that the medieval world had to depend upon Latin translations for its knowledge of the Greek originals. In translation there existed a portion of the *Timaeus,* done by Chalcidius, and scattered fragments of the other dialogues of Plato, most of which, if known at all, were known by title only. But Chalcidius' commentary gave also some idea of pre-Socratic teaching and some of the doctrines of Aristotle and of the Stoics and Neo-Platonists. Of Aristotle's works, only the logical treatises *De Interpretatione* and the *Categories* were known in translation, supplemented by Porphyry's *Introduction to the Categories,* which, as has already been remarked in discussing Porphyry, had great influence upon medieval thought. Generally speaking, then, Aristotle was known only as a logician, and as such incompletely.

Of the Roman philosophers, some works or fragments of Cicero, Seneca, and Lucretius were at hand, as well as a few late Latin commentaries and treatises dealing with Porphyry, the Neo-Platonists, and the Hermetic writings. Some of the Greek Fathers were also known in translation, and the works of Augustine and the pseudo-Dionysius exercised great influence. But above all, scholars turned to the more recent compilations of Boethius and Cassiodorus.

Such was the mental equipment that philosophy found at hand in the ninth and tenth centuries. Little was added to it in the next two hundred years, except further portions of Aristotle's *Organon* and some scattered Latin renderings of Byzantine and Arabian thinkers, as well as the medical writings of Galen and Hippocrates.

A glance at the political set-up of the new era may also not be amiss. The coronation of Charlemagne as Roman Emperor in 800 celebrated the emergence of order out of confusion and the laying of the foundations of modern continental Europe. In England, also, some consolidation of the warring Saxon kingdoms had taken place, and, in spite of the ravages of the Danes, the eventual unification of all Britain under Edward, son of Alfred the Great, was to take place in another hundred years.

II. ALCUIN AND RHABAN MAURUS

There is little sign in Alcuin of the reawakening of philosophic speculation. If he is the first of the medievalists, it is largely because he happened to be born a contemporary of Charlemagne. His chief claim to fame lies in the field of education. Charlemagne, alarmed and distressed at the lamentable illiteracy of the French clergy, and unable to recruit teachers and organizers from France itself, imported him, along with other scholars from England and Italy, to help found institutions of learning and to devise an educational system in and under which clerics might be trained. It is to Alcuin that we owe the final classifications of the so-called seven liberal arts into the *Quadrivium* of arithmetic, geometry, astronomy, music (and medicine), and the *Trivium* of grammar, rhetoric, and dialectic, and their introduction into the schools as the basis of a liberal education. This system prevailed for the next five hundred years and fell into disuse only with the coming of the Renaissance.

In the next generation Rhaban Maurus, among others, carried on Alcuin's work. He wrote an encyclopedic survey of extant knowledge, divided philosophy into two parts, according as it was concerned with earthly or heavenly things, and approached the problem of education in a broad-minded and humanistic spirit. He also denounced the extreme form in which the Augustinian doctrine of predestination was being revived at the time by the abbot Gottschalk. In his attack upon this doctrine he was joined by another monk, Hincmar, whose argument has come down to us. God, said Gottschalk, not only desires that some souls shall be saved; he *wishes* that others shall be damned. No, replied Hincmar, God desires that *all* men shall be saved. In Christ he has offered them salvation. Those who are damned are damned because they deserve to be. As the result of their labors two synods in succession condemned the doctrine of double predestination

III. JOHN SCOTUS ERIUGENA

The first original thinker of the Middle Ages is John Scotus Eriugena. Born and educated in Ireland, whose monasteries were at that time famous for their learning, he followed the drift of scholars to Paris (about 847) where his unusual learning and his wit quickly won for him a great reputation. He knew Greek, and perhaps Arabic, as well as Latin, and was well acquainted with the Greek Fathers and with the Neo-Platonists. But his mind was too restless to be confined within the limits of orthodoxy. Incited by Hincmar to join in the attack on the doctrine of double predestination, he showed in his discussion of the subject symptoms of the unorthodox doctrine that later was to procure his own condemnation.

Plotinian Interpretation of Christianity. In his philosophy, Eriugena returns to the Plotinian doctrine of emanation with all its pantheistic implications which had been repeated by the Neo-Platonists and the pseudo-Dionysius. The universe and the human soul are not created out of nothing by divine fiat. When we hear that God made the world, we should understand it to mean that God is in all things and is the ground of their being. All things proceed from him, and all things express his nature.

Four Stages of Divine Unfolding. In this divine unfolding four stages may be distinguished. We start with *the nature that is uncreated but creates*. This is the center, the essence, and the source of all things. It is beyond all the categories of finite experience, and is indescribable by any terms at our command. It is too high even to be conscious of itself and have knowledge of itself, since consciousness and knowledge make sense only under finite conditions. For example, if God knew himself he would have to think of himself under the categories that knowledge implies, and, among other things, would have to classify himself, since knowledge implies classification, as one among a number of other members of the same genus, that is, as one among many Gods.

But this Being, although absolutely transcendent, contains within itself the infinite possibilities of all existence, which it proceeds to actualize. It now both generates and knows form, and thus becomes a divine mind enshrining the intelligible structure of the universe, the second person of the Trinity, the Son, *the nature that both is created and creates*. This nature goes on, in the procession of the third person of the Trinity, to make manifest the form or intelligible structure of the universe in which God first becomes conscious of himself and knows himself. This manifestation is *the nature that is created but does not create*—the world of individual things, corporeal and spiritual, unfolded by the world-process in time and space. Hence the universe, also, is an emanation from the divine substance and consubstantial with the Father. In creating it God is creating himself.

Finally, having exhausted all the possibilities of existence and thus reached the limits of self-expression, God turns back to himself and re-enters into himself. Just as at the beginning of the cycle he was *the nature that is not created and creates,* so, as the journey's end in which he rests after his long voyaging, he is to himself and to us who are part of him and of his striving, *the nature that neither creates nor is created.*

Incarnation and Redemption. Man, even as he is put forth from God, may return to God and lose himself in the ineffable essence of the divine. Herein his salvation lies. Of this cycle of creation and salvation the historic Incarnation and Redemption are the local and temporal manifestations, and in their benefits not only man but the whole creation shares. As the eternal Logos, the Son, is the agent through which the universe is put forth from God, so Christ, its manifestation in space and time, is the way by which all things return to and are reunited with him.

Man, being free, interfered with the completion of the cycle, and from this his fall and all its consequences resulted. A long and gradual ascent is the condition of his salvation. Death frees him from the gross flesh with which the Fall has endowed him; the resurrection of the body restores to him his corporeal nature in its original incorruptible form. Little by little, this body may be transformed into spirit, and man may become a mind pure and simple contemplating the truth. And finally the soul may make the mystic flight, passing away into God as air shimmers away into light, yet it would seem in some way preserving her identity, though identified with him.

Reason the Criterion of True Revelation. In the matter of faith *vs.* reason, Eriugena ranges himself with the Alexandrian Fathers on the side of reason. Indeed, his system is in a way an attempt to rationalize Christian doctrine. Revelation, he feels, cannot antagonize reason, since it is the revelation of truth, and truth must be reasonable. Philosophical and religious truth are one and the same thing. Scripture is to be interpreted by the use of reason and in terms acceptable to reason. How much more, then, is reason to be used in dealing with the interpretations given Scripture by the Fathers of the Church! Their pro-

nouncements have no authority except in so far as they are reasoned
and reasonable. The only authority is that of truth, and the truth about
God and the universe can only be discovered by rational thinking
and founded on rational grounds.

This interpretation of Christian doctrine, championed by Eriugena,
was destined to persist in spite of all efforts to suppress it. But its
course was largely underground, with sporadic reappearances from
time to time, till finally it gushed forth again some four hundred years
later in the German mystic, Meister Eckhart.

Chapter XXV

THE QUESTION OF UNIVERSALS

I. THE REAPPEARANCE OF THE PROBLEM OF UNIVERSALS

With the death of Eriugena about 877 Christian philosophy again relapsed into a silence that lasted for nearly two centuries. Meantime, however, a problem suggested by Porphyry's introduction to Aristotle's *Categories* was beginning to worm its way to the front. Porphyry, in commenting on the *Categories,* had raised again the question of the nature and status of *Universals,* or general concepts and essences such as "animal," "mankind," "justice," "redness," "squareness," and the like. But this question he had left wide open. "Now," he says, "concerning genera and species, whether they be substances or mere concepts of the mind; and, if substances, whether they be corporeal or incorporeal, and whether they exist apart from sensible things, or in and about sensible things, all this I will decline to say."[1]

The Problem Raised by the Sophists. We may note that in this sentence Porphyry re-states the problem that had so agitated Socrates, the Cynics, the Cyrenaics, Plato, and Aristotle. It had been raised in Greek philosophy, we may remember, by the assertion of the Sophists that each man was the measure of his own truth, and, by implication, of his own good, and that therefore there was no such thing as universal and absolute truth and right. Callicles and Thrasymachus had applied this view to the field of politics and ethics. The former had asserted that the stronger have a natural right to rule and to impose their will upon the weaker; the latter had maintained that right and wrong, justice and injustice are purely arbitrary and conventional affairs reflecting only the whims of those who happen to be in power, and hence that they are reversible by legislation.

The Socratic Universals. Socrates had attacked the Sophists' teaching, and had tried to prove that there is such a thing as absolute and universal right and wrong. Justice, he said, and temperance and virtue

[1] Trans. Rickaby, *Scholasticism*, pp. 2, 3.

exist in and for themselves and are what they are quite independently of the diverse and fluctuating opinions of different individuals regarding what is just and temperate and right. For that matter, they really already exist in the minds of all men beneath the apparent diversity of individual opinions, since these opinions, if sufficiently analyzed, will be found to converge upon and eventually reveal a definition upon which all men, in all times and places, will agree.

The Platonic Ideas. Plato had then taken these Socratic Universals, had expanded them beyond the realm of ethics to include general natures and essences of all sorts, and had made ultimate Realities of them, far more real than the concrete, particular things that embodied them. Indeed, he conceived these Universals, or Ideas, as possessing an existence of their own apart from and independent of both the sensible objects that enacted and the minds that entertained them.

Universals Attacked. The Platonic view, however, was opposed by both the Cynics and the Cyrenaics, who maintained that so-called "Universals" were nothing but the impressions of similarity which individual things made upon our minds, and that therefore they did not represent anything existing outside our minds, in or apart from particular things. Indeed, the Cyrenaics went so far as to affirm that, since we had no direct acquaintance with one another's sensations and thoughts, we could never be sure that different individuals were impressed by external objects in the same way. I, for example, could not be certain that what I called a "red" object gave you the same color sensation as it gave me, or that the characteristics that in my eyes distinguished a "human" being from all other classes of beings were like those that you regarded as distinctive properties of the human species. Hence, they argued, not only were Socratic Universals and Platonic Ideas non-existent outside of individual minds, but we could have no assurance even that they existed in the mind as concepts having the same significance for a plurality of individuals.

The Aristotelian Forms. Again, Aristotle had also attacked the Platonic Ideas, denying that Universal types and natures existed in themselves apart from particular things. Only what is individual and concrete, he said, has substantial existence. However, Universal Forms were not merely impressions of similarity made by particular, concrete substances upon our intellects. They were *really* an integral part of the substance which determined and distinguished its species or genus. Every concrete thing is some species, or kind, of thing, and is united to all other things of the same class by the real possession of one and the same Form. This Form exists not only in our minds as a general concept. It exists also in all the individuals subsumed under the class-concept in question, as a real nature or essence common to them all.

Later Graeco-Roman and Early Christian Views. In later Greek, and in Graeco-Roman, philosophy the problem of Universals retreated into the background. What view one took of their status was largely inherited from Plato and Aristotle, or from the skepticism of the Sophists, Cynics, and Cyrenaics. Early Christian philosophers, influenced as they were by Plato and the Neo-Platonists, assumed an "ultra-realistic" position with regard to the status and significance of general concepts. They believed that Universals were real metaphysical entities existing in and for themselves independently both of the minds that conceived them and the concrete, particular objects that embodied them. But, unlike Plato, they believed that these entities were not uncreated and self-existent, but owed their being to God.

To be sure, some doubt had been cast upon the Platonic substantiality and independent existence of Universals by both Augustine and Boethius, who had spoken of them as potentialities which assumed actual and substantial form only in concrete, particular objects. But the question of their nature had not become, as it was now to become, a matter of bitter controversy which took precedence for the time being over all other philosophic problems. This controversy was precipitated in the last part of the eleventh century by Roscellinus' violent attack upon the ultra-realists' position.

II. ROSCELLINUS

Roscellinus' View of Universals. Roscellinus (circ. 1050-1122) was a canon and teacher at Compiègne. Universals, he flatly declared, far from being substances existing in and for themselves, as the ultra-realists maintained, had no being outside our minds. They did not even *exist* in particular objects. For all real existence and substantiality are individual and concrete in character. However, particular substances impress the mind as similar to one another, and their similarities appear to be common characteristics in which they share. In this way we come to *classify* objects and to subsume them under types, and to use generic and general names like "redness" or "mankind." But a *name* is merely a *word,* and a word, as Boethius had already pointed out, is merely a movement of the air produced by the tongue. Hence, Universals turn out to be nothing but *flatus vocis*—vocal sounds standing for and summarizing the similar aspects and properties of individual substances.

In short, in the language of the Medieval Schoolmen, or Scholastics, Universals exist neither *ante res* (prior to individual things) nor *in rebus* (in and as part of individual things). They exist only *post res* (in derivation from and posterior to individual things).

Nominalism Defined. The term nominalism has been used by some historians of philosophy to describe Roscellinus' teaching. But by others it is considered a misnomer. The term, the latter feel, is properly applied only to the doctrine, later advanced, that really *universal* and *general* concepts do not exist even *in* the mind. The intellect, according to this doctrine, is incapable of thinking without imagery, and always has to *picture* a so-called abstract and universal idea in a vague and undetailed, but nevertheless particular and concrete, sensible instance of the genus or species in question. The universal and common character of this image lies simply in the fact that it is a kind of composite photograph of many similar percepts, and is used by the mind to symbolize and stand for all of them.

Roscellinus a Realist. There is, however, no sure ground for attributing such teaching to Roscellinus. He seems rather to have believed that the mind can really abstract and contemplate in a purely *general* way the *common features* of particulars without *picturing* to itself in a specific and sensible image the common feature in question. We can, for example, *conceive* redness without *seeing red,* and entertain a general idea of mankind without the name's conjuring up before our eyes some vague and composite but particular image of a human being. *Universals* then *really* exist as such *in* our minds, although they do not exist outside them, either in themselves or in individual objects. Hence, it is argued, Roscellinus is more properly classified as a *realist,* though as a realist of an attenuated and very "moderate" sort.

The theological implications of this doctrine were at once perceived, and threw the medieval world into an uproar. The one, identical substance and godhead of the Trinity tended to dissolve into a superficial unity, existent only in our minds, of three really distinct and separate divine substances, united only by the similarity of their natures and of their power and will. The term "hypostasis," with which the Latins had equated the term "person," was, Roscellinus declared, also equivalent to *substantia,* or "substance." Hence, since all substance is individual in character, the three persons of the Trinity must be three distinct and separate substances, or, in other words, three distinct and separate Gods. To maintain that they are one substance was to confuse the persons and to deny any *real* difference between Father, Son, and Holy Ghost.

Roscellinus was promptly haled before the Council of Soissons in 1092, charged with teaching that there are three Gods instead of one, and forced to recant his heresy.

III. ANSELM

Common Nature of Objects. Among the bitterest opponents of Roscellinus was Anselm, Archbishop of Canterbury and a theologian and philosopher of high attainments (1035-1109). He accused Roscellinus of tritheism, and, bred as he was in the Neo-Platonic and Augustinian tradition, he maintained that our general concepts were of real universal essences and natures existing outside our minds. Roscellinus, he argued, failed to see that the resemblances between individual substances, which gave rise to universal ideas in the mind, were themselves due to the participation of these substances in universal essences, like mankind, triangularity, redness, etc., whose presence in them constituted their similarity and made them instances of one and the same class or genus. Different individual objects could not *look* alike, unless they *really were* alike. And they could not really be alike unless they possessed an identical nature in common.

Moreover, every *particular* substance is as truly and profoundly some *sort* of substance, endowed with a *universal* nature which it shares with other particulars of the same sort, as it is a distinct, particular thing existing apart from all other things of the same class. Substance is, then, a union of the universal and the particular, both of which are equally essential to its existence.

Theologically this conjunction of universality and individuality in substances means that the three individual persons of the Trinity, each one of which is God, are nevertheless one God, not three Gods. Though distinct from one another, they at the same time share, exemplify, and individuate one and the same Divine Nature. This single godhead is equally present in them all, and is as integral a part of each of the three divine persons as are the distinct individualities that make one the Father, another the Son, and the third the Holy Ghost.

Universals as Archetypes in the Divine Mind. Finally, Universals exist not only as general concepts in our minds but also outside our minds, as the common natures of individual substances. They also exist from all eternity, prior to both human minds and particular objects, in the divine intellect, as components of the general plan and Idea of the universe which God had in mind before he put that Idea into effect by creating the world of particular substances embodying it. First, the universe existed as God's unspoken, then as his spoken, word. The unspoken word, the system of Universals which forms the content of the divine mind and constitutes God's knowledge of himself, is the Logos, or Son, who is both the archetype and the agent of creation.

Faith and Reason. Anselm also devoted much time and thought to the problem of the relations between faith and reason. The two, he felt, are not antagonistic but one at heart. We must, he felt, have faith in the Christian verities before we can begin to understand them, and this faith is not dependent upon prior reasoning about them. The veracity of the content of revelation is not something to be established or rejected on rational grounds. "I do not," he says, "desire to know in order that I may believe." Rather, he continues, "I believe in order that I may know." Nevertheless, believing does not mean that we should not also seek to understand what we believe. It is the business of reason to show, as far as it can, that faith is reasonable, and by so doing to reinforce the claim of revelation to truth. Reason, however, must not criticize Christian doctrine. When it comes upon something revealed that passes understanding, then its proper course is not to doubt but to hold its peace and accept the truth on faith.

Proofs of the Existence of God. Having thus justified the use of reason in dealing with revelation, Anselm proceeds in his *Monologium* to probe with it even the most recondite of the mysteries of faith. We not only know by revelation that God exists. Dialectic also proves the fact. In the first place, the moral life is a search for goods of one sort or another, and of different degrees of goodness. But, differ as they may in kind and in degree, they owe their desirability to a common quality of goodness in itself, resident in them all. In order, then, that we should find anything good, there must exist an absolute and sovereign goodness or perfection.

Again, attacking the subject from another angle, all beings have a common quality of existence. To say that all beings are self-existent is to make them all share in a common capacity for self-existence to which they owe their several beings. To say that they endow each other with existence, or, in other words, are the causes of the things of which they are the effects and *vice versa,* is palpably absurd. Therefore, there can be only a single cause or ground of being from which all things derive their existence.

Finally, the idea of the higher and the lower, the more and the less complete and perfect in nature, forces us to one of two conclusions.

Either we must go on and on to infinity in an endless and fruitless search for that which is most high and absolutely perfect and complete, or we must admit that such an absolutely complete and perfect being exists. The first alternative is absurd. Hence we are logically compelled to accept the existence of such a being—that is, of God.

Gaunilo's Objections. This argument was at once attacked by Gaunilo. Anselm's arguments, he pointed out, *may* indeed necessarily lead to the *idea* of a single, complete, perfect being as the ground and cause of the universe. But they do not necessarily force us to the conclusion that this idea has its counterpart in the objective world. If it did, we could just as well argue the existence of a perfect island somewhere out in the middle of the ocean from the fact that we can imagine such an island to exist. In short, the *idea* of a perfect being does not necessarily imply the *existence* of a perfect being.

To Gaunilo, Anselm replied to his own satisfaction in his *Liber Apologeticus*. But the honors remained with his opponent. Anselm's so-called "ontological argument" was rejected by most of the later scholastics, including Thomas Aquinas.

The Nature of God. Having logically proved, as he thought, that God exists, Anselm turned the light of reason upon the divine nature. But thus directed and focused, the light failed wholly to illumine it, and revealed shadows which Anselm recognized but could not dispel. At first, to be sure, things seemed clear enough. The character of the less perfect indicates the nature of the more perfect. Therefore God will possess completely the qualities inferior beings possess incompletely, and hence will be spirit rather than body, and a spirit perfectly wise and powerful and good. These qualities, however, are not attributes *of* God, detachable so to speak from his being. They are the substance of God—are God himself.

At this point the trouble begins. A substance is nothing without attributes. Unqualified, it becomes vacuous. If, then, God has no attributes, but only substance, paradoxically enough he cannot be a substance. Again, how can a being conceived as simple and single be also conceived as spread through all space and time? How, if he is not in space and time, and therefore exists nowhere and at no time, can he be conceived as existing at all? He must, then, somehow exist both in and out of space and time. Or again, take the Trinity. Here, too, reason runs into insurmountable contradictions and difficulties. By and large, Anselm found himself obliged to confess that the nature of God is ineffable and transcends all the categories of human experience, including even knowledge and being. All our attempts to

describe the divine nature are at the best but poor approximations of
the truth.

So far as the creation of the universe is concerned, Anselm accents
the orthodox doctrine that it was called into being out of nothing by
divine fiat. To derive matter from God and to regard the universe as
an emanation of the divine substance are to conceive the world as a
deterioration of the godhead and the godhead, therefore, as a being
susceptible of corruption. The only way, then, in which a perfect
being can give rise to a universe is by simply willing it to exist.

Incarnation and Redemption. In his treatise, *Why God Became
Man,* Anselm seeks to explain Incarnation and Redemption. Adam's
misuse of free will and consequent sin and fall, in which the whole
human race is involved, constituted an act of willful disobedience to
God, and therefore logically necessitated a punishment that God, however merciful his inclinations, could not withhold without ceasing to
be just. But a just punishment for willful disobedience to the supreme
will must itself, by the logic of the case, be supreme. The honor of
God, then, could be satisfied only by the extinction or damnation of
the whole race. Such a course, however, would defeat the object for
which God created the world—to secure the happiness of man. The
logic of this situation offered and demanded but one method of escape.
Nothing that finite man could do could atone for his sin against the
infinite. But God, being infinite, could, if he substituted himself for
man and suffered in man's stead, give himself the infinite satisfaction
his honor demanded and thus atone for man's sin. This he did in the
Incarnation and Redemption. God's suffering in Christ acquired for
God an infinite merit demanding logically an infinite reward, which,
since God had no need of it, he transferred to man's credit and thus
made his salvation possible.

IV. WILLIAM OF CHAMPEAUX

Now that the theological importance of the question of Universals
was realized, the fat of the controversy over their nature was in the
fire, and William of Champeaux added fuel to the flames by an attack upon Roscellinus, the fury of which carried its author to the extreme assertion that the universal alone has real existence, that it is
wholly and exhaustively present in each particular example of itself,
and that the individuality of these examples is nothing but an accidental variation of the generic essence. The difference between you
and me, for example, is only skin deep. Underneath the skin we are

one and the same human being. This doctrine proved to be as heretical as the teaching of Roscellinus. Its implication was to revive the ancient Sabellian heresy that the three persons of the Trinity are merely three unessential modifications or aspects of the essentially unitarian nature of the godhead.

V. ABELARD

Both the extremely individualistic form of realism advocated by Roscellinus and the Platonic ultra-realism of William of Champeaux were called to account by Abelard (1079-1142), whose love-affair in his maturity with Héloïse, and life-long devotion to and correspondence with her after both had adopted the religious habit, have made him a great figure in the history of romance as well as of philosophy. He had been a pupil of both William of Champeaux and Roscellinus, but he could agree with the conclusions of neither of his masters.

Nature of Substance. Against William he reasserted the individual and concrete nature of substance, and denied that particular objects could be reduced to mere instances of universal types and Forms, to which they owed all the *reality* they possessed. On the contrary, over and above their generic natures as *kinds* of objects, they also, he maintained, possess a *real* individuality which makes each particular thing a substance in its own right, distinct from all other instances of the same universal class.

But with the extreme individualism of his other teacher, Roscellinus, Abelard was equally impatient. To be sure, Universals were not themselves substances as the ultra-realists maintained. But, on the other hand, they were not mere names we used to designate resemblances between individual things. When we predicated one and the same particular name of a number of individual objects, we gave to that particular word a generic significance indicating the concept of a class or genus to which we asserted the objects in question *really* belonged. We could not do this, however, unless the common natures we were predicating of them *really* existed. It would make no sense, for example, to state that Tom, Dick, and Harry are all *men,* unless there was actually such a thing as *mankind*.

In other words, we could not *predicate* common properties *of* particular substances unless these properties were already really there *in* the substances in question, and were really possessed by them. Indeed, we could not have any common names in our speech, or general concepts in our thinking, if in the external world there were no such things as common and universal characteristics.

Nature of Universals. But Abelard went still further. He felt with Anselm that Universals exist even apart from and prior to their particular instances, as well as independently of the human minds that entertain them as general ideas. They constitute the Form of the universe as it is conceived by the intellect of God, and are the patterns after which individual substances are created, and because of which these substances are the *kinds* of things they are.

To sum up in the terminology of the day used by Abelard, Universals exist at the same time *ante res* (as Ideas in the divine intellect), *in rebus* (as the common natures shared by individual substances) and *post res* (as the general concepts formed by human minds).

Abelard a Moderate Realist. This doctrine, which took a middle course between the extreme positions of William of Champeaux and Roscellinus is sometimes called *conceptualism*. But conceptualism, like nominalism, is now regarded by many historians of philosophy as a term more properly applied to later teaching, and Abelard is classified by them as a moderate realist—much more "moderate," needless to say, than Roscellinus. His view was later adopted, with some modifications, by Thomas Aquinas, and in the final form given it by the latter has become part of the philosophy accepted and promulgated today by the Catholic Church. But before it was given final shape, the nature and status of Universals continued to be a subject of spirited and bitter debate. To these further developments of the controversy we shall return in a moment.

Abelard's attitude towards philosophical and theological questions, like his doctrine of Universals, was moderate and liberal. He accepted revelation because he considered it in accordance with reason, and insisted that we should *believe* only what can be defended and supported on rational grounds. It was the business of philosophy to undertake such a defense and to make Christian doctrine intelligible. But to do so philosophy had to have a free hand in criticizing theology and in rejecting beliefs that it found contrary to reason.

Christianity a Way of Life. Of other religions than Christianity, Abelard was tolerant. He felt that Greek philosophers, like Socrates and Plato, of whom, to be sure, his age had scanty knowledge, were inspired, and that Christianity was the culmination of a double process of revelation Hellenic as well as Hebrew. He also thought that what entitled a man to be called a Christian was adherence not so much to the dogmas of the Church as to the moral precepts preached and practiced by Christ. Hence, men who lived before Jesus himself had appeared were nevertheless, in a sense, already Christians if they had followed the way of life he was later to expound and exemplify. Nearly two centuries later, Dante expressed much the same view in the *Divine Comedy,* and admitted the Emperor Trajan to Paradise on the ground that although he was a pagan he was a Christian at heart.

Morality and Conscience. Under the title *Know Thyself,* Abelard wrote an ethical treatise in which he maintained that the morality or immorality of an act has little or nothing to do with either the nature and consequences of the act itself or the thoughts and desires by which it is prompted. It is good or evil solely as it is well or ill *intended.* If ill intended, it is sinful; if well intended, it is not, whatever its objective character and subjective motivation. But he is careful to point out that there must be a standard of some sort for judging whether *intentions* are good or bad. Otherwise, anyone could excuse any act by pleading that his intentions were of the best.

This standard Abelard finds in a natural law of morality manifested in the *conscience* possessed by every man, and founded upon the will of God. To be sure, individual interpretations of this law may differ, and the conscience of one man may permit or prohibit behavior that the conscience of another does not. When such differences exist each individual must obey his own conscience, and can rest assured within himself that, if he has honestly done so, he has not sinned but has acted in accordance with the divine will. Conversely, anything a man does that is against his own conscience is sinful, no matter how much his act may commend itself to the consciences of others.

Effects of Abelard's Teaching. Abelard's view of the nature of Universals was ably seconded in the twelfth century by Hugo of St. Victor, Gilbert de la Porrée, Alan of Lille, and John of Salisbury, the last of whom was a liberal educator, a historian of philosophy, and an able psychologist, as well as a theologian. But it had to undergo further forging in the fires of controversy and tempering by a more complete knowledge of Aristotle before it finally crystallized in the teaching of Aquinas. One of its immediate effects, however, was the conversion of William of Champeaux from his ultra-realism. He did not, however, accept Abelard's own views, but became an *indifferentist,* and, indeed so extreme an indifferentist that he almost landed in the camp of Roscellinus.

VI. INDIFFERENTISM

The "indifferentist" theory of the nature of Universals, like the doctrine of Abelard, was an attempt to find a middle path between the ultra-realists on the one hand and Roscellinus on the other. It had a great vogue in the twelfth century, and· was developed and championed by the Englishman, Adelard of Bath; the Fleming, Walter of Montaigne; and William of Champeaux, after his conversion from ultra-realism.

The "indifferentists" agreed with Roscellinus that substance is individual and concrete in character, but against him they argued that each individual substance possesses *essentially* properties that it possesses *in common* with other individuals. I, for example, am *essentially* a distinct, particular, unique human being not to be confused with any other man. But I am just as essentially one man among others, undifferentiated from them so far as my *humanity* is concerned. Common properties, then, signify a real *non-difference,* or similarity, between individual substances, which is as much a part of their substance as is their difference from one another.

These respects in which particular objects are alike constitute *genera* and *species,* and are not modified by the distinctive characteristics of the individual. They are present without differentiation, or *indifferently,* in each of their particular instances. They really exist then *in rebus,* and not merely, as Roscellinus had taught, *post res.* But they do not exist, as Abelard maintained, *ante res.* Outside of our minds, they are located only *in* individual substances, and are no more than properties *of* individual substances.

William of Champeaux, however, in the zeal of his conversion from the ultra-realistic point of view, pushed *indifferentism* to an extreme that verged on the individualism of Roscellinus. Like other *indifferentists,* he taught that it is part of the essence of an individual substance to be like other substances in some respects, and that therefore Universals exist *in rebus* as well as *post res.* But he denied that common natures or properties exist without difference in different things. For example, two objects have a common property of *blueness.* It is part of the essential nature of them both to be like each other in this respect. But the blueness of the one is not the blueness of the other. It is the blueness of that one particular object and of no other object. Blueness is not then present altogether without difference, or *indif-*

ferently, in the two things. In the one case the "common" property is solely a property of *this* individual substance, in the other of *that.*

VII. NEW HERESIES

Meantime the Platonic realists were by no means discomforted, but if anything spurred on to new efforts. In the persons of Bernard and Thierry of Chartres they stoutly defended the extreme thesis that William of Champeaux had abandoned. Indeed, Thierry carried things so far as to verge on pantheism. Bernard accused Abelard of partitioning the godhead among the three persons of the Trinity, and Gilbert of applying an "indifferentism" to it that substituted similarity for identity. He argued with such effect that he succeeded in having their views condemned as heretical.

Pantheism. Such condemnations were inevitable. The Church was now in a state of intellectual ferment not unlike that which marked its first formative centuries, and a crop of new heresies, not to speak of some that were perennial, were bound to spring up. Among the latter we may note a persistent tendency towards pantheism fostered both by the intellectual dispute between the different kinds of realists and by frequent outbursts of mystic emotion. Nor should we overlook the curious mixture of Manichaeism and materialism revived in the twelfth century by the Catharists and the Albigenses, against whom Alan of Lille defended at length the immaterial, simple, and immortal nature of the soul with a zeal that ranks him with John of Salisbury as one of the first medieval psychologists.

But Alan, for all his denunciation of the Albigensian heresy, was himself in danger of pantheism, since in his teachings he moved towards a theory of the interpretation of God and the universe which verged on a derivation of the world from the divine substance.

At Chartres the pantheistic tendencies of Thierry became explicit in Bernard of Tours, who, returning to the Plotinian doctrine of emanation, regarded the universe as an offshoot of God. His pupil, William of Conches, was not quite so bold, but went so far as to identify the Holy Ghost with the Platonic world-soul, and, in the realistic tradition of the school, to reduce individual souls to aspects or modifications of it. Amalric of Bena, under the influence of Chartres, taught that all things are God, and that God is everything. In Belgium, David of Dinant maintained that matter, spirit, and God are identical at heart. Their teachings had an insidious and widespread influence. They became, for example, linked with a quasi-Adventist movement that expected every human being to turn into the Holy Ghost in the year 1210, and with the preaching by Joachim of Flora, in his so-called "eternal gospel," that the old dispensation was presided over by the Father, the present dispensation by the Son, and that a new order was imminent in which the Holy Ghost was to reign supreme.

The Inquisition. These heresies met with immediate rebuff from the Church. Unable to refute them by philosophic argument or to intimidate them by threat of excommunication, she resorted to stronger measures and for the first time invoked and received the aid of the civil authorities in a campaign of physical extirpation. Hitherto, heresy had been a purely ecclesiastical misdemeanor, subject only to spiritual correction, save for sporadic persecution at the hands of pious princes or mobs. In the twelfth century, however, heresy became a criminal offense punishable under civil law by death, on the theory promulgated by Pope Innocent III that treason to the Christian God was treason to the State. Burning at the stake, rare in the past, now became the recognized penalty for questioning the authority of the Church. Nay more, not content with taking cognizance of such cases as were brought to her notice, the Church commissioned the mendicant Orders, and particularly the Dominicans, with the duty of ferreting out heresy and reporting any suspects they might detect. Thus in the middle of the thirteenth century, the Inquisition was well established.

VIII. MYSTICISM VS. DIALECTICS

Meantime, the monastery of St. Victor at Paris was nurturing mystical tendencies, which, however, like the mysticism of Augustine, succeeded in keeping within the bounds of orthodoxy. The love of God, it was admitted, could never fuse us with him or destroy the limitations of our finite natures. Nor could it circumvent the discipline through which alone, aided by divine grace, the soul could advance step by step to realization of her beatific vision.

But the fires of untamed and consummated ecstasy, though banked, apparently continued to smolder, and found vent in a contempt for the dialectical hair-splitting to which the philosophers of the period were given, and even in a disparagement of serious metaphysical and theological speculation. Among the mystics of St. Victor we must number Hugo, with whom we are already familiar, and Richard, and more especially Walter who regarded philosophy and secular learning as a menace to Christianity and accused theologians of light-mindedness in their treatment of the ineffable mysteries of faith.

Among those he attacked was Peter Lombard whose *Sentences* contain a typical list of the questions with which philosophers were concerning themselves. Some of them are profound, as, for example, the query whether a God who foresees that he will create is not eternally determined to create; others, like the question why Eve was created from Adam's rib rather than some other part of his body, and why in the Incarnation God became man rather than woman, are trivial.

Chapter XXVI

THE ARABIAN AND JEWISH COMMENTATORS

1. MOHAMMEDAN KNOWLEDGE OF PLATO AND ARISTOTLE

Curiously enough, considering the Church's later acceptance of Aristotle as her official philosopher and of her adaptation of his teaching to her needs, the dangers arising from philosophic speculation were at first laid at his door, and his teaching and influence were regarded as pernicious. Indeed, the heretical utterances of David of Dinant were directly attributed to acquaintance with Aristotle's *Physics*. Let us, then, turn back for a moment and see how and when the Church gained her first knowledge of the Aristotelian philosophy.

Translation of Plato and Aristotle into Arabic. By the end of the fifth century much of Aristotle as well as some of Plato had been translated from the original Greek into Armenian and Persian, and the *Organon* and considerable Neo-Platonic material subsequently became available in Syriac. This material was passed on in the eighth century to the Mohammedan Caliphate at Bagdad, where its appearance in Arabic incited Arabian scholars not only to translate all the most important works of Aristotle, but to extend their knowledge of the Neo-Platonists. From Bagdad the ancient philosophers in Arabian guise accompanied the Mohammedans to Spain.

While, then, Christian philosophy was almost entirely in the dark as to Aristotle except for an acquaintance with his logic, the Mohammedans were basking in his light, and it was largely from them, through Latin translations of the Arabic translations, that twelfth century Christian thinkers were introduced to the Aristotelian metaphysics, physics, psychology and ethics. Some acquaintance, to be sure, came at first hand through the comments and direct translations of men like Grosseteste, professor at Paris and Oxford and later bishop of Lincoln, and John of Basingstoke. But for the most part it was to the collective labors of the groups of translators from the Arabic at Toledo and at the courts of Manfred and Frederick II in Sicily that the new knowledge of antiquity was acquired. To the results of their work we ought also to add Hebrew renderings of the Arabic made in the thirteenth century.

For the Arabs Aristotle had great fascination. But it must be remembered that their knowledge of him was only one degree less direct than the acquaintance they were to transmit to Europe, received as it was through the Syriac, and sometimes through Syriac and Hebrew. So their translations were bound to be garbled. Furthermore, they read him frequently in the colored light of commentators like Alexander of Aphrodisias and under the spell of the Neo-Platonic philosophers with whom they were already acquainted. These last led them to interpret the Aristotelian doctrine of the uncreated and eternal character of the universe in terms of the Plotinian doctrine of emanation and to incline to pantheism. Again, as we shall see in a moment, meditation upon Aristotle's somewhat difficult teaching with regard to the active intellect led some of them to reject the personal immortality of the soul.

Effect of Greek Philosophy on Islam. The stimulation of philosophic speculation created for Islam much the same problems as it had raised for Christianity. It necessitated attempts at reconciling the results of reason with the revelation in the Koran, and, where independent thinking conflicted with revealed truth, as it did when it became pantheistic or denied personal immortality, it plagued Mohammedan with much the same heresies as harassed Christian orthodoxy. Moreover, mystical movements appeared, as in Christianity, sometimes confined within orthodox limits and sometimes overleaping those bounds and passing into the pantheistic camp.

The labor of rationalizing the Mohammedan revelation was undertaken by the Mutazilites, of which group the first Arab philosopher, Ibrahim ibn-Nazzam, an ardent defender of the freedom of the will, was a member. Better known is Al-Kindi who lived some fifty years later and exhibited the encyclopedic tendencies prevalent in Europe at the time. A century later, belonging to the same orthodox group but showing some tendencies towards pantheism, came Al-Farabi of Bagdad. He wrote at length on Aristotle, and tried to reconcile Aristotelian with Platonic teaching.

II. AVICENNA

These earlier philosophers are all overshadowed by the great Avicenna (980-1036), who was also eminent in the medical world. His works, when translated into Latin, made a deep impression upon the Christian thinkers of the thirteenth century. A man of profound and universal learning, he read the *Metaphysics* of Aristotle forty times in an effort to overcome a difficulty eventually dispelled by chancing on a treatise of Al-Farabi's.

In his interpretation of Aristotle, Avicenna follows the Neo-Platonic lead. God emanates the universe from himself in a series of triads of mind, soul, and body, each one of which is identified with a heavenly sphere. This process terminates in the Aristotelian "active intellect," which governs directly the regions beneath the moon and transmits to all things their appropriate forms. From it human souls are also derived. Avicenna, however, stops short of absolute pantheism by preserving Matter as a principle of pure potentiality existing independent of God.

Avicenna also remains orthodox in defending the personal immortality of the soul and at the same time rejecting pre-existence and reincarnation. His psychology follows, with some complications, that of Aristotle. Against the triple division of the soul into vegetative, sensitive, and rational faculties he leans a five-runged ladder of knowledge mounting from mere potentiality of knowing to possession of the truth. To this he adds a final stage of Neo-Platonic and Plotinian, mystical ecstasy.

Avicenna also occupied himself with logic, which he treats as a method of philosophic thinking rather than as a part of philosophy itself. He divided philosophy into six departments, three—ethics, economics, and politics—"practical" in nature, and three—physics, mathematics, and theology—existing both as pure and as applied sciences. This division passed over into Christian Scholasticism.

III. AL-GAZZALI

The attempt to construct a Mohammedan philosophy met with a resistance similar in its nature and its grounds to that offered to Christian speculation by elements in the Church like the School of St. Victor. The leader of the opposition was Al-Gazzali (1058-1111). He denounced as rankest heresy the view, inspired by Aristotle, that the universe is eternal and Avicenna's doctrine of the procession or emanation of the heavenly spheres from God. Furthermore, he demanded an unconditional surrender of reason to faith and a complete submission of philosophy to the truth revealed in the Koran.

Like the monks of St. Victor, again, Al-Gazzali was a confirmed mystic, but, like them, he kept his flights and his ecstasies at the orthodox "ceiling" of aspiration and steered clear of disappearance into the pantheistic empyrean where the soul is engulfed again in the godhead from which she sprang. However, unlike the orthodox Christian mystic, and more in line with Plotinus, he regarded the final intuition of God, not as something beyond man's native powers and bestowed by divine grace, but as the natural and predictable result of an ascetic discipline open to every man and comparable to the scientific discipline by which the mind reaches intellectual clarity.

The mystical current in which Al-Gazzali was carried is known as Sufism. Its source lay in Mohammed himself, who was a man not only of practical genius but of ascetic temperament and mystic vision, and it seems to have tapped very early allied currents in Christianity, Neo-Platonism, and even Buddhism. Within three hundred years of the Prophet's death it had become an organized movement in the Mohammedan Church, submitted to a severe and ascetic rule of life and governed by a spiritual head. Al-Gazzali, however, poured into it theological and philosophical elements that made it one of the great waters of spiritual life in Islam. Henceforth mystical intuition was to rank officially with revelation and reason as a channel by which the Mohammedan verities are conveyed to the faithful.

IV. AVERRHOES

With the death of Avicenna the center of Arabian philosophy shifted from the East to Spain where, a hundred and fifty years later at Cordova, it produced Averrhoes (1126-1198), as great if not greater a thinker and commentator of Aristotle. He, too, was a doctor by profession, and his philosophy resembles that of Avicenna in many important respects, as, for example, the eternity of the universe and the procession from God of an hierarchy of intellects, each one of which is the form, and the cause of motion, of its particular heavenly sphere. His view of Matter, however, was more Aristotelian and less Neo-Platonic than that of the other Arabs, in that he regarded it as less negative in character. For him it was potentiality teeming with latent forms which were actualized by the prime mover, who is the first of the minds generated from God.

Last and lowest of the emanated minds is the human intellect, the mover of the lunar sphere. This, like Aristotle's active intellect, is the light of universal and eternal truth, one and the same for all men in all times and places, which, as contemplative reason, resides in each human individual independent of his other conscious operations. For

Averrhoes, as for his master, the activity of contemplation is wholly impersonal, and, in so far as each one of us attains to it, he escapes from his particular personality and ceases to be himself. Moreover, as Aristotle also taught, it is the only operation of human consciousness that is not supported by the body and that survives its dissolution. All, then, that is individual and personal in us is destroyed by death. The impersonal intellect in us alone remains unextinguished. There is no such thing as personal immortality.

Doctrines like the eternity of the universe, the emanation of the spheres, and the destruction and death of the individual soul were, as we have seen, as heretical in Mohammedan as in Christian eyes. Averrhoes knew it and sought to defend himself by a method not unlike one used later by free thinkers to avoid condemnation by the Catholic Church. There are, he said, two kinds or degrees of truth. One is philosophic, and, though not wholly in accord with the letter of the Koran, is not incompatible with an allegorical interpretation of it. The other kind is reached by theology, whose demands are satisfied by probabilities. It is grasped by simple religious faith which is satisfied with imaginative pictures and symbols. For example, the orthodox assertion that the universe has a beginning is the way in which minds confined within the limits of religious symbology and theological argument symbolize and image the philosophic truth that the universe is eternal.

This device gave rise in Christian Europe to the doctrine of the "two-fold truth," which sought to justify heretical doctrines on the ground that they were the conclusions at which human reason must necessarily arrive, and which all thinking men would accept, were it not for the other truth, the Christian verities revealed in the Scriptures. It met, however, with as little success in the one case as in the other. Christians and Mohammedans alike saw through the subterfuge almost at once, and, in spite of it, Averrhoes became a suspect and fell into ecclesiastical and political disfavor.

V. AVICEBRON

Before crossing the Pyrenees and re-entering Christendom, we ought to say a word about the progress of philosophy among the Jews, particularly as there was much reciprocal give and take between them and the Arabs. The two great Hebrew philosophers of the times, both of them belonging to the Jewish colony in Spain, were Avicebron in the eleventh, and Maimonides in the twelfth century. Avicebron drew his inspiration from Neo-Platonism, but, like the Arabs, he tried to stop short of out-and-out pantheism. His reservations, however, were different. Whereas the Arabs saved themselves by positing Matter or Potentiality as co-eternal with God, Avicebron began at the beginning and separated God from the universe by an act of free-will. From the ineffable One, which, as with Plotinus, transcends all characterization, issues the Will to create, and from this Will emanate, not only Form, but Matter understood in the Aristotelian sense of potentiality. These are the fundamental principles permeating all being from the world-mind in which they first appear down to corporeal substance.

But unions of Form and Matter are not only universal and general in character. They are also individual. Each particular thing, therefore, has not merely the form and matter of its species and its genus, but also a unique Form and Matter belonging to itself alone.

VI. MAIMONIDES

Revelation and Philosophy. Maimonides of Cordova, though influenced by Neo-Platonism, was dominated by Aristotle, but by an Aristotle of the Arab and particularly of the Averrhoistic type. Like Averrhoes, he was also concerned with reconciling the results of philosophizing with revealed truth. Revelation, he felt, must be so interpreted as not to conflict with truths or facts established beyond all uncertainty. At the same time, if a philosophical conclusion is no more certainly proved than a revealed truth, revelation has the right of way. For this reason Maimonides refuses to accept the doctrines of the eternity of the universe and of Matter, and holds to the theory that they had a beginning and were created by God. This is the teaching of the Old Testament and, philosophically, honors are even between it and the view that the world is uncreated and without beginning, since neither view can be established or disestablished on rational grounds.

Nature of God and the Universe. Since, however, we cannot prove that the universe is created, we cannot in Maimonides' opinion argue from its existence the logical necessity of a creator. The so-called "cosmological" proof of God's existence is then philosophically dubious. Here again, as in every case of philosophic doubt, we may trust the Scriptures. But we may also follow Aristotle and show that, though the existence of a creator cannot be proved, the necessary existence of some reason for the change and motion going on in the world can be philosophically demonstrated. Even though alteration and movement be as everlasting and therefore as uncreated as the universe, they can still be conceived as eternally inspired by the attraction of the divine perfection. If, then, the argument from efficient causation is unsound, the argument from final causation still holds. Therefore, we have philosophic as well as revealed assurance of God's existence.

When we come to discuss the nature of God, we find that he is even more transcendent than the Aristotelian deity. Like the Plotinian One he is ineffable. We can say what he is not but not what he is.

In his description of the universe Maimonides follows Avicebron and Averrhoes. From God proceeds a descending series of intellects presiding over the heavenly spheres and terminating in the active intellect that displays itself in human thinking. But Maimonides argues with Aristotle against Avicebron that these intellects are pure Form unmixed with Matter, and makes a sharp distinction between the matter of the heavenly spheres and that of things on earth.

Like Averrhoes he rejects personal immortality. To be sure, the impersonal active intellect, by actualizing the individual's capacity for thinking, endows him for a brief time with a mind of his own. But the capacity for individual and personal thinking disappears with the destruction of the body, and only the active intellect survives. At the same time, the individual in his present existence may increase his vision of the truth and his hold on the eternal, and thus identify his personal life with the operations of the active intellect. By so doing he attains peace and happiness and salvation and a sort of immortality here and now.

Chapter XXVII

ARISTOTLE VS. PLATO

I. FIRST CHRISTIAN REACTION TO ARISTOTLE

We can easily understand that a philosopher like Aristotle who denied that Matter and the universe had been created, who disbelieved in personal immortality, and whose views regarding the divine gave little support to belief in a personal deity, might not commend himself at first sight to the Church. Nor was the situation eased by the emanatistic and pantheistic glosses given the Aristotelian teaching by the Arabian and Jewish commentators, as his work passed through their hands. So it was that the *Physics,* to which the heresy of David of Dinant was attributed, was banned in Christendom in 1209, and the *Metaphysics* was suppressed six years later.

This condemnation, however, was of short duration, and by the middle of the thirteenth century Aristotle's physics and metaphysics were being officially taught, with expurgations, at the University of Paris, which had been founded some fifty years before. Here, and at its offshoot at Oxford, the renewed interest in the Aristotelian philosophy was centered. Further translations were made, no longer from Arabic, but from Greek, knowledge of which was being regained by the West, thanks to the Crusades and to more intimate relations with the Byzantine Empire. By 1260 William of Moerbeke, a friend of Aquinas, was undertaking a critical edition of the whole Greek text, with Latin versions of all the works hitherto untranslated. To him Europe owed its first acquaintance with the *Politics,* of whose existence the Arab scholars were unaware.

II. MODIFICATION OF PLATONIC TRADITION BY ARISTOTELIAN INFLUENCE

William of Auvergne. But the revived cult did not displace overnight the Platonic tradition handed on by Augustine and Anselm. The latter continued to claim its votaries, who, however, could not escape the ever-increasing Aristotelian influence. Among them we may mention William of Auvergne (d. 1249), Alexander of Hales (d. 1245), and Bonaventure (1221-1274). To the Augustinian teaching regarding God and the soul William of Auvergne adds little that is new. In his theory of knowledge, also, he clings for the most part to Augustine. But he knows his Aristotle and his Arabs, if only to criticize them. He argues against the eternity of the world and the teaching that Matter is the principle that individuates members of the same species from one another, and attacks the Neo-Platonic theory of emanation and the Arabian view regarding the procession of the intelligences and their spheres from God. He also dispenses with the active intellect and finds that the potential intellect is capable of producing forms by itself when stimulated by sense experience. Aristotle's physics, however, he is inclined to accept, in so far as the explanation of natural phenomena is concerned.

Alexander of Hales. Upon Alexander of Hales the hand of Aristotle lies more heavily. All beings save God, he tells us, are a mixture of matter and form, potentiality and actuality. God alone is pure form and pure actuality. Against both pantheism and emanation he sternly sets his face. God cannot be the substance or the source of the substance of all things, since things are made of different stuffs. Spiritual matter or potentiality is capacity for thinking but not for moving or changing; the matter or potentiality displayed by the heavenly bodies is capacity for motion but not for alteration; and the matter of terrestrial bodies is capacity for both movement and change. Although, then, matter is present in all created beings, it is not one and the same matter in them all. Hence there is no one substratum of any sort, divine or non-divine, created or emanated, of which they could be modes.

The Soul and the "Active Intellect." At this point, however, another question arises. If the soul is not pure form and a pure activity of thinking, but possesses a potential or unrealized capacity for thought as well, there must be an agent by which this capacity is realized. So it is that Alexander is forced to invoke the active intellect of Aristotle, though he has a hard time trying to work it into his Augustinian psychology and finds it a white elephant on his hands. It made trouble, too, for all the other philosophers of the Franciscan order who followed in his steps. Grosseteste tried to deal with it by interpreting it in terms of the Augustinian doctrine of the inner light by virtue of which the soul is able to grasp eternal truth. John of Rochelle, a pupil of Alexander's, identified it with God, and only saved himself by heroic efforts from the pantheism his view implied.

The Tripartite Soul. Another question, closely allied with the status of the active intellect, also comes to the fore in Alexander. Hitherto, following the Augustinian teaching, the soul had been generally regarded as a single unit expressing one and the same identical essence in the exercise of her various faculties. Aristotle, however, by his doctrine of three separate souls responsible respectively for the vital functions, the activities of the senses, and the operations of thought, had suggested that the Christian soul, at least, is not to be identified with them all. Alexander, for example, believes not the soul but a separate vital principle to be the source of life in the body. And in discussing the operations of knowledge he tries to limit the function of the active intellect to actualizing the Forms underlying the physical universe and contained in the potential intellect. Upon the active intellect thus degraded he superimposes the Augustinian faculties of the intellect that knows other created minds and the intelligence that by special illumination from God contains and grasps eternal truths and first principles.

Substantial Forms. Finally, in Alexander we come face to face with perhaps the most difficult and confusing of all the problems raised in the process of recasting Christian theology in Aristotelian mold—the question of *substantial forms*. If the soul is an actualization of potentiality, albeit spiritual, she must be a composite *spiritual substance* like any material substance in which Form and Matter are combined. Furthermore, the body, in so far as it contains potentialities capable of further realization, will not find them formulated and actualized in the soul, as Aristotle taught, but in a *corporeal* Form on the corporeal level of existence. In short, the soul will no longer be the Form and actualization of the body, and the body will no longer be the Matter of which the soul is the Form. Both body and soul will henceforth provide each its own Form and Matter, or in other words will possess each its own *substantial form*. In that case, however, the human being is no longer a union of Form and Matter but an association of two composite substances, in each one of which Form and Matter are conjoined.

III. BONAVENTURE

Disagreement with Alexander. Alexander, then, in fathering the doctrine of *substantial forms* had laid quite as embarrassing a question on the doorstep of the Franciscans as that of the active intellect. It was left to the ablest theologian of them all, the eminent Bonaventure, to take up these two obstreperous problems and deal with them as best he could. He began by denying outright the distinction made by Alexander between spiritual and corporeal Matter and Potentiality. The difference between spirit and body is one of Form alone. Matter is not only universally present in all created things, it is universally one and the same in them all. The basis of this sameness would seem to lie in the fact that in the mind of God there exists a single, universal concept of Potentiality as such.

Existence of Substantial Forms. Nevertheless, and here Bonaventure agrees with Alexander, *substantial forms* exist. Though spirit and body are formulations of the same Matter, they actualize different capacities it possesses. Actualizing each a different capacity, each contains within itself its proper potentiality as well as its proper form, and does not require any other level or kind of existence to support it. Both spirit and body, then, have *substantial forms.* It follows that the human soul, being spirit, is not the actualization of potentialities afforded by the body, but is an actualization of spiritual potentiality. Hence, she exists independently of the body and is immortal.

Still, Bonaventure contends, the fact that the soul is a *substantial form,* independent of the body, does not prevent her from also constituting in Aristotelian fashion, the "entelechy" or fulfillment, of the body in which she resides. True, the body has its corporeal *substantial form,* just as the soul has her spiritual one. But without the soul, the body could not realize its highest capacity, fulfill its highest purpose, and perform its crowning function—the capacity, purpose, and function of housing and feeding her. The *substantial form* of the body stands, then, to the substantial form of the soul in the Aristotelian relation of Potentiality to actuality.

Nature of Individuation. But what individuates one man or one soul from another and gives rise to a myriad particular instances of the actualization of the nature of the soul and of the human species? Is it Matter, as Aristotle taught, embodying over and over again one and the same human form? Or have Tom, Dick, and Harry not only a common human nature, but also each his own individual form, which adds their particular characters to their common humanity? It is, Bonaventure replies, neither the one nor the other, taken by itself. There is, he insists, no such thing as a form of the individual. The *essence* of the individual is always identical with the *essence* of the species. The deepest thing in Tom, Dick, and Harry, for example, lies not in what distinguishes them from one another, but in the *human species* which unites them and, in spite of their individual peculiarities, makes all three *men.*

But—and this is what makes real individuals of them—in Tom, Dick, and Harry there are actualized not only the Form of the human species, but other Forms as well—the Forms of the particular attributes and qualities, whose presence or absence in different combinations or degrees serves to set them apart and make them three distinct people. Although, then, they have no individual *essences* or Forms of their own, they each combine in a unique and unreduplicated way the human species with a lot of other Forms, and the composite result is particular, though all its ingredients are universals. In short, each individual is a composite substantial form mixing in a special way a number of other substantial forms and owing, like every substantial form, its existence neither to Form nor Matter alone but to the interaction of the two.

The "Active Intellect." The active intellect Bonaventure treats more summarily. Like Alexander, he limits its function to extracting from sensible experience and imagery the Forms embodied in sensible objects. Knowledge of one's self, of the eternal verities, and of God are the work of the Augustinian "inner light," with which the grace of God illumines the soul. Bonaventure is one of the great mystics of all time, and his description of the further reaches of knowledge, as it rises from cognition of the sensible world to apprehension of God, portrays the steps by which the soul, estranged from the good and blinded to the truth by sin, regains the beatific vision, the enjoyment of which is her supreme bliss and peace.

The Existence of God. The splendor of the created universe testifies to God's existence and reflects his glory. We may well then meditate upon the harmony and order and beauty of the sensible world. From them we may also argue the necessity of a being that accounts for its existence, its nature, and its motion. However, these intimations of God's presence and God's glory are as nothing compared to those we find when we look within ourselves. There, in the power to remember, which gives continuous existence and personal identity to the soul, in the power to know, which depends for its exercise upon the images retained by memory, and in the power to love, which without memory and knowledge we could not possess, we find the Trinity reflected and the generation of the Son by the Father and the procession of the Holy Ghost.

There, too, by the aid of a faculty of intellect, higher than the active reason which deals only with the structure of the sensible world, we find God's existence proved, as Anselm proved it, by the presence in the soul of the idea of a perfect being. Nay more, as Augustine had already pointed out, our minds could not entertain the concepts of eternal truths unless those truths existed, and those truths could not exist except in a divine mind, or be imparted to us finite and fallible beings save by divine grace. Knowledge, then, is a reception of God's likeness by the mind, not abstracted from experience, as the Forms of the physical world are abstracted from sense by the active intellect, but infused into us from above. God, in a word, is a necessary presupposition not only of our mere being, or *existence,* but of our being what we are, or *essence.*

Finally, we have the same direct intuition of God's existence that we have of our own. Still, we can have no intellectual concept of what God is like. Even the eternal truths are not apprehended as they exist in the divine mind, but obscurely and incompletely. This is due to our finite and created natures, and to the further blinding of our minds by the Fall. We occupy an ambiguous situation, placed as we are between the rest of the created universe and God, and drawing, as we do, upon both for knowledge, we find the certainties derived from one source clouded by the not so certain conclusions drawn from the other.

If, then, there is any further degree of approach to the divine, it must be made by other than intellectual means. Such a way exists—the way of all the great mystics. It is the secret and ineffable way of ecstasy. To tread it, Bonaventure tells us, we must pass from theological doctrine to the divine grace for our support. We must abandon study for prayer. We must cease to think and must only love. Then a burning flame will take the place of the divine light, whose heat will consume all our dross and leave in us God and God alone.

Avoidance of Pantheism. Bonaventure, however, remains an orthodox mystic, and never, in theory at least, allows himself to break down the barriers that separate the finite and the created soul from her creator. That there is a creator *separate* from the universe is proved by the fact that nowhere in it do we find anything whose nature or essence implies or necessitates existence. All its constituents, then, owe their being not to their own power of self-existence but to an eternal cause. Furthermore the created cannot be co-eternal with the creator, as Aristotle taught, but must have a beginning in time. This point Bonaventure argues at length, and here disagrees with his contemporary, Aquinas, who, like Maimonides, finds reason equally complacent to both theories, but revelation asserting a creation out of nothing by divine fiat.

Chapter XXVIII

THOMAS AQUINAS

I. THOMAS'S TEACHER, ALBERTUS MAGNUS

Triumph of Aristotle over Plato. With Bonaventure the Platonic tradition, which, as we have seen, was becoming more and more tinged with Aristotelianism, came definitely to an end in the Catholic Church. Side by side with him, Albertus Magnus (1206?-1280) and Thomas Aquinas were effecting the great synthesis of Christian doctrine, in purely Aristotelian terms, which was to become the Church's official philosophy. The foundations of this synthesis were laid by Albertus' encyclopedic work of collecting from the Greeks, Arabs, and Jews everything that bore on Aristotle, and of writing an exhaustive paraphrase and exposition of his works and a commentary upon them. His mind, like that of his philosophic master, was universal in its scope, his learning was profound, and his acquaintance with the physical sciences and mathematics of the day was thorough and complete. Indeed, his interest in natural phenomena and his sympathy with the new methods of observation, experiment, and inductive reasoning which were now beginning to make headway put him, one foot at least, in the very current of thought that was so soon to undermine the Aristotelianism of which he was so ardent a champion.

Born a German, Albertus took up soldiering as a career, only after a few years to become a Dominican monk. He traveled widely, taught at Cologne and other German cities, and spent three years in Paris. Eventually he became bishop of Ratisbon—which office he resigned in order to return to the Dominican monastery at Cologne and devote himself to his studies.

Aristotle and Revelation. Albertus was not only an encyclopedist and commentator, he was a philosopher of note. In dealing with Aristotle he tried to divest him of the glosses introduced by the Arabs and to recover his original thought. Nor did he try to read into him Christian doctrines. He took him as he stood, and, so taking him, regarded his teaching as the supreme achievement of the unaided human intellect. The natural light of reason could not be expected to discover

395

and make clear the trinitarian nature of God, or the why and wherefore of the Incarnation and Redemption. These had to be revealed
to the human mind from on high. They were not then matters to be
reasoned about but to be accepted as articles of faith, and as such they
were subjects not for philosophy but theology.

But, Albertus insisted, in her own field, thus sharply demarcated
from that of theology, philosophy had the right to speculate freely,
as Aristotle had done, and to come to such conclusions regarding the
nature of God and the universe as reason might indicate. If these
conclusions ran counter to revelation, then faith had the right of
way. Otherwise philosophy might proceed as far as she could.

Claiming this liberty for himself, Albertus anticipated in many respects the work of his pupil Aquinas. But in others he remained a
member of the old school. He maintained that spirits are a union of
Form and Matter, that the soul is a substantial form and inseparable
from all her faculties, including the vegetative, and he held to the
doctrine of "seminal reasons" or special predispositions to particular
Forms in Matter and to the mixture of Forms in individuals. He also
continued the argument against the eternity of Matter and of the
universe—though seemingly, like Aquinas, he regarded creation by
fiat as a revealed truth which reason by itself cannot establish. Like
Aquinas, again, he rejected the "ontological proof" of Anselm and
based his demonstration of God's existence upon inferences drawn
from the existence and nature of the world.

II. AQUINAS' LIFE

Thomas Aquinas (1227-1274) accomplished in his much shorter
life a philosophic synthesis as wide as and more profound than that
of his master. Born into the great family of the Counts of Aquino
near Naples, he was educated at Monte Cassino, and entered the
Dominican order. This he did against the will of his father, and so
much to the disgust of his brothers that they kidnapped him and held
him prisoner in the family stronghold at Roccassone for two years.
At last he escaped and made his way to Paris where he became a
pupil of Albertus Magnus. From Paris he followed Albertus to Cologne
and spent four years there. In 1252 he returned to the Sorbonne to
study theology, receiving his master's degree seven years later. The
rest of his life he spent between Italy and Paris teaching.

He was a prolific writer. He commented at length not only on
Aristotle but on the pseudo-Dionysius and on the *Sentences* of Peter

Lombard, and, in addition to many other treatises, wrote the two monumental *Summae,* the *Summa Theologiae* and the *Summa contra Gentiles.*

III. GOD AND THE UNIVERSE

Like Albertus, Aquinas delimits sharply the fields of philosophy and theology. The subject-matter of philosophy is restricted to everything that lies open to argument, and its purpose to the establishment of such truth as can be discovered and demonstrated by the use of human reason. The subject-matter of theology is the content of faith, or, in other words, is revealed truth, which reason is incapable of discovering and demonstrating and about which there can be no argument. Nevertheless, the two fields overlap. Since no truth can contradict reason, the "mysteries" of faith cannot be unintelligible but are simply beyond our finite, human understanding. They, therefore, can be reasoned about as far as reasoning will carry us, and prove to be, in part at least, within human comprehension. The existence of God, for example, can be proved by reason apart from revelation, as Aristotle showed. Other theological points, too, are susceptible of rational demonstration. Indeed, a good part of philosophy—the most important part in fact—is devoted to matters of theological interest and forms a *natural theology,* as Aquinas calls it, to be distinguished from *revealed theology.*

IV. PHILOSOPHICAL PROOFS OF GOD'S EXISTENCE AND NATURE

Existence of God Proved. Turning now to the most fundamental of all problems, the existence of God, Aquinas holds that we cannot argue his existence from the existence in our minds of an idea of him, for we can have no definite idea of the infinite, let alone its implication of necessary existence. Nor can we demonstrate his existence on the ground that we need a creator to account for the existence of the universe. Philosophically speaking, the Aristotelian view that Matter and the universe are uncreated and eternal is every whit as sound as the view that it is created by God out of nothing. The honors then are even, in so far as natural theology is concerned, and we must appeal to revealed theology to turn the trick in favor of special creation and a creator.

However, the absence of revealed light and the belief that Matter and the universe are eternal and uncreated, did not prevent Aristotle from proving the existence of God. He showed that the perpetual actualization of Potentiality and formulation of Matter, to which all the activities of the universe may be reduced, become intelligible only on the supposition that there is an unmoved and therefore uncreated, self-existent and wholly actualized Form of being whose sheer perfection sets the whole world moving in pursuit of it. Add to this proof the arguments for a cause of motion at the beginning of the series as well as at the end of it, for a reason why things are necessarily what they are, and for an explanation of the order and the harmony in the universe, and we can rest assured that God exists.

Philosophical Knowledge of God's Nature. Have we also any "natural light" respecting the *nature* of God? Yes, the Aristotelian argument for his existence shows us that he is the sole example of pure Actuality and therefore a single being, that he must be immutable and without alteration or shadow of turning, and that he must be absolute perfection and therefore supremely good. Furthermore, he must be infinite, and therefore must possess to an infinite degree the good characteristics, like intelligence, knowledge, and benevolence, freedom and power, found partially displayed by finite creatures.

But how can such a being account for the existence of a world in which there are not only many individual things, but many Forms, and in which there are movement, change, and imperfection. To answer the first query, Aquinas is obliged to desert the Aristotelian view that God knows only his own Form and to inject into the divine mind the world of Platonic Ideas. God's self-knowledge is therefore a knowledge of the whole formal structure of the universe, which, as Augustine and his followers had taught, constitutes in the divine mind a plan or model in accordance with which the world is created.

Explanation of Imperfection. In explaining the imperfection of the universe, Aquinas would seem once more to part with Aristotle and to lean toward Neo-Platonism. First he invokes "metaphysical evil," or the doctrine that whatever is not God must of necessity be imperfect and that the Forms of created things constitute a ladder of descending degrees of perfection. Aristotle, it should be said, also admitted such an hierarchy. Below God comes the hierarchy of angels. Being pure spirit, they are, in Aquinas' opinion, devoid of Matter and Potentiality. Here he disagrees sharply with both Alexander of Hales' view that there is a spiritual matter distinct from corporeal matter, and with Bonaventure's doctrine that Matter, though universally the same, possesses a capacity for taking on the Form of spirit as well as that of body. What differentiates the angels from God is that their natures are not self-existent but created, or, in other words, that their essence and their existence are not identical.

V. FORM AND MATTER

Men and Angels. There is one odd but, as we shall see in a moment, extremely significant consequence of the purely formal nature of angels. All Forms, and here Aquinas is thoroughly Aristotelian, are Universals. The most particularized Form is at least that of a species. There are no Forms of individuals, as Plotinus maintained. If, then, the angels are pure form, no angel is, properly speaking, an individual. Each is a species unto himself. Herein angels differ from human beings, each one of whom is not a species unto himself but a particular instance of the species "man," which he shares with all his fellow-men.

Man and Matter. But why this difference between an angelic and a human being? The answer lies in a kind of Siamese-twin of the assertion that all Forms are Universals—the Aristotelian doctrine, also adopted by Aquinas in defiance of Scholastic tradition, *that Matter is the principle that individuates all particular objects from one another*.

Human beings, unlike angels, are not pure Form. They have bodies as well as souls, and are therefore a mixture of Form and Matter. In them the Form of the human species actualizes Potentiality in the different ways that we call Tom, Dick, and Harry. But there is no such thing as a Form of Tom or Dick. Their souls, or individualities, or personalities, are just particular actualizations by the human species of Matter's capacity for being worked into that Form. The distinction, then, between human individuals, as between all other particular objects, is not due to the possession of separate Forms, for all men have only one Form, the human. It is due rather to the indeterminate nature of Matter which lends itself to a variety of determinations by the same Form. Matter, therefore, is the reason why there are *many* men or *many* anything. Incidentally, its indeterminate character accounts for its failure to register finished and flawless instances of the Form in question. To it all the physical imperfections of the universe, as well as the multiple and extended character of the world, are to be attributed.

No Plurality of Substantial Forms. Furthermore, Aquinas thinks, Bonaventure's teaching that the individual can have more than one *substantial form* is incorrect. Substantially, a thing is simply what it is and nothing else. All Forms, then, other than that which defines its essence, will be conjoined with it simply as *accidental* properties. They will in no wise mix with it and become ingredients in what makes it *substantially* what it is. They can be put on or off without affecting its real self. We cannot, then, appeal to different mixtures of substantial forms as the principle of individuation. Once more we must have recourse to Matter.

But how can one and the same universal Form by actualizing one and the same absolutely indeterminate Matter produce different particular determinations of that Matter? It cannot. When, for example, the Form of the human species actualizes individual men, we must not think of it as actualizing an indeterminate possibility of anything and everything. We must think of the soul rather as an actualization of Matter already prepared to form the individual in question.

VI. THE STATUS OF UNIVERSALS

Finally Aquinas has to deal with the old question of the status of Universals. Here, as we have already seen, he has deserted the Aristotelian position that Forms exist only in particular objects, and made them ideas and archetypes in the divine mind. Still, since this is not to say, as Plato did, that they exist in themselves, independent of any mind whatsoever, Aquinas criticizes Plato and regards his own position as not incompatible with Aristotle's teaching. The Forms are also immanent in the universe, and are inseparable there from the particular objects that embody and enact them. However, they may be abstracted by the mind from other particular instances, in which they appear as common qualities and resemblances, and may be dealt with without reference to the particular conditions under which they occur. As concepts of the mind they are no more separable from the intellect, which entertains them, than they are, as Forms of material things, from the things which materialize them. The object of knowledge, in so far as it is known, becomes a mode or thought of the thinking subject. The Forms, then, are at once God's ideas, the formal structure of the sensible world, and concepts formed by and forming the human intellect. But they are not *merely* any one of these.

In this doctrine Aquinas writes journey's end to the middle way chosen by Abelard in avoiding the extremes in the controversy over the status of Universals. It comes as near the Aristotelian doctrine as the exigencies of Christian orthodoxy, and the consequent concessions to the modified Platonism of Augustine, would permit.

VII. PSYCHOLOGY

The Active Intellect. In his view of the functions and dignity of the active intellect Aquinas restores that faculty to the position that Aristotle had assigned it, and from which William of Auvergne and Alexander of Hales had degraded it. It is, he says, the highest faculty of the soul, the possession of which makes man but little lower than the angels. It is a ray of the inner light, of the divine illumination, which, according to Augustine and his followers, enables the soul to grasp and to unite herself with eternal truth. Its nature is to actualize within her the system of Forms that constitutes the intelligible structure of the universe. Were it pure intellect like the angels, it would see truth face to face. But, since the human being is a composite of Form and Matter, of Actuality and Potentiality, the truth is not completely and once and for all realized by his mind. His vision of it is partial, obscure, intermittent, and laboriously attained. In other words, his mind is in great part only an unrealized capacity for knowledge, or a passive and potential intellect.

Furthermore, man has a body, and senses, and sensible experience crowded with individual data, and it is through perception that he gets his first contacts with the external world and his first incentive to think. His intellectual processes are not self-initiating and self-supporting. Sensible experience pushes the button that sets the active part of the intellect to work realizing the truth it potentially contains. This operation consists in abstracting from the particulars of sense-experience their common and universal characteristics—in other words, their Forms.

To some extent the preliminaries to the formation of universal concepts have been performed by the senses themselves. Acted upon by external objects, they absorb the sensible characteristics, or species, of these objects, abstracted, to be sure, from their matter, but still sensible in character. We *perceive,* for example, not only a blue cup or a blue plate, but the color blue, which is a *sensible species* present in both objects.

The Process of Understanding. Sensible species, however, do not help us to *understand.* To understand we must, as we say, reduce things to *intelligible* terms. Here the active intellect enters upon the scene. Stimulated by the sensible species, it proceeds to make them intelligible by abstracting from them, or, in other words, by actualizing in itself, the universal laws and types and natures which they exemplify

and suggest, and which the potential intellect, or our capacity for
knowing the truth about them, already contains. Thus, little by little,
by a process that is, on the one hand, a progressive discovery in things,
and, on the other, a progressive actualization in the mind, of ever
more inclusive and more fundamental Forms, the nature of the sensible
world is comprehended and the intellect's power of comprehending
it is realized. Finally, the whole intelligible structure and ultimate
explanation of the universe, abstracted from the sensible medium in
which it is first conveyed to us, fills the intellect and fulfills the intellect's capacity for knowledge, enlightening it with the vision of
absolute truth, in so far as a finite and embodied mind can be enlightened.

Immortality of the Soul. For Aquinas, as for Aristotle, the active
intellect alone survives the dissolution of the body. The sensitive and
vegetative functions of the soul, depending as they do upon the body
for their activity, perish with it. However, Aquinas modifies the Aristotelian doctrine to meet the Christian demand for personal immortality. For Aristotle the active intellect was as impersonal in character
and as devoid of particular location as the universal truth it enshrined.
For Aquinas, the whole substance of the soul, to which both personality and will are essential, share in the deathlessness of the active intellect with which she is endowed. *We,* then, do not perish with the
body. Not merely the vision and the contemplation of truth survives
death; *your* vision and *my* vision, *you* and *I* also endure after the body
has collapsed beneath us.

It was difficult to reconcile such doctrine with the assertions that
Matter is the principle of individuation and that therefore the angels,
being disembodied, must be species not individuals. It was no less
hard to reconcile it with the view, upon which not only Aristotle but
the Christians themselves insisted, that the human being is constituted
by a union of Form and Matter, of soul and body, and therefore, when
deprived of a body and reduced to soul, pure and simple, must be
incomplete. Theology, however, came to the rescue with the revealed
teaching of the resurrection of the body and its eventual reunion with
the soul.

VIII. ETHICS

Knowledge of God the Highest Good. Knowledge, as we have just
seen, is an activity. It is a search for truth, an attempt to reach God.
God, therefore, is the end for which knowledge strives. But to have
a direction and a terminus is to have volition and love. The soul natu-

rally desires and wills what she seeks. Her will and her love have, then, the same end as her knowledge. All desires and all affections converge upon God. God is her supreme good, just as he is supreme truth. But just as truth is first seen through a sensible medium as in a glass darkly, and the Universal is found only in its individual instances, so the supreme good is not apprehended and loved immediately, but broken and distorted and obscured in different degrees by a myriad individual goods and a variety of particular desires and affections.

Thus the moral problem arises of which course to choose between alternative desires and goods. Those most in accordance with the sovereign good, or, in other words, most pleasing to God, must be discovered and followed. All morality, all law, all obligation, are based upon God's will. Ethics studies the alternative courses of action with which we are confronted and seeks to discover among them those which lead to a realization of the end of human life. The results of its investigations counsel self-control, the subjugation of the passions by reason, the avoidance of vice and the pursuit of virtue, and the development of the contemplative life. They establish the institution of the monogamous family and the right to possess private property as God-given. They demand that the sovereign power in the state shall be exercised for the well-being of the whole community.

Happiness Not on Earth but in Heaven. Still, the most scrupulous observance of God's ordinances and the most painstaking cultivation of the moral and intellectual virtues cannot give the soul complete peace and happiness in this life. She is by nature supernatural, and her destiny can be fulfilled only on the supernatural plane. No matter how exemplary her conduct, or how concentrated upon God her thoughts may be while she is on earth, it is beyond death that she must look for the attainment of her sovereign good. At the most she can but prepare herself here below for her true life beyond the grave. But that preparation is of tremendous import, for it unlocks the doors to heaven or to hell, according as the soul has followed or has spurned the discipline imposed by God.

Free-Will of Self-Determination. It is within the power of the soul to make this choice, to accept or to reject, and herein lie human freedom and moral responsibility. At the same time, Aquinas does not attribute to the soul an absolute "indifference" of the will in the face of alternatives. The will is naturally and necessarily directed towards the good. We cannot exercise volition except at the incentive of desire and towards its satisfaction. If the will, then, were enlightened by an accurate knowledge of the true good, it would spontaneously, necessarily, and freely prefer, choose, and pursue it. No alternative course would be present or possible to it. Still, because of its essential self-determination to the good, this inability to entertain or to follow, or in other words, to *will,* any other course, does not destroy our liberty of volition but rather expresses it.

For example, God, Aquinas insists, who is himself the sovereign good and has absolute knowledge of it, *cannot* will other than the absolute good. No alternative to doing good is possible in his case. He *cannot* choose or will evil. Being himself good, he *must* will the good. His choice and will are not uncaused and undetermined. They proceed by inexorable necessity from his nature. But to be completely determined by absolute goodness and to will only the absolute good is perfect freedom.

By thus attributing to God freedom, not of indifference, but of self-determination, Aquinas placed himself emphatically in the rank of those who held that the divine character is prior to the divine will, and that a wholly sufficient and completely determining reason for what God *does* is to be found in what he *is.* Since he is absolutely benevolent, just, wise, and intelligent, his volition and his behavior must necessarily express these qualities. This teaching of the priority of the intellect over the will in the divine nature was, as we shall see in a moment, bitterly attacked by Duns Scotus.

Self-Determination and the Choice of Goods. Descending now to man, we find that he, too, is self-determined to the good. He cannot choose or will any course of action that he does not think, at the moment, will attain a desired end and satisfy a want. But unfortunately the human will, unlike the divine, is not enlightened and determined by an accurate knowledge of what the truly desirable end and the deepest wants really are. Because of his material nature and its attachments to the physical and temporal world, man has no clear vision and no undivided love of the sovereign good. His eye is caught on every side by relative and contingent goods, satisfactions of the moment, gratifications of the senses, worldly successes, and the like, which divide the love of which God is the proper object, and scatter it in a thousand conflicting drives upon as many different satisfactions.

Therefore man, unlike God, is always confronted with alternative choices and courses of action between different goods and different ways of attaining them. His problem—the problem that makes him a moral being—is to select, under the guidance of reason rather than of passion, the alternatives designated by the intellect as best calculated to attain the highest and deepest good. Since we have only an indirect knowledge of its nature, gained by reasoning and by revelation, our choices must often miss the mark and lead us away from God rather than towards him. Even so, choice of the wrong course is dictated by the desire to satisfy a want and attain a *good,* and is therefore not imposed upon us by an outer force, but is determined by the impulse to pursue good, which is the very essence of the will. An evil choice is simply a mistaken choice, a choice of a spurious good—good, because it satisfies desire, spurious, because it satisfies desires that alienate the soul from God. Since, then, all alternatives present themselves under the general form of the good, whichever alternative is chosen is willed under no compulsion save that of our own self-determination. Our choice of it is therefore a free choice, for which we are morally responsible and for which we merit punishment or reward.

IX. PHYSICS AND ASTRONOMY

The World-Process. Aquinas' physics follows closely that of Aristotle. The world-process is essentially an increasing actualization and exhaustion of Potentiality in a ladder of Forms, and each new substance to which the union of Form and Matter gives birth is double-faced. It is Form in as far as it has realized possibilities latent in less highly organized beings, but it is at the same time stuff or Potentiality for further formulation and actualization.

His insistence upon the graduated nature of the process of ascent leads Aquinas to reject the widely accepted Augustinian theory of "seminal reasons" or "predispositions" for all sorts of Forms, innate in Matter itself. It is only by being first actualized in a given Form that Matter can become predisposed to receive further formulation.

The Heavens and the Earth. Again, Aquinas follows Aristotle in sharply contrasting the more perfect matter of the heavenly spheres, infected with spatial movement but immune from qualitative change, with the matter of the terrestrial elements which is corrupted by both potentialities. Moreover, celestial matter is endowed with superior, spherical motion, whereas the terrestrial elements tend to follow straight lines as befits their inferior substance. Incidentally, Aquinas accepts the Aristotelian geocentric astronomy as corrected and amplified by Ptolemy and other later astronomers, but he admits that it is only a provisional hypothesis, not necessarily true, which may some time be supplanted by some other explanation of the perceived movements of the heavenly bodies.

As we have seen, while Aquinas admitted that the "cosmological" arguments for the existence of God are inconclusive, he accepted as logically necessary Aristotle's postulation of an unmoved Mover, making the world go round out of sheer love of perfection. Like Aristotle, he regards the initial circular movement of the outer heaven as the source of all the motion and of the processes of generation and corruption that go on in the sublunar sphere.

Man. The apex of the sublunar aspiration and movement from Potentiality to Actuality is man, in whom Matter is at last formulated to such a point that it can support an immortal soul. In a way that anticipates somewhat the modern discovery that the gestation of the embryo briefly recapitulates the evolution of the species, Aquinas points out that the unborn human body passes through a number of intermediary and preparatory actualizations before it is ready to receive its soul from God.

In man, too, the nature of the final causation by which God moves the world is at last made manifest. Man is made to glorify God by contemplating and loving the divine handiwork, even as God himself contemplates it and finds it good. The whole movement and direction of his being is motivated by the love of God and proceeds toward the vision of God. As it is with man, so is it with the whole creation from the humblest actualizations of Matter to the sun and the other stars.

X. MINOR OPPONENTS AND CHAMPIONS OF AQUINAS

Attacks on Aquinas. Aquinas thought and wrote in an atmosphere of bitter dispute. He trod on many toes and aroused much determined opposition during his lifetime, which led shortly after his death to the temporary condemnation of certain of his views at both Paris and Oxford. The philosophic storm center his philosophy created was to persist for five hundred years, and was only finally dissipated when in 1879 Leo XIII directed that his teaching should be made the basis of all Catholic theological and philosophic teaching.

In the first place, he encountered the ill-will of the mystics, then chiefly centered in the Franciscan order. Bonaventure, for example, must have felt his ecstatic ardors chilled by Aquinas' assertion that hope of attaining the beatific vision in our earthly life is vain, and that here and now we had better cultivate the virtues and the perfections realizable in our present estate and be content to postpone mystical consummation of the love of God till after death.

In any case, the Franciscans took to the war-path and were joined by some of the Dominicans. The Thomistic doctrines especially under attack were the denial of the plurality of substantial forms and the deprivation of the angelic intelligences of their matter and therefore of their individualities. In England the anti-Thomistic campaign was led by two successive Archbishops of Canterbury, Kilwardby and Peckham, and the condemnation at Oxford was largely their work.

Siger of Brabant. The attack on Aquinas was facilitated by the fact that despite his efforts he could not free Aristotle from the Neo-Platonic glosses of Averrhoes or prevent him from convincing some thinkers that the universe and Matter are uncreated and eternal and that there is no such thing as personal immortality. Thus Siger of Brabant, who was a contemporary of Thomas, defended the impersonality of the active intellect, the non-existence of personal immortality, the impossibility of a first cause, and the uncreated character of the universe. These doctrines he aired at Paris under cover of the "twofold truth," and succeeded in defying the university authorities and scandalizing the Church for some thirteen years. They were, however, eventually condemned.

Aquinas' advocacy of a philosophy that lent itself to such interpretations was utilized by his enemies to strike at him. The result was that the condemnation of Averrhoism was extended, at Paris, to the Thomistic view that Matter is the principle of individuation and, at Oxford, to the teaching among others that Matter is passive and the human soul a single entity.

Defenders of Aquinas. But Aquinas did not lack defenders. He had left many disciples who rallied to his support, and the aged Albertus Magnus hastened to Paris to defend his dead pupil. The condemnations, which were of only local authority and extent, fell to the ground, and his influence steadily increased. His prestige is nowhere better seen than in Dante's *Divine Comedy,* which not only sings his praises personally but solves on Thomistic lines every theological and philosophical problem it raises. Also, Dante draws largely upon Aquinas for his famous plan set forth in *De Monarchia* of pacifying the clashes between Pope and Emperor, which followed inevitably from the growth of the Papacy as a secular and a political power. The temporal and the spiritual power, he maintains, should be clearly distinguished. There should be a universal Empire, just as there is a universal Church, each with its well-defined province. The Emperor should be the supreme civil authority, the Pope the supreme spiritual authority. Neither should trespass upon the domain of the other.

Under such an arrangement the two, instead of incessantly quarreling, will cooperate.

Raymond Lull and Godfrey of Fontaines. The Thomistic philosophy produced not only ardent followers and ardent antagonists. It also gave birth to attempts to mitigate its more extreme and forthright positions and to reconcile it with other currents of thought. We find, for example, Raymond Lull (1235-1315) endeavoring to elaborate the principles and the ideas common not only to philosophy and the Christian revelation, but to Christianity and Mohammedanism, and from these to deduce logically the truth of the Christian position. More directly related to Aquinas is Godfrey of Fontaines (d. 1303) who, while accepting Thomism in principle, differs from him in many important points. He denies, for example, the distinction between the essence, or character, of a thing and its existence. He returns to the doctrine of substantial forms and maintains that an object, instead of possessing only one substantial form, possesses as many as the characteristics predicated of it. He also accepts the further consequence, with which we are already familiar, that the principle of individuation lies neither in Matter, nor in an Idea, or Form, of the individual, but in the different mixtures of substantial forms.

Henry of Ghent. Henry of Ghent (d. 1293), while agreeing with Aquinas in many respects, also differed from him so sharply in others as to make him the forerunner of Thomas' most redoubtable critic, Duns Scotus. He could not agree that the eternity of the universe was even thinkable. Matter, he felt, is not the principle of individuation. Since essence involves existence—and here he shares Godfrey's opinion—it is of the nature of Form to be individualized. And since it is also of the nature of Form to be what it is and nothing else, its particular manifestations must display a similar self-identity and difference from one another. Most important, however, are Henry's rejection of Aquinas' theory of the supremacy of the intellect over the will and his enthronement of the will as supreme. Whereas the intellect is passive, the will is originally active and acts without any determination whatsoever. To be sure, it must be presented with an occasion for its exercise, such as is supplied by a desirable object, but its activity is not caused or determined by the presence of the object. Freedom is, therefore, not self-determination to the good but absolute indifference or indeterminism. This teaching, like Henry's theory of individuation, leads us directly to Duns Scotus.

Chapter XXIX

DUNS SCOTUS

I. LIFE

The most important and acute critic and opponent of Aquinas was Duns Scotus. Indeed in philosophical ability and acumen he was second, if not equal to Thomas himself, and ranks along with Roscellinus and Anselm and Abelard, as one of the great figures of the Scholastic period. He was born towards the end of Aquinas' life, it may be in the year of his death. Probably English, though perhaps Scotch or Irish, he entered the Franciscan order as a young man, studied and taught at Oxford, and went in 1304 to Paris. After spending four years there he left for Cologne where he died the same year (1308), cut off even more prematurely than Aquinas. Critical by nature, he fought with his contemporaries and criticized his predecessors, but always impersonally and often without naming them.

II. DISTRUST OF REASON

From the mystical tendencies of the Franciscan order Scotus gets perhaps a certain distrust of philosophy, which leads him, on the one hand, to put theology entirely out of the reach of philosophic speculation by restricting it to the supernatural and to revelation, which admit of no discussion, and, on the other, to cast positive doubt upon the possibility of rationally demonstrating even the existence of God, the providential direction of the world, and the immortality of the soul. Reasoning to be conclusive must, he thinks, be *a priori*—a logical deduction from first principles of their necessary consequences. Reasoning *a posteriori* from effects or consequences to what causes them is inconclusive and of secondary importance. Hence proofs of the existence of God, of his providential government of all things, and of immortality, arguing as they do from effects to causes, cannot have the validity assigned to them by Aquinas. These questions belong entirely to theology, and the only certain light we have with regard to them is cast by revelation.

At the same time, Scotus holds that there are philosophical reasons for believing that God exists. The idea of God, of a complete and perfect being such as Anselm talked of, is not self-contradictory. It is therefore an idea possible for us to entertain, and is entertained by us as an idea possible of enactment. In having the idea of a perfect being, we are unable to find reasons why such a being should not exist. Hence, if such a being does not exist, the idea is both possible and impossible—which is a self-contradiction. Therefore the non-existence of God is self-contradictory. It follows that God exists.

But if such a being exists, he must be infinite. He must be an infinite cause to produce an infinity of effects; infinite intelligence to contain an infinity of intelligible Forms; infinite good to explain the endless aspiration of the will towards a final good.

III. RELATION OF GOD'S WILL TO HIS INTELLECT

Still, the intelligible Forms compassed by the infinite intellect of God are not essential or primary elements of the divine essence. Neither are they models or archetypes which determine what the created universe shall be like. They are chosen and evoked in the same instant and by the same fiat of the divine will as brings the universe into being. The Forms or natures of things, then, are not prior to the things themselves. They are God's thoughts or knowledge of what he creates. His will that such should be his knowledge and that such should be the things he knows is a single act of volition.

It follows that, far from the divine reason or, for that matter, the divine goodness determining God's will and activities, as Aquinas had maintained, the divine intellect and benevolence are what they are because God chooses that they should be so. In other words, his will is not the expression of his character, his character is the expression of his will. So, too, his act of creating at one stroke the Form and the Matter of the universe and the individuals resulting from their union, is not motivated by any desire to realize what is already intelligible and good in his eyes, but by his simple "so be it." For nothing is good and intelligible in himself or in his creation except as he wills it. Finally, right and wrong have no absolute character apart from his volition. God does not will that things should be because it is right that they should be. They are right because he so wills them. He is governed by no moral law; the moral law—what shall be right and what shall be wrong—rests upon his "say-so."

But the divine will knows one master—the law of self-contradiction.

God does not will the impossible, as, for example, that squares shall be round. Nor can he will himself to be a mad intellect and to create a chaotic universe composed of incompatible Forms and things. Again he cannot without contradicting himself alter the commandment that his creatures shall have no other God but him. He cannot leave unpunished those who flout, and unrewarded those who love and obey, him.

IV. RELATION OF UNIVERSALS TO PARTICULARS

Since the Universal has no priority over the individuals that embody it but is created along with them, the universe comes into being as a system of Forms already enacted in their particular instances. In other words, it is of the very nature of the Form itself to be particularized. Tom, Dick, and Harry, then, are not due to an individuation by Matter or by a Form of man whose nature it is to be simply and purely a Universal. Nor are they the embodiments of Ideas of individuals existing in addition to the Form of man. They are due to the fact that it is inherent in human nature to be not only mankind but *men*. To be sure, to *think* of men is to think of mankind. For thought the individual always presents a universal aspect. But to *be* man, implies being *a* man. To possess *the* human form implies possessing *a* human Form, the Form of Tom or Dick or Harry. *Individuation, in short, is necessary to the complete expression of Form.*

As with man, so with all things. All essences and species are both universal and individual. As concepts which God's mind and our minds form of things they are Universals. In the things of which we form concepts, they are groups of individuals.

This implication of individual existence on the part of Forms and Universals is called by Scotus a "contraction" of essence. Tom, Dick, and Harry, for instance, are "contractions" of the human essence and Form. They concentrate and bring to a point the species and give to it the finishing touch and added perfection of their separate individualities.

"Quidditas" and "Haecceitas." But the distinction we make between individual "contractions" of the same essence cannot be reduced to the kind of distinction we make between things whose Forms and essences also are different. Tom, Dick, and Harry do not differ from one another in the same way as they differ from a litter of kittens. Nor do they differ from one another as different concepts the mind forms of Tom and Dick may differ. Their difference is of another sort, resting upon the fact that each individual "contraction" of a given

Form is necessarily *this* individual. Tom, for example, possesses not only *whatness* (*quidditas*) which makes him human, but *thisness* (*haecceitas*) which makes him Tom. But it is the nature of "this" to be "not that." Logically and formally, then, "this" is "not-that." Tom by virtue of being Tom is logically not Dick. In short, the difference between Tom and Dick is a difference not of *matter* (as with Aristotle and Aquinas) or of *essence* and nature (as in the case of Aquinas' angels) or of *individual forms* (Plotinus) or of mixture of *substantial forms* (Alexander of Hales and Bonaventure). It is of a new sort original with Scotus—the formal and logically necessary difference of any "this" from all "thats" or, in other words, of any one *individual "contraction"* of a given Form from all other contractions.

This kind of difference which Scotus calls "formal difference with respect to the thing" is not confined to the distinction between members of the same species. It is also the sort of difference that distinguishes God from his attributes, the absolutely indeterminate material substratum from its different formulations, the soul from her faculties. There, too, we have not merely difference of nature and form, such as exists between Universals, but the formal difference between this and that individual thing which distinguishes me from you. The universal application of this new "formalistic" principle is one of the distinguishing characteristics of Scotus, and is one of his chief claims to original thinking.

V. MATTER

Scotus also differs somewhat from Aquinas with regard to Matter. Thomas, following Aristotle, had regarded absolutely undetermined Matter as a limit, constantly approached as we strip away Form, but never reached. Everything *real,* he had said, is to some degree a formulation of Matter and an actualization of Potentiality. Scotus, though admitting that we never find pure Matter and potentiality devoid of all Form whatsoever, regards it as a real limit which God, if he chose to remove all Form, might create formless and void.

The first formulation of Matter takes the form of quantity, which is the basis of the multiple and extended character of the universe and of all locomotion and change. This prime Matter enters into all created beings, angels and human souls (who are many in number), as well as physical objects, and is one and the same in them all. Upon prime Matter rests a hierarchy of formulations in which each substance, constituted by the union of the Form of its species with Matter and individuated according to the principle of "formal distinction with respect to the thing," provides the possibilities for still another step upward and onward. Finally the familiar Aristotelian pyramid terminates in its apex, man, whose bodily form prepares Matter for the reception of the immortal soul, which the Scriptures tell us he possesses, but whose existence is incapable of rational demonstration.

The pyramidal structure of the universe as a whole is repeated throughout its parts. Each individual substance comes to a point in the individual Form distinguishing it formally "with respect to the thing" from all other individuals, and it rests upon an ever-widening base of the Forms and levels of being that make it possible. All these supporting Forms show the characteristic "double-face" of actualizing the potentialities of the next lower level and of thus providing new capacities for actualization in the next higher Form.

VI. THE SOUL

When, however, Scotus reaches the human soul, he denies the Aristotelian doctrine of triple composition and of the Matter-Form relation of the three parts. The soul is one and indivisible, and cannot be identified with any of her faculties or activities. Her difference from them is the final "difference with respect to the thing" that distinguishes one object from another. Nevertheless, while she is in the body her intellectual activity of knowledge is conditioned by the faculty of sensation, and its objects are limited to the Forms enacted in the sensible world.

The Augustinian theory of knowledge as a divine illumination from above Scotus rejects entirely. *All* our concepts, however abstract, universal and lofty they may be, have a sensible foundation. Still, the intellectual faculty is intrinsically capable of entertaining the Forms of all being whatsoever, not only sensible but supersensible. It is, then, by God's will that our reason is limited to the sensible universe for the object of its meditations, and by God's will its scope might conceivably be enlarged. For that matter, though God has limited the field of the intellect, he has endowed it with certain guiding concepts and judgments that it cannot but use in thinking about what it perceives. For example, although the intellect cannot prove the existence of God, it must judge that he exists.

VII. ETHICS

In the human soul, as in God, the will is prior to the intellect. Its choices are not determined by an imaged good. Indeed, we may, as Ovid remarked, see and approve the better course and yet deliberately choose and follow the worse. Our freedom is not freedom of self-determination, but freedom of power to choose undetermined by any motive, apart from what we are and apart from what we judge to be our good. The will must, it is true, have an incentive for its exercise in an object of desire recognized and known to be such, but what we shall find and recognize as desirable depends upon our will. We will to know this rather than that, and to consider this rather than that our good. Again the will is active and self-originating, whereas the intellect is receptive and gets its content from without. Finally, moral error, which lies in willing the wrong course, does not spring from misjudging what the right course is. Misjudging is itself a wrong choice of the idea or object to be contemplated or pursued, for which an absolutely undetermined decision of the will is alone to blame. We are as morally responsible for our thoughts as for our deeds, for what we want to do as for what we decide to do.

Chapter XXX

THE FALL OF MEDIEVAL
SCHOLASTICISM

I. GENERAL CHARACTERISTICS OF THE FOURTEENTH CENTURY

Rise of Individualism. The fourteenth century was an epoch of
unrest and transition in which the human mind, still rooted in the
medieval past, was becoming dissatisfied with the old order and was
reaching out towards something new. In art, the century saw the substitution of flamboyant for perpendicular Gothic, and of a more highly
individualized, personal and emotional sculpture for the calm, the
impersonality, the austerity, and the symbolic character of earlier
medieval work. In society it marked the breaking up of the corporate
spirit and of the over-arching and all-encompassing community of
thought, interest, and will, which not only had subordinated individuals to the two great Universals, the Church and the State, but
had so knit together successive generations that it was natural and
instinctive for each one to content itself with continuing or completing what its predecessors had begun, and with leaving what it had
started or continued to others to perfect. The individual was now for
the first time in many centuries beginning to feel self-sufficient and
self-assertive, and to center his work and his achievement about himself rather than about institutional and corporate centers of gravity.
This world, to be sure, was still overshadowed by the supernatural
order, and the individual still looked to a life beyond the grave for
the final fruition of his personal destiny. But we can see that it needed
but another step for him to focus his interests upon his life on earth,
and to demand and work towards self-fulfillment here and now. In
short, the fourteenth century had almost but not quite made the
Renaissance discovery of the capacities of the natural man and the
possibilities of life before death.

Emphasis on Practical Education. In the educational field emphasis
on quality was fast giving way to a passion for quantity. Universities
multiplied themselves with great rapidity, each one of which found
it paid to confer more and more degrees. Students frequented these

institutions for the purpose of getting, not an education, but a diploma, which they demanded in the shortest possible time, with the least amount of work, and with their eyes on the ecclesiastical job to which the master's degree in theology was a necessary preliminary. Naturally they were particularly irked at having to take the course in liberal arts, up to that time a requisite for specialization in theology. The pressure they brought to bear succeeded in shortening the period devoted to a liberal education and in enabling them to begin their professional work without sufficient general preparation and background. Even the University of Paris succumbed to these influences and became a degree factory. The result was the prevalence of superficiality, ignorance, lack of culture, absence of vision, and impatience with sound learning among university graduates.

General Situation. Politically speaking, the century was mediocre, save for the sudden sweep of the Black Death that decimated the population of western Europe. Everyone was at war with everyone else. But there were few great leaders and no spectacular and map-rending changes. Scotland brought to a final decision her long wars of self-preservation from the English, and England also lost all her French possessions save Bordeaux and Bayonne and Calais. The Swiss confederated and became, if not an independent nation, at least an autonomous portion of the Empire, and the Hanseatic League came into being. France lost Flanders and plunged into her Hundred Years' War with England, with its varying fortunes. And through internal discontent and insurrection both countries moved a step further towards the freedom of the individual. Meantime the Popes were in "Babylonish Captivity" at Avignon.

The effects of this general let-down were disastrous even in the higher circles of learning. Scholastically, it was a second-rate age, productive of little erudition and original constructive philosophic thinking. Its original thinking spent itself not in conceiving new systems but in attacking those that existed. The most Scholastic philosophy could do was to help demolish itself by its criticisms of both Aquinas and Scotus, while the persistence of Averrhoist pantheistic heresies and of mysticism and the increasing interest in the natural sciences completed its destruction. But the work of destruction produced two great mystics and great advances both in the formulation of scientific method and in the investigation and understanding of the physical universe. The critical and scientific achievements of the epoch were brilliant.

II. NOMINALISM

Extension of Roscellinus' View of Universals. At the end of the eleventh century, we may remember, Roscellinus had attacked the doctrine that Universals and Forms have a real existence independent of the minds that entertain and the objects that enact them. Nay more, he maintained, they stand for nothing real in the objects themselves. Essentially individuals are unique, and the resemblances they bear to one another are accidental and superficial, and do not indicate the possession of a common nature. General concepts, then, entertained by the mind, are purely mental entities to which nothing in the external world corresponds.

By some historians of philosophy, as we saw, the doctrine of Roscellinus has been called Nominalism, but others, because Roscellinus apparently believed that the mind can abstract really *general* ideas from particular objects and entertain really *universal* concepts, have felt that the term should not be applied to him. Now, however, a truly *"nominalistic"* theory of the nature of thought and knowledge appeared upon the scene, which did away with any distinction between *conception* and *perception,* and reduced so-called abstract and universal ideas to terms of sensory experience. At the hands of this new teaching Universals as such simply vanished from human thinking as well as from every other form of existence. This new doctrine, totally destructive of Universals, is known as *Terminism.*

Durand and Aureoli. Its great exponent is William of Occam, but his way was prepared by Durand of Saint Pourçain, a Dominican, and Peter Aureoli, a Franciscan, both of whom taught in the first quarter of the century. Durand started as a Thomist, Peter as a Scotist, but their similar temperaments and the similar difficulties they found in their respective masters led them to almost identical conclusions.

Both were empirically and skeptically minded, and were distrustful of entities that they could not observe. Both, moreover, were free-thinking, not indeed to the extent of rejecting the supremacy of revelation over reason, but sufficiently so to assert the supremacy of reason over the purely human authority of the Fathers of the Church, and to demand complete freedom of thought in criticizing their teaching.

This freedom they proceeded to exercise. Plato and Aristotle, the Church Fathers, and the Scholastics, might, for all they cared, preach the reality of Universals and Forms. The fact remained that the only

reality with which we had any acquaintance was individual and concrete. We observe and deal with particular men and horses and chairs,
never with abstract human or equine nature or chairness, either apart
from individuals or in them. Universals, genera, species, substantial
forms and the like exist only in the mind. But in the mind they exist
only as a kind of composite and confused image produced by the
overlapping of individual percepts, which records and merges the
accidental resemblances in a blurred and vague, so-called "common
concept." The more general the concept, the less specific the resemblances to which it is sensitive and hence the more indeterminate and
meaningless its content and its outlines.

The same is true of so-called "sensible species" like the color red.
We never see red, we see red objects. "Red" is just as much a composite image as "mankind" or "beauty." Only, since it simply records
successive impressions of single points of resemblance, it is more
clearly defined than vaguer images, like "being" or "matter" or "form."

A New Theory of Knowledge. If there are no such things as Universals, obviously it cannot be the function of the intellect to abstract
them from the external world. Still, the problem of knowledge remains. If the intellectual processes of abstraction and classification and
reduction to least common denominators, by which we discover, as
we say, the natures of things and the laws governing their behavior,
really lead us further away from the truth, what is knowledge and
how can it be gained?

Peter Aureoli had his answer. The composite image called a concept is after all a representation of *things*. We do not perceive sensations, we do not think about perceptions. We perceive and think about
the outer world, and our composite and long-range images are as immediately records of objective individual reality as our close-range
ones. *Universals, in other words, are composite and superimposed
sensations.* Between thought and sense-perception there is no difference of kind, but merely a difference of the degree of accuracy with
which we observe the individual. What has heretofore been called
knowledge leads us away from reality into pale abstractions and dulls
and blurs observation instead of sharpening it. What we need is a
method of knowledge that will rid itself of Forms and Universals,
will concentrate upon the individual, and will find means of sharpening and giving more depth and precision to our observation of its
being. Progress towards discovering such a method was made by
William of Occam.

III. OCCAM

Philosophy as Inference from Observed Data. Occam, an English-man, was born on the threshold of the fourteenth century and died in 1350. He studied at Oxford, where he was influenced by the rapidly rising interest in science and mathematics and in their bearing upon philosophical problems. He shares the empirical tendencies of Durand and Peter Aureoli, and demands that philosophy shall concern itself with the observable and with inferences rigorously drawn from and confined to the observable. All true propositions either state or treat of what is self-evident, or are inferred from it and verified by it. We may, to be sure, make true propositions involving the relations between abstract ideas, as, for example, "God is good." But the truth of that proposition no more indicates that God exists than the truth of the proposition "the chimera has three heads" indicates that the chimera exists. The only true propositions stating the *existence* of their terms are those dealing with sensible experience or, as Occam calls it, with intuition.

It follows that we cannot explain the sensible world by supersensible entities like Forms or even God. For to establish the relation of cause and effect, the cause must be no less perceived than what follows from it. One sensible object can, then, so far as philosophy is concerned, be caused only by another sensible object. Moreover, since experience presents us only with particular things and never with Universals and Forms, always with men and never with mankind, the individual alone can be asserted to be real.

"Occam's Razor." Thus armed, Occam slashes at Aquinas and Scotus with what is known in the history of philosophy as *Occam's razor*. *Entities are not to be multiplied except as may be necessary.* Away, he cries, with universals, essences, substantial forms, and the like as principles of explanation and as metaphysical realities. Away, too, with the philosophies founded upon the assumption of their existence. Universals exist only in the mind as the last or family names of things, born of our habit of dealing with particulars *en masse* and of per-ceiving their superficial resemblances before distinguishing their in-dividualities and calling them by the first names that designate what is real and ultimate in them. Standing as they do for any one of a number of individuals and for no one in particular, general terms express a confused "concept" of any particular object to which they are applied. Indeed the two names, general and particular, do not designate different kinds of being, as the formalists maintain. They designate merely two aspects, one confused and "general," the other distinct and particular, of the same individual.

For example, the proposition "Tom is a man" simply states that an object, taken at a distance and confusedly to be something that might be either Tom, Dick, or Harry, turns out on closer inspection to be something that can only be Tom. Predicating the "man" of him no more adds anything to him that he did not already possess, or enlarges our knowledge of his real self, than does writing his family name Brown after Tom. As Tom Brown he is no more and no less of a person than he is as Tom, but Brown is the less intimate and revealing of the two terms and indicates less acquaintance with him personally.

Convenience of Universal Names. Nevertheless, "universal terms" have their uses. They are, to be sure, individual names and sounds, but they are names that may indicate and be substituted for indefinite numbers of individuals. They deliver the mind from the necessity of enumerating all the members of a group when referring to them *en masse.* For example, if I wish to indicate all the people in a city I do not have to read through the directory out loud. I can simply make the sound and utter the word "population."

Philosophically, too, the fact that we have "general" terms, or words that can be used to indicate indifferently large numbers of individuals, saves us a lot of bother. It makes it quite as unnecessary for the mind to entertain a mysterious concept or universal called "mankind" in order to grasp and deal with individual men, as it does for individual men to enact a mysterious form or essence of human nature in order to be human beings. Neither the mind nor the external world requires such supersensible instruments. All that exists in external reality is individual objects. All that exists in the mind is individual impressions of these objects more or less clearly distinguished from one another. All that the mind needs is two sets of names with which to indicate whether its experience of an individual is general and confused or particularized and distinct. In short, Universals of the Platonic-Aristotelian type are just so much metaphysical junk.

Revelation the Basis for Belief in God and the Soul. For all his destructiveness and his opposition to Aquinas and Scotus, Occam remained in his own opinion a good churchman. But he paid his price. Since we have no direct experience of the existence of God, or of one God rather than many, or of the divine attributes, or of the immortality of the soul, or of a first cause, or of a prime mover, or of the finitude or the infinity of the universe in time and space, we can have no certain knowledge regarding them save that vouchsafed by revelation. For that matter, we have nothing but the authority of the Scriptures for the very existence of the soul. We experience, or "intuit," to be sure, things like sensations, emotions, pleasures, pains, desires, volitions, and processes of thinking, but we do not "intuit" any immaterial substance, any thinking or willing entity, behind them. The only possible *philosophical* attitude towards all these questions must be noncommittal and skeptical, and certainly must never go beyond assertions of seeming probability or improbability.

So, too, if it were not for revelation, we should be entirely in the dark with respect to the existence and nature of moral principles. We can no more reason out what is right and what is wrong than we can reason out what the divine nature is like. In the one case as in the other, the use of reason is of no avail. We must simply bow before the moral law as an expression of God's will. Good is good, evil is evil, because God wills them to be so.

Nor can we assert that the divine decrees express an immutable distinction between good and evil imbedded in the divine nature. Occam not only agrees with Scotus that all so-called "principles" are the unmotivated, arbitrary, and reversible wishes of the deity, but he goes beyond him in maintaining that God can flout even the law of self-contradiction and make it our duty to disobey the first two commandments and to hate the Lord our God with all our heart and all our soul and all our mind, and turn to other gods than him.

Bradwardine and Mirecourt. A more extreme exaltation of the divine will, even to the point of annihilating human freedom, was undertaken by Thomas Bradwardine (b. 1290, d. 1349), professor at Merton College, Oxford, and later Archbishop of Canterbury. The divine will not only determines what God shall be and do; it determines also what man shall choose, when he is, as we say, acting freely. To be compelled by God is perfect freedom. To be motivated by anything except the divine will, as, for example, the pressure of external circumstances, the solicitations of the senses, or even the representations of intelligence and reason, is to will under duress.

Bradwardine apparently saved the moral responsibility of the individual in these circumstances by attributing to him the power to listen or not to listen, as the case might be, to the voices of the world, the senses, and the intelligence, and to obey or not to obey the spontaneous, or divinely directed, welling up of pure, unadulterated volition within him. Another theologian, John of Mirecourt, scorned any such reservations. We, he pointed out, have no say in the matter at all. We do not will, God wills in and through us. Therefore it is not we who sin, but God who sins in and through us. Hence sinning is not sinful.

IV. BURIDAN AND NICHOLAS OF AUTRECOURT

Buridan and His Ass. In contrast to those views, however, John Buridan (b. about 1300, d. about 1358), professor at the University of Paris, maintained that the will is subservient to the intellect and must necessarily choose what seems the better course of action. To illustrate his point, or to illustrate what was considered by his opponents its absurdity, either he or they invented the famous story of the ass that starved to death when placed midway between two equally attractive bales of hay. Buridan, however, did his best to extricate human beings from this situation by endowing the human will with the power of suspension of judgment till further deliberation had worked out a clearer and more reasoned picture of the truly better course. Furthermore, since deliberation never ends in a dead center, but always shows one alternative to be preferable, man is in no practical danger of becoming involved in the donkey's predicament.

Autrecourt's Attack on the Concepts of Substance and Causation. Of all the disciples that Occam's theories rallied to his banner, perhaps the most eminent was Nicholas of Autrecourt (d. about 1350), who also was a professor at Paris. He did his best to explode the two fundamental concepts of *substance* and of *cause and effect,* by arguing that both can be denied without self-contradiction. The seeming *production* of one event by another will not hold logical water. There is nothing in a given event—which is simply what it is—to necessitate an antecedent from which it springs or a consequence flowing from it. Hence there is no necessary link between any two events, and therefore no demonstrable *causation* of the one by the other. In that case, however, the concept of *substance* also goes by the board, since we mean by substance something that gives rise to the qualities it displays. For example, the substance of the apple is regarded as the *reason,* or *cause,* for its color, shape, taste, etc. But if no such connection is logically necessary, we cannot with any certainty argue from accidents and qualities to the existence of a substance underlying them.

All in all there is no more to *cause* and *substance* than what we directly experience. We experience the repetition of certain sequences, and on that basis are entitled to expect, or, in other words, to consider it probable, that the occurrence of certain events will be followed by the occurrence of certain others. So, too, in the case of substances, we experience our own souls and what we call external objects. These we may call substances, if we like, remembering always that we have no warrant for asserting the necessary existence of anything underlying and backing our experiences.

It follows that there is no necessity of invoking God as a first cause and no possibility of proving his existence by so doing. Nor can we prove it from the necessity of a most perfect being, since so-called degrees of perfection are, logically speaking, simple differences of kind, and in the distinction or difference of "this" from "not-this" there is no more or less. A thing is simply "this" or "that." All things, then, being equally existent and equally themselves and nothing else, are equally perfect. Hence the existence of God, like that of an external world, and of substance, and causality, remains an undemonstrable proposition.

Both Autrecourt and Buridan have other interests and other teachings, which place them, one foot at least, in the rising tide of interest and progress in the natural sciences that in the fourteenth century was already seriously undermining the Scholastic edifice. We shall have occasion to return to them when we take up the history of this movement.

V. THE MYSTICS AND THE AVERRHOISTS

We have now to note briefly cross-rips set up by the persistence of currents of thought that flowed almost equally at odds both with the orthodox Aristotelianism of the Church and with the attacks directed by the new science against Aristotle in general. The followers of Averrhoes' interpretation of Aristotle had never been silenced, and mysticism, with its ever-attendant leanings toward Neo-Platonism and pantheism, had more than held its own. The fourteenth century brought them into the open. Indeed, its opening was marked by an outburst of pantheistic mysticism in Germany, which cannot but remind us of Scotus Eriugena.

Meister Eckhart. Meister Eckhart, the originator of this mystical revival, was born near Gotha in 1260. After joining the Dominican Order, he took his degree in theology at Paris in 1302, and taught at Cologne till his death in 1327. His reaction to Aristotle and to Thomism was as violently negative in its way as that of Occam and his followers, and he turned back to Neo-Platonism and to Eriugena and Dionysius the Areopagite for his inspiration.

God, Eckhart insisted, is ineffable and indescribable in any of the terms at the command of the human mind. In him all things live and move and have their being. Out of his unknowable and infinite depths arise the Word, or Son, in which the archetypes of all created things are contained, and the Holy Ghost, and finally the created universe. This outgoing movement in the divine life is supplemented, as with Eriugena, by a return of God to himself, in which the human soul is the chief participant. United to him more intimately and profoundly than any other creature, her salvation lies in loosing herself from all other bonds and in losing herself in him. She must divest herself of all worldly attachments, all loves, all desires, save the desire for God alone. Her goal lies higher than virtue, higher than good works, higher than religious observances, higher than anything given in prayer or sacrament. She must become the absolutely poor—stripped even of herself. Then, and then only, having surrendered everything that separates her from God, she and the God in her will return to their source and be swallowed up in its unspeakable bliss and glory.

A movement to have Eckhart formally condemned by the Church was already on foot before his death, and shortly afterwards his views were proscribed. It is perhaps for this reason that other mystics of the time, like Tauler (1300-1361), the Admirable Ruysbroeck (1293-1381) and Suso (1300-1365) are less daring in their doctrine and more eager to avoid the reproach of pantheism.

Nicholas of Cusa. At the beginning of the next century Germany produced another mystic as daring as Eckhart and no less open to the charge of pantheism, Nicholas of Cusa, cardinal and bishop of Brixen. Cusa is also noteworthy for his interest in the natural sciences, for his advocacy of the view that the earth revolved upon its axis, for his revival of atomism, and for his prevision of the relativity of motion. He was moreover greatly influenced by the skeptical spirit of the times and, indeed, founded his mystical doctrine on a despair of reason.

The nature of God is, he said, unknowable, since in him all contradictions are combined and all essences are merged. No concept, no term, no essence that we entertain and use, can possibly cover or describe his nature. This recognition of the unknowableness of God, this "learned ignorance," is the beginning of wisdom. All that we can ever reach or touch by ordinary experience is the universe of created things and of matter with its diverse forms in which the divine nature is unfolded. Were it not, therefore, for mystical intuition which transcends reason, we could never reach the ineffable reality underlying the "theophany," or manifestation of the divine being in the unfolded world.

Man is the being in which the world-process culminates, the nearest return to God that it can effect. He is possessed of an immortal soul endowed not only with reason, but with the gift of intuition by the exercise of which she overcomes and passes beyond all the insoluble contradictions in which reason ends, and is united and absorbed in God.

Cusa, as we shall presently see, links the last mystics of the medieval epoch with the first great mystic of the Renaissance, Giordano Bruno.

John of Jandun. We pass now to the Averrhoists. Their attack both upon the anti-Aristotelians and upon what seemed to them, not without reason, the distortion of Aristotle by Aquinas, was carried on at Paris by John of Jandun. He does little but repeat the already familiar theses of the eternity of the world, the impersonality of the active intellect, and the mortality of all that is personal and individual in the soul. These views, combined with his political hostility to the Papacy, got him into difficulties, and he was forced to fly from Paris and take refuge at the court of Louis of Bavaria. His doctrines, however, were enthusiastically received at the University of Padua, which remained the great center of Averrhoism well into the Renaissance.

VI. THE RE-AWAKENING OF THE SCIENTIFIC MOOD AND INTEREST

We turn, at last, to the most formidable opponent with which Scholasticism had to contend—the re-awakening in Europe of Aristotle's scientific mood and interests, and the turning of them against his teachings and authority, not only in the realm of metaphysics, but of science itself. The Arabs, as we have already noted, had fallen heir to his interest in the natural sciences, though they had not challenged his conclusions. It was acquaintance with Aristotle's scientific work that fostered, if it did not actually beget, the nascent scientific curiosity already astir in Christendom in the early part of the thirteenth century.

Hence it is, perhaps, not a matter of chance that what we may call the first modern physics, founded on observation and formulated in mathematical terms, was proposed by Grosseteste with whom we are already acquainted as one of the first translators of Aristotle from the original Greek and one of the first imbibers of Neo-Platonic and Arabian teaching from its original sources. His theory, in brief, was that all matter and extension, including animate as well as inanimate bodies, may be reduced to terms of light radiating from a central point, and that all motion and process are governed by such geo-metrical necessities as a straight line being the shortest distance be-tween two points, the sphere being the primary form of radiation about a fixed point, and the most effective exertion of force being that exercised by the apex of a pyramid. We have here, it will be noticed, not only an analysis of qualitative difference and change into terms of quantity and movement in space, but implicitly at least, a substitu-tion of mathematical necessity for purposes and final causes as the explanation of the nature and behavior of physical phenomena, in-cluding living bodies.

VII. ROGER BACON

Revolutionary Views of Philosophy and Theology. The great prophet, however, of modern science, who broke directly and em-phatically with the authority of Aristotle, was Roger Bacon, a pupil of Grosseteste's, whose long life spanned almost the entire thirteenth century. His views were so revolutionary that, though he was a mem-ber of the Franciscan order and took the precaution of writing much in cipher, he was under suspicion of heresy and harassed by the Church throughout his whole career. Indeed, he spent fourteen years in prison, and was saved from a worse fate only by his sharp distinction between the light thrown by science and that vouchsafed by revelation, and by his devout adherence to Catholic doctrine so far as things super-natural were concerned.

Philosophy, too, he was careful to subordinate to theology. She was the forerunner of revelation in pre-Christian times and its handmaid and interpreter since the Incarnation. But this service is not servitude, since revelation and reason are in accord. Philosophy, like revelation, is a divine illumination of the mind, a ray of the Augustinian inner light. Indeed, it is the working within us of the active intellect, which Bacon regards as introduced into the soul from without, and as the presence in us of God himself.

To agree that the function of science and philosophy is to confirm the findings of theology does not, however, force us to agree that the scientific and philosophic methods and theories in vogue, as, for example, Aristotle's, are necessarily the correct ones. Nor does the supremacy of theology place her own methods and results beyond criticism. For that matter, theology is a grievous sinner. Not only does she trespass upon subjects that do not concern her, but she tres-passes blindly, relying upon the less important sciences and ignorant even of them. Again, within her own province she falls back upon the authority of glosses and interpretations rather than of the Scriptures themselves, and, when she does turn to them, she contents herself with the bad Latin translation of the Vulgate, too lazy and too ignorant to study them in the original tongues.

Theology must, then, reform herself by learning the languages in which her documents are written, and by founding her conclusions upon first-hand rather than second-hand knowledge of revelation. Philosophy is in the same fix. She is ignorant of her own history. Before she can talk intelligently of Plato and Aristotle, the Neo-Platonists, and the Jewish and Arabian philosophers, she must read them as they wrote, in Greek and Hebrew, Chaldee, and Arabic, and not in translations, and incorrect translations at that.

The Necessity of Squaring Philosophy with "Experience." But direct, untranslated acquaintance with philosophic and theological sources is only the first step. Much knowledge, to be sure, is gained by a study of the true history of theology and philosophy. But nothing could be more stultifying than blindly to accept the authority of the ancient philosophers and the Fathers of the Church, however correctly understood, before weighing their claims in the balance of intelligence and *reason*. History is still in progress. Aristotle, for example, may have been the last word in human knowledge and reason in his day, but that does not make him the last word for all future time. To regard him as such, to bow before him after the fashion of Hales and Albertus Magnus and Aquinas, is to doom the world to perpetual ignorance. For that matter, Hales' knowledge of Aristotle is so scanty that he does not understand what he is accepting as gospel truth, and Albertus and Thomas read their Aristotle with no sense of his historical context and no acquaintance with the progress of science since his day. It never occurs to them to check his observations and statements with observations of their own. It never occurs to them that his philosophy must be squared with *experience* before it can be accepted as authoritative.

Furthermore, their ignorance is colossal of the new instruments that knowledge now has at its command, notably the application of mathematics and the discovery that the passive observation of nature can be supplemented by deliberate *experiment*. On the importance of experiment Bacon cannot too strongly insist. It reveals truths that neither reasoning nor observation could ever discover of themselves. It is the only means of verifying scientific hypotheses in any field. It enables us to reconstruct the past and to calculate what will happen in the future. All in all, then, unless reasoning is founded on up-to-date observation amplified by experiment, and employs the mathematical method in its operations, the mind, even be it the intellect of an Aristotle, can get us nowhere.

Father of the Experimental Method. Such was Bacon's vision, recorded in his *Opus Majus,* his *Opus Minus,* his *Opus Tertium,* and the *Liber Sex Scientiarum.* Unfortunately we have only a part of the *Opus Minus* and the *Opus Tertium* and fragments of the *Liber,* so that our knowledge of this vision in its completeness is far from adequate. It was not, indeed, a sudden or a clean break with the past. The discontent it voiced with things as they stood was already in the air. Curiosity regarding nature was everywhere abroad. The insistence that a knowledge of mathematics is an indispensable condition to understanding the universe had already been suggested by Grosseteste. But Bacon's comprehension of the possibilities of mathematics and of its fundamental role, not only in science but in philosophy, goes far beyond Grosseteste's position. His appeal to *experience* as the origin and justification of all philosophy and science, and as the final court before which their claims to validity must be tried, is novel. And his discovery that experience can be deliberately enlarged and deepened by *experiment* is original with him. He is the first thinker in recorded history to use the phrase "experimental science," and may be regarded as the father of the experimental method.

Father of Invention. In a sense, too, we may regard him as the father of European *invention.* To be sure, the discoveries attributed to him, as, for example, the telescope, the burning glass, spectacles, and gunpowder [1] are doubtful, and in any case were not followed through. But the *spirit* of invention was there. In the Middle Ages, it is fair to say, man had submitted to nature as he found her. It had not occurred to him that he could control her and, by harnessing her to his uses, improve his natural lot. Or when the possibility of such control did enter his mind, it appeared as magic, and all attempts to actualize it were promptly condemned by the Church as an invocation of Satan's aid against God's purposes and as the practice of a black art. But now the discovery that nature could be manipulated at will by experiment and thus made subservient to human ends was sure to be followed by the discovery that her forces could be mastered and her ways altered by man to suit his preferences. This awakened sense of power over nature

[1] Gunpowder and many other things commonly regarded as western invention tions were in use in China before Europe "invented" them

went hand in hand with the sense of the self-sufficiency and dignity of the natural man, which was one of the great characteristics of the Renaissance. Bacon shares this feeling, and in this, as in other ways, his face is turned towards the dawn of a new day.

VIII. THE PROGRESS OF SCIENCE

Occam's View of Motion. We can easily understand how great an impetus the scientific movement must have received from the teachings of Occam, and, conversely, how readily his followers must have come under its influence. So we shall not be surprised to find both Buridan and Nicholas of Autrecourt caught in and contributing to its current. Occam himself had been interested in natural phenomena, and part of his criticism of Aristotle had been devoted to the latter's contention that the existence and nature of movement demands the intervention and guidance of external causes. To this doctrine he opposed the theory that bodies simply *are* in motion of themselves and that it is the nature of motion to continue indefinitely. Given, then, the mere fact of motion, no external cause is needed to keep bodies moving or to determine their trajectories.

Buridan's View of Motion. Buridan carries the analysis of motion still further, concerning himself particularly with the movement imparted by one body to another, with the observed tendency of bodies so moved to lose their motion and come to rest, and with the acceleration of falling bodies. These phenomena he explained by trying to establish a relation between the persistence of movement and the mass and velocity of the moving object, and by noting the retarding influence of weight, and of the friction of the medium through which the body is passing upon the initial impetus with which the body is moved. Applying his conclusions to astronomy, he pointed out that the heavenly spheres stood in no need of unmoved movers to keep them moving. Free as they were from the brakes of friction and weight, a single, initial act by God was enough to set them whirling world without end.

Autrecourt's View of Physics and Immortality. Nicholas of Autrecourt dealt more particularly with the nature of the world-stuff, and supplemented his rejection of causality and substance as conceived by Aristotle with a frank acceptance of the Democritean and Epicurean atomism, hitherto anathema to the Church. All change, he maintains, may be reduced to change of spatial position. Growth and alteration are not, as Aristotle taught, due to the coming and going of different

Forms in an underlying substratum. They are due to the spatial move-ment and the shifting spatial arrangements of the atoms of which bodies are composed. It is their coming together that "forms" a body, their varying relations that alter it, their dispersion that destroys it. Incidentally, his teaching that light is material and corpuscular and is transmitted, not instantaneously, but at a certain speed, was quite at variance with the accepted doctrine of the day and anticipatory of modern science.

His views on immortality were equally defiant of ecclesiastical con-vention. The soul, or rather the two "spirits," intellectual and sensible, of which she is composed, do indeed survive death. But they get their moral characters from the atomic arrangements in the bodies with which they have been associated. After death they will be rewarded or punished, as the case may be, by being united with new aggrega-tions of atoms congenial to their good or evil tendencies and con-ducive to their salvation or damnation. This theory Autrecourt ad-vances tentatively. It is, he remarks, as reasonable as any other theory of immortality heretofore advanced, and may be held provisionally till something better turns up. The Church considered these views a "foxy" subterfuge and condemned them accordingly.

Albert of Saxony's Study of Physics. Another of these ecclesiastical *enfants terribles,* wise beyond their years, that the fourteenth century produced is Albert of Saxony (d. 1390), rector of the Universities of Paris and Vienna and bishop of Halberstadt. Albert carried on Buridan's work by further analysis of the nature of weight and of the space-time aspects of velocity. Every object, irrespective of its shape, possesses, in addition to its geometrical center, a point within it to-wards which its bulk tends to press and about which therefore it tends to cohere. Hence all things on earth tend to press towards the earth's center of gravity and to unite their centers with its. They also resist every effort to separate them from that center, and, as soon as the resistance is overcome, immediately return towards it. In this way we explain weight and the habit bodies have of falling. So far as the problem of velocity is concerned, Albert worked out its proportional relation to the space traversed by the body, but hesitated with respect to the time equation.

Mathematics of Nicholas Oresmus. Greater than any of his prede-cessors was Nicholas Oresmus, bishop of Lisieux (d. 1382). To him we owe the beginnings of analytical geometry and the first plottings of curves and graphs. Taking up the unfinished work of Albert of Saxony, he established the space-time ratio in motion, formulated the movement of falling bodies with mathematical exactitude, and equated uniform acceleration with uniform speed. He also argued for the view, now becoming more general, that the earth turns upon its axis, and that the heaven of fixed stars is stationary.

From the formidable array of the opponents of Thomism, and for that matter of Scotism, we must not conclude that these systems collapsed or even tottered under the battering they received. Both Aquinas and Duns Scotus had able supporters, who gave almost as much punishment as they took in the free-for-all theological scrimmage, and Thomism, far from being knocked over the ropes, was, at the end of the fourteenth century, still the fittest of all the fighters in the ring.

IX. GENERAL ACHIEVEMENTS OF THE FOURTEENTH CENTURY

The year 1453, the year in which Constantinople fell into the hands of the Mohammedans, is conventionally regarded as the date that announces the end of the Middle or "Dark" Ages and the beginning of the Renaissance. But we can now see that any such sharp line of demarcation between the two epochs is artificial, and that the Middle Ages were not dark but abounded in intellectual activity. Nor, even granting their darkness, did the night disappear and the new day dawn with tropic suddenness.

For the fourteenth century is as much a prologue to the Renaissance as it is an epilogue to medieval thought. It was astir with the naturalism, scientific, moral and philosophical, that was to color and direct the thinking of the next two centuries. It was groping towards the great discoveries in astronomy and physics which were so soon to be made and which were so profoundly to influence the new speculation. It had prepared their advent and their acceptance by breaking in large measure the shackles of the past. It had sown the seeds of doubt respecting the necessity of reckoning with anything supernatural in the conduct and the salvation of human life. It had asserted the power of the unaided human reason to work out satisfactory solutions of the manifold problems with which humanity was confronted. It had continued and emphasized the thirteenth century's ecclesiastical interest in Greek and Arabic and Hebrew, and had thus prepared the way for the recovery of the secular treasures of antiquity and for the devotion they were so soon to inspire throughout the western world. In the voyages of Marco Polo it had embarked upon the explorations that not only radically altered man's conception of the face of the earth and the westerner's illusion of the uniqueness and primacy of his particular civilization, but, in conjunction with the new astronomy, necessitated a reweighing of the place and importance hitherto assigned to humanity in the universe. We enter, then, the Renaissance, not with our faces, but our backs turned towards the rising sun of the modern world.

MODERN PHILOSOPHY

Chapter I

THE RENAISSANCE

I. THE RENAISSANCE SPIRIT

In the introduction to the *Discourse on Method* Descartes remarks that, after studying in the school of book-learning, he betook himself, for further instruction, to knowledge of himself and of the great book of the world. In so doing he was but following the example set him by the Renaissance. In the latter part of the fifteenth and in the sixteenth century the West, we might say, left the medieval home in which it had been brought up and began to study at the new university of human life opened by the extraordinary changes in orientation that the hundred and fifty years following the fall of Constantinople effected in man's outlook on himself and on the universe.

Enlargement of Spatial and Temporal Perspectives. During this period western Europe recovered and re-read in the original almost all the Greek and Roman literature, philosophy, and historical and scientific treatises of which we are possessed today. The voyages and geographical explorations and discoveries of the epoch acquainted it with the shape and a large part of the map of the world. The scientific interest in the operations of nature, awakened in the fourteenth century, was by now thoroughly aroused, and was beginning its startling revolution, particularly in the field of astronomy, of man's concept of the universe and of his position in it. And the vistas disclosed by these vastly enlarged horizons of space and time invited and impelled him to one of the greatest outbursts of reflective and creative activity that has ever occurred in the history of mankind.

Humanism and the Renaissance. Incidentally to the rediscovery, exercise, and enjoyment of its powers, the human mind was incited to explore and meditate upon itself. These explorations and meditations were guided and inspired in large part by the newly acquired vision of the life of antiquity. The Greeks and the Romans were now seen to have lived for many centuries a good and happy life, and to have built up an enduring and magnificent civilization, without the aid of revelation and supernatural sanctions and of faith in a privileged origin and destiny for man. Actuated by this disclosure of Graeco-Roman culture and by the general excitement of the times, man's interest and attention tended to shift from the question of what might become of him after death to that of what he might become and accomplish in his present life on earth by the exercise of his native talents.

Thus it was that western Europe awoke to the possibilities latent in the natural man, and that the individual became acutely self-conscious and engrossed with his own particular temperament and capacities and with the problem and the means of expressing them to the utmost. For this reason the epoch is known as the Renaissance, or period of re-birth, and its preoccupation with the development of human self-realization here and now, in this world, within the limits set by birth and death, has given to its spirit the name of *Humanism.*

II. THE RISE AND SPREAD OF HUMANISM

The Spread of Humanism. The western world was fortunate in having at the time rulers who were captivated by the new outlook and made their courts centers for its diffusion. First to be caught up by it were the "culture-mad" despots of the Italian cities, the Medici at Florence, the Gonzaga at Mantua, the d'Este at Ferrara, the Sforza at Milan, Frederick of Urbino, Alfonso of Naples, and Popes like Leo X at Rome.

From Italy the movement spread to France under the patronage of Francis I, where it produced the sculptor Jean Goujon, the architecture of the newer French châteaux and of the Louvre in Paris, the poetry of Ronsard and the prose of Rabelais. It spread to England, thanks to the interest of Henry VII and Humphrey, Duke of Gloucester, and to the migrations from Oxford to Italian centers of learning. Brought back to the universities, its spirit invaded once more the court, partly through the mediation of Sir Thomas More, the author of *Utopia,* and seized upon the nobility. And insensibly it merged into the *floreat* of the Elizabethan Age.

German scholars returned from Italy imbued with the Renaissance. The Emperor Maximilian, Frederick the Wise of Saxony, and the prince cardinal Albert of Mainz, among others, felt its contagion. Strasbourg, Nuremberg, Augsburg became centers of learning. The Rhenish and Danubian academies at Heidelberg and Vienna were instituted. German art was stimulated, though not sensibly modified, by Italian influence. In religion and ethics the movements that culminated in the Protestant Reformation were reinforced and accelerated.

Spain for all her intense Catholicism could not escape the spirit of the times. It impregnated her with Loyola, the militant founder of the Jesuits and one of the great figures of the "Counter-Reformation" within the Church. It excited Spanish architecture and painting, resulting in the cathedral at Granada, the town hall at Seville, and the work of El Greco and later of Velasquez. It assumed literary form in the dramas of Lope de Vega and Calderón, the *Don Quixote* of Cervantes, and, across the Portuguese border, in the *Lusiadas* of Camoens.

The Central Part Played by Florence. Of this ever-spreading light Florence was the central sun. Already in Dante she had consciously asserted the worth of modern achievement and measured it on equal terms with that of antiquity. Dante dares what no one in the centuries immediately preceding him would have dared—to rank himself as a poet with Homer and Virgil. In Petrarch and Boccaccio, also, Florence had begun in the fourteenth century to perceive and meditate upon the richness and the worth of human life in this world, and the possibilities of self-fulfillment that lay hidden in the "natural" man, beneath the medieval deposit of supernaturalism. Furthermore, fascinated by the memories of ancient Rome, from which Italians had never forgotten their descent, both Boccaccio and Petrarch had hunted and discovered the manuscripts of many of the "lost" works of classical Latin authors, as, for example, Cicero and Tacitus; and the great chancellor of the Florentine Republic, Salutati, had sought, not unsuccessfully, to conduct his diplomatic correspondence, not in the modernized Latin of the day, but in the ancient Ciceronian style.

III. THE BOOK AND BOOK-LEARNING

The Study of Greek. Passing now to the "humanistic" curriculum of the Renaissance we pause at the "book-learning" in which antiquity was discovered and published throughout Europe. Already, thanks to Salutati, Florence in the last years of the fourteenth century had received her first lessons in Greek from Chrysoloras, and in the first years of the fifteenth had come into possession of many manuscripts of the Greek historians and poets. Then, too, some thirteen years before the fall of Constantinople, Gemisthus Pletho, a Greek delegate to the Council of Florence, which had been convoked as a last attempt to unite the Eastern with the Roman Church, had been retained by Cosimo, the father of the Medicean dynasty, and had founded a Platonic Academy.

Meantime, at Ferrara and at Rome professorships of Greek had been instituted, and Pope Nicholas V had begun the famous collection of Greek manuscripts now preserved in the Vatican Library, and had planned a complete translation of the Greek classics into Latin. In Rome, also, was the Cardinal Bessarion, himself a Greek and a pupil of Gemisthus Pletho, to whom all the Greek scholars in Italy looked as their chief patron and protector. In Naples, and later in Rome, Laurentius Valla had interested himself in the restoration of classical Latin, had disclosed errors in the Vulgate translation of the New Testament, and had tried his hand at translating for the Pope portions of the *Iliad* and of Demosthenes, the whole of Thucydides, and parts of Herodotus. A host of other scholars, both in Rome and other Italian cities, were engaged at Nicholas' behest in similar tasks.

Patronage of Greek Scholars and Hellenic Culture. The collapse of the Byzantine Empire added a flood of refugees to the Greeks already resident in Italy. Many of them gravitated towards Florence, where Lorenzo the Magnificent, Cosimo's son, no mean poet and an enthusiastic patron of learning in all forms, welcomed them to the "garden" of great men with whom he loved to walk. Among them were illustrious scholars, followers of Aristotle as well as Plato, and the conflict between the Platonic and the Aristotelian points of view, which had become sterile in the Church, regained freshness and vigor, and generated a new interest in philosophy whose growth and expansion could no longer be constricted by ecclesiastical prohibitions and commands.

The Florentines took like ducks to water to the new language and to the new vistas it disclosed. All Italy followed suit. The educated learned Greek as a matter of course, and the passion for things Hellenic permeated all classes from princes like Cosimo and Lorenzo de' Medici, Alfonso of Naples, Frederick of Urbino, and Ludovico Sforza at Milan, to their humblest subjects. Indeed, one of the distinguishing characteristics of the Renaissance in Italy is that, whereas elsewhere the gifts of its spirit were confined largely to the cultured and aristocratic classes, the greater part of the Italian population worshiped at its shrine. All classes were transfigured by the love of knowledge, the sense and the pursuit of beauty, the feeling of life as a fine art, the devotion to the amenities and urbanities of daily living, and the aspiration toward individual self-fulfillment and perfection. Even the Church in Italy bowed momentarily before the vision, and, while repeating the letter of the Christian liturgy, worshiped in spirit for a brief space the way of life revealed by the Hellenic world. Nicholas V, Julius II, and Pius II prayed in what we might call side-chapels, but Leo X and his entourage knelt before the high altar of the ancient gods.

Such patronage from above and popular support from below forced Humanism in Italy to rapid and complete flower. The inclusion of the culture and achievements of ancient Rome within its scope, aroused interest in archaeology, and the ruins of antiquity, which hitherto had served as stone quarries, were now preserved and admired. Art galleries and museums came into being. Libraries, where manuscripts were eagerly collected and copied as fast as the human hand could write, multiplied throughout the land. The invention in Germany of the printing-press, though at first deprecated by the connoisseurs of the fine art of calligraphy, led little by little to the substitution of the book for the manuscript and to an easier and quicker broadcasting of the new learning.

IV. THE BOOK OF THE WORLD

Voyages and Discoveries. Meantime, the book of the world was also opening page by page. On the horizons of the medieval world the Far East and the fabled wealth of Cathay and of Ind had hovered like a mirage. Now, Columbus, inspired by the belief that the earth was round, sought a western passage to these lands, and discovered America. Five years later Vasco da Gama, despatched by the Portuguese Government to find the realm of "Prester John," rounded the Cape of Good Hope and eventually landed at Calicut on the Malabar coast, and founded a trading-post there. Within twenty years, Magellan, following Columbus' example, had discovered the western way to India, and, dying in the Philippines, had left his expedition to complete the circumnavigation of the globe.

Interest in Foreign Lands. The suspicion that the earth was not flat but round, condemned by the early Church as heretical, but harbored by Albertus and Aquinas and strengthened by the translation of Ptolemy, was confirmed. The reports brought back of the newly discovered peoples and civilizations aroused great interest. For centuries, to be sure, European rulers had been accustomed to receiving gifts of strange animals from the potentates of the Near East, but now zoological and botanical gardens came into being, actuated by a scientific interest in natural history. Rare plants and trees and animals were eagerly sought by the Italian cities, in the same spirit as inspired the collection of manuscripts and scholars and artists. Naples boasted of her zebra and giraffe, Leo X of his rhinoceros and elephant. The elephant, particularly, was a pet of the Roman people, and had its portrait painted. Its death, which threw the city into mourning, was celebrated by a magnificent funeral and obituary verses from one of Leo's poets. This interest was soon applied in many ways. The Italian menu was expanded by new fruits and vegetables, the pharmacopoeia by new medicines. Flower gardens were planted for the express purpose of pleasing the eye. Studs were established, of which the most famous was maintained by the Gonzaga at Mantua, and the breeding of thoroughbred horses began.

This awakened interest in the novel, rare, and curious products of nature went hand in hand with an aroused sense of the beauty of the physical world—a sense that during the earlier Middle Ages had been dormant, but had shown signs of awakening in St. Francis of Assisi and Dante and Petrarch. The loveliness of nature was now perceived with wide-open eyes. Landscape was loved, described, painted. Country life acquired charm. Picnics, expeditions to woods and lakes and streams, were popular. Travel for its own sake—a thing almost unheard of in earlier centuries—became a diversion. The globe-trotter had at last appeared.

V. THE BOOK OF HUMAN NATURE

Shift from the Supernatural to the Natural Man. The startling suggestions from the sudden and immense widening of the horizons of time and space set man thinking about himself. The book of human nature, also, had been opened, and therein he read with amazement and enthusiasm of the powers and opportunities with which nature had endowed him. The supernatural world retreated into the background. The pressure of heaven and the threat of hell paled in comparison with the prospect of the success or failure of his earthly career. This life was not a preface to life beyond the grave. It was a complete story in itself. It was to be seized, manipulated, exploited, refined, perfected to the full extent of the materials that nature had laid before him and of his capacity for dealing with them. In short, human life as a natural event within a natural setting was not something to be died to daily; it was something to be *lived*.

For the first time, too, in some seventeen hundred years man felt himself able again to confront and undertake the task alone. Like the Greeks to whom he looked for fellowship and inspiration, he felt competent to compass the nature of the universe and grasp the truth by the use of reason alone. His native intelligence could dispense with commandments from on high in figuring out the nature of the good and the conditions of human happiness, and his strength of mind and will was sufficient to raise him to perfection without calling upon divine grace for help. He was master of his salvation, and salvation lay in making the best of himself as he found himself.)

The Ideal Natural Man. Man eagerly took to the task of testing his new-found powers and perfecting himself in the mold in which nature had cast him. He became possessed of the ideals of completeness and finish, of polish and distinction and dignity, of a studied refinement of appearance and manner and taste and conduct. The concept of the *gentleman* was born. In *The Courtier,* Castiglione has given us a kind of fashion-plate illustrating the style of human living that the Renaissance man wished and tried to follow. The "well-dressed man" must be a good all-round athlete. He must ride well and dance to perfection. He must be at home in several languages, with Latin and Italian as an absolute minimum. He must be acquainted with literature and the fine arts, and have some knowledge of music. He must excel at the art of delicate love-making. He must be calm, dignified, independent. All these qualities must be interwoven and expressed in a single harmonious pattern of courtesy and good breeding.

In Italy the ideal of the gentleman, like the spirit of the Renaissance, was not restricted to the upper classes but was shared by the population at large. It broke down the distinction between the noble and the burgher. This, it should be said, had never been so marked in Italy as elsewhere, because of the democracy of the Italian priesthood, and the town, rather than castle or country, life of the Italian aristocracy. The princes of the Church might spring from the humblest origins, the peasant might become a Pope In the cities the noble and the bourgeois families lived much the same lives, had much the same interests, and were constantly thrown into friendly contact with one another. What snobbishness there was, was not then difficult to overcome. It was generally agreed that birth and wealth mattered little. True nobility is nobility of accomplishment alone, and that nobility is open to every man.[1] The only true class distinction was that between those who had acquired, in passable measure at least, the manner, the bearing, the accomplishments, and the culture of the "gentleman" and those who had not. The so-called "aristocracy" of the English and the French nobility, whom the Renaissance had not as yet reached, was held up to ridicule, and their unurban, isolated life of hunting and hawking

[1] Cf. Poggio's dialogue *On Nobility.*

was reckoned but a degree less boorish than that of the German robber-barons.

Interest in Culture and the Arts. Reflection upon "copy" provided by the spectacle of human life bred a flair for history and for literary and dramatic comment. The archaeological interest in antiquity was supplemented by a cult of "national" shrines and monuments, of the supposed birthplaces and tombs, not only of classic heroes, but of the contemporary great. The vision of future generations and of an immortal fame in time to come took shape, and writers and artists composed their work with an eye to the judgment of posterity. History and autobiography and satire became popular, as well as tragedy and comedy.

The desire to perfect the individual outwardly as well as inwardly raised dress and deportment and diction to the level of fine arts. Insistence upon embellishing the daily surroundings in which he moved created architecture, civic and private, of great magnificence. And against this imposing background, to delight the eye in moments of relaxation and festival, ballet and pantomime and pageant were lavishly presented.

We have not time to dwell upon the *floreat* of the arts which is one of the glories of the epoch. In the long procession of genius we may single out the poets Ariosto and Tasso; the historian and political observer Machiavelli; Benvenuto Cellini, sculptor and worker in precious metals, author of the famous autobiography; Leonardo da Vinci, to whom we shall return in a moment; Michelangelo, poet, painter, sculptor and architect; the architects Brunelleschi, Bramanti and Palladio; sculptors like Sansovino and Donatello; painters like Botticelli, Raphael, Correggio, Giorgione, Titian and Tintoretto. But in mentioning them we have only noted a fraction of the famous artists the Italian Renaissance brought forth.

The Morals of the Renaissance. The Renaissance, however, was by no means an altogether Golden Age. In its eager and passionate aiming at the Hellenic ideal, its bolt flew wide of the mark and missed the core of sound ethics about which Greek thinking and the fine art of Greek living centered. Its passion for perfecting the individual ignored the essentially social character of human life and the multiple restraints imposed upon the individual by his particular "lot" in the social complex, upon which the Greeks laid such stress. Its quest of universality and complete self-realization overlooked the "moderation in all things," the balance and the harmony, by which the Hellenic vision of the self-fulfilled human being was clarified and given focus.

Its cult of the natural man worshiped a being above the discipline of the limitations imposed by nature upon humanity and committed the unforgivable sin against the Hellenic spirit, denounced by the Greeks themselves as the quintessence and the source of all human misdoing —the sin of "hybris," of insolence, of overstepping the bounds.

So it was that the Renaissance was a corrupt, licentious, ruthless, revengeful age in which men shrank from no deceit or violence, however dishonest or highhanded, in gaining their ends and attaining their personal self-realization. The individual had got out of hand and was running amuck. Of the ethical deficiencies of the Renaissance, the Borgias have become, doubtless with exaggeration of their crimes, the traditional horrible example.

Absence of Hypocrisy. There was, however, one sin conspicuous by its absence in the Renaissance. The epoch was without hypocrisy. It was free from cant or smugness. Men did not rationalize their personal desires and picture to themselves their schemes for getting their own way as thoughtfulness for the good of others. They ran naked and unashamed in their race for success, and were frank in their intention of using any means to sweep aside everything and everybody that interfered with their winning the prize they coveted. Their vices were open and aboveboard, concealed never from themselves, and from others only so far as good taste demanded.

The Standard of "Honor." This lack of hypocrisy may have been a reflection of the one moral standard to which the age was really held—the ideal of "honor," which was supposed to govern the conduct of the "gentleman." But the sentiment of honor, then as now, was less concerned with what should or should not be done than with a manner of doing whatever one did. A man could act in all matters "nobly," like a gentleman, or vulgarly, like the common herd. Honor, then, would permit much that ethics would not. Still, the sentiment had ethical significance in that it recognized a better and a worse and prescribed the better. Behavior condoned by it was on the whole morally preferable to the behavior it condemned. The discipline it imposed upon action was considerable and salutary.

Renaissance Morals Criticized. It should be said, moreover, that thoughtful and well-poised observers noted and deplored the preoccupation with personality and the excess of individualism that threatened the social and moral structure of the epoch. To quote from Burckhardt's classic work, "It was not one of those methodistical moralists who in every age feel themselves called to declaim against the wickedness of the time, but it was Machiavelli, who, in one of his most well-considered works, said openly: 'We Italians are irreligious and corrupt above others.'"[2] Machiavelli was certainly no saint, and his *Il Principe* is commonly held up as an example of realism and cynicism in politics; though it is only fair to add that the regimen laid down for the would-be successful prince is not unlike the prescription written for the tyrant by Aristotle, in his severely medical and dispassionate discussion in the *Politics* of how every form of government may best preserve its health and escape the ever-threatening germ of revolution.

Savonarola. Nor were the times without their reformers whose excesses were scarcely less marked than those against which they declaimed. Preachers and prophets, drawn largely from the monastic orders, or from self-instituted hermits, ran up and down the land, summoning the people to put aside their wickedness and be saved. Greatest and one of the earliest was the Dominican Savonarola, whose eloquence so converted for a time the whole population of Florence that for four years (1494-1498) he had the whole city, then in temporary revolt against the Medici, not only in his spiritual but also in his political power. His exhortations he supplemented with an elaborate spy system, which kept the private life of the Florentines under constant surveillance, reported delinquencies, and even went so far as to confiscate by force all books and works of art that did not meet with his approval. The climax came in 1497 in a great public burning of books and manuscripts of authors like Boccaccio and Pulci and Petrarch, of articles of adornment, of playing-cards and other games, of musical instruments, of paintings and statues, ancient as well as modern, and of everything else, taken by force or piously offered, that was not in accordance with reformed ideals. A year later, Savonarola himself, excommunicated by the Church, deserted by the fickle populace, and condemned by a new, hostile administration, was burned on the same spot.

VI. LEONARDO DA VINCI

Leonardo's Predecessor, Alberti. It is said that during one of Savonarola's sermons in the Duomo a man was seen leaning against a pillar, heedless apparently of the storm of emotion that beat about him, busily making random sketches of the facial expressions of the frenzied congregation. This man was Leonardo da Vinci. Leonardo is perhaps the most fascinating and enigmatic human being that has

---

[2] Burckhardt, *The Renaissance in Italy*, p. 432.

ever appeared upon the earth. In him the Renaissance became incarnate. He had had, indeed, his prophet in Leon Battista Alberti (d. 1474), who was endowed with the same universality of interest, talent, and practical accomplishment. The facets of Alberti's versatility are not, indeed, so numerous. Neither do they shine so brilliantly, or with so deep and clear an inner fire as burns within the pure diamond of Leonardo's genius. Still, in describing the stuff of which Leonardo was made we are describing that which in lesser measure entered into the making of Alberti.

Universal Genius. Strong, handsome, skilled in all athletic exercises, an accomplished musician, completely a man of the world, the friend of kings and princes, and endowed with an extraordinary personal charm and magnetism, Leonardo would by these qualities alone have satisfied the standards set for the perfect "courtier." Clad, however, in this outward magnificence, walked probably the most universal genius of all time. Of his painting there is no need to speak in the presence of *The Last Supper*, *The Gioconda* (*Mona Lisa*), *The Virgin of the Rocks*, and *The Virgin with Saint Anne*. Scarcely less admired was his colossal equestrian statue of Francesco Sforza, unfortunately destroyed. As an architect he assisted in the building of the cathedrals at Como and Pavia and in the construction of a dome for the cathedral of Milan. His manuscripts show the care with which he studied the architectural problems of stresses and strains and loads, the principles of the supporting arch, and even the question of acoustics. He organized and directed the great spectacles and pageants in which the court of Milan delighted. He planned on paper cities scientifically laid out, with elevated highways above the streets, and with the elements if not the gadgets of modern sanitation.

He also brought the fortifications of Milan up to date. He had imagined many military innovations, such as exploding fire, siege mines and methods of destroying them, had improved scaling-ladders, catapults and pontoon-bridges, and for naval warfare had proposed gas bombs, fire projectors, and rams moved by levers. He also busied himself with the manufacture of cannon, worked out the principles of ballistics, and invented explosive shells and something, not unlike the machine-gun, designed to spray bullets in every direction.

Civil and Mechanical Engineer and Inventor. To the needs of peace and the necessities of everyday life he devoted himself with the same zeal. He devised a system of canals for irrigating the Lombard plains and at the same time preventing disastrous floods. For digging them he invented dredges, and locks to make them navigable.

Swamps he proposed to drain by siphons. He experimented with different methods of utilizing water-power, among them the first turbine. The power of steam also fascinated him. He speculated as to the possibility of working pumps and moving boats with it, and invented a cannon in which it was the projective force. He also tried his hand at machines for rolling metal, boring and planing wood, and sawing wood, marble and stone; at devices for clipping, at spinning-machines with spindles and bobbins; at ships' logs and speedometers and odometers and rain-gauges; at methods of improving ropes; not to speak of levers and jacks and arrangements of pulleys for dealing with heavy weights, and even revolving cranes.

Finally, we should note his efforts to invent flying-machines, submarine boats, and devices for enabling man to walk on water. To this end he devoted himself to studying the structure and the movement of fishes and birds, and their ability to support themselves and keep afloat and aloft in the water and the air. His manuscripts contain many notes and designs dealing with these matters. Having only man-power as a source of driving energy, he could not succeed. But had he possessed the internal combustion-engine, the first airplane might have taken off from the Lombard plain just as Columbus was discovering America.

Interest in Pure Science. Leonardo was not simply a supreme artist and inventive genius. His inventions, like his art, were incidental to a consuming curiosity regarding the structure and operations of nature, the mere satisfaction of which was to him an end in itself. By disposition he was a pure scientist, seeking the truth for its own sake, and the desire to grasp and possess it was his dominating and perhaps his only real passion. Nor could he in his practical applications take advantage, like modern inventors, of principles already discovered and knowledge already consolidated. Nature, whose inmost secrets he so ardently yearned to uncover, still lay, despite the scientific stirrings of the thirteenth and fourteenth centuries, wrapped in a thousand years of Platonic, Aristotelian, and Christian tradition.

Leonardo, then, had to read as he ran and to discover and develop largely by himself the principles he applied. So it is that we find him accompanying his painting and his sculpture with an investigation of the laws of perspective and chiaroscuro, and with detailed physiological and anatomical studies that pry deeply into the secrets of the human body, and boldly anticipate the discovery of the circulation of the blood, the structure of the nervous system, the localization of the optical and olfactory centers in the brain, and the way in which the eye functions as an organ of vision. His architecture and his engineering, civil, mechanical, hydraulic, military, and naval, go hand in hand with speculations in pure physics that lead him to the verge of the laws of inertia and acceleration, the molecular theory of liquids, the undulatory theory of light and of sound, the correlation of reflection and echo, and the grouping together of light, sound, and the radiating waves set up by a stone thrown into water.

Ranging further afield, his insatiable curiosity dealt with geology and astronomy. The discovery of fossil sea-shells on the hill-tops suggested to him the elevation of continents from the sea, the succession of geologic periods, and the place of erosion in molding the landscape. The Ptolemaic astronomy he rejected on the ground that the crystalline spheres would destroy each other by friction. The earth he believed was round, and not the center of the universe but a star. The light of the stars and of the moon he regarded as sunlight reflected from seas that covered them in part as they did the earth. And afar off and dimly he caught a glimpse of the principle of gravitation.

Insistence on the Mathematical Basis of Pure and Applied Science. But this was not all. Leonardo's generalizing power and the vast sweep of his imagination inspired him with a concept of the nature and method of science in all fields. Herein he was doubtless aided by reading the manuscripts, as yet unpublished, of Archimedes, who in the third century B.C. had correctly divined and had begun to develop the scientific implications and the possibilities of the atomic theory. In any case, Leonardo reached back across the centuries and took up the torch of the physical sciences where it had fallen from the dying hand of Archimedes and lain so long neglected. Aided by its light, he had already set forth the principles of modern mechanics a hundred years before Galileo, and, a hundred and fifty before Descartes, had made a universal application of mathematics to mechanics and a sweeping and unqualified application of the mechanical theory to the whole of nature. No human investigation, he tells us, can call itself science unless it proceeds by mathematical demonstration. Of all branches of investigation, mechanical science he considers to be the most useful and the most noble, since all the movements of all moving bodies, animate as well as inanimate, take place according to mechanical principles. Mechanical motion is the cause of every life and the mainspring of every activity.

Insistence on the Empirical Basis of Scientific Knowledge. At the same time Leonardo, for all his devotion to mathematics and pure science, was true to the empirical spirit. His scientific imagination, however high it might soar, and however far it might circle, always took off from the field of fact and returned to it to be checked up and refueled with experience. Upon the necessity of the fidelity of scientific theory to experience and of its constant verification by experience, he cannot too strongly insist. All knowledge, he tells us, begins in sensation, and all wisdom is the daughter of experience. All science is vain and full of error that is not born from experience and does not end in experience, and whose beginning, middle and end do not deal with data transmitted by one of the five senses.

To draw valid inferences from these data continual observation and experiment are necessary. Above all, the scientist must keep an open, detached and impartial mind, fearless of any conclusion to which his investigation may lead him, and of any shock to his pious preferences and ideals it may administer. Edification has no place in science. Of suppression and distortion in the interest of faith and morals, Leonardo will have none. All hindrances placed in the way of discovering and publishing the truth turn themselves into penances. A lie is so ignoble that even though it should say great things of God it would detract from his divinity. Truth is so excellent that it ennobles the humblest thing it praises.

Exaltation of Knowledge. For Leonardo science also spells happiness and salvation. Knowledge is desired for its own sake. It is the ornament and sustenance of the human mind. It fortifies us against the ravages of time and old age. Contemplation of the truth is man's supreme joy. Nay more, it is only by facing the truth that man can make the best of his other interests and activities and learn how to live. Knowledge teaches him what things can and what things cannot be; where and when to acquiesce in the inexorable necessities of the natural order, and where and when he may manipulate and conquer nature, and mold her to his desires.

But acquiescence in what must be acquires an almost religious exaltation from the awe-inspiring impersonality and impartiality of the rigid determinism that governs every movement of the universe from the orbits of the stars to the fall of the sparrow. Marvelous and stupendous, Leonardo exclaims, is necessity. Necessity compels every event to proceed inevitably from a cause and to produce as inevitably its effect. Necessity is the mistress, the governor, the theme, the curb, the eternal and unbroken law of nature, the order that, living infused in her, makes her rational and enables us to understand and deal with her.

At the same time, the analogy of the organism vies with that of mechanism in seizing upon Leonardo's imagination. Man is the model of the universe. The operations of nature are to be understood in terms of his desires, his eagerness, his impatience, his welcoming of the new. The earth is a living being, a work of art of which nature is the creator. Its skeleton is rock, and within it the waters circulate like the blood in the human being.

Attitude Towards the Church. Although he lived and died at peace with the Church, Leonardo, like many another man of the Renaissance, took his Catholicism with a grain of salt. By temperament a spectator, and free from reformatory impulses, he was amused or disgusted rather than outraged by the abuses that were so soon to precipitate the Protestant and the Counter-Reformations. But he openly expresses his contempt of the monks, of the cultus of the Virgin and the Saints, and of the sale of indulgences, discredits the story of the Flood, and apparently denies the divinity of Christ. His whole attitude is well summed up in his remark that, if we are doubtful of the evidence of our senses, we may well be still more doubtful of things of which there is no sensible evidence, like the being of God and the soul and other such things about which people are always disputing and contradicting one another.

Inner Solitude. Leonardo, however, paid the price for the universality of his genius. Attuned not only to the rich, many-keyed, and infinitely complicated music of the life that throbbed and flowed about him, but also to the austere harmonies of the outer spaces and of distant times long gone and yet to be; sensitive, subtle, complex, and conscious of his keener ear, his profounder and wider vision, and his greater power to understand what he saw and heard; aware of his supreme artistic capacity for perceiving and creating beauty, and of his immense inventive flair for grasping the practical applications of what he understood; he was imprisoned in the solitude to which all men of high genius are condemned. Kindly, humane, tolerant and compassionate as Leonardo always was in dealing with his fellows, and much as those who knew him loved him, there was always between him and them the barrier of his inner detachment and isolation, which could not be broken down.

Again, there was more in him struggling for fruition than could be harvested within any single finite mind. Only a god could have realized together harmoniously and to their fullest the myriad potentialities with which he was endowed. So in Leonardo the scientist was perhaps purchased at the price of the artist, though the complexity of his genius gives his painting an ambiguous and subtle fascination. Certainly the artist in him was purchased at the price of the scientist, since, had he not been diverted from scientific research by his painting and sculpture, he might, for example, have discovered the steam-engine.

Summary of Leonardo's Character and Life. Generally speaking, his manifold talents diffused his energy and stood in the way of his making the best of any one of them. And all of them were troubled by the sense of the unknown and by the overmastering curiosity to penetrate its mysteries, before which he was forever driven. Like some venturous sailor of the western seas, he abandoned the sure, sheltered Mediterranean coasts of thought for the boundless and mist-clouded Atlantic, following the lure of its ever-receding horizon, and sighting as he went the dim outlines of island after island, which his pursuit of what might lie beyond left him no time to land on and explore. The most he could spare was a moment to sketch their outlines and to guess and prophesy their fertility. He left it to future generations to colonize and exploit them.

Finally it may be that Leonardo paid a price in happiness for all that he was and did. And yet, who would not rather, like Odysseus, hear the intolerable sweetness of the Sirens' song, lashed though he be to the mast of finite existence, and knowing that abandonment to it spells death, than row like the multitude, with stopped ears, untouched and untroubled by its enchantment?

Such was Leonardo da Vinci, courtier, athlete, musician, painter, sculptor, architect, hydraulic, civil, mechanical, military and naval engineer, inventor, mathematician, physicist, astronomer, geologist, biologist, botanist, physiologist, philosopher, "a mind forever voyaging through strange seas of thought alone." He was born in 1452, the illegitimate son of a Florentine lawyer, studied painting in Florence under Verrocchio and attracted the attention of Lorenzo the Magnificent. He lived at Milan from 1483 to 1499 at the court of Ludovico Sforza and passed a year at Rome in the service of Cesare Borgia, and twelve years more in Florence. Finally he accompanied Francis I to France, and four years later, in 1519, died and was buried at Amboise on the Loire.

Copernicus and Galileo. Leonardo proved to be the precursor of continued scientific discovery, chiefly in the field of astronomy. Early in the sixteenth century, Copernicus (1474-1543), by his reading of Ptolemy and by studies of the heavens made with the naked eye, had become convinced that the Ptolemaic astronomy was incorrect and that the earth revolved about the sun. This theory was borne out by

Galileo (1564-1642), whose improvements of the telescope revealed the reflected character of moonlight, the moons of Jupiter, the phases of Venus, the rings of Saturn, the occurrence of sunspots and the rotation of the sun upon its axis. Galileo is also famous for his experiments in mechanics, his studies of the law of acceleration, and of the principle of the pendulum. For his "heresy" respecting the revolution of the earth about the sun Galileo was brought before the Inquisition and forced to recant his error. It is said that as he rose from his knees after solemnly abjuring his opinion, he was heard to murmur, *"E pur si muove,"* "Nevertheless it [the earth] *does* move."

Tycho Brahe and Kepler. Meantime Kepler (1571-1630), inspired by Tycho Brahe's work, and attempting to explain the incompatibility of the observed orbit of Mars with the theory of circular revolution, confirmed the heliocentric hypothesis of Copernicus and Galileo, and shattered once and for all the Ptolemaic spheres by his discovery that the paths followed by the planets as they revolved about the sun were not circular but elliptical. He worked out the other two great laws of planetary motion, that in equal times the planets cover such portions of their elliptical orbits as help enclose equal areas pivoted upon the sun, and that the squares of the periods of their revolutions are proportional to the cubes of their mean distances from the sun. He also studied comets, ascribed the tides to the attraction of the moon, and to some extent anticipated the Newtonian discovery of gravitation in his theory that the revolution of the planets was caused by magnetic influences radiating from the sun.

Scientific Progress. While this great astronomical assertion was in progress, upsets were occurring in other fields of scientific investigation. Under the leadership of Vesalius (1514-1564) medicine and anatomy threw off the authority of Galen; botany and natural history made great strides under Gesner (1516-1565); Porta (1575-1615) by his discovery of the *camera obscura* took the first step in the direction of modern photography; and Gilbert (1544-1603) interested himself in magnetic and electrical phenomena.

The shock administered philosophy, as well as theology, by the work of Copernicus, Galileo, and Kepler was tremendous. It destroyed all outer evidence of man's focal and privileged situation in the universe, upon which in his philosophical and theological systems he had preened himself so long. It shattered the crystalline spheres that had sheltered and revolved about him, and that had substantiated his claim to supreme importance in God's eyes by making him also the physical center of the world. Nay more, the solar system, of which he now found himself inhabiting a small and incidental fragment, became itself a physically insignificant incident in a universe to which no bounds could be set.

So it came about that whereas the earlier philosophers of the Renaissance had been mainly influenced by the recovery of ancient philosophy, almost in its entirety, in the original texts, the thought of the late sixteenth century was shot through and through with the excitement of the new scientific vision. Henceforth, too, the ancients were to be read in the light of the new knowledge. But before returning to philosophy, we must review the other great upheaval of the times—the Protestant and the Counter-Reformations.

Chapter II

THE REFORMATIONS

I. THE PROTESTANT REFORMATION

Italian Tolerance of Ecclesiastical Corruption. In Italy the corruption into which the Church had fallen alienated the respect of the thinking classes, just as the intellectual movement of the Renaissance had alienated their belief, and her hold upon the entire population had been weakened by the spectacle she offered. But, although the Italians found the behavior of the Church revolting, they also found much in the situation to tickle their sense of humor, appeal to their irony, and titillate their intellectual cynicism; at any rate, not enough to drive them to rebel. Moreover, Catholicism was too interwoven with the life of the Italian people, and the Church was too profoundly a part of the fabric and pattern of their society to be easily ripped from their existence. Things like the sale of indulgences, the veneration of miracle-working images, the prevalence of miracle-mongers, and the conspicuous irreverence, venality, and immorality of the priests and monks, and particularly of the mendicant friars, were publicly derided, satirized, scorned, deplored and denounced. But the general gesture of revolt was a shrug of the shoulders, an aversion of the eyes, a tolerant sigh that the clergy, after all, were human and that humanity, after all, was frail. Even the Franciscan preachers of contrition and reform, or Savonarola with his eloquence, could not at the moment succeed in arousing moral tempests of more than teapot size. It needed the tremendous shock from the north and the loss of half of Europe from her fold to arouse the Church to an effective sense of her condition and to determined and drastic action.

Growing Resentment of Ecclesiastical Corruption in Germany. This shock had been long preparing and was now imminent. In Germany men were less sophisticated, less gifted with the sense of irony and drama, less the cynical spectator, less tolerant of life's shortcomings; more readily shocked, more prone to moral indignation, more easily pushed beyond shrugs and satirical jests to active reform. Moreover, political resentment against the tyranny and the exactions of the clergy had steadily been increasing among the German masses during the fifteenth century. The wealth of the Church was constantly and generally denounced as amassed at the expense of the peasants, and there were mutterings that it should be confiscated and divided among the poor. In the early years of the sixteenth century discontent had reached the proportions of a smoldering revolution, constantly flaring up in scattered peasant insurrections, which, however, were sternly extinguished before they could burst into full flame. It needed only the touch of a poker or the breath of a bellows to produce a general conflagration.

Luther's Attack. These were provided by Luther (1483-1546), an Augustinian monk. He had long shared the discontent with Aristotle, and had further suspicions that the Church underestimated the part played by faith and divine grace in the work of salvation. Indeed, in his opinion, she was untrue to the teaching of St. Augustine, and her unfavorable attitude towards the doctrine of predestination was in error. Moreover, he felt, the reliance she placed upon the sacraments was an almost blasphemous substitute for direct recourse to the mercy of God. Particularly shocking was the granting of indulgences, which might seem to flout the decrees of divine predestination and to imply an arrogation by the Church of a power to pardon sinners that belonged to God alone. That she should furthermore put this power up for sale and barter in her remission of sins for money was a scandal that could not be endured. So it was that on November 1st, 1517, Luther boldly posted his ninety-five theses against the sale of indulgences upon the door of the Church in Wittenberg, the town where he was teaching.

The news traveled like lightning to Rome, where its implied challenge of the Pope's full powers as Vicar of Christ was at once perceived. Summoned before the Diet of Augsburg the next year, Luther refused to retract. Moreover, his attention was now consciously turned upon the Papacy, and further reflection and study led him to deny its divine origin and authority. He was now well started upon the warpath. He denied that the clergy were set apart by their office from other men, and exempt from secular jurisdiction; that they alone were competent to interpret the Scriptures correctly, and then only when convoked in Council by the Pope. These views he advanced in three addresses to the German nation, and supplemented them by calling upon the temporal authorities to undertake the reformation of the Church.

The Diet of Worms and Its Results. The effect was catastrophic. At the Diet of Worms in 1521, Luther received so much support that the imperial edict condemning him, instigated by the Papal nuncio, fell flat, and Luther remained undisturbed and free to continue his campaign. Many of the clergy as well as the laity flocked to his banner, and the more radical among them now began to denounce monasticism, the celibacy of the clergy, the "idolatrous" veneration, as they deemed it, of the Virgin Mary and the Saints, and of the Host. Monks deserted their monasteries, priests got married, churches were invaded, images were broken, the ritual was parodied, and Melanchthon, one of Luther's most ardent supporters, along with others proceeded to celebrate the Lord's Supper and administer the communion, the wine as well as the bread, to himself.

With the further developments of Protestantism in Germany and the north we are not concerned. Suffice it to say that Scandinavia had been Lutheranized in the first half of the century, though in Sweden it was not officially established till 1592. No less early, Protestantism had firmly established itself in Switzerland, under Zwingli, and had set up under Calvin a theocracy at Geneva, marked by the burning of the "heretic" Servetus, who expressed anti-Calvinistic and anti-Trinitarian views. It got temporarily a strong enough hold on France to provoke civil war and win toleration for nearly a century only to be proscribed for another hundred years by the revocation of the Edict of Nantes (1685). It became part of the struggle for freedom of the Netherlands against Spain, and, thanks to William of Orange, it was partly cleansed in the Low Countries of the intolerance which so often marked its spread elsewhere, and became synonymous there with truer liberty of religious thought and expression.

Crossing the Channel, we find Calvinism transported from Geneva to Scotland by John Knox. In England the Reformation was more political than religious, fostered as it was by the Crown's resentment of the Roman control of the clergy, and precipitated by the determination of Henry VIII to divorce Catherine of Aragon and to marry Anne Boleyn. In 1534 the Anglican Church was formally declared independent of the Roman. But the revolt against Roman doctrine, ritual, and practice was moderate, and without Lutheran entanglements or such iconoclastic excesses as marked some other aspects of the Reformation.

The Reformation and Freedom of Thought. The cause of freedom of conscience, thought, and speech had, however, even less to hope at the moment from the Reformation than it had from the Church. The Reformation was far more hostile in spirit to the liberating influences of the Renaissance. Indeed, a part of its quarrel with the Catholic Church lay in what it considered the "paganizing" of Catholicism by the new culture. Nor did its rejection of the authority of the Church involve any immediate liberation of philosophical speculation from Christian doctrine, or make the way of the free thinker easier. Persecution grew with the same vigor in Reformed as in Catholic soil, and woe to the individual who aired any doctrinal differences from the tenets of the Protestant sect under whose domination he happened to find himself.

But, indirectly and in the long run, the Reformation was of great service in establishing and ensuring the liberation of philosophical speculation from subservience to religious dogma. Its insistence on the right of the soul to immediate access to and communion with God, without benefit of clergy, forced eventually the recognition of the right of every man to think as he chose, without interference, in matters religious and philosophical. And its equal insistence on the depravity and sinfulness of the natural man and of his complete dependence upon divine grace for salvation was instrumental in provoking the great reaction of the eighteenth century in favor of the essential goodness of the human soul. The literalness with which it took the Scriptures could not but provoke skepticism regarding not merely the content but the fact of revelation, and the substitution of sectarian dissensions for the pondered dictum of Rome was calculated to bring any and every assertion of the authority of theology over philosophy into disrepute. Then, too, the power of authority to impose itself was weakened by division, while the general uproar of the battle between Catholic and Protestant and of Protestants with each other aroused the mind both to a renewed interest in philosophic problems and to thinking independently of theological restrictions.

The Reformation and the Renaissance. In these respects the Reformation reinforced the liberating work of the Renaissance and helped re-establish the worth and the dignity of the natural man, his ability to work out his own salvation without supernatural help, and his capacity for seeking and attaining truth by the exercise of his native reason without recourse to revelation. So, too, in the long run, it fostered freedom of thought and speech and contributed to the rescue of philosophy from her thousand years of bondage to Christian dogma. However, before noting the revival of comparatively free philosophic speculation, we must pause to consider the housecleaning within the Church of which the Reformation was not, indeed, the cause, but may have been, in part, at least, the occasion. Let us, then, glance at the Counter-Reformation.

II. THE COUNTER-REFORMATION

First Attempts at Reform Within the Church. Before Luther's attack upon the laxity into which the Church had fallen, pious Catholics were showing their alarm over her condition. In Spain, where religious practice was peculiarly passionate and severe, under Ferdinand and Isabella and the great Cardinal Ximenes the Inquisition was established, the monasteries were reformed, discipline was imposed upon the clergy, and the study of Aquinas was revived. The Mohammedans and Jews were expelled from the country, and the measures were initiated that ended a century later in the banishment even of those infidels who had been prudently converted to Christianity.

But this rising tide of reform was not destined to engulf Italy as yet. To be sure, Leo X, in whom the spirit of the Renaissance had been momentarily enthroned in the chair of St. Peter, and under whom the Reformation had broken loose, was succeeded by Adrian VI, who had been tutor to Charles V and co-regent of Spain with Ximenes during the Emperor's minority, and later Inquisitor General. He was an earnest and pious man, who, called to account by the Lutheran catastrophe, made, so to speak, a plenary confession of the sins of the Church. But he was too weak and too short-lived a Pope to do much to correct them. To him, however, came Loyola for the commission that established the powerful Jesuit order, which increased its numbers with astonishing rapidity and did much to restore ideals of learning and discipline to Catholicism and to help it resist Protestant undermining.

The Sack of Rome and the Council of Trent. It needed, for all that, the political disorders under Clement VII, the sack of Rome by the troops of Charles V, and the threat of the secularization of her territories to bring the Church to a full realization of her sins, for which her tribulations were now regarded as divine punishment. She was shocked into pulling herself together and setting her house in order once more. By the middle of the sixteenth century she was able to face the world again at the Council of Trent with a conscience cleared in many respects of the charges hurled against her. She overhauled her discipline and administration, started the index of prohibited books, revised the missal and the breviary, prepared a catechism for the use of the priesthood, proclaimed the supremacy of the Pope, thus helping clear the way for the eventual proclamation of his infallibility, decided various points of doctrine, and presented a unified and bold front to the Reformation which enabled her to shift from the defensive to the offensive. The more fundamental abuses were, indeed, passed over for the most part, but the machinery had been set in motion for their eventual correction.

Divine Grace and Molinism. Meantime the question of the place of divine grace in the scheme of salvation, which the Reformation had brought to the fore, was agitated once more in Catholic circles. The Thomists stood by the doctrine of Aquinas, who had accepted the Augustinian teaching but applied it with moderation and common sense. Even so, it seemed too severe to the Jesuits. A member of the order, Louis de Molina, invented the doctrine known after him as Molinism, which pictured the average man as free and able to perform of himself a set of ordinary duties, for whose omission he was therefore responsible. God was sensible and did not expect too much of human nature, and hence should be met half way. Since God was reasonable and man was free, failure to fulfill one's moral obligations could not be put off by the excuse that God was too harsh or man too weak. Moreover, in perplexity the individual had only to appeal to his spiritual adviser for instruction as to what his duties were and how best to perform them. There was no need for too much introspection and soul-searching. The priest was a kind of doctor, who could tell him how to keep his spiritual health and how to restore it when it had been impaired by some moral imprudence.

This view carried on the Catholic tradition in ethics, and its prescription of recourse to spiritual advice and to the confessional served both as a prophylaxis and a remedy against too great moral perplexity, anxiety, and remorse. Still, the Jesuit doctrine invited grave abuses. Seeking, as Aristotle thought the judge should do, to modify the generality of the law to fit it to the particular case, the spiritual adviser was only too likely to find himself informing his charge as to just how far he could go without getting into difficulties. Or he became like a doctor who, instead of laying down the rules of health and prescribing cures for disease, should make it his chief business to enumerate the liberties the patient might probably take with his particular constitution without doing it too much harm.

This is not to say that much advice of this sort is not part of good counsel. The lawyer points out what the law permits as well as what it forbids. The doctor does his best to combat an excessive amount of precaution in his patient. The wise spiritual adviser warns against exaggerated conscientiousness, as well as against lack of scruple. But in excess, and too much to the exclusion of all else, such advice becomes vicious. In the mouths of the Jesuits it tended to establish a minimum standard of conduct and quantity of virtue necessary to absolution and salvation, and exposed them to the reproach of *casuistry*.

Jansenism. We ought not to take leave of the Counter-Reformation without mentioning its aftermath of Jansenism; all the more as the Jesuit practice, and particularly the outlook on human life inspiring that practice, played an important part in originating the movement. Jansen (1585-1638), Bishop of Ypres, complained, like the Reformers, of the tendency of the Church on the one hand to fall into formalism both in thought and worship, and on the other of the too lenient view she took of man. Like Luther and Calvin, he reverted to Augustine for inspiration, and insisted on the essential depravity and helplessness of the soul since the Fall, and on the uselessness of mere works unless they were accompanied by an acceptance of God's saving grace and by a conscious and fervent love of him. The implications of the Jesuit attitude, that man was a free agent capable of availing himself of the salvation proffered by Christianity, without determination thereto by the divine will, was abhorrent to him. At the same time he himself hesitated before the implications of predestination, and refused to set limits to the divine mercy or absolutely to cut off the most recalcitrant sinner from all hope of salvation. Furthermore, he rejected the Protestant doctrine of justification by faith. To be saved, a man had to do more than call upon the Lord Jesus Christ; he must justify that call by a long and arduous process of Christian living.

Jansen was as opposed to the Reformation as he was to what he considered Catholic laxity. Salvation was possible through the Catholic Church alone. But in spite of his submission to the Catholic faith, his views, which became the subject of a long and bitter controversy with the Jesuits, got him and his disciple Arnauld into difficulties. They were condemned by the Church, and for the next century the Jansenites were subjected to almost continuous persecution and were all but stamped out.

Chapter III

CONTINENTAL PHILOSOPHY
TO DESCARTES

I. THE ITALIAN NEO-PLATONISTS

We may remember that prior to the fall of Constantinople a Platonic Academy had been founded in Florence, that among the Byzantine refugees there were adherents not only of Plato but of Aristotle, and that the old conflict between the Platonists and the Aristotelians broke out afresh. It was, however, now carried on with a difference. The contestants were not so strictly umpired and held to order by the Church, and had at their disposal the original Greek texts of the two philosophers. So it was a new Plato and a new Aristotle that entered the ring.

Marsilio Ficino and Pico della Mirandola. The emergence of the rediscovered Plato in the authentic Greek created comparatively little disturbance. He inspired Marsilio Ficino (1433-1499) to undertake a new translation of his works, which was quickly followed by the first translation of the complete works of Plotinus into Latin. Like the Medieval Platonists, Ficino was still able to find in Plato a philosophic prop for Christianity, designed to convince the intellect by rational argument of the truth of revelation, which, following the Platonic tradition in the Church, he regarded as essentially reasonable. Thirty years younger, Pico della Mirandola, a student of Plato and the Neo-Platonists, was captivated also by the mystical, esoteric teachings of the Jewish Kabbala in which Pythagorean, Neo-Platonic, and Gnostic ideas were fantastically fused with symbolism and allegory. Under the influence of this "theosophy," which sought to penetrate the mysteries and grasp the occult forces of nature and to lift the veil from the face of God, Pico embarked upon a Christian mysticism which found in the Kabbala a key to the arcana of revelation. But like Ficino, he managed to confine his speculations within the limit of orthodoxy.

Impregnated, also, by the new scientific hope of controlling nature, this mysticism turned to magic spells and incantations as a means of forcing her to comply with human desires. Her occult powers were invoked, spirits good and evil were summoned, even the dead were raised to impart knowledge of her secrets and to endow man with the power to utilize them. Great expectations were aroused of finding the philosopher's stone able to turn the baser metals into gold, and of discovering fountains or manufacturing elixirs, to drink of which would restore youth to the old, or confer upon young and old alike the power to live forever. Fantastic as these speculations and researches were, they took, in alchemy, the first steps towards modern chemistry.

Paracelsus. Alchemy found its most famous exponent in Paracelsus (1493-1541). A Swiss by birth, an omnivorous student, an indefatigable traveler, and a doctor by profession, he spent most of his life a wanderer, hounded from one place to another by the suspicions he aroused. His medical ideas were revolutionary. They broke entirely with the great authorities of the past and were bitterly critical of contemporary medicine. His concept of the field and method of medicine was far ahead of his time, but his system was so infected with alchemy and magic that, except for his perception of the natural propensity of the body to cure itself, and of the use of chemical preparations as drugs, it advanced very little upon the theory and practice it denounced.

The Nature of God and the Universe. Not only, however, was Paracelsus under the spell of magic, alchemy, astrology and the like, he had a philosophy typical of the mysticism and magic generated by the commerce of Neo-Platonism with the new scientific interest. God is the first cause and essence of all things. The Father is the center, the Son the radius, and the Holy Ghost the circumference of the divine being. Creation is the self-expression of the divine will, and takes place by a process of division of the divine essence and by a multiplication of creative principles. First to appear is chaos or matter, the formless substratum of which all things are made. Within this the four elements are separated out, and of them all individual things are composed.

But these principles are not dead. They are infused with life and spirit. The whole universe, therefore, is animate, as a whole and in every minutest part. Everything—be it astral, terrestrial, animal, vegetable, mineral—has its spiritual principle, and its particular soul-forms

or invisible living beings inhabiting it. These soul-forms are intermediate between pure spirit and matter, and are embodied in an
ethereal matter.

Man and the Universe. Man is the culmination of the process of
creation, and in him are concentrated all the forms and forces that go
to make the world. He is in miniature (microcosm) what the universe
is in its entirety (macrocosm). His mind is part of the universal mind.
His soul is akin to the soul-form of the stars, and is clothed with an
invisible astral body. His terrestrial body is composed of the four
elements and contains within itself the whole essence of primordial
matter. It follows that he is *en rapport* with the whole of nature and
potentially in possession of all her secrets and master of her hidden
forces. These he may learn to penetrate and to utilize by the study
and the practice of magic and alchemy. By tapping the hidden resources of the spirit, he may manipulate the soul-forms of all things,
utilize the influences of the stars, reconstitute astral bodies, summon
the souls of the elements, and even of human beings, transmute the
elements, heal the sick, and perform many other wonders.

Such magic, Paracelsus protests, is not sorcery. It is white, not black.
It is the practice of powers given man by God for his salvation, not
lent him by the Evil One to ensure his damnation.

III. THE NEW ARISTOTELIANISM AND POMPONAZZI

We have noted that the recovery of the "real" Plato and the "real"
Neo-Platonists revealed nothing shockingly inconsistent with the traditional Platonism and Neo-Platonism of the Church. The case was
different with Aristotle reintroduced in his true guise. Re-read in the
original Greek, he proved different from the Aristotle upon whom
the Church had so long pinned her faith.

Aristotle on Immortality. Pomponazzi (1462-1525), doctor of medicine and professor of philosophy at Padua and Ferrara, argued that a
reading of the original texts quite disproved the assertion of Aquinas
and the other Scholastics that Aristotle's teaching supported the immortality of the soul. The case was quite the reverse. Nay more, Pomponazzi began to have doubts of his own in the matter. He rejected
as superstitious and derogatory to the nature of good men the so-called
proofs of immortality based upon the contention that, if God is to be
justified and a moral government of the world vindicated, there must
be a future life in which the rewards and punishments, so notoriously
lacking here below, are at last meted out. Virtue is its own reward,

vice its own punishment. There is then no moral need of heaven or of hell. Nay more, such concepts are detrimental to true morality, since to be virtuous from fear of hell or hope of heaven is not to be truly virtuous.

Aristotle and Christian Doctrine. Such doubts bred others no less serious. Turning once more to Aristotle in the Greek, he found there no warrant for the idea that there can be interferences with the natural order, or in other words, for the occurrence of miracles. So, too, Aristotle is a broken reed to lean on when it comes to reconciling God's precise foreknowledge of what is to be with his purpose to bring things to pass and his providential direction of their course, not to speak of reconciling a providential government of the world with human free-will. Aristotle re-read is no less at sea in these matters than the theologians who looked to him for support.

To have this illusion shattered about one who had so long been her official guide, philosopher and friend, was bad enough. But it was adding injury to insult to have him publicly quoted in opposition to a cardinal article of her faith like immortality. So it was that Pomponazzi was haled before Leo X and charged with heresy. He exculpated himself by the device of the two-fold truth. He believed, he said, in immortality because the Church asserted it.

But the real Aristotle had been too thoroughly exposed to be again ecclesiastically fig-leafed. Pomponazzi's opinions continued to be held, discreetly half-veiled for the most part by the same subterfuge, but so shamelessly by Vanini (1584-1619) that he fell into the hands of the Inquisition and was burned at the stake.

IV. RECRUDESCENCE OF PANTHEISM AND NATURALISM

Meantime, the Aristotelians and the Platonists were beginning to compose their differences in a way that led towards pantheism, and the scientific movement was fast unfolding into a full-blown naturalism and mechanicalism. Both these tendencies were accelerated by the possession and translation of the original Greek texts of the early Ionian philosophers and of the Stoics and the Epicureans, not to speak of the publication (1544) with Latin translation of the works of Archimedes, of which Leonardo had read the manuscripts. Their first fruits were Caesalpinus, the botanist, who evolved a pantheistic system along realistic rather than the usual mystical lines, and Telesio (1508-1588), who tried to reduce the entire universe to matter acted upon by the expanding and contracting forces of heat and cold. The cele-

brated physician Cardano (1501-1576), the candor of whose autobiography is a monument to the freedom of the Renaissance from hypocrisy, was on his way working towards a naturalistic theory of evolution.

V. FIRST FRENCH AND GERMAN PHILOSOPHY

In France the first philosophical repercussions of the Renaissance
were negative rather than positive, inspiring as they did Montaigne
(1533-1592) to a generally skeptical attitude. Nevertheless, Montaigne's
self-analysis, to which his *Essays* are admittedly devoted, make him
one of the founders of introspective psychology.

The renewed commotion caused by the fall of Constantinople was
carried by Reuchlin (1455-1522) to Germany. He had studied under
Pico della Mirandola at Florence, and was thoroughly imbued with
his master's enthusiasm for the Kabbala and conviction that it contained the key to the mysteries of the Christian faith. He devoted himself to the study and teaching of Hebrew, and was at one time or
another professor at Tübingen, Stuttgart, and Heidelberg. But his
pro-Semitic sentiments kept him in continual hot-water, and he was
always moving on. Thanks, however, in part to him, the way was
prepared for the Protestant Reformation.

The great northern figure of the Renaissance was, however, the
Dutch scholar and priest Erasmus (1466-1536). Well-versed in Greek,
he helped edit and translate into Latin many of the Church fathers,
and his famous edition of the Greek New Testament revealed the
inferior and often false translation in the Latin Vulgate, which was
used and regarded as authentic by the Church. Endowed with a keen
wit and a sarcastic tongue, he lashed out at the ignorance, the greed,
and the corruption of the priesthood and the monasteries. But for the
violence of Luther, his somewhat younger contemporary, he had as
much contempt as he had for stupidity within the Catholic fold. Nor
did he spare the civil authorities. His equal antipathy to the abuses
of the Church and to the excesses of the revolt against them, and his
unwillingness to be drawn into the quarrel, gained him the ill-will
of both parties, which, however, never jeopardized his safety or even
curbed the freedom, the frankness, and the barbed wit of his speech.

VI. GIORDANO BRUNO

Life. Returning to Italy, the next philosopher on our list is Giordano
Bruno. Born near Naples in 1548, he appeared upon the philosophic

scene late enough to be influenced not only by the Neo-Platonic mysticism, the new Aristotelianism, and the pantheistic and naturalistic speculations which had accompanied the Renaissance, but also by the revelations of the new astronomy regarding the nature of the physical universe.

He began his career as a Dominican monk, but soon became skeptical of the Catholic faith. Protestantism he found no more satisfactory. The restlessness of his disposition, and his hostility to Catholic and Protestant alike, kept him moving, suspected by the religious authorities wherever he went. In Paris, he might have had a professorship but for his refusal to attend Mass. Crossing to England under the protection of the French Ambassador, whose friendship he had gained, he spent two years in London and Oxford, but was disgusted with English manners and with the narrowness and pedantry of university life. Returning to France, he was forced by his enemies to flee the country. For a while he wandered in Germany and Switzerland. In 1593 he was so foolish as to accept an invitation to visit in Venice, where he had already published some of his books. The Inquisition promptly snapped him up. After a long imprisonment in Rome he was burned at the stake in 1600 in the Campo de' Fiori, where recently a statue of him has been erected to commemorate his martrydom.[1]

Oneness of God and the Universe. As we have said, Bruno was captivated by the new astronomical vision of the universe, which he accepted without misgiving or reservation. He was also influenced by Nicholas of Cusa and by Telesio, as well as by Lucretius, the Stoics, and the Ionian philosophers. Let space be infinite, he cries, let there be an infinite number of universes, let man be infinitesimal, let there be no Paradise beyond the stars, tenanted by God and his angels. Reality is all the more sublime. God and the infinite universe are one and the same thing viewed under two different aspects. We call it God, when we think of it as the all-inclusive unity, the one thing from which all things spring and in which they all live and move and have their being. We call it the universe when we think of the infinite number and variety of manifestations, which, in its division into many particular things, the one all-inclusive thing assumes. To express this difference of perspective, Bruno uses the terms *natura*

---

[1] The chief works of Bruno are *Della Causa, Principio ed Uno; De Monade, Numero et Figura; De Triplici Minimo et Mensura; De Immenso et Innumerabilibus;* and an allegory entitled *Spaccio della Bestia Trionfante,* in which Christianity is attacked and the Old Testament stories are placed on a par with the fables of Greek mythology.

naturans, or creative nature, and *natura naturata,* or created nature. These terms were later adopted by Spinoza to denote essentially the same distinction.

Monadic Character of the Universe. Also, in emphasizing the one and indivisible character of the universe in its role as creative nature, Bruno employs the word *monad,* suggested perhaps by the Atomists and Cusa, which we shall find also figuring in Leibnitz' system. God is the monad of monads, the principle of unity which also displays itself in the unified character of individual objects, each one of which repeats and reflects, in the unique and unreduplicated nature of its particular being, the oneness of the Reality of which it is a part. We may also, if we like, speak of God as the *stuff* or *matter* of all things, since he himself provides the possibilities that he actualizes, and is the origin from which all things spring, the substratum in them which persists unchanged through all their changes, and the principle into which they are eventually resolved.

Creation is the unfolding of the divine essence, the displaying of the nature of things. Being determined by the nature of God and nothing else, it is a process in which the opposition between freedom and necessity is meaningless. God reveals himself in the system of laws and relations that bind all things together, and in the endless wealth of types and individuals embodying those types, entering into those relations, and exemplifying those laws. He is equally present in all things. He is all things. And yet he is more than their sum. He transcends each and all, and his nature cannot be described by such terms as law, or substance, or type, or kind. He is ineffable.

The Nature of the Mind. The outgoing of God from himself which develops him into an infinite plan and panorama and kaleidoscope in space and time, culminates in the human soul. In mind the nature of God achieves its most complete expression. But if God is as truly intelligent and living as he is material, then there is some portion of life and intelligence in everything. Mind, moreover, represents the end of God's outgoing from himself, and a reverse movement of withdrawal into himself. Our thinking and philosophizing and striving after truth are a movement away from the multiplicity, the variety, the change, and the motion of God as manifested in the world to the unity, the simplicity, and the unchangeableness of God as he is at heart.

Man, standing as he does at the point where the process of withdrawal and of thinking emerges from the process of outgoing and of physical evolution, in which it has hitherto been latent, is a privileged being. He occupies a position midway between God as *natura naturans* and God as *natura naturata*. At death he may hope that his soul will still be carried on the current of God's return into himself, of which her activities have been a part, and that she will eventually become one with *natura naturans,* rather than be swept away in the outgoing stream of change, of which the dissolution of the body is an incident, and lapse again into *natura naturata,* into new forms of which beings of undeveloped soul are resolved when they are destroyed.

Bruno's Break with Christianity. Bruno's system, though founded on the new scientific discoveries, has much in common with the mystical philosophies of Eriugena and Meister Eckhart. It is interesting to note, however, that there is no attempt to square Christian theology with it; no endeavor, for instance, to make it explanatory of the doctrine of the Trinity, after the fashion of the Christian mystics. Bruno had broken too completely with his early faith for that. He did indeed use his distinction between *natura naturans* and *natura naturata* to defend himself against the charge of atheism. He loved to describe himself as "God-loving," just as Spinoza, who, as we shall soon see, resembled him in many important respects, was called "God-intoxicated." But with Christianity he would make no compromise. His is the first important system boldly and without subterfuge to defy the theological restrictions to which philosophy had so long been subject. It marks the definite breaking of the thousand years of bondage. Philosophy was no longer the handmaid of Christianity. She was once more her own mistress, free in spirit, though she still had to fear persecution, to think and to say what she chose. Henceforth she was to defend this liberty against all comers with a conscience cleared of theological qualms.

VII. TOMMASO CAMPANELLA

Certainty That the Self Exists. In the early years of the seventeenth century a number of widely different philosophic movements were in progress. The Italian Campanella (1568-1639), though a devout Catholic and a Dominican monk, was nevertheless disgusted with Aristotle, and attracted, as Bruno had been, by the naturalism of Telesio. Sharply differentiating the philosophical results of reasoning from the truth vouchsafed by revelation, he proceeded to work out a system which in some respects anticipates Descartes.[2] Our senses, he points out, deceive us, and hence their seeming reference to an external world and the account they give us of its nature cannot be trusted. Nor can any reasoning founded on their reports give us certain knowledge. The only trustworthy feeling that I have is that of my own existence, and the only knowledge I can obtain must be acquired by reasoning out its implications.

The Self and God. As certain as my awareness of my own existence is my consciousness of that existence as part of a larger whole. And I can argue with assurance that this larger reality, which includes and limits me, is the cause of my sensations. I can also argue that, since my consciousness is a part of Reality, it must be representative of the nature of the Real. I find that I myself am a unity possessing power and will and knowledge in limited degree. Therefore, the whole of which I am a part must be a unity possessing these attributes completely. Therefore God exists.

However, there must be other degrees of imperfect manifestation of God's nature besides my own. Above me and more godlike is the hierarchy of the angels. Below me and further removed from God is the corporeal world. But this, again, exhibits different grades of perfection. Nearest to reason, human and divine, comes the intelligible or mathematical plan of the universe. Below this is the world of bodies embodying that plan, and finally we have the superficial, sensible order of the moving, changing phenomenon produced by these bodies. Since, however, all these worlds are progressive degradations of the qualities exemplified perfectly by God, knowledge, power, and will are present to some degree everywhere.

The love of God and the desire to return to him, which are the essence of religion, are correspondingly omnipresent. The inertia of physical bodies, the tendency to persist and to resist destruction, is a kind of religion on their part. So, too, is the instinct of self-preservation in animals. Finally, there is the religion of reasonable beings who consciously love God, seek to know him and to do his will, and to unite themselves with him.

The Ideal Commonwealth. In his work, *The City of the Sun,* Campanella constructs an ideal commonwealth. His vision is drawn largely from Plato, and incorporates the community of property and wives, the state control of human breeding, the military training, and the pro-

---

[2] For Campanella's philosophy, cf. his *Universalis philosophiae sive metaphysicarum rerum juxta propria dogmata partes III,* particularly Part I.

visions for educating a guardian class entrusted with supervision of the lives of its citizens, advocated in *The Republic*. He was also an ardent champion of the supreme authority of the Pope, not only in religious but in temporal matters. In fact, he exalted the sovereign pontiff to the position of political king of the whole world. The arguments of Campanella bear interesting witness to the bitter struggle of the Church at the time to assert her authority over Catholic rulers. The attempted exercise of such dominion had already provoked the separation of the Anglican from the Roman communion, and the issue remained a constant source of irritation in France for centuries.

VIII. JAKOB BOEHME

God Felt Not Known. In Germany, this time under Protestant and Lutheran auspices, Jakob Boehme (1575-1624), a poor shoemaker of Görlitz not far from Prague, voiced another great outburst of Christian mysticism, in the mode of Eriugena and Meister Eckhart. His thought is difficult to fathom, as, in addition to the obscure style in which it is set forth, it changed from time to time. We may, however, describe its essentials as follows. It is not the head but the heart that finds God. God is felt, not known in the sense of being grasped and defined by reason. To feel him we must merge ourselves in his Holy Spirit and abandon ourselves to its ineffable revelation of the divine nature.

So experienced, God is the abyss, the boundless, at once the Nothing and the All. In the depths of his being moves blind, primordial will, the Father from whom all things proceed, groping after self-expression, and finding its fulfillment and manifestation in the Son, who is the will become conscious of itself and of its goal, and enlightening itself with this consciousness. From the interaction of this blind, outgoing energy and of its reflection upon itself, springs the World-Soul, the Holy Ghost, the Lord and Giver of life.

God the Creator. God is now aware of himself as creative, as entertaining an abstract and still virgin and unproductive plan of creation, or wisdom, and as a living source of possible further life. This plan must be realized and turned into a living being, if God is to become completely self-conscious, since self-consciousness involves a contrast of one's self with something recognized as not one's self. Therefore the life of God is a ceaseless striving to impregnate the virgin and as yet barren form of creation. It is a travail to bring forth the universe, to incarnate the Son, to give embodiment to the life which is the Holy

Ghost, in order that God may have something besides himself to know and love, and may thus experience the full meaning of love and knowledge.

From this travail and this divine agony are born the worlds, which repeat the nature of the Trinity, in the conflict of outgoing expansion and ingoing contraction and of the natural energies and motions springing from their battle. Through this conflict nature in her turn becomes half-conscious of herself and of her goal. Her aim is to overcome the struggle of opposing forces and to produce out of them new levels and crystallizations of existence, just as the divine travail, engendered by the outgoing and the ingoing will, brought her forth. The Incarnation and the Passion of the Son must lead to his Resurrection. Complete self-consciousness must arise in nature even as it does in God. This takes place in man, whose free will stands over against the divine will, and may oppose it or be harmonious with it.

The Relation of Man to God. But the creative operations of nature, it will be observed, involving as they do a stilling and a stabilization of the battle of opposing forces, are also returns of nature towards the primordial unity of God. In their way they are acts of self-abnegation, of submission to the primal will, which both underlies and is above the conflict. This submission becomes complete when man freely resigns his own will to the divine will and consequently identifies his separate self with the one that is higher and deeper than will itself.

Such resignation brings with it a more profound insight than that of reason. Reason reveals to us only the barren virgin, the empty form of the universe, grasped by an outgoing act of knowledge towards an external object. But with the resignation of the human will to the divine, comes a mystical, immediate, inner *understanding,* as Boehme calls it, of the very heart of God.

This understanding, however, is not passive. Neither does it withdraw the soul from life, or obliterate her distinction from God. On the contrary, it is active and creative, and in its light the soul repeats within herself the divine process of creation, projecting and incarnating the image of her own self-fulfillment, and bringing forth a life all the richer and more abundant for the struggle that constitutes it, and a triumph all the sweeter for the battle by which it is won.

The Problems of Evil and Free-Will. Here we have perhaps the thought underlying the various attempts that Boehme makes to work the origin of evil into his scheme. He began, apparently, by simply dramatizing it, under the allegory of the fall of Lucifer, as incidental to the fundamental division of the will and to the conflict of God with himself that inexplicably occur within the abyss. Later, apparently feeling that he had thus made God morally responsible for evil, he tried to justify its existence by invoking the conflict and interdependence of contraries which are a necessary condition of the existence of the universe. Finally, he seems to have fallen back upon the argument that God introduces evil into the world as a foil against which to make his glory, his goodness, and his mercy the more manifest.

The same vacillation appears in his treatment of the problem of free-will. Sometimes he regards the existence of opposed and struggling wills, each one of which is not only pitted against the others but is divided against itself, as a primary manifestation of the nature of the primordial will. At other moments, he looks upon individual freedom as expressly created by God to provide himself with other wills to love or hate, and thus to complete his own consciousness of freedom.

But whatever the part played by evil and by man's free will in the life of God, their part in human life is plain enough. It is incumbent upon man to ally himself with light against darkness, with good against evil, and, since he is a free agent, he is responsible for his choice. His life, then, is truly his own to make or to mar, and his creation of himself is as original, as spontaneous, and as profound, as God's eternal act of self-creation.

IX. PIERRE GASSENDI

Revival of Epicureanism. In France, meanwhile, within the Catholic fold, the Epicurean atomic theory and a modified Epicurean ethics were being revived by Pierre Gassendi (1592-1655), mathematician, scientist, and priest. Early in life he fell under the influence of the anti-Aristotelian movement in France, fostered in the sixteenth century by the logician Ramus, and became interested in the discoveries of Galileo and Kepler. He inclined, also, as far as the restraints of his religion would permit him, to the empirical view that the intellect is wholly dependent upon the senses for information, and that reasoning can do no more than work over the material they present. In these circumstances it is not surprising that he found Epicureanism the most congenial of the ancient philosophies.

His work consisted largely in re-writing Epicureanism, not indeed as a metaphysics, for he deals severely with the Epicurean theory of the gods and accepts without questioning the whole Christian and Catholic background of the universe, but as a logic, physics, and, with some reservations, an ethics. His revamping of the atomic theory of the nature of matter and his empirical theory of knowledge brought him into bitter controversy with Descartes. In his ethics he defends the Epicurean theory that pleasure is the good. It is the natural end at which all sentient beings aim. It is not opposed to virtue, but is rather the crown and the sign of a well-lived life. Nor is hedonism a selfish doctrine. Nature, indeed, instructs us to pursue our own pleasure, but in instructing us she also implies that we should love everything from which we naturally derive pleasure—our family, our friends, the human society of which we are a part.

Freedom of the Will. Finally, like the Epicureans, Gassendi defends the freedom of the will against determinism. There can be no gainsaying the feeling of freedom. We are directly aware of being able to choose. But, whereas for them the problem was to work freedom into the mechanical theory of the movement of the atoms proposed by Democritus—which they did, we may remember, by endowing the atoms with a spontaneous deviation from their perpendicular fall through space—for Gassendi the difficulty was to reconcile freedom with God's foreknowledge.

Chapter IV

EARLY ENGLISH PHILOSOPHY

I. ITALIAN INFLUENCE ON ENGLAND

We may remember how the spirit of the Renaissance had been introduced in England early in the fifteenth century by Humphrey, Duke of Gloucester, a son of Henry V, himself a collector of classical manuscripts, a patron of learning in touch with Italian scholars, and a powerful influence in the revival of learning at Oxford. From his time on, there was an increasing migration of English scholars to Italy, who returned imbued with the ideals and the results of the new learning. Humphrey's nephew, Henry VII, was friendly with the Dukes of Ferrara and Urbino, and an admirer of Italian culture. He took many Italians into his service, and during his reign the ideal of the all-round man, pictured by Castiglione in *The Courtier,* became fashionable with the English nobility. Italian masters of the manly arts were imported, Italian literature was studied, and Italian became the polite language of the day and was habitually used at the court of both Henry VIII and Elizabeth.

There was also an immigration of Italian artisans and artists, merchants, and bankers, and the influence of Italian commercial knowledge and methods is still remembered in terms like cash, bank, bankrupt, and ditto, and the signs £. *s. d.,* derived from *liri, soldi* and *denari.* The political ideas of Machiavelli were also whispered in the ears of English statesmen, and were listened to by Wolsey and later by Cromwell. The effect of Italian upon English literature is notorious, and dates back to Chaucer. Petrarch was much admired, and the sonnet-form was introduced into English poetry. Spenser was under the spell of Ariosto and of Tasso, and Shakespeare found in Italy the inspiration for some of his plays.

Sidney and More. The Italian ideal of universality received English incarnation in Sir Philip Sidney, handsome, brave, soldier, courtier, traveler, humanist, acquainted with the new science, well versed in French, Spanish and Italian literature, and himself a stylist in poetry and in prose; also, more philosophically, in Sir Thomas More, admirer

of Pico della Mirandola, a lover of music, and of learning, an omnivorous reader and brilliant conversationalist, author of *Utopia,* and a
brave and conscientious opponent of Henry VIII in the matter of
the divorce of Catherine of Aragon—a daring that brought him to
the block.

In the *Utopia,* More is prophetic of many social and economic
changes some of which have come to pass, others of which still await
realization. He dreamt of compulsory education, laws regulating labor,
improvement in housing and lodging, the prevention rather than the
punishment of crime, and the tempering of punishment to suit the
offense. He also advocated religious toleration and liberty of conscience, and advanced the idea of a natural religion to supplement
Christianity.

The Cambridge Platonists. A century later the same Platonic and
Neo-Platonic influences that produced della Mirandola and Ficino in
Italy, and through them Sir Thomas More, helped produce the little
group of Platonists at Cambridge, of whom Henry More and Cudworth are the best known. These men were liberals in thought, who
endeavored by the aid of Plato and Plotinus to rationalize religion,
and at the same time to imbue it with Platonic and Neo-Platonic
mysticism. They endeavored to revive the Platonic Ideas in the shape
of eternal and immutable principles of reason and of morality, and
Cudworth went so far as to resurrect the Platonic World-Soul in his
concept of the "Plastic Medium" to whose operations the natural
world was attributable. Henry More was even more mystical, and
turned to Neo-Platonism more than to Plato himself for his inspiration. But the movement was not only an echo of the Platonism of
the Renaissance. It was more directly a reaction against the naturalism,
also a product of the Renaissance, which had already seized hold of
Francis Bacon, and at the moment had Hobbes in its grip. To these
philosophers we must now lend an ear.

II. FRANCIS BACON'S LIFE AND CHARACTER

Rise to Power. Francis Bacon (1561-1626), the son of Sir Nicholas
Bacon, Lord Keeper of the Seal under Elizabeth, was born with a
silver spoon in his mouth, through his kinship to the great Cecil
family. Graduated from Trinity College, Cambridge, in 1575, he
studied law, entered politics, and became a member of Parliament,
thanks in part to the patronage of the Cecils and Walsingham and the
Earl of Essex. Under James I his preferment was rapid. Attorney

General in 1613, Lord Keeper of the Seal four years later, Lord Chancellor in another twelvemonth, he was raised to the peerage as Baron Verulam in 1618, and in 1621 was created Viscount St. Albans.

Fall and Retirement. But Bacon was not an altogether admirable character. He had always been something of a toady and a time-server, and his willingness to prosecute his former friend and patron, the Earl of Essex, who had fallen into Elizabeth's disfavor, was little short of treacherous. As Lord Chancellor he was accused of accepting bribes and of corruption in the conduct of his office. A Parliamentary investigation was held, and Bacon confessed to irregularities. He was deposed from office, given a heavy sentence both in fines and imprisonment, most of which, however, was suspended. But he was barred from Parliament and temporarily banished from court. He returned to his country estate at Gorhambury for the few remaining years of his life. The story of his death is well known. Being interested in the problem of preserving meats by the application of cold, he got out of his carriage one day to gather snow with which to stuff a chicken. He himself caught pneumonia, but as he himself wrote on his death-bed, "The experiment succeeded, excellently well."

Bacon had, however, the virtues of his vices. His cool, prudent, dispassionate, time-serving and ungenerous nature, which proved his moral undoing, was favorable to the realism, the patience, the perseverance, and the dogged experimentation, upon which his enunciation of scientific method was founded.

Works. Throughout his political career as well as after his retirement he pursued his scientific and philosophical interests and wrote and published almost continuously. By some people he is credited not only with the works bearing his name, but with having also composed what we are accustomed to call the plays and poems of William Shakespeare. His *Essays,* published in 1597, gave him an immediate literary popularity, and remain one of the masterpieces of English literature. Among his other works we may mention the *Advancement of Learning* (1605), published first in English and later in enlarged form in Latin; the *Novum Organum* (1620), of which a preliminary sketch entitled *Cogita et Visa* had appeared in 1607; and various scientific essays, which, along with the *De Augmentis Scientiarum* (the Latin version of the *Advancement of Learning*), the *Organum,* and other works projected but not written, were designed to form a comprehensive project to be known as the *Instauratio Magna.* Besides these we may mention the *New Atlantis,* in which Bacon describes his political utopia, the *History of Henry VII,* and the *Apothegms,* which is a collection of jokes and anecdotes.

III. BACON'S PHILOSOPHY

The Baconian Method. Bacon is a child of the new hope which dawned with the Renaissance, of discovering the whole truth about the universe by the use of reason. This hope we have already seen working in Leonardo da Vinci, and we shall presently have occasion to note it in Descartes, fortified in his case by his perception of the possibilities of mathematics. Bacon, however, is content to develop a method of discovery and to leave to others its utilization. His mind was less speculative than Leonardo's and more empirical than Descartes'. For him the great instrument to understanding is *invention,* or the abandonment of random discovery for deliberate research. So, too, the first purpose of *invention* is practical—the domination of nature by man. Knowledge, he tells us, is power. The condition of invention is acquaintance with and right interpretation of nature. Paradoxically, we conquer her by obeying her.

The "Idols" and Their Demolition. But obedience is not so easy. It is hard to approach nature with an open mind and without preconception or prejudice. As a matter of fact, we habitually approach her, blinded by four outstanding kinds of preconception, or, as Bacon calls them, *Idols.* In the first place there are the *"Idols of the Tribe,"* which are settled habits of perceiving and thinking rooted in all human beings, such, for example, as our tendency to introduce purposes or final causes into natural operations and to explain things by their results rather than their antecedents. Secondly, there are the *"Idols of the Cave,"* or the prejudices of the individual, born of his particular character, education, and environment. Thirdly, there are the *"Idols of the Market Place,"* or the deceptions due to the looseness and misuse of language and to the employment of words, without stopping to consider and define their meaning. Finally, there are the *"Idols of the Theater,"* whose worship is the blind acceptance of tradition and authority. One of the ugliest and most baneful of these idols is Aristotle, against whose dominance of logic and scientific thinking Bacon, like his earlier namesake Roger Bacon, vehemently protests. Aristotle, he tells us, has sterilized logic by his preoccupation with the syllogism, and has vitiated his science by the employment of a faulty and hasty method of inferring general laws from particular instances. The syllogistic form of reasoning is unfruitful even in theoretic sci-

ence; the Aristotelian manner of observing and inferring from experience is of no help in inventing practical means of controlling
nature and subjecting her to our ends.

Before we can begin to think correctly, we must demolish the Idols.
We must oppose authority with observation of nature and with independence of spirit in drawing conclusions from that observation.
We must cut loose from meaningless terms and expressions. We
must discount, as far as we can, our personal preferences and prejudices. We must correct as far as possible the errors of the senses and
of faulty reasoning.

If we will do all this, look nature in the face as she is, observe her,
and experiment with her, we may hope to discover what Bacon calls
the *forms* of things. By *forms* we are not to understand the scholastic
or Aristotelian forms, but rather the latent structures and processes in
nature, which are reached, not through generalization, but through
analysis of phenomena into their simpler constituents.

The Inductive Method. How, then, shall we go about our task?
The answer is the Baconian method of *induction*. First, in any collection of phenomena under investigation, we must carefully compare
the instances in which it does or does not appear. In this way, we
extract essential aspects and conditions from those which are non-
essential. If, for example, we are investigating a case of food-poisoning
at a picnic, we try, by comparing what the different people have eaten,
to exclude certain dishes as innocent, that is, as *negative instances,*
and to fix upon others as possibly guilty. The next thing to do, as
Bacon remarks, is to compare those instances in which the phenomenon
is present in greater or lesser degree, or, in the case of our picnic, to
see if we can correlate the degree of the poisoning in different individuals with the comparative amount they have eaten of this or that
suspected food.

Upon the importance of *negative instances* Bacon dwells at some
length. No conclusion can be established till the possibility of negative instances is excluded. For instance, we may feel reasonably sure
that the poisoning has been caused by a certain dish, but we must be
sure that *all* the people who ate it were made ill, before we can announce confidently that we have discovered the cause of their illness.
If someone present has partaken of it, and *not* been poisoned, then
we are still doubtful whether we have really run the offending article
to earth. In Bacon's words, our experience, which was first *empirical*
because of doubt, must remain *critical* because of continued doubt.
It is just the absence of the critical spirit and the tendency to jump

to unwarranted conclusions, Bacon says, that are the cause of much credulity and superstition.

Finally, having proceeded by a cautious and critical *induction* from instances to forms, we must *verify* our results by continued observation and *experiment*. Here, however, a difficulty arises. In dealing with nature as a whole, we can never be sure that a negative instance will not turn up and invalidate our conclusions. Furthermore, an enormous number of instances would seem to be necessary to warrant our drawing any conclusions at all.

The Use of Prerogative Instances. These difficulties are partly obviated in Bacon's opinion by choosing for observation and experiment *prerogative instances* in which the phenomena under investigation may be considered typical, as we should say, or striking, and singularly free from adulteration with accidental or irrelevant aspects. He enumerates twenty-seven varieties of such instances. One, the *solitary instances,* as he calls them, which have next to nothing in common except the phenomena under investigation, will do for an example. Color is best studied in things like dew-drops, crystals, prisms, etc., where it is not complicated by the presence of other common characteristics in the objects compared. Again, Bacon remarks, the use of *analogies* is very fruitful. We may remember that the waves radiating from a stone thrown into a pool suggested to Leonardo an *analogous* theory of the nature both of sound and of light.

Once more, however, the use of these instruments must be attended by extreme caution. There must be no jumping, no flying away. We must proceed laboriously, step by step, from particulars to our inferences regarding them. The solid truths, which are of most concern to us, lie half-way between rules of thumb, or minor axioms, and the most general, highly abstract axioms or hypotheses. To keep our feet on these intermediate axioms, our understanding needs to be weighted down by attention to fact, rather than buoyed up by vain speculations.

Bacon's Metaphysical Preferences. Bacon's mind, as we may judge from the list of his works, is by no means confined in its interests to natural science. He was interested in the spectacle of human life, in history, in mythology, in the philosophy of politics, in poetry. Nor could he escape altogether some speculative adventure. Metaphysically, he seems to have inclined towards materialism, and he preferred openly the theories of the Ionian philosophers and of Democritus and Lucretius to the systems of Plato and Aristotle. Indeed, his criticism of the Atomists was to the effect that their atoms were not sufficiently tangible and physical. At the same time, the caution of his temperament led him to be careful in avoiding the reproach of irreligion and atheism. He professes faith in God and in what we might call the principles of natural religion. He makes no attack upon Christianity, but he disapproves strongly and openly of the fanaticism and persecution that have marked its history.

IV. BACON'S THEORY OF POETRY

Bacon's theory of the nature and function of poetry is also well worth noting. It is the business of science to conquer nature by obeying her; it is the function of poetry to conquer her by releasing the mind from bondage to her and permitting it to escape into a world of its own in which nature is remolded to suit the heart's desire. "Therefore poetry was ever thought to have some participation of divineness, because it doth raise and erect the mind, by submitting the shows of things to the desires of the mind, whereas reason doth buckle and bow the mind unto the nature of things." [1]

Since conquest through obedience depends upon observation not only of the present, but of the past conserved in the memory both of the individual and the race, history contributes to the experience from which science springs and by which it is checked and verified. But it also provides rich material with which the *imagination* may work, and out of which it may build its magic reconstruction of the world.

Narrative, or epic, and dramatic poetry both present their imaginings in historic form, as taking place in time past or present. But there is another form—the parabolic—which pictures the significance or underlying form and structure of events in allegory and symbol, and is therefore more akin to science; as, for example, when it conveys scientific truths or teaches practical lessons by means of parables. But parables and allegories may also be woven about the unknown, the mysterious, the divine; in which case they produce a mythology, or, in other words, a symbolism which gives imaginative equivalents for the objects with which religion deals. The god Pan, for example, is a symbol of the universe taken as a whole; Eros, the oldest of the gods, the symbol of the atom; Prometheus, the allegory of human inventiveness; Narcissus, the image of self-love. Bacon applies this allegorical method to classical mythology with an excess of fancy bordering on the fantastic.

[1] *Advancement of Learning*, II, 13.

V. THOMAS HOBBES' LIFE AND CHARACTER

It is said that Bacon in the last years of his life at Gorhambury was sometimes attended in his walks by a young man who took down his thoughts from dictation. This young man was Thomas Hobbes, by whom Bacon's naturalistic and materialistic leanings in science were given metaphysical and systematic form. Born at Malmesbury in 1588, the son of a boorish and ignorant country parson, who was eventually forced to flee his parish after a brawl at the church door, Hobbes was precipitated into this world some two months before his time by the fright his mother shared with many other people in England at the approach of the Spanish Armada. At fifteen he entered Oxford, then according to contemporary accounts a place "where the young were debauched to drunkenness, wantonness, gaming, and other vices," and where he proved an idle student. But a trip to the Continent, after graduation, as tutor to one of the Cavendish boys. aroused his enthusiasm for scholarship, and especially for the study of the classics. A second and a third trip to the Continent at a much later date acquainted him with mathematics and brought him into personal contact with Galileo at Florence and with the mathematician Mersenne in Paris. Returning to England in 1637, he decided at the age of fifty to develop a philosophic system.

Residence in France. His meditations, however, had almost immediately to be transferred back to Paris. The Civil Wars in England were brewing, and Hobbes, fearing lest his political views should get him into trouble, fled to France once more. There he remained for the next eleven years, working on his system and, incidentally, disputing with Descartes. It may be remarked in passing that he was the worst of mathematicians, and was engaged all his life in controversies with men much more able than himself, by whom he was continually worsted. His somewhat cantankerous temper also embroiled him with the English universities, upon whose antiquated system of education he was unsparing in his attacks.

Writings. The fall of the Stuarts in 1645 apparently incited him to write his most famous work, *Leviathan,* published in 1650-1651. The political views he expressed in it angered the royal exiles in Paris, because of their apparent justification of Cromwell's usurpation, and offended both the French and the fugitive English clergy. Once more, fearing for his safety, Hobbes fled home to London, where he was not molested. He now published, among other works, the *De Corpore* and the *De Homine,* in which he set forth his metaphysical views.

Old Age and Death. In 1660, the Stuarts were restored, and Hobbes not only regained the royal favor, but became a personal friend of Charles II, who was himself an intelligent, cultured, and mellow man, much interested in the natural sciences and particularly in chemistry. But he still had to bear the brunt of accusations of blasphemy and atheism hurled at him by the clergy. He was now an old man, but he still had many years to live. His activity, too, both mental and physical, was indefatigable. He walked every day—and sang every night—for exercise, and at the age of seventy-five still played an occasional game of tennis. At eighty-four he wrote his autobiography in Latin verse, and in the next two years translated the whole of the *Iliad* and the *Odyssey.* At ninety he was still writing. The last part of his life was spent at Chatsworth, the seat of the Devonshires, where in December, 1679, he died in his boots of a paralytic stroke, aged ninety-one.

He was over six feet tall, red-haired, irascible, generous, witty, a good conversationalist. He had been drunk, he said, about a hundred times in the course of his life, and he had an illegitimate daughter, for whom he provided amply.

VI. HOBBES' METAPHYSICS AND PHYSICS

Philosophy and Knowledge. Philosophy, Hobbes tells us in the opening paragraphs of the *De Corpore,* consists in the knowledge we gain of effects by arguing from causes, and of causes by arguing from effects. Its end is practical and lies in the usefulness of such knowledge in the conduct of everyday life. Its method consists in using the shortest way of procuring such knowledge. This we may do either by a *synthetic* construction of universal types, laws, and the like, out of particulars, or by an *analysis* of the particular into the more universal elements entering into it. Both methods are useful, but philosophical knowledge, or knowledge of the *causes* of things, can be gained only by analysis.

Before we can proceed further, we must ask what knowledge is. Reasoning, Hobbes replies, is a process of adding our percepts to one another or subtracting them from one another, and getting the results. This we could not do without speech and words, which we can employ as signs or symbols of large numbers of percepts, and use as means of communicating our percepts to others. These words, however, stand for nothing "universal" either in nature or in thought. All there is in nature, for example, corresponding to the word "man" is particular men; all there is in our mind is a particular image or picture of a man which we make the sign of all other individual percepts of the same sort.

True and False Propositions. If now we join two names together in such wise that the second is the name of the same thing as the first, we get a proposition. Propositions are *true* when the predicate is the name of everything of which the subject is predicate. By this token the proposition "the chimera has three heads" is as true as the proposition "man has two legs." How then are we to distinguish true propositions from false, and those which refer to facts from those which deal with fancies? Error, Hobbes replies, arises when an anticipated fact fails to fit the name we expected to apply to it. It is deception with respect to what might have been the case but turns out not to be so. Herein it differs from nonsense or absurdity, which asserts the impossible by combining names that designate contradictory particulars, as when we talk of an immaterial substance or a free will.

The distinction between propositions about facts and propositions about fancies can be drawn, Hobbes thinks, by demanding that all names shall be reduced to their least common denominators before being coupled. For example, if we dissect the chimera and its three heads, we shall find it made up in our mind of the same percepts as constitute for us what we call facts, and shall be able to reduce it by further analysis to the least common denominators into which all percepts may be resolved. Hence it will be expressible in the names and propositions that hold good for all experience, and that, in Hobbes' opinion, have objective validity and reference.

The Constituents of Reality. So fortified, we approach the philosophic problem. What are the least common denominators of all our percepts? They are space, body, and motion.[2] All things are extended and resistant, and alter their spatial relations to one another. Motion is the name by which we signify and understand their successive and simultaneous relations to one another.

"Spirit," in the sense that the theologians and theologically minded philosophers use it, is ruled out of the discussion. The word, Hobbes tells us, can only be used properly as the sign of two things, first, of a very attenuated body like air or gas, and second, of some adjectival quality, as when we speak of a peaceful or a warlike spirit in a nation, or of a person as being high-spirited. Used as the sign of a so-called

[2] Cf. *De Corpore*, Part II.

"immaterial substance," it stands for nothing at all, and denotes a contradiction in terms like "bodiless body."

The Root of Religion. At the same time, Hobbes refrains from attacking theological entities. They may exist; indeed, God must exist as the cause of the universe. But what he is like is undiscoverable by any process of analysis or reasoning, and his nature, therefore, cannot be made a subject of philosophical research or argument.

The root of religion Hobbes finds in man's natural curiosity about nature and his demand for an explanation of natural phenomena. Man is also afraid of these phenomena, since he does not understand them, and is in particular awe of seemingly chance occurrences. Also, he is much impressed by dreams and apparitions, which give rise to a belief in ghosts. Thus he comes to personify natural forces, to regard the immediate causes of all things as beings like himself, to propitiate them with prayers and ceremonies, and to consult them with omens and divinations. The weaknesses of a developed religion lie in the self-contradictions it exhibits in its doctrines, in the hypocrisy and selfishness that arise in a priestly caste, and in its reliance for its authority upon alleged miracles, which, when they are found to have natural causes, recoil upon those who have invoked them to bolster up religious dogma.[3]

The Universe Nothing but Matter in Motion. Space and time are attenuated images or "phantasms" of body in motion. If I imagined the corporeal aspects of the world annihilated, they would leave these images behind them. At the same time space and time have a filling, a stuffing, which we call *substance*. Moreover, the changes in bodies are continuous. Motion is imparted by the impact of a contiguous body. It makes no jumps. Cause and effect are the names we use to signify the passing on of motion from one body to another. Since Hobbes rejected the notion of the void, he was obliged to think of the spaces between the smallest particles of solid matter as filled with an insensible ether, through which the motions of one body are conveyed to another and produce seeming action at a distance.

In a word, the subject matter of philosophy is bodies and their motions. Reflection upon it suggests to Hobbes a fourfold division of philosophy, or, as we might say, four fundamental philosophic sciences.[4] First, we have *geometry*, which treats of the relations of motion to space, and deals simply with the movements of bodies. Next, we have *physics,* which is concerned with the effects produced by one body

[3] Cf. *Leviathan*, I, 12.
[4] *De Corpore*, I, 6.

upon another incidentally to their motion. Passing now to bodies endowed with consciousness, or the power to represent things in sensations and images, we get *ethics,* which deals with the mental motions, or the conscious processes of the body, and *politics,* which deals with the effects and interactions of minds upon one another set up by their collisions and communications.

VII. HOBBES' ETHICS (PSYCHOLOGY)

Sensation and Images. With the very simple essentials of Hobbes' physics we are sufficiently acquainted. We have now to study the capacity possessed by some bodies for perceiving, imagining, and reasoning.[5] This capacity, as Hobbes conceives it, is in no way a break with the activities of physical nature. Our sense-organs are jarred by different sorts of movements, and the shock administered to them is conveyed to the brain. Sensation is the motion thus set up in the body. It is not, therefore, of an order different from motion in general. An inanimate body hit by another body simply *quivers;* a body capable also of representing the shock *feels.*

Just as purely physical movement dies away because of the interruption and interposition of other motions, so perceptual movement also tends slowly to fade, for the same reasons. This fading or "decaying sense," as Hobbes calls it, is memory and imagination. Not only, however, do single images persist, but whole trains of sensuous representations continue to vibrate, in the order in which they were presented, and a fresh stimulus may revive the almost quiescent motions of similar or associated images experienced in the past.

In this way, we get associations of images, play of fancy, and trains of thought, which in some cases are seemingly haphazard, in others are threaded on some desire or design and are therefore deliberate and inventive. Since man is naturally an inquisitive animal, much of his thinking is regulated by the desire to answer the question "why" and to represent to himself the causes of things. Herein lies the basis of science and philosophy.

Good and Evil and Free-Will. The mention of desire directs our attention from the perceiving and thinking movements of the body to its motor and volitional responses. Stimulation of the senses not only makes an impression upon the body; it gets an answering kick out of it. This kick, or "endeavor," as Hobbes calls it, may be of two

[5] Cf. *Leviathan,* I.

sorts. If the stimulus is beneficial, it carries us towards the stimulus, is attended by *pleasure,* and is called *appetite,* or *desire,* or *love.* If the stimulus is harmful, we tend to kick it away, and our motion of *aversion* is *painful* and is called *hate.* To these simple roots may be traced all the luxuriant flowering of the passions and the emotions, as well as the distinction between *good* and *evil.*

Again, these activities may be either voluntary or involuntary. They are voluntary when they are accompanied by images of the end towards which the movement is directed and of the means for attaining it. Voluntary movement, however, is commonly complex. It is the component of an alternation of appetites and aversions, hopes and fears, images of the good or evil consequences of doing or refraining, and is therefore vacillating and *deliberative.* We feel *free,* as long as the see-saw continues. Eventually, a component of forces is reached, we make up our mind, and the response occurs as an act of *will.*

VIII. HOBBES' POLITICS

Self-Assertion a Natural Fact and Right. *Ethics* has revealed the basis of *politics.* All men are actuated by an appetite for self-preservation and self-expansion just as every body tends mechanically to pursue the line of its original direction. Men, then, naturally desire power. This appetite and this tendency to assert himself can no more be bred out of man than the first law of motion can be bred out of a moving body. It can only be taken away in the one case as in the other by force. Every man, then, is free to use, as far as he can, his own power and momentum towards the furthering of his own interests; or, to express this natural fact in terms of *politics,* he has a *right* to do so.[6]

However, just as the natural tendency of moving bodies to pursue the line of their original direction brings them into collision, so the assertion of the freedom and the right of each individual man to preserve himself brings him into conflict with the exercise of the same freedom and right by his fellows. Wills clash even as bodies in motion run headlong into one another. The result, therefore, of the unlimited exercise of natural *rights* is a *bellum omnium contra omnes.* In fact, the natural condition of mankind is one in which all men are at war with one another, and thereby find their natural rights curtailed and stultified in part.

All Men Practically Equal in Power. Power in human beings is not a matter of brute force alone. It is a matter of cunning and in-

[6] For Hobbes' political theory cf. *Leviathan,* I, 13 ff.; II, 1-21.

telligence, with which the physically weaker are often more liberally endowed. To all practical intents and purposes all men are equal in power, and it is impossible for any one individual to assert his will by crushing the wills of the others. Compromise is the only way out, if complete social chaos and stultification of the natural right to life and liberty and happiness are to be avoided.

This compromise takes the form of a deliberate quest for peace, called by Hobbes the *first law of nature*. Peace is attained by the acquiescence of the individual in the *second law of nature,* expressed in his willingness to refrain from exercising his full freedom and natural right, and to "be contented with so much liberty against other men as he would allow himself." Such "mutual transferring of right," Hobbes continues, "is that which men call contract."

The Necessity and Duties of Government. But, we ask at once, how is this covenant to be enforced? How are naturally hostile individuals to be held to their contractual obligation to relinquish a portion of their natural right to assert themselves without regard for others, and how are they to be forced to content themselves with the same liberty in enforcing their will against their fellows as they allow their fellows against themselves? The answer is that somewhere in society there must be lodged an agent empowered to enforce the social covenant. In other words, there must be a government endowed with sovereign powers and armed with the means of asserting its authority. What, then, are the specific functions and the limitations of sovereignty, and under what form of government is it most effectively exercised? Its prime function is to ensure the well-being of the state by defending the members of the commonwealth against one another, and the commonwealth against other communities. More specifically, its business is to coerce, to define, and administer justice, to make laws, to appoint agents, to confer honors, to choose and regulate the religion of the community and to censor all doctrines publicly taught.

Subject and Sovereign. It is the duty of the subject to obey the sovereign in all respects, since to it, and to it alone, he owes his rescue from the natural state of war, his protection against the predatory impulses of his neighbors, and his opportunity to go his own way and carve out his own career in peace, as far as the compact with others allows. On the other hand, sovereignty is not without its limitations. It owes, to be sure, no specific duties towards the subject, since obligations or duties arise only where there is a covenant, and covenants are possible only between subjects, not between the subject and the sovereign. Nevertheless, there are some things the sovereign cannot do, and some things it must do. It cannot deprive the individual of his right to self-defense and self-preservation. No man, Hobbes tells us, can be properly bound by any covenant or coerced by any authority to injure himself, to be a witness against himself, to undergo hazards, or stoop to dishonor, except under conditions of national emergency. For the sovereign to attempt any of these things would be an abuse of sovereign power. Moreover, the subject is free to act as he chooses when and where the sovereign has failed to lay down rules for the guidance of his behavior.

Finally, obedience to authority is a return for its fulfilling the function of ensuring the safety and happiness of the subject. For the sovereign is sovereign only in so far as it fulfills this function. The interest of the governing agent, *qua* ruler, must be identical with that of the subject. The moment this identity ceases to exist, a government is misusing its sovereignty.

It follows that there can be no such thing as binding international law or treaties. For there is no international super-sovereign to enforce contracts between nations. International peace, then, is really an accident. "The law of nations," says Hobbes, "and the law of nature is the same thing." The natural relations of nations must always be what normal inter-individual relations would be without the social compact —a state of war.

Sovereignty Best Exercised by Absolute Monarchy. Under what form of government is sovereignty most effectively exercised? Hobbes answers, Under an absolute monarchy. To be sure, democracy seems to be the original and primitive form of government; but in its pure, town-meeting character, it is workable only in small and simple communities. The moment a community grows, there has to be delegation of sovereignty to some sort of representative agent and the establishment of permanent governmental machinery. Recurrent assemblage of the citizens, or of representative parliaments, with executives empowered to carry on in the interval, take the place of the original government by continuous democratic pow-wow round the camp-fire. It becomes, then, merely a question of expediency to what or to whom sovereignty, which in any case has to be delegated, should be delegated. The best delegate is one man rather than many, or, in other words, an absolute monarch.

Absolute monarchy, Hobbes continues, has in no respect more disadvantages than other forms of government, and in many respects it has less. The caprices of a king are no worse than those of a popular assembly. Nor is his tendency to favor and enrich private individuals and interests at the expense of the public any more marked than that of parliaments. The difficulties sometimes presented by the hereditary principle, when an infant succeeds to the throne and a regency becomes necessary, are no greater than those which regularly accompany the effort to introduce continuity into democratic government.

On the other hand, an absolute monarch can more easily identify himself with the common good. In him private and public interest more readily coincide than they do in democratically elected governing agents. He can ask advice wherever and whenever he wishes. He can consult experts and follow their counsels. He can arrive secretly, and unaffected by popular clamor, at wise and scientific decisions. Democracy can do none of these things. Last but not least, he is above party and political factions. He takes no sides, has no irons in the fire, has nothing to gain or lose. His view of the public welfare is unprejudiced, non-partisan, and long-range. The moment it fails to be such, the moment he opposes his own interest to the common good, he can himself be rightly opposed. Thus there is always a check upon unwarranted exercise of power.

The Stir Created by "Leviathan." The *Leviathan,* in which Hobbes sets forth his views on the nature of the individual and the state, is probably the greatest work on political philosophy produced in the seventeenth century, and one of the greatest written in modern times. It provoked an immediate storm, as we have seen, which estranged him from all parties alike, Royalist and Cromwellian, Anglican and Puritan. It was largely responsible for the accusations of heresy, blasphemy, and atheism, which we have already noted. Its influence was profound and wide-reaching and still affects our theories of sovereignty and government today.

Chapter V

DESCARTES AND THE OCCASIONALISTS

Education and Character. René Descartes (1596-1650) came of the lesser nobility of Touraine. His father followed the law, and was a member of the local parliament in Brittany. His mother died in giving him birth, and from her he inherited a delicate constitution. At the age of eight he entered the famous Jesuit school at La Flèche, founded by Henry IV for the sons of gentlemen, where he was put through the usual curriculum not only of studies, but of discipline, manners, and social polish. His poor health won for him certain exceptions and favors, among them permission to lie abed mornings, which became with him a life-long habit. He was a precocious child and an obedient and bright scholar, inclined towards mathematics, and especially towards geometry. With algebra, which had just been introduced, he was as yet unacquainted.

After eight years at school, and a dull year in the country, he was let loose in Paris by his father, with plenty of money and a valet to look after him. For a youth of seventeen he behaved himself extraordinarily well in the circumstances. Indeed, Descartes was all his life a man without vices. His great diversion was gambling, but, as he gambled prudently and for stakes within his means, this can hardly be called a vice. It was, however, comparatively easy for him to keep his head, for, young as he was, he had already developed the inner detachment, the love of solitude and retirement, and the dislike of society, that always characterized him. He plunged not into dissipations, but into study—a course in which he was aided by meeting an old school friend, Mersenne, now a priest and mathematician, who introduced him to Mydorge, the most celebrated French mathematician of the day.

Enlistment in the Army. But Descartes was also restless and eager to travel and see the world, and in those days there was no better way of seeing it than by enlisting in one of the numerous armies that were forever campaigning about Europe. Descartes chose the service of Maurice of Nassau, son of William the Silent. At that time Holland, having won her independence from Spain, was one of the richest, the most liberal, and the most civilized of European countries. Moreover, Maurice himself was a remarkable man, who reflected in the variety of his interests and the breadth of his outlook on life something of the universality of the spirit of the Renaissance. Besides being a great strategist and well-versed in military engineering in all its branches, he was a student of science and mathematics, and had gathered about him in his camp at Breda a distinguished group of scientists. Here Descartes settled himself from 1617 to 1619, and to this period belong his first writings—a treatise on music, various mathematical studies, and his *Pensées*. At this time, too, he passed through a curious mental crisis. He made, he said, his "great discovery," which consisted apparently in a sudden intuition of the possibility of applying algebra, with which he was now acquainted, to geometry. In other words, he discovered analytic geometry.

Life in Paris and Holland. In 1619 the Thirty Years' War broke out, precipitated by the revolt of the Protestants in Bohemia, and Descartes joined up with the Catholic army. The Catholics were successful, and with them Descartes entered Prague. But he soon tired of soldiering and returned to Paris, where he spent the next three years. Here he was much sought after by the brilliant society that was so soon to come to full flower in the great age of French literature. Corneille was a stripling. Mademoiselle de Scudéry was just out of the baby-carriage. Molière, La Fontaine, Pascal, Madame de Sévigné, Bossuet, were about to enter it before Descartes left Paris again, this time for good and all, except for brief visits. Racine still lacked some ten or more years of being born. This pregnant and expectant brilliance Descartes tried to dodge, but in vain. He even went into hiding, but was unearthed.

Finally, in 1628, he took refuge from its importunities in Holland, where he lived first in one place, then another. He could now devote himself without interruption to his favorite studies, astronomy, physics, chemistry, anatomy and medicine. Now, too, he wrote his *Rules for the Direction of the Mind,* and a work on the *World,* which he withdrew, however, on hearing of the condemnation of Galileo. In 1637 the *Discourse on Method* appeared, and in 1641 the *Meditations.* To this epoch belongs his solitary love affair. He had a mistress, who bore him a daughter.

Descartes' philosophy was now known, and he had an enthusiastic following, centered for the moment at the University of Utrecht. He was also in correspondence and in controversy with Hobbes, Gassendi, the Jansenist Arnauld, More the Cambridge Platonist, and others. But these academic tempests in the philosophic tea-pot soon boiled over into scalding controversies of more serious proportions. The rectorship of the University of Utrecht fell into the hands of Voët, the most prominent of the Dutch Reformed theologians, who, alarmed at the popularity of the Cartesian system, and particularly shocked by its suggestion that the earth moved, launched an attack upon its author. Indeed, attempts were made to proscribe the teaching of it at the University, which might have succeeded, had Descartes not appealed directly through the French ambassador to William of Orange, at whose behest the States-General intervened and shut up his persecutors.

Friendship with Elizabeth of Bohemia. The most romantic of Descartes' admirers at the moment was the Princess Elizabeth of Bohemia, granddaughter on her mother's side of James I of England, and daughter of the King Frederick, whose flight from Prague to refuge at The Hague Descartes in his modest capacity of soldier had helped precipitate. A brilliant, melancholy, brooding woman, much interested in philosophy, she was the chief ornament of the fashionable little court held by her widowed mother at the Dutch capital. Descartes, whose birth and means, as well as his fame, made him a welcome guest, attended it frequently and struck up a life-long friendship with the Princess. They talked, they wrote to each other, Descartes directed her reading, sent her his own manuscript to peruse, and dedicated to her the *Principles,* published in 1644.

The Hague, however, offered other attractions. There, too, was the court of the King, William of Orange, and the aristocratic assemblage of the States-General. Holland was in the toils of her particular Renaissance. The artists Rubens and Van Dyck were but just dead, and Rembrandt was coming into his own. Freedom of thought and speech were greater there than anywhere else in Europe. All in all, The Hague vied with Paris as the intellectual and artistic center of the western world.

Christina of Sweden. But Descartes was not destined to end his days in halcyon calm. He had a friend named Chanut, who was French minister to Sweden. Among other things, Chanut wrote him of the extraordinary personality of Christina, the Swedish Queen. His accounts can scarcely have been exaggerated. Disappointed and angered at the fact that his heir turned out a girl rather than a boy, her father, the great Gustavus Adolphus, tried to get even with fate by correcting through education nature's mistake in sex. His success was beyond all expectations. Brought up by the Regency in accordance with her father's wishes—Gustavus died while she was still a child—she developed into one of the most astonishing characters of the day. A woman-hater, she habitually wore masculine riding-clothes and "reformed" such feminine apparel as sometimes she had to don. She was excessively hardy, an excellent shot, and could spend ten hours at a time in the saddle without undue fatigue. Her mind was as strong and enduring as her body. She studied twelve hours a day, had a great talent for languages, knew French, Italian, Spanish, German, Greek and Latin, and read Tacitus, that most difficult of Latin prose authors, as a relaxation. Also she governed.

Journey to Stockholm and Death There. Descartes was much intrigued by Chanut's description of this extraordinary female and of the interesting intellectual circle she had gathered at her court. Christina's curiosity, also, was aroused by the ambassador's account of his friend, the great Descartes. They began to correspond, and the Queen added his works to those of Tacitus as light literature with which to beguile herself in moments snatched from business of state and hunting. Eventually she invited him to Stockholm. She wanted to get his philosophy first hand. Also she had it in mind to found a Swedish Academy, modeled after the French Academy. Descartes accepted.

He arrived in Stockholm in October 1649, in the dusk of the approaching Swedish winter. He had his audience with Christina, where he learned, with what secret horror we may well imagine, that the only hour she could spare for instruction in Cartesianism was five o'clock in the morning. Gone were the happy days of lying snug abed till noon, writing and meditating. She insisted that he put his literary "remains" in fit shape to be published—which he did. At her command he also drew up rules of procedure for her projected Academy. These proved to be his death warrant. The winter was especially severe. Chanut was down with pneumonia, and Descartes, whose lungs were the weak point in a generally delicate constitution, was unwell. He returned from the matutinal interview with the Queen at which he submitted his plans, sickening himself, as it proved, with pneumonia, and took to his bed. His medical studies had made him distrustful of doctors, and he would have none of their bleedings and other antiquated ministrations. He held out for ten days. On February 11, 1650, he died, tended by Chanut, who had by this time recovered from his illness, and fortified by the rites of the Church.

Buried first in Stockholm, his body was later removed to Paris, where it was first placed in S. Geneviève du Mont. Still later it was transferred to the church of S. Germain des Près, where it now reposes.

In appearance, Descartes was slight, but well-built, with a large head and a pale complexion, a big nose, and a wart on his cheek. Being bald, he wore a wig. He was very particular about his dress, and always wore a scarf, a sword, and a feather in his hat. The inner man was good-tempered, serene, abstemious and regular in his habits, indifferent to uninteresting people, kind and generous to his servants, avoiding excitement and worry, devoted to his garden, a lover of riding and walking, never rich, but always well off. His generosity prevented his amassing money during his lifetime. His household was comfortable and well-ordered.

II. SOURCES AND DIRECTIVES OF THE CARTESIAN PHILOSOPHY

The Scholastics and the Renaissance. The Cartesian philosophy springs, generally speaking, from two sources. On the one hand, Descartes received at the hands of the Jesuits a thorough training in Scholastic logic and metaphysics; on the other, inspired by the spirit of the times, he grounded himself thoroughly in the new science of the day, and particularly in mathematics. Like Leonardo and Bacon he had a vision of the possibilities of a novel scientific method, and perceived the fundamental role that mathematics was to play in scientific investigation and in the formulation of scientific hypotheses. His metaphysics bears many evidences of Scholastic influence. Like Augustine he falls back upon the principle of inner certitude as his starting-point, and his deductions from that principle follow in many respects the line of the Augustinian and Scholastic argument. At the same time, he seeks to reinforce Scholasticism with the precision of mathematical science.

Rules for the Mind and for Daily Life. Already, in his early work, the *Rules for the Direction of the Mind,* he had laid down the method he intended to follow. This he condensed and restated in the *Discourse.* He will, he says, confine his thinking to fields in which certain and indisputable knowledge seems possible of attainment. He will not take other people's opinions, or accept as a starting-point anything short of an *intuition,* or mental content, so clear and so distinct that there is no avoiding it. Building upon this intuition, he will keep his superstructure anchored and riveted to its foundation by constant analysis and review and verification of his procedure. No difficulties will be skirted or left unresolved. The foundations will be frequently re-examined and retested by subjecting even the seemingly self-evident to searching criticism. Last, but not least, he will do his best, as he says in a letter to Henry More, the Cambridge Platonist, to avoid what we today call "wishful thinking." "Nothing," he writes, "removes us further from the pathway of truth than to establish certain things as true of which no reason, but our will alone, persuades us."[1]

In the *Discourse on Method*, Descartes adds some rules of provisional practical conduct to be observed in his pursuit of truth. He will, he declares, continue to lead a normal, well-balanced daily life, avoiding extremes and eccentricities. He will adhere to Catholicism, and he will respect public opinion and convention. He will avoid the vice of vacillation. His course will be firm and resolute, founded on probability where certainty is impossible. Nor shall it be plagued by the "repentings and remorses that disturb the consciences of feeble and uncertain minds." His third maxim "was to endeavor always to conquer myself rather than fortune, and change my desires rather than the order of the world." To this end he would discipline his mind to acquiesce in the changes of external fortune, and would seek to render himself indifferent to them.

III. CERTAINTY THROUGH DOUBT

Descartes now proceeds to apply his method. He will begin by *doubting* everything that can be doubted. His experience of the external world of space and time, of his own body, of his own life from day to day, may all be dream and illusion. But in any case the dream is there beyond all possibility of doubt. He is dreaming, he is experiencing, he is thinking. Therefore he, at least, exists. *Cogito, ergo sum. Je pense, donc je suis.* I think, therefore I am.

Proof of Existence. If, now, *cogito, ergo sum* is undeniably true, there may be discovered in it a criterion for establishing further truth. This Descartes found in its *clearness*, or inescapable presence, and in its distinctness, or definite and unmistakable character, not to be confounded with anything else. Wherever, then, I can find anything else as *given*, and as *distinctly itself and nothing else* as my own existence, I can claim for it equal truth. But I am as clearly and distinctly *not* the author of all of my experience, as I am the author of some of it. I can therefore conclude that a being more perfect and more complete than myself exists. It may be argued, however, that after all

[1] Correspondence, Vol. I, p. 402. Cf. Haldane, *Life of René Descartes*, p. 328.

in our dreams we move in a seemingly objective world, which, nevertheless, does not really exist outside us, but is spun out of ourselves. To dispel this lingering doubt, Descartes invokes the ontological argument of St. Anselm that the idea of perfection or completeness logically involves existence, and that we, imperfect beings that we recognize ourselves to be, are not sufficient reason for the idea of perfection we entertain, or for that matter, for the nature and the difference of the other ideas that occur to us. Nor can we doubt without implicitly asserting the existence of an objective standard of reality and truth.

Again, turning to arguments of a cosmological sort, we are not sufficient reason for either the fact of the continuance or existence of ourselves. We are not self-created or self-existent. We must then have a cause.

Furthermore, we are in a position to deduce the nature of that cause. Nothing less than an intelligent, rational, moral cause can be sufficient reason for our own thinking and moral nature. Therefore, the perfect, complete being, whose existence is as indubitable as our own, must be a supremely intelligent, rational, and moral being. In short, God exists.

The deduction of an external, sensuous, physical world is now easy. My senses testify to its existence, since I cannot control them at will, and refer them to an external object or cause. Their immediate cause cannot be God, since God is revealed as an incorporeal mind or spirit. It cannot be myself, since in that case God would be deceiving me by making me feel that my sensations come from without; and deception is something of which God, being perfect, is by definition incapable. Therefore, an external physical world exists. To be sure, my senses deceive me as to its nature; but God, in giving me my reason, has endowed me with the means of seeing through that deception and figuring out the true nature of the physical order.

IV. ERROR AND EVIL

The Nature and Cause of Error. But my reason itself frequently is at fault. How can error occur in an instrument naturally attuned to truth and given me by God for the express purpose of correcting error? To answer this question, let me first look within myself. There I find that many of my ideas present themselves to me as unclear and indistinct. Still, if they present themselves as such, I can be in no error regarding them. I recognize their doubtfulness and my own ignorance and uncertainty. It is only when I take an unclear and indistinct idea to be clear and distinct, that I fall into error. But how can I feel an idea to be true, which presents itself to me as doubtful?

Descartes answers that I am a creature of impulse and volition as well as understanding, and my will is not subject to the distinction between true and false, certain and doubtful, made by the understanding. In this mere jumping or assenting of the will to this, that, or the other idea, there is, to be sure, no more error than there is in the entertainment by the understanding of ideas it recognizes as unclear and indistinct. But sometimes the will impels us to give a mental assent to certain ideas to which the understanding, isolated from the will, does not assent, and leads us to regard ideas as true which in our more rational moments we should feel were indistinct and unclear and insufficiently thought out. When we do this, and allow our will rather than our intellect to determine what seems true and what seems false, we fall into error. It is the business, then, of the seeker after truth to confine the assents of his will within the circle of ideas that present themselves to his intellect as clear and distinct. Moreover, since man is a free agent, he may justly be blamed for letting his wishes run away with him, and may be held responsible for the loose and erroneous thinking that results.

The chief causes of our assent to unclear and indistinct ideas as clear and distinct, lie in unanalyzed and uncorrected childhood impressions of the nature and importance of our sensations and the character of the external world, too deeply ingrained to be shaken off even by mature reflection. Again, our attention tires so easily, particularly when occupied with entities not immediately presented to sense or imagination, that it is wont to abandon the search for such truth as is not immediately perceived, and to take the easiest way out. Finally, we are the victims of ambiguous words or phrases, which we do not stop to analyze, and which express our ideas inaccurately.

Evil. The problem of error raises the problem of evil. How can error find a place in a perfect world, created by an omnipotent and morally perfect God? Descartes' answers are conventional. We must trust God. Moreover, it is the nature of a finite being to be imperfect, and therefore to err. The imperfection of the part may contribute to the perfection of the whole. Free-will—which is in itself a perfection —involves the possibility of misuse.

V. FREE-WILL

In his theory of free-will Descartes tries to work both the theories of self-determination and of "indifference" into his scheme. God's will is "indifferent," as the Scotists taught. It is a spontaneous act arbitrarily determining what is good and what is evil. But man is naturally inclined to follow the good, and his reason is naturally directed towards the truth. Following the dictates of the nature given me by God is perfect freedom. "But the indifference of which I am conscious when I am not impelled to one side rather than another for want of a reason is the lowest grade of liberty, and manifests defect or negation of knowledge rather than perfection of will; for, if I always clearly knew what was true and good, I should never have any difficulty in determining what judgment I ought to come to, and what choice I ought to make, and I should thus be entirely free without ever being indifferent." [2]

His clerical opponents at once accused Descartes of attributing the "lowest grade of liberty" to God. To this he replied that the standard of goodness and truth to which we naturally seek to conform ourselves is set for us by God, but that this standard was freely willed by him undetermined by *any* motive, and therefore without hesitation or choice between motives such as is implied in the lower form of liberty. The problem of reconciling human free-will with divine foreordination, he dismissed as involving a mystery too deep for our finite minds to fathom, and therefore as insoluble.

VI. SUMMARY OF THE CARTESIAN SYSTEM

Mind and Body. Descartes is now ready to undertake, in the first part of his *Principles,* a formal statement of his philosophy. Our minds are in contact with objects and their qualities, and with eternal truths. Objects divide themselves into two classes, thinking things and extended or physical objects. The qualities or affections we attribute to objects are the result of the interaction between mind and body. The essence, or substance, of the mind is simply to think; the essence, or substance, of the body is simply to be extended. Neither body nor mind, however, should be called substance in the strict sense of the term, since neither is self-existent and self-explanatory. God alone can lay claim to that title.

[2] *Med.,* IV, trans. Veitch.

Universals. Universals, Descartes insists, have no real existence of their own. For example, things like duration, order, and number either are modes of physical existence, or, when abstracted by the mind and emptied of their content, are modes of thinking. But, even as modes of thinking, general ideas are founded on resemblances, and are simply signs standing for groups of similar particulars, not for a common nature pervading them.

The mind does, however, think in certain categories. It distinguishes relative substances like mind and body from the absolute substance, God. It distinguishes substance from its modifications, or even essential attributes from substance; the stone, for instance, from its shape or even from its duration or persistence. It thus forms general notions like genus, species, differentia, property, accident.

Inadmissibility of Final and Formal Causes. Purposes or final causes are ruled out by Descartes as explanations of the existence and the behavior of the universe. Generally speaking, we can form no notion of the end to which God made the world, since the divine purpose is unfathomable. Therefore, we have no business to account for the existence of the world by imputing to God some special reason for creating it. Such guessing becomes doubly ridiculous when we fancy ourselves and our happiness to be the end God had in view, and proceed to explain and evaluate the processes of nature as means for producing man. It becomes positively puerile if we suppose, as some people do, that the reason for man's existence lies in God's desire to be flattered and praised by human worship.

Bad enough in metaphysics, Descartes feels, teleology in physics is worse than useless. Final causes—explaining things by their results instead of their antecedents—have no place in the physical sciences. Even in biology and physiology they are inadmissible. We do not explain the presence or the structure of an organ by saying that it exists *in order* to perform a certain function. Organs do, indeed, perform their functions admirably, but we are not, therefore, entitled to assert that they have been created by God expressly for that purpose.

The old substantial forms of the Scholastics are equally unsatisfactory as explanations. They are bad metaphysics in the first place, and in any case science would never get very far by invoking them as explanations. To say that a thing acts as it does because it is its nature to do so does not very greatly further the search for the causes of events.

VII. PHYSICS

The Nature of the Physical World. Having thus in the *Discourse* and portions of the *Meditations* and the *Principles* established his metaphysics, Descartes turns to his physics and tackles the problems of the nature of the physical world and of the relations of mind and body in man.

Give me extension and motion, he cries, and I will construct a world.[3] The nature of matter is his first concern. He strips from it, at once, all its qualities such as weight, impenetrability, color, and the like, and reduces its essence to extension alone. Furthermore, denying the possibility of the void, or empty space, he rejects the atomic theory which Gassendi was reviving and defending. All space is filled, or, in other words, space and matter are identical. Remove all bodies from space, and space would collapse and shrink and vanish, for without body there would be nothing to separate and hold apart its different points and places.

Again, location, or place, is a relative term, defined with respect to an arbitrarily chosen fixed point. The boundaries, or surfaces, of any one chunk of space are set by the chunks that immediately surround it. These form the place or space *outside* the chunk in question. Consequently, so-called change of place is a misnomer. Objects do not pass from one place to another in the sense of occupying first one portion of space and then another. Being identical with the space they fill and the place they occupy, they carry their space and their place and their boundaries with them, wherever they go. They are said to have changed their place, when their place has changed its external boundaries by bringing its surfaces into contact with the *superficies* of new chunks of space. When, however, we abstract the extended from the other aspects of matter, and construct a geometrical, spread-out manifold of fixed points in fixed relation to one another, we represent to ourselves this shift of surfaces that occurs when the parts of space slide away from the parts with which they have been in contact, and come into contact with the boundaries of other places, as the passage of a body *through space* from one fixed location to another.

But can motion be conceived as taking place in a solid space? Descartes answers this question by invoking the infinite divisibility of matter. Space does not come in solid blocks. It has large chunks and

[3] *Disc.,* V. *Traité du Monde,* 6.

small, and the bigger pieces are bathed, so to speak, in a sea of tiny corpuscles. Through these they can move, much as fishes of all sizes or shapes swim through the surrounding water without losing complete contact with it for an instant.

Matter, or extension, is, in Descartes' opinion, essentially inert and motionless. We must suppose, then, that God in creating it introduced motion into every part of it. This motion, once introduced, can never be destroyed, short of an act of God. It can only be transferred. Furthermore, we must also assume certain laws—the law of inertia, according to which each thing tends to preserve any given state of motion or rest unless disturbed by an outer force; the law of least action, according to which motion tends always to transmit itself in a straight line; and the law of action and reaction, according to which, when two bodies meet, the lesser loses its direction but not its motion, the larger none of its direction and only as much of its motion as it imparts to the other body.

Cosmology. Supposing that under these conditions God has introduced motion everywhere into extension, what will happen? Everything will tend to start off in a straight line from a given point, or to expand about a given point. But by collision these rectilinear movements will be transformed into circular, revolving motions, and innumerable vortices will be formed. Friction will tend to break up extension into corpuscles of various sizes and to rub them down into spheres. In this way matter of different degrees of density will come into existence. The smaller and less resistant particles will be driven towards the center of the vortex, where they will globulate and constitute suns and fixed stars; and the coarser and less polished chunks will compose the planets. The planetary masses will move in the vortex about the central suns, and, revolving at the same time upon their axes, will create a vortex of their own, and throw off satellites.

The condemnation of Galileo, however, made Descartes hedge. The earth itself does not move around the sun. It is carried in a vortex that so moves. In the same way, a boat, floating on the surface of a stream, does not move relatively to the current that carries it past objects on the shore.

The mechanical explanation adopted in physics and astronomy is carried by Descartes into every department of natural life, including biology and physiology. He was thus led to his theory that animals are automata without consciousness, whose apparently conscious and even intelligent behavior is to be explained mechanically as the reaction of an excessively complicated machine. This theory, however, was not original with Descartes. It was held before him on theological grounds, by the Jesuit Pereira, who felt that to attribute consciousness to animals complicated both the question of human immortality and the problem of evil. Descartes' view provoked immediate protest and he was severely taken to task for its inhumanity by Henry More.

The Interaction of the Human Mind and Body. Descartes, however, could not regard human beings as automata. In them thinking substance was obviously conjoined with extended substance. But how? The human body, being part of the mechanical order, was itself a mechanical apparatus whose every reaction could be explained without invoking consciousness. Moreover, if one tried to introduce conscious interference into it, how could the mind control the body without exerting physical force and thus augmenting the fixed quantity of motion created by divine fiat? Finally, how could an immaterial, unextended substance like the mind, having nothing in common with matter, be conceived in any sort of contact with it?

Faced with this difficulty, Descartes made an ingenious attempt to cope with it. The mind, he asserted, merely *directs* the course of the currents of motion flowing through the body, without in any way altering their volume. He located the soul's point of contact with the body in the centrally situated pineal gland, buried deep between the two hemispheres of the brain. This, his anatomical and physiological studies of the sensory apparatus and the nervous system suggested, was a kind of bottle-neck through which the incoming sensory currents of "animal spirits" passed, and in which they were transformed into outgoing impulses terminating in muscular movement. Here, then, was the natural spot for the mind to intervene and switch the trains of movement set up by sensory stimulation to the appropriate volitional and motor, or outgoing tracks.

The weakness of his attempt was obvious. The mind could no more alter the *direction* of the flow of motion in the body without exerting physical energy than it could alter the quantity, supposing even that the quantity were alterable. The problem, then, of the interaction of mind and body was raised rather than solved by Descartes, and remained a major philosophic perplexity. It was one of the chief inspirations of the systems of both Spinoza and Leibnitz, as we shall presently see. But, before turning to them, we shall do well first to examine the attempts to deal with it made by the so-called *Occasionalists*.

VIII. THE OCCASIONALISTS

General Theory. The Occasionalists, rejecting Descartes' attempt to explain interaction, held that any direct and natural communication between mind and body was impossible and invoked supernatural aid to effect it. God, they said, acted as an intermediary. On the *occasion* of the body being stimulated, God aroused in the mind the appropriate sensation and response. And on the *occasion* of that response, God set the body moving in an appropriate reaction. This seemingly cumbersome business was short-circuited by the divine omniscience. In a single instantaneous act of combined omniscience and omnipotence, God was aware of the situation in the nervous system, had aroused the corresponding sensations in the soul, and had produced in the body the motor reactions to which the mind was inclined by such stimulation.

Geulincx. Geulincx (1625-1669) of Antwerp, for a time professor of philosophy and medicine at the University of Louvain, and a French priest, Malebranche (1638-1715), the chief exponents of this view, took it, however, in different perspectives. Geulincx argued that since the essence of the mind is to think, all our unconscious and involuntary activity takes place, not in the mind, but in the body, and therefore is to be identified with physical motion. The activity, however, of a purely thinking substance cannot be reduced to physical movement, and therefore cannot interact with it. Nevertheless, such interaction seems to take place. Feeling and volition seem to cause movements of the body. The only way out of this dilemma is to suppose that conscious states are simply the *occasions* of these movements, and that God is their real *cause*.[4]

Malebranche. Malebranche both expanded Geulincx' assertions, and supplemented them by maintaining that God is the cause of our conscious experience as well as of the bodily processes. Matter, being passive, can neither initiate nor transmit physical motion of itself. All movement, whether or not corresponding to mental states, needs the constant intervention of God to set it and to keep it going. But in that case, how account for sinful movements and for the apparent subjection of the mind to bodily appetites and impulses? By the Fall, Malebranche answers, which obscures our vision of the true relations between things. Salvation consists in regaining that vision, which we have lost.

[4] Cf. particularly Geulincx's *Metaphysica vera et ad mentem peripateticam.*

The question now arises how we come by vision, or consciousness, or knowledge of any sort. There are three possible sources of knowledge—material objects, the soul, and God. Material objects cannot implant knowledge, since their images or messages, even before they reached our senses, would become confused and mixed in traversing space, and, when they finally did stimulate our bodies, would set up physical movements, not conscious states. Furthermore, the transformation of bodily into mental activity is inconceivable. The mind, however, can no more account for mental processes than can the body. Being finite, it cannot create them out of nothing. It cannot, as we have just seen, create them out of bodily states. For that matter, consciousness cannot even refer to physical objects or represent them in mental terms, since it is impossible to represent or refer to what has never been present or given us so much as an inkling of its existence. Hence, seeming experience of an external world cannot be even a mode of consciousness, much less its creation.

We are left, then, with God as the only possible source of our experience. Even so, we cannot suppose that he simply implanted potential knowledge in the mind, and then left the mind to develop this knowledge little by little, running, so to speak, under its own steam. A finite mind is not capable of containing, even potentially, the infinity of ideas deployed by consciousness. Hence God must be continually imparting to the mind every minutest item of experience separately and one by one.

Pursuing this train of thought still further, Malebranche is led to conceive an intelligible extension, in which ideas co-exist, parallel to the physical extension of objects, and to regard the mind of God as the spiritual "place" in which all finite minds have their dwelling. All "vision" is "vision in God"; all experience and knowledge, even of the so-called external world, are experience and knowledge of God's ideas, which are modes and limitations of his being. All desires, being directed towards an imagined good, are forms of the love of God.

IX. THE SCHOOL OF PORT ROYAL

Pascal. Before passing on to Spinoza we ought to mention the School of Port Royal, originally a Cistercian abbey near Paris, which under the famous Marie Angélique Arnauld, became the great stronghold of the Jansenists and the rallying point for a number of famous men, among them Blaise Pascal (1623-1662), the author of the *Pensées* and the *Lettres Provinciales*. Pascal was greatly influenced by Mon

taigne, and by Montaigne's skeptical attitude, or, as he called it, Pyr-
rhonism. But with Pascal skepticism and a thoroughgoing Jansenism
went hand-in-hand, since the impossibility of supporting the content
of the Christian revelation by reason and the doubts raised by reason
as to the credibility of that revelation testified to the completeness of
man's fall, and rendered faith the only possible means of salvation and
of attaining a knowledge of God. Belief, then, in the truth of Christianity is wholly a matter of faith, and, conversely, faith has no ground
except the fact of revelation.

But Pascal has other claims to fame than those afforded by the
Pensées and the *Lettres*. He was also one of the most eminent mathematicians and scientists of his time. At the age of sixteen he wrote a
classic work on conic sections. He made extensive studies of the
cycloid curve, then much in dispute among mathematicians, laid the
foundations for the calculus, and was the creator of the theory of
probability. In science he made valuable experiments in hydrodynam-
ics, established the fact that air possesses weight, and invented the
barometer.

Chapter VI

SPINOZA

I. LIFE

Education and Excommunication. The outward life of Spinoza presents a striking contrast to that of Descartes. Born in Amsterdam in 1632, of one of the Jewish families that had sought refuge in the Netherlands from Spanish persecution, he, too, received a broad and thorough education. From the Synagogue he learned his Talmud and his Maimonides and the other medieval Jewish theologians. He also became acquainted with the mystic lore of the Kabbala, which, in spite of his profound contempt for it, seems to have influenced him, and is perhaps responsible for the traces of Neo-Platonism some writers find in his system.[1] Latin he acquired thoroughly from Francis Van den Ende, a learned and free-thinking physician, well versed also in the natural sciences, who incidentally was later hanged by the French for taking part in a conspiracy against the monarchy. With Greek he was less well acquainted. Spanish, and perhaps Portuguese, as well as Hebrew, were native tongues, and he knew also French and Italian, and, it may be, some German. Van den Ende also introduced him to the writings of Giordano Bruno and Descartes, and probably grounded him in science. Also, following the Rabbinical imposition of a handicraft upon every Jew, whatever his other education, Spinoza learned the trade of making lenses.

By the time he was twenty-three he was showing signs of rebellion against both the letter and the spirit of the orthodox Jewish faith. Apparently, this rebellion soon became open, for, a year later, after an unsuccessful attempt to bribe him into outward conformity and an equally unsuccessful attempt of some orthodox fanatic to assassinate him, he was formally accused of heresy and excommunicated from the Synagogue. Henceforth he no longer existed for his community, his friends, and his family, and had to begin a new life, alone.

Removal to The Hague and Death. Spinoza received the news of his extinction as a Jew calmly, with the remark that it was only what

[1] Cf. Caird, *Spinoza* (Blackwood, 1899), pp. 39 ff.

he expected. He changed his given name, Baruch, to the Latin equivalent, Benedictus, and went on his way. Fortunately, he had Gentile friends, belonging to the suspected but tolerated Remonstrant sect, with whom he was stopping at the time of the excommunication, and with whom he continued to make his home. For a living he had his lenses to fall back on. Four years later he moved to a suburb of The Hague, and eventually, in 1670, to the city itself. There he took lodgings and worked at his trade till his death, which occurred from consumption in 1677.

Philosophical Works. In 1663 Spinoza had published a summary of the second part of Descartes' *Principles,* and, the year of his arrival at The Hague, this was followed by the *Tractatus Theologico-Politicus,* a book so liberal in tone that he deemed it prudent, even in comparatively tolerant Holland, to issue it under a fictitious name and to see that it was not translated into Dutch. Even so, complaint was at once made by the Dutch Synod to the States-General, and the work was prohibited. The Catholics speedily followed suit and placed it on the Index. However, it won for Spinoza, whose authorship became known, celebrity in learned and emancipated circles and a call to the chair of philosophy at Heidelberg, where he was promised complete liberty of teaching, provided he would not disturb the established religion. Spinoza refused on the ground that teaching would cut too much into his time, and that the restrictions laid down would probably get him into difficulties.

Hereafter Spinoza published nothing. But he carried on a voluminous correspondence with learned friends and started the unfinished work *On the Amendment of the Understanding.* Last but not least, we may imagine him every evening, after he closed up shop, working away on the *Ethics.* The manuscript was finished by 1674, and was shown to several of his friends, including Leibnitz. He had, indeed, thought of issuing it in 1675, but the mere rumor that he was about to publish another "atheistic" book raised such a rumpus among the clergy that he let the matter drop. So, after his death, it was found in his room along with his letters and other unpublished work, and a few personal belongings. These comprised his entire estate.

Character. Of Spinoza it may be truly said that he was beloved by all who knew him. Frugal and simple in his living, he just managed to make both ends meet, month by month, but he never complained and was always cheerful, friendly and kindly. Nor was there any pride of the intellect about him. He was as affable with the humble as with his learned friends, and among his sincerest mourners was the family with whom he lodged. Nor did he try to make converts to his teaching, but in this, as in all other matters, he was content to live and to let live.

II. EXTERNAL SOURCES OF SPINOZA'S PHILOSOPHY

The external influences on Spinoza's philosophy are a matter of dispute. His Jewish philosophical heritage comprised a knowledge of the medieval commentators, as, for example, Maimonides and Avicebron, who themselves inherited Arabic Aristotelianism and Neo-Platonism and the Arabic cult of the "active intellect" and the inclination to interpret the Aristotelian doctrine of the eternity of the universe in the light of the Neo-Platonic pantheistic theory of emanation. With Bruno, too, he was acquainted. We know also that he had at one time been much impressed with Descartes, whose enthusiasm for the uses of mathematics he shared but with whose conclusions he had come totally to disagree.

Nor can he have been ignorant of the advances and discoveries in empirical and experimental science that were going on about him, though they may have seemed to him an inadequate substitute for the power, in which he so firmly believed, of a mathematically disciplined reason to solve all the problems raised by the question of the nature of Reality. We can seemingly see all these factors at work in his thinking, but not in such wise as to detract from the independence and originality of his thought. Of that there can be no doubt.

III. REFERENCE OF FREEDOM OF THOUGHT

An indispensable condition of sound philosophic speculation is, Spinoza feels, complete freedom of thought and expression for the individual in all matters. Over such freedom, he claimed in the *Theologico-Political Tractate,* neither Church nor State should exercise any restrictions whatsoever. To ensure this, it is above all necessary that civil government should be liberated from all ecclesiastical domination or interference, and to effect this liberation the claims of the Church and of religion in general to revealed and divine authority must be demolished.

The Eternal Good. Such demolition Spinoza tries to accomplish by a criticism of the pretensions of the Bible to divine inspiration. He challenges the accuracy and reputed authorship of the books of the Old Testament and the boast of the Jews to be the "chosen people."

Religion, he points out, is not to be confused with theology or any one religious system. The miracles upon which theologians rely as evidence of their particular faith are inconsistent with the concept of a divine order, and are therefore self-contradictory. Belief in them is, however, natural enough, and has perfectly good natural explanations. So, too, the whole Christian scheme of the Redemption is incredible. Jesus was a man like other men, but a man whose mind was peculiarly attuned to the order of the universe, and whose will was directed towards the eternal good.

In the unfinished essay *On the Amendment of the Understanding,* found along with the *Ethics* among his effects, we get further light as to what this eternal good is. It lies not in riches or fame, which are transitory, but in fixing the affections upon an object in which there is no change or decay. This object is found in the knowledge of the union existing between the mind and the whole of nature, in other words, in the knowledge and acceptance of the true nature of the Real.

Next, Spinoza proceeds to lay down the criteria for distinguishing this true and adequate knowledge, in which the mind finds its fulfillment and its peace, from inadequate and confused ideas. But as this portion of the essay is repeated in the *Ethics,* we need not concern ourselves with it now.

IV. GOD

Necessary Characteristics of Reality or God. In the *Ethics* Spinoza attempts the task of setting forth a complete philosophical system in the form of a geometry in which each proposition is supposed to follow from its antecedents with the same necessity as governs the deduction of one Euclidean proposition from another. He begins by laying down a series of *definitions,* resting upon broad necessities and distinctions of thought and experience. In applying these definitions to the universe and developing the resultant series of propositions we must be guided by certain *axioms,* like the laws of self-contradiction and excluded middle, the principle of sufficient reason, and the assumption that the nature of the Real is rational and, conversely, that reason is the test of truth.

From these it appears that we can accept as ultimately real only what we can conceive as *self-caused, self-existent, free* in the sense of being self-determined, and *eternal,* or unaffected by time. Thus prepared, Spinoza plunges into a geometrical demonstration, proposition by proposition, that the universe, or totality of existence, alone fulfills the specifications reason demands for what it will consider real, and that only one such universe or Reality can be conceived and therefore exist. Such a being we will call God. All else, Spinoza goes on, we must define either as an essential quality of the Real, which we will call an *attribute,* or as an unessential modification or *mode,* whose reason for existence is found in some preceding object or event.

Incidentally, Spinoza's use of the term God is apt to be confusing, since for us, because of the Christian tradition, the word "God" immediately and inevitably suggests a personal being; whereas, for him, as we shall see in a moment, it has no such connotations. Indeed, we shall understand him better, if we substitute in our minds a neutral term without personal implications, like Reality, or the Real, or, to use his own word, *Substance.*

The Attributes of God. If, next, we ask what is the nature of Reality, reason perceives that it is both a *thinking* and *extended* being. In other words, and here Spinoza finds his solution for the Cartesian problem of the relation of thinking and extended substance, mind and matter are not even derived and dependent *substances* as Descartes thought. They are rather *attributes* or essential characteristics of the nature of the Real. God, the only true substance, is as really an extended, spatial order of physical objects as he is an immaterial, unextended system of thoughts.

But, if God is as truly physical as he is mental, and *vice versa,* and if his essence is expressed with equal completeness in both attributes, then every modification or expression of his nature must have a double manifestation. There will be, nowhere in the length and breadth of infinite space an occurrence without a mental "correlate," nowhere in the infinite richness and variety of God's thinking a thought that is not linked with a physical "other half." These "correlates" do not *cause* each other, any more than the concave side of an arc causes the convex, or *vice versa.* But just as the concave and the convex everywhere accompany and involve each other, so Thought and Extension must be conjoined in a one-to-one correspondence. In short, we have in Spinoza a complete "psycho-physical parallelism," which obtains throughout the entire universe.

The Infinity of Attributes. But this is not all. Since the Real must necessarily be conceived as unlimited and infinite, its nature must be expressed in an infinite number of ways besides the two that our minds are able to perceive. Not only, therefore, is God infinite Extension and infinite Thought, but he is also infinite in an infinity of other attributes of whose nature we can have no inkling. "God, or substance, consisting of infinite attributes, of which each expresses eternal and infinite essentiality, necessarily exists." [2] The humblest object that we touch is infinite beyond all comprehension, turning to us, as it does, but two of its countless facets.

The doctrine of infinite Attributes has given rise from the beginning to difficulties and to varying opinions as to Spinoza's meaning. Especially perplexing is the relation of the unknown Attributes to the Attribute of Thought which, in us at least, knows only the Attribute of Extension. To an objector named Tschirnhausen Spinoza wrote in terms suggesting that each Attribute was apprehended by a corresponding form of thinking—which might suggest that within thought itself there is an infinite number of thinking Attributes, each of which stands to some one of the Attributes unknown by us as our thought stands to the Attribute of extension which it alone knows. [3] Or he may mean simply that, since the Real is rational, the unknown Attributes, though they lie beyond the grasp of *our* minds, are nevertheless intelligible. But with this disputed question we have no time to deal more fully.

The Activity of God. "From the necessity of the divine nature," Spinoza continues, "must follow an infinite number of things in infinite ways—that is, all things which can fall within the sphere of infinite intellect." The fecundity of the Real is limited only by the law of self-contradiction and the bounds of logical possibility. Somewhere everything possible has actual existence. God, then, is the cause of all things.

But things do not proceed from God as from a creator existing outside and prior to them. Nor do they exist at the command of his will or to fulfill a purpose on his part. Spinoza is no less outspoken than Descartes in his rejection of final causes as explanations. To attribute purposes to God is to transfer to him our own interests, prejudices, and desires, and to destroy his perfection by representing him as pursuing unrealized ends and therefore as incomplete.

We say, for instance, that God is *good,* meaning thereby that he likes what we like. We announce that he is without *evil,* meaning thereby that he lacks those qualities that happen to be obnoxious to *us.* We assert that there is a divine *order,* or, in other words, that God has created things in such wise that they are most easily remembered and pictured by mankind; and we denounce as *disorderly* whatever puts any tax upon the human memory or imagination. So, too, im-

---

[2] This and other quotations from and references to *Ethics* are from the Elwes translation.

[3] Cf. *Epistles,* 63, 64, 65, 66.

posing our own preferences upon nature, we speak of things as absolutely *beautiful* or *ugly,* and believe that God must share our esthetic as well as our moral tastes. But "things are not more or less perfect, according as they delight or offend human senses, or according as they are serviceable or repugnant to mankind." This should be sufficiently attested by experience, which shows "by infinite examples that good and evil fortunes fall to the lot of the pious and the impious alike," and that the Real, therefore, is not actuated by ethical considerations. In short, "the perfection of things is only to be reckoned from their own nature and power."

Teleology Inadmissible in Scientific Explanations. Finally, teleology is death to scientific investigation, since whenever it runs up against a difficulty and is in want of an explanation, it gives up the search for the natural causes of the event and appeals instead to the "will of God—in other words, the sanctuary of ignorance." For example, men are prone, when surveying the intricacies of the human body and the way in which all its organs work together, to conclude, because of their ignorance of the causes of so great a work of art, "that it has been fashioned, not mechanically, but by divine and supernatural skill, and has been so put together that one part shall not hurt another. Hence anyone who seeks for the true causes of miracles, and strives to understand natural phenomena as an intelligent being, and not to gaze at them like a fool, is set down and denounced as an impious heretic by those whom the masses adore as the interpreters of nature and the gods."

V. THE RELATION OF THE UNIVERSE TO GOD

The Universe the Necessary Expression of God's Nature. But if God is neither an efficient nor final cause of the universe, how does he cause it? By logical necessity, Spinoza replies. The existence and nature of the universe follow from the nature of God, just as the existence and equality of its radii follow from the nature of the circle. God and the universe are one thing. As the immanent nature and essence of all things, determining each modification of the attributes of thought and extension to be what it is, and to occur when, where, why, and how it does, God may be called, as Bruno called him, *natura naturans.* As the aggregate of Attributes and *modes,* or particular mental and physical events that articulate and segment the Attributes of Thought and Extension—and the other, unknown Attributes as well—he may be called *natura naturata.* But the difference between the two is simply the difference between an object regarded in its entirety as a single, coherent whole and the same object regarded as the sum of its parts with the accent on their multiplicity and dispersion.

If, then, we inquire into the cause of any particular physical or mental event, we find that the reason for the occurrence is twofold. The *immediate* cause lies in some antecedent and contiguous event. But the reason why particular events have the causes and the effects they have, and no others, lies in the nature of the universe of which chains of efficient causation are part. The constitution of the Real is such that the modifications of the Attributes *must* occur in a certain order and no other. Hence a given physical or mental event *must* be preceded by *this* antecedent and followed by *this* consequence. Thus *efficient* causation is an expression of the logical, formal necessity of God's being the kind of being he is and expressing himself as he does.

In such a Reality there is no room for freedom in the popular sense of the word. "Things could not have been brought into being by God in any manner or in any order different from that which has in fact obtained." Our motives are inexorably engendered by preceding conditions, and our volitions follow as necessarily from our motives as physical effects follow from physical causes. Freedom, as we shall presently see, means to Spinoza something different from liberty to act undetermined by antecedent motives and circumstances.

Substance and Attributes. There is, however, one difficulty we must refer to before proceeding. How, it has frequently been asked, does Spinoza conceive the relation of the Attributes to the infinite Substance whose essence they reveal? Does he think of Substance as a substratum underlying the Attributes, which would still be there if the Attributes were removed? Or does he think of it as completely exhausted and contained in the sum of the Attributes? The answer seems to be that Spinoza at least meant to think of Substance, not as something underlying its Attributes, but as fully taken up and expressed and exhausted in them.[4] At the same time, the propensity to think of a thing as having more to it than its qualities is so strong in the human mind that we may wonder whether he could entirely rid himself of the notion of a substratum which would still be there even if its Attributes were taken from it. However, this perplexity need not further detain us.

The Infinite Modes. We have noted that God and the universe are for Spinoza, as for Bruno, one and the same thing looked at in two

---

[4] Cf. Pollock, *Spinoza*, pp. 152 ff.; Joachim, *A Study of the Ethics of Spinoza*, pp. 14 ff.; McKeon, *Philosophy of Spinoza*, pp. 187 ff.

different ways. So, too, we may take a double view of both of the Attributes. Extension may be regarded either as a single indivisible nature, or as the infinite collection of particular extended objects in which that nature is displayed. Regarded in the latter fashion it is called by Spinoza "the face of the entire universe," and is designated as an "infinite mode." The same designation is applied to motion and rest, which are universal characteristics of Extension, and are the source of its diversification into individual extended objects. In like manner, the activity of Thought which, accompanying rest and motion, produces the individual modes of thinking corresponding to physical events, is called by Spinoza an "infinite mode of thought," or "intellect absolutely infinite." There is some uncertainty whether he distinguished another infinite mode of that Attribute consisting of the aggregate of its individual modifications, and corresponding to the "face of the entire universe." But some critics feel that he had this in mind, when he spoke of the "infinite idea of God." [5] However, as the "infinite modes" play little part in his system, we need not discuss them further.

VI. NATURA NATURATA

Spinoza is now ready to proceed from God as *natura naturans,* or the one Substance of whose nature all things are the co-equal and co-eternal manifestations, to God as *natura naturata,* or the sum total of events in which that nature equally deploys and displays itself in space and time. To the human modifications of his nature, God, as we have just seen, manifests himself as two correlated systems, one of interconnected physical events, the other of correspondingly intercon-nected *ideas.* These two systems must run exactly and completely parallel to each other, since they are two ways of exhibiting one and the same nature each one of whose modes is simultaneously expressed in all its Attributes. Hence any modification of that nature will be simultaneously registered in its entirety in the two Attributes that fall within our ken. "The order and connection of ideas is the same as the order and connection of things."

Just what Spinoza meant by these *ideas,* and how he conceived the mental correlates of bodies and of their motions and changes, is a question that has provoked difference of opinion. Since there are *ideas* of inanimate as well as animate physical objects and processes, *ideas* can scarcely be regarded as individual psychical entities, like souls or minds for example, attached to all particular things. Nor, since for

[5] Cf. Joachim, *op. cit.,* pp. 83 ff.; Pollock, *op. cit.,* pp. 100 ff., p. 176.

Spinoza, as we shall see in a moment, the infinite intellect of God is impersonal, can they be the *thoughts* of a self-conscious mind reflecting upon the order and connection of physical events. One is tempted rather to think that the *idea* meant for him what we should call the *truth* about each particular physical event—and this all the more so, as the infinite intellect of God, which comprises the totality of *ideas* that modify the Attribute of Thought, seems to mean the whole truth about the entire universe, entertained by a mind unconscious of itself as a thing apart from that truth. In any case, we must avoid many of the connotations the word *idea* has for us, and shall do better to substitute for it in our minds a non-committal term like *mental correlate*.

VII. THE HUMAN AND THE DIVINE MIND

The Nature of Man. We turn now from the general characteristics of *natura naturata* to one of its incidents—*man*. Since man is one of the infinite number and variety of the modifications of the divine Substance, he will, like all else, share not only in its Thought and its Extension, but in the myriad of other Attributes that lie beyond our ken. Our minds and our bodies are but two segments of the immensity of our being. They are not superficial appearances, for they cleave to its center and to the center of Reality. But beyond and about them, radiating from that same center, is the infinity of what we are as modes, also, of the other Attributes of God. We all of us, then, live and move and have our being in countless other worlds besides our own, undreamed of and inconceivable. Our every act and thought register in terms of extension and consciousness a modification occurring simultaneously throughout the endless number of all the other, unknowable forms of our existence.

Like all else, we are, so far as God exhibits himself in us in terms of Extension and Thought, a correlation of a physical and a mental event. The "idea" correlated with a human body is a human *mind*. There can be no interaction between them, but the parallelism between them is complete. Nothing can occur in the body without a corresponding registration in the mind, nothing in the mind without a correlated change in the body. Changes in the body are occasioned in the body only by physical causes, changes in the mind only by antecedent modifications of consciousness. But the two chains of causation are interwoven link by link, so that to all intents and purposes one psycho-physical situation causes another psycho-physical situation.

Self-Consciousness. The *idea* correlated with the human body has a characteristic that we do not observe in the mental correlates of other than human bodies. It not only reflects the make-up, native activities, and modification by other physical events of the physical organism of which it is the registration in the Attribute of Thought; it also reflects *itself,* and in so doing reflects *upon* itself. In Spinoza's phrase, it is not only an "idea of the body"; it is an "idea of the idea of the body," or "idea of the mind." In short, it is *self-conscious.*

Whether the mental correlates of other bodies, animate or inanimate, are also self-reflective and self-conscious is a question Spinoza does not raise. By implication, the *ideas* of so-called *inanimate* bodies would seem, in his opinion, not to be so. The nature and status of *animal* consciousness is not discussed. In man, however, self-consciousness is an observed fact, and it is with man alone, and with his relation to the universe, that the rest of Spinoza's philosophy is chiefly concerned.

In any case, only a particular and partial modification of the Real can be self-conscious. For self-consciousness can accompany only an *idea* that reflects both its own body and *other* physical events by which that body is surrounded and with which it is in *contact* and *conflict.* Without such registration within itself of the existence of an *external* environment, an *idea* would have nothing from which to distinguish and set apart both itself and the body with which it was correlated. Hence it could not recognize itself as one event among others, as *this* event rather than *that* and as *itself* rather than something else. But it is precisely such recognition of apartness that constitutes the "idea of the idea," or, in other words, the self-reflective character of the "idea of the human body" which makes that idea a self-conscious mind.

Self-consciousness and "personality" are, then, for Spinoza, the mental correlates of limited and finite beings and are expressive of the alienation of the part from the whole to which it belongs and from which it draws its true significance. They are centered in and about the particular location, situation, and fortunes of a particular event, and reflect the importance and central position in the universe each such event necessarily assigns to itself precisely because of its partial and circumscribed character. Hence they are associated, not with the essential characteristics and relations that unite the mode with the whole of nature, but with the special idiosyncrasies and interests that sever it from and oppose it to the necessary order and connection of events in which it occurs and that emphasize its particular and fragmentary character.

Human and Divine Intellects Contrasted. Conversely, the infinite intellect of God must be impersonal. For, instead of being associated, like the human mind, with a particular body, surrounded by other bodies of which it is not the correlate or "idea" and by other "ideas" associated with these bodies, it has as its physical correlate the content of all space and time. It has, therefore, no environment from which to distinguish and with which to contrast itself. In short, it is free from the *intellectual* conditions of self-consciousness.

Moreover, having no particular body, and being associated with no particular part, it feels none of the passions, interests, prejudices and personal loves and hates that reflect the contact, the conflict, and the modification of a particular human mode with and by other modes. For how should a whole, all of whose parts are equally expressive of itself, love or hate or favor any one of them above another? The mind of God, then, being without desire, will, preference, or any emotional disturbance, is as free from the "affective" as it is from the intellectual conditions of self-consciousness and personality.

Of Spinoza's insistence that to think and know as God thinks and knows is to transcend self-consciousness and personality, there can be no doubt. That he so taught was recognized at once, and immediately gave, as it still gives, rise to the charge of atheism. His doctrine cannot but remind us of the Aristotelian "active intellect" which thinks impersonally in each one of us, and, in flooding our minds with the light of truth, obliterates our consciousness of our separate selves and identifies us with the object we are contemplating. With the Aristotelian teaching Spinoza must have been familiarized by Hebrew commentators, like Avicebron and Maimonides, in whose systems it played so important a part. However that may be, the view that God is impersonal occupies a central position in his philosophy.

The Essential Impersonality and Impartiality of the Human Mind. Although a human mind and the particular body with which it is correlated constitute a fragmentary, local, and ephemeral modification of Thought and Extension, they nevertheless partake of and display the universal and unchanging essence of these Attributes. Hence, since the Attribute of Thought is *essentially* a comprehension of the truth, the whole truth, and nothing but the truth about the constitution of the universe, the human mind also is *essentially* a complete understanding of the true nature of the Real. Personality and self-consciousness are *accidental* obscurations of its essence by its particular association with a particular body. And, since the Attribute of Thought is coextensive with the Attribute of Extension, the human mind is capable of extending in its thinking and point of view its physical base from the particular body of which it is the mental correlate to *all* the bodies that constitute the physical universe. It is thus able to conceive itself as equally correlated, like the infinite intellect of God, with all objects and events instead of with one of them, and as viewing all that occurs from the standpoint of the universe as a whole rather than from that of a single incident in the universe.

Human Happiness and Truth. Since it is the essence of the human mind to know the truth, we naturally strive after knowledge, and to the degree that we attain it we are realizing our true selves. Hence the progressive identification of the human mind with the infinite intellect of God is accompanied by an ever greater sense of happiness. Knowledge of the union of the mind with the whole of nature is, then, as Spinoza pointed out in *On the Amendment of the Understanding,* man's only true and unfailing good. And it is the application of this knowledge to our dealings with the rest of nature, and particularly with our fellow-men, that is the basis of the *good life* and of *moral conduct.* Furthermore, since such knowledge makes us at last at home in the world and at peace with ourselves and the rest of nature, its attainment spells salvation. By it we are delivered from bondage to our specifically human estate and made one with the divine mind.

The Obstacles to Knowledge and Happiness. A large part of the *Ethics* is devoted to discussing the obstacles that stand in the way of our transcending the self-consciousness and self-centeredness imposed upon us by our position, as one event among others, in the necessary order and connection of things, and to describing the means of overcoming them. The two fundamental obstacles responsible for our shortcomings and unhappiness are *error* and *passion.* The human problem, then, is that of freeing our minds and hearts from them. To solve it Spinoza launches upon a detailed review of the human situation in the universe.

VIII. PHYSICS, PSYCHO-PHYSICS AND PSYCHOLOGY

Man, being a body as well as a mind, is subjected to all the conditions to which the physical universe is subjected. In his description of those conditions, Spinoza is in essential agreement with Descartes. He notes the laws of motion and the persistence of structure and identity through change and growth, accepts Descartes' identification of matter with space and his corpuscular theory of its constitution, and holds that the human body, being part of the physical order, must partake of the nature of matter, and, in its inner processes and give-and-take with other bodies, must be governed by physical laws. The biological functioning of the organism, therefore, is mechanical in character and explicable in minutest detail by efficient causation. Furthermore, the body, though an individual modification of the Attribute of Extension, is articulated into a complexity of organs, and these organs into an indefinite number of constituent parts.

Passing now to psycho-physics, we find that "the idea which constitutes the actual being of the human mind is not simple, but compounded of a great number of ideas," each one of which has its particular physical correlate. Moreover, just as the organs composing the body are divisible into material corpuscles, so these "ideas" are themselves compounded of registrations of physical ultimates. Finally, the same laws of causation hold for the order and connection of ideas as hold for bodily processes. Trains of thought are no more to be explained by the conclusions at which they arrive than are physical sequences. They, too, are motivated by their antecedents, not by their results.

From psycho-physics we pass to psychology. Since, according to the laws of physics, any modification of the body tends to persist until stopped by some new modification, so its mental correlate will persist until stopped by a new idea. Hence the mind retains images of past events and *remembers*. Furthermore, since every modification leaves some trace of itself in the physical organism, new stimulations of that trace will call up the old image associated with it, and the mind will *recall*. So, too, images may persist which are not referred to the past, in which case the mind *imagines*. Finally, if two modifications have occurred together, the recurrence of one will also recall the image of the other; that is, there is *association* of ideas.

IX. KNOWLEDGE OF THE EXTERNAL WORLD

With these preliminaries in mind we turn to the problem of knowledge and error. Our first question is that of the possibility of knowledge itself. If a man's mind is the mental correlate only of his own body, how can he know anything but his own body and the "ideas" correlated with it? The answer is that his pyscho-physical state at any given moment is always a composite of both the nature of his own particular body and mind and of the nature of the external environment by which he is being influenced and modified. Hence his mind.

in knowing itself, will register, also, the "ideas" of the objects by which he is being conditioned. Furthermore, in proportion to the number and sensitiveness of his body's contacts with its physical environment, his experience is enriched, and the scope of his acquaintance with the nature of the Real is enlarged.

But, since there is no interaction between mind and body, and since our experience of the external world does not come into the mind from the outside, but wells up from within, how can the mind know when the ideas of which it is compounded are adequately representing the physical world and occupying their proper place in the necessary order and connection of ideas, and when they are not? In short, how are we to distinguish *true* from *false* ideas? For that matter, why should we even make the distinction between adequate and inadequate ideas?

Spinoza's answer is Descartes'. Some ideas are in themselves clearer and more distinct than others. A clearer and a more distinct idea is *intrinsically* a truer registration of its subject than a blurred and distorted one. We do not have to compare it with its subject to know that. And, since "the order and connection of ideas is the same as the order and connection of things," we can be sure that an idea which is perfectly clear and distinct in itself is correlated in our minds solely with its parallel event in the Attribute of Extension, and is covering that event completely and adequately. Moreover, such an idea will of necessity be occupying its proper place in "the necessary order and connection of ideas" that constitutes the truth about the universe.

X. THE NATURE AND SOURCE OF ERROR

If, however, it is the *essential* nature of the mind to entertain adequate ideas, how is error possible? We should expect the mind to distinguish its component ideas from one another, to correlate each with its parallel physical event, and to place it where it belonged in the Attribute of Thought. Plainly, then, error is not native to the intellect. It must be an interference from the outside with the natural and normal operation of our reason.

The source of this interference cannot be laid at the door of the *will,* as Descartes thought, for the will and the understanding are not two separate faculties operating independently of each other. Simply to entertain an idea is already to have *assented* to it and to have accepted it as clear or unclear, distinct or indistinct.

Error, rather, has its roots in the fact that our sensible experience—

or, as Spinoza calls it, our *imagination*—registers the nature of our own body as it is being modified by its environment, and the nature of other bodies as they are modifying our own. Hence it cannot give an exhaustive and adequate account either of our own organism as it is apart from its modifications by external bodies or of external bodies as they are in themselves apart from their effects upon us. Therefore, sensible images, whatever their stimuli, not only fail to distinguish and articulate clearly and distinctly the different factors co-operating in the modification of a human organism by external events, but also fail to spell out in their entirety the total natures of these factors.

Nor are generic ideas, or "universals," in Spinoza's opinion any improvement upon sensible images as instruments of true knowledge, for they themselves are nothing but blurred and confused and sensible composites of blurred and confused sensible presentations. They are useless, therefore, as means for analyzing images into their elements, and for assigning those elements correctly to their proper physical correlates, and thus placing physical and mental events in their *true* places on the maps of Thought and Extension.

The human mind, then, would appear to be dependent for its information and knowledge concerning the nature of the Real upon what Spinoza calls "knowledge from the mere suggestions of experience," and upon the confused and inadequate ideas these suggestions are bound, in the nature of things, to suggest. True, its essence is knowledge of the Real. But can it manifest that essence under the handicaps imposed upon its operations by its association with a particular body and by the limited and muddled mentality consequent upon such association? Spinoza thinks it can.

XI. INTELLECTUAL MEANS OF ESCAPE FROM ERROR

Error Is Misplaced Truth. In the first place, it may already have dawned upon us that there is no such thing as absolute error, since even the most fanciful presentations, such as illusions and hallucinations, have, after all, their proper physical correlates, and, once they are referred to these correlates, turn from inadequate to adequate, from false to true, ideas. For example, says Spinoza, the sun appears to be about two hundred feet away. This idea is an inadequate mental correlate of the external physical situation, but it is an adequate idea or representation of the state of a body like mine when modified or affected by an external body of the real size and at the real distance of the sun. So, too, the feeling of free-will is an adequate or true correlate of the confused and hidden character of the causes that determine our actions; it is an inadequate idea if referred to a real absence of determining factors.

Plainly, then, error consists merely in what we might call misplaced truth. It lies in correlating an idea with more or less than its actual counterpart in the Attribute of Extension, and it may always be corrected by discovering the physical datum of which the idea is the mental Siamese twin.

The Nature of All Thought and All Extension. Moreover, the means of correction are within our grasp. Even on the level of sensible presentation there occur certain indications of absolute truth useful to the mind as a handhold and foothold for climbing out of the spatio-temporal trap in which it is seemingly snared by its association with a particular body. Within its own finite nature and the finite nature of its physical correlate it finds characteristics that pertain to all Thought and all Extension in all times and places. For example, the laws of motion and the mathematical structure that we can infer from studying our particular portion of space and time necessarily hold good, in Spinoza's opinion, for the entire Attribute of Extension; and the laws that govern the rational operations of our own mind give us the structure of the entire Attribute of Thought. Furthermore, once in possession of these adequate ideas, the mind can deduce from them other ideas equally true and necessary, since "whatsoever ideas in the mind follow from ideas which are therein adequate, are also themselves adequate."

The mind, therefore, can overcome its finite handicap and know the absolute truth about the nature of both Thought and Extension. This truth is the basis of *science*. By reducing the complexity of presentation to the least common denominators provided by these adequate ideas, we can *understand* it and thus dispel our erroneous attribution of ideas to correlates with which they do not belong. Nay more, we can understand our errors, seeing how in the nature of things they must come to pass, and we can thus find place for them as natural facts in the natural world. For example, once we know the laws of physics and optics and apply them to the sun and to the human eye, we can understand how a body like the sun, modifying from a given distance a body constructed like the human eye, *must* produce the modification of the physical organism of which the seeming size and distance of the sun are the mental correlate or "idea." In short, we can give a scientific explanation of the discrepancy between the real and the seeming situation, and in so doing turn that which, if taken at its face value, would be error into an enlightening example of scientific fact.

XII. INTUITIVE KNOWLEDGE

Understanding and Intuition. However, the mind's power to know is not exhausted by *scientific understanding*. We *understand* individual events by assigning to mental and physical occurrences their proper correlates, and by connecting psycho-physical situations with their proper *causes* and *effects;* that is, with the *antecedent* and *contiguous* situations that, in the necessary order and connection of events, determine their particular occurrence and location, and with the particular *subsequent* and *contiguous* situations whose occurrence and location they in their turn determine. But, no matter how far we carry this correlation and this connection in any direction, we find ourselves merely explaining one event by connecting it with another, without being able to explain further *why* that connection should be what it is, or *why* situations should have the causes and effects they have rather than others. Although, then, we may discover *how* any particular event fits into the necessary order and connection of things, we do not as yet grasp the necessity of that order's being necessary. We know the modifications of the Real only in terms of one another, not in terms of the whole of which they are parts, and of whose essence their causal relations and their order and connection are the necessary expression.

The Nature of Intuition. To bring knowledge to its full fruition we must, then, explain the modifications of God by referring them directly to his essence, as well as to one another, for their cause. To do so we must, so to speak, look down from above upon the universe as a whole, as well as along its surface from part to part. Thus seen, the Real reveals itself as a single, all-inclusive system of interrelated and causally interconnected events, in which the way these events determine one another to existence and modify one another's character and course is itself determined by the nature of the system in question.

The power to look down upon the universe as well as along it, to grasp its nature as a whole, and to explain the part not only by its connection with other parts but as a necessary expression of the divine essence, the human mind possesses by virtue of its essential identity with the infinite intellect of God. And its ability to exercise that power, in spite of its fragmentary, local, and ephemeral character, is due, like its ability to understand, to the fact that every modification of the

Attributes of Thought and Extension exhibits their essential and universal characteristics. Hence, our minds are able not only to *understand* the particular causes of particular events, but also to construct from so much of the Real as falls within our ken an adequate idea of the universal Plan or Pattern to which *all* the modifications of both Attributes throughout infinite space and time must conform. In Spinoza's own words, "The human mind has an adequate knowledge of the eternal and infinite essence of God." This knowledge it can discover and develop within itself, if only it will set itself to the task, and in attaining it, it recovers its birthright of vision "under the aspect of eternity."

XIII. ERROR AND THE PASSIONS

Self-Assertion and Preference. But is it within the power of the human mind to set itself to the task of shaking off its errors and attaining vision under the aspect of eternity? Hitherto we have been treating human beings as if they were static and stationary fragments of Thought and Extension, in *contact,* to be sure, but not in *collision* with other bodies. And we have dealt with error as due merely to mixed and confused experiences correlated with modifications of the human body from without, by which the human mind might be perplexed, but was not otherwise disturbed.

The human body, however, like all other modifications of Extension, possesses inertia and changes its state or place in accordance with the universal laws that govern all alteration and locomotion. Hence, like all other bodies, it tends to persist in any given position or motion, and to resist any interference with that position or motion by the action of other bodies upon it. The mental correlate of this obedience to what we now call the first law of motion is self-assertion and volition. We *wish* and *endeavor* to preserve ourselves, and to have and go our own particular ways. And we naturally *prefer* those modifications of our own bodies, and the bodies to which those modifications are due, which further our self-preservation and self-assertion. Them we *seek, welcome,* and *embrace,* whereas we naturally *avoid* and *combat* those other modes of the Real whose action upon us is harmful or obstructive to our self-preservation and self-assertion.

The Influence of Value Judgments on Truth Judgments. So it is that the ideas of which the human mind is compounded differ in *pleasantness* as well as in clearness and distinctness. Some are most grateful, others extremely distasteful, to us. And their pleasantness or

unpleasantness becomes confused with and substituted for clearness
and distinctness and the reverse in our minds. Our impulse is to feel
that *agreeable* ideas are more adequate representations of the true
nature of Reality than *disagreeable* ones, and to discredit and reject
as confused and indistinct, and therefore erroneous, ideas that we do
not *like*. Hence, we tend to conduct our thinking, not impartially and
according to the laws of logic, with a view to discovering what ideas
are *true,* but according to our particular, self-centered preferences and
prejudices with a view to establishing the truth of those ideas that we
find *agreeable* and flattering to ourselves. In short, our attribution of
ideas to their proper objects is not hampered solely by the intellectual
confusion associated with the physical confusion of bodily modifications. It is vitiated also by "wishful thinking," which, for the sake of
satisfying desire, assigns objects to ideas and ideas to objects in the
correlation most pleasing to our self-esteem, our loves and hates, our
hopes and fears.

Of this confusion Spinoza has already given major examples. We
want to be free, and therefore we see in our feeling of freedom the
correlate of an objective liberty, rather than the ignorance correlated
with the inability of body and mind to record distinctly the causes of
their behavior. We *want* to think that we are the darling of the gods
and that the universe is run for our benefit. Hence we correlate everything in it that benefits our body and pleases our mind with a divine
purpose rather than with a mechanically determined and necessary
order and connection of events.

XIV. THE EMOTIONS

The Nature of Emotion. Plainly, then, we must investigate this
affectional, emotional, volitional aspect of the mind, to the end that
we may discover both the part it plays in the production of error and
any suggestion it may make as to how the errors for which it is responsible may be corrected. So it is that in Book III of the *Ethics,*
Spinoza develops his theory of the emotions. He begins with definitions and axioms that define *activity* and *passivity* as respectively conditions in which both mind and body are determined to action by
their own natures or by the natures of external things, and that therefore equate them on the mental side with *adequate* and *inadequate*
thinking. He also notes the capacity of the body for being "affected
in many ways, whereby its power of activity is increased or diminished,
and also in other ways which do not render its power of activity either

greater or less." And he defines *emotion* as "the modifications of the body whereby the active power of said body is increased or diminished, aided or constrained, and also the ideas of such modifications." When emotion arises connected with our "adequate" causation of our behavior, it is an activity; otherwise it is a *passion,* or state wherein the mind is being acted upon.

Furthermore, the mental correlate of an increase of the native activity of the body through beneficial external stimulations is *pleasure,* and of the reverse, *pain.* Under the influence of the one the organism enjoys also a feeling of general well-being, or "merriment" as Spinoza calls it; under the influence of the other it becomes depressed and "melancholy." The natural search for beneficial stimulations and avoidance of harmful ones is correlated with love or hate of external objects and of their mental representations, according as those raise or lower the state and sense of well-being.

Derivation of All the Emotions. Out of the three elementary emotions of desire, pleasure, and pain, taken in conjunction with the laws of association, Spinoza develops the whole body of emotions by which the mind is affected. In connection with memory and anticipation, they beget feelings of hope and fear, of confidence and despair, of relief and disappointment. Through the workings of association, love and hate are extended from the external causes that heighten or lower our pleasure and well-being to the things that benefit or damage these causes; and, once more, to whatever helps or harms these things, and so on. Hence we naturally rejoice, in ever-widening circles, over the well-being of what brings us good and the downfall of what brings us ill, and we sorrow over the opposite. Nay more, we tend to reproduce and imitate in ourselves the emotions under which we see other beings like ourselves laboring, though these beings are neither loved nor hated by us.

The mere sight, then, of pleasure and pain and of well-being and misery in other human beings will arouse similar feelings in ourselves. Therefore we feel pleased and perfected by pleasing and benefiting others, and pained and harmed by paining and harming them. So it is that men are naturally imitative and social and altruistic, and that their loves and hates, their envies and their pities are motivated by crowd psychology, the approvals and disapprovals of their fellows, and sensitiveness to public opinion. We estimate ourselves in terms of what other people think of us. By association we tend to love or hate whatever is loved or hated by our friends. And our natural hatred of those who hate what we love gives rise to class and sectional and national antipathies. Still, we can never utterly rejoice at the destruction of what we hate, since the idea of destruction is in itself a painful idea. Conversely, we can feel joy in remembering past evils. This ambiguous interrelation of hate and love enables us to overcome hatred and to turn it into love, or to diminish it by associating it with other causes than the hated object. Moreover, the more inevitable and necessary these causes seem to be, the less the hatred they engender. Complete understanding of the necessity that makes the hated object what it is transforms hatred into compassion or into detached scientific interest. Incidentally, this possibility of converting hate into compassion or scientific interest is of great importance in Spinoza's system. Without it salvation and the attainment of the eternal good would be impossible.

So far, the emotions with which we have been dealing have been passions connected with the modification of our body and mind by external things and their ideas. If we add to them passions like gluttony, drunkenness, lust, avarice, and ambition, which are exaggerations of our natural affections for certain classes of outer objects, we have perhaps discussed them sufficiently to indicate Spinoza's treatment of the subject.

Besides the passions, there are certain pleasurable or painful states or emotions that accompany the essential activity of the mind unmodified by the pressure of the outer world. These emotions, correlated as they are with the exercise of reason, will be themselves, not irrational, like the passions, but rational, and will exhibit strength of inward character. They are courage, or desire for self-preservation and self-assertion governed by the dictates of reason, and highmindedness, or generosity of nature, which lies in aiding and loving one's fellowmen as a man motivated entirely by reason should.

XV. HUMAN GOOD AND EVIL

It must be plain from what we have just been saying that *good* and *evil, right* and *wrong,* are purely relative to human interests. What in the necessary order and connection of events *benefits* the preservation, self-assertion, and self-realization of the human race we call *good;* those modifications of the Real that tend to destroy, or harm, or interfere with human self-expression we call *evil.* So, too, human action is *right* or *wrong* according as it tends to further or obstruct the self-fulfillment of human life. The human moral order, then, is centered upon and revolves about that particular mode of the Real we call *man.* By implication, other self-conscious modes, differently organized and situated from ourselves, and with other interests than ours, might conceivably be the centers of moral values and systems at variance with one another and with human ethical standards.

But the distinction between good and evil, right and wrong, does not exist as such in the infinite intellect of God. Seen "under the aspect of eternity," all things, in whatever relation they may stand to our particular human interests, and all human actions, whether virtuous or sinful from the human point of view, are equally complete, adequate, and perfect expressions of the nature of the Real. Hence, neither human moral distinctions nor the particular good and evil of any other mode of Reality can be conceived as receiving special cosmic sanction and support. God fulfills himself as clearly and distinctly, as adequately and perfectly, in the ways that harm us and in the harm they do us, as in the ways that benefit us and in the benefit they do us. What is good or evil, right or wrong, from the point of view of the part, is merely and equally *necessary* from the point of view of the whole.

XVI. THE GOOD LIFE FOR MAN

Man's Pursuit of His Good. Nevertheless, man, in learning to view things from the standpoint of the whole, will not thereby become himself *indifferent* to his own particular interests and to the distinction founded upon them, between what is good and evil, right and wrong for *him*. For he will see that it follows from an "adequate knowledge of the eternal and infinite essence of God" that he, as a special modification of the Real endowed with the drives and desires characteristic of that modification, must live his particular form of life in a certain way, if he is to preserve and assert himself and realize his desires. He will, to be sure, learn to accept what he must in the nature of things. But he will also be encouraged to utilize to his advantage what he can modify in such wise as to aid his self-preservation and self-assertion, and to destroy that which is destructive to them, or, when he cannot do so, to protect himself against it. For the nature of the Real necessitates such self-assertion on the part of all its modifications according to their several natures. Hence, that man, also, should so act is a part of the necessary order and connection of things, and the condition of his continued existence as an expression of God's essence.

The Criteria of Good and Evil. In the third and fourth books of the *Ethics,* entitled respectively *Of Human Bondage* and *Of Human Freedom,* Spinoza discusses human good and evil, and the means of

promoting the one and of overcoming the other. The distinctive character of the human modification of the Real lies in its power to *know*
of its union with the whole of nature, and to survey all the modifications of that nature, including itself, "under the aspect of eternity,"
in their proper places in the necessary order and connection of events
in which the infinite and eternal essence of God is displayed. Hence
that in man which he will endeavor and desire above all else to preserve and assert will be his capacity for *knowledge*. It follows that
such emotions and activities as foster the power to *know* will be *good*
emotions and *right* behavior, and that such as impair it will be *evil*
and *wrong*. As we have just seen, this distinction coincides with that
between the emotions and behavior we call *active* and those we call
passive and the conduct motivated by them. They coincide, furthermore, with the emotions and conduct we call *rational* and those we call
irrational.

Implications of Human Morality. To establish what is right and
wrong we have only to ask specifically what benefits us, or, in other
words, what is most harmonious to us. That is most harmonious with
which we have most in common. What we have most in common
with is our fellow-beings. Therefore, the interest in our fellow-beings,
with which the psychology of the emotions has shown that we are
necessarily endowed, is a *good* interest conducive to the expression
of the rational part of our nature. Altruism and social harmony are
the natural goods of a rational being.

In so far as men live in obedience to reason, they necessarily agree
and by their agreement render their common exercise of reason easier
to maintain and their common joy in knowledge of the truth the more
secure. Dissension among men arises only when and in so far as they
are a prey to their passions. True, in the absence of reason the fear of
being harmed is an emotion strong enough to control the impulse to
harm others. But a rational being has no need of such restraint. His
exercise of his sovereign, natural and inalienable right to self-preservation and self-assertion, his competency to judge for himself what is
right and what is wrong for him, his necessary pursuit of what is
useful and his innate propensity to cherish what he loves and to
destroy what he hates, cannot bring him into conflict with his fellows,
since what is *truly* helpful or harmful to the self-preservation of one
man is helpful or harmful to all men alike.

The state comes into being as an aid to the life of reason. It imposes certain restrictions upon the indulgence of human passion, disobedience to which we call *sin,* obedience to which acquires *merit* for

us. But, were man not a prey to his passions, and were he completely
free to express his rational nature, the state and the restrictions it
imposes on us would be unnecessary. Men would live in spontaneous
harmony with one another, and there would be no sin and no merit.

XVII. THE CONTENT OF THE GOOD HUMAN LIFE

The All-Inclusive Character of the Good Life. In what kind of a
distinctively human life will, then, the prevalence of reason in the
individual and the state permit and encourage man to express his
modal and finite characteristics? The answer is that the life of reason
will be liberal, rich, and well-rounded. Its physical activities will be
as complete as possible. The more capacities for experience and action
the body has, the greater, Spinoza insists, is the mind's capability of
perception and of activity. Moreover, "pleasure in itself is not bad but
good; contrariwise, pain in itself is bad." Therefore, life is to be lived
and enjoyed to the utmost, not denied. Again, if the mind is to be
strong and healthy, the body correlated with it must be so, too. The
man who is actuated by reason will therefore care for his body and
give proper exercise to all its functions.

Finally, social life is not to be regarded as a mere means to the
better exercise of the activity of knowledge. It is pleasant in itself, and
as such its amenities are an essential part of the good life. Part of virtue
is to laugh and to make merry, for "assuredly nothing forbids a man
to enjoy himself save grim and gloomy superstition." Indeed, "the
greater the pleasure wherewith we are affected, the greater the perfection whereto we pass; in other words, the more must we necessarily
partake of the divine nature. Therefore, to make use of what comes
our way, and to enjoy it as much as possible (not to the point of
satiety, for that would not be enjoyment) is the part of a wise man.
I say, it is the part of a wise man to refresh and to recreate himself
with moderate and pleasant food and drink, and also with perfumes,
with the soft beauty of growing plants, with dress, with music, with
many sports, with theaters and the like, such as every man may make
use of without injury to his neighbor." For thus the body is kept in
condition "for performing all the actions which follow from the necessity of its own nature," and thus the mind is kept open and "capable
of understanding many things simultaneously." LUKE 12:19

At the same time, our enjoyment must always be checked and mod-
erated by reason. There is no such thing as excess of joy or being too
happy. Pleasure is always a good. Pain and a severe and dour outlook

on life are always bad. But it is also bad to become too addicted to one pleasure to the exclusion of others. Moreover, pain and grief may often be useful and therefore good in restraining overindulgence and in preventing an isolated pleasure from becoming so excessive as to hinder rather than heighten the activity of the body as a whole.

The Passive and Evil Emotions. We have now to mention the passive emotions which interfere with the exercise of reason and with rational living. First of these comes hatred of our fellow-men, and its evil brood of envy, derision, contempt, anger, revenge, and the other passions it begets. "Whatsoever we desire from motives of hatred is base, and in a state unjust." Fear and hope, overesteem and disparagement, pity, humility, and repentance, overweening pride and too great dejection, and desires aimed, not at the pleasure and well-being of the whole, but at the satisfaction of some single craving regardless of the best interests of the entire man, are either useless or positively detrimental to true happiness. They are, therefore, irrational passions. Some of these passions, too, reflect the false perspective of time with its consequent overemphasis of the present as against the future and the past.

Naturally, it is of the essence of reason to resist them, and to preserve itself and keep its head in their midst. So far as we act rationally, for example, we tend to correct the false perspective of time and to give equal weight to ideas regardless of their temporal reference. We detect and discount the importance spuriously added to an event by its presence or subtracted from it by its futurity, and when confronted with a choice we prefer and pursue a greater future good rather than the lesser present one at which the unthinking and the vulgar clutch.

Again, reason casts out that arch-enemy of human happiness, fear in all its forms. The behavior of the rational man is actuated by the pleasure he takes in living rationally. The good life is an end in itself. To live it from fear of living otherwise and in order to escape evil is the mark of an irrational mind. A morality, therefore, founded upon fear is a false and dangerous morality. "Superstitious persons," Spinoza remarks, "who know better how to rail at vice than how to teach virtue, and who strive not to guide men by reason but so to restrain them that they would rather escape evil than love virtue, have no other aim but to make others as wretched as themselves." Wherefore, he adds, "It is nothing wonderful if they be generally troublesome and odious to their fellow-men."

Furthermore, reason rids us of our obsession about death. The wise man, free from all fears and occupied with realizing to its fullest life while it lasts, has no time or emotion to waste over thoughts of death. "His wisdom," says Spinoza in one of his most famous phrases, "is a meditation not of death but of life."

The Good Life a Free Life. We are now able to say that the rational life is a *free* life determined, not by our passions and opinions, but by the activity of our essential being which is complete, unclouded, and unhampered union of our minds with truth. The man whose views and whose actions are determined only by reason, that is, by himself, hates no man, "is angry with no man, envies no man, is indignant with no man, despises no man, and least of all is proud." It is "ever first in his thoughts that all things follow from the necessity of the divine nature; so that whatsoever he deems to be hurtful and evil, and whatsoever accordingly seems to him impious, horrible, unjust and base, assumes that appearance owing to his own disordered, fragmentary and confused view of the universe. Wherefore he strives before all things to conceive things as they really are, and to remove the hindrances to true knowledge, such as are hatred, anger, envy, derision, pride and similar emotions. . . . Thus he endeavors . . . as far as in him lies, to do good and to go on his way rejoicing."

XVIII. LIBERATION FROM HUMAN BONDAGE

Control of the Passions. We now know how the good man should live, and what the obstacles to living the good life are. These obstacles are the passions or "emotions contrary to our nature" with which we are assailed by the external world, and which impair our "power of arranging and associating the modifications of our body according to the intellectual order." We have now to ask whether it is possible for us to overcome the "emotions contrary to our nature," or whether the good life must remain forever a mere counsel of perfection.

Plainly, the passions are more difficult to deal with than simple intellectual error. The latter can be dissipated by recognizing the confused and inadequate nature of an idea, by distinguishing its constituent elements whose confusion makes it erroneous, and by assigning those elements to their proper physical correlates and thus to their proper place in the necessary order and connection of ideas. But the passions cannot be overcome merely by understanding them. To be sure, they can be understood, like any other modification of our body, and "an emotion, which is a passion, ceases to be a passion as soon as we form a clear and distinct idea thereof." For to understand a passion is to remove it from us by seeing that it is not part of us and does not originate in us, but is a modification of our real essence in a way contrary to our nature.

Nevertheless, the real understanding of a passion, in such wise that it is overcome and removed, necessitates more than an intellectual apprehension of its character and causes. We may have a knowledge of good and evil and know that we are doing wrong, without being impelled thereby to mend our ways. We may approve the better course but follow the worse. If we are to follow as well as to approve the better course, we must *prefer* it. We must *desire* and *will* the good, must *hate* and *shun* the bad. In Spinoza's own words, "a true knowledge of good and evil cannot check any emotion by virtue of being true, but only in so far as it is considered as an emotion." The point in question thus becomes that of determining whether in the nature of things it is possible to invest the knowledge of good and evil with sufficient emotion in favor of the good to make it efficacious.

Love of Knowledge Strongest of All Loves. Spinoza believes both that such knowledge is in the nature of things necessarily accompanied by an emotion that makes it efficacious, and that he can prove mathematically and mechanically that this is the case. Granted that "any emotion can only be controlled or destroyed by another contrary thereto, and with more power for controlling emotion," the *desire* to know and the emotion attending the acquisition of knowledge and the application of it to our daily lives, are naturally and inevitably the strongest desire and the most powerful emotion with which a human being is endowed. For an idea is vivid and the emotions it arouses are correspondingly strong in proportion to the *number* of ideas associated with it, and to the *degree* in which these ideas are *present* experiences rather than memories or anticipations and are felt to be *necessary* rather than merely possible. Now, an idea that is *understood* is in complete possession of all these qualifications. It is seen in its proper relation to *all* the other ideas that fall within the scope of the divine intellect, and as a *necessary* expression of the nature of the Real and as part of a whole *present* in its entirety to the mind.

Hence, when a man understands and intuits, he is modified not by some portion of Reality confusedly experienced and inadequately represented, but by the whole of Reality adequately represented. But an adequate idea of the whole must necessarily modify man more profoundly than does an inadequate idea of the part. Hence the emotion and the driving power connected with understanding and intuiting will be in themselves greater than the passions or impulses arising from partial and confused modification by any part or combination of parts not understood. We conclude, therefore, that since the desire to understand and to know is the most profound and powerful reaction that any modification of our being can arouse in us, it can be successfully pitted against any other desires such modification may awaken.

XIX. THE INTELLECTUAL LOVE OF GOD

Our Love for God. This overpowering desire to know the nature of the Real, which is the one human desire that cannot be indulged to excess, and this disinterested love of such knowledge for its own sake, which is the one love than which no man hath greater, are synonymous for Spinoza with the love of God, and their satisfaction means human salvation. "The more we understand things, the more do we understand God," and the more we understand the more we love him. "This love towards God cannot be stained by the emotion of envy or jealousy: contrariwise, it is the more fostered in proportion as we conceive a great number of men to be joined to God by the same bond of love." It is of the nature of reason to desire to share its knowledge and its vision with others. Nor can anything separate us from the love of God. "No one can hate God" or help loving him, since for a man to hate or even to be indifferent to knowing the true nature of the Reality of which he is a part would be self-contradictory. The love of God is also completely disinterested, without thought of favor or expectation that God will love man in return. For to ask love from God would be to desire that he should not be the infinite and eternal Reality equally expressed in all things, but a private and personal being like ourselves. But so to conceive God would balk our essential desire to unite our minds with Reality, and would bring pain and frustration instead of joy and peace.

At this point Spinoza reiterates the assertion, already made in discussing the infinite intellect, that the Real is impersonal in character. "God is without passions, neither is he affected by any emotion of pleasure or pain." Nor does he love or hate anyone, as a person loves or hates. He is all things, the truth about all things, and an infinite mind lost in the contemplation of that truth; in whose sight all space is here, all time is now, and the content of all space and of all time is neither good nor evil but equally existent, equally necessary, and therefore equally expressive of and participant in the nature and the perfection of the Real. At the same time, it is part of that nature and that perfection that the mind should love truth, and that the vision of the truth should be the most interesting, the most exciting, the most desirable, and the most lovable of all things. As Spinoza puts it, "God loves himself with an infinite intellectual love," and our love of him, and our union with him in the vision of all things "under the aspect of eternity," may be fitly described as "part of the infinite love wherewith God loves himself."

The Love of God Not Antagonistic to a Love of the World. Our love of God, however, and our union with him are in no way antiphysical and ascetic. They create no dualistic opposition between the soul and the body, and, indeed, not only are compatible with, but encourage and are fed by our enjoyment of the good things the world has to offer and by our participation in worldly affairs. The wider and more varied and rich our experience, the more we understand, and, as we have just seen, the more we understand, the better we know what God is like. And "he who possesses a body capable of the greatest number of activities possesses a mind whereof the greater part is eternal." The attainment of the beatific vision and the consummation of the intellectual love of God do not disembody us. On the contrary, they enlarge our body through an ever-widening and deepening understanding of its modifications and relations, till it becomes, as it were, the whole order and connection of the modifications of the Attribute of Extension which constitute the body of God.

XX. IMMORTALITY

Nature of Immortality. Needless to say, there is no such thing as personal immortality in Spinoza's system. "The mind can only imagine anything or remember what is past, while the body endures," and the whole range of experience connected with personal existence disappears with the body. *My* mind, the localized point of view that makes me *me,* is centered in and radiates from one particular modification of the Real, which is surrounded by other bodies and marked off from them. It, therefore, ends when the physical circumstances come to an end that support it and permit within it the distinction between itself and other things.

At the same time, though I myself, body and mind, have a beginning and an end in birth and death, nothing can destroy the fact of my existence. Nothing can remove *me,* as a distinct person, born at a certain time, living a certain life, and dying at a certain date, from the nature of the Real. From all eternity I am part of history, one event in the infinite order and connection of events, which nothing can displace or replace, and to all eternity I shall so remain.

If, then, I view myself "under the aspect of eternity" and contemplate myself simply as part of the truth about the world, I lift myself, body and soul, and every tiniest incident of my life, clear of time altogether, and see myself as an eternal fact forever present in the Real. In this sense I am immortal. But this immortality is not a *quantity* of existence. The vision that confers it does not add one instant to my ephemeral duration in time. It does not defer or abolish my death. It does not give me any power to go on existing after my allotted duration on earth is over. That duration is all there is to *me*. But even so, it is time enough for me to transcend time and to invest my brief life, while it lasts, with the *quality* of eternity. Here and now, on earth, in this body, for the span of its duration in time as a mode of the Real, this corruptible may put on incorruptibility, this mortal may put on immortality, if only it will fill mind and heart with deathless truth and good.

Deathlessness of the Mind. But there is also something more to immortality. The kind of immortality we have been describing is shared with all other things. To me, viewing existence "under the aspect of eternity," not only my mind but my body and all other physical events appear as modifications of God's being that nothing can alter or erase, and that therefore are timeless and deathless. "In God there is necessarily an idea which expresses the essence of this or that body under the form of eternity." But, though the majesty of the Attributes of Thought and Extension is co-eternal, their glory is not quite co-equal. The order and connection of physical events, to be sure, is no less timeless in God than the order of ideas. Both are equally objects of intuitive knowledge, and both are equally invested with the deathlessness of truth. To the mind alone, however, belongs the power of *perceiving* their eternity. In short, the mind is not a merely contemplated object, as the body is. It is also an *activity* of contemplation. And this activity, being essentially contemplation under the aspect of eternity, "depends on the mind as its formal cause, in so far as the mind itself is eternal." It is deathless, and therefore something to which the death of the body, momentarily correlated with it, cannot put an end.

"The human mind," then, "cannot be absolutely destroyed with the body, but there remains of it something which is eternal." But the "something which is eternal" and survives the death of the body is precisely the *impersonal* activity of the mind, which, even while we are alive, extinguishes as far as possible the *personal self-consciousness* from which we suffer because of the correlation of human thinking with a particular body surrounded and modified by other bodies.

Morality and Immortality. Incidentally, Spinoza rejects the argument that, were it not for belief in personal immortality and hope of heavenly reward for virtue and fear of hell-fire awaiting the wicked, mankind would go to the dogs. That may be, he says; but, if such is the case, it is a slur upon true piety and religion and a founding of morality upon man's passions and inadequate and confused ideas rather than upon his rational nature and his acquaintance with the truth. To say that the man who does not believe in personal immortality has no incentive to right living is "not less absurd" than to suppose that "because he does not believe that he can by wholesome food sustain his body forever," he "should wish to cram himself with poisons and deadly fare"; or that "because he sees that the mind is not eternal or immortal, he should prefer to be out of his mind altogether and to live without the use of reason; these ideas are so absurd as to be scarcely worth refuting." Blessedness in this world or the next "is not the reward of virtue, but virtue itself." Salvation is not a heavenly crown that awaits in the future those who have controlled their lusts. It is a way of living here and now which automatically frees us from them.

XXI. SALVATION

The Union of the Mind with Nature. We come at last to the propositions in which Spinoza proclaims the saving power of the "something which is eternal" in our thinking, and of the vision "under the aspect of eternity" to which it elevates the mind. Their gist repeats and sums up much that we know already. The alpha and omega of our redemption lie in the statement that "our mind, in so far as it knows itself and the body under the form of eternity, has to that extent necessarily a knowledge of God, and knows that it is in God and is conceived through God." That this "knowledge of the union existing between the mind and the whole of nature" is the true and eternal good for which our whole being is athirst and in which we find our peace is now plain beyond doubt. All temporal loves and pleasures are a yearning for an object not as yet possessed and a passage towards a perfection still unattained. But the intellectual love of God is not a pursuit, but a possession and a consummation, and the felicity or "blessedness" that attends it must consist "in the mind being endowed with perfection itself."

Our Love of God Indestructible. To the indulgence of this love there are no stumbling-blocks save the misunderstanding of passion and evil. "There is nothing in nature which is contrary to this intellectual love, or which can take it away." No catastrophe, however great, can befall us which cannot be understood, and which, when seen under the aspect of eternity, does not take its place in the necessary order and connection of events as one of the infinity of co-equal witnesses to the rational character of the Real. So understood and so seen, it puts off the bitterness wherewith it affects the finite and passion-bound, personal and self-centered part of the mind which clings so stubbornly to its particular place, and time, and body, and makes them the all-important centers about which the other modifications of God revolve, and in relation to which their perfection and his are judged. The eternal part of the mind, whose essential activity has no center and is bound up with the interests and the fortunes of no one modification of the Real more than another, must rejoice equally in comprehending whatsoever comes to pass. Hence it will acquiesce in suffering and misfortune, not sullenly and hopelessly, but as evils necessarily to be endured. It will acquiesce in them joyfully as manifestations of the higher necessity and perfection to which it is attuned, towards which its love is directed, and from which it can only be separated by ignorance and failure to understand. Nothing, then, can occur in God's infinite and eternal essence that does not the more inflame our love of him.

Final Freedom and "Blessedness." Therefore, from him who loves God and unites his mind with the vision of God's infinite and eternal nature, all that harasses finite human life falls away—all hatred, all discontent, all frustration, and all fear. Even death, the last enemy, is trampled under foot, since to understand death, to see that it is a natural event necessarily implied in the essence of the Real and that its occurrence can rob us of nothing that a rational being should fear to lose, is to take away its sting. The power of the mind to achieve the vision under the aspect of eternity and to acquiesce in the destruction of the body is its power to attain "to being of such a nature that the part thereof which we have shown to perish with the body should be of little importance when compared with the part which endures."

So, at last, man attains redemption. From a passive he becomes an active being. From determination by the other modifications of Reality he passes to determination by the eternal part of himself, which is one with the whole of Reality. From bondage he escapes to freedom. Out of restlessness and unhappiness he creates blessedness and peace.

The winning of salvation is a long and arduous task, accomplished
only by unremitting discipline of the spirit. Nevertheless, though "the
way leading to it seems exceedingly hard, it may . . . be discovered.
Needs must it be hard, since it is so seldom found. How would it be
possible, if salvation were ready to our hand, and could without great
labor be found, that it should be by almost all men neglected? But
all things excellent are as difficult as they are rare." *Omnia praeclara
tam difficilia quam rara sunt.*

Chapter VII

LEIBNITZ

I. LIFE

Early Years and Diplomatic Career. Among those of Spinoza's admirers who visited him, and who were shown the manuscripts locked in the drawer of his desk, was, we may remember, a young German, Gottfried Wilhelm Leibnitz, destined to be the third of the great Continental philosophers of the seventeenth century. Born in 1646, the son of the professor of moral philosophy at the University of Leipzig, he was a precocious child. His father died when he was six years old, and, before he was ten, he had been turned loose in his father's library, where he absorbed most of the Greek and Latin classics. He entered the university at fifteen, already interested in philosophy and critical of the Scholastic doctrine of substantial forms. Two years later, he was studying law in Jena and at Altdorf, where his brilliant attainments procured him the offer of a professorship, which he refused. We next hear of him in Nuremberg, where he joined the mystical brotherhood of the Rosicrucians, and where a friendship he struck up with one of the secretaries in the diplomatic service of the Prince Bishop of Mainz got him the job of helping revise and codify the law of that city. He so favorably impressed his princely and episcopal employer that at the age of twenty-four he was sent to Paris on a delicate diplomatic mission, which he himself had suggested. He was to try to convert Louis XIV's evil designs on Germany into a virtuous crusade against the Turks, by pointing out to the King that the mercantile power of Holland, with which France was then at war, could best be threatened by a campaign in the Near East and the conquest of Egypt.

The mission was not a success, since the King, who really did toy with the idea, eventually decided that Crusades may have been all very well in the time of St. Louis, but were no longer *à la mode*. However, Leibnitz fell in with all the scientific and literary lights of Paris at the time, among them Malebranche, Arnauld, the Cartesians, and Huyghens, with whom he studied the higher mathematics. One result of all this intellectual ferment was the invention of the integral and the differential calculus, which was also worked out independently by Newton. His stop in Paris was interrupted by a brief visit to London, where, it seems, the ideas leading up to the calculus first entered his head.

Work in Hanover. The death of the Prince Bishop of Mainz in 1673 threw him out of a job. But he found immediate employment under the Duke of Brunswick, and soon moved to Hanover to become the librarian of the ducal library, which post he held for the next forty years. His position, however, was not confining and allowed him to roam over a great part of Europe in the fulfillment of his duties. Honors were showered on him thick and fast. He was offered the librarianship of the Vatican Library, but declined the necessary condition of conversion to Catholicism. He founded the Academy of Sciences at Berlin, and planned a similar Academy at St. Petersburg, and also at Vienna, where, however, the Jesuits put a spoke in his wheel. He was made a privy councilor by the Electors of Brandenburg and Hanover and by Peter the Great, and in Austria was created an imperial privy councilor and a baron of the Empire. Towards the end of his life, however, he fell into comparative obscurity, and died in 1716, a forgotten man.

Varied Interests and Writings. Leibnitz' interests were as varied as his activity was prodigious. Enchanted by his discoveries in mathematics and formal logic and the algebra of logic, and convinced that he had found in them a kind of philosopher's touchstone, he bubbled with ideas of the inventions to which he conceived they might lead in every conceivable field, not to speak of new notions in politics, government, law, and theology, most of which came to nothing. But he actually did invent a calculating machine which he put through its paces before the Royal Society in London. He also wrote at length on diplomacy, international law, ordinary law, politics, mathematics and physics. He proposed a universal language. He was interested in China, whose spirit of religious tolerance and conciliation, as reported by the Jesuit missionaries, appealed to him, and he advocated the compilation of a dictionary of Chinese, which he thought might be the mother of all languages. He defended the doctrine of the Trinity, and published a system of theology in which he sought to find a common basis for Catholicism and Protestantism. He devoted himself to gathering material for a history of the House of Brunswick. He fought with Newton and with Boyle, and wrote the *Theodicy* and the *New Essays* to refute Boyle's skepticism by proving on rational grounds that the universe is rational and that God is good. His other more important philosophical works, composed in intervals of leisure between other occupations and with the conviction that he was reconciling all previous systems, are the *New System,* the *Monadology,* and the *Principles of Nature and of Grace.*

II. CRITICISM OF DESCARTES AND SPINOZA

Although Leibnitz admired Spinoza's philosophy, he quarreled with it for several reasons. In the first place, he could not accept the mechanical causation which played so prominent a role in both the Spinozistic and the Cartesian systems. Chains of so-called causes and effects merely describe the order in which things occur, but they do not explain why things are what they are or happen as they do. To say, as Spinoza does, that it is the nature of Reality to exhibit itself in the sequence of events that actually takes place, does not throw any light upon what that nature is. Furthermore, Spinoza did nothing towards solving the all-important problem of the relation between mind and body raised, and so unsatisfactorily treated, by Descartes. To say that they were two sides or aspects or attributes of one and the same thing was no answer, particularly if the thing was nothing but its sides, and if Reality, which was supposed to unite the two attributes, was, as Spinoza said, nothing more than the attributes it was supposed to weld together. In the Spinozistic system extension and thought remained as completely divorced as Descartes had left thinking substance and extended substance. Both philosophers had reduced the essence of matter to extension and nothing else, and the essence of mind to nothing but a thinking activity. In that case, there could be nothing incorporeal about the body, nothing unconscious about mind. But, Leibnitz thought, such a view runs contrary to observed fact. Apart from the propensity of the mind to insist that matter must be an extended *something,* matter possesses inertia in and of itself. This Descartes himself had admitted in his theory that matter tended to remain as it was until God introduced motion into it from the outside. But this inertia, this tendency to maintain the *status quo,* is not passivity on matter's part. It is activity, it is *force.* Hence matter is, at the very least, extension *plus* Force.

If now we look at thinking substance, what do we find? Its essence is not exhausted by being conscious. If it were, what would become of the mind when we are unconscious? Hence, Leibnitz concludes, there is more to thinking substance than just the thinking. It possesses the power of persisting through states of more or less consciousness and of surviving lapses into unconsciousness. In other words, the mind, too, possesses a kind of inertia, a tendency to remain mind, even when unconscious. The mind, then, is a *force,* as well as a state of being conscious.

But if Force is present in both mind and matter, it is a least common denominator in them both. It is the substance of which thought and extension are the attributes. It is the Reality of which we are in search. If it is the Real, it is also ultimate. It fulfills the Spinozistic requirement of being "that which is in itself and is conceived in itself; in other words, that of which a conception can be formed independently of any other conception."

III. THE NATURE OF FORCE

Force and Monads. Force, then, is the pre-supposition and explanation of all things, the object of all our mathematical computations, and the object that seems to run, if you like, mechanically. It is a *metaphysical principle.*

How now are we to conceive Force in itself alone and independently of any other conception? Since it is that which remains in matter, over and above extension, it must be *unextended* and therefore *indivisible,* and therefore *simple,* and therefore *fundamental.* It is in all times and places what it is. It does not change or become. It cannot be conceived as created or destroyed, except perhaps by divine fiat. Therefore it is *eternal.*

Force, however, is not one. It cannot be one. It is a many, each one of which is equally possessed of all the prerogatives we have just been describing. This multiplicity of Forces is proved by an examination of both mind and matter. The spread-out, extended aspect of space means that each point in space *resists* being encroached upon and interpenetrated by the other points. Two bodies, as we say, cannot occupy the same space at the same time. If each point in space did not tend to hold its own, space would crumple up, collapse, contract, and vanish. Each point of space, then, may be regarded as a center of force.

Or again, take the mind. I am not you. I am I. I am unique. We are not only different minds, but we are minds absolutely shut off from one another. Each mind resists the encroachment and interpenetration of another mind, just as each point of space resists being identified with any other point. There are, then, as many Forces as there are *individuals.* But, according to the principles of the calculus, the number of any units regarded as ultimate cannot fall short of infinity. Therefore, the number of unique individual Forces constituting Reality must be infinite.

These Forces, as we have seen, fulfill, severally and collectively, the specifications laid down for *substance*. We may also call them *units*, provided we do not confound them with mathematical units, which are divisible. To avoid this confusion, we may describe them as *points*. But here, too, we must be on our guard against thinking of them in terms of mathematical points, which have no real existence, but are purely and simply conceptual in nature. Perhaps, then, we may define them as *atoms*, but certainly not as physical atoms, which are not only divisible but extended. Nor can we use the term *qualitative* atoms, or ultimate units of qualitative rather than quantitative difference. For qualities are accidents of substance, whereas in these metaphysical ultimates there is no distinction between accident and essence. Each ultimate *is* what it is, and all that it is. It has no accidental properties or predicates. To avoid these possible confusions, let us adopt the term *Monad*.

With the concept of the Monad Leibnitz feels that he has overcome the Cartesian dualism of mind and body, refuted the psycho-physical parallelism and pantheism of Spinoza, destroyed atomistic materialism, reconciled the Scholastic nominalistic view that the individual alone is real with the realistic contention that universals also have real existence, and combined Plato and Aristotle. For the Monad, besides being the least common denominator of mind and matter, is individual and concrete but also possesses a Form and exemplifies an Idea, of which, being unique, it is in itself the only example and instance.

IV. THE DEDUCTION OF MATTER AND MIND FROM FORCE

Force and Consciousness. Having thus inferred the existence of the Monads from an inspection of the nature of extension and of thought, Leibnitz proceeds to deduce consciousness and space from force as he has conceived it. Activity, or Force, makes each thing what it is and gives it its form or nature. But what do we mean by a thing's nature? We mean by our own nature or character the way in which we *represent* ourselves to ourselves. When, then, we talk of things as they are *in* themselves, we mean the thing as it would represent its nature to itself if it were conscious. Things *in* themselves are things *for* themselves. Again, we speak of the Monads as tending to persist in their own being. But the idea of effort is drawn from our inner feeling of tension and striving, and the term is meaningless except as representing that feeling. Existence and Force, then, imply an inner life within the Monad, akin to consciousness. In ourselves we are viewing the Monad from within, as it is in and for itself.

But how about objects that we call inanimate and unconscious? The principle of continuity involved in the calculus now comes to Leibnitz' aid. This leads him to believe that there are no hops, skips, and jumps in nature, but rather a mincing progress by infinitesimal steps from zero to infinity. Man is not a miracle and an interference with the natural order. Hence the self-representative character of Force revealed in his consciousness and will is not an exception. Either there is no self-representation and no life anywhere—which is disproved by the existence and nature of man—or there is self-representation and life everywhere. Hence the so-called inanimate and lifeless world is merely a lesser degree of what we find in man, and absolute lifelessness and lack of consciousness are in the nature of a limit constantly approached, the lower down the scale we go, but never reached. The Monads that constitute the inanimate world are less endowed with perception and appetition than those which lie at the heart of living beings. They may be said to be in a sort of stupor, and their self-representations, or existence *for* themselves, may be called *perception,* or "little perceptions" (*petites perceptions*), in contradiction to the *apperception* of the higher Monads.

The Monads and Consciousness. The calculus also extricates Leibnitz from another difficulty. If the Monads are all unextended, indivisible, simple, fundamental, and eternal, how are we to distinguish one from another? Qualitatively, formally, and substantially, they are all alike, and, since they are unextended, they cannot even be distinguished from one another by saying that they occupy different points of space. They would seem to be indiscernible from one another, and there would seem to be no reason why they should occur in any one order rather than another. But, according to Leibnitz' own theory of the *identity of indiscernibles,* we should then have no ground for believing the Monads to be many and different, but should rather be obliged to regard them as one and identical. The calculus, however, enables us to avoid this contradiction by regarding the Monads as differing from one another in the *degree* to which they represent to themselves one and the same thing. Thus they can all be Forces and all possess the same characteristics, and yet be discernible from one another and therefore many and different.

Matter and the Monads. We pass now to the deduction of the phys-ical world from the nature of Force. Extension cannot be the result of an interpenetration of the Monads or of any co-operation between them, since, as we have seen, they resist any encroachment upon their na-tures and conversely cannot encroach upon the natures of their fellows. Hence they cannot interest or influence one another. The physical world is rather the sign and symbol by which they represent to them-selves their *exclusion* of one another. The prime characteristic of mat-ter is the *impenetrability* of one part by another. This Leibnitz calls *materia prima*. But what do we mean by impenetrability? We mean that two bodies cannot occupy the same *space*. In other words, the Monad must represent to itself exclusion and impenetrability by rep-resenting bodies as side by side occupying different spaces. Extension, therefore, is a secondary characteristic of matter expressive of its es-sential impenetrability. We may call it *materia secunda*. Leibnitz has inverted the doctrine both of Descartes and Spinoza. Instead of ex-tension being the essence of matter, body, impenetrability, and re-sistance, matter is the essence of extension.

We may sum the situation up as follows. The metaphysical unique-ness and independence of each Monad, or at least of all the higher Monads, appear in two ways. Each Monad represents to itself that uniqueness *subjectively* in the feeling of individuality and separate personality. It also represents its independence to itself *objectively* in the apartness of its body from all other bodies. Space, which is the condition of such apartness, is not, then, an external thing. It is a form of the *inner* experience of each Monad. It is a mode of representing confusedly and on the level of *petites perceptions,* or purely physical existence, precisely the same fact of which self-consciousness, and per-sonality, and a plurality of selves distinct from one another, are the representations on the level of mind.

V. THE CONSTITUTION OF REALITY

The nature of the Real is now clear. Reality is constituted by an infinite number of Monads representing to themselves, in degrees ranging from zero to infinity, the essential nature of things, or, as we may now say, the same universe. A zero degree of representation is non-existent, since its existence would be equivalent to non-existence. It is a limit which is more and more closely approached but never reached. Infinity, however, is reached and realized in the mind of God, the Monad of Monads, as Leibnitz calls him. The divine intellect is a complete, absolutely clear, completely articulated, and wholly intelligible representation of the nature of all things, actual and possible. Below God, in an infinite series of Monads differing infinitesimally from one another, the content of the divine mind is reflected with almost imperceptible degrees of growing confusion, indistinctness, and intelligibility, in a descending hierarchy. This hierarchy lapses through man and the different grades of animal and vegetable life, and of complexity in inanimate substances, towards the absolute zero in which all representation, and with it all existence, would be extinguished, if it were ever reached. Though the gradations are continuous and without break or jump, they fall roughly under three heads. At the bottom of the scale lie the *petites perceptions* of the "swooning" Monads that constitute the physical world by representing to themselves their individuality as spatial apartness. Above them come the Monads possessed of simple feeling and memory whose activity is expressed in the consciousness of animals, and finally we rise to Monads in which reflection, self-consciousness and reasoning power are added to feeling and memory. These are the souls of men.

Since God is pure spirit, the divine Monad exists in isolation. But in human beings and animals, the soul Monad has Monads of a lower order clustering about it. In other words, men and animals have *bodies*. They are physical as well as conscious entities, and therefore represent their unique individualities in terms not only of mental but of bodily difference. My body is not your body, just as my conscious self is not your conscious self.

Furthermore, inorganic bodies—anything that holds together as a unit—also have a dominant Monad about which lesser Monads "cluster" and to which the aggregate owes its form and its cohesion. The self-representation of the dominant Monad, however, remains on the level of *petites perceptions*. The Monad sleeps but not quite so deeply as the others that cuddle about it. Hence the aggregate of the self-representations of the inorganic group is reflected in the consciousness of a higher Monad, like the human soul, as a single complex thing, rather than as a mere collection of unrelated units.

VI. PROOFS OF THE EXISTENCE OF GOD

Reason for Existence of Our Particular World. The reasons Leibnitz gives for the existence of God differ somewhat from the proofs with which we are already familiar. The cosmological argument, based on the necessity of a first cause, cannot be invoked in its usual form. For

Leibnitz, in criticizing Descartes and Spinoza, has already gone on record as saying that causality does not explain *why* things exist and behave as they do, but only describes *how* things act. Moreover, his account of the Monads shows no cause why they should not all be absolutely uncreated and eternal beings. Again, this is not the only possible world, and it is logically possible to conceive of the Monads as representing to themselves a different kind of universe from that which they actually do represent. There must, then, be some reason why the Monads behave as they do and not otherwise. This reason cannot be found in them, since, if they themselves could account for their behaving in this way rather than that, they would *necessarily* be what they are, and no other universe would be possible. Therefore, the explanation for their representing this particular universe rather than some other, must lie outside themselves. The requisite explanation is found in God.

Nature of "Windowless" Monads. Leibnitz' next proof rests on one of the most interesting and the most difficult points in his system. The Monads, we remember, are unique, and resist any encroachment upon or modification of their individuality by other Monads. No two of them can simultaneously occupy the same space, or, on the higher level of representation, be the same self. On the physical level, the Monads resist one another and hold one another off. On the mental level, their inner lives are absolutely private and incommunicable, except in so far as that part of their inner experience which they call the external world enables them by its behavior to represent indirectly, in terms of their own experience, what may be taking place within the other Monads.

The fact that each Monad is thus held *incommunicado* and is unable to interact or directly communicate with its fellows is freely admitted by Leibnitz. "The Monads," he tells us, "have no windows through which anything could come in or go out." [1] Each one is hermetically sealed up within itself. Still, the fact remains that a large portion of this hermetically sealed self-representation appears to reflect an external world with which we seem to ourselves to interact. And yet, if the consciousness of the Monad represents only itself to itself, how can the impression of an external world and of other selves arise? Why should I ever think that there is a universe outside me, of which I am a part? At this point, God is invoked to explain the principle of *pre-established harmony*.

[1] All quotations from Leibnitz are from Latta's translation.

The Pre-established Harmony and God. God, he tells us, has so arranged it that when certain changes and developments take place within one Monad, appropriate changes will take place in the inner experiences of the other Monads, representing and referring to these developments and giving to the other Monads the feeling that they are observing something going on in a world external to themselves. Leibnitz uses the illustration of two clocks keeping perfect time with one another, not because the mechanism of the one is geared into that of the other so that they interact; or because God is constantly setting the one clock by the other, as the Occasionalists taught; but because they have been so constructed and wound up and set going, once and for all, in the beginning, as to be always synchronous. Such clocks, without interaction and without intervention from the outside, will always tick simultaneously, strike simultaneously, and register the same second, minute, and hour simultaneously.

It follows that God must exist, not only to explain why the clocks are of the make they are rather than of some other, but to account for their being so perfectly timed that they appear to interact.

Had the technique of moving pictures been invented in Leibnitz' time he might have found in them another analogy for illustrating *pre-established* harmony. He might have likened the Monads to an infinite number of individuals hermetically sealed, each in a separate room outfitted with a projector and a screen, before whose eyes one and the same picture representing the doings of all the individuals was being shown. The films would be so "cut" and the projectors so synchronized that when the occupant of any one room did anything, what he was doing would be simultaneously thrown on the screens in all the other rooms.

Furthermore, if we imagined the screens to differ infinitesimally in size from an infinitesimal point to infinite bigness, the picture would be presented with an infinite number of degrees of clearness and completeness, ranging from an infinitesimal blur and flicker of light, in the case of the "swooning" physical Monads, to the completely inclusive, clear and distinct showing, from which no detail, however minute, was omitted, that takes place in the divine Monad.

VII. CREATION BY "FULGURATION"

The divine Monad, however, is responsible not only for the *pre-established* harmony and synchronization of the behavior and experiences of the other Monads but for their existence as well. In dealing with the question of their creation Leibnitz found himself in a quandary. Considerations inspired by the calculus demanded that the "created" Monads should differ from God not in kind but in degree only, and hence should be really consubstantial with him and distinguished from him only in point of possessing a lesser *quantity* of the same substance. In that case their creation would be in the nature of a procession or emanation from God. But, on the other hand, the orthodox Christian doctrine, which Leibnitz had no desire to challenge, was that God created the universe out of nothing by fiat, and that the nature of the created differed from the nature of the Creator not only in degree but in kind as well.

Confronted with this difficulty, Leibnitz tried to reconcile the opposing points of view. He needed a term that would not too much connote an emanation theory of the origin of the Monads and range him along with Eriugena and Bruno, who taught that the created was consubstantial with the Creator. On the other hand, this term must somehow avoid the defiance of the calculus implied in creation *ex nihilo*. Such a term Leibnitz thought he had found in "fulguration." The lesser Monads are "fulgurated," or sparked and struck off, by and from the divine Monad. A process of "fulguration" might seem to hover somewhere half-way between emanation and creation by fiat, and to make the lesser Monads sufficiently consubstantial with God to allow of the application of the calculus, and yet not sufficiently so as to rate as an unorthodox method of deriving them from God.

VIII. BIRTH, DEATH, AND IMMORTALITY

At this point a few minor questions pop up, which it will be well to dispose of at once. How do things like birth, growth, death, and immortality fit into the picture? In principle there should be no real birth and no real death for any Monad, since all alike should be conceived as "fulgurated" once and for all, before all time, from the divine Monad, and as indestructible except by divine fiat. In that case, coming into and passing out of existence would be relative, and would signify simply increase or decrease in the degree of the Monad's self-representation. Also, needless to say, change of quality and place, growth and decay, and the like, will be internal processes, in which only the content and degree of each Monad's self-representation are altered in accordance with the metaphysical "clusterings" of lesser Monads, first about one dominant Monad, then about another. On the inorganic level the metaphysical shifting will appear as the transformation of one physical object into another. In vegetable life the dominant Monad will wake up sufficiently to represent the shifting as a process of organic growth and decay. In animal life it will be aroused to the point of representing these changes as alternations in its own state of consciousness, and to becoming wider and wider awake as its body grows. In the same way, when a living being grows old and dies, the cluster of sleeping Monads that forms its body is gradually dispersed, and as gradually the dominating Monad, to whose superior degree of self-representation the cluster owes its organic unity, relapses to the sub-conscious level.

Leibnitz had, however, to except man from this general rule, both at the beginning and at the end of his earthly career. To conform to Christian teaching he had to conceive human soul-Monads as specially created, or "fulgurated," at the generation of each human individual, and not as pre-existing before birth. To ensure the personal immortality as well as the indestructibility of the human soul he could not permit her to lapse into a sub-human and sub-conscious degree of self-representation when the inferior body-Monads were dispersed by death. Therefore, he held that God detached her intact from her earthly body when it was destroyed, and preserved her throughout everlasting time in the fullness of her self-conscious, personal, rational, and moral degree of self-representation.

IX. ALL IS FOR THE BEST IN THE BEST OF ALL POSSIBLE WORLDS

Our Particular Universe Best. One question, however, still hung fire. Why did God choose to create or "fulgurate" this particular universe instead of some one of the other possible worlds conceived by his mind and equally capable of enactment? God, Leibnitz replies, is good. Therefore he chose the *best* of all possible worlds. However, in choosing he could not flout the law of self-contradiction. He could not pick all the best things out of all possible universes and run them together and make a world out of them. For the universe to be logical and consistent, he could only weave together things that logically could be realized together without contradiction and combined into a single rational whole. The best possible world, therefore, is limited by what Leibnitz calls the *compossibility* of its elements. Of course, there are many arrangements of compossible elements, but this is the combination in which "is obtained as great possible variety as possible, along with the greatest possible order," and thus "as much perfection as possible." We may, therefore, come to the conclusion that all is for the best in the best of possible worlds.

The Problem of Evil. Leibnitz, however, realized that his optimism might be challenged unless he could satisfactorily dispose of numerous indications that all was not for the best, and explain why the best of all possible worlds seemed so inferior in quality. So it was that he undertook to solve the problem of evil. To facilitate his solution, he divided evil into three kinds, *metaphysical, physical* and *moral*. Metaphysical evil is the limitation and lesser degree of perfection necessarily imposed upon every created Monad by virtue of not being God. Logically, everything that is not God must be imperfect. Physical and moral evil are the ways in which the created Monads must represent to themselves their limited and imperfect character. Physical evil is essentially a sense of being constricted and hampered by the external world. Moral evil is essentially a sense of being limited by the weakness and the incapacity of our own selves. Suffering and sin then must necessarily exist, if there is to be any created universe or anything in existence except God.

This logical justification of evil Leibnitz supplements with a moral justification which proceeds along familiar lines. Evil in the part does not detract from the perfection of the whole. On the contrary, it contributes to it, as the shadows in the picture and the discords in a musical composition enhance the perfection of the work in question. More generally, the contrast of evil everywhere throws the good into higher and clearer relief. The afflictions and sufferings of the present moment are means to our greater perfection, and, as compared with it, are nothing. Pain and misfortune are a salutary punishment for sin, and, when they befall the righteous man, they test his character and afford him an opportunity for showing his strength.

Moral evil, being the twin of error and born with it, as Spinoza also insisted, from confused and inadequate thinking, may be dispelled. Even when we choose the worse cause, we choose it because of its momentarily satisfactory and therefore good quality. All acts are performed with a view to procuring some benefit. Pleasure accompanies the natural expansion of the Monad to a greater degree of self-representation. Pain is the sign of some interference with its development. Hence we are naturally inclined to pursue the pleasanter course, since we are self-determined to the good.

X. THE FREEDOM OF THE WILL

Freedom, for Leibnitz, lies in liberty to follow the determinations imposed upon us by our nature, not in ability to act without determination. In his essay *On the Ultimate Origin of Things* he states that God possesses this freedom to perfection, "for he acts from a principle of wisdom or perfection." The so-called freedom of indifference "springs from ignorance." It means not that the will acts without motivation, but that, because our ideas are confused, it hesitates between various courses of action. Our final decision, however, is always determined by what we think, correctly or incorrectly, to be for the best. "The wiser a man is, the more he is determined towards that which is most perfect."

However, the process of deliberating and thinking things over is not entirely a play of conscious thought, as Spinoza believed. Our attitudes and our decisions are in part the work of our unconscious mind, and it is largely their contribution to our choices that makes us vacillate and gives us the sense of not being determined by anything to choose the course we do. In Leibnitz' own words in *New Essays,* "It is the *petites perceptions* which *determine* us on many occasions without our thinking it, and which deceive people by the appearance of an *indifference of equilibrium,* as if, for instance, we were completely indifferent whether to turn to the right or to the left."

For the same reason we do not always choose and act *logically,* as beings actuated only by clear and adequate perceptions would. Probability is a sufficient motive for action. Moreover, the alternatives and choices thus presented make us moral beings, and our incentives to action appear not as determining causes but as ideals or ends which we may or may not pursue. Were we wholly dominated by reason, then we should be absolutely free. But in that case we should no longer be in a position to choose between good and evil, and should have transcended human morality and have become like God.

XI. LOGIC AND LANGUAGE

The general interest in logic and the philosophy of language during the first half of the present century has placed Leibnitz in a somewhat new light as a philosopher. Whereas he had been traditionally assessed largely in terms of his metaphysics, he is now studied mainly as a logician, without question one of the most original in the entire history of the formal sciences. Unfortunately Leibnitz withheld most of his logical treatises from publication and it was not until the last turn of the century that they were brought before the public. If he had been less secretive with his ideas, the development of modern non-Aristotelian logic probably would have been considerably accelerated.

Logic and Metaphysics. For the historian, the most interesting facet of Leibnitz' logic is his partial deduction of the basic principles of his monadology from logical premises. The subject-predicate structure of propositions is the basis for his important conception of substance. A substance is that which is always a subject and can never be a predicate, of which predications can be made but which can never be predicated of anything else. It is that which persists through change. This insures the genuine individuality of the monads, the foundation of Leibnitz' metaphysical pluralism. His pluralism, moreover, is related to his mathematical interests in the infinitesimal calculus. The view that every predicate belongs eternally to its subject implies, as Leibnitz recognized, "that the individual concept of each person includes once for all everything which can ever happen to him." This is basic to the description of the monads as reflecting internally the structure of the world and is involved, therefore, in the doctrine of pre-established harmony as well as in the theory that freedom is compatible with determination.

The Universal Language. Leibnitz' broad interests in the sciences, law, history, and social and cultural pursuits generally, as well as in numerous technological problems, combined with his intense rationalism and concern for exactness and certainty in knowledge to produce a general theory of a logical language that he hoped would be accepted as a basic instrument of knowledge. His *Universal Characteristic,* which he discussed on numerous occasions with varying emphases, was intended to be the key that would unlock countless mysteries and bring to an end the seemingly interminable controversies of philosophers. It was a symbolic language that would permit the intricate calculation with propositions that is available to mathematics, but a language into which the propositions of ordinary discourse would be translatable. "Whence it is manifest that if we could find characters or signs appropriate for expressing all our thoughts as definitely and as exactly as arithmetic expresses numbers or geometric analysis expresses lines, we could in all subjects *in so far as they are amenable to reasoning* accomplish what is done in Arithmetic and Geometry." In this grandiose vision Leibnitz established the ideals not only of symbolic logic but of the unity of science, ideals which inspire the twentieth century more than they did his own.

Chapter VIII

LOCKE

I. REACTION AGAINST RATIONALISM

Periods of great constructive activity in philosophy are apt to be accompanied or followed by skeptical movements which doubt the ability of the human intellect to grasp the nature of Reality and challenge systems founded upon a belief in the infallibility of reason. At the very beginning of the history of European philosophy two centuries of construction in Ionia and Magna Graecia were called into question by the destructive criticism of the Sophists, and the re-building of Plato and Aristotle was accomplished in the face of the skepticism of the Cynics and the Cyrenaics. A little later, Stoicism, Epicureanism, and Neo-Platonism developed and consolidated their respective positions under continuous bombardment by Pyrrho, Arcesilaus, Carneades, Aenesidemus, and Sextus Empiricus. Again, even the crystallization of Christian dogma, backed though it was by revelation, was fractured here and there with doubts, and the faith of the Middle Ages was followed by the free thought of the Renaissance.

The Renaissance, however, challenged faith in revelation, only to oppose to it faith in the power of the unaided reason to reach and grasp the truth, and this faith inspired the systems we have just been considering. Bacon, Hobbes, Descartes, Spinoza, and Leibnitz were all certain that the Real was constructed according to mathematical and logical principles, and that the human mind, by strict adhesion to the scientific method and obedience to the laws of mathematics and logic, could reason out its nature. The objections that they urged against the Scholastics and the ancients were *rational* objections, and their defense of their own systems was a *rational* defense. But just as in the past this assumption of the infallibility of reason had been repeatedly questioned, so once more it was to be called to account. The point was again to be raised whether the very nature of the human understanding and the conditions under which it operated were not such as to render it an instrument of limited powers and of doubtful 'efficacy so far as the discovery of the nature of Reality was concerned. Foremost in this skeptical movement was the Englishman, John Locke.

II. LIFE

Education and Character. Locke was born in 1632, at Wrington, not far from Bristol, of a middle-class yeoman family. Educated, after attending a grammar school in Bristol, at Westminster School in London, he would not have had to budge very far or clamber very much, to attain, along with his schoolmates, what must have been the ambition of every high-spirited seventeen-year-old boy at the moment—some really good point of vantage for observing the decapitation of King Charles I. In 1652, he got a scholarship at Christ Church, Oxford. Little is known of his undergraduate days, but they were sufficiently satisfactory to get for him a tutorship at Christ Church after his graduation and later the post of lecturer in Greek and rhetoric.

Locke was a man of many interests. He was attracted at first to theology, but soon turned to medicine, and practiced for a while as assistant to an Oxford M.D. He was also drawn to physics and chemistry and to the study of religious and political problems, and, as early as 1666, was writing his *Essay Concerning Toleration,* in which he already exhibited the broad-mindedness and the tolerance which characterized him throughout his whole life. In it he condemned persecution, argued for civil and religious toleration, and advocated the reunion of the Church of England and the Nonconformist bodies on a basis large enough to include and satisfy all shades of opinion.

Political Career. In 1666 he received a diplomatic appointment as secretary to the British Ambassador at the Court of Brandenburg. Returning to London, he met by accident Lord Ashley, later Earl of Shaftesbury and the greatest political figure under Charles II. Upon him he made so favorable an impression that he was offered the post of tutor to Ashley's son. About the same time, he was also elected a Fellow of the Royal Society, which had been incorporated in 1662. In 1672 Shaftesbury was made Lord Chancellor, and Locke, who had become a confidential friend, was appointed Secretary to the Board of Trade, a post which he held for the next three years.

Always delicate, Locke suffered much from asthma, and, when a temporary eclipse of Shaftesbury's prestige involved a reverse of his own political fortunes, he seized the opportunity to spend four years on the Continent traveling for his health. Two of them he spent at

Montpellier in the south of France, and one in Paris. Meantime he was preparing his *Essay Concerning Human Understanding.*

In 1679 Shaftesbury returned to power, and Locke to England and to public life again, but not for long. The question of excluding from the succession the King's Catholic brother, James, Duke of York, afterwards James II, was being hotly debated, and pressure was brought to bear by Shaftesbury and others upon Charles II, to legitimatize his illegitimate son, the Duke of Monmouth, and make him heir to the throne. Charles refused, and Shaftesbury, who still supported Monmouth, was accused of treason but acquitted. Monmouth was arrested, and Shaftesbury, again under accusation, had to flee to Holland. Locke followed him. Because of his connections with the Monmouth party he was deprived of his University post and stipend by order of Charles, and his extradition from Holland was later demanded by the British Government on the ground that he was plotting against James II, who had succeeded his brother in 1685. For a while he had to remain in concealment and live under an assumed name. His time he divided between Cleves, Rotterdam and Amsterdam. All the while he worked at the *Essay.*

With the deposition of James II and the accession of William and Mary in 1688, he returned again to England and to prominence in politics. He was offered, but refused, the ambassadorship at Brandenburg, and was made Commissioner of Appeals. There followed a burst of publication—the *Letter Concerning Tolerance* in 1689, and a year later *Two Treatises on Government,* the *Essay Concerning Human Understanding,* and a *Second Letter for Toleration.*

After a couple of years in London he made his permanent home with some friends named Masham, who lived at Oates in Essex. Lady Masham was the daughter of Cudworth, the Cambridge Platonist, of whom we have already spoken. Here he rode and gardened, went on with his writing, and kept up with his circle of learned friends. Nor did his retirement in the country deprive him of political position. In 1696, he was appointed Commissioner of Trade and Plantations, but resigned it four years later, because of his failing health. In 1704 he died at Oates, at the age of seventy-two.

Political and Religious Views. Up to the last, however, Locke's literary activity was unremitting. The ideas that he had advanced both in his treatises on *Tolerance* and *Government* and in the *Essay* were controversial and shocking to many people, and he was kept on the *qui vive* defending his views from attack. Indeed, the great *Essay* was condemned by the authorities at Oxford for its skepticism. The letters on *Tolerance,* which expounded the position of the so-called "Latitudinarians," who denied the authority of the Church, the Fathers, and the Councils and demanded that the Bible be interpreted in the light of reason, naturally raised the ire of all those who bowed before ecclesiastical authority or insisted on taking the Bible literally as interpreted by their particular sect. So, too, the *Treatises on Government* argued at length against the divine right of kings to rule independently of the consent of the governed, and, while accepting much of Hobbes' political theory, advocated constitutional government, and insisted that it was not only the right but the duty of the subject to rebel and depose a sovereign who defied the will of the people as expressed in Acts of Parliament. Locke also advocated a frequent revision of the contract upon which government rests so as to bring it into accord with the new needs and circumstances of the times. In the *Treatises,* again, he advances such interesting economic views as the worthlessness of gold and silver coinage, except as convenient medium for the exchange of true wealth, which lies in the products of labor.

III. "INNATE" IDEAS

No Innate Ideas. As a champion of freedom of thought and speech on all subjects within the widest possible limits, Locke found himself obliged by his philosophic meditations to include among those limits certain bounds to thinking imposed by no external censorship, but by the very nature of thinking itself. Granted that a man were permitted by Church and State and all other restrictive forces to think as he pleased and to say what he thought, to what extent would the censorship exercised by the peculiarities of his mind permit him to grasp and to describe the true nature of the universe? In the *Essay Concerning Human Understanding* Locke sets himself to answer this question by inquiring critically into the powers and limitations of the human mind.

His first doubts regarding the unlimited powers of reason arise in connection with the Platonic theory that the mind comes into the world already in possession of certain innate truths—a theory, as we have seen, handed on to medieval thought by Augustine, and accepted by Descartes, Spinoza, and Leibnitz. There are, says Locke, no such things as innate moral, or mathematical, or logical principles, already fortified by which the intellect begins its operation of thinking about the world. On the contrary, we are born with perfectly blank intellects. At birth the mind is a *tabula rasa,* an absolutely blank sheet of paper with no watermarks of any sort in its texture, and all our ideas without exception are derived from the writing of experience upon its virgin surface. The first book of the *Essay* is devoted to refuting all arguments to the contrary.

All Ideas Derived from Experience. Locke begins by attacking the contention that all men agree in thinking in certain ways and in holding certain ideas, which, therefore, arising as they do in all human minds independently of the peculiarities of individual experience, must be inborn. To this Locke replies that, no such common agreement, or *consensus gentium,* can be shown to exist, and that, if it did exist, it would not prove innateness. Nor is there any way for distinguishing such truths as are innate from such as are learned.

Finally, the process of learning reverses the procedure we should expect if there were such things as innate principles. We recognize the truth of specific propositions before we accept general maxims. Many of the most necessary and valid propositions are not recognized until our attention is drawn to them, and then only if we have been so trained by previous education as to be able to understand them.

Turning now from the intellectual to the moral field, we find that there are no universal and self-evident moral principles. Moral standards, ideas of right and wrong, are relative to time, place, and circumstance, and have always to be explained and defended. We can always ask *why* this is right, or *why* this is wrong. Even conscience, that supposedly infallible guide to right conduct, is fickle and self-contradictory, imposing conflicting courses upon different individuals and upon the same individual at different times.

So, too, with religious beliefs. The central idea of all religions, the idea of God, is not innate. It is not universal, and where we find it, we find, not a single concept common to all who entertain it, but many conflicting and contradictory ideas.

Balancing up the sheet in the other column, we can discover no reason why all the ideas held to be innate should not be suggested by and derived from experience. Even such seemingly "necessary" truths as the logical principles of self-contradiction and identity do not have to be revealed. They may be learned from ordinary, everyday experience.

IV. THE DERIVATION OF IDEAS FROM EXPERIENCE

We must now show *how* the mind learns these ideas from experience. We come by all our ideas, Locke tells us, through *sensation* and *reflection.* First we perceive and feel, then think about what we feel and perceive. Perception presents us with *simple qualities,* derived in some cases from a single, in others from a multiple, source. Color, for example, comes through the eye alone. A quality like solidity, however, is a combination of sensations of touch and resistance.

The perceptions thus written upon the blank sheet of the mind do not disappear immediately or all at once. Many of them fade slowly. They leave their mark. They are retained and *remembered.* This persistence enables the mind to *contemplate* them, to *discern* their similarities and differences, to *compare* and *distinguish* them, to *compose,* in imagination and fancy, their elements in arrangements not immediately given in sensation, and to *abstract* from them so-called general ideas. In his description of abstraction Locke follows Hobbes. The so-called general idea is a particular image of the class in question, taken as representative of all the other particulars belonging to that class. This power of abstraction, in Locke's opinion, is not possessed by the lower animals but by man alone.

The senses present us not only with *simple* ideas but with *complex* ideas compounded and combined in various ways, as in ordinary objects where various qualities are conjoined, or in collections where many objects are herded together. To these, through the power of imagination, the mind is able to add an infinity of new ideas. Nevertheless, in spite of their variety and number, all *complex* ideas fall under three heads. They suggest to us either "distinct *particular* things subsisting by themselves," as *substances;* or things considered as not subsisting by themselves, but "as dependencies on, or affections of, substances," like "triangle, gratitude, murder, etc.," which we will call *modes;* or *relations* of various sorts in which the ideas stand to one another.

V. NEGATIVE IDEAS. INFINITY AND POWER

Having described the processes by which the mind derives its ideas from experience, we are at last ready to analyze all our ideas into their constituent perceptual elements. But we are now faced with the fact, in itself an apparent refutation of Locke's refutation of innate ideas, that many of our ideas do not seem to be given in experience at all. For example, we never experience *infinity,* and yet we have an idea of infinity; we experience, not *substances* in themselves, but only their qualities, and yet we have the idea of substance. These are but two of a number of other ideas that transcend the field of sense-perception.

But how can ideas that are derived from experience refer to things that are not perceived?

Nature of Infinity. To answer this question, Locke analyzes these ideas, one by one. Let us begin with the idea of infinity, spatial and temporal. Our idea of space, says Locke, is derived from combined visual and tactual sensations, which give us the ideas of figure or shape, and place. Incidentally, he combats the Cartesian identification of space and matter, and maintains that there is nothing self-contradictory in the idea of a vacuum. Time, or duration, is an idea founded upon the flow of our inner experience. Time in the abstract is "the consideration of duration as set out by certain periods, and marked by certain measures or epochs, like the periodical reappearance of the sun and the moon."

Now, the succession of visual and tactual experiences by which we go on enlarging our perception of space, and the succession of states of consciousness that constitutes duration, are both such that we cannot conceive them as coming to a stop of themselves. The ability to go one step backward or forward in space and time carries with it the ability to go on indefinitely. Here, then, lies the secret of the idea of infinity. It is not a positive idea. It is a negative one. It expresses simply the inability of the mind to derive from its perceptions of extension, duration, and the process of counting, any idea that interferes with an indefinite continuance of those perceptions.

Nature of Power. *Power* is another idea that seems to have no sensible basis. We say that fire has the power to melt gold, or that the sun has the power to bleach wax. But we never perceive either the fire or the sun *doing* what we say they do. Neither do we perceive the gold or the wax being acted upon. All that we perceive is the gold melting or the wax turning from yellow to white when heat or light is present. Again, perception gives us no idea of the initiation of motion implied in the idea of power. No material object sets itself in motion. A billiard ball is set in motion by the cue or by the impact of another ball. It is acted upon, instead of active, and when it hits another ball, what we see is a *transference,* not a *production,* of motion. Production of power and initiation of motion are only perceived in ourselves, in our acts of volition. Our idea of power in the physical world is an unwarranted application of this perception to a field in which no such experience occurs. Therefore, it is a confused idea.

VI. POWER AND FREE-WILL

Power and Choice. Furthermore, Locke insists, such power as we *experience* in willing is not power to choose, but simply power to act according to our choice. This observation leads him to discuss at this point the freedom of the will. Freedom is not indetermination, for when confronted with alternatives, we cannot help *preferring,* and therefore wishing and willing, one course rather than another. Nevertheless, compulsion of this sort does not involve any question of freedom *vs.* necessity. Liberty consists in being able to do what we want and will to do; necessity in being hindered from putting our volition into execution. The so-called freedom of the will is, then, not freedom, or power, to *choose,* but freedom, or power, to *act* in accordance with our choice. Wills are not free; *men* are free.

Choice and Determination. Furthermore, there *must* be determining reasons for our preferring and willing what we do; we also can easily see how our will is determined to be what it is.

To push this point home, Locke analyzes the mechanism by which volition is determined. The first determining condition of volition is a feeling of uneasiness and desire—an impulse to remove and satisfy a want. If the uneasiness is not there, the *bare contemplation* of the satisfactions that allay it is not sufficient to determine the will and set us to work. Moreover, the greater the uneasiness, the more powerful the urge. Therefore, what we prefer and will must always be the removal of the most intense and pressing uneasiness, and the satisfaction of the most imperative desire, at the moment. But the simple absence of a good, however good we may regard it in theory, does not weigh against the immediate urge to remove present pain and satisfy immediate needs. Hence, we frequently do not will what is best for us in the long run, and, perceiving and approving the better course, prefer and follow the worse one.

However, all volition is aimed at happiness, and, if we sufficiently dwell on our true good, it may become an object of immediate desire, and its absence may create a major uneasiness and incite the will to pursue it. This is facilitated by the power the will has "to *suspend* the execution and satisfaction of any of its desires," pending a closer consideration, examination, and weighing of the value of the desired objects.

Freedom and Suspension of Choice. It is this power "to suspend the prosecution of this or that desire" that is the source of all liberty; in this "seems to consist that which is . . . improperly called *free-will*." Improperly called, Locke thinks, because suspension of choice is itself the inevitable result of the conflict of the uneasinesses in the mind, and the "indifference" of the will before the final choice is only valuable in so far as it permits that choice to be "the last result of a fair examination" and to be determined by a final judgment of good and evil emerging at the end of a series of reasoned and deliberate judgments, rather than by the impulse of the moment.

Both the Human and the Divine Will Self-Determined. On this point Locke is explicit. Power to choose undetermined by our "last judgment of good and evil" would be as great a misfortune and imperfection as lack of power to refrain from action till we have chosen. The more compelled we are to choose and pursue the greatest good, the freer we are. This is shown by the fact that "those superior beings above us, who enjoy perfect happiness, are more steadily determined in their choice of good than we; and yet we have no reason to think they are less happy, or less free, than we are." Nay more, "God himself *cannot* choose what is not good; the freedom of the Almighty hinders not his being determined by what is best."

Psychologically, too, determination of this sort is not attended with any feeling of compulsion. "The constant desire of happiness, and the constraint it puts upon us to act for it, nobody," Locke thinks, "accounts an abridgment of liberty, or at least an abridgment of liberty to be complained of. God Almighty himself is under the necessity of being happy; and the more any intelligent being is so, the nearer is its approach to infinite perfection and happiness."

VII. SUBSTANCE AND CAUSATION

Substance. Another idea, constantly in our minds but apparently lacking any foundation in sense-perception, is the idea of *substance*. We never see or feel a substance. All that we experience is a group of qualities. How, then, is the notion of substance derived from sensation? In attacking this question we notice at once that many of a substance's qualities are not believed to be inherent in the substance itself. We recognize that they are effects produced by it in us. For example, color, sound, taste, smell, tactual qualities and the like are, as we say, subjective, and cannot be said to exist in the external world. The various ways in which the object affects *us,* Locke calls *secondary qualities*. Nevertheless, in a sense the secondary qualities are not merely in our minds. They are in the perceived object as *powers* possessed by the object of affecting us as it does. "Yellowness is not actually in gold," says Locke, "but is a power in gold to produce that idea in us by our eyes."

Certain of its perceived qualities, however, Locke conceives as belonging to the object itself, and as inseparable from it. Things-in-themselves are solid, extended, possess shape, are in rest or motion and are many in number. These qualities, which inhere in objects and are there, whether or not we experience them, are called by Locke *primary qualities*. It is the primary qualities that affect us with the secondary qualities. Indeed, Locke intimates that were our senses ultra-microscopic in acuteness, the secondary qualities would be resolved into their primary constituents. Color, for example, would disappear, "and instead of it we should see an admirable texture of parts of a certain size and figure."

Nature of Substance. So far, then, the idea of substance is bound up with three sorts of ideas, *primary qualities, secondary qualities,* and *powers* to affect or be affected by other substances. If we add to it the ideas associated with a soul or spirit, or immaterial substance, which is just as easy to conceive as a material body, we see how complex the idea of substance really is. But there is even more to the idea than that. It indicates also *"something besides* the extension, figure, solidity, motion, thinking, or other observable ideas. . . ."* And yet, if we ask what this *something besides* the qualities is, we find ourselves in the same case as the Indian "who, saying that the world was supported by a great elephant, was asked what the elephant rested on; to which his answer was—a great tortoise; but being again pressed to know what gave support to the broadback tortoise, replied—*something, he knew not what."*

In a word, the idea of substance as *something besides* its qualities is, like the idea of infinity, not positive but negative. It stands for nothing except a particular collection of perceived qualities *plus* an inability to *"conceive how they should subsist alone nor one in another,"* which makes us "suppose them existing in and supported by some common subject." But of the nature of this supposed support we have no positive or clear or distinct idea whatsoever.

Closely allied to the ideas both of substance and of power is the idea of *cause and effect,* which conceives one event, simple or complex, as *producing* or *being produced* by another.

Nature of Causation. But whether causation be the *creation* of something new, which never existed before, or the *generation* of one thing by another, or the *making* of a thing by an external cause, as in the case of manufacture, or the *alteration* of a thing, we have no positive idea of how the so-called cause produces the so-called effect. Once more we are dealing with a negative idea—an observation of sequence *plus* an ignorance of how the seemingly connected links are actually interwoven.

VIII. THE MEANING OF IDENTITY

Characteristics of Identity. In the idea of cause and effect we have passed from ideas of substances and modes into the field of relations. The most interesting of these is the relation of *identity*. The idea is highly complex, both in its various applications and in the ideas that go to constitute it. In the first place, identity involves the ideas of space and time. The *same* object cannot be in two places at the same time. By the same token, it excludes all other objects from the place it occupies. *Different* objects cannot occupy the same space. Again, the idea of identity excludes the idea of two beginnings for one and the same object, or of one beginning for different objects.

These considerations enable us to solve the old problem of the principle of individuation. Individuation, says Locke, is involved in the very nature of existence itself, "which determines a being of any sort to a particular time and place, incommunicable to two beings of the same kind." In other words, points of space are unique and cannot be confounded with one another. We can only pass *from* one *to* another. This takes time. Hence no one individual can be in two places and no two individuals can be in one place at the same time.

As we have said, the idea of identity is very diversely applied. We have *identity of substance,* which means that the *same* substance is continuous with itself in time and space. It does not skip intermediate points in passing from place to place, or intermediate instants in passing from moment to moment.

Besides identity of substance, we have *organic identity,* such as a plant or animal exhibits in its growth. Here there is a constant change of substance. Yet we speak of a changing body as the *same* body. Why? Because in this case identity means unbroken continuity of arrangement and of relation between the different parts of the body.

Identity of the Individual and of the Person. In what does a man's identity consist? Not, replies Locke, in the identity of his soul or personality, since in that case, supposing there is transmigration of souls, we should be obliged to call the successive reincarnations of one and the same soul the same *man*. But if we were certain "that the *soul* of

Heliogabalus were in one of his hogs," would we say that this "hog were a man or Heliogabalus"?

We are now faced with the interesting question of determining what *personal identity* is. Such identity, Locke tells us, is purely a matter of consciousness, and rests upon the continuity introduced into consciousness by memory. "In this alone consists personal identity, i.e., the sameness of a rational being; and as far as this consciousness can be extended backwards to any past action of thought, so far reaches the identity of that person; it is the same self now as it was then. . . ." Therefore, we might add, even supposing that there were reincarnation, the reborn soul, though the same thinking substance, would not even be the same *person* any longer, since in this incarnation she has forgotten her former lives.

Personal Identity Possible. A number of subsidiary points have now to be considered. Can this continuity of consciousness and memory be preserved, when the substance underlying it is changed? Locke replies that since the body can be mutilated and altered and even completely renewed without interfering with personal identity, continuity of consciousness is not dependent upon permanence of organic constitution. So, too, there is no reason why it should not be independent of changes in thinking substance, or the soul. Nay more, there is no certainty that one and the same consciousness and personal identity might not be "transferred from one thinking substance to another," in which case "it will be possible that two thinking substances may make but one person. For the same consciousness being preserved, whether in the same or different substances, the personal identity is preserved."

Suppose, however, "I wholly lose the memory of some parts of my life beyond a possibility of retrieving them . . . yet am I not the same person that did those actions, had those thoughts that I once was conscious of, though I have now forgot them?" No, Locke replies, you are the same *man,* but not the same *person.* One and the same man might be a number of different persons "if he had distinct incommunicable consciousness at different times." It is probable, Locke thinks, that personal consciousness "is annexed to and the affection of one individual immaterial substance." But we cannot be certain.

The Person Not the Man Morally Responsible. It is, Locke adds, with the *person* not the *man* that justice human and divine is concerned. Happiness and misery, reward and punishment are bound up with our consciousness, and only with external objects so far as they affect our consciousness. We do not hold a man responsible for what he does when not in his right mind, or punish him for it. And we

determine that for which he is responsible and accountable in so far
as his consciousness "owns and imputes to itself past actions, just upon
the same ground and for the same reason as it does the present." Indeed, at the Last Judgment, God's sentence, to be just, must be "justified by the consciousness all persons shall have, that *they themselves,*
in what bodies soever they appear, or what substances soever their
consciousness adheres to, are the *same* that committed those actions,
and deserve that punishment for them."

It is now obvious that ideas like substance, power, cause and effect,
infinity, identity, and the like are far from being clear and far from
being adequate representations of the things to which they are supposed to refer. They are obscure and confused in themselves and are
partial and incomplete pictures of their objects. Much of this confusion
arises from the ambiguity of the *words* we use as symbols of our ideas,
which only too often do not fit them exactly and suggest other ideas
besides those of which they are the name.

IX. THE AMBIGUITY OF ABSTRACT, UNIVERSAL TERMS

The part *words* play in thinking is so great that Locke devotes the
whole of the third book of the *Essay* to them. Most of them, he points
out, are general terms or family names, signifying classes of things
rather than particular objects. We are, therefore, confronted with the
age-old problem of the status of universals or *essences.* Locke deals
with this question by differentiating between *nominal* essences and
real essences. The nominal essences of things, expressed by their common name, rest upon the experienced resemblances that cause objects
to fall into different groups and to receive different appellations. But
they are so vague and fluctuating that we cannot relate them even to
hypothetical groups in nature. Nature produces innumerable particulars, freaks, monstrosities, ambiguities, and the like, to which it is
well-nigh impossible for us to assign a class and give a specific name.
Underlying these nominal essences, to be sure, there may indeed be
real essences, or some objective, underlying similarity of constitution in
various individuals which gives rise to their superficial resemblances
and to our application to them of a common name. Such essences
would stand for real groupings, independent of our experience, but,
since they are unknown and purely hypothetical, they have no bearing
upon knowledge.

Knowledge then must content itself with *nominal* essences, or "those
abstract complex ideas to which we have annexed distinct general

names." But in so doing it must not forget that they rest, not upon *all* observed qualities, but upon a few of the more obvious ones. They are not exhaustive, and the more general the idea, the more incomplete and partial it is. They mean different things to different minds. And they are expressed by words, whose imperfections and abuses are notorious.

The first step towards clear understanding is to remedy these deficiencies in general ideas and abuses of words so far as we can. This we may do by meaning something when we speak, and by saying what we mean. We should use words in their ordinary signification and be careful to define what we signify by them. We should also illustrate what we mean by them. We should not vary the meaning we give to them, or, if we do, we should note and explain our change in usage.

X. KNOWLEDGE AND ITS LIMITATIONS

Nature of Knowledge. At last we ask ourselves, What is knowledge? Locke's answer is that it is *"the perception of the connection of and agreement, or disagreement and repugnancy, of any of our ideas."* This perception of agreement or disagreement of ideas takes place in four fields. First, we perceive it with respect to their *identity* or *diversity;* second, in the field of their *relations;* third, regarding the *co-existence* and *necessary connection* of qualities in things; and fourth, touching the question of *real existence* of things.

These perceptions may be actual and immediate, or they may be habitual, by virtue of our power to remember. Memory preserves both immediate, intuited ideas and demonstrated ideas from which the successive steps of the demonstration have been dropped. The reliability of demonstrated ideas rests upon the fact that what has once been shown to be true holds good whenever the subject-matter recurs. All knowledge, then, rests upon primary intuitions which are known to be what they are. Their presence and nature are unescapable. In demonstrated ideas we perceive agreement and disagreement, not immediately, but through the intervention of other ideas, whose certainty we have successively experienced. And the idea finally demonstrated must seem as obvious and as immediately certain as the idea with which we started.

Finally, besides intuitive and demonstrated knowledge, we have what Locke calls "sensitive knowledge." We cannot help referring our experience to an external world.

Knowledge and Experience. We have now to ask how far we can trust our so-called knowledge. Only, replies Locke, in so far as it concerns itself with things experienced or demonstrated from experience. The application of this test shows that we can have absolute certainty throughout all our experience of the *identity* or *difference* of our ideas. We experience directly things as like or unlike one an, other. But the relations between things are so numerous and complex that both our intuitive and demonstrative knowledge goes only a little way. So, too, as regards co-existence and necessary connection, we can know *what* the qualities of an object are, but we cannot know *how, why,* and *by what* they are tied together. We can see things acting and being acted upon, causing others or being brought into being by others, but we have no knowledge of the *connection* between the so-called causes and their so-called effects, or of the method by which power is *transferred* from one object to another. We have no experience, and therefore no knowledge, of spirits or souls or of the real nature of the external world. We have not any absolute certainty that the external world exists, though experience insistently suggests the presence of a "something I know not what" behind the perceived qualities whose combination makes up an object.

Truth and Error. Still, may we not make valid inferences from this suggestion? To answer this question, we must first discuss what we mean by *truth* and *error*. Truth and error, Locke tells us, come into being when we begin to make *propositions* about things. The ideas conjoined by propositions are in themselves neither true nor false; they are just *there*. When, however, we conjoin them, and predicate one thing of another, we raise the question of truth or falsehood.

Universal Synthetic Propositions Untrustworthy. Then we find that the truth of a proposition consists in *"the joining or separating of signs, as the things signified by them do agree or disagree with one another,"* and that falsehood is the reverse. We can make true or false propositions about fanciful objects like chimeras or centaurs, but such propositions add nothing to knowledge, and may be left out of account.

Another difficulty now confronts us. The propositions that are useful are universal and synthetic propositions. We make general statements to the effect that certain ideas are everywhere and always conjoined, and that certain things are universally true of experience. What warrant have we for this assurance of "everywhere" and "always"? We have no warrant, Locke replies, "unless we know the precise bounds and extent of the species its terms stand for." Therefore it must be admitted that we can make no certain universal propositions about substances as they really are. For their *real* essences are unknown. Nor can we make such propositions even about *nominal* essences, since, even in things as we experience them, we are unable to understand how and why their qualities hang together as they do. Hence we cannot say that these qualities *must* everywhere and always occur together.

We can, however, make certain universal propositions and have real knowledge where we can ourselves determine our definitions and meanings in the realm of fruitful propositions. Thus we can be certain of the truth of mathematical propositions. So, too, we can have real knowledge of moral laws and ideas, since they, too, are such that we can perceive how their elements hang together and involve one another.

The Existence of Our External World. Having at last set the limits to certainty and knowledge, so far as the nature of things is concerned, we return once more to the question of their existence. What can we certainly know to exist, except our perceptions and ideas? The insistent suggestion of our senses that perceptions are produced in us by external objects, cannot, as we have seen, be verified. However, though not so certain as intuition or the results of the deductions of our reason, it is nevertheless "an assurance that deserves the name of *knowledge.*" To all practical intents and purposes, the suggestion of an outer world is sufficiently certain to enable me to trust it. But it gives us no inkling as to the nature of those objects, or even of their continuous existence in the past. We can, however, trust our memory and believe that just as in the past we did have certain experiences, so in the past objects giving rise to those sensations actually did exist. But "this knowledge also reaches no further than our senses have formerly assured."

Of the existence of finite spirits or souls, we have no certain knowledge. We can only take them on faith.

We conclude that we can make no universal propositions about concrete objects with absolute certainty. The only propositions regarding them that have the value of knowledge are particular propositions.

Certainty of One's Self. There is, however, one thing, besides my ideas, of whose existence I have immediate and intuitive certainty. That is myself. I am as sure of my own existence as I am of the pain I feel or of the doubts I entertain. Our own existence, he says, "we perceive so plainly and so certainly, that it neither needs or is capable of any proof."

We may now sum up the whole situation. "No existence of anything

without us, but only of God, can certainly be known further than
our senses inform us."

We have, Locke thinks, a *demonstrative* knowledge of the existence
of God. The proof is as follows. I actually exist. Since something cannot come from nothing, I must be produced by something. This something cannot come from nothing. Hence what causes me must have
always existed, and be eternal. It must also be the source of all power
in the universe, and therefore most powerful. Again, I am a thinking
being. Mind cannot have been produced out of nothing. Nor can it
be an effect of matter, since matter is an unthinking substance, and
it is as difficult to conceive thought arising from the unthinking as it
is to conceive matter produced by nothing. Indeed, there is nothing
in the concept of matter to account even for the existence of motion.
For the same reason, matter *plus* motion cannot be conceived as giving
rise to mind. Thinking, therefore, must be at least as eternal as matter,
and the cause of my mind must be this eternal mind.

Still, may not this thinking Being *"also be material"*? The question,
Locke answers, is really not important, since God, whether pure mind,
or mind and body, in any case exists. Still, since attributing a body to
God might encourage materialism, it is best to show the folly of such
a supposition. As we have seen, thought cannot be conceived as arising from or located in matter. Taken severally or collectively, the
particles of which matter is composed are not thinking beings. No
one of them, and no organization of them, whether at rest or in motion, can ever produce anything but physical situations. Therefore,
God's thinking has no material cause or ground. God is an immaterial
being.

But may not matter be co-eternal with God and uncreated by him,
as many philosophers have maintained? This Locke denies, but his
argument against it is an act of faith. Creation of spirits and bodies out
of nothing by God is something that exceeds our powers of comprehension. Nevertheless it is a fact.

Respecting the immortality of the soul, Locke is cautious. He accepts it as a matter of faith, but we have neither intuitive nor demonstrative knowledge of it. Indeed, the *pros* and *cons* of the question
whether the soul is material or immaterial are so evenly balanced that,
if a man weighs them, "the difficulty to conceive either will, whilst
either alone is in his thoughts, still drive him to the contrary side."

In his *Reasonableness of Christianity* Locke argues that immortality cannot be inferred from the ideas of identity and personality, or regarded as part of the essence of the soul. It is an additional gift, granted us by God's grace. It may, therefore, be withheld, if it so pleases God, and perhaps it is denied to those who have not made themselves worthy of it by virtuous and Christian living here below.

XII. THE NATURE AND LIMITS OF DEMONSTRATION

Most Demonstration Only Probable. The last chapters of the last book of the *Essay* are devoted to a further consideration of demonstration, which Locke has invoked to prove the existence of God, but of whose character he has given no detailed discussion. First of all, we should note that much of our thinking is "wishful." We cannot, indeed, avoid seeing things upon which we have turned and to which we have opened our eyes, but we can turn and open them upon such experience as we please. Again, we may note that since absolute certainty is so scarce, we have to base a large part of our thinking and acting on *probability,* and to make use of judgments founded on a *presumed* agreement or disagreement between ideas, rather than of propositions grounded upon actual perception of this relation. Most of our judgments, therefore, have only partial and fallible validity. But there are laws of evidence, which set limits to probability and involve degrees of credibility. These we must now examine.

Presumption and probability, and the weighing of evidence, rest in the first place upon the conformity of the reported event with our experience and upon the credibility of the witnesses reporting it. Thus the more conformable an event is to our own experience, and the more universally it is testified to by other men, the greater its probability and the easier our assent to it. Conflict of testimony creates less probability in the event and more doubt in our minds. In evidence that counts we must include the testimony of history, remembering always the distortion that arises from handing down reports either by word of mouth or by copying.

Again, analogy is of great assistance in establishing the probable nature of the operations and processes in nature that escape experience. So, too, is experiment. Here again, the most probable analogies are those which agree most closely with experience. For example, by analogy we may argue from the continuous and orderly nature of the experienced world that the rest of the universe exhibits the same continuity and gradual ascent from the lower to the higher. Our faith in miracles, however, must not be disturbed. Their contrariness to experience and consequent improbability are more than offset by the testimony of revelation.

Uselessness of Syllogistic Reasoning. The fact that so much of our thought and action is based upon probability leads Locke to point out how inevitable a great diversity of opinion on all subjects must be, and how necessary it is for us to be charitable and tolerant in dealing with such differences.

Turning now to the processes of reasoning which underlie demonstration, Locke expresses grave doubts as to the utility of the syllogism and of traditional logical methods in the acquisition of knowledge. Probabilities are not established, neither is knowledge enlarged by its use. The weaknesses of reason are due, not to a failure to cast its thinking in syllogistic mold, but to the restricted number of ideas with which it can deal, to the obscurity of many of the ideas we do possess, to the inability of the ordinary mind to perceive the connecting ideas immediately intuited by men of genius, to starting from false premises, and to the misuse of words. The most certain knowledge we have is prior to reasoning of any sort, and if, in the progress of demonstration from idea to idea, we stop long enough for each new link in the chain to become immediately and intuitively certain, we shall arrive at correct conclusions, syllogism or no syllogism.

Moreover, most of our knowledge is only probable, and upon the judgments and assents involved in such knowledge no amount of syllogizing could confer any additional certainty. Sound argument uses only "proofs drawn from any of the foundations of knowledge on probability."

Acceptability of Revelation. Probability must also govern our attitude towards matters of faith and so-called "revealed" truth. "Revealed" truth cannot have the same certainty as demonstrated or intuited truth, since certainty is bound up with direct experience. In no case can we accept a revelation *"if it be contradictory to our clear intuitive knowledge.* Because this would be to subvert the principles of all knowledge, evidence, and assent whatsoever; and there would be left no difference between truth and falsehood, no measures of credible and incredible in the world, if doubtful propositions shall take place before self-evident."

The objects of faith may be above reason in the sense of lying beyond the reach of our present experience, but they cannot be contrary to reason. Reason must always be followed, so far as it affords us certain knowledge. Revelation may indeed run counter to *probability,* but, if we are to accept its improbabilities, they must still be such that, if they were experienced, they would prove intelligible. Finally, we should never accept revelation as a substitute for reasoning, when it is possible by the use of the unaided intellect to attain certainty. We should only take on faith what is incapable of being known at all, or what belongs among those things of which our knowledge at the best gives only probability.

The Influence of Wishful Thinking. People, however, are apt to believe what they want to believe. "They are sure because they are sure; and their persuasions are right because they are strong in them." What they believe *"is a revelation, because they firmly believe it; and they believe it because it is a revelation."* And, "when once they are got into this way of immediate revelation, of illumination without search, and of certainty without proof and without examination, it is a hard matter to get them out of it." Supernatural light, however, does not extinguish the natural light of ordinary intelligence. God commands our assent to truth by making it reasonable. *"Reason must be our last judge and guide in everything."*

As it is, reason has troubles enough of its own. It is prone to assent in its judgments to that which is not true and to fall into intellectual error. Since assent is grounded on likelihood and has probability as its proper object and motive, it is interesting to ask *"how men come to give their assents contrary to probability."* The causes of error fall under four heads. In the first place, we often assent to propositions without examining even such evidence of their probability or improbability as lies close at hand. Or we misuse the evidence we have, for want of skill in weighing testimony. Or we are simply too lazy to examine it. Or, in examining it, we are swayed by other than rational considerations, as, for example, by principles that we have been taught by others to accept as true, received hypotheses, or established explanations, or individual ruling passions, prejudices, and preferences, and finally deference to authority of one sort or another. We refuse to be convinced by unwelcome views or to go on with any inquiry that seems to be leading to results damaging to our preconceived views, and we may decline to employ our faculties in the search of any truth. In this way we protect ourselves against the acquisition of unwelcome knowledge. But in the end truth will win out, since we have eventually to accept willy-nilly the views that have the greatest intellectual probability on their side.

Chapter IX

BERKELEY

I. LIFE

Childhood and Education. Locke, for all his skepticism, considered it so probable as to be practically certain that our perceptions of the external world referred to and were caused by material substances possessed in themselves of the primary qualities of "solidity, extension, figure, and mobility." Berkeley's skepticism regarded the existence of any such substances as not only undemonstrable, but impossible, and his main argument is concentrated upon demolishing the being of the material world.

Of Berkeley's ancestry and early life we know very little. He was born in 1685 in a farmhouse that constituted the only habitable portion of Dysert Castle, otherwise in ruins, near Thomaston, twelve miles from Kilkenny in Ireland. His father is said to have been a kinsman of Lord Berkeley of Stratton. He was a precocious and imaginative child, and was early haunted by a sense of the unreality of the material world. His education was received at Kilkenny School, the Eton of Ireland, where he studied classics and mathematics, and at Trinity College, Dublin, where his eccentricities and enthusiasms won him the distinction of being considered either the greatest genius or the greatest dunce in the College. There he came under the influence of Locke and the Cartesians. He was much interested in philosophy, and was already working his way towards the main principle of his system, which eventually burst suddenly upon him as a kind of revelation, in much the same way as the principles of analytic geometry suddenly occurred to Descartes.

In 1707, he was elected a tutor at Trinity, and two years later was ordained a deacon and then a priest in the Anglican Church. At this time, he also published his *Essay Towards a New Theory of Vision,* in which he attacked Locke's theory that primary qualities are objective, not subjective. This was followed almost immediately by the *Treatise Concerning the Principles of Human Knowledge.* Meantime he had been promoted to the office of sub-lecturer and junior Dean, and in 1712 was made junior Greek lecturer.

Life in London and Abroad. The next year he went to London, where he was introduced by Swift, an old schoolmate, to his cousin, Lord Berkeley, by whom he was presented at the Court of Queen Anne. He was thus made free of London society, which at the time was brilliant and counted among its members Steele, Addison, Pope, Prior, and the great Deist, Clarke. He wrote essays in the *Guardian,* Steele's paper, attacking the free thinkers, and published the *Dialogues.*

The sojourn in London was followed by a journey to Italy, as secretary and chaplain to Peterborough, who had been on an embassy to the King Amodeus of Sicily. His trip was interrupted by the death of Anne and the recall of Peterborough, and he returned to England. A few years later, we find him abroad again as tutor to the son of the Bishop of Clogher. It is probable that he met Malebranche at this time, and there is a story that he hastened the philosopher's death. He visited Malebranche, so the story goes, when the latter was ill with pneumonia, and the violence of their dispute was so great, and Malebranche shouted so much, that the inflammation of the lungs was aggravated and resulted in death. A little later, Berkeley was once more in Italy, in Rome and Naples and Calabria.

The year 1720 saw his return to England, which he found in the throes of the panic induced by the bursting of the "South Sea Bubble" —a scheme for underwriting the national debt by exploiting the reputed riches of the South Seas. The shares went to £1000, the directors sold out, the stock collapsed, and many people were ruined. To this epoch belongs the essay *De Motu,* a study of power and causation. From England, Berkeley went back to Dublin as chaplain to the Duke of Grafton, where he was given the degree of D.D. by Trinity and appointed a Senior Lecturer and University Preacher. Shortly afterwards he was made a Dean and elected to the lectureship on Hebrew.

Life in Rhode Island. Also, he came into money. Swift had an ardent admirer in the famous Vanessa Vanborough, who had willed him all her fortune. Discovering his secret marriage with Stella, she revoked this will, and left half her property, a sum of about £4000, to Berkeley, and then conveniently died. Also, at this time he had a vision. He was much shocked and saddened by the state of English society and dreamt of one more perfect which might be founded in far-away America, then invested in the eyes of many visionaries with a halo of romance as the home of the noble and unspoiled savage, a child of nature as yet uncorrupted by civilization. The Bermudas, at the moment, exercised a special fascination. They were to Europe what the Hesperides were to the Greeks. There, it seemed to Berkeley, a college might be founded with the double function of educating the clergy and converting the Indians. He set about soliciting subscriptions and obtained a charter from George I. These were difficult days for him. There was litigation over the Vanborough estate and much red tape in connection with the charter. Then, too, he was courting Anne Forster, a lady of a good English-Irish family.

At last all difficulties were smoothed out, and in September 1728 he set sail with his bride for Rhode Island, where he landed at Newport in January 1729. Rhode Island, since the days of Roger Williams, had been the asylum of the oppressed, and thither most of those had betaken themselves who could not get on with the Puritans of Massachusetts. Furthermore, the merchants and sea-captains of Newport had amassed considerable fortunes, and the combination of a liberal tradition with wealth had produced a gay and pleasantly worldly society, given to fox-hunting and other amenities of existence, and patterned somewhat after English country-life. Berkeley was hospitably received in Newport, and spent two years there, living first in town, and then in a country house called Whitehall—which is still standing —about three miles inland. Here his first child was born, and here he busied himself with his scheme for the Bermuda college and with writing the *Alciphron* dialogues. He also took a great interest in Yale College and carried on a philosophical correspondence with its President.

Elevation to a Bishopric and Death. Things, however, went badly with the Bermuda project. The Walpole ministry balked at contributing the £20,000 promised earlier by the state, and Berkeley abandoned all hope of realizing his dream. He went up to Boston with his family and took ship for England. The next two years he spent in London— from which death had taken Steele and Addison, and Ireland had reclaimed Swift. In 1734 he was made Bishop of Cloyne, an episcopal seat in County Cork, not far from Queenstown. Here he spent the next twenty years attending to his diocese—with one break only in his routine when in 1737 he went to Dublin to sit in the Irish House of Lords. He was much interested in the social condition of Ireland and in improving matters in his diocese. Liberal and kindly, he was only too glad to cooperate with the Roman Catholics. The literary fruit of this epoch was the *Siris,* the famous essay which, beginning with a disquisition on the medicinal virtues of tar-water, ends with a discussion of the Trinity, after having dealt on the way with the vital principle, the nature of space and time, free-will and necessity, matter and form, the soul, and the nature of God.

Berkeley's eldest son was now ready to go to Oxford, and had matriculated at Christ Church. The family followed in order to be near him. For some time the Bishop had been in bad health and had suffered from gall-stones. At the end of the first year in England he died suddenly in January 1753.

II. THE DOUBLE PERCEPTION OF SPACE

The Perception of Distance. Berkeley seems to have been started on his skeptical path by Locke's own doubt, expressed in a passage in the *Essay,* as to whether a man born blind and acquainted with a globe and a cube only by touch, could, if his sight were suddenly given him, distinguish the globe from the cube by his eye, without again handling them. This doubt was raised in Locke's mind by a question put to him by his friend Molyneux, which suggested that our perception of shape and magnitude is double, and combines those qualities as they are given by touch and as they are given by sight. The same question perhaps had already occurred to Berkeley, but the hint thrown out by Locke helped crystallize his doubts as they appeared in the *Essay Towards a New Theory of Vision.*

In this work he concludes that not only shape and magnitude, but the distance and the relative situation of objects, are not perceived directly by the eye, but are judged only after visual have been associated with tactual sensations and with experiences of movement. That *distance* is not given by sight Berkeley argues, first, from the absence of any means within the eye itself for estimating the nearness or the remoteness of the sources of the rays of light that impinge upon it. Pictures are cast upon the retina in the flat, and contain no suggestions as to which of their features are nearer, which farther away. Nor can distance be judged by the degree of the convergence of the two eyes, since no one consciously computes the angle or is conscious of the lines of convergence. Even if he were, there would be no reason in the activity of vision itself for associating a sensation of less convergence with more distant objects, of greater convergence with objects closer at hand. Therefore, Berkeley insists, distance is perceived *mediately,* not immediately. It is *learned* through long association of objects of touch and experiences in reaching and walking, with objects of vision.

Magnitude and Situation. Coming now to *magnitude,* we find that the same considerations hold true. We have size as it is given to touch and size as it is given to the eye. These two sorts of sizes are quite different and often contradict each other. "Nor will it be found that great or small visible magnitude hath any necessary relation to great or small tangible magnitude—so that the one may certainly be inferred from the other." [1] Again, visual size differs with the distance of the object—remoteness or nearness. To overcome these discrepancies we invent standards of measurement in terms of tangible magnitude. But they are artificial and arbitrary.

Or take *situation.* Our perception of situation is excessively complex and curious. In the first place, since all images are inverted on the retina of the eye, external objects are given upside down. Again, visible and tangible situations differ and sometimes confuse each other. Only long association enables us to correlate visual with tactual and motor right and left, up and down, and the like. A man blind from birth, if suddenly given his sight, would have no idea of visible up and down, right and left.

The upshot of the whole matter is that *"the extension, figures, and motions perceived by sight are specifically distinct from the ideas of touch called by the same name; nor is there any such thing as one idea or kind of idea, common to both senses."*

Primary and Secondary Qualities Equally Subjective. These conclusions seemed to Berkeley to knock the bottom out of Locke's distinction between primary and secondary qualities. For, if we say that objects actually possess in themselves solidity, extension, figure and mobility, we may properly be asked which sort of these qualities do they possess, tangible or visual?

Nay more, the so-called primary qualities are just as subjective, just as much effects produced on our senses, as are the so-called secondary qualities like color, taste, sound, temperature and the like. They are complexes of visual, tactual, and locomotor sensations. There is no more reason for believing that they are really in the external object than for believing that color and taste and smell are in it. Like the secondary qualities, they are effects produced by the object upon our minds. We are left, then, with an external world possessed of *no known qualities whatsoever,* since all qualities and properties, primary as well as secondary, are effects produced by that world upon the kind of sense-organs we have.

[1] All quotations are from Fraser's edition, Oxford, 1871.

III. THE IDEA OF MATTER

At the most, then, the term *matter* can signify no more than this unknown something, of which we can predicate neither size, nor shape, nor extension, nor motion, nor rest. But can it signify even that? In other words, can we so much as have an *idea* of matter as something more than the combination of sensible qualities we call an "object"?

Berkeley's approach to this question is made through his discussion of the nature and origin of abstract ideas set forth in the introduction to his *Treatise Concerning the Principles of Human Knowledge.* Here, again, Berkeley follows Locke and allies himself on the side of the "nominalists." *Things,* he tells us, are experienced as groups of qualities. Though the qualities are not *experienced* in isolation, we can isolate them for purposes of thought and consider them separately.

Moreover, the mind, in comparing the combinations of qualities it perceives, notes points of resemblances and common features. Thus the ideas of these qualities or combinations of qualities acquire a *general* reference and significance. The picture may be vague and ill-defined and without reference to any particular instance of the idea under consideration, but it is nevertheless particular, not universal, concrete, not abstract.

It is the particular image, taken as a sign or representation of everything falling within the class of objects under consideration, that constitutes the so-called *abstract idea.* Universals, then, are not names of real abstract natures, but of relations in which individuals stand to one another. So-called abstracting and generalizing does not lie in getting rid altogether of particularity and concreteness, but in making one particular concrete image or picture stand for a whole class of objects.

It follows that general terms or names do not signify one idea, as they are commonly and erroneously supposed to do, but a multitude of ideas. The name "horse," for instance, signifies a myriad different images of a horse called up in a myriad different minds by hearing the word. But the name equally signifies all these images, since it stands for certain aspects which they have in common.

Names, then, do not *limit* the ideas for which they stand. "There is no such thing as one precise and definite signification annexed to any general name, they all signifying indifferently a great number of particular ideas." They also arouse passions as well as evoke ideas, and

acquire halos of value which frequently do not illuminate their meaning. Hence the magic and the authority attributed by the Schoolmen
to universals is quite absurd. Abstract and general terms in no wise
enlarge our knowledge, except as convenient symbols for representing and communicating the images of particular things. They arise
from experience and terminate in experience. Apart from their reference to sense-perception they have no meaning or use.

With these considerations in view, let us look once more at *matter*.
What is in our mind when we have the idea of "matter" in general?
The answer is obvious. We have nothing but the image of some
vaguely extended, and resistant, particular object of indefinite shape
and size, either moving or resting, faintly stained with color or hardness or softness or other "secondary" characteristics. The only difference between this image and the picture of any other "material" object
is that we make it representative of all other experiences exhibiting
the same "material" qualities. Matter, in a word, doesn't *mean* anything except complexes of sensations. Where, then, is Locke's "substance"? Where is the "something I know not what" underlying and
supporting the combinations of qualities we call material things?
Nowhere.

IV. THE DIALOGUES BETWEEN HYLAS AND PHILONOUS

Non-Existence of a Material Substratum. This position, reached by
Berkeley in his youth, remained till the end the core of his system.
We have now to follow him in the reiteration and elaboration of his
main thesis, to which the *Dialogues* are devoted. In the first series of
Dialogues Berkeley appears in the character of Philonous arguing with
Hylas, a believer in the reality of Locke's substances. The first *Dialogue*
covers familiar ground. The distinction between primary and secondary qualities is destroyed and all alike are agreed to be subjective
and experiential in character. Hylas struggles a little against abandoning the notion of Sir Isaac Newton that there is an objective and absolute space, time, and motion existing independently of sensible extension, movement and duration; but he is soon convinced by
Philonous' argument that such absolutes are merely abstractions from
particular sensible instances. He is next dislodged from the idea of a
substratum, to which he still clings. He is prodded with Locke's story
of the elephant and the tortoise and with the impossibility of finding
any final substratum except at the end of an infinite regress, and he is
thrown into confusion by being asked to explain just how such a sub-

stratum, if it could be found, should be conceived as "supporting" its qualities.

Existence and Experience. The college bell is about to ring for prayers. As Hylas and Philonous part Philonous suggests that *no ideas can exist without the mind*. This thought so staggers Hylas that he is not sufficiently recovered from it to face Philonous again till the next afternoon. Then the conversation is resumed in the second *Dialogue,* and once more Philonous has the upper hand. Hylas is soon driven to admit that even his own body and his own brain, the supposed organ of thought, are nothing but complexes of perceptions existing in his own mind.

But Philonous, it soon turns out, has not the courage of his convictions. Hylas, quite properly, confesses himself converted to a thorough-going skepticism regarding the real existence of anything but his own experience. So it is that we now find Philonous accepting the intimations and external references of our perceptions as valid, in spite of the skeptical doubt that could properly be urged against such an acceptance. To Hylas' remark that Philonous by rights is as much of a skeptic as he is, Philonous objects. He has, he says, denied only the reality of sensible things, considered as existing absolutely "out of the minds of spirits, or distinct from their being perceived." But that does not prevent them from existing in some other mind, as for example, in the mind of "an infinite omnipresent Spirit, who contains and supports them." In support of the existence of such a mind Berkeley adduces much the same arguments as Locke brings forward in favor of an external cause of our sensations.

Hylas, however, still remains obdurate. Supposing that there is a God, is it not still possible, as the Cartesians maintain, that besides spirits and ideas there is a material world, and that this world is the "subordinate and limited cause of our ideas"? Or may not Malebranche be right in his theory of "vision in God," according to which the soul, "incapable of being united with material things, so as to perceive them in themselves . . . perceives them by her union with the substance of God" and by knowing the ideas or representations of material objects existing in the divine mind? Philonous replies that the arguments against the possibility of our ideas representing non-mental objects hold true for the divine mind also. As for *matter*— how can matter *cause* immaterial ideas, or what need has God of it as a subordinate *instrument* for *occasioning* ideas in us?

Existence and Spirits. Hylas, shaken in his beliefs, begs for time off to run things over in his thoughts, and suggests that they meet the

next afternoon for the third *Dialogue*. The day after finds him plunged
in gloom. He is convinced that *material substance* is no more than a
false and groundless hypothesis, but he cannot quite see how things
can exist simply as ideas in the divine mind. Nor can he understand
how it is any more possible to have ideas of spirits, which Philonous
himself has admitted to be "a sort of beings altogether different from
them," than it is to have ideas of material things. To say that "there is
spiritual substance, although you have no idea of it; while you deny
that there can be such a thing as material substance, because you have
no notion or idea of it" seems to him to be not quite fair dealing.
"To act consistently" Philonous "must either admit matter or reject
spirit."

Philonous replies that the idea of material substance is inconsistent
in itself and that no reason can be brought forward for believing in
the existence of matter. I am not conscious of either its existence or
its essence. On the other hand, although I have no direct intuition of
my own spirit and no immediate evidence or a demonstrative knowledge of the existence of other finite spirits, the existence of spirits in
general is not self-contradictory, and I do have reflective knowledge
of my own soul. I know "that *I myself* am not my ideas, but somewhat else, a thinking, active principle that perceives, knows, wills and
operates about ideas."

The Divine Mind and Experience. Hylas, however, still objects.
Common sense insists that *"to be perceived* is one thing, and *to exist*
is another," and that objects have a being of their own apart from
being experienced by any mind. Also, how are we to distinguish between fact and fancy? How are we to absolve God from being the
direct "author of murder, sacrilege, adultery, and the like heinous
sins"? And must we not say that God suffers the same pain and uneasiness in himself as are often connected in our minds with these
same ideas when he implants them in us? To these objections, Philonous replies that there is nothing in the external reference of a man's
ideas which is repugnant to the Christian religion or denies that their
object, "existing without his mind, is truly known and comprehended
by [that is, *exists in*] the infinite mind of God." As for ideas representing the various sorts of moral evil, such ideas are produced, not
by the infinite mind, but by the free activity of our own spirits. Again,
pain and uneasiness are *understood* by God, but are not *felt* by him.
He knows what they are, but, being without those complexes of ideas
which represent the bodies, passions, and parts, and with which the

sensations of pleasure and pain are connected, he cannot himself *experience* either suffering or enjoyment.

But Hylas continues to struggle. Appealing to the Cartesian argument, he asks whether God would implant in us so strong a suggestion that a physical world exists if there were really no such thing as matter. That would be deceiving us. The answer is, says Philonous, that God does not deceive us. All that he suggests is that an *external* world exists. This suggestion is trustworthy. He does not suggest that the external world is *material*. The materialistic hypothesis is self-deception on our part, and can easily be dispelled by the use of the intelligence with which God has endowed us.

"Sameness" of "Similar" Objective Impressions. But how, continues Hylas, can we ever perceive the *same* object. There will be as many so-called experiences of the same object as there are spirits, plus God's experience which is supposedly the *real, external* object that the other spirits are perceiving. But wherein lies the *sameness* of all these distinct ideas, which all the spirits, including God, are entertaining? There would seem to be merely as many experiences, or objects, as there are spirits, human and divine, without any single and common point of reference to make them, though different, perceptions of the *same* thing.

Philonous, now on the defensive, asks what we mean by *same,* and what difference does it make what we mean. Identity is a very loose term. Suppose, for instance, a house were all pulled to pieces and rebuilt inside, so that only its outer walls remained unaltered. Would that house be the same or not the same? You might say, "Yes"; I might say, "No"; but we should nevertheless "perfectly agree in our thoughts of the house, considered in itself." Anyway, the materialists are in the same boat. They, too, experience different objects. There are as many ideas of an object as there are materialists thinking that they are looking at one.

"Not at all," Hylas replies. The materialists believe that their several ideas of an object have some "archetype" or point of reference outside their minds, which makes their several complexes of sensations, ideas of one and the same object. Philonous retorts that the Berkeleians believe exactly the same thing. Your idea and my idea do refer to one and the same object existing outside both our minds: to wit, God's idea.

But how, Hylas asks, can an extended world exist in an unextended mind? Since the mind is unextended, replies Philonous, nothing can exist *in* it, literally speaking. The phrase "in the mind" is merely a figure of speech, to designate the activity of experiencing. Very well, but how are we to reconcile the Biblical account of creation with this transforming of things into ideas? That is easy to explain. There is nothing in Genesis inconsistent with supposing that God first created finite spirits and then implanted in their minds that complex of his ideas we call the universe.

"Esse = Percipi." We may now sum up Berkeley's philosophy in the famous phrases of his own choosing. *Esse* is *percipi* or *percipere*. Nothing exists except perceiving or being perceived. Spirits and their ideas —that is all there is to existence. Reality, then, is constituted of immaterial thinking substances and their experiences and thoughts. One of these thinking substances, God, is eternal and infinite, the others are created and finite. In finite spirits there are experiences and ideas of two sorts, some produced by their own perceiving and thinking activities, others (which we call the external world) imparted to the finite minds by the infinite mind through the process that we call knowledge. Matter is nonexistent as a substance or substratum. At the most, it is only a convenient name for those complexes of perceptions or ideas which we call physical objects. These objects, to be sure, are external to the finite spirits, but in so far as they exist outside the finite minds, they exist in the mind of God and nowhere else.

V. THE "ALCIPHRON" DIALOGUES

Ethics. The *Alciphron* dialogues add little that is new to the point of view we have just set forth. Their tone is predominantly theological and moral. In them Berkeley fills in with the conventional Christian idea of God his philosophically outlined picture of an infinite mind whose thinking creates and supports the universe. He is particularly concerned with confuting atheists and free thinkers and in defending revelation and a system of absolute morality based upon supernatural foundations. With this end in view he sets up a group of "minute philosophers," as he calls the free thinkers, and gives them their say. He then proceeds to demolish the arguments he has put into their mouths against any morality or for a naturalistic ethics, and against all religion or for a natural one.

The content of Berkeley's ethics, such as it is, is not particularly noteworthy. It does, however, seem to have changed somewhat as time went on. In his earlier work, he had defined happiness as the greatest amount of pleasure and the least of pain in the long run. Only an intelligent being is capable of achieving a balance of pleasure, since the use of reason and intelligence is necessary in estimating the comparative value of pleasures and pains past and future, and in devising the means of ensuring a maximum of enjoyment in life, rather than of suffering. In the *Alciphron* dialogues, however, he has become less hedonistic. Man is now regarded as exclusively *rational* in his essence. Therefore, only rational pleasure is distinctively *human*. Sensuous pleasure remains the natural and essential good of the lower animals, and in as much as man also has an animal as well as a rational side, it solicits his lower nature and is an object of desire. But true happiness is to be had only from the satisfaction of our reason, which to Berkeley means obedience to the will of God.

Epistemology. Again, in the seventh and last *Alciphron* dialogue, and in the *Siris,* Berkeley's theory of knowledge has become less empirical and nominalistic. He uses, to be sure, his doctrine that general concepts and abstract ideas are particular images used as signs or symbols to rebuke the scientists for supposing that their concepts are clearer or more comprehensive than those of theology. We can, for example, form as clear an abstract idea of grace as we can of force— which is not to say that either of the ideas is clear. Both are confused and inadequate, but the one is not more so than the other.

At the same time, knowledge has become for him more than perception, and the understanding is beginning to emerge as a faculty distinct from sensation. Abstract ideas are coming to be regarded as so remote from percepts as to be almost detached from them, and their origin, it is hinted, is to be found, not in sensations, but rather in the mind's reflection upon its own activities. In other words, there is a tendency to derive mathematical and scientific truths from the nature of *spirits* rather than from *ideas.* But these tendencies never came to a head.

Chapter X

HUME

I. LIFE

Education and Character. David Hume, the third and last of the great British empiricists, was born at Edinburgh in 1711, of the family of the Humes of Ninewells, related to the Earls of Hume. Losing his father in his youth, he was brought up by his mother, who was a woman of great force of character. At twelve years of age he matriculated at the University of Edinburgh, where he received a thorough education in the classics and became acquainted with Greek and Roman philosophy.

The six years after his graduation he spent between Ninewells and Edinburgh, reading, studying, and thinking. He was preparing for the bar, but he was also beginning to work out his philosophy. By this time, too, his essential temperament displayed itself. He was prosaic, with little sense of the romantic or the beautiful and no appreciation of art and music. Music he considered mere noise, Gothic architecture a heap of confusion and irregularity, and Shakespeare a disproportionate and misshapen giant. The last criticism may have been motivated in part by his Scotch dislike of the English, for Hume was a thorough and typical Scot. These clouds, however, had silver linings. Though he lacked esthetic sense, he had a keen sense of the ridiculous and a wit and humor which were always kindly. He was an acute observer and critic, and his mind was broad, tolerant, and fair.

Hume, however, never went to the bar. His studies produced in him a curious crisis of mental revulsion and of disgust not only with the law but with philosophy as well. He was suddenly seized with a yearning for the practical and got a job in a merchant's counting-house in Bristol. The experiment did not work. He could not stomach either the town or the counting-house. So he broke away altogether, crossed to France and settled down for two years at La Flèche, where Descartes had gone to school, and wrote the *Treatise of Human Nature*.

152

In 1737 he returned to London with the manuscript and got it published two years later. He had hoped the book would make a stir.
But it did not cause a ripple. It fell, as Hume himself said, "dead-born"
from the press, without reaching such distinction as even to excite a
murmur among the orthodox. In his disappointment he abandoned
philosophy, turned to history and economics, and in 1741 published
his *Essays, Moral and Political.*

By this time Hume was becoming known and was gathering round
him a little circle of brilliant friends, of whom the most noted was
Hutcheson, the moralist. He tried also for the chair of moral philosophy at Edinburgh. But the *Treatise* had not fallen altogether still-
born, and the University turned him down because of his opinions.

Diplomatic Career and Life in Scotland. In 1745, he passed a disagreeable year attached to the service of the crazy Marquis of Annan-
dale, and the next year had an equally abortive adventure as secretary
of a projected expedition under St. Clair against the French in Canada,
which ended in a fizzle with a naval raid on the Breton coast. But St.
Clair took a fancy to him, and, on being chosen chief of a military
embassy to Turin and Vienna, invited Hume to accompany him as his
secretary. Hume traveled with him through Holland, up the Rhine
to Frankfort, thence to Ratisbon and Vienna, and back by the Tyrol
and Italy. But he had no eye for scenery or tradition, and was wholly
immersed in the politics and human affairs of the countries he visited.

In 1748 he published his *Enquiry into the Human Understanding,*
in which he revised and condensed the *Treatise* in a manner more
acceptable, as he thought, to the public. A year later, his mother died
and he returned to Ninewells to continue the revision of the portions
of the *Treatise* dealing with ethics. This appeared in 1751 under the
title of *Enquiry into Morals.* It was followed within a twelvemonth
by his *Political Discourses.* Once more, he tried for a professorship—
this time, the chair of logic at Glasgow—and once more his opinions
proved too shocking for a virtuous and respectable university to
stomach. However, he did get the job of librarian of the Advocates'
Library in Edinburgh, though even in this case there was some opposition because of his views. He held the post for six years. Meantime he
was always writing. His *History of Great Britain, containing the
Reigns of James I and Charles I,* appeared in two volumes in 1754 and
1756 and succeeded in offending everybody. A year later came the
Natural History of Religion.

Resigning his post at Edinburgh, Hume spent a couple of years in

London, writing as usual. The fruits of this period were his friendship with Edmund Burke and the *History of England under the House
of Tudor* (1759).

Life in France. In 1763, the war between Great Britain and France
being at an end, a British Ambassador, Lord Hertford, was sent to
Paris, and Hume was made secretary of the embassy. At court and in
French literary and philosophical circles Hume received a tremendous
ovation, like that which later was tended to Benjamin Franklin.
Many of his works had been translated into French, and his wit, his
irony, and his refined skepticism, which outraged British respectability,
were congenial to the spirit of the Enlightenment, then at its height
in France. He was feted by the Dauphin at Versailles, and—a rare
honor for a philosopher—listened to three eulogies recited by three
little future kings, the Dauphin's children, later the ill-fated Louis
XVI, Louis XVIII, and Charles X. He enjoyed Paris and all the flat-
tery immensely and much preferred the French to the English. But he
was not taken in by their adulation. He also made friends with
D'Alembert, the celebrated mathematician and philosopher, with
Diderot, the editor of the great *Dictionnaire Encyclopédique,* and also
with Turgot, the economist, later Minister of Finance under Louis
XVI. After Hertford's recall in 1765, he was left as *chargé d'affaires*
at Paris for a time. A little later Hertford, on being appointed Lord
Lieutenant of Ireland, asked Hume to accompany him to Dublin.

Return to Edinburgh and Death. Hume refused. Instead, he returned to England, accompanied by Rousseau, whom he had be-
friended, and with whom he later quarreled violently and still later
was reconciled. The next year (1766) he went back to Edinburgh,
where he was made Under Secretary of State for Scotland. The re-
mainder of his life was quiet and uneventful. He bought a house in
Edinburgh, where he lived quietly with his sister. In 1775 his health
began to fail, and, knowing that his disease was fatal, he wrote his
autobiography entitled *My Own Life.* The next year he died.

There has been considerable discussion of the comparative merits
of the *Treatise* and the *Enquiry* as an exposition of Hume's philosophy. Hume himself preferred the *Enquiry.* On the other hand, the
champions of the *Treatise* point out that much of great value has
been altogether dropped in the later work, or has been so condensed as
to lose in large measure its original force.

II. THE DERIVATION OF IDEAS FROM EXPERIENCE

Impressions and Ideas. In the flow of conscious experience, Hume tells us, we distinguish two sorts of things. On the one hand, we have *impressions,* in which are to be included not merely our sense-perceptions but feelings like love, hate, desire, will, etc. On the other hand, we have *thoughts* or *ideas.* Hume, it will be noted, restricts the term "idea," used by Locke and Berkeley indiscriminately of all experiences, and employs it in the more usual and modern sense of the word. The distinction between *ideas* and *impressions,* he continues, lies in the greater degree of force and vivacity accompanying *impressions.* In comparison, *ideas* are pale and cold. This is because the *idea* is the work of *memory* and *imagination,* and only mediately of direct *impressions.*

Hume, however, is as insistent as Locke and Berkeley that all our ideas, though they seem sometimes to transcend experience, are derived from impressions. The so-called creative power of the mind "amounts to no more than the faculty of compounding, transposing, augmenting, or diminishing the materials afforded us by the senses and experience." No idea whatsoever can be found that is not decomposable into terms of experience, and, wherever sense-perception is lacking, the corresponding ideas are lacking also.

The Derivation of Ideas from Impressions. Hume has, then, on his hands precisely the same problem as confronted Locke. How are we to derive *from* experience ideas that seem to *transcend* experience? To answer this question, he begins, as Locke began, by giving an account of the way in which all ideas are built up. The construction of ideas is due to *association.* Impressions, as they occur, arouse memories and images of *similar* impressions, or of *contiguous* impressions that happened near by or at the same time, or of impressions considered their *causes* or their *effects.* Whole blocks of impressions given together are revived together in connection with the circumstances of their occurrence. Thus we come by *complex* ideas, like those of *substance, modes* or qualities, and *relations.* Among the relations of importance to philosophy are *resemblance, identity, spatial* and *temporal arrangement, quantity, degree, continuity,* and *cause and effect.*

Of modes and substances, Hume disposes in short order. He dispenses with Locke's "something I know not what" and insists like Berkeley that we have "no idea of substance distinct from that of a collection of particular qualities." But the idea is more than a mere aggregate of qualities or modes. It comprises also "a principle of union," based upon contiguity and causation. "The simple ideas, on the other hand, of which modes are formed, either represent qualities, which are not united by contiguity and causation, but are dispers'd in different subjects, or if they be all united together, the uniting principle is not regarded as the foundation of the complex idea."

Nature of Abstract Ideas. We cross now into the field of relations. In doing so, we must keep in mind that there is no such thing as an absolutely *abstract idea*. Hume agrees with Berkeley that all ideas are particular and concrete. They are images or pictures made to stand for and signify a host of other particular things whose images are like or associated with the representative image.

Words or names, in being generally applied, do not have to recall all the images associated with them. They simply revive the "custom we have acquired of surveying them," or a sort of vague composite photograph of the general features in which all the particular images are potentially present. "A particular idea becomes general by being annexed to a general term; that is, to a term which from a customary conjunction has a relation to many other particular ideas and readily recalls them in the imagination."

With these considerations before us, we turn back to the task of deriving from experience such abstract ideas as seem to transcend it. We begin with *space* and *time*. The idea of their infinity and infinite divisibility, which had bothered Locke and had been defined by him as a negative idea, Hume disposes of in short order. We have no idea of infinity, he says. Ideas are drawn from experience and are adequate representations of experience. Spatial and temporal experience never presents itself as infinite or its objects as infinitely divisible. Therefore there can be no such thing as infinite space and infinite time.

Again, empty space and time are nonexistent. The idea of extension is the idea of an extended *content* of some sort or other.

In like manner, "the indivisible moments of time must be filled with some real object or existence, whose succession forms duration and makes it conceivable by the mind." Moreover, that object must be a changing object, since experience of an unchanging content would give us no idea of succession and therefore no sense of the passage of time.

Time, however, is not an idea added to the ideas of the separate events that occur in succession. If I hear five musical notes, I do not have *six* impressions, composed of the impressions of five sounds *plus* an independent, sixth impression called "time." The notice I take of time is only a notice "of the *manner* in which the different sounds make their appearance," or, in other words, an abstraction of an idea of *succession* from successive events.

It follows from what we have been saying that there is no such thing as absolute, mathematical space or absolute motion and time. Geometry is not an exact science. "It takes the dimensions and proportions of figures justly; but roughly and with some liberty." Again, since the notions of equality and of "greater than" and "less than" are relative, we cannot devise any absolute standards or instruments of measurement. So, too, no exact means of estimating comparative velocities can be found. All standards of measurement both of extension and duration are at the best approximate.

III. MATTERS OF FACT

Matters of Fact and Belief. All objects of knowledge may be divided into two kinds, *relations of ideas* and *matters of fact*. The relations of ideas are worked out according to the laws of logical implication. Matters of fact are not connected logically, since the contrary of any fact is conceivable. They are connected by cause and effect.

But how do we distinguish what we call *facts* from what we call *fancies?* This distinction involves a mental attitude of *belief* in *facts, disbelief* in *fancies*. Belief, Hume defines as "a lively idea related to or associated with a present impression." It is, he adds in the *Enquiry,* "nothing but a more vivid, lively, forcible, firm, and steady conception of an object than what the imagination alone is ever able to attain. . . . It consists not in the peculiar nature or order of ideas, but in the *manner* of their conception and in their *feeling* to the mind." This feeling is sense of *reality*. What we believe in we consider to be a *fact.* "I confess," says Hume, "that it is impossible perfectly to explain this feeling or manner of conception. . . ."

But why is it that some ideas inspire and are accompanied by *belief,* others not? In the first place, Hume replies, belief is founded upon impressions. Impressions are sensations. They are *there.* We cannot get away from them. Nothing could be more *real* than they. So it is that they, and the memories of them, are bound to be more vivid and living than ideas about them or pictures of them constructed by the imagination.

Fact and Fancy. But no *idea* of any object, however vivid it may be, actually presents that object to our senses and makes us believe in its *existence.* To *believe* in the *existence* or reality of a horse or a centaur, for example, we must *see* one. Illusions and hallucinations are, after all, deceptions of the *senses*. But generally speaking, we do *see* horses; we do not see centaurs. It is the corroboration of the idea of the horse by the *impression* of the horse that gives the idea factual value, and it is the failure of experience to support the idea of the centaur with an impression or perception that makes the centaur a fancy.

Still, some people occasionally do *see* hallucinations which awaken in them a very lively *belief* in their *reality*. What of them? If we all saw centaurs with the frequency and the regularity that we see horses, they would be just as *real* and would excite the same belief. But we don't. A further and perhaps final distinction between matters of fact and fancies and illusions is that the impressions we call matters of fact constantly *recur* and keep recurring in the same context of associations and circumstances. Thus the belief which any impression, even a hallucination, inspires, is reinforced and strengthened, in the case of matters of fact, by the continued repetition of the impression.

As to the origin of our sense-impressions Hume is noncommittal. "Their ultimate cause is," he thinks, "perfectly inexplicable by human reason, and 'twill always be impossible to decide with certainty whether they arise immediately from the object [Locke], or are produced by the creative power of the mind [Leibnitz], or are deriv'd from the author of our being [Berkeley]."

IV. CAUSE AND EFFECT

The Causal Relation. We pass now quite naturally to *cause and effect,* since the belief that matters of fact are causally connected is almost as strong as the belief in their reality. We spontaneously ask *why* any given matter of fact occurs, and as spontaneously answer that it is *caused* by some other matter of fact. What, then, is the ground of this belief? There certainly seems to be no necessity for such a belief. Causes do not announce themselves as such. They have always to be discovered. Or again, from a quite novel impression we can get no idea of how it will behave and what it will give rise to. Certain impressions are the *causes* of certain others only because they have proved *de facto* to be so. Until the particular effect has been produced the so-called cause is not the reason for its production.

Nor can we argue for the necessity of causation on the ground that its opposite is logically inconceivable. It is not inconceivable that nothing should exist. Therefore, the existence of the universe is not logically necessary and does not require a reason. But if existence as a whole does not have to be explained, why should the existence of a particular object at any one time or place have to have a cause?

The Earmarks of Causality. What, then, are the earmarks of the causal relation? In the first place, a so-called cause and its effect must be *contiguous*. There can be no spatial gap between them. There can be no action at a distance. Again, the cause must *precede* its effect, and the effect *follow* its cause in time. But here again, the effect must be contiguous to the cause, must immediately follow it. Causality can no more jump gaps in time than it can gaps in space.

But "an object may be contiguous and prior to another, without being consider'd as its cause. There is NECESSARY CONNECTION to be taken into consideration; and that relation is of much greater importance than any of the other two above mention'd." We feel that any impression considered to be the cause of another simply *must* be followed by that other, and that any event considered as the effect of another *must* succeed whatever is regarded as its cause. It is this sense of *must* which distinguishes causal connection from coincidence. In coincidence, the contiguous and prior event *need* not be followed by its sequent. Its sequent is not its consequence but has its explanation elsewhere.

The feeling of *necessary* connection is often expressed by saying that the cause *produces* the effect, and that the effect *is produced* by the cause. But we never experience the process in which one event is *produced* from another, nor do we perceive in any one impression any *power* to bring another into being. For that matter, we do not even experience any power or any process of production in our own inner experience, as Locke maintained. We will, to be sure, that our arm or leg should move, and it does move. But we do not perceive the link between our volition and the ensuing movement. We do not perceive our will *making* the arm or the leg move as it desires.

This conclusion holds good not only for the causation or production of one body by another and of bodily movement by human volition, but also for any causal and creative activity we may try to impute to God. We are "equally ignorant of the manner or force by which . . . even the supreme mind operates either on itself or on body." For "we have no sentiment or consciousness of this power in ourselves" and "we have no idea of the Supreme Being but what we learn from reflection on our own faculties."

The *necessity* implied in the idea of causation is neither an *a priori* necessity of logic nor an obvious *a posteriori* inference from experi-

ence. It is an outcast from the only two fields in which knowledge is
possible, relations between ideas and relations between matters of fact.
But, although we cannot know that such necessity exists, we can,
Hume thinks, show how the *feeling* of necessary connection between
impressions arises from experience. To this he now applies himself.

The Feeling of Necessary Connection. The key to the situation he
finds in the *association* of ideas. Not only does the flowing character
of impressions make the mind expect that any present content of ex-
perience· will be followed by something or other, but the fact that
impressions occur over and over again in *similar* sequences, and that
one specific event is invariably followed by another specific event, gets
the mind into the habit of looking for certain sequents and no others,
when certain antecedents occur. This habit of leaping forward to and
expecting the sequent associated with the antecedent becomes so ingrained by continual repetition of their conjunction as to make the
mind feel that when the one event occurs the other simply *must*
follow it. Conversely, in looking backward from any event, the mind
feels that the impression *must* be connected with the antecedent with
which it has hitherto been invariably associated. Events so habitually
conjoined and associated as to be accompanied by this feeling of *must*
are called *cause* and *effect,* and the relation of simple sequence is turned
into one of *causation* or *production.*

A cause, then, we may define as "an object precedent and contiguous
to another, and so united with it, that the idea of the one determines
the mind to form the idea of the other, and the impression of the one
to form a more lively idea of the other." So, too, with the feeling of
necessity. "The necessity or power which unites causes and effects lies
in the determination of the mind to pass from one to the other."

The Causal Relation Subjective. It follows that the causal tie and
the necessary connection supposed to subsist between cause and effect
exist, so far as knowledge is concerned, entirely in the mind. They
cannot be said to exist in the external world, because, in the first place,
we have no certain knowledge that such a world exists and no knowledge of what it is like if it does exist. Nor are they in themselves impressions or qualities of impressions, as we have already pointed out.
Our ideas of them are drawn from a *feeling,* which arises from a
custom or habit of association. But it *guarantees* nothing. We cannot
know for certain that in the past or in the future given antecedents
will have the consequences they now have. There is, therefore, no
a priori impossibility of miracles, though in weighing the evidence for
them, we must establish a greater *probability* of their occurrence than

of error or deception on the part of those who testify to them. But this opens up a new question. What do we mean by *probable,* and where do we get that idea?

V. PROBABILITY AND CHANCE

The idea of probability is intimately bound up with that of causation and of its opposite, *chance.* In pure chance the mind expects no one thing to occur more than another. If, for example, I throw a pair of unloaded dice, or a single die, I feel that the chances are equal that any one of the sides may turn up as the result of the throw. To feel it more *probable* that one side rather than another should turn up, there must be some admixture of feeling of causation, which makes it customary for me to expect that event. And my feeling of probability will become stronger as *feelings* of causation connected with the situation become more numerous. Nevertheless, since there is a large admixture of chance, that is, of ignorance of determining causes, I experience more or less doubt as to the outcome, which I express by saying that the chances of its occurring are greater or less.

But why does a feeling of probability accompany a superior number of chances? It is not a necessity of thought that it should do so, nor is it a quality of one or of any number of impressions taken in themselves. Hume explains it as follows. Take, he says, our die, and mark two of its sides with one figure, and the remaining four with another. We throw the die, and consider the "turning up of each particular side as alike probable." But, finding that the number marked on four sides of the die does, as a matter of fact, turn up more often than the number marked on two the mind forms the habit of expecting the figure inscribed on the four sides of the die to turn up more frequently than the figure inscribed on two, and a more intense feeling of probability attends the superior number of equal chances.

In estimating the *probable* causes of events, or in predicting their probable effects, the same considerations hold true. The feeling of probability is intense in proportion as events have been found to go together, though in complicated situations where a variety of causes are at work allowance must always be made for the intervention of other causes in producing the effect. Our predictions of natural events are no whit different in principle from our predictions of how the dice will fall. We base them upon the occurrence of similar events in the past, to which we give weight in proportion to frequency.

VI. FREE-WILL

Having disposed of causation and probability, Hume in the *Enquiry* takes up at once the question of free-will, treatment of which in the *Treatise* is postponed to the book on the *Passions*. Since among men we observe the same uniformity of behavior as in nature and find the same motives always producing the same actions, both in our midst and in the past as recorded by history, we must assume the same necessary connections in the conduct of human beings as in the occurrence of physical events. Since, however, human individuals are infinitely varied in character, we do not expect "that all men, in the same circumstances will act precisely in the same manner," especially as "such uniformity in every particular, is found in no part of nature."

By liberty, then, when applied to voluntary actions we can only mean *"a power of acting or not acting according to the determination of the will;* that is, if we choose to remain at rest we may; if we choose to move we may." To maintain a free-will of indifference, is to make freedom "the same thing with chance; which is universally allowed to have no existence."

So far Hume has gone hand-in-hand with Locke. Now he proceeds to point a moral to his tale. The ethical consequences of a free-will of indifference are exactly opposite to what its defenders suppose they are. Such freedom, instead of making men responsible for their actions, really makes them irresponsible. For, if a person's choices and actions are not determined by his character, they are no index to his character and acquire for him neither praise nor blame. Hence "it is impossible he can, upon their account, become the object of punishment or vengeance."

Hume's consideration of liberty leads him still further afield into a discussion of the relation of human freedom to divine foreknowledge and providence and of the relation of sin and evil to the divine benevolence. He points out that those who uphold the omnipotence and the universal providence of God find themselves in a dilemma. If God foresees and foreordains all things, then either evil and sin do not really exist, or God is not really good. The argument that all things are really for the best and that the imperfection of the part contributes to the perfection of the whole, may be all very well in theory, but it is weak and ineffectual in practice. Far from being a consolation in time of misfortune and suffering, it is calculated to' exacerbate our woes. "You would surely more irritate than appease a man lying under the racking pains of the gout by preaching up to him the rectitude of those general laws which produced the malignant humors in his body . . . where they now excite such acute torments." Nor, where moral relations are concerned, does a man who is robbed of a considerable sum "find his vexation for the loss anywise diminished by these sublime reflections."

On the other hand, it is impossible "to explain distinctly how the Deity can be the mediate cause of all the actions of men, without being the author of sin and moral turpitude. . . . To reconcile the indifference and contingency of human actions with prescience; or to defend absolute decrees, and yet free the Deity from being the author of sin has been found hitherto to exceed all the power of philosophy."

VII. BELIEF IN THE EXISTENCE OF AN EXTERNAL WORLD

External and Real Impressions Distinguished. Returning now "with suitable modesty" from "these sublime mysteries; and leaving a scene so full of obscurities and perplexities," for "her true and proper province, the examination of common life," philosophy finds herself confronted with one more common and deep-seated belief that needs explanation—*the belief in the existence of an external world*. This belief incidentally must not be confused with the belief in the *reality* of impressions, which is the basis of our distinction between fact and fancy. For the superior vivacity and warmth, which make impressions *facts,* do not account for the feeling of *externality,* of existing *outside* our minds, in which we also put our trust.

The belief in the existence of an external world contains two factors, a faith that objects exist distinct from and external to ourselves, and a faith that objects continue to exist even when unperceived by the mind. These two beliefs are distinct because there is nothing in the faith in the *external* existence of an experienced object that necessarily carries with it a faith in its *continued* existence when unexperienced. Believing that an external object is there when I am experiencing it is not the same as believing that it goes on existing when I am not experiencing it.

The Senses and the "Self." How do these beliefs arise? Neither of them, any more than the belief in causation, has any foundation in sense-impressions, which never present us with either the continued or the external existence of objects. Our sense-impressions of any one object are frequently interrupted in all sorts of ways, and while they are interrupted the object certainly is not present to us. Nor do they acquaint us with the externality of the object. To perceive a thing to be *outside* us, we should have to perceive *ourselves* to be outside the thing. To do that we should have to have an impression of our "self." This, however, raises the difficult question of "how far we are *ourselves* the objects of our senses." Hume replies that the problem of the self is one for the most profound metaphysics to deal with. The senses no more give us a "self" behind the flow of our perceptions and feelings than they give us a substance behind a group of "objective" qualities or a "necessary connection" between events. " 'Tis absurd, therefore, to imagine the senses can ever distinguish betwixt ourselves and external objects." All our impressions, "external and internal, passions, affections, sensations, pains and pleasures are originally on the same footing."

Reason is no better foundation for the belief. There is no *logical* ground for believing in an external world. On the contrary, it is just reason and logic that undermine our naïve faith in its existence and cast skeptical doubts upon our unsophisticated attribution of external, objective existence to what are really internal, subjective impressions.

External Objects and the Imagination. Where, then, is the seat of this belief? In the *imagination,* Hume answers. We neither perceive nor infer the existence of an external world; we *imagine* it to exist. Even so, how does such a belief attach itself to imagining? The component parts of all imaginings are provided by sense-impressions, and the belief has no foundation in them. For not only are all sense-impressions just experiences and nothing more, but "external" experiences are no more involuntary and violent in character than "internal" ones, Descartes and Berkeley to the contrary notwithstanding.

There are, however, two reliable peculiarities of such impressions as are imagined as external and as continuing to exist even when they do not impress us. In the first place, they "have a peculiar *constancy* which distinguishes them from the impressions, whose existence depends upon our perception." They recur, after interruption, just, or almost, as they were.

"This constancy, however, is not so perfect as not to admit of very considerable exceptions." Still the general context is there, and the changes are such as I can explain. In spite of some inconstancy, the recurrence of my impressions is *coherent,* and their *coherency* is the second distinguishing characteristic of impressions believed to be external.

We now "proceed to examine after what manner these qualities give rise to so extraordinary an opinion" as continued existence. So far as *coherency* is concerned, it seems at first sight to be on the same footing as necessary connection. It is based upon repeated associations of ideas, *plus* an extension of that association to fill in the gaps in my perceptions. Our habit is to interpolate a succession of images between past and present and to imagine their continued existence in the unperceived interval between the two perceived moments.

Nevertheless, the idea of continued existence differs in certain important respects from causation. The idea of causation arises from a regular succession of perceptions, and does not suggest a *greater* regularity than that which is perceived. But the idea of continued existence bestows on objects a greater regularity and a more enduring connection "than what is observed in our mere perceptions." We are, therefore, confronted with the difficulty of understanding how we can imagine *more* regularity and coherence in our perceptions than that which we actually perceive.

Similarity, Sameness, and Constancy. Furthermore, why does a recurrence of *similar* impressions give rise to the idea of the *same* object? After all, in connecting up the past with the present impression, all I do is to interpolate a series of *similar* images that *resemble* the impression I remember and the impression I now have. Why should I believe, then, that an object preserves its *identity* and its *distinct existence* rather than believe that the old object ceases to exist, and a new, absolutely similar one takes its place? There is no more *reason* for the one belief than the other, and the latter belief is really more consistent with experience, which only gives me a recurrence of *similar* impressions.

To deal with this difficulty we must appeal to *constancy*. And to explain constancy we must invoke duration. When we trace time back moment by moment in our imagination and imagine the content of each moment to be similar to that of the next moment, or to change so continuously and explicably as to produce no violent interruption in the train of images, we are able to extract that content from time, and to talk of it as *one*—and the *same*—object persisting *through* time. The *same* object, in a word, is an *invariable* or *constant* content of the several moments of time imagined as *uninterrupted*.

Still, actual impressions give us only the invariableness or constancy necessary to the idea of identity. They do not give us the continuity. Constancy is continually being interrupted. How, then, is the idea of uninterruptedness derived from interrupted impressions? Why do I consider that the constancy has *persisted* while the impression was not there, and believe that the object has remained, and remained the same object, while it was not only not constantly present, but not present at all?

Similarity and Identity. The gist of Hume's reply is that the imagination is lazy and follows the line of least resistance. When there is a rapid succession of similar impressions, their resemblance "conveys the mind with an easy transition from one to the other," which approximates "one constant and uninterrupted perception." It is more difficult for the imagination to distinguish these impressions from one another than to "mistake the one for the other" and allow them to coalesce into a single picture.

We now see how mere *likeness* gives an image of *identity*, when similar impressions are repeated in rapid succession. But what are we to say when the intervals between the recurrences are much longer? Here again, Hume answers, it is easier for the imagination to regard the new impression as continuous and identical with the old ones than as discontinuous from and merely similar to them. The mind is upset by contradictions and interruptions which derail it from the line of least resistance, and it seeks to avoid and bridge them if it can, and it is much less difficult for the imagination to picture a continuity of existence filling the gap between two similar impressions than to picture the gap as unfilled. Hence we "remove the seeming interruption by feigning a continu'd being, which may fill those intervals, and preserve a perfect and entire identity to our perceptions."

We cannot *know* that objects have *not* existed in the interval, just as we cannot *know* that they have. We must imagine, or "feign," as Hume calls it, in any case, and we must "feign" the one thing or the other. So, naturally, we "make believe" the thing which is pleasanter and less jolting and less startling to the imagination.

Feigning and Faith. But this is not quite all. We do not merely "make believe" that objects continue to exist when unperceived, we *believe* it in sober earnest. How is it that *feigning* becomes *faith?* The reply is that the "matter-of-factness" of an impression is more easily imagined as continuously accompanying the "feigned" perceptions interpolated between the past and the present impression, than as not so accompanying them. To imagine it as interrupted would jar the mind, whereas to imagine the interpolated impressions, also, to be matters of fact makes smooth and comfortable the transition of the imagination from the object as it was last experienced through the "feigned" perceptions of it to our present experience of it. Hence the imagination is able to impart all the warmth and vivacity and reality of my present perception of an object to my "make believe" of its continued existence when unperceived by me. In this way, my imagination renders the *fiction* of the object's continued existence when *unperceived* as believable and as real as the *fact* of its *perceived* existence here and now.

This belief is transferable by analogy to new objects, whose constancy and coherency we have not had time to test, provided "the manner in which they present themselves to our senses resembles that of constant and coherent objects." As most of our objective experience presents itself in this manner, we come to feign and to believe in the continued existence of an external universe.

VIII. THE IDENTITY OF ORGANISMS, REFASHIONED AND ESSENTIALLY CHANGING OBJECTS, AND SELVES

Hume has so far been dealing with identity of *substance*. He next takes up the identity of organisms, in which the substance is constantly renewed and the structure subject to a process of birth and decay, and the identity of objects, in which great changes are effected, as in the constant repairing of a ship or the rebuilding of a church. In spite of the magnitude and often the sudden and revolutionary nature of change in such instances, we still speak of the object as identical. How can we do this?

In the case of organisms, the answer is easy. The changes involved in growth are so slow and so insensible from moment to moment, that the "make believe" by which the imagination retraces their path is almost as smooth and easy as the path between approximately similar impressions. Hence the vivacity and reality of the present perception are conveyed without difficulty to the images "feigned" between it as it is now and it as it is remembered.

Again, in case of considerable and drastic changes, the idea of the end or purpose of an object, which is an element in the complex idea of the object as a whole, is made dominant, and the attention is fixed upon it. Since the purpose is not altered by the other changes that take place, the imagination is once more able to "make believe" the continued existence of that purpose throughout the process of addition and renovation, and to endow its "fictitious" continuance with the same weight and believableness as attends the actual perception of it.

Finally, it is the nature of some objects, like a river, for instance, to change and move. So, here again, the introjection of images of change and movement is possible without jar to the imagination, and we can speak of the continued existence of the *same* river.

Personal identity is no exception to the rule. "The identity, which we ascribe to the mind of man is only a fictitious one, and of a like kind with that which we ascribe to vegetables and animal bodies." We neither can perceive a bond uniting our successive impressions nor demonstrate from reason its existence; any more than we can perceive or demonstrate a material substratum, or a causal nexus, or an identity, in our objective impressions. My subjective impressions are just as broken and interrupted, by sleep or a swoon, for example, as my impression of so-called outer objects, and I "feign" the continued existence of a "self" or identical personality during these interruptions by the same methods and for the same reasons as I feign the continued existence of the external world. While I sleep my *self* is no more a *present* impression than my body or my bed.

Were it not for memory we should have no more basis for feigning personal identity than for feigning identity in objects. "Memory alone acquaints us with the continuance and extent of this succession of perceptions" constituting the self, which is causally connected and believed to be the *same,* in spite of changes of character and disposition. And we can "feign" the continuance of our "selves" through those periods of which we have no memory, just as we "feign" the continued existence of an external object through those periods when we are not perceiving it. And "make believe" becomes belief in exactly the same way. Thus "we can extend the identity of our persons, beyond our memory, and can comprehend times, and circumstances, and actions, which we have entirely forgot, but suppose in general to have existed."

IX. CRITICISM OF THE PRETENSIONS OF METAPHYSICS

Criticism of Arguments for the Existence of an External World. Armed with these arguments, Hume launches an offensive all along the line against the pretensions of metaphysics. He attacks first of all the common inference made from our *belief* in the continued existence of an external world to the *fact* that such a world exists. The reasons for the one, he points out, are not arguments for the other. There is no reason to suppose that our impressions are supported by a material substratum. But there is no more reason to suppose that our impressions have a subjective support in a self, or an objective support in a divine mind. All we perceive and all we can demonstrate is the existence of *our* perceptions, not perceptions of external objects, whether material or divine, but just perceptions.

This skepticism, Hume insists, is not inconsistent with all he has said about the inevitableness of *belief* in an external world of some sort. All he is maintaining is that the existence of such a world is a matter of *faith,* not of knowledge. But, he adds, if at the moment he were forced to choose between discounting that faith and attributing to it the certainty of absolute knowledge, he would say, "I am more inclin'd to repose no faith at all in my senses, or rather imagination, than to place it in such implicit confidence."

Criticism of Realism, Materialism and Idealism. Plato and Aristotle, the Scholastics, the Cartesians, and Locke are all taken roundly to task for exhibiting this implicit confidence. Ideas, forms, matters, substances as distinguished from accidents, the distinction between primary and secondary qualities, are all dismissed as something of which we can have no proof. Hume then turns upon those who believe in the real existence of spiritual substances, spirits, souls, or whatever one chooses to call these non-material entities. To begin with, the idea of such entities is riddled with self-contradictions. It is quite as difficult to explain the relation between a spirit and its ideas and perceptions, as it is between a material substance and its qualities. The assertion which the immaterialists emphasize, and with which Hume agrees, that our impressions and ideas and feelings are immaterial, is no argument in favor of the "spiritualistic" hypothesis. It only renders the hypothesis the more untenable for those who, like Descartes, the Occasionalists and Spinoza, believe also in bodies, since it makes any conjunction or interaction or parallelism of the soul with its body or with the material world utterly unintelligible.

Criticism of Spinoza and the "Theologians." Nay more, the immaterialistic hypothesis, together with the theism founded upon it, is really "a true atheism, and will serve to justify all those sentiments for which *Spinoza* is justly infamous." Spinoza's "hideous hypothesis" that God is a single simple substance of which both extension and thought are the attributes, and of which all particular objects and ideas are modifications, is, Hume remarks, singularly like the theological hypothesis that the impressions which we call natural phenomena "also are modifications, and modifications of one simple, uncompounded, and indivisible substance," the mind of God. If we drop from the Spinozistic system the universe of unknown and incomprehensible *external,* physical entities corresponding to our impressions, we get a result practically indistinguishable from the view Berkeley and other theologians uphold.

Again, as Bayle pointed out in his *Encyclopédie,* all the objections urged against Spinoza apply equally forcefully to the theism of the theologians. If we urge against Spinoza that matter is not an attribute but a stuff of which physical objects are made, we can with equal right urge against the theologians that mind is not an attribute of God but a substance in itself, albeit immaterial, of which perceptions are made.

Nor, if we object to Spinoza that one and the same simple substance cannot be conceived as taking on contrary and incompatible forms, is it any easier to see how God's mind or our minds can contain at the same time incompatible ideas. Nor, again, is it any easier to see how an immaterial substance like soul can entertain different and contradictory *activities* of perception and motion without violating its simplicity and its unity, than it is to see how a material substratum can act in many different and contradictory ways and yet remain single and simple.

Matter, Mind and Causation. Finally the argument that matter cannot give rise to mind assumes that effects must *resemble* their causes —an assumption for which there is no warrant in the succession of impressions. There is just as much and just as little apparent connection between motion and thought as there is between the position of bodies and the movements which are said to result from it. "Tho' there appear no manner of connection betwixt motion or thought, the case is the same with all other causes and effects." If, then, we argue that bodies cannot think, we are bound logically to argue also that they cannot move, "since there is no more apparent connection in the one case than the other."

As a matter of fact, both conclusions are contrary to experience, in which the different dispositions of the body are observed to "cause" changes in our thoughts and sentiments, quite as clearly as they are observed to "cause" bodily motions. Whence "we may certainly conclude that motion may be, and actually is, the cause of thought and perception," in the same sense and to the same extent that any impression can be said to be the cause of another.

The upshot of the whole matter is that we cannot both have our cake and eat it. We must either deny causation where the mind does not *perceive* the necessary connection between impressions, or we must accept it for what it is—a customary connection which in actual experience obtains between impressions of the most diverse sorts. To choose the former alternative is to deny causation altogether, since the necessary connection is never perceived, and to leave the universe itself without "a cause or productive principle, not even the Deity himself."

On the other hand, if we accept causation in the only sense of the word that means anything, then, since all matters of fact, without exception, are "susceptible of a constant conjunction," it must follow "that, for aught we can determine by mere ideas, anything may be the cause or effect of anything."

In the Appendix to the *Treatise,* Hume confesses to doubts regarding his treatment of personal identity and the self. He feels that, in spite of his criticism, the self somehow *is* put together again in defiance of all logic, by certain principles that, say what we may, *do* "unite our successive perceptions in our thought or consciousness." But what these principles are, or how they operate, he admits that he has no idea, and adds that he can form no satisfactory hypothesis on that point. It is perhaps significant that, when he came to condense the *Treatise* in the *Enquiry,* he omitted the whole discussion.

Relation of God to Universe. In the *Enquiry* Hume adds somewhat to his discussion of theism in the *Treatise.* He points out that the entire concept of God as the *author* of anything is extremely dubious. Our whole argument from cause to effect is founded upon the connection of one indefinitely large group of constantly repeated and similar impressions with another group of impressions, similar to one another, succeeding the first group with unfailing regularity. One instance of a succession is not sufficient to establish a *necessary connection.*

By rights, therefore, to establish a causal connection between God and the world, we ought to have recurrent impressions of a Deity followed over and over again and with unfailing regularity by the impression of a universe.

In the *Enquiry,* also, and in the *Dialogues on Religion* he points out that even granting we could infer the existence of God from the universe, we should have no right to ascribe to him more wisdom or goodness or power than is actually displayed in the universe, which is his work. We never can have any reason to *infer* any attributes, or any principles of action in him but so far as we know them to have been exerted and satisfied. As the universe stands, it does not suggest the existence of a Deity both all good and all powerful. Nor can we assume a God whose benevolence is limited, since such an assumption evades the question. It is not drawn from experience, which fails to suggest the existence of even a benevolent, if partially powerless, God.

Criticism of Immortality. The idea of immortality is also criticized by Hume. Metaphysically, the idea involves the notion of a spiritual substance or soul, about which enough has been said already. Moreover, even if such substances could be shown to exist, the fact remains that we can forget and do go to sleep on occasion, and hence can be conceived as losing memory and consciousness for good and all. Moreover, there is just as valid a reason for supposing that animals possess these thinking substances as that men do, and just as much reason for believing that our souls exist before birth as that they survive death. But we remember nothing before birth. Why, then, should we remember anything after death? Persistence of personal identity, however, is a matter of memory. If we remember nothing of this life after our death, we cannot be said to have personal immortality.

The moral argument that we must survive death in order to receive the punishments of vice and the rewards of virtue withheld in this life is also fallacious. Vice and virtue are in the long run dealt with in a sufficient manner by society, which is quite capable of protecting its own interests without calling upon a hypothetical heaven or hell for aid. The structure and disposition bestowed upon us by nature determine the human good and suggest that it is something to be realized in this life, not in the next. Nor can we have any ideas of what God wants us to do save those founded upon what we want to do ourselves. Moreover, most of us are such mixtures of good and evil that we deserve neither heavenly rewards nor hell fire. Then, too, what would become of dead infants? They have had no chance to do either good or evil and therefore to *deserve* anything at all!—certainly not heavenly bliss or infernal torment.

Finally, coming down to matters of fact from these speculations, the evidence of perception and experience, which never acquaints us with a disembodied consciousness and suggests the disappearance of the mind along with the body, is *against* immortality.

The Origin and Growth of Religion. In the *Natural History of Religion* Hume places the origin of religion in superstition and ranks the primitive gods men create in their own images on a par with elves and fairies and gnomes and similar supernatural imaginings. These anthropomorphic gods get themselves clothed in philosophic concepts and moral ideals, and the history of religion exhibits a constant vacillation between the anthropomorphic and the philosophic poles of thought. Theology is a bad mixture of the two elements. Polytheism is more consistent with experience than monotheism, and is much less intolerant. A monotheistic god is jealous of all other divinities, and the votaries of such a deity are always bent on persecuting the followers of any other god than their own. Thus all religions based upon devotion to a particular god tend to become cruel and fanatical. They impute to their particular deities sentiments and behavior men would be ashamed of in themselves, and they encourage their devotees to curry favor with the objects of their worship by all sorts of superstitious devices rather than by humane and upright living.

X. HUMAN PASSIONS

The Primary and Secondary Passions. The second and third books of the *Treatise* are devoted to a discussion of human passions and of morals—subjects which were later given a more condensed treatment in the *Dissertation on the Passions* and in the account of morals given in the second book of the *Enquiry*.

Corresponding to impressions and ideas are primary feelings, like pleasure and pain, and reflective impressions or passions founded on these sensations. The passions may be calm or violent and direct or indirect. Direct passions are feelings like "desire, aversion, grief, joy, hope, fear, despair and security"; among the indirect we may "comprehend pride, humility, ambition, vanity, love, hatred, envy, pity, malice, generosity and their dependants." The indirect or secondary passions are built up out of the primary passions and out of each other by the same laws of association and of the smooth and easy transition of the imagination as govern the processes of the understanding. The primary passions, again, attend, some of them like pleasure and pain, upon the natural appetites of the organism, others like aversion and desire, upon the pleasure-pain complex. For instance, an organic impulse *plus* pleasure or pain gives rise to attraction or repulsion.

The secondary passions may be divided into the pleasurable and the painful and into those which concern the self and those which concern other people. Any pleasurable or any painful passion tends to excite all the other passions of the same affective tone, one after another. "Grief and disappointment give rise to anger, anger to envy, envy to malice, and malice to grief again, till the whole circle be compleated." So, too, joy starts a whole cycle of associated feeling such as love, generosity, pity, courage and the like.

Again, when concerned with the self or with other people, they induce, if pleasurable, either self-satisfaction or love for others as the case may be; if painful, the reverse. This suffusion of both one's

interest in one's self and one's interest in others with both pain and
pleasure gives rise to a complicated system of selfish and social emotions, like family affection, esteem of the rich and powerful, benevolence and compassion, envy, malice, and contempt, and last, but not
least, the "amorous passion."

Curiosity the Basis of Philosophy. Finally, Hume takes up the "passion" of general curiosity, or, in other words, the passion for discovering the truth, which is the driving power of philosophy and of the
pure sciences. He remarks that the passions for the chase or for gambling and the passion for philosophy very closely resemble one another. In all three cases the pleasure arises primarily from the activity
itself, and the value imputed to the stakes or to the quarry is secondary
and part of the general pleasure of the game. Thus we pursue truth
only in part for any extrinsic value it may have, and primarily for
the fun we get out of discovering it. At the same time, to take full
pleasure in the game, we must be playing it with a view to winning
something useful to us. Half the pleasure is gone unless we are playing for money or for a prize of some sort. Pheasants and partridges
are better game than crows and magpies because they are good to
eat. In the same way, philosophizing is satisfactory because it combines
the pleasures of just hunting or gambling with the satisfaction of
bagging or winning something we may put to use. The same is true
of our love of mathematics, algebra, morals, politics, natural philosophy
and the like, all of which present a game to be played with a stake to
be won.

But this is not quite all there is to philosophy. A powerful incentive
is also found in the passion for prying and peeping which keeps busy-
bodies always delving into other people's affairs. This passion, which
is quite different from the love of hunting and gambling, attends upon
the fact that the unknown produces less vivid and therefore less pleasurable ideas than the known. Hence we seek to remove pain by acquiring knowledge of the event. So it is that men pry into their neighbors' affairs, wonder what can be the causes of startling and novel happenings, and are always speculating as to what is going on behind
the scenes in the universe.

XI. MORALS AND POLITICS

Morality Artificial and Conventional. Passing now to a consideration
of morals, Hume finds himself in agreement with Hobbes, in regarding morality as an artificial rather than a natural state of mankind.

Moral behavior is directly instigated neither by reason, which is power-less to motivate action of any sort, nor by immediate impressions. There are no absolute and unmistakable moral ideas and principles which impose upon us *a priori* ethical obligations. Nor, if there were, could reason, which is concerned only with truth and falsehood, ever discover them of itself. What ought to be is founded upon what is. Morality is rather a matter of sentiment and rests primarily upon a feeling of pleasure and satisfaction experienced in some situations which we therefore call *good,* and a feeling of pain in others which we therefore call *bad.* There are no essentially and naturally right or wrong impulses, nor is there any innate sense of right and wrong. Moral sentiment is artificial and conventional and is determined by the circumstances in which human beings find themselves. These circumstances create a "common interest" and "a kind of convention or agreement" between individuals that they will all promote that interest.

Man Naturally Altruistic and "Sympathetic." This agreement, how-ever, does not, as Hobbes maintained, conflict with the natural pro-pensities and first condition of mankind. "Limited generosity" is part of man's native self-interest, and we are endowed with the "natural virtues" of affection and kindliness towards our family and friends. We naturally, too, are grateful and compassionate creatures. We take *pleasure* in loving and benefiting those to whom we are attached. But under strictly natural conditions the circle to which we are attached and which it gives us pleasure to benefit is necessarily small and lim-ited. We have no instinctive affection for humanity as a whole, or desire to benefit all mankind. Nor could we ever develop such affec-tion and desire out of our instinctive and *pre-moral* affections (which are also displayed, incidentally, by the non-moral animals) and attain to a sense of general, *moral* obligation, were it not for *sympathy,* or an instinctive interest in other things and other persons existing distinct from our particular affection for some of them. This is capable of in-definite extension, and through its action, our natural "confin'd gen-erosity," or positive affection for a few other persons, is broadened out so as to include all mankind. *Sympathy,* then, is an indispensable factor in creating the idea of a public interest and in transforming our pre-moral, instinctive virtues into the artifice and convention of morality.

Such an artifice and convention must arise so early in human history that man's "very first state and situation may justly be esteem'd social." It has its rudiments in the necessity, in which even a savage finds himself, of cuffing his offspring into some sort of peace among themselves. Therefore, although society is in a sense artificial, it is an artifice to which man is driven by the needs of his nature.

Sympathy and the Public Interest. Since self-interest forces social organization upon men and of necessity becomes identical with the public interest, we are made uncomfortable by the opposition of unrestrained private interest to the public interest, and experience satisfaction when we see the two identified. The one pains, the other pleases us. We approve the one, we disapprove the other. Hence our *sympathies* lie with the assertion of the public interest against unrestrained exhibitions of private interest, and thus give rise to moral standards.

The Origin of Government. But Hume, like Hobbes, finds it necessary to establish somewhere in society a power to enforce justice and preserve order, since the common interest in the observance of justice is not a strong enough emotion to hold in check "the solicitations of our passions, which always plead in favor of whatever is near and contiguous." Thus government, or the lodging of power to uphold society in the hands of a few disinterested persons, arises. Government not only executes and decides justice, but imposes it. In this way the sovereign, besides correcting injustice, prevents it and affords men "a security against each other's weakness and passion as well as against their own."

Government, Hume emphatically asserts, is not always necessary, nor is it impossible for primitive societies to live without it. Moreover, it is not necessarily founded upon the consent of the governed (as Rousseau and other political philosophers were maintaining); neither are all men created free and equal. Nor again, is the "duty" of allegiance to it founded on a delegation of sovereignty to it by the people. Though the "duty" of allegiance may have originated in such a delegation in the beginning, the sentiment of loyalty has become so entwined with other sentiments, and its absence contributes so greatly to the general uneasiness out of which moral disapprobation arises, that the reasons for considering loyalty a *virtue* have become far more complex than any mere promise, expressed or tacit, to obey the sovereign.

In the same way, the foundations of government and the reasons for its sovereignty and stability rest upon a far broader basis in human nature than the simple consent of the governed. The authority of government is, to all practical intents and purposes, derived from force and custom and historic continuity and the disapprobation aroused by the attempt to subvert by force any system of authority standing for law and order, no matter how tyrannical it may have become. So it is that "men may be bound by *conscience* to submit to a tyrannical government against both their own and the public interest." Nevertheless, there may come a time when these supports are broken down by tyranny, and more moral uneasiness is occasioned by the retention than by the overthrow of government. In that case a society feels it has a moral "right" to rebel, and when it *feels* it has a *moral* right, it has one.

International law, Hume remarks, necessarily is less binding upon nations than the civil law of a state is upon citizens. Since any state is generally able to secure by itself the welfare of its subjects, "the *natural* obligation to justice among different states is not so strong as among individuals," and hence "the *moral* obligation, which arises from it, must partake of its weakness." Therefore, the same sanctity can never attach to international treaties as attaches to contracts between individuals.

XII. LOGIC

The Problem of Induction. Hume was neither a mathematician nor a logician, and he failed to appreciate or understand many of the problems occasioned for philosophy by these disciplines. Nor was he entirely consistent in matters of logic. He was critical, for instance, of Aristotle's syllogistic method, yet was committed to it in his own argument. However, it was Hume's great merit to raise one of the most crucial problems in logic and methodology, the question of induction, of whether it is possible to infer general statements from particular instances. Although his own conception of induction, derived from Bacon, was somewhat deficient, and his arguments therefore defective, Hume recognized that inductive inference is impossible. It is impossible since on the one hand it does not yield a logically necessary conclusion and on the other hand it cannot be justified by experience because such a justification would be circular. Knowledge, therefore, of the kind sought by science—that is, general and predictive knowledge—is theoretically impossible.

Empiricists today give full support to Hume's position that factual knowledge cannot be deduced from *a priori* premises. However, they regard his skepticism as a product of his own allegiance to the seventeenth and eighteenth century rationalists' criterion of certainty in knowledge, a criterion which demands that anything less than certainty be rejected. Empiricists are now more likely to adopt a probability conception of knowledge that permits them to accept the critique of induction and yet avoid scepticism.

Chapter XI

MINOR EIGHTEENTH-CENTURY BRITISH THINKERS

I. GENERAL UNREST OF THE CENTURY

Locke, Berkeley and Hume, although they were the only stars of first magnitude in the British sky during the eighteenth century, were by no means the only luminaries. They were surrounded by a host of stars of lesser magnitude and of various colors. The century, both in England and on the Continent, was reaping the harvest of the Renaissance. Thought along all lines was still breaking loose from the ancient fetters. New ideas, ethical, social and political, were astir. A political philosophy supporting the growing democratic movement was in process of formulation. Religious skepticism and free thought, which formerly had meant revolt against Christianity, now appeared within Christianity itself, in attacks upon the doctrine of the Trinity, in the spread of Unitarianism, and in the general attempt to square Christianity with a rationalistic and free-thinking position and to regard it as one offshoot, among many, of an underlying "natural religion" whose creed was confined to acknowledging the existence of a personal God and the immortality of the soul. This separation of theism from its orthodox Christian setting gave rise to the *deistic* movement. Again, the naturalism and materialism of Hobbes had its heirs and followers. The entire century, both in England and on the Continent, was agitated by the most diverse and conflicting ideas and ideals in every department of human thought.

II. INFLUENCE OF CHINA ON EIGHTEENTH-CENTURY EUROPE

Jesuit Reports of Chinese Civilization. An interesting contribution to the unrest of the times was made by China. European acquaintance with China had dated from the travels of Marco Polo (1254-1324), whose accounts of the court of Kublai Khan aroused the wonder and piqued the imagination of the medieval world. But it was not till the end of the sixteenth century that the reports of Jesuit missionaries at

Peking began to turn China from a fable into a fact. These reports were somewhat disquieting to European and Christian complacency. The Jesuits were not only struck by the material civilization of China and by the advanced character of many of her economic and social institutions, but they were particularly impressed by the purity of the Chinese religion and morality and, above all, by the religious tolerance of the government, which stood out in striking contrast to the bigotry, the intolerance, and the sadistic love of persecution that lay like a canker at the heart of so-called Christian charity. Also, they were puzzled to find that the history of China was not amenable to the chronology revealed in the Bible and recorded events occurring, if not before the creation of the world, at least before the Flood, which, according to the word of God, Noah and his family were the only human beings to survive. How the Chinese could have gone on making history under water was something of a problem for the theologians.

Chinese and Christian Ethics Compared. Such stories proved congenial to the new spirit aroused in Europe by the Renaissance, and a century later were becoming one of the inspirations to the Enlightenment. The Chinese accounts of eclipses that took place before the Flood were confirmed by the new European astronomy and helped foster the attack on the credibility of the Bible and further the general offensive of the Enlightenment against the idea of supernaturally revealed religion. The high order of Chinese morality and religion tended to depose Christianity from the ethical and theological pedestal upon which it had placed itself and to destroy its self-constituted monopoly of true faith and pure morals. Indeed, it might seem that in some respects at least, as, for example, charity and tolerance, the Chinese had succeeded better, despite their ignorance of revelation, than the Christians.

In the last part of the seventeenth and the early years of the eighteenth century indications of Chinese influence are specific. Leibnitz, we may remember, regarded Chinese as the mother of all written languages and urged the compilation of a Chinese dictionary. Also, Malebranche, in answer to an appeal from the Jesuits for a metaphysics of Christianity that might prove palatable to the discriminating intellectual palate of China, composed his *Entretien,* which takes the form of a conversation between a Christian and a Chinese philosopher.

Admiration of Chinese Culture. In the eyes of the Enlightenment, the virtues of Chinese civilization vied with the Arcadian simplicity of the noble savage as a picture of the goodness of the natural man. Voltaire pointed to them as a refutation of Rousseau's argument that civilization is a regress from perfection, not a progress towards it. And the French economist Quesnay (1694-1774), one of the founders of the "physiocratic" school of economics, to which we shall have occasion presently to refer, held up Chinese economic organization as a rebuke to European conditions.

These influences of China upon Western thought were supplemented by even more obvious effects upon Western art. The architecture, landscape-gardening, furniture, wall-papers, and household ornaments of the period all bear witness to them.

III. NATURALISM AND DEISM

Collins and Bolingbroke. Among the chief exponents of naturalism and deism were Toland (1670-1721), Clarke (1675-1729), Collins (1676-1729), Bolingbroke (1678-1751), Hartley (1704-1757) and Priestley (1733-1804). Clarke [1] used the rationalistic method of deism and the stock arguments for the existence of a God as a prop for Christianity and even for the probability of a divine revelation. Collins,[2] on the other hand, devoted himself to demolishing the credibility of revelation, and thus to discrediting orthodoxy, by pulling the Bible to pieces and showing up its inconsistencies and particularly the nonsense, as he regarded it, of the prophetic vision of the coming of Christ attributed to the Old Testament writers. Bolingbroke [3] was even more violent in his assaults upon revealed religion, which were also directed against all metaphysics as well as against theology. Moses, Plato, the Cambridge Platonists, Descartes, Leibnitz, Clarke and Collins were all fools in his opinion. Their arguments for the existence of God and their admissions at the same time that there is real evil in the world, were as calculated to throw doubts upon the existence and the beneficence of the Deity as were the arguments of the atheists. Both the atheists and the clergy were in a kind of tacit con-

---

[1] *A Discourse Concerning the Being and Attributes of God,* etc.

[2] *The Scripture Doctrine of the Trinity; Essay Concerning the Use of Reason, etc.; A Discourse of Free Thinking; A Discourse of the Grounds and Reasons of the Christian Religion; Inquiry Concerning Human Liberty; Liberty and Necessity.*

[3] *Concerning the Nature, Extent and Reality of Human Knowledge; On the Folly and Presumption of Philosophers; On the Rise and Progress of Monotheism; On Authority in Matters of Religion.*

spiracy to disprove God's existence by the combined stupidity of their demonstrations.

Toland and Hartley. Toland,[4] after passing through Catholic, Protestant, and deistic phases of belief, arrived eventually at a system of materialistic pantheism. Matter, he said, is not only extended and impenetrable, but is also capable of thought under certain conditions. But, and here Toland severely criticizes Spinoza, its thinking is not co-extensive and parallel with its physical properties. It only thinks in spots, and these spots are animal and human brains. Consciousness is therefore a function of the brain and, when the brain is destroyed, the mind is destroyed with it.

Hartley,[5] who became a physician because rational scruples stood in the way of his becoming an Anglican priest, always remained in his own opinion a good deist, if not a good Christian. He did not indeed go so far as to maintain, like Toland, that the mind was the offspring of the brain. There is a soul, separate from the body, but the soul is a particular, subtle form of matter, acting upon the brain and acted upon by it. Thought and will and feeling are bodily vibrations set up by the soul. There is no distinction of kind between matter and spirit. God is the cause of all things, and the order of the universe is established by him with the same inexorable necessity as appears in the system of Spinoza. Since God is good, all things are for the best, and the ultimate happiness and perfection of all beings are foreordained.

Priestley. Priestley [6] was an ardent defender of the Unitarian position, and maintained that the development of Christian theology was a progressive corruption of primitive Christian belief. He also found it not inconsistent with Christian teaching to regard the soul as material, and made a lengthy attack on the idea of spirit, claiming that there is nothing the soul can do which the body cannot be equally well conceived as doing, and that therefore the notion of a spiritual substance is superfluous. God himself is a material being, though his matter is of an unusual and privileged sort. In explaining God's relation to the universe, Priestley made use of the favorite analogy of the Continental deists—the analogy of the watchmaker and the watch. God constructs and winds up the mechanism of the world, which, once created, runs by its own momentum, in a manner determined by its

---

[4] *Letters to Serena. Pantheisticon.*

[5] *Observations on Man, etc.*

[6] *Disquisitions Relative to Matter and Spirit; The Doctrine of Philosophical Necessity; Free Discussions of the Doctrines of Materialism.*

springs and cogs. Priestley also managed to believe in the immortality of the soul, in spite of his materialistic conception of its nature.

IV. MORAL AND SOCIAL SYSTEMS

Dispute Between the Relativists and the Absolutists. Hartley and Priestley wrote much on ethical and political matters, and bring us back to the most important aspects of eighteenth century British thought. Before, however, mentioning their views, we must turn to the very end of the seventeenth century and name a few of the more important of their predecessors. Generally speaking, we may note at once that the increasing inquiry into moral and social questions was of two sorts. On the one hand, it followed the tendency initiated by Hobbes and later developed by Hume to dispense with *a priori,* absolute and immutable principles of conduct and to derive moral standards from experience and particularly from the basic qualities of pleasure and pain. On the other, it sought to defend such principles and to establish them with the same certainty as attends mathematical truths. This reaffirmation of absolute morality frequently appears as a protest against the empirical tendencies of the age.

Clarke. The deist Clarke, following the reasoning of the Cambridge Platonists, insisted that the propositions governing moral conduct are self-evident and furthermore are capable in themselves of determining human behavior. In other words, knowledge of the good is sufficient to ensure our pursuit of it. We cannot truly know and approve the good and decline to follow it. But, being a theist, Clarke also sought to show that, though morality has a natural foundation in human reason, it has also a supernatural foundation in the will of God and is therefore properly subject not only to human but to divine rewards and punishments.

Cumberland and Shaftesbury. Cumberland [7] (1632-1718) and Shaftesbury [8] (1671-1713), on the other hand, were more concerned with establishing morality on a rational and naturalistic basis by dwelling on the instinctive and fundamental character of our altruistic impulses. They were opposed to Hobbes' view that human behavior, so far as it is unselfish, represents a compromise adopted for the express purpose of securing each individual as much self-assertion as the clash and reciprocal limitation of one will by another will permit. Public is not, then, fundamentally opposed to private interest, and the concessions

---

[7] *De legibus naturae.*
[8] *Inquiry Concerning Virtue and Merit.*

the individual makes to others do not involve any essential self-sacrifice. Our moral sense arises from the fact that not only do we naturally love our fellow-beings and express that love in various ways, but we also, by transference, come to love that love itself and to delight in its manifestations—in other words, to love virtue for itself.

Mandeville vs. Butler. This view was adopted by Joseph Butler (1692-1752), who used it as a weapon against the cynicism of Mandeville (1670-1733). Mandeville, in *The Fable of the Bees, or Private Vices Public Benefits,* published in 1724, argued that morality is wholly artificial and is introduced by the political powers-that-be to coax or to threaten the vain and silly masses into obedience, and that it is an open question whether its inhibition of the natural passions and desires is really good for society as a whole. To Mandeville and to Hobbes, whom he treats as sharing the same view, Butler opposes the fundamental character of the altruistic impulses and maintains, after the fashion of Aristotle, that pleasure, far from being the end at which moral action is aimed, is the reward accompanying the attainment of the natural goal of human striving—which is happiness. We are, so to speak, wound up to perform certain functions and to pursue certain ends, which we should pursue and perform whether or not pleasure resulted. Those operations bring us satisfaction, or "happiness," which is different from pleasure. The moral sense, being founded on activity of this sort, has a natural authority. Conscience is the voice of a rational and pondered love of self-fulfillment.[9]

Butler, however, is perhaps most famous for his *Analogy* in which he seeks to defend orthodox Christianity against the Unitarians and the deists. Starting from the basis of "natural religion" as a common ground of agreement, he argues first the necessity of supernatural standards and sanctions of morality and of free-will and moral responsibility, and infers therefrom the necessity of the Christian revelation and of the Incarnation and the Atonement. Given, he says in effect, the theistic assumption of a just and benevolent God, such a being could not have acted otherwise than Christianity reveals him as acting. There is no middle course between Christian theism and atheism. Nor, if we reject the revealed character of the Scriptures, have we any other alternative than the hypothesis that they are a deliberate imposture.

Hutcheson. Hutcheson [10] (1694-1747), who had considerable influence on Hume, follows in Butler's and Shaftesbury's footsteps, so

[9] *Fifteen Sermons.*
[10] *Essays.*

far, at least, as his ethics is concerned. He, too, insists that man is naturally a kindly animal, endowed with good-will towards his fellows, and draws the distinction, later repeated by Hume, between the calm and the violent passions. With the calm emotions, he associates universal benevolence and the moral approbation it excites. He insists against Hobbes that this benevolence is entirely disinterested and unselfish and is exercised, not for the purpose of procuring pleasure, but because it expresses and realizes our nature. Pleasure may, indeed, result from it, as it may result from any natural function, but it is not the end of our altruistic any more than it is the end of our self-centered impulses. Our criterion for judging good actions is double. Their results must be beneficial and their intention benevolent. Beneficial results are to be computed in terms of the greatest good of the greatest number. Here Hutcheson is the forerunner of Bentham and modern "utilitarianism."

Adam Smith. A contemporary and friend of Hume's was the famous economist, Adam Smith (1723-1790), author of the *Wealth of Nations*. But he was also interested in ethics, and his *Theory of Moral Sentiments* is a major contribution to the moral speculation of the period. Like Hume, Smith dispensed with a "moral sense" and regarded "sympathy" as the common element in moral sentiments. Sympathy comes from imagining ourselves in the other person's position, and, being a social emotion, is in itself pleasurable, even when we sympathize with the sorrows of others. Furthermore, when we see one person kind to another, we take pleasure in the kindness of the one party, the pleasure his kindness gives the other, and the sentiment of gratitude felt by the other towards his benefactor. If we can also sympathize with the motives that inspire the friendly deed, and therefore can feel that the gratitude it inspires is proper and well-grounded, we experience a feeling of approval and impute merit to the person and the act that arouse the feeling. The sense of the *propriety* of the situation is the basis of our approval and is present in all judgment that an act is morally good and right.

Sympathy extends still further. In judging our own behavior we endeavor to estimate it as it would appear to an outside, ideal spec·tator, and in the light of the feelings it would arouse in him and of the approbation he would bestow upon it. It is the judgment of this ideal spectator that constitutes our *conscience*. His voice we come to respect, even as we respect the voices of other persons, and his words of praise or blame give us a sense of inner self-respect or unworthiness, as the case may be. These words represent general rules of behavior constructed by our feeling of propriety and meritoriousness, and obedience to them is what we call *duty*.

Hartley's Ethics. Meantime, Hartley, whose naturalism we have just been discussing, had published his *Observations on Man*, even before Hume's *Enquiry* had appeared. In it, he proceeded to develop self-interest and sympathy and the moral sense out of pleasure and pain by the laws of association. Upon the fundamental, physical pleasures he erects a hierarchy of higher enjoyments, such as the pleasures of imagination, esthetic pleasure, the intellectual and ethical pleasures engendered by the activities of thought and moral behavior, and finally the pleasures of religious experience.

V. REACTION AGAINST HUME

Price and Reid. The rumpus raised by Hume's skepticism and by his flat denial that moral principles can be either directly intuited or rationally demonstrated led to a reaffirmation of absolutism in ethics. Price [11] (1723-1792) reasserted the position taken by the Cambridge Platonists and Clarke that moral verities are self-evident truths, and that right conduct must be motivated by the moral law and is the more meritorious in proportion as it involves a struggle against the natural impulses of our nature.

Reid [12] (1710-1796), also, divided human nature into a rational half and a half composed of habits, appetites, desires, and affections. Against Hume, he argued that reason rather than the natural appetites and desires should decide what ends we ought to pursue, and should devise the means for securing them. Knowledge alone can tell us what is good. To know the good is to desire it. We have an intuition of right and wrong, and this intuition is sufficient to motivate right action. The emotion accompanying such intuition is one of sympathy and benevolence towards good men. In judging our own behavior, it takes the form of an approving or disapproving conscience. Very much the same view was set forth by Reid's disciple, Dugald Stewart (1753-1828).

Besides attacking Hume's ethics, he also combated Hume's intellectual skepticism, which, he felt, was the logical result of the doubts

[11] *Review of the Principal Questions in Morals.*
[12] *Enquiry into the Human Mind on the Principles of Common Sense; Essays on the Intellectual Powers of Man; Essays on the Active Powers of the Human Mind.*

thrown by the Cartesians upon the interaction of the mind and the body, and therefore upon the ability of the mind to know an external world—doubts, moreover, that had been further and consistently developed by Locke and Berkeley and carried to their inevitable results by the Scottish thinker. The place to combat them was the place of their origin, and so it is that we find Reid reasserting the validity of the "common-sense" belief that the objects of our experience are not perceptions and ideas but external entities. We do not see visual sensations; our visual sensations are a seeing of objects outside ourselves. We do not know concepts; our concepts are a knowing of external reality.

Impressions and Experiences. Reid puts up little argument for his contention beyond insisting that our belief in an external world is implanted in us by God, and that, if it were not valid, God would not have implanted it in us. He did, however, criticize Hume's pulverization of the continuity of experience into discrete, unconnected particular impressions and ideas, and maintained that the connections and relations between events are as immediately sensed as the impressions themselves. The mind does not proceed to construct a world out of sense-data by introducing relations among them; the world it first meets is an already constructed world, outfitted with relations and connections, towards which its primitive reaction is not one of perception but one of *judgment* about perceptions. I experience the causal connection between two events just as directly as I experience them. The suggestions which thinking and perceiving carry with them, that there are a thinker and an external object thought about, are just as integral a part of experience as the sense-impressions from which these suggestions emanate. For example, when I perceive an object I am no less sure of my own existence as something more than an experience of it, and of its existence as something more than my experience of it, than I am of the sensations that constitute my *perception* of the object, but do *not* constitute either me or it. In a word, *common sense,* upon which Reid lays great stress, and to which he is always appealing, presents us with a subject experiencing and knowing an object. All the elements of that presentation, subject, object and the perception of the one by the other, are equally trustworthy.

VI. THE REVOLUTIONARIES

Priestley. Priestley, besides attacking orthodox Christianity, was also in revolt against the established social and political order. A disciple of Rousseau, whom we shall have occasion to discuss in a moment, he was an ardent champion of the natural goodness of mankind and as ardent in denouncing the corruption brought upon it by so-called civilization. He was also well to the fore in the hue and cry of the democratic movement, and got ahead of Bentham in announcing the principle of *laissez-faire*. Inspired by an invincible faith in progress as a panacea for all human ills, he felt that, if men could only be freed from regimentation and planned economic and government control, they would be quick to realize the millennium by means of their released energies and their unhampered goodness of heart.

Paine and Godwin. Priestley was naturally prominent among the liberals in England, who supported the grievances of the American colonies and the propriety of the American Revolution. Along with him were Price and Paine, who later were to share his joy in the revolution in France. Paine has his place, also, as a great atheist, and his *Age of Reason* still ranks as one of the most famous attacks ever made upon orthodox Christianity. Paine was followed by Godwin, Shelley's father-in-law, whose *Inquiry Concerning Political Justice* first appeared in 1793. A spiritual offspring of the French Revolution and the Age of Reason, he carried the revolutionary movement to its extreme conclusions. Philosophically, he turned the tables on both Locke and Hume by subjecting the term "mind," which both of them had used familiarly and uncritically, to the same skeptical analysis that they had applied to substance and personal identity and causation. Minds, he pointed out, no more exist than do bodies or spirits. Just as substance means only the presence of groups of qualities, so mind means nothing but the presence of impressions. The groupings and successions of conscious states are fundamentally the same in all men and follow the law of logical procedure. Hence, we may be called essentially reasonable beings. But rational procedure is obscured and is given a different complexion in different individual streams of consciousness by the influence of environment, social, political, educational, traditional and the like.

Godwin's Anarchism. Therefore, to restore all men to their natural and common rationality, and to enable their conduct to be regulated by reason alone, all these hampering and diversifying influences must be removed. Since, in his opinion, pleasure is indicated as the natural good at which all men aim, all obstacles to its pursuit must be swept away. In removing them Godwin makes almost as clean a sweep of established standards and institutions as did the Cynics and Cyrenaics. Nothing must interfere with the exercise of pure reason. Away, then, with all irrational sentiments and ties—with filial piety and gratitude and friendship, except as these are justified by the hedonistic calculus. This is not to say, however, that man is naturally altogether selfish. He is naturally altruistic. But his generous emotions must no more be allowed to overstep the bounds set by reason than his selfish ones. Again, general rules and laws are only to be obeyed when they are reasonable. Moral judgments based upon other than coldly rational grounds are of no account. All forms of government have irrational foundations and therefore should be swept away. All laws are pernicious. All coercion is wrong. Reasoning is the only weapon we should ever use with others. All co-operation is silly. Marriage is an unnecessary burden. The possession of property, however, seems reasonable to Godwin, and, on that account, should not be interfered with, in spite of the inequalities it fosters. These inequalities would disappear, like all other evils, if only man could be restored to the sweet reasonableness which is the essence of his nature.

VII. DEFENSE OF ORTHODOX CHRISTIANITY

Paley and His "Evidences." Meantime, orthodox Christianity was not wanting for defenders to protect it against both the Unitarians and the deists, as well as against the atheists. The most famous of them was Paley (1743-1805), who was also a moralist, as well as a theologian. His main argument as given in his *Evidences of Christianity* is based upon design, and is itself obviously designed to protect its readers against the influences of the new discoveries in geology and biology, which were prophetic of the doctrine of evolution and were already casting doubt upon the belief in the fixity and special creation of species and upon the Biblical chronology. The chronology, however, Paley is willing to abandon. As long as we admit that God created the universe, the question of how long ago he created it does not matter. That there is a creator, we infer from the existence of the universe, just as we infer the existence of a watchmaker from a watch. And, just as we infer from the mechanism of the watch the intelligence of its contriver, so we must deduce the wisdom and the power and the goodness of God from the marvelous interadaptation of the parts of the universe, and particularly from the adaptation of biological structures to their functions.

In his moral speculations Paley insists that right conduct is determined by God and that its rewards, like its sanctions, are supernatural. Standards of right and wrong are given both by reason and revelation.

The rational and revealed good is the general happiness of all God's creatures. This happiness can be obtained by the individual only through observing the general laws and cultivating the habits which have been found useful in securing it. Generally speaking, the goodness of human behavior is determined on a utilitarian basis, and thus Paley takes his place with Bentham as one of the founders of utilitarian ethics.

Chapter XII

FRENCH AND ITALIAN
ENLIGHTENMENT

I. FRENCH DEISM AND EMPIRICISM

Voltaire. In the Continental Enlightenment, as in eighteenth century British thought, Locke was an important influence. The *Essay* had been published in French in 1700. Voltaire had further popularized him in the *Lettres sur les Anglais* published in 1734, and again some thirty years later in the *Dictionnaire philosophique portatif*. Voltaire (1694-1778) was the most prominent of the French deists and a bitter critic both of orthodox Christianity and of the established political and social institutions of his time. He was a master of irony and satire, and the wit with which his free thinking sizzled made him doubly disagreeable to those whom he attacked and helped raise the temperature of the hot water in which he was forever splashing. His *Candide* mercilessly lampooned the optimism of Leibnitz and ridiculed from every angle its assertion that all is for the best in this, the best of all possible worlds. In *Zadig,* he made fun of the metaphysicians and the moralists, and in *L'Homme aux quarante écus* he paid his respect to the political and social institutions of the day. Also, he was unsparing in satirical attacks upon the Bible. At the same time, he could not go the whole hog with the contemporary French materialists, whom he also castigated, and he clung tenaciously to a deistic type of theism and to its creed of the watch and the watchmaker.

Voltaire's point of contact with philosophy, however, was but one of his many contacts with life. He was a poet, a dramatist, a storyteller, and a historian. The follies and the foibles of the philosophers and the theologians were simply scenes in the great *comédie humaine,* in every incident of which he found something to amuse him and something upon which to exercise his talent for criticism and irony. Every phase of human life was grist for his mill, and human speculation in matters of philosophy and theology was poured into the hopper —and ground exceedingly fine—along with everything else.

Condillac's Derivation of All Ideas from Experience. It remained for Condillac (1715-1780) and Diderot (1713-1784) to translate Locke's skepticism into Gallic fashions of philosophic thinking. Condillac, in his *Traité des sensations,* adopted Locke's view of the mind as a blank tablet upon which the senses write their messages, and Locke's apparatus of memory, association, comparison, differentiation, and abstraction as the means by which complex, universal, and abstract ideas are built up out of sense-perceptions. There is nothing in thought that is not derived from experience and resoluble into it.

To drive this point home, Condillac turned himself into a philosophic Pygmalion and created a statue which he brought to life, still encased, however, within a veneer of marble and sunk as yet in complete unconsciousness. He then chipped away the veneer from the tip of the statue's nose and held a rose to its nostrils. The slumbering statue is awakened by a smell—its first and, for the moment, its only *sensation.* When the rose is removed, the sensation lingers as a *memory.* The memory occupies the entire consciousness of the statue and therefore engages its *attention.* We hold now a little asafetida before the uncovered nostrils. The statue has another experience in addition to the memory of the rose. It *compares* the two, and for the first time discovers by means of the comparison that the smell of the rose is *pleasurable* or *agreeable,* the odor of asafetida *painful* or *disagreeable.* The statue now *loves* the scent of the one and *hopes* and *desires* that it will be repeated; it *hates* the smell of the other and is *averse* to and *fears* a recurrence of the *repugnant* experience. In short, *volition* has come into being within its marble breast. Other odoriferous objects are now placed before it for it to sniff. Its experiences and memories are multiplied and variegated, attended to, compared, discriminated, loved or hated, willed or not willed, according as they are pleasurable or painful. General ideas resting upon resemblances and differences are formed, and judgments of likeness and unlikeness are pronounced. Finally, the carrying over of sensations by memory links them up with present experiences and gives the statue the impression of a single, individual stream of consciousness, that is, of its *self.* The statue is now self-conscious.

In this way Condillac built up an entire mental life out of smells alone. As we chip away the marble from the other sense-organs, experience and the ideas to which it gives rise become more and more complicated. But it is not until we have enabled our statue to receive *touch* sensations that its impressions and ideas can acquire the significance of *objects* existing *outside* itself. The sense of *externality* is bound up with experiences of size, shape, solidity, extension, and the like. Touch, therefore, is the most important and fundamental of the senses.

Condillac's Skepticism. Condillac, however, shares Locke's skepticism as to the power of the mind to discover the real nature of outer objects. Whether the external world is material as Descartes taught, or composed of unextended monads as Leibnitz claimed, is something we cannot know. Hence, neither of these philosophers, he tells in his *Traité des systèmes,* nor yet the Occasionalists, or Spinoza, have any foundations for their pretensions to certitude or for the systems to which these pretensions lead them. At the same time, Condillac himself feels quite certain that Locke's suggestion is wrong that no sound reasons against the body's thinking can be adduced, and he believes with Descartes that we must regard consciousness as the activity of an immaterial substance. The passivity of the soul, he also feels, may be due to the Fall. Condillac was a priest and an abbé and never allowed his skepticism to trespass upon his theology.

Helvétius' Psychology. Helvétius, like Condillac, tried in his *De l'Esprit,* to show that all the operations and contents of the mind are derived from sense-perception. But he is chiefly interested in this conclusion as a preliminary to the construction of an ethical and political theory. Just as our intellectual processes and ideas are developments of perceptions, so our moral ideals and standards are all developed out of the primitive sensations of pleasure and pain. From these two sources arise all the passions by which the private life of the individual is agitated and motivated. Our feeling of liberty, and here Helvétius closely follows Locke, is a feeling of freedom from outside constraint. As long as we can do what we desire and choose to do, we are free. The question whether we can choose otherwise than we do choose he turns over to the theologians. To attempt to discuss it philosophically would be, he says, like trying to write an essay on causeless effects.

Helvétius' Ethics and Social Theory. The individual is actuated by self-interest, interpreted not economically but in the larger sense of interest in everything he finds agreeable or disagreeable to him. His judgments of good and evil, approbation and disapprobation, are founded upon those impressions. The same is true of society, which is a group of individuals. Social favor and disfavor are therefore dictated by utility, and conduct is deemed virtuous or vicious according as it is useful to society at large. We approve ideas that flatter our self-importance. We disapprove ideas that do not agree with our own, and we condemn as immoral those who hold them. Altruism is based upon the fact that the sacrifice of private to public interest brings more pleasure and is therefore more useful than its opposite. It is not spontaneous but calculated. Ideas, however, of what is useful and therefore of what is right vary with the times. Hence there is no absolute right and wrong, and all moral standards are relative and changing.

Since we are all actuated by the same passions and we all possess them to about the same degree, all men are naturally alike and naturally equal. Apparent inequalities are due, not to difference of structure, but to differences in ambition, which again depend upon differences of training. Education is therefore all important if the general level of intelligence, which is mediocre, is to be raised, and if humanity is to realize its undeveloped capacities.

Against the established political, social and religious order in France Helvétius inveighed with all the bitterness and something of the irony of his friend and master, Voltaire. Himself a deist, as impatient as Voltaire of theologies and metaphysics, he got into difficulties with the Church, especially with the Jansenists and the Jesuits, and fell into disfavor at court. In spite of his protests and retractions, his book was condemned and burned by the hangman, and he was deprived of a lucrative office he held from the crown. But the notoriety of his case helped make him famous, and turned *De l'Esprit* into one of the best sellers in every country of Europe.

II. FRENCH MATERIALISM

Diderot and De la Mettrie. Diderot, the author of the *Encyclopédie,* gave a distinctly materialist twist to Locke's skepticism. He quite agreed with Locke's view that there could be no *a priori* certainty of the body's not thinking and of the necessity of a soul to explain mental activity; though he seems to have felt that the materialistic hypothesis could not easily account for the unity of experience and for self-consciousness. However, in spite of his avowed skepticism he inclines to a belief in the reality of matter and in the possibility of reducing all things, conscious and animate as well as inanimate, to materialistic and mechanical terms. All mental processes, he insists, are mechanically directed. Our behavior is determined by the kind of machine we are, and our feeling of freedom is an illusion.

Meantime, a thoroughly materialistic point of view was also in process of formulation. Here, too, Locke's skeptical admission that, for all we know, it may be the body that thinks, and that therefore the concept of a soul is unnecessary, was not without its influence. Of this point of view De la Mettrie (1709-1751) is one of the earliest exponents, best known by his *L'Homme Machine* in which he defends the thesis that the human organism is through and through a mechanism. The differences between the so-called higher and lower forms of life are, he maintained, of degree, not of kind, and consist solely in more or less complex structure. Desire is the mainspring which makes the wheels of all forms of animate being go round, and, the more powerful and the more numerous the wants of an organism are, the "higher" it ranks in the scale. Man, therefore, is the highest of all the animals.

Consciousness is a function of matter and needs no soul to explain it. The body feels and thinks. Mind grows, matures, decays as the body moves along its appointed path from the cradle to the grave. The senses, and here De la Mettrie agrees with Locke and Condillac, are the sources of all our ideas.

When it came to such questions as the existence of God and of immortality, De la Mettrie was silent.

In his preparation of the *Encyclopédie,* Diderot had as an associate the celebrated French mathematician D'Alembert (1717-1783). D'Alembert ranged himself with the deists and impartially attacked both the Jesuits and the Calvinists. His chief interest, however, lay always in mathematics and science, and his part in theological and philosophical controversies was only incidental.

Holbach's Attack on Christianity. Another contributor to the *Encyclopédie* was Holbach (1723-1789), who in *Le Système de la Nature* —a work due in part to the advice and help of Diderot—expounded a system of atheistic materialism. In it, as in a somewhat earlier work, *Christianisme dévoilé,* he denounced not only Christianity but all religion as purveyors of fear and credulity, ignorance and superstition, and found in the idea of God a sanction for tyranny and persecution and oppression and most of the ills to which humanity in general, and the contemporary French nation in particular, were the heirs. Emphatically rejecting the existence of a Deity, he reduced Reality to terms of matter moving in accordance with mechanical principles and laws. There is no such thing as soul or spirit. It is the brain and the nervous system that are conscious, and their activities of sensation and thought are governed by the same necessity as obtains in the rest of nature. Free-will, in the sense of lack of determination, is nonexistent.

Since all events are mechanically determined, purposes are ruled out as explanations. Seeing is not the reason for the existence of the eye. The ear does not exist in order to hear. Man's whole organic structure is produced by the movements of matter, and the functions it performs are the results, not the explanations, of its organs, which are developed out of antecedent conditions through antecedent causes. We see because we happen to have eyes; we hear because we happen to have ears. Had the movements of matter produced a different sort of organism, our functions and activities would be different from those we possess. Naturally, since we have no souls, we can only be as immortal as our bodies, and our bodies are patently mortal and perishable, like all other individual objects. Matter and motion alone are eternal.

Holbach's Ethics. Holbach's ethics was utilitarian. Happiness is the good after which all men strive and towards which all else, including virtue, is a means. To expect mankind to purchase so-called virtue at the expense of happiness, or to refrain from so-called vice at a price of unhappiness, is worse than useless. Nothing can be truly virtuous that makes for unhappiness. If vice makes a man happy he should pursue it. A sound morality must be scientific, based upon human desires as they are and upon a knowledge of the natural environment in which they operate. Man is naturally motivated by self-interest. It is the business of a rational ethics to enlighten that self-interest, to show man where his true good lies and the means best adapted to attaining it. The superstitious "Thou shalt nots" of religion and all other supernatural sanctions must be swept away, and rational rules must take their place, founded upon an investigation of what really is naturally good and what really is naturally bad for a being endowed with the desires and drives we happen to possess.

Holbach was also in the van of the political revolutionary movement and a trenchant critic of contemporary systems of government. Like Helvétius, he was a champion of the rights of the French masses and had a somewhat dogmatic faith in the power of education and of reason to restore all men to their birthright and to establish their natural equality and dignity.

His honesty and straightforwardness and nobility of personal character commanded great respect and commended him as a friend to many who could not stomach his views. Holbach's atheism, indeed, proved too much for even the tolerance of Voltaire, who rushed to the defense of God and wrote an article about him for the *Encyclopédie*.

Cabanis. Holbach was followed by Cabanis (1757-1808), a French doctor, who drove home the materialistic hypothesis, particularly in so far as it affected man. Starting from Holbach's conclusion that matter and motion, acting in accordance with mechanical principles, are all that exist, and that human consciousness and behavior are purely natural facts on a par with all others, he developed a thoroughly mechanical and materialistic psychology in an essay on the relations of man's physical organization to his intellectual and moral faculties.[1] In this essay he insists, like Holbach, that it is the body that is conscious and that wills and thinks. The term "soul" is simply a way of expressing the sentient character of the physical organism. It does not designate a separate entity. The brain, he says in a phrase that has become famous, secretes thought as the liver does bile. Or again, the brain reacts to impressions conveyed to it by the sensory nerves just as the stomach reacts to the food we swallow. The one begins to think, when stimulated; the other to digest. Cabanis' own thinking, we may remark, was carried on under circumstances congenial to its mental digestion by others. The French Revolution, in which Cabanis played a considerable part, was in progress. God had been dethroned in France for the time being, and the Goddess of Reason was enjoying her brief interregnum in his stead.

Later, Cabanis seems to have retreated somewhat from his materialism à l'outrance. In his Lettres sur les causes premières, not published till some years after his death, he expresses the opinion that life is an infusion into the organism of an immaterial, vitalistic principle, possessed of will and intelligence, which is omnipresent in the world. The indwelling of this principle in us constitutes the self, which is an immaterial entity able to survive the dissolution of the body.

III. THE DAWN OF THE THEORY OF EVOLUTION

Early Evolutionary Suggestions. The biological speculations of the Enlightenment are also colored by the dawn of the theory of evolution. In England, Locke had noted the imperceptible gradations separating man from animals, the animals from vegetable life, and living from inanimate matter. He had also pointed out the arbitrary character of our classification of animal life into genera and species, which, he said, was dictated by our own convenience rather than by the organic lines of differentiation suggested by nature.[2] And he had explained the structure of the human body as an adaptation of the organism to environment, not, to be sure, evolved, but rather bestowed

[1] *Considérations générales sur l'étude de l'homme et sur les rapports de son organisation physique avec ses facultés intellectuelles et morales.*
[2] *Essay III*, 6, 22 ff.

by God. Hume, also, had brought forward as a possible alternative hypothesis to special creation the notion that the universe grew into its present shape as an individual organism grows.[3]

In France these ideas assumed a more definite and a more advanced form. Diderot looked upon matter as a moving, changing, quasi-animate substance whose forms, including animal species, are in a process of generation and transformation no less constant than that of individual objects. He points out, like Locke, the indeterminateness of the boundaries that separate the animate from the inanimate and hints that the one may have developed out of the other. The continuity of human with animal structure was also emphasized by De la Mettrie and Helvétius. Holbach regarded man in his present state as the product of a long evolution from a primitive stock, though he declined to commit himself as to how the first ancestors of the human race originated. These thinkers were at one in excluding all idea of design or purpose from the process of development and transformation and in maintaining the purely mechanical determination of its origin and direction.

Early Precursors of Evolution. Among other early precursors of the evolutionary hypothesis, we may mention De Maillet (1656-1738), Maupertuis (1698-1759), the natural historian Buffon (1707-1788), Robinet (1723-1789), and De Bonnet (1720-1793). Robinet regarded all species, including the human, as variations of a single underlying type. He worked out, moreover, a detailed system of parallelism between mental and physiological processes and even went so far as to locate the moral sense in certain nervous tissues. De Bonnet suggested that the animal and vegetable species existing today are not as God created them in the beginning but have undergone modifications that would render them unrecognizable to their first parents. And as early as 1735 De Maillet had considered the possibility that existing species might be developed out of earlier extinct ones and had insisted upon the importance of the study of geology as a means for reconstructing the past history of the earth.

IV. THE REVOLUTIONARIES

General Revolutionary Atmosphere. We have noted the keen interest taken by the eighteenth century philosophers in political and economic questions and the part many of them played in commend-

[3] *Dialogues on Natural Religion*

ing and advocating the spread of the ideal of democracy, which was then in progress throughout all western Europe. In England the revolution had been to a large extent forestalled by the liberties and rights the British people had already wrung from the crown and the nobility, and its eighteenth century episodes, with the exception of the loss of the British colonies in America, were not marked by violence. But in France, conditions were different. The movement towards democracy was retarded. More had to be accomplished within a briefer space of time, and what had to be done had to be done by violence. Passions were enflamed. Resentment at the contemporary situation ran high and turgid, and its waves, beating against the established order, cast high into the air a foam of idealistic hopes and visions of a human society in which all individuals, freed from the odious tyranny that now oppressed them, should be free, equal, perfect, and happy. French political philosophy reflected the tenseness of the French atmosphere heavy with hatreds and enthusiasms, and, however skeptical it might be in some respects, its faith in the perfectibility of human nature and the future of the human race was unbridled and unbounded.

Montesquieu. There were, to be sure, cooler heads like Montesquieu (1689-1755) whose *Esprit des Lois* is one of the greatest of the French political contributions to the eighteenth century and is remarkable for the sanity and the moderation of its liberal views on politics and religion. Indeed, it was not advanced enough for men like Helvétius and Voltaire, and the friends—among them Helvétius—to whom Montesquieu submitted the manuscript for criticism advised him not to publish it. He ignored their advice, and the book scored an immediate success and acclamation.

Condorcet. Among the more prominent of the enthusiasts we may mention Condorcet (1743-1794), another contributor to Diderot's *Encyclopédie,* and a friend of Voltaire and D'Alembert and of the French economist and minister of finance, Turgot. Condorcet also made valuable contributions to the mathematical theory of probability. But it is upon his *Esquisse d'un tableau historique du progrès de l'esprit humain* that his fame chiefly rests. In this work he sketches the progress of man from primitive barbarism to contemporary times. In human history he finds an advance towards equality between individuals and between nations and towards human perfection. During this advance the chief enemy of progress has always been political and ecclesiastical tyranny, which he believes is about to be overthrown by the exercise of human reason. The moment is at hand when there will be no more tyrants or slaves or priests, and when all men will be equal and all men will be equally enlightened.

Possibility of Perfecting Human Nature. The present inequality among men rests in his opinion largely upon the uneven distribution of wealth, the advantages bestowed by the inheritance of wealth, and the unequal opportunities and results of education. These inequalities cannot be wholly done away with, since they are rooted in nature and their destruction would violate natural human rights. But they can be diminished by political and educational measures and reduced to the basic inequalities of intelligence and capability, which no means at human disposal can wholly eradicate.

Even so, however, no limit can be set to the perfectibility of human nature, and the measures for further approximating perfection are obvious. The sciences may be improved, both in their exactitude and the extent of their application. Medicine will make enormous strides, both in the prevention of disease and its cure. Indeed, death itself may in the end be the result only of accident or of old age, and the expectancy of life may be so increased as to make man little short of immortal. The practice of eugenics will progressively improve the human stock. Equality of the sexes in all matters will be attained. War will be abolished. Education will be perfected. The fine arts will flourish. A universal language will be invented. Man is on the march upward and onward forever. In contemplating his glorious future the philosopher may well forgive and forget the errors of his past.

V. ROUSSEAU

Character. But of all the political and sociological thinkers of the eighteenth century, Jean Jacques Rousseau (1712-1778) is by far the most important and the most interesting. In character Rousseau was full of contradictions. He was infected with petty meannesses, and fortified with great nobility. He was hard-headed where he should have been soft-hearted, and soft-hearted where he should have been hard-headed. He was emotional, temperamental, sentimental to a high degree, but he was also capable of profound insight and of clear and cool reasoning. His life, too, was characterized by alternating episodes and vicissitudes. Born a Protestant, he embraced Catholicism and reverted to Protestantism again, though at heart he was a typical eighteenth century deist. Very susceptible in a rather namby-pamby way to women, he passed from one mawkish love-affair to another, married, if he really did marry, one woman completely unsuited to him, lived with her nearly thirty years on and off, and had by her five children, all of whom he left on the doorsteps of foundling asylums and deserted so completely that his descendants have never been traced.

Life. His youth was one of vagabondage, trying his hand at this, that, and the other. From Geneva, where he was born, to Italy, to France, back to Italy, back to France, to England, and back to France again—now reasonably well off, now in dire poverty, now driven by restlessness to the city, now driven back to the country for the consolations of solitude and of the pastoral scene for which he had a sentimental and shallow passion—such was his life. In some of his wanderings, too, he was driven by that bitter persecution with which the established order, be it political, economic, social or religious, greets the appearance of new ideas. Religion was to the fore in this hounding, and Catholics and Calvinists alike were hot upon his trail. But he had also his admirers and supporters, not always sympathetic but at least tolerant, among the more liberal and enlightened men and societies of the time. The English welcomed him, and Frederick the Great, whom he had bitterly attacked, was great enough to extend him asylum in Germany.

Unfortunately, however, he had a genius for quarreling with his friends, for making mountains out of molehills, and for imagining petty and personal animosities to be formidable organized conspiracies directed against him. Among those who were at one time or another his friends or in contact with him, though many of them fell out with him later, were Voltaire, Diderot, the Duke of Luxembourg, the Prince of Conti, D'Alembert, Mirabeau, Hume, Gibbon, Boswell, Prince Henry of Prussia, the brother of Frederick the Great, and George III. But he was too stormy a petrel to avail himself of these safe landings. In spite of his profound longing for solitude and an Arcadian life, it was trouble that he really sought, and trouble that he always found his whole life long.

If we may trust his own account, the ideas that made him famous burst upon him suddenly like a revelation. In the years 1749 and 1752 the Academy at Dijon offered prizes for two essays—the first on the influence of science upon the purification or corruption of manners, or, as we should say, morals, and the second upon the origin of inequality among men and whether it is authorized by natural law. Rousseau saw the first of these competitions advertised in the newspapers, and then and there his revelation took place. In reality there was a long subconscious preparation for the event, for, as we may gather from his *Confessions,* he had been for some time revolving stray questions connected with political problems. But their eventual eruption into the foreground of his mind was like the unexpected and violent outburst of a volcano. The lava-flow solidified in the two *Discourses*—the first of which won the academic prize.

Civilization a Corruption of Man's Native Goodness. In this *Discourse,* Rousseau set himself squarely against the accepted view of his time, held as we have seen by Condorcet almost as a divinely revealed dogma, that the sciences and the arts foster the progress and are the mainstays of the happiness of mankind. On the contrary, Rousseau argues, it is to them that the real fall of man is due. History shows that the most primitive and the least advanced peoples are the happiest and the least corrupt. Nor is that to be wondered at when we consider the obvious effect of art and science upon human character. They lead to luxury, and luxury to the undermining of all the simple and essential virtues. Furthermore, they breed inequalities among men and distinctions of class and of wealth, which are the root of economic and social evil and the great breeders of human unhappiness—ills that are minimized or altogether absent in primitive societies. Far, then, from being the saviors of mankind, the arts and sciences are the serpents in its original Eden—where ignorance is bliss and the fruits of the tree of knowledge are rightly forbidden us by a wisdom that foresees the disastrous results of tasting them.

In the second *Discourse,* which won honorable mention but not the prize in the Dijon competition, Rousseau elaborated upon the perfection of the state of nature, drew a characteristic picture of the "noble savage," which became all the rage, and then described at length the fall of man. The "noble savage" is not, as Hobbes had maintained, in a state of war. He is naturally social by nature, full of pity for and sympathy with his fellows. Happily exempt from family associations and from romantic love, and casually reproducing his species here and there as the passing desire of the moment dictates, he is free from all the selfishness, the possessiveness, and above all the jealousy which are love's bitter fruits.

This idyllic state, however, was too good to last. Man began to forestall and circumvent nature by inventing tools, and thus his ruin began. Under the new conditions inequalities of talent revealed themselves, the stronger differentiated themselves from the weaker, differences of wealth and poverty arose, sympathy gave way to self-aggrandizement, and the strong and the rich became dominant and organized society as it now exists for the purpose of eternally keeping themselves on top and the poor in servitude.

"Le Contrat Social." But the *Discourses* are only a prelude to Rousseau's greatest and most famous work, *Le Contrat Social*. Here we have a discussion of how the development of society *ought* to take place, if it is to minimize the evils of inequality and loss of primitive individual liberty, which inevitably attend its growth. The prime business of all legislation is to preserve liberty and equality—not indeed to an absolute degree, which is impossible—but sufficiently to keep individuals from doing violence to one another by the exercise of their superior powers, and from being able to buy others or being forced to sell themselves to others, because of too great differences of wealth.

Society is founded upon an agreement between individuals who associate for the purpose of offsetting as far as possible the evil consequences of the fall of mankind from its primitive perfection. It rests upon a social contract. But, if this contract is to be effective, there must be power to enforce it lodged somewhere in the body politic. In other words, there must be sovereignty. So far, it will be seen, Rousseau agrees with Hobbes, save that for Hobbes selfishness and the warfare of individual interests are the primitive condition of society, whereas for Rousseau they represent a fall from an original state of peace. The pressing question, then, for Rousseau, as for Hobbes, becomes where sovereignty is to be lodged.

Sovereignty Inalienably Lodged in the People. It is in answering this question that Rousseau lays the basis of the revolution. Hobbes had conceived of sovereignty as not only delegated but absolutely relinquished to a single person, to be exercised by him in the interests of the whole state. Rousseau, however, declared that sovereignty resides in and is inalienable from the people as a whole, and must be exercised by them and by none other if the purposes of the social contract are to be realized. It cannot be divided and portioned out. Law, he continues, is simply the expression of the common will of the sovereign people with regard to matters of common interest. Strictly speaking, the sovereign people should always legislate as a whole and not through elected representatives. Representative government is a curtailment of popular liberty. The only true democracy—or government by the sovereign people—must take the form of the Athenian Ecclesia, or, we might add, of the New England town meeting, where the whole people gathers together and legislates directly. Such government is only possible in a small community, and therefore Rousseau, remembering his Plato and his Aristotle, limits the ideal state to ten thousand individuals.

Government Rests on the Consent of the Governed. But direct action of this sort is impossible in actual fact where states are larger. There fore the sovereign people establishes a form of government through which it governs itself. But the people is always sovereign, and the power of the governing agent is derived solely from the consent of the governed and may be exercised only for their convenience and in their service. Since the perfect and only really democratic form of government is impracticable in large states, and since the device of representative government by temporarily elected parliaments is excluded by Rousseau as a subterfuge of which he disapproves, the agent can only be a monarchy or an aristocracy. Monarchy has too many disadvantages. Hence the best agent of the sovereign people is an aristocracy; not hereditary—for that, in Rousseau's opinion, is the worst possible governmental agency—but elective. In this way only can the people secure the best possible class of public servants.

But, whatever the governmental agent employed, the moment it ceases to register the will of the sovereign people and begins to arrogate sovereignty to itself it should be overthrown. The right of the people to change the form of government at will, which is the right to revolution, is as inalienable as its sovereignty.

Finally, Rousseau considers the relation of religion to the state. The state will certainly not support nor countenance anything like either Catholic or Protestant Christianity. But it will not only countenance but drastically impose natural religion, or, in other words, belief in God, in immortality, and future rewards and punishments. Unbelievers in these "natural" dogmas will be banished, and apostates from them must be put to death.

Theory of Education. Democracy, then, is the best political device for recapturing the equality, the simplicity, and the straightforwardness that the noble savage, as yet uncorrupted by civilization, spontaneously enjoys. But, if it is to be successful, it must be supplemented by revolutionary changes in the education of the individual. These changes, Rousseau sets forth in his *Emile,* which carries the ideal children, Emile and Sophie, from their own cradles to a cradle that their united efforts are about to rock when their education is at last complete.

Present methods of training Rousseau finds wrong from start to finish. They create an artificial child, instead of permitting and encouraging the noble savage to develop. Infractions of the state of nature begin at birth with swaddling clothes, and are continued in all sorts of restrictions that tend to cramp and distort the primitive, untrained, unspoiled, unperverted human nature, frank, honest, direct, and unfearing, with which the child is born. Parents, nurses, tutors, schools all conspire in the unholy work of instilling into the child "conditioned reflexes," as we might say, of every undesirable sort—fears, inhibitions, vanities, selfish desires, distorted habits, and false ideas about almost everything.

How then should children be brought up? They should be left as free as possible in all respects. The words "obey" and "command," "duty" and "obligation," should be left out of their vocabularies. Physical obstacles alone should be put in the way of too untrammeled or dangerous self-expression. Punishment, reproof, moral appeals, only harm the child to whom morality is as yet meaningless, and whose impulses are naturally good.

In a word, early education should consist in the greatest possible lack of so-called education. As it is, children will learn evil enough from their parents and imitate the lack of honesty and frankness, the vanity and the selfishness, of their elders. But, if they can only be sufficiently shielded from their parents' vices and from the artificiality of the world during their formative period, they will reach the age of reason, adolescence, and independence, sufficiently fortified by the unhampered development of their native goodness, courage, honesty, and unselfishness to resist the destructive influences of their environment and to cope successfully with life.

Little Sophie's upbringing will not differ from Emile's except as the natural virtues in need of fortification differ in her case somewhat from those of men, and as woman's place in the world needs a different equipment. She is by nature less rational and less intellectual than Emile and therefore at a disadvantage for which she has compensations in her female charm, intuition, and taste. The cultivation of these virtues and of a knowledge of masculine character enables her to dominate men's hearts and thus their actions.

Rousseau's *Emile* had great and immediate influence upon educational theory. It inspired Pestalozzi and Froebel, whose insistence upon the importance of a study of child psychology and the development of the natural activities of the child still motivates much of modern education. And in other ways, it has had important indirect effects.

VI. VICO

While we are still on Latin soil we should mention the Italian and Neapolitan philosopher Vico (1668-1744).[4] Vico was born and bred a Roman Catholic and always remained a good son of the Church. But his system exhibits great independence of the scholastic tradition. He was a lawyer by profession, greatly interested in the philosophy of jurisprudence, and his devotion to the law colored his general outlook.

Truth Created, Not Discovered, by the Mind. Truth, he tells us, is not something external to the mind. It is not *found* by our own intellectual activities. What we call the process of discovering it, is really a process of manufacturing it. Its fabric is spun, its pattern is planned, its measurements are taken, its shape is determined by the mind whose intellectual activities it suits. In knowing, as in doing, we make things come true, for all knowing is essentially doing, and all the mind can know is what it itself does. For example, in mathematics the mind creates the elements with which it deals, lays down the conditions under which it works, and produces out of these elements, according to these conditions, the edifice of mathematical truth.

God, by actualizing the potentialities of existence he contains and by combining them as he does, at once generates and knows the absolute and flawless truth about the universe—the Word, the Son, and then brings into being out of nothing the truth or fact that a universe exists, and thus creates the world. God's truth is the standard by which we measure the truths created by human minds. These truths are necessarily incomplete, because of the inferior creative power of our intellects. Nevertheless, within the limits set upon that power, our minds in so far as they create coincide with the creative activity of God, and the truths they generate coincide with the absolute truths produced by him. Therefore the truths created by human intellects are not relative and individual but eternal and immutable. Only, since our intellects are finite and restricted in their scope and power of creation, we cannot bring forth complete truth and make for ourselves a knowledge that, being all-inclusive and certain through and through, equals God's.

Certainty Without Knowledge. We can, however, have *certainty* without knowledge, as when we improperly substitute dogmatic certainty of mere opinion for the truth we can and ought to create, or properly supplement with faith truth that it is beyond our power to

[4] Vico's most famous work is his *Principii di una scienza nuova.*

create. On the certainty that attends erroneous or dubious opinions, there is no need to dwell. Intellectual advance lies in converting certainty of that sort into the certainty that accompanies truth. This we do by testing our opinions with a view to discovering how far they can be really said to have been made by the activity of our minds, and how far they have other causes. An example of the justifiable certainty which may still persist when knowledge is impossible, and truth cannot therefore be created, is the certainty we have of God's existence. Man cannot *know* that God exists. He cannot feel that God's existence is certainly *true*. For to know him would be to create him, and man cannot be the maker of God. But though he cannot *know* him, he may *feel* certain that God exists. No human being, then, can assert the *truth* of God's existence. Only God can do that, and in so doing he creates himself. Human beings are limited to asserting the *certainty* of his existence, since mere assertions of certainty do not *make* truth as assertions of *knowledge* do.

So it is that Vico rejects all attempts like those of Descartes and Spinoza to find the criterion of truth in self-evidence and certainty. The criterion of truth lies in our having made it, as is shown by an examination of the "true" concepts of mathematics and science.

In insisting that absolute truth was generated by God Vico disclaimed the Scottish doctrine that it is the product of an unmotivated and "indifferent" act of the divine will. On the other hand, he was equally unsympathetic to the Thomistic doctrine that God's will was determined by his nature. Both points of view, he felt, distinguished the divine intellect from the divine will, and divided into two what was really one. The intellect and the will were one thing, just as knowing and creating, or willing, the truth were a single activity.

The Creation of the Universe. So much for the process by which God generates eternal and immutable truth. But how does he make a fact and a truth of the universe? In other words, how does he create a material world? In God, Vico replies, exist the powers and possibilities of all things. These powers are actualized as "metaphysical points" of force. The points of force exert themselves and so produce the physical phenomena of extension and motion which are the least common denominators of material existence.

Life, according to Vico, is a purely mechanical event and animals are automata. In man consciousness is added to life in the shape, first, of self-determining impulses to self-expression which work through the mechanical vital principle, and second, of reason, which is God thinking and creating within us.

Theory of Society and History. In generating truth God generates the natural laws by which the physical universe is regulated and the moral law which governs human behavior. He has implanted in human beings conscience, which is an innate sense of justice. Upon conscience and justice all man-made laws are based. Man is naturally and from the beginning a social being. Society is not artificial and not the result of any deliberate compact. The anti-social human being is no longer human. The development of civilization is a progressive clarification of conscience and of man's social nature. The successive stages of history are variations and amplifications of the same law as we find under the most primitive conditions.

History Vico divides into three periods, based upon the expression that law assumes. In the primitive period, law manifests itself as religious authority, customs and usages; in the second period, as authority exerted and regulations formulated by absolute rulers, such as kings and aristocracies. In the third and final period, called civil or human law, it is expressed in authority and legislation resting upon a philosophic understanding of the principles upon which law at all times rests, and from which in all its stages it springs. After coming to maturity, law and civilization decay and relapse to the primitive stage, and then the cycle repeats itself. This scheme of repeated cycles of three stages Vico applies to all the history he is familiar with and especially to the Graeco-Roman period.

Out of his discussion there arises a concept of the philosophy of history. Such a philosophy, if it is to be sound, must be drawn from a knowledge of human nature, since all history is made by man. Naturally, this knowledge must include an acquaintance with the past. But it must do more than that. It must be accompanied by an imaginative ability to put ourselves in the place of primitive peoples and to see whatever period we are studying through the eyes, not of our time and place, but of those who lived in it. Our failure to deal with primitive human life in terms of itself and our tendency to read into it our own sentiments and conditions lead to errors, like the contract theory, for example. If, however, we can see others as they see themselves, we shall find that primitive beliefs and customs are not based upon ignorance and superstition, but are rather a kind of "poetic wisdom" which grasps in its naïve and imaginative way precisely the same truths and principles as more mature civilizations exemplify in a more reflective and sophisticated manner.

Chapter XIII

GERMAN ENLIGHTENMENT

I. LIBERALISM OF THE PRUSSIAN AND AUSTRIAN GOVERNMENTS

Maria Theresa and Joseph II. We cross now into Germany. There too, we find the Enlightenment, or *Aufklärung,* in full swing, though under political auspices different from those that prevailed in France. East of the Rhine the long-drawn-out struggle between Prussia and Austria was in progress, and the opposing figures of its last forty years were Frederick the Great and the great Empress Maria Theresa, whose reigns began in the same year, 1740, and ended with their deaths in 1786 and 1780, respectively. Both rulers, while heading despotic governments, were liberal and humane and instituted many important reforms. Indeed, Maria Theresa's son, the Emperor Joseph II, was almost radical and attempted experiments in social reform inspired by the ideals of the Enlightenment. He did his best to break the power of both the clergy and the nobility. He issued an edict of religious tolerance, and, in spite of a personal visit of protest from the Pope, he closed innumerable monasteries, instituted governmental regulation of those that remained, lifted the heavy hand of Rome from the Austrian priests, devoted the wealth taken from the churches to education, exercised strict control over the relations of the peasantry to their overlords, and abolished serfdom.

Frederick the Great. Frederick the Great, himself a child of the Enlightenment, was exposed from his earliest youth to French influences, which were eagerly welcomed by the native intelligence, broad-mindedness and humanity of his outlook. He was interested in history and philosophy, in art and music. He corresponded with many of the eminent Frenchmen of the day, and was for a long time a friend of Voltaire, with whom he kept in touch both by letters and by frequent visits of the philosopher to his court. Not only did he establish religious liberty, but he tolerated the freest criticism of himself, although it was often bitter and unjust. Rousseau, we may remember, who had violently attacked him, was offered asylum in Germany from the persecution of the French and Swiss authorities. His government, too, was conducted on enlightened principles. He abolished torture, purified the administration of justice, and was himself always accessible to such of his subjects as had real grievances to lay before him. One of the great generals of all time, he increased the boundaries and established the power of Prussia and made her supreme among the German states and the center of gravity about which the non-Austrian ones were henceforth to circle.

Conditions, then, in Germany were at the moment most favorable to liberal and humane thought. Furthermore, since the greatest of all the German princes was himself on the side of political reform, German thinking was less obsessed by political and social problems and freer to devote itself to science and philosophy.

II. RELIGIOUS LIBERALS

Reimarus. East of the Rhine French deism had its representative in Reimarus (1694-1768), who not only attacked the belief in the special inspiration of the Bible and discredited the alleged miracles it recorded, but rejected the possibility of miracles and of supernatural revelations altogether. God, he maintained, does not use such means to manifest himself to mankind, nor does he choose one religion rather than another for that purpose. The true Scriptures are the book of nature, and to that book all men of all times and places, be they learned or ignorant, barbarian or Greek, Jew or Christian, have always had equal access.

Mendelssohn. Somewhat the same position was maintained by the Jewish thinker, Moses Mendelssohn (1729-1786). He protested, to be sure, against the current materialism, and wrote a dialogue entitled *Phädon,* modeled after Plato's *Phaedo,* to prove the immortality of the soul. This won him the title of the German Socrates. But, when engaged in religious controversy by a contemporary Christian thinker, Lavater, who sought to convert him to Christianity, he replied in his *Jerusalem* that no religion had a monopoly of truth, but that all were true and all were good in proportion as they inspired men to lead the good life. Judged by this standard Judaism was as true as Christianity or any other form of belief, and he was content to adhere to the faith of his fathers.

Lessing. Interesting in themselves as examples of the German *Aufklärung,* both men gain a further importance from their influence on Lessing (1729-1781), who is perhaps the most distinguished German representative of the period of the Enlightenment. He is, it is true, overshadowed by Goethe, but Goethe, though only twenty years younger, outlived him by fifty years and belongs as much to the first third of the nineteenth as he does to the last part of the eighteenth century.

Lessing was first and last a poet, a dramatist, and an art critic. His earliest interest was in the stage and, with the exception of the *Laokoon* in which he sets forth his theory of art, it is by his dramas that he is known. At the same time, he was a man of wide culture and liberal tendencies, which made it all the easier for two incidents to bring him into the arena of theological controversy and to enlist him as an avowed champion of religious freedom. The first of these incidents was the friendship he struck up with Moses Mendelssohn. The second was the entrusting to him of the manuscript of Reimarus' book, which had not been published during the author's lifetime. Lessing published portions of it in his essays *On History and Literature,* and was roundly taken to task by the orthodox theologians for his impiety in so doing. He replied, and the controversy that ensued was violent and bitter, and ended only when the government of Brunswick, which was less tolerant than the Prussian, suppressed the offending literature at the instigation of the clergy, and shut Lessing up.

Not to be suppressed, however, Lessing took to the drama as a vehicle of self-expression, and, adapting the opinions of his friend Mendelssohn to the stage, wrote his famous play *Nathan der Weise.* In this he tells the famous story of the three rings to illustrate the point that, if it is by their fruits ye shall know them, Christianity, Judaism, and Mohammedanism are all true religions because they have all produced noble and upright men. From now on, Lessing was engaged in ceaseless religious controversy as a constant champion of the liberal cause. He sought to free religion from the fetters of miracle and history and to found it upon a natural and rationalistic basis. He distinguished sharply between the original religion preached by Christ and its later developments. At the same time, he was sympathetic to the doctrines of the Trinity and of eternal life, both of which he regarded not only as basic Christian beliefs but as essentially reasonable in character. In the one he saw a statement of the outgoing and creative nature of God and of the essential divinity of man; in the other, an expression of the truth that the human race is in a state of evolution towards a higher and more perfect state. Upon the concept of development he laid great stress. The universe is in a state of continuous and progressive evolution, and God is forever revealing himself more and more completely, as the history of religion shows.

III. CLASSICISM VS. ROMANTICISM

Winckelmann. In the *Laokoon,* Lessing lays down the limitations with respect to the subject matter and method of representation imposed upon poetry, on the one hand, and upon painting and sculpture, on the other, by their different natures and situations. Herein he shows the influence of a revival of the Renaissance enthusiasm for antiquity that swept German men of letters in the last half of the eighteenth century. This return to Greece and Rome was led by Winckelmann (1717-1768), a critic and historian of art, whose sojourn in Italy aroused in him a passion not only for the art, but for the whole life and point of view of the ancient world. The perfection of Hellenic art, fostered, like the perfection of the Hellenic intellect, by the ideal conditions under which the Greek lived, lay in its cultus of pure beauty. To Winckelmann, the secret of Greek sculpture lay in its impersonality and its emphasis upon the presentation of ideal and universal types of perfect proportion and balance and harmony, from which all individual idiosyncrasies and variations from type were excluded.

Herder. The joint influence of Winckelmann and Lessing, combined with the lectures of Kant and a reading of Plato and of the British and French philosophers of the Enlightenment, fathered the ideas of Herder (1744-1803), who reacted against the classical revival and allied himself rather with the romanticists. He was obsessed by the idea of growth and development and is one of the founders of comparative religion, comparative mythology, and comparative philology. In his philosophy of history, he approaches at moments the Darwinian theory of evolution, though his general point of view is Aristotelian in that he regards the successive stages of animal life, not as successive stages through which humanity has passed in emerging from an animal ancestry, but rather as a ladder of forms of which man has always been the topmost rung. However, he seems to have felt that this ladder represents the animal species that have survived in the struggle for existence and have succeeded in establishing themselves through their superior power of adapting themselves to their environment.

Goethe. Lessing's great "classical" successor was the poet Goethe (1749-1832), in whom an Italian journey aroused much the same enthusiasms as it did in Winckelmann. But Goethe was not untouched by the romanticism of Rousseau, and he had to carry his classicism through the fire and smoke of the French Revolution and of all the unrest it created in the contemporary world, which Lessing did not live to feel. Like his Faust, he had himself yearned for experience for experience's sake, and had had his spiritual as well as his physical *Wanderjahre*. His classicism in consequence tended to become a romantic ideal for him, to be pursued not so much with a view to attaining it as because without a noble quarry there would be no pleasure and no sense of self-realization in the chase. The real end and justification of life lay in just living, but without objects to live for there could be no life to live.

Goethe also made valuable contributions to the advance of the theory of evolution, though by the time they were published in 1820 the theory had already outgrown them.

IV. FAITH VS. REASON

Hamann and Jacobi. In the meanwhile, skepticism was beginning to give rise in Germany to a faith founded upon a despair of reason. Hamann (1730-1788), for example, revolted against logic and abstraction and took refuge in pietism and mysticism. We must *feel* Reality, in which all logical contradictions are reconciled. The processes of knowledge can never discover God. God can only be found in naïve and childlike belief. Somewhat the same point of view was more elaborately held by Jacobi (1743-1819). He, too, argues that the processes of reason can never demonstrate the existence and nature either of the sensible world or of God. Indeed, the logical conclusions of exact reasoning must, as Spinoza's system admirably shows, be atheistic and fatalistic. The only terms in which we can *understand* the universe are mechanistic and deterministic. Free will, being undetermined by causes, cannot be explained. God, being infinite, cannot be comprehended. For our acquaintance both with the external world and God we must rely upon faith. Sense-perception carries with it a conviction that it represents objects existing outside ourselves. In other words, the senses "reveal" the existence of an external world as an immediate fact which cannot be gainsaid in spite of our inability to prove its truth. So, too, we have a supra-sensible, intellectual feeling or conviction which "reveals" to us God's existence as an immediate fact, although the moment that we try to *demonstrate* the truth of that fact we land in Spinozistic determinism and atheism. The two assurances, perceptual and intellectual, of the existence of the objects to which they point are equally trustworthy.

Wolff. There remains one philosopher to be mentioned, significant as the immediate and positive link that connects Kant with previous European philosophy. Moreover, he was the first German metaphysician of the new era, and his philosophy dominated German thought till its place was taken by the Kantian system. This philosopher was Wolff (1679-1754). Wolff was a follower of Leibnitz, with whom he had become acquainted as a young man. In these circumstances he was naturally opposed to the skeptical and empiricist views in process of development in England by Locke and his successors. He held to the doctrine of innate intellectual and moral principles, and believed in the power of reason to attain and demonstrate truths that escape the senses. Furthermore, reasoning, guided especially by the law of self-contradiction, was the only means of reaching Reality, and the demonstrable and rational character of a hypothesis was the sole criterion of its validity.

This rationalism got him into difficulty with the clergy, which at Halle, where he was teaching, was to the fore in the Pietistic revolt against the intellectualism and the dogmatism, as they were then considered, into which Lutheranism had fallen. Religion from this point of view was a matter of the heart rather than of the head, in which the claims of reason were subordinate to those of feeling and emotion, and the revelations vouchsafed the individual in his private devotions counted above any theology that consistent and scientific thinking might produce. For that matter, no one was entitled to be a theologian who had not shared in the Pietistic religious experiences which centered about conviction of sin, repentance, and conversion.

Out of this dominant sense of unworthiness, sin, and alienation from God, the Pietists evoked a morality of a puritanical sort. All forms of amusement, such as games, dancing, theater-going and the like, were condemned as worldly and ungodly. The primitive text of the Bible was taken literally as a guide to life.

Wolff's insistence that theology and morality were based upon reason and that their hypotheses and prescriptions, like those of any other science, must be demonstrated with mathematical exactness, was highly obnoxious to the Pietists. Nor did he gain favor in their eyes by delivering a eulogistic address upon "The Practical Philosophy of the Chinese," and pointing to the ethics of Confucius as testimony to the possibility of constructing a satisfactory ethics upon reason alone, without the aid of divine revelation and the experience of divine grace.

He was indeed so successfully persecuted by the Pietists that in the end he had to leave Halle for a time, and take refuge in Saxony, until he was eventually recalled to his former post by Frederick the Great, and a year or two later was installed as chancellor of the university from which he had been expelled.

Influence of Leibnitz. Wolff's own line of reasoning led him to adopt the system of Leibnitz with considerable modification. From Leibnitz' theory, suggested by the calculus, that the soul-monads and the body-monads differ only in degree, he returned to the old dualism of a difference in kind between mind and matter, echoed in a dualism of sense-experience and intellectual knowledge. In this way Wolff revived for himself the old difficulties of explaining the interaction between mind and body and between the operations of the intellect and the material provided by the senses. This perplexity he dispelled by invoking the Leibnitzian doctrine of pre-established harmony in the somewhat attenuated form of a miraculous arrangement made by God between mind and body and thought and sense. He denied, however, the inner self-sufficiency and self-justification with which Leibnitz had endowed the monads, and maintained that everything was to be explained as a *means* to the furtherance of something outside itself. In accounting for the existence and activity of objects we must look, not for that which might be useful to the thing in question, but for that in it which might be useful to other objects. Man, in his opinion, is the end to which everything else in the universe is the means.

The theory of external uses and the habit of explaining all things as means to human life and happiness pervade his whole system. In nature the inanimate is a means to the animate; the animate is a means for giving the soul a body. Philosophy itself is a means for enlightening the mind, and an enlightened mind is a means to human happiness. The universe is the means by which God reveals himself. Purpose is all pervading. The universe is designed by God and its parts are designed by him to work together. This is the reason why the universe exists and why every minutest event happens as it does. In the divinely regulated order miracles and special revelations may occur; but, if they do, they must be recognizable as part of that order and not as exceptions to it. Such was the philosophy to which Kant was at first addicted.

Chapter XIV

KANT

I. LIFE

Early Education. Immanuel Kant is the great homebody among philosophers. Of Scotch descent, he was born at Königsberg in 1724. He died at Königsberg in 1804. He lived there all his life. Nor during his whole life did he go more than forty miles from the city. He was even less traveled than Socrates, who, except as a soldier, never set foot outside of Athens. His father was a strap-maker, his family of the Pietistic persuasion. His first education was received at a Pietistic school, from which he went on to the University of Königsberg at the age of sixteen. There he had almost entirely to support himself. By the time he was twenty-two, both parents were dead, and, cut off from even such small help as they could afford to give him, he now, along with his three sisters and one brother—the survivors of nine children—had to make his own way as best he could. He was equipped with an excellent knowledge of Latin, less Greek, and a thorough training in mathematics and physics.

The next nine years he picked up a living by tutoring. Then he returned to the university, took his doctorate, and became an instructor, lecturing mainly upon physics. Finally, in 1770 he was appointed professor of logic and mathematics. This post he held till his retirement in 1797—an act inspired by the censorship to which the expression of his religious opinions, which had long since broken with his childhood faith, was subjected by the Pietistic and reactionary successor to Frederick the Great. During the last years of his life his mind appreciably failed.

Character and Habits. The regularity of his life has become a byword. He never married, and the proverbial setness of a bachelor's ways was reinforced by a methodical temperament. He was awakened at five every morning, and not once in thirty years, his servant testified, did he fail to respond to the call. He worked all the morning and dined promptly at one o'clock at a restaurant, which he varied in order to escape from the sightseers who came to stare at him after he had become the most noteworthy monument of the town. Every afternoon at four, rain or shine, followed by his manservant carrying an umbrella, he took an hour's walk, so punctually that the citizens of Königsberg, it is said, set their watches by his appearance at the door of his house. On returning, he puttered about till twilight, and then abandoned himself to meditation, gazing abstractedly at the tower of a neighboring church. Every night he went to bed before ten o'clock. Once, some fast-growing poplars in the foreground suddenly blotted the spire from sight, and the construction of the Kantian philosophy, deprived of its ecclesiastical source of inspiration, was temporarily held up till the obliging owner of the trees topped them at Kant's request.

Another mainspring of the clock-like ticking of his life was his anxiety about his health. He was not only a bachelor and excessively methodical, he was also a hypochondriac. He stuck to a prescribed and restricted diet. He was afraid of sweating. He always breathed through his nose, under the impression that nothing invited disease like an open mouth. This fussiness was not altogether foolish. He was delicate, undersized, flat-chested, with one slightly deformed shoulder. He was always a little ailing, but never really ill. Like the proverbial New Englander, he "enjoyed" bad health.

Possessed of all the moral virtues, but not in any way a prig, Kant was a man of somewhat cool affections and of nearly stone-cold esthetic sense. He had little eye for natural beauty and no ear at all for poetry and music. He was, however, a great reader, except, curiously enough, of philosophy. He knew, to be sure, his Voltaire and his Rousseau, and he was well up in contemporary British literature, secular as well as philosophical. But his knowledge of the history of philosophy in general was meager and spotty.

He was keen on geography, and loved to listen to the stories of those who traveled and to gather information from all sources about the four quarters of the globe. Politics, too, attracted him, and books on politics and the newspapers seduced him from his more serious intellectual activities, just as detective stories are said sometimes to beguile the labors of the justices of the Supreme Court. There was also a certain sprightliness in Kant's make-up that gave a sparkle to his wealth of information and helped make him an agreeable conversationalist, ever welcome in the homes of his friends. It also helped make him an admirable lecturer, able to make dry bones live.

Unfortunately, however, there is no sprightliness in his philosophic writings. They are among the driest in the annals of philosophy and

contain the hardest bones to crack. Nevertheless, the Kantian system
is one of the great monuments of philosophic achievement. No system
in the history of philosophy has had so immediately widespread and
profound an effect. The next hundred years were almost completely
dominated by it. The most significant philosophy of the nineteenth
century was inspired by it, and reveals, beneath the superficial alterations suggested by Kant's successors, its essential structure, fundamentally unchanged. It is safe to say that no one can understand
philosophy since Kant unless he knows his Kant.

II. EARLY VIEWS

Influence of Science and Mathematics and of Wolff. Kant's interest
in philosophy, however, developed out of an earlier predilection for
science and mathematics. His first writings were concerned with
physics and astronomy, and his later philosophical works were interspersed with excursions into the field of the physical sciences. Of his
scientific works, *A General Natural History and Theory of the
Heavens* (1755) is perhaps the most important, though, owing to the
failure of the publisher and lack of distribution, it remained almost
unknown. In it Kant applies Newtonian principles to the fixed stars,
develops a mechanical theory of the whole sidereal universe, and suggests for the first time the nebular hypothesis of the origin of planetary
systems. His other scientific writings ranged over such subjects as the
action of the tides on slowing up the rotation of the earth, the influence of the earth's rotation upon winds, the causes of earthquakes,
the different races of man and the beginnings of human history, the
volcanoes on the moon, and the influence of the moon upon the
weather. In his discussion of the human race, he had already developed an idea which he never abandoned, that, although the different races of man have developed from a common origin, the human
species, like all others, is fixed and has not evolved from lower forms
of life. At the same time, he speculates whether in certain circumstances the anthropoid apes might not develop human characteristics,
and thus, without change of species, attain a quasi-human level of intelligence and culture.

Kant's first philosophic views were those of Wolff, and, through
Wolff, of Leibnitz. He was thus predisposed to rationalism and to
confidence in the ability of the mind to deal with metaphysical problems. But soon these views were shaken and modified by disturbing
influences. The spirit of the Enlightenment and of the Age of Reason,

while reinforcing his rationalism, seems to have undermined the Pietism of his early training and to have converted him from an evangelical Christian into a rationalistic free thinker. But his rationalism in its turn was undermined by the skepticism of Locke and particularly of Hume. He was, as he himself said, roused by the latter from his dogmatic slumbers.

The Influence of the British Empiricists. At the same time, he found himself inclined to be as critical of the British empiricists as they had made him of Wolff and rationalism. He felt that, in spite of their desire to resolve everything into, and derive everything from, experience, they had invented a new metaphysical entity, the *mind,* which underlay and supported experience in much the same way that the spiritual and material substances they rejected supported physical qualities and mental activities. Nay more, they had attributed to mind a highly complex organization that *forced* it to behave in certain ways. It was of the *nature* of mind to perceive, to remember, to associate its impressions along certain lines, and to establish certain relations between them.

The British empiricists, then, had, in Kant's opinion, taken back with one hand what they gave with the other. They might deny innate ideas, but they ascribed to the "mind" innate predispositions to react in certain invariable ways to the experience presented to it by the senses. The mind at birth was not the blank sheet of paper they claimed it was; it was water-marked with a complicated pattern that showed through the moment experience began to write upon it. When scrutinized, the pattern looked strangely familiar. It was ingrained with everything that the empiricists denied of the external world,—with substantiality, and identity, and power, and necessary connection, and all the rest. This water-mark was not stamped upon the mind by experience; it was simply brought out by experience. It was the preliminary condition, not the result, of knowledge. Knowledge, then, was not derived from experience, except in so far as it depended upon experience for its material. It was an *a priori* activity of an entity, called *mind,* which, also, was more than the experience with which it dealt.

Critical Attitude Towards the British Empiricists. To Kant the difficulty in which the empiricists had landed themselves suggested a new idea. Suppose that experience really did have an innate structure which necessarily determined it to perceive, to think, and to feel as it did. In that case its inability to represent the nature of what lay outside it—and here Kant was willing to go the whole hog with the skeptics—would not necessarily render all truth relative and the conclusions of all science and all reasoning invalid and uncertain. Truth would still be absolute, and reason would be trustworthy, *within the realm of experience*. For, if human thinking had a fixed character, then, in all times and places, whenever and wherever it occurred, and whatever the sense-experience presented to it might be like, it would always obey the same laws, follow the same lines, and construct its world according to the same plan.

Moreover, Kant was inclined to give to our irresistible *belief* in the *existence* of a self and an external world, which was admitted by the empiricists, the same weight as Reid had attributed to it. Even if we could never know what stimulated the mind from the outside and what responded from within to that stimulation, the implication in our thinking that such a stimulus existed, and that there was something which, when stimulated, did the perceiving and the knowing, was as unescapable as the fact of experience itself. The *existence* of a perceiving and knowing *subject,* which provided the *forms* in which experience must appear, and of an *object,* which provided *material* to be experienced in those forms, was a necessary presupposition of the existence of experience and thought. Thus reason will be able to attain *certainty* rather than *probability* in dealing with the data presented to it, and will be able to assert that the content of our consciousness *must* behave as it does and *must* have the structure and the relations it exhibits. Upon these *"musts"* can be securely founded an absolute knowledge and a universally valid science of Reality *as it appears to the human mind.*

Critique of Pure Reason. This would seem to be the central idea amplified by Kant and worked out in great detail in the *Critique of Pure Reason.* His approach to it was gradual, and we can to some extent trace his development from the earlier Wolffian and rationalistic attitude, evinced in his first publications, through the influence of the British School towards his eventual position. This had been partially worked out by 1770, when he published a dissertation on the form and principles of the sensible and intelligible world. The next eleven years were devoted to perfecting it. In 1781 the *Critique of Pure Reason* was published.

Kant describes his philosophy as "transcendental." By this he means that he is not concerned with the *content* of experience but only with the *forms* or ways in which the human mind, by virtue of its constitution, is obliged to react, in perception and in thought, to any and every content the touch of an external world may stimulate within it.

whatever the nature of our sense-organs and our sensible experience. These *transcendental* forms of mental activity are also *a priori*. That is, they are not built up from experience or influenced by it, as the British empiricists maintained. On the contrary, existing independently of experience and *prior* to it, they are the agents by which experience is influenced and built up into the shape in which it is presented to us. Our question, then, becomes the problem of enumerating and describing these forms and procedures, and to this task Kant now sets himself.

III. TRANSCENDENTAL ESTHETIC. SPACE AND TIME

Space and Time "a Priori" Forms of Intuition. We begin with sensations as such. Are there, we ask ourselves, ways in which sense-experience, whatever its character and content may be, simply *must* present itself? Yes, answered Kant. No matter what our sense-experience was like, it would necessarily be smeared over *space* and drawn out in *time* by a mind constructed and geared like ours. Its episodes and events, however different they might be from those presented by the sense-organs we actually possess, would still *co-exist side by side* or *come one after another*.

Time and *space,* therefore, are not part of the *stuff* of experience. Neither are they *ideas* derived from experience. They are *a priori* forms of intuition, or, as we should say, of *perception*. Their study is the study of what Kant calls *transcendental esthetic,* using the term "esthetic" in its original Greek meaning of that which pertains to sensation. Space is the form of the *external sense,* or in other words, of our perception of outer objects; time, of the *internal sense,* or of our perception of the flow of our consciousness.

At the same time Kant is careful to point out that space and time are wholly relative to *our* type of mind. Conceivably, beings outfitted with another type might not "intuit" and perceive spatially and temporally, but in some other way. Moreover, since these forms are relative to our kind of mind, we have no right to extend them beyond our experience and to predicate them of the external world. For that matter, there is nothing in sensible experience that can give us any hint of the nature of things as they are in themselves.

The Synthetic Activities of the Perceiving Subject. Just, however, as the fact that there is sensible experience suggests the existence, though it does not reveal the nature, of something external to ourselves, so the spatial and temporal forms in which experience is presented suggest the existence and the activity of a perceiving subject, though they give us no hint of what that subject is like. Already, in the smeared, successive, spatial and temporal manner of "intuiting" or perceiving, we catch it preparing to unite and join together and *synthesize* sense data and to make of them a single whole.

We may, then, suspect that the prime function of the perceiving and knowing subject is to make *one* consistent world out of the manifold of sense impressions. This suspicion will be confirmed, and the nature and conditions of the activity of synthesizing and unifying will be more completely grasped, by an examination of the operations of *knowledge,* to which we now pass.

It is these operations that give significance to the spatio-temporal content of experience. Our sense-perceptions would remain meaningless unless they were further worked over. On the other hand, without percepts the mind would have nothing to think about, and there would be no *knowledge.* "Thoughts without content are empty, intuitions [perceptions] without concepts are blind. Therefore it is equally necessary to make our concepts sensuous, i.e., to add to them their object in intuition, as it is to make our intuitions intelligible, i.e., to bring them under concepts. These two powers or faculties cannot exchange their functions. The understanding cannot see. The senses cannot think. By their union only can knowledge be produced." [1]

IV. TRANSCENDENTAL LOGIC

Transcendental Analytic and Dialectic. The study of the mechanism and operations of the understanding is called by Kant *transcendental logic.* Whatever we are thinking about, be it sensible representations or intelligible concepts, our thought has an *a priori* structure of its own which it expresses in its reasoning. Transcendental logic is the investigation of this structure. It has two divisions, *transcendental analytic* and *transcendental dialectic.* The former is a search for the *a priori* structure of the understanding, and the "principles without which no object can be thought." The latter deals with the tendency of the mind to regard its structure as the structure not only of thought but of external *being.* We believe that the categories by which we unify experience, as, for example, substance and accident, unity and plurality, cause and effect, and interaction, apply also to things as they are in themselves. Because we cannot *think* these things in any

[1] In the discussion that follows the quotations are from *Critique of Pure Reason* (trans. Max Müller, 2nd ed.).

other way we conclude that they cannot *exist* in any other way. To conclude however, that things cannot exist in themselves except as they exist in thought is to fall into illusion, and is to turn logic into a semblance of metaphysics, or, as Kant calls it, a *dialectic*.

This tendency to turn the ways of the mind into metaphysical entities existing outside the mind is reinforced by the fact that we can say beforehand that experience cannot contradict the laws of logic and be *true*. But that does not mean that the laws and categories of correct thinking force all logically true propositions to hold true of experience as well. They may, indeed, be contradicted by experience. For example, the proposition "apples are blue" is, formally and logically, a true proposition. Still, the logical possibility of blue apples does not force us, or even enable us, to grow apples of that color in our orchards.

Although, then, the content of experience must be capable of being logically arranged and cannot exhibit logical self-contradictions, it need not exhibit everything that is logically consistent. What the *stuff* of experience is like can be determined only by consulting experience. But, if the mind cannot even use its categories and laws to determine what the sensible manifold of its experience shall be like, how much less can it use them to determine what the things-in-themselves which provoke this sensible manifold are like! It is the task of *transcendental dialectic* to point out the folly of trying to transform what is true of an object so far as we are concerned into something true of the object as it is apart from us and in itself, and to explain, criticize, and curb the mind's "sophistical illusion" of ability to extend knowledge beyond experience and to know things as they are in themselves.

V. TRANSCENDENTAL ANALYTIC

The Categories of Thought. Let us now proceed to the analysis of the mind's structure undertaken by *transcendental analytic*. The mind's mental activity of synthesizing and unifying experience expresses itself in *judgments* about sense data. These judgments follow certain fixed lines and assume certain fixed forms. We may assert *quantity, quality, relations,* and *conditions of existence,* or *modality,* of everything that occurs in the sensible manifold. Each one of these four forms of judgment is moreover a trinity. For instance, in asserting quantity we state that what we are dealing with is either *one* or *many,* or one aggregate or *totality* of many constituents. In our qualitative judgments, we make positive (*real*) statements, or *negative* statements, or cautious, *limited* statements about things. Again, our assertions of relation fall under three heads. We say one thing is the property of another, thus putting the two things in the relation of *substance* and *accident;* or we say one thing is the *cause* or the *effect* of another; or we say that co-existent things act upon and react to one another (*reciprocity* or *community*). Finally, we make statements regarding the conditions or *modality* of a thing's existence. We say "such and such is *possible;* such and such is *impossible;* this *exists* or this does *not exist;* this could not be otherwise and is *necessary,* or this might be otherwise and is therefore *contingent."*

These four trinities, making in all twelve fundamental concepts or Categories, exhaust the entire machinery of syntheses. Everything that occurs in the sensible manifold falls under some one of them. We are *obliged* to think in these terms. But that obligation is not imposed upon us by the content of experience. It expresses *a priori* and *transcendental* necessities of thought inherent in the structure of the knowing apparatus. These ways of thinking are then *pure categories of the understanding.* It is the synthesizing by the Categories of the manifold of sense-experience "intuited" under the forms of space and time that turns it from an irrational and chaotic welter of sensations into an intelligible and orderly world of interrelated objects.

The Necessity of Gearing Sensible with Intellectual Operations. But how does this synthesis take place? The Categories are the source neither of the existence nor the nature of the sensible manifold. The ways in which we understand things are not responsible for there being anything to understand. Nor is the sensible manifold in itself in any way the source of, or responsible for, the intelligible form given it by the mind. How then can the Categories and the sensible manifold ever get together? Where is their meeting-point, and how can they intercommunicate if and where they do meet? To answer these questions we must consider in some detail the unifying operations of the mind. Then, after we have shown how the mind constructs an intelligible and orderly world out of the sensible manifold, we can go on to show up the self-contradictions and errors into which we fall when we seek to bring the Categories into contact with things-in-themselves and to regard the ways in which Reality must appear to us because of the peculiar constitution of our particular type of mind, as ingrained in its nature as well.

VI. UNIFYING OPERATIONS OF THE MIND

The Transformation of Sense-Perception into Objects. The connecting up of the mind machine with the sensible manifold is called by Kant the *Deduction of the Pure Concepts of the Understanding.* If, he says, we examine the sensible manifold we discover at once a fact of fundamental significance. Being given in space and time, experience is not presented in isolated bits. It is given in chunks of co-existent and enduring percepts. In other words, there is no datum of experience that is not a manifold, and that therefore is not a conjoining or, we might say, a *synthesis* of elements. Still, since these syntheses are decomposable into constituent elements and are therefore "constructions" built up out of sensible stuff, they cannot be accounted for by experience itself. They represent a reaching down of the synthetic activity of the mind into experience, and are the results of *apprehension* working on the level of sense-perception.

These sensible syntheses are remembered and associated and imaged, and their recurrence in sense-perception recalls analogous "manifolds" intuited at other times and places. In this way the manifold of sense is transformed into a manifold of *"imagination"* in which invariable sequences and co-existences and other relations now appear. Stable and enduring "images" are abstracted from the procession of appearing and disappearing percepts. *Objects,* or steady and reliable syntheses of experience, are constructed, and are distinguished from haphazard and "subjective" experiences. Since this unifying of sense data into objects has to take place within the frame of space and time, physical objects are represented as *extended,* shaped, impenetrable by one another, etc., or, in other words, as *bodies.* Sense-experience now becomes a sensible *world.* But this *reproduction,* as Kant calls it, of sense-experience by the imagination is not the product of that experience. It is another manifestation of the *a priori* and *transcendental activity of apprehension.*

"The Transcendental Unity of Apperception." Again, in thus unifying the manifold of sense-experience into a single, organized world, the mind is betraying and displaying its own oneness. For only a single, unified mind could recognize its experience as one and the same coherent content of consciousness. This unifying principle binding together consciousness is not derived from experience but is a necessary presupposition of our ability to synthesize the manifold of sense into an intelligible whole. Kant calls it *the transcendental unity of apperception.*

In unifying all the representations of experience, the subject is also *conscious* of its own unity. In fact, the mind could not make one experience and one world of the manifold of sense-perceptions unless it at the same time were conscious of its own oneness and self-identity. Self-consciousness, therefore, and the consciousness of a unified, intelligible world go together.

However, self-consciousness is not consciousness of that which does the perceiving and the knowing. It is consciousness of that which is known. In the act of self-consciousness the self becomes an object to itself. Therefore, just as I know external objects, not as they are in themselves, but as they are presented to me colored and formed by the kind of mental apparatus I possess, so I know myself, not as I really am in myself, but as I am presented to my real or *transcendental ego,* the knowing subject, after being worked over and reformulated by the machinery of that same apparatus. In short, what the knowing subject is really like in itself is just as unknowable as the real natures of the things it perceives.

We have now partially examined the mechanism by which the mind works over the sensible manifold and makes a world of it. But we are as far as ever from discovering the point of contact and communication between the sensible manifold and the mental processes. These processes must have some affinity with sense-experience in order to get hold of it, and, on the other hand, sense-experience must have some affinity with them that makes of it a stuff with which the mind can work. The search for this affinity now becomes Kant's chief problem.

VII. THE SCHEMATA

The object of his search, Kant finds in space and time. Images, he tells us, like sensible percepts, are presented under the forms of space and time and therefore have a form as well as a content. This purely spatial and temporal form may be abstracted from their particular content. But, taken the other way round, such a form represents the concept of the thing submitted to spatial and temporal conditions. This form is not a *pure* concept since it is still outlined in space and is therefore outlined in a *particular* way. Nevertheless, it is a *general* representation, which holds good, like the concept, for all the objects of a given class. It is *conceptual* because it is a universal, emptied of all particular content, but it is *sensible* because it is an *outline* presented in space and time. This outline is called by Kant a *schema*, and, hovering as it does midway between the pure concept and the sensible particular by virtue of possessing the characteristics of both, it affords the point of contact and communication between the operations of the intellect and the presentations of sensible experience.

Kant enumerates a few of these *schemata* by way of illustration. The Category of *quantity* appears under the forms of space and time as the schema of *number,* which represents simply "the successive addition of one to one," without taking any account of the particular contents or natures of the units so manipulated. The Category of *reality* is "schematized" by the image of filled time, without reference to what fills it; of *negation* by the image of time thinned out and emptied of content in general, either in part or whole. *Substance* finds its schema in the representation of time as always full notwithstanding the changes that occur in the character of its filling. *Cause* is represented by the invariable successions that occur in the manifold, *reciprocity,* or *community,* by the invariable behavior of the elements of the manifold when occurring together. *Possibility* and *impossibility* appear as the inability of opposites to apply simultaneously, and their ability to apply successively, to the same object. The *necessary* is that which appears at all times.

<h3 style="text-align:center">VIII. ANALYTIC AND SYNTHETIC JUDGMENTS</h3>

Universality of Analytic Judgments. Having thus brought the sensible manifold and the Categories of the Understanding into contact, Kant proceeds to a discussion of the activity of judgment, the exercise of which with respect to perceptual experience this contact makes possible. Judgments are of two sorts, *analytic,* which analyze a concept and affirm or deny of it only that which is already contained in or excluded from it; and *synthetic,* which add to a given concept something that is not given or necessarily implied in it.

The truth of an analytic judgment is, Kant tells us, easily determined by the law of self-contradiction. Nothing can be part of the concept of a thing that contradicts that concept, and everything must be true of it that is logically implied by its definition. But absence of self-contradiction does not establish the truth of synthetic as it does that of analytic propositions. The truth of synthetic propositions has to be tested by a further requirement of conformity to the content of experience.

But in that case how can synthetic propositions establish *universal* truths even within experience itself? All positive truth about experience must apparently be drawn *a posteriori* from an observation of its actual content, whereas the actual content of experience open to our observation is limited and interrupted. No one of us should be able to argue regarding the nature of even the phenomenal world further than his particular experience of it carries him.

Kant attacks the problem as follows. We are agreed that if universal synthetic propositions about experience are true, they must be applicable *a priori* to all *possible* experience that might be presented to the mind. Any so-called law of nature, for example, that is *universally* valid must be applicable, not only to our particular section of space and time, but to *all* phenomena throughout infinite time and space.

The Structure of Experience. Has, then, experience as such any characteristics in the absence of which it would cease to be *experience?* If it has, we can lay down certain conditions of all *possible* experience. Kant thinks that such characteristics exist. Unless experience were *coherent* and *intelligible,* it would relapse into a "meaningless rhapsody of sensations," more *unreal* than dreams and hallucinations, to which the term "experience" would not apply. All possible *experience,* or, at any rate, all possible *real experience,* must be articulated and intelligible.

But what is it that gives coherency and *reality* to experience and therefore makes *real experience* possible? Precisely the same structure as determines how the mind shall think. The possibility of experiencing a world and the possibility of thinking or understanding a world are one and the same possibility. Nothing can be conceived which it is formally impossible to perceive, and conversely nothing can be perceived which it is impossible to form a concept of. Experience, in order to be even *possible, must* be so constituted that we are able to assert *a priori* the existence of "things" throughout its entire breadth and length; to know *a priori* that at all times and places things will be before or after, below or above, to the right or the left, of one another; to have *a priori* certainty that they will possess size, shape, number, and sensible qualities which may be predicated of them; that they will have causes and produce effects; and so on and so on. Hence, universal synthetic judgments *a priori* can be made of *all* experience, and may therefore be objectively true, in that they give us real knowledge of how the content of experience, whatever it may be like, *must* be constituted.

IX. NECESSARY CHARACTERISTICS OF ALL POSSIBLE EXPERIENCE

Characteristics of Experience. If now we turn to that content, what are the characteristics that may be universally predicated of it? In the first place, it is *axiomatic* that all experience must be *extensive* in character. It is a totality of co-existent parts or qualities placed side by side, and presented all together at the same moment. Furthermore, any quality of experience may vary in *degree* and intensity. We can therefore have a universally true objective knowledge that in all times and places the content of experience will have not only *extensive* but *intensive* magnitude.

Furthermore both co-extensive and intensive experience are continuous, since any space, however large or small, is divisible into nothing but spaces, and any time, however long or short, is divisible into nothing but times. So, too, *intensive quantity* is continuous, since it is impossible to have in the gradation from presence to absence any gap in which the quality in question is not present, and present to the degree that fits in between the next higher and the next lower amount of intensity. It is this continuity in the combinations of the manifold of phenomena that gives us the idea of a *whole* as contrasted with that of an *aggregate*. A "whole" is produced by the uninterrupted continuation of synthetic activity. An "aggregate" is the result of momentary, repeated acts of combination.

Time is a *permanent* form in which the sensible manifold is presented as successive and changing. Its permanence is experienced as a certain durability in phenomena underlying their alterations in time, or, we might say, as a *substance* which endures, while its *modes* or *accidents* change.

Temporal Sequence Irreversible and Causal. Temporal succession, though it may be conceived or even pictured as reversed, is always *experienced* as irreversible. It *must* be so experienced if experience is to be an orderly and intelligible *experience* and not insanity. Furthermore, a merely higgledy-piggledy succession of events, even if it were never thrown into reverse, could not constitute anything we could call *experience*.

All possible experience must also be so constructed that certain events can only occur in it after others, and that therefore to reach event B, whatever it is, I *must* first pass through event A, whatever it is, and *cannot* reach A by first passing through B. In that case, we can say that A is the *necessary condition* or *cause* of the occurrence of B. *Causality,* being a form in which any sensible manifold *must* appear to the human mind, will hold true of everything that any human being at any time or place *can* perceive. Portions of our experience, however, can be apprehended in a reversible order and such portions exhibit *co-existence.* Indeed, the condition of co-existence is *ability* to reverse and alter the order in which its parts are presented; just as the condition of causation is *inability* so to do.

Spatial Experiences. Co-existence is as necessary a condition of all possible human experience as sequence and causality, since a sensible manifold in which it was impossible to pass to and fro from part to part would be just as incoherent and crazy as one whose temporal sequences suddenly reversed themselves, and whose events did not *necessarily* always follow one another in the same order. To the one as to the other the term *experience* could not properly be applied.

Furthermore, the elements of the manifold of a sane *experience* must interact, or, as Kant calls it, "commune." Nor can there be any action at a distance. The ties that bind events together must be continuous. Without these interconnecting ties phenomena would fall apart, and our experience of them would not be a continuous passage from one to another, but would occur in disconnected flashes which had nothing to do with one another. Substances, therefore, "must stand in dynamical communion, immediately or mediately, with each other, if their co-existence is to be known in any possible experience." Without *reciprocity* the manifold of sense could not become even stuff for a sensible *world*.

The Conditions of Possible, Real and Necessary Experience. There remain only the *modal* Categories of *possibility, reality,* and *necessity* to be considered. To be *possible,* experience must be, first of all, free from self-contradiction. Secondly, it must be consistent with the construction of space, which is a form under which all objective reality and possible *things* must appear.

To assert objective *reality* of a phenomenon, the phenomenon must be *perceptible* as well as conceivable, since "perception, which supplies the material of a concept, is the only characteristic of reality." At the same time, reality may be attributed to things as yet unperceived, provided these possible perceptions "hang together with some other perceptions according to the principles of their empirical connection." Hence "it is possible . . . even before the perception of a thing and . . . in a certain sense, *a priori,* to know its existence." On this fact rests our ability to make valid predictions regarding the future.

We pass now to the modal Category of *necessity.* Although all objects of possible or real experience are *necessary,* their necessity is determined neither by logic nor by any *a priori* nature of experience itself. Qualities could be combined in substances otherwise than they are, and substances could co-exist otherwise than they do, without running foul of either the law of self-contradiction or the conditions of possible experience. However, the sensible manifold, if it is to be *experience* and not mere madness, *must* have reasons for the particular arrangement and succession of its elements. These reasons are necessitated by *the law of causality,* which forces experience to behave as it does and occur in the sequences and connections we perceive. To be sure, what is the cause of what, and what the effect of what, can only be ascertained by observation. But we can *know* that every event has a cause and will have an effect, for, if things happened without causes and did not produce effects, "there would not even be such a thing as nature." We can, therefore, rule out *a priori* the occurrence both of chance and of "blind" necessity in the world. Everything that happens is *necessary* and that necessity is the condition of *intelligibility.*

Knowledge and Science Based on Experience. Since, then, the human mind has a fixed constitution, which determines what human experience *must* be like in all times and places, nature *must* be uniform throughout, and natural laws must be universally valid. Hence we can make universal synthetic propositions, and hence the *scientific* study of nature as a whole and *scientific* prediction of future events are fruitful and reliable. It goes without saying that science, like all knowledge, cannot transcend experience or make statements about anything but experience. But it can make absolutely and universally true statements about it.

The questions whether the field of possible existence is larger than that of real existence, and the field of real existence larger than that of necessary existence, Kant dismisses as interesting but unimportant. Even if there were other possible, non-spatial and temporal forms of perceiving and forms, other than our Categories, of making experience intelligible, they would be unintelligible to us and could never belong to our experience. We are only concerned with existence as it is for us and there we find the distinctions between the possible, the real, and the necessary largely academic.

X. THE NOUMENA

Noumena and Phenomena Differentiated. We are now confronted with a perplexing idiosyncrasy of thought. Although its Categories receive all their content from perceptual experience and cannot be extended beyond experience, nevertheless the mind persists in constructing out of experience an order of objects of thought and knowledge which transcends the objects of sense, and is possessed of an intelligible *content*. The mind regards them, not as its thoughts about sensible phenomena, but as non-sensible, intelligible *things* about which it is thinking and to which its concepts apply. Since these intelligible *things* are not presented to empirical or sense-experience, he calls them *noumena,* which is the Greek equivalent for intelligible object, as opposed to *phenomena,* which are given in sense-perception. We have now to ask what is their status and how the mind happens to construct them.

Being concepts of the mind they cannot exist independently of the mind. Nor can they have an *intelligible* content with which the mind is directly acquainted, since the only mental *content* is sense-experience, and all concepts are of sensible things. Nor, again, is there any such thing, in *human* experience, at any rate, as a *non*-sensuous *perception* or *intuition* of a *non*-sensuous object.

At the same time, the *noumena* are not fictions pure and simple, but have a basis in fact. The *existence* of a manifold of sense-experience *is not* due to the mind, although the *nature* of that manifold *is* derived from our particular kind of sense-organs, our spatial and temporal forms of perception, and the categories in which we think. Hence the mind, recognizing the external *origin* of experience, tends to think that experience itself must exist independently of our sense-perceptions.

Phenomena Conceived as Merely Existent. But independently of those perceptions a phenomenon can only be *conceived* as a bare something, stripped of all sensible qualities, but nevertheless still a *thing* capable of being "intuited" or perceived. Since, however, we can think of such a bare "something," we can *think* of the noumenon as *existent* (which does not mean that it actually exists), in spite of the fact that we can neither perceive nor form any concept of its nature.

Noumena, however, add nothing to our knowledge. They indicate rather the limit to which knowledge can go and where it must stop. All we can know of things-as-they-are-in-themselves is that they *exist*. What they are like *must* remain forever unknown because of those very conditions that make human knowledge possible within the realm of experience. The upshot of the whole matter is that "a real division of objects into phenomena and noumena and of the world into a sensible and intelligible world is . . . quite inadmissible," since noumena are not objects for thought, and an intelligible world without a sensible content is meaningless.

XI. THE IDEAS OF PURE REASON AND TRANSCENDENTAL DIALECTIC

Existence of Unifying Principles. However, the mind does not accept its limitations and is not content to conceive merely the *existence* of things-in-themselves. It seeks to conceive their *nature*—or, in other words, to fit them into the Categories that determine the ways of its thinking. But these Categories are only applicable to and valid for things, not as they are in themselves, but as they appear to us through sense-experience.

Furthermore, the mind is driven by its nature to synthesize and unify whatever it deals with. Science does this by reducing sensible phenomena to terms of the Categories, and thus *understanding* them. But the mind does not stop here. It attempts to unify into higher all-embracing unities the syntheses introduced by the Categories. In so doing it operates on a new level, above that of understanding—the level, as Kant calls it, of *pure reason,* and the absolute and ultimate unities it tries to establish are termed *Ideas of Pure Reason.*

The Soul, the Universe, and God. Since our world displays three aspects—a thinking and perceiving subject, which perceives and thinks under certain *a priori* forms of intuition and categories of thought; a world of phenomena intuited and known under these forms and categories; and, finally, just the existence of objects of thought in general—reason will strive to introduce absolute unity into each of these factors. So it is that we find reason in search of a *soul,* as the unifying ground of the activities of the mind; of a *universe* of simple indivisible substances causally and reciprocally interconnected, as the unifying ground of phenomena; and of a *Supreme Being* or First Cause as the unifying ground of all thinking subjects and all objects of thought. But such unifying grounds and explanations cannot be found *within* the activities of thought, in the manifold of phenomena or the field of objects in general, of which they are supposed to be the least common denominators. Hence reason, in its work of higher synthesis, tends to project into the realm of things-in-themselves the ultimate unities it tries to produce in experience and tends to regard them as ideas corresponding to ultimate entities *existing outside the realm of experience altogether.*

This projection, however, is even more illegitimate than the tendency of the mind to apply the Categories beyond the realm of sense-perception. The Categories, at least, are displayed in and supported by the sensible world, but experience exhibits no such unities as reason is endeavoring to establish. On the contrary, the experienced world conspicuously lacks them, and the mere fact that reason *must* try to accomplish these all-embracing syntheses is no guarantee that they actually exist beyond experience. Nor is there any warrant for believing that more unity prevails among things-in-themselves than reason can introduce into the experienced world.

The *Ideas of Pure Reason* are then purely *ideals,* and, recognized as such, they are useful lines along which to proceed in seeking to introduce the maximum unity possible into the work of the Categories on the sensible manifold. But as ideals supposed to be realized outside the sphere of the understanding and of experience in a world of things-in-themselves they are unjustifiable and unfruitful.

The Function of Transcendental Dialectic. It is the business of *transcendental dialectic* to expose the *transcendental illusion* that counterparts of the Ideas of Pure Reason necessarily exist, by pointing out the difficulties and self-contradictions in which this illusion involves us. We begin with the attempt to unify mental activities by means of the Idea of the *soul.* The difficulties in which this Idea lands us are called by Kant the *paralogisms* (or faulty conclusions) of *pure reason.*[2]

XII. THE PARALOGISMS OF PURE REASON

The Soul as an Immortal Substance. The Idea of the soul is derived from the fact that all experience and thinking, whatever it may be of or about, is *self*-conscious—which gives rise to the hope and the illusion that the *self* can dissociate itself from both its internal and external experiences and the Categories under which it thinks them, and know itself as a separate object, and for what it is in itself. But as we saw, in discussing the *transcendental unity of apperception,* I can only understand myself in terms of the same Categories as enable me to understand all other things. *Self*-consciousness is subject to the *a priori* and necessary conditions of all possible experience. Therefore, I can only know myself as a substance, as simple, as self-identical and personal—a knowledge which suggests to me that I may be immaterial and immortal, and that, as Berkeley maintained, the stuff of the sensible manifold originates *within* the mind. Unfortunately, however, as we also know, such knowledge does not catch the "I" that does the

[2] Cf. pp. 341-405 (M. M. pp. 279-327).

thinking. It only catches a "me," which is not the "I" as it is in itself, but merely as it must represent itself to itself. None of the Categories can be applied to it as it is in itself.

For instance, the *soul* is not a substance, since "substances" are organizations of "intuited" or perceived sensations. Even if it could be so described, we could come to no conclusions regarding its immortality, since there is nothing in the notion of substance to guarantee permanence and indestructibility. Objects are only verifiably permanent and indestructible for the length of time they happen to endure and survive in the sensible manifold.

Simplicity of the Soul. So too, the *simplicity* of the soul is not given in experience, nor have we any warrant for attributing it, or any other characteristic, to the soul as it *is* in itself. The "unity of apperception" we experience can no more assure us that the soul in itself is simple, than that the external substances apperceived as one and single are so in themselves.

Nor would the "simplicity" of the soul differentiate it in any way from matter. For all we know, matter in itself may be simple. It may be even conscious. All we can say is that the soul is not a body and not spatial. But it does not follow that a distinction exists between soul and body, or between the spatial and the non-spatial, in the world of things-in-themselves.

The Soul as Self-Identical and Personal. The attempt to predicate self-identity and personality of the soul also goes on the rocks. Self-identity is implied in the "unity of apperception," which makes my experience hang together in time, and makes it *my* experience. But I can no more transfer the coherence and identity of my *experience* to the soul than I can transfer to it other experienced qualities. Moreover, such self-identity would be a purely private affair. I could never *demonstrate* it to you or anyone else. But what cannot be demonstrated to anybody else's satisfaction can scarcely be said to be known as true even of all *experience*. There is, then, no way of proving the soul to be self-identical.

Nor is there any way of knowing that the soul is a single person. To be sure, I represent myself to myself as one and the same person from moment to moment. But this representation might conceivably be passed on from one thinking subject to another. There might be momentary thinking subjects, each one of which remembered what the other had experienced. In that case, the content of consciousness might be handed from one to another of a plurality of perceivers, and any one personal self-consciousness might be the child of many fathers.

The Soul and Material Objects. The idealistic argument that the existence of an external world is doubtful is also faulty. The existence of outer objects is no more doubtful than my own existence. Both I myself and the external world are known only as phenomena, not as things-in-themselves. What their existence as things-in-themselves is like we have no means of knowing. Idealism and realism are equally illegitimate as descriptions of things-in-themselves.

Nor can we ever solve the problem of the dependence or independence of the mind on the body, since such a solution would necessitate an extension of knowledge beyond the sphere in which knowledge is possible. This leaves the solution a matter of unsupported faith, but of a faith that conversely cannot be disproved.

So far as the interaction of mind and matter is concerned, the same criticisms hold good. Here, too, the *pros* and *cons* are equally invalid if asserted dogmatically. They both treat of matter in terms, not of a phenomenon, but of a thing-in-itself. Of the nature of the relations of the "I" to other things-in-themselves we can know nothing, assert nothing, and deny nothing. In a word, we have no right to extend to the realm of things-in-themselves the distinction between the ego's representation of itself as a soul and its representation of its other experiences as external bodies. In that realm there may be no dualism.

So much for the impossibility of ever knowing what the soul is really like, and what the real conditions of its existence are. We pass now to the second great illusion of reason, that we can know the real nature of the external, physical world as it is in itself and find its unifying principle. The vanity of this attempt is shown up by what Kant calls the *Antinomies of Pure Reason*.[3]

XIII. THE ANTINOMIES OF PURE REASON

The First Antinomy. Let us suppose that besides the experience we *call* an external world, there really *is* an external universe of material "objects." That universe obviously must be conceived as either infinite or finite in time and space. But if we conceive time as infinite, then an infinite past has been *completed* and brought to an end at the present moment. A past, however, that has been brought to an end is finite. Therefore the universe has a past which is both finite and infinite—which is a contradiction in terms. Hence the universe cannot be infinite in time.

Take now its spatial infinity. To be spatially infinite the universe

[3] Cf. pp. 426-571 (M. M. pp. 344-363).

must be temporally infinite as well, since an infinite space is a space that takes infinite time to traverse. Hence infinite space is involved in the self-contradiction of infinite time and the universe cannot be spatially infinite.

But a universe limited and finite in space and time is no less self-contradictory, for an absolute beginning to time or end to space would mean that the universe is limited by *nothing*. But limitation by nothing is self-contradictory and inconceivable. Hence the universe *must* be conceived as unlimited and infinite.

The Second Antinomy. The *second Antinomy* is that of the necessity of conceiving "material" objects both as infinitely *divisible* and as compounded ultimately of *indivisible* parts—which is a self-contradiction in thought.

The Third Antinomy. The *third Antinomy* has to do with causation. On the one hand, it is impossible to conceive of any first link in the chain of causation, since the Category of causation forces the mind to think of every event as preceded and explained by another event. On the other hand, we *must* conceive the chain as having a first link, for, if no *first* cause exists, there is no sufficient reason for the causal series, which is left without any ground for occurring as it does.

Again, since a first cause of this sort would be causeless, it would be an inexplicable event, undetermined by another event to exist, to have the nature it has, and to produce the effects it does. It will just occur spontaneously and act *freely*. But how can an event that is absolutely unaccountable and inexplicable in itself be invoked with any consistency to account for other things? An inexplicable explanation is no explanation. It follows that we cannot conceive a causeless or *first* cause standing at the beginning of the series of causes and effects. It is, then, as logically impossible as it is logically necessary to assert its existence.

The Fourth Antinomy. Still, and we come now to the *fourth Antinomy*—there must be some *necessity* for the existence and the particular nature of the phenomenal world—some compelling reason for the presence rather than the absence of this kind of world, or of any world at all. This reason, since there can be no reason for its being otherwise, *must* be what it is.

But the existence of such a reason is inconceivable. If we conceive it as the first link of a causal series, it is open to all the objections, just set forth, to the existence of such a cause. If we can conceive it as the totality of phenomenal existence, we are confronted with the fact that just as any particular event need not logically be what it is, but might be otherwise, so the totality of events might logically be different from what it is, and is not itself necessary.

Finally, if we try to think of the necessary condition of the existence of a physical world as itself outside the world, we are trying to think the impossible. For, unless the phenomenal universe had been created *at a given time* the creative principle could never have been *outside* the world-process. It would have been always a part of the world-process, a causeless first link of the causal chain. Still, if we suppose the physical universe to have been called into being *at some time* by an *outside* factor, then this factor must have existed *before* the world was, and again becomes a first cause, subject to all the disabilities thereof. A necessary object or event is inconceivable. Hence, with equally good reason, the physical universe both must have and cannot have a reason why it exists and is what it is.

The Solution of the Antinomies. The *Antinomies,* Kant continues, spring from an improper extension of the term "totality" beyond the limits set to its meaning by experience. Totality is not a concept applicable to the phenomenal world. It is one of the guiding ideals into complete conformity with which reason, for all its efforts, can never bring experience. We cannot effect an actual, all-embracing *synthesis* of past, present, and future, since the content of time is a process of accretion to the end of which we never come. Therefore, although we can have an *idea* of totality, we cannot predicate an *existent* wholeness even of the phenomenal order, not to speak of predicating it of things-in-themselves.

Once rid of this mistaken attribution of totality to experience, the *Antinomies* are easily solved. Since the phenomenal world is never complete, we cannot determine whether its totality is limited or unlimited. Nor can we determine from experience whether the parts which go to make up that totality are or are not infinitely divisible. The sensible world is neither finite nor infinite but merely *indefinite* in extent and duration. It is divisible neither into a finite nor an infinite number of parts but simply into an *indeterminable* number of constituents. It exhibits causal connections which determine the time and place of its component events, but its order is also an expression of things as they are in themselves, which is not governed by the Category of physical causation, and may therefore be an expression of a *free* causality interpenetrating the necessary order of physical causation. So, too, the contingent character of the events of experience, no one of which is *logically* implied or necessitated by its antecedents, might

go hand-in-hand with a necessary *logical* determination of the nature
and order of these events by the things-in-themselves.

His solution of the *third Antinomy* has, Kant believes, an important
bearing upon the problem of human free-will. Man has not only an
empirical character; he is also a thing-in-itself. In so far as he is a
member of the phenomenal order, his acts, like all natural events, are
subject to the laws of causation. But his acts, like all natural events,
are also *freely* determined by his nature as a thing-in-itself, or as Kant
calls it, by his *intelligible character*.

We can see this *free* causation at work in the way reason deals with
the universe. The activities of reason are not determined by the natural
order. On the contrary, they seek to conform the natural order to an
ideal order which we, as rational beings, feel *ought* to exist. This
ceaseless attempt to superimpose our rational ideals on experience does
actually modify experience. Without it the phenomenal world could
not have the significance it has. Reason does, then seem to introduce
something extra and novel into the temporal series. But the modifications it brings about in experience have no antecedent causes in foregoing occurrences. They appear in experience as uncaused events, introduced from the outside into the temporal and causal sequence of
phenomena, and determined by the nature of reason alone. Hence the
causality of reason appears, in its relation to the temporal and necessary connection of events, as *free* and *undetermined* causation. Why
reason determines itself as it does, and has the nature and the ideals
it has, is an insoluble problem.

XIV. THE IDEAL OF PURE REASON. GOD

The Existence of God Undemonstrable. We come now to the attempt reason makes to demonstrate the existence and to determine the
nature of an ultimate Reality from which both the soul and the universe spring and upon which all things depend. Its ideal is to attain
and to comprehend a Supreme Being, a God.

The idea of God Kant calls the *Transcendental Ideal of Pure Reason*.[4] He calls it an *Ideal* rather than *Idea,* because it transcends Ideas
like the soul and the universe, just as they transcend the Categories of
The Understanding which apply to experience. Its object is not only
beyond experience, but, unlike the existence of the soul and the universe, is not even thought of in terms suggested by experience. On the
contrary, it is supposed to exist independently of the conditions under

---

[4] Cf. pp. 567-704 (M. M. pp. 459-654).

which experience exists, and is in no wise describable by them. Space and time are not forms of its existence; nor can we confine it within the Categories. It is conceived as the ground of all possible being, and therefore cannot be conceived, as the soul or the universe might be conceived, as capable of non-existence. For how can I make an absolute negation of what I conceive to be the ground of all existence whatsoever, unless I have in my mind the idea of such an absolutely existing being whose very essence is to exist?

So far so good. But there is a great difference between asserting that God cannot be *conceived* except as existing and asserting that because we must *think* of him as existent he must therefore *exist independent of our conception of him.* Once more, we are dealing with an illusion, the greatest of all illusions entertained by pure reason, that the existence of God is demonstrable.

The Ontological Argument. How illusory such a hope is may be shown by an examination of the arguments used by the theologians. Take, for example, the famous "ontological argument" that since the concept of an *ens realissimum,* or all-perfect being, involves the notion of necessary existence, such a being must exist. To this Kant replies that, in the first place, we cannot predicate necessity of anything, even of Reality itself, since the existence of any and every subject together with its predicates can be denied without self-contradiction.

Moreover, all judgments involving existence, Kant continues, are synthetic, and add to the concept something not logically necessitated by it. Hence since the opposite of *any* synthetic judgment is logically possible, and since *any* synthetic judgment can be denied without logical self-contradiction, the proposition "God exists" may be denied without contradiction. There is nothing self-contradictory in saying "God, who must be *defined* as a necessarily existent being, does not necessarily exist."

Furthermore, *existence is not a predicate or a property.* It adds nothing to any concept. It merely determines the relation of the concept to experience. Concepts enacted in the world of experience are concepts of existent objects. The conceived dollar has as many pennies in it as the dollar in my pocket. In or out of circulation, its definition is the same. If putting the dollar in my pocket changed the value of the dollar, then either my idea of the possible dollar is defective and does not define the real dollar, or else the dollar in my pocket is not what I thought a dollar was. In a word, existence is not conceived; it is not an idea. It is perceived; it is an experienced fact.

The Cosmological Argument. The so-called cosmological proof of God's existence, which argues from the existence of the world to a *necessary cause* of the world, improperly argues that the cause *necessarily* exists, and thus identifies it with the *ens realissimum* and exposes it to the objections we have just noted as well as to all the objections against the idea of a first cause. Again, contingency and necessity are valid concepts only *within* the universe. They can be applied to particular objects and events, but not to the existence of the universe as a whole. The fact that there is a world is neither necessary nor contingent. The universe needs no reason for its existence rather than its non-existence, or for being this world rather than that. It is simply there, and is what it is.

Finally, we have the argument from design, which infers from so-called evidences of design the necessity of a supreme designer. At the best, this argument can lead us, not to the concept of an *ens realissimum,* but only to the notion of a kind of architect constructing the world out of matter already on hand. To make God the creator of the matter, as well as of the design, we have to invoke the cosmological proof—with what consequences, we already have seen. Again, we could not even infer from the evidences of design that God was a *perfectly* good workman, but only that he was a very good one. Hence the argument would not even establish his perfection as an architect, let alone his existence.

Finally, even if we could assert the existence of a first cause outside experience, we could never tell whether or not that cause was the supreme explanation of *all* experience, since all experience is not present to us. At the most, we could only say that it was sufficient cause for our experience here and now. Even then, however, we should be extending synthetic propositions beyond the realm of experience, where alone they are valid, and should be pretending to knowledge about things-in-themselves which are unknowable.

In a word, we have no rational proof that the soul, the physical universe, and God are more than ideas and ideals of thought, and that they refer to independently existing objects. The relation of these *transcendental objects* to our thinking is the same as the relation of physical objects to our perceiving. There may or there may not be things-in-themselves corresponding to them. To assert dogmatically the existence of such things lands us in the difficulties we have already recounted.

To be sure, in dealing with the world we act *as if* they were ultimate truths, and except on that assumption all our attempts to introduce unity into the world are meaningless.[5] And to act *as if* these suppositions were true is to act *as if* the Ideas of Pure Reason were ideas of *existing* objects. Still, even these assumptions cannot go further than the supposition *that* such objects exist. It does not presume to tell us *what* they are like. The nature of God or the soul or the universe is no more indicated by the assumption of their existence, than the nature of things-in-themselves is indicated by the forms in which they are perceived.

XV. TRANSCENDENTAL OBJECTS

"Categorizing" Things-in-Themselves. Kant, we may remember, found it necessary to establish in the manifold of sense points of affinity with the Categories that made it compliant and adaptable to them. These were found in the *Schemata*. The *manifold* nature of sense which enabled us to *enumerate* its parts and to subject them to arithmetical processes, made experience compliant to the Category of *quantity*. The *permanent* and *enduring* character of perceptions gave *substance* to them, and the *invariability* of their observed *sequences* lent itself to the application of the Category of *causality*.

Kant's task is now to find similar go-betweens connecting the Ideas of Pure Reason with the Categories.[6] For, if the world produced by the union of the Categories with sense-perception were not compliant to the Ideas of Pure Reason, we could never achieve a final unification of the universe through the concepts of the soul, the universe, and God.

However, the difficulty of finding *Schemata* connecting the Categories and the Ideas is quickly overcome. These *Schemata* are found in the nature of the Categories themselves, just as the *Schemata* of sense-perception were found in the nature of experience itself. The Categories, by virtue of their unifying and systematizing power, lend themselves to the further work of unification carried on by the Ideas of Pure Reason. Substance, causality, necessity, and the other Categories are as ingrained in metaphysical speculation as they are in scientific understanding. Hence we find reason in its turn producing a final world of *transcendental objects,* or things-in-themselves conceived in terms of the Categories, just as in the *Schemata* the Categories are perceived not only as general characteristics of sense-experience, but as necessary forms of thinking about sense-experience. These *transcendental objects* in which God, the soul, and the universe are thought of as substances

[5] Cf. pp. 642-704 (M. M. pp. 576-664).
[6] Cf. pp. 682 ff. (M. M. pp. 547 ff.).

with properties, and as substances in causal relation, are the *Schemata* of the ideas.

Transcendental Objects. For instance, between the Idea of the soul as an unknowable thing-in-itself underlying our conscious activity and the soul as the ordinary, everyday, "empirical" self given in self-consciousness there intervenes the soul as a *transcendental object,* or *Schema,* freed from any particular content of consciousness, and regarded as an unknown *substance* possessed of unknown *qualities.* Between the Idea of the collection of things-in-themselves that underlie the physical universe and the physical objects constructed by the Categories out of sense-experience, there hovers the *Schema* of the universe, a *transcendental object,* thought of in terms of *substance* and *causation.* Finally, God himself is *"schematized"* as a *substance* with *properties,* whose existence is *necessary* and whose relations to both soul and the universe are *causal.* Nay more, reason represents to itself the nature of the divine substance in terms of its own activities, and thinks of God as a supreme *mind* upon which the rationality and order imputed to things-in-themselves depend, just as the rationality and order of our particular experience depend upon the synthesizing activity of our particular minds.

There are, however, two drawbacks, Kant says, to "schematizing" God as a *mind.* Imputing unlimited wisdom to God tends to make us mentally lazy and prone to refer to it everything we cannot understand, without further attempting to discover things by ourselves. Furthermore, turning the ways in which we are obliged to conceive God into attributes of God himself breeds a perverted, anthropomorphic notion of God as a quasi-human person, whose arbitrary purposes govern the course of natural events. So, instead of investigating the course of phenomena to find out by observation what the aims, if any, of nature are, we judge *a priori* what God's aims are from our own prejudices and preferences, and then twist natural events into conformity with them. Under such circumstances, the Ideas of Pure Reason become hindrances rather than helps to the enlargement of our understanding.

XVI. THE DISCIPLINE OF PURE REASON

Criticism of the Rationalists. Pointing, as it were, a moral to his tale and applying all that has gone before to the tendency of philosophy to indulge in speculations that transcend experience, Kant gives a final word of warning both to the rationalistic philosophers who employ *a* *priori* arguments and methods, and to the empiricists who deny altogether *a priori* principles and derive everything *a posteriori* from experience. Both parties, he thinks, need to be subjected to the *discipline of pure reason.*[7]

The chief trouble with the rationalists, he feels, lies in their admiration for mathematics, and their belief that, like the mathematicians, they can make *a priori* synthetic judgments with absolute certainty and can argue from the particular and the contingent to the universal and the necessary in a way that cannot be refuted. If from the inspection of a single triangle we can infer universal truths which hold for all actual and possible triangles we could ever come across, why, they say, should we not be able to infer the nature of all experience from *our* experience, and demonstrate from it with absolute certainty universally valid *a priori* propositions regarding the nature of the universe?

The trouble is, Kant replies, that philosophy forgets that mathematical axioms and demonstrations rest, not upon the variable and contingent *content* of our experience, but upon the unchanging *forms* of space and time in which *all* human experience is given. Hence mathematics is able to regard each individual representation of its concepts as wholly representative of the concept in question. Thus every individual triangle illustrates the entire nature of triangularity. Any instance of $3 + 3 = 6$, or $3 - 2 = 1$, or $3 \times 3 = 9$, or $\frac{3}{2} = 1\frac{1}{2}$ is symbolic of something that will *necessarily* be true in *all* times and places.

The concepts of philosophy, however, have to take account of the *stuff* that fills in mathematical particulars, and this stuff is variable and contingent and presents individually different *things* in shifting relations to one another. No one physical object or thinking subject is exhaustively representative of *all* objects or *all* minds, as one triangle is exhaustively representative of all triangles. In dealing with her data philosophy has nothing *a priori,* nothing in the way of *necessarily* universal characteristics, to rely upon. For philosophy to have an adequate general concept of the universe in general, and to be able to say the world *is* beyond all doubt such and such, all that ever happened in space and time would have first to be observed.

Hence our philosophic estimates have no demonstrable or *apodictic* certainty, like those of mathematics. There can be no such things as philosophic axioms. Nor can any philosophic arguments be *demonstrations,* since reasoning founded on a changing and accumulating content of experience can never arrive at certainty, as reasoning can that is based upon the unchanging *forms* in which the changing content presents itself.

Criticism of the Empiricists. So much for the rationalists. The empiricists, too, should tread more carefully. Hume, for example, fails to distinguish between the synthetic judgments and concepts that rest upon the content of actual experience, on the one hand, and those, on the other, that are based upon the *a priori* conditions and forms of all possible human experience. He does not see that the concepts of substance and causality, for example, are not built up out of experience, but are ways in which the human mind by its very nature is forced to think of all the experience that may be presented to it. A similar confusion exists in Hume's mind between the provinces of reason and of the understanding. He mixes up the proper claim of the Categories to be valid for all possible human experience with the unjustifiable pretensions of the Ideas of Pure Reason, like the soul and God, to objective counterparts existing outside the world of experience in the realm of things-in-themselves.

The Nature of Legitimate Demonstration. The upshot of it all is that the concepts of philosophy are hypotheses pure and simple, whose function is to explain experience and whose propriety is estimated by their relevance to experience. If they do not stick to the conditions of all possible human experience in their conjectures about possible objects, they become idle fancies.

Legitimate proofs, however, can be made of concepts whose content is given in experience.

For example since *experienced* events always have to be thought of as originating in antecedent occurrences, there *must* be a causal connection between *experienced* events. Hence causation is a demonstrable fact. Or again, although the concepts of substance and attribute do not logically involve each other, in *experience* we cannot find things without qualities, or qualities detached from things. Hence we can demonstrate that substances *must* have attributes, that attributes *must* inhere in substances.

Furthermore these proofs do not rest upon circumstantial evidence. The truths they establish are not demonstrated *provisionally* from accumulating observation of particular events, and subject to the possibility of our finding, either now or in the future, events that contradict them. They are drawn immediately from the constitution of the mind. They are direct, necessary, and leave nothing further to be learned or known about the subject. Since all human experience *must* fall within the Categories, no experience could ever occur that would disprove them.

The fallacy of the so-called demonstrations of the existence of God lies in the fact that experience presents us with no instance of the idea of either a necessary or a most real being. Therefore, it is impossible to say beforehand whether or not a perceived instance of the concept of a perfect being, i.e., God, would exist necessarily or not.

One last word of caution is necessary, before we leave the subject of proof. We are prone to believe that proving the impossibility of demonstrating the truth of a proposition is proof that the proposition itself is false. This, however, is an unwarranted assumption. The impossibility of demonstrating that a proposition is true does not disprove the truth of the proposition in question. Hence though we cannot prove the existence of the soul, of an objective physical world, and of God, we are just as unable to demonstrate their non-existence.

XVII. GOD, FREEDOM, AND IMMORTALITY AS MORAL POSTULATES

Rationality of Moral Action. But, Kant continues, man's relation to the universe is not wholly intellectual. The world is a stage upon which we *act* as well as scenery which we *observe* and about which we *think*. It arouses desires, hopes, and expectations. Our behavior and our expectations, as well as our thinking, must be reasonable. Here, then, is another fertile field for the exercise of reason.

Now the Ideas of God and the universe and the soul, which are regulative ideas of our thinking, are regulative ideas of our conduct as well. The man who acts rationally is the man who acts *as if* there were a God, *as if* he were an immortal soul, *as if* his soul were free and morally responsible for its choices. In other words, reason imposes upon us obligations with respect to how we shall behave. It not only shows us how we *do* behave, and what *does* take place; it also tells us how we *ought* to behave, and what Reality *ought* to be like.

All our activity as rational beings, Kant continues, is focused upon three questions—What can I know? What should I do? What may I hope? The first question, which deals with the powers and limitations of the mind, has already been answered. The second, which is the practical problem of ethics, is about to engage our attention. The third is both practical and theoretical. We hope for what ought to be, just as we know what is. And just as our knowledge of *what is* leads us to the conclusion that there is an ultimate ground of all existence, so our knowledge of what *ought to be* leads us to the conclusion that there is an ultimate justification of our hopes.

We hope for happiness. Reason tells us that in order to realize this hope, we must *deserve* happiness. It would be irrational to expect happiness without meriting it. The reasonable conditions of attaining happiness are, then, what we call *moral* conditions. They are not derived empirically from an observation of experience. They are *a priori*. They are a presupposition of moral experience and action. They flow from the nature of reason itself. They render us moral beings inhabiting a moral world.

But plainly *if* the moral law is to be reasonable, and rewards are to be linked with deserts, there must be a moral and rational government of the world. Furthermore, since we do not get what we deserve in this world, there must be another life in which rewards are apportioned to our merits. In short, moral obligation is rational and explicable only on the assumption that we are immortal as well as free, and that there is a God who sees to it that our deserts bear their proper fruits, if not in this world, then beyond the grave. Hence, since moral obligation connotes God, freedom and immortality, whose existence reason cannot deny, we may feel morally, if not intellectually, certain of the being of God and of our own free and deathless nature.

The Categorical Imperative. These propositions set forth by Kant at the end of the *Critique of Pure Reason* were amplified and developed, after some years of further reflection, in the *Metaphysics of Morals,* published in 1785, and in the *Critique of Practical Reason,* published in 1788. In the *Metaphysics,* Kant discusses first what he calls the morality of common sense. He points out that nothing can be called absolutely good, except a good will. Unless the motive behind our action is pure, our behavior cannot be called meritorious and deserving of the reward of happiness. Furthermore, the good will is the only thing whose goodness is not the goodness of a means to some further end, but an end in itself.

To be truly meritorious, Kant goes on, we must act not from *inclination* but from *duty*. What, then, is duty? We can say at once that a dutiful action derives its worth, not from its consequences, but from some general law or principle. It is done because it is right in itself, not because it leads to something beyond itself. Can we, then, state the law of right behavior? We can, Kant replies. The rule of right behavior is always to act in a manner in which we should wish all other people to act. In a word, strictly moral behavior is always founded on a universally applicable maxim.

This maxim, Kant feels, is not derived from experience. As a matter of experience, we find that we are always falling short of our duty. The presence of the ideal, and the sense of *ought* and *duty,* are, therefore, not the product of experience which is not in itself ideal and as we would have it. We have a sense of right and wrong, which we apply to events, as it were, from above, when they occur.

The seat of this sense must be, not in the empirical content of volition, but in the *a priori* structure of the will, which is nothing but reason in action, or, as we might call it, *practical reason.* Since, however, right and rational behavior is hindered by immediate desires and interests in such wise that human conduct is never wholly reasonable and meritorious, the good will is never a realized fact, but appears in experience as an unrealized ideal, accompanied by a sense of the necessity or obligation of realizing it, which commands the will as *imperatively* as the ideals of pure reason coerce our thinking. These imperative commands are of two sorts. They enjoin certain behavior as the necessary means to some further end, or they order us to behave in a certain way because such behavior is an end in itself. In the latter case, we are acting according to what Kant calls the *categorical imperative,* and, since we feel it to be incumbent on everyone to do what is right, simply because it is right so to do, we are following the rule, *"Act as if the maxim of thy action were to become by thy will a universal law of nature."* [8]

The Universal Rule of Right Behavior. But it is not much use saying *do right* unless we can specify what it is right to do. Is it then possible to discover any one universally and everlastingly right, definite, and concrete kind of action, obligatory upon all men in all times and places, and applicable to all our fellow-beings in spite of their different temperaments, desires, and situations?

Kant answers in the affirmative. Moral behavior is behavior towards other *men,* each one of whom is rational, and finds his good in the conscious realization of his nature as a rational being. Rational beings have a value for themselves, which cannot be measured in terms of the relative value they may have for other people. Recognition in others of the same absolute worth as each one of us finds in himself is the basis of moral behavior and expresses itself in the general rule, or "practical imperative" of so acting *"as to treat humanity, whether in thine own person or in that of any other, in every case as an end*

[8] *Metaphysics of Morals,* p. 48 (trans. Abbot, Kant's *Theory of Ethics,* 5th ed., p. 39; subsequent quotations from this book are from the same edition).

withal, never as a means only." This is the concrete content of ethical action. This is *what* we should do, and *how* we should act in dealing with our fellow-men, if our behavior is to have a universal and absolute moral value and to be truly good.

This rule of action is not prescribed by our particular preferences, desires, and ends. It is derived, like the categories, from the nature of reason, and is, therefore, *a priori*. To put it in terms of volition, the truly moral or rational will prescribes its own law and its own imperative, with no other end in view than to express its own nature. Its obligation is self-imposed. Hence the moral will is self-determined and self-legislating, or, as Kant calls it, *autonomous*. When, then, we act morally, we are not only citizens of the world, to which, incidentally, considerations of prudence and expediency might better adapt us, but we are citizens of an ideal order, or "kingdom of ends" of which we are both the subjects and the monarchs, obedient in our actions to a law laid down by our own will.

There is no compromising with these ends, nor is there any equivalent for them as there is with the ends that have only an *extrinsic* value dependent on their ability to satisfy human desires. *Moral* action has an intrinsic value, and *dignity* which cannot be traded for a consideration, without depriving us of self-respect. Since the autonomous will is self-legislating and exercises its causality uninfluenced by anything except itself, it is *free*. Its acts occur independently of the causation we find in the phenomenal world. Its law of action, the Categorical Imperative, and the moral behavior inspired by that law, originate in the transcendental self in the world of things-in-themselves. How this intervention of the intelligible self in the current of sensible currents and this introduction of free acts into the linkage of physical cause and effect is possible we cannot know. But we are always behaving *as if* our wills were free and could dictate their choices. And, although human freedom is one of those things that can be neither proved nor disproved by argument, we can at least defend the hypothesis on rational grounds against dogmatic skepticism.

Three years later Kant returned to the charge in the *Critique of Practical Reason,* in which he reiterated and expanded the views advanced in the *Metaphysics of Morals*.[9]

God himself, he now adds, is subject to the moral law. But God is not harassed by alternative courses of action and the necessity of choosing between them. Since he cannot will other than the good, the moral law does not present itself to him as an obligation or duty

---

[9] *Critique of Practical Reason,* pp. 126-143 (A. pp. 105-120).

but as a spontaneous rule of action—as, indeed, it would to us, were it not for the conflict between our transcendental and our empirical selves. God's will is therefore above obligation and duty. It is *holy*. We may remark in passing that this holiness of God bears some analogy to *dignity* in man for which no equivalent can be found in the values of this world and upon which no price can be set.[10]

Human will, however, is *heteronomous,* as Kant now calls it, or subject to motivation by an object other than the expression of its own nature. Still, no goal save self-expression can *command* the will and put it under an *imperative* obligation. It is not our duty to be happy, but it is our duty to be good. Nay more, it is always within our power to be good, though it is not always within our power to be happy.[11]

XVIII. THE REALITY OF FREEDOM

Practical reason, we remember, from which moral activity flows, not only assumes the existence of a thing-in-itself, or soul, behind the empirical self. It assures us that this entity is a moral being, witness its self-expression in the moral law, which is not derived from empirical experience and does not belong to the "me," and yet is felt as directly as a color or a sound or any other element of the sensible manifold. We are *conscious* of moral obligation. We *feel* free. We *feel* responsible.

Freedom Is Self-Determination. Can we be sure, however, that our consciousness of possessing a free and responsible character is not an illusion?[12] As a natural being I am subject to the same determinism as the Category of causation imposes upon all nature. If I am to be free, then, I must be not only *in* the temporal series but *above* it, and must somehow manage to intervene in time from outside time. Can we make any sense of such a situation?

Kant thinks we can.[13] My acts, he says, may be as completely determined by antecedent causes as any other natural events are. But it must be remembered that the natural order as a whole, and the nature of the entire succession of events appearing in the relation of cause and effect, rest upon a world of things-in-themselves, which condition the sensible world to be the kind of world it is. Therefore, my entire career in time, although each of its moments is the outcome of what

[10] *Op. cit.,* pp. 143-144 (A. pp. 120-121).
[11] *Op. cit.,* pp. 146-156 (A. pp. 122-130).
[12] *Op. cit.,* pp. 157-175 (A. pp. 131-147).
[13] *Op. cit.,* pp. 225 ff. (A. pp. 188 ff.).

has gone before, is also conditioned to be what it is by the *intelligible character* I possess as a thing-in-itself, which expresses itself *freely* in all my actions. If the nature of my real character, laid up among the things-in-themselves, could be known, then all my actions in all circumstances could be absolutely foretold. But I should be none the less free, since my behavior, although absolutely predictable, would still be determined by myself, and would be foretold from a knowledge of *my* nature.

Suppose, however, we object that if we are created by a God our freedom and moral responsibility are thereby destroyed, since God has made us what we are. To this Kant replies that the question of who made us has no bearing on freedom.[14] Although God may be responsible for my existence, it is I who am responsible for how I behave, and it is the latter responsibility alone that has moral significance.

There is, then, nothing self-contradictory or contrary to reason in the idea of a free will expressing itself efficaciously in the deterministic stream of empirical causation and modifying the course of events. It follows that our consciousness of freedom and of the moral law is not necessarily an illusion, even from the point of view of pure reason.

XIX. THE AFFINITY OF THE MORAL LAW AND MORAL CONDUCT

The "Deduction" of the Moral Law. We have now to ask how the moral law, which cannot in any way be inferred from sensible experience and is so frequently opposed to its counsels, can be brought into any working relation to the desires and drives of everyday life. After all, it is these desires and drives that constitute the *content* of moral behavior. Without them the Categorical Imperative would be as void as the Categories of the Understanding would be without the manifold of sense to fill them and to give expression to them.

We see that we are confronted once more with some of the problems that faced us in the *Critique of Pure Reason*. We have, for example, to find some way of establishing a connection between the moral law and its content of everyday behavior, analogous to the so-called *deduction* of the Categories. There must be something corresponding to the *Schema;* some go-between linking moral consciousness and behavior with the *a priori* and transcendental moral law.

In the coincidence, Kant tells us, of the actual feeling of being free and responsible with the undeniable logical possibility that we may actually be what we feel we are, we find the "practical" equivalent of

---

[14] *Op. cit.,* pp. 232 ff. (A. pp. 194 ff.).

the deduction of the Categories. Just as sense-perception comes already prepared for utilization by the Categories, so the experience of freedom and moral responsibility, once shown to be not necessarily an illusion, can be linked up with a universal and categorically imperative moral law.

The necessary go-between corresponding to the *Schema* Kant finds in a certain *typical* form common to all our moral questionings about how to act in specific circumstances. Since this way of reaction to sensible and particular situations involving moral decisions is universal, we may call it as much a law of *nature* as the temporal continuities, persistences, and sequences of sensible experience. When we ask ourselves off-hand whether an act is good or bad, we are asking whether the act is something *we* are willing to do, irrespective of the number of other people who are doing it.

The empirical test, then, of the absolute *rightness* of an action would be its *universal* applicability to *all* people in *all* situations. Such a test is completely naïve. It is instinctively applied by persons who have never reflected upon moral problems, and who have no inkling of a categorical imperative or of an *a priori* universal moral law.

Here is a universal empirical test of concrete moral behavior in the everyday world, akin to the universal *sensible* characteristics, or *Schemata,* of sense-experience. And here is a common meeting-ground between experience and the *a priori* moral law, akin to the *Schemata* linking the Categories of the Understanding to their sensible content.

The "Transcendental Object" of Practical Reason. Practical reason is also analogous to speculative reason in that it has a transcendental object.[15] Just as our thinking about the world is governed by the ideas of God, the soul, and the universe, so our moral behavior in the world is governed by the idea of the *good*. Again, just as God, and the soul, and the real universe underlying phenomena, cannot be *known* in any of the terms provided by the sensible manifold or by the Categories, so the nature of the good is not determined by experience. It is, as Kant has already pointed out in the *Metaphysics of Morals,* the good will, expressing itself in the moral law.

Kant now proceeds to expatiate upon the moral sentiment of respect.[16] Our truly moral acts, he says, are often performed against our inclinations and produce disagreeable feelings in us. At the same time, they arouse our self-respect, which is the only truly moral sentiment. This sentiment of self-respect, being a subjective, empirical feeling,

[15] *Op. cit.,* pp. 176 ff. (A. pp. 148 ff.).
[16] *Op. cit.,* pp. 195 ff. (A. pp. 164 ff.).

gives the moral law a subjective, sentimental validity in addition to its objective, rational authority over our behavior.

Moreover, since respect is an emotion, it has the same driving power as the other emotions. It thus provides a motive for right action which is as empirically felt and as urgent as pleasure and pain, and it creates in us an *interest* which may go hand-in-hand with them. And, since self-respect *feels good,* it is a feeling that can be desired and loved. Hence duty is not grim. Respect for the moral law may also be *love* of the moral law. In fact, if we are not to be merely and grimly virtuous, we must love the moral law as well as respect and obey it. If we love the good then we are not only virtuous but holy, even as God is holy.

Still, to fallible beings like ourselves such love is a counsel of perfection. No human being can be expected to *love* doing right unreservedly and under all circumstances. Any human being who pretends that all his actions proceed from pure goodness of heart and are dictated by sheer love of humanity is a hypocrite and a fanatic.

XX. THE MORAL ANTINOMY

Happiness and Virtue. Finally, to complete the analogy between the active and moral side of our nature and its intellectual, thinking aspect, we discover that practical reason, like pure reason, has its Antinomies.[17] The moral good contains two elements. It involves *virtue,* or action in accordance with the moral law, on the one hand, and *happiness,* on the other. Virtue and happiness, however, do not logically involve each other.

Nor, in the world of experience, do we find any *causal* connection between them. Only too obviously, in this world at least, the righteous are cast down and the wicked flourish. The virtuous are not happy, and the happy are not virtuous. At the same time our moral nature demands that there should be a *necessary* connection between virtue and happiness, reward and merit. We feel it morally *obligatory* that virtue should be rewarded and rewarded in proportion to merit. Nay more, happiness is not the effect of moral behavior. Nor can it be the *cause* of it, since action inspired by any motive except the pure rightness or wrongness of the deed in question is not completely moral.

We are then confronted with the Antinomy that there both *must* and *cannot* be a *necessary* causal connection between virtue and happiness. In short, the attempt to make a thing-in-itself of the moral law

[17] *Op. cit.,* pp. 246 ff. (A. pp. 206 ff.).

is seemingly as self-contradictory as the attempt to make a thing-in-itself of the soul, the universe, or God. Can we resolve this Antinomy? Kant thinks we can.

The Solution of the Antinomy. In the first place, there is nothing self-contradictory in the idea that we can attain complete happiness. Virtuous behavior, however disagreeable it may be from some points of view, is accompanied by a feeling of self-approbation and self-respect, which *contents* us and which motivates behavior much as prospective pleasure does. To be sure, this contentment is never complete or unbroken, or attained and maintained without a moral struggle. However, we can imagine—in God, for example—a *contentment* which is not contrasted with and assailed by worldly desires and pleasures, but is maintained and enjoyed without effort. The divine felicity or *bliss* accompanies a spontaneous, continuous and complete identification of the divine will with the moral law. Hence perfect happiness is a conceivable and possible *experience,* and perfect virtue might conceivably and possibly be rewarded by it.

Furthermore, though, morally speaking, human beings do not, and because of their fallibility cannot, *justly* enjoy perfect happiness in this life, they might conceivably perfect themselves and make themselves worthy of enjoying complete felicity, if they had more time and opportunity to do so than is afforded them here below. Indeed to attain this complete accord between the will and the moral law, which is the necessary condition to a *deserved* complete felicity, an infinite progress towards perfection is necessary and such progress requires an endless duration of our personality.

The Moral Necessity of Assuming God, Freedom and Immortality. Provided, then, that we can assume immortality, we can see how the identification of virtue with happiness, necessary to the solution of the antinomy, is not only logically but empirically possible. But to convert this possibility into an actuality something more than ourselves is necessary. Since observance and love of the moral law are plainly not rewarded by happiness in this world, we are obviously incapable by our own efforts of creating a world in which this blessed event occurs. We can only do our best to further the moral order, and, indeed, it is part of the moral order that we should endeavor to promote it. But if the moral ideal is to be practicable, and if our effort to attain it is to have any chance of success and any meaning, there must be a principle that guarantees the possibility of our realizing it and that provides us with the infinite time necessary for its realization. In other words, there must be a God in whom the ideal after which we strive has actual existence, and who is able to create a universe in which we, also, in due time may be able to attain it and to partake of his holiness and bliss as the just reward of our merits.

On the assumption, then, that God, freedom, and immortality are facts, we can solve the moral Antinomy. Without them, it cannot be solved and morality remains without explanation, and the moral order is paradoxical and self-contradictory. In a word their *possible* existence, which reason permits us to assume, is transformed by the exigencies of our moral nature into real existence.

Kant, however, hastens to point out that it is not our *duty* to postulate their existence.[18] In other words, there is nothing *immoral* about disbelieving in God, freedom, and immortality. Duty and morality oblige us only to do our best to promote a connection between happiness and virtue and to deal justly with our fellow-men, even though we feel that in the universe in which we find ourselves our efforts can never be crowned with complete success. The assumption that, thanks to God, freedom, and immortality, our obedience to the moral law, has a cosmic meaning and justification, can never be more than a matter of individual *faith*.

Kant brings his *Critique of Practical Reason* to an end with a warning that we must not regard the practical necessity of assuming God, freedom, and immortality as in any way a theoretic or metaphysical argument in favor of their existence. From the point of view of metaphysics the question remains wide-open. Nor can we learn anything about the *nature* of God, freedom, and immortality, from the fact that their existence is a necessary *moral* postulate. To be sure, conceived in the interests of practical reason, God is *thought of* as an omniscient, omnipotent, and beneficent willing and thinking being, but these notions of the divine nature, which fit our moral needs, in no way constitute a *knowledge* of what God is really like.

XXI. THE ESTHETIC SENSE ("CRITIQUE OF JUDGMENT")

The Nature of Beauty. The true and the good are now disposed of. The beautiful alone remains to be considered. Kant tackles it in the *Critique of Judgment,* published in 1790.[19] Our judgments of *taste,* which distinguish the beautiful from the non-beautiful, are not, Kant tells us, logical or objective in character. They do not add to our un-

[18] *Op. cit.,* pp. 290 ff. (A. pp. 242 ff.).
[19] The references to and quotations from this volume are from the translation by J. H. Bernard, London, 1892.

derstanding or enlarge our knowledge of objects. Nor have they any-thing to do with the moral judgments we pass upon things. They deal merely with a certain sort of interest and satisfaction my representations arouse *within me*. That is, their content is *subjective*. Furthermore, the interest that provokes them is distinguishable from every other interest, and, if they are to be valid, must be kept unadulterated. The moment that I allow moral prejudices, or practical needs, or intellectual considerations, to influence my estimate of a work of art, my judgment is not a purely esthetic judgment, but is clouded by irrelevant elements. "We must not be in the least prejudiced in favor of the existence of things, but be quite indifferent in this respect, in order to play the judge in things of taste." In short, the satisfaction we take in beauty is a *disinterested* satisfaction. We like the beautiful object, not because it procures us further sensuous gratifications, or excites moral approbation, or increases our knowledge, but simply because its immediate presence pleases us in itself.

At the same time, although esthetic satisfaction is subjective, we attribute to it a *universality* that we do not attribute to other purely subjective feelings. The pleasure, for example, that we take in a certain dish or a certain wine we should not dream of imputing to everybody. But if I consider a picture or a statue *beautiful,* I expect you to share the pleasure I take in it and to agree with me as to its beauty. And yet I cannot exactly say that you *ought* to agree with me, as I could, were I inviting your attention to some scientific concept I considered true, or to some moral concept I considered good. Here, then, we have something that is at once purely subjective and yet universal, and something that is *universal* and yet not a *concept* or general idea of anything, but a *feeling* pure and simple. How can this be?

Beauty a Satisfaction not Striven for, Common to All. We can best answer this question by further examining the nature of the universal "feel" of beauty common to all those who experience it. In the presence of the beautiful object we have a sense of "purposiveness," as Kant calls it. Our will comes to rest just as it does when we have finished a good dinner or have accomplished something we *wished* to do. Beauty is, therefore, a satisfaction and fulfillment of the *will*. Nevertheless, it is impossible to discover any sense of unfulfilled desire or specific and conscious purpose that the sense of beauty satisfies. When we come upon loveliness, we have not wished or willed or purposed anything, in spite of our feeling that a demand of our will has been pacified. Our state of mind, then, is a consciousness of "purposiveness" without consciousness of purpose; a state associated with willing, and yet a state to which volition has not contributed, and in which desire and aim have played no part. This paradoxical feeling of fulfilled purpose in which no purpose has been fulfilled constitutes the universal element in beauty.

The disinterested, impractical, contemplative sense of beauty is not built up out of repeated experiences of beautiful objects, any more than the Category of causation is derived from repeated sequences of events. Like that Category it is *a priori*. Another mark of its universal and *a priori* character is the sense of necessity connected with it. The *pleasant* actually and as a matter of fact excites pleasure. "But the *beautiful* we think of as having a *necessary* reference to satisfaction." It *must* satisfy. This necessity, however, is not grounded either in the sensible content or in the intelligible form of experience. It must, then, be a purely subjective necessity, which we can only describe and talk about by saying that we all possess a common sensitiveness to whose authority we can appeal in judging that this or that object *is* beautiful, and that this sensitiveness is, therefore, a possible source of esthetic pleasure to all men in all times and places. That some people do not get esthetic satisfaction from an object we feel to be beautiful is, we say, a reflection, not upon its beauty, but upon their sensitiveness.

"Free" vs. "Dependent" Beauty. The charm and the emotional appeal of objects adjudged beautiful are not part of their beauty and vitiate any esthetic judgment they are allowed to influence. Nor has beauty anything to do with the *perfection* of an object. Perfection in an object implies realization by it of a specific form or ideal to which it should or does conform. The feeling of perfection, arising as it does from the object's fulfilling specifications laid down beforehand, is not the same as the feeling of beauty which "presupposes no concept of what the object ought to be."

At the same time, judgments of perfection may be accompanied by judgments of beauty that in a way depend upon them. The appeal, for example, a human being or a building makes to the esthetic sense is inseparable from our concept of the specific form or purpose a man or a church or a house *ought* to embody. Beauty so conditioned is called by Kant "dependent beauty." Such beauty is not "free," and our appreciation of it is not entirely and strictly esthetic. "Free beauty" is unadulterated with awareness of any purpose whatsoever. An instance of it is the beauty of flowers. The judgment that they are beautiful is a pure esthetic judgment into which no extraneous considerations enter.

Again, the moment we try to construct a standard or ideal of beauty by which to judge, we are fettering our esthetic judgments with non-esthetic conditions. "An Ideal of beautiful flowers, of a beautiful piece of furniture, of a beautiful view," or, in other words, of free beauty, "is inconceivable." No less so is an ideal "of a beauty dependent on definite purposes, e.g., of a beautiful dwellinghouse, a beautiful tree, a beautiful garden," whose justification and therefore whose "dependent beauty" lie in subservience to some external end.

The Sublime. The *sublime* is like the beautiful in that it is pleasant in itself and that the satisfaction it brings is neither intellectual, moral, nor sensual, but *sui generis*. The feeling of sublimity, however, is connected with boundlessness, whereas the feeling of beauty is connected with form and proportion.

Again, whereas the sense of beauty is disinterested, the feeling of sublimity positively defies and violates our sensible and imaginative interests. It overwhelms us with a size and might that neither our senses nor our imaginations can cope with. It agitates the will instead of pacifying it, as beauty does.

In short it is a sort of imaginative transcription of the idea of infinity. Since nature does not present us with experiences of infinity, natural objects cannot be said to be in themselves sublime. In themselves they are only beautiful. Their sublimity is imputed to them by the notion of infinity, also aroused in us by the more terrible, the more interminable, and the more chaotic and the more desolate aspects of the natural scene.

Finally, in the presence of the sublime we experience both pain and pleasure at the same time. The sublime makes us feel at once big and little. It fills us with awe at the vanity of our attempts to withstand the irresistible forces of nature. In a word, it *humiliates* our sensible and finite nature. Nevertheless, we should not feel this sense of abasement and of awe unless our reason was able to entertain the *idea* of the totality of existence, and to compute the infinite. The very essence of the sublime lies in its contrasting of the inability of sense and imagination with the ability of reason to cope with it, and, at the same time transmuting our pain at the powerlessness of the imagination to picture the ideas entertained by reason into a pleasure engendered by the feeling of the power and the majesty of our higher selves.

XXII. THE "DEDUCTION" OF ESTHETIC EXPERIENCE

No "Deduction" of the Sublime Possible. The *feelings* of beauty and sublimity, being *a priori,* must have, like the *Ideas,* the *Categories,* and the *Categorical Imperative,* a *deduction* that finds something in the nature of experience itself already congenial to their universal and necessary application to sensible phenomenon. For the sublime no such deduction is possible, since sublimity is, properly speaking, not referable to natural objects in themselves, which are always formed and finite, but arises rather from our power to entertain ideas that the sensible world is inadequate to represent. Still, this inability of the sense and the imagination to picture ideas that the mind can entertain is as universal as the *Schema* of sense-experience. Therefore, it affords the same support to universal and necessary judgments of sublimity.

Beauty Involves a "Universal" Judgment About "Particular" Objects. Beauty, however, which, unlike sublimity, is referred to external objects and not merely to our feelings, requires a real and more complicated deduction. In its case, we have to find something in the *positive* content of *experience* corresponding to the universal *a priori* validity and necessity of our esthetic judgments. This validity and this necessity, it will be noted, unlike the judgments expressive of the Categories of the Understanding, does not hold good for *all,* but only for *single* objects. For example, although I can declare beforehand that *all* flowers, past, present and future, *must* be substances possessed of qualities, and *must* have causes, I can only declare a priori that *this particular* flower, given here and now in my experience, *must* be beautiful for all other experiences as well. To state that *all* flowers are beautiful would not be an esthetic but a *logical* judgment, and a judgment moreover that could neither be made beforehand, like the judgment that all things *must* have causes, nor be verified by experience.

In a word, there is no *objective* principle of beauty in the sense that there is an objective principle of causation. The principle of beauty is *subjective.* It lies not in any claim that I can make upon all *objects,* but upon a claim I can make of all *subjects* in the presence of a given particular object. I cannot demand of all flowers that they shall be beautiful, but I can demand of all men that they shall find beauty in this individual flower.

The "Sense" of Beauty a Basis for Universal Esthetic Judgments. What, then, is there in esthetic *experience* that exhibits an affinity to this peculiarity of esthetic judgments? Kant finds the answer in the ability of the beautiful object to satisfy the will without having aroused any previous desire or purpose calling for satisfaction. This indicates that sense and imagination are able to present their content spontaneously and freely, already conformed to the law and order which the mind seeks through the Categories to impose upon the sensible manifold. In short, the beauty of sense-experience is a kind of spontaneous and innate *rationality* exhibited without their aid or intervention. Since every rational being is capable of recognizing and deriving pleasure from this "free," "uncategorized" exhibition of rationality in sensible representations, we may properly demand of him that he feel it when we feel it. Hence we may assert that judgments of taste express universal rules of judgment and are valid for everyone.

We are entitled, Kant thinks, to assume the existence of a communicable, common esthetic sensibility as part of the common sensitiveness, or "common sense," which enables us to communicate sensations of any sort to one another. It is as much a part of the *a priori* structure of the mind as the Categories or the Ideas, and the judgments founded upon it have the same authority as those pronounced by the understanding or by reason. Only, whereas the understanding and the reason create a common and communicable world by imputing *objectivity* to phenomena, esthetic taste creates it by imputing to each one of us the common *subjective* thrill and satisfaction felt by all of us in their presence.

As a matter of fact, esthetic satisfaction is rarely experienced in a pure state. Ordinarily it is mixed up with the social feeling of the necessity of actually communicating it to other people. Esthetic judgment also is prejudiced by considerations of propriety, as, for example, by the discovery that what we took to be a natural flower is an artificial one, or by moral or intellectual interests, or by charm.

XXIII. ART AND THE ARTIST

Artificial vs. Natural Beauty. So far, Kant has been only considering the beauty of nature. Now he takes up the beauty of artificial objects and the subject of art. Art, to be true art, must avoid all appearance of purpose and aim at giving the same sense of "purposiveness without purpose" as pleases us in the natural object.

To be able to do this and avoid the appearance of art is a mark of *genius* on the part of the artist. Artistic genius is an original capacity which produces spontaneously, and without consciousness of the origin of its ideas. Its works, while sufficiently true to nature as not to be nonsense, are not merely imitative of nature, but set up standards of taste and rules of esthetic judgment valid for other people. Artistic genius is, then, the creative counterpart of the receptive faculty of esthetic taste. It can produce what people with a sense of beauty are able to appreciate.

Kant sums up the difference between natural and artificial beauty by saying that the one "is a *beautiful thing,*" the other "a *beautiful representation* of a thing." It follows that, whereas in order to judge of natural beauty I need not have beforehand a concept of what sort of thing the object is to be, I must know what the artist is trying to portray.

In the production of beauty art has one paradoxical advantage over nature. Nature cannot make a thing both beautiful and ugly at the same time. But "beautiful art shows its superiority in this, that it describes as beautiful things which may be in nature ugly or displeasing. There is only one kind of ugliness which cannot be represented in accordance with nature, without destroying all esthetical satisfaction and consequently artificial beauty; *viz.,* that which excites disgust."

The creative genius of the artist has always to be checked by the esthetic taste he shares with his public, if the beauty of his work is to be communicable to others. He must be a spectator as well as a creator. He must also combine imagination with understanding. He gives to concepts and ideas, which the understanding uses only as instruments of knowledge, an added aura and iridescence of subjective value common to all men possessed of taste.

In doing this, the artist, in so far as he is a genius, sees something new in things, which has never been seen before. His vision is free and spontaneous, undetermined by anything except himself, and its result is unique and not to be reduplicated. His work cannot be successfully copied or imitated by other geniuses, but it may be an inspiration to the exercise of their originality.

The Hierarchy of the Arts. Of all the arts, Kant ranks poetry highest because of its superior power of expanding "the mind by setting the Imagination at liberty." After poetry comes music. "For, although it speaks by means of mere sensations without concepts, and so does not, like poetry, leave anything over for reflection, it yet moves the mind in a greater variety of ways and more intensely, though only transitorily." It is the language of the heart. Its mathematical structure is, as it were, its grammar, but "in the charm and mental movement produced by music, mathematics has certainly not the slightest share." For this reason, from a cultural point of view, in which appeal to the understanding is dominant, music occupies a low rank "because it merely plays with sensation." Furthermore, music has the disadvantage of obtruding itself upon us whether we like it or not. We can turn our eyes away from a picture we do not like, but we cannot stop our ears against noise.

Among the formative arts, Kant gives the palm to painting, partly because "as the art of delineation it lies at the root of all the other formative arts," and partly because of the wider extent of its power of representation.

XXIV. THE ESTHETIC ANTINOMY

At this point, the Kantian machine begins once more to whirr, and turns out an *Antinomy*. We do, and yet we cannot, dispute about taste. We do, and yet we cannot, claim for our esthetic judgment the necessary assent of others. On the one hand, esthetic judgments *do not* imply objective standards, since, if they did, any dispute about them could be settled by argument and proof. On the other hand, they *do* imply objective standards, since, if they did not, we should never even think of disputing about them or of expecting others to share our views.

This Antinomy, however, like the Antinomies of pure and practical reason, can be solved. Esthetic judgments do imply the existence of a standard, and do involve a general *concept*—the concept of a subjective feeling of purposiveness experienced in the presence of a beautiful object. At the same time, this concept or standard does not acquaint us with any quality in things that can be known or proved. *My feeling* that a thing is beautiful does not demonstrate that the thing *is* beautiful in itself.

In short, the general concept of the feeling of purposiveness affords sufficient ground for *asserting* the validity of esthetic judgments, but insufficient ground for *proving,* though not for *feeling,* that some display better taste than others. We may then quarrel over taste, although we cannot effectively dispute about particular tastes. The only way I can bring you to share my point of view is not by argument, but by educating your taste till it agrees with mine.

XXV. TELEOLOGY, PURPOSE AS A CAUSE

Beauty as Pleasure. Purposiveness plays so central a part in Kant's esthetics that it is not surprising that he should devote the latter half of the *Critique of Judgment* to a discussion of teleology and purpose in general. He begins to veer in that direction towards the end of the first division of the work. The beauties of nature, he tells us, suggest that "behind the production of the beautiful there is an Idea of the beautiful in the producing cause; *viz.,* a *purpose* in respect to our Imagination," just as the existence and order of nature suggest the Idea of a God as a reason for the presence of the universe. Still, there is much in nature that suggests, not a teleological, but a mechanical explanation of the occurrence of beautiful forms. This, taken in connection with the principle of not multiplying principles beyond necessity and with the purely subjective character of esthetic judgments, precludes us from using esthetic experience as an argument for the teleological constitution of the universe.

There is, however, reason for believing that in the supersensible world, esthetic, logical, and moral judgments have a common, though unknown, ground. The beautiful is closely allied to the good and the true. Beauty ennobles and elevates the mind above the pleasures of the senses. It is intelligible. It brings an immediate satisfaction which is an end in itself. The satisfaction it bestows is, like moral satisfaction, disinterested. It betokens freedom of the imagination. It is universal. All these characteristics point, like the moral law and the activities of pure reason, to a transcendent source numbered among the things-in-themselves.

Teleology Inadmissible as a "General" Explanation. We pass now to Kant's critique of teleological judgment, which deals with the scope and validity of *purpose* as a principle of explanation. Kant warns us at once against an undue extension of such explanation to everything and anything. There is nothing, he tells us, in "the universal Idea of nature, as the complex of objects of sense" to warrant our jumping to an all-embracing teleological conclusion. And, of course, it is quite out of the question to introduce purposes into the world of things-in-themselves, about which we know nothing.

Furthermore, *external purpose,* or accounting for things on the ground that they exist *in order to* promote one another's existence or well-being, may be ruled out at once as a principle of explanation. For example, neither experience nor any *a priori* necessity warrants human beings in thinking that what in nature they find beautiful or useful has been produced by nature in order to please or benefit them. Beauty and utility are wholly subjective and relative. *"It is I that introduce the purposiveness."* All inanimate objects and events are quite explicable on mechanical principles by efficient causation, and in their case at least, teleological explanations are out of place and inadmissible.

Teleology Necessary to the Explanation of "Organic" Phenomena. In the realm of biological phenomena, however, the situation is different. It looks very much as if in organic being *"every part"* were "reciprocally *purpose* [*end*] *and means";* and as if all the parts were "only possible through their reference to the whole," and existed for the sake of the whole. This interdependence of the natures and functions of the parts of an organism on each other, and their dependence on the character of the whole of which they are the parts, cannot be satisfactorily explained by our minds on mechanical grounds, try as we may so to explain them. For our minds are so constituted that in explaining things they must *begin* with the constituent elements and, by means of synthetic judgments, combine them into wholes. They cannot *begin* with the synthesis and causally derive its elements from it. To them the whole is, as Kant puts it, "the *effect* of the concurrent, motive power of the parts." [20] Our minds cannot reverse the process of explanation and understand how a body can be the *efficient cause* and motive power of the concurrence of the factors that enter into its constitution. The completed product comes *after* the process that builds it up, and the whole appears *after* its parts have been combined. And our Category of causation demands that causes should *precede* their effects. It is beyond the power of *human* minds, then, to apply the Category of causation to a process in which the completed product, *before* it is completed, influences and directs the process of its own completion, or in which a whole, *resulting* from a combination of parts, nevertheless *causes* the parts to combine as they do.

Still, a mind differently constituted from ours might conceivably be able to understand, in terms of efficient causation alone, how an organic body determines the nature and directs the activities of its various organs, and how these organs reciprocally support and determine one another's functions. It is because a mechanical explanation of organic phenomena is not *a priori* impossible that our minds go on trying to understand them in terms of efficient causation, in spite of the fact that for minds like ours efficient causation will not work as an explanation.

The Basis in Experience of Teleological Explanation. However, our minds demand an explanation of biological phenomena, and since mechanical, efficient causation will not work, they look elsewhere. Now, it is a matter of experience that the *representation* of a com-

[20] *Op. cit.,* II, 77, p. 323. The italics are mine.

pleted product does, as a matter of fact, cause and determine the process of completion, and that the *representation* of a whole may influence
the nature and arrangement of its constituent parts. This we see in
every department of daily life, in the fulfillment of every intention, in
art, in manufacture, in the planning and realization of a human career.

Furthermore, we find that when we do represent a product as the
cause of its own production, we are talking in terms of what we call
purpose, and asserting the efficacy of purposes. Since this efficacy,
which is undoubted, cannot be reduced by our minds to terms of
mechanical causation, we have simply to call it *final causation,* or causation exerted from the end rather than the beginning—by the pull of
the future rather than by the push of the past. This sort of causation,
which, since it is not comprised within the causal category we cannot
understand, we apply to biological phenomena. But, Kant warns us
again, simply because teleology is the only explanation of such phenomena that will work for our type of mind we are not therefore
entitled to attribute the behavior of nature as a whole to a purpose.

XXVI. THE TELEOLOGICAL ANTINOMY

Efficient vs. Final Causation. We are now confronted once more
with an *Antinomy.* On the one hand, the human mind is obliged to
judge that *"all* production of material things is possible according to
merely mechanical laws." On the other, it is equally obliged to judge
that *"some* production of material things is not possible according to
merely mechanical laws." [21]

This Antinomy, Kant feels, is rooted in a confusion of the operations
of the mind expressed in the guiding and regulative Ideas of Pure Reason, such as God, the universe, etc., with those expressed in the application of the Categories of the Understanding to the sensible world.
Judgments of the understanding that phenomena are causally connected demand that *all* objects and events be regarded as the necessary
products of antecedent causes, and therefore as *all* mechanically produced. But judgments guided by the Ideas of Pure Reason no less imperatively demand that we seek a transcendent cause for the existence
of the universe, whose relation to the world cannot be regarded as
mechanical, since mechanical causation holds only of the relation of
events occurring *within* the universe and capable of being *understood.*
Final causation, however, which involves a determination of the parts
by the whole, comes nearer to expressing the possible nature of the

[21] *Op. cit.,* II, 69, pp. 294-295. The italics are mine.

relation of the universe to its ground. Hence the reason for the existence of the world may more properly be described as a *purpose* or
final cause than as a mechanical or efficient cause.

Solution of the Antinomy. The Antinomy is easily disposed of in
Kant's opinion. For, supposing that things-in-themselves really were
purposively connected, there would be no contradiction in their appearing, under spatial, temporal, and sensible conditions, as also mechanically connected by the Category of efficient causation. After all, it
is merely a consequence of the particular constitution of our understanding "that we have to represent some products of nature as possible according to a different kind of causality from that of the natural
laws of matter, namely, that of purposes and final causes." If, then,
the really mechanical might underlie the apparently teleological, the
really teleological might underlie the apparently mechanical.

Again, there is no contradiction in an object's being both mechanically and teleologically produced, if we say that its mechanical structure and behavior have the same relation to its purpose as the mechanical constitution of the universe has to the reason why there is a universe and why the universe is what it is. Furthermore, we are not
forced to content ourselves with showing that mechanism and purpose
do not contradict and exclude each other as principles of explanation.
We are entitled to regard them as twin expressions of one and the
same *supersensible* explanatory principle which transcends them both.
Hence some production appears mechanical in character, some purposive, and we seemingly have two kinds of causation, final and
efficient, on our hands. But in reality there may be only one principle
and one kind of production, though what the nature of that principle
is we cannot know, any more than we can know the nature of things-
in-themselves.

XXVII. TELEOLOGY AND MAN

Warnings Against the Undue Use of Teleology. In an appendix to
the above discussion, added in the second edition of the *Critique of
Judgment,* Kant pursues further the question of teleology, particularly
in its relation to theology. He reiterates that the scientist can gain
nothing by employing the teleological method, and that it is his business "to pursue natural mechanism, in respect to the explanation of
natural products, so far as it can be done with probability." Where
mechanical explanations fail, the failure should be laid to our peculiar
type of mind, and should not be supposed to indicate that "it is impos-

sible *in itself"* to express the efficacy of purpose in terms of efficient causation.

Since, however, minds like ours are obliged to use not only efficient but final causes in explaining the behavior of phenomena, we must introduce method into teleology, just as we do into mechanical science, and ask what a phenomenal world run on purposive lines would be like. In the first place, we see that in such an order the mechanical aspects will be regarded as means to the expression of purposes.

Again, since the principle of economy governs teleological as well as mechanical explanation, final like efficient causes are not to be multiplied beyond what is necessary, and supernatural explanations are to be reduced to a minimum.

Man, the Final Purpose of Nature. Passing now to *external purpose* Kant asks whether nature suggests the existence of any *final purpose,* at which she aims, and answers that she does not. We are accustomed to say that vegetables exist for the purpose of being eaten by animals, animals for the purpose of being eaten by man, and *ergo* man is the purpose to which everything is a means. But, Kant points out, we can argue with Linnaeus in just the opposite way. Grazing animals exist in order to keep vegetables from killing each other off, carnivorous animals to keep the herbivorous animals from killing off vegetables, and finally man, by killing off lions and tigers, helps keep them from eating up the cows and goats that by their browsing help keep the vegetables from crowding out each other. "And so man, although in a certain reference he might be esteemed a purpose, yet in another has only the rank of a means."

Still, in spite of Linnaeus, and in spite of the seeming indifference and even hostility of nature to man in many respects, Kant feels that man in one sense is "not merely, like all organized bodies, a *natural purpose,* but also the *ultimate purpose* of nature here on earth; in reference to whom all other natural things constitute a system of purposes." As an *animal,* however, man has no prior claim over the other animals to be nature's darling. It is only if we regard man's earthly vicissitudes as a discipline for cultivating his higher, rational nature, and if we can describe that nature as self-justifying and a means to nothing beyond itself, that he can be regarded as the final end of creation.

Now, man actually has such a nature. He alone, in his subservience to the moral law and in the expression of his freedom in accordance with it, proves to be a self-legislating, self-determining being whose purpose is wholly set by its own nature, and wholly realized by the free exercise of its own essential activity, altogether independent of natural conditions. He, therefore, may be regarded as the "final purpose, to which the whole of nature is teleologically subordinated."

XXVIII. TELEOLOGY AND GOD, FREEDOM, AND IMMORTALITY

The Moral Argument for the Existence and Nature of God. We pass now to God and to such suggestions of his existence as a teleologically constituted universe may afford. On the whole, Kant agrees with Descartes that, though the order of nature justifies the concept of an intelligent cause of the world, it can in itself "disclose to us nothing of a *final purpose of creation*." Our data are merely empirical, and here, as everywhere, conclusions drawn from experience are not valid beyond experience. The natural order can only suggest the existence of a supreme being as the ground of the universe, but "with all our knowledge of nature it remains undecided whether that Supreme Cause is its original ground according to a final purpose," or produces events by a "mere necessity of its nature." *Natural theology* may, then, be dismissed from consideration.

The only workable theology, Kant concludes, must be founded on *moral* grounds. As we have just seen, we are entitled to regard man as the final purpose of a teleologically constituted universe, only because he has a moral nature. And the self-determining, self-legislating, and self-justifying character of a moral nature is applicable to a supreme being. Attached to it such a character becomes omnipotence, omniscience, and infinite goodness and justice.

Furthermore, since the supposition that the ground of all existence is moral is a necessary presupposition of the validity of our own moral activities, we are entitled to believe it to be such. However, it must be remembered that the necessity of admitting on moral grounds that there is a God, is not a *demonstration* of his existence. Nor does thinking about God in certain ways give us any *knowledge* of his nature. Moreover, we apply moral qualities to God from the analogy of our own finite experience. Finally the moral argument cannot flout rational self-contradictions and absurdities. It can never warrant us, for instance, in even *thinking* of God as a mystical being that confounds reason, or as a magnified human being, or as a being who can be experienced and influenced and who can influence us, or as a being who can be pleased and placated "by other means than by a moral sentiment."

The same restrictions are laid by pure reason upon practical reason's necessary assumption that we are immortal. Our liberty to go beyond reason in our belief in a future life is not license to go contrary to reason and the law of self-contradiction in our thoughts of what such a life may be like.

Can, then, the implications of teleology *convince* us of the existence of God, freedom, and immortality? On theoretical grounds and by rational arguments, *no*. But although we cannot be convinced on theoretical grounds of their existence, we can in a sense be *convinced* on practical grounds, if by conviction we mean *acting as if* such objects existed. Our moral life is action of this sort, and it is a permanent principle of the mind to assume as true such objects as make *moral action* rational and obligatory, even though they do not make *knowledge* of themselves obligatory or even rationally possible.

Curiously enough, freedom, the other supersensible postulate of moral behavior, is an objective reality as well, whose activity is actually displayed under the Category of causation, and whose effects are empirical and observable. Although we cannot *demonstrate* the existence of freedom, we can *experience* it in ourselves.

The Necessity of a Theology. Whatever, then, we may think of the moral argument for God and immortality, it is the nearest thing to a proof we have. At least, it lays the foundations for a theology with its "determinate *concept* of the Supreme Cause" as moral, and for *religion,* with its *"recognition of our duties as divine commands."* For this reason alone the moral argument renders us a great service. Theology may not have any objective validity. It may not give us knowledge of any sort. Nevertheless it is useful in that it systematizes our thinking about God.

Finally, although we cannot compass God with the Categories of the Understanding, which apply only to objects of possible experience, we may yet regard the qualities we have to attribute to him, if our moral life is also to be a rational life, as a kind of "cognition of God and of His Being." An ethical theology is, therefore, possible, founded on "properties and determinations of His causality merely thought in Him according to analogy." Such a theology has all the reality requisite for giving a supersensible and rational foundation to ethics and to right behavior. Conversely, ethics needs a theology, for, though the moral law can be observed without the aid of theology, we cannot see any rhyme or reason in ethical rules without invoking the final design theology contributes. To renounce theology is to renounce reason in conduct.

XXIX. THE MINOR SUCCESSORS OF KANT

Reinhold. The influence of Kant was immediate, widespread, and powerful. Its most noteworthy fruits were the four great German idealists, Fichte, Schelling, Hegel and Schopenhauer. But before passing on to them we shall do well to glance at other, minor disturbances created by Kant's views.[22] Naturally enough, they resolved themselves into a battle of the *pros* and *cons,* in which, however, the *pros* often modified considerably the standpoint they were defending, in a way, sometimes, that pointed towards absolute idealism. Thus Reinhold (1758-1823), for long professor at the University of Jena, was a moderate, and cautious, and somewhat critical Kantian. He felt that Kant had taken too much for granted the fact of consciousness, just as Kant felt that Locke and Hume accepted uncritically the presence and the activity of mind. Consciousness, Reinhold felt, immediately presented us with an internal form and matter of its own, and implied a perceiving and knowing subject and an external object by which the subject was affected. The subject contributed form to conscious presentations, the object, their content, though neither the one nor the other was to be confused with experience itself. In each act of presentation an object appears and a subject perceives in one and the same act.

Although the subject cannot know things-in-themselves, but only itself as affected by them, it cannot deny the fact that it is affected, and therefore cannot deny that things-in-themselves exist. Hence we do *know* that there *are* such things. Perception is itself a formalizing in terms of time and space of the matter provided by them. The resultant perceptual experience becomes matter for further formalizing by the understanding, and the categories and concepts which enable experience to assume an intelligible structure afford, in their turn, the stuff to which reason imparts the final form of an absolute unity and a single meaning.

Consciousness is, then, in a sense, a progressive actualization of certain possibilities of representation, sensible and intelligible, which it contains within itself. This actualization, however, implies that there is an *impulse* or *drive* in consciousness towards realizing them, which appears in consciousness as *desire*. Desire is twofold—on the one hand, to be affected by things-in-themselves and to receive the matter of experience and to feel pleasure; on the other, to express the mind's ca-

[22] The ensuing discussion is largely drawn from Kuno Fischer's *Geschichte der neuern Philosophie.*

pacity for giving form to the matter thus provided. The sensible desire to receive the stuff of experience Reinhold associated with our selfish impulses and, when controlled by reason, with the search for happiness. The desire to organize experience he regarded as governed by the moral law, suffused with a sense of duty, and as a quest for the moral good.

We may remark that Reinhold makes two significant shifts in the emphasis of the Kantian system. He accents the active side of knowledge. Experience is experiencing, knowledge is knowing. And he asserts that the *existence* of things-in-themselves does not lie beyond the province of knowledge and the powers of demonstration, but is *knowable*. His views, however, put forth though they were as a constructive interpretation of Kant's philosophy, were too radical to be stomached by those who swallowed Kant, hook, line and sinker. They were also seized on eagerly by the anti-Kantians as proof positive of the justice of their complaint that Kant was really a skeptic scarcely preferable to Hume.

Schulze. A noteworthy attack upon both Kant and Reinhold was made by Schulze, in a book entitled *Aenesidemus,* in which he accused Kant of not answering Hume and of becoming involved in fatal self-contradictions. Kant's treatment of causality, he says, is still open to Hume's objections. Willy-nilly, Kant ends by assuming in the *Critique of Pure Reason* that the necessary forms of our thinking are also the necessary conditions of the *existence* of objects; in which case things-in-themselves are *knowable*. For that matter, they must be. If things-in-themselves are really unknowable, then we have no business to assume that they exist, or to assert that they in any way *cause* or are the *ground* of experience, or, as knowing subjects, *cause* our judgments and categories to be what they are.

The same difficulties, in Schulze's opinion, beset Reinhold. He tells us that things-in-themselves *exist,* and are the *causes* of our experience. But in the same breath he tells us that they are unknowable, and, by so doing, implies that reality and causation, which are characteristics of *known* experience, have no application to them.

Obviously, *unknowable* things-in-themselves are a shaky foundation on which to build a philosophy. Reality must be *knowable* if it was to be *real*. It could be rendered knowable in two ways. Either philosophy could revert to *realism,* and maintain that our minds could know external and independent objects as they *are,* or it could branch out on a new line of thought, dispense with external objects altogether, and find in the nature and activities of consciousness the essence and ground of all being. This had already been attempted by Berkeley, but in a way that shattered the unity of Reality, left its fragments without a common ground, and raised grave difficulties as to their interrelations. An *idealism* must be sought which tied together all consciousness and found for it a single underlying cause.

Maimon. In directing philosophy along this novel path, the skepticism of Salomon Maimon (1754-1800) was instrumental. According to Maimon, things-in-themselves are meaningless. They are invoked only to account for the world as it appears. They can, then, be dispensed with if we regard the *cause* of appearances as not outside but inside consciousness. Still, such a cause is not *known* by us. If it were, we should have perfect knowledge. Hence knowledge is always irrational to some extent, and can never attain complete certainty, save in the sphere of mathematics—where certainty is possible, only because we are there dealing, not with the content of consciousness, but with unavoidable conditions of experience, like space and time.

The Kantian categories, however, can claim no such certainty, since they cannot impose more unity and connection upon experience than experience actually exhibits, and experience is not given in a completely connected condition. What we shall perceive and how we shall perceive it cannot be determined beforehand. Therefore, *no* certain synthetic propositions *a priori* can be made regarding it. For all we can *know*, experiences might turn up which were not caused and not substances or qualities or definable in terms of any of the "categories."

Beck. Maimon's skeptical conclusions suggested that, if an idealistic way out of the Kantian difficulties was to be found, consciousness must be further studied with a view to discovering how it produces its content. This task was undertaken by Beck (1761-1842). Beck begins by a criticism of the theory that knowledge is a kind of registration of external objects, and that ideas agree with or represent their objects. On such a theory of knowledge Kantianism is impossible. The only possible way of straightening out Kant is to regard as *activities* of consciousness the so-called *objects* given in experience. The fundamental presentations of consciousness are not facts but acts. Perceptions are *perceivings*. The same is true of the so-called formal aspects of consciousness. Space and time are not forms, they are deeds, doings, consciousness caught in the *act* of synthesizing and organizing its acts of presentation. So, too, the categories are nothing but the *acts* of reason, not *a priori* rules by which mental activity is governed. Concepts are *conceivings*. Reality is *realizing*.

Jacobi. Another, but somewhat different, criticism of Kant was made by Jacobi (1743-1819). He could see little use in a philosophy that was self-confessedly unable to penetrate the true nature of the Real. Nor could he swallow an interpretation like Beck's that tended to transform our perceptions or perceivings of things into the objects that were perceived. He stuck, then, to a belief in things-in-themselves. But he could not accept the Kantian view that these things were unknowable and yet the causes and grounds of our perceptual experience and our knowledge. True, no amount of *reasoning* could assure us of their existence or their nature. But reason was not the only avenue of approach. The existence of things-in-themselves is a matter of instinctive belief, and this belief goes just as deeply into the nature of the Real and is just as trustworthy as any results of reasoning could be. Therefore, whereas for Kant there can be only *practical* certainty of their existence, as necessary postulates of moral action, for Jacobi there can be also an equal *theoretic* certainty. Quite apart from ethical considerations, and relying simply upon the testimony of perceptual experience, we can be certain that things-in-themselves exist.

To be sure, Jacobi feels, we can see what Kant was trying to do. His doctrine of things-in-themselves was an attempt to rescue philosophy from going over the precipice towards which it had been headed ever since the time of Descartes, and from annihilating itself, along with the existence of an external world, in a purely *subjective* idealism which reduced the Real to nothing but a dream of the perceiving and thinking subject. At the same time, Kant himself, having rescued philosophy by the device of the things-in-themselves, also came near to reducing our entire experience and knowledge of things-in-themselves to a mere figment of the mind, and thus rendering his device useless.

These philosophies, though not of the first rank, pointed the way by their criticisms of Kant to the great idealistic systems to which we now turn.

Chapter XV

FICHTE

Early Life and Education. The first of the great German idealists, Johann Gottlieb Fichte, outlived Kant by only ten years. The period through which he lived was stirring, covering, as it did, the career of Frederick the Great, the American and French Revolutions, and the rise and fall of Napoleon. It saw also the rise of the democratic movement in Germany and the first steps towards her eventual unification.

Fichte was born in 1762 at Rammenau in Saxony of a middle class family in modest circumstances, which was descended from a Swedish soldier in the army of Gustavus Adolphus, wounded and left behind in the town during the Thirty Years' War. His father, a pious, upright ribbon-maker, had married above his station, and the Fichte family was not harmonious. With his mother, from whom Fichte inherited a quarrelsome disposition, his relations were always strained. He was a studious and independent child, endowed with an extraordinary memory, which attracted the attention of a nobleman living in the neighborhood, who undertook his education. He studied theology at Jena and Leipzig, with an interim of making his living as a tutor in a Swiss family in Zurich. Here he became engaged to be married, but his difficulties in making a living and financial reverses in his fiancée's family postponed his marriage for nearly nine years.

Rise to Fame. Meantime, Fichte had fallen much under Kantian influence, and particularly under the spell of *Critique of Practical Reason* and *Critique of Judgment,* which especially appealed to the moral earnestness and enthusiasms dominant in his character. He wrote an explanation of the latter volume—his first philosophical work —which was never published. Furthermore, he went to Königsberg and had an audience with Kant, by whom he was coldly received. Not to be rebuffed, he wrote in four weeks his first published work, an *Essay Towards a Critique of all Revelations,* and submitted it to the old philosopher. Kant was delighted with it, and with Fichte, and got it published. By mistake Fichte's name and the preface he had written were omitted, and the work was ascribed to Kant himself and highly praised by the critics. Kant corrected the error, revealed the true authorship, and Fichte became famous overnight.

In this essay, Fichte attempted to fit belief in a revealed religion into the Kantian scheme, using all the Kantian methods. Such belief, he says, bound up, as it is, with a supernatural interference with the natural order, cannot be based upon either pure or practical reason, both of which present to us universal laws, physical and moral, allowing of no exceptions. However, certain occurrences associated with profound changes in our moral nature, as, for example, the phenomenon of religious conversion, may *appear* to be of supernatural origin and to be direct and exceptional revelations from God. The supernatural halo does not emanate from the event itself, which is just a sensible event like any other. Neither is it bestowed by reason, which cannot prove or disprove that the event is of supernatural origin. It is rather a matter of the imagination. A revelation, then, is an event that dispels moral confusion and brings moral peace, imagined as directly and especially produced by God to that end. No necessity of our nature impels us to regard such occurrences as divine interventions. But it is natural and highly beneficial for us in certain circumstances to do so. In time we may outgrow the need for such beliefs along with the moral conditions they accompany. For the present they have their use in promoting obedience to the moral law.

University Career at Jena. Things now began to come Fichte's way. He got married, and published, anonymously, two interesting political essays inspired by the French Revolution, defending the view that the individual has certain inalienable rights, like freedom of thought and speech and the right to change or overthrow any form of government, which are part of the essence of our moral nature. Also, he was offered and he accepted in 1794 a chair of philosophy at the University of Jena, which at that time was the most famous university in Germany and a leader in the new philosophic and literary movements. Furthermore, it received additional light from the nearby court of Weimar, whose ruler vied with the princes of the Italian Renaissance in gathering about himself a galaxy of genius, in which Goethe stood pre-eminent.

Philosophically, the university was steeped in Kant, of which hitherto it had enjoyed the somewhat weak and tepid infusion supplied by Reinhold, Fichte's predecessor. The new and more fiery, more morally tinctured, and more emotional interpretation provided by

Fichte won immediate approval and enthusiastic support. His lectures on Kant, however, became more and more an exposition of his own maturing views, of which his various publications with regard to his *Wissenschaftslehre,* or *Theory of Science,* are a summary.

The system he set forth made many converts. Reinhold adopted it wholeheartedly. Jacobi, one of Fichte's most eminent contemporaries, was readily attracted by it, in spite of his skepticism regarding the power of reason to lead us to any but atheistic and fatalistic conclusions about the nature of Reality, and his consequent insistence upon the validity of intuition and immediate perception of truth. At the same time, Fichte made many enemies. The more conservative Kantians were aghast at the liberties he was taking with their master, and Kant himself was so annoyed by the Fichtean interpretation of his philosophy and so alarmed by the charges of atheism it provoked, that he publicly repudiated it.

In other respects, too, Fichte soon found his position at Jena becoming more and more difficult. His temper and his discretion were not of the best. His political views were suspect. His proposal to lecture on Sunday mornings, though at an hour that would not conflict with divine service, was hailed as an attempt to introduce the cult of the Goddess of Reason at the moment worshiped in France, and raised such a rumpus that, at the instance of the Weimar Government, the hour was shifted to the afternoon. Then, too, private efforts that he made to abolish student societies, or rather his public submission of the question to the university authorities, led to riotous manifestations against him which necessitated his withdrawal for a time to the country. Last but not least, he was accused of atheism, and, though he vigorously defended himself against the charge, he refused to be guided in any way by the university authorities, and thumbed his nose at the Saxe-Weimar Government. His threat of resignation was taken at its face-value by the Weimar Council, whose decision was concurred in by the Grand Duke, and in 1799 he was to all intents and purposes dismissed from Jena.

Move to Berlin. He had, however, powerful friends in Berlin, like Schlegel, the leader of the German Romantic school, and the theologian and moralist Schleiermacher, who arranged for him to come to the Prussian capital. This was done without difficulty. Kant's persecutor, Frederick William II, was dead, and his easy-going son, reassured as to Fichte's political innocuousness, dismissed the philosopher's asserted irreligion with the intimation that atheists were God's concern, not his.

At first, things went smoothly. He was on intimate terms with

Schlegel and Schleiermacher, and with the philosopher Schelling, whose views we shall presently describe. But in Berlin, as in Jena, peace was shortlived. In 1800 Fichte published his *Vocation of Man*. Its highly moral tone offended both the sentimental romanticism of Schlegel and the rationalism of the old guard, including Schleiermacher, who wrote bitter criticisms of it. Schelling, too, was drifting away from the Fichtean philosophy and setting up a philosophy of his own, and he and Fichte disputed with each other in increasingly acrimonious terms.

However, so far as the general public was concerned, Fichte had a huge success in Berlin. He had, to be sure, no university position, but the public lectures he gave were crammed with the best people. Nor were academic offers tardy in presenting themselves. The Russians called him to Kharkov, the Bavarians to Landshut, but he declined the proffered positions. Finally, it was arranged that he should teach summers at the University of Erlangen. He was also writing continuously. His Erlangen lectures were published under the title of the *Nature of the Scholar,* and were quickly supplemented by a series given in Berlin *On the Characteristics of the Present Age,* and *The Way Towards the Blessed Life, or Doctrine of Religion,* in which he vehemently denounced the corruption, as he saw it, of the times, and recalled humanity to what he considered its true destiny.

The "Addresses to the German Nation." The Napoleonic Wars had now burst upon Europe, and Prussia, deserted by the other German States, and facing Napoleon alone, was defeated at Jena. Fichte had volunteered as a lay chaplain, but had been refused. Now, with the government deserting Berlin, he went first to Königsberg, where he taught at the university, and then to Copenhagen, as the French invaded East Prussia. But within a year he was back in Berlin again, delivering his famous *Addresses to the German Nation* under the upturned noses and the somewhat contemptuous gaze of the French, who still occupied Berlin, and who felt, apparently, too secure to be bothered with suppressing such idealistic rantings.

The theme of the *Addresses* is the superiority of the German nation to all others. The Germans are the purest, the most homogeneous and the most vital of all races. The German language is the best of all languages. In the German Reformation the Christian religion attains its greatest height. In German philosophy the human mind reaches its greatest profundity. It is the mission of Germany to realize her cultural possibilities and to Teutonize the world.

To fulfill her glorious destiny Germany must unite. To unite she must rally round Prussia, her natural center of gravity. 'ı o maintain her unity, she must develop and impose a system of education which will bring her genius to fruition, inspire her people with a sense of their racial, historical, and cultural oneness, and arouse in them a burning love of the Fatherland.

Fichte's ideas on education received a new stimulation from the proposal to establish a university at Berlin. He was asked to submit proposals for a scheme of organization—which he did at length. But his ideas were too radical to be accepted. However, he was given a post at the new university, which was opened in 1810. He now attempted a new exposition of his system in lectures on the *Facts of Consciousness, Transcendental Logic,* and *Theory of Law,* which, however, were inferior to his earlier works and added little to them. His temper, too, was deteriorating, and he was again involved in academic disputes. Indeed, after a few months he resigned the rectorship of the University, to which he had been appointed, simply because he could not have his own way in everything.

Death. It was well perhaps that Fichte's life should be near its end. He was permitted to die, as he had lived, with his boots on, and to escape what might well have been years of decreasing power and increasing petulance.

The beginning of Napoleon's end was at hand, and his armies in retreat from Moscow were straggling in confusion through Germany. The moment for liberation had struck. In March, 1813, Prussia allied herself with Russia and declared war upon France. Fichte volunteered again, but was once more refused. His voice, however, was heard, extolling the justice of the Prussian cause and prophesying in the war a new means for hastening the unification of Germany under Prussian leadership.

Meantime, the wounded were pouring into Berlin in such numbers that an appeal was made for volunteer nurses. Fichte's wife responded at once and worked in the hospitals during the winter of 1813. Early in 1814 she was taken with a fever. Fichte, whose health had been failing for some time, tended her devotedly, passing the day at her bedside and postponing his lectures till evening. Just as she was recovering Fichte was stricken with the same disease. He lay in a coma for eleven days, and died on January 27th.

II. INFLUENCE OF KANT AND THE MINOR KANTIANS

It is fair, I think, to say that the theme of Fichte's philosophy is in the main a dramatization of *Critique of Practical Reason* and *Critique of Judgment,* in which some of the suggestions dropped by the lesser Kantians we have just been discussing were also adopted and organized. He agrees with Reinhold in regarding consciousness as essentially an activity busied with realizing its own potentialities. With Maimon he holds that things-in-themselves are not necessary to explain the content of consciousness, which can be derived from the thinking subject. Furthermore, he takes the hint dropped by the Jewish philosopher that consciousness is at heart a search for an ideal that is never attained. Again, he is sympathetic with Beck's contention that the objects and presentations of consciousness are really *acts* of the mind, in which it represents to itself its own nature, and that Reality is essentially a dynamic, not a static, affair, a process of *realizing* rather than a condition of realization. With Jacobi, too, he is ready to admit that *feeling* brings us closer than *reasoning* to the nature of the Real. The upshot of it all is that Fichte throws the unknowable *objective* things-in-themselves into the discard, and regards Reality as an absolute thinker or "ego" producing its own experience out of itself, and progressively organizing its experience in accordance with necessities imposed by its essentially moral and purposive nature.

In the *Wissenschaftslehre,* or *System of Science,*[1] Fichte works out this conclusion in a systematic and detailed manner. The goal of philosophy, he tells us, is to reduce all human experience and activity, all science and all knowledge, to a fundamental principle which shall be one, self-evident, absolute, exhaustive, all-comprehending, and all-explaining. By the degree of its approximation to this goal the value and truth of any particular philosophy must be judged. So tried, all *realistic* systems are found wanting. They lead to materialism and fatalism. They satisfy only lower types of intellect. They cannot explain the existence and nature of consciousness, and hence they leave the problem of knowledge without solution. Consciousness can be accounted for, and knowledge can be made intelligible, only on the hypothesis that consciousness itself is the active principle from which the whole universe is derived.

[1] The discussion of the *Wissenschaftslehre* is founded on Kuno Fischer's *Geschichte der neuern Philosophie.*

III. THE NATURE AND IMPLICATIONS OF SELF-CONSCIOUSNESS

The Ego and the Non-Ego. Let us now examine consciousness. We are struck at once, with the fact that every act of experience and thought involves the assertion of the existence of a thinker, or ego. Every "think" is an "I think." It is wrong, then, Fichte feels, to interpret Kant *realistically* and to look upon the things-in-themselves as entities existing independently of thought, unknowable in themselves. They rather represent ideal limits or goals of our thinking set by the activity of thought itself. To endow them with an existence over and above what they mean to consciousness is a faulty interpretation of their nature.

The existence, however, of the subjective thing-in-itself, the thinking subject or "ego," is a necessary postulate, or assumption, of all thinking, and therefore of all existing. But this assumption of the existence of a thinking subject is obviously an act of that same subject. When I say "I am," it is *I* who say it. It is *I* who assume my existence.

This postulation of its own existence by the ego is the first and fundamental principle of the Fichtean philosophy. Since it is a first principle, it cannot be proved. It can only be felt and lived. It can only be *acted upon* as if it were true. I cannot force a man to assume his own existence. I can only ask him to.

Now it is necessary to my *self*-consciousness that I should project a part of my experience outside my *self,* make of it an external object, and assume that it is not myself. Otherwise, I should have nothing to distinguish myself from and to contrast myself with. Since, then, the existence of self-consciousness depends upon a consciousness, also, of something not myself, *the ego,* says Fichte, *in postulating its own existence, necessarily assumes the existence of a non-ego.* This is the second principle of his philosophy.

However, the distinction between subject and object is still a distinction *within* experience. If, then, there were no ego to do the experiencing, there would be no non-ego to be experienced. On the other hand, if there were no non-ego for the ego to experience as something different from itself, there would be no object distinct from the thinking subject, and hence no thinking subject distinct from the object. Either aspect, therefore, is necessary to the existence of the other, and both are equally necessary to the existence of a self-conscious experience.

IV. THE ABSOLUTE EGO

Expressions of an Absolute Ego. But, in that case, both the empirical ego and the empirical non-ego—that is, both what I recognize in my experience to be myself, and what I recognize as not myself—must be two aspects of a transcendental "I," or ego, that thinks itself in these two ways in order to become self-conscious. This transcendental thinker, which creates an experience in which *selves* are distinguished from one another and from objects they assume to be external to them, is called by Fichte the Absolute Ego.

The division of the Absolute Ego into subject and object gives rise to another fundamental distinction, this time within the "me" part of my experience. In so far as I am acted upon and determined by the external world, I am a receptive and *passive* being, a mere *spectator* of existence. As such I am, in Fichte's words, *theoretic*. On the other hand, in so far as my experience and behavior are not simply *reactions* to external circumstances determined by the nature of those circumstances, but are my own *actions* determined only by myself, I am an *active* and *practical* being.

Behind this opposition of empirical activity and passivity there must be an absolute activity, which is not conditioned by a corresponding receptivity or passivity external to itself. On the contrary, it must be conceived as self-conditioning and self-supporting, and therefore as freely determining the opposition of activity and passivity within itself, just as it divides itself on its own initiative into the ego and the non-ego. In short, the Absolute Ego freely *wills* to be what it is.

We are now ready to "deduce" five fundamental forms of thinking and existing, *reality, negation, relation, causality,* and *substance.* When I say "I am" and thereby assert my own existence, I postulate myself as *real.* When I distinguish what is not myself from myself, I use for the first time the word *"not."* When I postulate both myself and what is not myself as interacting and interconnected in my experience, I *relate* the ego and the non-ego to each other. In regarding, as I must, the experience of which I am the passive and recipient spectator as also an experience originating in the creative activity of my own thinking, I am asserting that the passive and theoretic part of my nature is a *result* of which the practical part of my nature is the *cause.* Finally, in regarding both myself and what is not myself as two co-ordinate parts or factors of *my* experience, I am asserting both myself and the external world to be *modifications* of an absolute self or *substance* underlying both the experience I call *myself* and the experience I call outer and objective.

V. THE ANSTÖSSE OF THE ABSOLUTE EGO

The Development of the Absolute Ego. We see now *why* the Absolute Ego divides its experience into an ego and a non-ego reciprocally conditioning each other's existence. It does so *in order to become self-conscious.* But to become *self*-conscious, we must *reflect* upon our experience. Complete self-consciousness can only be attained on the level of reflective knowledge, which acquaints us with the truth about ourselves. It is the complete self-consciousness given in self-*knowledge* that the Absolute Ego is seeking to attain. And, since the postulation of the non-ego is the first condition of self-consciousness, such postulation, with the resultant universe composed of "me" and "not-me" in infinite profusion and variety, is a necessary means to the Absolute's knowledge of itself.

The development of absolute self-knowledge proceeds by a succession of definite acts, called by Fichte *Anstösse,* or thrusts. The first of these *Anstösse* creates mere unreflective sensation, which is a step above unconsciousness. The moment, however, that sensation appears, the Ego has limited itself by creating a definite and restricted content of consciousness.

The second *Anstoss* takes place when the Ego, in becoming *aware* of the fact that it is perceiving, differentiates itself from its perceptions and thus turns them into a non-ego *other than* itself.

The third *Anstoss* is accomplished when the Ego, by means of memory and imagination, turns its perceptions into a world of *objects* and its awareness of them into a consciousness of *things.*

At this point the categories come into play. The non-ego seems to be the *substance* of which different "things" are the *modifications,* and also seems to *cause* the subjective images which picture and duplicate within the ego the experiences we call the external world. At this point, also, we get space and time. Space is the principle that differentiates individual objects from one another, however alike they may be in all other respects, and that breaks the non-ego into a multitude of external objects reciprocally excluding and limiting one another. Time is the expression of the fact that these objects alter their spatial relations to one another in a certain irreversible order, which cannot be run backward.

The fourth *Anstoss* occurs when the Ego reflects upon the subjective images in consciousness, classifies them, abstracts general ideas from them, and thinks about them in general terms. The fifth comes to pass when the Ego again reflects upon these concepts, and by exercise of the faculty of judgment arranges them in logical relations to one another. Finally, in the sixth *Anstoss,* the Ego reflects upon its powers of judgment, recognizes itself as the originator of the laws that govern its thinking, and knows itself to be the basis of its own knowledge. Could I myself fully accomplish this step, I should know the whole truth about the universe, the whole universe would be wholly *within* my experience, the distinction between the ego and the non-ego would disappear, and I, the finite ego, should have become identical with and indistinguishable from the Absolute Ego. But in that case, I and the universe, and consciousness itself, would have disappeared, since all are dependent for their existence on an opposition between an ego and a non-ego.

VI. THE NATURE OF THE ABSOLUTE EGO

The Absolute Ego an Eternally Uncompleted Process, with God as a Goal. We have now further light upon the nature of the Absolute Ego. The Absolute Ego is not a substance. It is a *process.* It is a *striving* towards a goal. But *striving* implies a struggle against resistance. To be *striving,* then, is to find obstacles and limitations to overcome. Without these obstacles there could be no overcoming, no winning. Hence if the Ego is to *win* and to *attain,* it must impose limitations upon itself for the purpose of conquering and doing away with them. The world-process is like a game which can be played and won only by the aid of an opponent and of set rules regulating the moves.

Striving, moreover, implies *will*. So we are led back once more to the fact that the Absolute Ego is an Absolute Will. And we can now understand the distinction between the practical and the theoretic ego as a twofold *purpose* of this will. The will's purpose to be conscious of itself is the basis of the theoretic ego and the foundation of *knowledge*. Its *purpose* to translate this knowledge into action and to *enact* its ideal is the basis of the practical ego and the foundation of *morals*.

We have talked of the Ego as purposing and willing to know its own nature and to express that nature in action. But what is its nature? What is the ideal it is seeking to enact? Fichte's answer is that the goal the Ego sets before itself is activity for activity's sake; activity, free and spontaneous, such as we find in playing a game. For in a game our opponents and obstacles are not forced upon us against our will, but are freely chosen and welcomed, and we strive to win, not for the sake of winning, but because the striving to win is part of the game itself. This ideal of a completely free and spontaneous activity, indulged in and carried on for its own sake, is God.

God, however, must forever remain an unrealized ideal. For the Ego cannot attain to absolutely *free* activity without putting an end to that struggle *towards* freedom which is its essence. In the act of *winning* it would do away with itself, since its very self is a *process* and a *striving*—an attempt to win. We have already seen how the attainment of the ideal of absolute *knowledge* would abolish the distinction between ego and non-ego, and thus destroy consciousness. We have now to see that the attainment of the absolute moral *good* is for a like reason impossible.

VII. THE BASIS OF MORALITY

Morality a Struggle for Freedom. The eternal *struggle* to realize the ideal of absolute freedom and the equally eternal *failure* to do so, in which the life of the Ego consists, are seen in the situation of the finite egos, that is, of ourselves. To the finite egos, life seems cruel and harsh. The obstacles and the antagonists it opposes to our self-fulfillment appear as part of the non-ego and as an interference with our liberty, and our struggle with our environment and our fellow-men feels not like an exercise of freedom, but like a struggle against necessity. These limitations we cannot remove, neither can we *will* that they should cease to exist, for in so doing we should will our own destruction. We can, however, will to open our minds to the ideal at which the Absolute Ego is aiming. We can discipline ourselves to regard suffering and failure and misfortune and defeat, not as a thwarting of liberty by necessity, but as incidents in a *struggle* that we *welcome* and *freely* accept.

This self-discipline is a *moral* process. Its *purpose* is to enact the ideal of freedom in the life of the finite ego, so far as such enactment is possible. It is, then, an affair of the *practical* activities of the ego. It is, moreover, a discipline *freely* undertaken. It has to be if it is to be a *moral* process, for only that which we freely chose has ethical significance.

The Essentially Social Character of Free and Moral Action. But how can the finite egos possibly possess and exercise freedom of any sort, not to speak of choice? In so far as they are physical events—

different bodies as well as different selves—they are subject to the same determinism as governs the activities of all other physical bodies. And their wills seem to be constrained by drives, desires, and motives connected with their physical constitutions. In short, we appear as parts of a mechanically run universe subject to the causal law of necessary connection between events. The physical universe, then, seemingly affords no theater for moral conduct.

However, certain of the physical bodies by which I am surrounded and influenced do not *force* me to act. They rather invite and persuade me. These bodies behave towards me as if I were a free and autonomous being. But, if I feel that they are dealing with me as if I were free, I cannot but feel that *their* action, also, is freely, not mechanically, motivated. In other words, I feel that they are *fellow-men,* with egos inside them like my own ego. With such physical events my relations are not deterministic. My response to their influence is a *free* response. My interconnection with them is a *moral* relation. Moreover, only towards bodies of this sort can my behavior have any *moral* significance for me. In short, ethical conduct is essentially *social* in its origin and public in character.

VIII. SOCIETY AND THE STATE

The Function of the State to Guarantee Freedom. Since *moral* freedom is *social* in character, right, justice, and the like are dependent upon a *society* of egos. In the presence of other selves, each individual self has the *right* to be treated as a free, self-determining ego by its fellow-egos, and is under the *duty* of treating them as free, as long as they respect its rights. This right to be treated as a free being may be defended by force if necessary. But before using force, we must be certain that our rights have really been infringed upon by others. To decide this, appeal must be made to a neutral judge capable of giving a disinterested decision. In accepting his decision, I do not lose my freedom, since, if the decision is just and impartial, it expresses the will of all moral beings, including myself, and therefore fulfills my own will in so far as my will is moral and self-determined. Still, I cannot be expected to accept his decision unless I know the judge has the power to enforce it and to make others respect my rights. In short, there must be a state empowered to put the decree into effect.

The state is essentially a contract between individuals to respect one another's inalienable *rights* to self-preservation, property, and freedom from bodily violence, all of which are necessary conditions of the free development of the personality of the Ego. The enforcement of this contract must be delegated to a *government,* itself governed by law, and answerable to the people for the execution of laws made by the people. To preserve law and order the state must have force at its command to prevent and punish crime. It must also possess the means, military and economic, of protecting its citizens against the competition or aggression of other states. It is also the duty of the state to provide its citizens with a livelihood, not through charity, but by providing them with an opportunity to work.

The Private Freedom and Duty of the Individual. The life of the individual, however, is by no means exhausted by his membership in the state or his duties as a citizen. He has also a sphere of private life and private action in which he is free to express his individuality as he pleases. It is the duty of the state not to interfere, itself, with the individual's freedom of private life, judgment, and behavior, and to protect that freedom against infringement by other people.

At the same time, the sphere of private life is a sphere of private *duties* of the utmost importance. For example, the relations between the sexes and between parent and child are the most intimate means of developing the self-consciousness and freedom at which the Absolute Ego aims. Moreover, the family is the fundamental unit of society. Hence the state is justified in regulating these relations and in requiring the fulfillment of the obligations involved in marriage, the proper care and education of children, and the like.

Again, private morality enjoins conduct towards both one's fellow citizens and the citizens of other states that the state itself does not require of, and impose upon, the individual.

IX. THE RECONCILIATION OF MAN WITH NATURE

The Necessity of Freely Willing and Accepting the Natural Order. In the state, however, the attainment of freedom has not reached its last possible stage, and therefore the potentialities of the moral life have not been exhausted. The state, to be sure, introduces the maximum of possible freedom into the relations of the finite egos to one another, but there remains to be solved the problem of the relation of man as a whole to the universe—the non-ego—with which he is confronted and by which he is limited. How is the maximum of freedom to be attained in his dealings with it?

The formal conditions of the reconciliation of man with nature are easily enough described. The Ego must will *freely* the mechanical and deterministic order that limits it. The moment it does that it will become wholly aware of its own origination of its activities, and will overcome the conflict between freedom and necessity in a completely attained consciousness of its self-determination. In that event it would feel thoroughly at home in the world, and would see itself, its ideal, and all the rules and the moves of the game, enacted in its life.

Here, then, is the final problem of morality—to remake our actual world into a world of that sort, to conform the real to the ideal, and to reconcile the rules of the game with our desires, and our natural impulses with our spiritual cravings. With the solution of this problem, the real and the ideal, the mechanical and the teleological, would be amalgamated, and perfect freedom would be attained in perfect self-service. Conscience is the call of the ideal of freedom and completeness rebuking the incompleteness and partiality of our finite natures.

Attainment of the Moral Ideal Would Destroy Morality. *Complete* moral freedom, however, is as unattainable as complete *mental* freedom, and for the same reasons. To do away with the opposition between the ego and the non-ego in the moral world by realizing the ideal would be as fatal as overcoming it would be in the sphere of knowledge. Destroy the distinction in the one case, and consciousness itself would disappear; destroy it in the other, and morality would disappear. For moral activity, like consciousness, rests upon the Ego's contrasting itself with something not itself. Without the foil of vice and evil to contend with there could be no merit, no virtue, no moral worth. The annihilation of evil, then, which is the guiding ideal of moral action, would mean the annihilation of the moral good as well. Therefore *complete* moral freedom, like the complete mental freedom of absolute knowledge, must in the nature of things remain an ideal forever unattained, but nonetheless forever sought.

X. THE DUTIES OF MAN

Nevertheless, in spite of the fact that the moral law can never be completely enacted in our behavior towards either the limitations imposed upon us by our fellow-men, or those to which we are subjected by the non-ego, we must always conform our attitude and our conduct to its behests. We must always do right with no ulterior motive, simply because it is right to do so. We must do our duty, and do it solely for the sake of doing it. Being the sources of our deeds, we are responsible for them and for allowing ourselves to be motivated by other considerations than those of duty and right doing.

Behavior to be Moral Must be Rational. Moral action, however, is always *rational* action. It is rational, and hence moral, to subordinate the physical to the spiritual. But it is irrational and therefore immoral to *sacrifice* the physical to the spiritual, particularly if that sacrifice is motivated by love of power and fame rather than by pure love of doing what we think is right. We have certain *physical obligations* towards ourselves, and it is our *duty* to keep our bodies sufficiently strong and healthy to subserve their moral purposes.

So, too, our minds, which are the vehicles and the tools of the moral life, must be kept free and uncramped and unwarped, and their activities must be guided by the moral law and devoted to the attainment of the moral ideal of freedom. We are morally bound, also, to improve ourselves, to fulfill our duty as citizens, and to make the best of ourselves in our various walks of life and in our several professions.

XI. ART AND THE ARTIST

The Freedom of Beauty and Art. Beauty, like truth and goodness, is an expression of freedom. The artist in creating beauty feels free and undetermined by anything except his artistic genius, and the contemplation and enjoyment of the beautiful is shot through and through with a sense of liberation. Nay more, the free and spontaneous work of the artist is a direct revelation of the creative activity of the Absolute Ego fermenting within him. And the mind in its contemplation of the beautiful object not only receives a foretaste of absolute freedom, but is shown how a world that seems to exist independently of us may be in reality freely produced and fashioned by ourselves.

Beauty, then, is a *moral* value, and the activity of the artist is a *moral* activity. Still, the liberation effected by esthetic experience is not to be confused either with knowledge of the truth which makes us free, or yet with the practical moral activities by which freedom is won through struggle. The sense of beauty is a distinct avenue of approach to the ideal. For Fichte, as for Kant, the beautiful exhibits "purposiveness without purpose." Unsought for, it satisfies desire. Artistic creativity prescribes no ends to itself, but fulfills the supreme purpose of the will, which is to be free.

It follows that the artist is under a moral obligation to do the *best* that is within him and to exhibit the ideal. And a second-rate man, although it is not his fault that he is not a good artist, is under moral obligation not to produce for public consumption work that, because of his lack of genius, must in the nature of things be also second-rate.

Finally, the more free the whole man is, the greater the opportunity for the expression of the artistic genius in him. No one can be a good artist who is not also a good all-round human being. So, too, sound appreciation of art and judgments of taste cannot be had from men locked within the esthetic interest to the exclusion of all else.

Esthetic Experience Self-Justifying. Fichte notes the similarity between esthetic experience, which contemplates the beautiful object, and the contemplation of truth by the scientist and the philosopher. In both we have a contemplation of pure form which pays no attention to the other aspects and bearings of the object in which it appears.

Again, both sorts of contemplation are ends in themselves, and both confer freedom upon the spirit. The philosopher, in so far as he is a philosopher, cannot wish the truth to be other than it is. If he has got hold of what he thinks is the truth, his love of truth and his search for it are satisfied, whatever the truth may be. He cannot be committed beforehand to some particular point of view he would prefer to find true and would regret finding false. In the same way, a man in love with beauty cannot wish the beautiful object to be other than it is. He is content with the loveliness of what he is contemplating, whatever it may be. As a moralist or a scientist he might regret that so fair a thing should be frail or false but as a connoisseur of beauty he could not deplore that so frail or false a thing should be so fair. Beauty, like truth, whatever it pertains to, pacifies the will and enraptures the soul.

XII. THE REVISED SYSTEM

Solipsism Logically Necessary but Morally Impossible. The presentation of Fichte's system in the *Wissenschaftslehre* aroused a philosophic storm. Particularly, his doctrine that God is an unrealized and unrealizable ideal, and, at that, a state of being rather than a person, evoked the charge of atheism to which we have already referred. So it was that almost immediately he deemed it advisable to restate his views in a way that would make them clearer to the public as well as to his opponents. The most important work of this era of reconstruction was *The Vocation of Man,* published in 1800.

The earlier chapters of this work do little more than restate in a form more palatable to, and digestible by, the popular mind the main theses of the *Wissenschaftslehre.* We are *free,* Fichte reiterates, not only with a freedom of self-determination, *within* the causal linkage of events, but also because we freely *cause* the experienced world to which that linkage, along with space and time and the other categories, gives formal structure. For the so-called *external* world is still *my* world, a part of *my* experience and therefore also *within* myself. My consciousness of the outer world is, then, really a representative of myself to myself.

The *logical* conclusions to be drawn from these considerations, Fichte continues, are that I myself alone exist, and that the whole universe, including other persons, is the creation of my own mind. However, as a moral, practical, active being, I have to act *as if* other persons besides myself existed, and *as if* I were surrounded and limited by an environment of which I am not the creator. I have, then, at least *to believe* that other selves and that external objects exist.

Nature of Moral Obligations. Now the moral and practical situation which involves this *belief,* and the conduct based upon it, imposes upon me obligations towards the experiences I call my fellow-men. But, Fichte goes on in the last chapter of the *Vocation,* if these experiences represent merely dream personages and not other real selves like my own, the sense of *duties* owed them is ridiculous, and my practical life is a kind of delirium. A duty towards a mere figment of my imagination would rest on insanity pure and simple. To act morally would be an exhibition of madness. On the other hand, if other selves *really* exist independently of me, and the experience to which I attribute objectivity is *really* objective, my moral activities have significance. Furthermore, if truth and the pursuit of it are nothing but a figment of my imagination and a dream image, then so-called knowledge is madness too. The *assumption* of the existence of an external world is therefore an assumption without which we cannot act, or think, or even live. Nor can we avoid making this assumption. It is not a consciously and deliberately formulated hypothesis. It is rather unconscious, instinctive, implicit, and prior to thinking and willing.

The Eternal and the Temporal Orders. What is, then, the ideal bound up with the *faith* in an objective reality larger than ourselves imposed upon us by our moral nature? It is the *improvement* of the world. It is possible, and it is our duty, to *better* the world in many ways. Evils of all sorts, physical, political, economic, and moral, confront us and impose upon us an obligation to remove them.

The ideal world, which would result if they were done away with, presents itself to us in two lights. On the one hand, it is something that can only be realized in the *future*. It is a divine, far-off event, towards which the whole creation moves, but towards which it can be conceived as moving by a purely mechanical and material process. The world-process may be a blind, non-purposive progress in the course of which the things we find evil will be automatically eliminated. In that case, we are simply being swept helplessly along, willy-nilly, towards perfection. On the other hand, the ideal is something that can be realized in the *present,* by my own free will and act. I can cooperate with the natural process towards perfection, if such a process exists, and I can deliberately direct the course of nature towards the realization of human ends. I can here and now freely will the ideal to dwell in my own life, and can incarnate it in my own thought and action. In short, in the midst of imperfection I can live perfectly, and thus anticipate in my own self the goodness towards which the whole universe aspires.

But I can scarcely incarnate in my present life an ideal whose realization is only possible in the future. There must, therefore, already exist an ideal moral order of which at the present moment I am a member. This order which is equally attainable in the past, the present, and the future, is plainly something to which time and its divisions make no difference. It is lifted altogether clear of time. It is eternal.

Moral Action an Incarnation of the Eternal in Temporal Form. To live morally is to live irradiated by the vision of the eternal. Every good act is an incarnation of the eternal in temporal form. No good deed, however futile and fruitless it may seem to have been, is vain. Issuing from the eternal, it has made the eternal manifest in time, and has made the moment in which it was incarnate a portion of eternity. It may, indeed, seem ineffectual as a means towards bringing the ideal to pass in the future. It may be wrecked by the evil it is seeking to remove. But even so, it in itself, by the mere fact of its commission, realizes the ideal it seeks to serve.

This eternal order which justifies the moral will and is enriched by all good deeds, however wasted they may seem as efforts to redeem the world, is the expression of an infinite moral will, of whose striving for self-realization the world-process is the expression. This will is God. Of it and him our wills and minds are parts. What seems evil in it is merely an occasion for overcoming evil, and a testing of our power to overcome it. It is the necessary condition of the struggle, without which there would be no duties, no merit, no moral values, no good, and no God.

The World-Process the Self-Development of God. In *The Way Towards the Blessed Life or Doctrine of Religion,* Fichte continues in the lyric and mystical tone of the *Vocation.* In the first lecture, he points out that the world-process is an aspiration and a search for true existence. It has no true existence in itself. Hence love of the world

can never bring peace. Peace is only to be found in fixing our affections upon the eternal.

But how and where is the eternal to be found? Through thought
and knowledge, Fichte replies. We must *know* the truth, must *know*
God. By knowing the truth and contemplating the eternal our minds
put on eternity and become one with the source and ground of all
existence. In that knowledge the distinction between subject and object
is overcome, and God is all in all.

Having in the second and third lectures defined the object of all
true love and the means by which that love is consummated, Fichte
turns in the fourth lecture to a defense of his position. The first objection that will be made arises from the difficulty of deriving the multiple, varied world from the One that underlies it. Fichte replies that
the existent, in existing *in* itself, also must exist *for* itself. In the act
of being, God, then, must represent to himself the existence of his own
being. In this act of representation he becomes conscious. He *knows*
that he exists. In a word, God's being, which is one, eternal and unchangeable, can be apprehended by him and become a "self" of which
he can become conscious, only if it is characterized as a universe containing a plurality of selves and not-selves. In this way the many proceed from the One.

The Five Stages of Salvation. With an interlude of a lecture [2] squaring Fichte's view with Christianity, the rest of the work is devoted to
setting forth the stages through which the finite self must pass in
order to attain salvation. The path of knowledge leads us from sense-
experience to a rational order pervading that experience, and then to
an understanding of this order as a revelation of the being of God, and
to an apprehension of the human mind that understands it as an image
of the divine reason. Next, we see as in a glass darkly that our intellects
are really one with the intelligible order upon which they reflect, and
that the finite self is really one with God. Another step, and we see,
as it were, the truth and God face to face, and gain in abandonment
of our selves to God an immediate awareness of our unity with him.
Upon this supervenes the fifth and final stage, the enjoyment of the
Beatific Vision, in which the finite self is made one with God.

These five stages have their parallel in the practical and moral life.
Freedom can only be obtained by living and experiencing them all.
The sensible world, and the vision of Paradise that represents life after
death in sensible terms, set up as the moral ideal a happiness founded
on the natural life of man. The apprehension of an intelligible order

[2] Lecture VI.

in sense-experience is accompanied by a morality founded on reason, whose ideal is a Stoic calm and independence on external events. Both these ethics are uninspired and self-centered.

Ethics and the Inner Life. When, however, we understand that both our reasons and the rational order of the universe are the expression of a higher power, ethics becomes something warm and glowing. We are fired with the sense of a mission to perform, and in throwing ourselves into it and fulfilling it as best we can we find our happiness. But, even so, our ethics conceives the good as something lying in the future, to be attained by material accomplishments and "reforms" of one sort or another.

With the dawning sense of the unity of the finite self with God, our moral emphasis is shifted from worldly activities and ideals of material reforms, physical, social, economic and the like, to the inner life. We now perceive that our true mission is to live in the presence of the eternal and to enact it in our own selves. And finally, loving God with all our mind and all our soul and all our strength, we come by the moral path to the same Beatific Vision to which knowledge raised us. For God is love. He loves to exist, and he loves the world begotten by his awareness of his existence. And the world loves him in return, and we in our successive acts of reflection are impelled by love of him. "Love is therefore higher than all Reason; it is itself the fountain of Reason and the root of Reality; the sole creator of Life and Time—and thus," Fichte concludes, "I have finally declared to you the highest real point of view of a Doctrine of Being, Life and Blessedness—that is of True Speculation, towards which we have hitherto been gradually advancing." [3]

Contemporary Criticisms of Fichte. Besides the charge of atheism, which Fichte tried, as we have just seen, to refute, another objection to his system was made by his contemporaries and successors. He had reduced the non-ego, or nature, so they said, to a purely passive and negative creation of the ego. Such reduction was not true to experience. In experience nature does not appear as passive but as active, possessed of a highly complicated and highly dynamic structure, and endowed with a being and a power as real and as self-supporting as the being and the operations of the thinking subject. In experience the relations between the subject and the object are reciprocal, and object depends on subject as much and as little as subject depends on object. The body depends upon the soul no more than the soul upon the body.

[3] Lecture X (trans. Smith, *Fichte's Works*, London, 1873), p. 539.

Being may lie in being experienced, but to be experienced a thing must be.

The ego, then, cannot be regarded as even logically prior to the non-ego. Nor is there any warrant for supposing it creates the non-ego. Both, rather, appear to be produced by something more profound than either of them—something to which neither the term "subject" nor "object" can be applied. This point was at once brought up by Schelling, Fichte's friend and for a brief space his colleague at the University of Jena.

Chapter XVI

SCHELLING

I. LIFE

Influence of Fichte and Hegel. Friedrich von Schelling (1775-1854) was the son of a professor of Oriental Studies and Theology at Tübingen. He was early attracted by Kant and Fichte, and his earliest philosophical works were expositions of the latter's system, in which, however, he showed considerable independence of thought, and a growing interest in nature and science. This interest bore fruit in his *Ideas Regarding a Philosophy of Nature* (1797), and an essay *On the World-Soul* published in 1798.

That year he became a professor of philosophy at Jena, where Fichte still held a chair. He taught there five years, and quickly became the leader of the Romantic Movement in the university. Meantime he was becoming less and less sympathetic with Fichte's doctrine, and also with the view of Hegel, who was also teaching at Jena, and whose star was destined to be the brightest philosophic luminary of the nineteenth century. To this period belong further works on the philosophy of nature, his *System of Transcendental Idealism,* and his *Bruno.*

After leaving Jena, Schelling taught at Würzburg. His conceit made him many enemies there, as, indeed, it had at Jena. Eventually it got him into difficulties with the government. In 1804 he published a new statement of his philosophic views (*Darstellung meines Systems*) and other lectures in which he struggled with the problems raised by his criticism of Fichte and Fichte's criticism of him. From Jena he moved to Munich, where he lived quietly for the next thirty-five years. Shortly after his arrival, his work *On the Relation of the Fine Arts to Nature* appeared. After that he published little, but nevertheless went on developing his system.

In 1841 he was made a Prussian privy councilor and a member of the Berlin Academy, and began a course of lectures on the philosophy of religion. But, as his enemies succeeded in pirating the manuscript of his lectures before they were delivered and issuing them privately, Schelling abandoned the course. The nine last years of his life he passed in philosophic silence, and it was not till after his death that his final views were published by his sons, in four volumes dealing with the philosophy of mythology and the philosophy of revelation.

II. REHABILITATION OF THE NON-EGO

Criticism of Fichte. Schelling's system takes off from his feeling that Fichte had reduced the non-ego, or nature, to little more than the bare presence in consciousness of a something-not-myself-I-know-not-what. It stood simply for the fact that experience had *objectivity,* and thereby limited the amount of experience that I can call *me.* It was purely negative in character. Hence the Fichtean philosophy was without a cosmology. It not only failed to fit the operations of nature into the rest of its scheme, but it ignored them altogether.

The non-ego, however, Schelling insists, cannot be dismissed so lightly. An examination of the "external" experience we call the physical world reveals nature not as a mere passive limit to the activities of the ego, but as containing within herself an activity of self-limitation, similar to the self-limitation involved in self-consciousness. This activity is governed by a fundamental law of polarity, expressed in a struggle between the two forces of attraction and repulsion and in a resultant equilibrium. Matter, magnetism, electricity, chemical processes, light, and the fundamental activities of organic life are all manifestations of it. Furthermore, if we examine more deeply the self-limitation of the non-ego, we find that in physical nature, as in consciousness, we are dealing with a process that never absolutely fulfills itself and reaches its goal.

Again, there is a one-to-one correspondence between the stages of physical development, beginning with matter in its purely *quantitative* aspects, passing through its magnetic, electrical, chemical and luminiferous *qualities,* and culminating in the *vital* properties of organic bodies, with the successive *Anstösse,* or thrusts by which the ego develops self-consciousness. Finally, we may place the levels of both physical and mental evolution in a single graduated series leading from the lowest expression of the Real in spatial and material form to its highest expression in self-conscious spirit.

III. THE EVOLUTION OF THE NON-EGO AND THE EGO

The Law of Expansion and Contraction. Moreover, if we examine the higher, conscious expressions of the Real, we shall find that they, too, obey the law of attraction, repulsion, and resultant equilibrium, displayed in natural processes. To exhibit this new link between the ego and the non-ego is the purpose of the *System of Transcendental Idealism*. The expansion of consciousness, Schelling tells us, rests upon the fact that there *is* consciousness. Pure and primal consciousness is simply a registration of its own existence. But even this blank act of registration of mere existence by pure consciousness is consciousness of *something*. In performing it, consciousness becomes an object unto itself, and is now *self*-conscious. Since the object of which it is conscious is simply itself, the limitation of the subject by the object, of the "I" by the "me," is an act of *self*-limitation.

Let us start with sensation. Consciousness is a process of expansion and contraction, and sensation is the equilibrium resulting from the conflict of these two forces. Sensations are data of consciousness because they represent an expansive, outgoing activity of the self. But being involuntary and uncontrollable, as well as limits upon creative activity, they show also that the outpouring of consciousness which gives rise to them is continually checked and balanced by the contraction and return of consciousness upon itself.

Objective Experience and Reflective Thought. The next step in the evolution of consciousness is *perception,* which turns sense-data into perceived *objects* and sets these objects over against the self as an *external world*. The sense of the *outsideness* of objective experience, as contrasted with the *insideness* of subjective experience, expresses itself as *space;* the consciousness of the self as something distinct from the spatial external world, whose activity is not one of running round in space but of sitting at a fixed point watching the world *go by,* gives us *time*. In so far as our experiences are abstracted from time and change and considered solely in their spatial aspects, we perceive *substances;* in so far as we emphasize their temporal and changing characteristics, we perceive *accidental properties*.

If, next, we analyze the implications of *causation,* we shall find that the effect determines the cause as well as the cause the effect. Hence the temporal sequence, in which the cause precedes the effect, and in which the properties of one substance seem to produce or modify the properties of another, is really an expression of a *reciprocal* relation and interconnection between the substances underlying these changes. Here, once more, we see expansion and contraction at work.

Consciousness, having developed blank sensation into physical nature, now proceeds to reflect upon the situation. In contemplating nature as a thing apart, it abstracts itself from nature, and begins to reflect upon itself as the knowing subject and upon the *activity* of knowledge as something different from the *content* of knowledge. It now forms *concepts* and passes *judgments*. By so doing it differentiates its thoughts *about* objects from the objects themselves.

In thinking, as well as in perceiving, the law of polarity holds good. The expansive, creative power of the self, of which we are now aware, is still unable to make us *feel* that we create our universe. The universe is still a limit to our thinking, which contracts the self into a subject distinguished from its object. The ego and the non-ego remain for consciousness two independent and co-equal aspects of some underlying reality more profound than either of them in which their opposition is overcome.

IV. THE PRIMACY OF THE WILL

The Self-Determination of Moral Action and Artistic Creation. The nature of this reality Schelling, like Kant and Fichte, thinks is more adequately revealed in the moral life and in the will than it is in thought or in physical nature. The opposition, for example, between the *freedom* we experience within ourselves and the *necessity* that we run up against outside ourselves is overcome in the activity of *self-determination*. Here, we are, indeed, necessitated to act as we do by our own natures, but such determination, since it is inner, not outer, and is attended by no sense of external compulsion, means for us liberty of action. Furthermore, as we have just seen, we are forced to think of things as we do, not by any pressure exerted by the outer world, but by the constitution of the mind itself. Knowledge, also, is a free activity and is an expression of the general power of the self to determine its own behavior.

Again, in art we have another activity in which the opposition between conscious and unconscious creation is overcome. In the artist the self beholds itself as a spontaneous and untrammeled creator, whose works are not involuntary and uncontrollable, like sense-experience, but are self-imposed limits or goals. But such limitation is equivalent to self-determination and is attended by a feeling of freedom. Artistic creation shows not only how the inner limitations of one's own nature are compatible with liberty but also how in certain circumstances limitation from without is equivalent to freedom.

The Non-Ego a Limit to the Will, not to Knowledge. It is in the will again that the secret of our ability to attribute an external objective character to some of our experience is due. *All* sense-experience is *mine, is inside* me. *All* of it conforms to the demands of knowledge, which is also *mine,* and *inside* me. But *some* of it does not conform to my *will.* On the contrary, *some* of it is *against* my will, thwarts me, and arouses repugnance. Sense-experience, then, is really external to my will, although it is still contained *within* my consciousness. It *is* experienced by me, but it *is not* willed by me.

Yet again, the necessity for a plurality of thinking subjects lies in the volitional part of our nature. The fact that I am *self*-determined is in itself a limitation. It restricts *my* will to what *I* desire. But I cannot be conscious of my individual will without a recognition of *other* individual selves and wills.

To contrast, however, my will and my individuality with another's, and thus to be self-conscious, presupposes a common theater of action. Hence that which seems to my experience to be external must *really* be external, if self-consciousness is to be explained. In this way the assumption that our private worlds present us not only with *similar* but with *identical* objects of experience is validated.

Moral Activity the Reconciliation of the Ego and the Non-Ego. In so far as the will is self-determined it obeys a law that it itself lays down. This law is the moral law, the categorical imperative. Here, once more, the process of expansion and contraction is exemplified in the distinction between motives inherent in the nature of the will itself and motives excited by the outer physical world. The moral problem is to harmonize these physical and worldly impulses with the moral law, and happiness depends upon such reconciliation. All individuals must undertake this task, since it is only by submitting their personal and worldly inclinations to the control of the categorical imperative that they can realize their freedom without interfering with a similar realization on the part of their fellow-men.

History, Schelling feels, is a continuous progress in the direction of perfect freedom. Its goal is the establishment of a condition of affairs in which the moral law shall remain supreme, and in which the opposition between freedom and necessity, between conscious volition and unconscious impulse, shall be overcome. Indeed, history is a progressive incarnation of God, who is not a person but a perfected world. At the same time, Schelling, like Fichte, maintains that the realization of the ideal would be suicidal, since the complete removal of limits and obstacles would spell death to the exercise of freedom, to which there may always be more and more but never a consummation and an end.

V. THE NATURE OF THE ABSOLUTE

The Absolute and the Ego and the Non-Ego. Schelling had one final problem on his hands—the problem of describing the nature of the underlying unity or *Absolute,* of which spirit and nature, the conscious and the unconscious, are both alike the manifestations. This question is taken up by him in his *Statement of My System,* and his *Lectures on the Method of Academical Study.* The Absolute is an infinite and eternal Reason, in which the conscious and the unconscious, the subject and the object, the ego and the non-ego are *identical.* The Absolute Reason is one. Outside of it there is nothing. Within it there can be no distinction or difference or division, since if there were, the Absolute would not be one and infinite. It would be, rather, a collection of finite beings. It follows that from the point of view of the Absolute the finite is not real but simply an appearance, and that the distinction and opposition between the conscious and the unconscious, spirit and matter, the self and the not-self, are illusions. Stated in terms of the law of attraction and repulsion, the Absolute is the point of *indifference* or absolute equilibrium in which the expansion and the contraction underlying the ego and the non-ego exactly balance and cancel each other. Here, then, we have a Reality transcending the opposition between idealism and realism and describable as *neither* subject nor object, mind nor matter.

This description of the Absolute was not enthusiastically received. Fichte denounced a Reality so conceived as absolutely dead, and pointed out that the names Schelling applied to it, like unity, totality, self-equality, and nothingness were without meaning. Hegel, who by this time was developing and expounding his own system, remarked that it was like the night, in which all cows are black.

The Derivation of the Ego and the Non-Ego from the Absolute. Schelling, like Fichte in the same situation, sought to make his meaning clearer, and to avoid the objections brought against him. Although the Absolute is transcendent and inexpressible in terms of finite existence, the appearance of the finite within the Absolute presupposes a tendency, a will, stirring at the heart of all being, to become existent and to assume the forms with which knowledge occupies itself. This impulse or will to existence is felt by us as an infinite living spirit manifesting itself in a finite universe. Its realization is a *free* process, which does not deny liberty to its creatures, but rather imparts its own freedom to them.

The fall of the Absolute into finite existence and the resultant world-process is necessary to the transformation of the original *indifference* of the Absolute, which is *neither* subject nor object, ego nor non-ego, into an *identification* of subject and object in a mystical unity which is them *both*. To this end the distinction between subject and object must be first developed in order to be ultimately overcome. In the course of transforming indifference into identity, the Absolute becomes a personal God.

The generation of God lends itself to expression in terms of Christian doctrine. From the Father, the *indifference* which is the ground of all existence, is produced the Son, in which the Father becomes conscious of his existence and forms an idea of himself. And this *self*-consciousness of the Father, which is the Son, reacts upon the *indifference* at the heart of the Absolute, and gives rise to the third person, the will to create. The will to create is a will to transform *indifference* into *identity,* the real into the ideal, and for this purpose the world is formed. The resultant universe displays throughout its length and breadth and in every part a conflict between the two forces of procession and separation from God, on the one hand, and of re-identification with him, on the other. In so far as there is a breaking away from God, there are individuality and self-assertion; in so far as there is re-identification with God, all things are submitted to universal laws expressive of God's will. The assertion of the individual against the universal is the ground of all that is disorderly and irrational in nature.

The Place of Evil in the Absolute. In man, the conflict between the two principles gives rise to the moral distinction between good and evil. Sin is a defiance of the divine will by the individual human will. But we must be able to defy God, and, generally speaking, the individual must be able to assert itself against the universal, if God himself is to be realized. Without such assertion there could be nothing for God to love, nothing for him to redeem, nothing separate from his will and from his self to reconcile and identify with himself. In short, the existence of evil is a necessary condition of the divine self-realization, the final act of which is accomplished in the Incarnation.

But if God wills evil for the sake of his own self-fulfillment, how can he be absolved from responsibility for it? Evil cannot be dismissed as negative, since the self-assertion on which it is founded is a positive defiance of the universal will. To this difficulty Schelling replies that without the opposition upon which evil rests, there can be no self-consciousness and no self-realization of the Absolute. The Absolute is no less perfect for having to realize itself in evil ways.

Chapter XVII

HEGEL

I. LIFE

Education. We have already noticed that teaching philosophy at Jena, along with Fichte and Schelling, was a professor named Hegel. Though five years older than Schelling, he was slower in arriving at his philosophic maturity. But his system was destined, when completed, to dominate the nineteenth century, and to display its author as the most profound and the most brilliant thinker of that epoch.

George William Frederick Hegel was born in 1770 at Stuttgart, the capital of Württemberg, where his father occupied a minor government position. His schooling he received at the *gymnasium* of his native town and at the theological seminary at Tübingen. As a student, he seems to have attracted little attention. He was an ordinary, healthy, genial, good-humored youth, indistinguishable from the run of his fellow undergraduates. He disliked, moreover, the dullness of his teachers, and had frequently to be reprimanded for cutting his classes. He was, however, sufficiently to the fore to help his friend Schelling found a republican club devoted to discussing the ideas of the French Revolution and the unrest generated by it throughout Western Europe. He had also formed the habit of taking copious notes on everything that interested him. At the moment, his chief interest lay in classical literature, and especially in the tragedies of Sophocles. He hated the Romantic Movement and emotional extravagances of all sorts. His interest in philosophy was as yet dormant.

Philosophical Career. The next six years were the period of his philosophic awakening. These he spent as a private tutor, first at Berne, and then at Frankfort. Particularly, he studied and revolted against Kant. His theological education—he was destined for the church—and his enthusiasm for classical culture, and especially for Greece, were also contributing to the ferment of his spirit. He was also much attracted at the moment by the philosophical views set forth by Schelling. He sympathized especially with his friend's criticisms of Fichte, and with his idea of the Absolute as an *identity* of the ego and the non-ego. His first published work, indeed, was *On the Difference between the Systems of Fichte and Schelling* (1801). These sympathetic relations led in 1802 to a year's collaboration with Schelling in getting out a philosophical review, the *Critical Journal,* which he continued to edit, after the latter left Jena.

From now on, Hegel's rise was rapid. In 1803, he was made a *privat-docent,* and two years later a professor at the university. He was also rapidly developing his own views and coming more and more to disagree with his former collaborator. The period bore brilliant fruit in his *Phenomenology of Spirit,* published in 1807.

Before its publication, however, the victorious advance of Napoleon's army had forced him to flee from Jena. After a brief period at Bamberg, he settled down for the next eight years as a schoolteacher in Nuremberg, where he married and where his two sons were born. Here, too, his *Logic* first saw the light of day.

In 1816 he was offered and he accepted a professorship at Heidelberg, and in another two years moved on to Berlin to occupy the chair left vacant by Fichte's death. Here he spent the rest of his life, devoting himself to his lectures and his writings. The *Encyclopaedia of Philosophic Sciences* appeared in 1817, the *Philosophy of Right* in 1821, and the lectures given between 1823 and 1827 form the basis of his *Aesthetics, Philosophy of History, Philosophy of Religion,* and *History of Philosophy.* A band of disciples was fast gathering about him, and he was the recipient of many public honors—all of which was gratifying to his growing conceit and self-importance.

The first European cholera epidemic struck Berlin in 1831. Hegel moved his family out of town for the summer and devoted himself to revising the *Science of Right.* In the autumn, however, he returned to Berlin. He was suddenly taken ill with cholera, and a day later— November 14, 1831—was dead.

II. EARLY VIEWS

Enthusiasm for Freedom. The six years spent in tutoring and meditation immediately after his graduation had given Hegel the two leading ideas of his system. Like all young revolutionaries, he was inspired by the idea of *freedom,* and the idea had been strengthened in him by his Protestant theological training, with its opposition of the inner to the outer life, of conscience to external authority, and of the right of private judgment to the curbs upon thinking and upon action imposed by the Roman Church.

This enthusiasm for *freedom,* at first defiant and individualistic, became reconciled with social compulsions by Hegel's study of Rousseau and Kant. At the same time, he rebelled against the abstract character of Kantian morality. He revolted also against the ethics of the Old Testament, which seemed to him to rest upon commandments imposed externally upon man from on high and to give to morality an unhealthy and unnatural basis. Christianity, too, in its official forms he found unsatisfactory. It tended to segregate religion from life, to oppose the world to the spirit, and as a result to vacillate between the two. Greek ethics was in his opinion best, with its idea of destiny as governing a man's life not from the outside but from within, as part and parcel of himself. He would have agreed with Heraclitus that a man's character is his destiny. And he saw a great wisdom in the Hellenic ideal of moderation and restraint, and in the Hellenic sense of the necessity of submitting human life to the restrictions laid upon it by the structure of the natural order of which it is a part. Man conquers nature by obeying her. But his essential victory is not the Baconian one of practical advancement. It has a deeper, spiritual sense. It is found in a triumph over his destiny, which consists in accepting with joyful resignation the renunciations his fate exacts from him. Not to rebel against life, but to love it as it is, with all its limitations and vicissitudes, is to overcome fate and to transmute it into freedom.

Revolt from Fichte and Schelling. Hegel's second principle, in which we can see the influence of Schelling's idea of *identity,* and of Fichte's influence behind that of Schelling, is that life is an organic unity, a spiritual activity, in which all seeming antagonisms between man and nature are overcome, and the clash of opposing forces is stilled. Multiplicity, variety, opposition, antagonism, are all subservient to some higher principle in which they are ultimately identified, and to whose being—which is an activity of reconciling and fusing them—they are necessary.

Where is such a principle to be found? It was in answering this question that Hegel broke completely with Fichte and Schelling and incidentally completed the demolition by the German idealists of those parts of the Kantian system that they deemed superfluous. Fichte, we may recall, although he dispensed with the objective things-in-themselves underlying and provoking the sensible manifold and made the thinking subject the source of the content as well as of the forms of experience, nevertheless had retained a subjective thing-in-itself in his doctrine of the Absolute Ego. This Ego was something more than either the finite ego or the non-ego which it produced through the finite ego. It remained a kind of *substance* which *underlay* the finite ego.

For Schelling, too, the Absolute preserved the character of a Kantian thing-in-itself. It was neither an ego nor a non-ego, but something that transcended them both—a primal *indifference* out of which ego and non-ego arose in the course of transforming indifference into identity.

III. THE NATURE OF REALITY

The Absolute Is the World-Process. Hegel in his criticism of Fichte and Schelling simply knocked out altogether the idea of an absolute *subject* underlying experience and creating it out of the unfathomable depths of its being, just as they had knocked out the idea of an absolute, unfathomable *objective* source of experience. Schelling's Absolute, the night in which all cows were black, was in Hegel's opinion a purely negative quantity—an absence of all predicates. But if the Real is indescribable in any of the terms placed at our disposal by experience and thought, then we might as well abandon philosophy at once and for good and all. Furthermore, if the Real is *not* anything it seems to be, we have also on our hands the problem of explaining where all these things the Real is *not* come from. Certainly, the Real cannot account for their existence and their nature, and the whole world of experience is left hanging, with nowhere to come from and nowhere to go.

Moreover, any system, idealistic or realistic, that *opposes* Reality to appearance and denies to the Real its *experienced* characteristics turns the Absolute into a negation pure and simple, devoid of all perceivable and thinkable properties, and therefore the equivalent of nothing at all. But the least demand we can make upon the nature of the Real is that it shall *account for* appearance, and *explain* the multiple, varied, changing, kaleidoscopic spectacle of existence.

However, to explain experience the Absolute cannot be outside of, or above, or below experience. It cannot exist in any way *apart* from experience. It cannot be an Ego or a Mind whose thinking creates the world. An Ego or Mind apart from its thinking is nothing. An Absolute Ego or Absolute Intellect is simply the conscious *process* of experiencing and thinking, no less, no more. The Real, then, is a *Process,* not a substance. The sum of all that is experienced, then, tells all there is to know about the nature of the Real. The Absolute *is* the world-process, just as I *am* my career. The Absolute is a *life* and nothing more, just as I am my life and nothing more.

The World-Process Is a Career. But a career, or a life, has *cohesion* and *form*. Its totality expresses the development of a single self, and all its episodes are somehow taken up and worked together into a single coherent whole, just as the episodes of a novel flow together to form a single consistent plot. There is no moment and no incident in it that is not given significance by the nature of the process of which it is a part. In the same way the world-process is the living out, the making explicit, of a plan or character inherent in its evolution, which Hegel calls the Absolute Idea. But *self*-realization, if it is to have any meaning, implies *self*-consciousness. The Absolute Existence, which realizes and makes explicit the Absolute Idea, must therefore be conceived as a process of evolving self-consciousness, culminating in complete self-knowledge, or comprehension of the Idea which its development sets forth.[1]

Such complete self-knowledge becomes an intelligible and attainable ideal the moment we discard the antithesis between subject and object, mind and matter, thinking and being. *Thinking* and *being* are one and the same activity. I *am* what I *think* myself to be. Subject and object are identical. Complete self-knowledge consists in a conscious realization of that identity, which is, by virtue of the oneness of thinking and being, also an *act* of identifying the one with the other. The Absolute, then, may be defined as an Idea or Plan becoming conscious of itself. Or, to use a single term to express the process of self-consciously realizing an idea, we may say that the Absolute is *Spirit*.

Spirit and Nature. In the living, pulsating, self-realizing activity of Spirit there is no actual distinction between the Idea and the process of its self-fulfillment. However, for the purposes of philosophy we may conveniently separate the *logical idea* of things, which defines the possibilities of thinking and experiencing and therefore of existence, from *nature* in which those possibilities are given realization, and the form of the Absolute is given a concrete filling. When, however, we separate in our thinking form from content, we make the content *other than* and *external to* the form, and distinguish the several elements or parts of the content from one another, as spread out in *space* and *time*. At the same time we recognize the interconnection of the parts as *causality*. And finally we oppose our inner consciousness to an *outer* world.[2]

The distinction between Spirit and nature confronts us with an interesting situation. On the one hand, consciousness seems to evolve out of nature by a process of gradual rise and development from the

---

[1] *Phenomenology*, Preface and Introduction.
[2] *Encyclopaedia, Philosophy of Spirit (Mind)*, § 382.

inorganic, through the *vegetable* and the *animal* forms of organic life, in which an inner principle of growth realizes itself, and subordinates the special functions and purposes of the parts to the larger life of the whole, till it reaches the level of conscious thought.[3] At this point it reduces nature to terms of its own *experience* and turns natural events to its own uses, and then reflects upon that experience, and by so doing transforms nature into an intelligible order, in which the Idea is completely expressed.[4]

On the other hand, instead of Spirit developing out of nature, nature, being the experience of the Spirit, is produced by the Spirit and given by it her form and structure in the categories of thought. In thinking of itself as produced by nature, the Spirit is merely tracing the successive steps by which it itself produces the world. Its appearance in the bosom of nature is really its return to itself, its recoil from the creation of the universe within itself.

The Human Level of the Self-Realization of Spirit. In human consciousness the self-realization of the Spirit reaches higher levels. When we reason and reflect, the Spirit rises above, negates, and transcends its individual enactments, although it still uses the individual as a base. It is, to be sure, *we* who do the reasoning and the reflecting, but our thinking occupies itself not with the particular but with the universal, and becomes impersonal or superpersonal in its interests and its significance. We tend to lose consciousness of ourselves in contemplating the truth.

Moreover, at the human level the Spirit becomes conscious of its *freedom*. It realizes that its seeming dependence upon the external world and its apparent determination by the law of causation are in reality a captivity to circumstances and rules of which it itself is the author and which it freely imposes upon its own existence.

But, however high the Spirit may soar in human thought, it can never attain complete self-realization and self-knowledge in any finite experience. To reach those final peaks it must transcend and overcome finitude completely, and become Absolute Spirit. In a sense, however, we constantly are negating and transcending our finitude just in recognizing and knowing it. The very act and fact of thought is a recognition that the scope of our thinking is wider than its finite base and content and is capable of embracing the whole truth, or Absolute Idea, which it is forever striving to encompass.

---

[3] *Encyclopaedia, Philosophy of Spirit (Mind)*, § 382. Cf. *Phenomenology* C. V. also A, a.

[4] Cf. *Phenomenology*, A, I, II, III.

IV. SUBJECTIVE SPIRIT

Sensation, etc. If now we analyze the stages of the self-realization of Spirit more closely, we shall find that they are three, *subjective, objective,* and *absolute.* Under subjective Spirit we may first of all group the consciousness we share with the animals and the pre-conscious natural activities of the organism. Sentience, once awakened, means first the presence of immediate, particular sensations, not as yet referred to external objects. So, too, accompanying these first sensations are feeling-values in which the Spirit begins to sense its own being, without as yet attaining real self-consciousness.

The Spirit has now become an *attitude* towards its content. In reacting to its experience the Spirit claims its sensations and feelings as its own. But as yet there is no reflective self-consciousness. Nevertheless, the experience of the individual is acquiring a unity and a significance that transcend any particular moment. Through memory, association, and habit, the nascent self is being slowly freed from slavery to each new and separate sensation, is being fortified against the desires of the moment, and is developing a level of consciousness upon which thinking may be based. Subject and object are now fairly clearly distinguished, and the conscious organism asserts itself as a unified entity different from the rest of nature and possessed of a fixed constitution of its own.

Reflection upon the Ego and the Non-Ego. The Spirit has now laid the foundations for self-consciousness. Hitherto it has been busy developing the *content* of experience, without, however, having become clearly aware of the *operations* by which that content is evolved. Now it begins to consider its creative *activity*. This step is of vital importance. It is an indispensable condition, not only of the emergence of self-consciousness, but of the later abolition of self-consciousness in Absolute Spirit. For the Spirit by mere *willing* cannot master the physiological processes and involuntary experiences and reactions of its own body. To absorb the body and the external world into itself, and to reduce them to its own experience, the Spirit must reflect upon them, and rationalize them, and prove that their seeming externality cloaks a situation of its own creation. But such reflection and rationalization involve a consideration of the *act* by which the creation of experience is brought to pass. In other words, they provoke reflection upon themselves, as something different from their work.

The Spirit now enumerates to itself the stages through which it has passed: *sensation,* or the mere unwilled presence of experience; *perception,* in which floating sensations cohere as *things* upon which the attention is focused; and *understanding,* by which universals are abstracted from *things* and regarded as constituting their essences. Accompanying all these operations goes the "I think," the Kantian "transcendental unity of apperception," which encompasses my sensations, perceptions, and thoughts, and makes them part of one and the *same* world, and that world *my* world.[5]

The Recognition of Other Selves. But for the Spirit to recognize *itself* is to recognize also something that is not itself, and to draw at last a clear-cut distinction between *subject* and *object.* Furthermore, the *object* now presents itself as in part, at least, a world of other selves. Such a non-ego, comprising other egos with whom we can contrast ourselves and with whom we can communicate, is necessary to the Spirit's complete self-realization.[6]

These selves, although they exclude one another, figure in one another's experiences as *objects.* Furthermore, although each has its particular experience and world, all share a common experience and world. We live, as we say, in the *same* world, perceive and think about the *same* objects.

It is the myriad individual yet intersecting worlds of experience thus constructed which we must now seek to combine in some larger unity that will appropriate them all as *its,* just as I appropriate as *mine* all the different moments and aspects of my experience and all the different attitudes and acts of my self-consciousness towards its content.

Now, we can detect in ourselves Spirit in the act of building up this unity, in which the opposition of the ego to the non-ego is overcome, and can trace the steps by which the work of reconciliation is carried on. In the first place, the ego *likes* the non-ego, and draws from it much of its satisfaction and self-expression. Here, then, is a kind of identity, an identity of *interest,* binding together the subject and the object into a larger whole.

The Appearance of Social Consciousness. But this relation is one-sided. I like and desire the non-ego because it panders to my selfish interests. The non-ego is for me something to be exploited and to be enslaved to my own caprices. When, however, the non-ego is recognized as containing other *selves* like our own, the situation is broadened. The non-ego asserts its claims to be treated not merely as a means but as an end in itself, and my life, instead of battening upon

[5] Cf. *Phenomenology,* A, I, II, III.
[6] Cf. *Phenomenology,* B, IV, A

the outer world at will, has to recognize the existence of other individuals and to meet with opposition from them when its desires clash with theirs. *Self*-consciousness has now become *social* consciousness.[7]

Still, in its primitive form social consciousness is a consciousness of *opposition,* of conflicting and clashing wills at war with one another. This opposition can be completely overcome only by a self-conscious and voluntary identification of the private with the public self, and of the individual with the common interest. Meantime, however, a partial reconciliation is effected by the institutions of society and the state. By them the clash of individuals is, indeed, largely prevented, but prevented by means in which the individual does not as yet wholeheartedly acquiesce. Social organization, therefore, seems to exert *compulsion* upon individuals and to *force* them to conduct themselves in a way that is still against their will and a limitation upon their freedom.

V. OBJECTIVE SPIRIT

We have now reached the point where the transition from *subjective Spirit* to *objective Spirit* takes place. *Objective Spirit* is the fund of common objects, common interests, and common activities, which the Spirit has created in the individual experiences of different self-conscious subjects. In this way different individual worlds are given a single focus, and the experience of each separate self *means* a universe larger than itself and shared with other selves.

The passage from subjective to objective Spirit opens up new fields of reflection. The Spirit now meditates upon the human race rather than upon the individual. It thinks about the organization of society, about its origins and development, about the principles underlying social conduct. The result is the formulation of philosophies of society, of law, of morality, and of history.

The appearance of objective Spirit, moreover, reacts upon the individual subject, and turns him at last into a *rational* being. Only in society can we live the life of reason. For reason means an identification of the individual with the universal in which the universal is found to explain and perfect the particular. So, too, to act as a reasonable being is to act in a moral and social manner. Moral conduct is rational conduct. The anti-social and immoral individual is an irrational individual.[8]

We turn now to consider the nature and the conditions of the *rational*

[7] Cf. *Phenomenology,* B, IV, A. B.; BB, VI, A.
[8] *Phenomenology,* C, V, B.

activities of *Spirit,* made possible by the attainment of *objective* Spirit. Here again we have three aspects. In the first place, we have the processes of rational thought or *theoretic Spirit.* The conditions of reasoning turn out to be very like those of self-consciousness. We begin with *intuition,* in the Kantian sense, which in its turn is a triad of blank sensation, attention, and apperception. The intuited data are remembered, imaged, and reproduced—another triad, whose unity gives us *representation* and turns sense-experience into a world of perceived *objects.* Finally, we have the stage of thought, in which objects are understood, judgments are passed upon them, and we begin to reason about them.[9]

The second aspect of rational life is that of *practical Spirit,* or reason expressed in terms of desire, volition, action, and the like. Finally we have *free Spirit,* in which the theoretic and the practical are united in rational self-determination. With the free Spirit, to know the good is equivalent to willing it.

VI. ABSOLUTE SPIRIT

The Ultimate Syntheses. We rise now to the final level of spiritual development, that of *Absolute Spirit.* In the Absolute Spirit, the complete union and reconciliation of all the differences and distinctions manifested in the world-process take place. The absolute experience is made one with the absolute Idea. The opposition of form to matter, of subject to object, of self to the not-self is transcended, and the world-process is transfigured into the self-conscious life of the Absolute, which is both its own subject and its own object fused into a single completely harmonious Reality.

Once more it is by three steps that we rise to the heights of absolute Spirit. These are provided by *art, religion* and *philosophy.* In art, to be sure, we still have, in the difference between the artist and his work, a persistence of the distinction between subject and object, the Spirit and nature. But this opposition is already being overcome, since the artist's work appears as the creation of his genius and the expression of his purpose; or, to put it more generally, the object appears as the free creation of the subject, and nature as the product of the Spirit. Moreover, the natural, objective element is subordinated to the subjective, spiritual factor. The work of art is dominated by the Idea, and translates the Idea into sensuous terms. A fine statue or a fine picture,

[9] *Philosophy of Spirit* (*Mind*), §§ 444-469.

for example, are not imitations of nature. They are re-arrangements of nature which deliver the spiritual values and meanings with which she is pregnant.

Art. Art takes on the characteristic triple form. We have *symbolic art,* where the form employed is not adequate to the idea it seeks to express, and succeeds only in symbolizing the Idea. There is *classic art,* in which the natural form is regarded as completely adequate to express the Idea—which in the nature of things it cannot be. The defect of classic art lies precisely in its failure to realize that the Idea is transcendent and that no sensuous representation is able to manifest it in its entirety. Finally, there is the *art which synthesizes and rounds out the symbolic and the classic.* In this art the form, though an inadequate expression of the Idea, still succeeds in grasping and conveying it, so that the sensuous representation means and pictures the Idea to the beholder. Indeed, all beauty does precisely this. It is the sensuous body, so to speak, of the Spirit, in which the nature of the Spirit is indicated.[10]

Religion. In religion the synthesis of experience and the Idea is carried still further. Objective nature now becomes the manifestation of a companionable Spirit or self, akin to our finite selves, in whose image we are created. And her processes are interpreted as the workings of its purpose. Once more there are three aspects to religion—three ways of conceiving God. We may regard him as a pure unity, an abiding, changeless, eternal being transcending the world, and existing apart from it. This is exemplified by the Christian concept of the Father. Or we may conceive him as incarnate and immanent in the phenomenal world, or in Christian terminology, as the Logos or Son. Or we may look upon him as a return of the finite to the infinite, of variety into simplicity, of the many into the one, there to come to rest and to be fused and perfected. This aspect of God we may call the Holy Spirit.[11]

Philosophy. Philosophy, however, soars higher than religion. Indeed, she is the final synthesis of the attitudes taken respectively by art and religion. She combines art's glorification of the finite Spirit as a creator with the assertion of religion that the finite Spirit is itself a creation of Absolute Spirit. In this way she effects an identification of the finite with the absolute. Yet again the eternal triad appears. In regarding the return of Spirit into itself, we can start at any one of three points in a circle. We can have a philosophy that begins with a logical *form* or

[10] Cf. *Phenomenology,* CC, VII, B.
[11] Cf. *Phenomenology,* CC, VII, A, C.

Idea developing itself through nature into Spirit. Or, taking *nature* as our starting-point, we can see her developing the Spirit as a means towards assuming a rational form. Or, initiating the process with *Spirit,* we can watch Spirit realizing its form or idea in the evolution of nature.[12]

VII. LOGIC

The World-Process Governed by the Laws of Logic. We have now seen the Absolute becoming subjective and objective Spirit, attaining self-consciousness, diversifying its career with an infinite wealth of adventure, and, at the end, gathering again all the richness of its infinitely various and multiple experience into one, in its return upon itself as Absolute Spirit. These episodes, though they are unrolled before our finite eyes in temporal succession and as a progressive evolution, are in the Absolute raised altogether above time. In it they are all there all at once, a vision of itself under the aspect of eternity, in which the stages displayed to us in time appear as a simple analysis of all the levels and kinds of existence of which an absolute experience is capable, and of which it is the eternal and complete enactment. It is to a description of these levels and kinds of existence that Hegel turns in his *Logic,* X-raying, as it were, the flesh and blood of the Absolute, pictured in the *Phenomenology of Spirit,* and disclosing the skeleton about which the World-Process is built and by which it is supported.[13]

The Hierarchy of Syntheses. This skeleton is constructed of a series of superimposed ascending triads in which the seemingly antagonistic concepts revealed in experience by the *understanding* are reconciled and combined, or in Hegel's own phrase, *aufgehoben,* "taken up," by *dialectic* in higher logical concepts. These, in their turn, are finally united by *speculation* in a supreme synthesis in which all differences and seeming contradictions are fused and explained.

These syntheses do not evolve in time. They are rather derived from one another by logical implication, and form a logical hierarchy culminating in the all-embracing, all-reconciling Absolute Idea. The hierarchy is complicated and has many ramifications, and in it lower syntheses frequently re-appear on higher levels. Since *being* and *thinking* are identical, the laws of thought codified by logic will make manifest the constitution of the Real. To discover, then, the structure of the Absolute we have only to analyze our own mental processes and categories. Hegel's analysis is, however, so minute, so technical,

[12] Cf. *Phenomenology,* DD, VIII.
[13] The discussion here is based upon *Encyclopaedia* (*Logic*).

and so lengthy, that we can do little more here than describe its general features and results.

VIII. THE BASIC TRIADS

Being, Not-Being and Becoming. The most all-embracing concept of our minds would seem to be that of *being*. It is the least common denominator to which all things may be reduced. But pure unspecified *being* without a particular content of some sort is equivalent to nothing at all. It is indistinguishable from *not-being*. To assert, then, as a *thesis* that the Absolute is unqualified *being* is also to assert the *antithesis* of our statement, and to say that the Absolute is non-existent.

Can we then find some further concept that will overcome this contradiction and prove to be a *synthesis* of the ideas of *being* and *not-being?* Hegel finds such a concept in that of *becoming.* When a thing *changes,* it *is* what it *was not* a moment before, and it *will be* in another instant what it *is not* now. But, if it is to remain the *same* object throughout its changes, what it *is* must be somehow *identical* with what it *was not,* and with what it *will be.* In a *process,* then, the seemingly mutual exclusion of *being* and *non-being* by each other is overcome in a higher synthesis.

Since Hegel's Absolute is a Process and a Career, the concept of *becoming,* in which relative *being* and relative *not-being* are continually being related, *aufgehoben,* and synthesized, is the fundamental concept of his philosophy. It reveals, too, more clearly the ultimate *triad*—and with the threefold measure in which his thought is always appearing we are already familiar—to which everything that exists is reducible. *Thesis, antithesis,* and *synthesis*—these mark all movement, all change, all life, all thinking. *Becoming,* then, is the first *living* notion.

The Concept of Becoming. Let us examine further implications of *becoming.* We cannot think of *change* without also thinking of *quality.* For *change* is a play of qualities that come and go. Again, since there would be no change without a diversity of qualities, we cannot entertain the concept of *becoming* without also entertaining that of *diversity.* But this diversity must be strung on a *single* thread, for otherwise we should not have real *change* but rather the *substitution* of one episode by another in which there was no connected history. Hence, in thinking of *becoming,* we must also think of identity, and *singleness* or *unity,* as well as of *difference* and *multiplicity.* Furthermore, the concepts of *identity* and *difference* and of *unity* and *multiplication* are pairs of Siamese twins, in which the one cannot be severed from the other.

When, however, we think of the *quality* of *oneness* or *unity,* we are also thinking of a *unit* or of the basis of all *quantitative* measurement. In other words, we pass from the category of *quality* to that of *quantity.* But we find at once that the idea of *quantity* gives rise in its turn to that of *quality,* since it is applicable not only to spatial magnitudes but to *degrees* of intensity. But *intensity* and *degree* are meaningless except with respect to *quality.* Hence, the two concepts, although antithetical, are *synthesized* in the concept of *measure* or of the *amount* of quantity a thing contains—the amount being also a *quality* of the thing in question.

But *quality, quantity* and *measure* make no sense without the concept of *something* that possesses these characteristics. In short, there must be a subject or *essence* underlying them, of which they are the predicates or attributes.

IX. ESSENCE AND ITS IMPLICATIONS

Essence, Existence, and Change. In arriving at the concept of *Essence,* we have revived the concept of *being* and raised it to a higher level. Blank *being* has become *something,* and, in acquiring properties that define it, has become determinate. *Essence,* then, may be described as *being* determining itself to be *something,* and thereby negating and abolishing itself as bare indeterminate existence.

Nevertheless, we still distinguish the *essence* of a thing from its *existence.* Furthermore, we identify its *essence* with that which persists and remains the *same* throughout its changes, and thereby we create an opposition between *appearance* and *reality.* Finally, taken in connection with the idea of *essence* the concept of *becoming* seems to fall into hopeless self-contradiction. How can one and the same thing *really change* and yet remain *identical* with itself? Obviously we have here a number of pairs of *theses* and *antitheses* that call for a new *synthesis.*

The Syntheses Effected by the Concepts of "Ground" and "Force." This synthesis is found in part, Hegel feels, if we consider the essence the *ground* or *reason* for appearances. The reason or ground of an object or event is merely the object or event itself more completely understood. The chemical constituents or grounds of a phenomenon, for example, are merely an analysis of the phenomenon in question. In the same way all *appearance* is merely the logical outcome of its reasons and the manifestation of its ground. *Appearance,* then, is not opposed to *reality.*

In the same way another paradox to which the concept of *essence* gives rise—the necessity of thinking of it as a *whole* determining the nature of its *parts,* and at the same time as composed of *parts* determining the nature of the *whole*—is overcome in the concept of *force.* For a *force* is the equivalent of its expressions and identical with them. Its manifestations are not derived from it by dividing it, nor is it built up out of them.

Actuality, Potentiality and Fact. Nevertheless, the concept of *force,* though it may overcome the contradiction of *whole* and *part,* at once itself suggests the opposed concepts of *actuality* and *potentiality.* These concepts, however, are found to involve one another, since bare potentiality cannot be conceived without reference to the specific, actual thing it makes possible, and a floating actuality, divorced from that which makes it possible, would be a chance, *inexplicable* event, which our minds would refuse to accept as such.

This opposition is overcome in the concept of *fact.* For the conditions under which any fact *actually* occurs are also the conditions that render it *possible.* A *fact,* then, in being *actual* does nothing but express the *possibility* of its occurrence. Indeed, it may be defined as simply an actualization of all those potentialities that render its particular actualization possible. It is, then, a *synthesis* of the *possible* and the *actual.* It is its own potentialities realizing themselves.

X. THE RECONCILIATION OF FREEDOM AND NECESSITY

The concept of *fact*—that is, of *existence* plus a *measure* of *quality* and *quantity* that gives it a determinate character or essence; plus *identity* and *difference,* which enable it to grow and develop; plus a *reason* or *ground* for being what it is of which its *appearance* is the complete manifestation; plus a dynamic activity or *forcefulness* whose whole nature is expressed equally in its several expressions or *parts;* plus an *actuality* that merely absorbs, conserves, and realizes the potentialities that make it possible—suggests yet another example of *thesis* and *antithesis.*

On the one hand, we must conceive all facts as *necessary.* Given all the possibilities, the fact *must* emerge. What is, *must* be, because the conditions that enable it to exist could not produce any other fact.

On the other hand, facts have to be conceived as *free* events. For if we ask *why* certain possibilities should give rise to certain facts and to no others, we can give no reason and find no cause for the connection in question. We can only answer that it is the nature of things that certain events should have the effects they do. But since nothing outside it forces the nature of things to be what it is, and to exhibit itself in the specific realizations of potentiality and causal linkages it does, that nature *freely* and of its own self-determination establishes what shall cause what, and how possibilities shall be realized.

Such a situation, however, creates no opposition between the *freedom* and the *necessity* of the *fact*. On the contrary it synthesizes them and establishes their identity.

XI. THE RECONCILIATION OF SUBSTANCE AND ACCIDENT

When, however, we speak of a "nature of things" underlying and *freely* expressing itself in the *necessary* order and connection of events, we are thinking once more, though on a higher level, in terms of an *essence* and its *properties*. And we now are confronted with the thesis and antithesis of *substance* and its *attributes* or *accidents*. The difficulty here is that the substance both is and is not its properties. Take away all its properties and nothing is left, and yet we persist in thinking that something still remains. Otherwise, we should not be able in thought to distinguish the notion of *substance* from the idea of the sum of the attributes supposed to *inhere* in substance.

The difficulty, however, is overcome if we regard *substance* as the *cause* of its *attributes*. For a cause is a *cause* only in so far as it gives rise to an effect. And in producing the effect it loses nothing of itself. Conversely the effect is already *all there* in its cause, potentially present in the sum of the conditions that enable it to come into being. Otherwise the cause could not produce it, nor would the conditions in question be the potentialities of *its* existence.

Applying the relation of *cause* and *effect* to *substance* and its *attributes,* we can understand how a substance is completely exhausted by the properties that manifest its nature, but is at the same time *more* than those qualities, just as cause and effect, though completely present in each other, are nevertheless *different* from each other.

XII. THE SYNTHESIS OF EFFICIENT AND FINAL CAUSATION

Difficulties of the Concept of Mechanism. The concept of causation, however, involves us in another difficulty. It seems to imply an infinite regress in which no first or ultimate cause can be found. Such a regress can be avoided only if in our search for the cause we *progress* instead of *regress,* and make the so-called effect the cause of the so-called causes leading up to it.

Kant had pointed out that we seem actually to have causation of this sort, or in other words *final,* rather than *mechanical,* causation in the case of organic bodies, and of the *purposive* activities of conscious life. In organic bodies, we seem to have a *reciprocal* situation, where the whole, although built up out of parts, nevertheless seems to determine the relations of the parts to one another and to itself. Or again, in conscious purposive activity the end brought to pass by certain means also determines the means employed to accomplish it. And Hegel himself had insisted that the institutions and the character of a people *reciprocally* influence each other. Can, then, the concept of *reciprocity* be applied to the infinite regress of efficient and mechanical causation? In short, can the seemingly *mechanical* character of most of the world-process be regarded as really *organic?*

Difficulties of Conceiving Purposes as Causes. Kant, it will be remembered, had dealt with this question very cautiously, declaring that there was no *a priori* impossibility of a purely mechanical explanation of teleological phenomena, that final causation was undemonstrable even in the case of organisms, and that experience warranted no more than the assertion that the *representation* by the mind of a completed whole or of a goal ahead could cause the arrangement of the parts or the means for attaining it.

Moreover, if we examine the concept of *final* causation, we find that we are confronted with the difficulty of an infinite regress in reverse. Just as looking backward we could discover no *first cause* to the process of efficient and mechanical causation, so in looking forward we can discover no *final goal* to the process of final causation. Each end attained turns out to be the means to some further end, just as each efficient cause turns out to be the effect of some preceding cause. Can we, then, find any way both of avoiding the difficulties of *infinite regress* and *infinite progress,* and of synthesizing efficient and final causation in a concept that will embrace and harmonize them both?

Identity of Means and Ends. These difficulties can be overcome and the synthesis attained only if we can succeed in first synthesizing the *end* and *means* presented in *final causation* in the same way that we synthesized *efficient cause* and *effect.* We amalgamated efficient cause and effect by showing that they were not *external* to each other, but were two expressions of an underlying principle that was equally *both* cause and effect. In the same way, end and means might be conceived as two manifestations of an underlying principle that was *both* its own end and its own means.

Such a principle would be self-realizing and at the same time realized in and by the very process of self-realization. Neither end nor means would be external to it or distinct from each other. Since, then, both final and efficient causation present precisely the same problem, which is solved in precisely the same way by invoking in either case an identical principle, they may themselves be regarded as identical at heart, in spite of their outer contradiction. But, if they are both identical at heart, there can be no real contradiction between the mechanical, efficient causation of a whole by its parts and the teleological, final causation of its parts by a whole.

There is, moreover, yet another way in which the contradiction between efficient and final causation is overcome—this time on what we might call the moral plane. Whatever *is,* expresses the nature and purpose of the Absolute. Therefore the mechanical order of the world-process manifests the absolute purpose. In knowing itself and constituting itself as a process whose events are interconnected by efficient causation, the Absolute is at the same time realizing its end and attaining its perfection, since self-knowledge is its goal. But if self-knowledge is its goal, the truth about itself or, in other words, *absolute* truth is its good, and therefore is the *absolute* good. Hence, mechanism is not morally opposed to purpose, as something destructive to it, which blocks the attainment of the ideal. On the contrary, it is expressive of purpose, and is itself an ideal as well as a real order. The moral and the natural, the teleological and the mechanical, are no more contradictory ethically than they are metaphysically. In ultimate value, as in ultimate fact, they are identical.

XIII. THE NATURE OF THE ABSOLUTE

Identity of the Absolute and the World-Process. The *concept* we are seeking, which unites the two kinds of causation, is *becoming* raised now to a higher level, and indeed made the supreme Reality, the Absolute Idea. Only conceive the Idea as a *process* and all difficulties disappear. In a *process* we have something of which it can be equally said that the parts cause the whole and the whole causes the parts.

In a *process* you cannot vary the sequence and nature of its causes and effects without altering the nature of the process itself. A *process,* therefore, like an alphabet or a personal career, is something that both determines and is determined by its constituents. Furthermore, a *process* sets its own goal, which lies just in progressing and processing; by progressing and processing, it attains its end. In a *process,* then, end and means, cause and effect are one and the same thing. It is present in its entirety and fulfilled completely in each moment of the temporal sequence in which it manifests itself. And this complete self-realization, and this complete presence of its attained ideal in each of its parts, and episodes, and moments, makes each and all of its instants eternity in its sight.

In the concept of *process,* furthermore, all other contradictions are "taken up" and overcome. The opposition between *essence* and *existence,* and *form* and *matter,* and the *categories* and the *content* of thought is abolished, and the *actual* and the *possible* are united.

The World-Process Its Own Cause and Its Own Goal. Applying now the concept of *process* to the Absolute Idea, what do we find? The Absolute is more than *substance.* It is a *subject* developing and objectifying itself. It is more than *essence.* It is *essence* that also *exists* in and for itself, and completely expresses itself in existing. It is *universal,* but not universal in the sense of being a *general average.* The *Idea* is an Ideal, at once aimed at and realized. Within it other universals, like laws and types, appear as the first self-differentiations of the absolute universal. They are no less necessary to its wholeness than the many are necessary to the concept of unity. The limit of this self-differentiation and self-expression is the *individual,* in which particular existence is united with universality, or to put it Scholastically, in which *thisness* and *whatness* are combined. Furthermore, *what* the universe is accounts completely and exhaustively for the fact *that* it is. Every *possibility* of existence is exhausted and realized in *actual* existence. Outside of the all-inclusiveness of the existence realized in and by the Absolute there are no other possible worlds that might have been realized. In the fact or *thatness* of existence is comprised all the *whatness* of existence, all that existence conceivably *can* be.

Hegel ends the *Logic* with a reiteration of the warning that the world-process which constitutes the Absolute Life and Experience and which enacts the Absolute Idea, is *not* aimed at a goal *external* to itself. It is not seeking to be other than it is, either in its parts, its moments, or its totality. Its end is within itself, and is completely realized from and to all eternity by its being, at each moment and in each episode of its history, precisely what it is at that moment and in that episode. There is no divine, far-off event towards which the whole creation moves. There is, to be sure, a divine event, but it is found in the move-

ment itself, not in some distant climax and termination. It is not far.
off. It is taking place in our midst. It has always been present, and in
no future, however remote, will it be more present than it is here and
now. In short, the Absolute drives on, not for the purpose of getting
to some destination. It moves simply for the sake of moving, and its
end is attained in the complete self-satisfaction and self-realization it
finds in change and motion.

XIV. COSMOLOGY

Nature the External Expression of the Idea. We have reviewed the
logic by which Absolute thought and existence are governed. We have
seen that its fundamental principle is one of *thesis, antithesis,* and
synthesis, which involves a constant taking up and reconciliation of
pairs of contradictory concepts and experiences in higher, more comprehensive and penetrating ideas, until finally all oppositions are overcome in the all-inclusive, all-reconciling, and all-explaining Absolute
Idea. It now remains to see more fully how this principle is manifested
in the operations of physical nature, of human history, of the state,
of art, of religion, and of philosophy.

Nature, Hegel tells us, is coeval with the Idea. From and to all
eternity the Idea has been enacted in the world-process, and nature,
being that enactment, has no temporal beginning or end. She is the
external expression—the *outwardness* and *otherness,* as Hegel terms
it—of the Idea, and is therefore *spatial, temporal,* and *material.* Space,
time, and matter, however, without specific content are as empty concepts as that of not-being, and, as in the case of not-being and being,
are synthesized in the concept of *becoming,* which, on the physical
level, individuates nature into a system of changing, moving, diffused
individual bodies.

The Physical Level. The primary qualities of nature are quantitative—mass, velocity, gravitation, etc.—and are subject to mechanical
law. Gravitation is a physical exhibition of *thesis* and *antithesis,* and
the stable system that results, of *synthesis* and of *reciprocity.*

Physical objects, however, exhibit not only change of *external relations,* but also of *internal state,* as in light, sound, polarity, magnetism,
chemical reaction and the like. This level is much richer in triads of
thesis, antithesis, and *synthesis* and in examples of *reciprocity,* than
the mechanical. In chemical processes, in which the inorganic level
culminates, elements become fused into new wholes, and matter *becomes* more completely, by changing quality as well as place.

The Organic Level. Coming now to the organic level, we find bodies that are not merely *objects,* but *subjects* as well. Here the synthesis of the parts forms a *whole* that exists in and for itself and influences and directs its constituent elements. Organisms are true *individuals,* which preserve their identity throughout all their changes in such wise that at the end of their careers they are still *essentially* what they were at the beginning. In them the Idea expresses itself, not only as a moving and changing, but as a *living,* matter.

In *vegetable* life, the differentiation and reciprocity between the parts and the whole are only imperfectly developed. In the ascending series of *animal* organisms, they become more and more marked, till they reach their culmination in the human body, in which the *organic* possibilities of nature are completely actualized and exhausted. Here, at last, the Spirit has evolved a physical organ that permits it to become a self-conscious soul.

XV. ETHICS AND POLITICS

Nature of Morality. We now turn to a consideration of *objective Spirit* as manifested in human society and history. Social organization is an indispensable condition of the self-consciousness, self-expression, and self-determination of the Spirit, and therefore of its *freedom.* The objective counterpart of the exercise of freedom by any one individual is a recognition on his part of the *right* of other individuals, also, to be free and self-directing. Society, therefore, implies a reciprocal enjoyment of individual *rights* by its members, restrained and socialized by *duties* they owe one another. This interweaving of rights and duties with the free self-determination of the individual makes him a *person* whose freedom is expressed in a categorical imperative, demanding that he treat all persons, including himself, in the same way. Since personality is lodged in distinct individual selves, it implies a right to privacy and to private property.

The rights and obligations of persons towards one another, the limits imposed upon the expansion of their private personalities, and their reciprocal duties, are expressed in *contracts* by which individuals publicly *bind* themselves to perform certain actions and to refrain from others. Institutions like the family and the state rest upon covenants of this sort.

So far, however, these contracts appear as things imposed upon the individual from the outside. They seem to be restraints upon his freedom rather than expressions of it. In short, we have an apparent conflict between the *subjective will* of the individual and the common *objective will* of society, which needs to be overcome. The needed *synthesis* is supplied by the *moral will,* which identifies the private and the public interest and *welcomes* the restrictions laid upon it by the presence of the wills of others and by social organization. For it is only when we voluntarily accept and *will* the public good as our own good that our attitude and conduct can be said to be actuated by *ethical* considerations alone.[14]

Individual Freedom and Social Compulsion. Morality, as opposed to mere obedience to law, is pre-eminently a matter of intention and purpose, and moral guilt and innocence are determined on subjective grounds. But to decide what good and bad intentions are, we must first define what we mean by good. What is the human good, the attainment of which a good intention must set before itself? The answer is *happiness,* which, in its turn, may be defined as richness and abundance of life, which, on further analysis, turns out to be life lived in accordance with duty. For, only when we are doing our duty, are we truly self-determined and free in our life.[15]

We are now faced with a number of new difficulties. Duty and inclination do not coincide, and the attempt to identify the one with the other leads to a one-sided morality either of undue repression or undue license. Moreover, we cannot take conscience as our guide, since to do so would make it superior to the moral law, make morality purely subjective, and make the individual the final judge of right and wrong. How, then, are we to reconcile objective standards of morality with freedom of individual conscience?[16]

Man a Social Being. The synthesis and reconciliation of the objective and the subjective good Hegel finds in the morals of daily *living.* Individuals are born into a social and moral order, which is not in conflict with their individuality. In it, rather, their individuality is expressed. This order is not artificial. The individual is *naturally* social, *naturally* moral, *naturally* a family man, *naturally* a citizen. The restrictions the moral and social order lays upon him are not interferences with his nature. They are ways in which he freely determines himself as a human being. In the moral order, we have another example of an organic, living whole, which both determines and is determined by its parts, and whose parts reciprocally determine one another.

In the family, this organic, reciprocal unity is seen in the relations

[14] *Encyclopaedia, Philosophy of Spirit* (*Mind*), §§ 474-475.
[15] *Philosophy of Right,* Part II.
[16] *Phenomenology,* BB, VI, C.

of husband and wife and of parents to children. It appears again in the interdependence of the economic activities that minister to human material needs, and in the reciprocal support social institutions afford one another. It is seen in the industrial unions or corporations in which the workers combine in order to ensure themselves secure and decent living conditions and to build up the same sense of kinship and the same spirit of mutual aid as is found in the family. Finally, the organic character of the moral and social order is most completely manifested in the state.[17]

The State. The state is the whole that absorbs and synthesizes all other human institutions.[18] It is the expression on the social plane of the Idea, just as the natural order manifests the Idea on the physical level. Its function of ensuring the cohesion, the solidarity, and the reciprocal support, of the individuals that compose it is exercised in three ways, legislative, executive, and judicial. These activities are best and most efficiently carried on by a single individual, in whom sovereignty is lodged. To talk of the sovereignty of the people is to delude one's self. The people does not possess sufficient inner cohesion to possess a coherent popular will. The so-called "will of the people" is a myth. For that reason republican forms of government are unsatisfactory and inferior to monarchy.

But the monarch must not be a despot. He must perform his functions in the interest of the state as a whole, and to that end he must permit and encourage the utmost possible freedom in his subjects. He must foster liberty of thought and speech, that there may be a public opinion on all matters whose true meaning and worth he may understand and appreciate, after winnowing from it the chaff of folly, and ignorance, and prejudice. To this end there must be complete freedom of the press, and, generally speaking, every individual should be at liberty not only to speak but to write as he wills on matters of general interest. Such freedom must, however, not be abused, and some restrictions must be laid upon it. But the vilification to which the great are always subject is something that they must endure as a price of their greatness.

International Relations. International law, in Hegel's opinion, cannot have the same authority over nations as the laws of a country have over its citizens. The state is the ultimate unit of social organization, and there can be no superstate entitled and empowered to enforce

[17] *Philosophy of Spirit* (*Mind*), § 512; *Philosophy of Right*, Part III, §§ 142-256. Cf. *Phenomenology*, BB, VI, A.

[18] For Hegel: on the state, cf. *Philosophy of Right*, III, §§ 257-340.

contracts between nations. Nor is there any political force that can moderate strife between nations, as the state keeps the peace between individuals. International quarrels can only be decided by war. The only verdict as to which side is right in a war is the verdict of history.

XVI. PHILOSOPHY OF HISTORY

The Nature of History. We are thus led to Hegel's philosophy of history. History is the expression of the search of the finite spirit for freedom. The great men of history are the Spirit's vehicles. They are the agents by which progress is carried on, and the yardsticks by which progress is measured. Progress, however, is an empty concept without the content and matter given it by society and the state. It consists in successive transformations of the state in the direction of the expression of the Idea in terms of human, social activity and organization.

We may measure history by standards of both geographical and political advance. Geographically, civilization has spread westwards and, as it has pursued the setting sun, it has developed politically. Both advances have manifested three stages, the intermediate one of which may, however, be divided into two periods.

Three Stages of History. Human history begins in Asia. In Asiatic political institutions there is no individual freedom. The individual is completely subjected to the will of the ruler. He cannot even call his soul his own. Obedience is the law of his being, and where obedience to one central and completely dominant individual is lacking, all is chaos and turbulence. In Asia, then, we have the geographical cradle and the political infancy of the race.

The second, double epoch is staged in Greece and Rome and represents racial adolescence and maturity. The political institutions of Greece, which are aristocratic and democratic, manifest the growth of individualism and the conquest, in some measure by some people, of individual freedom, which, however, is not yet a common possession. The sterner, Roman maturity makes the idea of the nation supreme and subjects the individual will to the common needs of national security and growth. Now, too, a philosophical recognition of the *person* and of the rights and duties of the person arises. The individual, completely suppressed by the universal in Asia, and partially emergent from it in Greece, is reabsorbed into the universal on a higher plane.

This process is repeated in the last stage of the political manifestation of the Idea, which takes place in Western Europe. The individual, revolting against the objective and external pressure of the universal upon him, seeks escape in developing a private, subjective world of his own, in which he may move freely. Finally, the struggle between the outer and the inner and between the universal and the particular is overcome and harmonized in the constitution of a society in which the individual freely wills the universal good, and freely identifies his will with that of the supreme individual, the monarch, in whom sovereignty is lodged and by whom the common will is exercised.

This is the ripe old age of the world. It is a period not of weakness, but of strength. It represents on the objective, political level the return of the Idea into itself, enriched by the harmonious reconciliation of the political principles of absolutism and individualism, of despotism and democracy, and of national cohesion and private freedom. The synthesis begins with the history of Christian Europe, and is completed in Germanic culture.

The Infantilism of the Oriental Stage. So much Hegel tells us in the introduction to his *Philosophy of History*.[19] The rest is largely illustration of these points and expatiation upon them. Take the Orient. The infantilism of China is expressed in the patriarchal form of its government. It is also clearly manifest in the Chinese language, which sounds like baby-talk and is written with pictorial characters instead of an alphabet. India is not quite so childish. Its political institutions have advanced from the patriarchal to the caste system, in which all subjects no longer grovel equally before a single emperor, but have begun to develop distinctions of rank among themselves. The many are no longer blotted out by the one, but have begun to assert themselves.

The Hindoo temperament is still sunk in childish dreaming and make-believe. It lacks vigor and self-reliance. Hindoo ideas are mystical, fantastic, extravagant. Hindoo mentality is pre-adolescent. Hindoo physique is boyish. The beauty of the Hindoo women is languorous, fragile and unearthly. All in all, "the character of Spirit in a state of Dream" is "the generic principle of the Hindoo nature." [20]

Persia, Assyria, and Egypt have civilizations less removed from complete expression of the Idea. The individual now separates himself from the universal, but still considers himself dependent upon it. Politically the restrictions of caste are lifted. Assyria and Babylonia

[19] Cf., also, *Philosophy of Right*, III, §§ 341-360.
[20] The discussion that follows is based upon *Philosophy of History* (trans J. Sibree. George Bell & Sons, London, 1905).

exemplify advance in worldly magnificence and luxury. Egypt is striving for self-comprehension, and in that striving we may see Spirit seeking to reflect upon itself.

Graeco-Roman Youth and Maturity. History is now ready to enter upon its second great phase, exemplified in the two epochs of Greece and Rome. In the Greeks man first becomes conscious of his individuality, and reflects upon it. All Greek political and social institutions manifest this individualism. Typical, too, of the accent on individuality is the Greek love of form, finish, and balance. Again, if in Egypt we saw the emergence of the individual from nature, so in Greece we may see the return of the individual to nature on a higher plane, where man and nature are not in conflict but in harmony, and where nature appears as an appropriate stage setting for the realization of man's finite, distinctively human ideals.

Still, just because of its contentment with the finite and the human, Greek morality, in spite of its beauty, cannot be regarded as the culmination of the self-consciousness of the Spirit. It lacks infinite aspirations. It is not sufficiently introspective. It is too simple, too *youthful,* and too naturalistic. It has not developed an inner moral sense and made right and morality an affair of the private conscience.

So it is that the youth of Greece gives way to the maturity of Rome, where the individual is once more subjected to the universal, which now appears on a higher plane as an abstract freedom, expressed in constitutional government, dominating the particular man, and, at the same time, constituting him a *person* possessed of *rights.* Out of this new concept of the person and of personal rights, arises the whole edifice of Roman law.

In the Roman Empire, monarchy also returns, having completed one spiral of its upward course. The Emperor has been raised from the status of an Oriental despot to that of a repository of all the functions of the state. The caste system is abolished in the absolute equality before him of all citizens alike. Still, the Emperor's will is absolute, and government consists in harmonizing the will of all individuals with that of the sovereign individual.

The Spiral of Historical Development. Philosophically speaking, the many, who have asserted their independence in Greek life, are subjected again by Rome to the one, but on a higher level than that of Eastern despotism. They have become individuals and persons—which they were not at the Oriental stage of human development. And the one, whose slaves they now once more become, is, so to speak, one of themselves, and, like themselves, an individual and a person. In the person of the Roman Emperor the Spirit has gained as completely unlimited subjective self-realization as can be gained under objective, political conditions. But in so doing it has contradicted itself, and has really destroyed individuality. For, it is the nature of the individual to be not only one among other individuals, but to be one *on an equality* with others. It is his nature to be limited by them in will and power, rather than to be an absolute master of them, with no restriction upon the exercise of his volition and his strength.

If the monarch is really to rule, and not merely to domineer, the many must reassert themselves. The relations of the sovereign to the subject must be moralized and placed upon a basis of justice and equity. The monarch and his people alike must be participants in a constitutional government guaranteeing individual independence and at the same time binding all individuals together in the service of the nation as a whole. To the development of this final phase of objective Spirit, we now pass.

Early Christianity the Beginning of the Third Stage. It begins with the rise of Christianity. Once more the finite individual, now elevated to the rank of a particular person, begins to assert himself. But this time he does not reappear in opposition to the universal and the infinite, but rather as himself a *particular manifestation* of the infinite, the universal, and the self-existent, which he now recognizes as constituting his inmost essence. Spirit is now about to return to itself in a *synthesis* of its indeterminate manifestation in the Oriental epoch and its finite, determinate manifestation in the Graeco-Roman world. The approaching synthesis is signalized by the Incarnation in which the universal and the particular, the divine and the human, are fused in a single historic individual, the God-man.

The new era, however, dawns slowly. Apart from the historic Incarnation, God and Heaven are still regarded as external to human life. The authority of the two great medieval institutions, the Catholic Church and the State, is exerted upon the individual from without. Politically, the caste system returns, though in a higher, feudal form. Charlemagne, the first Holy Roman Emperor, is still the source rather than the vehicle of justice and might and government organization. His empire rests upon force and subjects other nations unwillingly, and by outer constraint, to its rule.

At last, however, the individual reappears, and the many proceed from the one—by three steps. Geographically and politically the empire of Charlemagne falls to pieces and the nations of modern Europe begin to form themselves upon its ruins. Men start rebelling against the feudal system and against their liege-lords, who govern by an outward force in which there is no intrinsic right. Little by little, sovereignty is built up about a supreme authority, who is a truly *political* power, In the sight of the sovereign his subjects are not only all equal, as they were in the sight of the Roman Emperor; they are all possessed of *equal rights*. And their wills are interwoven into a common interest. The *one* has now become a *whole* in reciprocal relations with all its parts. The transition to modern monarchy is taking place.

Meantime, to complete the triad of reactions against medievalism, the Church rebels against the world and the conditions of the time. She reaffirms the supremacy of the inner, spiritual life, and re-emphasizes the worth of the individual soul in the eyes of God.

The Culmination in the Reformation. The stage is now set for the final act in the development of objective Spirit. In Germanic culture the Spirit at last becomes fully conscious of its freedom and freely wills the identification of the individual with the true, the eternal, and the universal. The act is divided into three scenes. First there is the Reformation, which is the true sunrise whose approach was heralded at the end of the Middle Ages by the false dawn of the Renaissance. Then we have the period immediately following the Reformation, and finally the German Enlightenment.

The Reformation proclaims the freedom of man—his freedom to worship God as he chooses, and to make his peace with God directly without external ecclesiastical and political control, and his freedom to develop his social and political institutions without external direction. It fuses Church and State in the same moral and social order, and subjects them both to identical standards and laws. The Catholic distinction between the priesthood and the laity disappears, and all priests are men like others, and all men, men of God.

In the same way the contradiction between the position of the monarch and that of the subject is overcome. Petty principalities are merged into larger wholes. Fractious and semi-independent vassals are brought to heel. The power of the monarch is consolidated, and its exercise is "invested with an authority emanating from the State."

The French Enlightenment and the German "Aufklärung." The second phase is the phase of the Enlightenment, the French Revolution, and the Age of Reason. Man now *reflects* upon the situation, and seeks rational grounds for his increasing freedom. He unites himself once more with nature, as the Greeks did, only on a higher plane. He regards the laws of nature as *reasonable* and *good*. He draws from them the concept of the *rights* of man. In him Spirit is now recogniz ing its freedom and worth as an individual, but, for the moment, still as a particular opposed to the universal.

But not for long. Spirit is about to return to the universal and to unite the individual with it in the highest and final form of freedom—the rational freedom of the individual, expressed in disinterested public spirit and action, subject to the freely willed and accepted limitations of society and the state. In such circumstances the will is no longer actuated by impulse, be it selfish or benevolent, but simply by its own nature, or, in other words, by duty. But duty is no longer opposed to inclination. This self-legislation of the will, "will making itself its own object," is "the basis of all Right and Obligation—consequently of all statutory determinations of Right, categorical imperatives, and enjoined obligations."

Thus self-directed and fully free, the individual will subjects itself and its rights to the objective freedom found in a social organization based upon reason and morality. But the service of such an organization is the service of reason and right, and therefore of the individual will's own inmost nature. There is no longer any conflict between the subjective and the objective, the particular and the universal, the individual and society. On the contrary, they are reconciled and synthesized in a concept of freedom that identifies them. The attainment of this freedom is the work of the German *Aufklärung.*

XVII. PHILOSOPHY OF ART

The Nature of Beauty. The historical development of objective Spirit has now run its course and culminated in the political institutions of Germany. We rise now to the highest level of the expression of the Idea—the realm of *Absolute Spirit,* which manifests itself in art and religion and philosophy.

Before discussing the history of art, we must pause a moment to describe the nature of *beauty.*[21] Wheresoever the Idea is sensuously displayed we find the *beautiful.* Since the Spirit discovers much in nature that pleases it and that it regards as a congenial mise-en-scène for the exercise of freedom, it perceives *natural beauty* in the universe. But there is also much in nature in the way of unresolved contradictions that is either out-and-out disagreeable to the esthetic sense or that suggests possibilities of being made more pleasing. Where this is the case, the Spirit seeks through *art* so to reconstruct the material provided by nature that it conforms to the esthetic demand and becomes

[21] The discussion follows Hegel's *Aesthetics.*

beautiful. In so doing the Spirit, working through the artist, gives a more complete sensuous embodiment of the Idea than that afforded by nature, and brings *ideal beauty* into being.

Oriental Art and Its Symbolism. Coming now to the evolution of art, we find that it goes through the three phases of thesis, antithesis, and synthesis, and in so doing runs parallel to the unfolding of human history. Oriental art is *symbolic,* and is largely *unconscious* of the Idea it is striving to portray. In its most primitive phases the symbol and that which it symbolizes are not distinguished, but are confused and identified.

A step above this is *fantastic* symbolism in which the sensuous content and its spiritual meaning, though separated in name, still remain imaginatively confused, and confused in such a way that the symbol counts as a reality. Of this, Hindoo art is an example.

The Sublime. Finally, in Egypt we have a real symbolism, in which the symbol suggests that it means more than it is, but leaves the nature of this "something more" a *mystery*. It is with the sense of mystery that the sense of the *sublime* is associated. The sublime is that which defeats every effort of sense and imagination to picture it. It is that whose presence reduces all else to nothingness. It can be described only in symbolic terms. Even so, it defies every effort of the pictorial arts to symbolize it, and can be given only by poetry anything approaching adequate symbolic expression.

The Absolute, since it defies sense and imagination, is sublime. Religion symbolizes its sublimity in two ways, pantheistic and personalistic, according as we regard God as the universe itself, or as an individual transcending the universe. Based upon this dual symbolism of the Absolute, we have a double flight of the artistic imagination, particularly in poetry. On the one hand, we have mystical religion and art that are pantheistic in spirit, on the other, religion and art that deal with God as a person.

As soon as art and religion clearly recognize the inadequacy of the symbol to that which is symbolized, we get *conscious* symbolism, which either *illustrates* by myths, parables and the like, or uses *metaphor* as in allegory, simile, and symbolic painting.

The Human Character of Classical Art. The second great period of art, the classic, begins in a rude and primitive manner, with idealizations and personifications of natural phenomena in which moral character is attributed to natural forces, and the world-process is interpreted in terms of human interests and activities. Little by little the humanization of the universe is carried on by Greek religion and art, till we reach a culmination, in which the natural and the moral are brought into complete harmony, and the ideal world appears as a community of man-like gods and god-like men united by a common civilization. The gods, however, although they are represented as idealized human beings, are not without sublimity. They dwell apart from man on serene heights that raise them far above the clouds and storms of the human level of existence. They are carefree and deathless.

Under these conditions art takes the finite as subject matter and gives it a finite form. In dealing both with the human and the divine its aim is to depict the definite, the finished, the balanced and the harmonious, freed for the moment from the brooding shadow of the infinite. Its accent is upon the individual, not the universal.

Such art bears within itself only too obviously the seeds of its decay. It is one-sided. It is too preoccupied with the finite. It has created only statues, not flesh and blood men. In invading religion, and in making religion a cult of beauty, art has deprived the gods of any real objective existence and has transformed them into subjective ideals.

The Synthesis Effected by Romantic Art. So it is that classic art makes way for the third and final phase of artistic expression—the modern, romantic movement. Art now turns inward for its inspiration, and finds its material in the character and meaning of the inner life. It creates music and lyric poetry as new vehicles of its expression, and religious art is preoccupied not so much with the outward story of Christ as it is with the spiritual meaning of the episodes of his life. Again, on the secular plane, it finds its subject matter in adventure, in chivalry, in knighthood, in loyalty and honor, and in romantic love. The infinite and the universal return, but no longer opposed to the individual and the finite. On the contrary, they now complete and perfect it. In modern romantic art the *synthesis* of the Oriental and the Classic, the infinite and the finite, is at last accomplished.

Each period has its typical and dominant art. The typical art of the Orient is *architecture,* of the Graeco-Roman classicism, *sculpture,* of the modern romanticism, a trinity of *poetry, painting,* and *music.*

If we now examine the separate arts, we shall see them one and all exemplifying the *thesis, antithesis* and *synthesis* of the three periods. Oriental architecture, sculpture, painting and poetry are fantastic, symbolic, mysterious and inarticulate. Classic architecture, sculpture and literature are poised, serene, finite, finished. Then comes the Christian, romantic Gothic, soaring, aspiring, pointing beyond itself, suggestive of meditation and the inner life, yet wholly articulate and free from the monstrousness of Oriental architecture. So, too, Gothic and

Renaissance sculpture and painting, though finite and finished in outer semblance, express an inner life and experience. They depict not the body but the spirit within it. And lyric poetry, perfect in form, interprets the aspirations of the soul. In each separate art, as in art as a whole, the final, Romantic period reconciles the contradiction between the Classic and the Oriental.

Art, however, even in its final romantic phase, fails to effect a synthesis of *subjective* and *objective* in *absolute* Spirit. In its exemplification of the free creation of the object by the subject, it affirms only the Absolute Spirit's *subjective* activity. In this respect it is the *antithesis* of religion, which reaffirms the *objective* phase of Absolute Spirit by its insistence that the creative individual is himself created and depends upon a being external and objective to himself. To religion we now turn.

XVIII. PHILOSOPHY OF RELIGION

Since religion stands to art in the relation of thesis to antithesis, we naturally cannot look to it for an ultimate synthesis of the subjective and objective phases of Absolute Spirit.[22] The development of religion, however, like that of art, is a process of increasing reconciliation of the subjective and the objective within its own sphere. This process reproduces the stages, already noted, of the evolution of history and of art.

We begin with *natural religion,* in which man feels wholly dependent upon and subservient to nature. He is her creature and her plaything. He lies prostrate before inhuman, semi-monstrous, infinite forces over which he has no control. Such is the religious attitude of the Orient—an attitude expressed in three ways, in Chinese religion, in Hindoo religion, and in Buddhism.

As we travel west, however, we find this relation of utter subjection yielding to a dawning self-assertion of the individual and attainment of freedom. Man is no longer deifying external, natural forces only. He is beginning to find gods within his private, moral experience. Here, too, we have three manifestations of the new spirit. Persian religion opposes moral good to moral evil. Its gods represent not only natural but moral forces. The religion of Syria dwells upon the dying and the rising god, and finds a religious significance in suffering and death. The Egyptian religion is full of mystery. Its gods are symbols of unknown spiritual forces operating behind the veil of nature and of sense.

[22] The discussion follows Hegel's *Philosophy of Religion.*

Asia Minor and Egypt thus prove a spiritual as well as a geographical stepping-stone to Rome and Greece and Palestine. For the Hebrew, Greek and Roman cults form a trinity in the unity of the new worship of spiritual individuality and inner freedom, which now appears as the antithesis to the Oriental prostration before objective nature.

Judaism accents the transcendental individuality and personality of God, and invests him with sublimity. It also stresses his righteousness and justice and mercy and other *moral* qualities. Hellenism, the cult of humanity and beauty, asserts against the transcendentalism of the Hebrew Jehovah, the kinship of the gods with men. Man is on a familiar and friendly footing with them, and enters into every relation with them that he would with other human beings. In Rome, we have a religious expression of the notion of order. The gods are gods of the state. Their primary relations are with institutions rather than with individuals. They are, one might say, members of the state. Their worship is a political affair, and is dominated by the political order and by political considerations.

We are now prepared for the final phase of an absolute, all-reconciling religion, in which the antithesis between the universal and the individual is overcome. This is provided by Christianity, whose fundamental concepts effect the necessary synthesis. The doctrine of the Trinity especially is found by Hegel to be profoundly significant. The Father represents the pure identity of the Absolute. He is the Absolute Idea reflecting upon its essential unity. The generation of the Son by the Father is the final religious expression of the appearance of difference within identity. It is the Absolute Idea developing itself in the manifold variety and contradiction of the world-process and in the conflict and suffering that multiplicity and contradiction entail. In the Passion and Resurrection the suffering and conflict are conquered, sanctified, and glorified, and exhibited as essential to the richness of the Absolute Idea.

The Holy Ghost, proceeding from both the Father and the Son, is the manifestation under the form of religion of the return of difference into identity, and of the gathering up again of all the variety and multiplicity and contradiction of the world-process into the unity of Absolute Spirit. Thanks to its outpouring, the finite, individual spirit, enlightened by Christian teaching, is able to believe that the universe is good and the work of God, despite the seeming evil and discord of which it is so full.

Christianity, however, in spite of its synthesis of the objective and the subjective aspects of *religion,* does not completely reconcile the objective and the subjective aspects of Absolute Spirit. For all religion involves imagination, faith, and mystery; whereas a final synthesis of the subjective and the objective can only be attained by *understanding* and *rationally demonstrating* their unity and identity. This is the work of *philosophy.*

XIX. THE HISTORY OF PHILOSOPHY

In philosophical speculation, what was formerly a matter of imagination and faith now becomes the work of *reason.* We can *demonstrate* the reciprocal relation, one pole of which is emphasized by art, the other by religion. The Spirit, rising to its absolute level, realizes that all existence whatsoever, be it nature, or society, or the individual, is the creation of reason, and that the will of the individual, in so far as it is moral and rational, is one with the universal will and is fulfilled in the same common good. When by the aid of philosophy we *know* what on the lower levels of Absolute Spirit we have imagined or believed—that Reality is Reason and that all its manifestations are completely intelligible—then we also *know* that, in submitting our minds to the laws of logical and exact thinking and our wills to the moral law, we are attaining and exercising in common one and the same absolute freedom of self-expression. In that supreme, philosophical act of absolute knowledge and absolute will, all our differences are reconciled and *aufgehoben,* and subject and object, the many and the one, the particular and the universal, are synthesized, freed from all contradictions, in the living truth which is the Absolute Idea.[23]

The final synthesis, like the partial reconciliations effected by art and religion, is built up progressively. Philosophy, too, has a history,[24] and that history, also, exhibits thesis, antithesis and synthesis. Oriental metaphysics, we are told, true to the Oriental spirit, denies the being and worth of the individual and reduces the many and "becoming" to illusion. The general temper of Graeco-Roman philosophy is to revive the many, to affirm the existence of the particular, and to exalt the importance and value of the individual and of his subjective experience.

The distinctively Greek period has its three moments. Pre-Socratic philosophy concerns itself with nature, and with the problems of matter and form, motion and rest, the whole and its parts, and the like,

---

23 *Phenomenology,* DD, VIII.
24 *History of Philosophy,* Oriental Philosophy, A, B.

raised by an investigation of nature. Objective Spirit is rescued from the nothingness to which Orientalism condemns it, and at the same time the individual as a part of nature recovers his existence. The Sophists and Socrates place the emphasis upon the subject, and base the moral order on the individual. Plato and Aristotle seek in their systems to synthesize nature and the individual, the universal and the particular.

The Roman period, whose subjection of the individual to the state drives him back upon himself into his inner life for the exercise of freedom, is marked by Stoicism, Epicureanism, Skepticism, and Neo-Platonism. These philosophies find the moral good in an inner peace of mind, which the world can neither give nor take away, and in an inner approach to and contact with the Real. In this way, Rome, though destructive of Greek individualism, becomes the foster-mother of inner self-determination and of personal, private liberty of thought and attitude.

In medieval philosophy, dominated by Christianity, we begin the long and tortuous approach to the final period of modern thought. Christian dogma is given metaphysical backing, the new philosophy is systematized, Plato and Aristotle are invoked to support it and are interpreted in accordance with its needs, and the conflict between the particular and the universal breaks out again.

Then comes the Renaissance. Nature and the individual reassert themselves, aided by the discovery of the true Plato and the true Aristotle freed from the glosses given them by the Church. Human life and human individuality, regarded as parts of nature, are once more exalted as they were in Greece. Nature herself becomes deified in pantheistic systems. The individual recovers to some extent his objective liberty, and begins a free investigation of the external world, with which, however, the Church still tries to interfere.

Upon the Renaissance follows the Reformation, and with it modern philosophy appears. Its harbingers are Bacon and Boehme; Bacon because he establishes the scientific method and insists on its universal application, Boehme because he so clearly perceives the principle of contradiction and of the identity of opposites. Next, Descartes and Spinoza try, by applying the scientific method, to *understand* the world—an attempt which ends disastrously in setting matter and mind, the objective and the subjective, in irreconcilable opposition to each other. This provokes a period of skepticism, exemplified by Locke and Hume, in which the objective is largely reduced to terms of the subjective. Also we have attempts by Leibnitz and Wolff to heal the breach between the two principles. In France a naturalism reappears in which mind is reduced to terms of matter. Morally, there is a tearing down of established standards and beliefs. Freedom of individual thought and action is affirmed by Rousseau, subject, however, to the control of reason, and identified with rational thinking and conduct.

The stage is now set for German Idealism, initiated by Kant, continued by Fichte and Schelling, and brought to its climax in the Hegelian system by which all previous philosophy is *aufgehoben* and synthesized. The Absolute Idea is once and for all made manifest on the highest plane of its self-expression. Pure reason by pure reasoning has wholly laid bare its own essence, and, since thought and existence are identical, has in so doing revealed the essence of the Real.

Chapter XVIII

SCHOPENHAUER

I. LIFE

Early Education. The finality of Hegel's philosophy did not remain long without challenge. The gauntlet was at once thrown down by Schopenhauer. Arthur Schopenhauer was born in 1788 into one of the rich merchant families that constituted the aristocracy of the free city of Danzig. His people were well off, and his parents were cultured, traveled, and broadminded and liberal, religiously and morally. His father, particularly, was sympathetic and indulgent, ever respectful of the son's independence and right to develop his own opinions and carve out his own career.

When he was five years old, his parents, outraged by the annexation of Danzig by Russia, moved to Hamburg. At the age of nine he was placed for two years with a French family at Le Havre, in the belief that a knowledge of French would be valuable to him in the commercial career which it was hoped he would follow. For similar reasons he was left when he was fifteen with an English clergyman at Wimbledon near London, while his father and mother were making a tour of England and Scotland. He picked up English and with it a distaste for what he considered Anglo-Saxon cant and hypocrisy and the interminable round of morning and evening prayers inflicted upon him by the clerical household.

After three months of this he rejoined his parents, and was bribed out of an already developing distaste for his father's business by the promise of a Continental tour. He stopped for some time in Paris, and visited the south of France, Switzerland and Vienna. Finally, obedient to his promise, he returned to Danzig as a business apprentice, and then, returning to Hamburg, got a job in a mercantile house.

Financial Independence. In 1805 his father died. The estate, to be sure, had been somewhat depleted by the depression that followed the boom in Hamburg's prosperity created by the war between Prussia and France. Still, he inherited enough to be financially independent, and his father's death absolved him from his promise to go into business and left him free to follow his own inclinations. The family circle, moreover, was broken. His mother, who was a brilliant woman of considerable literary talent, and who found domestic ties in general, and her husband and children in particular, something of a bore, decamped at once to Weimar, where she embarked upon a literary career, made of her house a kind of salon, and proceeded to live her own life. Thither Arthur presently followed her, and was there impressed, if not carried away, by the enthusiasm for things Greek of which Goethe, now an old man, was the center and the chief exponent. His temperament, however, was incurably romantic and the serene influences of the Weimar circle, though they helped form in him a great admiration for Plato, could not make the leopard change his spots.

Idiosyncrasies. By now these spots were definitely marked. He loved philosophy. He hated women—an aversion rooted perhaps in his lack of sympathy with his mother, and fostered by her new and rather free mode of life and by the circle of friends she had gathered about her, most of whom he cordially detested. This aversion to his mother grew on him, so much so that later on he neither saw nor corresponded with her for many years. And his enmity towards her expanded into a contempt and repugnance for the whole sex, expressed in his famous *Essay on Women,* which his sporadic and temporary liaisons (for he never had a serious or lasting love affair) served only to intensify.

Again, the famous pessimism of Schopenhauer was temperamental, though doubtless it was exaggerated by his unhappy filial relations. As a youth he was abnormally sensitive to the spectacle of suffering in all forms and particularly to animal suffering. Its existence, he felt, could not be reconciled with any theory that affirmed a just and benevolent God, and was proof positive that existence is evil.

Philosophical Studies at Göttingen and Berlin. Upon attaining his majority and receiving his share of the paternal fortune, he entered the University of Göttingen. There his interest in philosophy was further stimulated by Schulze, whom we may remember as one of Kant's critics and the author of *Aenesidemus.* Under Schulze's guidance he became a devotee not only of Plato but of Kant. At the same time, he cultivated other things besides philosophy, notably his musical talent and the pleasures of society where he was perhaps not over-popular because of his self-assurance and his overweening ways.

From Göttingen, he migrated to Berlin and devoted himself to the natural sciences and particularly to medicine, psychology, and psychopathology. He attended Fichte's lectures and acquired a contempt for Fichte's teaching. Presently the retreat of Napoleon from Russia and the declaration of war by Prussia against France endangered Berlin. Schopenhauer departed first to Dresden, and then to Weimar, where he prepared his thesis for the doctorate at Jena. This was his first work, *On the Fourfold Root of the Principle of Sufficient Reason* (1814). Meantime he had had an interesting correspondence with Goethe over Goethe's attack on the Newtonian theory of light, which led to the publication in 1816 of his essay *On Vision and Color.*

The final break with his mother had taken place, and Schopenhauer was now living in Dresden. His system was taking definite shape in his mind. He had been reading the French materialists, Cabanis and Helvétius, and he had also been profoundly stirred by the Latin translations of the Upanishads, which had first appeared in 1801, and by other books on Hindoo religion and philosophy which had been written since that time. In 1818, his book was ready for the press, and at the end of the year was published under the title of *Die Welt als Wille und Vorstellung (The World as Will and Idea).* Like Hume's *Treatise,* however, it fell still-born from the press, and a second edition, twenty-six years later, met with little more success.

Life in Italy and Frankfort. Meanwhile, his life flowed along in an easy and uneventful fashion. While his book was still in the publisher's hands, he had left for Italy, where he spent the winter. On his return, he applied for and received an appointment as *privat-docent* at the University of Berlin—a city which he disliked heartily. Here, he and Hegel came immediately to blows. He had another fight, too, on his hands with the family firm at Danzig, which had gone bankrupt—a fight from which he emerged triumphant, with a considerable part of his modest capital still intact.

The Berlin episode was short, and Schopenhauer was off to Italy again. But after two years' absence he returned, not to teach but to work in independence. His bachelor habits were now firmly established. Long since, in Göttingen, he had initiated the series of poodles, which were his closest companions. His mother was wholly out of the picture, and another domestic row had estranged him from his sister. He learned Spanish, and in 1829, we find him trying to arrange with a British firm for a translation of Kant's works into English.

In 1831 came the great cholera epidemic, which carried Hegel off. Schopenhauer fled the city and removed to Frankfort, where he was destined to spend the rest of his life. Here he settled into a regular routine. After his morning tub—one apparently agreeable memory of his sojourn in the clerical family at Wimbledon—and his coffee, taken not too early, he worked the entire morning. At noon precisely he stopped, diverted himself for a half-hour upon the flute to relax his mind, and betook himself to the *Englischer Hof* for midday dinner. After dinner a nap and light literature till four. At four a rapid, two-hour walk with his white poodle, which all the children in the neighborhood called "young Schopenhauer."

Rise to Fame. After his walk, the "elder" Schopenhauer, at least, visited the reading-room to peruse the papers and reviews. Thence he went on sometimes to the theater or a concert. Supper followed between eight and nine, washed down by half a bottle of wine. An hour's reading, while he smoked his long pipe. And so to bed.

In 1836, Schopenhauer published a short work *On the Will in Nature*. Nothing came of it. He continued to be ignored both by the philosophers and the laity. He had a moment of high spirits when an essay dealing with free-will won a Norwegian prize, but these were immediately dashed when an essay on the foundations of morality was rejected at Copenhagen. Both these essays he published in 1841 as *The Two Fundamental Problems of Ethics*. Meantime his hatred for the successful Fichte, Schelling, and Hegel grew more intense.

Nevertheless, his day was just beginning to dawn. By an irony of fate, though he himself had scant sympathy with materialism and naturalism, the scientific spirit and democratic institutions, his views were invoked by the champions of these rising movements, and he began to find himself the center of an ever-widening circle of disciples. Furthermore, he was also being taken up in England, where his ideas proved a valuable ally to anti-theological and anti-clerical agitation. His British reputation was enhanced by an article in the *Westminster Review* praising his *Parerga and Paralipomena,* a book of essays published in 1851.

People at home and abroad now began to read him. Another edition of *On the Will in Nature* appeared in 1854, a third edition of *The World as Will and Idea* in 1859, and, just before his death, a second edition of *The Two Fundamental Problems of Ethics.* He appealed not only to the materialists and anti-clericals, but to the mystics, the spiritualists, and generally to all the cults and "isms" that still, today, rush to supposed Magi and Hindoo lore for inspiration. Curiously enough, the army, too, felt his fascination, and he numbered many officers among his disciples. And the hated women flocked about him. There were demands for his photograph. His portrait must be painted. Strangers flocked to the *Englischer Hof* to watch him eat. Even the

Universities sat up and began to take notice. Leipzig went so far as to offer a prize for the best essay on his system.

Schopenhauer had been unusually vigorous and healthy all his life. But now age was beginning to tell on him. His heart was not so good as it had been. His walks had to be shortened and taken at a slower pace. But nothing could daunt or restrain him or convince him that he was growing old. In the autumn of 1860 he had a slight heart attack, followed by pneumonia. He convalesced and was up and about again. One morning he had arisen and breakfasted as usual. A few minutes later, his doctor, dropping in to visit him, found him lying back in a corner of the sofa, apparently asleep.

II. CRITICISM OF FICHTE AND HEGEL

Acceptance of the Idealistic Hypothesis. Schopenhauer accepted along with Fichte and Hegel the analogy of a human career in describing the character of the Real. For him, as for them, Reality was an activity of willing and of thinking. He sided, moreover, with Fichte against Hegel in maintaining that the will is prior to the intellect, and that thinking arises incidentally to volition. But here the resemblance ends. Fichte and Hegel regarded the world-process as through and through moral and rational. Its aim was the expression of moral freedom or of intellectual clarity and consistence. The Fichtean Ego never swerved from its lofty moral purpose. The career of the Hegelian Absolute was governed by an unflagging reverence for the laws of the strictest logic, and an impeccable obedience to them.

Schopenhauer, however, was suspicious of the perfect rationality and morality attributed to the Absolute by Fichte and Hegel. In his doctoral thesis, *The Fourfold Root of the Principle of Sufficient Reason,* he had already cast doubts upon the efficacy of reason as an instrument for discovering the nature of Reality, and had insisted upon the importance of immediate, unrationalized experience and of volition. In *The World as Will and Idea* he developed this line of thought and subjected the content of consciousness to a sort of psychoanalysis, with a view to discovering its real character, and to inferring from that character the real nature of the Absolute.

Experience and Reason Expressions of the Will. The first book of *The World as Will and Idea* is devoted to an analysis and appraisal of the representational, perceiving, thinking aspects of experience. He agrees with the idealistic hypothesis that all knowledge is of perception, and with the idealistic division of experience into subjective and objective, and the distinction between sensations and ideas within objective experience. He accepts the Kantian view that space and time are not abstract ideas but *a priori* forms of the sensible manifold. They are, however, twin expressions of a deeper condition and principle of all sensible experience—the principle of *causation.* No event in the stream of phenomena can be experienced as causeless. It must have a reason why. This reason must be different from it. To be different from it, it must occur in a different *moment,* or occupy a different *place.* Space and time, then, are forms of causality.

Matter, again, is nothing but another form of causality. As the *content* of space and time, it is the expression of causal activity passing in *change* from one time and one place to another. Furthermore, it is a union of space and time, and enables us to correlate a particular spatial position with a particular temporal moment. In every material object "here" and "now" are conjoined.

Reason Secondary and Instrumental. Turning now to abstract ideas, we find that they are quite different from perceptions. They reflect or represent them. They are not caused by one another. They are *inferred* from one another. Nevertheless, chains of inference must always end in a concept founded upon experience. *Understanding* draws concepts from experience and keeps them applied to experience. *Reason* uses concepts without reference to the percepts upon which they rest. By detaching them from their anchorage in sensation it is able to voyage, to explore, to invent, to create, and to predict.

For instance, from any given example of cause and effect the *understanding* infers that the cause has produced the effect in question. But when we wish to *repeat* the observed effect, and when we deliberately repeat the cause in order to produce it, we use our reasons, not our understandings. For we are, in that case, acting in accordance with a concept of causation in general, without which we should be unable to feel that a repetition of the one event would be followed by a recurrence of the other.

Nor should we forget that it is reason that makes truth universal and communicable. On the level of understanding we could not pass on our knowledge to one another. I could not, for example, communicate to you my understanding of how a particular instrument works, unless I could compose my message to you in terms of the general principle of that instrument, applicable to all similar instruments in all experiences in all times and places, and comprehensible by all intellects.

The upshot of the whole matter is that all reason is *practical* and has to do with experience. It can give us nothing that is not found in experience. It adds nothing to our knowledge of Reality. All truth is directly or indirectly connected with experience. The concepts closest to experience are likely to be the truest, since the further a chain of inferences gets from perception, the greater are the chances of error creeping into it. There is nothing behind or beyond or deeper than sensation. All our so-called getting *behind* or *beneath* sensible experience is really constructing *upon* experience. Hypotheses, scientific and metaphysical, erected by reason, remove us, if anything, from the *felt* essence of the Real.

III. REALITY AS WILL

Knowledge and the Real. Still, Schopenhauer goes on, in the second book of *The World as Will and Idea,* there is more to experience than a kaleidoscope of sensations. Experience *interests* us. It *means* something that is *more* than what shows upon the surface. Our question now becomes, What is this *more?* The philosophers cannot answer this question, for they all disagree. Nor can the mathematicians and the physical scientists give an answer. Mathematics deals only with certain external relations between sensible phenomena. The physical sciences simply describe how experiences arrange themselves in space and time according to the law of causality. But they tell us nothing of the inner nature of the phenomena themselves. Plainly, since we *know* experience entirely *from without,* the *"more"* that we are looking for must be found by getting inside phenomena, and by feeling them from within. Can this be done?

Certainly not by the so-called process of knowledge, Schopenhauer replies. Knowledge deals only with the outer aspects of experience. It does nothing but synthesize and interrelate phenomena.

Will and Reality. We must, therefore, look elsewhere for the clue. Let us examine ourselves. We are phenomena like everything else. We have *bodies,* submitted like all other bodies to space and time and causality. We view ourselves, as we view everything else, from the outside. But, at the same time, I see other bodies and my own body *from within* my own body. In myself, then, I am aware not only of the external characteristics of all phenomena, including myself. I am also aware of the inner nature of a phenomenon. My awareness is neither perceptual nor conceptual. It has a peculiar warmth and intimacy. It is a living, glowing, dynamic experience. It is what we call *Will.*

Again, from the point of view of knowledge and reason all phenomena, including my own body, are on precisely the same footing. My body is no more and no less intelligible than any other body. No special accent of any sort is laid upon it. In short, as a pure intellect engaged only in *thinking* about things, I should have no means of claiming any one particular body as *mine* more than any other. It is my *will* that claims one among the many equal objects of sense and knowledge as *its*. It is my *will* alone that is *within* the body I call *mine,* but outside all other bodies. It is upon the will, not the intellect, that the distinction between the self and the not-self rests. It would seem, then, that so-called *rational* thought is in reality "wishful" and dictated by the nature of the will. Hence *reason* cannot be the essence of the Absolute.

But what is the relation of my *will* to my phenomenal self in which I appear as a spatio-temporal event experiencing and knowing a phenomenal world? The relation cannot be one of causation, since causation has to do only with the spatial and temporal phenomenal aspects of experience. The movements, for example, of my body, though expressive of my particular will, are not caused by it. They are, rather, my own *perceptions* of the way in which I will to act. They are, in Schopenhauer's phrase, objectifications of my volitions. So, too, my whole body, and myself as I exist for myself as phenomenon, may be regarded as my will become conscious of itself and visible to itself, that is, as an *objectification of my will*.

Escape from Solipsism. So far, so good. But can I be sure that anything exists except *my* will and *my* experience? The whole of my experience, including the entire so-called external world, may be, for all I can know or perceive, simply the objectification of *my* will. I may still be the Absolute and *you* may be a part of my cosmic dream. To show that this is not the case, we must show that all other bodies, like my own, are manifestations of a *will* actuating them from within.

To do this we must inspect more closely the nature of the Will. The Will, transcending, as it does, the world of phenomena, is a true thing-in-itself. It is above space, time, and causality, which are forms only of its outer, objectified aspects and not applicable to its inner character. It is one, since all multiplicity and individuation are due to spatial and temporal conditions of existence. Indeed, my own individuality, and selfhood, and existence as a distinct person, are superficial. I am one individual among many simply because I have a particular body, and my possession of a particular body is incidental to the space-time form in which the will objectifies and appears to itself.

It would be, therefore, absurd to suppose that the Will is more objectified and more intimately connected with the perceived phenomenon I call *my* body than with the perceived phenomena I call external bodies. All bodies are equally manifestations of an inner reality, and each one is as directly grounded in that reality as any other. Hence the Will must be regarded as no less *within* the external world than I feel it to be within myself. It must feel itself and recognize itself *internally* in other bodies besides mine, just as it views itself *externally* in them.

Metaphysical Characteristics of the Will. Since the Will is above space, time, and causality, it is self-caused and self-determining. Hence it wills *freely* to objectify itself in a world-process subjected to these conditions. In me, for example, it wills *freely* to become my body, my life, my career, and to subject its manifestation of itself in me to the same causal necessities as govern other phenomena. The laws of nature are the formal rules which the Will itself determines to follow in its behavior. Hence there is no conflict between the inexorable determination of one event by another and the undetermined nature of the Will itself.

IV. THE NATURE OF THE ABSOLUTE

The Irrational and Amoral Character of the Human Will. Schopenhauer has now set forth his reasons for believing that the Absolute is Will rather than Reason. It now remains to determine the nature of the Will. To do this we must examine the behavior of the Will both in ourselves and in the rest of the phenomenal world in which it objectifies itself.

A frank and fearless analysis, both of subjective individual experience and of the larger absolute experience which constitutes the world-process, shows that their motivations, far from being organized as a moral Will actuated and stabilized by a moral purpose, are disorganized, contradictory, and blind. In ourselves, the Will resolves itself into a welter of irrational, conflicting, and reciprocally stultifying desires, ends, and satisfactions to whose procession there is no end. Each seeming goal attained turns itself into a new dissatisfaction and a new craving. Human life has no goal, nor could it reach one, if it had it. Fundamental in ourselves, and driving us forever on, is a blind and diffuse craving just to exist, under any circumstances, anywhere, at any cost.

The Irrational and Amoral Character of the World-Process. If we now turn from an analysis of ourselves to an examination of the external universe and the world-process, what do we find? We note immediately that external forces and events conflict with one another and destroy one another. This is true of all grades of cosmic development. Inanimate objects smash one another up. Living bodies prey upon one another. Sensitive organisms inflict endless pain upon one another. Intelligent organisms are in a state of cut-throat competition and often of open and bloody battle. The world-process is one of endless suicide. All we can infer from it is a Will whose essence is discontent, and whose aim is simply, as we have already said, to be anything, anyhow, anywhere, at any price.

The Absolute, then, far from being the organized, unified, morally inspired affair that Fichte imagined it to be, is blind, irrational, and unmoral. It is *a will to be, a will to live,* no matter how. Its essence is simply to *affirm* itself, and to appear as a world-process, no matter what. In such a Will there is no purpose, no morality, no happiness, no good. Its motivation is insane, its fruit is suffering, and the universe created by its blind and conflicting cravings is an evil thing.

In its insensate striving, the Will follows a fixed line of development in which we may distinguish successive *grades of objectification,* rising step by step from a lowest level of the blind and inanimate events and forces of mechanical nature to a highest level attained in the conscious life of man. In these successive grades we find the nature of the Will objectively presenting itself with more and more distinctness and completeness, till at last in human beings we get our closest and most correct view of it.

Existence as Conflict, Suffering, and Evil. From our observation of the grades of objectification we also receive a valuable hint of the true relation of the intellect and of knowledge to the Will. In each individual thing the Will *aims* at preserving and maintaining itself as best it can against opposing phenomena. To this end it devises *means.* Such law and order and structure as obtain in the universe are but the strategic plan of the tragic battle of the Will with itself, which fills all space and time. Every object, animate or inanimate, is a weapon both of offense and of defense. In the inanimate world individual events affirm themselves and defend themselves against one another according to the law of inertia. Inorganic matter is all battering ram and resistant rampart. In vegetable and animal organisms we find all sorts of devices for attacking and for warding off attack. Living matter is all tooth and claw, all breeding one's own, and feeding upon every other form of life.

At last the Will creates in the human intellect its most efficient instrument of survival and destruction. The power of reason to generalize and predict gives the human mind a capacity for anticipating new situations and dealing with them in the light of former occurrences. Knowledge is a long-range gun that enables the Will both to kill at a distance and to lay down a barrage against advancing death before it comes too near. Reason, then, is only an instrument evolved like tooth and claw in the interest of self-preservation.

V. THE SEARCH FOR SALVATION

No Salvation in Western Ethics. Is there, then, any hope of salvation from such a universe? Scanning the world in which he lived, and contemplating its organization, its ethics, its religion, and its philosophy, Schopenhauer could find none. For all alike were bent on glorifying the Will to Live. All western civilizations sought salvation in more and more life, more and more satisfaction, in action, and progress, and so-called betterment of the world by good works. This self-perpetuation of the Will was justified by systems of morality that stressed the ethical value of suffering in the formation of character, by religious doctrines that sought to consecrate suffering and make it expressive of God's purpose, and by philosophies like Fichte's and Hegel's that found in contradiction and conflict indispensable conditions of the Absolute's perfection.

What we must do, or rather not do, to be saved, if salvation is possible, is clear enough. We must strike at the root of all evil and kill the Will to Live. We must stop desiring anything, stop willing anything, stop struggling, stop striving, cease from uplifting, cease from progressing. Thus and thus only can suffering be destroyed and peace attained. But does it lie within the power of the Will to turn upon itself in its entirety and to deny and extinguish itself?

The promise that this might be so and the hope of salvation that flowed from such a promise Schopenhauer found in Greece and in the East. Plato and the Buddhist sages were the harbingers of the dawn. The one might seem to promise respite from the Will to Live, albeit momentary, here and now. The others held out a hope of negating it once and for all.

Temporary Escape from the Will. The third and fourth books of *The World as Will and Idea* explore the way of salvation. From the phenomenal world, Schopenhauer continues, we have nothing to hope and everything to fear. For it is the phenomenal world that is the arena of desire, and struggle, and strife, and suffering. But let us take another glance at the forms and types and laws which constitute the Form of the universe, and the Truth about it. Like the Will itself, they are eternal, changeless, and above causality. They are beyond strife, harmonious with each other, and unaffected by the birth, the conflict, and the death at one another's hands of the phenomena that exemplify them. This hierarchy of Forms in which the Will *objectifies* itself Schopenhauer calls the world of Platonic Ideas.

These Ideas, though primarily created by the Will to Live as instruments of self-affirmation, also may be *contemplated* for their own sake and as ends in themselves. This power of *contemplation* arises, it would seem, from the fact that the intellect generates more power than it needs to perform its primary function of serving the Will, and that the excess is drained off by passing from the practical applications of the universal to the particular to an impractical, theoretic interest in the universal itself. Under certain conditions the theoretic interest may suspend the practical interest. When this takes place, knowledge is freed from subservience to the practical exigencies of the Will, and becomes an end in itself, and the pleasure attending it is not adulterated or followed by surfeit and pain. At such moments the Will is completely satisfied and ceases to desire.

Furthermore, when the intellect escapes the clutches of desire, the individual is freed from the bonds of his own particular nature and personality. His attention is freed from attending to the practical and particular bearings of things upon his own life, and becomes absorbed in their eternal and universal aspects. He forgets himself and loses himself in the object of his contemplation, and at the same time forgets what is temporary and accidental and insignificant in that object. Viewing "under the aspect of eternity" both himself and that which he beholds, he is no longer an individual and a person. He is a timeless, will-less, knowing subject, raised by identification with the eternal above the flux and strife of the phenomenal world and the tyranny of willing and desiring to the calm in which the Ideas dwell.

The Esthetic Escape from the Will. The pleasure attending the pure *contemplation* of the Ideas is *esthetic satisfaction*. The Ideas themselves, regarded now not as means to further striving, but as visions to be entertained for their own sake, become things of *beauty*. The *artist* is distinguished from other men by his peculiar ability to forget the *practical* bearings of the phenomenal world upon himself and others, and to penetrate and to contemplate the Ideas, and to express them and his joy in contemplating them to his fellow-men through his work. Thus he is in a way a savior, since in revealing beauty and arousing esthetic satisfaction he gives peace and cessation from desire.

VI. THEORY OF ART

The Beautiful and the Sublime. We are thus brought to Schopenhauer's theory of art. We may begin our discussion by pointing out that we are already in a position to distinguish the beautiful from the sublime. The sense of beauty is associated with the contemplation of phenomena agreeable and friendly to ourselves. In their presence we can lose ourselves spontaneously and without effort in the object of our contemplation. But when we contemplate the Ideas of phenomena hostile to ourselves, self-forgetfulness is difficult and requires effort in the face of the practical bearing upon our lives of the object in question. However, in rising above the hostile aspects of the phenomenon to contemplation of its Idea, we have a sense of triumphing over the terror inspired by its unfriendliness towards us. It is the injection of the sense of triumph into the pleasure of contemplation that gives us the feeling of the *sublime*.

The Constructive and Pictorial Arts. Passing now to the different arts, we find that they may be arranged in a hierarchy corresponding to the scale of ascending grades of the objectification of the Will. At the bottom of the scale are the blind, mechanical forces of nature. Architecture is the art that seizes and sets forth the Ideas manifested in the inanimate world. It contemplates the properties of matter, such as gravity, cohesion, rigidity, fluidity, and the reflection of light. And it builds with beauty according as it succeeds in revealing these material forces and properties in perfect harmony and balance. For this reason, Schopenhauer prefers classical architecture to all others. In it the equilibrium which holds the secret of architectural beauty is most clearly seen. Gothic architecture, on the other hand, he regarded as a mere makeshift, due to the inclemency of the northern climates. Snow and rain make high-pointed roofs and vaultings necessary, but they represent an interference with esthetic design by unfortunate but necessary concessions to practical exigencies.

A step above architecture comes landscape painting, which also reveals forms and laws lurking behind inanimate nature. In both it and architecture the liberation of the individual mind from the tyranny of the Will to Live counts for much more than any revelation these arts may give of the deeper significance of the phenomenal world. The Ideas first begin, as it were, to acquire depth when living beings are concerned, and it is by arts whose subject matter is animate that the more profound meanings of existence are brought out.

The most superficial of the deeper arts are animal painting and sculpture, which display the Ideas exemplified in the lower orders of animate things. Next come painting and sculpture of the human form. Sculpture catches the outward beauty and grace of the human being, but is not well adapted to seize and portray inner life and character. This is better done, though not adequately, by painting, and especially by portrait painting. Portraiture displays the nature and Idea of the individual person, in so far as it is possible to display it within the limitations of the materials, like paint and canvas, with which the artist is forced to work.

The great art for representing the Idea of man in all its complexity is poetry, which is able also in its descriptions to transmit the other Ideas. The highest kind of poetry is tragedy. For through tragedy we feel most intimately and directly the blindness of the Will and the strife and suffering with which its objectifications are infected.

Music. One art, music, remains to be mentioned. In Schopenhauer's opinion, it is unique. It is not, like the other arts, the manifestation of some definite Idea or Ideas. Nevertheless, it liberates the human mind more completely from servitude to the Will than does any other form of esthetic satisfaction. Why is this? The answer Schopenhauer finds in the peculiarly intimate relation music bears to the Will. Instead of revealing an Idea in which the Will is objectified, it reveals immediately the nature of the Will itself. Music is a direct *objectification* of the Will, parallel to the expression given the Will by the Ideas. Unlike the other arts, its works are not copies of copies but first-hand imitations of the original.

The parallelism between the direct expression of the Will in music and its indirect expression in the other arts by way of the Ideas is seen in the musical scale. The bass notes correspond to the forces of nature. The treble, which carries the air and motif, corresponds to the higher objectification of the Will in human life. Musical intervals run parallel to the grades of objectification. The variations from and returns to the key in a motif represent the restless striving and outgoing of man's experience and its ceaseless recoil upon itself. The different musical tempos reflect his various moods. Music, then, is the only art to penetrate to the core of the Will and to express directly its essence without the need of intermediary Ideas.

VII. DEATH NO ESCAPE

But the Will cannot find any enduring and final peace in the contemplation of what, after all, are means it has devised for living, and, in living, for craving, struggling, and suffering. The forces and forms of nature, the human body, the character of the inner man, the episodes of human life, with which art deals, are but assertions of the blind impulse to exist. Ultimate salvation must come, not by throwing sops to the Will to quiet it, but by extinguishing it altogether. The Will must turn upon itself and of its own volition deny and destroy itself. How this mystical act of self-renunciation is possible Schopenhauer learned from the Buddhists and expounded in the fourth and last book of his chief work.

The way of escape, he remarks at once, is not by the gate of death. The Will, being a thing-in-itself, lifted clear of time and change and causality, can never die. Only its individual manifestations come into being and pass away. It follows that just as our birth does not bring the Will to Live into existence, so our death cannot destroy it. In that sense, we are, if you like, deathless. But such deathlessness must not be confused with personal immortality. There is no survival and persistence of individuality. *I,* in so far as I am a person and an individual, belong to the phenomenal world, and, like everything else in that world, am transient and dissolving.

By my death, then, the *Will* is not freed from living, and the life that I was is succeeded by another. Nevertheless, death should have no terror for us. For it is precisely to the extent that we are individual and personal that we are enslaved to the Will, and therefore *live.* And *life,* as we know, is evil, is all restlessness and unsatisfied desire, all defeat and failure and suffering. The most happiness we can expect from it is some surcease from pain. Why, then, be terror-stricken by the knowledge that *my* life will soon be over, and that in a brief moment *I* shall be gone? For at least I have the assurance that when I am dead the Will can never again suffer in *me.*

VIII. TRUE MORALITY AND SALVATION

Intelligence and Existence. Since the death of the individual involves no renunciation of life in general on the part of the Will, we must look elsewhere for our hoped-for salvation. We turn once more to the intellect, which in its contemplative activities found even the structure of an evil universe beautiful, and succeeded by means of that beauty, albeit only for a moment, in denying itself. But these contemplative activities have also a *practical* use, since they enable us to *comprehend* the evil character of the Will to Live and its works, and to *reason out* the true way of salvation.

As *thinking* beings, for instance, we can be *intelligent* in our appraisal of the ethical situation, and can detect the errors of a moral system founded on the affirmation of the Will to Live. We begin our criticism by grasping the true nature of the eternal justice manifest in the world. Since the same Will affirms itself in both the criminal and the victim of his crime, all crime is futile. Every act of violence against another is really an act of violence against one's own deepest self. In the very commission of a criminal act the victim is avenged and the perpetrator is punished, since the Will, in instigating the violation of one of its manifestations by another, has done no more than to violate and inflict pain upon itself.

Again, the intelligent eye perceives not only the futility of wrong-doing, but the equal futility of remedial and practical right-*doing*. The so-called virtues only help the Will to continue its affirmations and thus prolong the evils of existence. So, too, the punitive and repressive measures inflicted upon the criminal by society as retribution for his evil acts seem unintelligent to the enlightened mind. Nothing could be more senseless and evil than taking *vengeance* upon wrong-doers, since in taking vengeance the Will is only adding to the sum of suffering and evil with which all existence is infected. Punishment for the sake of punishment is stupid and immoral.

Nor is *corrective* punishment in any better standing. Corrective measures aim at no more than the sinner's repossession of virtues that are not only valueless but are positive means to continuing the Will to Live.

The Intelligent Attitude Towards Evil-Doing. The intelligent attitude towards sin and crime, the attitude decreed by knowledge and understanding, should not be one of indignation and hatred and loathing. It should be inspired by the Buddhistic feeling of compassion for the sins and sufferings of the whole world. For all men are in their essence one and the same with their fellows. The sin of one is the sin of all. The suffering of one is the suffering of all. The same Will sins and suffers in them all. Every human individual bears vicariously the sum total of the evil which constitutes existence. The rain of the same compassion, then, should fall upon the good and the evil alike.

The way of salvation lies at last clearly before us. It is pointed out to us by Hindoo philosophy and especially by Buddhism. To tread it we must accomplish a complete revolution in the scale of moral values to which we have been accustomed. We must *renounce* the Will to Live and all its works and "virtues." We must withdraw ourselves through ascetic discipline from the world and worldly things, whether these things count as good or bad. *We must will not to will.*

Salvation by Denial of the Will to Live. This we can only do if we break every attachment of interest and desire that binds us to the phenomenal universe and to the Platonic Ideas that form its structure. All our natural impulses must be curbed and mortified. Particularly, the sexual instinct must be repressed and extinguished. For the sexual instinct is the strongest, the most fundamental, the most unruly, and the most dangerous of all the affirmations of the Will to Live. Then, too, if it could be totally denied, and if consequently the human race could die out, the intellect and knowledge and the more complicated and complete objectifications of the Will would pass away.

Nay more, with human consciousness all other grades of consciousness would disappear, as twilight disappears with the extinction of light. Abolition of knowledge and of the Platonic Ideas would involve the destruction of phenomena and of sensible experience, which can only exist under the forms provided by the Ideas. Finally, with the destruction of experience and thought and self-consciousness, the Will to Live, also, deprived of its expressions, would be laid at rest.

Furthermore, he who attains salvation for himself vicariously atones for the sins of the whole world and effects its redemption. The *whole* Will is denied by each saint and sage who enters what we may now call Nirvana.

The Spontaneous and Miraculous Character of Salvation. But, we may still ask, is salvation possible? Is not the Will bound by its very nature to affirm itself, to objectify itself, to strive, to struggle, and to suffer? In that case, no amount of renunciation and denial on our part can overcome the Will to Live, and no salvation is possible. Schopenhauer replies that there is nothing in the nature of things that renders our hope of liberation vain. We must not forget that the Will is *absolutely free*. Having no nature to determine it, prior to its objectification, it is not even self-determined to live and to express itself as it does. Its objectification and its appearance as a phenomenal world are a miraculous act for which no reason can be given. Conversely, there is no reason why the Will should not in a similarly miraculous manner refrain from objectifying itself, dissolve the phenomenal world into nothing, and cease to affirm itself and to live.

The act, then, by which the individual denies the Will to Live is mystical and spontaneous, arising, for no reason whatsoever, from something in him deeper than reason, deeper than existence, deeper than willing itself. Being spontaneous and unmotivated, it appears to be supernatural and effected, as it were, by a divine grace bestowed by some agency outside the individual himself.

The Positive Nature of Nirvana. One last difficulty. Is not the state of a Will that has ceased to affirm itself, and that has renounced and denied the very activity of willing, equivalent to nothingness? No. Nirvana, into which the Will, redeemed from affirmation and willing, at last enters, is, indeed, indescribable in any terms of our finite experience. We have no predicates or epithets at hand that we can apply to it, since all categories and epithets and attributes are drawn from and can be applied to the *affirmed* Will alone. Relatively to anything *we* can know, or perceive, or feel, or will, Nirvana is indeed nothing, and the state of the Will that has denied itself and entered Nirvana is, indeed, pure emptiness. But in itself it is not negative. It is a positive bliss beyond all thought and speech. To the Will that has become will-lessness and has attained this bliss, the relation is reversed. To it, *our* existence, *our* universe, with all its suns and stars and milky ways, *"ist als Nichts,"* is as nothing. For in relation to it, our world, the world of the affirmed Will, is a complete negation and emptiness of what is really real.

Chapter XIX

HERBART

I. KANTIAN BASIS OF HIS PHILOSOPHY

Life. Johann Friedrich Herbart was born at Oldenburg in 1776. He studied philosophy at Jena, under Fichte, and in the end was profoundly dissatisfied with the Fichtean interpretation of Kant. In this way he was led to undertake by himself an independent study of the *Critiques*. After receiving his degree at Jena, he was tutor for some years in a family in Switzerland, and put in his spare time working out his own system. In 1805 he was called to Göttingen to lecture on philosophy, and in 1809 accepted the chair at Königsberg, which Kant had formerly held. Here he remained till 1833. In that year he returned to Göttingen as professor of philosophy, and died there in 1841.

Attitude Towards Kant. Herbart accepts the Kantian, and, for that matter, the post-Kantian idealistic hypothesis that experience gives us only phenomena. He accepts also with Kant, but in contradiction to the idealists, the hypothesis of things-in-themselves existing independently of experience. At the same time, he realizes that the idealists have good ground for complaint against things-in-themselves and for discharging them from their systems. For, in his opinion, Kant had failed to show that experience necessitates an assumption of their existence, and conversely had been unable to demonstrate how, given such entities, experience could be deduced from them. Herbart proposes to succeed where Kant had, in his opinion, failed.[1]

We begin with *experience*. It does not in itself convey any *knowledge* of anything. On the face of it, it is unintelligible, since it is not self-explaining and self-supporting. Nor does it hang together systematically. Its transitions do not reveal their why and their wherefore. Still, it occurs in an orderly manner, and proclaims itself to be experience *of* something more than itself, even if it cannot tell what that something more is. Moreover, it does quite definitely state that experience is *not of* more experience. We do not perceive our perceptions. For, in that case, since perceptions are perceptions *of,* we should find ourselves

---

[1] Cf. Herbart's *Hauptpunkte der Metaphysik; Allgemeine Metaphysik.*

involved in an infinite regress of perceiving perceptions of perceptions of perceptions, world without end. Experience, then, must be *of* something that is not experience, which we will call the Real.

II. THE NATURE OF REALITY

Reality Simple, Changeless, Self-Sufficient. The question now arises whether experience and reasoning can give us any *knowledge* of the nature of this Reality. Herbart thinks they can. In the first place, since contradiction means unreality, to be *real* is to be free from contradiction. Again, what is *real* must be positive and *self-sufficient* and *independent* of everything else. It must be absolutely *simple,* since complexity and qualification of any sort require explanation. It cannot be quantitative or extended, since it cannot be divided or exist in varying amounts or degrees. It cannot change, or become, or move, since it cannot be or become other than it is.

Reality Many, Not One. Furthermore, we can *know* that the Real is *many,* not *one.* The multiple and variegated character of experience, and the unique and reciprocally exclusive character of its parts, can only be explained on the hypothesis that each incident is the appearance of a separate and unique Real. The number of these Reals, like the variety of experience, is indefinite.

Again, the *plurality* of the Reals, as well as their changelessness, is demonstrated by the fact that phenomena *do not turn into,* but *succeed,* one another in our experience. Since the Reals are not in time, this temporal succession of their appearances must be within our minds and due to a subjective relating of the Reals to one another on our part. The same is true of the apparent *causation* of one experience by another. Each experience and each property of a so-called "thing" is explained only by its particular, underlying Real, and the seeming causal interconnection of experiences is due to the mind's relating a plurality of Reals, each one of which accounts only for a single experience or property. So, too, the clustering of many qualities in a single object is an act of similar interrelation by the mind. The Reals themselves cannot become parts of larger wholes. Finally, we can deduce from the *variegation* of experience and the *difference* of the many qualities appearing in it, that the Reals, also, underlying this diversification, are *different* as well as many. However, the diversity that appears in the content of our experience can give us no hint of what the different natures of the Reals are really like.

III. THE MIND OR SOUL

We are now led to ask what *experience* is, and what the *mind* is. It would seem at first sight as if the mind's *relating* of the Reals had nothing to do with them, and as if experience, whose content and relations are purely subjective, was wholly irrelevant to the nature of Reality.

This difficulty Herbart meets by pointing out in the first place, that though our "relating" of the Reals does not influence the structure of Reality, the structure of Reality does influence the way in which we relate things-in-themselves as they appear in experience. Moreover, he continues, the mind, or soul, is itself a cluster of Reals and as such shares all the qualities of Reality—its simplicity, indivisibility, changelessness, etc. Our changing, moving variegated experience, which appears to be at variance with these characteristics, is merely the expression of the *resistance of a psychic Real like the soul to the disturbing influences of the other Reals*. The soul, like every other Real, seeks to *preserve* its unique character, and *experience* is its registration of the counterbalance it establishes in preserving itself unspotted by influence from without.

All the Reals tend to encroach upon and modify one another, and all of them *resist* encroachment and modification on the part of the others, and thus *maintain* their unique and simple natures. The nonpsychic Reals do not *recognize* this fact. The psychic Reals, that is, minds or souls, *register* it, and *consciousness,* or *experience,* is that registration.

IV. THE SIGNIFICANCE OF THE SPATIAL, TEMPORAL, CAUSAL AND MATERIAL ASPECTS OF EXPERIENCE

Nature of Space and Time. We are now in a position to understand more clearly the significance of experience, and to throw more light on the world of things-in-themselves. *Space,* Herbart tells us, is the way in which a psychic Real *must* represent in experience the existence of a *plurality* of Reals. The discrete, unique points into which its seeming continuity is divisible are our way of registering this plurality and the reciprocally exclusive character of things-in-themselves.

Time, with its concomitant *change* and *motion,* gives us another hint as to the nature of Reality. The discrete instants into which its flow may be broken up are another witness to the fact that Reality is many, but their succession, and the incidental change of place and quality that accompanies it, suggests that the Reals themselves, though immune to internal alteration, *shift* their relations to one another, or, in other words, the pressures they bring to bear upon one another and the resistance they offer to such pressures.

This situation in the world of things-in-themselves, which the nature of experience would seem to indicate, Herbart expresses by saying that the Reals are "together," and that their *togetherness,* or *Zusammenheit,* *varies in degree.* That is, the Reals *can be more or less together,* and exert more or less pressure, and offer more or less resistance, or none at all, among themselves.

Causality an Expression of Pressure and Resistance to It. The *causal* aspects of experience bear, in Herbart's opinion, further witness to this situation. Events in experience that *do not cause* one another are the conscious registration of Reals that are *not together* and that therefore are *not* pressing upon and resisting one another. Causal connections in experience mean that the Reals involved are *together* and are exerting and resisting influence upon one another.

In a way, then, the Reals themselves exhibit a relation of cause and effect. Their *togetherness* evokes *resistance* to one another. They influence one another *not* to be influenced by one another. The Reals, then, are not free and self-determining. They *force* one another to preserve themselves. Each Real is necessitated to behave as it does by the presence of the others with which it is *together.*

The temporal, antecedent and consequent character of causation in our experience has no place in Reality. The interaction between the Reals is immediate and simultaneous. So, too, the apparent *expenditure* of force in experienced causation is purely subjective. The Reals cannot *expend* force in influencing one another, since such expenditure would imply change and motion within themselves.

Nature of Matter. We come now to *matter*—to the fact that space and time have a stuffing or *content.* This, according to Herbart, throws more light on the nature of Reality and suggests a somewhat more complicated situation, involving as it does the *difference* as well as the *togetherness* of the Reals. The Reals are always as much *together* as they can be, but the degree to which they can "get together" depends upon the degree of their *likeness* to one another. This degree is represented in the experience of a psychic Real, or mind, by the degee to which experienced phenomena can and do coagulate, combine, mix, and fuse, or, in other words, by the degree to which they seem to occupy the same space and the same instant of time. Indeed, if all the Reals were exactly alike, their *togetherness* would be complete, in which case the spatial and temporal extension of experience would contract to a single point and instant, and vanish altogether.

The spatial points and temporal instants of the experience of a psychic Real are then *held apart,* or *forced apart* by the difference of the Reals underlying them. And this holding apart or *repulsion* of one point by another will be strong in proportion to the difference, and concomitant inability to *get together,* of the Reals these points register. Conversely, the similarity of the Reals and their consequent tendency to be *together,* will display itself in experience as an *attraction* exerted by one point of space upon another. And the total situation in the world of things-in-themselves, in which Reals of various degrees of likeness and unlikeness are proportionately influencing one another and resisting one another's influence, and tending to come together or to hold one another off, as the case may be, is represented in consciousness as by the tautness and tenseness of space and time and the shifting equilibrium of phenomena.

Space and Matter. But, when points of space exert and resist a pull upon one another, and by their attraction and repulsion hold each other firmly in place, they introduce a *rigidity* and *solidity* into extension, which we call *matter.* For example, a molecule represents a coagulation of Reals, which, cling and squeeze as they may, can never get entirely together because some of them are unlike. And when several coagulations of this sort start attracting and repelling one another, their reciprocal influences and resistances are represented in consciousness by larger corporeal masses. Matter, then, like space and time, can only appear when a psychic Real is together with a plurality of other Reals, and when some of these Reals with which it is together are different from one another.

Space, time, matter, and motion are not, then, entirely *subjective,* as Kant supposed them to be. They are, indeed, the necessary forms in which any conscious Real whatsoever must represent a plurality of distinct, independent things-in-themselves. But consciousness would not so represent a Reality that was not multiple and the relations between whose constituent parts were not shifting. Hence these forms of experience are dependent upon the *two* factors of a conscious thing-in-itself and of other things-in-themselves in variable relations with each other and with it.

The fact that the Reals *shift* their relations and *vary* the degree of their *togetherness* is ultimate. It can no more be explained, and requires no more explanation, than their plurality and their various degrees of likeness and difference. All we can say is that this is the sort of Reality which experience seems to indicate.

V. THE PLURAL CHARACTER OF THE SELF

Each Item of Experience Separately Conscious of Itself. Hitherto we have spoken of a psychic Real, or mind, as if it were itself a single, simple, unique thing-in-itself—a sort of Kantian or Fichtean *ego*. But we have no right or reason so to treat it. Not only does the hypothesis of a perceiving "self" separate from experience involve us in an infinite regress of perceiving that we are perceiving that we are perceiving, but the self-consciousness that accompanies one datum of experience cannot be identified with that which accompanies another, different datum. There are as many perceptions that we perceive as there are perceptions.

The "self," then, like experience itself, and like any of the *things* given in experience is simply a coherence of a plurality of experiences, and its multiplicity in unity may be explained in the same way that the co-existence of attributes in any object is explained. Just as in the case of a *thing* we are obliged to posit as many things-in-themselves as it has properties, and to base each quality upon a separate Real, so in the variety of my consciousness, or your consciousness, we must assume as many underlying things-in-themselves as there are items of consciousness. Each one of these items, along with the "I know" that accompanies it, represents a different psychic Real. The so-called Ego, then, is multiple. Nor does the self-consciousness attending any datum of sensation come any nearer to expressing the true nature of a psychic thing-in-itself than does the datum itself.

VI. THEORY OF KNOWLEDGE

Since the character neither of experience nor of self-consciousness can in any way picture the character of things-in-themselves, it might seem as if any knowledge of any sort of either the existence or the nature of the Reals was impossible, and as if the metaphysical inferences made by Herbart were completely unjustified. His answer is that knowledge does not lie in *picturing,* and that experience need in no wise *resemble* the Reals in order to be the basis of real knowledge about them.

Thus the inescapable presence of experience, its uncontrollable and unalterable character, and its persistent and inextinguishable external reference enable us to *know* that an external, independent Reality *exists,* and its unchangeable and invariable *order* enables us to *know* that Reality must be plural, of varying degrees of likeness and un-likeness, and of togetherness and apartness in its internal relations. So much we *must* infer from experience, but so much is all we *can* infer. How many Reals there are, in what their differences consist, and what the actual shifting of their relations is really like, are ques-tions upon which experience throws no light, and which we therefore can never *know.*

Incidentally "general" and "abstract" ideas have no metaphysical significance. They are mere abbreviations for groups of sense data, and do not in any way enlarge or deepen our knowledge. They come no nearer to describing the nature of the Real than do the experiences from which they are drawn.

VII. PSYCHOLOGY

The Nature of Volition. Herbart's psychology ties in with his meta-physics. He warns us against regarding consciousness as either an *activity* of a psychic Real or as a *passive* reception of impressions by it. Activity and passivity are forms of experience and cannot be predicated of things-in-themselves or of their relations to one another.

The *seemingly* active character of the psychic Reals, as evinced in the phenomena of desire, impulse, and volition, is an expression in experience, Herbart tells us, of the tendency shared by the psychic Reals with all other Reals to be in as complete as possible a state of *togetherness* and equilibrium with other things-in-themselves. But the mind, or soul, in experiencing, is *together* with non-psychic Reals both unlike itself and unlike one another, which are therefore more or less influencing it and one another, and provoking more or less re-sistance to such influence. Hence the items of experience registering this complex and shifting inter-relation of the Reals will tend to balance and check and inhibit one another just as the Reals they rep-resent are doing.

Seeing, however, that *togetherness* is always at a maximum, there will always be the least possible amount of inhibition of one item of experience by another. In other words, every perception and idea will seem as vivid as it can seem, and will appear in consciousness, not merely as a representation, but as a representation that *strives* to main-tain its vividness against the inhibiting influences of other experiences. Hence ideas will give the impression of competing with one another, and experience will be suffused with a tenseness and an awareness of struggle and effort. It is this tense, driving aspect of experience that we call volition.

Inhibition and "the Threshold of Consciousness." Again, and on this point Herbart is insistent, sensations cannot *destroy* one another. The utmost they can do is to *arrest* one another. But each sensation, though arrested, preserves itself, and when the pressure, which is always the least possible, is removed, it tends to reassert itself. And, according as the relations among the Reals vary, so sensations rise and fall in the intensity of their presentation and their clearness.

Herbart feels, moreover, that a thoroughly scientific statics and mechanics of consciousness can be established, and that exact mathematical formulae can be worked out for the equilibrium and the shifting of conscious data.[2] For example, the degree of pressure necessary to remove a presentation from consciousness, or, as Herbart put it in one of his most famous phrases, to "sink" it beneath *"the threshold of consciousness,"* is exerted by the inhibitory idea in inverse proportion to their respective strength. Again, the pressure lets up as the conscious data upon which it is exerted "sink," with the result that the velocity with which they approach the threshold of consciousness is retarded according to a set mathematical formula. Conversely, presentations driven below the threshold of consciousness by the pressure of other conscious data reappear when the inhibitions are removed, and in so doing bring with them, once more in a manner expressible in a mathematical equation, the other presentations with which they have been associated. The behavior of memory and of the association of ideas thus becomes subject to precise scientific determination.

Pleasure, Pain, Desire, and the Self. Upon this mechanical foundation Herbart builds up other states of consciousness. *Pain* is indicative of the fact that a given presentation is being batted back and forth by other presentations, some of which tend to sink it below the threshold of consciousness, others to raise it above the threshold. *Pleasure* means that the situation is generally favorable to its appearance in consciousness. When we *desire,* data are elbowing others out of the way that prevent them from rising to the surface and being experienced. When a group of presentations has become established in such wise that it suppresses re-emergent items that were not or will not be "together" with it, and attaches to itself re-appearing data that were or may be associated with it, we get a consciousness that remembers its own past and anticipates a future of its own. That is, we get a *self.*

[2] Cf. *Psychologie als Wissenschaft.*

There is, however, no one abiding, central presentation by which the self is constituted. On the contrary, the elements of the self-conscious mass are always shifting, as they keep step with the shifting relations of the plurality of underlying Reals. The ego is simply an abstract expression for the fact that, in spite of the shifting, the shedding, and the accretion that take place, the elements of the central core are congruous and "together" with one another, and in the aggregate resist disturbance and disintegration by external influences.

These conclusions were of great significance to the history of psychology. They helped break down the faculty-psychology which had hitherto dominated German thought, and whose influence is so patent upon philosophers like Kant and Hegel. The concept of the "threshold of consciousness" was later developed in the ideas of the unconscious, the subconscious, the subliminal, etc., which play so important a part in modern psychology. So, too, the "inhibition" of ideas by one another and the tendency of inhibited ideas to struggle against suppression, to reappear when the censor is off guard, and during suppression to set up obscure drives and conflicts and strains, are prophetic of the central concepts of the psychoanalytic school. Last, but not least, Herbart's attempt to study psychological phenomena in the same spirit and by the same methods that obtain in the physical sciences gave a great impetus to the development of psychology as an exact science and to its detachment from metaphysics. To him we owe our hope of subjecting mental occurrences to the minute and rigid analysis, the precise measurements, and the mathematical formulations, which have proved so successful in dealing with physical events.

VIII. ETHICS, EDUCATION, AND RELIGION

Ethics. For Herbart, *ethics* [3] is another expression of the metaphysical situation of togetherness, shifting relations, tendency to self-preservation and establishment of equilibrium, which are characteristic of Reality. Pleasurable and beneficial experiences, or, in other words, experiences more or less unanimously "voted in" by the central core of representations which constitutes the "ego," tend to be preserved by their "togetherness" with it. The more congruous the representations that push themselves across the threshold of consciousness are with the ego, the *freer* we feel our wills to be. The more varied and intense the representations than can occupy consciousness without disturbing the concentration of the ego the more self-realized and

[3] Cf. *Allgemeine praktische Philosophie.*

perfect and happy we are. The more "together" the representation of our own will can be brought with our representation of another's will the more *benevolent* is our disposition. When wills clash, we represent their "togetherness" and equilibrium under the concept of *right*. If an ego revolts against that equilibrium, we demand that it be re-subjected by meting out *retribution* to it. If the self tends to maintain the harmonious counterbalance, we speak of it as deserving to be praised and *rewarded*. Out of these representations and the relations underlying them the whole complex structure of ethics and social organization can be evolved.

At the same time, Herbart feels that, although valid general moral principles can be laid down, the applications of them to individual conduct must not be too rigid and must allow for the great variety and difference of human temperaments and circumstances. Each case should, as far as possible, be decided on its own merits. There must always be a compromise between the real and the ideal. The aim of education and of political organization should be to adapt the general to the particular and the particular to the general.

Education. The scientific tone of Herbart's psychology and ethics is reflected in his views upon education—a subject that deeply interested him. He could not see eye to eye with Rousseau and Rousseau's theory of allowing the child to develop along its own lines and in its own way. Nor could he agree with his contemporary Froebel, or with the older Pestalozzi, who were founding their systems of education to a large extent upon Rousseau's ideas.

On the contrary he felt that the child should be subject to discipline from the beginning. It is the function of education to mold the child, not to leave him to his own devices. It should supervise and direct his development with a view to making him as "all around" many-sided a man as possible, endowed with as many interests as can be inculcated and fostered in him. Above all, the teacher should seek to consolidate all these interests with which he is trying to imbue his pupils, in a unified moral character dominated by ethical ideals.

Religion. The chief function of religion is to reinforce ethics by giving, in the idea of God, a beautiful and appealing concrete expression to moral ideals, and by encouraging the hope and the belief that these ideals and the pursuit of them have some sort of cosmic backing. To be sure, it is within neither the power nor the province of philosophy to think up *arguments* favoring the existence of such backing, or generally to support theological hypotheses. Still, the behavior of the experience we call "nature," and particularly the purposive character of the activities of those phenomena we call "organisms," permit the *belief* that there may be among the Reals a divine Real that governs the shifting of their relations, and the changing degrees of their togetherness and apartness, with some end in view. The philosopher will observe and note the permissibility and possibility of such an inference. but it is not his business to try to validate it.

Chapter XX

MINOR EARLY NINETEENTH-CENTURY CONTINENTAL PHILOSOPHY

I. MINOR POST-HEGELIANS

Before crossing the frontier and examining elsewhere the philosophy of the first half of the nineteenth century, we have still to note commotions provoked in Germany by the Hegelian philosophy. Some of the philosophers whom we shall examine did, indeed, live on into or through the third quarter of the century, but for the sake of convenience we may deal with them now. As may be imagined, Hegelianism made a great stir, not only in metaphysical circles but among the theologians and the political thinkers. Its implications in all three fields were revolutionary in character, and calculated to provoke not only enthusiastic support but violent opposition. We shall deal with the metaphysicians first.

Beneke. Beneke (1798-1854) protested against the entire *a priori* method of the Kantian and Hegelian philosophizing. We must begin with experience and stick to experience, he said. Starting, then, with experience, what does it permit us to *know?* First, and immediately, the self, and by inference the existence of an external physical world and of other selves. Furthermore, the spatial and temporal forms of experience are not wholly relative to *human* consciousness. They are possible forms of all conscious existence and, therefore, of Reality itself. So, too, we directly *experience* causality, since we are conscious of ourselves as the reason why sensations and feelings are present to us. We can also infer, though not with certainty, the existence of God both from our moral needs and the fragmentary and partial nature of our experience.

As a psychologist Beneke ranks higher than as a metaphysician. Indeed, to some extent he shares the honors with Herbart as one of the founders of modern psychology. He supplemented his metaphysical assertion of the fundamental character of experience and of the self, with a scientifically conceived and applied study of consciousness that makes him an important figure in the development of the *introspective* method.

Weisse. Next to Schopenhauer and Herbart, however, the most eminent of the early anti-Hegelians was Weisse (1801-1866). He attacked Hegel for giving too much weight to the claims of logic in determining the nature of the Real, and not enough to those of art and religion. For that matter, art and religion bring us nearer to the heart of things than any amount of scientific and philosophical thinking can. If we followed out Hegel's doctrines to their logical conclusion, we should be forced to deny God, freedom, and immortality.

To these charges Göschel, a favorite pupil of Hegel's, replied with some warmth. A controversy ensued, Weisse publicly renounced Hegelianism of any and every sort, and in his *Metaphysics* once more denounced Hegel's determinism and godlessness and opposed to them his own conviction that men are possessed of free will and that there is a personal God. The Catholic Church, also, became involved in controversy in the person of a priest named Günther, who countered the idealism and the latent pantheism of both Schelling and Hegel with a dualistic conception of the Creator and the created, and, within the created, of mind and matter. Apparently, however, Günther's attack upon Hegel carried him beyond the bounds of strict orthodoxy, since his system was not altogether favorably received by the Church.

Schleiermacher and Strauss. The theological reverberations of Hegelianism were even more stirring. Schleiermacher (1768-1834) had already hinted that Christian theology was not so much a description of objective, metaphysical truth as a symbolic expression of man's subjective moral and religious experience, which is in itself inarticulate and inexpressible in any but figurative terms. This subjective appropriateness he did, indeed, feel to be so complete that we could not help believing also in the objective validity of Christian doctrine. But the accent had been shifted from the factual and historic aspects of Christian theology to its inner, emotional and symbolic applicability.

This question, the keen edge of which had been blunted by Schleiermacher's deeply religious nature and personal piety, was now sharply raised. Naturally it cut most deeply into the three central problems of Christian theology—the personality of God, the nature of Christ, and the freedom and immortality of man. And it drew the most blood from the first two.

In 1835, Strauss (1808-1874) published his famous *Life of Jesus,* in which he attempted to show that in the Gospels we have neither history nor deliberate invention, but unconscious poetry and myth, woven partly out of the Jewish expectation of a Messiah and partly out of the impressions Jesus made upon his disciples. The Gospels, then, give us not the man Jesus, but the Christ-myth of which he became the center. In raising Jesus to divinity, the poetic imagination was simply constructing a symbol of the essential divinity of all men.

The Hegelian Right and Left Theological Disputes. The uproar was terrific. The Hegelians fell apart, to use Strauss's own phrase, into a Left and Right, and the controversy soon spread from the Christological problem and involved the nature of God himself. The Left, accepting the teaching possibly implicit, if not explicit, in Hegel, that theological concepts are imaginative transcripts and illustrations of the nature and operations of the Absolute Idea, divided over the question of where the precise basis of the symbol was to be found. Strauss himself was pantheistic, and maintained that there is no God except the thought which is in all thinking beings, no attributes of God which are not the laws of nature, and that the word "God" is simply another name for the infinite totality of existence.

Feuerbach (1804-1872), on the other hand, was unwilling to ascribe any objective reference to the concept of God. Theological dogma is purely *subjective* in origin and crystallizes the *inner* aspirations, hopes, and fears of the human soul. These inner yearnings and questings override the bounds of reason and create ideal pictures of what they seek. The resultant idealizations of human life are the gods. God, therefore, is nothing but the picture of an ideal human being to whom we attribute all the qualities that we value, such as personality, love, sympathy, willingness to share our sufferings, and the like. But there is no objective reality in the external world corresponding to the picture. God exists only in so far as we succeed in realizing our ideals. Immortality, too, is a myth, not a fact. Bauer (1809-1882) was even more definitely "atheistic" than Feuerbach. He attacked Strauss's theory that the Gospels are unconscious poetry and mythology, and maintained that they were deliberately invented.

Hegelianism and Christianity. These views were vigorously combated by the Hegelian Right and Center parties, who upheld the compatibility of the Hegelian philosophy with religion and with the objective truth of Christian dogma. The conflict, not unnaturally, soon involved and turned upon interpretations of Hegel's metaphysics, particularly in so far as it had to do with the nature of *substance*. Heretofore, it had been assumed somewhat uncritically that he had regarded substance as subjective and conscious in character, and had looked upon the Absolute as a quasi-personal, spiritual being. In that case, the existence of a personal God could be defended on Hegelian grounds. Now, this interpretation and this compatibility with Christianity were challenged by the Leftist, anti-religious wing of the school.

Again, the question came up whether substantiality was regarded by Hegel as essential or accidental to a thinking subject. If essential, he could be invoked as a champion of personal freedom and immortality. If only accidental, the ground was knocked from beneath the feet of his Christian, religious disciples. Once more the Right and the Left divided.

Finally, the point was raised whether the Hegelian Absolute could without any self-contradiction manifest itself in a single human subject. Upon the way this point was settled hung the congruity of the Incarnation and the divinity of Christ with the Hegelian teaching. The Right wing maintained that these dogmas were confirmed, the Left that they were completely discredited, by Hegel's teaching.

The attacks of the Left upon Christian doctrine soon inspired doubts with regard to the place and value of Christianity even as a social institution. Rothe maintained that ecclesiastical organization could no longer express and embody the Christian life. The state alone could do that. In an ideal state religion would not be a thing apart, with a special, ecclesiastical setting, but would be absorbed into society and pervade a man's entire social and political life. In short, the Church is not a unique institution with a validity and an authority all its own. It is merely a symbol and focus of activities and ideals which suffuse and actuate all human existence.

Political and Social Reverberations of Hegelianism. The anti-Hegelians welcomed Rothe with open arms. Here was proof positive that Hegelianism led inevitably to a pagan deification of the state. But the state itself was soon to be brought under the fire of the Hegelian Left. The *Hallische Jahrbücher,* originally a conservative theological journal, edited by the Hegelian Right, and highly Prussian and aristocratic in its politics, began to develop Leftist symptoms. First it gave way theologically by publishing an essay of Strauss's, and accepting one from Feuerbach, which the censor suppressed. Then it changed its political front and started veiled attacks upon the Prussian bureaucracy. As its fever ran higher, it turned to extolling the French Revolution, the Rights of Man, the *Contrat Social,* and industrial democracy. Soon it was demanding freedom of the press and praising political democracy and radicalism. In 1843 its publication was prohibited by the Prussian Government. But the radical spirit was not to be downed. Sturmer and Daumer agitated for individualism and anarchy

Daumer, however, the author of violent anti-Christian diatribes, turned Catholic in the end.

Meantime, these social and political views were, as we might expect, vigorously resisted by the Hegelian Right and Center. They were also severely criticized by Karl Marx (1818-1883), the co-author with Frederick Engels of the famous *Communist Manifesto,* published in 1847.

II. DIALECTICAL MATERIALISM

Perhaps the most important development of the Hegelian Left was and is the theory known as *Dialectical Materialism.* This hypothesis was initiated by Karl Marx, and was promulgated by him in collaboration with Engels. Later it was reiterated by Lenin, who was a disciple of Marx, but who re-read Hegel on his own account, and whose annotated copy of Hegel's Logic is an interesting and valuable document for an understanding of the social and political fruition of the movement in Russia.

Karl Marx. Karl Marx (1818-1883) grew up under the influence of the conditions that produced the liberal movement in Germany and the revolution there of 1848, and was one of the most radical and strenuous partisans of the "Young German" party and its "advanced" ideals of social reforms. His entire life was spent in bitter opposition to the established order of his day, which he never ceased to attack with his pen and which he felt must be overthrown, if necessary, by the sword. The established order retaliated by doing its best to suppress him—so that, like Rousseau, a century earlier, he was in constant hot water.

He began his career by studying law in the university of Trier, his native city, but his interest soon shifted to philosophy, and particularly to the system of Hegel of which he became an enthusiastic advocate. Almost immediately, however, he came to feel that the "orthodox" interpretation of Hegel consecrated the political, social, and religious *status quo,* of which he was already a critic, and consequently he was soon to the fore in the group of "Young Hegelians" who were establishing the Hegelian Left, and either developing a naturalistic, materialistic and anti-theistic interpretation of the Hegelian philosophy or, at least, using it to undermine orthodox Christian doctrine. However, he was unable to agree with many of the conclusions of the other "Young Hegelians," as we shall see in a moment, which he considered either too temporizing and conciliatory, or too mechanistic and destructive of human liberty and opportunity for human progress.

Marx's Agreement with Hegel. Marx accepted wholeheartedly the Hegelian teaching that Reality is essentially a *process,* that this process is intelligible and congenial to the human mind, and that it moves with a "logic" of its own, according to the "dialectical" law of *thesis, antithesis,* and *synthesis.* He was also struck by the part that the Kantian and Hegelian category of *reciprocity* plays in the world-process. Causes produce effects, and wholes are built up out of parts, but effects *react* upon their causes, and wholes *react* upon their constituents, in such wise as to modify and partially determine their character. Any given set of conditions is, then, what it is, not only by reason of the antecedent conditions from which it has sprung, but also by reason of the resulting conditions to which it has given rise. Both Kant and Hegel had found this category best exemplified by organic and social phenomena, in the interdependence and interdetermination of the total structure and the component organs of a living body and in the reciprocal influence upon each other of the individual and the state. Applying this to the thesis-antithesis-synthesis triad, we find that theses and antitheses are both the cause and the effect of each other and that the synthesis is the new situation both created by, and, in the process of creation, creating their interplay.

Marx's Rejection of Hegel. But here Marx's agreement with Hegel came to an end. He rejected flatly the latter's view that these characteristics of the world-process indicated that it was the teleological unfolding of a design or Idea in the experience of an Absolute Mind or Spirit. The behavior of the world-process, he maintained, did not suggest guidance by a moral plan or purpose. Above all, its material and physical aspects could not be reduced to conscious content and regarded as mental in their essential character. On the contrary, they could only be explained on the supposition that matter in motion, extended in space and time, and existing in and by itself, independent of any mental awareness of or reflection upon it, underlay the phenomenal world.

Furthermore, the material substratum, being independent of mind, was in no wise due to it. Not only was it not mental content, it was not created by mind. On the contrary, there was every indication that mind was the product of matter in motion, that its appearance was dependent on certain physical conditions, and that its occurrence was purely incidental to the operations of physical nature.

Such being the case, the Hegelian insistence that the laws of being are an expression of the laws of thought, and can be discovered by analysis of the process of thinking, is founded on a false assumption.

Human thinking is rather an adaptation of the human mind to the movement of the universe of which it is a part, and its logical character is a reflection of the dialectical nature of that movement. But the "logic" of events is only discoverable by an observation of and meditation upon the operations of external nature and the course of human history as a whole—not by an analysis of individual consciousness.

Marx's Rejection of Idealism and Positivism. These considerations not only led Marx to reject all the idealistic interpretations of the universe, monistic and pluralistic, that had been proposed up to his time. They also made him critical of the contemporary "empirical" and "positivistic" attempts, which we shall take up in the next chapters, to reduce the Real to terms of phenomena alone, and to turn the nature and behavior of their supposed substratum into no more than a set of convenient descriptions and condensations of the flow of experience itself. And it impelled him to discard as superstitious and false all belief in the existence of supernatural, immaterial, and theological entities. The same negative attitude toward all non-materialistic interpretations of the appearance and behavior of the world-process has persisted as one of the cardinal points of *dialectical materialism*.

Marx had two more major objections to make to the Hegelian system. In the first place he felt that Hegel had made the world-process a closed circle in which the triad of thesis, antithesis and synthesis had already been completely accomplished and displayed. To cap the climax, Hegel had identified the final synthesis in all departments of life with the existing conditions of his own day, and had made them the ultimate expression of the Absolute Idea.

This struck Marx as nonsensical. The world-process is, to be sure, circular in that it moves continually through a repeated round of theses, antitheses, and syntheses. But it is not therefore a *closed* process —not to speak of human history having been closed by Hegel and his times. On the contrary, it is an *open* process. Its circular movement —and upon this Marx laid great stress—is *spiral*. It becomes *different,* as it goes on, though its new and different phases always exhibit its essentially dialectical character. So, too, humanity and human institutions continually *evolve,* as they dialectically revolve, and no stage or state can be regarded as conclusive or sacrosanct.

This belief in the *open* character of the world-process and of human history also made Marx critical of all materialism that was completely mechanistic and deterministic in its implications, and of all attempts to bolster up existing institutions—like Christianity or Hegelian idealism, for example—by reinterpreting them. All such points of view kept, or tried to keep, the cosmic and the historic circle closed, and therefore put a stop to *progress*. In a deterministic and mechanical universe there could be no real *reciprocity*. Man would be merely an effect of a cosmic and historic process upon which he himself could produce no effect and whose course he could not alter. He would be the slave of natural forces and of his own past, and could do nothing but accept his fate.

Nature of Dialectical Materialism. But, Marx maintained, once the human mind has been produced by nature, it becomes an active and causal factor in nature, and a co-determinant, to say the least, with natural forces in molding human destiny. It is able to alter the world-process to some degree, to modify its surroundings, and therefore to *improve* the human situation in the world. Man, then, is not the slave but the master of his fate. And the whole value and function of knowledge, scientific and philosophic, lies in making man recognize and exert that mastery, and in showing him how to change both his environment and himself for the better. Mere contemplation and understanding of the universe as it is get us nowhere. It is an emasculation of the mind's *essential* power to *act* and to *create*. The all-important thing is the *application* of knowledge. Any philosophy worthy of its name is a *practice,* a way of life. All science that is of any value is *applied* science. Theory and practice cannot be separated. They are to all useful intents and purposes one and the same thing.

Dialectical materialism, and sciences inspired and guided by it, are *active, creative,* and *applied* knowledge. Their grasp of the dialectical movement of the world-process and of human history enables them to *predict* what in the logic of events should occur, and therefore the course that man, in so far as he is intelligent, rational, and logical, should and, since he is a free active and creative factor in bringing things to pass, can follow. They naturally and inevitably put themselves into effect.

But to do so, dialectical philosophy and science require a *collective* united knowledge and effort on the part of all mankind as a whole. They cannot be applied by the individaul as such, but only by society pulling together as one man. Hegel, and here we come to the last of Marx's principal objections to the Hegelian system, had unduly exalted the individual at the expense of society. He had made society a *means* to the self-expression of the individual, which he regarded as the ultimate and complete expression in human terms of the Absolute Idea.

The Individual and Society. This, however, in Marx's opinion, is to invert the true relation of the one to the other. The individual is not an end-in-himself, but a means to the self-realization of society of which he is an integral part. He and his fellows, like the cells of a living body, stand in a relation of *reciprocity* to one another and to the community—all for one, one for all. Each may be the center of a separate life and activity, but each depends upon the others and upon the community for his existence and the performance of his special functions, and constitutes with them and it a single indivisible whole in whose maintenance and welfare his particular career finds its true self-expression, and his proper happiness is attained. Society, then, not the individual, is the real human unit. Hence, human thinking has got to be *collective,* human action *concerted,* and human resources *pooled,* if the common good of *all* human beings is to be attained. Otherwise we shall have in the future, as in the past and the present, dispersed and disunited individuals obtaining each a particular and isolated good, unshared with his fellows and only too often obtained at their expense.

What, then, does human history reveal in retrospect and in prospect, when viewed through the eyes of *dialectical materialism?* Looking backward we see that humanity hitherto has been at ceaseless war with itself. It has exhibited great differences and inequalities of individual opportunity, education, and possessions, which have given rise to *class* divisions and distinctions of various sorts. By and large, human society has been split into two opposing factions, the "haves" and the "have nots," the upper and the under dogs—a distinction whose bases have been largely artificial and fortuitous.

Economic Basis of Society. The most fundamental aspect of this cleavage is the economic aspect, since at the economic level we are dealing with the very bases and necessities of human life and survival, and with the minimum conditions of human progress and happiness. At the root of the economic situation lies the institution of *private property,* upon the possession of which the opportunity for individual self-realization has largely depended in the past, and by the possession of which the worth of the individual has hitherto been measured to a great extent. Human history, then, has been fundamentally a struggle for *wealth,* and wealth has tended to become more and more concentrated in the hands of the few to such a point that the many are left with a pittance barely sufficient to enable them to subsist, and often without that. Furthermore, the advantages that the possession of wealth bestows enable the few to dominate the many, to keep them in a condition of economic slavery, and to oppose successfully any attempts the many may make to obtain a larger share of wealth and to better their condition.

Up to the present, humanity, at least as a whole, has not been really conscious of the existence, the nature, and the significance of the economic situation. It has not sufficiently grasped the fact and the character of the conflict, or been sufficiently acquainted with what it portends and its dialectically inevitable outcome. But now, with the shift from agriculture to industry and the substitution of machinery for handicraft, the class warfare has become so acute that human beings no longer suffer dumbly its consequences. They have become conscious of the fact that there exists a clear-cut and bitter opposition between a laboring class, or *proletariat,* which *produces* material wealth and prosperity, and a middle class or *bourgeoisie*—which has supplanted the old aristocracies—which amasses, monopolizes, and enjoys them in the form of what we now call *capital.* The class struggle is, then, basically a conflict between *capital* and *labor.*

Of the all-important *thesis* and *antithesis* presented by this conflict, Hegel, who took little interest in economics, had, in Marx's opinion, taken almost no account. On the contrary he had *aufgehoben* and synthesized such political, social, and cultural oppositions as he had observed in human history in a so-called democracy dominated by a well-to-do middle class in control of capital, and therefore in a position to exploit the worker. And this synthesis he had invested with an air of grandiose finality.

The Abolition of Private Property. But in so doing he had reached only a partial and temporary synthesis which turns out to be no more than a *thesis* to which an *antithesis* has been slowly but surely developing since the dawn of human history. In any event, if the world-process and human history are spiral rather than circular, we should expect this to be the case. The dialectical method indicates that this *antithesis* must come to a head and enter into the final phases of its conflict with the *thesis,* in which the balance of power will pass to it. Hence logically we may expect the dictation of the *capitalistic bourgeoisie* to give way to a dictation of the *proletariat,* and the capital wealth amassed by mankind to pass from the hands of the few to the hands of the many, or in other words from the hands of the capitalists to those of the laboring class which has produced it. But this can only be accomplished if *private* property is abolished, and all property becomes *public* by being transferred from the possession and control of the individual to the possession and control of the community.

World-Revolution. Such is the course of events logically indicated by the dialectical process. But to put it into effect requires human *effort*. Man must cooperate actively with the dialectic of the world-process and of human history, in which he is an active force and to the development of which he is able to contribute. But human nature being what it is, we cannot hope that the *antithesis* will come to pass by peaceful means. The capitalistic bourgeoisie cannot be *reasoned* into handing over to labor or to the community the wealth for which it has been so greedy and on which it has so tight a hold. The proletariat will not come to the top unless it puts itself on top. It must then be prepared to take active, energetic, practical steps to overthrow the capitalistic bourgeoisie, to destroy the institution and distribute the substance of private property, and to put the sources of wealth, the means of creating and distributing it, and its ultimate benefits into the hands of those whose toil produces it.

In short, the proletariat throughout the world will have to *revolt*, actively and forcefully, against existing conditions, and must be willing to shed its and capitalistic blood, if necessary, to attain its ends. And it is the business of dialectical materialists to arouse the proletariat to a sense of its plight and its power, to instill it with dissatisfaction with its present lot, and to encourage, foment, and further by all possible means, throughout the whole world, a world-revolution.

The Classless Society. But the triumph of the world-revolution is only a means to a further end. It is only a successful assertion of the *antithesis* against the *thesis*. It is primarily a work of *destruction*. But its out-and-out battle with and triumph over the *thesis*—the capitalistic bourgeoisie—will be at the same time a work of *construction*. For it will be guided by the ideal of a new *synthesis*, and will make of that ideal a fact. This synthesis will take the form of a "classless society," in which there will be no class distinctions and no class warfare, no bourgeoisie and no proletariat, no rich and no poor.

In it individual interests will be reconciled, and all the inequalities of opportunity, wealth and education, and all the resultant envies and hatreds that have hitherto divided mankind itself, will be *aufgehoben* and overcome. Public interest will absorb and transfigure private interests. *Esprit de corps* will "take up" and transubstantiate individual ambition and initative and become the mainspring of human activity. Nationalism will become internationalism, and human allegiance will be to humanity as a whole throughout the entire world. All men will be comrades, laboring shoulder to shoulder, not each for his own self-aggrandizement, but all for the good of the great community of all mankind, and all will take joy in so doing. All will voluntarily pool the results of their labors for the common benefit. All will share in the enjoyment of the wealth acquired together and held in common, to such degree as the value of their respective services suggests. And the higher cultural values, which hitherto the masses have been too poor or too uneducated to enjoy, will now through community support and the diffusion of education be put within the reach of all alike. The emergence of this *synthesis* from the conflict between *thesis* and *antithesis* by which humanity is at present torn, may be a long and painful process, fraught with privation, suffering, destruction, and the shedding of blood, but it is the logical outcome of the present situation of mankind.

Marx's View of Religion. We may remember the commotion caused by the attack of the Hegelian Left on Christian theology. Marx shared the sentiments that inspired it, but he felt that it was too temporizing, conciliatory and weak. As he saw it, Christianity had to be extirpated root and branch, not only because *dialectical materialism* denied the existence of anything but matter in motion and its products, and was therefore opposed to *all* supernaturalistic systems, religious and philosophical, but also because Christianity, and for that matter all religions, had not only tolerated but sanctioned the existing social and economic organization of society, which was about to be overthrown.

Christianity had become the religious expression of the spirit of the *bourgeoisie*. It had approved the institution of private property, which was the root of all evil. It had connived at the concentration of wealth and power in the hands of the few, and at the exploitation of the many. Indeed, it had fostered the belief that the acquisition of private wealth by an individual was a sign of divine favor and a reward for meritorious conduct. Nay more, it proclaimed that things as they were, were as its god willed them to be, and that the oppressions and injustices, miseries and sufferings with which human society was infected were part of his divine plan, and therefore really just and really good.

Christianity, then, had to be overthrown, and its god destroyed for moral as well as metaphysical reasons. The capitalistic organization could not be conclusively and convincingly done away with, unless at the same time the philosophical, theological, and ethical sanctions it invoked in its defense were also disproved and discarded. Hence the world-revolution must be anti-theistic in general and anti-Christian in particular.

Such in outline was the cosmic and social philosophy underlying the views set forth by Marx, in collaboration with Engels, in the *Com-*

munist Manifesto, and later by Marx alone in *Das Kapital.* This philosophy, restated and reaffirmed by Lenin, became the guiding ideal of the recent social and economic revolution in Russia.

III. FRENCH PHILOSOPHY

Maine de Biran and Royer-Collard. Such metaphysical speculation as France produced during this period was not original, but was rather eclectic and reminiscent of the views of earlier thinkers. For example, Maine de Biran (1766-1824) avowed himself at first a disciple of Locke and Condillac, and, following them in their introspective, psychological method, finally worked out a point of view of his own. He now denied Condillac's doctrine of the passivity of consciousness, and substituted for it a philosophy of the self as an active, developing entity, rising through the stages of sensation and perception to a condition of reflective knowledge. To these he later added an activity of pure spirit which transcends the mental operations characteristic of human beings and brings the mind into direct contact with God and the supersensible world.

Along with Maine de Biran we may also mention Royer-Collard (1763-1845), who, inspired by Cartesianism, attacked Condillac and the sensationalists, and regarded consciousness as the activity of a spiritual substance. Again in Jouffroy (1796-1842) we find a similar emphasis upon the spiritual nature of the soul and a theistic conception of the universe.

Cousin. But perhaps the most prominent of the representatives of this way of thinking, and after Comte, the best known of the French philosophers of the period is Victor Cousin (1792-1867). Cousin bases his system on a complete and exact analysis of consciousness from which in his opinion nothing is omitted and in which nothing is slurred over. Such an analysis reveals that the development of the individual consciousness is paralleled by the development of the race, and that this evolution, as Hegel pointed out, has three stages. In the individual consciousness we may distinguish sensation, volition, and reason. To our sensations we assign an *external ground.* The will, which is spontaneous, self-sustaining, free, and prior to reflection and deliberation, is the essence of the *self.* Reason is an *impersonal* activity, like the active reason of Aristotle, union with which in the vision of truth raises the individual out of himself and makes him one with all other selves, all truth, and all reality.

By reason, then, we are lifted out of the domain of psychology into that of metaphysics. The two great concepts dominating rational thought—causality and substance—apply to an external world as well as ourselves. We now distinguish subject from object, the self from nature, and at the same time explain their existence and their relations, by referring them to a First Cause, God. The universe of minds and bodies is the result of God's absolutely undetermined, free and spontaneous act. Nothing in his nature necessitated his creating at all or creating the kind of world he does.

Applying these conclusions to history, we find the various stages and movements of consciousness mirrored in the external world. Humanity is first spontaneous and unreflective, preoccupied with and sunk in the external environment, and conscious only of the infinite of which it is a part. Then it becomes reflective, self-conscious, and individualistic, opposes itself to nature and occupies itself with its own finite character and destiny. Finally, it realizes and relates both the finite and the infinite. The East is devoted to the infinite, Greece to the finite, modern Europe to the union of the two. Government passes from the despotism of Asia through the individualistic democracy of Greece to the constitutional systems of modern Europe. Theology evolves from eastern pantheism into Greek polytheism, and from polytheism into Christian theism. Philosophy, differentiating itself into a number of individual distinct systems, each one of which is in partial possession of the truth, would find the whole truth in a reunion and fusion of all these opposing views into one.

All this sounds Hegelian. But Cousin was highly critical of German idealism. He disagreed with Kant's position that the nature of Reality is unknowable, and with Schelling's view that it is apprehended, not by reason, but by a kind of mystical intuition. Nor could he stomach the Absolute Idea of Hegel, or Hegel's principle of the identity of opposites, or his flouting of the law of self-contradiction, or the Hegelian application of the triad of thesis, antithesis, and synthesis to the world-process.

IV. ITALIAN PHILOSOPHY

Rosmini. Before leaving Latin soil, we ought to make a brief trip into Italy and brief mention of Rosmini (1797-1855) and Gioberti (1801-1852). Both were priests, and therefore their speculations were necessarily restricted. As it was, some portions of Rosmini's work were formally condemned. Both, again, were aroused by contemporary developments in France and Germany. Rosmini endeavored to restore an objective criterion of truth. The concept of existence he found to be not only universal and fundamental to all thinking, but also objective in its implications. It is more than an idea *in* the mind; it is an idea of something outside the mind. The existence of this something is not inferred but directly intuited. Truth and Reality, then, exist independent of being and thought.

Since the feeling of externality is trustworthy, we may also have confidence in the felt externality of our body and of the causes of our sensations. The externality of our body and of the grounds of our experience mean, moreover, that the self is different from the body and from its content of consciousness, and is, therefore, a *subject* opposed to an object. Being a subject, it must have an essence and attributes. If, now, we follow out the system of more and more general universals thus created, we arrive at last at the *summum genus,* or idea of *being,* in which all other ideas are contained—that is, at the universal and absolute truth about all things. This idea, however, is not built up out of other concepts in the process of knowledge. It is a presupposition of knowledge, and is therefore innate.

Gioberti. Rosmini was attacked by Gioberti, whose system is much more orthodox. Gioberti begins with the premise that God, whom he designates as *being,* creates out of nothing the universe, which he calls *existence.* From God comes all human knowledge, which is an implanted intuition of the truth, or, in other words, of God himself. Philosophy is reflection upon the nature of the truth thus intuited and revealed, and upon the relations of the created to the Creator. Morality and religion are a progressive expression of the truth by human life, and a redemption, so to speak, of *existence* by *being,* culminating in the Incarnation. Gioberti's violent attacks upon the Jesuits, however, led to an eventual condemnation of his philosophy.

V. KIERKEGAARD

Until recently there has been a general neglect in the English speaking world of one of the nineteenth century's most interesting thinkers, the Danish theologian and philosopher Søren Kierkegaard (1813-1855). Kierkegaard made an isolated one-man protest against Hegelianism and its impact upon European culture. A lonely and highly introverted person with an acute consciousness of guilt, an extraordinary literary genius who ill fitted the society about him, he launched an attack upon the industrialized society and the institutionalism of his time, particularly the established Church, and upon what he regarded as the soul-destroying factors in Hegel's philosophy, its intellectualism and its absolutism. Although not an effective force in his own place and time, Kierkegaard's efforts have borne important fruit in the twentieth century in the rise of existentialist philosophy and neo-orthodox theology.

Kierkegaard was an intense individualist who turned his hatred and irony upon everything that seemed to militate against the full expression of individuality. The extreme intellectualism that flowed from Hegelianism was, he insisted, the culmination of a philosophy and science that deal only in abstractions, such as man as a metaphysical universal, or man as collective society, or man as a biological species, but know nothing of man as a real, living, struggling, suffering being. It is only the individual who is genuinely real, because only the individual exists, and yet Hegelianism, in which philosophy was thought by many to achieve its maturity, cultivated a method that yields no knowledge of the individual, for such knowledge must be personal and subjective, and produced a metaphysic in which the individual is denied in the total reality. The individual loses his authentic reality when he is swallowed up by history, by associations, by the public, or by the age in which he lives. It is futile to expect the individual as an individual to appropriate the whole of existence. The whole is available only to that which stands outside of existence. The individual is the very meaning of existence.

It is rising above both the intellectual and esthetic to the ethical plane that authenticates concrete existence as an individual. Here it is the absolute decision of moral choice that counts. In his solitariness the individual must accept the responsibility for decision.

As a theologian, Kierkegaard insisted that the estrangement, despair, and anxiety of the individual can be met only by an act of faith, which affirms existence and accepts even what appears to the reason as ridiculous, that God was incarnate in Christ and that in him we have our salvation.

VI. CONTEMPORARY SCIENCE

Astronomy, the Physical Sciences and Mathematics. Excepting for the imposing development of philosophy in Germany, the first half of the nineteenth century is more marked by scientific than by metaphysical progress. In France mathematicians had been busy working out the possibilities of the calculus and of analytic geometry, and one of the results of the Revolution was the founding of the great engineering and technological school in Paris, known as the *École Polytechnique*. In astronomy the Newtonian celestial mechanics had been confirmed and elaborated by Laplace. The law of gravitation, it was felt, might prove universally applicable to even the minutest particles of matter. Chemistry, crystallography, and the theory of probability had made rapid advances. Sadi Carnot was laying the foundation of thermodynamics. And natural history had been raised to a new level by Cuvier, who shares with Laplace the honor of being the greatest French scientist of the early nineteenth century.

We may also permit ourselves to make a brief excursion across the Channel, while we are dealing with science. In Great Britain we find at the period, Herschel the astronomer, and the physicists and chemists, Priestley, Davy, Young, Dalton, Faraday, and Bell. In 1836 the British Association was founded. The Scotch universities were infected with the contagion of the Continental scientific spirit, though for the moment Oxford and Cambridge remained immune.

Again, if we cast a glance across the Rhine into Germany, we shall find there, also, great scientific contributions and advances contemporaneous with the speculations of the German idealists. Gauss and Jacobi were adding to mathematical knowledge. Liebig was occupying himself with organic chemistry. Humboldt was a great name in medicine and in the physical sciences. Von Bunsen was beginning his researches and inventions.

All this scientific ferment was also being crystallized and precipitated in great scientific generalizations and concepts. As we have already remarked, the Newtonian law of gravitation was being extended. The atomic theory of matter was reasserting itself. The mechanical hypothesis was coming into vogue once more. The kinetic theory of nature was in process of construction. The undulatory hypothesis of the character of radiant energy, suggested by Leonardo da Vinci, was being vindicated by Young and Fresnel. The concept of the ether was proposed. Thomson was working in thermodynamics along the lines suggested by Carnot. The notion of energy was being applied outside the field of thermodynamics to electrical, magnetic, and chemical phenomena.

Geology and Biology. Similar advances were taking place in the geological and biological sciences. Analogies between inorganic and organic matter and between plants and animals were in process of discovery. The cell was established as the morphological unit of life. The belief in recurrent, periodic cycles and overturns or catastrophes in the life of the universe was giving way to the theory of continuous geological and biological development. The science of embryology had been developed, and had revealed the "recapitulation" by the individual foetus of the characteristics of the embryos of lower forms of life—an observation which was later of great importance in helping confirm the Darwinian theory. Lamarck was suspecting that the structure of the organism might undergo important modifications caused by the environment. Chambers had said outright that the concept of development might be applied not only to the origin of the solar system and the earth but to the generation of animals, and even of man himself.

Such questions and considerations could not but arouse discussion as to whether there is really any essential difference between organic and inorganic matter. A controversy raged between the mechanists and the vitalists over this point—the one maintaining, the other denying, that life can be reduced to terms of chemical reaction and that the living cell is nothing but a highly complex chemical molecule. Finally, in 1859, Darwin published his *Origin of Species,* which administered as great a shock to thought as did Galileo and Copernicus by their destruction of the Ptolemaic geocentric astronomy. But of this more anon.

Psychology and Economics. Consciousness and its relation to the bodily processes were also brought under scientific scrutiny, and psychology, as we noted in discussing Herbart, began to set itself up as a science, backed, to be sure, for the moment by metaphysics, but in a fair way soon to detach itself from philosophy. The responsiveness of the nerves to electrical stimulation was discovered. The difference between motor and sensory nerves was recognized. The mechanics of sight and hearing were studied by Helmholtz. Herbart applied, as we have seen, mathematics to conscious behavior and thought he could describe it in exact formulae, analogous, for example, to the law of gravitation. In 1846 Weber (1795-1878) added his famous "law" governing the increase in stimulation necessary to produce an increase in sensation. Lotze was also attempting to bring all psychophysical phenomena within the bounds of a strictly mechanical theory.

Since the end of the eighteenth century economics, also, had been becoming more and more of a science. The French "physiocrats," Quesnay, Gournay, and Cortillon, and the British thinkers, Adam Smith, Ricardo, and Malthus, had attempted to establish exact "laws" governing economic activity, and their efforts were being supplemented and carried on by John Stuart Mill, to whom we shall return in a moment, and by others. In short, modern *economic theory,* like modern physics and chemistry, was in process of construction, and was destined to undergo much the same vicissitudes, overturns, and reconstructions as were to occur in the history of the other sciences.

In France the acceleration of scientific progress inspired the Positivism of Comte.

Chapter XXI

COMTE AND POSITIVISM

I. LIFE

Auguste Comte was born in 1797. His family was fervently royalist and Catholic, but by the time he was thirteen he had become both a religious and a political free thinker. He entered the *École Polytechnique,* and began also to read philosophy, particularly Hume and Adam Smith. He also studied with Lamarck and Cuvier, and was well abreast of all the scientific discoveries and movements of the day. In 1818 he fell in with Saint-Simon, the most prominent French socialist of the epoch, and became his ardent disciple. Overwork brought on a mental breakdown in 1826. Recovering from it, he became a teacher of mathematics at the *Polytechnique* and spent his spare moments in elaborating and publishing his philosophy, the first volume of which appeared in 1830. Twelve years later, the sixth and last volume of the *Positive Philosophy* fell from the press. Immediately he embarked upon another book—the *System of Positive Polity,* the four volumes of which were published between 1851 and 1854. Meantime, his early religious upbringing was reasserting itself, not however by restoring him to the bosom of Mother Church, but by inspiring him with a cult of humanity in which the great philosophers and scientists took the place of the Christian saints, and an organized devotion to the cause of humanity was substituted for the worship of God. Disciples gathered about him and formed a sort of church, whose tenets were set forth in the *Positivist Calendar* published in 1849. In 1857 he died.

II. SCIENCE AS RELIGION

Even his *positivistic philosophy* was, however, in a sense a scheme of salvation. Comte was alarmed at the mental anarchy of his time and by the general breakdown of the old standards. He felt that something must be done to remove moral confusion from the minds of his contemporaries, and that, if order was to be brought out of mental and moral chaos, the restoration of some sort of unified and coherent belief was necessary. Since the principal source of moral and mental unrest was the conflict between science and religion and between reason and authority, it was about this point that measures of relief must be concentrated.

Three possible ways of dealing with it presented themselves. An attempt might be made to reconcile science and religion. Or the authority of religion and the Church might be re-asserted. Or science itself might be turned into a religion, and its concepts might be so developed and popularized as to take the place of theology. History, however, shows that the battle between scientific and theological concepts is never-ending, and that therefore a reconciliation of the two is impossible. The second course is out of the question. The world cannot go backward. Copernicus, Galileo, the Renaissance, the present scientific awakening, have occurred. They cannot be effaced. Their results are part of history, and the revolution they have accomplished cannot be undone.

The third course alone is practicable. We can at least go forward, even if we cannot go back. The scientific method must be extended, the scientific point of view must be developed, and life must be reorganized on a scientific basis. Thus only can the world be saved. If this can be done, if we can become as scientific in our estimation of moral and social phenomena as we are in our dealings with physical events, then we may succeed in formulating a new, positivistic philosophy of life by which human beliefs and attitudes will be inspired and moral stability will be regained. What we need, therefore, is a *science* of social behavior to which men may pin their faith.

III. THE THREE STAGES OF THOUGHT

The Law of Growth. To found such a science, Comte continues, we must first study the development and nature of the scientific point of view. When we do this, we find that it invariably passes through three stages, or, in other words, exemplifies a *law of growth*. It expresses itself first in a *theological* form, next in *metaphysical* speculation, and finally in a *positivistic,* truly scientific manner. Its first phase represents a necessary point of departure from which all intellectual activity must start. The second marks a period of transition. The third is the fixed and final goal of all thinking. Such is Comte's celebrated *law of the three stages.* It will be found to hold good for the evolution of intellectual activity, both in the individual and in the race.

In the initial, theological stage all phenomena are explained by super-natural, arbitrary causes. The child finds reasons for the behavior of things by imagining them to be actuated by invisible beings similar to himself. In the same way, the race in its infancy explains its universe as the work of gods whom it creates in its own image.

At the metaphysical level both the individual and the racial mind have dispensed with quasi-human and personal causes of things. But they still find the explanation of phenomena in causes conceived as existing beneath the surface of events and as possessed of a superior reality to the appearances *grounded* in and upon them. Even science invokes all sorts of hypothetical entities which are just as "metaphysical" as the things-in-themselves the philosopher finds behind the sensible universe.

Positivism. The final stage, that of *positivistic* thought, is reached by criticism of the other methods. It involves a rejection of all hypothetical construction of entities regarded as existing apart from and beneath the sensible universe. The mind, as it progresses, comes to consider all such explanations as mystical and imaginary. But the dismissal of these "metaphysical" philosophies and scientific concepts does not reduce scientific thinking to a mere empirical observation of sense-data. Science does not consist in merely amassing facts, nor is its advance simply an enlargement of the field of vision. Science also infers from the behavior of phenomena certain *laws* which their behavior exemplifies and follows. It is a process of generalization.

These *laws,* however, are not regarded by positivistic science as governing and determining the behavior of the sensible world. They are not the *causes* of things. As long as science considers them such it has not as yet risen above the metaphysical level. *Natural laws* are no more than descriptions of *how* phenomena do behave. They are not explanations of *why* they behave as they do. Why things behave as they do is something we cannot know. The causes of things are unascertainable. This is true, not only with respect to the why and wherefore of the universe in general, but with respect to each particular phenomenon occurring in sense-experience.

IV. THE POSITIVISTIC VIEW OF SCIENCE

The Practical Nature of Science. It follows that science on its final, positivistic level is not in any way concerned with discovering the causes of events. It merely infers from phenomena concepts of wider and wider application, and its goal would be attained if it could discover some all-inclusive concept, or law, to which every phenomenon could be subjected. In that case, Comte thinks, the practical end of science, which is found in the *power to predict future events,* would also be realized.

He realizes, however, that in assuming the uniformity of nature and the universal prevalence of certain habits of action throughout all space and time, he is himself indulging in one of those *metaphysical* hypotheses that he condemns. He hastens to modify the dogmatism of his assertion. Laws are not *necessarily* absolute in the sense of being of necessity *universally* true. The establishment of absolute laws, which we could be sure held for everything in all times and places, would require a *complete* scientific observation of all phenomena whatsoever, past, present, and future, throughout the entire universe. Obviously such completeness is impossible.

Furthermore, scientific thinking is relative to the nature of the human organism. Sense data are relative to the kind of sense organs we possess, and the inferences we draw from them are conditioned by the nature of human mental processes. Organisms differently constituted from ours might have a different phenomenal experience, different methods of reflection upon sense data, and therefore different forms of scientific generalization. All in all, then, Comte admits, scientific laws are at the best approximations.

Science as Ability to Predict. Nevertheless, within the limited spheres of space and time with which we are familiar we can regard these laws as sufficiently absolute for our type of organic set-up to give us practical certainty in dealing with the natural world immediately surrounding us. We have practical certainty, for instance, that the law of gravitation is absolute for our solar system. Therefore, we can compute and predict the behavior of bodies within that system with mathematical precision. If we cannot know absolutely whether it describes also the movements of other heavenly bodies, we have the consolation of knowing that their movements do not concern us. We know absolutely all that we need to know absolutely.

We are now in a position to see what science does and what it can do. It organizes knowledge. It gives us the power of prediction and enables us to control nature in many ways and to harness her in the service of human progress and happiness. Surely, then, it should also be able to give certain *ideals* to humanity and to afford mankind *moral* guidance and inspiration.

V. THE BACKWARDNESS OF THE SOCIAL SCIENCES

If science is to do this, however, the social sciences, which deal with human progress and self-realization, must become scientific in their outlook. That they will eventually adopt a scientific attitude and find inspiration in the vistas opened up by positivistic science is suggested by the historical fact that all the others have either attained or are fast attaining the positivistic level. Indeed, we may arrange the sciences in an order of precedence determined by their successive attainments of positivistic finality. Mathematics was the first science to rise from the theological, through the metaphysical, to the positivistic grade. The next to follow suit was astronomy. Then physics arrived, followed by chemistry. Biology is on the way. Why, then, should not ethics and sociology also win out in the end, in spite of the fact that they are now cluttered and hampered by theological and metaphysical concepts?

Incidentally, we may note, the other sciences have attained a positivistic outlook in the order of their complexity and dependence upon their fellows. Mathematics, the simplest and most fundamental of the sciences, arrived first. Naturally, then, the social sciences, which are the most complex and cap the scientific edifice, may be expected to lag behind and be the last to reach the final stage.

In developing the biological and social sciences, we have, however, to adopt a different method from that used by the sciences dealing with inorganic phenomena. In the inanimate world the parts are better known than the whole, and science progresses by building up general concepts and laws from an observation of particular events. The subject matter of biology and the social sciences is, on the contrary, better first observed *en masse* than in the individuals that constitute the whole. In these sciences we progress from the whole to its parts. For example, we can only understand the individual man in his social aspects by first studying the nature and constitution of society.

Furthermore, the time element enters into the study of sociology. Society has evolved. It has had a history. In the course of its development it has accumulated and handed on a heritage of experience. The past has influenced the present, and the present status of human society cannot be understood without reference to the past.

VI. SOCIAL STATICS AND DYNAMICS

Social science may be divided into *social statics,* which investigates the enabling conditions of the existence and permanence of social organization, and *social dynamics,* which concerns itself with the enabling conditions of change and progress. *Statics* shows us that social equilibrium is maintained by a conflict of opposing attitudes. Egoism and altruism, both of which are original impulses in human nature, offset each other and hold each other in check. Intellectual vivacity and curiosity are counterbalanced by mental laziness. Brakes are put on progress by the dislike of change. Liberalism and conservatism wrestle with each other, and by the tension of their struggle keep each other on their feet. These conflicting attitudes of mind, and the system of checks and balances they set up, are indispensable to the stability of the social structure. It takes all kinds of individuals to make an orderly world. Nevertheless, the goodness of a society is measured by the strength of the nobler motivations of altruism and intellectual keenness, curiosity, and freedom. If society is to progress, these attitudes must be in the ascendant.

If we now proceed from the universal to the particular, we find that the units of which society is composed are not individuals but families. Upon the importance and fundamental position of the family in the social organization Comte cannot too strongly insist. Without it the individual would not be human. It provides, then, the bricks, so to speak, out of which the edifice of *human* society must be constructed.

We have already a hint as to the conclusions to which *social dynamics* will bring us. Moral and social progress are measured in terms of the growing preponderance of our higher over our lower activities, and of the increasing control of the lower by the higher. The higher activities are rational in nature. Therefore, progress lies in the development of reason and science in our attitude towards life and in our method of dealing with the ethical and social problems it presents. Only thus can we be just and fair and truly moral in our relations with our fellow-men.

If we turn back to history, we shall find that moral progress is identical with intellectual progress. The three stages of the evolution of thought have corresponding political phases. Theological, personalistic types of explanation of natural phenomena go with a militaristic organization of society. The metaphysical stage is associated with societies that make much of abstract legal considerations. The positivistic outlook is the natural attitude and support of the modern industrial age.

VII. THE WORSHIP OF HUMANITY

Voltaire said that if there were not a God it would be necessary to invent one. Comte having rejected God, along with theology and metaphysics, was forced to re-create an object to worship and to serve, acceptable to his Positivism. He felt a need of an external being whom man might adore and whose will he might do, and this supreme being, or *grand être,* he found in *humanity* as a whole. Mankind is the true God of the individual man, the "great being" whom he should seek to serve and whose perfection he should endeavor to ensure. We should love Humanity with all our mind and heart and strength and seek to do its commandments. We should love our neighbors as ourselves. Religion pure and undefiled is to express this love in honesty and justice towards our fellow-men, in honoring the family, and in infusing all the activities of society, economic, political and social, with morality.

This religion, like all others, demanded outward symbols and forms. It had to have its clergy. To provide them Comte adapted the sacraments and the ritual of the Catholic Church and instituted a priesthood. Chapels were acquired in which services were held. Comte seems even to have dreamt of a kind of theocracy. His clergy, chosen for their character, their intellectual attainments, and their knowledge of human nature and its problems, were to direct the life of the Positivist state. They were to oversee education, compose quarrels, and advise the rulers, as well as to perform their specifically priestly functions as ministers of the publicly established cult of the great being, Humanity.

Chapter XXII

BRITISH PHILOSOPHY 1800-1870

I. BENTHAM

Continental Influence on British Thought. We now cross the Chan-nel to Great Britain. We find there a somewhat complex situation, due to the convergence of widely different strains of thought. Kant's influence was making itself felt. Samuel Taylor Coleridge (1772-1834), who had studied Kant and Jacobi and developed an enthusiasm for the post-Kantian idealists, was lauding German philosophy and at the same time attacking contemporary British thought, which still was largely shaped by Locke and Hume and their successors. Out of the psychological and epistemological theories of the earlier British School the so-called *associational psychology* was developing, which, follow-ing their lead, tried to build up memory and imagination and the more abstract processes of thinking out of sense perceptions associated ac-cording to certain invariable laws. Eighteenth century British ethics was contributing to the formulation of *Utilitarianism* in the sphere of morals. Finally, to these inherited British and imported German influences we must add French ones emanating from the Positivism of Comte.

Utilitarianism. The link between the British ethics of the last half of the eighteenth and the first half of the nineteenth century, is to be found in Jeremy Bentham (1748-1832) whose mature years straddle equally the two epochs. It is to him that we owe the coining of the term *utilitarianism* to designate a theory of morals that had a profound effect upon the ethical thought of the early nineteenth century and that still claims many adherents. To him, too, we owe the adoption from Priestley, or from Hutcheson, of the phrase "the greatest hap-piness of the greatest number," which he made famous as the watch-word of the new movement. This, he tells us, describes the highest and ultimate moral good, at which all action, so far as it is considered ethical, must aim. The moral value of conduct, private and public, is to be measured in terms of its usefulness. And what is or is not useful will be determined, according as it does or does not contribute to the greatest good of the greatest number of people. Both the individual and the state must ask whether any proposed course of action will or will not be conducive to the happiness of the majority, and must judge it to be morally good or evil by this standard.

Happiness, Bentham defined as pleasure, and maintained that pleasure and pain are the mainsprings of human action. We instinctively avoid the one and pursue the other. They are, therefore, the natural bases of our distinction between good and evil. Since we can only judge what we ought to do on the evidence of what we, constituted as we are, actually do tend to do, we *ought* to seek pleasure and to shun pain. Pleasure is the moral as well as the natural end of action, and *right* behavior is behavior calculated to increase the amount and distribution of pleasure in and among human beings.

Bentham, however, was not interested so much in the strictly ethical implications of his doctrine as in its economic and political bearings. In the idea of utility measured in terms of general welfare and happiness he found a useful basis for criticizing existent social institutions and for making suggestions with regard to their possible betterment. Utilitarianism, as a system of morals, is most closely associated with the name of John Stuart Mill, of whom we shall have occasion to treat in a moment.

II. JAMES MILL AND THOMAS BROWN

Attack on the "Ego." Closely linked with Bentham, and in a way philosophically, as well as biologically, the father of John Stuart Mill was James Mill (1773-1836). Like Bentham, with whose utilitarianism he agreed, he was more interested in economics than in ethics. But he was also a psychologist of eminence, and his *Analysis of the Phenomena of the Human Mind,* published in 1829, was a feather in the cap of the Associationists.

Kant, it will be remembered, had maintained that our acts of perception and knowledge are attended by a transcendental "I know"—a *knowing* that I know or that I perceive, which synthesizes all our experience into a unity of apperception. Stewart and Reid had also upheld the existence of an independent faculty. James Mill on the contrary maintains that no such transcendental "I know" can be isolated from judging and perceiving and set over against them. The *self-conscious* element pervades all consciousness. Knowing that we know or that we feel is not superimposed upon the act of knowledge or perception. It is involved in it. A feeling is also a consciousness of that feeling. All consciousness is self-consciousness. All awareness is also an awareness of being aware.

In this way Mill undermined the notion of an "ego" existing apart from and behind experience, which had played and was playing so important a role in the Kantian philosophy and in the systems of the post-Kantian idealists. The subject, the self, was given *in* experience, and was no more than a certain quality that experience felt in itself.

Brown. Another important contributor to the Associationist school was Thomas Brown (1778-1820). Brown, like Mill, denied a special faculty of consciousness expressed in a transcendental "I know" accompanying the stream of experience. The self is a derivative state of mind, built up by memory which annexes past states to present ones and thus bestows upon the flow of experience a sense of self-identity. This sense is, however, unanalyzable. The belief in our self-identity is an original intuition and law of human nature, from which we cannot get away.

The same, Brown thinks, holds true of causation, and herein he differs from Hume, whom he criticizes at some length. Causation, to be sure, is based upon an observation of the occurrence of antecedents and sequents. But the belief in causal connection is not built up by repeated observations of the same sequences. It is an original intuition. Repeated observations form rather the basis for our distinction between mere coincidence and real causal connection, and thus enable us to scrape off the superfluous and irrelevant elements that attach themselves to the essential linkage between cause and effect.

III. HAMILTON AND MANSEL

Hamilton's Philosophy of the Unconditioned. From James Mill, we should, genealogically speaking, pass immediately to his son John Stuart Mill. But the younger Mill was philosophically the son of many fathers, with some of whom, like Kant and Comte, we are already acquainted. One of them, however, remains to be mentioned—Sir William Hamilton (1788-1856), a Scotch lawyer and philosopher who was for the last twenty years of his life Professor of Logic and Metaphysics at Edinburgh University. Hamilton was greatly influenced by Reid, whose works he edited, and also by Kant. Indeed, his system is largely a mixture of their views. His reputation as a philosopher was established early in his career by an article "On the Philosophy of the Unconditioned," which appeared in *The Edinburgh Review* in 1820. After his death his university lectures on metaphysics and logic were collected and published. He was a man of great and diverse learning, and had a keenly critical mind. He made valuable contributions to the Associationist psychology. But he added little original to the development of metaphysics.

Hamilton differs from both Kant and Reid, and agrees with James Mill and Brown in denying any transcendental basis or special faculty of consciousness to Kant's transcendental "I know." Consciousness of being conscious is not a separate act reflecting upon the activity of perceiving and knowing. All consciousness means not only awareness but a recognition of being aware. Consciousness is then essentially self-consciousness.

Consciousness a Conditioned Perception of Reality. But Hamilton agrees with Reid in holding that experience is immediately and directly *of* something external to itself. We do not perceive perceptions. Our perceptions are acts of perceiving an object outside and independent of the mind. We do not, then, have to argue and infer the existence of an external world. Nor is our sense-experience a subjective and second-hand representation of it. We are in direct contact with an external reality, and the sense of that contact is part and parcel of our perceptions, and is as immediately present and given as they are.

However, although we directly perceive an external world existing independently of our perceptions of it, we do not and cannot perceive it as it really is. Our sense organs and ways of thinking condition and distort its real nature. Nor can we know *ourselves* as we really are. We can only know ourselves as we appear to ourselves under the form of the internal sense, which presents us with a flow of experience in time. Here Hamilton is in agreement with Kant.

Still, although the content of experience is *phenomena* and not things-in-themselves, we cannot say that the sensible world is an illusion. On the contrary, we draw *within* the world of phenomena the line between the real and the illusory, waking and dreaming, sanity and madness. The phenomenal world is a real appearance of Reality to our minds, so far as they are able to apprehend it.

At this point we find Hamilton veering away once more from Kant. Kant had regarded the categories—substance, quality, causation, and the like—as *positive* forms impressed by our minds upon experience. Hamilton regards them rather as *weaknesses* of the mind, indicative of its inability to grasp the true nature of the Real. We must formulate experience as we do, because we are not strong or knowing enough to formulate it otherwise. The categories are not colored glasses. They are merely cloudy ones.

The Nature of Reality Inconceivable. This dim-sightedness of the human mind subjects it to what Hamilton calls *The Law of the Conditioned*. The human mind is so constituted that it limits the existent by the laws of self-contradiction and excluded middle. Hence, being unable to conceive the Real as *both* unconditioned and conditioned, absolute and relative, infinite and finite, one and many in character, it must think of Reality as *either* the one *or* the other. But since a conditioned and an unconditioned Reality are equally self-contradictory and unthinkable, the mind must conceive the Real as *neither* the one *nor* the other—which is also self-contradictory and inconceivable.

The only possible conclusion, Hamilton feels, is that, though we can know that the Unconditioned exists, we cannot know or conceive its nature. However, the mind is not therefore doomed to complete skepticism. We do not need to call, like Kant, upon moral postulates for aid. The intellect itself has its postulates, though the Law of the Conditioned prevents its verifying them. For example, the mind quite independently of moral motivation *believes* that there is such a thing as an uncaused, free act. But it cannot conceive such an act, since its experience is conditioned, and is given as a temporal succession of events and objects in which no first, unprecedented event or thing is ever found. Therefore, believe as we may and must in freedom, we cannot help *conceiving* of everything as caused. Or take God. We cannot help believing on intellectual grounds that he, as the unconditioned Reality, exists. But how he exists, our minds, thinking only in terms of the conditioned, are unable to understand.

Valid Knowledge of the Conditioned Possible. Within experience and the realm of the conditioned we may have valid and authoritative knowledge. The steps by which such knowledge is built up Hamilton describes at length. Experience *presents* us with an external world spread out in space and a self continuing in time. Memory and imagination retain and recombine sense presentations. In their work they are governed by the *law of redintegration,* to which Hamilton endeavored to reduce all laws of association. According to this formula the different elements entering into a mental state tend, when they recur separately, to recall the others.

Images and memories provide the food for the relating, comparing, connecting, judging activities of thought, which extract from them general ideas and by comparison subsume data under these ideas. In his view of universals, Hamilton follows the nominalistic tradition. General ideas are based upon and refer to particulars. There is no such thing as mankind apart from individual men. Though innate ideas do not exist, the mind follows certain *a priori* rules in thinking which supply what Hamilton calls the principles of *common sense.*

We may express these rules as follows: In our reasoning we do not feel that we have got down to bed-rock and reached *fundamental* rather than *derivative* notions, until we have analyzed everything that is complex into simple elements, and have reached that which seems necessary, universal, and incapable of further explanation. In endeavoring to reach rock-bottom we shall find our instinctive and safest guide in the Aristotelian dictum that the test of truth and existence lies in what appears true to all. That which is universally apparent is the *evident,* and sound evidence can be gathered, and reasonable certainties can be attained, only by obeying the rule of evidence, as Aristotle has expressed it.

Mansel's Theory of "Negative Knowledge" of the Unconditioned. Hamilton's disciple, Henry Mansel (1820-1871), Professor at Oxford and Dean of St. Paul's, endeavored to escape in another way the complete skepticism *The Law of the Conditioned* seemed to imply. While agreeing with Hamilton that *positive,* objective knowledge can be had only of the finite and the conditioned, he maintained that we may have what he called "negative knowledge" of what lies beyond experience. This "negative knowledge" is based upon the extension to the Unconditioned of such definite, determinate and relative qualities of the conditioned as one pleases, and then declining to limit or "condition" the attributed qualities by defining them in their ordinary human sense.

For instance, we may attribute to God *infinite* and *unconditioned* power, knowledge, benevolence, justice, mercy and the like, although we cannot possibly *know* what these qualities are like when removed from their conditioned context and human significance and given *unconditioned* status. God's power is still power, although not what we mean by power. He is righteous, but not what we mean by righteous. He is moral, but we cannot judge him by our moral standards— since *unconditioned* power and moral qualities escape our definitions of the terms.

IV. JOHN STUART MILL

Life, Works, and General Attitude. Like his father and Bentham, John Stuart Mill (1806-1873), to whom we now turn, was deeply interested in economic, political and social problems, and discussed them at length in his writings. His "classic" *Principles of Political Economy* appeared in 1848, his no less "classic" *Essay on Liberty* in 1850, his

Thoughts on Parliamentary Reform and his *Views on Representative Government* in 1859 and 1860 respectively. A year later he was discussing *The Subjection of Women.* To the next decade belong his more important philosophical works, with the exception of his *Logic* which appeared in 1843, and his *Essays on Religion,* which were published after his death. His *Utilitarianism, Examination of Sir William Hamilton's Philosophy, Comte and Positivism,* and the edition of his father's *Analysis of the Human Mind* were written between 1860 and 1870.

Metaphysical questions Mill was inclined to push to one side, partly because he was convinced that they were unanswerable, and partly, perhaps, because speculation did not appeal to him. He was in agreement with the skeptical contention that we cannot know what things-in-themselves are like. For that matter, we cannot even be sure that they exist. We have not the immediate perception of an external reality claimed by Hamilton and Reid. We are indeed haunted by the feeling that such a reality must exist as the ground and cause of our perceptions. But we have no means of testing its validity. For Mill, as for Kant, knowledge cannot be extended beyond experience.

Matter "A Permanent Possibility of Sensation." Why, then, do we *believe* that such a world exists? The belief is built up, he tells us, out of empirical experience by the aid of memory and the association of ideas. Our past experiences are recollected, and the laws of association lead us to expect them to recur in the context in which they were formerly perceived. There is no basis in our memory for any other expectation. Our belief is continually verified and strengthened by our daily experience, and comes to represent a *permanent possibility* of re-experiencing the same sensation. The possibility of such experience continues to exist in the absence of the experience itself. It assumes, therefore, an objective, external character, and becomes a kind of substance, of which the recurrent sensations, when they are again felt, figure as the manifestations and qualities. Indeed, what we mean by the *matter* or *substance,* which we suppose to *underlie* phenomena, is simply this *permanent possibility of sensation.*

The Self. Mill tries also to derive the consciousness of *self* from empirical experience. He was a thorough-going Associationist in psychology, and felt that the entire content of consciousness could be built up from sense perceptions by memory and imagination working in accordance with the laws of association. But here he ran into difficulties to which he himself confessed. Experience, as he viewed it, was a series of discrete impressions. Somehow, as these impressions flowed by, they precipitated a subjective belief in a permanent possibility of *having* more perceptions, just as on the objective side they precipitated the belief in the permanent possibility of their *recurring*. This belief, which accompanied the sequence of sense perceptions, became "materialized" as the idea of a soul-substance underlying the subjective aspect of experience.

Such an explanation, however, he regarded as by no means satisfactory. It involved the supposition that a succession of feelings could be aware of itself *as a whole,* and that therefore each moment in the series, although existing only in the present, could be conscious of past and future moments—a supposition that Mill admitted was very difficult to defend. Still, if it could not be defended, we were driven back upon the equally precarious assertion that the self was more than either actual or possible consciousness, and must be regarded as a spiritual substance. But spiritual substances were entities of which we had no experience whatsoever, and were quite impossible to conceive. We were, then, between the devil and the deep sea, forced to choose between two equally unsatisfactory hypotheses. We simply have to face them, admit them, and leave them as they are. All we can say is that in consciousness we just do have a series of feelings that does know itself as a whole inclusive of past, present, and future—how or why, we cannot tell.

Religious Views. Mill's metaphysical skepticism naturally made him noncommittal towards theological speculations. However, he regarded Hamilton's assertion that positive knowledge of God is absolutely impossible as altogether too dogmatic. There is no *a priori* impossibility, rooted in the limitations of the mind, of knowing what God is like—if he exists. The question of his existence and his nature is wholly a matter of evidence, to be treated and decided like any other hypothesis. Is there anything in experience that leads us to believe there is a God? If so, what does experience suggest with regard to his character?

The evidence of a God's existence, Mill seems to think, is certainly not conclusive one way or the other. We cannot prove or disprove it. Nor are the probabilities particularly *pro* or *con*. There is about as much to be said on the one side as on the other. It is largely a matter of opinion, about which men are free and certain to differ.

Certainly, however, there is no evidence whatsoever for a God who is both all-good and all-powerful. On the contrary, the evidence absolutely rules out such a being. The suffering and imperfection in the universe are sufficient proof that, if God is omnipotent, he cannot be benevolent, and that, if he is a moral being, his power must be limited

No *good* God can possibly be conceived as deliberately creating out of a plenitude of power a universe like ours. Mansel's doctrine of "negative knowledge" was particularly obnoxious to Mill. If God was to be called good, just, merciful, and the like, we must, when we applied those terms to him, mean by them what we meant when we applied them to our fellow men. If God was a moral being, he must come up to our standards of morality. We could not call him benevolent and loving, and then, on the ground that he was divine, excuse in him behavior that no benevolent or loving human being would for a moment contemplate himself or tolerate in other men.

If we exclude all metaphysical and theological questions from consideration, what have we left? Everything, Mill thinks, that is of real value. Here he is in full accord with Comte and the Positivists. We have science and we have morality, we have all the bases of human organization and happiness, none of which depends upon metaphysics and theology. Knowledge and science, though they may not extend beyond experience, are valid within experience, and create out of it an orderly, stable, and trustworthy world, if they are developed along the right lines and according to the right methods.

Rejection of Aristotelian Logic. We are thus brought into contact with Mill's most important philosophic work—his theory of logic and of scientific method. Here once more empiricism and the Associationist psychology are paramount in determining his views. For the old, scholastic, Aristotelian logic, with its syllogisms and necessary deductions, Mill has little use. Correct and fruitful methods of reasoning are always *inductive*. They start from the data afforded by experience, and proceed to build up general rules and truths regarding them. But general truths have no content or application outside of the particular instances upon which they are based. Nothing can be *deduced* from them regarding particulars except what the particulars have already contributed to them. In a word, all so-called logical *deduction* by syllogistic methods is really *induction*.

Take any instance of deductive syllogistic reasoning you please. The conclusion is not *deduced* from the major premise, it is *presupposed* in it. The major premise is inductively inferred from an observation of many particular facts *plus* an assumption that other facts occurring in like circumstances will exhibit similar characteristics.

The Proximate Validity of Natural Law. But have we any right to assume that these other facts in which the characteristic has not yet occurred will eventually exhibit it? Can we be sure, for instance, that just because all the human beings of whom we know are mortal, all those alive or yet to be born will also die? If we cannot be *certain,* then it is impossible to establish any general or universal truths, which are necessarily true in all places and at all times. The assertion of such truths is, at the best, the assertion of an hypothesis.

Mill is more than ready to admit this. All the so-called laws and uniformities of nature have only a proximate validity. They are true descriptions of natural events so far as we have observed them. But their unbroken persistence, while observed data accumulate, leads us to believe that all the operations of nature are uniform and regular, just as our observation of death in human beings leads us to infer that "all men are mortal." Again, just as we base all our dealings with our fellows upon the assumption that they are mortal, so we make of the uniformity of nature in general a principle of induction in general. *If* nature *is* uniform and regular in her behavior, we can infer the universality of her laws from our partial observations of her workings. *If* nature is *not* uniform and regular, the whole process of induction goes by the board, and we can infer nothing with any certainty, and have nothing that we can properly call knowledge. Experience hitherto and everywhere has supported the principle of uniformity, and has validated our faith in it by confirming the inferences and predictions we have made in accordance with it. We have been able to build up an exact and reliable body of scientific knowledge, which stands as yet uncontradicted by the course of events.

The Observed Uniformities of Nature. Proceeding now to investigate these uniformities, what do we find? We find space and time; we find the principles of mathematics, which, in Mill's opinion, are not *a priori* but derived from experience; we find the laws with which the physical sciences deal; and above all we find the law of causation, which is practically the law of uniformity itself. Causation rests upon an observation of invariable antecedents and consequents, *plus* an assumption that whenever the same antecedents occur they will have the same consequents.

We cannot, however, accept antecedents and consequents at their face value. Otherwise we might mistake what merely comes *after* for what occurs *because of.* It is the business of science to separate consequences from mere sequents by detecting the circumstances that *under all conditions* precede a given event and without which *under no condition* the event occurs. When we have discovered them, we have discovered the antecedents with which the event is *necessarily* connected. Indeed, we can mean by necessity no more than *unconditional* sequence.

The Laws of Experimental Induction. As a means of precipitating everything that is accidental and conditioned from a series of events and of leaving in it only what is necessary, unconditional, and truly causal, Mill advances his famous *laws of experimental induction*. First, we pick out such antecedents as are *common* to the events whose cause we are seeking. This is the *method of agreement*. We then precipitate from these antecedents those whose presence or absence makes any *difference,* so far as the absence or presence of the events is concerned. This is the *method of difference.*

Again, to exclude the possibility of the event's being connected with antecedents other than those already suggested by the method of agreement and difference, we may appeal to other experiences of similar situations to show that there is at any rate a *residue* in the event that *is not* habitually connected with antecedents other than those already indicated, and that *is* habitually connected with them. This is the *method of residues.* Finally we seek to determine whether a greater or lower degree or quantity of the event is proportionate to the degree or quantity of certain of its antecedents. This is the *method of concomitant variations.*

When an antecedent can pass all four of these tests, so far as its relation to a sequent is concerned, it is regarded as a *cause,* and the sequent in question is called its *effect.*

All the while, however, we are also using *deductive* reasoning. We are familiar with the sequences of events, and if we meet with certain occurrences we *deduce* that they are caused by such and such antecedents. But these deductions have always to be *verified* by experiment, and observation, and analysis.

We must, however, be on our guard against regarding causes as metaphysical entities. The cause of one phenomenon is nothing but another phenomenon, whose unconditional connection with it we have established by the rules we have just been discussing. To know the causes of things is not to penetrate beneath the phenomenal world. It is simply to apprehend what events in the phenomenal world always occur together.

Free-Will and Necessity. Mill's definition of necessity leaves, he feels, both the determinists and the advocates of free-will little real to fight over. Man, being a part of nature, is subject to her uniformities. His behavior proceeds according to the law of causation. His acts are determined by the interaction of his character and his environment. Knowing what a given individual is like, we can predict with reasonable certainty what he will do in given circumstances. All our dealings with our fellows are based upon the assumption of human uniformities, just as our dealings with the physical world are based upon the "axiom" of the uniformity of nature as a whole.

There is then as much *necessity* in human behavior as there is in physical nature. But in neither case can we detect any *compulsion*. There is no such thing as a fate or destiny which forces us or nature to behave as we do. We, like nature, act in an orderly and predictable way. But the fact that we so behave does not deprive us of our feeling of liberty. *We* ourselves initiate our actions. *We* are the source of them, *we* are responsible for them. *We* play an active part in the molding and development of our own characters and careers. My desires and ideals direct my behavior and *cause* me to be what I am. I can do what I *want* to do with myself. What more could one ask in the way of freedom?

Utilitarian Ethics. But what are our desires and ideals? What do we want to do? In short what is the *good*? In answering these questions Mill displays himself as the foremost and the most systematic of all the champions of Utilitarianism. Like his father and like Bentham, he finds the moral good in the greatest happiness of the greatest number, and defines happiness in terms of pleasure. But he also departs in some ways from their teachings. Bentham, for example, in the "hedonistic calculus" he tried to construct for computing the relative value of a pleasure, had not taken account of the *quality* of the pleasure under consideration. He had simply judged it in relation to its intensity, presence, duration and the like. Mill, however, insisted that some pleasures are preferable simply because they are *higher*. Intellectual pleasures, for instance, are *intrinsically* better than sensual pleasures. No intelligent man would sacrifice his intelligence, even if he were assured that if he were more stupid he would be more contented.

Again, whereas Bentham sought to reduce our altruistic feelings to self-interest, Mill recognizes the primitive character of social impulses and founds the social character of the good—the greatest happiness of the greatest number of people—on the gregarious instinct. We are naturally altruistic and self-sacrificing. We naturally find our individual happiness indirectly by directly promoting the happiness of the group.

The Dangers of Altruism. At the same time, Mill felt that unselfishness can be carried too far. The individual is himself a member of the group whose greatest and most widespread good he is supposed to be promoting, and is himself a repository of the happiness of the greatest number. He must, therefore, always reckon himself as an end as well as a means, and must weigh, in an absolutely scientific and rational manner, the contribution made by his own happiness to the greatest good of the majority against that made by the happiness of others. He will yield to others when by yielding he adds to the sum of human happiness. He will demand that others yield to him when getting what he wants is in his judgment more in line with the general good than is the satisfaction of his neighbors' desires. Reason must rule and check our altruistic as well as our selfish impulses. We must love our neighbor *as* ourselves, not *more* than ourselves. Doing as we would be done by, means subordinating our desires to the welfare of others to the *same* extent, neither more nor less, than we feel others should sacrifice themselves to us. Only thus can society be reasonable and just.

"Laissez-faire." The greatest happiness of the greatest number is attained under conditions of the greatest possible individual freedom. It takes all kinds of people to make a world, and the more room the world has in it for the self-development and expression of different individual characters, the better chance everyone has to be happy. Paternalism, regimentation, socialism—anything and everything that tended to destroy the freedom of the individual—were intensely distasteful to Mill. In his *Principles of Economics* he advocates the "laissez-faire" policy. In his *Subjection of Women* he demands that women be given the same rights and opportunities for self-expression as men enjoy. All control is to be deplored, except such as is necessary to subject the individual's pursuit of his own happiness to the well-being of the community as a whole. As men become better educated and more wise, we may hope that moral, social and economic problems will solve themselves and will call for less and less social interference and control. In any case, the social, moral and economic ideal lies in the greatest amount of individual freedom and self-expression compatible with the greatest good of the greatest number.

V. DARWIN

The Theory of Biological Evolution. While Mill was developing his philosophy a young man named Charles Darwin (1809-1882) had attached himself to a natural history expedition which cruised around the world in the *Beagle* collecting and studying biological data. The fruit of this voyage, maturing after some twenty-five years of further observation and reflection on Darwin's part, was *The Origin of Species,* published in 1859. In this work he advanced the hypothesis that living matter is plastic, rather than cast once and for all into fixed forms and species, and that the types it assumes represents its successful adaptation to its environment. As he saw it, life from the first has to struggle for existence against many disadvantageous conditions. In the course of that struggle it assumes a variety of forms. Forms that are not adapted to the circumstances in which they find themselves are killed off, and those which succeed in adjusting themselves survive. The species of animals existent at the present time have come to be what they are as the result of a long process of development in the course of which their structures have been profoundly modified. And they owe their being to the fact that they have proved the fittest to survive in the struggle for existence.

The implications of this theory were at once plain. There was no reason for excepting man from the process of *evolution* by which all other forms of life had been molded into their present shape. He, too, represented a *survival of the fittest* in a *struggle for existence* in the course of which his nature, psychological and physiological, had undergone enormous changes. Further research and meditation convinced Darwin that man had evolved from some species of monkeys akin to the existent anthropoid apes, and that his more remote ancestry was merged with their genealogical tree. His superiority over his simian cousins could be sufficiently accounted for by the principles governing the evolution of all living things. The struggle for existence had eventually sharpened his wits and had conferred certain physical advantages upon him which enabled him to cope successfully with the hostility of other species and to modify his environment to his own advantage. These conclusions were embodied in the *Descent of Man* published in 1871.

The Stir Created by the Darwinian Theory. Just as Copernicus and Galileo, in displacing the earth from its central position in the universe and converting it into a planet of the solar system, had deprived man along with it of all astronomical centrality and importance, so now the Darwinian theory went on to deny him any special biological privilege among the various forms of life that had originated on the earth. He had started from scratch like the others, and like the others he was simply and solely what he had succeeded in making himself.

This new biological concept produced the same stir and provoked the same reactions as did the new astronomy three hundred years earlier. It aroused controversy among the scientists and, at the start, was condemned by most religious bodies.

But the accumulation of evidence since Darwin's time has tended to confirm the evolutionary hypothesis, and it is now generally upheld by scientists. Probably, too, its acceptance by the lay mind today is as widespread as was the popular acceptance of the Copernican astronomy seventy-five years after its promulgation—if not more so. But it is only fair to say that neither it, nor, for that matter, the helio-centric astronomy and the sphericity of the earth, is universally accepted today. Indeed, the teaching of the evolutionary hypothesis, so far at least as man is concerned, is still discouraged in certain institutions of learning.

The hypothesis itself has undergone considerable modification since Darwin's time. Doubts have been raised whether the struggle for existence and the survival of the fittest are sufficient explanation for the process, and whether further determining factors must not be sought. And the *continuous* character of evolution has also been questioned. Considerable evidence has been brought forward to show that it is not an orderly progress step by step, but proceeds by hops, skips, and jumps, in which unforeseen mutations or "sports" occur and establish themselves.

Chapter XXIII

THE EFFECT OF SCIENCE ON PHILOSOPHY

I. SPENCER AND BAIN

Reality Unknowable. The advances in the physical sciences and the doctrine of evolution influenced greatly the further developments of philosophy. Thus in England they conspired with the skeptical, empirical views expounded by Mill and his predecessors to produce the system of Herbert Spencer (1820-1903). Spencer agrees with Hamilton, Mansel, and Mill in regarding the nature of Reality as a mystery which it is beyond the power of the human mind to grasp. Try as they may, both metaphysics and religion come up against a stone wall which they cannot penetrate, and only trip themselves up in logical contradictions and absurdities when they kick at its impenetrability.

But Spencer will have none of Hamilton's assertion that God must exist despite our powerlessness to comprehend him, or of Mansel's doctrine of "negative knowledge" of him. Nor can he admit, with Mill, that God is not inconceivable, but simply a being whose existence may not be inferred from the evidence at hand. The implication of the relativity of all human knowledge to perceived phenomena, which are themselves presented only in relation to one another, is that the absolute and the unconditioned must be, in the nature of things, forever *unknowable*. We may, indeed, trust our instinctive feeling that behind phenomena there is a Reality in which they are grounded. But what that Reality is we shall never *know*. To be sure, we may call the Unknowable the *cause* of the phenomenal world, and describe it as a *power*, but such terms can be at the best no more than vague approximations.

Philosophy and Science Concerned Only with Sensible Experience. The province of knowledge, and therefore of science and sound philosophy, is the field of phenomena. The methods of philosophy and science are the same. Both seek by observation and induction to reach general ideas descriptive of the behavior of the sensible world, and thus to achieve unified visions of the totality of the field in which they work. The difference between science and philosophy is only one of scope. The sciences observe and infer within limited and sharply defined ranges of research. Philosophy seeks to unify the concepts arrived at by the special sciences and to weave them into one consistent whole, in which everything that happens in the universe shall have its part and receive its final explanation.

If we collate the findings of the special sciences we shall discover certain general principles which may be regarded as ultimate, relatively, at least, to the phenomenal universe, and which may therefore be called *philosophical*. These least common denominators are such things as the sense of a Reality behind phenomena, the general division of experience into subjective and objective aspects, and the co-existence, sequence, impenetrability, and shifting nature of experience out of which the notions of space, time, matter, motion, and force arise. To these we may add ideas like the conservation of energy, the indestructibility of matter, the law of least action, the impossibility of action at a distance, and the like, which may be deduced from the fundamental concepts.

Evolution and Dissolution. Finally, all those first principles about which the sciences cling are themselves threaded on an ultimate law of development which runs through all things whatsoever. Everything, without exception, that occurs in the universe is part of a process in which matter is being either integrated or disintegrated, and in which motion is being concurrently either dissipated or absorbed. Everywhere things are being built out of simpler, scattered, and incoherent elements into more complicated, more unified, and more coherent and stable structures, and everywhere such motion and energy as are not lost in the process undergo a parallel transformation into more diversified and complicated forms. This is *evolution*. Eventually the limit of the integration of matter and the diversification of motion is reached. Then the reverse process of *dissolution* sets in. The complex, integrated structures are broken down, and energy is lost and becomes unavailable.

This formula, laid down in his *First Principles* (1862), Spencer proceeded to apply generally. Two years later he had covered with it all biological phenomena. In the *Principles of Biology* he finds that organisms are more complex integrations of matter than inorganic substances, and that life is a process in which the inner structure of a body is being continually adapted to an environment. Bodies that effect a continuous adjustment of internal relations to external relations *live*. Given this capacity, the entire process of biological evolution can be explained and can be shown to be simply an example of the ultimate cosmic law.

The next thing for Spencer was to bring psychology within the fold. The first edition of his *Principles of Psychology* had been published in 1855, and followed fairly closely the Associationist doctrine. Now, *mind* had to be worked into the general evolutionary scheme. The processes by which ideas were built out of simple sense data lent themselves readily to the formula of integration and increasing complexity. And in general the parallelism of conscious states with physiological conditions and changes in the nervous system, brought the stream of consciousness within the general formula of evolution.

This, however, is not to say that consciousness can be reduced to terms of physical energy. It cannot. It *accompanies* physical energy under certain conditions. That is all we can say about it. But, Spencer reminds us, mind is itself a phenomenon. It gives us no more clue to the nature of the Real than does the material world.

Sociology. From 1876 till the time of his death, Spencer was busied with the publication of his *Principles of Sociology* and his *Principles of Ethics* in which he sought to reduce all social and moral phenomena to the general law of evolution. History, he tells us, displays a process of integration of families into tribes, tribes into settled communities, and of communities into larger and larger political units—a process which is accompanied by a progressive diversification and dissipation of human activity. Complete integration and diversification would be reached in a wholly stable and orderly social organization in which all individuals were free to express themselves and to live their own lives without interfering with the self-expression and individualism of their neighbors. Individuals, then, have a *right* to self-preservation, to liberty, and to happiness. Since, however, the welfare of the individual is bound up with the welfare of the group, and the community cannot be harmed without injury to the individual, individual rights are rightly abridged when the safety of the group is threatened and can be maintained only by their abridgement. But when the peril to the community is removed these rights are automatically restored.

Spencer goes on to argue at length against socialism and paternalism on the ground that they interfere with individual self-expression. The state, he holds, exists for the sake of the individual, not the individual for the sake of the state. The sole business of the state is to keep the peace, by preventing, through the exercise of its police power, its citizens from coming into internal conflict with one another, and by protecting them from attack from without. For the state to interfere further with personal freedom is to trespass upon individual rights. Moreover, whatever impedes unduly the exercise of individual liberty and the pursuit of individual happiness recoils upon the general welfare, which after all is nothing but individual welfare. That government is best which governs least—understanding by "least" the minimum of control consistent with peace and order.

Ethics. Underlying Spencer's social theory are his views on ethics. Ethics is the science of human conduct. Some conduct we call good, other bad. In other words, we attribute *moral* value to it. But what is *moral* conduct, and on what basis do we distinguish between *right* and *wrong?* To answer these questions we must first study the nature of conduct in general. Conduct, properly speaking, is activity aimed at ends. It involves an adaptation of behavior to ideals. Right conduct lies in adjustment, wrong conduct in maladjustment, to the ends and ideals at which human beings naturally aim.

But what are the ends and ideals in question? Spencer's reply is hedonistic and utilitarian. The desired, desirable and ideal life is one attended by the greatest amount of agreeable feeling. Good deeds, then, will be acts whose intention is to secure the maximum of agreeable feeling for the greatest number. Evil deeds will be acts which detract from it.

To be sure, ethical principles like these assume that a surplus of agreeable over disagreeable feeling is attainable by living beings. Otherwise, we shall be obliged to admit that life is not worth living, and that a morality whose aim is to ensure life and liberty and the pursuit of happiness is topsy-turvy and deluded. But the assumption that life is worth living is, Spencer feels, a reasonable supposition. Most people, at any rate, seem to find it so, seeing how they cling to it, and how impossible it is to uproot the instincts leading to its maintenance and preservation.

When Spencer approaches the problem of applying his moral principles to the complexity of the human situation, his hedonism and utilitarianism depart somewhat from standard. The moral ideal at which we directly aim is not based upon a "hedonistic calculus," in which pleasures are consciously estimated, and weighed, and compared. It lies rather in establishing a social condition, expressed in the general, evolutionary terms of adaptation to environment, in which the maximum amount of agreeable feeling will automatically occur. Since pleasure is a sign of adjustment, the more adjusted life is to its surroundings the more pleasurable and the happier it will be. Among human beings the environment is largely social, and it is the inter-

adaptation of individuals that counts most in securing the widest diffusion and the greatest amount of pleasurable feeling.

The Evolution of Morality and Religion. The history of ethics reveals, Spencer thinks, a continuous progress, in accordance with the
general law of evolution, towards a state of complete interadaptation
of individual interests in which all conflicts will be resolved, and
selfishness and unselfishness will be indistinguishable. Little by little
the sense of solidarity develops, and restrictions which were at first
external and compulsory become internal and spontaneous. Conscience
appears as a curb upon behavior, but even the conflict between conscience and impulse will be eventually overcome in spontaneous interadaptation and right doing.

As it is, hostility of attitude, he maintains, is giving way to friendship. War is yielding to amicable settlement of differences. Justice,
whose basis lies in the law of nature that all living things shall reap
what they have sown, has become humanized by a recognition that all
may sow as they will, provided they do not interfere with one another.
Upon this principle of equal liberty of self-expression for all individuals, with its corollary that none may do as he would not be done
by, is erected the whole edifice of human rights and laws. When each
individual succeeds in making it the rule by which he lives, the moral
ideal will be attained.

In his sociological discussions Spencer gives considerable space to
the evolution of religion. Its root lies in dreams and visions, in which
the dead reappear and thus impress the primitive mind with a belief
in their continued existence. In this way ancestor worship arises, which
Spencer regards as the seed from which all religion has grown. Indeed, primitive religion is essentially fear of the dead. From it prayer
and placation naturally spring, and are quickly given ceremonial and
institutional form.

It needs but another step to people the whole natural world with
ghosts or spirits akin to ourselves and to crystallize in fixed and elaborate rites man's attempts at appeasing their wrath and enlisting their
help. The fear of the living, which is the beginning of social and moral
organization, is now supplemented and reinforced by the fear of the
dead, which provides supernatural sanctions for ethical conduct. So,
step by step, religion *evolves* and in its evolution follows the general
law of increasing integration and complexity, accompanied by diversification of activity.

Bain. Almost contemporary with Spencer was Alexander Bain (1818-
1903). Bain was a psychologist of the familiar Associationist type, with

an added interest in the interconnections of psychology and physiology. He also shared the distrust of metaphysics evinced by Mill and Spencer, and was uncompromising in his assertion that it is impossible to know that an external world even exists, let alone what it is like. All the primary qualities, as Locke called them, such as shape, extension, solidity, and the like are nothing but internal sensations, given by the eye and the muscles. So, too, the self is nothing but a bundle of sensations, including those of pleasure and pain, desire, motivation, and the movements in which motives are discharged into behavior and by which desires are satisfied. Since all behavior is motivated and all motives have their grounds, there can be no such thing as freedom. But lack of freedom does not undermine the bases of morality. Morality arises out of the compulsion exercised upon us by social organization. Experience teaches us that rebellion against this compulsion brings social disapproval and even punishment. Experience shows what kind of behavior gets us into trouble, and the association of such conduct with disagreeable social consequences is the basis of the moral sense of right and wrong, and becomes articulate in the still, small voice of conscience.

II. GERMAN NATURALISM

Trendelenburg. The empirical, skeptical, positivistic and naturalistic way of thinking which we have now been following so long, was not, however, by any means confined to Great Britain. It had also a strong foothold in Germany and in France. Just at the turn of the half-century Friedrich Adolf Trendelenburg (1802-1872), though by no means carried away by the naturalistic current, was sufficiently influenced by it to maintain that motion was the least common denominator of both thought and being and therefore the universal principle which it is the business of metaphysics to seek. From motion he tried to deduce space, time, and the categories, all of which he regarded as forms both of thought and objective existence.

He denied, however, that motion is purely mechanical in its behavior. It is, he says, purposive, and it contains within itself a principle of design and self-determination, which expresses itself in organic life and comes to self-fulfillment in conscious selves. This teleological principle points to the existence of an ideal which is forever realizing itself in the world-process. A governing ideal presupposes, in its turn, intelligence and will as the origin of motion. Hence intelligence and will afford the best description we can give of the nature of the absolute and the unconditioned, which some of our categories probably do not fit at all and of which none can give a really satisfactory concept.

German Materialism. Although Trendelenburg had only one foot in the empirical, naturalistic, materialistic current, there were others who were in it head over heels. Among these were J. Moleschott (1822-1873), L. Büchner (1824-1899) and E. Haeckel (1834-1919). All three were agreed that consciousness could be reduced to terms of matter and physical energy, and that the universe was a mechanism, which, being self-existent and self-maintaining, stood in no need of a God to explain its existence and provide it with a purpose. Freedom and immortality naturally shared the fate of God. Büchner's book, *Force and Matter,* published in 1855, had great popularity, as did also Haeckel's *Riddle of the Universe,* which appeared in 1899.

The extreme materialistic position was, however, avoided by W. Ostwald (1853-1932), who tried to reduce both mind and matter to interconvertible forms of energy. It was also looked upon askance by F. A. Lange (1828-1875) and E. Mach (1838-1916).

III. LANGE

Reality Unknowable. Lange, a professor at Zurich and Marburg, started from the Kantian position that the categories of the understanding alone give to experience the forms under which we must think about things, if we are to call them *true.* All valid knowledge is therefore necessarily scientific in character. But the categories into which experience must be cast before it is regarded as intelligible necessarily turn it into a deterministic system subjected to the category of causation and to mathematical formulae. In short, we must *think* in terms of mechanism if we are to think at all. The only possible scientific and *intelligible* view of the world is the mechanical view.

But the mechanical concept, though the only *true* description of the phenomenal world, cannot be extended beyond human experience to things-in-themselves. Of the nature of Reality we can know nothing. We have no more right or reason to assert that it is matter than we have to proclaim that it is mind. Nay more, the mechanical concept and the categories upon which it rests cannot be regarded as *a priori* in the full Kantian sense of the word. They are not imposed upon experience from the outside. They are products and parts of the very nature to which they give a mechanical form, and are developed in accordance with the same laws as govern all her provinces. It is from the point of view of the materialistic and mechanical hypothesis as a philosophic method rather than a metaphysical description of Reality that Lange's well-known *History of Materialism* is written.

The Possibility of "Value Judgments." However, Lange believes, like Francis Bacon, that, although knowledge buckles and bows the mind to a naturalistic interpretation of the world, the imagination erects and ennobles it by submitting the shows of things to its desires. We create in our fancy ideal orders of various sorts, not necessarily mechanistic, which have esthetic, moral and religious *values* for us. We cannot know whether anything corresponding to them has real and concrete existence, and therefore we cannot compare them in point of their *truth*. But we can compare them in point of their relative goodness and ideality. We cannot, for example, argue that one religion is truer than another, but we may argue that it is more satisfactory. We may, in other words, substitute value judgments for truth judgments in dealing with the ideal world.

IV. MACH

The Theory of "Neutral Entities." The same Neo-Kantian caution as restrained Lange, also kept Mach from joining the out-and-out materialists in their splashings. First, professor of physics at Prague, and then of philosophy at Vienna, he adopted an attitude towards the nature and limitations of philosophy not unlike that of Mill and Spencer. However, he did not feel that an investigation of the problem of the relation of mental to physical phenomena involved an excursion beyond the phenomenal world and the limits of sound scientific thinking.

In dealing with the question he went off on a new tack and tried to steer a neutral course between the materialists and the idealists, which would avoid the difficulties that arise when we attempt to reduce either mental to physical, or physical to mental, phenomena. The complex of experienced qualities—colors, sounds, tastes, smells, tactual and muscular sensations, etc., which make up the sensible world and which we persist in regarding as both inside us and outside us, is, he said, neither internal nor external. The content of experience is neither subjective nor objective. It is simply *there,* or, as he called it, *neutral.*

The contents of experience, however, exhibit interdependence and what we call causality. Certain phenomena do not appear except in connection with others. One condition of the presence of sensations is that they shall be in relation to special groups of phenomena which we call the sense organs of organic bodies. Another condition is that they shall be linked up with other phenomena, which are not organic. Take, for example, color. It depends both upon the eye and upon light. When the eye closes, or when night falls, it disappears. It is inside me in its relations to my eye, outside me in its relations to reflected light. If the light is shining and my eye is open, it is both a mental and a physical fact at the same time, split by its dual reference into a kind of double vision of itself. In so far as it is hooked to the phenomena we call a nervous system, it appears to be an inner, subjective picture of itself. In so far as it is hooked to the phenomena we call light it appears to be an outer, objective replica of itself.

The Various Conditions of Phenomena. Here is the secret of the distinction we make between the mental and the physical. In so far as any sensible quality is viewed in relation to the sense organs upon which it is partly dependent, we call it *subjective*. In so far as it is supported by other, inorganic complexes of qualities, we call it *objective*. When a nervous system ceases to be attached through its sense organs to other entities, it becomes unconscious, as when we fall asleep, and the phenomena with which it was in contact, and which composed its conscious content, lose their *subjective, mental* character. But, as long as they remain hooked up with entities other than the nervous system in question, they remain *objective, physical* facts, retaining, in spite of not being perceived, all the characteristics they present to the waking organism. If, however, they lose touch not only with the organism but with the rest of their context, they lose their objective, physical status and become purely *neutral*.

For instance, color along with all other entities ceases to be present to the sleeping nervous system, and therefore ceases to be a *mental* phenomenon. When night falls, color also ceases to be a *physical* phenomenon, since its *physical* character is dependent upon the presence of light just as its *mental* character is dependent upon the presence of a nervous system. But the disappearance of color from an object, when light fails, leaves all the other characteristics of the object *objectively* there, since they are no more affected by the sun's setting than by the organism's falling asleep.

But when a nervous system dreams, what happens? In spite of its having seemingly lost all contact through its sense organs with objective entities, other entities are nevertheless *present* to it, and appear to it as real and vivid and objective as its waking experiences. Mach replies that in dreams the organism really is in touch with other phenomena. But, when an entity is dreamt about, it remains hooked up *only* to the nervous system, and is floating free of all attachments to all other entities. It is in contact *only* with the sleeping organism, and like that organism has lost contact with surrounding phenomena, and its behavior is influenced solely by the nervous system to which alone it is anchored. Hence, having slipped its objective, physical moorings, it has become a purely *subjective, mental* entity, whereas waking experience, being anchored both to the nervous system and to other phenomena, is *both* objective and subjective, physical and mental.

From this point of view we have no business to speak of phenomena being inside or outside the *mind,* or, for that matter, of an entity called the mind at all. So-called mind and consciousness are simply one way in which phenomena group themselves; so-called physical bodies are another. But phenomena are not thereby divided into two sorts that cannot be interchanged—soul and body, mind and matter, mental presentation and external objects. On the contrary, one and the same phenomenon may pass from one grouping to another, may be now a dream, now a perception of external reality, now an unperceived physical fact. This theory of neutral entities, in themselves neither physical nor mental, but on occasions either or both, has played and still is playing an important part in present philosophical speculations.

Objective References of Scientific Concepts. But Mach had also brought to a head a new difficulty. Heretofore skepticism had found its victims in metaphysical concepts, like God, substance, the soul, a material substratum and the like. Such entities transcended experience. They were not phenomena. Therefore, if knowledge could not be extended beyond phenomena, it was impossible to know whether or not such entities existed.

Mach and his successors, however, extended positivism and skepticism from metaphysics to the results of science itself. The scientist, it proved, was as great a sinner as the philosopher in laying claim to a knowledge that transcended phenomenal experience. The entities he posited as underlying phenomena were not experienced. They transcended experience as completely as did the entities conceived by the theologians and metaphysicians. Nevertheless, the scientists talked of them as if they were not only things-in-themselves existing behind phenomena, but as if their nature could be validly inferred from experience and made the object of accurate scientific knowledge.

But how could either the philosopher or the scientist maintain with any consistency that it was invalid to argue beyond experience to the existence of God, but valid to argue beyond it to the existence of the atom or the ether? Or how could he assert that, although it was impossible for us to know whether any objective reality corresponding to the concept of the soul existed, it was quite possible to test the concept of the ether vortex or the magnetic field, and know whether it represented a real object?

V. THE DOCTRINE OF THE RELATIVITY OF SCIENCE

Scientific Acceptance of Mach's View. Posed with these questions, a large and important group of philosophers and philosophically minded scientists admitted at once that metaphysics and science were in the same boat, so far as their knowledge of unexperienced entities was concerned. In Germany, Emil Dubois Reymond (1818-1895) and his brother Paul, G. R. Kirchhoff (1824-1887), H. Herz (1857-1894) and Avenarius (1843-1896), all announced more or less decisively the impossibility of extending scientific knowledge beyond phenomena and attributing objective reality to the fundamental entities conceived by science. Besides the great field of phenomena as yet unexplained but not necessarily inexplicable, there are certain scientific problems—like the real nature and cause of matter, motion, force, and consciousness —that are essentially insoluble. Confronted with them, Emil Dubois Reymond proclaimed, we must resign ourselves to the fact that we can never know the answer and must remain forever ignorant.

In England this view was shared by James Clerk-Maxwell (1831-1879), W. K. Clifford (1845-1879), and Karl Pearson (1857-1936). In France its great champion was Henri Poincaré (1857-1912). According to him, the concepts that science regards as fundamental not only have no validity outside experience but no sole and absolute and permanent authority within it. We regard the axioms of Euclid or certain principles of mechanics as if they were the laws of the Medes and the Persians. But a space of four or more dimensions is perfectly conceivable and perfectly consistent. Non-Euclidean geometries can be worked out in which the axioms of Euclid do not hold. So, too, other mechanical principles can be conceived.

The "Truth" of a Scientific Concept. A number, then, of alternative mathematical and physical systems are conceivable and workable. Certain ones, however, prove simpler and more convenient than others in dealing with observed phenomena. For instance—to choose an example of our own—it is still possible to work all celestial phenomena into the old geocentric, Ptolemaic astronomy and make the earth the fixed center about which everything else revolves. But the complications and inconveniences of so doing are enormous, and the resultant astronomy is unwieldy beyond description; whereas everything becomes comparatively simple and easy to follow and handle in the Copernican system.

Still, it is impossible to assert as an absolute fact either that the earth and the other planets go round the sun or that the sun and the planets go round the earth. It depends entirely upon where we take our stand, and we take our stand wherever we see things in the simplest and most convenient perspective. It is quite possible that as time goes on, new astronomical data will make the heliocentric astronomy as unwieldy as the observations of Kepler and Galileo and Copernicus made the geocentric system. In that case, we shall shift our point of reference to whatever point in space the new discoveries indicate as best adapted to give us the easiest and least confusing view of sidereal behavior.

The same holds of the concepts of the other sciences. They cannot, according to Mach, pretend to an ultimate and final character. They are merely the most suitable way at the moment of viewing the data at present available. New data may come along that they no longer fit, and then our concepts will be altered to suit the new situation.

VI. THE "CONCEPTUAL SHORTHAND" THEORY

But, if the ultimate concepts of science do not refer to anything existing beyond phenomena, and, even within the field of phenomena, are wholly relative to present observation, what is their status? What do they refer to? How do they arise? What is their exact relation to phenomena? The answer to such queries involved what we might call a philosophy of science. This was now forthcoming. Concepts like the atom, the ether, the magnetic field and even the axioms of mathematics are all of one feather with the Ptolemaic or the Copernican systems in astronomy. They are, as Pearson expressed it in his *Grammar of Science,* a *conceptual shorthand* for taking down in brief and succinct form the longhand writing of sensible experience. They stand for nothing, refer to nothing, mean nothing but sensible phenomena; just as the shorthand symbols stand for nothing, refer to nothing, and mean nothing but the longhand words and sentences. Without them we could never condense experience into workable, scientific shape, just as without shorthand the stenographer could never do anything but copy, or set down, in all its original voluminous, tedious, and unmanageable length, the long-winded screeds or dictations of her employer.

Again, just as there are different systems of shorthand, so there may be different systems of mathematics, geometry, physics, etc. Which scientific theory is best will be decided by the same rules as determine which system of shorthand is best. In the one case as in the other, the preferable system is that which does the neatest, briefest, simplest job of expressing in the least possible number of symbols the greatest number of longhand data. But no matter how ultimate and perfect a system of scientific stenography may be, its symbols and concepts never stand for anything but those data. They do not read anything additional into them or in any way enlarge or alter their sense. They do not introduce, so to speak, new words, different from those visibly and audibly spoken. They simply record in condensed form what phenomena say and write.

The same will be the case with all metaphysical and theological concepts. They will be merely useful *methods* of summarizing the value experiences, esthetic, moral, religious and the like, given in concrete individual feelings. They will not be intimations of an "objective" reality supporting these values. God, for example, is no more "existent" than the atom, but is simply a convenient shorthand method of condensing and simplifying the phenomena we call religious experience. And the varieties of religious experience will require each its most suitable shorthand, to condense and simplify its peculiarities and differences.

A large body of scientists and philosophers have accepted the Mach-Pearson view of the limitations of science and the shorthand characters of scientific concepts. But there are also many others who reject it.

VII. SCIENTIFIC ADVANCES

Physics, Chemistry and Mathematics. Meantime, the conceptual shorthand of science was changing with extraordinary rapidity. Helmholtz, William Thomson (Lord Kelvin), Clerk-Maxwell, and many others were developing the undulatory theory of light and of radiant energy, the concepts of the conservation of energy and of entropy, and the vortex theory of matter. The same hands carried on the researches into the nature of electricity made earlier in the century by Volta and Ampère and Faraday. The fields of electrical and magnetic phenomena were consolidated, and a common formula connecting them with the phenomena of radiant energy was sought. Physical chemistry was initiated by Kohlrausch and Arrhenius, and its growth has had great influence upon present theories regarding the constitution of matter.

Already, too, doubts inspired by the failure of the Michelson-Morley and Morley-Miller attempts to detect the motion of the earth relatively to the ether had suggested to Fitzgerald and Lorentz that the dimensions of a body might depend upon its velocity, and that it might become shorter in the line of its direction, proportionately to its speed. The way for Einstein's theory of relativity was thus opened.

These advances in the physical sciences were accompanied and facilitated by new discoveries in the field of mathematics. The concepts of real and irrational and imaginary numbers were developed by Cantor, Dedekind and Weierstrass. Lobachewsky and Gauss, inspired by the unverifiable character of Euclid's postulate with regard to parallel lines, worked out successfully new geometries based upon other postulates. In this they were followed by Riemann and Helmholtz, who suggested that *observed* physical space lends itself as readily under certain conditions to a non-Euclidean as to an Euclidean interpretation. Both sorts of geometry are merely two different conceptual shorthands, of which the Euclidean has generally proved the more convenient.

The Biological Sciences and Psychology. In biology similar strides were made. The cellular theory of living matter, which dated back to the beginning of the century, was now firmly established and threw new light upon the nature of reproduction and organic growth. The mechanism of heredity was investigated, and the dispute over the inheritance of acquired characteristics arose. Weissmann denied such inheritance, and maintained that hereditary characteristics are carried by the germ-plasm which perpetuates itself in the individual organism, immune to any modifications of the organism from without, and is handed on to the next generation untouched by such alterations. The chromosomes were also discovered, and their role as carriers of inherited traits was studied. Weissmann's theory of the germ-plasm has, however, been criticized by Delage and Driesch, and the question of heredity, and generally of reproduction, is still wide open. The subject was further scrutinized by Galton and Pearson and Mendel by means of statistics, and Mendel's law of dominant and recessive characteristics was formulated.

At the same time evidence supporting the theory of evolution continued to pour in from fresh discoveries in the fields of embryology, physiology, and paleontology. The struggle for existence and the survival of the fittest were extended from the conflicts between life and its natural environment, between different species, and between different individuals within the same species, to a possible conflict within the individual organism between its different tissues and organs. Also, it was suggested by De Vries that evolution, instead of being continuous and gradual, is at times subjected to sudden mutations productive of freaks, or sports, some of which may prove fit candidates for survival.

Mental phenomena as well as biological were brought within the sphere of evolution, and thus the question of man's spiritual as well as biological solidarity with all other living beings was raised. Wallace tried to save the soul from humble origins, by supposing a special infusion into man alone of a new spiritual element. Similar devices are used by those who, while accepting evolution so far as the human body is concerned, balk at extending it to human consciousness.

Psychology also forged ahead under Fechner (1801-1887) and Wundt (1832-1920), who continued Weber's efforts to subject the phenomena of consciousness to exact scientific measurement, and sought particularly to bring them into connection with the fields of physiology and physics. They tried to expand Weber's law and to make it more precise. And they founded their researches upon extended experimentation under laboratory conditions. To them we owe the emergence of psycho-physics and the development in psychological form of the idea of psycho-physical parallelism.

VIII. DURKHEIM

The "Collective Mind." Sociology, too, underwent an elaborate development at the hands of Emile Durkheim (1858-1917), who endeavored to establish the priority of group consciousness over individual self-consciousness. The group, he tells us, has a mind of its own, more primitive, more fundamental, and more compelling than indi·vidual minds. Out of this deeper crowd-consciousness, detached, individual people, with particular minds of their own, eventually develop as independent selves. But the collective mind is still dominant in them, and reasserts itself on all occasions. Since the collective mind is deeper and earlier than individual minds, it cannot be described as a mere *collection* of particular centers of consciousness, or as a result of their interaction. It has a real existence of its own, over and apart from aggregates of particular selves.

A social group, then, is an organism, not a mechanism, a whole that determines the relations and activities of its parts, not a whole built up out of its parts and determined by them to be what it is. We feel this determination at every instant of our lives in the power exercised over us by the intangible forces of social habits, conventions, and duties. A society controls every one of its members, and from that control there is no escape.

Standards of Truth. A society, being a psychological organism, has to be treated as a fundamental unit irreducible to terms of the individuals composing it. In its collective mind, not in individual minds, we find the basis of social values. Morality is one expression of group consciousness. What we believe to be good and right does not emanate from a transcendental conscience or categorical imperative directed from on high. Neither is it the result of a deliberate computation of the greatest happiness of the greatest number, or the outcome of an enlightened estimation of his own self-interest on the part of the individual. It is a manifestation of the collective mind and will controlling individual ideals and behavior. Since the collective mind of one group may differ from that of another, different communities do not necessarily subscribe to the same moral standards. Since the collective mind is an evolving, changing thing, the ethical point of view of one and the same community may alter with time and circumstance.

Even what we shall regard as reasonable and true is determined by group consciousness, not by categories and "inner lights" cast from behind the scenes. "Pure" reasoning and scientific thinking are not detached and impersonal. They may discount, indeed, the bias and provinciality of individual preferences, but they cannot escape the prejudices and predilections of the crowd. They reflect its idiosyncrasies at a given time and place. Truth, in a word, is no more absolute and universal than are right and wrong. There is no such thing as one self-identical truth, forever the same everywhere for all persons. Truth is a social product which varies in different epochs and localities. Like goodness and beauty, it is based neither upon a supernatural reality, nor upon the mind of the individual, but upon the herd consciousness of the community to which it appeals.

By realizing the social origin of all values, intellectual as well as moral and esthetic, we free them both from theological and metaphysical implications and from Protagorean individualism, and convert them into a subject matter that can be scientifically studied and analyzed. We can understand why one system of truth, philosophical, scientific, or theological, has truth value for one group of people, and why a directly opposite system is equally true to another. So, too, we can see how what is considered absolutely right here and now may be considered absolutely wrong across the street or tomorrow. When thus studied and understood, clashes of metaphysical systems, theological beliefs, scientific hypotheses, moral ideals, and canons of taste no longer distress us. We perceive the necessity and the basis of their relativity.

Chapter XXIV

BRITISH AND CONTINENTAL IDEALISM

I. GREEN

Attack on Utilitarianism and Empiricism. Powerful, however, as was the influence of science upon philosophy, post-Kantian idealism continued to cling to its positions and to extend its battle-lines. With the immediate German reactions to Hegel's teachings we have already dealt. Also, we have noted how Coleridge in England fought for idealism, and particularly for Schelling, and attacked contemporary British empiricism and skepticism. But the idealistic movement did not cross the channel in force till 1865, when Stirling published his *Secret of Hegel*. Once landed on British shores, it rallied to its banner enthusiastic and powerful adherents, among whom T. H. Green (1836-1882) and F. H. Bradley (1846-1924) are the most noteworthy. Green waged war on both the ethical and the metaphysical fronts. On the one hand, in his *Prolegomena to Ethics* ne attacked Utilitarianism, which at the time was being ably defended by Henry Sidgwick (1838-1900). On the other, he opened fire against the positivism and naturalism of which Spencer was for the moment the chief exponent. His heavy artillery he found in the argument that the ways in which we think things and the relations we establish between the elements of experience cannot be derived from sense perceptions, Hume and Mill and the other empiricists to the contrary notwithstanding. To connect sense data with one another and to weave relations between them, there must be something over and above experience—to wit, a rational self.

The Nature of the Absolute. So far Green went with Kant. But, like the German idealists, he could not see eye to eye with him so far as things-in-themselves were concerned. Sense-experience is not impressed upon the self from without, it is produced from within. To attribute it to an external source would be to *relate* it to that source. But relations always connect sense data, and cannot be conceived as subsisting between experience and something that is not experienced.

However, an experience that means a larger reality of which we are a part cannot be created by a finite self. Moreover, the relations by which any one finite experience is hooked together have attachments beyond that experience. They apparently link us to other selves, to an external world, and to a history in which we are incidents. Therefore, the ultimate source of experience and of the relations it exhibits must be an absolute mind of which our finite minds are parts. The content of this mind is the whole world-process. But the Absolute transcends the whole system of relations and the whole content of its cosmic experience, just as we, individually, feel that we transcend our sensations and the various ways in which we connect them.

Not only, however, do the implications of our thinking betray our transcendent character. So does our will. Our consciousness is shot through and through with desire, as well as with sense perceptions. Just as the rational organization of sensible experience reveals to us a self behind it, so the organization of our desires implies a self of which we are conscious, and whose *will* we do, in all our dealings with them. In other words, we have an ideal, which we regard as our true self. Realization of this self is desirable and good. Its realization, as contrasted with the fulfillment of particular and incidental desires, is the *moral* good.

The will of the higher self to subject all desires to its realization is God revealing himself within us as a moral being, just as our relating and connecting of experience is the manifestation of his rational and intelligible character. Truth, goodness, and beauty are all upheld and given an absolute character by an absolute, infinite, and eternal mind.

II. BRADLEY

Concepts and Entities. Bradley launches a wider offensive, not only against the naturalistic-positivistic-empirical point of view, but upon idealisms of the Berkeleian type and all forms of pluralism generally. Take, he says, a so-called thing. It is *there,* and it is something. That is, it has qualities. We treat it, moreover, as if it were more than its qualities, and call it a substance. But *what* is this substance? Is it identical with its qualities? In that case, we are denying the distinction between subject and predicate and rendering sentences and discourse mere meaningless babble. There is no sense in *predicating* qualities *of* a substance if it is nothing but these qualities. Is the substance then different from its qualities? In that case, when you say, for instance, that the apple is red you are stating that it is what it is not. Do you say that the distinction of the apple from its redness lies in its being also round? But roundness is not redness. Therefore, if the apple is an apple by virtue of being round as well as red, it is an apple by virtue of combining two logically contradictory qualities, red with not-red, and round with not-round.

Suppose, however, the empiricists reaffirm the position that a thing is nothing but the sum of its qualities, and reinforce their contention by maintaining that so-called substance, in which qualities inhere, is to be regarded as merely the togetherness of those qualities. It is a *relation* between them. Very well. But we must then admit that the subject or substance "apple" is spread out over all the qualities which are together. It is equally there in its redness, its hardness, and its roundness. In that case, however, when we say the apple is round and hard, what do we mean by "apple"? Plainly we are restricting the apple to its redness, which we have no business to do, and turning "round" and "hard" into qualities of that redness—which also we have no business to do.

In the same way we can box the compass, by saying the apple is red and round—in which case we locate the "apple" in its hardness and assert its hardness to be red and round; or by saying the apple is hard and red—in which case we identify it with its roundness and regard red and hard as adjectives predicated of that roundness. All the qualities that are together may be treated both as subjects and predicates, and the relation between them remains as a third something, different from any of the qualities it relates. But, if it is different from them, how can it relate them without itself being related to them by something which is neither it nor they?

The Nature of Reality. Along with the apple we have to dismiss everything empirical, scientific, metaphysical, and theological that has anything to do with *things, qualities,* and *relations.* Matter and motion, space and time, cause and effect, selves and egos, Gods and Absolutes, are all riddled by the same contradictions. There does remain, however, a kind of core which is positive. Reality must be free from contradictions. It must somehow include all appearances. It must somehow make sense of all their nonsense, since otherwise it would lose its own consistency. To make sense of them it must itself be a single system in which everything is related. It must be an experience of some sort, since being is meaningless apart from being perceived. It must be one experience, not many, since a plurality of centers of consciousness would put it back in the apple-cart.

Furthermore, our own experience is immediate, and a multiplicity in unity. It is an overcoming of incompleteness—though by methods that involve *us* in self-contradictions. Our knowledge is a thing of degrees. The moral life lifts us from the lower to the higher. Esthetic experience suggests reaches of beauty beyond what is immediately felt. The manner, then, in which the Absolute Experience includes us and our experiences, would seem to be one in which the higher contains the lower, the greater degree the smaller, the more real the less real. Appearance is a manifestation in a lesser and varying degree of something truer than we can know, more beautiful than we can feel, better than we can be. Our "higher" experiences lie nearer to the heart of things, and them we might know and feel again, were we perfect even as God is perfect. The "lower" being more partial, must receive in the Absolute a supplementation such that, felt as God feels them, we should not know them.

III. BOSANQUET

The Nature of the Real. Along with Bradley and Green we should mention Edward Caird (1835-1908), for many years Master of Balliol College, Oxford, and deal briefly with Bernard Bosanquet (1848-1923). Bosanquet rebounded from Bradley, to whom, however, he was heavily indebted, towards Hegel. Human reason, whose pretensions Bradley had so badly riddled, was rehabilitated at his hands and presented as the most complete intimation we possess of the nature of the Real. The Absolute is a systematic, rational totality of all experience, the whole nature of which is expressed in every part, and in whose wholeness every part finds its explanation and its completion. Moreover, since only that which is wholly self-existent, self-sustaining, self-defining, and self-fulfilled is truly *individual,* the Absolute is not only an individual but the only real individual. It is, Bosanquet says, a *concrete universal.* All other so-called individuals, be they particular sense data, or particular selves, are not wholly concrete and wholly existent.

Such being the case, all empirical philosophies, which base themselves upon sense-experience as an ultimate fact, turn things topsyturvy and transubstantiate the accidental into the essential. So, too, do systems which regard the existence of the *self* as the bed-rock of philosophic thinking. The human "ego" or personality is not truly concrete, individual, and real. It is an incidental and partial manifestation of the Absolute Individual, upon which it is wholly dependent for its existence and character.

To this dependence and incompleteness every department of human life bears witness. The self is bound up with the experiences we call the body and external nature, and appears to be an incident in this larger whole. Sensation, thought, moral action, esthetic contemplation —all reach beyond themselves to a reality, a truth, a goodness, and a beauty, which complete and perfect them. Man is a social being, whose individuality is forever merging itself in larger social interests and organizations. In short, our whole nature points to the conclusion that our destiny can be fulfilled and our peace can be attained only by foregoing our self-centeredness and our belief in the importance of our private and individual personalities. Salvation lies in throwing ourselves into the spirit and meaning of the cosmic drama, and in humbly accepting and losing ourselves in the incidental roles its plot assigns to us.

The Dramatic Character of the World-Process. We use the terms "role," "drama" and "plot" literally, not metaphorically. For to Bosanquet all the world's a stage, and the whole world-process is a play. The unity and harmony of the Absolute is conceived by him dramatically as well as logically. The Absolute is an artist—a playwright, actor, stage-manager, scene-painter and scene-shifter rolled into one—who himself takes all the parts and recites all the lines in the universal drama he has imagined.

It is interesting to note the appearance of this new variation of the idealistic interpretation of Reality in terms of a personal career. Fichte had thought of the world-process as the career of a fundamentally *moral* being; Hegel, as the career of a fundamentally *rational* being. Now Bosanquet turns to the *artist* for his inspiration and sees in the Absolute a being guided by as great an interest in *dramatic* effect as in logical coherence. This concept of God as essentially an artist has become popular in contemporary idealistic thought.

Since suffering, and sin, and misfortune present no more difficulties to the logician, and are, if anything, rather better "copy" for the playwright, than virtue and happiness, the problem of evil is easily solved by Bosanquet. Sin and suffering do not outrage an absolute reason, and they add to the satisfaction of an absolute artist. They have a tremendous dramatic value and add enormously to the richness of the cosmic drama. The sublimity and compelling quality of great tragedy and the "catharsis" of the emotions it brings about testify to that. But the greatest tragic drama a human being ever conceived sinks into insignificance beside the tragic grandeur and magnificence of the world-process.

Part of the human individual's conquest of his own sin and suffering lies in his ability to take this dramatic interest in his own fate, and to judge it, not by what it brings him, but by what it contributes to the dramatic perfection of the whole. But man is not only a dramatic critic, he is an actor. As an actor, the humblest individual has a chance to play the role of the tragic hero, who, by battling with misfortune, enduring pain, and expiating sin, triumphs over them even though they slay him. It is within the power of every man to acquit himself nobly in this role. In so doing he is conscious of enhancing and sharing the glory of the Absolute—and that consciousness is his beatific vision.

IV. MC TAGGART

Perhaps the most original system in British Idealism was that of J. M. E. McTaggart (1866-1925), who constructed on a foundation of Hegelian dialectic a closely reasoned theory, distinguished from the usual forms of idealistic metaphysics by its atheism as well as its extreme pluralism. Nothing exists for McTaggart except spirits, or persons. The Absolute is the total system of persons or selves as these are related to one another in a community of love. Moreover, every self is an autonomous being, uncreated, unchangeable, and indestructible.

Other British idealists who resisted the onslaughts of Realism and Pragmatism during the early decades of the present century were Andrew Seth Pringle-Pattison (1856-1931) and the personalistic psychologist James Ward (1843-1925).

V. RAVAISSON AND BOUTROUX

Ravaisson. The idealistic movement in France did not spring so directly, as it did in England, from the German post-Kantians. It returned rather to Kant himself, so far as its origins were Kantian, and it also drew largely upon native sources provided by Cousin and by Maine de Biran, who in their turn were inspired by the Cartesian tradition and by Condillac. The two most prominent exponents of the native way of thinking were Felix Ravaisson-Mollien (1813-1900) and Emile Boutroux (1845-1922).

Ravaisson was largely inspired by Maine de Biran who had infused Condillac's cold statue's passive reception of sensation with a consciousness of effort and will. But the statue was not yet fully awakened. Ravaisson aroused it completely, and turned its will into desire. Consciousness, Ravaisson maintained, was essentially love, yearning, aspiration. It envisaged an ideal and was forever striving to realize an end.

It was active, not passive; creative, not recipient. In consciousness regarded as a creative activity, Ravaisson thought he had found the
inmost nature of the Real. Everything is the product of spirit. The
physical world is only spirit present in lower degree.

As to the relation of the lower degrees of spirit to its complete
manifestation in God, Ravaisson is vague. Apparently he wanted to
reduce all differences of spirit to differences of degree and, at the same
time, avoid pantheism. But he makes one suggestion destined to be
of great significance. He regards the habits we form as a kind of
hardening of our spiritual arteries, and looks upon the completely
uniform behavior achieved by the physical universe as senile and
fossilized volition. This suggestion we shall presently find taken up
and expanded by Bergson.

Boutroux. Boutroux found further confirmation of Ravaisson's doctrine of creative spirit in his studies of *necessity*. These led him to
the conclusion that we had no right to speak of logical and mathematical necessity, or *a priori* necessary categories of thought, or even of
necessary causal relations between events. On the contrary everything
was contingent. It might happen or be otherwise. The postulates of
mathematics and the principles of science *might* be different from what
they are. There *might* be other sense data and other ways of arranging
them. Events *might* occur in other sequences and connections. There
was then no predetermining reason why we should have the postulates,
principles, categories, causal connections, etc., that we did. We just
happened to have them. That was all.

From the contingency underlying all these seeming necessities,
Boutroux did not, however, argue the existence of a real, irrational
factor of *chance* in the universe. He turned rather at this point to
Ravaisson and argued that contingency in nature pointed to the existence of a free yet orderly Spirit, whose activities were governed by final
causes and tended to become fixed habits.

VI. RENOUVIER

Reality is Experience. The philosophies of Charles Renouvier (1815-
1903) and of Jules Lachelier (1832-1918) were indebted not only to
the French tradition but largely to Kant. Renouvier starts on a frankly
empirical basis. Knowledge deals with phenomena, and is limited to
phenomena. Like Mach, however, he suggests that phenomena are
neutral and that their subjective and objective connotations are a matter of the perspective in which we view them. Still, the feeling that

experience is *of* something is part and parcel of experience itself. But we must not therefore suppose that this reference is to objects existing outside and independent of experience. It is rather an affirmation on the part of experience that it itself is the ultimate reality. Experience is *of* itself. Phenomena represent themselves. The activity of consciousness is a fusing of the active and the passive participles. Each item of experience is in itself a representing of something, and a something that is represented. Like the traditional serpent it lies coiled with its tail in its mouth.

All reality, then, is within experience. To discover its nature we have only to consult the ways in which experience behaves and the aspects it presents. Such inspection reveals nine general characteristics. Experience exhibits *relations*. It is spread out in *space* and drawn out in *time* into parts and moments that can be *numbered*. It is a complex of *qualities*. It *changes*. Its changes occur in *causal sequences*. It is a *personal* experience, and it aims at *ends*.

Truth and the Sum Total of Human Interests. As they stand, however, these categories do not fall together into a harmonious whole. They are rather like the bits of a picture-puzzle scattered on the table. In order to put them together, and thus discover what the picture is really like, experience must apply in the first place the principle of contradiction, which shows the pieces that simply will not go together, and which pieces may go together. Which pieces *do* go together or, at least, do *most probably* go together is a matter of *belief*. Belief is an experience of the willing, desiring aspects of experience. It rests upon the *force* with which certain representations and combinations of representations thrust themselves forward in consciousness, and upon the general *satisfaction* with which their presence suffuses experience as a whole. We *believe* in that which engages and satisfies the whole man.

What we call *certainty* and *truth* goes with *belief*. We regard as the *truest* picture of Reality the picture that appeals with the least amount of self-contradiction and the greatest all-round force to the greatest number of human interests. We must not, indeed, allow our desires and emotions to run away with our reason. But, on the other hand, we must not allow the intellect to suppress our moral and religious needs.

What picture of the Real do we piece together when we judge its truth by the satisfaction it gives the whole man? We get a Reality that is ethical, moral personalities that are free and immortal, and a personal, finite God. This picture is drawn not from conjecture or by argument, but directly from the features of experience itself. We *experience* moral demands made upon us by the universe and our response to those demands. We *experience* our moral personality. We *experience* free will. We *experience* a personal God. We *experience* our aspiration toward immortality. The force of these representations and the satisfaction they give our total nature are more than sufficient to counterbalance any intellectual difficulties they may present—provided, of course, we deal with them in as rational a manner as we can. Moreover, the intellect can never *prove* that they are illusions.

VII. LACHELIER

Lachelier's system reminds us more of the German idealists. Starting, like them, from Kant, he argues with them that the mind itself produces the experience which it organizes, by means of the categories, into a systematic and intelligible order. Like Hegel, he exalts the part played by reason over that played by the will in creating and manipulating experience, and insists that experience is, first and last, rational in essence. Hence the laws of logic are the laws of being, and our reason, rather than our wishes and our "hunches," is the last court of appeal in deciding what the Real is like.

Lachelier's views were set forth in his *Foundation of Induction,* and an essay on *Psychology and Metaphysics.* He argues there that the mental nature of the Real can be demonstrated both by induction from experience and deduction from the mere existence of thought. Proceeding inductively, an inspection of experience shows two things. It shows in the first place that experiences are only considered real in so far as they are explained and rendered intelligible. We suspect a phenomenon we do not understand. We feel that it must have a place and an explanation in a causal and therefore rational sequence of events. Until we fit it into its place in that order, its presence is disquieting. Experiences, in a word, tend to occur and to hook up with one another in a way *congruous* with the demands of logical thinking. Furthermore, since the so-called external and physical world can be reduced to a manifold of internal sense data, its source and the reason for its rational character must be sought in consciousness, not outside it. But, if the presence of the external world is presence to consciousness, and the objective reality of our experience is synonymous with its being thinkable, then the fact of experience needs a mind to explain both its existence and its nature.

Given the existence of the thinking activity presupposed by sense-experience, we can deduce *a priori* the necessity of a phenomenal world from the blank *being* of such an activity. To be is to be something.

To be something is to have an intelligible form and structure, which Lachelier finds in space, time, causation, matter, and the mechanical principles, generally, in terms of which we arrive at a scientific *understanding* of events and things. To attain complete being, however, thought must enact these principles in a concrete, individual, pictorial manner and thus create a world of sights, sounds, and other sensible representations exhibited in space, time, and causal connections. But the story is not yet finished. The mind must *reflect* upon its handiwork, and, in the act of reflecting, must become conscious of itself and of its own free, spontaneous and creative activity. These three stages are the bases, respectively, of science, art and religion.

In the mind of God all truth is enshrined. Finite selves are created by God, and attain to perfect knowledge and freedom in so far as they unite their minds and submit their wills to his.

VIII. FOUILLÉE AND GUYAU

As we leave France, we may mention in passing Alfred Fouillée (1838-1912) and his pupil Jean Guyau (1854-1888). To Fouillée both idealism and materialism give equally one-sided and unsatisfactory pictures of the nature of Reality. It is impossible to reduce the physical world to terms of subjective experience pure and simple. It is equally impossible to reduce consciousness to terms of matter in motion. Nevertheless, the dualistic opposition of the one to the other must be overcome. Fouillée effects this by supposing that the mental and the physical are both manifestations of one and the same impulse to self-expression, which is the essence both of thinking and physical activity. To these self-realizing entities he gives the name of *idea-forces*. In our own conscious activities we get an immediate experience of their nature. We are entitled to read processes of a similar sort into the external world, and to regard the Real as composed of evolving impulses towards self-fulfillment.[1]

Guyau attempted a similar reconciliation of the mental and the physical. But he found his least common denominator in a drive towards synthesis and unity. This, in his opinion, constitutes the core of Reality. It is manifest through all physical activity, all vital processes, and all psychological phenomena, and reaches its most complete expression in morality and social institutions.[2]

---

[1] Fouillée's chief work is *L'évolutionnisme des idées-forces*.

[2] For Guyau cf. *Esquisse d'une morale sans obligation ni sanction* (1885); *L'irréligion de l'avenir* (1887).

The Absolute an Integration of all Human Interests. In Italy, the philosopher-statesman Benedetto Croce (1866-1952) was a vigorous advocate of Absolute Idealism through the first half of the present century. A major influence in every department of culture from esthetics to history, Croce made an equally important impact on Italian life and politics by his defense of liberalism through the Fascist period and his participation in establishing the republic following the Second World War. His philosophy of freedom was expressed in his lifelong civic activities.

For Croce, Reality is spirit, developing, as with Hegel, through a conflict of opposites. But the logical and the dialectical movement is not, as it was for Hegel, both the root and the flower of the world-process. The root is the living, moving, developing character of spirit, not an absolute Idea that finds in process and progress a means to self-expression. And rationality is only one of several independent ways in which the spirit flowers. The Absolute is as multiform and rich an experience as these ways indicate. Its various aspects do not have to be reduced to one another. We do not have to seek a logical basis for artistic creation or for natural phenomena. The different activities of consciousness are self-justifying. The bond that unites them lies in their common subservience to the single and undivided life of the spirit.

Within that life, however, we may make the time-worn distinction between contemplation and action. We perceive and know, and we also do. The perceptive side of experience presents itself in intuition on the one hand and intellectual knowledge on the other. Intuition is more than the mere occurrence of sense data. It includes memory and imagination and feeling, and the spread-out, drawn-out spatial and temporal way in which they are given. It includes, in short, all that is *immediate* and concrete. And it gives us, for all its primitive and innocent nature, a true knowledge of the nature of the Real.

Intuition, Knowledge and Volition. Moreover, intuition is not a passive content of impressions and images. It is warm, glowing, gesticulatory, meaningful, a sort of talking to one's self preparatory to expressing one's self in articulate speech.

This articulate speech comes with concepts, and consists in passing judgments on things. Some judgments and concepts sum up and mean universal aspects of all experience under which every individual item falls. These are the instruments of logical and philosophic thinking. Others, such as scientific concepts, deal with restricted fields of experience, and constitute an artificial shorthand for dealing with their data in the most concise and convenient manner. Their function, unlike that of universal concepts, is not to see into the nature of experience, but to enable us to manipulate it in accordance with our practical needs. They are, so to speak, an extension of the will into the realm of knowledge, and a coloring of knowledge by desire.

The active, willing side of experience, by which we adapt experience to our own ends, instead of adapting ourselves to its nature as we do in our intuitional and intellectual activities, has also its two sides. We set before ourselves ends whose attainment is either useful to the individual or beneficial to all alike. In pursuing aims of the first sort we are actuated by expedient, "economic" motives. In hitching our wagons to the star of what is desirable and good in itself for all men under all circumstances, we are acting from moral considerations.

The Four Expressions of the Absolute Spirit. Thus we reach the four great expressions of the spirit, the *beauty* that irradiates intuition, the *truth* that enlightens the intellect, the *utility* that gives value to "economic" activity, and the *goodness* that suffuses moral conduct. These four forms of the Absolute Life interpenetrate one another in such wise that everything that exists has a value of some sort, which cannot be annulled by its lack of value in other fields. What is immoral or untrue or useless may yet be beautiful. The evil and the ugly may have their practical uses, or be intelligible. For that matter, nothing can be entirely bereft of every value, since nothing valueless can exist.

In this way we are able to reach a synthesis and reconciliation of the opposites that divide each field into two camps. Where the Absolute is unable to make the unintelligible intelligible, it may yet make it beautiful. It may bring intelligibility into ugliness even when it cannot bring beauty out of it. It may harness evil to practical use though it cannot convert it into moral good. The Absolute always in some way triumphs over every negation, since what is negative to one aspect of its existence is positive to another.

Upon the significance of history Croce is no less insistent than Hegel. The Absolute is a history—a history that combines activity with knowledge. The Absolute enacts the world-process and at the same time reflects upon it. So, too, in human history we have both events and a knowledge and evaluation of them. The events themselves were human deeds guided by the knowledge of those who performed them. We, if we would also know what has *really* happened, must enter into the past and see it through the eyes of those to whom it was present, and at the same time re-assess it in the light of the future to which it led and in which we now live. The historian both enacts his subject from moment to moment and yet surveys it as a whole—as the Absolute does. He is in his own right the profoundest of philosophers. History needs no philosophy of history, since history is itself a philosophy of the nature of the Real.

X. GENTILE

The Absolute a Unity-in-Plurality. Giovanni Gentile (1875-1944) reverts towards a more orthodox Absolute Idealism. To be sure, he contends, Reality is measured in terms of experience here and now. And in all times and places experience is being remolded by our so-called reflection upon it, which is an activity not of simple reception but of creative reconstruction. At the same time, the emphasis is shifted from the individualistic and multiple aspects of consciousness, which Croce had stressed, back to its unity and singleness.

We human beings are all vehicles for the self-expression of a single absolute thinker. This thinker has an absolute Idea, changeless and eternal, of which the world-process is the expression, and by which our individual remodelings of experience are motivated. Again, the Absolute Idea, as in Hegel, is a plurality in unity. It is creative and created, subject and object, all at the same time, just as the self-conscious self is at once an "I" and a "me." It goes out from itself and creates, as an artist paints his picture or as a poet writes his epic or his drama. Indeed, art is the human expression of its outpouring. In religious experience and aspiration it presents itself to itself as the object, the *me,* of which it is conscious. Finally, in philosophical systems it seeks to unite the "I" and the "me," itself as subject and itself as object, in a vision of its self-creative and self-conscious nature. But once again, the world-process as it occurs is Reality. History is the self-revelation of the nature of the Absolute to itself. Therefore history is the vision of truth. That is, it is philosophy.

Chapter XXV

GERMAN PHILOSOPHY SINCE 1850

I. FECHNER

The scene now shifts to Germany once more. We begin with G. T. Fechner (1801-1887), whom we have already mentioned as a psychologist and as a notable contributor to psycho-physics. Though he spent the greater part of his life in the first half of the nineteenth century, his more important works appeared after 1850. His philosophic speculations led him to the conclusion that the physical and the psychical are one. The physical is the form in which one conscious entity appears to other conscious entities. My body is how I look to Tom. Dick and Harry. My consciousness is what I am in and for myself. This is true of all organic bodies, in which the whole determines and dominates the arrangement of activities of the parts. All such bodies conceal souls.

However, since Fechner extends the organic analogy to the whole universe, nothing exists that is not part of an animated body. Not only do plants and animals possess souls, but the earth and the stars possess them too. Finally, there is a universal world-soul whose body is the total physical universe. This cosmic soul, of which all other souls are parts, is God, in whom all things live and move and have their being.

II. LOTZE

Nature of Truth and Reality. Far more important as a philosopher, and, indeed, the most distinguished metaphysician of the German group we are now considering, is Rudolf Lotze (1807-1881). Self-confessedly he owed much to Leibnitz and to Weisse, who, it will be remembered, attacked Hegelianism because of its overemphasis of the head and insufficient recognition of the claims of the heart. But Lotze had also studied medicine and physiology and physics, and was convinced of the importance to philosophy of scientific method and scientific theory. He saw, however, that scientific knowledge was itself an act of faith in the existence of truth and in the power of reason to attain it. We could not *prove* this faith, any more than we could prove the validity of our conviction that phenomena exist, or of our belief that values like beauty and goodness are real.

Lotze was disposed then to take a wide and eclectic point of view, and to give to esthetic, moral and religious values equal weight with the results of science in determining his system. Indeed, he felt that the business of philosophy was to show how the demands of phenomenal fact, of logical truth, and of moral value can all be met by one and the same world.

The Concept of Mechanism. The demands of science are met by the concept of mechanism. For that matter, the universe must be thought of as running like a machine, if its behavior is to be rendered intelligible. The mind cannot exempt anything from the operation of mechanical principles, not even itself, if it is to *understand* things. Biology and psychology are mechanical sciences, like physics. Vital and conscious processes can only be explained by the same laws as govern the movements of the stars and chemical reactions. Upon these points Lotze cannot insist too strongly.

Can we reconcile the mechanical hypothesis, which we must accept if the world is to be made intelligible, with the experienced facts of the case, and with our esthetic, moral, and religious demands? In answering affirmatively the first part of the question Lotze ranges himself with the idealists. The concept of mechanism does not commit us to materialism. It may be a description of how *consciousness* behaves. Our spatial, temporal, and causal ways of viewing phenomena are forms of sensible intuition. So-called matter and force are not even that. They can be shown to be secondary ideas derived from the forms of space, time, and causality. We have no need to go outside the mind to discover the stuff of which the mechanism is made. Reality is mental in its essence.

At the same time, Lotze disagrees with the absolute idealists. Reality is not to be thought of as an absolute thinker, of which finite selves are aspects. It is rather to be conceived after the organic analogy, as an interconnected whole composed of semi-independent centers of consciousness who bear much the same relation to the whole as the cells of which it is composed bear to the total organism. The mechanical hypothesis is the form under which these centers of consciousness make their relations to one another intelligible to themselves.

When we say this, we are also suggesting how the mechanical nature of the world can be reconciled with the values it displays. When we look at a machine, we find ourselves asking not only on what principles, but *for what purpose,* it runs. What, we say, is it *designed* to do? This question we may also properly ask of the mechanical constitution of Reality. For what purpose and to what end do the centers of consciousness of which the Real is composed interpret their experience mechanically, and make it appear as bodies moving in space, changing in time, and affecting one another according to the law of causation?

To answer this question, let me examine my own experience. I find in it my body, which is peculiarly *mine* and which I feel from *within.* At the same time my body is also outside me and belongs to an external world of bodies in general, to whose laws it, like them, is subjected. My body, then, mediates between me and the outer world. Furthermore, without my body and my sense organs and their causal, mechanical connections with the phenomena I call other bodies, I could not get into contact with other centers of consciousness. May we not say, therefore, that the *purpose* of the mechanical construction of my body and of its being geared up mechanically with other bodies is to permit my soul to interact with other souls, through the mechanical enmeshing of my body with their bodies? May we not further say that the purpose of the universal mechanism is precisely to enable all the conscious components of the Real to interact and intercommunicate with one another?

Interaction Between the Centers of Consciousness. The problem of whether and how the mind can interact with the body, does not trouble Lotze. The method by which interaction of any sort is effected, is, he thinks, a mystery. But how the soul acts on the physical organism, and how the physical organism influences the soul is no more mysterious than how one body acts upon another. All interaction is of one piece. In certain circumstances certain things do happen, whether it be one billiard ball set in motion by another, or the sensation of light "caused" by the impact of light upon the retina, or a muscular movement initiated by a conscious volition.

Having thus established the fact that the "monads" have windows through which messages to and from an outer world do go in and out, we can better understand the nature of construction of experience. The qualities we perceive outside us are relations with other conscious centers, established by means of our sense organs. The spread out, spatial character of experience, and its tendency to coagulate into separate clumps of qualities incapable of' interpenetration and of occupying the same space, indicate the plurality and the individuality of the separate "souls" which constitute the Real. The messages we re ceive suggest, moreover, that in addition to finite centers there is a universal mind which creates and preserves them and supports the external universe as a whole. Individual souls are somehow both parts of this cosmic mind, and at the same time separate persons.

We can now understand the relation of mechanism to the world of values. Mechanism not only satisfies our demand for an intelligible world, but, as the means of interaction and intercommunication between souls, it is a means to realizing moral and social and religious values, which rest upon a *fellowship* between the conscious centers of which Reality is composed. Its *purpose* is to make goodness, and beauty, and communion with God operative among men.

Self-Consciousness not Dependent upon a Plurality of Selves. Lotze attacks Fichte's view that there can be no ego without a non-ego, and that therefore interaction and intercommunication are necessary to personal self-consciousness. On the contrary, he maintains, self-consciousness is bound up with the mere fact of existence in and for itself, whether or not the thing so existing has a non-ego with which to contrast itself. Hence he concludes that the personality of God is not dependent upon and conditioned by interaction with other persons and limitation by them. In other words, an infinite person may exist— and this God is. For us, however, who are finite and whose personalities are incomplete modes of the divine life, the contrast and the give and take between the ego and the non-ego are indispensable conditions of approximating in our lives the goodness, the beauty, and the peace which are God's completely and always.

III. VON HARTMANN

Will and Idea Two Aspects of an Underlying Reality. Besides Lotze, there are two other men who figure prominently in the German thought of the period. They are Eduard von Hartmann (1842-1906), and Friedrich Nietzsche (1844-1900). Von Hartmann sided with Schopenhauer against Hegel in maintaining that the Real is not essentially rational, and that the world is Will as well as Idea. But he could not swallow Schopenhauer's assertion that the world is more Will than it is Idea, not to speak of Will's being the essence of Reality. The intellect, he claimed, cannot be subordinated to the Will and be a mere instrument evolved by it as a means to self-assertion and self-fulfillment. For it is inconceivable that a Reality whose essence is blind and aimless striving should assume a fixed and intelligible form like Schopenhauer's world of Platonic Ideas. The most that Will can do is to will to exist, but how it shall exist and what form it shall assume are determined by what Hegel called the Idea. Will and Idea, then, are distinct principles, neither of which is derived from or subordinate to the other.

At the same time, these two principles are not grounded in two separate metaphysical entities. They are rather—and here von Hartmann agrees with Schelling—two separate aspects of one and the same reality, which is neither Will nor Idea, nor any form of consciousness whatsoever, but is best described as *The Unconscious*. Out of the Unconscious, consciousness arises as an irrational, purposeless Will that there shall be a universe, accompanied by a coherent, logically framed representation or Idea of what the universe shall be.

The process of creation is a process of becoming more and more conscious, in which the Idea is made clearer and clearer, and its opposition to the irrational Will appears more and more pronounced. First, the Unconscious displays itself as a material, mechanical world in space and time. Then, in the course of the evolution of the earth, it prepares the way for living manifestations of itself, and so eventually for man, in whom it becomes self-conscious.

Since all activities spring from the Unconscious, all the aspects and levels of existence are bound together by mysterious bonds of sympathy which explain much that would otherwise be inexplicable. For example, in the Unconscious are rooted our instincts, our impulses, our desires, the interactions of mind and body, and the social ties that bind men to one another. Out of it spring the affinities of love, the thrill of beauty, and the ecstasies of mystical religious experience.

Existence an Evil. In becoming self-conscious, the Unconscious is made aware of the situation it has created—a situation that von Hartmann, like Schopenhauer, regards as essentially evil. Willing and existing are infected with pain and frustration and discontent. Hence it would have been far better if the Unconscious had remained unconscious, and had never become, as Will and Idea, a world. However, if it had to become a world, it could not have become a better one. It has built up a structure calculated to secure the least possible amount of evil and the greatest possible amount of good. It has provided the anesthetic of grateful sleep for all conscious beings. It has drugged youth with carefree enthusiasms. It snuffs out old age with kindly death. It condemns nothing it creates to the curse of endless existence, but relieves of its being everything that is born, and so shifts the otherwise intolerable burden of existence from generation to generation, and sees to it that each new individual upon whom the burden is imposed shall bear it but a little while.

Redemption an Acceptance of the Will to Exist. Nor is the Unconscious cut off from final and complete redemption. But it cannot be saved, as Schopenhauer suggested, by the practice of private asceticism and denial of the will. We must rather run our race and fight the good fight, shoulder to shoulder with all else that lives and suffers. We must not only renounce vain hopes, like the hope of happiness here or hereafter for the individual or the race; we must spread the Gospel of renunciation. We must immerse ourselves in the suffering that the Unconscious has brought upon itself by willing to exist. We must not seek the partial escapes from it or the mystical denial of it advocated by Schopenhauer. We must rather accept it, and welcome it, and experience it to the fullest. For suffering is the instrument of our salvation and of the salvation of the whole world. Through it the Unconscious expiates the crime of willing to exist, and only by accepting our share of that suffering can we contribute our due to the oblation made by the Unconscious for the sin of having become a world. When that oblation shall be complete and acceptable, then there will be no more consciousness, no more pain, no more existence, and the Unconscious will enter once more into the bliss of Nirvana, in which it dwelt before the foundation of the world.

IV. NIETZSCHE

Life. Friedrich Nietzsche (1844-1900), one of the most influential of the post-Hegelian German philosophers, was born in Rocken in Thuringia. He was descended on both sides from a long series of theologians, and was brought up accordingly. But temperamentally he was a born rebel, emotional, passionate and visionary. He was also at heart a poet, and in much of his work, which is, so to speak, sung rather than spoken, it is hard sometimes to hear the words for the music.

During his student days at the Universities of Bonn and Leipzig he broke completely with the family tradition. Through his studies in philology, which was at that time his chief interest, he fell under the spell of ancient Greece, whose way of life at its best struck him as vastly superior to that developed in Europe under the influence of Christianity. And a chance purchase of *The World as Will and Idea* made Schopenhauer thenceforth a dominant factor in his thinking and clinched his dissatisfaction with western civilization.

While still at Leipzig, he was offered a professorship in philology at the University of Basel, in Switzerland, which he occupied until increasing ill-health and decreasing interest in philology induced his resignation. The greater part of his philosophical work was done under adverse conditions due to his invalidism. In 1888 he went completely to pieces, and the next year had to be confined in an insane asylum, where he died ten years later.

Disgust with Western Civilization. Nietzsche's revolt against the modern world was perhaps intensified by the contemporary spectacle. The social and economic revolution through which Germany was passing in his youth, in a transition from feudalism and agriculture to industrialism and the attendant rise to power of a *nouveau-riche* middle class, was in Nietzsche's opinion no advance. If anything, the bourgeois theory and practice of life only illustrated all the more clearly the defects that from the beginning had vitiated western Christian ideals, standards, and institutions, and the philosophies that reflected and rationalized them.

From the beginning, he felt, the Germans had been the arch-enemies of Graeco-Roman culture and the instigators of western decadence. They had overrun and destroyed the Roman Empire; they had nullified, with Luther and Protestantism, the revival of classical culture and ideals by the Renaissance; they had warred ceaselessly against those countries in which the Graeco-Roman tradition still lingered. And now the Germans, as a result of the revolution, were unifying themselves under Bismarck for the purpose of extirpating the last traces of European culture inherited from the Greeks, and were completing the wreck of western civilization which they had already almost ruined with Christianity.

To liberate, before it was too late, humanity from the degradation to which the Christian, and especially the Teutonic Christian, outlook upon and way of life had reduced it, a radical spiritual, and for that matter moral and social, revolution was necessary and imperative. The nature of this revolution was indicated by Schopenhauer, revised and corrected in the light of a revised and improved version of the Darwinian theory of evolution.

The Will for Power. Nietzsche agreed with Schopenhauer and other German idealists in rejecting the notion of a material substratum, or things-in-themselves underlying phenomena, and with Schopenhauer in relegating intellect and reason to a position subordinate to that of the will. The essence of the universe is, as Schopenhauer had pointed out, a *Will to Live*. But, in Nietzsche's opinion, Schopenhauer had left the will to live a vague concept empty of concrete content. Further analysis, he felt, shows that the will to live is an exhibition and *utilization* of power. To be is to be *strong,* strong enough to exist, to survive, to assert, to affirm, to hold one's own and go one's way. The will to live is, then, essentially a *Will for Power*.

The *Will to Live* Schopenhauer had depicted as assuming many forms blindly at war with one another. The *Will for Power* Nietzsche broke up into a multiplicity of "quantities of force" in a state of conflict and tension with one another. They are the "substance" of the Real, and the tensions they set up constitute its structure. However, the play of forces, of which the universe is composed, is not mechanical. Nothing is absolutely predetermined. Nor are the "quantities of power" everlasting. They arise out of nothing, they are constantly threatened by disintegration and annihilation, and they return to nothing when their course has been run. But while they exist they are essentially efforts to resist annihilation, to defy their mortality, and to postpone the lapse into the nothingness that perpetually threatens and eventually engulfs them, but out of which new "quantities of power" are ceaselessly creating themselves *ex nihilo* to replace them.

Organic and Conscious Power. In their unremitting exertion of the power to exist, they utilize one another as a means to self-perpetuation and self-development, and the stronger dominate the weaker and reinforce their own strength from them. When these "quantities of power" attain the status of organisms, they evolve all sorts of devices of offense and defense with which to cling to life, and we have the Darwinian struggle for existence and survival of the fittest.

At length, organisms become aware of themselves and develop conscious will and intelligence, the most advanced existent forms of which, so far as we know, are human minds. But just as there are no material substances or metaphysical things-in-themselves underlying the stream of physical phenomena, so there is no immaterial entity or thing-in-itself, such as a soul, or self, or ego, underlying the stream of consciousness. Each individual "self," like each individual object, is a complex of forces and tensions, of strivings to exist, interrelated with the all-embracing complex of "quantities of power" that constitutes the universe.

The Eternal Return. Time is infinite, but the possible diversifications of the Will for Power, and their possible combinations and tensions are finite in number. Hence in the course of infinite time the same tensions and combinations are bound to recur, bringing with them the same world, and repeating its history. But since nothing is pre-determined and the recurrence is not mechanical, the repetition is not stereotyped and the return may be spiral, not cyclical. You and I, for example, will be raised from the dead an infinite number of times, and will live our lives over and over again. We shall be born in each new existence on the level on which we died in the preceding one. But we are free always to make the life we have inherited stronger and richer than when we lived it last, and to carry this added strength and richness over into our next reappearance, and thus be reborn on a higher level and repeat our lives on a grander scale. It behooves us, then, to live our lives here and now as we would wish to re-live them, refraining from all that we would not care to repeat and pursuing and exploiting the experiences we would.

Criticism of Schopenhauer's Pessimism. Since each human being is a manifestation of the Will for Power, his fundamental necessity and desire is to be strong—is to exert and exhibit power in all its manifestations. The profoundest and highest exhibition of power lies in the moral and spiritual strength to accept without evasion or complaint Reality for what it is, and to face human destiny without flinching and make the best of human life as it has to be lived.

At this point Nietzsche broke completely with both Schopenhauer and Darwin. While accepting the harshness of the universe and the tragic character of human life from which Schopenhauer drew such pessimistic conclusions regarding the character of existence and the way of human salvation, he could not agree that existence was therefore essentially evil, and that salvation lay in escaping from it and in destroying the Will to Live.

The weak man, indeed, may quail from and vituperate both the actual world and actual human nature, and seek salvation by backing away from and severing his connections with the one, and inhibiting, suppressing, and mortifying in himself the other. And he may concoct in his religion and philosophy excuses for this attitude and behavior. But for the *strong* man life in spite of, or rather because of, its essentially brutal, terrible, and tragic character, is essentially good. The strong man *loves* the possession of body, passions and parts, the exertion of power, the rough and tumble character of existence, and the struggle and the conflict it imposes upon him; even the blood, the sweat, and the tears that are the elixir of conscious existence. The affirmation of the Will to Live, then, which Schopenhauer had regarded as the root of all evil, is really the source of all good, and its negation, which Schopenhauer had proclaimed to be the way of redemption, was in reality the damnation of man.

Criticism of Darwin. Darwin had erred in much the same way. For him the struggle for existence was a struggle on the part of the organism to adapt itself, or in other words to *submit*, to its environment, and the fittest to survive were those whose adjustment was the most complete, or whose submission was the most abject. For Nietzsche the struggle for existence is a struggle *against* the environment, a struggle to adjust not the organism to the exigencies of its surroundings but those surroundings to the exigencies of the organism. And the fittest to survive are those who are *strong* enough to cope with the environment and submit it to their desires and needs. For that matter, survival is not an automatic affair as Darwin had imagined it to be. Nothing survives that does not actively *want* to survive, and the fittest are those in whom the Will to Live is most powerful.

Escapes from Reality in Dreams and Illusions. In its human manifestations the Will for Power expresses itself in two contrasting ways. It fulfills itself most profoundly and completely in passion, emotion, deep and exuberant feeling, action, and a fighting spirit. But man is a spectator as well as an actor, an intellect as well as a will, a poet and a dreamer as well as a warrior. He yearns for peace and tranquillity in a world better, more beautiful, more orderly and more rational than the actual world. So it is that he dreams dreams and sees visions in which he *pretends* that existence is not what it is, and thus in his imagination humanizes the inhumanity of the universe.

It is in these dreams that the weak and the over-intellectual take refuge from existence. But their dreams reflect their dislike and their fear of the turbulence and harshness of the actual world. They are opiates that the weak concoct for the express purpose of drugging themselves with a peace of mind ignobly bought by a surrender of the Will for Power and by a retreat from Reality. Moreover, the weak *substitute* the dream world for real existence. They deceive themselves into believing on the one hand that their falsifications of the world as it is represent its true essence, on the other, that those aspects of the universe which their weakness impels them to falsify are neither final nor profound.

The illusions and self-deceptions of the strong, on the contrary, reflect an affirmation of the Will for Power and an exultation in the actual world. They falsify life in the interest of strength, not of weakness. They enshrine the ideal of a universe more completely accepted for what it is, without evasion, palliation, or excuse of its inhumanity, and of a mankind endowed with more power to deal with it, to find value in it, and to feel at home in it, as it is. They picture cosmic power at last successfully confronted and defied by human power, and by virtue of that defiance allied with it.

Again, the strong do not *substitute* their illusions for Reality, as do the weak. They do not confuse the real and the ideal. They see that the illusion can cease to be an illusion, and that the ideal can be realized, only through their own efforts and an intensification of their own powers.

Such illusions, so cherished, act as tonics, not sedatives, to human virility. They excite the Will for Power instead of debilitating it. They enrich, rather than impoverish, human experience. They make the strong still stronger. They are weapons of offense, not of defense.

The Secret of Greek Superiority. As Nietzsche developed this train of thought, he found evidence for his conclusions in the various aspects and activities of human life. In the first place it gave him his clue to the superiority of Greek civilization. Admirers of antiquity, like Goethe and Winckelmann, had attributed to the Greek a cool, statuesque, and somewhat vacuous serenity, poise, and sweet reasonableness, supposedly originating in a successful negation of, and detachment from, all that is turbulent and disorderly and savage, both in the universe and man. This, according to Nietzsche was rank nonsense. The greatness of the Greeks was to be found in the fact that they were powerful enough to meet head-on the universe and the fate it had imposed on man, to recognize and contemplate without fear the dangers and horrors of the human situation, and to open their minds and their hearts to existence as it is. They were *strong,* and they did not have to emasculate Reality in order to deal with it.

Dionysus and Apollo. Both Greek religion and Greek drama bore witness to this. The Greeks worshiped both the calm, all-seeing, all-knowing Apollo, the deathless one, of easy and painless life, the serene patron of the Muses; and Dionysus, the leader of the wild Bacchantes in their frenzied dance, the god of intoxication and orgy and ecstasy, of passionate self-surrender and passionate enjoyment—the god, moreover, who not only lived with supreme and divine intensity, but who also suffered and died, as man did, and rose again triumphant, to become once more, by decree of Zeus, the lord and savior of the world.

So, too, Greek drama at its greatest succeeded in investing with a *tragic* value the most terrible examples of what man suffers at God's hands. Thus it turned them into things of *beauty,* which man could contemplate with serenity and esthetic delight, and a quickened sense of his own strength and dignity. In so succeeding, great Greek tragedy harmonized and fused all that Apollo stood for with all that Dionysus exemplified. It took the raw *stuff* of life, turbulent, terrible, and full of suffering, and gave it *form* and *plot* and *magnificence*.

The reason for the decline of Greek civilization was now evident. The Dionysiac and the Apolline, which had been associated and fused at the moment of Greek greatness, became dissociated and opposed to each other, and the Apolline, instead of giving articulation, form, and order to the Dionysiac, supplanted and suppressed it, and thus became an expression of the negation, not the affirmation of the Will for Power. For this, in Nietzsche's opinion, Socrates and his followers were largely responsible. Thanks to their addiction to knowledge and logic, and analysis, and to their undue exaltation of the intellectual over the emotional and volitional activities, everything the Greeks experienced or did became "sicklied o'er with the pale cast of thought." They began to say "nay" rather than "yea" to the tougher and rougher features of life, and to reformulate the universe in terms that sought to excuse such negation.

Art. These considerations suggested to Nietzsche a theory of the nature of art and the function of the artist, in general. Art is generated by and gives expression to two impulses, the Dionysiac and the Apolline. The Dionysiac provides, or should provide, its inspiration and its subject-matter; the Apolline should canalize this inspiration and arrange and articulate this subject-matter in a definite form. The fusion of the two, which takes place in great art, transforms existence from something demanding primarily *action* of some sort into an object of serene and sustained *contemplation,* but without thereby eviscerating it of any of its characteristics, even the most terrible. This transfiguration of existence, including man's lot in the universe, frees it from its "tensions," and by so doing converts it into a source of esthetic satisfaction and a thing of beauty. Hence a work of art makes its subject-matter, however dreadful, congenial to man and a source of human value.

However, the esthetic transfiguration of the terrible aspects of existence can be effected and appreciated only by the *strong,* who in their practical relations to the universe are not frightened or shocked by anything, and who accept everything as an integral part of the world and a natural episode of human life. The weak, who try in every way to hush up everything the existence of which they are too cowardly to admit and face, will denounce as ugly and esthetically revolting all works of art that depict anything they dread or of which they "morally" disapprove.

In investing with beauty *all* existence, no matter how horrible and hostile, man is hurling the greatest of his defiances against the ways of God to man. He is daring to *avenge* himself on nature for her treatment of him. In the work of art he shows her to herself as she is, dreadful in her features and savage in her gestures. But he also shows her the strong man, not panic-stricken by them as she might expect, but deriding them, as it were, by taking pleasure in contemplating them, and pride in that with which she thought to humiliate him.

By thus clothing the naked terror of existence with the value of beauty—a value which without the intervention of the artist it would not possess—great art proves itself the most potent of the illusions by which the strong man lives. It is the supreme test of his strength, and the mightiest instrument of his salvation. For art possesses, like love, the power to invest the beloved with an added and fictitious beauty which erases all defects. Again, both the artist and the lover draw added strength from their infatuation, and their passions and their determination to possess are all the more inflamed by the contemplation of the beauty they have imputed to the object of their love, be that object a mistress or existence as it is.

Furthermore, the artist can deceive others into pretending that the source of his inspiration and subject of his portrayal, whatever it may be, is as beautiful as he himself finds it. By enabling them to see and feel whatever he depicts as he himself sees and feels it, the great artist can make anything he chooses valuable *esthetically* to all those who are strong enough to receive and appreciate his work. Here it is, in its power to make *everything* seem beautiful, however terrible it may be, that the secret of the superiority of art over all other forms of self-deception lies. For neither religion nor philosophy can create in the strong man, at least, the illusion that everything, however terrible, is *good*. Nor can science deceive him into believing that the disorder and turbulence of existence are orderly and rational. In a word, the esthetic value is the only value the strong can impute to the *whole* of existence, and art is the only means man possesses for humanizing in its *entirety* the inhumanity of the universe.

The Decadence of Western Civilization. These meditations upon art were only part and parcel of an all-inclusive reflection upon western Christian civilization, the depths to which it had degraded man, and the means of redeeming him from it. As Nietzsche saw it, to the decadent, Socratic search for *logical reasons* for the spontaneous, non-logical, non-rational, violent play of power that actuates the universe and motivates human conduct—a search that had been responsible for the downfall of Greek culture—Christianity had added a still more decadent demand for *moral justifications* for everything man and the universe did. Subjected to the paralyzing effect of this double scrutiny by the Socratic intellect and the Christian conscience, Reality was completely emasculated, and all the strength, the zest, the guts, and the joy of living were taken out of the western way of life. The Dionysus within us was slain, and the Apollo, now assimilated to the effeminate Jewish-Christian God, provided not only the shape but the inspiration, the sum and the substance of human living.

What was needed, then, to save western civilization, if indeed it was not past redemption, was a resurrection of Dionysus in the human heart, a recovery of virility, a reaffirmation of the Will for Power, and a new fusion of the Dionysiac with the Apolline. A new ethics and a new religion were necessary, expressive of this fusion, which instead of reprobating and inhibiting, would encourage, sublimate, and canalize the great driving forces of human life, would restore the dignity and grandeur of man's destiny in the universe by recognizing the reality and the immensity of its tragedy, and would reinstate man in the complex of conflicting powers and tensions which lie at the heart of all existence.

Such a regeneration of humanity did not seem impossible to Nietzsche. Indeed, he believed that in the field of art its beginnings could be seen in Wagner's defiance of the old Apolline musical forms, in the unprecedented passion, exuberance and magnificence of his music, and in his harking back to the mighty warrior gods and heroes of the pre-Christian Germanic theology for the subject-matter of his operas. For a time Nietzsche much admired Wagner, and this admiration led, while it lasted, to a warm friendship between them.

Moreover, the doctrine of eternal recurrence suggested that a rebirth of Dionysus was at hand. Man, at the moment, could scarcely be imagined as more abject and impotent. The cycle must, then, swing upward, and the Will for Power, denied for the last two thousand years, must reaffirm itself.

The Superman. At this point a new idea which greatly excited him suddenly flashed into Nietzsche's mind. The "eternal return" was spiral, not a closed circle. The universe *evolved*. Hence the reaffirmation of the Will for Power must surpass all former affirmations of itself. It must be accompanied by a further *evolution* of the human race. From the man of the present must spring a being endowed with greater strength than humanity has as yet possessed—a being capable of living more deeply, more richly, more passionately and more exuberantly, of enjoying and suffering more intensely, of hurling more majestic defiances at the universe, and of humanizing and transvaluating its inhumanity with a splendor hitherto unachieved. Man will and must beget the *Superman,* to whom all races will contribute the blood of his body and the latent powers of his soul, and who will be a more splendid instrument of the Will for Power and temple of the risen Dionysus. Indeed, the whole evolution, so far, of the universe and of man may be regarded as a preparation for the advent of this glorious being.

The Superman will rejoice in the possession and exhibition of strength in all its forms, in the brute and terrible natural forces with which he must contend, and in his struggle with them. He will despise every sort of weakness, physical, mental, and moral. But he will not use his power to do violence to and exploit the weak. For physical violence is a weapon only of the weak and a puny weapon at that. The Superman will be magnanimous. His greatness will be greatness of soul. His strength will be an inner strength of character—the strength of daring to live completely and magnificently, shrinking from nothing, undaunted by nothing that can befall him. He will live the part of the hero of a great tragedy, and will transcend the weaklings of today as such a hero transcends the actors in a cheap and vulgar melodrama.

The Abjectness of Christian Ethics. To beget the Superman humanity must forswear all the values it now lives by and create new ones in their place. This transmutation of all values will involve the destruction of the timid, namby-pamby, killjoy Jewish-Christian morality which is the supreme negation of the Will for Power and which for centuries has made humanity spiritually impotent and sterile. Jewish-Christian ethics is a "slave-morality." It is the work of creatures too weak to face life as it is, too fearful of it to fight it, too feeble to enjoy it, and too spiritually flabby to work out their own salvation from its terrors and its dangers. It has preached and praised a mawkish humility, meekness, turning of the other cheek, pity, gentleness and loving kindness. It has denounced pleasure and enjoyment. It has discouraged and persecuted freedom of thought, action, and art, and all sane, robust and liberal living. And to "justify" its pusillanimous precepts and practices it invented the illusions of sin and hell and future rewards and punishments meted out by the hands and according to the standards of a puritanical God.

Such ethics is founded on the *resentment* the weak feel at any exhibition of powers they themselves do not possess. It is designed to keep the strong and the superior under their thumb and at their level. In fact, it was invented by the down-trodden Jews, who had in some way to compensate for their inability to withstand their enemies, and could imagine none better than that of calling them bad names and pretending to themselves that the superior qualities of their conquerors were sinful. This method of justifying weakness by vituperating strength was imported from the Old Testament into the New by Paul, who was afraid of himself, of the natural man, and of the natural world, and therefore had a holy horror of them all.

The Greatness of Christ. Christ, in Nietzsche's opinion, was not responsible for Christianity and its degradation of man. These were the work of Paul. Christ was strong, not a weakling. He neither feared nor resented the actualities of existence, human and cosmic, as did Paul and the Jews. He was one of the great tragic heroes of the human drama, who faced the terror of the universe and the tragedy of human life without rancor, without whining and without cringing, and with a triumphant serenity born of a profound and mystical sense of being at home in, akin to, and at one with all existence as it is.

Indeed, Christ now became for Nietzsche, along with Dionysus and Apollo, a name and a symbol for something eternal and universal. Humanity at its highest had effected in the Greeks a fusion of the Dionysiac with the Apolline, and for that matter with the Socratic. It had felt and examined the Will for Power, and in its thinking, its conduct, and its works of art, it had faced and dealt with the real world. In the Superman this fusion of exuberant emotion and passion with intellectual clarity, ethical sanity, and artistic honesty, would return with the added magnificence of a fusion with the Christlike. The new Dionysus and the Christ would rise together triumphant over the death both had suffered at the hands of Christianity and of Graeco-Roman decadence. There would be a glorious resurrection of the will and the power to live more fully and richly and joyously, and with greater heroism and tragic grandeur than ever man had done. And Christ's profound sense of oneness with the whole universe, a sense that embraced and transcended human good and evil, would become the universal heritage of the new race.

"The Transmutation of all Values" and the "Twilight of the Gods." This double resurrection will be accompanied by a "transmutation of all values" whose portents will shake the world. All the illusions and the self-deceptions by which the weak have been living, and the standards and institutions and ways of life expressive of these pretenses, will be destroyed. And there will be violence and bloodshed fomented by the weak.

In this tremendous "Twilight of the Gods," the Christian god will at last meet his doom. In creating him to sanctify the negation of the Will for Power, man created a god who has slain humanity. Now man must arise and kill the god who killed him. A new god, born of the Will for Power, and cradled and fostered by its enormous forces, conflicts, and tensions, must be brought into being—a god who accepts, as it were, full responsibility for all that is, and reinstates as an integral and accepted part of the Real everything that the Jewish-Christian god was forever denouncing or forgiving, or seeking to wash his hands of.

Beyond Good and Evil. This god, like his creator, the Superman, will be "beyond good and evil." For the Superman will find nowhere in the whole length or breadth of existence—not even in the tragic destiny the universe has allotted him—anything to fear, anything to hate, anything to pity, anything to forgive, anything to vituperate, anything to justify, anything to reject as alien to himself. In him Power conscious of itself will have embraced and been embraced by the entire complex of cosmic Powers, from which it sprang, from which it has been so long estranged, and to which it has at last come home. Of the exultation of the Superman in identifying the whole of himself with the whole of existence as it is, in all its terrible and inhuman majesty, the new god will be the expression and the symbol.

Nietzsche and Fascism. Nietzsche attracted at once a large following. Also, at the present moment he seems to be pre-eminent among the very few philosophers since Schopenhauer whose prestige has increased with the passage of time. It should be noted that the Nazi-Fascist movement publicly adopted him as its official philosopher, and Hitler once made a pious pilgrimage to the house in Weimar where Nietzsche died, and was there solemnly received by his sister. This is not surprising, since certain of Nietzsche's ideas can be so construed as to lend themselves to the support and justification of the Nazi-Fascist ideology. For instance, his glorification of the Will for Power as the sum and substance of the universe; his praise of strength and virility as the essence of human virtue; his insistence upon the decadent character of the Christian cult of meekness and weakness and upon its destructive influence on western culture; his appeal for the regeneration of western society by liberating the Will for Power from its bondage to Christian "slave-morality"; and his prophecy of the coming of the Superman in whom the Will for Power will be given free play—all these can easily be turned into grist for any fascist mill.

But it can also be argued that such grist can be obtained only by lifting passages and portions of Nietzsche's teaching from the general context of his thought, and deliberately ignoring others, and by perverting the general character and trend of his philosophy in the interests of wishful thinking and to suit special needs. For he can be quoted in condemnation of such fundamental Nazi-Fascist tenets as anti-Semitism, the superiority of any one race over all others, and the domination of the individual by the state. Furthermore, Nietzsche's concept of the Will for Power is metaphysical and ethical rather than physical and political in its nature and implications, bound up as it is with his view that the Real is a complex of energies, activities and tensions. And the human manifestation of this Will, in the strength of the strong man here and now and in that of the Superman in times to come, lies in the possession and exercise, not of superior brute force, but of superior moral stamina to face and to embrace exultantly, without fear, prevarication, or hypocrisy, the universe as it is in all its sublime indifference to human good and evil. Of the possession and exercise of this inward Will for Power the great virtues of the strong man and the Superman —generosity and magnanimity—are the outward and visible signs in the realm of human relations.

Nietzsche and Existentialism. It is at least an open question whether the Nazi-Fascist ideology was not discredited rather than supported by Nietzsche's philosophy as a whole. But there is abundant evidence of his influence elsewhere. Oswald Spengler (1880-1936), for instance, whose philosophy of history was in many ways attractive to the Nazis, owed much to Nietzsche in his method and basic insights. It is recent existentialism, however, especially as cultivated by Jaspers and Heidegger, that best perpetuates Nietzsche's influence. Together with the Danish theologian Kierkegaard, Nietzsche was the main foundation for the technical development of the existence philosophy. A separate chapter will be devoted to this movement.

V. THE NEO-KANTIANS

The Marburg School. The mixed philosophical beverages served during the last half of the nineteenth century were bound to displease an old-fashioned palate. Moreover, most of them claimed to be fortified more or less heavily with Kant. The adherents of pure Kantianism— and they were not lacking—could not stomach these new concoctions.

So it is not surprising to find a revolt against them and an advocacy of a return to the triple-sec of the three Critiques, uncut, uncolored, and unflavored, for philosophical refreshment. This movement was headed by Hermann Cohen (1842-1918) and Paul Natorp (1854-1924), both of whom held chairs of philosophy at the University of Marburg, and it was directed especially against the innovations of their colleague, Lange. Its followers were known as the "Marburg School."

But the old wine did not keep well in the new bottles. It lost the "body" given it by the thing-in-itself, the sparkle of metaphysical speculation, and the bouquet of God, freedom, and immortality. It became dry and critical and somewhat flat. It was Kant, to be sure, but Kant with the metaphysics and the things-in-themselves left out. Philosophy became a comment upon the processes of rational thinking, of ethical behavior, and of esthetic sensitivity and creation, and an attempt to fit them into one another in their proper order.

Cohen. At the same time, the Marburg school could not help tinkering in its turn with what it kept of Kant. Cohen and Natorp revised the categories, and formulated anew the principles of logic, which they regarded as more fundamental than those of ethics or esthetics. Cohen tried also to construct a logic of ethics. He reformulated the Kantian categorical imperative in political and legal terms. He enshrined it in the state rather than the individual, and made of it a kind of social or national will scientifically crystallized by the science of jurisprudence into rules and regulations for the conduct of the individual. These rules it is the *duty* of the individual to obey. In obedience to them his whole duty to God and man is fulfilled. When he has rendered to the state, there is nothing of any real worth left in him to render elsewhere. There are no private values. There is no moral will in the individual that is not absorbed into the public will.

Natorp. Natorp differed little from Cohen. He, too, rationalized and socialized morality. He regarded ethics as a science dealing with and defining the logical way in which we as rational beings *ought* to act, and found that way in the subjection of the individual will to the will of the community. All virtue is eventually social virtue. There are no real values in the individual that cannot be expressed in his activities as a citizen.

Also, we may remember that Natorp was one of the promulgators and defenders of what we called the "one-story" theory of the status assigned by Plato to the Ideas.[1]

The views of the Marburg school, exalting as they do the state, and

[1] Vol. I, p. 80, note 2.

tending to strip the individual of private worth, are significant. They are straws testifying to the rise and the direction of a wind that for a time blew a full gale.

Windelband. The revamping of Kant was now in full swing again, and the original tended to be lost to view in the emendations. Wilhelm Windelband (1848-1915), like Renouvier, talked of truth as an inner value and "feel" which experience has for us, and made of the universality we ascribe both to it and to the values of goodness and beauty an argument for the existence of a universal thinker. The universal mind expresses itself in a logical order; then, in a moral order in which the individual will submits itself to a social ideal; and then again in an esthetic order in which there are spontaneous creation and cessation from struggle. Finally religion seeks to bridge the gap that exists everywhere between the real and the ideal, and to achieve *perfect* truth, *perfect* goodness, and *perfect* beauty. Human history is the unfolding of the successive stages of this process.

Dilthey and Eucken. Much the same point of view was held by Wilhelm Dilthey (1833-1912), who regarded human history, and particularly the succession of the great typical ways of looking at life and estimating its significance, as a progressive manifestation of the wealth and splendor of the spirit we feel within us.

Rudolf Eucken (1846-1926) also seized upon this point of view to embellish his heritage from Fichte and to give added significance to his assertion that living is *doing* and that the fortunes and the aspirations of man are part of the process by which a universal mind strives toward and wins self-realization.

Cassirer. The eminent scholar Ernst Cassirer (1874-1945), a student of Cohen at Marburg, continued the Neo-Kantian tradition but went beyond it in his interpretation of the nature of scientific knowledge. After teaching at the University of Berlin he became professor at Hamburg and rector of the University. He resigned this position when the Nazis came to power and became a Swedish citizen, later, in 1941, joining the faculty of Yale University. A philosopher of vast erudition and great versatility, Cassirer pursued the problem of knowledge in relation to the historical development of philosophy and science in the modern era, writing extensively on mathematics, physics, epistemology, the nature and function of language, art, religion, and cultural theory. Cassirer advanced the thesis, idealistic in character, that the mind's activity integrates the totality of experience, embracing scientific knowledge, religion, and art, a process that transmutes the passive objective world into a world of "pure spiritual expression," an expression of mind itself.

In his anthropology Cassirer advanced the thesis, somewhat similar to that of the American pragmatist C. S. Peirce, that man is differentiated by his capacity for employing symbols and should be defined, therefore, as a symbolizing animal.

Chapter XXVI

PHILOSOPHY IN LATIN AMERICA

Latin American philosophy is sometimes accused of being unoriginal and repetitive of foreign, especially European, thinking. This may be true to some extent. But any lack of originality is compensated by both the quality and the quantity of its reaction to outside influences, by the interest these influences aroused in the educated classes, by the eagerness with which they were adopted and adapted, and by their embodiment in social and political practice. It is only recently that philosophy in Latin America has become a thing apart and its teaching a specialized profession. "Philosophers" in the restricted sense of the word are a modern invention there. With few exceptions, until lately, the cultivation of philosophy, both within and outside institutions of learning, was carried on by men of more and varied interests, eminent also in the sciences, theoretic and applied, in the arts, in literature, in social and political affairs. They were, moreover, frequently men of great learning and of encyclopaedic minds, well acquainted with the classics and, from the eighteenth century on, at least, with all the phases of modern European culture, and sufficiently independent in their point of view not to become servile adherents of what they favored. Indeed, Latin American philosophy throughout most of its history has been so interwoven with other intellectual and practical activities that it is hard to disentangle it from them and from the general pattern of the culture in which it figures so notably. Hence its history has to be in part an account also of the weaving of that larger pattern. Its content is so rich and so extensive in space and time that it is impossible to do it justice in the number of pages that can be allotted to it.

I. THE SCHOLASTIC PERIOD

Philosophy in Spain. The Latin American conquests took place at the beginning of the Golden Age of Spanish power, wealth, and achievement in all the arts of which we have already spoken in discussing the influence of the Renaissance. There was a revival of classical learning, especially of Greek, with an awakened interest in the un-varnished Aristotle it disclosed, due to the influence of the Renaissance; and there was an interest in the sciences—mathematics, physics, geog-raphy, metallurgy, botany and natural history—due largely to the prac-tical necessity of navigating long voyages and of investigating and utilizing the fauna, flora, and mineral resources of the newly discovered territories. Spanish science, however, still regarded Aristotle as an authority. And Medieval Scholasticism, still more submissive to him, though affected by the recovery of the classics and the renewed interest in Greek, proved impervious in Spain and Portugal to the new scientific discoveries and methods and to the new philosophical systems for which science was largely responsible and which elsewhere in Europe the Renaissance had created and fostered.

Nevertheless, in Spain, philosophical speculation was active within the bounds imposed upon it by Scholasticism. The University of Salamanca ranked along with Paris, Oxford, and Bologna, the other three great centers of European learning, and like them was agitated by the scholastic controversies of the times. The partisans of Aquinas and those of Duns Scotus were at swords' points, and both were attacked by the nominalistic followers of Occam. The learned Dominican Fran-cisco de Vitoria (1480-1546), graduate of Paris and professor at Sala-manca, succeeded in substituting Thomism for nominalism as the philosophy taught at Salamanca, but it still had to be defended against the attacks of the Scotist Franciscans.

To these controversies within was added the excitement caused by the Reformation and by the Humanism of Erasmus. His works were widely read in Spain and his views found an ardent advocate in Juan Luis Vives (1492-1540), born in Valencia and later professor at Louvain and Oxford. Vives was a man of great piety and learning and so "advanced" in his ideas that by some he is considered prophetic of Bacon and Descartes. But he was violently attacked by the clergy, and the Counter-Reformation, the Council of Trent, and the condemnation of the Humanistic aspects of Erasmus' teaching put an end to Human-ism in Spain and reasserted the old Scholasticism as the only permissible philosophy.

Luis de Molina. The Scholastic situation was again shaken up by the arrival of the Jesuits on the scene about the middle of the sixteenth cen-tury, and particularly by the liberal views advanced towards its end by Luis de Molina (1535-1600), professor of theology at Evora in Portugal and later at Madrid, and Francisco Suárez (1548-1617). Both were influenced by the spirit of the times that prevailed east of the Pyrenees, and both were concerned with reconciling human free will with divine foreordination and improving, so to speak, the relations between God and man, which the doctrine of predestination had rendered unpleasant. Aquinas had accepted the Augustinian teaching on the subject, and the Thomists still held to it, though not in too rigorous a form. Even so, it seemed too severe to Molina and Suárez, who tried to mitigate it, each in his own way.

Molina held that God neither desires nor wills the damnation of the sinner, but rather his salvation. Divine grace is offered to all. But it is for the individual of his own free will, which he can exercise without divine aid, to decide whether he will be saved or damned. God, however, foresees what the decision will be, and hence with whom grace will be efficacious and on whom it will be wasted. He therefore can be said to offer it, or withhold it, himself, according as it is accepted or rejected, and thus to foreordain the fate of the individual by foreseeing how the latter will freely choose.

Francisco Suárez. Suárez, who taught at various universities, including Salamanca and Rome, disagreed with Molina, and argued that the latter's views made the exercise of human free will too independent of God. In his doctrine of *congruism,* he maintained that though divine grace is at the disposition of all who will freely choose it, God's help is necessary in doing so, and is offered in different degrees to different individuals, according to their circumstances and needs. His aid is a necessary coefficient in the free acceptance of grace, and he foresees with whom it will or will not be efficacious, and dispenses it accordingly. Those to whom it is offered must freely will to avail themselves of it. They cannot, when *freely* willing, reject it, as Molina thought they could.

In either case, God was conceived as lenient and not disposed to be too exacting in what was demanded of human nature, and a man's misgivings as to whether or not he was fulfilling the duties imposed upon him could be cleared up by consulting his spiritual adviser. Thus the individual could be spared much unnecessary distress, confusion of mind, and even terror and despair, which might beset him if he was left without moral instruction.

Suárez was also noteworthy as a philosopher. A man of great learning, well versed in Aristotle and in the history of Scholastic philosophy, he tried to disentangle purely philosophical from theological views and make philosophy an independent "science"—all this, of course, without denying the superior authority of revealed truth. Though a good Thomist, he did not hesitate to differ from Aquinas on certain points.

In their political philosophies both Suárez and Molina, the latter first and most emphatically, denied the doctrine of the divine right of monarchs to rule, lodged sovereignty by the grace of God in the people, and asserted the right of the latter to rebel against and if necessary overthrow by force their rulers when dissatisfied with them. This right had also been suggested by Aquinas.

The Jesuits also accepted the doctrine of *probabilism,* originated by Molina. According to it, when a man holds strong and reasonably well-founded opinions, but lacks exact knowledge, he is entitled to them, even if they seem less probable than opinions to the contrary. And he can properly act in accordance with them. Even a priest may absolve a penitent, if the reason for doing so is sufficiently good, although there may be seemingly better reasons for denying absolution. In other words, even the confessed sinner should be given the benefit of the doubt whenever possible.

Church Controversy. These views created an uproar both in Spain and elsewhere. The Dominicans and the Jansenists within the Church, and the Lutherans and Calvinists outside it, attacked the teaching that grace is freely conceded to all who sincerely seek it, with (Suárez) or without (Molina) God as an auxiliary factor in their choice. The Calvinists, committed to the doctrine of the total depravity of man since the fall and of an ironbound predestination, and the Jansenists, who shared the same view to a lesser degree, were especially bitter.

The Jesuits retorted, and the dispute became so violent that Pope Clement VII enjoined silence on both parties in Spain, pending investigation of the matter by a commission. And later, when the commission failed to decide between the Jesuits and the Dominicans, Pope Paul V forbade further discussion.

Probabilism also was denounced by the Protestants, the Dominicans, the Jansenists, and Pascal, not only on theological grounds but as encouraging laxity of conduct. To it the Dominicans opposed *probabiliorism,* according to which a man was bound to think and act in the way that seemed *more* probably true and right. The Lutherans and the Calvinists dealt even more severely with the doctrine. However, the controversy was finally compromised by allowing choice only between probable opinions and courses of action that seemed *equally* well substantiated.

The denial of the divine right of kings and the affirmation of the sovereignty of the people and of their right to revolution had immediate political repercussions, and more important ones later on. From London James I wrote a violent letter to Philip III of Spain, accusing the latter of being a traitor to his class for allowing one of his subjects to express such views.

Philosophical Isolation of the Colonies. The philosophical isolation of Spain and Portugal from the rest of Europe lasted till the end of the seventeenth century; and, since during that period the Iberian peninsula was a bottleneck through which all knowledge of what was going on east of the Pyrenees reached Latin America, the Colonies were kept in the same ignorance. They were allowed to trade only with the mother countries and thus were cut off from one important access to the outside world. Also there was a strict censorship by Church and State of the books they were allowed to import, to print, and to read, and of the ideas they were allowed to discuss and even to entertain. This religious and political watching and warding of colonial thought and the restriction of philosophy to Scholasticism persisted for nearly two hundred years. It was only released when the aloofness of the Iberian peninsula itself broke down, and what had been taking place in the philosophical world during the last two centuries became common knowledge there.

Philosophy Reaches the Colonies. Philosophy, escorted by the Scotist Franciscan and the Thomist Dominican friars, discovered the New World with Columbus and, with the Augustinians and a little later the Jesuits added to her retinue, took possession of it along with the Conquistadores. Already in 1505 the Franciscans had established a college in the city of Santo Domingo on the island of Hispaniola (today divided between the republics of Santo Domingo and Haiti), and in the same city a college founded by the Dominicans was in 1538 raised to the rank of the University of St. Thomas Aquinas. After the conquests the settlement of Spanish America was so rapid that by the middle of the sixteenth century most of its present principal cities, endowed with educational institutions, already existed. In 1553 the two great universities of colonial times, the Pontifical in the City of Mexico and that of San Marcos in Lima, Peru, were founded, though San Marcos, because of disturbed conditions, remained a Dominican college and was not full-fledged until 1575.

The Beginnings of Philosophy in Mexico. In Mexico, philosophy had a distinguished beginning. Its first professor, the Augustinian Alfonso de la Vera Cruz, was a graduate of the University of Salamanca. There he had become learned in Thomistic theology, interested in mathematics, and acquainted with the Humanism of Erasmus; he knew Aristotle in the original Greek and commented on the Categories. His successor in the chair, the Dominican Ledesma, was transferred to San Marcos in Lima. A graduate of the University, the Dominican Tomás

Mercado, made a new translation of Aristotle's works on logic with a commentary. The professor of rhetoric, Cervantes de Salazar, was a disciple of Vives and through him of Erasmus; and the first Archbishop of Mexico, Juan de Zumárraga, incorporated whole pages of Erasmus in his writings. The first Bishop of Michoacan, Vasco de Quiroga, was acquainted with the *Utopia* of Thomas More.

The Jesuits and Education in the Colonies. With the advent of the Jesuits, for the most part Suaristic, education to its own advantage passed largely into their hands as they founded new colleges and infiltrated the universities. As an Order they were characterized by common sense, worldly as well as divine wisdom, intellectual curiosity, comparative independence of thought, a willingness to compromise when possible, and a charitable and acceptable view of God's ways to man. And they excelled in the art of teaching. Their liberal Suaristic Thomism proved a formidable rival to Dominican fundamentalism, and both easily outstripped Franciscan Scotism.

Among the first colleges the Jesuits founded were those at São Paulo and Bahía in Brazil. And the first and foremost exponent of Scholasticism in South America was Father Anchieta. These colleges soon ranked almost as universities, and, aided by the fact that the Brazilians were great readers, put the culture of Portuguese America on a level with that of Spanish America.

The Native American Culture. An original intention of many of these institutions was the conversion and education of the Indians, who, in Mexico and Guatemala at least, proved apt pupils quick in assimilating the subtleties of Christian dogma and Scholastic disputations. It should be remembered that the Spaniards had conquered not primitive peoples, but ancient and in many ways advanced civilizations, superimposed upon cultures even more ancient and perhaps as advanced. The Mayans and Aztecs, beside their magnificent architecture, sculpture, painting, metal work, ceramics, and weaving, had carried astronomy to the point of constructing elaborate calendars, the Mayan calendar being as accurate as the one we are using today. The Mayans had discovered the zero and the principle of position in arithmetic some five hundred years before the Hindus did and a thousand years before they were introduced into Europe by the Arabs. There were even premonitions of metaphysical thinking in the Aztec and Mayan religions; certainly in the fifteenth century the King of Texcoco, Netzalhualcóyotl, allied with Montezuma, warrior, moralist, lawgiver, engineer, astronomer, poet, and observer of human life, had thought out for himself a monotheism to which he adhered in private, wisely unwilling to force it upon his subjects.

In Peru, in spite of its great engineering and artistic achievements, the situation was different. The Incas had amalgamated with the primitive animism of their subjects a worship of the sun, behind which lurked the idea of an invisible creative power. But instead of accepting Christian doctrine and taking to its theology, the Indians were recalcitrant to the new religion and difficult of conversion.

Whether or not the Indians had souls and were to be regarded and treated as rational human beings was a debated theological question. They found able defenders in Alfonso de la Vera Cruz, in Zumárraga, in Vasco de Quiroga, who tried to organize the Tarascans according to the precepts of More's *Utopia,* and in the Bishop of Chiapas, Bartolmeo de las Casas, who advocated against the forcible conversion favored by the Franciscans an appeal to reason as a basis of faith. Largely due to their influence, both Church and State tried to deal humanely with the Indians. The Spanish Government promulgated exemplary laws in their behalf, but these proved difficult of enforcement and were frequently more honored in the breach than in the observance. This was especially true in Peru and Bolivia, where a system of forced labor in the mines, supported theologically by the argument that the Indians were irrational and soulless, prevailed throughout the colonial period. In Paraguay, however, the Jesuits instituted a benevolent socialism which lasted till their expulsion two hundred years later.

During the greater part of the seventeenth century, philosophy marked time in Latin America and was only prevented from falling asleep on its feet by the Suaristic Jesuits. Both in Spain and the Colonies the Inquisition retained its stranglehold and allowed little or nothing to be known of the new philosophies and the new scientific discoveries and methods that were agitating Europe beyond the Pyrenees. Generally speaking, too, now that the excitement of discovering, conquering and colonizing new, strange, and rich worlds was over, the colonial way of life had become provincial and lethargic. To be sure, two new universities of note were founded by the Jesuits, one in Quito in Ecuador in 1620, the other in Chuquisaca (later Sucre) in Bolivia in 1624. The latter was one of the most distinguished centers of learning in South America and proved to be one of the last strongholds of Scholasticism.

Góngora and de la Cruz. In Mexico, however, the last half of the century produced two notable exceptions to the times, Carlos de Sigüenza y Góngora and Sor Juana de la Cruz. Both in their different ways would have been at home in the Renaissance, possessing its typical

universality of mind—a universality, as we have already noted, not
infrequent in Latin America. Sigüenza y Góngora was Professor of
Astronomy and Mathematics in the Pontifical university, a poet, a
cartographer of the Valley of Mexico, an assistant to the Viceroy in
planning the drainage and fortifications of the city, an archaeologist
learned in pre-conquest history, a reconstructor of the Aztec calendar;
he was honored by Louis XIV of France with an invitation to join the
French court, and by Charles II of Spain with the title of "Royal
Cosmographer." Juana de la Cruz, an infant prodigy avid for knowledge, an omnivorous reader, and known as the Tenth Muse because of
her poetry, was lady-in-waiting to the Vicereine, astounded the learned
with her own learning, became a nun, and devoted herself to the study
of mathematics, geometry, music, the reasons for the differences between individuals of the same race, and even the properties of eggs and
sugar in cooking. If, she said, Aristotle had spent more time in the
kitchen, he would have written much more. Her library of four thousand volumes was one of the best collections of mathematical treatises
of the century, and she had also a large collection of musical and
scientific instruments. Finally, it is possible that she knew something of Descartes and the Cartesian philosophy, and it is certain that
Sigüenza y Góngora did.

II. KNOWLEDGE OF THE NEW PHILOSOPHY

Arrival of the New Philosophy. It is clear that, despite sacred and
secular efforts to the contrary, the new scientific and philosophical views
engendered by the Renaissance were at last becoming known in the
Iberian peninsula and in Latin America. By 1687, they were being discussed in Madrid by the educated classes and the aristocracy, by learned
societies, and especially by the doctors, and they were being accepted
in so far as they could be reconciled with revelation and Catholic
dogma. Philosophy, ancient and modern, thus began to be freed from
theological bondage and application and to be studied in its own right,
and in estimating and combining the comparative truths of different
systems consistent with revealed truth, *probabilism* was helpful. All
this, of course, could not but bring into question the authority of
Aristotle, the Church fathers, and even of Aquinas.

At first the clergy were up in arms and denounced the Renaissance
philosophers as mere amateur, anti-clerical, lay nobodies, ignorant of
philosophy. The Dominican fundamentalists were particularly alarmed.
The partisans of the new ideas in their turn called the old-guard

Scholastics narrow-minded and cloistered. From the intelligentsia and the upper classes this knowledge soon spread to the world in general, all the more quickly as some of the defenders took to writing in Spanish instead of Latin.

From the beginning, moreover, members of the clergy were numbered among those interested in the new philosophy. More and more persons became infected with the general intellectual unrest and began to revolt against the dominance of Aristotle in philosophy and science and against the Scholastic curriculum and method of instruction in those subjects. Now, Cartesian doubt, and reason, experience, and experiment, in so far as their use and conclusions did not conflict with the Catholic faith, were pitted within the Church itself against the "die-hard" Aristotelians, who bitterly fought any departure from fundamentalist Scholasticism.

Revolt Against Scholasticism. The revolt was spearheaded by the Benedictine monk Feijóo (1676-1764). Well acquainted with the French philosophers and with Bacon and Locke, and inspired by Bayle's *Dictionary,* he launched in his *Critical Theatre* and *Learned Letters* a prolonged attack upon prevalent popular beliefs and superstitions. In these articles he ridiculed the Scholastic methods of teaching, deflated Aristotle as a final authority, and praised Bacon and the Baconian scientific method.

The changing situation in the mother countries had immediate repercussions in the colonies. Hitherto prohibited books, now permitted to the clergy for the purpose of refutation, came into general circulation; books were smuggled into the colonies by foreigners and colonials returning from abroad, and even peddled by travelling salesmen or sold under false titles by the book shops. Then, too, there was an increasing influx of foreigners with pernicious religious and philosophical ideas, especially after the accession of the Bourbon dynasty in Spain. There were even Free Masons about, and the cook of the Viceroy of Mexico was denounced as one of them. The Inquisition found it impossible to stem the tide.

So it was that by the middle of the eighteenth century, philosophy in the colonies, as in the Iberian peninsula, was pretty nearly abreast of the times. Bacon, Locke, Newton, Descartes, Spinoza, the Occasionalists, Leibnitz, and Bayle were common knowledge, and Hume, Condillac, and the French Encyclopaedists were looming on the horizon.

Feijóo played a major part in disseminating the new ideas in the Colonies. His popularity there was immediate. He personally corresponded with the learned Barnuevo in Lima, where, as in Ecuador as well, Descartes, Leibnitz, and Newton were discussed and ten years later Locke was to be advertised by Verney, a Portuguese well-known throughout the Colonies. Another decade and Zapata was advocating in Peru the Baconian method and the observation of nature as the proper source of knowledge, and the Universities of Cuzco and Huamanga were falling into line. In Mexico the Jesuit Guevara had taken up the cudgels and was arguing furthermore for free discussion of metaphysical as well as scientific matters after the fashion of Descartes, Bacon, and Locke. Indeed, in Mexico, at least, some of the Jesuits allowed themselves to be carried away by the new ideas to an extent that, particularly in the case of the sensationism of Locke and then of Condillac, seemed inconsistent with even a liberal Thomism.

Reforms in Education. With the accession of Charles III, a great grandson of Louis XIV of France and second of the Bourbon dynasty in Spain, all restrictions upon the cultural relations between the outside world, the Iberian peninsula and the Colonies were removed. Educated in France, cosmopolitan and broad-minded, much influenced by the "Enlightenment," and in favor of the new science and philosophies, he encouraged their teaching in the Universities, whose educational methods he overhauled and reformed. He raised completely the ban upon the importation of books into Spain and Spanish America and sent scientific expeditions to explore further the animal, vegetable and mineral resources of his overseas possessions. He clipped the claws of the Inquisition, though he could not well interfere with the power of the Church to ban books it considered subversive. Even so, philosophical works, including now those of Pascal, the Port Royal School, the Jansenists, whom the Jesuits detested, and the Encyclopaedists, poured into Latin America, and could be read and talked about without fear of other than religious disapproval and penalties. As an example of the extent of importation, we may note that in 1785 a single consignment of books passing through Callao, the port of Lima, numbered 37,612.

Following the instructions of the King, the Viceroys in Mexico, Lima, and Buenos Aires and the Captain General of Guatemala put the reforms into effect in Spanish America. In Lima the Viceroy ordered that at least one course in modern philosophy and science should be taught in the universities and colleges under his control, and that students should have complete freedom in choosing and combining systems as they pleased. In 1771 not only Descartes but Gassendi, Newton, and Condillac were in the curriculum, and in the same year Aristotelianism was attacked and the Baconian experimental and inductive methods were advocated in Cuzco. In Venezuela, Valverde went so far as to denounce Aristotle as a pagan and to deny his influence on Aquinas.

In Mexico the great advocate of reform was Benito Díaz de Gamarra, a Mexican priest of the Congregation of the Oratory. Born in 1745, he had graduated with high honors from the College of San Idelfonso in the City of Mexico, taken his Doctorate at Pisa, and received from the Pope a high ecclesiastical post. His sojourn in Europe had converted him, heart and soul, to the new ideas, and on his return to Mexico he championed them and tried to put them into effect in the curriculum of the College of St. Michael the Great, an institution whose prestige equalled that of the University. A man of great learning, he dealt in his *Elements of Modern Philosophy,* his *Errors of the Understanding,* and other writings not only with philosophy in all its branches, but with geometry, physics, electricity, optics, and the nature of animal souls, and with contemporary intellectual, moral, social, and hygienic conditions in Mexico and the ways of improving them. His *Elements of Modern Philosophy* was adopted as a textbook even by the conservative University. He insisted that philosophical hypotheses should be founded on experience and reason, should be critical in attitude, and not subservient to any one system. Doubt should restrain them, and conclusions should not be jumped at just because they looked simple. As for his own views, while going along with the moderns in many respects, he still preferred the Aristotelian view of the relation between mind and body to the theories of Descartes, Malebranche, and Leibnitz, but favored the atomic rather than the Aristotelian view of the nature of matter.

His opinions and proposals roused a storm of opposition and he himself ran into rough weather. He got into difficulties with the Inquisition and had to resign his chair of philosophy and the rectorate of the College, to which, however, he was later restored. At his death, while still in partial disgrace, his library was found to contain many prohibited books not licensed by the Holy Office, including the *Henriade* of Voltaire, perhaps the most annoying, in the eyes of the Church, of all the Encyclopaedists.

Another influential Mexican in the anti-Aristotelian and anti-Scholastic campaign was the priest Antonio Alzate. He too was interested in and well acquainted with physics, astronomy, biology, natural history, chemistry, meteorology, and their practical applications, as well as modern philosophy. From 1788 to 1795 he conducted in his *Literary Gazette* a running attack on Scholasticism, satirizing its devotion to Aristotle, its blindness to what was going on in the world, and its refusal to have anything to do with reason, experience, and experiment in its methods. Another attack along the same lines had been made by Ignazio Bartolache in 1772, a distinguished mathematician, chemist, and doctor, in his *Flying Mercury*. In the last decade of the century, the *Peruvian Mercury* edited by Hipolite Unanue, physicist and naturalist, and the *First Fruits of Culture in Quito,* directed by Francisco Santa Cruz Espejo, a doctor of many interests and an admirer of Feijóo, continued in similar vein. And in the first years of the nineteenth century there appeared in Bogotá the *New Granada Weekly* headed by the physicist and naturalist Francisco de Caldas.

In Cuba there appeared during the last decade of the eighteenth century in the Havana *Periodical* two anonymous articles, one on "Physics," the other "A Philosophical Discourse," in which "modernism" in philosophy and science was championed. These have been attributed to the priest José Agustín Caballero, who in 1795 proposed liberalizing the curriculum of the University of Havana by including courses in the new style on physics, chemistry, mathematics and anatomy. In any case his *Philosophía Electíva* advocated the same reforms, set up philosophy as an independent science, and was sympathetic to the new philosophies. He is regarded as the father of modern education in Cuba, and as the initiator there, though perhaps indirectly, of anti-Scholasticism and of modern philosophy.

But Caballero's fame rests not only on his learning, his proposed educational reforms, and his leaning towards the new ideas. He was also a statesman, deeply interested in the relations of Cuba to the mother country, critical of conditions in Spain, and, influenced perhaps by the American Revolution, in favor of some degree of Cuban autonomy. All in all he ranks as one of the great men of Cuban history.

The students' theses of the time also bear witness to the trend. They attack the authority of Aristotle and even of the Church Fathers, advocate Cartesian doubt and Baconian experiment and induction, insist on sensible evidence as the criterion of truth, and discuss and criticize Descartes, Spinoza, Occasionalism, Locke, Condillac, and Berkeley with a freedom restrained only by theological prudence. Indeed, there was a kind of revival of the practice of the "Twofold Truth"—of stating what we should have every reason to believe from the evidence of experience and experiment were it not for divine revelation to the contrary.

The discovery of the new sciences was accompanied by their practical application. Already, a century earlier, painting and sculpture and architecture were being taught in Quito. Now were founded the School of Mines and the Botanical Garden in Guatemala, the Botanical Garden and Astronomical Observatory in Bogotá, and a little later a School of Navigation in Buenos Aires.

The fundamentalists, however, were not idle. They succeeded now and then in having "progressive" professors of philosophy removed under accusation of heresy. Locke and Spinoza were their special targets, the one because of his implication that matter might be the basis of consciousness, the other because of his pantheism. For a brief space, too, they were in the ascendant. The expulsion for political reasons of the Jesuits from the Iberian peninsula and possessions (1759-1767) had returned education to their hands. And Charles IV, who acceded in 1788, alarmed, as were his royal "cousins," by the American and French Revolutions and by the ideas that had inspired them, forbade the importation into Spain and the colonies of all books in foreign languages, all histories and descriptions and documents dealing with the French Revolution, and all the works of the Encyclopaedists. He had no use for philosophers, he said. He wished loyal subjects, and the more ignorant the colonials were, presumably the more loyal they would be.

III. THE INFLUENCE OF THE ENCYCLOPAEDISTS

The Rebellion of the Colonies. But the supposedly ignorant and therefore loyal colonists proved to be neither ignorant nor loyal. Besides the long list of other philosophers, they knew already the Encyclopaedists, the British moralists Bentham and Paine, and perhaps Jefferson and Franklin. Banned books continued to circulate. The "Declaration of the Rights of Man" promulgated by the French Revolutionary Assembly was translated into Spanish, printed secretly in Bogotá, and widely disseminated. In Peru Pablo de Olavide issued a manifesto to the Spanish nation calling for rebellion in accordance with the guiding watchwords of the French Revolution. In remote Chuquisaca prohibited books were found in private libraries and in that of the rector of the University, and passed from hand to hand in town. And the students, also, knew very well what was going on. In 1776 the Academia Carolina was instituted—a kind of "law club" in which would-be lawyers practiced unofficially their profession. Its meetings began in orthodox fashion, but ended in secret discussions of forbidden topics, like the Encyclopaedists and Rousseau; this, in spite of the Archbishop San Alberto's thunderings against all revolutionary ideas in his pastoral letters. And Villara, the District Attorney of Chuquisaca, whose great preoccupation was the plight of the Indians and the abolition of forced labor, was spreading revolutionary political ideas, as did also Monteguardo in the Argentine. And the University, now thoroughly infected with the "Social Contract" of Rousseau, proved a center of the Independence movement in South America. Moreover, had not Suárez and Molina and even Aquinas denied the divine right of kings to rule and asserted the right of their subjects to revolution?

The Colonies were now ripe for independence. They were self-sufficient and had developed a national self-consciousness of their own. In population and culture they were ahead of the United States. The City of Mexico was not only the largest city in the New World, but, according to the eminent European scientist Humboldt, who had travelled widely in the Americas, the foremost in the cultivation and application of the sciences. Nor, in his opinion could any European botanical library equal that of Bogotá. And Spanish surpassed Anglo-Saxon America in its interest in, and knowledge of, philosophy. It had at its finger tips ancient, scholastic, Renaissance, "modern," and "contemporary" European systems—Aristotle, Aquinas, Suárez, Bacon, Hobbes, Locke, Descartes, Spinoza, Leibnitz, the Occasionalists, Pascal, Condillac. The growing independence of thought thus fostered had prepared it to assimilate and put into practice the social and political philosophies that had just provoked and inspired two great revolutions. With such examples to follow, a third could not be long postponed. Indeed, in Europe political independence was being openly proposed by Miranda, a Venezuelan refugee, who tried, though unsuccessfully, to interest the British and French governments in the cause.

Revolution was precipitated when Napoleon invaded the Iberian peninsula and dethroned both the Spanish and Portuguese dynasties. Spanish America now owed allegiance, if to anyone, to a government in exile. The ties with the mother country had become too weak to stand the strain. Venezuela broke away in 1810, and sixteen years later, under the leadership of Bolívar in South America and Hidalgo in Mexico, the independence of the colonies, except for Cuba and Puerto Rico, was, after many vicissitudes and considerable bloodshed, a *fait accompli*.

That of Brazil was more tardy and pacific in execution, the work, indeed, of the ruling house of Portugal. The Court had fled, bag and baggage, to the New World and established itself in Rio de Janeiro in 1808. After the downfall of Napoleon and the return of the King to Lisbon, it was his son, left behind as regent, who severed the connection with Portugal and became the first Brazilian Emperor. The transference of the Court had benefited the country. Within eight years the Schools of Navigation, of Surgery, and of Fine Arts, the Zoological Garden, the Public Library, and the Royal Theatre had been established in the capital, and a Medical School in Bahía. To this epoch belongs also the first outstanding Brazilian philosopher, Father Mont' Alverne.

IV. INFLUENCE OF UTILITARIANISM AND DESTUTT DE TRACY

Andrés Bello. The leading figures in the independence movement were well educated and philosophically minded. Intellectually and philosophically the most eminent was the Venezuelan Andrés Bello, probably the most distinguished and erudite figure in the three Americas at the time. Sent with Bolívar to London in 1810 to plead the cause of the Colonies, he remained there for nineteen years. He knew personally Bentham, whose illegible manuscripts he copied, James Mill, and Hamilton, and was attracted by Berkeley's pluralistic idealism, and later by the eclecticism of Cousin. His writings, many of them published abroad, helped spread further knowledge in America of contemporary European philosophy and science, especially of Berkeley, and of the utilitarian movement in Great Britain. On his return to South America he became legal adviser to the Chilean government, drew up the civil code of the country, and organized the new University of Chile, of which he became the first rector. He was a many-sided writer. Besides his *Philosophy of the Understanding,* in which he set forth the views of the Scotch School and of Berkeley, he composed a Spanish grammar, wrote on international law and the use of metre in poetry, and, no mean poet himself, translated from Horace, Plautus, Byron, and Victor Hugo.

Democracy as a Social Ideal. The Revolution was not only political; it was also social, in theory at least. Liberty, Equality, and Fraternity were now the great dream to be realized. Democratic forms of government, modeled largely upon the Constitution of the United States, were set up without regard to their applicability to the conditions of time and place. Slavery was denounced and by 1854 had become unconstitutional everywhere in Latin America except Cuba and Puerto Rico. Freedom of religious and philosophical thinking was proclaimed, and in many countries the Catholic Church was disestablished and deprived of much of its property, and the monasteries and convents were closed. But the Independence was destined to inaugurate, rather than liberty, equality, and fraternity, a long period of disorder, usurpations of power and local revolutions in the countries into which the Spanish Empire fell apart.

Educational Reforms Favoring Philosophy. Education was immediately overhauled. The content and method of Scholastic instruction was completely discarded. The University of Chile was suspended in 1842 and reopened in 1843 with Bello as rector. That of Havana (1728) was modernized in 1842. The Universities of Buenos Aires and Montevideo were founded in 1821 and 1832, those of Colombia and Costa Rica in 1843. And institutions of learning multiplied in Brazil.

The teaching of philosophy under the new dispensation was much influenced, not only by Bello, but by José Joaquim Mora, another exponent of the Scotch School and of Utilitarianism. Mora was a Spaniard, called in by the Argentine government as an educator. Troubled political conditions kept him on the move from the Argentine to Chile, to Bolivia, in whose constitution the ideas of Bentham had been incorporated by Marshall Sucre, a collaborator with Bolívar in the Independence, to Peru, and finally back to Spain. In Lima he published in 1832 his *Course on Logic* and his *Course on Ethics According to the Edinburgh School*. The latter, particularly, was popular in Latin America. In Mexico Utilitarianism was championed and popularized by another Mora, Dr. José Maria Luis Mora (1794-1850); in Argentina and Uruguay by Esteban Echevarría (1805-1851), Juan Bautista Alberdi, who combined it with nascent eclecticism and idealism, and by Sarmiento, President of Argentina, who earlier had aided Bello in reforming education in Chile. In Chile, also, José Victoriano Lastarria under its influence was on his way towards the Positivism of which he became one of the great Chilean exponents.

Socialism. Then, too, the socialism of Saint-Simón was gathering disciples. It had influenced Simón Rodríguez, the "master of the liberator" Bolívar, who in Chuquisaca had tried to set up a model school on socialistic lines. It had its repercussions in Argentina and Uruguay in the thought of Sarmiento, Echevarría, and Alberdi. In Chile, Santiago Arcos founded a "Society of Equality." In 1828 the English philanthropist, Robert Owen, the first to establish cooperative societies, was called in by the Mexican government to try out a socialistic colony in Texas, which, however, did not succeed. And young Mexican intellectuals, such as Pantaleón Tovar (1828-1876) and Juan Diáz Covarrubias (1837-1858) favored it. In Brazil in 1845 there was being published in Rio de Janeiro a *Socialist Review*. Meanwhile, in contemporary Europe Karl Marx was developing "dialectical materialism," which was soon to take its place as one of the Latin American philosophies.

Destutt de Tracy. However, another important influence was that of the Frenchman, Destutt de Tracy, a disciple of Condillac. He was of no great account himself, but his *Elements of Ideology,* in tone rationalistic, sensationistic, naturalistic, anti-religious, and optimistic as to the perceptibility of human nature, had already been acclaimed in the colonies before the wars of Independence broke out. Now, in Bolivia, the *Elements of Ideology* were made obligatory reading in all the institutions of learning. In Argentina it was recommended by Lafinur and Agüero. In Cuba it partially inspired the reform of the teaching of philosophy in Havana undertaken by Father Varela, whose *Lessons in Philosophy* were adopted by some colleges in Mexico. But in Mexico Destutt de Tracy was perhaps best known through the writings of a Spanish admirer, Balmes. The *Ideology* also helped popularize the materialism of Gall's phrenology with its localization of the different aspects and functions of consciousness in different parts of the brain.

V. THEOLOGICAL REACTION AND ECLECTICISM

Revival and Reaction—Theistic Philosophy. The imposition of the *Ideology* on education in South America was denounced everywhere by the clergy and the lay conservatives as legally unconstitutional and as equivalent to a prescribed teaching of irreligion, materialism, and atheism in the schools. It lasted only a short while and was abolished in Bolivia, at any rate, in 1845. The revolt of the conservatives received much spiritual aid and comfort from a similar anti-naturalistic and "back to religion and God" movement in France. Theologically, this movement was headed by the ultra Catholics, De Maistre, Bonald and Chateaubriand; philosophically, by Maine de Biran and Jouffroy, and by the Italian, Vico. Their works were widely read in Latin America and inspired a revival both of Catholicism and theistic philosophy. Another anti-naturalistic influence we should perhaps mention was that of a minor German philosopher, Krause, a prophet not without honor save in his own country and in France, who was popular in Spain in the nineteenth century. His harmonious rationalism reflected in pious and theistic form the ideas of the great German idealists. It was diffused from Spain in varying degrees throughout Latin America, where especially Krause's views on natural human rights and his conception of law as not only a protective device but an instrument for enabling, and if necessary, compelling man to do his utmost to realize moral perfection, had some vogue. This philosophy of natural rights and law seems to have been particularly influential in Bolivia and Chile.

Eclecticism. But the most important factor in the philosophical reaction was the eclecticism of Victor Cousin. Cousin attracted a wide following, more so perhaps in South America than in Mexico. To him also Latin America owed its first direct acquaintance with Kant and the German Idealists and its interest in the history of philosophy and the philosophy of history. In Brazil, Mont'Alverne found in eclecticism a possible reconciliation of Locke, Condillac, the Edinburgh School, Kant, and Catholicism. His pupil, the poet Gonçalves de Magalhães, who had also studied in Paris under Jouffroy, developed a somewhat romantic version of Berkeley's pluralistic idealism. In Bolivia, some of Cousin's works were translated into Spanish, and he found faithful disciples in the jurist Terazas, one of his translators; in Ortiz, Rector of the University of La Paz; in Velasco, professor of law at Chuquisaca (now renamed Sucre); and in Villa and San Román at Cochabamba. Velasco was also influenced by Kant. In Chile the *pros* and *cons* of eclecticism were vigorously debated. Bello favored it, and was criticized as inconsistent by Lastarria, who likened Cousin to a hummingbird sipping one flower after another.

Eclecticism was also attacked by one of the most distinguished philosophers of the time, the Cuban José de la Luz (1800-1862). Another "universal mind," educated in the College of St. Charles and the University of Havana, he travelled in the United States and widely in Europe, where he studied with the famous naturalist and paleontologist Cuvier in Paris, interested Humboldt in Berlin in the establishment of a magnetic observatory in Havana, and, himself an accomplished linguist, attended lectures by the great philologist Cardinal Mezzofanti in Rome. On his return to Cuba he went into politics and educational reform, became rector of the College of Carraguayo, and later founded that of El Salvador near Havana. He was an admirer of Locke, Bacon, and Newton, an opponent of Maine de Biran and Cousin, and, though not irreligious, he was suspicious of metaphysics and absolutes in matters theological. But what he most disliked in Cousin was the latter's philosophy of history as essentially a social, political, religious, and philosophical program onward and upward towards the eclectic ideal. Cousin, however, did not lack adherents in Cuba, of whom the most eminent were the brothers Gonzales de Valle, professors in the University of Havana.

VI. INFLUENCE OF POSITIVISM

The Scientific Spirit. Philosophy seems to swing like a pendulum, more or less rapidly and with more or less wobbling, between affirmation and denial of the validity of metaphysical speculations and of hypotheses that transcend inductions from experience. Though the first half of the nineteenth century saw a swing away from the naturalistic influence of Destutt de Tracy, the pendulum was already wobbling and hesitant. As early as 1837 Comte had promulgated his Positivism. This, we may remember, was inspired by his distress at the confusion of the times and his search for a remedy. The answer was suggested by the rapid advances being made by the sciences in all fields, including now psychology, economics and sociology, and by their apparent power to cope satisfactorily with all questions that mattered. Metaphysical and theological speculations had proved useless, and could be discarded as primitive and outworn methods of solving human problems. And this suspicion was soon to be re-enforced by the Darwinian theory, the easy and simple materialism of Haeckel, Moleschott and Büchner, and the "scientific" philosophy of Herbert Spencer. The only reliable measures of truth and guides to sound thinking and rational human conduct were, then, scientific hypotheses founded upon experience and attested by the scientific method.

Positivism and the Problem of History. In Latin America the unstable and drifting political, social, and intellectual conditions of the day had given rise to much disillusion. Who or what was to blame? The Spanish inheritance and the Colonial tradition? Lastarria answered "yes" and Bello "no." Should Latin America remain Latin or should it imitate the United States? Or should it strike out on a new path of its own? Two philosophies of history were also involved. Was the course of history predetermined by God or Fate to proceed everywhere along fixed lines, as Hegel, Herder, and Vico maintained? In Chile, Bello favored this view and defended Spain, the Conquest and Colonialism as part of the pattern. Or was history an open process in which the individual was free to mold his own destiny, and the present not captive of the past, as Lastarria maintained? And what was the future role of the Indian according to either theory?

Positivism—with some accretion of utilitarianism and socialism, and a little later with the accent on Herbert Spencer, perhaps, rather than on Comte—seemed to Latin America the solution of its problems. Get rid of metaphysical, theological, romantic, and moralistic methods of dealing with the situation; apply the scientific point of view and scientific treatment, and all will go well.

Opposition to Positivism. Needless to say, Positivism met with hostility and opposition from the same quarters as had fought the *Ideology* of Destutt de Tracy. What must have seemed particularly offensive to them was its apostolic mission as a new *religion* destined to uproot the superstitious cult of a God and supplant it with a rational worship of glorified humanity—a worship, at that, conducted with a ritual largely plagiarized from the Catholic Church. This apotheosis of humanity, with its temples, saints, and ceremonies, never caught on in Spanish America, where, however, Positivism in its scientific aspects did tend to be accepted as a dogma of faith. But as a religion it made headway in Brazil, and Rio de Janeiro still has, or had as lately as 1940, a temple dedicated to the cult of the Great Being, Humanity.

Positivism in Brazil. Of all the Latin America countries, Brazil was the most and the longest impressed by Positivism. It was known there as early as 1853, but it was only in the 1870's that it became widespread. In Rio de Janeiro it was first taught by Benjamin Constant Botelho de Magalhães, Miguel Lemos, and Texeiras Mendes, three of its most distinguished apostles in that country. Lemos embraced it primarily not as a scientific movement but as a religion, and devoted himself to the propagation of the new faith. Positivism had been introduced into northern Brazil by Tobías Barreto, of whose philosophy, as we shall see in a moment, it was but a passing phase. But its most outstanding advocate was the doctor and surgeon Luis Pereira Barreto (1840-1923), who had become converted to it while a medical student in Belgium. However, he disavowed its religious aspects and was excommunicated from the Positivist Church by Lemos because of his apostasy. An ardent republican, he took part in the abolition of the monarchy in 1889. The new constitution, of which he was one of the framers, was drawn up under positivist auspices, just as that of Bolivia had been under the influence of Bentham, and the motto "Order and Progress" became that of the republic. He was a member of the first Senate, and, anticlerical and blaming the Catholic Church for the past backwardness of the country, he fought for a reform of education along positivist lines. But he became disgusted with politics and retired to his medical practice near São Paulo. There, besides introducing antisepsis into his surgery, studying yellow fever, and almost discovering its cause, he interested himself in introducing the cultivation of coffee into his part of Brazil, in wine-growing, and in studying and combating a parasite that attacked the grapes. Also, he published two volumes of a projected work on Comte's law of the three stages, which he found exemplified in the passage from conservatism (theology) through liberalism (metaphysics) to Positivism (science) that marked the evolution of Brazil.

Positivism in Mexico. In Spanish North America, Positivism appeared first in force in Mexico in 1867, introduced by the mathematician Gabino Barreda, who had attended Comte's lectures in Paris. Appointed Director of the National Preparatory School by Juárez, who had become President of the restored republic after the downfall of Maximilian and the expulsion of the French, he proposed to revise Mexican education in accordance with Comte's program. This, he felt, would correct over-specialization, provide a comprehensive view of all the natural sciences studied in their proper order, and thus produce trained and rounded-out minds capable of carrying out dispassionately the necessary social reforms. But the program proved in some respects superfluous for specialization in certain fields and had to be amended, although when fairly intact it governed education in some of the states till 1914. Again, Positivism met with considerable competition from the eclecticism of Cousin and the followers of Krause. The clerical opposition was negligible, as the Church, which had favored Maximilian and been favored by him, was in ill-repute with the new regime. All in all, Positivism dominated the thinking of the educated and governing classes in Mexico till Porfirio Díaz was deposed in 1911. Indeed, the group that surrounded him was known as "Los Scientíficos."

Positivism in Spanish South America. In Spanish South America the full impact of Positivism was more delayed, in some cases by almost a generation. In Peru its most eminent exponents were Mariano Cornejo (1866-1942), diplomat, statesman and at one time Minister of the Interior and President of the Council of Ministers; Manuel Gonzales Prado (1848-1918); and Manuel Vicente Villaran. In Chile it was espoused by Lastarria, who, however, criticized its dogmatic tone and rejected its exaltation of the state and humanity above individual men. In Valentin Letelier, also, it had a liberal supporter. More orthodox in their adherence were the brothers Jorge and Juan Enrique Lagarrigue, the latter also a somewhat advanced socialist.

In Bolivia, La Paz and Chuquisaca (Sucre) were the two important centers of Positivism, where its way had been prepared by the persistence throughout the metaphysical and theological reaction of an appreciable current of naturalistic, materialistic, and atheistic thinking carried over from the *Ideology*. The head of the movement in Sucre was Benjamin Fernández, professor of constitutional law. Positivism also became the philosophy of the liberal party. This alliance with politics

brought the State as well as the Church into the fray, and invited violent denunciation by Mariano Baptista, conservative President of the
Republic, who was ably seconded by the Archbishop of Sucre, Miguel
Taborga. However, with the overthrow of the conservatives in 1899
by the liberal party, Positivism, now with the emphasis on Spencer,
was installed, as it had been in Mexico, as the official philosophy of the
nation, and education was secularized and remodeled to conform with
its precepts.

In Argentina the Normal School of Paraná was the center of diffusion. Introduced by an Italian professor of paleontology, Pedro Scala-
brini, Positivism was taken up by his pupil, J. Alfredo Ferreira (1863-
1935), who became one of its most distinguished exponents, and tried
to reform education along its lines. It had been brought into Uruguay
by Alberdi, Echevarria, and Sarmiento when they took refuge in
Montevideo from a revolution in Argentina, and there it was perpetuated by Andres Lamas. In abeyance during disturbances culminating in
a military dictatorship, it was partly revised under the dictator Latorre
by José Pedro Varela as an educational plan, and it found disciples in
Carlos Maria de Pena and others.

VII. MODIFICATION OF POSITIVISM

With time and diffusion and application to different national conditions in Latin America, not to speak of the increasing prestige of
Herbert Spencer, Positivism departed in many aspects from the faith
of its founder. It allied itself more or less in some cases with socialism.
It became critical of the dogmatic attitude of Comte, and of itself as a
final and closed system. It was not so sure that metaphysics and theology were all nonsense, and it was ready to make concessions in that
respect.

Positivistic Concessions to Metaphysics in Argentina. We pass now
to a group of Positivists illustrative of these concessions. Most eminent
among them, perhaps, was the Argentinian José Ingeneiros (1877-1925),
prominent in politics, a doctor interested especially in mental disorders,
and incidentally an admirer of Ralph Waldo Emerson. Instead of
disparaging metaphysical hypotheses, he considered them legitimate
under certain conditions. Transcending experience as they do, and
incapable of verification by it, they must not pretend to give knowledge. They are purely speculative, concerned with possibilities, not
certainties. They are simply more or less probable according as they
are more or less logically consistent internally and in accord with

experience. And the points on which different systems agree are more probable than those upon which they disagree. Furthermore, metaphysical hypotheses must be antidogmatic, flexible, and inclined to change as experience, from which they take flight, goes on being enlarged and more deeply analyzed. If conducted within these self-imposed restrictions, they may hope to free themselves in the future from their conflicting dogmas and substitute for a multiplicity of closed systems at war with one another, a single open system, comprehensive in scope and continually evolving. Such a system will be an impersonal, not a personal, creation, the result not of the unrestrained speculations of the individual, but rather of the harmonious collaboration of many minds working on the same problems and comparing, reconciling, and synthesizing their conclusions.

Positivism in Cuba. Another thinker who took his Positivism with a grain of salt was the Cuban, Enrique José Varona (1849-1933), considered not only the greatest philosopher that the island has so far produced, but its most outstanding all-round figure and one of the great men of Latin America. An advocate of the independence of Cuba, he was its representative in the Spanish parliament and later an active participant in the revolution headed by the patriot José Martí. He was made Secretary of Education once the republic was established, and later was elected Vice-president.

As Secretary of Education he further reformed the University of Havana and the scholastic curriculum generally in Cuba. But, as time went on, his philosophic attitude towards all problems became more skeptical in tone, and more and more pessimistic with respect to discovering satisfactory and final solutions. At the same time his increasing sense of disillusion, instead of inducing apathy and resignation, convinced him all the more that the fight, though its outcome was always dubious, was worth fighting and that the world could at least be bettered by human will and effort, even if it must always fall short of the ideal.

Martí (1855-1895), with whom Varona collaborated, means for Cuba what Hidalgo and Bolívar mean for Mexico and Spanish South America. Not only a great patriot, but also prose writer, orator, poet, and social and political philosopher devoted to the ideals of democracy, he lived a stormy and agitated life, part of it in the United States. He was incessant in his denunciation of Spanish misrule and his advocacy of Cuban independence. At the end he died fighting in the field in the revolution that, aided by the United States, freed Cuba from Spanish dominion only to exchange it, for a long time at least, for North American domination.

Positivism in Puerto Rico. His contemporary, Eugenio María de Hostos (1839-1903), occupies a similar place in the struggle for Puerto Rican independence. Devoted to freedom, not only for his own country but for Cuba as well, he was incessant in agitating for their autonomy. In New York he was a member of the Cuban Revolutionary Junta. He travelled widely in South America, where he wrote and spoke in favor of admitting women to the universities, and was one of the proponents of the trans-Andean railway. After the Spanish-American war he went to Washington to try to get for Puerto Rico rights equal to those of the states of the Union, and failing this, returned to the island and continued to work for Puerto Rican independence. He had also a philosophic background for his views and activities. He started as a fairly orthodox Positivist and disciple of Comte, and later was much influenced by John Stuart Mill and Herbert Spencer.

Positivism in Bolivia. In Bolivia, Luis Arce Lacaze (1872-1929), professor of law at Sucre, writer and statesman, though at first orthodox in his admiration for Comte and Spencer, was also impressed by Pascal, Ingeneiros, and the pragmatism of William James. We must, he said, take into account the reasons of the heart as well as of the head as sources of knowledge, and judge the truth of an idea by the all-round satisfaction it gives. Since religious experience had this quality, he admitted its validity without, however, committing himself to any particular hypotheses regarding its significance and its source.

His near contemporary, Daniel Sánchez Bustamonte (1871-1933), professor of law at La Paz, was one of the founders of the radical party and had a brilliant political career. In his *Principles of Law,* published in 1905, he outlined his philosophical ideas. He distinguished Spencerianism from Utilitarianism, supplemented the struggle for existence with the moral struggle for the realization of ideals, and gave that struggle a metaphysical basis in Spencer's Unknowable. This, the Infinite Power that underlies the mechanism of the phenomenal world, also creates within us our moral ideals. Their presence demands guidance of our affections and emotions by reason. Conduct, to be moral, must be rational; in our ability to submit to reason lies our freedom and moral responsibility.

A similar moderate departure from Positivism characterized Ignacio Prudencio Bustillo (1895-1928), professor and director in the Faculty of Law at Sucre from 1918-1921. He published in 1923 his *Essay on the Philosophy of Jurisprudence,* in which he expounded his philosophy.

Bustillo believed firmly in the positivistic scientific method as the only way of dealing with the knowable, but, influenced by Ingeneiro, he admitted the validity of metaphysical speculation provided it based itself on the latest scientific hypotheses inferred from experience. Morality must be scientific, drawn from collective social conditions. So-called inalienable natural rights do not exist. They are the product of changing social points of view and change with them. They rest upon the imperative impulses to self-preservation and the perpetuation of the species. Bustillo felt that intuition, as advocated by Bergson, had its place, but, uncontrolled by positivistic, scientific restraints, it was an untrustworthy and dangerous guide, subject to caprice and leading to purely imaginative, unfounded metaphysical hypotheses.

VIII. RETURN TO METAPHYSICS

Meantime, while becoming self-critical, Positivism was also being criticized philosophically as well as theologically from without. It had still to contend with Kant and the German idealists, whose influence was by no means dead, and new threats, as we shall presently see, were already looming on the horizon. Its position, weakened in its orthodox aspects from within, was also threatened in increasing degree from without.

Bolivia. In Bolivia the foremost nineteenth-century opponent of Positivism was Manierto Oyola Cuellar. He studied law at Cochabamba, was professor and director of the college in his native town of Santa Cruz, senator and prefect of the department of Beni, and finally member of the Court of Justice in Santa Cruz. His philosophy was founded on Descartes, whose rationalism he opposed to Kantian skepticism regarding the nature of things in themselves, to Hegelianism, to Materialism, and to Positivism. Locke's sensationism and empiricism he regarded as the source of all evils, and he had no use for Berkeley and Hume. All these philosophies, with perhaps special emphasis on Hegelianism, he criticized at length from the point of view of a fervent Catholic. In Descartes' "I think, therefore I exist" he found the basis of his faith. From our own existence and nature we can infer, as Descartes did, the existence and the attributes of a Creator. But he blamed Descartes for not extending Cartesianism to the moral and social order, and made its rationalism in part responsible for the revolutionary views of the Encyclopaedists. An examination of ourselves shows us that we are subject to an absolute moral order for which we are not responsible and which, therefore, must be attributed to a moral government of the world by a moral as well as an intelligent personal God. But in Bolivia, Oyola Cuellar proved a voice in the wilderness not preparing the way of the Lord. The liberals triumphed in 1899; as we have seen, education, religious as well as secular, fell under the control of the State, and the teaching of religion and Christian doctrine in the schools was forbidden in 1913.

Uruguay. In Uruguay, Positivism was attacked by Prudencio Vázquez y Vega who denounced it as atheistic and immoral and contributary to the bad state of affairs in the country. And Angel Solla accused it of being divided against itself in separate sects whose views cancelled out one another. But it withstood its enemies and in 1910 became as in Bolivia and Mexico the official philosophy of the University and the State.

Brazil. The most eminent nineteenth-century Brazilian philosopher, Tobías (not Pereira) Barreto (1839-1899), also broke with Positivism. He studied first in a Catholic seminary, abandoned it for the profession of law, and eventually became Professor of Law at Bahía. First a disciple of Cousin, then of Comte, he revolted against them and against the influence in general of French philosophy in Brazil and became ardently pro-German in his views and a partisan of Haeckel and of the Darwinian Theory. However, influenced by Kant, Schopenhauer, and von Hartmann, he transformed the material aspects of the world-process governed by efficient causation into the expression of a blind and irrational will to live that burst through its mechanical activities in the voluntary, purposeful behavior of man. But he also considered religious experience valid and referred it to a "numinous" something above and beyond the will—a God unattainable by thought but accessible through immediate, quasi-mystical intuition. With Catholicism, Christian dogma, and theologies of any kind, he would have nothing to do, though on his deathbed he returned to the Church, whether because really converted or to please his wife is uncertain. In his teaching of law he was also equally critical of the pretensions of Comte and Herbert Spencer to make of sociology a science, of the view that man has been endowed from on high with inalienable rights, and of the contract theories of their origin advanced by Hobbes and Rousseau. Rights are simply changing products of a changing social organization, and they vary with it.

In connection with Tobías Barreto we should mention his admirer and disciple, the writer, professor of law, government attorney, and diplomat, José Pereira de Graça Aranha (1869-1931), one of the founders of the Brazilian Academy of Letters. Man, he said, is essentially a child of the earth, a social being, and an integral part of the universe. As such he accepted himself in the beginning and was happy. But now he denies his earthiness, opposes the individual to society, and regards himself as an exception to the cosmic order. This setting himself apart from that of which he is a part is the original sin from which all his troubles, anxieties, perplexities, and fears—moral, social, theological, and metaphysical—have sprung. To overcome them and find peace he must regain the lost sense of oneness with all things. This cannot be accomplished by moral, theological, and metaphysical means, which are tortured activities forever seeking and never reaching unattainable goals. In the esthetic sense, however, he comes nearest to solving his problems. He is content and at rest contemplating the beauty and majesty of the ever-changing spectacle of all time and existence, in which he is both actor and audience. What projects it he can never know. Appearance has to be reality for him. Contemplating the spectacle and identifying himself with it in esthetic union, he finds himself once more in communion and at peace with mother earth, with his fellows and with the undiscoverable ultimate nature of things, and both thinks and acts accordingly. These views he set forth in his novels and plays and in his *Esthetics of Life, The Modern Spirit,* and his incomplete autobiography, *My Own Story.*

Contemporaneous with Graça Aranha, though shorter-lived, was Raimunde de Farías Brito (1862-1917), a lawyer, poet, teacher of mathematics in his youth and professor of logic at Pedro II College in Rio de Janeiro. Solitary and pessimistic by temperament, barely earning a living, and with few friends, he sought consolation in philosophy. This he could not find in the prevailing Positivism, Spencerianism, and Materialism of the times, which he considered a blind alley in Brazilian thought. Acquaintance, however, with Kant, Schopenhauer, von Hartmann, Spinoza, and Leibnitz suggested a solution of his own, which he proposed in his *Purpose of the World, The Physical Base of Spirit,* and *The World Within.* He rejected Kant's view that things-in-themselves are unknowable and agreed with Schopenhauer and Hartmann that their nature, though obscured by the external world, is revealed in the essential character of the perceiving subject. But he parted from them in maintaining that this character is not the blind will to live or the unconscious, but is self-conscious personality. Hence the thing-in-itself, the reality underlying phenomena, must be mental and self-conscious. In that case the Spinozistic Attribute of Extension, with all its so-called physical content, can be reduced to terms of the Attribute of Thought. Leibnitz was more to the point with the theory of Monads whose varying degrees of consciousness constituted matter both inorganic and organic, and all mind. But the Monads must not be regarded as separate entities, given independent existence when created. They, spirits as well as bodies, like the rest of the universe, are merely the thoughts of God. Whether human souls are immortal or not; in other words, whether God continues to entertain the ideas that are spirits after he has ceased to entertain the ideas of their bodies as living things, was a point on which Farías Brito would not commit himself. Though a freethinker, he was sympathetic to all religions and looked forward to one that would combine the best in both oriental and occidental beliefs.

The last important Brazilian philosopher, spiritually if not temporally, of the epoch under consideration, was Jackson de Figuerido (1891-1928). Educated in a Protestant preparatory college, he turned materialistic, mechanistic, Darwinian, and agnostic while studying law at the University of Bahía. But there also he fell under the influence of Pascal, Carlyle, and Nietzsche. Arriving in Rio de Janeiro in 1913, penniless and unknown, his attractive personality at once won him many friends. Among them was Farías Brito, by whom he was so impressed that later on he wrote two books about him. But his admiration did not mean agreement. Pascal had taught him that the heart as well as the intellect has its reasons, and that these defy logic and rest upon faith. But since hearts beat differently and their reasons suggest different faiths, a criterion is necessary for distinguishing tenable from untenable beliefs. This criterion Jackson de Figuerido found in Catholicism, to which he was converted while desperately ill during the influenza epidemic of 1918.

Once converted, Figuerido became an ardent defender of the Catholic Church. Tertullian's famous saying, "It is believable because it is absurd; it is certain because it is impossible," became his watchword. But his philosophical views must have verged upon being unorthodox. He proclaimed himself a neo-Kantian, and identified God with the *noumenon,* the rest of existence with *phenomena.* He inclined to the Plotinian view that the phenomenal world represents a fall of the divine from itself into imperfection and suffering, and that its evolution from the inorganic to the organic to the conscious, and to the human soul, is motivated by an aspiration to reunite itself with its source. This point of view he expressed in his *Pascal and Modern Uneasiness.*

In his political views, Jackson de Figuerido was much influenced by the French reactionary Maurras. He upheld the authority not only of the Church over the individual conscience, but that of the State over individual liberty, and fought hard on the conservative side against democracy, individualism and liberalism, denouncing them as the evil consequences of Materialism and Positivism. And Positivism he twitted with owing its success to being a religion, though a fake one.

Though put on the defensive, Positivism by no means succumbed to these attacks. As we have seen, its temple still exists in Rio de Janeiro, weekly services are held, and its doctrines are seriously studied, discussed, and upheld. Its most distinguished exponent is Ivan Lins, a man of great learning, a prolific writer in the philosophical field, and still a devoted and even fundamentalist disciple of Comte.

Chapter XXVII

LATIN-AMERICAN PHILOSOPHY IN THE TWENTIETH CENTURY

We are now lapping over into the twentieth century, in the first years of which the influence of Kant and the German idealists was being supplemented and supplanted by an influx of new philosophies, largely French. Boutroux, Ravaisson, Renouvier, Bergson, and Lachellier, with the Italian Croce and the North American William James, were helping to inspire Spanish American thought, and contributing to the decline of Positivism. Already we have seen these new influences cropping up in some of the philosophies we have been discussing. And in those we are about to discuss we shall find them more and more obvious.

I. PERU

Deústua. We turn first to the Peruvian, Alejandro Deústua (1849-1945), whose long life spans the whole of the last half of the nineteenth and nearly the first half of the twentieth century. During the one he was indebted to Krause and was the one Latin American philosopher of any note who was Krause's disciple; during the other, to Bergson. A graduate of San Marcos, he was appointed professor of esthetics in the Faculty of Letters, and for the next fifty years played a prominent part in the University as teacher, Dean of the Faculty of Letters, and Rector. He was also Director of the National Library in Lima, held important political positions, and was especially interested in improving education from the bottom to the top throughout Peru.

Deústua approached philosophy through esthetics. Art creates beauty by combining freedom and order. Both factors are indispensable. This is true also of economic, social, scientific, moral, and religious achievement. On every level of human life we find free creative activity expressing itself in orderly fashion. But only in esthetic creation is complete liberty obtained, untrammeled by the order of which it is the source. For in art alone the free creative activity generates a continuously evolving order that keeps pace and is wholly harmonious with it. On the economic, scientific, and religious levels the orders to which it gives rise tend to crystallize into comparatively inflexible social and economic organizations, scientific hypotheses, laws and religious dogmas. These, instead of evolving *pari passu* with it, as do the forms of art, lag behind and retard the creative impulse, and obstruct rather than express its free exercise.

Deústua's chief works are *The Ideas of Order and Liberty in the History of Human Thought,* and his *General Aesthetics* and *Applied Aesthetics.*

II. URUGUAY

Rodo. In Uruguay, the brilliant writer, essayist and critic, José Enrique Rodó (1871-1917), while opposing, like Barreda in Mexico, too great specialization in education and approving the positivistic program and the ideals it was supposed to promote, viewed with alarm the results of its popularity. The mediocre minds of the great majority of the people, he felt, lost sight of the nobility and spirituality of these ideals, and converted Positivism into a justification of the pursuit of purely utilitarian, material and sensual ends.

Ferreira. Carlos Vaz Ferreira (1873-   ), a practicing lawyer, voluminous writer on all subjects, and successively professor of philosophy, rector of the University of Montevideo, and Director of the Faculty of the Humanities, also broke away from a positivistic point of view in which John Stuart Mill had perhaps figured more prominently than Comte or Spencer. His objection to it was but one expression of his dislike of dogmatic thinking in all fields, economic, sociological, moral, as well as scientific and philosophical. He was suspicious of hide-bound logic and in his *Living Logic* delighted in showing up the absurdities resulting from its use. Equally suspicious of experience as a guide, he warns that its rules of thumb may come by repeated invocation to be regarded as self-evident, eternal truths. Human thinking, intuitive, emotional, and conceptual, must be flexible and continually adapt itself to an ever-changing world.

Nor can we get rid of metaphysics, as the Positivists think. Scientific hypotheses are not accurate and final descriptions of reality, but provisional and symbolic. And *why* things behave as they do cannot be excluded altogether from scientific attempts to describe merely *how* they behave. After all, philosophers as a rule know something about science, witness Renouvier, Bergson, and James. Why then should not scientists know something about metaphysics, of which only too frequently they know nothing? At the best, it is impossible to make a hard and fast distinction between the two. Since metaphysics of some sort is unavoidable, a good metaphysics is the only cure for a bad one, and here scientists who know something about it could be of great help. Both the eclectics and the dogmatic partisans of a single point of view make a mess of it, since the "evidence" from which both scientific and metaphysical conclusions are drawn is always changing, and never warrants more than tentative opinions.

III. ARGENTINA

Korn. In Argentina, the outstanding representatives of the new movement are Alejandro Korn (1860-1936), Alberto Rougès (1880-1945), and Francisco Romero (1891-   ). Korn, a doctor in Buenos Aires specializing in psychology and mental disorders and the head of an insane asylum, interested himself in philosophy, abandoned his practice, and became a professor in the Faculty of Philosophy and Letters of the University. A principal factor in his conversion was Schopenhauer, who set him on the track of the Oriental and then of the European mystics. But he found in Kant the starting point of his own thinking. His philosophy he expounded in the three volumes of his *Works*. Conscious activity, he tells us, is all that exists. It has two aspects, subjective and objective, both equally real and irreducible to each other, but without "substance" such as matter and spirit underlying them. "Substance" is simply a general concept describing the continuity of the stream of consciousness, which is the only reality, the absolute, and is essentially a process of *becoming,* with no permanent substratum. Objective experience is a spatio-temporal order of sense data, whose present is determined mechanically only by its past. Subjective experience, on the contrary, goes on in time only. It is an affair of feeling, passion, emotion, desire, will, and reasoning, determined purposively by the future. It is always looking and moving forward to the realization of ideals that its free and creative activity engenders.

The two aspects of experience conflict. The free creative will of the subject is checked by his objective experience, to whose order he must in part submit if he is to survive. In part, however, he can control it and thus attain a modicum of "economic" freedom and material well-being. Also, he can and must control his subjective desires and impulses, and in mastering them freely creates a moral law and order for himself whose service is perfect freedom. He can also freely disobey what he has freely created, in which case he will be punished as certainly as if he had defied a physical law.

This punishment is not one of "economic" disaster or social disgrace on earth. Nor is it deferred to another world or to reincarnation in this. Supernatural punishments are hypotheses unwarranted by experience. The totality of experience, subjective and objective, is beyond good and evil, which are mere names we apply to its bearing *pro* or *con* upon the exercise of our creative freedom. To regard that totality as wholly good is to leave its evil aspects unexplained. To regard it as in itself both good and evil is to split it into two coeternal streams of consciousness—a God and a Devil. Neither of these hypotheses, apart from their logical self-contradictions, is suggested and supported by the nature of experience, whose only essential cleavage is between subject and object. The real punishment for disobedience to the moral law is the disobedience itself, which involves an internal degradation of freedom, a loss of the creative subject's mastery of his liberty, and a disloyalty to himself.

In the aspiration towards freedom we come closest to knowing the true nature of the experience that constitutes all existence. To fulfill that aspiration requires morality of a high and heroic order, necessitating the sacrifice not only of passion and desire and material welfare, but also of much that is properly held dear. It may even call for opposition and disobedience to the prevalent popular moral standards of the time and place and invite martyrdom. Nevertheless only by maintaining its absolute liberty and autonomy, come what may, can creative personality become identified with its source, of which its freedom is the highest expression.

Rougès. We turn now to Rougès. Though he studied law, he never practiced it, and, though called now and then into public service, he avoided politics and lived a retired life. However, he was active in the intellectual activities of his native city and province of Tucumán, and was one of the founders of its University in 1914, and a member of the governing board. In 1944 he was invited to teach there, and a year later, just before he died, was made Rector.

A sincere Catholic, he was restrained in this thinking by Christian dogma. But he was thoroughly acquainted with British and French philosophy and contemporary science. And his Catholicism was not so much Scholastic as Augustinian, Platonic, and neo-Platonic in inspiration.

Like Korn, Rougès divided experience into the subjective and objective and contrasted its two aspects as Korn did. But experience did not for him exhaust the existent. It implies, he says in his *Hierarchies of Existence and Eternity,* both a physical order underlying the phenomenal world, and a soul or spirit underlying subjective experience. The material and the spiritual differ radically in their relation to *time.* The physical world, whether regarded as purely sense-data or as also subphenomenal, *is* at any given time only what, when, and where it is at that time. Its past is dead, its future as yet unborn. It passes from one point of space, instant of time, and quality to another, each one of which totally excludes the other. Subjective experience, on the other hand, includes in its present moment of time both the past and the future, looking back to the one and forward to the other. It overarches and interrelates them as does a sentence, for example, in which each word is what it is because it completes those that it follows, is incomplete without those that follow it, and does not make sense without this fusion of past, present, and future intention.

This reciprocal interpenetration of past, present, and future in the "spiritual" now raises it partly out of time into eternity—not a static, timeless eternity, however, but a dynamic one in which past, present, and future exist as such, and yet form a single whole. Complete eternity, however, is found only in the mind of God, which contains, contemplates and interrelates in its ever-present "now" all that was, all that is, all that shall be. And so surveyed, all the hierarchy of existence, with its successive steps from the physical through the spiritual to God, posts the way to eternity.

Romero. We pass now to Romero. His family emigrated from Spain to Argentina while he was still a child. He took up soldiering as a profession. But he embarked, also, on a literary career and made a name for himself as a critic and writer on esthetics. The University of Buenos Aires offered him a temporary professorship, and on the retirement of his friend Korn, the chair of metaphysics. This he resigned in 1946, to teach in the Free College of Advanced Studies.

For him the two opposed characteristics of existence on all its levels, the inorganic, the conscious and the spiritual, are *immanence* and *transcendence.* All things are both what they are and something more. The world process is an *upward thrust,* obstructed by the inertia of *immanence,* in which the lower transcends, while retaining, its own immanent characteristics and adds to itself those of the next higher level. This upward thrust becomes more intensive and extensive as it proceeds from the lower to the higher, "colonizing" each new plane with all its possibilities and immediately discovering new worlds to conquer, until at last it attains its final objective and complete expression in *spirit*.

In spirit, however, there is still immanence to be overcome. Spirit is now self-conscious and conscious of all it has transcended, and *evaluates* all things including itself in terms of truth, beauty, and goodness. But, lodged in individual psychophysical organisms, it is involved in the struggle for existence, actuated by the "instinct" of self-preservation, and impelled to self-assertion at the expense of others. To the individual, things and other individuals possess value only as they are valuable to *him* and subserve *his* particular interests. Truth, for him, is what is practically useful in getting *him* ahead, morality for all is whatever *he* thinks it good and right for *himself* to do. And even God he regards as a supernatural individual who can be placated and flattered into doing what he wants done.

This immanence in individuality must be transcended before spirit can come into its own. It must become a *person*. As such it becomes centrifugal rather than centripetal, altruistic rather than selfish. The *person* now seeks truth honestly and disinterestedly for its own sake and willingly conforms with it, even when it discredits his wishful thinking. He does this because in transcending his individuality he has imposed upon himself an *obligation* to free his scientific and metaphysical thinking from individual bias. Moreover, he has also imposed upon himself the *obligation* to deal with his fellows "altruistically" with a view to their own best interests, to identify himself with the welfare of others and of society, and to aspire towards the divine with no ulterior motive. Egotism—intellectual, economic, social, moral, and religious—is the root of all ignorance and evil; altruism—respect for, and cooperation with, others in all those fields—is the source of the attainment of truth and goodness. All efforts to better mankind resolve themselves into attempts to turn the aggregate of amoral individuals, naturally at war with one another, whose peace is a precarious negotiated truce based upon fear, into a community of moral persons naturally at peace with one another, with no fear of one another, and united by a common moral purpose of realizing in their lives the values in which the transcendent upward thrust of the world-process comes to full fruition.

The distinction between the person and the individual, transcendence and immanence, is not always clear. Self-righteousness may disguise itself as the moral law, and selfishness as unselfish concern for the good of others—witness in international affairs imperialism masquerading as a missionary. Conversely, honest altruism may be tricked into a blind self-sacrifice of the altruistic person to the egotistical individualism of his neighbors and thus contribute to their selfishness.

Moral creative personality is, then, the final and highest achievement of the existent. But Romero warns the reader that his interpretation of the world process is only tentative and provisional. It is not his habit to dogmatize and assert mere probabilities as certainties. And he reserves to himself the inalienable right of all philosophers to doubt even their own systems.

Romero has written extensively. Among his works we may note *Contemporary Philosophy, Philosophy of the Person, Philosophical Papers (Papeles para la Filosofía)*, and *Philosophers and Problems.*

IV. MEXICO

Sierra. We now go northward into Mexico and backward in time to the first decade of the twentieth century. The Pontifical University in Mexico City had been abolished in 1883 as antiquated and useless, and its place had been taken by separate schools organized along modern lines. On its reorganization as the National University in 1910 by the humanist, statesman, and educator, Justo Sierra, the pressure of a group of young men known as the Youth Athenaeum *(Ateneo de Juventud)*, organized in 1908, was instrumental in establishing in the School of Advanced Studies a chair of the History of Philosophy. This group had begun, under the influence of Pedro Henríquez Urena, to doubt the positivistic creed in which it had been brought up. In his inaugural address, Sierra formally disestablished Positivism and dedicated the chair to the study of all philosophies up to date, including Bergson and William James; he left theists, pantheists, and atheists alike free to express their opinions, and the students at liberty to choose whatever views most appealed to them. Among the young men of various interests and callings who made up the Athenaeum were the two outstanding Mexican philosophers, so far, of the twentieth century, Antonio Caso (1883-1946) and José Vasconcelos (1882-   ).

Caso. Caso studied and for a while practiced law. But he found his true vocation in teaching, and taught in the Preparatory School and the School of Jurisprudence prior to the revival of the National University. After it was reconstituted he became professor of philosophy in the Faculty of the Humanities, a chair he occupied for thirty years. He was a voluminous writer and a great teacher beloved by his students. His prestige extended beyond the walls of the University, the frontiers of Mexico, and the shores of the Americas, not only as a

philosopher but as Mexican ambassador to various Latin American
governments. Among his chief works are *Existence as Economy, Dis-
interestedness and Love, Principles of Aesthetics, The Human Person
and the Totalitarian State*. In them he tells us that there are two classes
of philosophers, the heroic, creative, imaginative, intuitive ones, and the
discreet, critical, and cautious thinkers who will not go further than
reasoning permits. It was the heroic type that Caso admired, and his
philosophy, which owed much to Boutroux, Ravaisson, Bergson, James,
and others, was enlisted on the heroic side.

According to Caso there are three grades of being, the inorganic, the
organic or individual, and the personal. The inorganic can be divided
without changing its nature, but the organic individual dies and loses
its distinctive character if broken up. However, the efficiency both of a
machine and of an organism consists in obtaining the maximum results
with the minimum expenditure of energy. Operating on this principle
of *economy*, it is the nature of the human being, as of all individual
organisms, to reach out and appropriate everything he can, both organic
and inorganic, and assimilate it to his own selfish uses, with the least
possible effort on his part.

However, on the individual level more energy is generated than is
absorbed by practical needs. Even in the lower animals it spills over
into play just for the fun of it. In human beings it takes on other
disinterested forms. In doing so it creates and pursues *values*. It spontaneously seeks truth and beauty and the good of others for their own
sake. It expresses itself in *charity*, in the all-embracing Christian sense
of loving one's neighbor as one's self. Inspired by it, the human organism has ceased to be merely an *individual* and has become a *person*.

However, there is no sign that the human *race* as a whole is evolving
towards personality. Human history is *not* a record of *progress*. Physically the *race*, if anything, is deteriorating, and it is perhaps becoming
less attractive esthetically. Its morals and its art are no better than they
were the first day. Its only collective advance has been in science, which,
however, has only increased the ability of the individual to get the
better of nature and of other individuals. It is in the *men* of all times
and places, not in mankind as a whole, that the *person* keeps emerging
from the *individual*. To be sure, there are also great epochs of history,
as well as great men, but their level cannot equal that of the *persons*
whom they produce and to whom they owe their greatness. For this
reason Utopias are illusions, encouraging, at that, only the abolition of
economic misery and suffering, which would leave humanity still indi-

vidualistic, and indisposed to sacrifice material comfort in order to attain the higher, disinterested values.

But the distinguishing mark of the *person* is precisely his impulse to sacrifice not only his material comfort and welfare but his life, if necessary, in the service of those values. And the formula of sacrifice is the opposite of that of *economic* activity. Sacrifice combines a maximum expenditure of energy with a minimum of individual economic return. It is inspired not by a Kantian categorical imperative or sense of *duty* imposed from without, but by a free creative drive from within generating moral value and impelling the person to realize it in himself, cost what it may. This drive is not a Nietzschean will to power over others but a will to moral conquest of oneself.

Hence totalitarianism is as opposed as anarchical individualism to the emergence of the person. Sacrifice imposed willy-nilly by force by the state upon its members is not the voluntary self-sacrifice for the good of others that distinguishes the person from the individual. The state should not be a kind of super-individual extorting what it can from the individuals that compose it, but a free association of *persons* working together in spontaneous self-imposed service of the higher values. It should deal with its members, and with other states, as persons treat persons. To its failure to do so we owe the present conflict of individuals with individuals and with the state, and of the state with individuals and with other states.

It is in art, in which he was deeply interested, that Caso found the most untrammeled exercise of the free creative activity of the person. The artist does not have to explain and find reasons for things or turn them to extraneous purposes. He contemplates and treats them, not practically or theoretically, but simply as he *perceives* them. For him they *are* what they are *seen* to be. And this perception of them without preoccupation regarding their why, wherefore, and what for, reveals them also as they are in and for themselves.

The aspiration towards and pursuit of moral values is sustained by hope, which implies an order in the world that makes prediction of the future in terms of the present and the past possible, even if for our minds it has to be uncertain. The physical and the biological sciences assume such an order in their respective fields. The *person* also may assume a moral order and law that make sense of his creation and pursuit of values and of the *sacrifice* he must make in order to attain them. Furthermore, sacrifice in their service is an expenditure of energy that contradicts and cannot be explained by its mechanical and biological expressions. Such energy seems to be self-sustaining and survives all attacks upon it. May we not then hope that the *person* will also survive the death of the organism by which he is supported but not caused? May we not hope that he will live on, incorporated in the world of values he has created and, now freed from the necessity of self-sacrifice, will enter into beatitude?

Finally, the human person, however great, falls short of the human ideal. The values to which he aspires and his aspiration towards them can only be explained by postulating an omnipotent, omniscient, free and morally perfect person—God.

Vasconcelos. We turn now to Vasconcelos. He studied law and was one of the most brilliant, active, and restless members of the Athenaeum, in prophecy of his future many-sided and agitated career. He fought under Madero against Díaz, was rector of the University and later on minister of education under Obregón. During the ascendency of Calles, both as President and power behind the throne, he ran for the presidency against Calles' candidate. Defeated in what he declared a fraudulent election, he tried vainly to head a revolt and had to take refuge in the United States and then in South America. After his return from exile, he was for a while Director of the National Library, but he has not been active in politics. He has always been an uncompromising and forthright opponent of foreign interference, for the most part Anglo-Saxon, in the internal affairs of Latin America, and of the adverse influence of the Protestant, industrial, and materialistic aspects of the mentality of the United States upon Latin America. Left to develop along its own lines, free from such contamination, it may create, he believes, out of its mixture of Iberian and Indian blood a new "cosmic" race—the great race of the future.

Philosophically, Vasconcelos began as a Positivist and has returned to the Catholic Church. It is his intervening thought that concerns us. This is "heroic" in inspiration and intention, supplementing reason with intuition and aspiring to an all-embracing inclusiveness. Schopenhauer first detached him from Positivism, and the dynamic, anti-materialistic, and mystical movements in Greek philosophy, along with Leibnitz, Kant, Nietzsche, Bergson, and later, after his adherence to personal theism, the Personalists have helped mold his thinking. Perhaps he is most indebted to Plotinus.

In the world-process, whose essence is energy, he discovers two opposed currents, one descending from, the other ascending to, its source. On the one hand, the universe is running down and coming to a standstill through the degradation and dissipation of energy according to the law of entropy. But on the other, there is a reverse process of stepping up and liberation of energy—a passionate desire of the universe, as it were, to reunite itself with that from which it has proceeded. This upward struggle is observable on the inorganic level in the behavior of certain metals, in chemical affinities, and in the action of catalyzers, where energy is apparently increased without loss. This increase and liberation becomes more marked and extensive as we rise to the organic level, mount through vegetable and animal life to sensation, and, through developing consciousness, to spirit. However, the process is one not of continuous evolution, but of jumps in which a new form of energy suddenly appears, irreducible to and inexplicable by its antecedents and endowed with wholly new properties. For example, with the appearance of the organic there is a sudden shift from efficient to final causation. The advent of sensation is another such jump, and still another is the capacity of consciousness to retain *images* of experience and react to them emotionally. Imagery converts the physical into a mental world and enables it to survive there the constant dissolution of material existence. Experience can now, thanks to imagery, be evaluated and reflected upon, and the physical can thus be transubstantiated into a spiritual universe.

Already, and here Vasconcelos follows Kant, consciousness has imposed upon the stuff of experience a spatio-temporal layout and now reflects upon it in accordance with the Categories of the Understanding and the Ideas of Pure Reason. But they leave us with unknowable things-in-themselves on our hands. The nature of the real must then be intuited, since it cannot be reasoned out. And it can be intuited in the meaning and the value we *feel* in the world of images and ideas, into which we have transformed the sensible world. Here we are conscious both within ourselves and in the objective world of the passionate desire to return to its source that animates the upward thrust of the world-process.

Thus, in ethics, the moral is that which identifies us with the ascending, increasing current of energy. It is aspiration to unite not only ourselves but, through our transformation of the material into a mental universe, the whole of nature with the absolute. The immoral is that which involves us in the dissipation and degradation of the outflowing descending current. We do not distinguish which is which by reasoning but by emotional evaluation, by a *sense* of right and wrong, by conscience. Our free will may identify us with the one tendency or the other. If we choose to sink, the spiritual energy in us is degraded and dissipated, and we may lose, or in any case deserve to lose, our souls and perish as the lower animals perish. If we choose to rise with the ascending current, we may be carried by it beyond physical death.

Most ethical systems, ancient and modern, fail to realize the nature of the true good in which the ascending current finds both its beginning and its end. They are earth-bound and anthropocentric. Their highest value has to do with the *person*. But the person is not and should not be treated as an end in himself, but as a means to something beyond himself. Personal existence must be negated and transcended in mystical union with the Absolute, which alone is truly valuable in and for itself. This is recognized negatively by Buddhism and the Vedanta. But in Christian ethics alone it is positively proclaimed, enacted in the monastic and ascetic life of self-abnegation, and imposed as a duty—the only real moral obligation—upon all men alike. Negation and transcendence are obstructed by the descending current in us, in which all sins, the worst of which are cruelty and tyranny, have their origin.

As regards the best social organization in this world, there is much to be said for Socialism. But Capitalism, Fascism, and Communism are equally evil because of their despotic enslavement of the many by the few, or by an inhuman State.

The mystical re-entry of spirit into its source has its closest counterpart in religious conversion. It is spontaneous, sudden, a complete change and overturn of all that has gone before. The spirit is all at once no longer a separate being, no longer a person, but one with the One.

Esthetic experience is the nearest approach to it on the personal level. Here man *feels* immediately the oneness of the ascending current within him with that of all nature. This feeling half appeases his longing for complete unity with the One, and he rests for a moment almost satisfied. Half-forgetting himself as a person, he anticipates the total forgetfulness of himself in the final, mystical ecstasy of reunion with the ineffable source of all existence. It is in this satisfaction, this half-forgetfulness, this sense of anticipation, that the esthetic value resides, and things are beautiful insofar as they provoke it.

The genius of the artist lies in his sensitiveness to the coincidence and accord of the ascending spiritual rhythm of his own being with that of the rest of nature. He is thus enabled to translate into terms of his own rhythm all in nature that is not on the downgrade and that can be given spiritual significance. The resultant feeling of unity with the universe and the esthetic satisfaction that is given by overcoming separation from it—these the artist's genius enables him to communicate to others by his works, and thus he rescues from destruction for all men and all time the ephemeral, dissolving content of sense perception and the spiritual meaning, the aspiration toward the divine, the beauty he has discovered in it.

Upon this basis Vasconcelos erects an elaborate discussion of the fine arts in which Nietzsche's distinction between the Apollonian and the Dionysian plays a considerable part. Generally speaking, the arts may be divided into three kinds, the plastic, the emotional and symbolic, and the mystical and the religious. The religious and the mystical enlist and combine the others in the service of religious ceremonial—of liturgy —which is the supreme art, and the supreme manifestation of beauty.

V. PRESENT TENDENCIES

At the present moment, the interest in philosophy is perhaps more widespread than ever in Latin America and is integrated, as in the past, with the culture of the educated classes. We cannot, however, because of limitations of space, continue to follow it in the work of individual philosophers. It is not that they do not deserve special mention, but rather that they deserve more than can be given them. And to pick and choose between them is impossible. Moreover, most contemporary systems are in the making and may have a long future in which their authors may frequently change their minds. To pin them down to the present moment is to do them an injustice. Let us, then, simply note contemporary tendencies—with apologies to individuals for not giving them the attention they merit.

At the moment Latin American thought is open and responsive, as it always has been since its emancipation from Scholasticism, to all the current philosophical movements abroad in the world today. It is receptive of all the present "isms" and all the current "neo's." Dilthey, Husserl, Scheler, Brentano, Hartmann, Heidegger, Cohen, Natorp, Stammler, Kelsen, Bergson, and others have contributed largely to it— and this largely through the medium of Ortega y Gasset. Moreover, his perspectivism and his insistence that the proper task of philosophy is to study the circumstances out of which its various systems arise, rather than to claim objective validity for them, is much in vogue.

So it is that in Latin America we find a deep and widespread interest in the perspective of the Latin-American person—in discovering his distinctive angle and what makes him, to vary the figure, tick differently from, let us say, the Anglo-Saxons or the Chinese. This general perspective is fragmented into different national perspectives, and even local ones, that constrain the person to think as he does. For instance, *Lo Mexicano,* what makes a Mexican what he is and determines what he thinks, is the interest of perhaps the most influential school of philosophic thought in present-day Mexico.

This return of philosophy to anthropocentrism and to what we may call "patriocentrism" is, however, but part of a prevalent swing, everywhere apparent in philosophic thought, away from metaphysics to a combination of neo-positivism, neo-humanism, and naturalistic personalism. The whirligig of time has its revenges. What its next revenge will be in the world at large and in Latin America in particular remains to be seen.

Chapter XXVIII

RECENT SPANISH PHILOSOPHY

In the meantime, Spain had produced two of the most important philosophers of the first half of the twentieth century, Miguel de Unamuno and José Ortega y Gasset, both of them eminent also in the political, educational, and literary life of their country.

I. UNAMUNO

Life and Education. Unamuno (1864-1936) was professor of Greek in the University of Salamanca and later its rector. Dismissed because of his opposition to the monarchy and the dictatorship of Primo de Rivera, he left Spain, to return only after the latter's fall, when he became a member of the Constituent Assembly of the Republic, with which, however, he fell out just before his death in 1936, on the eve of the Spanish Civil War. First and last a patriotic Spaniard, he reflected at length upon the history, the vicissitudes, the virtues, and the short-comings of Spain, and upon the distinctive characteristics of the Spanish temperament and outlook on life. These he found to be a mixture of commercialism, formalism, blind faith, and intolerance on the one hand, and a restless, Utopian, adventurous, revolutionary, impractical nature on the other, the symbol of which was Don Quixote. In a combination of Don Quixote and Sancho Panza, the symbol of the practical point of view—a combination dominated by the former—Unamuno saw the future and the salvation of Spain.

He was a voluminous writer both in prose and verse, and expressed much of his philosophy in his novels and his poetry. Philosophically, Unamuno is in some respects a precursor of the Existentialists. He was born and brought up in the Catholic Church. But while a student in Madrid he underwent a religious crisis. The "reasons of the heart" still impelled him to believe in the teachings of the Church, but now in the reasons of the head he could find no rational ground for be-lieving in them. Thus he became involved in an unending conflict within himself—an emotional conflict all the more devastating because he had a veritably obsessing horror of death and a passionate desire to believe in immortality and in God as a guarantee of it. Of this horror of having to die, and of the search for means of circumventing extinction, his philosophy is fundamentally the expression.

Learned in the classics, in theology, and in the history of philosophy, he was most attracted by Pascal and Kierkegaard and to a lesser degree by Schopenhauer, Nietzsche and William James, all of whom in their several ways had stressed the equal, if not superior, importance of the subjective, the passionate, the emotional, and the intuitional, to the objective and to cold logic and reasoning as accesses to truth. Of reason left only to its own devices, whether used by science, theology, or philosophy, he despaired. Positively and constructively used it can assure us of nothing. Negatively and destructively employed, it casts doubt upon everything, and only induces skepticism with respect to the validity of the systems founded upon it. We are left then with the reasons of the heart to give human life the supernatural extension and significance without which it is futile, meaningless, a mere tragic interlude between nothingness and nothingness. But the reasons of the head and their skeptical implications cannot be banished by the reasons of the heart. They are always there, continually challenging the latter, questioning the ability to take anything on faith and undermining belief with unbelief.

Faith and Reason. From this everlasting conflict between faith and reason, between the desire to believe and the haunting inability to do so, there results an agonizing conflict within us between the two which gets us nowhere and leaves us in perpetual suspense. At the same time we cannot remain suspended and inactive in thought and action. We must take sides, and in order to give meaning to life and rescue ourselves from despair, we must commit ourselves to faith; we must will to believe in the reasons of the heart, and create, in order to believe in him, a God who loves us and whom we love in return. Otherwise our lives are without significance, and the universe itself is equally so, resolved into the nothingness from which we emerge and into which we so soon expire. And to prevent this extinction we must also create immortality in order to believe in it, and thus assure ourselves that death does not end all for us.

In doing so we run tremendous risks—the risks pointed out by reason. Moreover, these risks are not merely of *belief* but of *conduct*. We must stake our whole lives on faith, and live and love as if there were a God who loves us, and as if we were immortal, though we cannot know, here and now at any rate, and perhaps will never know, whether or not the risk has been worth taking. But it must be taken unless we are to surrender to reason and live in continual bondage to reasonable doubt and consequent moral despair.

Nevertheless, Unamuno could not altogether free himself of this doubt and despair. Rejecting the reasons of the head adduced by the Catholic Church in support of its dogmas, he found also that the latter, along with their conception of God, failed to satisfy the reasons of his heart. He longed to be a Christian and he found in Christ on the Cross the supreme embodiment of his own conflict between faith and doubt and of the loneliness not only of himself but of all men in that struggle. But he could go no further. Religious dogma was as unacceptable as scientific "truth."

But there should be no indecision in the ordering of a man's life. This is an adventure to which he must commit himself and which he must carry through one way or another. He must be a person, must develop his personality, must be himself, and be true to himself, come what may. He must have, love, and serve an ideal, though it might prove imaginary and impracticable, and might come to naught or to grief. Like Don Quixote, he must have a Dulcinea, however idealized; must tilt at windmills; mistake the imaginary for the real; right wrongs, whether real or fancied; and be, if necessary, considered crazy by the rest of the world for committing what seems to them follies and absurdities which, in the long run, may turn out to exhibit a wisdom and a charity greater than theirs.

Unamuno's chief philosophical works are *El Sentimiento Trágico de la Vida, La Agonía del Cristianismo,* and *La Vida de Don Quixote y Sancho Panza.*

II. ORTEGA Y GASSET

Life and Education. José Ortega y Gasset was born in Madrid in 1883. Educated in his youth by the Jesuits, he studied at the University of Madrid and then in Germany at Berlin and at Marburg under Cohen. For a time, too, he was influenced by Unamuno, but broke with him in 1909, the year before he was made professor of philosophy at Madrid. Politically he was prominent in the establishment of the Spanish Republic and a member of the Constituent Assembly. After the Spanish Civil War he lived abroad for a while, but later returned to Spain and resumed his chair of philosophy. Well read in the entire history of European philosophy and science, he was at first particularly influenced by Renan, under whose guidance he discarded the Jesuits and Christianity and turned skeptic; then, by Kant and the German idealists and contemporary German thought, with the emphasis perhaps upon Scheler and Heidegger; but above all, later on by the philosophy of history of Dilthey. A great orator and prolific writer not only in the field of philosophy but in those of history, sociology, politics, art and literature, he has helped diffuse in Spain knowledge of contemporary science and philosophy, especially that of the Germans whom he much admired, and has had great influence upon present Spanish and Latin American intellectual life.

I Am I and My Surroundings. To his early period belongs the famous theme upon which the development of his philosophy plays variations: *Yo soy yo y mis circunstancias (I am I and my surroundings).* The one cannot be separated from the other. They are interrelated and interlocked. But under neither of them is there any underlying substance. I am not a thing, a soul, a mind, a spirit. Nor have my surroundings a material substratum. Both are confluent in a stream of consciousness, subjective and objective, that nothing transcends or supports. Reasoning or intuition that tries to establish anything above or below it leads only to self-contradictory philosophical, religious, ethical and scientific concepts. Vitalism—Bergson, for example, with his *élan vital*—is equally unsatisfactory. For it surreptitiously introduces the existence of forces, or energies, or drives, as cosmic principles actuating both me and my surroundings.

What then am I? The answer, mediating between rationalism and vitalism, is that I am my whole life, which includes my surroundings. I am a *career,* a *life,* a *history,* which makes itself from moment to moment, which is in perpetual flux and alteration, and never stable. This history is continually interpreting and reinterpreting itself in projected philosophical concepts, theological and moral beliefs, and scientific hypotheses about itself, which, in the heat of the present moment, it regards as valid also for all other moments past and future, that is, as *absolute.* But as my content of consciousness, subjective and objective, changes, and as my life goes on, the interpretations of it, to which absolute validity is attributed, change also, and the absolute truth and right of one moment become the absolute error and wrong of the next. In short, all so-called absolutes turn out to be such relatively to the moment alone in which they are regarded as such. There is no such thing as an *absolute* absolute, valid for all in all times and places. My *total history,* my *total life,* then, that constitutes and comprises me and my surroundings and projects these shifting "absolute" interpretations of its content is, as Ortega y Gasset says in another well-known phrase, nothing but a particular *perspective,* and not the only perspective.

The Real as Perspectives. For other individuals exist, each one of them with his own life history projecting its appropriate "absolutes" and constituting another perspective. But these perspectives, although they in part exclude, in part include one another. I figure in you and your surroundings, and you in me and mine. We have a common "objective" world of shared surroundings, though even this varies in different perspectives relatively to our respective physical idiosyncracies. And also, to a great extent, large groups of perspectives interpret themselves in the same way and project similar "absolutes," philosophical, religious, scientific, and ethical. But, since none of these projections succeeds in transcending the perspective in which it occurs, *all we can say of the Real is that it is a collection of perspectives, of partly similar, partly dissimilar, content, and is, as far as we can ascertain, nothing more.*

But why should and do groups of perspectives agree? Why do the individuals "sharing" similar spatial or temporal surroundings tend to think, to some extent, in the same way and have the same outlook on and way of life? Ortega y Gasset finds the answer in Dilthey. Our histories are shaped by the larger current of human history, in which wider, inclusive perspectives or cultures built up out of individual perspectives are created and destroyed. And these, of longer or shorter duration, and greater or lesser geographical extent, color and focus *en masse,* allowing for racial and national peculiarities, the truths, the goods, and the gods projected in the individual perspectives of those exposed to them. You and I, then, are what we are and think, believe and behave as we do because of the geographical, topographical, historical, linguistic, semantic, national, provincial and domestic "surroundings" that are part of our total selves. Participant in other cultures and with different "surroundings," our perspectives would be other than they are.

Cultural Relativism. The ways of life, thought, and belief of these cultures are incommensurable. No culture is better or worse, superior or inferior to another. None can be judged by the standards of another. Each, to be sure, tends to regard its interpretations of its own life as absolute, applicable to, and valid for other cultural ways of living, thinking, and believing, and for other standards of evaluation. Hence each culture, like each individual *I,* praises or condemns others according as their interpretations of their *yo y mis circunstancias,* are found to agree with its interpretation of its own. And it will even seek to impose its particular perspective by force, if necessary, upon other contemporary ones. But in so doing, each is extolling no more than a phantom truth, a phantom God, a phantom universe, a phantom good and evil, of its own making, without objective existence or authority, absolute relatively to itself only, and so only in its own fancy.

But though all metaphysical, theological, ethical and scientific speculations are equally subjective and relative to the time, place, and circumstances of those who indulge in them, philosophy still has a legitimate task to perform. Abandoning all claim to objectivity, it may properly and fruitfully confine itself to studying the conditions, cultural and individual, by which its successive, various and contradictory speculations have been determined to be what they are. It can philosophize about the history of philosophy. But it can do this only when it has liberated itself from *faith* of any sort, and has ceased to believe in its own beliefs. This liberation, in Ortega y Gasset's opinion, is already taking place. From a culture dominated by faiths in the power of metaphysics, theology, and science to attain objective truths and moral standards, we are passing, or have already passed, to a culture of universal skepticism regarding them and their conclusions.

Ethics. In his *Rebellion of the Masses,* Ortega y Gasset expressed his concern at the submergence of all guides to conduct in a rising tide of vulgarity, lawlessness, and barbarism, and at the consequent demoralization and disorientation of everyone, especially of contemporary youth. But one must have some guide, or one's career and history and perspective will be chaos. What then is the *ethics* suggested by perspectivism? We cannot appeal to duties and obligations imposed as absolute from outside the individual, from earth, or from on high, for there are no such things. Morality is a purely subjective affair, originating *within* each particular perspective and expressive of its particular "slant," and since the slant of one individual is not that of another, the moral code of one is not applicable to another. Ethics is as multiple and variegated as humanity is.

The business then of each individual will be to live his *own* life, make his *own* history, pursue his *own* career, develop his *own* perspective—in short, fulfill *himself.* His morality will be *vital,* will arise spontaneously out of the evolving *living* process which is himself, and will be obedient only to his particular varied and complex desires and drives and to the ideals they project. It will evolve with him as he and his surroundings evolve, suggesting, appropriately to his particular perspective, his dealings with each episode in the great adventure and voyage of discovery that every life is. And, since each new episode and discovery in his adventure may call for a new method of meeting them, individual morality will be flexible. But as long as he faces and copes with them and carries on, he is *moral;* if and when he fails to do so, he is *immoral.* There is no middle ground of action which is neither the one nor the other. The individual must commit himself and stick to it. To do this he needs no fancied transcendent incentives, sanctions and norms. In all this, Ortega y Gasset approaches the atheistic existentialist point of view.

Chapter XXIX

NEO-SCHOLASTICISM

I. THE DECLINE OF MEDIEVAL SCHOLASTICISM

The decline of the scholastic philosophy from the fourteenth century to the nineteenth was the product of complex causes involving the impact of broad cultural trends as well as certain traits characteristic of the philosophy itself. Scholasticism was by no means the whole of Medieval philosophy, and even at the moment of its most general acceptance, the beginning of the fourteenth century, the prime achievement of Scholasticism, the synthetic philosophy of Aquinas, was not without vigorous and widespread opposition. From within the scholastic fold, the nominalism of Occam and his followers was a major blow at the fundamental realism of Aquinas, while from without, the resurgence of mysticism with its monistic and Platonic bias and also the increase of pantheism weakened the intellectualistic, individualistic, and Aristotelian framework of Scholasticism generally. Moreover, the opposition of Averroism, strong in the thirteenth century, was still a significant force in the fifteenth. The fifteenth cenury humanistic movement, with its concern for the literary forms of antiquity, branded the inadequate language and style of the traditional Latin Scholasticism as boorish if not barbaric, while the excessive, lifeless formalism of the writers in the scholastic tradition, lost in their interminable distinctions, made that philosophy entirely unattractive to a world that was gaining a new sense of the creative power of human thought.

In the sixteenth century the Protestant reform movement, which drew part of its strength from the anti-scholastic reaction, contributed much to the breakdown of the respect for the authority of the past, which respect had become necessary to the fortune of Scholasticism, not only because of the principle of authority established within the philosophy itself, but because of the habit of its own adherents of a slavish subservience to the past and an increasing reliance on its authority.

Finally, it was the spirit and achievement of the new science, in the sixteenth and seventeenth centuries especially, that effected a complete eclipse of Scholasticism and rendered it almost if not totally negligible as an intellectual current until the nineteenth century. The new physics clearly demonstrated the erroneous character of numerous basic conceptions in the medieval science that was intimately associated with and presumably founded upon the Aristotelian metaphysics that was the groundwork of scholastic philosophy. The discrediting of the science resulted in widespread rejection of the philosophy and philosophical method with which it was so closely associated. Meanwhile the scholastic philosophers, with their minds on the past, remained for the most part ignorant of contemporary scientific developments, vigorously opposed the inquiring spirit that moved the new science, and did nothing to save their philosophy from its demise. Indeed, lacking the imaginative insight and creative initiative requisite to a reorientation of the philosophy in relation to science and a redefinition of its fundamental principles in the light of contemporary conditions, they persisted in a course of opposition to science that led to the discrediting of scholasticism within the ranks of Catholicism as well as without. The entire enterprise of philosophy, non-Aristotelian as well as Aristotelian, suffered considerable opprobrium as a consequence of the scholastic attitude.

It would be an error to identify Scholasticism during this period of its decline and eclipse with Catholic philosophy generally. A positive interest in the new science was not uncommon among Catholic philosophers, who engaged in the common debate of rationalism *versus* empiricism and, influenced by Bacon, Descartes, Locke, and Condillac, attempted to salvage philosophy within the Church both for its own sake and for its service to science and theology.

II. RISE OF THE NEW SCHOLASTICISM

Scholasticism, of course, did not disappear. At the highly important sixteeenth century Council of Trent the *Summa Theologica* of Aquinas had occupied a place alongside the scripture on the altar, and at the Council's close in 1567 Pius V had proclaimed St. Thomas a Doctor of the Church. It was promoted in France by Jacques Bossuet (1627-1704) and Barthélemy des Bosses (1688-1738), while in late sixteenth-century Spain it enjoyed a genuine revival, especially under Gabriel Vasquez (1551-1604) and Francisco Suárez (1548-1617). Within a very few years the major work of Suárez, the *Disputationes Metaphysical,* went through twenty editions. It was the last important constructive work in scholastic metaphysics until recent times. It was followed by a long period of commentaries which showed little independence of Aristotle or medieval thought. The French revolution and the Napoleonic wars dealt serious blows to Scholasticism. By the close of the eighteenth century and during the first half of the nineteenth, Catholic philosophers pursued philosophy more or less independently of an established system and to a large extent under the influence of idealism. Scholasticism had become almost entirely non-creative and for a period quite unimportant.

Nevertheless Scholasticism, especially in its Thomistic form, was deeply entrenched in Catholic thought, particularly in the Dominican order, and the effort of the Church to achieve a philosophical synthesis capable of incorporating science and revealed truth resulted in the nineteenth century in its successful resurgence. Several factors conspired to breathe new life into the thirteenth-century philosophic forms. A general increase in interest in medieval culture, encouraged in both France and Germany by the romantic literary and philosophical movement, brought Thomism into fresh focus. The threat of Cartesianism, Kantianism, Hegelianism, Positivism, and Materialism to the fundamental positions of Catholicism encouraged a return to Thomism, a return that received the blessing of the Church. Cajetano Sanseverino (1811-1865) in Italy, Cardinal Zephryrinus Gonzalez (1831-1892) in Spain, and the Jesuit Joseph Kleutgen (1811-1883) in Germany contributed to its revitalization and popularization. Pius IX, one of the most influential popes of modern times, recognized its promise as a philosophy for the Church because of its apparent or real agreement with the main body of Catholic dogma. In the *Syllabus of Errors,* 1864, he had condemned the proposition that "The method and principles by which the old scholastic doctors cultivated theology are no longer suitable to the demands of the age and the progress of science."

But it was the encyclical *Aeterni Patris* of Pope Leo XIII, issued August 4, 1879, and published in 1880, that firmly established Thomism as the foundation of Catholic thought. The *Aeterni Patris* celebrates the virtues of scholastic thought generally, but its specific exhortation to the bishops of the Church is "to restore the golden wisdom of St. Thomas, and to spread it far and wide for the defense and beauty of the Catholic faith, for the good of society, and for the advantage of all the sciences." But as a caution against a too slavish attitude toward the past, the encyclical advises that "if there be anything [in the philosophy of Thomas] that ill agrees with the discoveries of a later age, or, in a word, improbable in whatever way, it does not enter Our mind to propose that for imitation to Our age."

Not all Catholic thinkers adhered to Thomism even after the encyclical of Leo. Especially in France neo-Kantianism contended for acceptance among clerics as well as among the laity. The competition was gradually reduced to a minimum, however, as Thomism was made the foundation of all Catholic education and its study was encouraged at leading Catholic institutions of higher learning, such as Louvain, Fribourg, Rome, Ottawa, and the Catholic University of America at Washington. Under the sponsorship of Leo XIII the Leonine edition of the works of Aquinas was published in Rome in 1882, followed by definitive editions of other scholastics, including Duns Scotus.

A most important development was the establishment in 1891, at the instigation of Leo XIII, of the Institut Supérieur de Philosophie at the University of Louvain in Belgium under the leadership of Désiré Mercier (1851-1926), later Cardinal Mercier. Dedicated to the study of philosophy as philosophy and not simply in its relation to theology, and to the pursuit of both the natural and social sciences, the faculty of this institution, which has included the distinguished historian of medieval philosophy M. De Wulf (1867-1947), has been a major factor in establishing Neo-scholasticism in its present position of strength. This position was dramatically affirmed in 1923, on the six-hundredth anniversary of his canonization, when Pius XI crowned Thomas the chief non-apostolic teacher of the Church.

An important factor in the Church's interest in Scholasticism has been, of course, its belief that the synthetic character of this philosophy, in its ability to embrace both science and religion, would protect Catholic orthodoxy from the disintegrating influences of modern ideas and attitudes. It was not only the impact of nineteenth-century physics and evolutionary biology, together with materialistic and positivistic philosophy, that threatened the structure of orthodoxy, but the popularity of idealism and the increased historical and social knowledge as well. In particular the "higher criticism," or literary-historical study of the Bible, was an immediate threat to the traditional conception of the scripture. Finally, a growing democratic conscience became an open threat to the authority of the Church in its dominion over both conduct and thought.

It was to stem this tide of modernism that Pius IX in the *Syllabus of Errors* condemned the opinion that scholastic method and principles are out of date. In the encyclical *Pascendi Gregis*, Pius X in 1907 reaffirmed the instruction of Leo XIII and ordained "that scholastic philosophy be made the basis of the sacred sciences" as the first remedy against modernism.

III. CHARACTER OF NEO-SCHOLASTICISM

Recent scholastic philosophy has been concerned with a large area of problems, ranging from physics, biology, and psychology, through metaphysics, theology, ethics, and social philosophy. In opposition to Kantian agnosticism, nineteenth-century positivism, and twentieth-century logical empiricism, it has defended the possibility of metaphysics. It has defended classical logic in the presence of the current development of non-Aristotelian logic, and has been a strong advocate of the classical substance-attribute metaphysics. It has opposed epistemological realism to all forms of subjectivism, with special objection to Cartesianism, and has fought nominalism in both metaphysics and ethics with its theory of universals.

The neo-scholastics have attempted to retain the thirteenth-century foundations of their thought and find a compatability between these and modern science, while at the same time renovating the scholastic method by abandoning the slavish adherence to the syllogistic technique and creating new linguistic and literary forms. Though it constitutes the foundation for Catholic theology, scholastic philosophy is pursued to some extent in independence of its theological connections and has in recent years found numerous non-Catholic adherents, especially among those attracted to a broad philosophical synthesis that supports doctrines of natural law, authority, or value absolutism against modern relativisms. Not the least of its attractions has been its involvement in the study of cultural history, the structure of modern culture, philosophy of history, and the philosophy of education. It has made a strong appeal to those who believe that modern problems can best be solved by rethinking them in the light of an earlier wisdom.

IV. JACQUES MARITAIN

It is in the work of the French Thomist Jacques Maritain (1882-) that Neo-scholasticism has achieved a ground for maturity that goes beyond commentaries and eclecticism. Maritain, a convert to Catholicism who had studied with Bergson at the Sorbonne, undertook in his earlier works a re-examination of the nature and function of philosophy and thereafter has constructed his system on what he considers to be solid Thomistic foundations but not as a commentary on the philosophy of Aquinas or that of Aristotle. His *The Degrees of Knowledge* (1932) is the foremost neo-scholastic work presenting the principle of the unity of knowledge on the basis of which physics, mathematics, and metaphysics are related and in terms of which a satisfactory concept of the relation of science to religion is sought.

The foundations of Maritain's philosophy are an epistemological realism that opposes the subjectivity of Kantianism, romanticism, and idealism in general, and a metaphysical realism that asserts the reality of universals against the nominalistic persuasion of modern empiricism. Whether he is concerned with natural science, law, politics, or ethical theory, Maritain champions the independent reality of the external world, both the physical and moral orders, the objectivity of truth, and the absoluteness of value, and declares that these are discoverable by human reason. The criteria of truth and falsity are in the world, not in the mind. The function of reason is to discover the nature of the real, not to prescribe for reality, and it is only when this role is adequately realized that a genuine unity of knowledge will be approached or the moral truths upon which the security of human society depends be discovered.

In his effort to advance Thomism as a philosophy for the modern world, Maritain argues that as a theocentric humanism it embraces the values recognized by the modern humanistic tradition, while at the same time it enjoys the profoundest insights into the existential condition of man, insights that challenge those claimed by the typical existentialists. For existence is apprehended, he insists, by the intellect itself, and a true existentialism requires no recourse to the non-rational or irrational.

Chapter XXX

IDEALISM IN THE UNITED STATES

I. COLONIAL THOUGHT

American and European Thought. Until the close of the nineteenth century, American philosophic thought was a loyal colonial of Europe. It is not that the youthful nation had no creative genius of its own. It had an almost passionate spirit of inventiveness that gave to its people a historic sense of destiny and the promise of a better world. But this originality was an affair not of the mind, but of action; it was the combined creativeness of youthful statesmen who in their inexperience had the moral courage to believe in freedom and equality, of the pioneer with his eyes and heart fixed always on a farther western horizon, of the entrepreneur who dreamed so effectively of commercial conquest and exploitation in a virgin empire, and of the technologist, whose artless delight in his early conquest of nature was to become so soon an evil foreboding of world destruction.

And even here it was more than anything else the spirit and the occasion that were unique. The political philosophy in terms of which the new government was being so successfully constructed was essentially an inheritance from Locke and the liberal British empiricists and from the French Enlightenment; the rugged economy of individualism that sanctioned the expanding industrial and commercial empire justified itself by a theory also from Locke, through Adam Smith and Ricardo; American technology was the application of a new daring and inventiveness to British and Continental physics and mathematics; and even the restless feet of the pioneers were in large part moved by the desire for expansion and the quest for a new life that brought an incessant flow of immigration from western Europe.

But to say this is simply to say the obvious, that America was in its adolescence and youth; not withstanding two wars, one matricidal and the other fratricidal, its adolescence glowed through its idealism and unbridled optimism; its youth was an unbounded energy and self-determination. Culture is not created in a day, and for two centuries and more the mind and spirit of the new world were nurtured from the table of Europe. In religion, art, literature, and morality, and in philosophy and science, America lived on its ancestors or borrowed generously from the rich relations of its forebears. Yet always while adopting it adapted, and the end product was impressed indelibly by its own characteristic genius of practicality.

Jonathan Edwards. In philosophy, the American mind was under the dominion of its earliest and not least brilliant expression, Jonathan Edwards, whose Calvinistic theology, virtually breathing the spirit of a decadent old world, ruled men's minds, whether positively or negatively, until it was exorcised by the scientific spirit that closed the nineteenth century. Edwards' puritanism in theology and morals was not simply a new edition of Calvin's divine sovereignty and human depravity; it was Calvin with a vengeance, plus Augustine and Plato. Moreover, as a vigorous reaction against New England's loss of the sense of sin, it depended not entirely on the thought of the past, but supported itself by Locke, Berkeley, and Newtonian physics. It was this orthodox philosophical theology that became the great tradition in American religion, morals, and philosophy.

Enlightenment Philosophy. In the colonial period, Samuel Johnson had outlined a philosophical polemic against Calvinism and had defended the freedom of the will, but it was the representatives of the Enlightenment, Franklin, Jefferson, Paine, and Palmer, who offered the most vigorous, though indeed somewhat shallow, opposition— an opposition made effective by their leading participation in the founding of the Republic. Jefferson and Paine especially combined their fight for freedom and social advancement with a militant hatred for Calvinism. Theirs was a religion of humanity and moral optimism, of middle-class virtue and an unbounded faith in the power of reason to destroy superstition and evil and to create a better world. Their rationalistic deism was an attack on the abject pessimism of Calvinism, and taken with their political philosophy was a stroke for secular and civic institutions against the abuse and domination of the church. It marked the beginning of the scientific spirit in American life and institutions.

II. THE TRANSCENDENTALISTS

The Rise of Unitarianism. As in Europe at the end of the medieval period, there was in America a revolt and a reformation within the Christian fold itself that helped prepare the way for the liberation of philosophy from ecclesiastical domination. Just as the authority of the

Roman Church had been defied by Luther and Calvin, so evangelical Christianity in New England was challenged by a protesting Unitarian movement.

In the case of this lesser, as of the greater Reformation, the contribution to the enfranchisement of philosophy was indirect. The rise and spread of the Unitarian movement made unorthodox and comparatively free thinking in religious matters (though not in ethical) socially safe, comfortable, respectable, and, in New England at least, aristocratic. Thus an atmosphere was created favorable to the eventual escape of philosophic speculation from all theological restrictions whatsoever, and to the restoration of free and independent investigation and discussion of the nature of the Real.

Transcendentalism. The principle that every movement generates a counter-movement found no exception in the American Enlightenment. American thought in the first part of that century was strongly influenced by Comte and Cousin in France and by Hamilton and Mill in Great Britain. But as German, French, and English romanticism replied to the European Enlightenment, with its background of empiricism and deism, so Transcendentalism was the New World response to its own Age of Reason. Against skepticism, empiricism, reason, and the devotion to science, the Transcendentalism of Channing, Emerson, Thoreau, Parker, Alcott, and Margaret Fuller arose to dominate the middle of the century. Grounded in the romanticism of Rousseau, Kant, Goethe, Herder, and Coleridge, and with a carefully guarded heritage of Platonic metaphysics and Neo-Platonic mysticism, Transcendentalism was a true moral awakening, a revival of ethical puritanism freed from its morass of commercialism and applied to the issues of human freedom and social betterment. But it was more than that. It was at once an intensive emphasis on the dignity and worth of man and an esthetic delight in the divinity of nature. With its idealistic metaphysics and intuitive methodology, Transcendentalism was a reformed religion for intellectuals and a poetry for mystics.

Emerson. Of the transcendentalists, Ralph Waldo Emerson (1803-1882) was the most eminent. Emerson had only the vaguest of philosophic systems, and in it various influences lay confused. He had been dosed with Locke and Berkeley and Hume at Harvard, disliked their empiricism and found them dull. He had sought relief at the Unitarian fount, which he found too chilly for his stomach. With the German philosophers, he was conversant almost entirely through Coleridge, but what he knew of them suited better his romantic constitution. Through reading the Cambridge Platonists he had discovered Plato, in whom, more than in any other, he found spiritual healing. But what attracted him in Plato was not so much the intellectual as the emotional and mystical strain seized upon and emphasized by the Neo-Platonists.

The Over-Soul. These influences, positive and negative, were combined in his point of view. Not reason but intuition is for Emerson the key to the nature of the Real. Nature is the outer appearance and symbol of an inner spiritual fact. This inner spiritual essence, creating and supporting all things, of which man's mind is part, is the Over-Soul. Within the universal mind nature lies as a harmonious whole, the parts of which are all interrelated so as to express the divine purpose and to subserve man, the supreme manifestation of deity. Science and religion —and Emerson was well read in the science of the day—alike testify to the glory of God. Both interpret the divine ideas, innate in the human mind, of which all experience is the reminiscence. To enter the kingdom of heaven we must become like little children, and spontaneously and trustfully accept the revelation of which nature is the vehicle.

Decline of Transcendentalism. But Transcendentalism could hardly have hoped to survive as a philosophy for America. It was more than anything else a spiritual and moral attitude. It was for the most part indifferent to science; it had an inadequate and ambiguous metaphysic, and its immediate ties to Continental spiritualism, idealism, and romanticism gave it an exotic air that could never become native to a people engrossed in the practical issues of a youthful nation. Besides, the rumblings of something new were already being heard with the publication in 1859 of *The Origin of Species,* and America, which had produced little science and few scientists, was already becoming exposed in its philosophy and spirit to the contagion of European positivism and scientific materialism.

III. NEO-HEGELIANISM

The St. Louis School. Yet the idealism of Transcendentalism received strong support from the Hegelian absolutism that had invaded America, indirectly through the mediation of England, and directly by way of German immigrants and American students in the period when European study was considered indispensable to a liberal education. The imported Hegelianism, intended to support speculative thought in opposition to the agnosticism, naturalism, and positivism of Spencer and the continental materialists and positivists, flourished for a time under the leadership of William T. Harris (1835-1909) and eventually achieved its definitive American statement in the temperate absolutism of Josiah Royce.

Hegelianism was introduced to America by Harris and others of the St. Louis School two years after Stirling published his *Secret of Hegel* in England. Hitherto, we may remember, acquaintance with German thought had been, thanks to Coleridge, mainly acquaintance with Schelling. Harris had himself been instructed in Hegelian doctrines by Henry Brokmeyer, a German immigrant under whose direction the *Logic* had been imported and studied by an enthusiastic group. In 1867, *The Journal of Speculative Philosophy* was founded by Harris, and devoted to spreading the new gospel. In its pages Peirce, Howison, James, Royce, and Dewey found a forum for the ideas which were to become the flowering of American culture. Under its auspices, also, translations not only of Hegel but of other German philosophers were made. Kant, also, was read in the original in the numerous philosophical clubs that appeared throughout the country. Upon this main stock of Hegelianism were grafted ideas contributed by the Concord Transcendentalists, and the men of St. Louis, in their turn, helped introduce Hegelianism to Concord. Bronson Alcott lectured in the West on Platonism and Neo-Platonism, Harris in Concord on ideas derived from the Germans. So it was that St. Louis became for the moment the philosophic center of America and the conveyor in particular of the German message.

The "New Thought" Movement. The German "transcendental" influence had interesting ramifications. At the time of the Italian Renaissance, we may remember, the doctrine, derived from Neo-Platonism, that nature veiled the face of God and symbolically revealed his essence had given rise to a belief in occult influences and in the hidden existence in man of an ability to exercise occult powers. This belief expressed itself in astrology and alchemy and magic rites for summoning spirits and raising the dead. Now, in the same way, the Transcendentalists' assertion that the universe is a symbol, and that the interrelation and the interaction of its parts and events rest upon a cosmic hidden sympathy, fostered once more a sense of occult forces— a sense intensified by the phenomena of mental suggestion, and by the study and practice of hypnotism, or "mesmerism," as it was called, which were being introduced from France. The mind, it might seem, had in reserve mysterious powers over the body and the physical world, far in excess of those which it ordinarily wielded, and minds might, even at a distance, project upon one another through occult channels curses or blessings, health or disease.

Itinerant hypnotists and mental healers engaged the public attention. Of the latter, Quimby was the most famous; and justly so, for he had developed from observations of his patients a really scientific theory of the nature of hypnosis. Some contend, moreover, that it was his destiny to be the forerunner of the founder of Christian Science. He had already preached the fundamental ideas upon which Mrs. Eddy seized, that all is mind and all is good. It has also been suggested that Mrs. Eddy may well have read one of the early American books on Hegel. In any case the whole New Thought movement, including Christian Science, is in its philosophy a ramification, in part at least, of Neo-Hegelianism. So, too, the "transcendental" atmosphere proved congenial to revivals of Oriental mysticism and to the rise and spread of theosophy.

IV. INFLUENCE OF EVOLUTION AND NATURALISM

But Transcendentalism and Hegelianism had strong opponents. Whereas European thought in the nineteenth century was determined in considerable part either positively or negatively by physics, the scientific impact upon American philosophy, due mainly to the latter's predisposition to favor religion and morals, came first in the attire of Darwinian biology and the attendant naturalistic philosophies of Huxley, Spencer, and others. Darwinism was both opposed and proposed on scientific grounds. The biologist and geologist Louis Agassiz (1807-1873), the most celebrated American scientist of his time, opposed evolution on the ground that species are immutable. On the other hand evolution was defended in brilliant debates by such outstanding scientists as the botanist Asa Gray (1810-1888) and the geologist James D. Dana (1813-1895). Most important was the work of the Harvard mathematician and scientist Chauncey Wright, an enthusiastic disciple and correspondent of Darwin whose positivistic persuasion was in sharp contrast to the speculative inclinations of most American thinkers and whose famous essay *The Evolution of Self-Consciousness*, combining Darwinism and utilitarianism, was an important contribution to empirical psychology and to the foundations of naturalistic pragmatism.

But the most pronounced surface repercussions were felt in religious circles, where the doctrine of special creation was sacred to orthodoxy and the idea of cosmic purpose had been based on the concept of an essentially static universe. The religiously oriented American philosophy of the period undertook, in the persons of James McCosh (1811-1894), Noah Porter (1811-1892), and John Fiske (1842-1901), to reconcile the ways of God to evolution through the instrumentality of a new world view which conceives purpose primarily in terms of the future of a dynamic universe. As a popular adaptation of the system of Spencer, Fiske's *Outline of Cosmic Philosophy* (1874) was widely read and exerted a broad influence.

The religious disposition of these authors met strong opposition in the naturalistic leanings of the works of Henry Draper (1811-1882) and Andrew D. White (1832-1918), both of whom wrote on the conflict of religion and science in a manner that accused religion of obstructing scientific progress.

V. ROYCE

In 1882 a young Californian, lately graduated from Johns Hopkins at Baltimore, went to Harvard to teach philosophy. He was Josiah Royce (1855-1916), in whom American Hegelianism bore its ripest fruit.

The Object of Experience—More Experience. In *The World and the Individual* (1900-1901) Royce expounded the essence of his system. He built up his metaphysics in his own way, and came to conclusions that differed in many respects from the views of the great British Hegelians, Green and Bradley. Experience, in which we must begin our quest for Reality, is not, he tells us, self-contained. It is experience *of* something more than what is given in its content. The question now becomes—what is this something more? The object *of* experience cannot be independent of experience, since in that case experience could not be *of* it. Nor can experience simply return upon itself and be of itself, since such experience would be meaningless. It would not signify anything. Finally, we cannot do as Mill and the other British empiricists did, and locate that to which experience refers in the mere *possibility* of more experience. For how can my experience be *of* a mere possibility? I cannot experience a *possibility*. I can only experience actual data.

These difficulties leave us no alternative but the theory that the object of any particular experience is more experience. Every item of experience, every idea, means, intends, yearns, and gropes for a wider experience in which its meaning shall be fulfilled and it itself shall be made intelligible. The object of an idea, then, is that which would realize the idea's significance.

The Nature of the Absolute Experience. The significance of an idea, however, rolls away from it in an ever-widening circumference of meaning. Nothing short of an absolute and infinite experience embracing the totality of existence can entirely exhaust what an idea intends and tries to say. There must, then, exist an absolute mind to which the secret lying at the heart of every experience is laid bare, and by which it is understood. In that infinite understanding the meanings of all things conspire to give a final, single, and complete meaning to the Real, in which all intentions are fulfilled, all questions answered, all searchings pacified.

This overarching Absolute contains us and all our experiences, but it contains much more besides. It comprehends the infinite content of all time and space as a single completed fact. All that is, all that was, and all that shall be are present to it in their entirety, just as the successive notes of some haunting musical phrase pass, and at the same time linger as a whole. By it all our errors are understood and thereby corrected. So, too, sin and evil find their place in it—not as partial aspects of a wider good, but as things with which the Absolute struggles, even as we struggle, and over which it triumphs even when we do not. We ourselves, though our minds are parts of the Absolute, are not thereby deprived of real individuality and uniqueness. Somehow we remain separate selves and personalities, in spite of our partial nature.

The Self-Repetitive Character of the Absolute Experience. All this infinite wealth of experience—the magnificence of the world-process, the splendor of human history, all selves, all sensations, all passions, all emotions, all loves and hates, all aspirations and disappointments, all ecstasy, all suffering, all failure, all sin—are experienced and understood and brought within the focus of a single meaning by the absolute mind. But this is not all. The Absolute not only knows the infinite collection of experiences, which constitute the totality of existence and the content of its mind, but, since that collection is grasped as a single completed fact, it knows its own knowledge of it, and so on *ad infinitum*. It knows, and knows that it knows, and knows that it knows that it knows, etc., thus multiplying without end the initial magnificence of its vision, just as reflecting mirrors repeat indefinitely the same scene.

But, even this piling of infinity upon infinity does not destroy the ultimate completeness and the finished and perfected character of the Absolute's life. Contemporary mathematics, with its theories of transfinite numbers, suggested the possibility that an infinite collection like the ordinary ordinal series, 1, 2, 3, etc., might, for certain purposes and under certain conditions, be regarded as a completed whole and made the number 1, or ω as Cantor called it, of a new infinite, *transfinite* series of a higher order. Royce seized upon this mathematical theory as a means for overcoming the difficulties that beset the infinitely self-repeating character of the Absolute's self-consciousness. Just as the infinite ordinal series may be thought of as a completed unit, so the infinite series of acts of reflection with which the Absolute knows itself may be regarded as closed, and therefore as consistent with the all-embracing, finished and perfected nature of the absolute mind. The Absolute not only sees the infinite content of all space and time as a single unified, finished experience. Its infinitely repeated act of being conscious that it is conscious of that experience is also seen as a completed fact of perfect self-consciousness.

In his later years Royce gave more and more attention to moral and social problems. Since the significance of the life of the individual infinitely transcends his individuality, goodness lies in his self-identification with this larger meaning. He must be loyal to the aims and purposes in which he finds his wider significance expressed. Above all he must be loyal to the principle of loyalty in itself. For loyalty is the supreme principle—the categorical imperative, as it were, of the moral life. By obedience to its call, we help realize the meaning we have in and for the life of the Absolute.

VI. HOWISON

Pluralistic vs. Monistic Idealism. The monistic Hegelian idealism of Royce may have dominated the idealistic camp, but it by no means domineered over it. At the University of California George Howison (1834-1916) expressed in no uncertain terms his dissatisfaction with Royce's conclusions, and developed in opposition to them a pluralistic idealism of the Berkeleian type. He contended that Royce, for all his assertions to the contrary, failed to save the reality of human individuals, and reduced them to mere aspects of the Absolute. Furthermore —and here Howison agreed with Fichte and disagreed with Lotze— a plurality of selves is an indispensable condition of self-consciousness. No ego without an alter. If I am I, I am not you—to and from all eternity.

Moreover, moral relations can only obtain in a society of real, independent selves, each one of which is endowed with freedom and self-determination. To reduce these selves to parts of the life of an Absolute is to deprive them of their liberty, since their wills become so many expressions of one and the same absolute will, just as their consciousness of themselves becomes an expression of one and the same absolute consciousness. Absolute idealism, then, in destroying the possibility of the interaction of independent free wills, strikes at the very root of a moral order.

The Real a Society of Moral Personalities. To keep the Real moral and self-conscious we must suppose it to be composed of uncreated and indestructible moral personalities in social relations with one another. These selves are bound together in a common subservience to the same ideal. This ideal of completely perfected self-hood endowed with perfect wisdom and perfect goodness is enacted in a divine self. God is one person among others. He does not create the other selves. He is not their efficient cause. They are uncreated, uncaused, and eternal. But, actually enacting as he does all that they would like to be, he holds out to them a vision of achieved perfection, which moves them, after the fashion of Aristotle's God, as the beloved moves the lover. By the power of attraction and by final causation he binds them to one another and to himself in a common allegiance to his supreme perfection.

These views Howison first brought forward in a public debate with Royce in 1895 at the University of California. He expressed them more completely in his *Limits of Evolution, etc.* (1901). A similar tendency to save and exalt the individual self was displayed by Thomas Davidson (1840-1900).

VII. CARR

A pluralism of a somewhat different type was also advanced by H. Wildon Carr (1857-1931) of London University and the University of Southern California, who was greatly influenced both by Leibnitz and by Bergson. Reality for him is composed of non-spatial, non-temporal Monads, which are active, living and conscious. Spatial, temporal and physical phenomena exist only as the experience of these Monads. The Monads are, moreover, windowless. We can never break through the periphery of our own sensation and knowledge. Hence we can never experience, in perception or conception, a reality existing independent of ourselves. I am conscious only *of* my perceptions and ideas. My perceptions and ideas are not a consciousness of something existing beyond and independently of them.

However, the experience within which each Monad is necessarily confined *means* a common and external world. Within my private world I find and deal with experiences that the very activity and nature of my consciousness forces me to treat as other people and outside objects. But so dealing with my conscious content means *living*. It does not mean sitting by and looking on. It is only insofar as I am an *actor* that my inner world assumes an outer and a social significance. The moment that I try to stand off from it and survey and analyze and reflect upon it, I devitalize everything in it that means and represents other persons and other things, and reduce it to *my* conscious content and nothing more. In other words, if my knowledge, whose only object is my own experience, is to represent to me an external world, it cannot be purely contemplative and descriptive. It must be infused with warmth and vitality and activity. It must be a *behaving towards* and a *living with*.

Away then with matter and with essences, with subsistence and with existence, and with everything else that is static and frozen. Both to *subsist* as a Platonic Idea and to *exist* as a concrete substance mean to be changelessly and eternally what one is. Existence and subsistence are alike epitaphs. They are conditions of death, not of life. Reality is living. Every Monad of which it is composed is pulsing, changing, evolving. *Real* things neither subsist nor exist. They *become*.

VIII. PERSONALISM

The Growth of Personalistic Thought. Personalism is perhaps most conveniently regarded and treated in connection with American philosophy. To be sure, it had a long period of European incubation, and many influences contributed to its making. Philosophic movements of different sorts and motivations had at different times attributed different degrees of social, moral, epistemological and metaphysical importance to the individual human being, and had thereby adumbrated the fundamental importance in the scheme of things assigned him by contemporary personalistic thought. Also, the words "personalism" and "personalistic" had been used by some European neo-Kantian idealistic thinkers to characterize the emphasis their systems gave to the self-conscious, volitional, moral, social, creative and active aspects of the human mind. And the French philosopher Renouvier adopted the term "personalism" to express the gist of his philosophic views.

Nevertheless, it was in the United States that "personalistic" doctrine first emerged as a definitely organized school of thought whose adherents, however much they might differ on some points, were all in communion with one another with respect to certain fundamental ideas, and were as one in adopting "personalism" as their common name. The word and the philosophic opinions it stands for were first introduced into America by B. P. Bowne (1847-1910), long professor at Boston University.

Bowne. Bowne emphasizes free, moral, and responsible personality as the central fact and prime constituent of the real. Persons are unique. They are, at least when they are once started, self-existent and self-supporting. The supreme reality of the self-conscious person is revealed immediately in experience. Personality is creative, produces experience, and molds it into the categories which give it substantial, causal, self-identical and unified form. At the same time, what we call the external world is not a figment of the finite mind. It exists independent and apart from us as the rational experience of a divine mind who creates and sustains it, and thinks it in the categories that we, also, discover within ourselves. The real, then, consists of a supreme person surrounded by other individual personalities, with whom, as in the Berkeleian system, the experience we call nature is his method of communication. The finite persons are caused by him, but are distinct from him and from one another. They are free and morally responsible, and their deepest relations both with him and with one another are moral relations.

Belief in God is above all demanded, as Kant maintained, by the exigencies of the practical and moral life. Without God morality would be meaningless, and our practical needs would remain without response. Christian dogma has its basis in these needs and may therefore be held as true. Still, Bowne did not insist on too great unanimity in the statement and interpretation of it. On the contrary, if religion is to be kept vital and abreast of the times, Christian dogma requires new expressions in the language and phraseology of the religious experience of the day.

The metaphysical hypotheses set forth by Bowne are accepted in the main, with some modifications, variations, subtractions, and additions, by most members of the contemporary personalistic movement. But personalism is still so elastic in its scope, and so generous in claiming as its own so many thinkers, not only modern but scattered throughout the history of philosophy as far back as the fifth century B.C., that it is difficult to deal even with its contemporary aspects in a way satisfactory to all of its present-day adherents.

Emphasis on the Personal, Creative, Free, and Moral Essence of Mental Activity. However, what would seem to distinguish personalism from other variants of pluralistic idealism is, in the first place, the overwhelming importance it attributes to the *moral* and *personal* characteristics and activities of the individual centers of consciousness,

which, with their experiences, constitute Reality. Since these characteristics and the values associated with them are the *highest* properties of
consciousness, they are therefore also the *deepest,* and indicate most
clearly the nature of the real. Reality, then, is essentially and primarily
a plurality of *personal experients and experiences.*

Again, personalism is insistent upon the continuously *creative* nature
of the activities of the persons constituting the real. God, the supreme
person, and the origin of all existence, is forever originating the experience we call the external world. This he continuously imparts to
the finite centers he creates and supports, but they, in their turn, as
continuously re-interpret, re-mold, and, in a sense, re-create it as they
receive it from him and act upon it. Besides thus cooperating with
God in the production of the external experience shared by them all
in common, each person is also the creator of a wealth of private and
unique experience of his own.

Another point emphasized by personalism is the *freedom* of the
creative activity and behavior of each individual center of consciousness. Each person is the sole originator of his own activities and the
sole molder of his own life, and he, and he alone, is ultimately responsible for what he does with himself and the character he develops.

Personality and an Essentially "Moral" Order. Since the highest values displayed by personal existence are *moral* values, we may infer that
reality is as profoundly moral as it is personal. The universe, we
may be sure, is founded on moral principles, and the world-process is
governed by a moral purpose and aimed at the realization of a moral
ideal. This ideal is the *free* production, on the part of each finite
center, of moral character expressed in a life lived in accordance with
the moral law. Moral laws are as universal and inexorable as so-called
natural laws, and their defiance is as inevitably followed by disaster
as is defiance of the operations of nature. Since the freedom necessary
to the possession of moral responsibility and the production of moral
character may be expressed in disobedience as well as obedience to the
moral law, and since suffering in its various forms is incidental and
even necessary to the highest development of the individual, the existence of evil is compatible with the fundamentally ethical and teleological nature of reality.

Persons are social by nature, and the higher and deeper aspects of
morality rest upon social relations. Hence a personal reality will be
a social system, and the strongest ties binding the finite centers both
to one another and to God will be social in character. But such ties
are not bonds. They in no wise destroy or impair the unique value of

each separate person, and in no wise restrain him from the maximum of individual development and expression of his particular and unique moral nature. Indeed, the production of the maximum wealth of value possible to each individual is God's purpose with regard to man.

Flewelling. Among Bowne's successors, Ralph Tyler Flewelling (1871-   ), at the University of Southern California, has attempted a marriage of personalism, relativity, and quantum physics and has brought the principles of personalistic metaphysics and ethics to the interpretation of history and the analysis of culture.

Flewelling has insisted that for the most part contemporary philosophy has failed to adequately appreciate the philosophical implications of the breakdown of the mechanical patterns of classical physics and is dominated unjustifiably by the materialistic metaphysics historically associated with strict causal determinism and the old conception of the nature of matter. Relativity and quantum theory have revolutionized not only physics but metaphysics as well, and those who can read the handwriting on the scientific wall should recognize that not only is the new physics not hostile to personalistic principles but actually demands that reality be interpreted as fundamentally personal in character. Flewelling, one of the most vigorous American exponents of theism, and much influenced by the tradition of liberal religion, has repeatedly argued that the moral quality of society is adversely affected by materialistic metaphysics.

In his philosophy of history, developed in part as an argument against Spengler's cyclical and fatalistic thesis, and in relation to a theory of the tragic factor in human existence, Flewelling has described the development of western culture in terms of the gradual unfolding and implementation of a democratic personalistic moral ideal. Opposed to the optimistic view that progress is automatic and inevitable, he has held that it is nevertheless real, and that a genuine cultivation of the spiritual quality of personality should open new vistas of human achievement. Although the Orient has been dominated by totalitarian and authoritarian principles, the recognition of the supreme intrinsic worth and the creative power of the individual person is deeply embedded in its spiritual life and offers itself as a basis for a reconciliation of the profound cultural differences between East and West.

Chapter XXXI

RECENT CONTINENTAL VITALISM

I. BERGSON

Reality Given in Experience, Not by Reasoning. In many respects akin to pragmatism is the philosophy of Henri Bergson (1859-1941) who was professor at the Collège de France from 1901 to 1921. Bergson is easily the outstanding thinker of the present century in France, and is perhaps the most eminent of recent philosophers.

Like the modern empiricists, Bergson insists that experience is Reality, and Reality experience. To discover the nature of the Real we have only to consult experience. Moreover, that nature is not inferred from experience, it is given in it. Nature is what we experience it to be.

If now we look at experience, what do we find there? We are first of all struck by the familiar oppositions of subject and object, the inner and the outer, flux and stability, mind and matter, sensation and thought. At the same time, those oppositions are all oppositions *within* experience and seem interrelated and interdependent. We have, therefore, to ask how they are related, and whether they do not display some least common denominator, and on which side the heart of the Real is situated.

Again we note that immediate perceptual experience does not pass into complete oblivion as it passes away. It is no longer consciously present, to be sure; nor for that matter is it consciously past. Still it does not evaporate when and where it falls. It rather seeps beneath the surface and is all retained and conserved in an underground reservoir in which much of it is forgotten temporarily or for good, but from which some of it bubbles up, often unaccountably and fantastically, as *conscious* memory.

Memory plus Experience the Basis of Useful Ideas. Conscious memory does not, however, except under abnormal conditions, well up haphazard from the subterranean water-table of pure memory. We dig for it, so to speak, and only pump to the surface as much of it as suits the needs and purposes of present experience. Mingled with appropriate memories, immediate experience becomes *useful*. It becomes an experience that reconstructs a coherent and orderly past and is able to anticipate the future. Thus it becomes an instrument of survival and of progress. It enables the organism both to adapt itself to an environment and to devise means for adapting the environment to its own organic impulses and aims. It is of the nature, then, of everyday perception to be forward-looking. The very curdlings of sense-experience into objects represent ways in which the organism acts in and towards the situations in which it finds itself involved. When I say, "Thus I have done in the past and so I will do in the future," I am talking about a "thing." Sense perception is not of things. Things are useful and reliable manipulations of sense perception.

So, too, the "ideas" to which the commingling of memory with immediate sensations gives rise are practically motivated, and the ordinary workaday world with its "fixed" quantities and qualities is a convenient shorthand method of dealing with the rough and tumble of perceptual experience. The same is true of our more abstract concepts. They are signals of how we should act in a given situation. The more "remote" the concept is from the concrete situation, the more objective, disinterested, precise, and therefore useful are the directions it gives. For example, mathematics, mechanics, logic, and the like, tell us *exactly* what to do under certain circumstances. We reject their advice at our peril. Therefore, the "purer" and more "theoretic" a concept seems, the more practical it really is.

The Understanding and the Real. Paradoxically enough, however, the better an idea works in teaching us how to cope with external experience, the worse it works as a teacher of what we ourselves really are. For thinking distorts and fails to give the whole of experience, just because it must select and emphasize those experiences which are most *useful* and must construct its world of them. It therefore necessarily falsifies the Real.

Moreover, reason, being an instrument for adapting the experience we call ourselves to the experience we call an external environment, envisages, approaches, and handles things from without. This is true of its dealings with us as well as with the outer world. When we *reflect upon* and try to *understand* ourselves, we are dealing with ourselves in terms designed to stabilize and crystallize situations outside us in a shape that enables us to get a foothold and a handhold on them. We are not dealing with ourselves in terms suitable to express the unstable, uncrystallized, infinitely varied and fluid character of our entire experience as we feel it from within.

This, however, is not to cast a slur upon the intellect. Reason is an indispensable instrument in enabling us to realize the infinite possibilities of experience, since an environment that is crystallized and solid enough to grasp affords us more opportunities of doing things with it than an environment so fluid and inchoate that it slips through our fingers. Order is a better theater than chaos for the free exercise of the inventive and histrionic powers of the actor. To the free and complete self-expression of experience it is as necessary that its stage should be set as that its lines should be spontaneous and improvised. In setting and ordering the stage and arranging the objective accessories of action, the intellect invites experience to endless and free experimentation. It holds up all sorts of possibilities. It suggests innumerable plots and plans to which the stage lends itself. It hints at ways in which the furniture and the scenery may themselves be altered and the arrangements changed.

The Real Given in Experience as an "Élan Vital." Still, the fact remains that the intellect cannot give us the whole of experience, or experience without falsification, or experience sensed from within. *Intuition* alone can give us that. To get at the *reality* of experience, we must undo the work of the intellect. We must escape from its "useful" categories. We must relapse into the richness and vitality of the freedom and flux of immediate feeling. We must substitute the "real duration" in whose sparkling waters we splash and swim for the clock-time on whose dead current we are helplessly carried. We must revitalize the panorama of nature with all the wealth of detail ignored or erased in the "useful" map compiled by the intellect and the sciences.

When we have done this, and have *intuited* experience from within rather than *known* it from without, what do we find? We find that its essence is an *élan vital,* a thrusting and pushing and flinging of itself forward and an expansion outward to which no limit can be set. But thrusting and pushing and expanding are *efforts,* and efforts mean *resistance.* This resistance cannot come from the outside, since experience is all there is. It must be, therefore, of the very nature of the *élan vital* to create resistance in order to overcome it. The *élan vital* gives rise to what we call matter. Matter is the basis of everything that appears habitual and mechanical and static.

Against this tendency in itself to relapse into fixed and lazy ways, the *élan vital* is always struggling. That it is only partially successful is shown by the existence of experience that we call an external, material world. That it is not wholly unsuccessful is shown by the emergence of the living from the inanimate, and by the development of instinctive and intellectual levels of experience as instruments for adapting organisms to their environment, and for thus preparing the way for more complete self-expression of the *élan vital*.

The Physical World as Dying Spirit. The physical universe, then, which the *élan vital* is forever peeling off from itself, is spirit from which vitality and spontaneity and gaiety and freedom have departed, and which has become merely the husk of its true self. But the life of the spirit is intensified and brought to the height of its activity by the effort of sloughing off the bonds of matter and unleashing to its fullest length the freedom it is forever craving and winning for itself.

At the same time the physical portion of experience, as well as the spiritual, is in a state of uninterrupted growth and evolution. From moment to moment the material world is being built up and crystallized and thrown off by the onward-moving, living essence of experience, as the *élan vital* precipitates from itself the solidified and formalized consciousness and the mechanical habits of behavior into which its free activity is forever condensing.

God. The central, animating point, from which the *élan vital* radiates is God. From God experience surges outward and ever outward in ever widening circles, driven ceaselessly towards increased richness and spontaneity and creative freedom. It creates and outgrows matter. It creates life. It focuses itself a myriad times over in individual human consciousness. It unites the new perspectives it gains after this fashion in the wider vistas afforded by social ties and institutions and moral activities. Its evolution is the creation of bigger and better opportunities for action and for cooperation. It breaks down and overcomes the distinctions it creates between one self and another, between the inner and the outer, between man and the universe. It merges the individual with his fellows and mankind with nature, and reveals to them their essential oneness.

But God dwells not only at the center. He is also the centrifugal urge, the "up and away" in search of ever fresh adventure, that is the breath of life to all existence and to all experience. God is not a *fait accompli*. He is in the making, as all things are in the making, and to the making of him as of them there is no end. He is inexhaustible activity, he is limitless freedom. He is an ever-opening and ever-widening vista of more and more to be done, and of more and more energy and vitality at hand for the doing of it.

No philosopher has been more influenced by the life sciences than Bergson, and certainly none has succeeded better than he in cultivating a new and original insight into the nature of reality.

II. VAIHINGER

Concepts as "Fictions." In Germany we find another system that has something in common with pragmatism. This is Hans Vaihinger's (1852-1933) philosophy of the "as if." Vaihinger is in step with the Mach-Pearson theory of scientific concepts as conceptual shorthand, and in sympathy with the pragmatic applications of it. He extends it from the concepts constructed by the physical sciences to theological, moral, and social ideas and ideals. But he carries the theory a step further. These concepts and ideas, he tells us, are not even true to *experience,* not to speak of being valid beyond experience. On the contrary they are falsifications of experience in the interest of greater convenience and edification. They are *fictions*—stories that it is pleasanter or more profitable to tell ourselves about the facts than to accept and transcribe the facts as they are.

For example, we might say, it is more convenient and it pays better to act *as if* the universe were an orderly and determined affair. Therefore, in spite of its experienced disorder and contingency, we invent a story about it to the effect that it is as we wish it to be. We create the "fiction" of natural laws, atoms moving about in space in a predictable manner, and the like. Again, it is comforting to believe in a God who is all powerful and all good. This is an illogical inference from the kind of world in which we live. So we create the fiction that there is such a God, and deal with him *as if* he existed. Or it may be that for one reason or another we find it convenient to view our fellow-men *as if* mankind was essentially depraved or essentially good. As experienced, they are perhaps neither. Therefore we "make believe" the doctrine of original sin, or draw an expurgated portrait of the noble savage.

All objects are subjected to the falsification of the *as if.* They are viewed neither as they are experienced, nor in accordance with the demands of pure logic. They are fictions about experience invented to bring it into conformity with certain values and ideals. These values and ideals arise out of biological needs and the exigencies of the economic struggle. Hence our entire systematized universe—scientific, moral, theological, and metaphysical—is a sort of novel or romance, written about experience, to be sure, but subjected to all sorts of falsifying alterations and expurgations in order that it may suit our preferences and prejudices, which, being dictated largely by biological and economic interests, are for the most part bourgeois.

Chapter XXXII

PRAGMATISM

I. PEIRCE

Life and Work. It was in the logical realism, Platonic idealism, and pragmatism of Charles Sanders Peirce (1839-1914) that American thought first came of age and declared itself in a measure independent of Europe.

Peirce was the son of a leading Harvard mathematician, who gave him a rigorous education in mathematics, logic, physical science, and the history of philosophy. He was himself a professor at Harvard for a brief time, and later held other academic appointments, but during much of the creative period of his life he served the United States Coast Survey. His late years were spent largely in seclusion and poverty. Peirce's scientific work was not unimportant, but it was as logician and philosopher that he left a permanent impress upon American thought. Very little of his philosophical work was published during his lifetime, but six volumes of his papers were published from 1931 to 1935, with a promise of more to come. In this great profusion of highly original writings, the content and significance of which are only now becoming generally known and appreciated, Peirce contributed to the foundations of symbolic logic, constructed the outlines of a cosmic metaphysics and ethics, analyzed the problems of meaning and signification, and advanced a symbolic theory of the mind. His philosophy promises to stand for a long time as the chief ornament of new-world originality.

Tychism. In his constructive thought Peirce was at times inclined toward idealism, but his philosophy was not entirely systematic, and it combines idealistic with realistic and pragmatic factors. Peirce was an intellectualist, but a militant advocate of experimentalism in opposition to intuitionism and a priorism; he at times argued as a positivist, yet enjoyed the pleasures of speculative metaphysics. At a time when philosophy in America was still largely the enterprise of the clergy, he championed empirical science as its necessary foundation. Peirce wanted less "seminary" and more "laboratory" philosophy.

Like most thinkers of his time, Peirce was greatly influenced by Darwinism and was responsible in part for the large and permanent impact of biological theory upon American thought. He was attracted to the spontaneity, life, and variety of the world, which prompted a cosmic evolutionism that made chance, or "tychism" central in all process. Deviations, large and small, from the apparently established patterns of nature, were evidence for him that absolute chance or freedom is a foundation factor in the universe, the first category of existence, accounting for the infinite variety and development of all things. For Peirce, not only does natural law evolve and multiply, but even the principles and forms of logic, however immutable they may seem, are evolving according to the principle of vitality. The world process is a gradual shaking down of a disorderly, undetermined, and haphazard chaos into a crystallized, orderly system.

Logic and Knowledge. In problems of logic especially, Peirce was a vigorous advocate of realism. He deeply resented the subjectivistic and sophistic tendencies of the pragmatic conception of truth that was developed in part on foundations supplied by him. The problem of truth, he insisted, is not to be confused with the problem of knowledge. Truth has an objective status; it is discovered, not created, by science. Peirce believed that genuine knowledge is possible, knowledge that is communicable and public, but he argued with great skill for a doctrine of fallibilism, the position that no statement can be assumed to be infallible. He defended this view on linguistic, logical, and psychological grounds, holding that in effect, every proposition is a hypothesis and no knowledge can be taken as final. To say of a proposition, for instance, that it is true, is to say that all of its implications are true. But these are infinite, or at least indefinite in number, and there is no logical or theoretical justification for holding them to be true.

Realism. As a philosopher of science as well as a metaphysician, Peirce defended a realistic theory of universals and vigorously opposed the nominalistic tendencies of both empirical science and pragmatic philosophy. Science was regarded by him as a progressive approximation to the truth; but it is not a search for a truth about particulars, or even collections of particulars, but rather of universals. Scientific knowledge is of general principles that are genuinely operative in nature. In his doctrine of universals Peirce was much influenced by the late medieval philosophers, particularly by Duns Scotus.

In his interest in symbols, Peirce not only made fundamental contributions to symbolic logic, but advanced an amazing number of highly suggestive ideas with reference to the whole theory of language and communication and the problem of meaning. Two decades after his death the most advanced semantics was to recognize in him one of the most creative thinkers in the history of that discipline.

Peirce and Pragmatism. The greatest immediate impact of Peirce on recent thought, however, has been his influence on the foundations of pragmatism. Influenced somewhat by Kant's interest in the relation of logic to action, of thought to experience, as well as by the biological context of thought suggested by Darwinism, he held that the meaning of concepts is to be found entirely in their application to existence, that the "rational purport of a word or other expression, lies exclusively in its conceivable bearing upon the conduct of life." Accordingly, "if one can define accurately all the conceivable experimental phenomena which the affirmation or denial of a concept could imply, one will have therein a complete definition of the concept." It was this theory of meaning, developed by Peirce in discussion with his Cambridge associates during the seventies, that was converted by James into the theory of truth that is basic to his pragmatism, a theory later refined and tempered by Dewey.

European Influences on Pragmatism. To understand pragmatism, we ought, however, to go further back than Peirce's influence on James. Back in the sixties, Lange, it will be recollected, had distinguished judgments of truth from judgments of value. Although, he said, we could not make valid comparisons of different religions in point of their truth, we could properly compare them so far as their satisfactoriness was concerned. A little later Mach, and then Pearson, had pointed out that scientific concepts, or in other words, scientific *truths* were not revelations of entities existing beyond and independent of experience, but were simply *conceptual shorthands* for summing up and organizing in brief, convenient and simple shape great numbers of experienced events and objects. These shorthands were *truer* insofar as they were *better* for the purposes of the scientist. In a word their truth lay in their *usefulness*. So long as a theory was useful, it remained true. The moment it outlived its usefulness, and some more convenient and simple theory was found to do its job, it became false. Truth was itself a value.

Renouvier also was insisting that the scientific interest could not be divorced from other human interests, and that therefore the truth of a theory lay in the general satisfaction it gave to the whole of human nature, including moral and religious demands. Plainly there had been amassed a number of suggestions which called for organization in a new philosophy.

II. JAMES

Pragmatism proper, the most native and characteristic American philosophy, the most significant contribution of America to intellectual culture, and possibly the most important philosophical movement of the first half of the present century, was fathered by William James (1842-1910), the founder in America of experimental psychology. James, educated in medicine, physiology, and psychology as well as philosophy, was professor at Harvard from 1880 to 1907, during the most creative period of American thought. He expanded Peirce's pragmatic theory of meaning into a theory of truth, laid the foundations of a physiological science of mind and a philosophy of radical empiricism, and against a background of moral and religious interests advanced a pluralistic conception of reality. A student of the biological sciences, James' psychology and philosophy were oriented in Darwinism, on the basis of which he cultivated an instrumental theory of the mind as an agent in the service of the life of the organism.

James's View of Experience. James, like the British empiricists, founds his theory of knowledge upon the revelations of sense-experience. But his study of consciousness leads him to far different conclusions. For one thing, it permits him, as we shall see in a moment, to have a metaphysics. For another, it leads him to reject altogether the view that the content of experience is atomic in nature. Experience is not made up of separable, discrete data fitted together like the bits of a mosaic into a pattern from which the relations between the component parts of the pictures they present can be abstracted and regarded separately. On the contrary, it is a flowing, continuous affair in which there are no cracks and joints, either spatial or temporal. Things shade and merge into one another both in space and time. Nothing is self-contained. Everything tends to spill over. To be sure, experience is continually curdling and thickening into what we call things or substances, but these curdled spots melt and run at the edges into a liquid "transitive" stuff, which thickens immediately into some new "substantive" aspect. The content of consciousness then, though infinitely multiple and varied, is *one,* not many as the earlier empiricists taught.

If we view experience as an affair of this sort, the old, hidebound distinctions between matter and form, substance and relation and activity, and the like, all collapse and are dissolved in the stream of consciousness. Sense data cannot be precipitated from the relations in which they occur and from the activities in which they are engaged.

They are *given* with a "fringe" of prepositions relating them on all sides, and they are given *doing* something. They are immediately and fundamentally *in relation* to one another—of, by, with, beside, before, after, passing into and out of, one another. They can no more be torn apart from their relations than an octopus can be torn away from its tentacles. Strip a thing of its relations and you have nothing left.

Effect of Attention and Volition upon Experience. But why does experience curdle in spots? Why is it thicker and more solid here, thinner and more running there? How can it "stay put" and constitute a world, and why should it constitute this world rather than that? How does it give rise to "ideas" about itself? And why should we call some of these ideas "true," and others "false"? Such are some of the questions we must now answer.

James's reply is that consciousness displays what we call "interest" and "attention." It is volitional as well as sensory. It not only feels but it likes some of its feelings, dislikes others. It selects, attends to, and dwells upon a part of its content; rejects, neglects, pushes away, and forgets the rest. What is selected and attended to is made real and vital. What is rejected and pushed away thereby becomes relatively unimportant and unreal. The world of things, therefore, is largely of our own making.

But the content of consciousness is not exhausted by data immediately present to it. Besides the experience with which we are here and now *acquainted,* we entertain "ideas" which memory and imagination enable us to draw from sense perceptions. These "ideas" refer beyond what is directly present, and afford us indirect *knowledge about* experience that is past and experience that is yet to come.

The same volitional, selective influences as govern the attention we give to our sensations also operate in connection with our ideas. Some ideas engage our attention, monopolize the footlights, dominate the stage, and make the rest of the mental cast insignificant by comparison. Moreover, since every idea, because of its active, transitive side, is a motor-idea and discharges itself in action, unless inhibited by other ideas, the concepts that dominate our thought are also the concepts that inspire our behavior.

Truth an Expression of Purpose. But by what principle is the selective activity of consciousness motivated? By the total *purpose* of the consciousness in question, James answers. We attend to and promote what gives our total nature, including our emotions and yearnings and aspirations, the greatest satisfaction. The ideas that interest us are *previews* of situations that have bearing upon the achievement of that satisfaction. They are not mere memories of situations that are dead and gone. When we *think*, we are not dully looking over photographs of the past. We are trying to paint a portrait of *future* experiences that will answer to our desires and fulfill our total purpose. These experiences are the "objects" to which ideas are supposed to refer.

Furthermore, and here we come to James's *pragmatic* view of the nature of truth, the "feel" of *truth* which some ideas have is simply the feeling that they do anticipate the desired and satisfying experience. They "correspond" to their objects by producing them. Conversely, the falsity of an idea is the feeling that the experience it pictures is undesirable or unlikely to occur. Since true ideas are regarded as forecasts of agreeable and satisfying experiences, they are in themselves agreeable and satisfactory to entertain. Nevertheless, the proof of the pudding is in the eating. For the idea to be truly true, it must "work" not merely by being pleasing in itself, but by anticipating or producing the satisfactory experiences it promises. As long as it continues to "work" in this way, it remains true. When it ceases to yield satisfactory results and no longer "works," it becomes false, and goes into the scrapbasket of outworn creeds, outgrown hypotheses, and discredited theories.

Plainly, then, for James, *thinking* is secondary to *willing*. Idea reflects impulse, and reflects it as it wants to be reflected. The will determines how and what we shall think. Ideas, insofar as they satisfy or disappoint the expectations of the will, envisage truth or error. The truth of an idea has nothing to do with anything outside experience, or even with any permanent form and constitution of experience. It denotes simply that the idea is working satisfactorily at the moment as a means of getting out of experience what we now *want*. To be true an idea must continually *come* true.

Experience and Reality. How much metaphysics will such a theory of the nature of knowledge and truth enable us to get out of experience? It will certainly not permit us to look outside experience for metaphysical entities. We have no right to assume anything existing *beneath* consciousness. Transcendental unities of apperception, ego, souls, spiritual substances, are all out of the picture. They are unnecessary now that it has been shown that relations are not introduced from the outside into the manifold of sense-experience, but are part and parcel of it. Nor has self-consciousness any need of external support. It, too, is simply there in the stream of consciousness, floating as it were upon its surface, and handed on, along with the other content, from one moment to another. The continuous, unbroken, flowing character of all experience is sufficient to account for its continuity, without invoking the intervention of a transcendent self.

In all these matters, James is, as he himself terms it, "a radical empiricist." Reality is nothing but experience. It has, we might almost say, no third dimension of thickness, such as the "transcendental" philosophers and the old-school metaphysicians attributed to it. It is only a flowing, extended *surface*.

The Fringed, "Open and Close" Nature of Experience. But on this surface, and in the two dimensions of length and breadth, there may exist all that we need. Among the ideas that "work" are those that indicate the existence of a plurality of streams of consciousness and of other selves like our own. Practically and pragmatically, we find ourselves dealing with a world of fellow-men, with whom we are in experienced companionable and moral relations. Furthermore, the spread of any individual's consciousness is a curious affair. It expands and contracts, it has tentacles and fringes. It is subject to all the baffling occurrences of abnormal psychology. It opens upon extraordinary vistas, sometimes revealed in split personality, in hypnotism, in telepathy, in clairvoyance, and in the "metapsychical" phenomena investigated by "psychical research."

This "open and close" peculiarity of the field of consciousness should be enough to convince us that our individual streams of experience are really currents in a great sea of more experience that encompasses us on every side. Ordinarily and normally they flow within the limits of what we call prosaic, everyday consciousness. But on occasions they fan out over the surface of the "more," and become confluent with new waters; only, however, to shrink again to their "normal" volume.

Religious Experience vs. Marginal Nature. There is, however, one sense of contact with the "more" that has been usual and well-nigh universal throughout human history. Man has always and everywhere had *religious experience*. He has felt around and about his consciousness the presence of another experience, akin to his own, sympathetic to his aspirations, fighting with him against evil in the service of the good, and inexhaustibly able and willing to encourage and comfort him. Upon this larger presence he is forever falling back in communion and in prayer. Nor does it ever fail him. Here is an experience that escapes and passes beyond the ordinary kind of data given in connection with the senses, and that yet remains *experience*.

It is in exploring and interpreting this "more" that metaphysical speculation is justifiable and of positive value. In dealing with it we must be guided by the same method as inspired our trafficking with sensory experience. In the one case as in the other, the test of the truth of an idea will lie in how it *works*. If it prefigures the occurrence of experience that brings to our whole nature comfort and happiness and peace, we may regard it as true. Judged by pragmatic standards, the most soul-satisfying and therefore the *truest* way of interpreting religious experience is to suppose it to come from another personal consciousness like our own, with which we commune as a friend, who loves us and desires to help us. In other words, theism best stands the pragmatic test of truth.

Nature of the God of Religious Experience. But not every kind of theism. For the theism that conceives God as infinite and omnipotent James has no use. If God can do as he pleases, and has been pleased to create the kind of world we live in, it is impossible to conceive him as a moral and friendly being. No God who is worth his salt can be good, as we understand goodness, if he so much as tolerates our universe as it stands, not to speak of creating it deliberately by fiat. Far from satisfying him, it must disgust and pain him beyond words. No humane God can be truly happy, James says somewhere, as long as a single cockroach suffers from an unrequited love.

No, the useful God, the God we need and turn to, must be a God who is limited and thwarted, who suffers, and fights, and does the best he can, like ourselves. Only with such a God can we cooperate in any intelligible sense of the word. If the world as it stands is the creation of the divine will and is good in the divine sight, there can be no such thing as helping God better it, since it completely fulfills his purpose and manifests his power, as it is. Nay more, there is no room for real freedom, real novelty, and real experiment in such a world. The universe is a *bloc* universe, achieved, finished, and closed, in the very act of its creation.

The Universe Tychistic. We must therefore conceive God and ourselves as fighting shoulder to shoulder to perfect the universe. The odds against the success of our common task are heavy. God must contend with the stubbornness of our free wills, which by refusing to cooperate may retard or even wreck the working out of his scheme. He and we have also to reckon with a factor of pure *chance* in the universe. James, we see, here agrees with the *tychistic* view advanced by Peirce. Plan as we may, we have always to take into account an unpredictable element in things, which may upset and defeat our calculations at any moment. The world-process, in a word, is a gamble, involving an enormous stake and tremendous risks. But the risks are worth taking. The game is worth playing. It is exciting in itself, and we are playing for a prize beside which all the material wealth of the world is as nothing. If we and our partner, God, win, we shall have won the salvation of the universe.

The Will to Believe. In a Reality so conceived we may also hope for immortality. We have, James feels, possible intimations of it in the phenomena observed and studied by psychical research. But even without them, we should be justified in believing in it because of its pragmatic, practical value. To be sure, ideas like God and immortality can never receive the same matter-of-fact corroboration by experience, as, say, our anticipations of an eclipse or a concept like the law of gravitation. We cannot see God face to face as we can a falling apple or the moon obscuring the sun. He is too "marginal," too much on the "fringe" and in the "beyond" of our experience for that. Nevertheless, belief in him and in immortality satisfies our moral and esthetic and emotional demands. A world of which God and immortality are believed to be a part is a more livable and workable world than one from which they are excluded. We *want* to believe in them. We are happier all around if we believe in them.

Since, however, their existence is not clearly corroborated and is open to argument, we are bound to be assailed by doubts. To dispel these misgivings, we have to make an effort. We have to "will to believe," as James puts it, in a famous phrase. This "will to believe" is a vital factor in our ability to help God win the game. Disbelief in him and in the value of the game is precisely one of the things we have to fight against. It paralyzes our efforts and renders us less efficient. To be at our best and to do our best, we must unremittingly *sustain* our faith that God exists, that his game is worth playing, that the risks are worth taking, and that there is a good chance of our winning—if only we so will.

III. SCHILLER

With many of James's conclusions F. C. S. Schiller (1864-1937), of Corpus Christi College at Oxford and for some years professor of philosophy at the University of Southern California, was in agreement. Some of them he developed independently, in others James's influence may be seen. Like James he was interested in psychical research and in the bearing its discoveries might have on such problems as that of immortality. He also defended vigorously the concept of God as a finite, struggling, fighting being like ourselves. He was a radical empiricist —in a way even more radical than James. Also, like James, he was an indeterminist, and believed that experience harbors spontaneous and chance events, which cannot be predicted, and for which no predetermining causes exist. He accepted the pragmatic criterion of truth. The truth of an idea for him, as for James, lay in its utility and workableness as tested by its all-round satisfactory results; not in its correspondence to any unseen order and constitution of the world. Ideas were true as long as they enabled us to cope with experience. When they lost that power they turned false.

But Schiller, as we have just said, was even more radical than James in some respects. He dwelt upon the fact that ideas and beliefs which "work" for one man will not "work" for another. What is one man's meat is another man's poison. Every individual tends to construct out of the flow of experience, the reality, sensible and intellectual, that suits himself. He colors and interprets experience in terms of his own personal predilections and idiosyncrasies. He builds his own particular world. He almost, we might say, *creates* his special, private truth. So-called knowledge is not a registration of something already existing independently of it. It is a process of producing and building up a world congenial to the knower in question.

Experience lends itself to any and every form in which the individual creative personality cares to mold it. Hence there is no common *original* experience with a form and a cast of its own. On the contrary, there are as many experiences, as many realities, and as many truths as there are individuals. But since every individual experience, if it is to "work," must be a *social* experience in which other individuals play a part, the rough edges of our private worlds and realities get rubbed off, and certain experiences and ideas prove, as a matter of practice, to work for most individuals. In this way, a *derivative,* common experience, embodying "public" concepts workable and "true" for all alike, is built up out of the social aspects of our original private experiences.

This public truth, however, is purely pragmatic. It is only true for me as long as it works for me. When it ceases to express and satisfy my purpose it becomes false so far as I am concerned. I am then clapped into an insane asylum, or dubbed an eccentric and scorned as out of step. Sometimes, however, my truth eventually comes to "work" for other people as well as for me, gains public acceptance, and becomes common property. In that case, public opinion is reversed. I am no longer considered out of my head, as my contemporaries thought me, but a prophet far in advance of his times.

Because of the stress his system laid upon the creative aspects of individual thinking and the private and particular nature of truth, Schiller preferred to call his philosophy, not pragmatism, but *humanism*. A modern sophist, Schiller insisted that Protagoras' aphorism, "Man is the measure of all things," is the beginning of philosophic wisdom.

IV. DEWEY

Background of Dewey's Thought. Pragmatism came to its maturity in the thought and extensive writings of John Dewey (1859-1952), long professor at Columbia University. Dewey's pragmatism was developed against a background of biology, psychology, and sociology, a concern for life and living experience. It became essentially a moral philosophy, directed toward the actual achievement of personal and social well-being through the instrumentality of social action and the educational process, and supported by a technical apparatus in the form of a biological theory of the mind as organic and symbolic function, an experimental logic defined as the theory of inquiry in problem solving, and a theory of instrumental ethics that undertook to achieve a science of morality by the employment of factual propositions relating means to ends. In all, Dewey's philosophy has the character of a highly refined genetic social psychology. More an attitude and method than a system, it attempts to avoid traditional metaphysical issues and expresses its author's profound belief that human felicity will be achieved only through the extension of scientific attitudes and methods to the solution of human problems, and his optimistic faith that the achievement of a genuinely humane knowledge is possible.

Professor Dewey developed his thought against a background of social and political unrest and transition, conditions wrought in part by the growth of industry, the trend toward urbanization, and the exhaustion of free land. To what extent his early social experience in New England shaped his later thought cannot be determined, though it is not unlikely that his concern for a better world and his utilitarian attitudes in general derived in part from his puritan environment as well as from the empirical social philosophy of nineteenth-century England.

Although in his earlier years he faced the emotional problems generated by a traditional religion encountering natural science, Dewey's evangelical background had only a negative effect on the development of his socially oriented scientific humanism, a product of respect for experimental method combined with an intense social consciousness.

While he found in the formalism of Hegelian absolutism a unity and wholeness that was intellectually pleasing, he turned reluctantly to the concrete, particular, and practical, determined to overcome the extreme atomistic and over-individualistic concept of society that plagued both social thought and practice, by drawing his materials from living social experience rather than from books or abstract thought. The subsequent development of his thought was in part an objection against absolutes, whether moral or doctrinal, and a critique of the religiously inspired idealism that has been a principal nourishment of these absolutes.

Dewey and Darwinism. The influence of Darwin upon Dewey was twofold. As Dewey himself pointed out, the major intellectual impact of Darwin is not seen in the conflict of science with fundamentalist religion, but is found internal to the discussions of science and philosophy themselves, the question whether the world is a construction of immutable forms or species or is genuinely changing and dynamic. Dewey accepted the verdict of Darwin against Aristotle and founded his philosophy squarely upon the fact of change.

A second influence of Darwin, mediated to Dewey through the physiological psychology of James, was the suggestion that the mind in a sense is an organic function determined by its survival value, and that thought processes are to be interpreted, therefore, with reference to the concrete problems of the organism's efforts to achieve environmental adaptation. Dewey's experimental logic, based in part upon this concept of mind, assumes, accordingly, that ideation is instrumental to life rather than descriptive of an external order of reality. Experience as the interaction of the organism with its environment became his nearest approach to a metaphysical principle as he entered the controversy over the nature of reality and of knowledge engendered by the realists *versus* the idealists and later the neo- *versus* the critical realists.

The influence of Peirce's pragmatic theory of meaning and of James's extension of pragmatism to a theory of truth are evident in the development of Dewey's own experimental concept of meaning and his substitution of the notion of warranted assertability for the logical propositional values of true and false.

Mind as Symbolic Function. Further, mention may be made of Dewey's highly abstruse theory of mind as a symbolic functioning of events, a concept developed in part on foundations laid by Peirce. Peirce had approached the problem of the nature of signs or symbols not only from the standpoint of logic, or the relation of signs to one another, and semantics, their relation to that which they signify, but also in terms of what has come to be called pragmatics, the relation of signs or symbols to their users. He identified thoughts with signs and at times went even to the extreme of defining man not only as a user of signs but as the sign which he uses. In fact, Peirce enlarged his conception to cosmic proportions and described the world itself as a system of signs. The permanent impact of Peirce at this point was his idea that since all thought must be in signs the mind must be conceived essentially as something that functions symbolically.

James and Dewey both entertained symbolic conceptions of the mind, but in Dewey, influenced by Peirce on the one hand and biology and psychology on the other, the theory achieved its mature and most satisfactory formulation. Here mind is conceived as a twofold function, an instrumental problem-solving function relating to the organism's interaction with its environment, and a symbolic functioning of events. Symbols occur when the natural interactions of the organism with the world are "directed towards anticipated consequences." Such interactions have the quality of intelligence. Knowledge, for Dewey, is always mediated by symbols, and the meanings of symbols, a symbol being a thing or event that stands for another thing or event, are always grounded in a behavioral context involving experienced difficulty.

Ideas as Instruments of Successful Action. According to Dewey, thought has no object outside of experience, and no being of its own apart from experience. Thinking is not of a different order from perceiving. Ideas are anticipations of perceptions. For that matter, things are only what they are perceived to be. They exist only *as* they are experienced.

The function of thinking is not primarily to construct general images and ideas out of remembered perceptions or to anticipate in a general way general situations. Ideas are specific in character, are aroused by specific circumstances, and anticipate a particular occasion. They are practical *instruments* for dealing with each specific situation as it arises. They are *responses* to that situation, and their business is not to indulge in generalities, but to attend to it and to it alone. Insofar as they prove effective *instruments* in dealing with the situation that evokes them they are true of it. If they fail to work in any particular case, we have made a *false* estimate of the situation in question.

Every case has to be met and judged on its own merits, so there can be no hard and fast universal ways of dealing with experience. We live in the midst of an evolving, changing experience to which knowledge is an act of adaptation, and of adaptation to which a *true* idea is the sign. But knowledge, like experience, is in constant flux, since it involves continuous readjustment to changing circumstances, and an idea signifying adaptation at one moment may mean quite the reverse at the next.

Again, if an idea operates upon a situation with an unsteady hand, we call it an "hypothesis." It trembles with "if" and "perhaps." It is conjecture. It becomes a "fact," however, the moment that it stops shaking and gets down to working firmly and steadily for the time it continues to work.

The Social Basis of True Ideas. Upon man's social nature and the importance of his social activities in producing knowledge and truth, Dewey was insistent. A great part of the environment to which knowledge is an adjustment is social in character, and the truth of an idea is correspondingly a mark of its social acceptance. The mental processes productive of social truth—in other words, productive of the body of ideas that "work" for the experiences of most people—are what we call the processes of *reason,* and express themselves in the rules of *logic*. But there is nothing sacrosanct and immutable about these ways and rules of thought. What man considers reasonable and intelligible and logical at any time is the product of the collective thinking of that time. Society, which does the collective thinking, is in a state of constant development. Its relations to its natural environment change, and its individual components are ceaselessly being readjusted to one another. Hence the common instrument called social truth is experimental in character and subject to uninterrupted revision and refinement.

The Fluidity of Truth and Good. In the same way, standards of rationality and principles of logic are what they are at a given epoch because they embody the most successful *experiments* in thinking, up to date. They have evolved because they have "worked," and they owe such authority as they possess to their instrumentality in helping us solve the problems that confront us now and here. Their "necessary" character is contingent upon their good behavior. Under new conditions and in the face of new problems they might prove ineffective and useless; in which case they would no longer be good logic but bad.

We are concerned only with the present, not with the past. Let the dead bury the dead. In any case, let not the dead hand of past truth seek to dictate what shall be true for us who belong to another generation and live in another, newer world. To be sure, many past truths are also present ones. They continue to live. But the only real life in them belongs not to their past but to their present applicability.

They hold true today, not because they were good enough for our fathers, but because they happen to be still good enough for us. *We* are the only judges of what works and is true for *our* experience. Though we may hold fast to so much of our legacy of past ideas as helps us to meet our modern conditions, we must not hestitate to reject everything that no longer measures up to our needs, and that therefore, so far as we are concerned, has ceased to be true and become false.

In fine, truth must be kept pliant and supple, if it is to serve mankind. The moment it is allowed to become stiff and unyielding—as it does when it is crystallized in conventions and legalisms and moral and religious dogmas—it is no longer a help but a hindrance and a positive danger to the furtherance of human purpose. It is no longer truth; it is error. It behooves us to be vigilant in keeping truth up with the times, and in bringing it up to date, since only by being kept burnished, and rustless, and unblunted, and keen, can it always prove instrumental in enabling us to deal with the problems of the present.

This is, to be sure, a counsel of perfection, which falls largely upon deaf ears. We none of us heed it, and in consequence are always behind the times and stagger along under a burden of ideas, inherited from the past, which no longer fit our needs and hence are false to the conditions of the day. The world, in Dewey's opinion, is a junkyard of outworn creeds of every sort, among which we still stumble.

So it is that we find him an active reformer, seeking to clear away what he considers the rubbish, and to introduce in its place the ideas that in his opinion will work under modern conditions and are therefore true of them. This advocacy of reform extends itself into many fields, social, political, economic and moral, in which he is well known for his "advanced" ideas. Furthermore, he has in some cases been able to test his views in the laboratory; most notably in connection with the education of children, whom he would teach pragmatically by leading them to find out things for themselves by experimentation, and to learn by doing.

The Uselessness of Metaphysics. Pragmatism, or *instrumentalism,* as Dewey preferred to call it, is primarily an epistemology, or theory of the nature of knowledge, and an ethics, in as much as it is also a plan for living. In metaphysical and theological problems Dewey has little interest. He would agree with Schiller and James in ruling out as useless and false any metaphysics and any theology that tried to transcend experience and to reach objects existing independently of it and incapable of being incorporated in it. Reality is for him experience and nothing else. We have to take experience as we find it. Its presence makes us want to do certain things and presents us with certain ends. Whether experience is actuated by chance or is purposive, raises for Dewey a question that he believes to be unanswerable. Certainly it is not of the *bloc,* deterministic, mechanical type. It is not a shuffling over and over again of the same old cards. New cards apparently are constantly turning up in the pack.

Religion. Emotional needs are too private, too various, and too conflicting, personal religious experiences too diverse, to precipitate ideas that can be worked in common by all men alike. The innumerable contradictory and antagonistic theologies and concepts of God bear abundant witness to that. Religious beliefs, being private, do not lend themselves to membership in a public truth shared by and useful to society as a whole. But the truth that really counts for Dewey is precisely the social truth—the truth that emerges from the cooperative search of mankind for ideas which all individuals can handle together as instruments for promoting the welfare of the race. Experiences that we do not and cannot share with others cannot give rise to ideas which are socially workable. But only such ideas can lay claim to "universal" validity, and only such ideas can be made the subjects of fruitful investigation.

Accordingly, Dewey conceives of religion in social rather than private terms. In his *A Common Faith,* a classic of humanistic religion, he distinguishes between "religion," the great diversity of historical religious faiths and practices, and "the religious," a quality of experience that may belong to political, moral, artistic, or scientific experiences that are ordinarily more or less sharply distinguished from religion. "The religious" is not a unique experience but is a quality of experiences that can be shared. It is what an experience "does in and to the processes of living" that indicates its religious quality. Religion for Dewey is non-dogmatic, experimental, and free from all supernaturalism. It is a moral faith in ideal ends, and the power of religion is the "power of an ideal," the power to unify the self and achieve perspective, to dispel fear and induce a sense of the dignity of human nature and human endeavor. The word "God" may be used, but it is divested of its traditional associations and indicates the union in thought and action of the ideal and the real.

Instrumentalist Ethics. Of major concern to Dewey was the problem, old as Socrates, of whether knowledge of values is possible. Perhaps no philosopher has analyzed this problem more thoroughly, or with more serious intent, in the interest of creating a genuine moral intelligence. There is no such thing as knowledge of end values or intrinsic values.

The very nature of knowledge precludes this as a possibility. But of course there can be and is knowledge of means-end relationships, of what means are necessary for the achievement of specified ends. Such knowldge is genuinely scientific, belonging especially to the social sciences and psychology. Its cultivation is a requisite for intelligent social action.

To the objection that this would mean that there could be no knowledge of the truth of categorical imperatives, that only conditional statements, indicating the relation of means to ends, could function in a moral science, Dewey readily concurred. But, he insisted, nothing is lost thereby. For many of the major ills of human society are caused by the absolutistic morals set forth in categorical fashion, with no genuine respect for the actual circumstances of particular moral experience. Ends or intrinsic values should not be considered independently of the means for achieving them. Value judgments are possible on a rational, intelligent basis only when means and ends are taken together. There are no ends that are not also means, and ends therefore do not escape intelligent appraisal. When this is done, Dewey insisted, the whole gamut of human knowledge is relevant to the moral life. The means-end relationship is genuinely existential, and the hypothetical or conditional value judgments expressing it may rest securely on scientifically acceptable empirical propositions, capable of being tested by observation. Moral knowledge of this variety, then, is possible.

Chapter XXXIII

NEO-REALISM IN GERMAN AND AUSTRIAN PHILOSOPHY

I. REVOLT AGAINST IDEALISM

Through most of the nineteenth century and into the twentieth, Idealism in one form or another, monistic or pluralistic, subjective or objective, voluntaristic or intellectualistic, dominated much of the philosophic scene. But its natural enemy, Realism, was far from dead, and seemed to await only the propitious moment to arouse itself to a new life and a vitality such as it had not known since the middle ages. From the beginning of the present century it appeared at every turn, the champion of "common sense," setting itself against Idealism, Pragmatism, and Vitalism alike. The realists were unconvinced that Reality was fundamentally mental in character, and that nothing existed except centers of consciousness and their experiences. Consciousness and experience, they maintained, were *essentially* consciousness and experience *of,* and *of* something external to and independent of mental activity, which, if all minds whatsoever were extinguished, would still be there. Reality, in a word, refused to be experience, to be wholly experience and nothing but experience.

In reviving Realism, however, its champions have revived it with a difference. The older modern realisms tended to locate the independent objects of sense and knowledge in enacted concrete existence, material or immaterial, like atoms or souls. The new realisms have extended the field of entities whose being is independent of being perceived or conceived to include unsubstantial objects, such as essences like redness and oneness and beauty and goodness, and even logical propositions and logical absurdities. In this respect the neo-realists show a Platonic turn of mind. Plato, it will be remembered, attributed to the Ideas a being that was neither physical nor mental but either purely logical and ideal, as some commentators claim, or simply *sui generis.*

549

II. BRENTANO AND MEINONG

Mind as Intentional. In the German-speaking countries, Neo-realism stemmed largely from the empirical psychologist Franz Brentano (1838-1917), who exerted a strong influence on the leaders of the school, Alexius Meinong (1853-1921), Edmund Husserl (1859-1938), and Nicolai Hartmann (1882-1950). Brentano's theory of the mind was developed under Aristotelian, scholastic, and Cartesian influences and centered on the scholastic concept of "intentionality." The mind is differentiated from physical reality by its ability to intend or refer to something beyond itself. The preposition *of*, which dangles from experience, is not so much a hawser anchoring it to an external object as a kind of tentacle reaching out and groping for objects both existent and non-existent. The strength and vitality of experience goes into this tentacle, which simply *must* attach itself to an object of some sort, real or imaginary. Awareness of being aware of an object, reflection and self-consciousness, are pale and secondary in comparison with the primary consciousness of *things*. "We can define psychical phenomena," says Brentano, "by saying that they are phenomena which intentionally contain an object in themselves."

Experience an Awareness of Independent Subsistent and Existent Objects. Meinong calls his philosophy *Gegenstandstheorie,* or theory of objects. The independent objects upon which the "of-ness" of consciousness lays hold are, he tells us, by no means limited to physical existences. They include things like the Platonic Ideas—mathematical entities, essences like blueness or goodness, logical propositions, and self-contradictions like round squares. In a word everything that can be thought about or mentioned is equally independent of being thought or talked about. To distinguish abstract, logical objects from the concrete, physical objects, Meinong uses the term "subsist," instead of exist. Concrete things *exist*. Logical essences *subsist*. Logical absurdities are neither existent nor subsistent. Nevertheless they are in a sense *there* and have being, since we can refer to them. None of these objects would be destroyed if consciousness were destroyed. Physical things would still be there, essences would remain intact, some propositions would still be true and others would still be absurd—ready and waiting for a newly born consciousness to come along and perceive them and conceive them and recognize their valid or self-contradictory characters.

There are even "subsistent" objects of *opinion* as well as of knowledge. If for example, I say, "I *think* that the weather will be fine," or "I *take it* that this man is honest," *that the weather will be fine* and *that this man is honest* are objects of opinion. If I can say, "The weather *is* fine," or "The man *is* honest," both propositions are objects of knowledge. Doubt enters into one of these pairs of statements, conviction into the other. In the one case I *assume,* in the other I *judge.* But both kinds of propositions are equally objects that consciousness is *of.*

Values Independent of Consciousness. Objects, though heterogeneous, may be arranged in a hierarchy. Certain objects give a foundation to others, and are indispensable conditions of their existence or subsistence. For example, the subsistent proposition, *the weather is fine,* could not subsist and be an object of knowledge unless there were such things as weather and fine days. Thus increasingly complex and superior objects are built up out of comparatively simple and inferior ones.

Only objects of judgment or opinion can be regarded as good or bad. I can indeed immediately feel the pleasurableness of pleasure and the painfulness of pain, but I cannot sense the goodness of the one or the badness of the other. *Values* pertain only to propositions, and may run counter to immediate feelings. For instance, I may judge that something, however disagreeable, is good, or something, however pleasurable, is bad. Some propositional objects *ought* to exist or *ought not* to exist, whatever felt pain or pleasure their existence may involve. Such objects have *dignity.* We also *desire* to enact or to annul some propositions, whatever their pleasure-pain content may be.

Nevertheless, goodness and badness are not altogether independent of evaluation in terms of pleasure and pain. The good "propositional" object, whether or not it brings a painful or a pleasurable sensation, is an object the knowledge or opinion of whose enactment gives us at the moment a feeling of pleasure. For example, it is a satisfaction to propose to one's self a painful operation. If the proposition were unsatisfactory, we should not entertain it and act upon it. The operation in question would be undesirable or ought not to be performed. But, being satisfactory even though its performance entails pain, it is something we desire to have done and feel ought to be done.

It follows that value inheres in propositions and is quite as independent of consciousness as the propositions themselves are. Whether or not minds exist or bodies exist, the proposition "a diseased appendix is an appendix to be removed" is a satisfactory and *good* proposition. So, too, quite independently of the existence of body or mind, the proposition "men are nothing but cannon-fodder" is a *bad* proposition in itself. It is neither *dignitative,* nor *desiderative,* to use Meinong's terms.

Objective Reality and Experience. The relation of objects to minds is in a way equivocal. The object is both in the mind and outside it. Whatever the nature of the object may be—whether it is a round-square which can neither *exist* nor *subsist* in itself, or a proposition that *subsists,* or a physical fact that *exists,* or a future or a past event—it is present and existent *in* the mind of which at the time it is the object. It is part of the *content* of that mind's consciousness. But it owes neither its subsistence nor its existence to being *in* the consciousness in question. Still, even its independent being can never be out of the reach of the mind. Even when it is unperceived it must be perceivable, and when it is not entertained it must be entertainable. An entity that was essentially such that it could never become an object of sense or thought or reference would be non-existent and non-subsistent. It would be worse off than a square circle, since it would have no self to contradict. Objective reality must therefore be congruent to the mind and *before* it as an object of possible entertainment, even when it is not *in* it.

III. HUSSERL

Phenomenology. Husserl, to whom we now turn, agrees with Brentano and with Meinong in regarding consciousness as essentially a set of tentacles attached to objects. Hence there can be no such thing as a study of consciousness as such, detached from the objects to which it is affixed. To study consciousness is to study awareness of something beyond consciousness, which inserts itself into and becomes part of conscious processes. This description of consciousness of objects, Husserl calls "phenomenology."

But can such a description be undertaken? If all consciousness is awareness of *objects,* how can there be any left over for the investigation of that awareness? However, fortunately for phenomenology, consciousness is not merely a mass of tentacles wrapped about and adherent to objects. It is also reflective and self-conscious, and hence can be aware not only of objects but of itself—remembering always that the self is essentially a consciousness of things other than itself.

Still, in studying itself, it has to anesthetize and immobilize itself and loose its hold upon its objects. Phenomenology, therefore, cannot *feel* the nature of consciousness from *within* and experience its *contact* with its objects, or even, like psychology, observe its ordinary functioning, since that functioning also is in abeyance. It can only make a post-mortem examination in which the tentacles are as dead, so to speak, as the objects to which they are attached, and the objects, being on a par with the tentacles, appear merely as a prolongation of them. Instead of really and sensitively touching its object, consciousness merely sees from the outside that its nature is to be in touch with objects, and that its desensitized tentacles are in contact with them.

Analysis of the Nature of Experience. The particular interest of phenomenology is to investigate the general character of that contact. This it can do in a perfectly detached and "objective" way, thanks to the temporary withdrawal of the *inner* consciousness and activity from the subject-object relation, and the concentration of attention upon that relation as seen from the outside. All that phenomenology does is to see from the outside and to describe to the by-standers what it so sees. Furthermore, its descriptions will be exact, since they are mere anatomical charts. And they will have universal validity, since they deal with the formal structure of consciousness in general.

What, then, does our phenomenological anatomy of consciousness reveal? It reveals consciousness as the preoccupation of a subject with an object, expressed in a variety of attitudes towards a content of sense perceptions and images which are *of* an object that can be known and characterized. Preoccupation with an object is equivalent to *meaning* that object. Attending to it is *intending* it, and intending it to the exclusion of other objects. Hence consciousness can be defined as *meaning* or *intending* an object. Meaning involves someone who means something. He expresses his intentions in the way he behaves towards this "something." He likes it, dislikes it, reflects upon it, manipulates it according to what it means to him. But this is not all. Experience also signifies to him the existence of an external object which has meaning for him, and which can therefore be known and practically dealt with and made the object of his meaningful activities generally.

Objects as Meanings. Objects, therefore, must be capable of meaning something. They are what they can mean to us. However, when we are not there, their possible significance is not destroyed. Hence they continue to exist. We can, to be sure, never exhaust their whole meaning. We see them now from one side, now from another, in a series of perspectives. Hence we can never be exactly and wholly sure what we do mean by them, and what they can mean to us. So it is that we fall into error regarding them.

Our "phenomenological" study, however, confining itself to the universal aspects of the given, and never meaning and trying to see more than it does actually see, is exact and trustworthy. What we *perceive* of the object is true as far as it goes. The universal concepts we draw from that perception are also true and reliable, since they give us the fixed forms and essences exhibited by what is observed, and give them as they completely are. These essences, since they are self-existent objects of thought, are not constructed from sense-experience. They are directly intuited.

Take, for example, any *existent* object. What do I *mean* by it, and what does it *mean* to me? It means to me and I mean by it something I like or dislike, something that has for me various qualities varying in different perspectives, something that may be described in terms of chemical elements and of the entities of physics. It means finally something existing independently of myself. To you it may have different meanings, according as you like or dislike and see it in other perspectives, or perceive other qualities in it, or hold another opinion regarding its chemical constitution or the nature of the physical elements of which it is composed.

What, then, *is* the object in itself? It is all you and I mean by it, and all it means to you and me. Those meanings may be increased by other minds who find in it significance that escapes me, or I may add to them myself as I continue to explore it. We have not so far exhausted those meanings. That is to say our knowledge of it is incomplete. We may read into it meanings it does not possess. In that case we are mistaken and in error about the object. But the meanings we discover were there before we discovered them. And the meanings we falsely read into it were never there in the object at all. So too the meanings we now find in it, would remain in it in our absence. The object in itself is everything it can mean to everybody. Only a portion of those meanings are what any one person means by it.

Take, however, a *quality* of the object. Here I mean a universal essence or nature that is what it is, and that does not differ in this object and in that. The particular object in one perspective may be round, in another, oval. But roundness cannot be circular in one perspective and oval in another. In universals we have objects whose meanings we can immediately exhaust, and that mean to us at once and directly everything that they are. Such objects are given in one fell swoop, and given exactly as they are and in exactly the same way to all minds. Though I may not mean by the object exactly or wholly what you mean, I do mean by roundness precisely what you do. Nor can the meaning of roundness be added to or altered, once we have meant what we do by it. Furthermore, roundness would not be meaningless, if our minds were blotted out. It would not become nonsensical, simply because consciousness of it no longer existed. It would still have meaning

in itself and continue to subsist even if there were nobody to mean anything by it, and even if there were no existent objects to enact it.

Phenomenology as a Movement. In recent years Phenomenology,
grounded in Husserl's "phenomenological method," has had some success, in both Europe and America, as a more or less independent philosophical movement. Husserl's disciples have attempted to employ the
method as a technique of analysis and description not only in psychology, which was the master's main interest, but in such widely diverse
areas as metaphysics, mathematics, history, art, sociology, and religion.
The ideal of Phenomenology has been the achievement of philosophy
as an exact and autonomous science which will yield absolute knowledge in such a manner as to achieve a general unification of the sciences.
The phenomenological method in Husserl is defined as an *a priori*
method that abstracts the object from the content of experience and
obtains thereby an intuitive grasp of pure essences rather than existences.
It is a twofold technique: (1) *Eidetic reduction,* which seeks the essence
or defining form of the object by ignoring the particular circumstance
relevant to its uniqueness, and (2) *Transcendental reduction,* which
"brackets" or eliminates the objects of all existence judgments in favor
of the pure stream of consciousness.

IV. HARTMANN

The A Priori Character of Value. The foremost moral philosopher
of continental Neo-realism and Phenomenology has been Nicolai Hartmann, late of the University of Berlin, whose three-volume *Ethics,* published in 1925, was a major contribution to the analysis of the problem
of value. Hartmann's position is grounded in two propositions, (1)
that values are absolute and (2) that there is *a priori* knowledge of
them. The values are independent of the things that are valuable and
it is by virtue of them that such things are valuable. And knowledge of
these values comes not from an experience of valuable things, because
these can be judged as valuable only in terms of a previously known
standard, a value that is immediately discerned or felt. Otherwise judgments of value would become involved in an endless regression of instrumental or contingent "goods."

Values as Essences. The absolute values, which have a status over
and above and independent of all experienced good objects, are eternal
essences. They are presupposed in every instance of valuation, in all
moral willing or judging. "The apriority of values," says Hartmann,

"floats, as it were, in the air." But there is an *a priori* access to the value essences, the inner and autonomous voice of conscience, which, unsummoned and with an emotional mystery, is the "ideal world" speaking to the moral consciousness, determining its moral decisions or convicting it of guilt.

Chapter XXXIV

BRITISH NEO-REALISM
AND ANALYSIS

I. FROM IDEALISM TO ANALYSIS

Realistic Reaction to Idealism. The Absolute Idealism that dominated British thought at the close of the nineteenth century was destined to decline in the face of the inevitable resurgence of a philosophy more indigenous to the native British temper. For that Idealism was largely an adaptation of Hegelianism that had its roots in a logicism and rationalism and an absolutistic and speculative persuasion that were basically foreign to the traditional British ways of thinking. Those ways, nominalism, utilitarianism, a suspicion of speculative metaphysics, a pronounced tendency toward agnosticism, and a profound respect for empirical and analytic techniques, reaffirmed themselves in the rise of a new Realism in opposition to Idealism.

Whereas in the United States the chief enemy of Idealism was Pragmatism, which was fashioned in part as a polemic against absolutism, in the British Isles Pragmatism itself was not entirely divorced from Idealism and was never successful in establishing itself on broad and permanent foundations. But Realism, with unpretentious beginnings, lacking a well defined charter for its efforts, and quite without the polemizing spirit of the pragmatists, but with great logical and analytical skill and a firm attachment to the sciences, transformed the character of British thought during the first decades of the present century and brought to a full expression its native philosophical talents.

Method of New Realism. The result was not a new system to replace the old absolutism, nor for that matter was it a clearly defined philosophical school in any sense. Certainly it was far from a unified movement. It was rather a new insistence upon an old method and a new respect for an old attitude, the empirical method and scientific attitude. The realists refused to regard philosophy as a way of knowing independent of science. On the contrary, philosophy cannot be divorced from science, and all genuine knowledge is obtained by scientific techniques. But the problems of philosophy have a greater generality, and unlike science philosophy may venture hypotheses beyond the reach of supporting evidences. But again like science it analyzes, takes apart to understand the world piece by piece, rather than synthesizes it as a vast system knowable not empirically but as a rationally intuited complex intersection of ideas.

Logic and Mathematics. More than any other group of philosophers, the new realists were influenced by the new developments in mathematics as well as logic. They pursued these disciplines in independence of other philosophical considerations but with important results for their metaphysics.

The strength of the idealistic metaphysics was in its rationalistic assumptions and in its logic. That whatever satisfies the intellect is real and true and that it can be satisfied only by a consistent, harmonious, all-inclusive whole was a foundation of Bradley's Hegelianism. Against such an assumption and method the realists threw the weight not only of the method of natural science but that of the new relational logic as well. With such a logic, widely cultivated by the realists, the Hegelian notion that the all-inclusive character of the whole makes it possible to infer from the nature of a particular thing its relations to other things was eliminated by atomistic logical conceptions. The untenability of Hegelianism was also argued on the logical ground that the world of appearance, of space, time, and relations, is not self-contradictory and therefore does not require supervention by a different order "reality."

The newly developed symbolic logic, moreover, was, in the hands of such realists as the logicians Russell and Whitehead, a powerful instrument for the analysis of scientific ideas, especially in the physical sciences, and for the determination of their philosophic implications.

Finally, the theory of logic and mathematics led some of the realists into the acceptance of a form of Platonism in their theory of universal or abstract entities, and insulated them against an extreme form of empiricism in their theory of knowledge.

Natural Science. British Realism has been affected by physics, biology, and psychology, but it has by no means concerned itself importantly with problems of the social sciences. In physics it has been influenced especially by the theory of relativity in its denial of absolute time and absolute space and its employment of a space-time manifold in the description of events. Physics has also favored the realistic theory of knowledge by the discovery that through the employment of the tensor calculus the subjective element in the observation of physical phenomena can be eliminated. The new conception of matter as events rather than stuff was brought to bear on the mind-body problem and was employed by Russell, especially, as evidence in favor of the new theory, shared by Mach and James, that reality is a neutral entity, neither mind nor body.

The impact of Darwinism resulted in a strong interest in development and process among the realists, as evidenced in Samuel Alexander and Lloyd Morgan. But it was psychology that figured prominently among them as a common interest. For the realists were obsessed with the importance of solving the problem of knowledge, and to this end they provoked endless debate on the psychology of sense perception. For at least two decades every person in Britain who wanted to try his wings in philosophy was expected to produce something original on perception.

Religion and Moral Philosophy. While British Realism has affiliated primarily with science rather than religion, the increase in speculative and metaphysical interests since the first war has indicated a considerable concern for cosmology and for problems basic to the philosophy of religion. Developments in Realism, moreover, have had a noticeable effect upon religious thought with respect to both the theory of knowledge and metaphysics, with the result that in recent years British and Scottish theologians have been less inclined toward the idealistic pattern than has been the case with their German and American colleagues. Since the beginning of the realist movement, moral philosophy has received a fair share of attention, particularly from those realists who represent the analytical tradition. Though they have for the most part refrained from elaborate value theories, these have endlessly analyzed the structure of value language and the meanings of the basic concepts of value theory and ethics: value, goodness, right, duty, and obligation.

Analytical Philosophy. The story of British Realism is in large part the story of British Analysis, or analytical philosophy, for the realists have frequently been analysts and, indeed, at times their analytical method has been the chief characteristic of their philosophy. G. E. Moore (1873-   ), who was the chief figure in the rise of Realism, was also the prime mover of the analytical school, which centered first at Cambridge but was eventually to dominate the entire scene of British philosophy, invading even the precincts of Oxford, the stronghold of Idealism.

In 1903 in the preface of his *Principia Ethica* Moore laid down the program of Analysis. "It appears to me that in Ethics, as in all other philosophical studies, the difficulties and disagreements, of which its history is full, are mainly due to a very simple cause; namely to the attempt to answer questions, without first discovering precisely *what* question it is which you desire to answer. I do not know how far this source of error would be done away, if philosophers would *try* to discover what question they were asking, before they set about to answer it. . . . But I am inclined to think that in many cases a resolute attempt would be sufficient to ensure success." In this program Moore and his associates were following a tradition native to their country, for Hobbes, Locke, Berkeley, and Hume had each taken a similar stand, that philosophy should be pursued in plain and simple language and its problems reduced to simple and clear proportions. But no one before had so faithfully committed himself to this ideal as did Moore, and never before had it been the foundation of an entire movement.

The task of philosophical analysis is to determine what the questions are and whether they are meaningful or meaningless. Supplying the answers may or may not be a philosophic enterprise; the chief role is the critique of abstractions. For Moore this is not the whole of philosophy, but it is the major part. In this the British analysts have agreed with the continental and American logical empiricists. Ludwig Wittgenstein, who belonged to both movements, asserted in 1922 in his *Tractatus Logico-Philosophicus* that "The object of philosophy is the logical clarification of thoughts." But whereas the logical empiricists have attempted to do their clarifying through logical analysis, employing especially symbolic logic, the British analysts have favored the everyday language as sufficient for expressing meaningful questions.

With its twin brother Realism, Analysis has been passionately empirical, with a robust suspicion of systems, speculation, and metaphysics. Thoroughly committed to the methods of science, it has been satisfied with piecemeal studies and probable results. Above all, it has been a defense of the common-sense knowledge of the man in the street, seeking in sense data the indubitable grounds for that knowledge.

II. MOORE

Unlike most of the British realists, Moore came into philosophy through the classics rather than through mathematics or the natural sciences, although he became a careful student of logic and was influenced by Russell's work in the theory of mathematics. For the most part his efforts have been expended on ethics and the theory of knowledge approached through his questioning analyses of ideas, concepts, and propositions. Although essentially realistic throughout, Moore's position has altered from time to time, moving somewhat in the direction of Humean phenomenalism. Knowledge for Moore is the immediate apprehension of the real object, where the object is neither the product of perception nor represented to the mind by a copy that is present in consciousness. In our very act of being conscious we affirm, not only the independent existence of an object of which we are aware, but the fact that the object is not in any way influenced or changed by our consciousness of it. Our senses do not color and distort the nature of what they perceive. They give us the object precisely as it is, and precisely as it would continue to be if they ceased to operate. Nevertheless, some things, such as toothaches, he agrees, have their being only in being perceived, while others, like the moon, in no way depend on being perceived. A sense datum is not a mental image of the real object; it is that very object, or at least a part of the object. From this a knowledge of the whole object may be inferred, but it is an inference from a part or aspect to the whole, not from a mental copy to an original thing. Does an object as not perceived, therefore, have the same qualities, e.g., color, as when perceived? At least, according to Moore, who is not dogmatic in this matter, or in any other, this is a possibility, for there is nothing illogical in supposing it to be true.

Moore does not accept the Mach-James-Russell view of consciousness as simply one arrangement of the same items that in other contexts constitute physical objects. Our consciousness of objects is more than their mere presence in connection with and dependence upon our bodies. It is an additional and superimposed *meaning* that the objects acquire in certain circumstances. When red is seen, it is not simply *there*. It *means* red to us. We, so to speak, *intend* that red shall be red and nothing else.

In Ethics Moore has advocated a position consistent with his epistemological Realism. In addition to persistent efforts to clarify the meaning of ethical questions, he advanced at an early date the notion that the values things possess in our sight, like goodness, badness, beauty, and the like, are just as truly qualities of the object, and just as inherent in it, as its color or taste or smell. They do not depend in any way upon us and our attitudes. They, too, are there in the object, whether or not we are there to see and deal with it. Moreover, such objectively existing qualities are indefinable. Goodness is, like yellow, an unanalyzable quality of the object which possesses it. Goodness is a simple quality. It is itself only and cannot be broken down into constituent elements. Ethics is, therefore, an autonomous discipline. Moore refuses to ground it in metaphysical foundations, either naturalistic or idealistic.

III. RUSSELL

By far the most prolific writer among the British realists and the most widely known of all modern British philosophers, Bertrand Russell (1872-   ), was influenced profoundly by Moore, whose philosophic method turned him from Hegelian Idealism to Realism, and by the continental Positivism of Mach and the Realism of Meinong. From his student days in 1890 until 1916, and again in recent years he was at Cambridge University. Not only is Russell one of the most eminent philosophers of the present century, he is perhaps its most distinguished logician. He arose to his highest stature as a contributor to logical theory, symbolic logic, and the theory of mathematics, thereafter turning his attention to the philosophy of the natural sciences. Between the two wars he wrote numerous popular and semipopular works on science and sociopolitical problems, in the latter identifying his complete contempt for subservience to dogma and institutionalized custom and authority. His technical treatises of this period were on the theory of the mind and the nature of matter. His more recent technical writings have dealt with the problems of meaning and the nature of knowledge and truth.

Russell has been far too creative and independent to give final pronouncements in philosophy. His position and arguments have shifted frequently and without hesitation, a fact which accounts for not a few contradictions in his writings. This is not to say that his philosophy is on the whole without a fundamental unity. It does mean, however, that to summarize Russell's thought is almost impossible unless it is treated at considerable length in terms of its actual development. The major transition in his thought was from a conception of philosophy as an *a priori* science similar to mathematics in its deductive procedure and in its concern with abstract concepts and with the world of logical possibility, to a more traditional notion of philosophy as concerned with the actually existing spatial-temporal world and including among its interests a wide variety of subjects.

Mathematical Logic and Its Application to Philosophy. In his creative work as logician and mathematician, Russell was influenced by the new mathematical developments of such men as Cantor, Frege, Schröder, and Peano. His merit as a logician consists not only in his contributions to specialized problems of logic and the general theory of mathematics and logic, but as well in that he more than any other person has been responsible for bringing what had heretofore been the work and possession of a few mathematicians to the attention of philosophers as well as scientists on a broad front. In this alone he has had an enormous impact upon the thought of the present century.

As a logician, Russell has been interested primarily in deduction, but he has recognized the importance of inductive inference for the whole of thought processes and the pattern of knowledge. Among his many contributions to formal logic and analysis have been his concept of *propositional function,* his *theory of types,* and his *theory of descriptions.*

The theory of propositional functions was developed in the analysis of general propositions in their universal and particular forms, such as *All men are mortal* and *Some men are mortal.* It says in effect that *All men are mortal* means that if anything is a man then that thing is mortal, but does not assert that there is a thing that is a man. On the other hand, *Some men are mortal* means that there exists at least one thing that is a man, and it is mortal. The universal sentence is a propositional function rather than a proposition, since it contains a variable and is therefore neither true nor false. It says, "For all values of *x,* if *x* is a man, then *x* is mortal." The assignment of a determinate value to *x* would convert the sentence into a proposition, as in the case "John Jones is mortal." Russell regards this principle as having great importance for the history of metaphysics. Aristotle, for instance, failed to recognize the non-existential character of a universal sentence and therefore supposed, according to Russell, that "All men" is the subject of *All men are mortal* in the same sense that "John Jones" is the subject of *John Jones is mortal.* This led him to suppose that "All men" denotes an entity in the way that "John Jones" does, which resulted in his assumption that a species is a substance.

Russell's theory of types was invoked as a technique of avoiding certain kinds of logical paradoxes that arise from assuming that a collection may contain members that must be defined by means of the collection as a whole. The theory states that "Whatever involves *all* of a collection must not be one of the collection." This has the effect of saying that a proposition cannot refer to itself and thereby saves many arguments from involvements in a vicious circle. Thus the skeptic who asserts that he knows nothing does not refute himself because the original assertion cannot be included in the total class of propositions to which it refers. Or the man who says "I am lying" does not contradict himself and therefore speaks the truth because his assertion cannot be turned upon itself without violating the theory of types. It belongs to a different type from those to which it refers.

The theory of descriptions, or, more accurately, the theory of definite descriptions, has importance for the analysis of conversational language, particularly in instances where the sentence structure suggests or indicates existent entities. To employ an example of Russell's, for instance, the sentence "The golden mountain does not exist" seems to suggest that there is such a thing as a golden mountain which does not exist. The theory of descriptions overcomes this peculiar difficulty, among others, by eliminating phrases of the form "the so-and-so" when they appear, in favor of a construction that overcomes the difficulty of employing the existence of non-existent things. Thus the sentence "Scott was the author of *Waverley*" means "One and only one man wrote *Waverley,* and that man was Scott." This can be stated "There is an entity *c* such that the statement '*x* wrote *Waverley*' is true if *x* is *c* and false otherwise; moreover *c* is Scott." This sentence states that the author of *Waverley* existed. Now when this analysis is employed, "The golden mountain does not exist" means: "There is no entity *c* such that '*x* is golden and mountainous' is true when *x* is *c,* but not otherwise." This overcomes the original difficulty and, according to Russell, in principle "clears up two millenia of muddle-headedness about 'existence,' beginning with Plato's *Theaetetus.*"

Russell's most important systematic work in logic was his elaboration, with Alfred North Whitehead in the *Principia Mathematica* (three volumes, 1910-1913), of the theory of logistic, the unification of logic and mathematics accomplished by the deduction of pure mathematics from the principles of logic. This monumental work was directly influenced by the prior efforts of Peano to employ symbolic logic in the analysis of the nature of mathematics, and the earlier success of Frege in deducing arithmetic from logical premises. Russell's proof that mathematics derives from or is a part of logic consists essentially in showing that natural numbers, the positive integers, are definable in terms of logical concepts and that mathematics as a whole is reducible to the theory of natural numbers.

The unification of logic and mathematics not only produced a symbolic and mathematical logic, but permitted and stimulated new mathematical concepts, as for example the theory of fluxions and of the continuum, which have enabled us to overcome the paradoxes of Zeno and to bring the logical concepts of space and motion into accordance with the perceived facts. In this way the old contradictions and antinomies connected with the idea of the infinite have been cleared away. It is the application of this new logic to sense-experience that inspired Russell to construct his own system. It appeared to him possible to bring generally the principles of logic into conformity with the data of sense, and to combine them in a concept of Reality in which "transcendental" and metaphysical factors are not necessary. This he tried to accomplish in his own philosophy, in which he employed an extensive knowledge of the history of the physical sciences and their latest developments and a devotion to an almost Humean empiricism.

Reality a Totality of Existent and Subsistent Entities. Russell believes that objects exist independently of any experience of them, and that they include not only physical things, but such objects as relations, mathematical entities, and the like. These entities also exist independently of one another and can be referred to and meant separately. For instance, a relation has existence and meaning apart from the particular items it relates. Reality is therefore pluralistic and discrete, and may be called "logically atomistic" in nature.

This, however, does not imply physical atomism. Believing as he does that logical relations of the same sort are independent of the terms they unite, Russell also rejects the view that logical propositions are ultimate entities. They can be pulverized into constituent items, and either one of the terms related can be replaced by a new one without depriving the rest of the proposition of its original meaning. For example, if, instead of saying *Socrates is mortal,* I say *Plato is mortal,* I do not change the significance of the *is mortal* part of the proposition. And if I alter *Theaetetus is sitting* to *Theaetetus is flying,* I do not disturb the *Theaetetus is* portion of the statement. Such changes do not put a whole new proposition in place of the old. They merely revamp the old one, leaving it as it is except for the altered term. Propositions are, then, atomic in character.

Point-Events. The particular items of which Reality is composed fall together into systems. These systems are grasped by logical thinking, of which they are the objects, and are expressible in logical and mathematical formulae. The data that are thus systematized are given in sense-experience. They are not, however, given as a passive stuff. They actively *occur* from moment to moment. They are better described as *events* than as things. To emphasize the active, *occurrent* character of sensory stuff, Russell, and, as we shall see in a moment, Whitehead, describes what is experienced as *point-events* taking place in *space-time.* Their time-aspects, as *happenings* which pop in and out, and prolong and sustain themselves, are no less important than their spatial, spread-out, side-by-side character.

Sense is an *acquaintance* with these point-events, which enter into relations, exemplify forms and laws, and exhibit mathematical principles. Logical judgments *describe* these data by interpolating the relations that bring them within classes and systems and that introduce a structure of some sort into their existence. Perception, we might say, gives us the matter of which experienced Reality is composed, logic the forms; remembering always that the material items and the forms are *objects* and exist independently of one another and of any mind that perceives or knows them.

The Identity of Mental, Physical and Logical Data. For that matter, and here we are reminded of Mach and James, *mind* is merely one arrangement or system of the same sensory stuff and logical forms that in other relations constitute the physical world. It is of the nature of this stuff to appear. Reality is appearance. Systematized appearances form physical objects. When further and more subtly ordered by means of mathematical and logical principles, they are construed as the physical sciences conceive them. But the entities that the physical sciences conceive are not concrete and sensory. They do not, in Meinong's phrase, *exist*. They rather *subsist* as logical constructs.

But it so happens that some of the systems we call physical bodies not only introduce order and relations into the sense data of which they themselves are composed, but also give additional focus and another frame of reference to the sense data constituting other bodies. Sense data thus doubly controlled will appear in two bodies at the same time—in a body *of* which they are appearances and in a body *to* which they are appearances. In that case the same item of experience figures as the experience of one body by another. The ability of one body to provide an additional focus and frame of reference to the sensory stuff organized by another body is expressed by the possession of a nervous system and brain (which are themselves complexes of sensory items) on the part of the body in question. And the consequent appearance of the qualities of one body in connection with another thus outfitted we call *consciousness* and *mind*.

The Nature of Mind. In the presence of a conscious body the sensory stuff of which other bodies are composed, and the logical systems by which their constituent items are related and given form, owe a double allegiance. On the one hand, they are attached to the objects they constitute, on the other, to the bodies that, as we say, *perceive* and *conceive* them. Their attachment to the one makes them *physical* facts; to the other *mental* facts.

One and the same appearance, then, may be both physical and mental at the same time or only mental or only physical at a given moment, depending upon conditions. It is physical insofar as its presence is dependent upon the system *of* which it is an appearance. It is mental insofar as its presence is dependent upon another system, of which it is not the appearance but *to* which it appears. Such a sensory-item is physically an *aspect,* mentally a *perspective.*

Since it is doubly moored, either its physical or its mental anchor may be tripped without setting it adrift. Floating free of its physical mooring, it is a dream or an image fastened to and caused only by the brain. Detached from the brain, it remains anchored to the external body as a sensory item that is still *there,* although the other, *conscious* body is not on deck to perceive it. Secured firmly fore and aft, it is one body's perception of another body, or, it may be, its conception of a logical system. Severed, if that were possible, from all relations whatsoever, it would be neither physical nor mental. It would neither be an appearance of anything nor an appearance to anybody, or, if it were a concept, it would revert to the status of an essence that was neither enacted in any physical system nor entertained by any mental one.

Sensory items are attached to their physical moorings by the chain of ordinary, physical causation, whatever a linkage of that sort may really be. They are, however, anchored to the brain of a mentally constituted body by a cable, woven of Meinong's and Husserl's "meaning." When they appear as a mental perspective, they are what we *mean* by other bodies. What we will mean by them, and what they shall mean to us, is of a complicated weaving, the strands of which are drawn from our particular memories and associations of ideas and habits of thought and action. The same objective-datum may appear in one perspective to you, in another to me, or in different perspectives from moment to moment to either of us. The bewildering differences and shiftings of our mental perspectives and meanings are due to the different ways in which the strands of mental or, as Russell calls it, "mnemic," causation are intertwined in different people.

Language and Reality. At an early date Russell had declared that logical analysis is the essential nature of philosophy, and his work in logistical theory and the solution of logical paradoxes was an important contribution to the instruments of analysis. In his recent work, after an extended excursion into the natural sciences, he has returned to the problem of analysis as such with discussions of the nature of meaning and truth, the theory of language, and the relation of language to reality. While refusing to accept its strict anti-metaphysical dicta, he has identified himself in both spirit and method with the logical positivists. He has tempered his empiricism with the insistence that the general propositions necessary to empirical science can be established only with the aid of general logical propositions whose validity is *a priori.* Pure empiricism, he has held, would not permit us much of that general knowledge which we undeniably possess. Nevertheless the foundation of factual knowledge is basic propositions which are connected directly with non-verbal experiential occurrence. Here Russell defends the realists' correspondence theory of truth against the coherence theory popular with idealists and some positivists, and against the pragmatic theory. Against the pragmatists also he refuses to define truth in relation to knowledge. For Russell, moreover, in opposition to the positivists, a proposition can be true or false not only in the absence of knowledge of its truth value but even though there is no possibility in principle of describing a method by which its truth value might be determined. This results in Russell's holding as meaningful many of the sentences that logical positivists would discard as meaningless.

Russell holds that to a limited extent it is possible to infer something about the nature of the world from the structure of language, in particular that there are objective relations that correspond to relation terms and that there are real universals and not simply general words.

Ethics and the Good Life. In his early writings, Russell held with Moore that value resides intrinsically in objects, and at times he has suggested a realistic theory of the subsistence of value universals, that goodness and beauty have the status of timeless essences. In recent years, however, he has been committed to a positivistic approach to value, a subjectivism that identifies value with desire and insists that "outside human desires there is no moral standard." Except for discussions of the relation of means to ends, there can be no science of values, since value judgments are essentially expressions of emotion. Value statements referring to intrinsic values, those concerning ends rather than means to an end, are exclamations in the optative mood rather than assertions in the indicative. They have, therefore, no factual significance. Ethics is a matter of opinion or taste rather than fact, and conclusive ethical argument is impossible. In matters of morals, disputes are decidable only by persuasion and compulsion.

This has not meant for Russell that ethics should be abandoned, or that a moral life is impossible. On the contrary wisdom in moral choice and a heroic pursuit of the good life have been of major importance to him. Science, he maintains, has quite clearly indicated the falsity of traditional religion; there is no ground for belief in God or the reality and immortality of the soul. But goodness and beauty are not less good and beautiful because there is no God. The moral life must be grounded in human experience, not in the sanctions of religion or of tradition and convention. Men should seek the highest good for its own sake, indifferent to promise of rewards or threat of punishment and undeterred by the fact that their values have no support from the cosmos, no guaranteed status beyond the reality which they are given by the moral yearnings, strivings, and imaginings of men. But it is better to face reality than to seek aid and comfort in delusions. We must accept life for what it is and alter it for the better when and where we can, promoting life, growth and creativity, justice and peace, freedom and community. The free man, the man who has broken the shackles of ignorance, superstition, and fear, must stand alone without gods and in a universe cold and indifferent. Yet he can know the companionship of his fellow sufferers and, even if only in imagination, he can contact the eternal world of values which "brings a strength and a fundamental peace which cannot be wholly destroyed by the struggles and apparent failures of our temporal life."

IV. ALEXANDER

Emergent Evolution of the Universe from Space-Time. To S. Alexander (1859-1937), for some time professor of philosophy at Manchester, England, Reality presents itself as a process of emergent evolution in which different levels and orders of being are superimposed upon one another. Each level is the necessary condition of the next higher, and therefore each new order presupposes the existence of all the lower ones, upon the topmost of which it directly rests. But the higher orders, though dependent on the lower for their existence, cannot be resolved into terms of the lower. Every level represents a novel, irreducible development. For example, life, though dependent upon physical bodies for its appearance, cannot be reduced to terms of mechanical motion. Neither can mind, which cannot appear except in organic physical bodies, be reduced to terms of organic and vital activity.

The rock-bottom of the Real is space-time. This is the stuff of which all things are made. Space and time cannot be separated from one another except in artificial abstraction from one another by the mind. In reality they form a single entity whose one and only property is motion. Space-time in motion presents certain universal characteristics which permeate its entire length and breadth and which we designate as categories. For instance, space-time is, so to speak, mottled and pockmarked with *places*. In other words, the motion of space-time is here *this* motion, here *that*. It is everywhere *something*. Everywhere something can be said to exist—that is, to be itself in contradistinction to something else.

Moreover, the places remain fixed in their contours and differentiated from one another, although their tenants may move in and out. Thus we get what we call a *substance* enduring and preserving its identity despite the changes that occur in it. Furthermore, these spots of distinguishable motion move about and congregate in galaxies which have a movement of their own. These distinguishable moving galaxies of spots tenanted by distinguishable motions are *things* divisible into constituent elements and parts. Because of the nature of space-time, things occur within, outside, above, below, beside, before, after one another, etc. In other words, they are in *relations* to one another. Finally motions merge into one another in such wise that one is the prolongation, or *effect,* of the other. Such motions exhibit *causal* connection. In short every perception, and for that matter every conception, is an aspect or form of space-time.

The Successive Appearance of Non-Organic, Organic, and Conscious Matter. In some of these spots primary qualities appear, and space-time becomes geometrically describable. When such spots stand others off and resist penetration by them we have solidity and matter. They then are physical bodies. Some of these bodies, again, exhibit what we call secondary qualities. They are colored, resounding, hot, cold, and the like. Of these bodies there are some that have an organic and living character, and of these again some that are conscious and think.

Why these different levels should appear in the order of dependence that they do is a question we cannot answer. The lower levels cannot account for the appearance of the higher. To be sure, without them the higher could not exist, but in them there can be found no reason why the higher should exist. We simply have to accept as ultimate the fact that they do exist, and that the lower are the condition, though not the cause, of the higher. It is the nature of the Real to be like that—and that is all there is to say.

Organic bodies provide a specific condition for the appearance of consciousness, which we call a nervous system and nervous activity. Not all nervous activity is also conscious. Some of it is, however, and when we have a nervous system or nervous currents that possess the added characteristic of *awareness* we have *mind*. Mind is a nervous system that is conscious. Once more, why consciousness attaches to certain nervous systems and not to others, and why the same nervous system is now conscious, now unconscious, as when we wake and sleep, is an unanswerable question. It is part of the ultimate nature of the Real that such should be the case.

The Nature of Consciousness. Consciousness is awareness and knowledge *of* an external world existing independently of the observant nervous system. This awareness of an external object involves consciousness of the act of awareness itself, just as the consciousness of *doing* anything is a consciousness, not only of *what* we do, but of the doing of it. To be conscious of the activity of being conscious of something is self-consciousness. In this awareness of the act of consciousness *what* we are conscious of is "compresent" with our awareness of the act, just as we could not very well know we were doing anything unless at the same time we knew, however vaguely, what we did. In this way I have an immediate, inner *experience* of the external world as well as of myself. I directly "enjoy" what is outside me no less than what is inside me. I am immersed in it. I am not contemplating it from the outside. I am *living* it.

However, the consciousness of the act as well as of the object of consciousness discriminates between the act and the object. While involving the object in the act, as anything that is done is involved in the doing of it, awareness also separates the object from the act and makes it external. Although in my immediate experience the object acted upon is part of the sensation of acting, it can also be *contemplated* as something apart from that sensation. When I am not *living* the act of being conscious of something, but am *contemplating* the content of consciousness as something external to my awareness of it, I have *knowledge* of the object, not immediate experience of it. Incidentally, Alexander thinks that the *living* quality of awareness rests upon special movements in the brain, which differ according as consciousness is "directed" toward different objects.

Higher Possible Reaches of Emergent Evolution. But we are not yet done with the Real. The highest level that *emergent evolution* has reached, as far as observation goes, is human mind. However, we have no right to suppose that evolution has stopped and that its highest level has been reached. We may believe that our minds are simply flying fields from which Reality will "take off" for still higher flights, and that each new ceiling of existence it attains will prove a floor from which it will soar once more into the empyrean. We may foresee supermen, gods and super-gods, as the Real continues to build higher and richer levels of existence upon the basis of the lower, transcending eventually even mind itself. The vista that opens before us is infinite. The *emergent evolution* necessary to enact the vision it discloses is endless. The everlasting upward thrust of the Real and its ceaseless appearance at new levels—these are God. God does not *exist,* since to say that he exists would be to say that Reality has already risen to its utmost heights. He is in the making.

We must remember, too, that the Real does not rise evenly like some vast flat continent from the sea of space-time in whose depths it has its bed. Rather is it elevated in islands with flat shores and abrupt inland plateaus from which, as a foundation, its peaks shoot up in isolation from one another. God is being made in spots, and each new upheaval of deity takes place only in and from the loftiest strata of being that have emerged at any given time. It may be that elsewhere the Real has achieved levels higher than our minds. But our minds mark the greatest altitude to which it has risen in so much of the universe as we know about. In our world, it is from ourselves that the hierarchy of heaven will spring. To feel the divine upward thrust within ourselves, to consecrate ourselves to preparing the ground for the next emergence, is to have religious experience.

V. WHITEHEAD

Alfred North Whitehead (1861-1947) of Trinity College, Cambridge, and later professor of philosophy at Harvard, was not only a mathematician and logician of first importance, but also a metaphysician of great prominence. With Bertrand Russell he authored the monumental *Principia Mathematica,* but in his later years turned his attention increasingly to metaphysics, to which he brought a broad and profound learning in the sciences. By the time he died, Whitehead had expressed himself on a broad range of subjects, including the history of science, philosophy of history, theory of education, aesthetics, and philosophy of religion. His main work in metaphysics, *Process and Reality,* was delivered as the Gifford Lectures in Edinburgh in 1927-1928 and first published in 1929.

The Actual World an Enactment of Essences in Point-Events. Like Russell, Whitehead considered the sensory stuff of which experience is composed to consist of *point-events* in *space-time* which occur and exist independently of a perceiving mind. These occurrences he called *occasions.* Over and above them there exists a world of essences, or *eternal objects,* which intersect one another in any given *occasion,* and thereby make it *this* thing rather than *that.* Thus every actual event represents one of an infinite number of ways in which essences might be combined, and the concrete, actual world is a multiplicity and *togetherness* of events selected from an infinity of other possible worlds. The actual universe is what it is because in each one of its constituent occurrences the eternal objects have come together as they actually have, rather than in any other one of the infinite number of possible combinations into which they might have entered. The actual, both in whole and part, is a limitation of possibility.

Since events, or, as we may now call them, *realized experiences,* are *together,* they are in relation to one another, and these relationships enter into and form part of them. Events enter into one another's essences and become part of one another. They have temporal and spatial relations. They are together in ways expressed in the categories. Moreover, their relations exhibit an order of increasing abstractness. Relations are themselves eternal objects, and the entry of an event into relations, and of relations into an event, is part of the *togetherness* of the essences that congregate in that event.

Events, and here Whitehead agrees with Russell, are not passive, but active. They are in flux and becoming. They are processes of focusing eternal objects. As processes they have a past consisting of the events from which they have emerged and in relationship to which they are still bound, and a future consisting of the subsistent, but as yet unenacted, essences to whose combination the process of becoming will lead.

The Nature of Mind and Consciousness. Consciousness and mind are not entities apart from events. Every event is an item of experience, with two poles, one mental, the other physical, between which it fluctuates. Consciousness is an ordering and unifying of events such that the whole appears as more than the aggregate of its parts and as a new unit of occurrence. It is not analyzable into a succession and collection of event-experiences. The totality of these experiences constitutes itself a single event, and is therefore an experience of *itself* as well as of the occurrences that constitute it. It is a *reflective* experience, a report *to* itself *about* itself. Our personal, individual, self-conscious minds are such events.

But minds are no more isolated and independent than are the items of event-experiences entering into them. They are in relationship to one another and to all else. Outside patterns are interwoven with their patterns. They know both themselves and a universe in the midst of which they are set, because event-experiences occurring in other contexts can also enter into them, and because the content and conformation of other wholes can intersect them. So it is that the content of *my* consciousness is also an experience of events happening outside and independently of myself.

But this is not to say that *I* exist independently of *them.* On the contrary, the content of my consciousness, or in other words, the consciousness of which I am *self*-conscious, is filled with occurrences that belong also to other complexes. *I* could be withdrawn and yet leave those events unaffected so far as their other contexts are concerned, although in that case they would no longer be *my* experience. But if *they* were withdrawn, there would be nothing left for me to be aware of, and therefore no awareness to report to itself anything about itself. Since every conscious subject is simply a unified awareness of some aspects of other events, there can be no such thing as an independently existing individual thinking subject.

Description of the Real. Let us now take a look at Reality as we have so far developed it. It is an infinite capacity and potentiality for the occurrence of event-experiences. It is also an indefinite actualization of this capacity in a world of realized experiences and occurrences, which, however, far from exhausts the realm of the potential. Here and now the actual world might be different in part or whole, so far as possibilities are concerned.

Again the universe of actualized event-experiences does not take place simply *here*. It takes place *there* as well. It is spread out—that is, in *space*. Nor does it take place simply *now*. It transcends *now* as well as *here* and is therefore in *time* as well as spatial.

Finally, if we examine point-events happening in space-time, we find that in occurring they exemplify *character* of one sort or another. Indeed, their occurrence is a getting together of qualities and essences and relations which in themselves do not change, but simply are disclosed for what they are as long as the event continues to display them. These characters constitute a world of "eternal objects," manifested in sense-experience but transcending it and subsisting independently of it.

But Reality is more than this. As we have seen, events are *processes,* and by being related in all sorts of ways they enter into one another and form an interconnected *world*-process. In the unity of the world-process not only are experience-events brought together and made part of one another, but the eternal objects, in themselves isolated and reciprocally exclusive, are also brought together. Although they have nothing to do with one another as pure essences, they get together in the occurrence called an object.

The Rational Nature of the Selecting and Enacting Principle. Furthermore, there seems to be a tendency to an increasing richness and value in event-experiences. Potentiality is actualized not helter-skelter, as it might have been so far as the mere potentiality of occurrent experiences is concerned. It is *possible* for the universe to happen indiscriminately. But the world does *not* happen indiscriminately. It happens in a way limited by the exigencies of logic, by the conditions imposed by certain relations, and by the restrictions laid upon an event by virtue of possessing a specific character of its own. It looks, therefore, as if the actualization of the possible and the unification of the actual take place in accord with some sort of *standard,* conformity to which is productive of *value.*

If this is the case, however, the Real must contain some principle of selection and limitation at work in the actualizing of *possible* occurrences into *real* event-experiences. Since the activity of such a principle produces, as a matter of experience, a world that we call rational, we may regard it as the reason why the universe is a rational order and the reason but for which the universe might quite *possibly* have been an irrational chaos. This reason we may call God. It is not a concrete thing, but simply that in the Real which brings rationalized concrete existence to pass.

There is, however, a further question that metaphysics cannot answer. Why, we may now ask, does Reality happen to contain this selective, rational principle? Why does *this* particular limitation upon the actualization of the possible exist rather than some other? For that matter, the universe seemingly might have been different without being less rational. It seemingly might have been different and morally more satisfactory. Why then *this* universe and none other? Potentiality, which is indifferent to the rational or the irrational and lends itself indiscriminately to the actualization of any and every world, cannot answer. Neither can the eternal objects, which, so far as they are concerned, might as easily and logically meet together in other ways. Neither can the principle of selection itself. That principle simply *is* there. No reason can be found for its being there, since it itself is the only reason for anything being there and being what it is. In a word, the presence of a God in the structure of the Real is something that nothing and nobody, not even God himself, can account for.

Chapter XXXV

AMERICAN NEO-REALISM

I. THE REALISTIC CRITIQUE OF IDEALISM

Decline of Idealism. In the United States, Realism was a compara-tively neglected and unimportant philosophic position until the early decades of the present century. Metaphysical speculation and theory of knowledge had been cultivated largely with a religious interest, a fact which accounts in some measure for the immense popularity of the various forms of Idealism, while the most immediate impact of science, in the form of Darwinism, contributed mainly to the founda-tions of Pragmatism. It is not that American thought was devoid of realistic tendencies, or even of explicit realistic argument. But the Neo-Scholastic Realism of the Catholics was hardly noticed at this time, while the Scottish Realism that had been established especially at Princeton University had largely spent its force. Both Chauncey Wright and Charles S. Peirce had been strong advocates of a realistic conception of scientific knowledge, but Wright had died at an early age and the brilliant work of Peirce, who argued extensively against the nominal-istic tendencies of the natural sciences, was largely unpublished and not widely known. Besides, Realism on the whole had been sporadic, unpretentious, and quite unorganized. At the turn of the century, however, a serious and militant Realism began to take shape, as the more scientifically minded were challenged by the growing profusion of idealistic systems and in particular by the massive structure of Royce's Absolute Idealism.

Rise of Realism. The early development of Realism in the United States paralleled that in Great Britian but there was no important impact of one upon the other. Although they had much in common, both in their polemic against Idealism and their interest in the advance-ment of a metaphysics and epistemology geared to the sciences, they followed somewhat different paths and maintained at most a rather condescending interchange of ideas. On the other hand, partly because many Americans had received their advanced education in Germany, there was a measure of influence from the German realistic critiques of Hegelianism. This situation was enhanced by the realists' involvement in psychology, for American psychology was strongly influenced by the Germans.

In the first volume of his major work, *The World and the Individual* (1900-1901), Royce criticized vigorously the basis of realistic epistemology, that the object known exists independently of its being known, on the ground, dear to the hearts of idealists, that the knower can know only the content of his own mind and that therefore there can be no knowledge of the realist's independent "real." The immediate response to Royce was by no means overwhelming. Articles by Ralph Barton Perry and William Pepperell Montague (1873-1953) were the first explicitly realistic replies to Royce. Gradually those who questioned the justification of the large speculative superstructures of the idealists and at the same time sensed the need for a more adequate realistic metaphysical orientation of science itself, to say nothing of their feeling that common sense was outraged by Idealism, began to make themselves heard in the journal literature.

II. THE NEW REALISM

The Ego-Centric Predicament. Among the leaders of the movement were some who had studied with William James and who had been especially impressed by the strong realistic component of his otherwise pragmatic philosophy. In particular the realists took a stand on James' famous essay "Does 'Consciousness' Exist?" as speaking for them in their reaction against the traditional solutions of the mind-body problem.

In 1910 an article by Ralph Barton Perry, "The Ego-Centric Predicament," dealt a broadside against Idealism reminiscent of G. E. Moore's "The Refutation of Idealism" in Great Britain. Perry's argument was not intended primarily to refute Idealism, but rather to dispose of the traditional argument of the idealists that because knowledge is always of states of consciousness, the thing known is in some way dependent for its reality upon its being an object of knowledge. We are involved, he insisted, in an "ego-centric predicament" which makes it impossible for us to know anything without that thing being in some way involved in our consciousness. But that the idealistic inference is unwarranted is indicated by the fact that even if the object did exist independently, it could not be known in its independence.

Epistemological Monism. Also in 1910 there appeared a succinct and significant document entitled "Program and First Platform of Six Realists," fathered by E. B. Holt, W. T. Marvin, W. P. Montague, R. B. Perry, W. B. Pitkin, and E. G. Spaulding. The importance of this piece lay not alone in its role of articulating the realistic uprising, but as well in the fact that it represented a serious effort of philosophers to cooperate like scientists, searching for areas of agreement, rather than compete in the manner usual in philosophy. Moreover, again like scientists, there was a conscious attempt to treat the issue at hand by isolating individual problems. Whatever the success of this effort, it was an interesting beginning of a movement which has since reached important proportions and is an important characteristic of contemporary philosophy. It is among logicians and philosophers of science, however, that the ideal of cooperation has been most nearly realized.

In the "Program and First Platform" and later in the cooperative volume *The New Realism* (1912) by the same authors, the basic arguments of Realism were set forth. The new realists, as they have been called, were advocates not only of epistemological realism that holds to the independent reality of the known particular object, but also of logical or metaphysical realism, that defends the real status of essences or universals. They were in a sense, therefore, modern Platonists, though they differed greatly with one another and from Plato at numerous points. The reality of *subsistent* universals was argued on the same basis as the reality of *existent* particulars, that they can be explained without reference to consciousness, and that mental activity, therefore, in no way produces them. That they are known only as objects of consciousness is irrelevant to their real status.

The most distinctive feature of the New Realism was its *epistemological monism,* or *presentative realism,* which distinguished it clearly from the early epistemological dualism of Descartes and Locke. The dualists had insisted upon the numerical distinction between the real object and the object as known in the consciousness, the known object being a *representation* of rather than a *presentation* of the real. The monism of New Realism identified the object known with the real object, insisting that on any other theory it is impossible to account for genuine knowledge.

III. MONTAGUE

William Pepperell Montague (1873-1953), for a half-century professor at Columbia University, was the most influential exponent of the New Realism. Born and reared in the puritan atmosphere of a small New

England town and educated at Harvard during its golden age of philosophy, he was touched by the moral enthusiasm of William James and inspired by the idealism of Royce.

Rejection of Pragmatism, Idealism and Positivism. But Montague rejected the pragmatism of James and Dewey, insisting that it was an illegitimate application to the problem of truth of the utilitarian relativism acceptable in values but abominable in logic. To regard the *good* as the "expedient or satisfactory in the way of conduct," and thus accept moral relativism, is one thing. But it is quite another to deny the absolutistic and objective character of *truth* in favor of "whatever satisfies individual beliefs." "Facts," said Montague, "are *good* only when they conform to subjective needs," but "ideas are *true* only when they conform to objective facts."

Montague's philosophy breathes much of the spirit of Royce's idealism, but he could not accept the subjectivism in epistemology upon which that idealism depended, nor the absolutism that engulfed the individual. Idealism, Montague contended, results from an argument involving an ambiguous middle term, *idea,* where, in the major premise "Ideas are incapable of existing apart from a mind," *idea* refers to the process of perceiving, while in the minor premise, "Physical objects insofar as they are perceived or known at all are certainly ideas," *idea* denotes the object of perception. The illicit combination of these propositions yields the idealistic doctrine that no physical objects can exist apart from a mind.

In his later years Montague became a vigorous opponent of what he termed "this negativism called positivism." He regarded logical positivism as barren and narrowly reductive in its method of analysis. He insisted upon both the theoretical possibility and the practical advisability of constructing a metaphysics, whether ontological or cosmological. Philosophy, he argued, is a vision, and upon it depends the progress of thought. Let philosophy *propose,* and science *dispose.*

Epistemological Monism. Montague's philosophy was grounded in a careful working of the problem of knowledge and a theory of the nature of consciousness, but it was essentially an effort to construct an animistic cosmology that seems to have been inspired largely by a religious interest.

As one of the authors of *The New Realism,* Montague opposed what he regarded as the agnosticism of the representative theory of knowledge in favor of an epistemological monism that identified the real object with the object as known. He opposed, however, the tendencies in New Realism toward behaviorism and objective relativism. He objected to the first on the ground that physiological behavior taken alone cannot account for the abstract features of real knowledge, or its time-transcending quality. He refused to accept objective relativism, which describes the object of perception in terms of the relations in which it stands to the perceiver, on the ground that it forsakes Realism for a positivistic or physicalistic type of phenomenalism.

Theory of Universals. Montague's Realism was an affair of metaphysics as well as theory of knowledge. Influenced somewhat by Santayana's doctrine of essences, and having an almost Pythagorean respect for mathematics as involving something both real and beautiful, he advanced a theory of subsistent universals that combined important elements from both Platonism and Aristotelianism. Universals *subsist,* timeless and spaceless, while particulars *exist* with a definite space-time location. But the universals must not be abstracted totally from the matrix of particularity. In this Montague was an Aristotelian. Yet they must be recognized as having metaphysical priority over the particulars which actualize them in space-time. In this he was a Platonist. Universals are not additional particulars, nor are they simply thoughts or concepts in a mind. They are real entities that subsist as in an ideal realm, sometimes exemplified in space-time particulars and sometimes not, known only to the mind of man, but in no way dependent upon it for their reality. An object can be blue only because *blueness* is genuinely and objectively real, and an act can be just only because *justice* is real. Universals are the potentiality as well as the attributes of the particulars. If they were not *really* real, the particulars would not be objectively what the realist regards them as being. When the universals intersect one another in space-time, particulars are actualized.

The Ways of Knowing. In his classic work *The Ways of Knowing,* Montague examined the fundamental problems of methodology and the theory of knowledge. Nowhere can one find a more brilliant or incisive critique of authority as a technique of establishing knowledge, or a more lucid exposition and analysis of reason, experience, and intuition as methods of knowledge. He attempted a "federation" of the ways of knowing, holding that the contenders, *authoritarianism, mysticism, rationalism, empiricism, pragmatism,* and *skepticism* all have special merit and are all in some ways and in some measure compatible with one another and mutually corrective and supplementary and are capable of shifting combinations to fit varying circumstances and problems. Moreover, the particular methods have a fitness for the various "domains" of the objects of knowledge. Thus authoritarianism applies to a knowledge of those objects experienced by others but not by ourselves;

mysticism or intuition is appropriate to the domain of ultimate non-instrumental values; rationalism is the method proper to the analysis of abstract relations; empiricism is necessary for knowledge of concrete facts and relations; and pragmatism belongs to the domain of individual and social conduct. The role of skepticism is to remind men that knowing with absolute certainty is impossible. All in all, Montague favored a combination of rationalism and empiricism with "just a touch of mystical experience."

The Nature of Consciousness and the Question of Immortality. Montague's cosmology was in a sense an enlargement of his theory of consciousness. From his childhood he had had a consuming interest in the problem of the existence and nature of the soul and he refused to accept the common decision that such a concept must be abandoned by both psychology and philosophy. He felt that in a profound intuitive insight he had "discovered the soul in its hiding place," and attempted to develop a theory of its nature through four stages, psychological, epistemological, biological, and cosmological.

Against the scientific arguments of recent decades, Montague insisted that the soul or mind exists as a genuine substantive and is not simply an adjective of the body. The physical brain simply is not the kind of thing that can serve as the sole ground for the body. In particular, it cannot account for the various types of self-transcendence: *prospective transcendence,* in which purposiveness is evident and which accounts for freedom in behavior; *retrospective transcendence,* the temporal continuity of the past and present; *spatial transcendence,* the mental dimension effecting reference to spatially removed objects; and *logical transcendence,* the abstract reflection evident in the consciousness of meanings and symbols. On this and other grounds Montague insisted on at least the possibility, if not the probability, that the soul is real, and expressed a strong and reasoned hope for its immortality.

The mind and its states were conceived by Montague as "forms of energy related physically and quantitatively to the atoms and their motions." The mind's energy is potential rather than kinetic, a system or field that imposes structure upon and interacts reciprocally with the physical body in a manner analogous to the physical influences of a magnetic field. The evolutionary process is an emergence of the field into four levels, mechanical, vital, sensory, and personal. In every degree of development there emerges in animal mind certain tertiary qualities that are irreducible to and incapable of explanation by any non-mental reference, being relations internal to the psychic field alone. Such are the qualities of fear, pleasure, curiosity, anger, and tenderness, on the sub-human level, as well as the human qualities distinctive to a moral and spiritual nature. The question of immortality is "whether a system of energy-forms consisting of tertiary or non-quantitative qualities can translate its full nature (at death) into the purely quantitative energies of the decaying nervous system." To the extent that the mind has a substantive independence of the body, rather than constitutes simply an adjectival description of the body, it appears to be something like the traditional soul and is something that may survive death.

Religion and Morals. Montague made a strong demand for the liberation of morality from its traditional bondage to religion. Although religion should not be identified with morals, and good religion cannot be divorced from either esthetic or moral values, morality must be required to stand upon its own two feet, without a religious sanction. Morality must be independent, and constitute its own sanction, the sanction of life setting its own supreme ideals of love and beauty and demanding of itself the enthusiasm requisite to their achievement. Moral duty is the demand of the ideal upon the real, of the higher self upon the lower self. It is not the imperious command of a divine lawgiver.

Promethean Religion. In his philosophy, Montague banished from religion the authoritarianism which robs men of the freedom of their souls, demands that they look backward rather than forward, and implies a "thoroughgoing subordination of what ought to be to what is, of value to fact, of right to might, of ethics to religion," and yields a "morality of commands and taboos, instead of a morality of ideals." He opposed also the otherworldliness and asceticism that he so commonly found in the religion of his childhood, and made a strong stand for a religion that affirms rather than denies life.

Montague attacked with equal vigor the orthodox identification of religion with the crude myth and superstition of the past, and its equation, at the hands of sophisticated liberalism, with moral idealism. Religion, he insisted, is neither a "traffic with demons" nor belief in an "ultimate ideal." It is a "momentous possibility—the possibility, namely, that what is highest in spirit is also deepest in nature, that the ideal and the real are at least to some extent identified, not merely evanescently in our own lives but enduringly in the universe itself. If this possibility were an actuality, if there truly were at the heart of nature something akin to us, a conserver and increaser of values, and if we could not only know this and act upon it, but really feel it, life would suddenly become radiant. For no longer should we be alien accidents in an indifferent world, uncharacteristic by-products of the blindly whirling atoms; and no longer would the things that matter most be at the mercy of the things that matter least."

Religion for Montague issues from the quest for joy and happiness amidst the tragedies of life; it is the finite soul yearning for fulfilment in the infinite. Religion does not make a man better morally, for it is not the basis of morality and atheism is not badness. Religion simply gives his life the radiance that is the precious possession of those who are saved from an otherwise "incurable sadness and loneliness."

In confronting the problem of evil, the bête noire of the philosophy of religion, Montague reflected the influence of James' pluralism and finitistic theology and of Peirce's tychism. If our evil is not God's evil, and our good his good; if he does not suffer in our sufferings and delight in our joys, he is not real or is not the God of religion. Evil cannot be reasoned out of existence by a superficial teleology; it is an awful fact in a universe that is filled with tragedy, a universe in which life itself has been marked with a curse "worthy of a primordial demon's genius, of having to feed upon itself, and carry on by murder and betrayal of its very own."

In the presence of such evil, moral men cannot and should not believe in an omnipotent God, for such a God would be one who subordinates right to might and violates everything sacred in human personality. Prometheus is Montague's symbol of religion, the symbol of a life-affirming religion that glories in the free intellect and has a hatred of whatever destroys the integrity of men's souls.

But atheism is no theoretical escape, for it fails to solve the problem of good, just as absolutistic theology fails with the problem of evil. The world's moral good, as the capstone of the emergence of life, sentience, rationality, and conscience, cannot be taken simply as the product of mechanism or chance. There are no grounds for dogmatism, but there is a respectable probability that God is real, "not as an omnipotent monarch, a giver of laws and punishments, but as an ascending force, a nisus, a thrust toward concentration, organization, and life." It is this probability that justifies religious belief, belief in a living God who is the soul of the physical universe and whose life contains and sustains us.

IV. CRITICAL REALISM

Critique of New Realism. For several years following the publication of *The New Realism,* criticism of its theory of consciousness and its monism claimed much of the energy of professional philosophers in the United States. By some, at least, of the new realists consciousness was described as an external behavioral response of the organism to the stimulus of the object known. This behaviorism was unsatisfactory to their critics, who argued that it failed to account for the abstractive powers of the mind and also that when taken in conjunction with the objective relativism implied by their monism it made impossible the explanation of error. Objective relativism was the position that objectivity must be attributed to whatever appears in perception, including the objects regarded by common sense as illusory as well as those considered to be genuinely real or veridical. A disc observed from different angles by different persons is, according to this view, elliptical as well as round, for the object is what it is relative to the organism of the observer, though not dependent upon the mental activity of the observer.

Epistemological Dualism. At any rate, the critics of the New Realism insisted that its epistemological monism, while presumably accounting for knowledge, was unable to account for error. The outcome was the publication in 1920 of a second cooperative volume of arguments for Realism, *Essays in Critical Realism* by seven authors, George Santayana, C. A. Strong, A. K. Rogers, A. O. Lovejoy, R. W. Sellars, J. B. Pratt, and Durant Drake. While differing among themselves in matters of metaphysics, these advocates of *critical* Realism united in their front against the epistemology of Idealism, Pragmatism, and the New Realism. While defending the independent reality of the object on the same ground as their predecessors, they advocated a return in principle to the dualism of Locke, that the object known to consciousness is not identical with the real object, but in some way represents it. They thus were willing to run the risk of being unable to adequately account for genuine knowledge in order to explain the possibility of error. The object in the consciousness is a mental state or idea. The real object in the material world is inferred as its cause, and is therefore known always as represented by it, and never directly.

V. SANTAYANA

No less eminent as a poet, an essayist, and a master of English prose than a philosopher, George Santayana (1863-1952), a Spaniard educated in the United States, once professor at Harvard, and resident afterwards for many years in Europe until his death in Rome, gave Realism a naturalistic and materialistic interpretation.

Essences and Animal Faith. We are, according to Santayana, immediately conscious, without distortion or falsification, of the nature of the real. We experience directly qualities, general characteristics, mathematical truths, etc.—*essences,* as Santayana calls them—exhibited and combined in various concrete, "objective" ways. These *essences* would *subsist* as possible conscious content, even if and when consciousness ceased to entertain them, or were completely blotted out. Furthermore, experience *feels* as if it were of something more than essences—of something that enacts them when we are not conscious of them, and combines them in so-called physical objects existing apart from entertainment by the mind. To be sure, we cannot prove that this feeling is valid and that material substance really exists, since we are immediately acquainted only with essences and their combinations. But we do business with the world of concrete objects as if the feeling were trustworthy, and on the assumption—or "animal faith," in Santayana's phrase—that we are dealing with a world that does not owe its being and its nature to our awareness of it. Were it not for this "animal faith," we should have no criterion for distinguishing between the combinations of essences both entertained by consciousness and considered to exist independently of it, and those merely entertained by consciousness and regarded as works of the imagination lacking material embodiment.

Why This Universe Rather Than Another. Again, without an enacting substratum of a certain sort that determines what essences and combinations of essences shall be embodied, there is no reason why those materialized in our particular world should be selected for entertainment by consciousness and for concrete exemplification in preference to all the other possible worlds in which other essences unknown to us, and other combinations we can imagine of those known to us, might equally well have been displayed. The reason cannot lie in the essences themselves, since they are all equally possible of enactment, nor can it be in the mind which is potentially capable of entertaining them all and all combinations of those given in experience. It must then lie in the nature or disposition of this something more to the universe than essences or consciousness.

But what disposes this something to select as it does? Certainly not, as some suppose, a benevolent and rational purpose. For essences frequently come in patterns and sequences not only ill-planned, uneconomical, and illogical, but frequently destructive of human existence and happiness. To try to impose such a purpose on a universe whose perceived behavior contradicts it simply makes the whole world-process unintelligible. Experience indicates that the operations of substance have no moral or logical aims, intents or purposes, but in their enactment of essences proceed rather on "mechanical" lines. The concept of substance and its behavior suggested by our observation of the world-process is that of matter in "mechanical" motion, actuated entirely by efficient causation.

While leaving the nature of matter to the physicists, Santayana hazards an opinion as to its presumable properties. It is, he thinks, spatio-temporal, dispersed, with parts moving relatively to one another and perhaps subject to internal alteration of character as well. Presumably, too, it is continuous and persistent in quantity, and the bodies and systems it generates are more or less enduring and for the most part, at least, the uninterrupted prolongations of antecedent processes. The structures and patterns assumed by matter in motion in displaying the total nature and career of an object or event Santayana calls *tropes*. And the invariable sequences in which frequently they are indefinitely repeated we consider natural laws, on the basis of which we predict successfully the future and act accordingly. But these laws merely describe, not prescribe, the natural course of events. The occurrence of one trope does not necessitate that of another. The past is no guarantee of the future. Matter may at any moment cease to be uniform and orderly in its behavior, or even simply cease to exist. Indeed it is quite possible that tropes keep occurring in the flux for which no "cause" can be found, and whose "effects" cannot be predicted.

The Psyche. Some of these tropes assumed by matter in motion are also organic and animate. Bodies that live as well as exist sustain themselves by feeding on other bodies, are able to regain their internal balance and repair themselves when disturbed or damaged, and to reproduce their distinctive patterns and tropes in other bodies proceeding from themselves—characteristics lacking in inorganic bodies. It looks, then, as if matter were potentially animate and organic, and becomes so when its parts happen to become related in a certain way. This way, or trope, which makes of inorganic matter a living body with powers and drives of its own that interact with the rest of the physical world and modify to some extent the enactment and combination of essences, constitutes a *psyche*. And once patterned as a psyche, a body is potentially conscious.

Spirit. In some living bodies, thanks to certain organic conditions that do not happen in others, this potentiality is actualized. They are then *aware* of being alive, are *aware* of their proper natures, functions and impulses, and of an external environment with which they are in dynamic relations and which they can alter. They now possess spirit or mind. This, however, is not a thing or a substance, any more than is motion or alteration or life. Like them it is a state or activity exhibited by matter under certain conditions. Nor is it a power or an agent. It does not direct or influence, but merely notes and records the nature and operations of the body. But it is not an "outside" observer whose presence or absence makes no difference to that nature and those operations. It is implicated in them as part of a psychophysical situation, neither constituent of which can be altered, impaired, or removed without altering, impairing, or removing the other. And this total situation is a dynamic and effective agent contributing to the course of events.

Again, the body's awareness of its nature, impulses and powers, and of its relations and interactions, propitious or unpropitious, with the rest of nature, is not passive but active. It is pleasure, pain, passion, emotion, desire, volition. A body conscious of itself not only tends like inanimate matter to preserve itself; it wants to preserve itself, and it wants to reproduce other bodies of a similar trope and psyche. It wills to do what it does. It pursues as well as moves towards the propitious, and fears and shuns as well as rebounds from the unpropitious. It rearranges in imagination essences in new and more advantageous combinations and seeks to enact them in the environment. It has aims and ideals, and endeavors to better its situation by making them come true.

The Realm of Truth. All this involves a distinction between fact and fancy. And one of the most imperative of the human organism's impulses and ideals is centered upon sorting out the actually enacted combinations of essences from the ones merely entertained by the imagination, and thus upon ascertaining what we call the truth which makes the universe intelligible. To fulfill this desire we should have to be omniscient—that is, acquainted with all the essences, their combinations, and the interrelation of these combinations, that are, have been, and ever will be given factual existence in the world-process. Such knowledge is an unattained ideal, forever pursued by the human mind.

The desire to know is only in part aroused by the practical necessity of acquainting ourselves with the nature of things sufficiently to survive, to adapt ourselves to our environment and to modify it, when possible, to our advantage. Truth is also sought just for the pleasure of knowing it, and the pursuit of it is a disinterested activity exercised for its own sake. Moreover, it is unperturbed if what it in fact discovers disappoints and fails to substantiate what our moral and religious interests hope it may discover in order to give substance to their long-

ings for a reality more concerned with human welfare than it appears
to be. What poisons as well as what nourishes them is food for thought,
and is equally capable of satisfying the understanding.

To be sure, our ideals and our aspirations may serve as incentives
and guides to bettering ourselves and our surroundings, which are
already in themselves good enough in many ways. We may partially
enact them in our lives, and our environment, and thus make them
come true and become existent. But the only existence they will then
possess apart from their partial embodiment by matter is that which
we give them. Still, the temptation to attribute to them more existence than their actual enactment warrants often proves irresistible.
The desire to know things as they are is always in danger of being
sidetracked and misled by false scents laid down by what we would
like and hope to find true, and often insist must be true, appearances
to the contrary notwithstanding. As we shall see in a moment, morality,
religion, and metaphysics are frequent enticers to these paths of
speculative dalliance with the nature of the existent.

The danger of being seduced by them is doubly great because even
the disinterested search for truth for its own sake is hampered by
ignorance and error. Knowing only a portion of the realm of essence
and only some of the patterns enacted by matter, we are liable to
mistaken conjectures regarding the extent and degree of their enactment and their interrelations. And we are subject to the perspective
of a particular time, place, and type of organic structure. Hence the
realm of truth is riddled with chinks and gaps, easy to fill in and
patch up with pleasant and consoling hypotheses unwarranted by and
even contrary to experience.

The Realm of Spirit. However, there are other realms, in which the
spirit, freed from the necessity of seeking and telling the truth, may
falsify and improve upon it in order to remold it to the heart's desire.
These, equally legitimate if properly defined and confined, are the
realms of art, of moral aspiration, or religion. And they also provide
a playground for metaphysics and theology when the latter are cut
loose from logical inferences from experience and indulge in hypotheses divorced from it. Taken together with that of truth, these realms
of fancy constitute the total *realm of spirit.*

Within them the spirit is at liberty to *picture* as concrete and existent
the beauty and the goodness it worships. It may *imagine* moral perfection enacted in a divine objective being. It may repaint the actual
world with the colors of a terrestrial paradise in which all is planned
and directed for the best. There is no harm in its doing so if it does

not forget that these pictures are only *imaginary,* not actually enacted, combinations of essences, and that to attribute to them substantial existence is to deform truth. Nor should it forget that their value is not enhanced by such attribution. Goodness is no better, beauty no more beautiful, for being materialized. Their essences remain the same whether merely entertained subjectively by the spirit, or also objectively enacted. The simple contemplation of them, like knowing the truth, delights and satisfies. The one uplifts our hearts to the heavens, the other keeps our feet on the earth. To mistake the one for the other turns the world upside down, or downside up.

But theology and metaphysics sometimes forget all this. They materialize the heavenly vision, supported by and supporting human aspirations, as an "immaterial substance"—which is a self-contradictory concept. They make it materially responsible for and therefore include in it all that it ideally excludes and negates—which involves a moral self-contradiction. They not only introduce aims and purposes as explanations of the operations of nature, sufficiently explained by efficient causes, but aims and purposes that make these operations inexplicable. They purchase religious satisfaction and moral support at a price of intellectual clarity. The same confusion of mind is betrayed by the moralistic attempt to censor and even suppress art and science when what they discover and express is unedifying and displeasing to moral assumptions.

The Life of Reason. The light of reason, however, will dispel this confusion. The enlightened mind entertains impartially, without fear or favor, all essences and all combinations of them whether enacted or merely imagined. Its overall desire is to distinguish and arrange them in such wise that they *make sense* of experience. If this necessitates a discipline of thought and imagination galling to overhasty inferences and the unbridled exercise of fancy, reason will be none the less satisfied. The man dominated by reason will discount as far as possible his preferences and prejudices, or at least will own up to them as such, in interpreting experience. He will recognize the different origins and directions of the interests that enter into and determine his total reaction to it. He will see through their pretensions, assign them their proper spheres of contemplation and action, and keep within bounds determined by reason as a whole, not by any one of them, their tendency to interfere with and influence one another. He will not expect beforehand that what satisfies his desire to know will also satisfy his moral and esthetic senses and aspirations. He will not be disturbed by finding the immoral often esthetically pleasing and suitable material for art, or the moral at times a bit drab. Nor will he be surprised or ashamed at finding his imagination recombining enacted essences in ideal worlds in ways satisfactory to his esthetic, moral and religious interests.

Sense can be made of all this by putting things in their places and seeing them in their proper relations to one another. Theological and metaphysical concepts cease to make experience unintelligible and make sense, once they are regarded as poetic recombinations of essence in ideal forms, and not as descriptions of enacted fact. But because they are not true to the world as it is, their ideal portrayals of beauty and goodness will not be disparaged. The reasonable man will not love them less because they do not happen to be enacted. Nor will he love truth less for telling him so. Once stripped of their false claims, referred to their proper origins, confined to their proper spheres, and seen in their proper relations to one another, science, religion, art, morals, and all the other expressions of the complex totality of human interests, can get along amicably in a rational mind. Thus harmonized, they will contribute their due quotas to making sense of the diversity and complexity of human experience and constitute a life of reason.

Chapter XXXVI

LOGICAL EMPIRICISM

I. THE RISE OF LOGICAL POSITIVISM

The Scientific Philosopher. One of the most interesting and important developments in modern philosophy has been the appearance in the twentieth century of a new kind of philosopher, the logician-scientist-philosopher who turns his back upon most of the philosophic endeavor of the past, with its speculation, systems, and involvement in value considerations, and aims primarily at the clarification and elucidation of meanings in the interest of advancing scientific knowledge. Akin in many respects to American Pragmatism and British Analysis, the movement variously designated as "Logical Positivism," "Scientific Empiricism," or "Logical Empiricism," is the chief expression of this development. Viewed historically, Logical Empiricism appears as a serious effort to construct a theory of meaning and a theory of knowledge that reconcile the valid elements of rationalism and empiricism and subscribe to the principles of logic and the procedures of the natural sciences. To this great task it brought especially the technical equipment of mathematical logic and a knowledge of the procedures of experimental and theoretical physics uncommon to philosophers, to say nothing of an unusual ability in philosophical analysis. In general the movement has been characterized by the method of logical analysis, an initial concern for the problem of meaning, a predisposition in favor of the type of cooperative effort typical of scientists, and an insistence that all genuine philosophical problems are scientific in that they can be solved with universal agreement. It has inherited the empiricism of Hume that requires sensory impressions as the foundation of all factual knowledge, and the rationalism of Leibnitz with its interest in a universal symbolic language and in the achievement of a unity of all knowledge.

The Program of Logical Empiricism. Although the content of Logical Empiricism has been various, complex, and changing, it has maintained a quite constant interest in certain definite problems. These

591

may be roughly summarized as an effort to establish an adequate theory of propositional meaning based on empirical verifiability, a critical theory of the syntactical structure of language and its semantic function in representing non-linguistic data, and a logically perfect language to which all the propositions of science can be reduced. Implied by these is a concern for the formalization of logic, the theory of induction, the general theory of symbolization, the problem of the truth value of empirical propositions, the nature of theory construction, and an interest in the problem of the unity of science. In recent years Logical Empiricism has developed rapidly, frequently abandoning old arguments and theses for new, a fact which makes it impossible to give a brief and full statement of its tenets.

The Vienna Circle. Although it is now largely an American movement, due especially to the migration of German-speaking philosophers to the United States after the rise of Nazism, the origins, foundations, and early development of Logical Empiricism were for the most part European. At the center of the movement has been the Logical Positivism that centered in the Viennese Circle at the University of Vienna in the nineteen twenties. There, under the leadership especially of Moritz Schlick (1882-1936), Rudolf Carnap (1891-), and Otto Neurath (1882-1946), a group of thinkers representing mathematics, logic, the physical sciences, psychology, and social thought pursued investigations into the philosophical foundations of their disciplines against a common background of positivistic persuasion inherited in part from the earlier positivism of Ernst Mach.

The members of the Vienna Circle maintained working relations with logicians, scientists, and scientifically oriented philosophers at various locations throughout Europe. In particular they were supported in their positivism by the work of the Polish logicians and semanticists in their studies of logical theory and the theory of signs, and the activities of the so-called Berlin Group, at the University of Berlin, whose members explored in detail the foundations of empirical knowledge with special concern for the problems of induction and probability and for the nature of scientific theory.

In an effort to achieve a broad association and cooperative effort among scientific philosophers, the logical positivists undertook in the late twenties and thirties a program of publications and international congresses directed especially to the promulgation of a general attitude favorable to the unity of all scientific knowledge and the solution of detailed technical problems relating to the problem of knowledge. The rise of Nazism in the German-speaking countries, however, brought an end to the Vienna and Berlin groups and seriously curtailed the activities of the positivists. The consequent migration of European scientists and philosophers to England and America permitted the continuation of cooperative work and brought Positivism into a closer contact with British analytical philosophy, to which it was already related, and with American empiricism, especially Pragmatism, with which it has in a measure joined hands in a broad affiliation under the banner of Logical Empiricism. Although the early orientation of Pragmatism was in the life sciences, biology, psychology, and sociology, and that of Positivism in mathematics, logic, and physics, the two had much in common in their empiricism, probabilism, suspicion of metaphysics, and their interest in the problem of meaning.

In their conception of philosophy, as in other matters as well, the Viennese positivists were much influenced by Ludwig Wittgenstein (1889-1951), whose highly suggestive *Tractatus Logico-Philosophicus* formed the foundation of much of their discussion. "Philosophy," says Wittgenstein, "is not a theory but an activity." Its object is the "logical clarification of thoughts." It does not produce knowledge of its own, as do the natural sciences, but "consists essentially of elucidations." The time-honored conception of philosophy as the pursuit of knowledge of reality and values was completely abandoned. In its place appeared the discipline of logical analysis and the consignment of all knowledge to the sciences. For the most part this conception of philosophy has continued to dominate not only those who regard themselves strictly as logical positivists, but also those others as well who affiliate with Positivism in the somewhat broader movement now known more commonly as Logical Empiricism.

II. THE VERIFIABILITY THEORY OF MEANING

The Analysis of Propositions. Logical empiricists generally have followed the logical positivists in the basic orientation of their theory of meaning. The positivists' primary interest has been in cognitive or "knowledge" meaning. Such meaning, they have insisted, is borne by propositions. A proposition is genuine, that is, it has cognitive meaning, if it is either true or false. Only propositions are true or false, and anything that is either true or false is a proposition. Propositions are not to be identified with sentences, as some sentences, e.g., imperatives, are not true or false, while different declarative sentences, differing in their symbols or syntax, may express the same proposition, that is, have the same meaning. Moreover, propositions are not identified with facts.

Facts are neither true nor false; they simply are. The facts make the propositions either true or false. Two propositions are said to be identical or to have the same meaning if the same fact or set of facts establishes them both as true or both as false. "To understand a proposition," said Wittgenstein, "means to know what is the case, if it is true."

The logical empiricists have followed the traditional distinction, recognized by Hume, Kant, and Leibnitz, between analytic and synthetic propositions, though their analysis, unlike that of Kant, has conformed to the requirements of modern relational logic which does not, like Aristotelian logic, describe all propositions as subject-predicate in structure. An analytical proposition is one whose truth or falsity can be established by an examination of the proposition itself, that is, by an analysis of its syntactical structure, the semantic meanings of its symbols, and the logic of the language in which it is expressed. In Wittgenstein's classic comment, "It is the characteristic mark of logical propositions that one can perceive in the symbol alone that they are true; and this fact contains in itself the whole philosophy of logic." A "true" analytical proposition, or what is called simply an analytic proposition, is a tautology. It is necessarily true; it is true in every possible case and cannot possibly be false. Its opposite, a "false" analytical proposition, one which is false in every possible case and cannot possibly be true, is a contradiction.

Synthetic propositions, on the other hand, are those which may or may not be true in any possible case, whose truth or falsity can be shown only by an examination ultimately of non-logical, non-linguistic fact. Their truth or falsity is not a matter of logic. They express possibility rather than necessity or impossibility. They are true only in certain cases and state, therefore, that one or more of the possible cases is under consideration.

Propositions, Science, and Knowledge. The logical empiricists' theory of cognitive meaning is founded on the distinction between these two types of propositions. Analytic propositions, tautologies and contradictions, have formal or non-factual meaning. These are the propositions of the formal sciences, logic and mathematics, or logistic. Synthetic propositions, whether true or false, have non-formal or factual meaning. These are the propositions of the non-formal, that is, factual or empirical sciences, physics, biology, psychology, sociology and their variants. Sentences which are neither analytic nor synthetic do not express genuine propositions, since they are neither true nor false. They are, therefore, cognitively meaningless, making no assertion of fact or form, and express, therefore, no knowledge. In the early development of the new Positivism sentences having no cognitive meaning were ordinarily described as meaningless, or nonsensical. In more recent years, however, some attention has been given to the problem of noncognitive meanings, such as affective, pictorial, or volitional meaning.

The criticism of factual knowledge depends on the determination of the nature of a genuine synthetic proposition. Recent metaphysics, the logical empiricists point out, has depended heavily on the Kantian principle of the possibility of synthetic propositions *a priori,* of the possibility of genuine propositions that express matters of fact quite independently of experience. Metaphysical statements are roughly defined by them as non-scientific statements of fact, for statements not based on experience are not scientific and those based on experience are physical rather than metaphysical. That Kant should have defended *a priori* factual statements is attributed by the empiricists to such considerations as the intellectual demands of his time relevant to the need for solving the problem of induction, and to the common assumption that Euclidean geometry, an *a priori* discipline, is descriptive of observable space. But on the basis of post-Kantian developments, especially in mathematics and theoretical physics, contemporary empiricists and positivists in general agree that Kant was wrong, that the development of mathematics and natural science during the past century has meant the destruction of the *synthetic a priori.* Pure mathematics is regarded as *a priori* but *analytic.* Applied mathematics, as employed in the natural sciences, is *synthetic,* since it is descriptive of matters of fact, but its application depends upon ostensive definitions that assign factual meanings to the symbols. This process of defining introduces an experiential factor with the result that the propositions are now *synthetic* rather than *analytic,* but are *a posteriori.*

The Verifiability Criterion. The verifiability theory of meaning, which has appeared in several forms, is the positivistic critique of factual meaning and is the foundation for the elimination of metaphysics. In brief, this theory, or criterion, simply states that to be cognitively meaningful a sentence must be verifiable, and that sentences purporting to assert matters of fact that are not verifiable are not genuine propositions and therefore are not statements of fact. Among such pseudopropositions, which pretend to be assertions of fact, being descriptive of states of affairs or of the universe, but which are actually cognitively meaningless, are most of the sentences of speculative metaphysics. Much of what most philosophers have had to say is therefore meaningless.

When first converted to Positivism by a study of Wittgenstein,

Schlick held that factual meaning depends upon the actual possibility of verification, that is, of determining by actual experience whether or not the proposition is true or false. A more generous interpretation of verifiability became obviously necessary, however, in view of the meaning demands of some statements which cannot be verified, such as, for instance, Schlick's now famous example, "there are mountains on the other side of the moon," it being assumed that the other side of the moon will never be observed because of practical difficulties. Accordingly, Schlick adopted the criterion of *verifiability in principle,* which was eventually presented as the theory that factual propositions are genuine if there is the logical possibility in principle of their verification or if they are logically deducible from propositions for which there is in principle the logical possibility of verification. A fact or process is logically possible "if it can be described, i.e., if the sentence which is supposed to describe it obeys the rules of grammar we have stipulated for our language."[1] Meaning, he feels, must ultimately be established in terms of experience. "All the questions that can in principle be answered (including those that may at any one time or place be technically insoluble) are always answerable in one way, namely by reference to some *observation* (be it of nature or of ourselves) or by any scientific method which always pre-supposes observation; i.e., the occurrence of some sense impressions—in short, by experience."[2]

Carnap, Ayer, Reichenbach and others rejected the claim, implicit in the verifiability theories of Wittgenstein and Schlick, that factual propositions are in principle definitely verifiable as true or false, in favor of the position that they are empirical hypotheses, confirmable in future experience, their truth value being designated in terms of probability. With regard to the factual meaning of a proposition, moreover, Ayer rejects the question, "Would any observations make its truth or falsehood logically certain?" in favor of "Would any observations be relevant to the determination of its truth or falsehood?"

Operationism. The American physicist, P. W. Bridgman, in the interest of clarifying the concept of meaning for the elimination of pseudo-problems and the explication of scientific procedure, has defined the meaning of a concept as the sum of the physical operations performed in the application of that concept in a particular situation, a position that derives from the pragmatic principle of Peirce that identifies the meaning of a concept with the totality of its consequences.

---

[1] "Meaning and Verification," *Philosophical Review,* 45: 349.

[2] "A New Philosophy of Experience," *College of the Pacific Publications in Philosophy,* Vol. I, p. 114.

Non-empirical propositions in the interest of whose verification operations cannot be performed are, therefore, meaningless, a verdict essentially similar to that of the positivists.

III. POSITIVISM AND METAPHYSICS

The Meaning of Positivism. The rigorous form of Logical Positivism under discussion may be defined in two ways, one affirmative and the other negative. Affirmatively described, Positivism holds that scientific knowledge, formal and factual, exploits all possible knowledge. Negatively, Logical Positivism holds that metaphysics is an impossibility.

Logical empiricists in general have convicted statements which they regard as pseudo-factual on some such grounds as that they have no empirical reference, being composed of constituent words for which no ostensive meanings can be determined, or that they are ultimately contradictions, or violate the syntactical rules of the language. They are revealed by logical analysis to be pseudo-propositions masquerading as genuine by virtue of their grammatical structure.

The Elimination of Metaphysics. The elimination of metaphysics is accomplished on the basis of the claim that all metaphysical assertions are non-empirical and that therefore no empirical method can be defined for their verification or confirmation. The traditional efforts of metaphysicians to find meaning in their statements on the basis of non-empirical methods and criteria, e.g., by combining the intuition of self-evident truths with deductive method, or by postulating the groundwork of metaphysical systems as necessary presuppositions of experience, are rejected. Whatever their existential claims, neither logical demonstration nor experiment is in principle, it is maintained, capable of determining such sentences to be true or false, since their grammatical structure proposes them as statements of fact, whereas logical analysis reveals the presence of non-empirical terms, a fact which makes their reduction to elementary experiential propositions an impossibility. Such statements are, therefore, nonsense.

The new positivistic opposition to metaphysics, based on the meaninglessness of its statements, must be distinguished from the traditional positivism of the agnostic variety. This distinction is immediately evident, for instance, in the case of the metaphysical statement in non-animistic theology "There is a God," where the term God lacks ostensive reference in that it is not defined in terms of observable phenomena. By the theist the statement is considered to be a genuine meaningful proposition and true. For the atheist it is a genuine proposition and false. For the agnostic it is a genuine proposition the truth value of which cannot be determined. For the Logical Positivist it is neither true nor false and is not, therefore, a genuine proposition; it is meaningless.

The Elimination of Normative Science. The verifiability theory of meaning holds a similar negative implication for normative ethics, where that discipline is defined in terms of statements expressing the notions of good, right, or moral oughtness or their correlates, statements undertaking to establish norms or ends or to determine intrinsic values. The logical positivists regard the statements of descriptive ethics, propositions describing moral practices or belief and the like, as genuinely meaningful, being in principle verifiable, but these are assigned to the factual sciences such as social psychology or anthropology, rather than accepted as a body of moral philosophy. Moreover, definitions of normative terms are accepted as meaningful but are classified as analytic or formal. Their use, therefore, constitutes a logic of ethics which is a legitimate philosophical pursuit but says nothing about actual values. Moral commands and imperatives are regarded as cognitively meaningless since they are not assertions of fact and only indirectly convey knowledge. They belong, therefore, neither to science nor philosophy. Value judgments, such as "killing is evil" constitute the crux of the problem. From their grammatical form they appear to be factual assertions. However, the positivists insist that they do not satisfy the verifiability criterion of meaning and are, therefore, either disguised imperatives or expressions of emotions. Whatever meaning they may have is emotional or volitional. The presence of a normative ethical symbol in what may be an otherwise empirical context contributes nothing whatsoever to the factual meaning of the statement but rather is simply an evidence of a certain feeling of moral approbation or indignation on the part of the speaker.

Logical empiricists in general have concurred in the position, long advocated as well by Russell and others, that there can be no science of normative ethics, the determination of end values of necessity being made on non-rational, volitional, or emotional grounds. It is significant, however, that the logical positivists, who, with the exception of Schlick, have produced little in the field of ethics, accepted in principle the empirically oriented ethical theory of Dewey, which is based on an instrumental theory of values and the denial of all absolutes. Dewey's effort to construct a science of instrumental ethics which denies the dichotomy of ends and means was an attempt to overcome the same radical dualism of fact and value which Positivism encouraged, and which he described as "probably one of the chief sources of the malad-justments and unendurable strains from which the world is suffering."

IV. LANGUAGE AND REALITY

Wittgenstein. In the *Tractatus Logico-Philosophicus,* Wittgenstein, influenced by Russell's doctrine of logical atomism, which asserts that "in a logically perfect language the words in a proposition would correspond one by one with the components of the corresponding fact,"[3] advanced the theory maintaining that the world is a construc-tion of discrete atomic facts, which facts are experiential and can be pictured by propositions by virtue of an identity of structural form. Propositions are thus pictures of reality, and those which cannot be shown by experience to picture reality, i.e., to represent the existence or non-existence of atomic facts, are meaningless. This theory involved the positivists on one hand in a kind of knowledge absolutism, since every meaningful statement is verified in "final indubitable 'facts' given in immediate experience," and on the other hand in methodological and linguistic solipsism. The solipsism arises essentially from the fact that the quale of perceptions cannot be communicated and further from Wittgenstein's own view that it is impossible to construct a meta-language that can communicate the logical structure of propositions. Much of the work of Carnap and Neurath has been an effort to over-come these difficulties.

Protocol Sentences. Carnap and Neurath rejected the existence of atomic facts on the ground that they are neither found in experience nor logically inferable without circularity from the existence of atomic propositions. They denied that propositions can be compared with non-linguistic reality. They replaced the principle that "Every proposition must be decidable as true or false," by the principle that "every propo-sition must be 'decidable' with a certain degree of probability." Proposi-tions are to be compared only with other propositions. Verification, or confirmation, consists therefore not in referring statements to ex-periential facts but in comparing them with protocol-sentences, sentences which report experience and "contain words referring to what is directly observed by the asserter of a proposition." Such primitive protocols must be present in the structure of a science to guarantee its empirical reference, but theoretically a protocol itself is incapable of an absolute verification and its nature is determined in part by scientific convention. Thus verification deals not with the observation itself but with the

[3] Russell, "The Philosophy of Logical Atomism," *Monist* 28: 520, Oct. 4, 1918.

results of the observation: i.e., sentences containing observation words. Neurath's formula for a proper protocol is as follows: "Otto's protocol at 3:17 {Otto's word-thought at 3:16: (In the room at 3:15 was a table perceived by Otto)}."

Russell, who has held a modified doctrine of atomic facts in his theory of basic sentences, sentences which correspond to objective non-linguistic fact and to which propositions to be verifiable must be capable of reduction, has objected that the theory of protocol-sentences deserts empiricism, fails to explain the possibility of knowledge, and substitutes a deficient syntactical or coherence theory of truth for the more satisfactory and realistic semantical correspondence theory. Carnap has insisted, however, that knowledge is only of the communicable and that it is found, therefore, only on the level of language, not of perceptions. Propositions, not sensations, are its basic facts.

Carnap's Formal Mode of Speech. Carnap's reply to Wittgenstein's solipsism was the construction during the early thirties, of a formal or syntactical theory of language intended at once to indicate the possibility of the communication of knowledge, detect pseudo-problems, and make possible the reduction of all meaningful statements to a common language. An initial distinction was made between (1) "real-object" statements, i.e., statements that are the product of empirical inquiry and concern objects and the relations that obtain between them; (2) "pseudo-object" statements, i.e., statements that appear to concern real objects but in fact are concerned only with language; and (3) "syntactical" sentences, i.e., statements which refer to the syntactical relations between sentences and are therefore about language. Carnap's example of (1) a "real-object" sentence is "The rose is red," which is a genuine factual sentence, verifiable in experience, and belongs to the empirical sciences. But (2) the sentence "The rose is a thing" is a pseudo-object sentence of the type traditionally employed in metaphysics and responsible for the pseudo-problems of philosophy due to the fact that it refers to such a non-experiencable entity as "thing." It is both meaningless and dangerous and must be discarded unless it can be translated into a syntactical sentence, such as (3) "The word 'rose' is a thing-word." This sentence is meaningful, on the level of language, asserting nothing about the non-linguistic world. This is Carnap's "formal mode" of speech as contrasted with the "material mode" of "real-object" and "pseudo-object" sentences. It is the domain of philosophy, expressing by analytical sentences the syntactical analysis of language. All genuine problems which are not factual, and therefore do not belong to the sciences, are formal only and belong to philosophy, to be resolved on the level of language.

It is the formal mode of speech, according to Carnap's theory, that makes the communication of knowledge possible and thereby overcomes the privacy of solipsism. This follows from the fact that the objects referred to in the formal mode sentences are protocol statements rather than private sensations. In recent years Carnap's views have altered considerably in his treatment of the knowledge problem.

V. PHYSICALISM AND THE UNITY OF SCIENCE

The thesis of physicalism, advanced first by Neurath and followed by Carnap, asserts that every significant statement is either a physicalistic sentence or is translatable without loss of meaning into a physicalistic sentence. A physicalistic sentence is defined as a sentence in the formal mode which expresses quantitative determinations or qualitative determinations reducible to quantitative, in terms of simple location in space and time. The protocol languages which report individual experiences and the languages of the special sciences are declared to be sub-languages of the physical language, which is intersensory, intersubjective, and universal. On the theory of the physical language all factual sentences are declared to have physical reference and all sciences to become thereby united as physics, a synthesis of physics, non-vitalistic biology, behavioristic psychology, statistical sociology, and descriptive ethics. Here, it is hoped, is Leibnitz' universal language that, as a common foundation for the structure of all theoretical science, can recall men from their philosophic disputations and bid them to calculate. The thesis of physicalism was intended to serve the program of the unity of science by a twofold route: providing a language common to the sciences, and facilitating the construction of a comprehensive system uniting the laws of the natural sciences. The first effort has proved more successful than the second.

VI. THE CRITIQUE OF LOGICAL POSITIVISM

Since 1930 a large body of literature has accumulated assailing Logical Positivism with almost every conceivable type of criticism, both responsible and irresponsible. It has been described as a crime against culture and a presumption against the great tradition of philosophy, that it should declare as meaningless most of the major issues that have occupied the creative genius of mankind; or as a morally irresponsible

attitude that has at the historical moment of greatest need sabotaged
man's effort to solve raionally his most crucial practical problems by
declaring normative judgments to be cognitively meaningless. Its existence has been accounted for as a natural periodic resurgence of skepticism, nominalism, and nihilism; as a reaction against the absolutism of
religion; as a confusion of logic, mathematics, and physics with philosophy; as the issue of that unadventurous temperament which favors the
purity of barrenness to the risk of error; as the ideational by-product of
disruption in European politics and economy; or as the technical foundation of a sensate and decadent culture. On logical grounds it has been
charged that the neo-positivistic conception of philosophy is arbitrary,
ambiguous, self-refuting, and impossible in practice; that the true nature
and conditions of experience are ignored in its empiricism, and that the
strict formality assumed in its logic is a myth; that the repudiation of
metaphysics is accomplished by a question-begging and self-refuting
argument, and that the positivists have admitted at the back door the
metaphysics ejected at the front; that the verifiability theory of meaning
is entirely arbitrary. Some critics insist that all knowledge is personal,
normative, purposive, and valuational, and that formal analysis deserts
the world of real problems for the pseudo-solutions of language. Others
argue that positivism's physical reductionism is a major distortion of
reality and threatens the progress of science with arbitrary theoretical
strictures, and that the ideal of the unity of science is a linguist's impractical dream of neither worth nor interest to the scientist. It is, in
brief, declared that Logical Positivism has been a major attempt at
philosophic suicide.

There is no doubt that in the vigor of its youth the new Positivism
was an extremist. Its extremes were the dogmatism and the iconoclastic
and destructive enthusiasm of a new movement. But the empiricism
upon which it was based is a serious and persistent attitude, the attitude
of those who prefer "intellectual asceticism" to "intellectual profusion."
Most critics, after the first flush of denunciation, have recognized this
and have with some approval acknowledged the service of Positivism
in purging philosophy of much of its lavishness and demanding more
rigor in its self-criticism. Moreover, Logical Positivism has been its own
most severe critic and there are clear signs that in recent years its
destructiveness and reductionism have been yielding to a maturity of
broad and constructive philosophic endeavor.

Chapter XXXVII

EXISTENTIALISM

I. THE EXISTENTIALIST MOVEMENT

At the opposite pole from logical positivism, with its emphasis on sensory empiricism, objectivity, behaviorism, logic, and science, Existentialism has been a reaction in favor of individualism, subjectivity, introspection, and feeling. It is a philosophy not of things, but of the human situation. As against idealism it is an objection to the liberal doctrines of optimism and progress. As a champion of the concrete against the abstract, of life as opposed to logic, of the non-intellectual and irrational in contrast to intellectualism, and of freedom as against mechanism and determinism, Existentialism has much in common with romanticism, pragmatism, personalism, Bergsonism, and voluntaristic and vitalistic philosophies generally.

With historical roots deep in the culture, Existentialism has an ancient heritage, the outlines of which have become plain especially since the work of its chief technical philosopher, Martin Heidegger. Socrates, the psalmists, Paul, Augustine, and Pascal contributed to its foundations. But in its modern technical form it is grounded in the psychology and theology of Søren Kierkegaard, the philosophy of Nietzsche, and the method and ontology of the phenomenologist Husserl.

There is no single existentialist position. The philosophy varies with its proponents, some of whom insist that they are not existentialists at all. But there is a common fund of doctrine that identifies them, nevertheless, and indicates quite clearly their relation to the classical philosophic tradition. Their major and differentiating thesis is the metaphysical pronouncement that "existence is prior to essence," while in the established tradition "essence is prior to existence." What this means for the existentialist is that human nature is determined by the course of life rather than life by human nature.

In its theistic form, Existentialism has been an important factor in the neo-orthodox awakening that has marked theology since the first war. Its emphasis on the negative qualities of man, on human estrangement and the tragedy of human existence, have supported the resurgence of the dogma of original sin and the entire structure of eschatological theology. Secular, or what is often called atheistic, Existentialism has been popularized especially since the second war by numerous expressions in fiction, drama, and poetry, particularly by its French partisans under the leadership of Jean Paul Sartre (1905-   ). In its technical formulations recent Existentialism is largely a German product, its foremost representatives being the Protestant theologian Paul Tillich (1886-   ) and the philosophers Karl Jaspers (1883-   ) and Martin Heidegger (1889-   ). To some extent the recent rise of Existentialism must be attributed to the destruction and human desolation attending the two world wars and the anxieties that stem from the continuing unrest in both world and domestic affairs. As such it is a product of large-scale social failure. But it is also an expression of the psychological and moral tensions that hold the individual in their grip in any age and in any society.

II. JASPERS

Karl Jaspers was a student of law at Heidelberg and Munich and later studied medicine at several German universities. Early in his career he made important contributions to pathological and psychiatric research. From 1921 until the Nazi regime he was professor of philosophy at Heidelberg. He returned to Heidelberg after the war but has been at Basel since 1948. His philosophical activity was from the beginning influenced by careful studies of Kant and Hegel, but Kierkegaard and Nietzsche have dominated his thought by directing it constantly upon the problem of the human condition. His philosophy has been more than anything else an attempt to answer their question of the nature of human existence. His answers reflect his Kantianism.

Philosophical Method. Jaspers' major completed work is *Philosophie,* published in three volumes in 1932, in which he undertook a detailed examination of philosophical method, and related Existentialism to the main scientific and philosophical streams of the culture. There he differentiated three fundamental methods, each supplementing the other and each fruitful within the context of its legitimate employment: (1) *philosophical world-orientation* directed to a knowledge of being-there; (2) the *elucidation of existence,* concerned with a knowledge of being-oneself; and (3) the *way of metaphysics,* the way of knowing being-in-itself.

Philosophical World-Orientation. *Philosophical world-orientation* is the method of grasping the objectively real world by scientific intelligence. It is a search for certainty and total reliability, knowledge that has both universality and necessity. It is an effort at complete systematization and unity. But although it is the proper and necessary starting point of any serious philosophic quest and although it can achieve clarity and precision, such scientific knowledge, because it is empirical and inductive and therefore probable, cannot arrive at a comprehensive unity. Unless augmented by the other methods it must fail to give the full picture of being, for the philosopher himself is involved in all three realms of being. Philosophy here encounters and must recognize the limits of scientific knowledge, its relative character, the partial and incomplete perspectives that are available to it. Knowledge, moreover, is only of phenomena, not of all reality.

Elucidation of Existence. It is in the analysis of the second method, the *elucidation of existence*, that the characteristic Exentialism of Jaspers appears in its most complete form. In his concern with the full nature of being the philosopher must return from the object world of things to his own situation, to himself, not as an object to be known with other objects, but as existing being, involved in concrete predicaments, in particular and peculiar circumstances. Here he does not find universality, objectivity, or knowledge. These are available only to the abstractive intellect in its contemplation of the empirical world.

The ancient injunction "know thyself" is misleading. Man cannot know himself; he is his own greatest mystery. We have a knowledge of what we are not, but not of what we are. In his freedom man has an awareness of his humanity. He has no other essence than free choice. It is the task of the existential method to bring about the consciousness of freedom and of the absolute responsibility which it entails. It must bring the individual to a realization also of the existence of others by effecting communication with them. In the subjective search of his private consciousness, man finds crisis, freedom, and decision; these are existence. The existent self is not a being who is free and makes decisions. The self is the very freedom and the decisions which are made. It is self-determining, determined by its own choice, which is both original and absolute.

The Way of Metaphysics. But man's freedom, which is destroyed by every attempt to achieve scientific knowledge of himself as a whole, is not separable from his consciousness of his finite nature. His finiteness is the finiteness of all living things, a dependence upon natural environment and natural process, the finiteness of whatever must die. It is the finiteness of dependence upon perceptual experience in human knowledge.

When man becomes aware of his finiteness he transcends it by a consciousness of infiniteness, for his potentialities seem to have no limit. He realizes that he has not created himself and positively seeks the one being, the absolute, which is the goal of metaphysics. In the face of insecurity, suffering, despair, conflict, violence, guilt, and death, which are the lot of the existing being, man yet goes forward with his eyes open and undeceived but with a faith that enables him to transcend the world and his situation in it, to achieve being-in-itself. Such transcendence is the total perspective that is gained not by objective knowledge but by genuine participation in life. For Jaspers the achievement of transcendence does not involve God or salvation in the Christian sense. Yet it is not totally unlike the Christian faith; and if it is not a positive theological doctrine in the traditional sense, it at least is not atheistic.

III. HEIDEGGER

The technical formulation of the central doctrine of Existentialism, that existence precedes essence, was the work chiefly of Martin Heidegger. Heidegger's academic career was mainly at the University of Freiburg, where he succeeded Husserl in the chair of philosophy in 1929 and became Rector in 1933. He resigned the following year and has since been in semi-retirement. Heidegger's major, though uncompleted, work, *Sein und Zeit* (Being and Time), was hailed by some as the fulfillment of Husserl's quest for a general ontology and as the most significant metaphysics since Hegel.

Born a Catholic, Heidegger cut his teeth on Thomism and on a profound encounter with the Christian religion. Thoroughly immersing himself in the history of philosophy, with special interest in Kant, he undertook a search for the nature of being, insisting that the major task was to escape from the burden of traditional dogmas and return to the genuine ontological insights of Aristotle, Plato, and the pre-Socratics. Heidegger's approach to philosophic history and metaphysics, which for him necessarily involve each other, was influenced by Husserl's phenomenological method, which attempts to abstract from the particular and individual and achieve a general knowledge based on the immediacy of inner experience. Heidegger attempted to avoid rationalism and intellectualism by coming to grips with the very content of

experience, though most empiricists have little patience with his extreme
subjectivism.)

Ontology. Heidegger has attempted to escape the designation of
existentialist on the ground that his concern is with being in its unity
and totality rather than with existence, but he quite clearly is a major
factor in the whole existentialist movement. The Greeks, he has insisted,
were admirable ontologists in their efforts to discover the meaning of
being, but they were severely limited by a consuming interest in the
world of things, the individual things that appear and are perceived in
ordinary experience and which they described by the application of the
various categories. *Being* was therefore always approached by them in
terms of some particular kind of being. Heidegger, on the contrary,
attempted to find being not as a derivation from the individual existent
but as *being in itself,* revealed in a context far more fundamental. His
beginning point was the analysis of *Dasein,* an attempt to answer the
question "what is man?" *Dasein* is, in Heidegger's usage, a term not
entirely translatable that refers to the mode of human existence.

Dasein. *Dasein* was analyzed by Heidegger especially in its temporal
or historical character, for only there, he insisted, is its true nature to be
found. *Dasein,* which is always *My Dasein,* and is indefinable and indescribable, must be radically distinguished from existent things, designated as "vorhanden" or "at hand." The existent things always belong
to a genus and have describable qualities. It is possible, therefore, to
determine their essence. But with *Dasein* there is no essence. *Dasein* is
being, or "being there." It expresses only existence. It is not given; it is
possibility. Man exists through his choices, and his being, therefore,
is entirely indeterminate. Animals and inanimate things "are there,"
because they are localizations in space and time, but they do not "exist."
Only man exists, because only man has a conscious awareness of his
existence. To exist, to have an authentic being, is to reflect on oneself,
to be concerned about oneself. True being is self being, involving not
only consciousness, but responsibility and free decision as well.

However, the individual is not in total isolation. Human existence
is a *being-in-the world;* the self is in relation to the not-self, a not-self of
other persons and things. The very structure of the individual is constituted by this relation with others and with the world. There is no escape
from some involvement in social relations. To effect such an escape, to
achieve anonymity, would destroy authentic existence by destroying all
possibilities, all freedom, and all choice. This would reduce the self to
a thing.

Temporality. Moreover, the real nature of *Dasein* is revealed in its temporality or historicity. The Greeks failed, in Heidegger's view, properly to assess time other than as a sequence of presents. But man is not simply his present. He is his past and his future. Man is forever oriented to his future, to his possibilities. He is projected toward the future, toward something yet to come, and this inspires *anxiety* and, to use a term which Heidegger has filled with meaning, *care*. Man transcends himself toward the future. He lives continually ahead of himself. His very being is temporality.

Dread. The individual is aroused from inauthentic existence and achieves an awareness of his authentic existence in *anguish* and *dread*. The experience of dread, like the "sickness unto death" of Kierkegaard brings one to the profoundest level of human emotion. Unlike fear, which is always of some specific and threatening thing and therefore has a definiteness about it, dread is an indefinite "feeling about," but not about any particular thing. It is not anything in the world, but the fact of being-in-the world that produces dread.

By dread we are held in suspense, and it is in this suspense that *Dasein* is apprehended, for dread demands a choice between inauthentic impersonal existence and the genuine existence of self-determination; it demands of a man that he take upon himself his own destiny. Here we are revealed as partial, relative, and finite—cast out upon a world in which all is worthless, homeless, hopeless, and forlorn, beings that have no reason for being, whose existence is a "being for death."

Death. For Heidegger, man is the being that knows he is going to die. He dies not only at the end of life, but every day of it. Death is certain, yet indefinite. Because it is inevitable it marks the contingency of life. Life is cast up between nothing and nothing. Death is its boundary and is its supreme possibility. To freely accept death, to live in its presence, and to acknowledge that for it there is no substitute and into it one must go alone, is to escape from all illusions and to achieve genuine dignity and authentic existence.

Nothingness. In an unusual essay entitled "What Is Metaphysics?" Heidegger examined the foundations of ontology and reached a quite startling conclusion. Science attempts the investigation of what is, and rejects any consideration of what is not, or *nothing*. But if the question, what is metaphysics? is asked, the answer must be that it is an enquiry into nothing. By a peculiar logical difficulty, we cannot rationally investigate nothing; but there is, nevertheless, a mood in which it is known face to face. Dread is the experience of nothing. But nothing is not merely the negation of something. It can be experienced, and its experience is an experience of naked "is-ness," being devoid of all meanings and free from all the disguises heaped upon it by the reason. "We, ourselves, confirm that dread reveals nothing—when we have got over our dread. In the lucid vision which supervenes while yet the experience is fresh in our memory we must needs say that what we were afraid of was 'actually' nothing. And indeed nothing itself, nothing as such, was there." In dread our *Dasein* projects into nothing, but it is only in the transcendence of *Dasein* as projected into nothing that pure being is revealed. As Hegel had said, pure being and pure nothing are one and the same. Nothing is a primordial being, the ground from which everything comes and to which it must return.

IV. TILLICH

A vigorous and highly original religious Existentialism has been set forth by the Protestant philosophical theologian Paul Tillich. Born in Germany in 1886 in the province of Brandenburg, Tillich was educated at Berlin, Breslau, and Halle and taught at several German universities including Berlin, Marburg, and Frankfurt. During the Nazi regime he came to the United States and in 1954 was appointed to a professorship in Harvard University. His writings show clearly the influence of Nietzsche, Husserl, and Heidegger.

Tillich's major work, *Systematic Theology,* the first volume of which appeared in 1951, was the groundwork of an existential analysis of being within the framework of a Christian theology that stands in clear opposition to the idealistically oriented liberalism that has pervaded Protestant thought during the past century. In a later work, *The Courage to Be,* Tillich analyzed the nature of anxiety in a manner that illumines this important corner of existentialist thought.

Anxiety. Accepting the familiar description of the post-war era, both for Europe and America, as an "age of anxiety," Tillich describes anxiety as fundamentally the "existential awareness of nonbeing," the "awareness that nonbeing is a part of one's own being." The awareness of one's own transitoriness and of one's own having to die produces a natural anxiety, an anxiety of ultimate nonbeing. Naked anxiety, which belongs to the nature of being as such and is an experience of unimaginable horror, strives vainly to convert itself into fear, because fear has an object and can therefore be met and overcome by courage. But anxiety itself has no object.

The Anxiety of Fate and Death. Anxiety appears in three forms, dependent upon the direction in which "nonbeing threatens being." The *anxiety of fate and death* proceeds from the threat of nonbeing against man's "ontic" affirmation. It is basic, universal, and entirely inescapable. The contingency of man, that the causes which determine him are without any rationality or ultimate necessity, yields the relative anxiety of fate. The fact of death, present with man during every moment of life as well as at the moment of dying, produces an absolute anxiety of nonbeing. The basic question of courage is whether there is a *courage to be* in the face of this absolute threat against being.

The Anxiety of Emptiness and Meaninglessness. The second type of anxiety is in its relative form the *anxiety of emptiness* and in its absolute form the *anxiety of meaninglessness*. Emptiness is the product of a threat to participation in creativity. Meaninglessness, which lies always in the background of emptiness as death lies always behind fate, is the loss of a spiritual center for life, the loss of an ultimate concern, of the meaning fundamental to all meanings. This anxiety is the threat of nonbeing to the spiritual life, a threat that follows from man's finitude and estrangement and leads to despair. To escape it, one attempts an escape from his own freedom and thereby sacrifices his genuine existence.

The Anxiety of Guilt and Condemnation. The third type of anxiety issues from the threat of nonbeing against man's self-affirmation, in its relative form, the *anxiety of guilt;* in its absolute form, the *anxiety of condemnation*. Man as finite freedom is free to determine himself in the fulfillment of his destiny. The anxiety of guilt and condemnation is produced by the failure to realize one's potentiality. It is a self-rejection, a despair in the loss of proper identity. Despair is the product of the three anxieties, interrelated to foster and support one another. Despair is the complete absence of hope. By suicide one might escape the anxiety of death, but he would be caught in the anxiety of guilt and condemnation.

Anxiety and Cultural History. Life, Tillich holds, is largely an attempt to avoid despair. From it there is no escape, yet most people experience it in its intensity only infrequently if at all. In the history of western culture the three types of anxiety have always been present, but each has dominated one of the three major eras. The classical era, the era of absolutism and tyranny, was characterized by the anxiety of fate and death, and ended with the attempt to achieve the Stoic courage. The Middle Ages, under the influence of the Judeo-Christian (Moral) religion, was brought to a close under the domination of the anxiety of guilt and condemnation, induced by the breakdown of the unity of religion. Today it is the anxiety of emptiness and meaninglessness that casts its shadow over a world that has lost its spiritual content.

V. SARTRE

Existentialism had been introduced to France from Germany prior to the second war, but it was nourished in the French underground during the German occupation, playing a not unimportant role in resistance politics. After the war it became a major factor in contemporary French culture, developing into something of a cult and expressing itself in artistic forms, particularly fiction, drama, and poetry, as well as in philosophical and theological studies and psychological analyses. Theistic Existentialism, best represented by Gabriel Marcel (1889-   ) has flourished in Catholic circles, while secular Existentialism has become popular among the artists and literati and has made some headway in academic philosophy. American Existentialism has on the whole derived more directly from France than from Germany.

The high priest of the secular existentialist movement in France, and in a measure responsible for its popular vogue, has been the dramatist, novelist, journalist and philosopher Jean-Paul Sartre (1905-   ). His major work, *L'Etre et le Néant (Being and Nothingness)*, published during the war, drew heavily upon the phenomenological method of Husserl, the atheism of Nietzsche, and the metaphysics of Heidegger. Formerly a teacher of philosophy at LeHavre and Paris, Sartre had studied Heidegger's thought in Germany.

Existence and Essence. Sartre takes his stand on the orthodox doctrine that existence precedes essence, by which he means that man is not defined by a common quality of human nature but rather is what he conceives and wills himself to be after his "thrust toward existence." Since there is no God, a fundamental postulate of Sartre's ontology, there is no concept of man in the mind of God which constitutes man's essence. Man does not come into the world ready-made; he is simply what he makes of himself, and is never made but always in the making.

Man as Freedom. It is here that a major emphasis of Sartre is founded, his doctrine of freedom. Man is free because he cannot be otherwise. He cannot escape his freedom, which becomes for him, therefore, a dreadful responsibility. But not only does one determine himself in his free choice; he also determines all others, for every decision he makes legislates for all men. Man is involved inevitably in anguish because his decision is never grounded in an external authority upon which he can rest the responsibility for his action. He must bear it alone. And when Sartre says alone, he means absolutely alone, for not only is there no God to share the burden, but there is no structure *a priori* for values to rest upon. Man's forlornness is his all-aloneness in which he must face the issue of his own freedom. For Sartre, that God does not exist is a dreadful fact that makes an ultimate difference to the world and to man.

To the common criticism that Sartre's philosophy, and indeed Existentialism in general, is pessimistic, he replies that such a charge can come only from those who are fearful of the truth that life is genuinely difficult. "Existentialism," he has written, "is nothing else than an attempt to draw all the consequences of a coherent atheistic position." The discovery that there is no God and that man is alone is the beginning of a genuine humanism that dignifies man as the free creator of all values and of whatever meaning there is in human existence.

POSTSCRIPT AND PROSPECT

It is more than twenty-five hundred years since Thales, by his efforts to interpret the world in terms of itself, marked the beginning of definable philosophy in the West. Philosophy is old, very old. And unlike any other discipline, it carries with it always the burden of its past. The philosophy of today is in a very real sense an accumulation of the centuries. In every era something new was added, and something old was lost. Yet the basic problems are still with us. With us, also, are the profound insights of those who have attempted their solution.

But although it is venerable with age, and its cultivation, therefore, demands scholarship and erudition, philosophy today has a freshness and vitality about it that makes it also an exciting and open adventure. New things are happening, in philosophy and around it, and there is real promise that the future will be more than simply a repetition of the past. Most important, perhaps, are the fundamental changes in the sciences, for philosophy, for all its conservatism, is a sensitive indicator of the trends of science. The recent past has seen two simultaneous revolutions in science, one in physics, the other in psychology, which may well be as fraught with consequences important to the future of philosophic thought as were the Copernican and Darwinian upheavals.

In physics, Einstein's theory of time as a "fourth dimension," of the relativity of motion, of the non-Euclidean nature of space, and of the equivalence of the mass of a body with its momentum, have brought into question many of the fundamental principles of the old physics. To this has been added the development of the *quantum* theory, based upon the discovery that energy, far from delivering itself in a continuous flow, comes in irregular beats and puffs for whose separated and capricious occurrence no reason can be found or even conceived.

Further examination of this disorderly situation has revealed to Heisenberg and Schrödinger a state of affairs described by the "principle of uncertainty." According to this principle it is impossible to determine simultaneously with mathematical precision both the exact position and the exact momentum of an electron, and to increase the accuracy of either measurement necessarily decreases the accuracy of the other. The physicist thus finds himself between the devil and the deep sea. Every step towards the attainment of the one goal, he knows beforehand, must of mathematical necessity carry him further away from the other. The electron has a disconcerting way of changing orbit and position without warning, and it refuses to cooperate with any attempt at measurement in the interest of predicting its behavior.

These discoveries appear at the moment to outmode the stock-in-trade of the conventional physics, and many insist that they call for a radical reformation of philosophical ideas deriving from physics. It seems that the old classical concepts of space and time, of mass and motion, of the conservation of energy and the indestructibility of matter, of causation and necessity, and of the amenability of physical occurrences to mathematical formulae, are no longer fundamental and reliable. On the contrary, the old concepts would seem to be superficial and inadequate.

Any philosophy, then, which finds in the nature and the conduct of the physical world some indication of the character of the Real can scarcely avoid a revision of the inferences it has hitherto been drawing. Reality, so far as the physical sciences introduce us to it, can no longer be thought of as the orderly, stable, uniform, causally determined and mathematically calculable affair it was of yore. It rather suggests a core of caprice, chance, spontaneity, and indeterminism, in whose sheer madness there is no method. The solid, ponderable aspects and the ponderous and calculable movements that constitute its grosser physical aspects are superficial and shallow. They are a lava-crust of dubious depth floating on a sea of molten, tossing, bubbling and seething being, if such it can be called. Or at least this is the claim of those who see the traditional cosmologies turned topsy-turvy by the physicists.

The second revolution, which is of equally great import, is the overturn in psychology effected by Freud and the psychoanalytic school. Formerly, mind was regarded as essentially reasonable and moral. But those days seem to be over. Under psychoanalysis it has revealed quite a different nature, and a nature, curiously enough, not unlike that revealed in matter by the probings of the new physics—that is, its rational and moral aspects tell only part of the story. They represent, indeed, only what the censor permits to be published of an autobiography that is essentially capricious, blindly impulsive, unmoral and irrational in the original text and in the spirit in which it is composed.

It may be argued that the new physics and the new psychology are not revolutions, but mere rebellions which will be put down without permanent damage to our hitherto established ideas. Perhaps. But at the moment there is no reason to suppose that their revelations will be more easily discarded and any less lasting and profound in their effects upon our thinking than those of the Copernican and Darwinian theories. It may well be that the physicist and psychologist of the future will be as little able to ignore or to reject them as the astronomer of today is able to pass by Galileo and return to Ptolemy, or the contemporary biologist to flout the doctrine of evolution and maintain the theory of special creation of fixed species. In that case philosophy will have to make startling and far-reaching adjustments.

There is evidence that such adjustments are already being made. The traditional cosmologies have for the most part collapsed, and there are stirrings of something new in their place. And in the rise of Existentialism, promising to bring a full articulation to the individualistic and subjectivistic facets of Western thought, there is very clearly the influence of the new psychology. If metaphysics must abandon the world of the classical machine, it is also being forced to look inward as well as outward. The past's preoccupation with man as a universal, or as a species, or as society, is yielding to an interest in man in his individuality and in his solitude. The ideal descriptions of man as the rational animal are now more commonly tempered or replaced by the picture of man as irrational, impulsive, and emotional.

In recent years, philosophy has moved progressively closer to science, not only in general interests and affiliations but even in method and content. Today it is taken for granted that serious creative participation in the philosophic enterprise requires a generous measure of scientific competence. Few would doubt that science is and will continue in the foreseeable future to be the major determinant of the character of philosophy. But what of the influence of philosophy upon science? The impact of philosophy upon the various elements of culture is subtle and difficult to assess. Theoretical science quite surely is importantly affected by basic, though often unexpressed, philosophical assumptions as well as by large-scale cosmological speculations. However, it is no doubt true that the influence of philosophy upon the course of science is far less pronounced today than in earlier eras. Of course, the line between science and philosophy is at some points not clearly drawn. The creative edge of science has a philosophical character, and very often the two disciplines are well represented in the same individual. Yet moderation in the estimate of philosophy's effect upon science is unquestionably the wisest counsel. On the whole, it is not likely that the scientific world today gives as much attention to philosophy generally or even to the philosophy of science as many philosophers would like to believe.

When we inquire into the present relations of philosophy and religion, we find that here, also, the times have changed. Philosophy no longer draws its major inspiration from religious interests, and proportionately there are fewer thinkers than formerly who might be regarded as philosophers of religion. A few decades ago, the impact of philosophy upon religion was largely productive of liberalism or modernism. Today the effect is more likely to be a naturalistic humanism. This is true in spite of the fact that religion seems to be enjoying something of a renascence and the philosophy of religion is increasingly popular in academic circles. The new vitality of religion is mainly the vitality of biblical orthodoxy. Except for its relation to Existentialism, this orthodoxy is largely non- or even anti-philosophical. What the future will bring, no one knows. But it is a safe conjecture that the reactionary trend of the present will eventually yield to a more reasoned and philosophical religion.

Of course the affiliations of philosophy are many and various. As always, it is related closely to art, morals, literature, education, and politics. But in recent years, there have been new emphases that promise to affect its course in the future. Ever since the First World War, which destroyed the easy optimism that had pervaded the nineteenth century and had become a prominent character of liberal thought, there has been a growing interest in the fundamental questions relating to the nature, meaning, and processes of history. This in turn has been intimately involved with both descriptive and normative analyses of culture, with the result that the philosophy of history and culture has become an important segment of the total philosophical enterprise.

The political and economic events of the past few years have made the Orient and Occident acutely aware of each other and have led to large movements that are a response to the demand for increased intercultural understanding and appreciation. Philosophy, as the discipline that relates to fundamentals, has been, as might be expected, affected by this new cosmopolitanism. The assumption that the academic pursuit of philosophy does and will play an important role in the future of world affairs is a common one. There is much disagreement, however, as to what that role will be, or should be, and perhaps even more disagreement in the matter of whether and how it can or should be implemented.

We have been engaged in the study of Occidental philosophy, as it arose in the Greek colonies and has affected the course of Western culture to the present. Nothing has been said about the intellectual history of Russia, and no effort has been made to acquaint the reader with the great deposit and tradition of philosophic thought in the Orient. In

India, metaphysics in particular achieved both maturity and cultural importance at a very early date. The main *Upanishads*, which underlie the philosophic tradition of both Hinduism and Buddhism, were produced as early as the sixth century before the Christian era. In China, parts of the *Tao Te Ching* and the *Chuang Tzu* were probably composed as early as the fourth century B.C., while the *Six Classics*, upon which the great tradition of Chinese ethics is largely based, are older than Confucius.

The story of Western philosophy is only a part of the history of philosophy. Indian and Chinese thought have a rich and varied past, as does the Islamic philosophy that underlies the culture of the countless millions of the Near East. Their study is far more interesting and rewarding than most Westerners suppose. The future quite surely will see a large cultural interchange between the East and West, and every serious student of philosophy will be confronted by the ideas of the world rather than by only those of his own tradition.

Finally, a word should be said about what may well be the most important and far-reaching development in philosophy in recent years, the orientation of philosophic thought as philosophy of language. There is nothing new in principle in the current interest in problems of language. It is found throughout the history of Occidental philosophy—in Plato, Occam, Locke, and Leibnitz. Nor do the profound insights of these suffer in comparison with recent analyses or theories. But never before has language played such a large role in technical philosophy or attracted such wide popular attention. This has been a language-conscious era. Its products range from the solid creative work on symbolism, meaning, and method, of thinkers of the first calibre, like Peirce, Russell, Whitehead, Wittgenstein, Carnap or Cassirer, to the popular treatments of semantics and pseudo-semantics that have had the dubious effect of convincing the philosophical dilettantes that all problems are language problems. At least two important trends, positivism and analysis, have been rooted in the interest in language. But more important are the new ways of looking at art, religion, and even science, that have derived from it. It seems safe to say that the philosophy of the future, whatever other qualities it may have, will reveal clearly the permanent impact of the language theory of the past half-century.

This history opened with the question, "What is philosophy?" It must close with the same question. Today philosophers and teachers and students of philosophy are subjecting the philosophic enterprise to a rigorous reassessment. They want to decide on its proper role in education, in moral living, in the practical affairs of the community, the nation, or the world. They want to know more about its function in the culture. Is it an important determinant of culture, or is it simply a by-product of the material facets of life and society.

They are asking, "What is the legitimate nature of philosophy? Is there such a thing as philosophical knowledge? Should philosophy be metaphysics, or ethics, or is it simply logic? Is philosophy contemplation, or action? Is it speculation, or analysis? Is it construction, or criticism?" Perhaps it is all of these, for philosophy is far too rich and varied in character and content to be defined so simply. But whatever else philosophy may be in the future, we may be quite sure that it will not forsake its ancient task, the *reflective and reasoned attempt to infer the character and content of the universe*. And we may be sure that wherever genuine philosophy is found, there also will be found that everlasting disagreement that is the surest sign of freedom of thought and inquiry.

Appendix I

READINGS ON THE HISTORY OF WESTERN THOUGHT

This listing includes only works available in English language editions. The dates indicate the year of publication in English.

1. *General History of Philosophy and Science*

E. T. Bell, *The Development of Mathematics*, 2nd ed., 1945.
George Boas, *The Major Traditions of European Philosophy*, 1929.
Bernard Bosanquet, *History of Aesthetics*, 1892.
C. D. Broad, *Five Types of Ethical Theory*, 1930.
Florian Cajori, *A History of Mathematics*, 2nd ed., 1919.
—— *A History of Physics*, 1899.
Frederick Copleston, *A History of Philosophy*, 2 Vols., 1946.
William C. Dampier (formerly Whetham), *A History of Science and Its Relations with Philosophy and Religion;* 3rd ed., 1942.
T. J. DeBoer, *The History of Philosophy in Islam*, 1903.
J. L. E. Dreyer, *History of the Planetary Systems from Thales to Kepler*, 1906.
James H. Dunham, *The Religion of Philosophers*, 1947.
Johann E. Erdmann, *A History of Philosophy*, 3 Vols., 1910-1913.
Rudolf Eucken, *The Problem of Human Life*, 1909.
Vergilius Ferm, ed., *A History of Philosophical Systems*, 1950.
W. T. Jones, *A History of Western Philosophy*, 1952.
Arthur O. Lovejoy, *The Great Chain of Being*, 1936.
S. G. Martin, G. H. Clark, F. P. Clarke, and C. T. Ruddick, *A History of Philosophy*, 1947.
Hugh Miller, *An Historical Introduction to Modern Philosophy*, 1947.
William P. Montague, *Great Visions of Philosophy*, 1950.
Erik Nordenskiöld, *The History of Biology*, 1928.
Hans Reichenbach, *The Rise of Scientific Philosophy*, 1951.
Arthur K. Rogers, *Morals in Review*, 1927.
—— *A Student's History of Philosophy*, 1928.
Bertrand Russell, *A History of Western Philosophy*, 1945.

C. Singer, *A Short History of Science*, 1941.

Newton P. Stallknecht and Robert S. Brumbaugh, *The Spirit of Western Philosophy*, 1950.

D. Sherwood Taylor, *A Short History of Science*, n. d.

Frank Thilly, *A History of Philosophy*, revised by Ledger Wood, 1951.

Radoslav A. Tsanoff, *The Moral Ideals of Our Civilization*, 1942.

—— *The Great Philosophers*, 1953.

Friedrich Ueberweg, *History of Philosophy*, 2 Vols., 1889.

Alfred Weber, *History of Philosophy*, with *Philosophy Since 1860* by Ralph Barton Perry, 1925.

W. Whewell, *History of Inductive Sciences*, 3 Vols., 1837.

W. P. D. Wightman, *The Growth of Scientific Ideas*, 1951.

Wilhelm Windelband, *A History of Philosophy*, 1910.

2. Greek and Roman Philosophy and Science

R. Adamson, *The Development of Greek Philosophy*, 1908.

Cyril Bailey, ed., *The Legacy of Rome*, 1923.

J. I. Beare, *Greek Theories of Elementary Cognition*, 1906.

A. W. Benn, *The Greek Philosophers*, 2 Vols., 2nd ed., 1914.

John Burnet, *Early Greek Philosophy*, 1930.

John B. Bury, *A History of Greece*, 1911.

John F. Callahan, *Four Views of Time in Ancient Philosophy*, 1948.

Benjamin Farrington, *Greek Science*, 2 Vols., 1949.

B. A. G. Fuller, *History of Greek Philosophy*, 3 Vols., 1923-31.

Heinrich Gomperz, *Philosophical Studies*, Part I, 1953.

—— *Problems and Methods of Early Greek Science*.

Theodor Gomperz, *Greek Thinkers*, 4 Vols., 1905.

Thomas Heath, *Greek Astronomy*, 1932.

—— *History of Greek Mathematics*, 2 Vols., 1921.

Werner Jaeger, *Paideia*, 3 Vols., 2nd ed., 1945.

E. Kapp, *Greek Foundations of Traditional Logic*, 1942.

R. W. Livingstone, ed., *The Legacy of Greece*, 1921.

Arnold Reymond, *History of the Sciences in Graeco-Roman Antiquity*, 1927.

Léon Robin, *Greek Thought and the Origins of the Scientific Spirit*, 1928.

George Sarton, *Ancient Science and Modern Civilization*, 1954.

—— *Introduction to the History of Science*, 1927.

—— *A History of Science: Ancient Science through the Golden Age of Greece*, 1952.

J. M. Warbeke, *The Searching Mind of Greece*, 1930.

W. Windelband, *History of Ancient Philosophy*, 1901.

E. Zeller, *Outlines of the History of Greek Philosophy*, 13th ed., 1931.
—— *Philosophy of the Greeks*, 6 Vols., 1903-1922. (German. Available in English only in part.)

3. *Greek and Roman Religion*

J. Adam, *The Religious Teachers of Greece*, 2nd ed., 1909.
Franz Altheim, *A History of Roman Religion*, 1938.
Cyril Bailey, *Phases in the Religion of Ancient Rome*, 1932.
—— ed., *The Legacy of Rome*, 1923.
E. Bevan, *Later Greek Religion*, 1927.
Edward Caird, *The Evolution of Theology in the Greek Philosophers*, 1904.
L. Campbell, *Religion in Greek Literature*, 1898.
Jesse B. Carter, *The Religious Life of Ancient Rome*, 1912.
F. M. Cornford, *From Religion to Philosophy*, 1912.
A. Fairbanks, *Handbook of Greek Religion*, 1910.
L. R. Farnell, *Cults of the Greek States*, 5 Vols., 1896-1909.
—— *Outline History of Greek Religion*, 2nd ed., 1921.
—— *The Higher Aspects of Greek Religion*, 1912.
W. W. Fowler, *The Religious Experience of the Roman People*, 1911.
W. K. C. Guthrie, *Orpheus and Greek Religion*, 1952.
William R. Halliday, *Lectures on the History of Roman Religion*, 1922.
Jane E. Harrison, *Prolegomena to the Study of Greek Religion*, 3rd ed., 1922.
Werner Jaeger, *Theology of the Early Greek Philosophers*, 1947.
R. W. Livingstone, ed., *The Legacy of Greece*, 1921.
C. H. Moore, *The Religious Thought of the Greeks*, 1916.
Gilbert Murray, *Five Stages of Greek Religion*, 2nd ed., 1925.
Martin P. Nilsson, *The Minoan-Mycenaean Religion and Its Survival in Greek Religion*, 1927.
—— *A History of Greek Religion*, 1925.
—— *Greek Popular Religion*, 1940.
H. J. Rose, *Ancient Greek Religion*, 1946.
—— *Ancient Roman Religion*, 1948.
—— *Primitive Culture in Greece*, 1925.
—— *A Handbook of Greek Mythology*, 5th ed., 1953.
T. Zielinski, *The Religion of Ancient Greece*, 1926.

4. *Pre-Socratic Philosophy*

A. W. Benn, *Early Greek Philosophy*, 1908.
John Burnet, *Early Greek Philosophy*, 4th ed., 1930.
—— *Greek Philosophy*, Vol. I; *Thales to Plato*, 1914.

Edward Caird, *The Evolution of Theology in the Greek Philosophers,*
 1904.
H. F. Cherniss, *Aristotle's Criticism of Pre-Socratic Philosophy,* 1935.
Benjamin Farrington, *Greek Science,* Vol. I; *Thales to Aristotle,* 1944.
Kathleen Freeman, *The Pre-Socratic Philosophers,* 1946.
B. A. G. Fuller, *History of Greek Philosophy: Thales to Democritus,*
 Vol. I, 1923.
T. Gomperz, *Greek Thinkers,* Vol. I, 1905.
K. S. Guthrie, *Pythagoras,* 1919.
W. A. Heidel, *The Heroic Age of Science,* 1933.
Werner Jaeger, *The Theology of the Early Greek Philosophers,* 1947.
M. T. McClure, *The Early Philosophers of Greece,* 1935.
R. M. Scoon, *Greek Philosophy Before Plato,* 1928.
E. Zeller, *A History of Greek Philosophy from the Earliest Period to
 the Time of Socrates,* 2 Vols., 1881.

5. The Sophists, Socrates, and the Socratics

Francis M. Cornford, *Before and After Socrates,* 1932.
M. M. Dawson, *The Ethics of Socrates,* 1924.
G. Grote, *Plato and the Other Companions of Socrates,* 4 Vols., 1888.
Paul Elmer More, *Hellenistic Philosophies,* 1923.
A. K. Rogers, *The Socratic Problem,* 1933.
A. E. Taylor, *Varia Socratica,* 1911.
E. Zeller, *Socrates and the Socratic Schools,* 1885.

6. Plato

F. C. A. Anderson, *The Argument of Plato,* 1934.
E. Barker, *Greek Political Theory, Plato and His Predecessors,* 1918.
—— *Political Thought of Plato and Aristotle,* 1906.
R. S. Brumbaugh, *Plato's Mathematical Imagination,* 1954.
John Burnet, *Platonism,* 1928.
Harold F. Cherniss, *The Riddle of the Early Academy,* 1945.
—— *Aristotle's Criticism of Plato and the Academy,* Vol. I, 1944.
F. M. Cornford, *Plato and Parmenides,* 1939.
—— *Plato's Cosmology,* 1937.
—— *Plato's Theory of Knowledge,* 1935.
R. Demos, *The Philosophy of Plato,* 1939.
Warner Fite, *The Platonic Legend,* 1934.
B. A. G. Fuller, *History of Greek Philosophy: The Sophists, Socrates,
 and Plato,* Vol. II, 1931.
T. Gomperz, *Greek Thinkers,* Vols. II and III, 1905.

G. Grote, *Plato*, 1865.

Alexandre Koyré, *Discovering Plato*, 1945.

Paul Elmer More, *Platonism*, 1931.

T. Nettleship, *Lectures on the Republic of Plato*, 1914.

C. Ritter, *The Essence of Plato's Philosophy*, 1933.

Richard Robinson, *Plato's Earlier Dialectic*, 1953.

David Ross, *Plato's Theory of Ideas*, 1951.

Paul Shorey, *Platonism Ancient and Modern*, 1938.

J. A. Stewart, *The Myths of Plato*, 1905.

—— *Plato's Doctrine of the Ideas*, 1909.

A. E. Taylor, *Plato*, 1927.

—— *Platonism and Its Influence*, 1927.

E. Zeller, *Plato and the Older Academy*, 1888.

7. Aristotle

J. Burnet, *The Ethics of Aristotle*, 1909.

S. H. Butcher, *Aristotle's Theory of Poetry and the Fine Arts*, 1927.

Harold F. Cherniss, *Aristotle's Criticism of Pre-Socratic Philosophy*, 1935.

B. A. G. Fuller, *History of Greek Philosophy: Aristotle*, Vol. III, 1931.

Theodor Gomperz, *Greek Thinkers*, Vol. IV, 1912.

G. Grote, *Aristotle*, 2 Vols., 3rd ed., 1883.

Thomas Heath, *Mathematics in Aristotle*, 1949.

Werner Jaeger, *Aristotle*, 1934.

Jan Lukasiewicz, *Aristotle's Syllogistic*, 1951.

G. R. G. Mure, *Aristotle*, 1932.

W. D. Ross, *Aristotle*, 2nd ed., 1930.

A. E. Taylor, *Aristotle*, 1943.

E. Wallace, *Outlines of the Philosophy of Aristotle*, 3rd ed., 1908.

E. Zeller, *Aristotle and the Earlier Peripatetics*, 2 Vols., 1897.

8. Stoicism, Epicureanism, and Skepticism

E. V. Arnold, *Roman Stoicism*, 1911.

Cyril Bailey, *The Greek Atomists and Epicurus*, 1928.

E. R. Bevan, *Stoics and Sceptics*, 1913.

N. W. DeWitt, *Epicurus and His Philosophy*, 1954.

R. D. Hicks, *Stoic and Epicurean*, 1910.

J. Masson, *Atomic Theory of Lucretius*, 1884.

—— *Lucretius, Epicurean and Poet*, 1907-1909.

Paul Elmer More, *Hellenistic Philosophies*, 1923.

N. Nicoll, *The Greek Sceptics*, 1869.

M. M. Patrick, *The Greek Sceptics,* 1929.

H. D. Sedgwick, *The Art of Happiness, or the Teachings of Epicurus,* 1933.

—— *Marcus Aurelius,* 1921.

St. G. Stock, *Stoicism,* 1908.

A. E. Taylor, *Epicurus,* 1911.

W. Wallace, *Epicureanism,* 1880.

R. M. Wenley, *Stoicism and its Influence,* 1924.

E. Zeller, *The Stoics, Epicureans, and Sceptics,* 1892.

9. Neo-Platonism

J. Adam, *The Vitality of Platonism,* 1928.

C. Bigg, *Neoplatonism,* 1895.

T. H. Billings, *The Platonism of Philo Judaeus,* 1919.

F. H. Colson and G. H. Whittaker, *Philo.*

J. Drummond, *Philo Judaeus,* 2 Vols., 1888.

B. A. G. Fuller, *The Problem of Evil in Plotinus,* 1912.

E. R. Goodenough, *An Introduction to Philo,* 1940.

W. R. Inge, *Plotinus,* 1918.

—— *The Philosophy of Plotinus,* 2 Vols., 3rd ed., 1929.

Joseph Katz, *Plotinus' Search for the Good,* 1950.

Philip Merlan, *From Platonism to Neoplatonism,* 1953.

R. B. Tollinton, *Alexandrine Teaching on the Universe,* 1932.

T. Whittaker, *The Neo-Platonists,* 2nd ed., 1918.

H. A. Wolfson, *Philo,* 2 Vols., 1947.

10. History of Christian Thought

S. Angus, *The Mystery-Religions and Christianity,* 1925.

—— *The Religious Quests of the Graeco-Roman World,* 1929.

L. Bertrand, *St. Augustine,* 1914.

E. Bevan, *Hellenism and Christianity,* 1921.

C. Bigg, *The Christian Platonists of Alexandria,* 1888.

Edwin A. Burtt, *Types of Religious Philosophy,* rev. ed., 1951.

Carl Clemen, *Primitive Christianity and Its Non-Jewish Sources,* 1912.

C. N. Cochrane, *Christianity and Classical Culture,* 1944.

C. M. Duncan-Jones, *An Outline of Church History from the Acts of the Apostles to the Reformation,* 3 Vols., 1938.

W. Fairweather, *Origen and Greek Patristic Theology,* 1901.

George P. Fisher, *The Beginnings of Christianity,* 1891.

—— *The Reformation,* 1906.

—— *History of Christian Doctrine,* 1896.

—— *History of the Christian Church*, 1915.

T. R. Glover, *The Conflict of Religions in the Early Roman Empire*, 2nd ed., 1909.

E. R. Goodenough, *The Theology of Justin Martyr*, 1923.

K. R. Hagenbach, *History of the Church in the Eighteenth and Nineteenth Centuries*, 2 Vols., 1869.

—— *Text-Book of the History of Doctrines*, 2 Vols., 1861.

William R. Halliday, *The Pagan Background of Early Christianity*, 1925.

Adolf Harnack, *The Mission and Expansion of Christianity*, 2 Vols., 1908.

—— *History of Dogma*, 7 Vols., 1894-1899.

—— *What Is Christianity?*, 2nd ed., 1901.

Edwin Hatch, *The Influence of Greek Ideas and Usages upon the Christian Church*, 1907.

F. J. Foakes-Jackson and K. Lake, *The Beginnings of Christianity*, 5 Vols.

J. H. Kurtz, *History of the Christian Church*, 3 Vols., 1888.

Kenneth S. Latourette, *The First Five Centuries*, 1937.

—— *A History of Christianity*, 1953.

Jules Lebreton and J. Zeiller, *The History of the Primitive Church*, 2 Vols., 1942, 1944.

F. Legge, *Forerunners and Rivals of Christianity*, 1915.

H. R. Mackintosh, *Types of Modern Theology: Schleiermacher to Barth*, 1937.

J. McCabe, *St. Augustine and His Age*, 1902.

A. C. McGiffert, *A History of Christian Thought*, 2 Vols., 1932, 1933.

—— *Protestant Thought Before Kant*, 1936.

—— *The God of the Early Christians*, 1924.

—— *A History of Christianity in the Apostolic Age*, 1897.

—— *The Rise of Modern Religious Ideas*, 1915.

Wilhelm Moeller, *History of the Christian Church in the Middle Ages*, 1893.

H. Richard Niebuhr, *Christ and Culture*, 1951.

Reinhold Niebuhr, *The Nature and Destiny of Man*, 2 Vols., 1941.

A. D. Nock, *Early Gentile Christianity and Its Hellenistic Background*.

Anders Nygren, *Agape and Eros*, rev. ed., 1953.

Robert L. Ottley, *The Doctrine of the Incarnation*, 4th ed., rev., 1908.

Otto Pfleiderer, *The Development of Christianity*, 1910.

—— *The Development of Theology in Germany Since Kant, and Its Progress in Great Britain Since 1825*, 1890.

—— *Primitive Christianity*, 4 Vols., 1906-1911.

Hastings Rashdall, *The Idea of Atonement in Christian Theology*, 1920.

Albert Schweitzer, *Quest of the Historical Jesus*, new ed., 1948.

R. Seeberg, *Text-Book of the History of Doctrines*, 2 Vols., 1905, 1 Vol. ed., 1952.

Rudolf Sohm, *Outlines of Church History*, 1895.

R. H. Tawney, *Religion and the Rise of Capitalism*, 1926.

Paul Tillich, *The Protestant Era*, 1951.

J. Tixeront, *History of Dogmas*, 3 Vols., 1910.

Ernst Troeltsch, *The Social Teachings of the Christian Churches*, 2 Vols., 1931.

Max Weber, *The Protestant Ethic and the Spirit of Capitalism*, 1930.

Paul Wernle, *The Beginnings of Christianity*, 2 Vols., 1904.

E. M. Wilbur, *A History of Unitarianism: Socinianism and Its Antecedents*, 1945.

11. *History of Jewish Thought*

Jacob Agus, *Modern Philosophies of Judaism*, 1941.

Salo W. Baron, ed., *Essays on Maimonides*, 1941.

—— *A Social and Religious History of the Jews*, 7 Vols.; by Dec., 1954, only Vols. I-II, "Ancient Times," 1952.

Norman Bentwich, *Hellenism*, 1919.

—— *Philo Judaeus of Alexandria*, 1910.

E. R. Bevan and C. Singer, eds., *The Legacy of Israel*, 1928.

A. B. Davidson, *The Theology of the Old Testament*, 1904.

Louis Finkelstein, ed., *The Jews: Their History, Culture, and Religion*, 4 Vols., 1949.

Abraham Geiger, *Judaism and Its History*, 1911.

Erwin R. Goodenough, *By Light, Light; The Mystic Gospel of Hellenistic Judaism*, 1935.

Heinrich Graetz, *History of the Jews*; 11 Vols., 1853-1875; 6 Vols., 1891, 1949.

Samson Raphael Hirsch, *The Nineteen Letters of Ben Uziel*, 1836, 1899.

Isaac Husik, *A History of Medieval Jewish Philosophy*, 1916.

—— *Philosophical Essays*, 1952.

Mordecai M. Kaplan, *Judaism as a Civilization*, 1934.

—— *The Meaning of God in Modern Jewish Religion*, 1937.

Kaufmann Kohler, *Jewish Theology Systematically and Historically Considered*, 1918.

Moritz Lazarus, *Ethics of Judaism*, 2 Vols., 1900, 1901.

Duncan Black Macdonald, *The Hebrew Philosophical Genius; A Vindication*, 1936.

Henry Malter, *Saadia Gaon, His Life and Works*, 1921.

G. F. Moore, *Judaism in the First Centuries of the Christian Era*, 3 Vols., 1927-1930.

David Neumark, *The Philosophy of the Bible*, 1918.

—— *History of the Dogmas of Judaism*, 2 Vols., 1913, 1919.

—— *Essays in Jewish Philosophy*, 1929.

Max Radin, *The Jews Among the Greeks and Romans*, 1915.

Jacob S. Raisin, *The Haskalah Movement in Russia*, 1913.

Solomon Schechter, *Studies in Judaism*, 3 Series: 1896, 1908, 1924.

—— *Some Aspects of Rabbinic Theology*, 1909.

Gershom G. Scholem, *Major Trends in Jewish Mysticism*, 1941.

Emil Schürer, *History of the Jewish People in the Time of Jesus Christ*, 5 Vols., 1886-1890.

Nahum Slouschz, *The Renascence of Hebrew Literature* (1743-1885), 1909.

Nahum Sokolow, *A History of Zionism*, 2 Vols., 1912.

Hermann L. Strack, *Introduction to the Talmud and Midrash*, 5th ed., 1920, 1931.

Meyer Waxman, *A History of Jewish Literature*, 4 Vols., 1930, 1933, 1936, 1941.

Harry A. Wolfson, *Philo; Foundations of Religious Philosophy in Judaism*, 1947.

David Yellin and Israel Abrahams, *Maimonides*, 1903.

12. *Medieval Philosophy and Science*

Henry Bett, *Johannes Scotus Eriugena*, 1925.

Meyrick H. Carré, *Realists and Nominalists*, 1946.

Frederick Copleston, *Medieval Philosophy*, 1952.

C. G. Crump and E. F. Jacobs, eds., *The Legacy of the Middle Ages*, 1926.

M. C. D'Arcy, *Thomas Aquinas*, 1930.

S. C. Easton, *Roger Bacon and His Search for a Universal Science*, 1952.

E. Gilson, *The Philosophy of St. Thomas Aquinas*, 1929.

—— *The Spirit of Medieval Philosophy*, 1936.

—— *Moral Values and the Moral Life*, 1931.

—— *Reason and Revelation in the Middle Ages*, 1938.

M. J. Grajewski, *The Formal Distinction of Duns Scotus*, 1944.

C. R. S. Harris, *Duns Scotus*, 2 Vols., 1927.

Charles H. Haskins, *Studies in the History of Medieval Science*, 2nd ed., 1927.

I. Husik, *A History of Mediaeval Jewish Philosophy*, 1941.

Ernest A. Moody, *The Logic of William of Ockham*, 1936.

Joseph Rickaby, *Scholasticism*, 1908.

J. M. Rigg, *St. Anselm of Canterbury*, 1896.

M. Rule, *The Life and Times of St. Anselm*, 2 Vols., 1883.

George Sarton, *Introduction to the History of Science*, Vol. II, 1931.

D. E. Sharp, *Franciscan Philosophy at Oxford in the Thirteenth Century*, 1930.

J. G. Sikes, *Peter Abailard*, 1932.

H. O. Taylor, *The Medieval Mind*, 2 Vols., new ed., 1949.

Lynn Thorndike, *A History of Magic and Experimental Science*, 6 Vols., 1934-43.

S. C. Tornay, *Ockham: Studies and Selections*, 1938.

W. J. Townsend, *The Great Schoolmen of the Middle Ages*, 1922.

A. C. Welch, *Anselm and His Work*, 1901.

Wulf, M. de, *History of Medieval Philosophy*, 2 Vols., 3rd ed., 1935-1938.

F. W. Woodruff, *Roger Bacon*, 1938.

13. *History of Modern Philosophy and Science*

E. N. da C. Andrade, *Science in the Seventeenth Century*, 1938.

N. Berdyaev, *The Russian Idea*, 1948.

E. A. Burtt, *The Metaphysical Foundations of Modern Physical Science*, 1927.

H. Butterfield, *The Origins of Modern Science*, 1949.

Mary Whiton Calkins, *The Persistent Problems of Philosophy*, 5th ed., 1925.

Ernst Cassirer, *Substance and Function*, 1927.

—— *Philosophy of the Renaissance*, 1927.

—— *The Problem of Knowledge*, 1950.

A. D'Abro, *The Evolution of Scientific Thought from Newton to Einstein*, 2nd ed., 1950.

Albert Einstein and Leopold Infeld, *The Evolution of Physics*, 1938.

C. W. Eliot, *English Philosophers of the Seventeenth and Eighteenth Century*, 1910.

R. Falkenberg, *History of Modern Philosophy*, 1893.

Kuno Fischer, *History of Modern Philosophy*, 1887.

Philipp Frank, *Between Physics and Philosophy*, 1941.

—— *Foundations of Physics*, 1946.

Étienne Gilson, *The Unity of Philosophical Experience*, 1937.

J. A. Gunn, *Modern French Philosophy*, 1922.

Harald Höffding, *A Brief History of Modern Philosophy*, 1912.

—— *History of Modern Philosophy*, 2 Vols., 1924.

—— *Modern Philosophers*, 1915.

C. E. M. Joad, *Introduction to Modern Philosophy*, 1924.

Lucien Levy-Bruhl, *History of Modern Philosophy in France*, 1899.

Ernst Mach, *The Science of Mechanics*, 1919, 1942.

K. Martin, *French Liberal Thought in the Eighteenth Century*, 1929.

T. G. Masaryk, *The Spirit of Russia*, 2 Vols., 1919.

George H. Mead, *Movements of Thought in the Nineteenth Century*, 1936.

John T. Merz, *A History of European Thought in the Nineteenth Century*, 4 Vols., 1896-1904.

Rudolf Metz, *A Hundred Years of British Philosophy*, 1938.

J. H. Muirhead, *The Platonic Tradition in Anglo-Saxon Philosophy*, 1931.

P. N. Milyukov, *Outlines of Russian Culture*, 1948.

R. B. Perry, *Present Philosophical Tendencies*, 1912.

—— *Philosophy of the Recent Past*, 1926.

O. Pfleiderer, *Development of Theology in Germany since Kant*, 3rd ed., 1909.

H. T. Pledge, *Science Since 1500*, 2nd ed., 1946.

J. H. Randall, Jr., *Making of the Modern Mind*, rev. ed., 1940.

A. K. Rogers, *English and American Philosophy Since 1800*, 1923.

Josiah Royce, *Lectures on Modern Idealism*, 1919.

Guido de Ruggiero, *Modern Philosophy*, 1921.

George de Santillana and Edgar Zilsel, *The Development of Rationalism and Empiricism*.

E. A. Singer, *Modern Thinkers and Present Problems*, 1923.

William R. Sorley, *History of English Philosophy*, 1937.

Leslie Stephen, *History of English Thought in the Eighteenth Century*, 2 Vols., 1876.

Lynn Thorndike, *A History of Magic and Experimental Science*, 6 Vols., 1934-43.

J. Wahl, *The Pluralistic Philosophies of England and America*, 1925.

Alfred N. Whitehead, *Science and the Modern World*, 1925.

Abraham Wolf, *A History of Science, Technology, and Philosophy in the Sixteenth and Seventeenth Centuries*, 1935.

—— *A History of Science, etc., in the Eighteenth Century*, 1938.

W. K. Wright, *A History of Modern Philosophy*, 1941.

V. V. Zenkovsky, *A History of Russian Philosophy*, 2 Vols., 1953.

14. *The Renaissance and Reformation*

A. Armitage, *Copernicus, the Founder of Modern Astronomy*, 1938.

W. Boulting, *Giordano Bruno*, 1916.

J. Burckhardt, *The Civilization of the Renaissance in Italy*, 1937.

E. A. Burtt, *The Metaphysical Foundations of Modern Physical Science*, 1936.

E. Cassirer, P. Kristeller, J. H. Randall, Jr., *The Renaissance Philosophy of Man*, 1948.

J. H. M. D'Aubigne, *History of the Reformation of the Sixteenth Century*, 5 Vols., n. d.

W. K. Ferguson, *The Renaissance in Historical Thought*, 1948.

George P. Fisher, *The Reformation*, 1906.

H. A. L. Fisher, *Renaissance, Reformation, Reason*, 1935.

E. M. Hulme, *The Renaissance, the Protestant Revolution, and the Catholic Reformation*, rev. ed., 1924.

T. M. Lindsay, *A History of the Reformation*, 2 Vols., 1928, 1936.

H. S. Lucas, *The Renaissance and the Reformation*, 1934.

E. McCurdy, *The Mind of Leonardo da Vinci*, 1928.

A. C. McGiffert, *Protestant Thought Before Kant*, 1936.

J. L. McIntyre, *Giordano Bruno*, 1903.

N. A. Robb, *Neoplatonism of the Italian Renaissance*, 1935.

Ralph Roeder, *Man of the Renaissance*, 1933.

Preserved Smith, *The Age of the Reformation*, 1920.

J. A. Symonds, *Renaissance in Italy*, 1908.

R. H. Tawney, *Religion and the Rise of Capitalism*, 1926.

Henry Osborn Taylor, *Thought and Expression in the Sixteenth Century*, 2nd ed., 1930.

W. H. Woodward, *Studies in Education During the Age of the Renaissance*, 1906.

15. *Continental Rationalism*

Samuel Alexander, *Spinoza and Time*, 1921.

David Bidney, *The Psychology and Ethics of Spinoza*, 1940.

H. W. Carr, *Leibniz*, 1929.

Kuno Fischer, *Descartes and His School*, 1887.

A. B. Gibson, *The Philosophy of Descartes*, 1932.

E. S. Haldane, *Descartes, His Life and Times*, 1905.

H. H. Joachim, *A Study of the Ethics of Spinoza*, 1901.

S. V. Keeling, *Descartes*, 1934.

J. Maritain, *The Dream of Descartes*, 1944.

R. McKeon, *The Philosophy of Spinoza*, 1928.

S. H. Mellone, *The Dawn of Modern Thought*, 1930.

J. Merz, *Leibniz*, 1884.

F. Pollock, *Spinoza, His Life and Philosophy*, 1912.

R. Roth, *Spinoza*, 1929.

Bertrand Russell, *A Critical Exposition of the Philosophy of Leibniz*, 2nd ed., 1937.

Norman Kemp Smith, *Studies in the Cartesian Philosophy*, 1902.

H. F. Stewart, *Secret of Pascal*, 1941.

C. C. J. Webb, *Pascal's Philosophy of Religion*, 1929.

H. A. Wolfson, *The Philosophy of Spinoza*, 2 Vols., 1934.

16. *British Empiricism*

R. I. Aaron, *John Locke*, 1937.

S. Alexander, *Locke*, 1908.

F. H. Anderson, *The Philosophy of Francis Bacon*, 1948.

R. W. Church, *Hume's Theory of the Understanding*, 1935.

K. Fischer, *Francis Bacon of Verulam*, 1857.

A. Campbell Fraser, *Berkeley*, 1899.

—— *Locke*, 1901.

James Gibson, *Locke's Theory of Knowledge and Its Historical Relations*, 1937.

Charles W. Hendel, *Studies in the Philosophy of David Hume*, 1925.

G. D. Hicks, *Berkeley*, 1932.

G. A. Johnston, *The Development of Berkeley's Philosophy*, 1923.

W. Knight, *Hume*, 1905.

B. L. Laing, *Hume*, 1932.

John Laird, *Hobbes*, 1934.

—— *Hume's Philosophy of Human Nature*, 1932.

B. Landry, *Hobbes*, 1930.

C. R. Morris, *Locke, Berkeley, and Hume*, 1931.

J. Nicol, *Bacon*, 1888-1889.

H. H. Price, *Hume's Theory of the External World*, 1940.

Norman Kemp Smith, *The Philosophy of David Hume*, 1941.

L. Stephen, *Hobbes*, 1904.

A. E. Taylor, *Hobbes*, 1908.

John D. Wild, *George Berkeley*, 1936.

17. *Continental Romanticism and Idealism*

G. E. Abraham, *Nietzsche*, 1933.

R. Adamson, *Fichte*, 1881.

A. F. Amiel, *Jean Jacques Rousseau*, 1922.

Crane Brinton, *Nietzsche*, 1941.

Edward Caird, *Critical Account of the Philosophy of Kant*, 1877.

—— *Hegel*, 1896.

Ernst Cassirer, *Rousseau, Kant, Goethe,* 1945.

A. Cobban, *Rousseau and the Modern State,* 1934.

F. Copleston, *Friedrich Nietzsche, Philosopher of Culture,* 1942.

A. C. Ewing, *A Short Commentary on Kant's Critique of Pure Reason,* 1938.

Kuno Fischer, *Arthur Schopenhauer,* 1893.

E. Forster-Nietzsche, *The Lonely Nietzsche,* 1915.

W. T. Jones, *Morality and Freedom in the Philosophy of Immanuel Kant,* 1940.

A. D. Lindsay, *Kant,* 1934.

W. Lowrie, *Kierkegaard,* 1938.

J. M. E. McTaggart, *A Commentary on Hegel's Logic,* 1931.

G. R. G. Mure, *An Introduction to Hegel,* 1940.

F. Paulsen, *Immanuel Kant: His Life and Doctrine,* 1902.

Herbert Marcuse, *Reason and Revolution,* 1941.

Herbert J. Paton, *The Categorical Imperative, A Study of Kant's Moral Philosophy,* 1947.

—— *Kant's Metaphysic of Experience,* 2 Vols., 1936.

H. A. Prichard, *Kant's Theory of Knowledge,* 1909.

A. S. Pringle-Pattison, *From Kant to Hegel,* 1924.

D. Sevenson, *Something about Kierkegaard,* 1941.

Norman Kemp Smith, *A Commentary on Kant's Critique of Pure Reason,* 2nd ed., 1929.

W. T. Stace, *The Philosophy of Hegel,* 1924.

E. B. Talbot, *Fundamental Principle of Fichte's Philosophy,* 1906.

R. Thomte, *Kierkegaard's Philosophy of Religion,* 1948.

C. C. J. Webb, *Kant's Philosophy of Religion,* 1926.

T. D. Weldon, *Introduction to Kant's Critique of Pure Reason,* 1945.

A. Wolf, *The Philosophy of Nietzsche,* 1915.

H. Zimmern, *Schopenhauer, His Life and Philosophy,* 1932.

18. *Scottish Realism, Utilitarianism, Positivism, and Marxism*

H. P. Adams, *Karl Marx in His Earlier Writings,* 1940.

V. Adoratsky, *Dialectical Materialism,* 1934.

E. Albee, *Utilitarianism,* 1902.

I. Berlin, *Karl Marx, His Life and Environment,* 1948.

M. M. Bober, *Karl Marx's Interpretation of History,* 1927.

N. I. Bukharin, *Historical Materialism,* 1925.

E. Caird, *The Social Philosophy and Religion of Auguste Comte,* 2nd ed., 1893.

R. L. Hawkins, *Positivism in the United States,* 1938.

S. Hook, *From Hegel to Marx,* 1935.

—— *Towards the Understanding of Karl Marx*, 1933.

V. I. Lenin, *Materialism and Empirio-Criticism*, 1908.

—— *State and Revolution*, 1917.

L. Lévy-Bruhl, *Philosophy of Auguste Comte*, 1903.

J. McCosh, *Scotch Philosophy*, 1875.

J. S. Mill, *Auguste Comte and Positivism*, 4th ed., 1891.

W. R. Sorley, *History of English Philosophy*, 1937.

L. Stephen, *The English Utilitarians*, 3 Vols., 1902.

J. Veitch, *Hamilton*, 1882.

J. Watson, *Comte, Mill, and Spencer*, 1895.

19. Latin American Philosophy

William R. Crawford, *A Century of Latin American Thought*, 1944.

Institute of Latin American Studies, *Inter-American Intellectual Exchanges*, 1943.

—— *Intellectual Trends in Latin America*, 1945.

John T. Lanning, *Academic Culture in the Spanish Colonies*, 1940.

Monelisa Lina Pérez-Marchand, *A Critical Study of Some Currents of Contemporary Philosophical Thought in Latin America*, 1940

Patrick Romanell, *The Making of the Mexican Mind*, 1954.

Aníbal Sánchez Reulet, *Contemporary Latin-American Philosophy*, 1954.

José Vasconcelos, *Aspects of Mexican Civilization*, 1926.

20. Neo-Scholasticism

Charles R. Baschab, *A Manual of Neo-Scholastic Philosophy*, 1923.

Gerardo Bruni, *Progressive Scholasticism*, 1929.

Charles A. Hart, ed., *Aspects of the New Scholastic Philosophy*, 1932.

Désiré Joseph Mercier *et al.*, *A Manual of Modern Scholastic Philosophy*, 2 Vols., 1916-1917.

Joseph L. Perrier, *The Revival of Scholastic Philosophy in the Nineteenth Century*, 1909.

R. P. Phillips, *Modern Thomistic Philosophy*, 2 Vols., 1934.

James H. Ryan, *A Student's Library of Neo-Scholastic Philosophy*, 1928.

Claude L. Vogel, ed., *Psychology and the Franciscan School*, 1932.

John S. Zybura, ed., *Present-Day Thinkers and the New Scholasticism*, 1926.

21. Logical Empiricism

Gustav Bergmann, *The Metaphysics of Logical Positivism*, 1954.

Joergen Joergensen, *The Development of Logical Empiricism*, 1951.

Victor Kraft, *The Vienna Circle*, 1953.

Hans Reichenbach, *The Rise of Scientific Philosophy*, 1951.
George de Santillana and Edgar Zilsel, *The Development of Rationalism and Empiricism*, 1941.
L. S. Stebbing, *Logical Positivism and Analysis*, 1933.
J. R. Weinberg, *An Examination of Logical Positivism*, 1936.

22. Existentialism

H. J. Blackham, *Six Existentialist Thinkers*, 1952.
James Collins, *The Existentialists*, 1952.
P. Foulguié, *Existentialism*, 1948.
M. Grene, *Dreadful Freedom*, 1948.
Ralph Harper, *Existentialism*, 1948.
E. Mounier, *Existentialist Philosophies*, 1948.
G. Ruggiero, *Existentialism, Disintegration of Man's Soul*, 1948.
Jean-Paul Sartre, *Existentialism*, 1947.
Alfred Stern, *Sartre, His Philosophy and Psychoanalysis*, 1954.
R. Troisfontaines, *Existentialism and Christian Thought*, 1950.
Jean Wahl, *A Short History of Existentialism*, 1949.

23. American Philosophy

Joseph L. Blau, *Men and Movements in American Philosophy*, 1952.
M. R. Cohen, *American Thought*, 1954.
Merle Curti, *The Growth of American Thought*, 2nd ed., 1951.
Marvin Farber, ed., *Philosophic Thought in France and the United States*, 1950.
R. L. Hawkins, *Positivism in the United States*, 1938.
V. L. Parrington, *Main Currents in American Thought*, 3 Vols., 1927-1930.
I. W. Riley, *American Thought*, 1923.
Herbert W. Schneider, *A History of American Philosophy*, 1946.
H. G. Townsend, *Philosophical Ideas in the United States*, 1934.
W. H. Werkmeister, *A History of Philosophical Ideas in America*, 1949.
P. Wiener, *Evolution and the Founders of Pragmatism*, 1949.

24. Miscellaneous Works on Recent and Contemporary Philosophy

G. P. Adams and W. P. Montague, eds., *Contemporary American Philosophy*, 2 Vols., 1930 (personal statements).
I. Benrubi, *Contemporary Thought in France*, 1926.
P. A. Bertocci, *The Empirical Argument for God in Late British Philosophy*, 1938.
W. Brock, *An Introduction to Contemporary German Philosophy*, 1935.

M. Farber, ed., *Philosophic Thought in France and the United States,*
 1950.

R. F. A. Hoernlé, *Studies in Contemporary Metaphysics,* 1920.

W. T. Jones, *Contemporary Thought in Germany,* 1931.

H. M. Kallen and S. Hook, eds., *American Philosophy Today and
 Tomorrow,* 1935.

O. Külpe, *Philosophy of the Present in Germany,* 1913.

A. O. Lovejoy, *The Revolt against Dualism,* 1930.

G. H. Mead, *The Philosophy of the Present,* 1932.

J. H. Muirhead, ed., *Contemporary British Philosophy,* 2 Vols., first
 series 1924, second series 1926 (personal statements).

Santayana, G., *Winds of Doctrine,* 1913.

Stebbing, L. S., *Pragmatism and French Voluntarism,* 1914.

—— *Philosophy and the Physicists,* 1937.

Appendix II

SOME CONVENIENT ANTHOLOGIES
OF PHILOSOPHICAL LITERATURE

The following titles are anthologies of important source materials in philosophy. They are given for the convenience of the student, but are not intended to divert him from the complete works of the major philosophers. Complete works are often available in numerous and sometimes definitive editions and are easily accessible in the libraries. Collections of selected writings of the major individual philosophers are available, some in inexpensive editions, but are not included here.

1. History of Philosophy

Charles M. Bakewell, *Source Book in Ancient Philosophy*, 1907.

D. J. Bronstein, Y. H. Krikorian, P. P. Wiener, *Basic Problems of Philosophy*, 1947.

E. A. Burtt, *The English Philosophers from Bacon to Mill*, 1939.

G. H. Clark, *Readings in Hellenistic Philosophy*, 1940.

Irwin Edman and H. W. Schneider, *Landmarks for Beginners in Philosophy*, 1941.

Kathleen Freeman, *Ancilla to the Pre-Socratic Philosophers*, a complete translation of the Fragments in Diels, *Fragmente der Vorsokratiker*, 1948.

G. Kennedy, *Bacon-Hobbes-Locke* (selections), 1937.

Richard McKeon, *Selections from Medieval Philosophers*, 2 Vols., 1930.

Milton Nahm, *Selections from Early Greek Philosophy*, 3rd ed., 1947.

W. I. Oates, *Stoic and Epicurean Philosophers*, 1940.

Benjamin Rand, *The Modern Classical Philosophers*, 1924.

J. H. Randall, Jr., J. Buchler, and E. U. Shirk, *Readings in Philosophy*, 2nd ed., 1950.

Daniel S. Robinson, *An Anthology of Modern Philosophy*, 1931.

T. V. Smith, *Philosophers Speak for Themselves*, 1934.

—— and M. Grene, *From Descartes to Kant*, 1940.

2. *Contemporary Philosophy*

James L. Jarrett and Sterling M. McMurrin, *Contemporary Philosophy*, 1954.

Daniel S. Robinson, *An Anthology of Recent Philosophy*, 1929.

Dagobert D. Runes, *Twentieth Century Philosophy*, 1943.

3. *Science and Philosophy of Science*

Cambridge Readings in the Literature of Science, 1924, 1929.

Herbert Feigl and May Brodbeck, *Readings in the Philosophy of Science*, 1953.

—— and Wilfrid Sellars, *Readings in Philosophical Analysis*, 1949.

John W. Knedler, Jr., *Masterworks of Science*, 1949.

H. Shapely, S. Rapport and H. Wright, *A Treasury of Science*, 1943.

Ivor Thomas, *Selections Illustrating the History of Greek Mathematics*, 2 Vols., 1939.

Philip P. Wiener, *Readings in Philosophy of Science*, 1953.

4. *Religion and Philosophy of Religion*

Henry Bettenson, *Documents of the Christian Church*, 1943, 1947.

Salo W. Baron and Joseph L. Blau, *Judaism: Postbiblical and Talmudic Period*, 1954.

Daniel J. Bronstein and Harold M. Schulweis, *Approaches to the Philosophy of Religion*, 1954.

F. M. Cornford, *Greek Religious Thought*, 1923.

Frederick C. Grant, *Hellenistic Religions*, 1953.

Charles Hartshorne and William L. Reese, *Philosophers Speak of God*, 1953.

John A. Mourant, *Readings in the Philosophy of Religion*, 1954.

5. *Ethics and Esthetics*

Ruth N. Anshen, *Moral Principles of Action*, 1951.

A. I. Meldon, *Ethical Theories*, 1950.

H. D. Oakeley, *Greek Ethical Thought*, 1925.

Melvin Rader, *A Modern Book of Esthetics*, rev. ed., 1952.

Benjamin Rand, *The Classical Moralists*, 1909.

Selby-Bigge, *British Moralists*, 1897.

Wilfrid Sellars and John Hospers, *Readings in Ethical Theory*, 1952.

Eliseo Vivas and Murray Krieger, *The Problems of Aesthetics*, 1953.

6. *Logic and Language*

Max Black, *Philosophical Analysis,* 1950.

A. G. N. Flew, *Logic and Language,* First Series 1951, Second Series 1953.

Irving J. Lee, *The Language of Wisdom and Folly,* 1949.

Leonard Linsky, *Semantics and the Philosophy of Language,* 1952.

7. *American Philosophy*

P. R. Anderson and M. H. Fisch, *Philosophy in America,* 1939.

Joseph L. Blau, *American Philosophic Addresses, 1700-1900,* 1946.

Max H. Fisch, *Classic American Philosophers,* 1951.

Walter G. Muelder and Laurence Sears, *The Development of American Philosophy,* 1940.

Appendix III

SUGGESTED READINGS IN THE
HISTORY OF PHILOSOPHY

An acquaintance with the history of philosophy can be attained only by reading the leading works of at least the major philosophers. *Reading about philosophy* should never be accepted as a substitute for *reading philosophy*. The following works are recommended to the serious beginning student.

1. *Ancient*

Heraclitus, *Fragments*.
Parmenides, *Fragments*.
Democritus, *Fragments*.
Plato, *Symposium, Phaedo, Republic, Theaetetus, Parmenides*.
Aristotle, *On the Categories (Organon), Metaphysics, Nicomachean Ethics, Poetics*.
Epicurus, *Letters* and *Fragments*.
Lucretius, *On the Nature of Things*.
Plotinus, *The Enneads*.
Epictetus, *The Discourses*.
Marcus Aurelius, *The Meditations*.
Origen, *First Principles,* Books I-III.
Sextus Empiricus, *Against the Dogmatists*.

2. *Medieval*

Augustine, *The Confessions, The Enchiridion, On the Trinity*.
Boethius, *The Consolation of Philosophy*.
Anselm, *Proslogium, Monologium*.
Maimonides, *Guide for the Perplexed*.
Aquinas, *Summa Theologica,* Part I, Questions 1-43; First part of Part II, Questions 49-89.
—— *Summa Contra Gentiles,* Book III, Chapters 1-113.

Occam, Selections on logic, theory of knowledge, metaphysics, etc., edited by Stephen C. Tornay.

3. *Modern*

Copernicus, *Concerning the Revolutions of the Heavenly Bodies.*

Bacon, *Novum Organum.*

Galileo, *Dialogues Concerning Two New Sciences.*

Hobbes, *Leviathan.*

Descartes, *Discourse on Method, Meditations.*

Pascal, *Pensées.*

Spinoza, *Ethics, Tractatus Theologico-Politicus, Correspondence.*

Locke, *An Essay Concerning Human Understanding, Reasonableness of Christianity, Two Treatises on Government.*

Newton, Selections on natural philosophy, etc., edited by H. S. Thayer.

Leibniz, *Monadology, New Essays on the Human Understanding, Discourse on Metaphysics, Correspondence with Arnauld.*

Berkeley, *The Principles of Human Knowledge, Three Dialogues Between Hylas and Philonous.*

Edwards, *The Freedom of the Will.*

Hume, *A Treatise of Human Nature, An Enquiry Concerning Human Understanding, Dialogues Concerning Natural Religion.*

Rousseau, *The Social Contract.*

Kant, *Critique of Pure Reason, Prolegomena to Any Future Metaphysics, Fundamental Principles of the Metaphysic of Morals.*

Bentham, *An Introduction to the Principles of Morals and Legislation.*

Fichte, *The Vocation of Man.*

Hegel, *The Philosophy of History, Lectures on Esthetics, The Phenomenology of the Spirit.*

Schelling, *System of Transcendental Idealism.*

Schopenhauer, *The World as Will and Idea.*

Comte, *Positive Philosophy* (selections).

Mill, *System of Logic, On Liberty, Utilitarianism.*

Darwin, *Origin of Species.*

Kierkegaard, *Concluding Unscientific Postscript, The Concept of Dread.*

Marx, *The Communist Manifesto.*

Nietzsche, *Beyond Good and Evil.*

4. *Recent and Contemporary*

Peirce, Selected writings edited by J. Buchler.

James, *Pragmatism, A Pluralistic Universe.*

Bradley, *Appearance and Reality, Ethical Studies.*
Bowne, *Personalism.*
Bosanquet, *The Principle of Individuality and Value.*
Royce, *The World and the Individual, The Philosophy of Loyalty.*
Bergson, *An Introduction to Metaphysics, Two Sources of Morality and Religion.*
Alexander, *Space, Time and Deity.*
Dewey, *Experience and Nature, The Quest for Certainty, A Common Faith, Logic: The Theory of Inquiry, Theory of Valuation.*
Husserl, *Ideas.*
Whitehead, *Science and the Modern World, Process and Reality, Adventures of Ideas.*
Santayana, *Life of Reason, Scepticism and Animal Faith.*
Schiller, *Humanism, Studies in Humanism.*
Unamuno, *The Tragic Sense of Life.*
Croce, *Aesthetic as Science of Expression and General Linguistic, History as the Story of Liberty.*
Russell, *Our Knowledge of the External World, An Inquiry into Meaning and Truth, Human Knowledge: Its Scope and Limits.*
Montague, *The Ways of Knowing, Belief Unbound.*
Moore, *Philosophical Studies.*
Cassirer, *Essay on Man.*
Perry, *Realms of Value.*
N. Hartmann, *Ethics.*
Ross, *Foundations of Ethics.*
Buber, *Eclipse of God.*
Maritain, *The Degrees of Knowledge, True Humanism.*
Lewis, *An Analysis of Knowledge and Valuation.*
Jaspers, *Man in the Modern Age.*
Ortega y Gassett, *The Modern Theme, Revolt of the Masses.*
Broad, *Scientific Thought.*
Wittgenstein, *Tractatus Logico-Philosophicus.*
Heidegger, *Existence and Being* (essays).
Carnap, *Meaning and Necessity.*

Appendix IV

SOME OF THE WORKS OF RECENT AND CONTEMPORARY PHILOSOPHERS

1. *American Philosophers*

R. Carnap, *The Logical Syntax of Language,* 1934.
—— *Meaning and Necessity,* 1947.
—— *Logical Foundations of Probability,* 1950.
J. Dewey, *The Study of Ethics,* 1894.
—— *The Significance of the Problem of Knowledge,* 1902.
—— *Studies in Logical Theory,* 1903.
—— *Essays in Experimental Logic,* 1916.
—— *Democracy and Education,* 1916.
—— *Human Nature and Conduct,* 1922.
—— *Experience and Nature,* 1925.
—— *The Quest for Certainty,* 1929.
—— *A Common Faith,* 1934.
—— *Art as Experience,* 1934.
—— *Logic, The Theory of Inquiry,* 1938.
—— *Theory of Valuation,* 1939.
—— *Knowing and the Known* (with A. Bentley), 1949.
G. H. Howison, *The Conception of God* (with Royce and others), 1897.
—— *The Limits of Evolution and Other Essays Illustrating the Metaphysical Theory of Personal Idealism,* 1901, 1904.
W. James, *Principles of Psychology,* 1890.
—— *The Will to Believe,* 1897.
—— *Varieties of Religious Experience,* 1902.
—— *Pragmatism,* 1907.
—— *A Pluralistic Universe,* 1909.
C. I. Lewis, *Mind and the World Order,* 1929.
—— *An Analysis of Knowledge and Valuation,* 1946.

G. H. Mead, *Mind, Self, and Society*, 1934.
—— *Philosophy of the Act*, 1938.
W. P. Montague, *The New Realism* (with others), 1912.
—— *The Ways of Knowing*, 1925.
—— *The Ways of Things*, 1940.
R. B. Perry, *General Theory of Value*, 2nd ed., 1950.
—— *Realms of Value*, 1954.
J. Royce, *The Religious Aspect of Philosophy*, 1885.
—— *The Spirit of Modern Philosophy*, 1892.
—— *The Conception of God* (with Howison and others), 1897.
—— *The World and the Individual*, 2 Vols., 1900-1901.
—— *The Philosophy of Loyalty*, 1908.
—— *The Problem of Christianity*, 2 Vols., 1913.
G. Santayana, *Life of Reason*, 1905, latest ed., 1932.
—— *The Sense of Beauty*, 1896.
—— *Character and Opinion in the United States*, 1924.
—— *Dialogues in Limbo*, 1925.
—— *The Genteel Tradition at Bay*, 1931.
—— *Interpretations of Poetry and Religion*, 1905.
—— *Three Philosophic Poets*, 1935.
—— *Scepticism and Animal Faith*, 1923.
—— *The Realms of Being*, 4 Vols., 1927-1942.
—— *Dominations and Powers*, 1951.

2. British Philosophers

S. Alexander, *Moral Order and Progress*, 1889.
—— *Space, Time and Deity*, 2nd ed., 1927.
—— *Beauty and Other Forms of Value*, 1933.
B. Bosanquet, *Logic*, 1888.
—— *History of Aesthetic*, 1892, 1904.
—— *The Principle of Individuality and Value*, 1912.
—— *The Value and Destiny of the Individual*, 1913.
F. H. Bradley, *Ethical Studies*, 1876.
—— *The Principles of Logic*, 1883.
—— *Appearance and Reality*, 1891.
C. D. Broad, *Perception, Physics, and Reality*, 1914.
—— *Scientific Thought*, 1923.
—— *Examination of McTaggart's Philosophy*, 2 Vols., 1933-1938.
—— *Ethics and the History of Philosophy*, 1952.
G. E. Moore, *Principia Ethica*, 1903.
—— *Ethics*, 1912.

—— *Philosophical Studies,* 1922.

W. D. Ross, *Foundations of Ethics,* 1939.

B. Russell, *A Critical Exposition of the Philosophy of Leibniz,* 2nd ed., 1937.

—— *Principles of Mathematics,* 1903.

—— *Principia Mathematica* (with A. N. Whitehead), 3 Vols., 1910-1913.

—— *Our Knowledge of the External World,* 1914.

—— *Analysis of Mind,* 1921.

—— *Analysis of Matter,* 1927.

—— *An Inquiry into Meaning and Truth,* 1940.

—— *Human Knowledge, Its Scope and Limits,* 1948.

F. C. S. Schiller, *Riddles of the Sphinx,* 1891.

—— *Humanism,* 1903.

—— *Studies in Humanism,* 1907.

—— *Logic for Use,* 1929.

—— *Must Philosophers Disagree?* 1934.

—— *Our Human Truths,* 1939.

A. N. Whitehead, *An Inquiry Concerning the Principles of Human Knowledge,* 1919.

—— *The Concept of Nature,* 1920.

—— *Science and the Modern World,* 1925.

—— *Religion in the Making,* 1926.

—— *Process and Reality,* 1929.

—— *Adventures of Ideas,* 1933.

—— *Modes of Thought,* 1938.

L. Wittgenstein, *Tractatus Logico-Philosophicus,* 1922.

—— *Philosophical Investigations,* 1953.

3. *Continental Philosophers*

H. Bergson, *Time and Free Will,* 1889.

—— *Matter and Memory,* 1896.

—— *An Introduction to Metaphysics,* 1903.

—— *Creative Evolution,* 1907.

—— *Two Sources of Morality and Religion,* 1932.

B. Croce, *Aesthetic as Science of Expression and General Linguistic,* rev. ed., 1922.

—— *History, Its Theory and Practice,* 1919.

—— *History as the Story of Liberty,* 1941.

von Hartmann, *Philosophy of the Unconscious,* 1886.

N. Hartmann, *Ethics,* 3 Vols., 1932.

M. Heidegger, *Existence and Being*, 1949.

E. Husserl, *Ideas*, 1913.

K. Jaspers, *Man in the Modern Age*, 1933.

—— *Philosophie*, 3 Vols., 1932.

—— *The Way to Wisdom*, 1950.

H. Lotze, *Microcosmus*, 1884.

—— *Logic*, 1889.

—— *Metaphysics*, 1884.

E. Mach, *The Science of Mechanics*, 1893.

—— *The Analysis of Sensations*, 1914.

J. Maritain, *The Degrees of Knowledge*, 1932.

—— *True Humanism*, 1938.

—— *Man and the State*, 1951.

Appendix V

CHRONOLOGY—I

fl. = flourished
c. = approximately

Thales—fl. c. 585 B.C.

Anaximander—fl. c. 560 B.C.

Anaximenes—fl. c. 546 B.C.

Xenophanes—fl. c. 530 B.C.

Pythagoras—fl. c. 530 B.C.

Foundation of Pythagorean Order 532 B.C.

Heraclitus—fl. c. 500 B.C.

Parmenides—fl. c. 475 B.C.

Zeno—fl. c. 475 B.C

Anaxagoras—fl. c. 460 B.C.

Empedocles—fl. c. 450 B.C.

Melissus—fl. c. 440 B.C.

Leucippus—fl. c. 430 B.C.

Protagoras—481-411 B.C.

Gorgias—c. 483-375 B.C.

Socrates—469-399 B.C.

Democritus—fl. c. 420 B.C.

Antisthenes (founder of the Cynic School)—c. 444-365 B.C.

Aristippus (founder of the Cyrenaic School)—c. 435-356 B.C.

Plato—427-347 B.C.

Aristotle—384-322 B.C.

Pyrrho (founder of the Skeptical Movement)—c. 360-270 B.C.

Zeno (founder of Stoicism)—c. 350-258 B.C.

Epicurus (founder of Epicureanism) 342-270 B.C.

Arcesilaus (Skeptic)—316-241 B.C.

Chrysippus (Stoic)—280-206 B.C.

Carneades (Skeptic)—214-129 B.C.

Panaetius (Stoic)—c. 180-111 B.C.

Posidonius (Stoic)—c. 130-50 B.C.

Cicero (Eclectic)—106-43 B.C.

Lucretius (Epicurean)—95-52 B.C.

Aenesidemus (Skeptic)—fl. probably some time between 50 B.C.-100 A.D.

Philo (Jewish Platonist)—c. 20 B.C.-54 A.D.

Seneca (Stoic)—4 B.C.-65 A.D.

Plutarch (Neo-Pythagorean)—c. 46-120 A.D.

Epictetus (Stoic)—c. 60-120 A.D.

Fourth Gospel (beginning of Christian philosophy; Platonic influences)—written c. 100 A.D.

Marcus Aurelius (Stoic)—121-180.

Irenaeus (Christian)—130-202.

Clement of Alexandria (Christian) —c. 150-220.

Tertullian (Christian)—c. 155-222.

Origen (Christian)—c. 185-254.

Plotinus (Neo-Platonist)—204-269.

Sextus Empiricus (Skeptic)—fl. c. 300.

Council of Nicaea (Doctrine of the Trinity formulated)—325.

Iamblichus (Neo-Platonist)—died c. 330.

Julian the Apostate (Neo-Platonist) —331-363.

Augustine (Christian)—354-430.

Proclus (Neo-Platonist)—c. 410-485.

Boethius (Christian?)—480-524.

Closing of the Schools of Athens. End of ancient philosophy. Philosophy in servitude to Christian theology for the next nine centuries. 529.

Mohammed (founder of Islam)—c. 569-632.

John Scotus Eriugena (Christian)— c. 800-877.

Avicenna (Moslem)—979-1037.

Anselm (Christian Platonist)—1033-1109.

Avicebron (Jewish)—fl. c. 1050.

Roscellinus (Christian) — c. 1050-1122.

Abelard (Christian)—1079-1142.

Averrhoes (Moslem)—1126-1198.

Maimonides (Jewish)—1135-1204.

Albertus Magnus (Christian Aristotelian)—1206-1280.

Aristotle condemned by the Church —1209, 1215.

Roger Bacon (Christian)—c. 1214-1294.

Condemnation of Aristotle retracted —1237.

Bonaventure (Christian. End of Platonic supremacy)—1231-1274.

Thomas Aquinas (Christian Aristotelian)—c. 1225-1274.

Meister Eckhart (Christian) — c. 1250-1329.

Duns Scotus (Christian)—c. 1274-1308.

William of Occam (Christian)— died c. 1349.

John Buridan (Christian)—c. 1297-1358.

The Italian Renaissance. Beginning of liberation of philosophy from servitude to Christian theology. 1453.

CHRONOLOGY—II

Fall of Constantinople. Beginning of the Italian Renaissance, of the liberation of philosophy from Christian theology, and of independent speculation. 1453.

Leonardo da Vinci (Italian)—1452-1519.

Savonarola (Italian)—1452-1498.

Machiavelli (Italian)—1469-1527.

Copernicus (Polish astronomer)—1473-1543.

Luther (German reformer)—1483-1546.

Montaigne (French)—1533-1592.

Molina (Spanish)—1535-1600.

Giordano Bruno (Italian) — 1548-1600.

Suárez (Spanish)—1548-1617.

Francis Bacon (English)—1561-1626.

Galileo (Italian astronomer and physicist)—1564-1642.

Campanella (Italian)—1568-1639.

Hobbes (English)—1588-1679.

Gassendi (French)—1592-1655.

Descartes (French)—1596-1650.

Pascal (French)—1623-1662.

Geulincx (Belgian)—1624-1699.

Spinoza (Dutch Jewish)—1632-1677.

Locke (English)—1632-1704.

Malebranche (French)—1638-1715.

Newton (English astronomer and physicist)—1642-1727.

Leibnitz (German)—1646-1716.

Vico (Italian)—1668-1744.

Feijóo (Spanish)—1676-1764.

Wolff (German)—1679-1754.

Berkeley (Irish)—1685-1753.

Voltaire (French)—1694-1778.

Jonathan Edwards (American)—1703-1788.

De la Mettrie (French)—1709-1751.

Reid (Scotch)—1710-1796.

Hume (Scotch)—1711-1776.

Rousseau (French)—1712-1778.

Helvétius (French)—1715-1771.

Condillac (French)—1715-1780.

Holbach (German)—1723-1789.

Kant (German)—1724-1804.

Alzate (Mexican)—1729-1790.

Gamarra (Mexican)—1745-1783.

Bentham (English)—1748-1832.

Guerara (Mexican)—1748-1811.

Fichte (German)—1762-1814.

Maine de Biran (French)—1766-1824.

Hegel (German)—1770-1831.

Caballero (Cuban)—1771-1835.

James Mill (Scotch)—1773-1836.

Schelling (German)—1775-1854.

Herbart (German)—1776-1841.

Bello (Venezuelan)—1781-1865.

Mora (Spanish)—1783-1864.

Hamilton (Scotch)—1788-1856.

Schopenhauer (German) — 1788-1860.

Cousin (French)—1792-1867.

Rosmini (Italian)—1797-1855.

Comte (French)—1798-1857.

Gioberti (Italian)—1801-1852.

John Stuart Mill (Scotch)—1806-1873.

Balmes (Spanish)—1810-1848.

Kierkegaard (Danish)—1813-1855.

Ravaisson (French)—1813-1900.

Renouvier (French)—1815-1903.
Lotze (German)—1817-1881.
Karl Marx (German)—1818-1883.
Spencer (English)—1820-1903.
Haeckel (German)—1834-1919.
Mach (Austrian)—1838-1916.
Peirce (American)—1839-1914.
Tobías Barreto (Brazilian)—1839-1899.
Pereira Barreto (Brazilian)—1840-1923.
Hartmann (German)—1842-1906.
James (American)—1842-1910.
Nietzsche (German)—1844-1900.
Bradley (English)—1846-1924.
Bowne (American)—1847-1910.
Bosanquet (English)—1848-1923.
Varona (Cuban)—1849-1933.
Deústua (Peruvian)—1849-1945.
Vaihinger (German)—1852-1933.
Meinong (Austrian)—1853-1921.
Royce (American)—1855-1916.
Bergson (French)—1859-1941.
Alexander (English)—1859-1938.
Dewey (American)—1859-1952.
Husserl (Austrian)—1859-1938.
Korn (Argentine)—1860-1936.
Whitehead (English)—1861-1947.
Brito (Brazilian)—1862-1917.

Mead (American)—1863-1931.
Santayana (Spanish, educated in America)—1863-1952.
Unamuno (Spanish)—1864-1936.
Schiller (English)—1864-1937.
Croce (Italian)—1866-1952.
McTaggart (Scotch)—1866-1925.
Flewelling (American)—1871-
Russell (English)—1872-
Ferreira (Uruguayan)—1873-
Moore (English)—1873-
Montague (American)—1873-1953.
Cassirer (German)—1874-1945.
Gentile (Italian)—1875-1944.
Rougès (Argentine)—1880-1945.
Maritain (French)—1882-
Hartmann, N. (German) — 1882-1950.
Vasconcelos (Mexican)—1882-
Jaspers (German)—1883-
Caso (Mexican)—1883-1946.
Ortega y Gasset (Spanish)—1883-
Tillich (German-American)—1886-
Heidegger (German)—1889-
Wittgenstein (Austrian)—1889-1951.
Romero (Argentine)—1891-
Figuerido (Brazilian)—1891-1928.
Carnap (German-American)—1891-
Sartre (French)—1905-

Appendix VI

GLOSSARY OF
COMMON PHILOSOPHICAL TERMS

The technical vocabulary of philosophy is comprised largely of commonplace terms employed often with uncommon and highly specialized meanings. In most instances the following definitions are not exhaustive. The student should rely neither on glossaries nor dictionaries, but determine the meanings of terms within the context of their specific usage.

Absolute. Unconditioned, unqualified, unrelated. In metaphysics, reality considered as a single entity, having no environment or relations to anything external to it. Cf. Parmenides, Spinoza, Hegel, Bradley.

Absolute idealism. Theory that reality is a single unconditioned and unrelated entity, spiritual, ideational, rational, or personal in character. Cf., Hegel, Bradley, Royce.

Absolutism. Opposed to relativism; indicates independence of relations. In metaphysics, theory that reality is an absolute. In ethics and aesthetics, theory that values are objectively real. In politics, doctrine or practice of unconditioned sovereign power.

Abstraction. Process of considering a part or aspect of something exclusive of attention to the whole or the total context. That which is so considered. Concept resulting from attention to common properties of particulars.

Accident. Something contingent, not necessary, non-essential, or that might not have been. In Aristotle's logic, one of the predicables.

Activism. Any philosophical position that describes reality in terms of activity or otherwise emphasizes action. Opposed to intellectualism.

Aesthetics. Theory of beauty and ugliness. Study of art values and principles of art criticism.

Agnosticism. In the theory of knowledge, the view that in any particular area knowledge is impossible. In theology, that it is impossible to have knowledge that God does or does not exist.

Analysis. As a method, the resolution of a compound into its elements, or a complex situation into its constituents. In contemporary empiricism, *logical analysis* indicates the application of logical principles in the determination of meanings. *Analysis* indicates the type of philosophy current at Cambridge and Oxford universities directed to the determination of meanings especially by the examination of language.

Analytic proposition (judgment). In traditional logic, a proposition in which the predicate is logically implied by the subject to which it is attributed and therefore gives us no new information about the subject, as, for example, "The radii of a circle are of equal length." (The radii of a circle *must* of their very nature be of equal length. If they were not, they would not be the radii of a *circle,* but of an ellipse or an oval.) A proposition that is true by definition.

In modern logic, a proposition the truth of which can be established simply by an examination of the proposition, i.e., by examining the meaning of the symbols and the logic of the language. A proposition that is logically true. A tautology. A non-factual proposition, one whose verification requires no recourse to experience. A statement that is necessarily true, i.e., that cannot possibly be false. A proposition whose denial would be a contradiction. Opposed to *synthetic proposition, q.v.* Cf. also *contradiction.*

Antinomy. Generally speaking, any real or apparent conflict between conditions producing the same result, or between the consequences of two equally demonstrable and convincing lines of reasoning. Used by Kant of the contradictions that arise from our ability to demonstrate with equal cogency that the universe must be both finite and infinite, caused and causeless, wholly determined and yet admitting of freedom, or the like.

Anxiety. In contemporary existentialism, a rough synonym for *anguish* and *dread.* Usually an awareness by a being of non-being. A consciousness of the threat of non-being, death, or nothingness. A psychological state induced by awareness of contingency, finiteness, guilt, or meaninglessness. Differs from *fear* in having no object.

A posteriori. Descriptive of knowledge and principles regarded as derived from or dependent upon experience. By positivists and most other empiricists, all factual or synthetic propositions are regarded as a posteriori. Opposed to *a priori, q.v.*

Appearance. That which is presented to the mind, especially in sensation or perception. In some systems distinguished from reality or from the thing-in-itself. Synonymous with *phenomenon, q.v.*

A priori. Descriptive of knowledge and principles of thinking that are not derived from experience and cannot be explained by experience, even if their only application is to experience. Cf. the Kantian categories. Such knowledge and principles being logically, though not temporally and psychologically, *prior* to experience, are considered a priori. Analytic propositions are generally regarded as a priori by both rationalists and empiricists. Opposed to *a posteriori, q.v.*

Archetype. The original, or model, of which other things are regarded as the copies, as, for example, the Platonic Ideas and the ideas of things existing according to Berkeley in the mind of God.

Atomism. Any theory that describes reality as a pluralistic system composed of separate, discrete, and irreducible entities. Employed also in recent logic, e.g., by Russell, to indicate theory of unanalyzable propositions. In social theory, the view that society is essentially a complex of individuals.

Attribute. In logic, that which is affirmed or denied of a subject. In metaphysics, that which is expressive of the nature of a thing; e.g., that which belongs to or inheres in a *substance, q.v.*

Axiology. Theory of the nature of value.

Axiom. Proposition assumed to be true without proof and taken as a basis for proof of other propositions. Traditionally regarded as self-evident; in modern logic, commonly taken simply as an assumption for the purposes of formal demonstration.

Basic proposition. In some contemporary empiricists, especially Bertrand Russell, a proposition resulting from a perception and demanding no further evidence in its support. Cf. *Protocol sentence.*

Being. As descriptive of metaphysical systems, often used to indicate opposition to change, or becoming. The category of reality. Whatever *is,* in and of itself. The most general predicate possible. In current existentialism, opposed to *existence, q.v.*

Categorical. Unconditional, non-hypothetical. Proposition that asserts unconditionally.

Category. A wide and universal concept in which the mind habitually formulates its thoughts and judgments. A basic way of viewing or experiencing the world. In Kant, categories are the a priori forms under which all experience must be subsumed by the understanding if it is to be intelligible.

Causal law. Law asserting invariable and universal behavior or strict conformity.

Cause. Various meanings. Usually, whatever is the ground, occasion, or agency for an event. Aristotle distinguished four causes of change and motion: material, efficient, formal, and final. Traditionally, cause has been identified as that which produces an effect. Since Hume, the notion of productive cause has often been replaced by causation conceived simply as an invariant relation, or universal conjunction, of events.

Certainty. In technical usage, a quality of a proposition established by logical demonstration or otherwise requiring no evidence. An objective state of affairs rather than a subjective state of mind. Cf. *certitude.*

Certitude. Commonly indicates the mental state of being sure or certain. A subjective state of mind. Unquestioned assurance. Sometimes described as *psychological certitude* as opposed to logical or rational *certainty, q.v.*

Class. Total group or collection of entities possessing a common property.

Coherence theory of truth. Theory that the truth of a proposition is a property of its logical coherence or consistency with a body of already accepted propositions.

Concept. An idea that is had by a mind. Distinguished from percept or sensation and from "Idea" in the Platonic sense.

Conceptualism. Any one of several theories describing the status of universals in terms of mental concepts and avoiding the extreme forms of both *realism* and *nominalism, q.v.*

Confirmation. Process of establishing, by evidence, a degree of probability for a proposition. Partial or incomplete *verification, q.v.* By some empiricists used to indicate *verification* where the achievement of absolute certainty for the truth or falsity of a factual proposition is regarded as theoretically impossible.

Contingent. Whatever can be conceived equally well as existing or not existing. Future events whose occurrence, though considered possible, is not regarded as necessitated and determined by the present existent situation. Propositions whose truth does not rest upon logic or the necessities of rational thinking, but which must be verified in and by experience.

Contradiction. A proposition the falsity of which can be established by an examination of the proposition itself; i.e., by an examination of the meanings of the symbols and the logic of the language. A proposition that is logically false. A proposition that is necessarily false; i.e., is false in every possible case and cannot possibly be true. Cf. *analytic proposition* and *synthetic proposition.*

Contradiction, law of. Traditional logical principle that "nothing can be both A and not A" and, when applied to propositions, that "no proposition can be both false and true." Cf. *Law of identity* and *Law of excluded middle.*

Correspondence theory of truth. Theory that the truth of a proposition consists in its correspondence to the fact or facts which it asserts, and that falsity consists in non-correspondence. There are various views on the nature of the correspondence. Sometimes called *semantic* theory of truth.

Cosmogeny. Theory of the origin or creation of the world.

Cosmological argument (proof). Inference of the existence of God from the existence of the world, founded upon the assumption that whatever exists must have a cause or reason.

Cosmology. Study of the constitution of the sensible universe as an ordered whole and of the totality of the general laws that sum up its behavior. The term *rational cosmology* is used by Kant to designate the totality of the questions concerning the origin and nature of the world regarded as a reality.

Datum. That which is given, e.g., in sensation. Something not accounted for within the context at hand.

Deduction. Inference from one or more propositions, taken as premises without denying or affirming their truth, to the conclusion logically implied in and necessitated by them. Used by Kant to designate the a priori applicability of the categories to sense experience, and called by him *transcendental* in order to oppose it to a discovery of the categories based upon the observation of experience. In modern logic, deduction is often taken as synonymous with logic. It is the science of determining what is necessarily the case if something else is the case. It is concerned primarily with validity rather than truth.

Deism. In theology, has the technical meaning of indicating the view that God transcends and is totally other than the world, his creation, and has no intimate relation to it. Contrasts with a theology of *immanence.* Designates a naturalistic religious trend strong in England and France during the seventeenth and eighteenth centuries.

Determinism. Theory that every thing or event is totally conditioned by antecedent cause. Theory of governance of the universe by causal law.

Dialectic. Various meanings relating to the process of rational thought. In Plato, the science of first principles. In Hegel, the process of reason indicating the structure of the real.

Discursive. A term applied to *processes* of thinking which reach their conclusions step by step through a series of intermediary operations.

Dualism. Any theory that in any field of investigation reduces the variety of its subject matter to *two* irreducible principles; as, for example, the natural and the supernatural, good and evil, will and intellect.

In metaphysics, a theory that reduces the universe to two fundamental kinds of reality, as, for example, mind and matter, or Platonic Ideas and matter.

In epistemology, a theory that regards the object of knowledge as not numerically identical with the object as known, i.e., as the content of the mind in the knowing relationship. Represented in Critical Realism, or in the knowledge theories of Locke and Descartes.

Dysteleology. Indicates the presence of factors in the world that oppose the notion of adaptation to good or desirable ends. Non-teleological; e.g., disease, death, or other so-called natural evils.

Eclecticism. In philosophy, the combining of elements derived from different philosophical schools or doctrines.

Egoism. In ethics, the theory that the highest good is one's own pleasure or well being.

Empiricism. In its rigorous form, the doctrine that all knowledge of fact must be validated in sense experience and that whatever is knowable is knowable directly by sense data or is capable of being inferred from propositions based on sense data. Opposed to *rationalism* and to knowledge by *intuition*. Opposed to "innate ideas," a priori structures of the mind and forms of thinking, entities, material or immaterial, transcending experience, and the pretension of reason to discover truths and beings existing outside and apart from sense experience. Empiricists commonly hold, therefore, that all genuine factual propositions are a posteriori. Many regard such propositions as empirical hypotheses, being incapable of verification as true or false with absolute certainty.

Entelechy. In metaphysics, the realization of the essence of a thing. Actuality. In vitalism, the productive life factor in living things.

Epi-phenomenalism. The teaching that consciousness is a mere accessory and accompaniment of physiological processes, whose presence or absence makes no difference to these processes, and whose activity is powerless to interfere with them and to influence them in any way whatsoever.

Epistemology. Study of the nature of knowledge, its origin, limitations, and possibilities and of the relation of the knowing subject to the known object. Concerns the problem of the validation of knowledge and the various ways of knowing, i.e., by reason, experience, or intuition, and is closely related to the theory of the nature of truth.

Essence. In metaphysics, designates that which makes a thing what it is and nothing else, in contrast with the qualities, or *accidents,* which attach superficially and for the time being to the thing and may be detached from it. Contrasted also with the *existence,* or factual being and "thereness" of a thing in and for itself, or its presence as an *experienced* fact. By some the essence of a thing is lodged in that which it shares in common with other things of the same sort, e.g., Plato; by others in that which makes it individual and concrete, e.g., Aristotle.

Eternal. Timeless, in the sense of having no duration, being outside of and independent of time. E.g., the Platonic Ideas, the Christian God, the Pythagorean theorem, or any "absolute truths," are held to be unaffected by the existence or non-existence of time. Used loosely as a synonym for "everlasting duration."

Ethics. Theory of the nature of the good and of how it can be achieved.

Eudaemonism. Ethical position that identifies happiness and general human well-being as the good.

Excluded middle, law of. Traditional logical principle that "everything is either A or not A," or, when applied to propositions, that "every proposition is either true or false." Cf. *Law of identity* and *Law of contradiction.*

Existence. Indicates the factual being and "thereness" of a thing, either independently of all actual and possible awareness and knowledge of it, or as an *experienced* fact. Opposed to *essence,* which merely describes the nature of a thing, but does not at the same time indicate that the thing described is "there" either in itself or in experience. Used by some philosophers in a narrower sense than *being,* to denote enacted, concrete, individual being in contrast to the being of universals, logical propositions and the like, to designate which the term *subsistence* is sometimes employed.

Modern existentialism, founded on the doctrine that existence is prior to essence, commonly ascribes existence only to human beings, on the ground that a conscious awareness of existence is necessary to authentic existence. Cf. *subsistence.*

Existentialism. Philosophical position based especially on the idea that existence is prior to essence. In application this means that a man has no fixed nature, but is what he does or chooses.

Explanation. Traditionally, the attempt to account for events by finding ultimate causes, reasons, or purposes for them. In modern empiricism, often synonymous with *descriptive explanation,* description of events by the identification of *proximate* as opposed to *ultimate* causes. For contemporary empiricists, explanation often consists in establishing a deductive relationship between the event to be explained and general causal laws and descriptions of circumstances taken as premises. The logical inverse of *prediction*.

External relations. Theory that relations are not dependent upon their terms, that the relations of a thing are external to it and not constitutive of its nature. Important in pluralistic metaphysics. Opposed to *internal relations, q.v.*

Extrinsic. In value theory, reference to the value of a thing in relation to something else. Opposed to *intrinsic, q.v.*

Fact. A state of affairs. That which objectively is. Not to be confused with a statement of fact or a factual proposition. Factual propositions are true or false. Facts simply *are*.

Fallibilism. Theory that it is impossible to attain absolute certainty in factual knowledge. Cf. Peirce.

Freedom. *Free will of indifference* (indeterminism). Indicates that the will exercises itself independently of all determination whatsoever, be it by instinct or impulse or passion or rational and moral motives or character or the *self*, and has no other "cause" than a blank, unmotivated power to decide and will, whose choices and volitions are explicable simply and solely by its mere existence and exercise, and require no other reasons of any sort to account for them. Often called "libertarian" concept of freedom.

Free will of self-determination. Decisions and behavior that the agent regards as determined by no compulsion of external forces, but simply by his own essential nature, or *self*. This *self* may be identified with reason and reflection and pursuit of the good, in which case ignorance, impulse, folly, passion, and the pressure of the instincts appear as external constraints upon volition and behavior expressive of the true self. But to establish moral and legal responsibility it is sufficient to show that the agent is not forced by anything *outside himself* to act as he does. Sometimes regarded as compatible with *determinism, q.v.*

Hedonism. Reference to pleasure or happiness. *Psychological hedonism* is the explanation of all motivation in terms of a desire to avoid pain and realize pleasure. *Ethical hedonism* is the moral doctrine that pleasure is the highest or only intrinsic good.

Humanism. Traditionally referred to the humanities or humane learning. In current philosophy, indicates especially naturalistic or nontheistic philosophy with positive emphasis on human values.

Hylozoism. Theory that matter is alive, or that life is a property of matter.

Hypothesis. A statement or idea whose truth is conditional, i.e., dependent upon the truth of another statement or idea. Often indicates tentative or probable explanation.

Idealism. In *metaphysics,* the theory that reality is of the nature of mind or of idea. May be monistic (absolutistic) or pluralistic, impersonalistic or personalistic. In *epistemology,* the theory that the known object is a product of its being known.

Identity, law of. Traditional logical principle that "If anything is A, it is A," or, when applied to propositions, "If any proposition is true, it is true." Cf. *Law of excluded middle* and *Law of contradiction.*

Induction. Usually, inference of a general proposition from observed particular instances or cases, where the general proposition refers to all instances of the type indicated, while the observation is of only some of those instances. E.g., the laws of physics are induced from the observation of physical phenomena. In typical induction, the observations yield premises which support the probability of the conclusion without necessarily entailing it. In "perfect" induction, or "complete enumeration," the generalization is inferred from observation of every member of the class which it describes. This is actually a form of deduction.

Innate ideas. Ideas or principles possessed by the mind independently of any experience, and incapable of being found in experience, though awareness of them may be occasioned by experience. E.g., Plato, Descartes, Leibnitz.

Instrumentalism. Dewey's pragmatism, based primarily on the theory that the mind is an instrument in the service of the life of the organism.

Intentionality. The mental intention of or reference to an object.

Internal relations. Theory that relations are dependent on their terms; especially in metaphysical absolutism, theory that all relations are internal to the absolute. Theory that the relations of a thing are constitutive of its nature. Opposed to *external relations, q.v.*

Intrinsic. In value theory, reference to value of a thing in and of itself. Opposed to *extrinsic, q.v.,* or *instrumental.*

Intuition. Immediate apprehension of the object. Direct, non-discursive, non-mediated knowledge.

Logic. Theory of inference. Often identified with deduction. Cf. *deduction* and *induction.* In absolute idealism logic is involved with or identical with metaphysics. In pragmatism logic is the theory of inquiry.

Logistic. Especially the theory that mathematics is reducible to logic. Sometimes synonymous with symbolic logic.

Materialism. Theory that the total universe, including all life and mind, can be reduced to and explained in terms of matter in motion. Applied also to systems that, although they regard consciousness as irreducible to terms of physical energy, still consider it dependent upon matter for its existence and find its processes explicable only when correlated with physiological processes and thus subject to the laws governing physical motion and energy.

Meaning. *Cognitive* or knowledge meaning is of two types, *formal* and *factual*. Statements having cognitive meaning, being assertions, are true or false. Non-cognitive meanings, e.g., emotive, affective, volitional, are sometimes identified.

Mechanism. Any theory that explains phenomena by reference exclusively to causation in terms of antecedent conditions, eliminating the notions of design, purpose, final causation, determination of the part by the whole, and of causation by occult powers.

Meliorism. Theory that the world is neither totally evil nor totally good and that there is a possibility of increasing the good. View that things can be made better. Opposed to optimism and pessimism.

Metaphysics. In its popular and general sense, investigation of the essential and absolute nature of reality as a whole or of the nature of being as such. Cf. *ontology.* The search for first principles. Originally meant "what comes after physics," and used originally of the works of Aristotle that followed his *Physics* in the collection made by Andronicus. Used by Aquinas to designate knowledge of *supernatural* entities; by the Cartesians, of *immaterial* entities; by Kant, of constructive attempts to know the nature of things as they are in themselves, and of theories regarding objects of faith, like God, freedom and immortality; by Bergson and other intuitionists, of the immediate acquaintance with the real given by direct intuition of its nature, as contrasted with the falsifications of the nature of the real by the intellectual processes.

Today a common distinction is made between *speculative metaphysics,* regarded by its opponents as an attempt to describe the world in the most general terms without adequate empirical grounds, and *reflective metaphysics,* that inquires into the assumptions, presuppositions, and methods of knowledge itself.

For current positivism, "metaphysics" indicates a theoretically unverifiable assertion of fact or a statement that purports to be factual but is cognitively meaningless.

Methodology. Analysis of the principles of inquiry, usually involving the problems of logic, evidence, verification, primary assumptions, etc. Used especially in relation to the methods of the sciences. Not to be confused with research techniques.

Monad. Usually, following Leibnitz, a simple living or sentient individual or atom, conceived as an elementary indivisible and irreducible unit of reality. A soul or self.

Monism. In *metaphysics,* the theory that all reality (1) is of the same kind, e.g., material or spiritual, and/or (2) is quantitatively one single entity rather than a collection of things independently real. Opposed to dualism or pluralism.

In *epistemology,* the theory that the object as known, i.e., the content of the mind in the knowing relation, is numerically identical with the object as objectively real. Represented in American New Realism and opposed to the dualism of Critical Realism.

Mysticism. The doctrine that the fundamental nature of reality is ineffable; that is, inaccessible through either the senses or the intellect, indescribable in any of the terms and categories at the command of ordinary human consciousness, and approachable only in and through a special state of *ecstasy* which transcends every form and activity, sensible, emotional, intuitive, volitional, and rational of normal human experience. In this ecstasy all sense of separateness, apartness, and difference of the self from the nature of the real disappears, self-consciousness is obliterated, and the individual is either actually merged and made one with the real, or engrossed in a beatific vision of it in which the distinction between subject and object, though still existent metaphysically, is no longer experienced.

The term is also applied to the special ascetic discipline regarded as a prerequisite to the attainment of *ecstasy.*

In a lower and more popular sense, it is also frequently extended to such attitudes and beliefs as rely upon ordinary human feeling, intuition, and experience of volition, rather than upon empirical observation and reasoning, as guides to the nature of the real.

Naturalism. Theory that the universe has no supernatural origin or ground and needs no supernatural explanation; that it is self-existent and should be explained solely by reference to itself; that its behavior is not teleologically explicable by final causes and purposes; that human life and behavior are in no way exceptional and outside the course of natural events, and are to be explained by the same principles as obtain throughout the rest of nature; and that human values, moral ideals, and conduct are determined entirely by the organic structure and needs characteristic of the human species.

Natural theology. Theology established on reason, or natural knowledge, as opposed to revelation.

Necessity. Indicates a situation that cannot be other than what it is.

Neutral monism. Theory that reduces both mind and matter to relations of neutral entities, i.e., that are neither mental nor material. Cf. Mach, James, Russell, and American New Realism.

Nihilism. Usually used loosely of theories that deny reality, values, knowledge, or, especially, moral distinctions.

Nominalism. Theory that universals are not real but are only names or words, and that reality is limited to particulars.

Normative. Relating to norms or standards, especially in ethics, aesthetics, or politics. Valuational in contrast to factual.

Noumenon. In Kantian philosophy, opposed to phenomenon, or appearance. Reality not known in perceptual knowledge. Cf. Kant.

Occasionalism. Theory of psycho-physical parallelism where mind and matter do not interact but correspond in their events as a result of a mediator, especially God.

Ontological argument (proof). Argument for the existence of God based upon the idea of God, i.e., the logical analysis and definition of his nature. The idea of a perfect being, it is argued, is necessarily the idea of an existent being, since a being that lacked existence would not be perfect. Reason demands the idea of an *ens realissimum,* of a complete, finished, sum total of being, lacking in nothing. Therefore logic and reason demand that this idea shall have enacted existence. Classic formulation by Anselm.

Ontology. The science or knowledge of *being* as such. Usually synonymous with *metaphysics* or with the central core of metaphysics as a theory of reality.

Operationism. Position in contemporary empiricism that the meaning of a term or concept is the set of operations performed on the occasion of its employment.

Panlogism. Theory that reality is reason or rational process. E.g., Hegelianism.

Panpsychism. Theory that reality consists of minds or psychic entities. E.g., Leibnitz' monadology.

Pantheism. The teaching that God and the universe are one and the same thing. Pantheism may be idealistic (Hegel, Fichte) or materialistic (Holbach, Diderot) or naturalistic (Spinoza) or moral (the Stoics) or mystic (Plotinus, Scotus Eriugena, Bruno), according to the view taken of the essential character of the real.

Paralogism. False reasoning. Employed by Kant to designate the incorrect reasoning by which the substantial, simple, and personal character of the soul is "demonstrated," and by which Berkeley's equation of *existence* with perceiving and being perceived is "established."

Parsimony, law of. Principle of economy in ideas, that explanation should employ as few ideas as possible. Cf. Occam's razor.

Particular. An individual thing or event. Opposed to *class,* of which it is a member, or opposed to *universal, q.v.*

Peripatetic. Pertaining to the philosophy of Aristotle.

Personalism. Pluralistic form of idealism that regards personality as the key to the explanation of reality as well as the locus of value.

Phenomenalism. Theory that knowledge and/or reality are limited to phenomena, i.e., to appearances.

Phenomenology. Especially the philosophy identified with E. Husserl and his followers which is described as a science of the subjective and its intended objects. Phenomenological method is an a priori method that seeks exact knowledge by abstracting objects from the context of experience.

Phenomenon. That which appears to consciousness, appearance. That which is perceived. Used sometimes of the "brute," fluid content of consciousness, sometimes of the facts, objects, and events into which this content coagulates. In Kant, designates any "object of possible experience," that is, everything that appears under the forms of space and time and in the ways determined by the categories of the understanding.

Physicalism. Theory in contemporary positivism that holds that only those statements are cognitively meaningful that can be expressed as physicalistic propositions, i.e., propositions designating observable properties. Important in the Unity of Science movement.

Pluralism. In metaphysics, any system according to which Reality is composed of *many* individual, independent, ultimate constituents, which cannot be reduced to terms of one another, or to aspects of some single common principle underlying them. Cf. Herbart, Lotze, James, Schiller, and others.

Positivism. Theory that equates all knowledge with scientific knowledge and regards metaphysics as impossible. *Logical positivism* regards metaphysical sentences as meaningless because they are in principle incapable of empirical verification.

Pragmatics. Study of the use and effects of signs. Distinguished from *semantics* and *syntactics; q.v.* Cf. *semiotic.*

Pragmatism. Philosophical position identified especially with Peirce, James, Schiller, Mead, and Dewey, based on a theory of the mind as an instrument for problem solving, and on theories of meaning and truth that emphasize the results or consequences of ideas.

Predicables. In Aristotelian logic, the predicates that a proposition may affirm or deny of a subject, e.g., genus, species, differentia, property, accident.

Predicate. That which is asserted of a subject. A term indicating a property. In metaphysics, an attribute of a substance.

Primary quality. Originally intended to indicate qualities regarded as belonging to objects taken independently of their being known. In Locke, solidity, extension, figure, motion or rest, and number. Often indicates quantitative characteristics of an object. Opposed to *secondary quality* and *tertiary quality, q.v.*

Probabilism. Theory that certainty in knowledge is not possible and that probabilities should be accepted in science and as guides for action.

Probability. In knowledge, a value less than certainty but more than ignorance. Has various technical applications in logic and methodology.

Property. In Aristotelian logic, an attribute or predicate of a thing that follows necessarily from its definition but does not indicate its essence. One of the five *predicables* in Aristotle's logic, *q.v.*

Proposition. That which is either true or false. Sometimes synonymous with *statement.* Not identical with *sentence.* A proposition is that which has meaning, either factual or logical.

Protocol sentence. In some logical positivists, especially Neurath and Carnap, sentences reporting the results of observations. Cf. *Basic proposition.*

Psycho-physical parallelism. The doctrine that every physical event is accompanied by and corresponds to a psychical event and *vice versa.* Cf. Spinoza. Used more particularly of the teaching that every psychical event accompanies and corresponds to a physiological event, but not that every physical event necessarily has a psychical concomitant. The relation between the two series of events is not regarded as causal, but simply as concomitant. Theory that mental states do not cause physical states, or *vice versa,* but that they merely accompany each other.

Rationalism. As a way of knowing, the method of establishing propositions by reason, or deduction, usually involving premises stating general ideas or principles. A priori method. Opposed to *intuition* and *empiricism, q.v.* Pure mathematics is the prime example of rationalism.

Realism. In *metaphysics,* usually any system that denies the possibility of reducing the universe to mind and thought, and that maintains that something would still exist if all consciousness whatsoever were extinguished. Used also of the Platonic doctrine that the Ideas are independent of and more real than sensible objects, and of the teaching derived from Plato, that universals exist independently of the particulars that enact them. In *epistemology,* the theory that the objects of knowledge and experience are real independently of their being known and experienced. *Realism* and *Idealism* are opposites when used in an epistemological context, but employed metaphysically they are not necessarily opposed.

Relational logic. Sometimes indicates non-Aristotelian logic, or logic employing propositions asserting relations other than traditional subject-predicate relations, e.g., symmetry, transitivity.

Relativism. Usually indicates the view that truth or moral and aesthetic values vary in relation to the knowing or experiencing subject or to other circumstances. Opposed to *absolutism.*

Scepticism. Theory that reliable knowledge is impossible.

Scholasticism. As a method, usually the subordination of science and philosophy to theology and the employment of deductive techniques in proving theses by reliance upon authorities. As a philosophy, especially the general type represented by Anselm, Abelard, Aquinas and Duns Scotus, culminating historically in the neo-scholasticism currently popular and approved in the Roman Catholic Church.

Secondary quality. Usually indicates qualities believed to belong not simply to objects as such, but rather resulting from their being perceived by the senses. In Locke, the powers of objects to produce in us such sensations as colors, sounds, tastes, etc., by their primary qualities. Opposed to *primary quality* and *tertiary quality, q.v.*

Semantics. Study of the signification of signs. Analysis of language meanings. Relation of signs or symbols to that for which they stand. Distinguished from *syntactics* and *pragmatics, q.v.* Cf. *semiotic.*

Semiotic. The theory of signs, including *semantics, syntactics,* and *pragmatics, q.v.*

Sense data language. In recent empiricism, language that describes, or purports to describe, sense data only, without referring to the properties of material objects. Cf. *sense datum.*

Sense datum. Used variously, but usually refers technically to the sensory content of the mind in sense perception, i.e., the sensation itself rather than the object sensed. Cf. *sense data language.*

Sign. Something that stands for or means another thing. Cf. *symbol.*

Solipsism. In metaphysics, a form of subjective idealism where an individual affirms that he alone exists and all other reality, the external world and other selves, is a product of his own mental operations, without independent existence. The interpretation of the world as our private sense data. In language, the view that significant propositions cannot be communicated because the significance of language is limited to possible experience. Linguistic solipsism has been treated as a problem especially in logical positivism.

Subject. That which experiences and thinks and unifies the multiple and varied content of consciousness into an objective world of *things*. In metaphysics, a synonym of *substance,* that of which qualities are predicated and in which they may be said to inhere.

In theory of knowledge, the knower, as contrasted with *object,* that which is known.

Subsistence. Employed by some modern philosophers to indicate the kind of being possessed by abstract entities, universals, logical propositions, formulae, types, laws and the like, as distinguished from the *existence* of concrete particular objects. Subsistence usually indicates a non-temporal, non-spatial reality, where existence indicates a space-time location. Used originally and more generally of the kind of being attributed to *substances* as contrasted with that of *qualities* and *accidents,* and of the duration and persistence of a thing despite the change and disappearance of its qualities.

Substance. That which exists in and by itself and not as a modification or relation of anything else. That which constitutes the essential nature of a thing, that makes a thing what it is. The *substratum* which stands under and supports the predicates or attributes, the permanent and self-identical support of the changes and of the different and successive qualities by which the thing is modified.

Substratum. A synonym for *substance* in the sense of a permanent, self-identical support for modes and accidents and changes. That which stands under the attributes and in which they inhere. Cf. Locke and Berkeley. Not synonymous, however, with *substance* in the sense of that which exists in and by itself.

Symbol. Often synonymous with *sign*. Sometimes sign that substitutes for other signs. Sometimes "conventional" as opposed to "natural" sign. Cf. *sign*.

Synoptic. Used to designate an act of thought or point of view in which a whole and all its constituents are grasped and seen together simultaneously in their entirety and in their necessary connection with, and implication of, one another. Cf. Spinoza's vision "under the aspect of eternity."

Syntactics. Analysis of syntax, or the formal relations of signs or symbols to each other in a linguistic system. Distinguished from *semantics* and *pragmatics, q.v.* Cf. *semiotic.*

Syntax. Formal arrangement of symbols in a symbolic system. *Logical syntax* indicates the formal rules of a symbolic system.

Synthesis. The operation and result of piecing together comparatively simple elements into larger and more complicated wholes. In Hegel and his followers the fusion of opposed ideas, thesis and antithesis, in a new "higher" idea or proposition in which their contradiction is overcome and their essential identity is revealed.

Synthetic proposition (judgment). In traditional logic, a proposition in which the predicate is not necessarily implied by the subject to which it is attributed, as, for example, "The orbits of the planets are ellipses." (There is no logical reason why planetary orbits should not be circular instead of elliptical. They are not elliptical by definition. Hence their elliptical form is not logically implied.) In modern logic, a proposition the truth or falsity of which cannot be established simply by an examination of the proposition itself, and which must, therefore, be verified empirically. A proposition which is not logically true. A factual proposition. A proposition or statement which is neither *analytic* nor self-contradictory. Cf. *analytic proposition.*

Teleological. Explanation of events not by their antecedents but by their results and purposes; that is, not by efficient but by final causation. The explanatory purpose may be regarded as external (argument from design) or internal (biological ends, entelechies). Indicates also attempts to explain the nature and arrangement of the parts by the whole of which they are the constituents, as, for example, in the case of organic bodies.

Teleological argument (proof). Inference of the existence of God from the teleology discoverable in the world, i.e., the operation of final cause, purposes, or adaptation to ends. Argument for an intelligent creator of the world baesd on the design alleged to be found in nature.

Tertiary quality. Sometimes indicates value qualities that belong not to an object but that result from the subject's relation to the object. Opposed to *primary quality* and *secondary quality.*

Theism. Religious philosophy asserting existence of God as a living being. Usually identified with monotheism. Theism is opposed to *pantheism, q.v.,* by holding that God is not identical with the world. Often used in opposition to *deism, q.v.,* as indicating that God is at least partially immanent in the world rather than totally transcendent to it.

Theodicy. Theory to justify the goodness of God in view of the evil in the world.

Theory. Usually an idea expressed by a hypothetical proposition or set of propositions. Sometimes erroneously employed to indicate an idea that is probably false. Also frequently employed erroneously in contrast to fact, *q.v.* Opposed to *practice*.

Transcendental. Transcending ordinary experience. Used by the *Scholastics* of attributes even more general than the Aristotelian categories, as, for example, unity, truth, goodness. Used by *Kant* of the a priori categories and other structures of the thinking apparatus, and also to designate attempts to extend the categories and procedures valid for human experience to the world of things-in-themselves, thus *transcending* experience. Also designates systems that consider experience to be governed by a priori forms and principles. Name applied to the Concord school of which Emerson was the chief representative. In theology, *transcendent* indicates the otherness of God in relation to the world, as opposed to *immanent*.

Tychism. Employed by C. S. Peirce to indicate his theory that *absolute chance* is a characteristic of the objectively real world and is evident in the world-process. In this theory chance means more than our ignorance of causes. It holds that many events actually have no causes, and happen for no reason whatsoever. Peirce considered biological processes to be obviously tychistic in character.

Types, theory of. Theory in modern logic, intended to avoid certain logical paradoxes, based on the principle that "whatever involves *all* of a collection must not be one of the collection." (Quoted from Russell and Whitehead, *Principia Mathematica.*)

Unity of science. Program of contemporary positivism and empiricism, inspired partly by Leibnitz, of achieving a unity of all scientific knowledge especially by formulating rules for an exact language for the statement of fact. Cf. *physicalism*.

Universal. In metaphysics, usually an entity which is apprehended by the intellect rather than by the senses and whose reality is independent of any exemplification in space and time. Opposed to *particular, q.v.* Cf. *Realism* and *Nominalism*.

Universal proposition. A proposition that asserts or denies a property of all the members of a specified class.

Utilitarianism. Empirical and altruistic hedonistic moral philosophy emphasizing the greatest happiness of the greatest number.

Validity. In logic, a proposition is valid if it follows necessarily from the accepted premises. When this is the case, the argument or reasoning is valid. *Validity* is not to be confused with *truth*. A valid proposition may or may not be true.

Verifiability. The possibility in principle of a proposition being verified, i.e., established as true or false. By some empiricists *verifiability* refers technically to *confirmability*. Cf. *confirm*. In current empiricism, e.g., logical empiricism, the *verifiability* (or *confirmability*) in principle of a factual proposition is the criterion of its cognitive meaningfulness.

Verification. Process of determining the truth or falsity of a proposition. In current empiricism often replaced by or identical with *confirmation, q.v.,* especially where absolute certainty regarding the truth or falsity of a factual proposition is considered theoretically impossible.

Vitalism. Theory that living things are identified by a property of life or a life force that is not reducible to physical or chemical processes. E.g., H. Driesch and H. Bergson.

Voluntarism. In metaphysics any position that places dominant emphasis on the will or volition as against intellect, reason, ideation, or feeling in its description of reality. E.g., Schopenhauer and James.

INDEX—I

Abelard, 375 f., 400; on ethics, 377; on the mind, 376; on universals, 376; realism of, 376

Abstinence (Porphyry), 332

Academics, influence of, on Stoicism, 265

Academy, Plato's, 125, 232 f., 274; Carneades causes rift in, 278 f.

Actuality, Aristotle on, 179

Adelard of Bath, 378

Aemilius, 331

Aenesidemus, on causation, 280; on ethics, 281; on sensation, 279 f.; on truth, 281

Agnosticism, of Protagoras, 104

Agrippa, 281

Alan of Lille, 379

Albert of Saxony, 430 f.

Albertus Magnus, 395 f., 407

Albinus, 296

Alcuin, 362 f.

Al-Farabi, 383

Al-Gazzali, 384

Al-Kindi, 383

Alexander, Aristotle estranged from, 172 f.; Aristotle tutor to, 171; death of, 173; epoch of, 228

Alexander of Aphrodisias, 383

Alexander of Hales, 390 f.

Alexandria, brilliance of, 229; skepticism favored in, 279

Alexandrian Jews, influenced by Plato, 299

Alfred the Great, 363

Amalric of Bena, 379

Ammonius Saccas, 306, 307 f.; Plotinus chief pupil of, 308

Analytic geometry, beginnings of, 430

Anaxagoras, 77 ff.

Anaxarchus, 93

Anaximander, 33 f.

Anaximenes, 35 f.

Ancient culture, maintained by Christian Church, 358

Angels, Thomas Aquinas on, 399 f.

Anniceris, 122

Anselm, attacked Roscellinus, 371; on creation of universe, 371; on God, 372, 373; on Incarnation, 374 f.; on Redemption, 374 f.; on universals, 371

Antichthon, 45

Antiochus of Ascalon, 278 f.

Antipater, 173

Antisthenes, 116 f.

Antonius, 269 f.

Apollonius of Tyana, 286, 291

Apuleius, 295

Aquinas, Thomas, 197, 376; and Aristotle, 398 f.; defenders of, 407; Duns Scotus critic of, 408 f.; life of, 396; on angels, 399; on ethics, 402; on God, 397 f., 402 f.; on happiness, 403; on man, 406; on matter, 398 f.; on mind, 401 f.; on physics, 405 f.; on the senses, 401; on the soul, 402 f.; on substantial forms, 399; on the will, 403; on universals, 400; on universe, 398; on Unmoved Mover, 406; opposed by Dominicans, 407; opposed by Franciscans, 406; opposition to, 406 f.; philosophy restricted by, 397; theology defined by, 397; works of, 396

Arabs, and Aristotle, 382; Aristotle pictured by, 384; preserved Greek philosophy, 382

Arcesilaus, 234, 274

Archelaus, 85

Archytas, 124

Arians, 335

Aristippus, life of, 119; influences Epi-

li

INDEX—II